ALSO BY

ELIA KAZAN

America America
The Arrangement
The Assassins
The Understudy
Acts of Love
The Anatolian

ELIA KAZAN

ELIA KAZAN

A LIFE

Alfred A. Knopf ✕ New York 1988

THIS IS A BORZOI BOOK

PUBLISHED BY ALFRED A. KNOPF, INC.

Grateful acknowledgment is made to Grove Press, Inc., for
permission to reprint excerpts from *Waiting for Lefty* from *Six
Plays* by Clifford Odets. Copyright 1935 by Clifford Odets.
Copyright renewed 1962 by Clifford Odets. Reprinted by
permission of Grove Press, Inc.

Library of Congress Cataloging-in-Publication Data
Kazan, Elia.
Elia Kazan : a life.
1. Kazan, Elia.   2. Motion picture producers and directors—
United States—Biography.   3. Theatrical producers and
directors—United States—Biography.   4. Authors,
American—20th century—Biography.   I. Title.
PN1998.3.K39A3   1988   791.43'0233'0924 [B]   87-40486
ISBN 0-394-55953-3

Manufactured in the United States of America

FIRST EDITION

TO
EILEEN
SHANAHAN

ELIA KAZAN

"W H Y are you mad?"

My wife asks me that, seems like every morning. Usually at breakfast, when my face is still wrinkled from sleep.

"I'm not mad," I say. "It's just my face."

I've said that to her ten times. She's my third wife and I'm happy with her, but she has yet to learn that I don't like to talk in the morning. Which is tough on her, a decent person, full of lively chatter, like bright pebbles.

Confronting me where I'm sitting at my typewriter is a small round mirror, clamped in a pretty but rickety Mex-made stand. It frames my face neatly, and sometimes when I work, I study my image. I certainly look mad.

The fact is I *am* mad, most every morning. I wake up mad. Still.

"Haven't you noticed that everyone is afraid of you?" my wife goes on, her tone gentle and sympathetic. "You're intimidating."

"Bullshit!"

"Ask your children. Or mine." She's brought me two blond stepchildren, nice kids. "They're scared of you too."

I'm rather good at concealing anger. Had to be in my old profession. But recently it's begun to show through. What I'm mad at nowadays is, for instance, mortality. I've passed seventy-eight and have only recently found how to enjoy life. For one thing, I've stopped worrying about what people think of me—or so I like to believe. I used to spend most of my time straining to be a nice guy so people would like me. Now I'm out of show business and I've become my true grumpy self.

I no longer hide it; it's out in the open, my perennial scowl. Which is why my smile, when it does appear, is so dazzling. The sheer surprise of it! That's supposed to be a joke.

S O M E T I M E S the image I see in the little round mirror shocks me. There he is—my father. I'm beginning to look like the man I feared most of my life and particularly during the years when I was growing up. I look away. I look back. He's still there, and his face still disturbs me.

My youngest son, who's only had twenty-five years to get used to my mug, is more direct. "What's the matter with your face?" he's said to me. Some nerve! Where's respect for your parents these days? "What's the matter with it?" I demand. "It looks like it's about to blow up," he says. "Like you could do something terrible any minute."

Which is exactly what I used to think of my old man.

Actually it's not the evidence of uncontrollable rage that worries me. That was useful when I was an actor in the Group Theatre and we did those semirevolutionary plays. Or when I played gangsters. The same expression did for both. It's another look, one that is there only occasionally, and when I see it I don't like it. It's my father's sly face. I call it the Anatolian Smile, the smile that covers resentment. And fear. I see the cunning in that smile. Father never wore that look at home; he was himself then. He kept that face for buyers. That's when I used to see it, when I worked summers at George Kazan, Inc., Oriental Rugs and Carpets.

Where did it come from—on me, I mean—that mask to hide a truer feeling? Whatever produces that smile, I'm not proud of. I'm moving the mirror back and out of line.

The thing about my face that disturbs me most is the clutch of crooked crosses on my forehead. I know how they got there. When I was separated from my first wife, Molly, I was very unhappy and used to sleep with my face clenched like a fist. I would grind my teeth too. My friend George Sferra, the dentist, warned me about that, so I made an effort to control it and did. But no one warned me that the creases on my forehead would not go away.

I SPEND a good deal of time in the country and have come to know the black snake. He is a courageous creature who asks no quarter, shows no panic. Confronted with a larger adversary—me—he moves away but just enough. It's his country too, and he's coiled at the side of the wood's path for his own good reason. I sense some kind of pride there. I may be pumping this empathy up, but it's there in me.

The black snake avoids man. We, who revere the scavenger eagle, scorn and despise the snake. If it slides onto a highway on an autumn afternoon and lingers to enjoy the heat that the blacktop has stored from the noonday sun, the next passing car will swerve enough to run it over. The first thing a snake learns is that man is the enemy.

Each spring I find a skin that a black snake has shed in its program of growth. Delicate as a butterfly's wing. I hold it in my fingertips, lift it to the sun, admire its color and fabric. I wonder about the life that skin contained. Would such a creature know regret? Or worry? Or guilt?

When I see the snake later with its glistening new skin, it is bigger and more confident—or so it seems—but no more friendly. It is still nature's essential outsider. But I know how vulnerable it is, that with all its hissing and writhing and snapping the air, a single strike across its back with a garden hoe will finish it. I've seen that and I've seen hawks stoop to pick up young snakes and carry them off, helpless. Their threatening aspect does not protect them.

So much for my angry look.

I've shed several skins in my time, lived several lives, and known violent and cruel changes. Generally I've understood what happened only after it happened. Events had meaning for me only in reverse chronological order.

I've known regret. And guilt. Also pride. Oh, yes, there've been days!

A writer, perhaps more than a filmmaker or a theatre director, lives off what he has stored up in the way of impressions and experiences. One thing we all learn is not to deny our violent feelings but to respect them. They are our material, as well as our bond with humanity. People generally try to forget the pain of the past, to lift themselves above it. They're protecting themselves where it hurt most. Artists know that they have to live differently than their neighbors, and that hurt is part of the game they've chosen to play. Our weaknesses, our faults, our sins, are what make us understand other living creatures. We don't look away when we look back.

The irony is that my face got its "look" when I was most successful. From the mid-1940s through the '50s and on into the first two years of the '60s, I was the most successful director at work in America, but I was in a turmoil of revolt, and it was against myself. I didn't like my public person. I wasn't the man I wanted to be. I despised my nickname, for instance: Gadget! It suggested an agreeable, ever-compliant little cuss, a "good Joe" who worked hard and always followed instructions. I didn't feel that way, not at all.

My publicity, which was constant during those years, plagued me. I got sick of seeing my name and picture in print. I shook off the excessive respect paid me and the praise for what I didn't myself esteem. It was suffocating. And it wasn't what I wanted to be. I told my friend John Steinbeck that I'd be happy never to see my name in newsprint again. He told me not to worry; that would happen. John was being roasted in the press through those years. He promised me my day would come.

O N T H E second of January, 1962, I flew to Stockholm with my wife Molly to publicize a film I'd recently completed, *Splendor in the Grass*. The big studios were still doing things in style in those years, and we stayed at a hotel where we were attended by servants who looked as if I should be serving them.

On the day after our arrival, I received a cable from New York City, informing me, by a prearranged code, that I had a new son by a woman not my wife. I can't remember that I was flustered. I went to a press conference and did my best to "push" my film.

Molly enjoyed the hotel, the excellent food, the service, our being alone together. She spent her afternoons playing solitaire and planning for the new apartment we'd bought, which was being prepared to her specifications. Since our children, all except the youngest, had gone their ways, Molly thought of this apartment as our last home and final resting place.

Molly, of course, knew nothing about the recent event in the city where our apartment was being prepared and what had led up to it. An expert dissembler, with a lifetime of practice, I'd covered my tracks perfectly. What had been most effective in the deception was that I no longer gave a damn if I was caught. The singular aspect of the situation was that I took it in stride. I'd become so accustomed to a life in layers that nothing could penetrate my indifference to personal danger and possible disruption. I'd anesthetized myself.

I H A D other problems, pressing just as hard. I'd agreed some months before to undertake, with Bob Whitehead, the position of coproducing director of the repertory theatre the Lincoln Center people hoped to set up as part of their clutter of cultural buildings on the Upper West Side. Almost as soon as I'd agreed to take the job, I wanted to be relieved of it. I've never been an office animal. I don't feel more powerful, wiser, happier, or more reassured sitting behind a desk. I certainly didn't want to play daddy to a drove of nervous actors—even though I was fond of them all individually. For a few weeks, fine. Permanently? No, thanks. Also, there are very few plays I like and never "period plays," never revivals. I knew all that about myself, but fought off my negative feelings, told myself they were nothing more than the doubts all directors feel the morning after they've signed to do a play—no matter how good it is.

The fact is I was silencing my instincts' protest. I thought my uncertainty improper for a man who'd turned fifty. I told Molly (who'd been urging me on, saying that this would be the apex of my career) that she was right. After all, my entire theatre training had prepared me for this job, to guide a permanent company of actors. So I silenced my heart, enjoyed the publicity, the power, the being sought after. I played the role of the theatre big shot perfectly.

My appointment was generally praised—at first. But I was soon to see for myself that the people who had criticized my selection were right. I had no experience in the production of classics. Or liking for that kind of theatre. I had strong feelings and a passably good eye but very little ear and a limited intelligence when confronted with a page of Shakespeare. I was skilled only in directing contemporary plays with contemporary themes that I subscribed to and with flavor (the talk) that I knew well. This was my special deficiency for the job at Lincoln Center.

When I felt a twinge of these doubts, I would dissemble. When Bob Whitehead reads this, even now, he may exclaim, "I had no idea!"

B U T   M Y   misery those years was deeper. I was in revolt against my way of life, my respectability and that of the wife I loved. Against our orderly and proper way of living. I longed for what I can only call chaos. I kept feeling I was in the wrong place, doing the wrong things with the wrong people. I had to strain to sit still across from the good friends Molly would invite to dinner, and would chafe at the conversation on culture, politics, and the arts that followed the meal. By the end of the evening, my smile had frozen. I felt that all the conversation we'd taken part in was the same as all the other conversations we'd taken part in, that all our friends were in constant and inevitable agreement on any and all subjects. I could always anticipate what they were going to say. They were, each of them, "on the side of the angels," and their views were fixed. No doubts were ever raised.

I, on the other hand, was on the side of the devil.

I'd drink too much and long for the taste of the streets again, of the gutter, the dark hotels, the cities where I was not known. Oh, to start over and live a totally different life! Some nights I'd break out of our home, looking for I never knew what, or where I might find it. More often than not, I'd end by calling my "girlfriend" (who was later to be my second wife), summon her out of her home. We'd walk the streets, sing and dance on the sidewalks, end by fucking in alleys, in the back rows of movie theatre balconies, and on park benches, in the summer on the roof of my apartment house, in the winter up against the radiator in the entrance of the building where she lived.

Was I hoping to be caught? I didn't care. Something had to happen, something dramatic. And soon! I was trapped in my "success." I hated the sound of cultured voices, heard them against the cries of anguished unrest within me.

I knew I needed help. I'd had the attention of one psychoanalyst a few years before, gone to him only because Molly said she'd leave me if I didn't. He was cultured and cuddly, and his wife drank too much. When she had to be assisted up the stairs and to bed halfway through dinner at his apartment, it caused me to wonder how a man who hadn't been able to help his wife could help me. I dropped out.

But now I knew I had to have help; my life was a mess. My second analyst was tall, grave, and austere and, as far as I knew, had no woman. At my urging, he was ruthless with me—that is, truthful. His observations sometimes reached the level of contempt. But I swallowed my resentment:

I'd asked for it. "How the hell did I get into this mess?" I demanded. "And why don't I like whom I've become? Tell me."

He did. He exposed my dissembling, small and large, pulled off my masks and kicked over my poses. He said I lied to myself, constantly, even as I told others the truth. He said I was constantly betraying my true feelings to please others, that most frequently I didn't say what I felt, only what was useful to say.

But he didn't condemn me. That wasn't his technique. He only did, and did thoroughly, what I'd begged him to do. He told me the truth as he knew it, and I accepted it.

One day he surprised me by saying that my longing to disrupt my life was the best thing about me. He said I'd spent my adult years (I was fifty) pleasing, winning, convincing, placating, selling others, doing what was asked and expected of me, never—not ever—doing what I wanted myself. Always others! No wonder I was angry.

He wasn't impressed with my professional achievements. (The first analyst I'd had said, in effect, "Why are you so concerned? After all, you're a completely successful man with a great career, a fine wife and family, and"—he didn't say this—"enough money to pay me every week.") I didn't defend my work. On the contrary, I said that the most painful thing about my situation was that I didn't like and no longer enjoyed my work, and that for some years I'd been unable to arouse any enthusiasm for the plays I'd been doing. I'd become a technician, very skillfully going through the motions and doing the job. Molly was fond of saying I could make a show out of the telephone book. I told the man how little I'd thought of MacLeish's *J.B.*, which I'd directed and which had won a Pulitzer Prize. "Then why did you do it?" he asked. "Molly liked it," I said.

After a few months, he told me that although I'd successfully impressed a great number of people with the plays and films I'd done, my best and truest material was my own life: my parents, my childhood, my dreams, my intimate life, the desperation and panic I felt. "And your past," he said. "You're not quite an American, are you? You've never spoken to me about that, of who you are. Why don't you look at it? Doesn't it interest you?"

I didn't know what to answer. Why had I never talked about that, why did I ignore those sources for films and plays and books? Those experiences were the ones I knew best, and felt deeply about. Why had I devoted myself to other people's themes and concerns and lives? These could not possibly be identical with my own, so how could I feel an emotion about them? He agreed; I'd just been going through the motions. I was guilty of the worst kind of betrayal: self-betrayal.

He left me like a jigsaw puzzle flung out over a table in disorder. Could I put it back together?

I didn't know if I could. I often felt painfully discouraged. But increasingly, as the weeks passed, he encouraged me to discover some respect for myself. One day, seeing that I was very low, he laid a compliment on me. "Under the ashes," he said, "there are still live coals." He diverted his interest, made new inquiries, began to ask about my parents in particular, what they were like and what I was like with them. "What went on between you?" he asked. "You never speak of them. It's unnatural."

I told him that while I was very close to my mother and would not have amounted to anything without her, I'd never in my life had a frank conversation with my father. My analyst wanted to know how that could be. I couldn't say, except that I was frightened of him.

"All your life?" he wanted to know.

"Even now. Today," I said. "And when you're frightened of someone, you resent him."

"But don't you owe him a great deal?" he said.

"What?" I said. "My fucked-up character?"

"What I meant was that he brought you to this country, didn't he? Where would you be now if he hadn't?"

I didn't answer.

He looked at the watch on his desk. He had a trick of letting our conversation collapse as we neared the end of the fifty-minute hour. He'd sigh, then rise, slowly, heavily, from his chair, a tall, gray man, neither kindly nor unkindly, neither friendly nor hostile.

I got up. "I'd probably be in some dusty alcove store in the Istanbul bazaar, waiting for customers." I laughed. It was ridiculous to imagine that now.

When I was sixteen, I bought an old car for twenty-five dollars—ever hear of a Maxwell? I knew my father would forbid it, so I kept it in a patch of woods at the bottom of our road. The Maxwell behaved erratically. When I'd turn off the ignition switch, its motor would continue coughing and pumping to fire its guts, stopping dead, then starting up again. I was like that with this analyst after I left his office; I'd keep on talking to him. "I know something you don't know," I said this time, "which is that the only good basis for a film or a play is a central character who's split, where there is a conflict within him and within the author about him. 'Ambivalence' is the essential word. I'm still scared of my father and you can't be scared of someone and feel compassion for him. I have only one emotion when I think of him, and it's not love."

Then I'd speak for my analyst, not present. "What makes you uncomfortable to talk about is what you should be writing about or making films about." "Fuck you," I answered. But he went right on: "You can always tell when a subject is good, because it disturbs you to talk about it. As the Jews say, 'Everything good hurts.'" "I don't want to write about my family," I said. "That's kitchen drama. *I Remember Papa*. Trivial!" Unfazed, he went on. "The most personal," he said, "is the most universal." He must have said that to me twenty times, and I still wasn't confident I knew what it meant.

At this time, my father was in the last year of his life. He'd developed Parkinson's disease, and his hand never stopped quivering. He no longer commuted to Manhattan, had given up his office there years before, so lost touch with his fellows in the rug trade. In New Rochelle, a friend with whom he used to play bridge regularly urged Mother not to allow her husband to play cards anymore because his mind was going and some of the men around the table were taking advantage of him. His old bridge associates had talked it over, the man said, and decided to find excuses for no longer inviting him to their games. Father didn't know their reason, and there was no way he could be told, so his suspicions mounted and his hostility. Suddenly friends of thirty years were "those damn Jews."

He found out that his wife was taking money for household expenses from his sons, and he considered it an insult. In a great burst of emotion, he yelled at me, "I don't want your money, I don't need your money, I have enough money!" I remember that despite the fact that his face became white and tense, despite that I knew his strength was going fast, I still felt the quiver of fear I'd known so often when I was a kid.

I remember when I was in my first teens, how I used to wait in my room at the top of the house, watching from my window until the taxi that he and his commuter cronies engaged to take them to the railroad station every morning had come by and carried him off for the day. Then, with the terror in the house lifted, I'd gallop down the stairs, gulp some breakfast, for it was late, then run the mile and a half to school. When I'd come back at three-thirty, the house was quiet and I'd read, but as the afternoon wore on and the time for him to return from business (or from the horse track) came close, the tension in the house returned. My mother would be in the kitchen making his supper, then in the cellar; I could hear her shaking down the ashes in our furnace and shoveling in more coal, while my brothers and I waited for the inevitable, Father's return at seven. If he'd had a good day with the out-of-town buyers (or at the track), he'd bring home a melon or some white seedless grapes, kiss "Sweet Abie," pinch my cheek between the knuckles of his first and second fingers, then fall into the chair at the head of the dining room table, where the ouzo bottle was uncorked. The drink was a relief and a lift, but it also showed how tired he was. He'd devour his dinner, while Mother stood attendance at the side of his chair until she was sure he was satisfied. My brothers and I would eat but not speak; talk wasn't allowed at the table, not from us. "What's your news?" he'd ask Mother. She'd answer, "The same, George; nothing, George." At breakfast he'd ask the other question: "*Tee-ee-neh-to, programma-sou?*" Of course, this was mocking too. He knew very well that she had no "program," except to do the same work she'd done the day before. That was the extent of the conversation. After his dinner and his coffee, he'd plunge onto the parlor sofa and sleep. For fifteen minutes. Then, in desperate need of relaxation and pleasure, he'd be off—if we were lucky—to play cards at someone else's house. And ours was quiet again. Mother and I would sit side by side, reading until we fell asleep.

Not until the end did I see his side of it. Only then did I ask myself how a man so chronically exhausted could possibly sit still to read a book or talk to his wife, or his kids. What would he talk to her about? His daily struggle to put some dollars in his pocket? What did Mother know about that life? What the hell did I, a boy so innocent of life as it was lived in the market-place, expect of him? What would he talk to me about—my Maxwell?

He had some modest savings, but they'd been salted down in life insur-ance, in Mother's behalf, which his sons were protecting against the day they knew was coming soon. He also had a safe-deposit box in the subcellar of the Empire State Building, which he'd go on about. After his death, we opened it; there was nothing there except expired insurance policies, some worthless stock, junk jewelry, and one locket that belonged to his grand-mother and had only personal value.

His protest against our money was his last great explosion. He gave up; he must have seen that it had been ineffectual. There was no way to tell what he felt, because when it was over he said nothing. But I could see that he'd surrendered his pride. From that day on he shrank. He slumped in his seat and seemed to be waiting for the end.

W H E N Father had first come to America, he must have felt that he was still in a hostile and threatening environment—after all, he could not speak the language—so he continued to behave in New York as he had among the Turks, guarding himself to be circumspect, always beyond criticism on the streets and in the marketplace, always ready with his smile of compliance. He'd learned to get by on his cleverness and never say anything that might be misinterpreted. He learned to survive by cunning, by guile, and by restraining his real reactions. He couldn't afford to behave truly on the streets or in his store. He had to please and flatter his customers. A sales-man has to sell himself before he can sell his goods. He preserved his life by pretending respect for what he feared and even despised. In Turkey, he'd learned what Anatolian Greeks learn: how it was necessary to be in order to survive.

All this technique of getting along Father had communicated to me by example. Despite everything, he'd been my model. As well as by the only spoken bits of advice he'd ever given me: "Mind your own business" and "Don't start up arguments" and "Walk away from a fight." Out in the world, Father couldn't afford anger. When someone tried to involve him in a con-troversy, he'd escape by saying, "I know nothing."

Of course, all this dammed-up anger had to come out somewhere, and it did, at home, against his wife and his offspring, particularly the one who'd disappointed him by not observing the tradition that sends the eldest son to his father's side in the family business. Rather, that damned fool boy had sought another way, which, at the time, appeared to be insane. When I told him I was entering the Yale Drama School, where I would study acting, his response was: "Didn't you look in the mirror?" I would resent that for years, just as he resented me for walking away from him when he needed me in his store. Even late in life, when he used to carry clippings about my shows in his pocket and make purposeless trips to New York on the commuter train so he could show these clippings to his old friends, I pitied him but still didn't love him. It would be years before I did, and it came about only when I'd made a voyage back to where he was born and brought up, and where I'd had something of the same experience that he'd had. But by then it was late, almost too late, and I was left with a persisting regret that I had never come to know my father.

I READ photographs; for many years that was my profession. Here is the first one I have of Athena Shishmanoglou, my mother. She is the determined-looking infant on her mother's lap. Notice her mouth. Do you detect a stubborn streak? It will serve her well.

This is the Shishmanoglou family a generation after they'd come to Constantinople out of Kayseri, in the backcountry of Turkey. Read the photograph with me. Isn't there something "Western" about this family? What is it? The clothes they're wearing? The quality of the background and furniture? Or the unclenched postures of their bodies? What struck me most was that they're all touching each other and especially that the eldest son's arm and hand are on his father's shoulder. Clearly there was love and trust there. Altogether you can see they were a devoted family, at ease with each other. In the U.S. now, the members of a family separate as soon as they can put together the airfare.

The head of the Shishmanoglous and his oldest son are wearing fezzes, the head cover of their Mohammedan oppressors. And indoors—which is the Mohammedan way. I've tried one on. A fez is hot. It doesn't protect the nape of the neck from the sun or shield the eyes from its glare. But all the Greek men of that time and place wore them. Why? A captive people since the fall of Constantinople in 1453, their tactic for safety was to blend in with the Turkish population. I've found evidence of deeper accommodations to the conqueror's culture. My mother's grandfather's first name was Murda. My mother's grandmother's "Christian" name was flamboyantly Turkish: Sultana. The family Bibles—I have one—were in Turkish. In Kayseri, the women stayed at home for the most part, but when they went out they covered their faces as did the Turkish women, and they stayed within the bounds of the Christian neighborhood.

The men, on the other hand, were everywhere on the streets, rubbing shoulders with the Turk, trading with him in the bazaar, competing with him and usually winning. But from the instant they walked out of their front doors, they said hello and goodbye in Turkish. On the streets they wore a mask of deference. They survived by "passing." The tactic persisted when some of these people came to America. In New York, many merchants in the rug trade had family names of Turkish derivation but concealed their Christian forenames, even in our polyglot city. By compressing them into initials. My father's brother, the man who brought us to America, was known in New York not as Avraam Elia Kazanjioglou but as A. E. Kazan. His nickname was Joe. What could be more American?

You who live in safety may call this self-betrayal. Don't be so superior. I've noticed the same kind of thing here among many other races and peoples who changed their names in order to "fit in." I've come to question last names. Many people in this democratic society still wear the fez.

The photograph of the Shishmanoglous was taken in 1889. The family had come out of Anatolia (you call it Asia Minor), I don't know precisely how many years before. *Anatolia* is the Greek word for "East," and from before Homer's time, people thought of the regions that darken before their own as mysterious and threatening. In the West, the golden light endures. Apollo, the sun god! Civilization!

Arriving in Constantinople, the men of the family prospered. The Greek Orthodox Church of the area had its headquarters in that city, and the Hellenic culture, industrious, international, mercantile, was the dominant one. Greeks were the majority of the urban population, and their cunning became legendary. The successful Greek traders of recent times (Onassis) came out of Anatolia or from the islands close to the shore of Turkey, but rarely from Greece proper. Their marketplace victories caused resentment as well as admiration; another reason for minimizing their differences and disguising their identities.

Mother's father is the man in the father's chair. His name, Isaak Shishmanoglou, is made up of a Christian forename and a Turkish descriptive package. Shish-man-oglou is a run-together of three Turkish words to mean "fat man's son." Isaak, of course, is out of the Old Testament. Athena's mother was Anna Karajosifoglou, which means, if you take it apart, "black" (Kara), "Joseph" (Josif), "son" (oglou)—Anna the daughter of Black Joseph's son. I knew my maternal grandfather for a few weeks when I was four years old, and I think of him as a gentle person. I didn't know my maternal grandmother, who'd died early, but to judge from this photograph, she was rather severe. Can you see that? The gentleness and the austerity?

The eldest son, Odysseus, standing behind his father, hand on his shoulder, didn't prolong his schooling but entered his father's business. That was the tradition, and he complied with it. The second and third sons were sent to German universities—in those years a German education was the most respected. When they graduated, they entered the family business. Importing cotton goods from Manchester and the English Midlands, they found outlets throughout Anatolia and quickly became affluent and respected.

Athena was born in Makrikeu, a predominantly Greek suburb of the capital city of Constantinople. *Makri* is the Greek word for "far." *Keu* is the Turkish word for "village." In this name, too, the cultures overlapped. Distant village? Distant as space was measured in their day but, when I made a visit in 1960, a twenty-minute cab ride from the center of Constantinople. The community, orderly rows of medium-size homes, sits on the shore of the Sea of Marmara and is about as far west as Turkey extends.

Athena was put to school with the nuns, young French and Italian women who wore soft gray vestments. As soon as she learned to read, she made reading a habit—in her very last years I recall her, always a book in hand. When she was a girl she read about America, and that roused a will to go there. But also something mysterious, an unexpected independence.

A kind of daring sparked in the girl. Her school building was on the edge of the sea, and it had a bathhouse at the end of a narrow pier, a small, square structure over head-high water. In the summer months, the young nuns bathed, changing in the windowless huts, then descending an interior ladder to where, shielded by a crosshatch grille, they dunked themselves without leaving the enclosure. But Athena and another student would pass through a trap exit and strike out for deep water. It was, in that culture, an act of bravado.

After Athena there'd been another pregnancy, Anna Karajosifoglou's seventh. She gave birth to a son, then died. I don't remember an explanation of what brought her down. People died more easily in those days.

After his wife's death, Isaak-pappou retired. Finding he no longer had a stomach for business, he threw it to his sons so he could spend his last years enjoying the ease he'd earned and the company of his favorite, Athena.

He'd wait until her school let out so they could do the family shopping together. Though it wasn't as quickly or as efficiently done at that hour, it was far more pleasurable. It often took the best part of an afternoon, but father and daughter were in no hurry, not in each other's dear company. They went from stand to stand, until they found fish pulled out of the sea that morning, gills still red, and octopus that quivered, and squid glistening with life. They studied the lamb carefully; it had to be freshly butchered. Isaak taught Athena how to tell if it wasn't. The stems of the vegetables and fruit had to be green, not withered brown. After which Isaak would take his daughter to the *zacharoplastion,* the sweet shop, and let her choose anything she wanted. Athena was to recall the *lokum* in pastel colors, with pistachios embedded in the transparent jelly.

At night, in the house, there was music. His Master's Voice on the gramophone. There'd be an occasional evening at a theatre. Those were the years when French operetta companies toured, coming up from the cultural capital of the Ottoman Empire, Gevur Izmir—"Infidel Smyrna," so called because, as the puritanical Turk saw it, most of the Greek population there lived for pleasure. "Oh, those cafés where women misbehave! Oh, those *thé dansants!*" Even the inside of the cathedral, Hagia Fotini, glittered shamelessly with rare metals and precious stones.

But for the Shismanoglous there were, above all, the pleasures of family life. Before radio and TV, people entertained themselves. Each meal was a prolonged party, enjoyed slowly to stretch out an evening with talk and stories, new jokes and old parables, fables told to make children laugh before bedtime. That society might have reminded you of the old South of this country. There were servants to do the drudge work, Turks instead of blacks. The middle-class Greeks loved their servants and vice versa. My mother was born into a kind of domestic paradise. But it couldn't last, and it didn't.

Athena was naturally and simply in love with her father, appreciated his loneliness and gave him the devotion he needed, the kind only a young girl has to offer, bright as her eyes and peppered with just enough mischief. Athena was trained to love. When, in the years that followed, she didn't have what she'd had then, it was a lack she felt as a deprival.

Isaak never had the need to remarry. Now, for contrast, look at my other grandfather's family, in a photograph taken in Kayseri, a meaner, dustier environment. After his first wife died, grandfather Elia, needing to be married, quickly found a sixteen-year-old girl and "bought" her from her parents, accepting her without a dowry. Here you see the woman after she'd borne six children. You can read what that cost her. Evanthia was younger than she looked.

I've studied the faces of my two grandfathers. On Elia-pappou's face, I see that he was determined, crafty, stubborn, cunning, unwavering in desire, tough-hearted. He'd lived his life with his back to the wall, and it shows. He had no time for gentle concerns. Kayseri was not a place for

culture; the struggle was too severe. Elia-pappou passed those traits on to his eldest sons; I cannot remember my father reading a book.

Equally I am the grandson of Isaak-pappou, a man who surrounded his children with love, who was, at one point in his life, glad to throw over a successful business so he could enjoy the more "human" things in life, a man for whom family came first and who enjoyed the life of conviviality.

What Elia-pappou was and what Isaak-pappou was are the two sides of my character. As you might expect, they have at times warred with each other.

THE YEAR came for Athena to marry; she was eighteen and her girl-hood days were over. Her father and her brother began to look around for a husband. In the tradition, it was their duty.

And so her fate was decided.

Tolstoi uses that phrase in connection with his heroine, Natasha, in *War and Peace*. I thought the phrase excessive when I read it. Her fate? But in that society, at that time, it was precise. A simple decision by her father and her brothers would determine, at one stroke, the rest of Athena's life. She had little to do with the choice—well, judge for yourself.

My father, at age thirty-two, having decided it was time to marry and begin a family, returned to his native land on a buying trip while, at the same time, looking for a wife. Greeks did this, went back to the "old country" to find their wives. George was a handsome man in his prime and doing well enough in his brother's business, the Kazan Carpet Company, Inc., where he was second in command, to take this drastic step.

Here is their engagement photograph. She is nineteen. You can read the independence and the sturdiness there; my father was lucky. He'd found a good woman.

This is how the union was arranged. I have their own words, recorded a few years before his death, while she was still in excellent health and he was still able to remember parts of his life. I taped this conversation in my country home on a warm summer's afternoon, in a room with open windows through which a soft breeze flowed. My mother was unusually happy that day, my father a bit sullen. He didn't like to talk about the past.

I asked Mother how she'd met Father.

"How did I first meet you, George?" she asked. Father wouldn't respond, so she went on. "My sister had a summer place on the island of Prinkipo." (Leon Trotsky was living there at the time.) "George, so it happened, was looking for a wife. I imagine he heard about me, so he and his mother came visiting. It wouldn't have been proper without his mother."

"She was not my mother," George said. "Not my true mother."

Then my voice comes on the tape. "What did you think of him, Mom?"

"I thought he was a nice-looking young man."

I remember she laughed; it's on the tape, a jolly, confident laugh. But my father, who was sitting at her side, close to the mike, made a grumpy sound.

My mother went on: "Then he went to Father, I suppose, and asked to marry me."

Father spoke up, and his voice trembled. He had the Parkinson's by then and his strength was fading. "Some ladies," he said, and his voice quavered, "made the remark that I should cut off my mustache. And she said, your mother, 'Never mind, it's fine, leave it.'"

"You liked that, Pop?" I asked him.

"Why not? That's the first thing I remember about her."

Then my mother: "So later, when the summer was over, my father and I went visiting to my sister. She lived in Kadiköy, across the bay from Constantinople. And George made a visit there, again with his mother. He'd just come back from America and everybody was asking how it was there and George spoke very well. I remember how we all listened. Then we went for a walk, first time alone, he and I, went to the boat station to see the boat from Constantinople come in. And there was his cousin, waiting to take the boat."

"Not my cousin," my father interrupted. He sounded impatient. "My brother Seraphim."

"George waved to them, his cousin and his friends, they were. But they didn't come near us. So later, George told me he asked his cousin, 'What you think of her?' And his cousin said, 'She looks fine—from behind.'"

She had to stop because she was laughing so hard. She used to laugh a lot at that time of her life, though I don't remember her laughing much before my father was sick. Only after time had pulled his teeth.

"Later," she said, "your father told me that, 'From behind.' Yes, it wasn't his cousin, I remember that now, George is right. It was his brother Seraphim."

"That's what I told you, damn fool," my father said. He turned to me. "Always has her own ideas on everything," he said.

"We got engaged," she said.

"How did you ask her, Pop?"

"He asked my father," Mother said.

"I didn't ask him," my father said. "She forgot everything. Her father was too old. I asked her brother Odysseus; he was head of the family at that time."

"So what did he say?"

"He said they'd think it over," Father said.

"And then?"

"They began making certain inquiries."

Mother laughed like a young girl.

"What you laughing all the time?" Father said on the tape. "Am I telling it wrong? Then you tell it, how it happened."

"You're telling it all right, George."

"What kind of inquiries, Pop?"

"I don't know what her people talked about. What was there to talk about anyway?"

My mother picked up. "I remember they had family conferences. They wouldn't let me go in there," she said, "so I don't know exactly what they said."

That was the extent and intimacy of their courtship.

"What's the difference?" Father said. "It's all finished now."

"How about your family, Pop? They had conferences too?"

"No. Nothing. We hadn't brought them out from Kayseri yet. My mother died long before. And Father married right away, a sixteen-year-old girl, damn fool. They had six children already, and he's waiting—I mean at that time he was waiting—for my brother and me to send money."

"You supported your father?"

"Fine man. But business? Kaput! Nothing! He was selling charcoal at this time. A few rugs maybe, here and there. But charcoal. Made from fruit pits and so forth. Imagine! Also God knows what kind small stuff. Meantime, six children. Who knows, maybe seven by now, damn fool. . . ."

"George, that was long ago. He's dead, George."

"I know. I know."

From the picture of that family you can see how backcountry Father's family was, compared with Mother's. Coarser stuff. But it was precisely this hungry, unsettled quality that drove them to America. Athena's family had a comfortable and secure life within the walls of their home, so they didn't press to leave Constantinople. They lived through the turmoil of two wars, survived by locking the doors and bolting the windows. Their descendants are still there.

But the Kazanjioglous, one and all, made it to America. Only a couple of years after the family picture was taken, and almost immediately after George's engagement to Athena, the two brothers brought their father, his second wife, and their six half-brothers and sisters to Constantinople, which was a stepping-stone to America and to safety.

Later on in the tape, my mother confesses, "Before George, there was another young man asked to marry me. But my brother Odysseus, he knew this man and he didn't want him. He said, 'I wouldn't give my sister to this man!' He was a nice-looking young man, but he wasn't educated. He didn't have the ability to read much. So then George came and they had this conference. I wasn't there, but after, Odysseus told me, 'Yes, George, he's a fine young man.'"

"And that was it?"

"That's how it happened. See, those days, the young lady had to like the young man, but first the family had to like him."

Athena loved her family, and that made her a dutiful child.

"They asked questions about my business," Father said sourly, and turned his head away.

"George had taken them all out to dinner, I imagine, because Odysseus said, 'He knows how to make the money and he knows how to spend the money.' I remember that; they all liked how George spent money."

"So then he brought you to America?"

"Oh, no, not while Father was alive. That was the agreement. Father made sure of that. The idea was that George should stay in Constantinople and buy rugs for his brother's store in New York. If George had to go there on business, you understand, he would go alone. There was no idea then that I'd go to America and stay there; oh, no, not then."

"Would your family have agreed to the marriage," I asked, "if they knew he would take you to America for the rest of your life?"

"Maybe no," Mother said. "Father wanted me close. But I knew the day would come when he wouldn't be there, and I made up my mind, when that happened, I would go. Well, what else could I do? George?"

He'd fallen asleep. There the tape ends. I had a tennis game.

Fifteen days after they married, George received an urgent letter from his brother in New York, ordering him to come back immediately. "Business reasons," Mother said.

What she didn't tell me, because nice Anatolian girls don't, is that when he left her to go to America, he left her pregnant. With me.

I've often wondered what she thought of his abrupt departure. For "business reasons"? The only evidence I have of her buried feelings is the expression on her face in another photograph, taken shortly after her husband left her. She looks stunned. It had certainly happened quickly! What her life would be—her "fate" for the next fifty-two years—had been determined. Irrevocably.

Was he there when I was born? Not necessarily. Those were the big growth years of the Kazan Carpet Company, Inc.

I was named, as tradition required, after my paternal grandfather.

In 1912, Isaak-pappou died and Father was free to move his wife as he wished. My uncle in New York had the notion of setting up a rug-washing plant in Berlin—then considered a safe place—and he sent Father there, with his personal baggage, Athena and their son, Elia, to set it up. Uncle Avraam already had such a plant operating in Long Island City, with great success. It not only cleaned carpets but left them with the glossy finish American homemakers favored.

Father took an apartment on Bambergerstrasse, I had a German nanny, my brother Avraam (now a psychiatrist) was born there. The first fluid he took was not his mother's milk but, as was the custom, a teaspoon of good brown beer. At the age of three, I spoke German.

There we had a stroke of luck—though it didn't appear so at the time. It had quickly become evident that the taste of Berliners was not the same as that of Americans; Germans liked the more primitive colors and the coarser textures of rugs as they came off the loom. The plant failed and was aban-

The author

doned. Father quickly decided to move his wife and two sons to New York City. There was a rumbling premonition that a great world war was coming. We were hustled back to Constantinople while Father went to New York to prepare for our journey and arrival. He secured an apartment on Riverside Drive, then sent one of his brothers, the same Seraphim who'd said Mother looked okay from behind, to bring us across the sea. We left Europe a short time before "that damned foolish thing in the Balkans." Our history is one of moving from place to place, just ahead of catastrophe.

The snapshot on the next page was taken on board the *Kaiser Wilhelm*, the flagship of the German passenger service, which brought us to America. It shows a sailing-away party; they often had them in those days. The frightened little boy in the white sailor suit is the author of this account. In the middle of the group, dressed in black, is his mother. She is still mourning her father, as are the other Shishmanoglou women. At the extreme left edge of the picture is Athena's older sister, Vassiliki ("Queenie"). After that day, the girls never saw each other again.

Behind Athena's right shoulder, dressed in white, with a rather unbecoming white hat, is her best friend, Lucy Palymyra. She is the only friend I can remember Mother having—I mean ever!—and she is going with us.

I recall her story now as through a mist.

When Athena was a young girl, living in the suburb of Constantinople, her constant companions were the three little girls next door. She remembered them all her life, and their names were Dolly, Nellie, and Lucy Palymyra. Dolly and Nellie died young, at sixteen and fourteen. The Armenian doctor who tended the girls gave their parents this explanation: "It was natural for them to die." The survivor, Lucy, became the companion of Athena's soul. Lucy's health was uncertain too, and her body frail. Athena remembered that she was about to marry when all the other girls did, at eighteen or nineteen. But she or her husband-to-be called it off. Lucy never married, never had children.

She had Athena and Athena's children.

When her husband informed Athena that he was going to bring her to

America, she was ready for an adventurous change in her life. Years later, she told me she was eager to go because she believed her sons would have a better chance to become something in the States.

She asked only one thing of her husband. Since she was being separated from her brothers and sisters, perhaps for a long time (it turned out to be forever), and since she had no friends in the new land and didn't speak the language (as her husband did), she asked if she could bring Lucy with her. Lucy, she pointed out, would help her with the two boys.

The reason she did not mention was that Lucy would give her someone to talk to. She also did not say that she hoped a change of climate and better medical advice might reconstitute her friend's health. From time to time, Lucy ran a fever that no doctor in Constantinople could explain.

I have, as one of my brothers has often pointed out, a shameful tendency to ascribe unflattering motivations to my father's actions. I've wondered why he agreed to take Lucy to New York. Perhaps since he was bringing his brother and one of his half-brothers into our Riverside Drive apartment to live, eat, and be served, he figured that Lucy's keep would be less than what he'd have to pay a servant.

I know this next will seem unfair too, but I believe it: Perhaps Lucy's being there would relieve him of the burden of making conversation with his young wife. They had little to talk about. Later in life, one of Father's favorite observations about someone, usually a woman, an Armenian, or a Jew, was: "He talks too much!" or "She don't close her mouth five minutes!" and he'd make a little clapper gesture with his thumb and forefinger. Lucy's presence would keep Athena satisfied and, once out of the kitchen, silent.

Then there were the two boys to take care of. And, no doubt, more on the way. Birth control? I doubt whether, at that time, it consisted of anything more than not doing it. I once found some condoms in my father's bureau, but that was years later. Very likely Athena would soon be expecting again. She was.

Lucy's chief charge was me. I can recall her from those years, a tall, delicately made woman with a proud bearing and a face sensitized by pain. She had innate culture. I can recall her lovely voice; it eased my night fears and gentled me to sleep.

No sooner had my father brought her over than he resented her being around the apartment. Perhaps she was secretly scornful of him, did her best to control it, therefore was overly polite. Which, in turn, he took as a criticism of his own blunt manners, as he must have caught Lucy's quick glance, then downcast eyes, when he summoned his wife to attend him. "*Ah-thee-nah!*" he'd shout, in the way he'd been taught to command a woman in Kayseri. Perhaps he thought Lucy had a bad influence on his wife. He must have resented how close they were, because Athena remembered, years later, that he said they were always "whispering in a corner."

Finally he lost all control—perhaps he'd had a bad day at the store or the track—and spoke his mind directly, letting his feelings run unchecked.

Lucy left. I'd say "quickly," except where could a lone woman go quickly in an alien society, with no money in her purse and an uncertain command of the language?

This I remember: Suddenly she was no longer there.

She died in her mid-thirties, at a place in Long Island where she'd taken a position as nurse to a family with many children. The American doctor did diagnose Lucy's illness: tuberculosis. Which must have been what her sisters had died of. Athena went to Long Island, packed Lucy's trunk, and shipped it back to her people in Constantinople. She did not describe the details of that day except to say that the people with whom Lucy had been living were "very kind" and loved Lucy.

I can only imagine what Mother felt as she packed her friend's trunk. Now she was alone in the strange country. She never complained about it until the day she died, but half a century later, when she described the event to me, I could feel the bitterness still in her voice.

She once told me that Lucy and she used to sing together. In all my memory, I can't remember hearing Athena sing.

With Lucy gone, Mother turned to me. We entered a secret life together, which Father never breached. That is where the conspiracy began.

C O N S P I R A C Y ? A word with criminal connotations. Do I mean that word means? Of course not. But what would you call it?

Mother wanted to send me to the Montessori school. This had been

Lucy's idea, a gift in parting. I don't know how Mother convinced Father that it was worth the extra cost. Perhaps he was so busy, therefore so indifferent, that he let her have her way to silence her. Those were his big years, the mid-1920s. After a quarrel with his elder brother, Father was doing very well on his own. He had all his heft then and the confidence that a steady flow of money gives. The one education he did want me to have was religious. I can't explain this; he didn't go to church himself, but he insisted I attend a Catholic service every Sunday and once a week go to catechism school. At intervals I was asked to tell my sins to an invisible priest through a dark screen. I didn't have any sins to tell, so I'd make them up—I'd stolen a candy bar, I confessed. I couldn't just sit there in silence, could I? And masturbation I couldn't talk about.

In our tradition, children were, up to a point, a mother's concern. That point came when the son was expected to begin "learning the business." One of the first things I can remember my father saying to me was: "Who going support me my old age, my boy?" To which I'd answer, "I will, Pop, sure thing, Pop, don't worry, Pop." That was a pledge spoken out of fear, which I never made good on and never intended to. My mother had other ideas. So did I—although I didn't know what they were.

He'd turn to me in the evening. "What you been doing all day, my boy?" I'm sure it seemed to him that he'd been knocking himself out to get up the wherewithal, while the rest of us did nothing to help carry the load. It was during these years that he gave me a nickname: "Good-for-nothing." "Hey, Good-for-nothing, bring your bicycle here for God's sake, go down delicatessen, buy half-pound ham, half-pound tongue, I give these Jews coming play cards something to eat after I take their money."

I remember the cardplayers—dark, well-fed Jews for bridge; sallow, tangle-haired Armenians for pinochle; black Irish from across the street for poker. I particularly remember one night when one of them, a Mr. Metzger, chose to compliment Father on his wife. I suppose the man thought it was his social duty, although most of the players barely acknowledged her presence in the house. I recall Father's response: "She's all right, minds her business." This angered me, but like all fez-wearers, I concealed my resentment.

While he napped on the sofa—"Wake me up, fifteen minutes sure"—Mother and I cleared the dining room, covered the table with a soft velvet cover, and placed four ashtrays around its circumference. While the cardplayers portioned out the chips or the pads and pencils, and cracked open the new packs of playing cards, Mother and I would do the dishes, she washing, I drying. The plates having been put away in the cupboard, we'd move to the living room, sit close together—the younger boys had gone to bed—and we'd read. I lived through the adventures of Tom Swift, then on to O. Henry and so to *Treasure Island* and *Les Misérables*. I can't remember what she read, only that she'd soon be asleep. I'd go to her and gently lift the eyeglasses off the bridge of her nose, where they'd left a pink print. As I went on reading, the gruff sounds from the other room faded until I couldn't hear them. I learned there that I could always find the comfort I needed in books.

It was during those nights that I became her special child. Perhaps I represented what she thought she might have been if she'd not been swallowed alive by a marriage. And although I didn't know it yet, I did know that some way, somehow, I'd find my own life. We never spoke our hopes; they were deeper than that.

So we waited, and when I was twelve and we'd moved to New Rochelle, I had a stroke of luck—the accident of my eighth-grade teacher. Her name was Miss Anna B. Shank, and as much as anyone, she influenced the course of my life. She was in her late forties, which I considered very old indeed, and she took to me. Observing that the other kids did not and that I was so shy that I drooped, head down, in the farthest corner of her classroom, Miss Shank made me her cause.

Actually my head was down for several reasons she would not have suspected. One was that I was looking at the legs of a girl named Jacqueline James, the leading lady of my erotic dreams that year, my eyes fixed where her knees protruded from under the plaid skirt and above her rolled stocking tops. Miss James was the first of a long line of my "unattainables." I can't remember ever speaking to her.

Another reason my head was lowered and my palm over my face was that my forehead was a rich field of eczema pimples. I'd spend the first minutes of every morning "milking" these and would go, anxiously, into the boys' room between classes to check on them.

Miss Shank saw me in a purer light. A deep-dyed romantic, she was the one who told me that I had beautiful brown eyes. Twenty-five years later, having seen my name in a newspaper, she wrote me a letter. "When you were only twelve," she wrote, "you stood near my desk one morning and the light from the window fell across your head and features and illuminated the expression on your face. The thought came to me of the great possibilities there were in your development and . . ." And so on.

Here is my photograph from my high school yearbook. Can you see what she saw there? Neither can I. The subject of this photograph has all the rigidity of a piece of primitive African sculpture. It's a mask, not a person.

Miss Shank set out zealously to turn me away from the eldest-son tradition of our people and the expectations of my father, to steer me off a commercial course that would feature bookkeeping and accounting toward an education in what they now call the humanities. It was she who suggested Williams College. I'd never heard of the place, my mother had never heard of it, and I doubt that Miss Shank knew much about Williams herself. It just sounded right to her. Since it was far from home and my father's authority and since the suggestion came from the only admirer I'd ever had, I sent for their catalogue.

Miss Shank made the effort to meet my mother. It took quite an effort, because Athena, still new to the area, rarely left home except to shop. Miss Shank passed on to Athena the conviction she'd formed about my special worth, and they fused their hopes. The two women, agreeing on possibilities that only they could see in me, struck up a partnership. This secret union is the one I call the "beautiful brown eyes conspiracy."

You can see why I called it a conspiracy. My mother knew as well as I did that if Father found out we were talking about anything as counter to his wishes as Williams College, he'd quickly quash it. What happened from then on took place where it had to, in secret. High school for me consisted not of the four years I spent in classrooms as much as of the afternoons I passed on the wicker rocker on Miss Shank's front porch, listening not to useless information about geometry and biology but to the expressions of hope and confidence that came from her, and talking about the books she gave me to read, what they'd meant to her and what they'd meant to me.

My mother's resolve that I'd go this other, better course grew stronger. Miss Shank provided coaching and eager encouragement. Perhaps these loving loyalties were why women have always meant everything to me. There were many others, later, who educated me in what was important in life and left me with a heart full of hope and feeling. Many of the men I've liked best have had strong "feminine" characteristics: Tennessee Williams, Clifford Odets, Bill Inge, Robert Anderson, Budd Schulberg, Harold Clurman, Marlon Brando, Jo Mielziner, and others have had those same sympathetic yielding qualities. I've never warmed to the so-called masculine virtues; I've lived apart from the male world and its concerns. Men, I've found, despite their swagger and bravado, are far less sure of themselves than women and need more affirmation and support. The competition through which they have to make their way is more intense, often brutal. Witness their locker room boasts about deals, scores, victories, and sexual triumphs.

In my own field, the actresses I've worked with are, with the exception of one man, Brando, better artists, and that is because their feelings are concerned with their intimate life. Men have to be constantly proving something that is often not worth proving—their muscles, their fearlessness, their affluence, the strength of their erections. Men's clothes are pathetic efforts to dramatize their strength, their potency, or their business reliability. Women's clothes usually have a simpler and more important purpose, as you can guess from the speed with which they throw them in tangles on a chair or even on the floor when that purpose has been accomplished. Oh, how they leap into bed then, ripping off the last garment as they do! Meantime, a man may be carefully folding his trousers across the back of a chair or turning his socks inside out to air them.

Of course, from the time the conspiracy around me started and through the four years of high school, I always felt guilty in my father's company. In his presence I was "underground," turning my head away when he looked at me, carefully noncommittal when he spoke to me. I knew I was conniving to betray him.

I'd moved my bedroom to the top floor of my parents' home—a kind of half attic—so that as little as possible about me would be known. I remember there were mice up there, gnawing behind the floorboards at night. Since I didn't see them, I was frightened of them as they must have been of me. I worried constantly about my hair falling out; twice a day I'd rub a tonic into my scalp, then examine the comb for fresh evidence of approaching baldness. My pimple problem seemed permanent. Was it connected with the frequent wet dreams I had at night? I tried to conceal my emissions by jumping out of bed after release, washing the sheets, and spreading them on chairs placed before large open windows to dry. Sometimes, in the winter, the sheets froze.

What do I remember about my four years at New Rochelle High School? Not a thing—except fantasies, dreams, and worries. I don't remember a single teacher, a single course, a single grade from those four years. It's as if I were struck over the head with a heavy rubber mallet in 1922, knocked unconscious, then came to in 1926. What I do remember are my feelings: that I was a secretive freak, full of unexpressed longings, unrevealed crushes, jealousies equally unexercised, fears of intangibles, hopes crushed—all unnoticed by anyone, not by Mother, not by Miss Shank, not by the two male friends I had.

I spent afternoons after school in the stacks of the New Rochelle Public Library, reading books that might explain the intimate problems of my life. Or in the movie houses. Movies became my passion. They were dreams, like my dreams. I didn't have money, so I found a way to sneak into Loew's New Rochelle. When the exit doors were opened and everyone was crowding out of the theatre, I would slip in against the current of the crowd. I was quick and I was slippery.

What did I want of life? Nothing noble. But, passionately, to be an American, to have what American kids had, a daily life like theirs, to be accepted by them, to enjoy what they were enjoying—each other's company, cars, bell-bottom trousers, summer places, a pocketful of pocket money, a varsity letter on my sweater, to dance with a girl, to dance well, to neck with her later—nothing very noble, you see. Just the most ordinary, the most common, and the most precious things.

I was convinced Father would be opposed to everything I wanted most. He'd found the Maxwell one afternoon parked at the side of the house and ordered me to get rid of it. I obeyed—and for forty dollars bought a Hupmobile, which I parked deep in the woods a quarter of a mile from home. There it was dismantled, all in one night, and its parts carried away. Served me right.

I generalized from this disaster that the most precious things in life were forbidden by authority (my father) and that everything I wanted most I would have to obtain secretly. I learned to conceal my longings and to work to fulfill them surreptitiously. I stopped feeling guilty about the beautiful brown eyes conspiracy. It was necessary. From that philosophical conclusion it was only a short step to this one: What I wanted most I'd have to take—quietly and quickly—from others. Not a logical step, but I made it at a leap. I learned to mask my desires, hide my truest feelings; I trained myself to live in deprivation, in silence, never complaining, never begging, in isolation, without expecting kindness or favors or even good luck. To do without good luck! What a fate! To never expect an improvement! To consider rejection inevitable!

But I learned to keep coming back, to persist. I hardened.

And since what I wanted most I didn't get, not nearly, I learned to live as an artist lives, empathically, observing, imagining, dreaming, all behind the mask.

In my high school yearbook, at the side of all the other names on my page there are lists of activities and achievements. Opposite mine, nothing. A blank. I was known for not being knowable. For not revealing anything. I was a boy with no activities.

So what? I didn't care. The conspiracy was working. I was saving money for the first tuition installment. I worked waxing floors—forty cents an hour. I worked at a small truck farm across the road—fifty cents an hour. I caddied every afternoon I could at the Wykagyl Country Club, carrying the bags of middle-aged women in long woolen skirts—a dollar a round. I spent nothing. I didn't take trolleys; I walked. Everywhere. I have strong leg muscles from that time.

Miss Shank, Mother, and I, preserving our secret, applied for admission and talked secretly about the contents of the college catalogue. Williams would be my liberated life; I'd be on the right track at last.

Father must have suspected that something was not going the way he'd have liked, because he became more insistent that I come to the store during the summer vacation and learn the rug business. He paid me twelve dollars a week, most of which I'd save. You could get a sandwich at lunch for five cents in those days. I adapted one of his discarded summer suits for myself, ripping open the back seam, doing it myself—I learned to use needle and thread as well as any sailor—sewing it together to eliminate the fullness over Father's belly, wearing it with the side pockets back around my buttocks. The trousers? I simply pulled them together at the waist into great pleats with a belt. I wore Father's straw hat from the year before, the one he was throwing away. I must have looked a fright. I can still recall Father's personal odor, with which the suit's cloth was permeated.

It must have been evident to everyone at the store that I was going to fail to honor the eldest-son tradition. I'd sit in the back with the largest ledger open in front of me and, concealed in its fold, Samuel Butler's *Way of All Flesh* or Somerset Maugham's *Of Human Bondage*. I got caught reading, was called to the floor and given a broom. "Sweep!" When I helped open the carpets to show customers, I seemed to be in a fog. Often, I was spoken to and didn't answer. Feeling my father's wrath building, I did my best to pretend some interest in rugs. But it didn't work. Father referred to me as "Hopeh-less case!" I said nothing. I was learning to take punishment without defending myself or fighting back. I still do that.

Father stopped introducing me to his customers. He no longer said, "Charlie"—or whoever—"meet my son Elia." I didn't blame him. I knew that I was an embarrassment to him.

I had a cousin who worked there, my mother's nephew Evangelos, who was especially scornful of me. He didn't conceal his contempt of me, and I thought my father tolerated it. Evangelos had a prime position in the store's hierarchy because of his penis. I never saw this dangling appendage, but I was told that it was of a phenomenal length. It became famous in the trade, and Evangelos was much envied. He didn't mind, when called upon, showing it to my father's best customers. It was an entertainment that Father provided for his important clientele. They'd follow Evangelos into the men's room and come out a few minutes later, marveling. Evangelos would look at me with a smile, and I felt my member shrink. Father was congratulated often on his nephew, never on his son.

But I didn't care. The conspiracy was working. I'd sent in the admission fee.

After work, so I wouldn't have to meet Father's eye, I would often spend the night at my Anatolian grandmother's place. Evanthia was an old woman who attributed her long life to eating three cloves of garlic, raw, every day, dropping the nuggets like dope. I'd urge her to tell stories about the old country. Oh, how I marveled! How I laughed! I was at ease with her. I've always been at ease with old women, always found special pleasure in their company. But in a room with girls my own age, I couldn't get out a sentence. I'd sit there like the piece of African sculpture I mentioned, looking threatening, with a quavering, pleading heart.

Then the news came. I'd been accepted at Williams, class of 1930.

And we had to tell him.

She told him. Mother. I couldn't open my mouth.

He hit her smack across the face, knocking her to the floor.

I don't know, actually, whether he knocked her to the floor or whether she chose to fall there; it was the safest place.

This happened in the morning. That's when we had decided to tell him: after his breakfast, when he was waiting for the taxi that would take him to the New York train. That way there wouldn't be a long, awful scene. And he'd have all day to digest the news.

There was the taxi. Calling for him.

The horn sounded again and he left the house.

Mother got up from the floor. She wasn't hurt. She was triumphant. When you're hit this way, it's a tremendous relief; you've found that it doesn't hurt as much as you feared.

And you're never again quite as afraid of that person.

Six months later, I came home from Williamstown for my Christmas vacation—I'd skipped Thanksgiving—and the first person I encountered was my brother George. "What happened here?" he asked. "What happened?" I said. "They're sleeping in different rooms now," he said. "I don't know what happened," I said. "I think," he said, "it was something about you."

W H E N I gave Barbara Loden, my wife at the time, the manuscript of my novel *The Arrangement* to read, she had a reaction I didn't expect. An actress who didn't spare herself exposures that would have embarrassed lesser artists, she asked me, when she'd finished the book, "Why do you have to be so intimate?"

For the autobiographer it's a basic decision: Will he reveal facts and episodes that embarrass him or discomfort other people; will he name all names? At this point in what I'm writing, I had to make that choice.

When I was fourteen, something happened I've not told; in fact, I was going to leave it out. But since it affected my whole life, I don't know how I could and pretend I was telling my story.

It started as a swelling in my neck. Then it went lower. One testicle, I found, was tender. Then it began to swell. Frightened, I delayed telling my mother. We did not discuss such matters. There was no one I could turn to or consult. My father? This development would only have confirmed the impression he already had, that I was in some way, perhaps in all ways, deficient. So I delayed reaching for help. I waited and hoped for deliverance.

When the swelling increased, I believed that it was my fault. I'd done something wrong. What? I had no idea. Desperately seeking enlightenment, I hustled three miles to the New Rochelle Library and hunted in the stacks. I found nothing—this was 1924—to help me understand the seriousness of the infectious disease called mumps.

Soon my scrotum was stretched to its limit. What would happen, I wondered, when it couldn't stretch further? I still hadn't said anything to anyone, but when it reached the girth of a grapefruit, in desperation I called my mother's attention to it. "Look," I said. And showed her.

Modesty in our family was Old World; it was pathological. (I had no sister. I'd never seen a naked female body, not even that of an infant. My mother appeared before us always fully dressed. I saw her exposed for the first time in a hospital a few weeks before her death; only then.) My problem was well beyond the range of my mother's experience or knowledge. She sent for a doctor—doctors made house calls in those days—then moved me down a flight to a bedroom where she could bring me food from the kitchen more easily and tend to me at night.

The doctor said I should stay in bed and that the room should be kept dark. I thought this ominous; apparently my problem was as serious as I'd feared. What the doctor was concerned about, of course, was that the infection might spread to the other side. "Lie still!" I remember how he stressed those words. And to my mother, he said, "Don't let him get up, don't let him go to the bathroom. Buy a bedpan." His final injunction was to keep my brothers away from me. That went for my father too—but less. I didn't understand any of it; but I was very frightened.

He instructed my mother to get me support for my load, which was now enormous. And he left. Mother hurried to a drugstore and brought back a sling. Of course, she didn't help me put it on, did not make sure it fitted.

After that, it seemed to be a wait-and-pray situation. So I waited and (in those days I "had religion") I prayed. My mother served me faithfully, and no one of my brothers came to see me. Or my father. I was a pariah.

When the swelling finally went down, the doctor was relieved to note that the infection had not passed to the other side. But there was bad news too. The original size of the stricken nut was that of a pecan; the mumps reduced it to a fraction of that. And it was dead. I was to live with only one source.

The doctor had not offered words of reassurance—I was convinced I would never have children. But that wasn't nearly as important as the confirmation of what I'd believed: that I was sexually undesirable and inferior to other boys. In the lingo of my father's rug store, I was damaged goods. It would require years of misadventures to assure myself that I was not less than others.

I was a smart kid, and reading was my solution. I read the lives of the great artists and discovered that many talented people had had some physical deficiency. Wasn't Lord Byron clubfooted? Didn't Somerset Maugham stutter? Wasn't Homer blind? And so on. And on. Until the day, years later, when I said to myself, "Cut it out, kid, you're breaking my heart!" and the fort of self-indulgence collapsed in laughter.

I still had the crush on Jacqueline James (she was always loving in my dreams). Then I heard rumors—oh, how they ate my heart!—that she "belonged" to Vin Draddy, the glamour boy of our football team. Sick with envy, I followed them when they walked down the halls, studied the looks that passed between them, cursed my "deficiency." I kept imagining them together and what they'd do—although I knew very little about sexual joining.

Here's what I knew: One day I'd found a thin pamphlet on the bureau in my bedroom on the top floor. It looked like something my mother would buy—demure, discreet, not explicit, unillustrated. Rather bashfully, it provided the minimum. Even I knew it was incomplete.

Then there was another rumor—the "Boys" was alive with them—that Vin was "doing it" with a Japanese girl in the class below ours. I studied Jacqueline for her reaction. "Oh, if I had you," I vowed to her (silently), "I'd never look at another girl!" I couldn't imagine how even a football hero, who could have any girl he wanted, would prefer another girl to Jacqueline James.

Bit by bit, the drama of sex was becoming the greatest drama of all for me. My imagination fed on it. All boy-girl relationships were magnified in my mind. But as for action? I choked. Anxiety played the game as a spectator sport. But what a passionate spectator I was!

I used to go to the movies most every afternoon after school; I never missed a show at Loew's New Rochelle or RKO Proctor, sneaking in as the first matinee crowd let out. I'd search up and down the aisles for a row behind one where the high school girls had swarmed, and I'd watch them frolic, whispering and giggling, squirming and hugging, crossing and uncrossing their long legs, their skirts far above their knees. I watched their pert, taunting profiles as they turned to whisper to each other, and I tried to make out what delicious secrets were being passed between them— while all the time pretending to watch Joan Crawford on the screen.

As I've said, I don't remember much about my life in high school, but I do remember clearly a scene in a suburban parlor to which my friend Bill Fenton had taken me. I remember sitting at one end of a long, darkened living room, with my arm around the shoulders—no, lower!—of a girl named Julie Webber. I remember she had her hair in very tight curls fixed in a kind of stiff jelly and that she exuded an antiseptic odor; a decent girl, she aroused nothing in me. At the other end of the darkened parlor, my friend Bill sat with Julie's younger sister, Marguerite, a blonde with that air of taunting mischief which devastated me. They were necking. And that is why I'd come along: to sit perversely frozen with Julie, watching her sister, Marguerite, for whom I was ravenous, carrying on with my friend Bill.

In a desperate attempt to gain prestige, I did something freakish: I went out for football in my junior year. It seemed to be the one sure road to social status. I weighed one hundred thirty-five pounds that year, and our coaches must have been either sadistic or very hard up for bodies, to accept me on their squad. I was assigned the position of substitute center on the third team and provided with equipment—reinforced pants that drooped halfway to my ankles and shoulder pads far too broad for me. At the end of a long afternoon, as the light of day was fading and after the first team had battered the second team into the ground and exhausted what resistance the sounder bodies of the third team could offer, I was inserted at center to be run over. I took my beating; I was always good at that. Finally someone in charge had a humane impulse, and I was made an assistant manager, whose job was dashing out on the field with a bucket of water and some towels every time there was a break in the action. I was happy for this privilege.

At the close of my junior year, I had a pleasant shock. A girl named Marjorie Valentine asked me to take her to the junior prom. My reaction to this invitation was equally delight and fear. I wasn't sure I was up to it; I was apprehensive about what Marjorie might call upon me to do. But Miss Anna B. Shank urged me to go, so I bought two tickets, put on my blue serge "Sunday suit," and called for Marjorie at her home. She was a girl with a reputation; she went with all the boys; it was a great drama that she'd turned to me.

After it was all over, I got the story. Marjorie had been unsuccessful in pursuit of the boy she wanted. She needed to be at the prom, where he'd certainly be, but didn't want to go with anyone who might cause him to doubt the disposition of her feelings. Going with me, I realized later, was the equivalent of going alone.

I can recall the moment when she asked me to wait at the top of the staircase leading down to the gym, where the prom was being held, while she went to the bottom and stood, legs parted, against the bright lights of the dance floor. "Tell me if you can see through my dress," she said to me. She stood against the flare of the polished floor for a moment, then looked up at her eunuch for his verdict. I was thrilled. It was the greatest intimacy I'd had with a girl during my three years of high school.

I hurried down to give her my judgment. Dropping my voice, I said,

"Yes, you can, I mean I could, I mean yes, I can." I was quite prepared to take her home and bring her back more modestly dressed. But, to my surprise, she strutted onto the dance floor and signaled for me to join her. We had one dance—awkwardly performed—and that was the last I saw of her that night. The single turn around the floor must have been to convince the big catch that she was with "nobody." I went home alone.

That was my sex life during my junior year.

My senior year, as far as girls were concerned, was a wipeout. I'd given up.

R I G H T in there, I suppose, was when the fix happened. I fixed on the type of girl the other boys had had in high school and I had not. They were the flirts I yearned for then and, for lack of confidence and general anxiety about my sexual worth, did not go after and could not have gotten if I had. After high school, this perverse yearning did not let up. It continued into college and into my time in the theatre and in films. I can't imagine why it remained so fixed and so strong and lasted so long that I can call it an obsession—except that it first hit me when I was most impressionable.

Even long afterward, when the girls I wanted came easily, a strange thing persisted. If I hooked up with a young woman who reminded me of the girls whose sexual activities were legend in the halls of New Rochelle High, my old uncertainty would reappear. The women I wanted most passionately I pleased least. The prettier they were, those near-adolescent, smooth young bitches who sent my heart hopping, the less capable I was sexually.

On the other hand, if the lady was dark, decent, intelligent, sympathetic, compassionate, understanding, sensible, modest, and every way "good"— then I was confident and at ease, for what reason was there to be anxious? I would perfectly satisfy those women while pleasing myself less. Indifference made me a "better" lover. I might be transported out of my head by a Lilith who'd throw me a glance of "no interest," then, having pursued her, seduced her, forced her, or bought her, I'd find anxiety swarming through me like a fever and I'd "perform" miserably. All a woman of this type had to do to arouse my desire was indicate a doubt whether, if she had me, she'd like me. I was attracted by the promise of rejection and unmanned that way too.

What assured me finally was the devotion of my first wife, Molly. She made me feel completely worthy. Months before we married she became pregnant—a better reassurance than anything a doctor would have said. Through Molly I gained self-esteem when and where I needed it most. But that was 1932; before that there had been eight years of unspeakable torture.

. . .

T W E N T Y - F I V E years later, a big shot who'd directed Pulitzer Prize
plays and could hold an Academy Award in each hand, I was busy turning
the tables.

One night I ran across a screenwriter in Chasen's, a movie colony restaurant. An old friend, he had an attractive girl at his side; he generally did.
I'd seen their names linked in columns. I thought my friend's manner with
the young woman patronizing. I could smell his eau de cologne; it was
heavy. She was an actress, clawing her way up. I noticed that her eyes were
slippery. I told my friend I was staying at the Beverly Hills Hotel, and I
told him my room number. I didn't look at the girl. I knew her date couldn't
help her in her career, and I knew that she knew I could—if I chose to. I
felt some sympathy for her; I thought her companion had demeaned her.

An hour later, she did what I expected she'd do. "Why don't you come
over?" I said, and hung up. When we were having intercourse, I suddenly
stopped and asked her to make a call. "He may be worried about you," I
said. She didn't hesitate. "Tell him you'll be home in an hour," I said. The
phone was at the head of the bed. We didn't have to disengage. She passed
a few pleasantries, told my old friend she was on her way home, and that
she loved him. This last particularly pleased me. When she hung up, we
resumed.

There was revenge enough—for both of us.

Remember that for years, when I was a very young man, every time I
entered a bed where a girl was waiting for me I'd be entering a courtroom
where I'd lost many decisions. Doesn't every culprit wish to turn the tables
on his judge, deflate his eminence, show him up, kill him? Wasn't it natural, since women had once held so much power over me, that when the
tables were turned and it was I who had the heft, I'd want to gouge the
situation for all it was worth?

Well, I did. I specialized in taking women away from men, particularly
those handsome young fellows who played leading roles in films, tall and
well muscled, every way confident or seeming so—war heroes, horseback
riders, fast-car drivers, publicity gods. I wanted to prove that Vin Draddy
wasn't able to please a woman or hold her, not when I wanted her.

And I liked Vin Draddy, I really did.

As for the women, I wanted to prove them not worthy of trust, traitor-
ous. I never forgave Marjorie Valentine or forgot that night of the junior
prom. I examined every member of the opposite sex I met for indications
that she would be, if the occasion was right, unfaithful. Needing to prove
this, I often did. My guess more often than not proved to be correct. This
pleased me.

The fact is that I've generally found women quicker to "do it" than men—if the door has a lock. Often, when I came to know them, I discovered that a sex adventure was all they had on their minds. I was continually amazed by what women would do, and when and where. My satisfaction was to egg them on.

Am I exaggerating?

What about the intellectual lady, six months pregnant, doing it with me on the spur of the moment in the bedroom of the apartment she shared with her husband? And with his picture on the bureau, smiling at us from under his spectacles. This woman, known among us all for her loyalty to the genial failure who was her husband, was often quoted as saying that "anyone who doesn't like Charlie has something wrong with them."

I found many women were working off the same kind of thing I was. They were getting back at squadrons of men, and would go to extraordinary lengths to play out their grudges. Sometimes I thought they actually preferred breaking the marriage laws in their own beds. And if an infant, the fruit of the union, slept peacefully through it all in a gaily painted cot at one side, or even in bed with us, I got a special charge out of it. It proved what I needed to have proved twice over.

Don't get mad at me. I'm not really worse than most of you. Admit it. Besides, I'm penitent now. And faithful.

There was a long stretch of my life, unhappily, when I was not able to be faithful to anyone, not to a single woman, not to the best woman I'd known, my first wife, Molly. I used to assert—this was my rationale—that I was faithful to her in every way except sexually (actually I was), and I used to say that those "other ways" were the important ones. Did I believe that? I did.

But I know now why what went on went on, and what old grudges I was working off. I know now how much energy I wasted doing what I was doing. I used to spend half of every day figuring out the logistics of liaisons. I behaved during those years like a crazy man. Love had nothing to do with it. I exhausted myself, the best of myself. I soured my life. Before and between rehearsals, on the way to a "shoot" in the morning, a quick stop at a girl's place or in the limo with an actress, in the lunch break, in the dressing rooms, in the theatre's boxes between acts, in every hotel in the Times Square district—they're all marked in my mind. It never let up.

The energy and the time I wasted that way!

I'm not proud of those days.

Now, finally, with my third wife, having lived through seventy-eight years, I am faithful and I'm at ease. Every day seems twice as long and twice as good. I am home free.

And contented. For sure? Yes, I'm contented. But the charm of life, if you dare allow it, is that final positions tend to melt like ice sculpture under the sun. Time is an anarchist, and I've learned to distrust absolutes, especially—since I know myself better than I know the rest of you—my own.

There are days, sometimes just hours, when I look back at my times of arrogance, squalor, and excess and don't think of those times as wasted. I remember what fun they were and how educational.

But I don't want them back.

I N J U N E of 1980, having been invited to be the speaker at the fiftieth reunion of my college class—a choice I found surprising—I drove to Williamstown and, in a benign mood, stood before my surviving classmates and asked, "Do some of you really have a memory so bright that you can recall me in those murky years, 1926 to 1930? Because I spent most every hour of our time locked in my room or in the stacks of the library. I carried no varsity letter, played no role in Cap and Bells, didn't make Gargoyle. An obvious neurotic, apparently without the faculty of speech, I was known to be completely silent for days at a time. Naturally I was not 'rushed' into a fraternity; that would have been like inviting a ghost to haunt a house. Socially I struck out; through four years of holidays and celebrations, I didn't dance, not once. At your house parties, I stood behind a table in a white coat splotched with grenadine pink, my heart rotten with envy, and served spiked punch to your dates. Don't feel sorry for me: I did that for myself."

Williamstown was pleasant enough that summer in 1980, but in the fall of 1926, when I saw it for the first time, it was enchanting. There was a soft, cool breeze that day, and the sky was a deep saturation of blue near purple over low, ever-moving, cotton-white clouds. Looking between the buildings—some classic Georgian, others great lumps of gray or reddish stone—the eye found, at the end of each vista, the softly scalloped Berkshire Hills, called "the mountains." They embraced a broad valley, making it home. The buildings on the campus were well spaced, and between them lay generous lawns, perfectly green after an untrampled summer's growth. Upperclassmen were everywhere, reawakening old acquaintance; trim and healthy, they seemed happy to be back. Many sported stiff-visored caps like those of German drinking clubs—were they the headgear of secret societies? I wondered. All the young men were dressed in casually pressed trousers, flannel or corduroy, and soft woolen sweaters—the frost comes early in northwestern Massachusetts. Some boys, especially fit and broad-shouldered, wore heavy-knit black sweaters with large purple W's across their chests. These were the lettermen, athletes of the teams. Everywhere there was an atmosphere of privilege and affluence; in a bay apart from the storm, the elite was gathering.

I arrived accompanied by my parents. I wore my blue serge Sunday suit, purchased for me by my mother at Rogers Peet and still stiff across the shoulders. I'd topped it, for a reason I've never understood, with a copper-colored snap-brim felt hat; the effect was to make my sallow complexion piss yellow. I had new brown shoes, varnished rather than polished; having replaced sneakers, they pinched.

My mother looked particularly Old World by contrast with the Yankees of New England. Wearing a modest dark dress and a small black hat with a pin through its top, she peeped curiously through her glasses at everything and anyone around her. I realize only now what a thrilling moment it must have been for her.

My father wore his business suit, cut full at the waist to contain his pot, and a high, hard collar, clutching a bow tie of blue polka dots. He looked what he was, a small cosmopolitan importer, uncomfortable out of his environment.

Having inspected the room assigned me under the eaves of a freshman dormitory, having thrown a swift look out of my single window, he was eager to leave. When I informed him what my curriculum was going to be— Latin, math, French, English, and astronomy—his question was: "Why you not learning something useful?" He pronounced the word "useh-ful." He was disappointed that I had not chosen to go to a business college, considering which—this I didn't recognize until much later—he was a good sport to pay part of my tuition of four hundred dollars and leave his business to make the train trip to Williamstown.

"Come, Athena, we go," he said suddenly. "I find taxi, don't worry," he said to me. My father had absolute confidence that whenever he needed a train, all he had to do was take a taxi to the nearest station and the train would be waiting for him, going where he wanted to go. After a brush of his lips across my cheek, he left. My mother followed. I didn't hold their headlong departure against them. I'm ashamed to say I was embarrassed by their appearance and eager to have them gone. I wanted to be alone and to jump into the swim with the Anglos.

I quickly spent the money my mother had left me to buy the books assigned for my courses, but what I studied were the accounts of football practice in the college paper and the stories about the first games. I learned the names of all the athletes. Afternoons I'd go to the practice on Weston Field, a solitary spectator sitting on the top plank of the field bleachers, and watch every move on the field. Later I'd recognize the stars of the backfield, follow them along Spring Street to the Gym Lunch, order a "western on rye" to have the privilege of sitting in a corner and observing them; or go into Bemis's, if I saw them there buying books—they had studies too— to overhear their conversation. How confident they were, how glamorous, how awesome. They looked as if their glory would never die.

Now I must confess my foolishness. I had actually expected to be invited to join a fraternity. I can't say why I expected this, being what I was, looking like what I looked like, and having none of the popular attributes, but I did. I expected to be "rushed" into a Greek letter society; I waited for that.

There came the big week, those crucial days when the most attractive first-year men, the "aspirants," were invited to look over the fifteen competing Greek letter fraternities and judge which was for them—while they, in turn, were being thoroughly inspected. The best of our class—a star football player, for instance—were fought over, they were pressed hard. All around me, I overheard the talk of who'd been asked to join which "house," particularly of who'd been chosen by the top-rank fraternities, Alpha Delta Phi and Delta Kappa Epsilon. Once you were elected by either of these, you were a BMOC, a big man on campus, already a success and set for life. That week the college rattled with tales and secrets.

But for me there was the sound of silence—which is a sound, as you must know very well if you've ever heard it: the sound of activity elsewhere, in the distance, echoes perhaps, that is all, whispers that drop away as you come closer or a phone ringing far down the hall in another room, you hear it through walls and over the hiss of steam escaping the radiators. Footsteps approach, then go past your door. The great clock in the gym tower tolls time's measured passage, and the whistle of the wind emphasizes the zone of emptiness around you. That autumn there was no message for me from the fraternity brothers except the message of silence.

Having since had my share of failures in films, plays, and books, I've learned that when you don't "make it," you don't hear the bad news; you hear no news. You're passed by as a dead body is. The thing to do is forget, and I've learned very well how to do that. Now, looking back, I laugh and tell myself I was lucky not to be "pledged," but how crushing that silence was in '26. It hurt for four dark, cold years, and in the blackest part of my heart I still haven't forgiven the men who rejected me.

I remember wondering what the hell was wrong with me anyway. My looks? My goddamn foreign looks? Those Anglos making the choices, what did they think? That I was a Jew boy? Yes, I looked like one. Was that it? Jews and blacks weren't taken into fraternities at Williams in 1926. Or was it something about my character? Was I clearly a freak of some kind? Was it something I couldn't see or understand that made me so absolutely unacceptable? My jittery sexuality—had they sensed that? Or was it something simple, like my bowlegs, my acne, my big butt? What?

I never found out. I only knew I'd been turned away and that the streets seemed darker at night. I'd have to "eat" what had happened and find my own way to get what I envied. I began to exercise violence in daydreams and in impulses that I thwarted: broke down doors, climbed through window guards, stole, ran, punched, kicked, slammed heads on hard wood floors. Above all, I realized that I now had to persist with my own strength and my special cunning. From that week in 1926 on, I knew what I was. An outsider. An Anatolian, not an American.

For the first year, if someone I recognized was walking up a sidewalk toward me and I was walking down, I'd cross the street before the encounter so there'd be no chance he'd not acknowledge my greeting. Later I improved this technique: I never said hello to anyone; others had to speak first. I kept my eyes straight ahead and usually on the ground. I became stoop-shouldered.

I didn't recall it then, but I do now, a favorite phrase of my father's, *Guzumuz yok*, which is Turkish for "We have no eyes." And that means: "We do not feel because we do not see slights, insults, and provocations. That is how we stay alive and continue here." At Williams I survived by *guzumuz yok*.

I lived alone that first year, had no friends. There was one good development: I decided to relieve Father of my dependency. I'd soon be asked to pay another bill at the Commons Club dining room. Father's feelings being what they were, I didn't want to elbow him for the money; I couldn't say, "Help me do what you don't want me to do." So I took the first step toward being free of him: I got a job waiting tables at the Zeta Psi fraternity. I learned how to clear a table six plates at a time.

This had another motive and another merit: It brought me into the company of others. Probably it was the only way I could have gotten with other boys just then, serving them their "shit on a shingle," corn muffins and apple jelly and the great pitchers of milk. It worked. I felt part of something for the first time; no matter that it was in a subservient position. I was still alone, but I found my own kind of swagger. Below-the-stairs pride—is that what the English call it? I wore as few clothes as possible and never a hat. My light overcoat, with no sweater under it, buttoned to the neck, I walked through snow in sneakers to serve the Zetes their breakfasts. Sometimes the wind-driven sleet stung like frozen tears, but I gloried in my ability to endure discomfort. I told myself I didn't want the raccoon-skin coats many of the other boys wore.

My clothes, my hands, and my hair smelled of dishwater and of souring garbage. When I'd mop the drip of a head cold by running a sleeve under my nose, I'd smell our kitchen. Perversely, I was proud of that too.

My salvation was the college library. I lived in the stacks, like a small animal finding refuge in a mass of brambles. I'd take out books by the bagful, read late at night and between classes in the day. Books were the solution to my life. I lived along with the authors of the great novels; by the light of their stories, I understood the drama of my own life.

Through all those days, I had one enduring friend, my mother. Every Monday I'd mail my soiled underclothing, socks, and shirts home in a laundry bag, and she'd mail them back, fresh and clean. That was the event of my week, the arrival of the laundry bag on Friday. In among my clothes there'd be bits of home cooking: baklava, white meat of chicken, grape leaves wrapped around spiced rice, brownies; always something. And a note: concern for my welfare, pride that I was where I was. And always a dollar or two, pocket money. She never failed me.

In time I began to see that I wasn't the only "freak" in Williamstown.

Others had taken the vows of solitude, lived in isolation and enforced celibacy, with only their animal pride for defense. Not that we quickly became friends; we were too wary for that. But it was good to know that they were there, a sort of underground.

There were three blacks in the class of '30. At graduation, one was our valedictorian, another our salutatorian; the third was number four in the class. They must have needed friends but seemed to be separated even from each other. I felt I understood them, both their need for others and their isolation. Years later, when my first book, *America America,* was published, on the dust jacket there was a quote from Jimmy Baldwin: "Gadg, baby, you're a nigger too." At Williams during those years, I was a nigger too.

The girls I dreamed about were at the Zeta Psi house party, the same girls I didn't have in high school. Now fully matured, they had an aggressive playfulness I rarely see in older women. They were far livelier, far bolder, as well as far prettier. Standing at service over the two punch bowls, one spiked, the other not, I'd select the girl I wanted most and keep my eyes on her all evening, observe where she went, whom she danced with, particularly those boys not her date. Did she like someone better than the big man on campus who'd brought her? Good! "Just you wait, kid! My turn's coming!"

Desire blended with anger. I'd do extra service, come back at dawn over the crackling snow crust and rearrange the dining room to serve breakfast. I'd find the girls, still in their party frocks, sprawled in disorder over the living room and in the corners under the stairs, the boys alongside, and everywhere the smell of stale applejack. I'd look for the girl whom I'd been following with my eyes the night before and from her position and company, re-create the story of her night. My face, serving breakfast, was the face Puerto Ricans call the face of stone. No one could have guessed what I was thinking and feeling. It wasn't friendly. I was quickly developing the mask that I was to wear the rest of my life.

It was there, I suppose, that revenge began to be a motive in my life. It was at these parties that my obsessive attraction to other men's women was born and my need—it amounted to that—to take them away. Looking back, it appears that most every girl I ever had belonged, when I took her, to another man. But then isn't every pretty girl someone else's when you meet her?

Lying in bed after the parties, I'd be humped over double, tensed by desire. How do you meet girls? I wondered. I considered finding a whorehouse, but I was too "well brought up" and finally too timid. What did I do? I went to North Adams, five miles by trolley, and entered the movie theatre there, which had "Five-Acts-Five" of vaudeville every Friday and Saturday. I felt comfortable in the mill town—no rich boys there, just mutts like me—and in the dark theatre, which had the musty smell of a bed whose sheets hadn't been changed for too long, I found the warmth I craved, that of human animals. The theatre was full of girls, and since I didn't know any of them, I could fantasize about them. The vaudeville and its performers had their special charm. And if the plump thigh of the girl sitting next to me slid over, was it intentional? Did it matter? Was she as lonely as I was? I'd sit without moving, and in the spasm of arousal, close my eyes. Sometimes I'd tremble. It was, for me, an enchanted atmosphere. But when I left the theatre, the night was cold and I was alone.

In my junior year, my appetite for revenge found an unexpected outlet: touch football. I was too small to go out for any varsity team, but where I did find a chance for some modest glory was in intramural sports. A waiter named Jack Bright and I were the stars of the Commons Club touch team— ringers. We ran the option play as well as I've ever seen it, and that year we won the intramural championship. The fact that all the good football players, three and four deep, were on Weston Field, playing for the varsity, did not deflate my euphoria. The next year, I had a triumph in basketball. At my weight, I could run sixty minutes without stopping. Height was not as prized on the courts then as it is now. In the crucial championship game, I was assigned the task of guarding a boy whose name was "Red" Putnam. He'd been declared ineligible because of poor marks, or he would have been playing varsity. I dug my teeth into that poor boy's butt for sixty full minutes and hung on like a pit bull. He scored only two baskets all told, and we won the championship. This meant more to me than the "A" I got in English.

When Father came up for my graduation—his second visit to Williams- town in four years—he was a changed man. The Crash had happened, and he was "eating capital." Mother told me he no longer went to the horse track every afternoon; he couldn't afford to lose now. I gave him my diploma and he kissed me. I could sense that he still wanted me to join him in his struggle for the dollar, but I had the fever of the malcontent now, and my sights were set on another course.

I walked into Chapin Hall with my fellow seniors for our final ceremony, sat with them shoulder to shoulder, and wanted what they had: their style, their looks, their clothes, their cars, their money, the jobs they had waiting for them, and the girls they had waiting for them. I wanted all that, and I wanted it soon. Every time I saw privilege from then on, I wanted to tear it down or to possess it. During those cold, dark years at Williams, the emotional groundwork for me to join the Communist Party was laid down. But what I wanted was not equality, not of any sort. I wanted the full re- wards of the system I'd been on the outskirts of for four years, the rewards I hadn't had. I wanted—as my political associates-to-be would say—to take over. And years later, for a time, I suppose I did "take over"—not with "comrades," but all by myself.

It took me many years to quiet this rage against my classmates, and those like them. Perhaps deep down in my black heart, I still haven't. I'm friendly, "civilized," and reasonable, but I notice still that every time I receive a request for money from the Williams Alumni Fund, I have a reflex to chuck it into the wastebasket, and usually do.

I think what got me over my hostility, to the extent that I have, was an encounter with a classmate some fifteen years ago. He'd been the center of our football team and its captain senior year. He was a member of the very best fraternity, Deke, and of the senior honorary society, Gargoyle. Of all the boys in the class of '30, I remember him as the perfect Williams man. Some forty years later, I met him at an alumni function to which the college had invited me. Unhappy at home at that time and deep in psychoanalysis, I'd been trying to understand my life—even as I am now, by writing this book. Curious about my college years, I went to the affair. When the program was over, I ran into my old classmate in the lobby and recognized him because of my interest in football. When I said my name, he knew of me. I asked what he was doing. He replied that his wife had just died. He looked forlorn, so when he suggested I come to his place for a drink, I went along.

His apartment was dark, and it did indeed look as if a life had just ended there. Over two great slugs of Scotch, I asked and he told me what had happened to the "big" athletes of our day, men I'd admired who'd had jobs on Wall Street waiting for them after they graduated. But their scores "downtown" had not been winning ones. Then he told me about himself. He'd had a job waiting for him when he left college, and over the years had risen to just below the top. But vice-presidents in the world of finance are listed by the dozen. Now he seemed terribly alone and wanted me to stay on when I said I'd better leave. I saw that he could not be envied and that there was nothing to "tear down." What I felt for him was sympathy and a kind of brotherhood.

Still another drink and he put a disk on his record player, dance music from our time, "Sweet Georgia Brown." We were both "loaded" by now. I lay back on the sofa, closed my eyes, and recalled the house parties where my classmates had danced to that tune while I served spiked punch. When I opened my eyes, he was on his feet, his right arm around the waist of an imaginary girl, and he was turning in place. His great hulk was graceful and his head tilted at the tender angle it must have had when he'd danced cheek to cheek.

BUT while, years later, I did not envy the boys who'd had jobs waiting for them at graduation, on that June day in 1930, sitting among them for the last time and hearing the fare-thee-well-and-good-luck speeches, I had to recognize that whatever I thought of their prospects, I had none, that my four years of study had left me unequipped to make my way, and if I had received an education, it was not one in the courses I'd studied but another education, one in spite of the curriculum and having to do with what I'd been forced to become as a young man, my character rather than any techniques or knowledge that I might have acquired.

I began then to question the educational system I'd passed through, the one that nails a kid to a chair at the age of six (I believe it's four now), demands compliance and obedience, keeps him submissive, makes that a habit, tames the kid so he is anxious to go along with the pronouncements of authority—his teachers—and never questions those judgments from above but believes that progress consists of learning to believe what the teachers believe and being able, when called upon, to repeat it. I suppose I'd learned (and have now totally forgotten) a little Latin, classical Greek, calculus, physics, economics, the history of Renaissance painting, American history, American government, astronomy, and the sources of Coleridge's "Ancient Mariner" and T. S. Eliot's "Waste Land"—all of which have been of no value to me. The college and the work in its classes had not provided me with what I needed most, a capability to find my own way in my own direction in a world from which I was already alienated and so to enjoy the independence that I'd learned to value so dearly. After four years, I had no remaining interest in any of the subjects I'd studied.

Practically speaking, I had to be educated again, to learn, in my father's phrase, something "useh-ful," useful to me. Because if I didn't, I'd very soon find myself selling my time and my energy and whatever talent I had, doing something I despised in order to pay the bills.

No, I didn't envy the boys of my class who had jobs in banks and broker-age houses, in the great corporations and the basic industries, waiting for them, nor did I envy those on their way to law school and medical school. But on that graduation day, as I walked out of the hall where degrees had been portioned out and where we'd been blessed twice, in lay phrases and in religious cant, I felt adrift. But the fact was that I had received an edu-cation in spite of my education. Four years at Williams had made a certain kind of man of me, not an agreeable man but a self-reliant, tough-skinned, resolute, and determined man, five foot six. I was going to find my own way, no matter what. I'd found I could live on very little, that by waiting on tables I could be independent of a nine-to-five job (the prospect I feared most). My marks at graduation had been *cum laude;* I thought perhaps I might get a scholarship somewhere and stall until I knew where I wanted to go and what I wanted to do. My goal in life was a simple one: to make a living doing something I enjoyed doing. I had no nobler ambition.

In my senior year at Williams, I'd had one teacher who did influence me. Mr. Dutton taught English lit, and I wrote a paper for him on "The Waste Land." He never spoke to me outside class, never knew I admired him. Mr. Dutton had a bad leg and an impaired walk, but, clutching his green cloth book bag, he strode the campus like a perfect man, asking for no sympathy, needing none. On that campus he was a freak, as were the four student friends I had. Mr. Dutton gave a special dignity to being exceptional and living outside general society. In class, it was his passion for what he was teaching that impressed me. In some way I don't quite understand, Dutton made me believe that perhaps, somewhere in the broad range of a life in the arts, there might be a niche for me and that I might well mark time until that niche appeared.

I learned one technique of behaving that, in time, would help me. Observe a writer at a gathering of intellectuals. You will believe what everyone else does: that he is a perfectly friendly and agreeable fellow. Then read what he writes about the affair. You'll find that he saw things you didn't and had reactions you didn't suspect. I acquired this technique from my waiter's job: to be a zealous listener, observe people sharply, form a private opinion—at that time often hostile and envious—but keep it all concealed. I learned the art of the masked observer in a waiter's white coat at the Zeta Psi fraternity house.

In those four years, I'd also found my way past hurt. Once I'd accepted the fact that I was and always would be an outsider, I was proud—like "Black is beautiful"—that I hadn't been chosen Gargoyle or by a fraternity, that I'd never seen the candlelit "goat room" or shared its secrets. I was delighted that there was a void opposite my name in this yearbook too. I gloried in my specialness, that I needed no one and nothing, no help, no sympathy, no friends except those, less than a finger count, of my own kind. I developed a swagger to tell the world around me that I was a freak and knew it, wore the same trousers for months and no socks, summer clothes in the winter, near naked in the summer, asserting in this way that I was part of the hard-skinned of the world. Not accepted, I made clear that I didn't want to be accepted. I was outside and liked it.

The other fellow is Alan Baxter.

My closest friend, Alan Baxter, a gentle outsider, had a true interest in the theatre—which I did not—and he'd been accepted at the Yale Drama School. When I found out I could get a job there operating a dishwashing machine to earn my meals, I decided to tag along. Teachers at Williams spoke up for me and Mr. George Pierce Baker, master of the Drama School, was generous, so I soon had a post at the stage door, pushing in pins opposite the names of students on the enrollment sheet when they entered the building and pulling them out when they left, which took care of tuition. All I needed was rent money for a bedroom. So Sundays during the sum-

mer I was back at the Wykagyl Country Club, toting golf bags around eighteen holes. Now it was two-fifty plus tip. I lived at home to save everything
I made.

When I told Father I was going to the Yale Drama School, he was bewildered. "Four years over in Massachusetts there," he told my brother, "looks
like he learn nothing."

At Yale I had no interest in what I'd be studying, had no real ambitions,
desire, or hope. I was like a man who'd chosen to incarcerate himself. I
knew that I had three years of leeway in a kind of detention area, three
years of sequestered freedom—that was the length of the course there—
but I didn't know why I wanted that freedom, what I might use it for.

At Williams I'd been part of a coterie of "freaks"; at Yale it seemed everyone was a freak, starting with the faculty. The "old man," George Pierce
Baker, was kindly and remote, a scholarly-looking old fuddy with pince-nez
glasses that hung by a black ribbon when they weren't clipped to his plump
nose. Most respectably married, he had a passion—completely unexercised, I'm sure—for the boy who drove him to work and back, a lithe La-
tino named Eduard Toledano. He simply adored this boy; anybody could
see that. We all agreed that the old man never looked happier than when
he was sitting at the side of his driver. Mrs. Baker looked precisely like a
Helen Hokinson cartoon; none of us had imaginations so lively as to fancy
him humping Mrs. Baker. He ran the school efficiently, but I can't remember anything I learned from him.

I did learn a good deal that was useful from the professor of directing,
Alexander Dean. He taught directing as an art of position, picture, and
movement, a technique useful for the direction of amateurs in college and
community theatres, where productions had to be cast with nonactors. The
stage positions and movements told the story of the scene and the relationship of the characters; in this way, behavior, feeling, and dramatic conflict
were suggested. There were emphatic areas on stage and those less so,
there were warm and cool spaces, there were strong movements, to downstage, and weak movements, to upstage and sidestage. The director's job
was to contrive a kinetic pattern that told what was happening. The actor,
as a vehicle of expression, was not to be relied upon. The stage picture, as
it developed, told the event. Rhythm and pace, "builds" and "drops," would
do the rest.

I remember one day watching one of Mr. Dean's rehearsals, leaning on the audience barrier at the back of the "house," when he came up
behind me and suddenly embraced me. He was a heavy man, given to
heavy perspiration, and it wasn't easy to slip out of his grasp. I had little
patience with his troubled soul then, but now I'm older and recognize the
desperation he was expressing. Dean was a devoted man; he isolated some
truths about directing for me and taught a particular craft of the stage,
which helped me later in my work. I learned from him what the directors

of the Group Theatre never learned: that directing a play should not be thought of simply as directing actors. Directing a play is an overall task, directing actors only a part of it. In the end, I valued Alex Dean and liked him.

The costume designer, Frank Poole Bevan, was a fine man and a superb teacher from whom I learned a great deal. He was married, and I liked his wife, Margo, very much. Whatever errant impulses Frank had—they were manifestly there—he kept to himself. He was scholarly, rigorous, and precise about his work, taught a very well organized course in the design and history of costume. I learned something priceless from him, although I didn't know it at the time: In another way, I was an outsider too, and I, too, would learn to rely on my work.

The other technical people—Don Oenslager, who taught scene design and did many shows on Broadway, and Stanley McCandless, a pioneer in stage lighting—were fine professionals, as were Phil Barber and Ed Cole, who taught scene building and stage mechanics. It seemed that these men who dealt with external and mechanical problems were more conventional in their personal lives. They did not have to deal with the storms of the soul. In time they all wrote books that were hardheaded, specific, and useful.

The acting teacher was a lady named Constance Welch, who lived with her sister and as far as I knew had no sex life. As I write this, I can't say why the faculty's intimate lives were so important to me; but they were. Constance was a lovely woman, with a soft face and a delicate complexion. Peach. She could have been quite desirable except for something curiously limp about her body, oversoft, like a beautiful flowering plant that does best indoors and requires a stake to hold it up. She taught acting entirely from the outside. The actor was to convey inner events by playing his "vocal instrument." Her method was the precise opposite of the "Method" later identified with the Actors Studio.

Constance had isolated the evidences of all the emotions in the voice and breath. She would assign her classes specialized exercises: anger scenes, scenes of jealousy, laughing scenes, crying scenes, scenes of fright, and so on, all to be conveyed with the use of certain vocal and breathing patterns. She believed that imitating the exterior would produce the interior feeling in the actor and in the audience. The result, it seemed to me, was mannered performances, without spontaneity and fun, or the heat of true passion.

Constance also taught "standard speech," to which she particularly hoped I'd devote myself since my speech was "so New York." I took this instruction as a joke. To go into a cafeteria on High Street late at night and ask the Greek waiter behind the counter for a cup of "hahf and hahf" (that is, coffee with a splotch of cream) was just too funny, a "camp."

No, I was determined to be myself. I balked altogether at what I was plunged into at Yale. I was being offered for a model the kind of theatre I liked least when I saw it: semi-English, classically sterile, mannered and polite, always properly controlled. The actors I liked—there weren't many: Jeanne Eagels—had feelings that shook the theatre when they were released. The potential in depth of the human psyche was never investigated at Yale.

Actually what I preferred during those years was the musical theatre. The Follies, George White's Scandals, Eddie Cantor, Ed Wynn and Tom Patricola, Marilyn Miller singing "Who?"—that was for me! That truly reached me and still does.

What I did take to at Yale was the scene shop—the smell of sawdust and the whirling power tools. I was interested in the technique of lighting a show and in the operation of a switchboard. Designated head carpenter, I built the turntable setting for A Winter's Tale, once staying up seventy-two hours without sleep. I'd never before been so committed to anything. Some way, it fitted in with my role in the kitchens at Williams and at the dish-washing machine at Yale. Building, lighting, costuming, stage manage-ment, the drills, the saws, the dye pots with their nostril-stinging tang: I liked all that. It struck me that I might make a living working backstage—not in the acting and directing side of the profession but in the "honest" crafts. I'd leave the rest to the kinks and the deviates. For the first time in my life, I'd found a genuine capability and perhaps one where I could do better than the other fellow. I was beginning to feel some confidence at last.

Later in life, when I'd become a furiously active theatre and film direc-tor, what I learned backstage at Yale served me well. No technician could tell me something couldn't be done; I'd very likely done it. I wasn't awed by the elite union carpenters or electricians in New York or in Hollywood. Many directors were.

There was also a sudden improvement in my sex life. At the end of my four years at Williams, I not only hadn't had a lover, I had no friends of the opposite sex; women's ways were a mystery to me. Something had even gone wrong between me and my mother, she who'd been my devoted ally. Unexpectedly I'd begun to resent her closeness, as if she were in some way responsible for making a proper relationship with a girl impossible for me. I've found an old diary from those days: "Why does she come into my room so much? I'm playing Beethoven and in she comes, sits there pretending to listen. She doesn't really like music. Then she'll fiddle with the dials, mak-ing the record too loud, and ask me if that's o.k.? What could I say? And why does she pinch my arm that way? What does she expect of me?"

I wonder now if she was aware that I was pulling away from her. My impatience was unfair. Mother was forty-four years old at this time and beginning to lose her hearing. She had no life with my father. Full of un-used love, she'd fallen to the status of a housekeeper. And there must have been another reason for her intruding on me; she must have felt that something was going wrong, and not knowing how she might help, she'd offer this inarticulate, sometimes clumsy support.

But once I was at Yale, relief came quickly, and from a surprising source. I was suddenly taken on by the wife of a rabbi, in whose house I'd looked for a room before deciding to move in with my friend Alan. This lady overcame my hesitations and my shyness, and turned up some passion in me. The connection didn't last long, since she was monitored by a devoted, older husband. But now I'd had a taste and began to look around for more.

My roommate, Alan, meantime had found a sweetheart in the playwrights class; her name was Molly Thacher. They were in love and delighting in each other. Alan's happiness depressed me. I was alone weekends. When there wasn't work in the shop or on stage, I'd have nothing to do but drink. My soul problems made it difficult for me to read. I'd go to a film by myself, then drink—by myself or at parties, where I was indifferent to everyone. There was as great a jumble of sexual preference among the students as among the faculty. They'd gather in masses, not couples, around a bathtub full of "alky" and spirits of juniper.

I can recall nights that spring when at two or three in the morning, dead drunk, I'd be leaning across the sill of my open window and crying in great, coarse-throat jags. I didn't know what was wrong with me. Despite my new interest in the backstage crafts, I was living a life without satisfaction and was given to black silences or murderous rages. I'd go to a party, behave sullenly, then leave to be alone in my misery. I was a vagabond in the city, wandering its streets at night without purpose or direction. Lovers passing left me sick. One night I dreamed I was born again, good-looking. My scalp itched constantly; I was convinced I would soon be bald. I passed out at a party from a bellyful of bathtub gin and woke at dawn lying on a garbage dump, five miles south of town. I was nearing the end of a road; you might have thought me beyond saving. I needed luck. Soon.

When school broke for the summer, Alan decided to go to Europe alone, and Molly drove off to her family's cabin on the shore of Blue Mountain Lake in the Adirondacks. I didn't think the separation odd until a few months later, when I looked back on it. I didn't want to go to my parents' home, so I took a job at the Toy Theatre in Atlantic City. It was a tiny place built over the swampy side of a bay at the southern end of the town. Its owner and operator was a rather mysterious Mexican homosexual, who'd saddled himself with the task of putting on a new production of an old "success" every week. A hell of a lot of work; he needed my help.

A photograph from that time shows me looking foreign but not "dashing."

It was the first directing I'd done out of school; I learned to get on a play in six days. It consumed my unused energy and gave me confidence that if I ever chose to, I could do anything I wanted in the theatre. I had not only to direct a pickup bag of actors but to provide some kind of setting and light it. I remember the first time I heard an audience roar with laughter at one of my directorial shenanigans; I began to get the idea that I could pull people into a theatre.

Naturally I took up with the pretty, blond leading lady. The affair continued until a day when I went to the theatre at a time not prearranged and discovered "my girl" in the grip of another young woman, deep in the rumble seat of her roadster. I was surprisingly unaffected by this romantic misadventure; I was accustomed to lesbians—the Yale Drama School had its share. I quickly found another actress, continued working without intermission. By the end of the summer I'd become proficient in marshaling a mediocre cast into a mediocre production, quickly and effectively.

Looking back, I seem to have been living at that time in an isolation no outside event could penetrate. The Great Depression was all around me. Those were the hungry years when there were long lines of the unemployed and the underfed in the big cities, and back in the hills, country people were eating wild greens. Bread lines, soup kitchens, uncontrolled floods, devastating droughts, migrant workers moving north and west, homeless families in urban slums, general despair, all meant nothing to me. A neurotic is so entirely concerned with his own problems, he can't look through the walls of the box in which he's locked himself.

I went back to Yale in September of 1931 because I had nowhere else to go and nothing better to do. I had the "I ain't got no money" blues. Alan returned from Europe and Molly came down from her lake in the Adirondacks. It soon became evident that there was trouble between them. I didn't know then and don't know now what it was about—they're both dead, so I can't ask. I became their go-between, carried notes back and forth, helping them to patch their quarrels. I became emotionally involved in their love affair.

Then it happened. I got lucky at last. Molly and I became friends. She wrote a play and put me in it. I got to know her better. She developed some kind of trust in me and, in so doing, woke what had been dying. One weekend we went to New York City in her Ford coupe to see a play, *The House of Connelly*. Driving back, I became aware of the way she was looking at me, with a longing more intense than any I'd ever seen. She'd fallen in love. This heartened me enough so I could feel too. And make a move. The following weekend, she and I drove from rehearsal into the country, stopping by the shore of a lake far out of town and off the road. We'd brought a picnic supper but didn't eat it. Night came as we lay on the shore; a lopsided moon rose. We were lovers.

I couldn't live with Alan now; I didn't want to be anywhere except in Molly's arms.

She told him what had happened and reported that he took it well.

I used to run from my classes to her apartment, clamber through the window because it was the shortest route to her embrace. I learned how precious is the love of another person. I learned the joy of being entwined in bed every night. Molly's roommate moved out—in celebration, not in resentment. Molly and I were living together.

One day when I was in the scene shop nailing corner blocks, Alan came in, drunk. He had a large screw in one hand and was scoring the top of his other hand with it. He showed me his bloody mitt. I didn't respond as he hoped; he was, I thought, behaving like a rejected lover—not hers, mine. I didn't like it.

Molly came as a miracle. It had taken me some time after my graduation from Williams to realize that the purpose of that college was not to instill information but to create a certain type of elite individual. Because of Molly, I began to appreciate the qualities of those Puritans: a live conscience, a stubborn mind, common decency, independence of thought, a lively and unremitting concern for our nation's future, respect for democracy as a political institution, plus an ideal of service in its behalf. Molly was the first person I'd met who lived with an obligation to causes bigger than herself.

What she meant to me was acceptance by an indifferent and foreign society, racial and social acceptance. She completely relieved me of the impression, ground into me over the years, that I was a member of an inferior group, lucky to be where I was, lucky to be accepted at all, a freak, a mutt, a boy whose clothes smelled of dishwater. When I was with Molly, I wasn't an outsider. In the words my mother spoke years later, after she'd come to know the girl, "Molly brought us into America." Mother meant our whole family, Molly had done that.

She was to become more than a wife to me; she was, for many years, a talisman of success. A deep and lasting artistic partnership was being born. I came to rely on her judgment in scripts. She made up for my lacks in taste and savvy. I gave her the energy and drive she needed. She was a person to whom, for many years, I felt I owed everything.

She loved me totally. And physically. She had long, slim fingers, tokens of delicacy and tenderness, but a body surprisingly voluptuous. What came to be between us grew out of desperate necessity—in her and in me. Need met need. Doubt sustained doubt. I didn't know I was capable of that kind of feeling. The corniest love songs sounded to me like responsible reporting. Her well and mine had no bottom. When it came to my "deficiency," she reassured me completely. *Axios! Axios!* Worthy! Worthy! Nothing else existed. Certainly not my studies. I was floating over the earth.

My acne disappeared. My legs were not bowed after all. When I walked I looked up off the ground at last, and what I saw looked good. Molly was my cure.

She believed I had talent. Beginning to believe it myself, I carried a pocket notebook and wrote down my observations and thoughts as if they were important. I kept a diary. I swore I'd never work eight hours a day; either twenty or nothing.

Molly had made up her mind in the first days of our acquaintance that I was gifted and bedeviled—and the man for her. She made it her duty on earth to encourage, protect, support, and—in the end—tolerate me in whatever I did. It nearly killed her, but she did not waver from her self-imposed duty, not once, not ever. From the day we became lovers until the day she died, in 1963, I was—and our four children became—Molly's whole life. I was never again to know a love so unwavering. I was luckier than I knew. Did I deserve it? I don't ask that question.

A T   Y A L E   I was going nowhere I wanted to go. Working on scenes that had been done hundreds of times and were worn thin, or on new plays that were imitations of old successes, stale even as entertainment, I saw that the work there would lead to teaching acting/directing at another college's dramatic department or to accepting a post as producer in a community theatre. That was not what I wanted. Molly also felt that two years with Baker were enough. A brighter and more experienced person than I, she'd been editor in chief of the Vassar *Miscellany* and, while spending two years as a social worker in the slum areas of New York City, had become involved in "progressive" causes. She heard Roosevelt speaking as if it were to her, wanted to get back into the struggle and use her gifts as a playwright to influence people. We both needed a passion and a cause; we both decided to move on.

Lee, Harold, and Cheryl in their prime

        I N the spring of 1932, I came down from the Yale Drama School to meet the directors of the Group Theatre. I was lucky; the first person I saw was Cheryl Crawford. Without the impression she made on me in her office in the now-demolished Forty-eighth Street Theatre— mid-America plain talk, no glamour crap—I might not have been able to get through my next encounter that day.

    "Sit down," she said. "The boys will see you soon." The "boys" were Lee Strasberg and Harold Clurman, then aged thirty years. I was twenty-two.

    When I walked into the murky, dormer-lit room where they were waiting for me, Lee was sitting in a corner reading a newspaper—not an editorial or the latest on the Great Depression; no, the sports page. He put the newspaper down with great reluctance when I entered, and throughout the interview that followed, he'd swivel his eyes in its direction. I'd interrupted something he clearly preferred to interviewing a saturnine young man of uncertain race without the visible qualities an actor needs to make his way even in a theatre as off center as the Group.

Harold, seated behind a table, was actually looking at me. Or was he? I couldn't tell. His eyes were turned toward me, but like an owl's at noon; they stared without blinking, and I wasn't sure they perceived. Then there was the curious behavior of his tongue; it kept poking around the inside of his cheek. To what purpose? To no purpose. It was as if there were a joke about me that he knew and I did not.

After the kind of pause directors learn not to allow, Harold said, "Well, tell us about yourself." Whereupon he pushed his tongue against the inside of his cheek, poked around a bit, then waited. Lee threw a greedy glance toward the sports page.

The "boys" were waiting for me to speak. I wondered if the theatre was the career for me. I couldn't remember anything about myself. Lee was now looking openly at his sports page. Harold was stroking the stubble of his blue-black beard. I heard him mutter, "Forgot to shave."

Does this sound like an exaggerated account, distorted by the day's anxiety? It is. Neither of the "boys" would have told it as I am. History is written by the last fellow at the typewriter.

Sometimes my bad temper saves me. I began to get peevish at the split attention I was receiving. I must have sounded resentful as I made the effort to tell the "boys" my personal history. I knew I was making a poor impression, but I hadn't expected that the man who'd directed *The House of Connelly*, a production I'd admired, would be so interested in box scores.

Then Lee surprised me even more. He spoke.

"Tell us what you want," he said. I thought his tone irascible.

"In a quick sentence or two, for chrissake?" I retorted. That to myself. What I said out loud was worse. "What I want is your job," I said. Out loud. Which was, to say the least, tactless. But I'd abandoned all hope by then. "I mean I want to be a director," the turtle said, retracting its head.

The effect of this bit of effrontery was startling. Harold's eyes focused. His tongue lay at ease on the bed of his mouth. Lee looked at me—a deadpan reaction, to be sure, but after all, I was not a box score.

In time I was sent back to Cheryl's office, a snug harbor after a heavy sea. "We'll be in touch," she said. Then an amazing thing happened. A week later, she got in touch. A letter informed me I'd been accepted as an apprentice at the Group Theatre's second summer camp. Signed, Cheryl A. Crawford.

I can recall my reaction: "They must be pretty hard up for apprentices if they took me."

There was a bit of information in Miss Crawford's letter that created a problem. I'd be required to pay twenty dollars per week for board and room. This sounds like a trifling sum today and it wasn't a hell of a lot then, except for a young man whose total savings on that day came to one hundred and twelve dollars and whose father's patience, with the Depression at its most brutalizing, was at an absolute nadir.

I decided to go anyway; I'd have five weeks sure; perhaps I'd find a way to improvise for the rest of the summer.

O N　J U N E　19, 1932, I checked in at Sterling Farms, Dover Furnace, New York, an apprentice at the Group's work camp. Alan Baxter arrived with me. Something in his character allowed our friendship to continue; in his place I couldn't have managed it. Assigned a room together, we threw our gear on the narrow twin beds and went out to see the sights.

I don't know why it was called Sterling Farms. Although it was verdant after the growth of spring, there was nothing of a work farm about the place. Central in a cluster of buildings was a handsome two-story structure, its white front mottled by the shadows of large maples. It contained a parlor, large for a farm's parlor but tight as a meeting place for a theatre troupe. Close by was a "barn," again not actually a working barn, but it did contain a large chamber, adequate for the company's rehearsals. There were two small dormitories—Alan and I were in one—a dining hall with a kitchen, and on a hill apart from the rest of the buildings, a cottage with a view. Perhaps the owner of Sterling Farms had once slept there.

People were rolling in, young actresses and actors, full of the joy of being alive and the anticipation of a summer of work. They'd been bonded together, some only a year and a half but many longer. To judge from the way they fell to catching up and teasing, they were delighted to be in one another's company again—and perhaps relieved that their theatre was continuing, not dissolving. None of the misery of the nationwide Depression was evident. These young artists were playful as puppies.

Now don't believe what follows. Don't believe that the month of May, which had already passed, and which is my favorite month because it is the burst of spring and the time of hope and promise, was three months long that summer, that it was May all summer that summer. The air of the place that May was sparkling and bright, as effervescent as soda. The camp twinkled with the games and the mischief of eager young artists. Don't believe that all the sounds that long, long May were mellow and intimate, that there were no voices raised in rancor or rage, that everyone liked everyone else, that the directors, when they spoke, never spoke that eloquently again, or that the buzz of the actors eating supper together was never again as congenial. Don't believe, if you are determined to be realistic, that there was an aura over all the people as they arrived, one that enlarged their talents and filled me with longing to become one of them. All that is how I remember my first summer with the Group and why I quickly made up my mind that no matter what it took in work and devotion, I'd hold on until I'd proved myself and become one of them. I had a passion at last.

Looking back now, I think of the people who were at Dover Furnace that summer as mature, experienced actors, and they were. But the fact is they weren't much older than I. I remember that when I realized this, it gave me hope.

We didn't know any of them, so Alan and I remained on the fringes of the clusters that kept forming, then bounding off into the buildings that contained their sleeping accommodations. I noticed that many of them were looking at Alan particularly, and for good reason: He was a tall, handsome young man, a "goy" to boot, who came across as a potential leading man. I looked as if I'd gotten off at the wrong station.

Something mysterious began to happen as I studied the arriving company. Despite feeling no confidence that I might be taken on as a member (what could they have thought of me except that I'd come to work as a waiter, grounds keeper, or janitor?), nevertheless, for the first time in my life, I didn't feel *outside*. Even though they were all from a world within which I'd never moved—Yale was never like this—still I felt that here were my own kind, a league of outsiders, people not assimilated by the society, rebels, a bunch who, below the surface, had their own off-center characteristics. They weren't "regular" any more than I was. Perhaps I'd found my own kind at last. If I had, my task was to make them feel I was their kind, before my one hundred and twelve dollars ran out.

I began to notice something else: that when I divested them of the glamour with which I and distance had clothed them, they were "ordinary" people. For instance, someone pointed out the boy—that's all he was at twenty-nine—who was going to play the leading role in *Success Story*, the play about to go into rehearsal and the production on which the future of the Group hung. He had the thrusting, determined look of a street kid, someone you might encounter on Second Avenue below Fourteenth Street, which is precisely where you might have met him—and walked right on by. It took some time before I found out that he was the crown prince of New York's Jewish theatre, who had spent his life on- and backstage, had all the stage confidence that that would provide, as well as another quality I came to learn was essential in a leading man: He made you wonder what he was thinking. But when I saw him for the first time, I judged him a rather ordinary person.

Reconnoitering the grounds, Alan and I found a swimming hole at the end of a path and, walking back, encountered a plump young actor with fawn-colored skin. Going to swim, he had a towel over his shoulder and an open book in his hands, which he was reading as he walked. When he looked up and nodded, I could see the title: *Left Wing Communism: An Infantile Disorder*. The author's name was unfamiliar to me. The actor walked on, reading.

A convertible of a bright color gunned up the dusty dirt road leading to the camp, then sliced across a field to the dormitory where Alan and I were to stay. I recognized the driver without recalling his name. He was hand-some as an Arrow collar ad, a beauty standard for men at that time. I'd seen him the winter before, playing the leading role in *The House of Connelly*. At his side was a golden-haired young woman, good-looking in an equally familiar way; she looked as if she'd been kidnapped and was enjoying the adventure. As he helped her out of the car and into their quarters, there was something mischievous about his expression, as if he were breaking a rule his elders had written. He reminded me of the fraternity cutups to whom I'd served spiked punch at Williams house parties. Now, without the dimension the play's drama had lent him, he seemed familiar to me, an-other "ordinary" person.

All this deflating gave me hope. As they arrived in camp, they stepped down into the world where I lived. It was as if I'd attended a circus per-formance, been dazzled by the extraordinary skills and stunts of the artists, then passed back into their living quarters, seen the performers out of cos-tume and at their most human, so not too different from me. But as these people became more like people I knew, they raised a new question: What was that mysterious thing called talent they all possessed? Did I possess it?

A long summer's twilight, and I came upon Harold Clurman stretched out on the grass at the feet of an actress. In that posture he, too, seemed— the word is not fair, but I was that surprised—ordinary. The actress was tall, with a handsome face built around a Semitic nose, which, years later, compelled by a desperate desire to become a Hollywood star, she would cause to be "bobbed," while, on the same impulse, she changed her name from Adler to Ardler.

Clurman, it was evident, was dotty as a slave dog about the woman; she was queen of the camp by his fiat. When she said something he—or she— thought witty, he'd burst into laughter, then look about anxiously to see if the others clustered around his idol appreciated her as much as they ought to.

I spent more time watching these two than anyone else. I had the im-pression that Harold was holding the actress rather against her will, that he believed he had to be constantly flattering. Was she as slippery as he seemed to fear? The anxious devotion he showed her gave him the aspect of a cuckold. The actors around the couple watched Harold with amuse-ment; he wasn't above them, he was one of them, as vulnerable to folly as anyone else in camp. In Stella's court, Harold was the clown and like a clown didn't seem embarrassed by his behavior. Was this man, I asked my-self, capable of directing the course of a theatre?

There was one exception to all my downgrading, and when the dinner bell clanged, I watched him walk down the hill from the cottage above— the living quarters, I'd gathered, of the camp's elite. Descending like Zeus from Olympus, the other man who'd interviewed me on the top floor of the Forty-eighth Street Theatre didn't greet those he passed. The camp had made him not more ordinary but more exceptional. He was accompanied by his mistress, priestess to his worship. He seemed anything but anxious about her, walked a little ahead as they strolled toward the dining hall at a pace he set. Apparently Lee Strasberg was still involved in what he'd been studying when the dinner bell had interrupted his work.

In the next few days I was to discover that this unyielding remoteness was habitual with Lee. He carried with him the aura of a prophet, a magician, a witch doctor, a psychoanalyst, and a feared father of a Jewish home. He was the center of the camp's activities that summer, the core of the vortex. Everything in camp revolved around him. Preparing to direct the play that was to open the coming season, as he had the three plays of the season before, he would also give the basic instruction in acting, laying down the principles of the art by which the Group worked, the guides to their artistic training. He was the force that held the thirty-odd members of the theatre together, made them "permanent." He did this not only by his superior knowledge but by the threat of his anger.

On the morning of December 7, 1941, when Pearl Harbor was sneak-bombed by the Japanese, Admiral Ernest King was quoted: "Well, they've got themselves into a war. Now they need a son of a bitch to fight it." He was speaking of his government and meant himself. Sometimes only a tough, unyielding man can do a job that's for the good of all. Admiral King was necessary after Pearl Harbor, and Lee Strasberg was necessary that summer in 1932. He enjoyed his eminence just as the admiral would. Actors are as self-favoring as the rest of humanity, and perhaps the only way they could be held together to do their work properly was by the threat of an authority they respected. And feared.

Clearly Lee thought so. He had a gift for anger and a taste for the power it brought him. No one questioned his dominance—he spoke holy writ— his leading role in that summer's activities, and his right to all power. To win his favor became everyone's goal. His explosions of temper maintained the discipline of this camp of high-strung people. I came to believe that without their fear of this man, the Group would fly apart, everyone going in different directions instead of to where he was pointing.

I was afraid of him too. Even as I admired him.

Lee was making an artistic revolution and knew it. An organization such as the Group—then in its second year, which is to say still beginning, still being shaped—lives only by the will of a fanatic and the drive with which he propels his vision. He has to be unswerving, uncompromising, and un-adjustable. Lee knew this. He'd studied other revolutions, political and artistic. He knew what was needed, and he was fired up by his mission and its importance.

T O M Y surprise, it was Harold who spoke on the first night, roaring defiance at the rest of the theatre world, relighting the fire for the members: what the Group meant, what it was destined to do, what position it must fill in American society. He was inspiring by the fervor of his passion as well as by the validity of what he said. New to this degree of emotionalism—Harold's face, as it filled with blood, looked as if it might burst—I was uncomfortable at first. Was this hysteria or was it inspiration? Was Harold showing off?

Looking back, having heard Harold speak again and again over the years, I do feel he enjoyed impressing people with how volcanic his emotions were, but I do not denigrate this; it was necessary. A theatre, particularly a company committed to permanence, stays together only by an act of faith inspired by its leaders. That year, idealism was our answer to the Great Depression. Comradeship buffered us in a society many of us, for one reason or another, considered hostile. The Group was possible because it came at a time of hardship, it offered dignity and faith to young actors, but also because there was no alternative—no soap operas, no TV films, no big-budget commercials, no voice-over quick bucks.

But it was possible above all because Harold was able to make us believe that a Group Theatre was the only course that would give our lives worth. He tore down the star system, proclaimed the theatre a collective art where all involved must work together toward a common goal. He called the theatre he advocated "an ideologically cemented collective." He taught ethics for the theatre artist, spoke words the masters of religion have used, railed in the grand manner of a visionary, calling into being what does not exist. I believed that a great theatre had been born and that it would be unlike any other that existed in this country. When he was through, I was an altered man.

It's said that Harold founded the Group Theatre. It's more accurate to say that he articulated the ideas that formed it. Someone else (Lee, Cheryl) did the day-to-day work; everyone in camp knew that and accepted it. In the next days, I was to find that Harold was rather looked down upon by the actors even as they admired him. He was a talker, they said, not a doer, and would never make it as a play director. Great rhetorical outbursts seem show-off when they aren't followed by action. If Harold was a prophet, he was not capable of making his visions come true—so it was believed. Cheryl and Lee had the same opinion the actors did. Lee patronized Harold, characteristically, by defending him, as if Harold could have status only because Lee stood behind him.

. . .

T H E   N E X T day, Lee put the Group people to work: the classes in the art of acting. Everything he taught was opposite to the instruction I'd listened to at Yale. Two young actresses, apprentices as I was, did a scene. When they were through, they looked to him for judgment. He said nothing. They waited. He stared at them. His face gave no hint of what he thought, but it was forbidding. The two actresses began to come apart; everyone could see they were on the verge of tears. Silence is the cruelest weapon when someone loves you, and Lee knew it. Finally one of them, in a voice that quavered, asked, "Lee, what did you think?" He turned his face away, looked at the other actors present. No one dared comment for fear of saying the wrong thing and having Lee turn on them. Finally, speaking quietly, he asked the stricken actress, "Are you nervous and uncertain now?" "Yes, yes," one actress said. "More than you were in the scene you played?" Lee asked. "Yes." "Much more?" "Yes, much more." "Even though the scene you did was precisely about such nervousness and you'd worked hard to imitate it?" "Oh, I see, I see," the actress said, getting Lee's point that now they were experiencing the real emotion whereas before they'd been pretending. He wanted the real emotion, insisted on the "agitation of the essence," as it was called, wouldn't accept less.

At his classes in the technique of acting, Lee laid down the rules, supervised the first exercises. These were largely concerned with the actor's arousing his inner temperament. The essential and rather simple technique, which has since then been complicated by teachers of acting who seek to make the Method more recondite for their commercial advantage, consists of recalling the circumstances, physical and personal, surrounding an intensely emotional experience in the actor's past. It is the same as when we accidentally hear a tune we may have heard at a stormy or an ecstatic moment in our lives, and find, to our surprise, that we are reexperiencing the emotion we felt then, feeling ecstasy again or rage and the impulse to kill. The actor becomes aware that he has emotional resources; that he can awaken, by this self-stimulation, a great number of very intense feelings; and that these emotions are the materials of his art.

Lee taught his actors to launch their work on every scene by taking a minute to remember the details surrounding the emotional experience in their lives that would correspond to the emotion of the scene they were about to play. "Take a minute!" became the watchword of that summer, the phrase heard most often, just as this particular kind of inner concentration became the trademark of Lee's own work when he directed a production. His actors often appeared to be in a state of self-hypnosis. When he directed a love scene, the "lovers" would seem to be not altogether aware of whom they were with but, instead, involved with their own inner state. There'd be no hint of how they proposed to consummate their love.

When Harold began, three years later, to direct the company Lee had trained, he had some difficulties. Once, when asked repeatedly by an actor what the motivation in a love scene was, Harold is said to have burst out with: "Why, you want to fuck her, that's your motivation." Harold was a complicated man, but he didn't choose to make things more complicated than they were.

During the summer of 1932, I completely subscribed to Lee's method. I used to collect my useful memories in a notebook, tabulating these experiences so I could look through them, as through a file, and find the emotion a scene needed and how to awaken it. This collection was called "The Golden Box," and I still have the notebook, with my store of emotions in it.

After an actor had played a scene, Lee would ask, "What were you trying to do?" Immediately the actor found himself on the defensive, with an explanation demanded. The judge at this trial was sometimes a "hanging judge." There was little joy in Lee's work—only guilt for the deviants and a kind of psychological restriction, which made a wild fling into experiment, humor, or fantasy impossible.

But that first summer, Lee and his method went unchallenged. When his judgment was questioned, his lips would tighten and the color would go from his face. Everyone could see that an explosion was coming. Often it did come. Actors succumbed to his emotionalism, even admired it. Facing his wrath, few would stand up for what they'd done. Gradually they became masochists; many seemed particularly to enjoy a good scolding from him. Lee was God almighty, he was always right, only he could tell if an actor had had it—the real thing—or not. To win Lee's favor and the reassurance it would convey was everyone's goal. No one doubted Lee those first months; I certainly didn't.

I W O R K E D like a beaver; every morning, happy and eager, I did my "sense memory" exercises like prayers at dawn; my "matins" they were: shaving without a razor or soap, feeling cold sitting in the summer sun, smelling a lemon, then smelling the space where the lemon had been held to my nostrils, still smelling the lemon . . . And so on. I did scenes with everyone who'd have me, asking everyone to work with me except those actors rehearsing *Success Story* with Lee. Fighting for my life, I was trying to impress the people of the Group, where I'd never tried to impress anyone before.

After a few weeks of work, I began to have an idea of what the artistic leaders there, the directors and the veteran actors, thought of me. The verdict was unfavorable: "Kazan has a great deal of energy but no actor's emotion." No emotion! A strange judgment to pass on a young man who was a closet hysteric. But I had it from a number of sources. It depressed me. Was I an emotional cripple? Was I inhibited from revealing the emotion that I certainly had in abundance? Why couldn't they see it? What was wrong with me?

While I was worrying about this, my one hundred and twelve dollars ran out.

I called Molly for advice. She was spending the summer in the cabin in the Adirondacks, trying to write a play. She sounded worried, told me to rush up there, she missed me, she missed me badly. I was tempted, of course. I'd been celibate for five weeks. I said I'd think it over and decide.

I decided. I told Harold I wasn't leaving the camp. His reaction, I was to learn, was characteristic: He showed no reaction. He left getting rid of me to others. He made no effort to help me stay. I suppose he had other problems and found it difficult to be tough. This gave me time. I went to the man who ran the dining room and kitchen, and I lucked out. He could indeed use another waiter. When Clurman looked up and saw me in a white coat, bringing him chopped liver, he took that as a matter of course too. Perhaps, I thought, he considers this a more suitable profession for me.

I determined to challenge the judgment that I lacked talent as an actor. I did more exercises to intensify my stage concentration. I did others to heighten my sensory awareness. I didn't let my "Golden Box" rest idle. I did voice exercises to rid myself of the specifically New York street accent. I did fencing, in case I might be called on to play Laertes. (Laertes! My God, was I crazy?) I never missed a body class. The person in charge of this training was Helen Tamiris. Her specialty was something called the pelvic thrust, an exercise she must have come upon during her bed games. On the down part of the movement, standing above me, she'd put her foot on my spine and press. Her footprint is still on my back. And I can still recall her voice screaming, "The floor is your friend!" as she pushed me down.

I sat at the feet of Lee and Harold, literally; wrote down everything they said. Harold opened my eyes to the importance of theatre in a society, that it had an obligation, particularly in our time of national emergency, which was to voice the concerns of the people in the audience. Theatre, he said, was not just a pastime between supper and bed. In the twentieth century, it must serve a purpose close to what it had in the pre-Christian Greek world, as a "pop" religion. It had to be an awakening and a reassurance for the masses when they saw their own dilemmas acted out.

Lee explored for us the work of a theatre I knew nothing about: the Russian theatre. In his cottage on the hill, he had a cell where a small man worked, a "slavey," who spoke to no one but Lee. This man was translating a series of books on the theatres of Vakhtangov and Meyerhold, both "studios," offshoots of the Moscow Art Theatre of Stanislavski. Lee was especially enthused over the work of Meyerhold, and he described to us, in scene-by-scene detail, the master's productions of *Camille* and *The Inspec-*

tor General. He showed us photographs and drawings of the unusual settings. I was fascinated. Theatre, I saw, did not have to be a realistic art. Leave that to films.

When he described a scene of courting lovers played from opposite ends of a seesaw as it stroked up and down, we all got the idea. Meyerhold did not depend on words. He spoke through bold inventions of theatre actions, close to dance. Lee quoted Meyerhold: "Words are decorations on the hem of the skirt of action." And another: "The actor no longer occupies the leading place upon the stage. The director will determine all life there." I was never to forget these two sentences. Lee also introduced me to the idea of what he called the "subtext," which describes what happens underneath and sometimes contrary to what is spoken. "The subtext is the play," he said. I repeated this fifty years later to the playwrights/directors group at the Actors Studio.

Above all, Lee expressed his own hopes to us, what he as a director hoped one day to do with the Group. It was a grand perspective. We would together create great ensemble productions with daring theatre visions that went far beyond realism and naturalism. We might have to develop these groundbreakers from plays that were often mediocre—but so had Meyerhold. The best that our contemporary playwrights could offer was short of Lee's visions of theatre. But we'd do it, create total theatre, combining all the arts of actors' techniques that we were learning as well as all the experiences of the great theatre of Russia, which he was studying and bringing to us.

There was an irony in this, which I didn't understand until later. Lee was a deeply introspective man and restrained in his physical expression, not flamboyant, not free. His directorial effects were intense, but they were always rigidly expressed. There was nothing of the circus about the man, and he was not, at that time, a performer himself. He had no facility for stage movement; the man he'd chosen for his ideal and his inspiration, V. E. Meyerhold, was his opposite. No choreographer was ever bolder. It's dangerous when an artist chooses a goal for which he is not equipped or temperamentally suited. But Lee persisted, year after year, planning productions in his mind that he could not and did not accomplish. Right up until his very last years, whenever I'd visit him at his Central Park West apartment, he'd find an occasion to pull me aside and speak of his hopes and dreams, unrealistic and poetic productions that he'd direct in daring ways that Broadway had never seen. As he'd tell me about his plans, I'd keep a straight face, while my feelings were concern and pity. I knew by then that nothing would come of Lee's visions.

Lee and Harold were men of size, and I owe both of them more than I can say; they gave a direction to my life when I was adrift. I learned a lot from them, directly and from observing them live out their lives. I admired one always and felt for the other always. At a crucial time in my life, I was lucky to have them as friends. I believe both died with a secret ache in their hearts, Harold from not having created the permanent theatre he'd spoken of so often and so eloquently, Lee from having become famous in a way that was not the way of his dearest dreams. Perhaps Lee didn't know this; I believe he did. So it goes in America: great plans in youth, realism at the end.

Y O U   M U S T be wondering about my strange way of telling a story, constantly shifting around, twisting back and forth in time even though my life has been lived as yours is being lived, in a progression of days. What I'm doing is unraveling a great tangle of twine, found in an old basket at the bottom of a dark closet. There are many strings, balled together. I pull on one; it yields, then binds. I pull harder; it gives a little more, bringing up with it another string, of another size, color, and texture. So the strands of my life intermingle; they cannot be separated into a succession of "and then I dids." I can only offer you various lengths extracted from various times in the jumble of my days, none completely free of all others, none unattached. Recounting bare events explains little; meanings come from connections— and from endings. Associations, turning up like the dummy card in stud poker, bring triumph, regret, and understanding. The links of meaning are always more relevant than those of time. For this reason, events that took place fifty years ago stand out vividly in my memory, whereas I can't remember what I did last week. I do not hope to untangle the whole ball; it is snarled and knotted and mildewed by time. To know it all . . . Whoever has? Who can?

I've often thought: Oh, if I could only have looked ahead and seen the consequences of what I was about to do. But the evidence of the cost of each step into the unknown—what might be gained, what lost—was all there, just below the surface. I didn't look long enough or hard enough, or I didn't dare look at all.

For instance, how did I come to marry a saint?

When I use that dreadful word "saint," I don't mean without fault. God, no! I mean a creature guided by a faith and committed to absolutes. Saints walk straight into a fire. Blind to alternatives, they are difficult creatures for their associates and for themselves. Especially the last, as you'll see.

In midsummer of 1932, this saint found herself pregnant and unmarried, a more serious matter in 1932 than in 1988.

She informed me of her condition over the phone to the Group Theatre's work camp. It hadn't been easy to get through from the Adirondacks, where she was vacationing with her mother. The Group's phone hung in the hall just outside the dining room, where, in my starched white coat, I was serving dinner to a fractious group of actors, so it was impossible for me to ask questions. She was able to tell me the fact and little more. Well, what more was there to tell?

A couple of days later, I received a letter. She'd been taking suppressed-menstruation pills. When I saw her later, she showed them to me. If they'd moved, I'd have believed them big black beetles; as it was, they suggested magic, not medicine. Molly said in her letter that she'd given up on them.

I knew how it had happened. A week before we left Yale and New Haven for good, she drove me to Poughkeepsie in her Ford coupe to show me Vassar College; she wanted me to know everything about her life there. There were no interstates in those days, and we made the trip over a winding blacktop without a center line. Happy, bubbling over, she was telling tales about her collegemates, then looking at me for my reaction, so she did not see the rabbit until the instant before she ran it over.

When she stopped and looked back, the animal was squirming around and around in one place, as if trying to free itself from the grip of something malignant it couldn't see. Molly didn't look back again.

I got out of the car and walked to where the rabbit lay on the black tar. I could see it was finished and didn't know what I could do for it except put an end to its pain. A rock out of a stone wall did that. I slid my foot under the warm, limp body and lifted it onto the turf at the side of the road.

Back in the car, I found Molly hysterical. She couldn't go on driving, so I took over, but her tears wouldn't stop. Was she taking the incident as an omen about us? She was shaking, so I pulled off the road and helped her out of the car. I led her over a wall of old gray stones; I remember we had to pick a way through a splendid stand of poison ivy and into a large open field. Two cows watched from a far corner. The spring of the year—May!—was in its glory, field flowers everywhere. An apple tree was sporting its blooms. We lay down under it. Overhead, bees were at work, and when Molly was quiet at last, we could hear their buzzing.

Her cheeks had their special high pink. When she opened her moist eyes, they glistened. She looked at me as women do when you're the only comfort they want.

I'd always been very careful, even when she'd wanted me not to be. This time her anguish held me to her and her arms. Then her legs clasped and lifted. When it came to that time, she wouldn't let go.

Two months later, when I had her letter, I felt—to use the word girls use—"caught." I regarded her pregnancy as a threat to my freedom. I resented it. I didn't want to leave camp; I'd scheduled scenes to show in class. A trip away would interrupt my voice and body work. I was straining to prove myself indomitable. The time for a verdict from the Group directors was coming near. I was grinding my teeth at night.

A friend had recommended an abortionist to Molly, and she went to see him. "I don't like the man," she wrote me. "He is little and cheap and lied to me. He wants all of $300 with $10 extra if I stay overnight. He doesn't urge this, says I could leave at four or five. But $300!"

Unhappy with the abortionist's character and his price, she went back to her friend. "I've been talking to 'A,'" she wrote, "she thinks she can jew the man down." (Molly's politicization was yet to begin.) "'A' says that guys in that game are a race apart, all call you 'dear' and most of them have dirty fingernails. This doctor, she says, has a long record of experience and is counted very skillful."

Abortions were illegal in the thirties, but they were tolerated by the rule of convenience. This particular man was what Molly didn't trust in a doctor—jovial. He made flippant remarks; to reassure her, I suppose. But he misjudged the girl; his manner had the opposite effect. Nevertheless she decided to go ahead with him and went to his office on West End Avenue for a preliminary examination. "The more I see of that damned doctor," she wrote me, "the less I like him. His office is dingy and the table covered with dust. I didn't know where to put my bloomers when I took them off. I hated his hands on me; he didn't wear gloves. I was nervous and mad at being in that position. Anyway, we made a date, Friday, at ten-thirty in the morning."

I wrote and asked if she wanted me to go with her.

"Yes, I do want you there and to stay through the next day, please," she answered. "I have to go to the Bowery Savings Bank first to get the cash. It's the one opposite Grand Central and I'll wait for you at ten o'clock by the side door. Then we'll go to where it's going to be done, at a 'sanatorium'—what's that?—10 West 123rd Street. Is that in Harlem? I keep thinking of girls with less money, what do they do?"

I met her outside the Bowery Savings Bank and she gave me the three hundred dollars to hold. Then we went uptown, where I waited in the anteroom. It was a hot day. My shirt was soaked through. "Why do you look so worried?" the receptionist said. Her legs were bulky in white stockings, and when she crossed them her skirt rode up, giving the place an air of impropriety. "It'll be over before you know it," she said.

It was quick. Molly couldn't wait to get out, and we left at four. We went to the apartment of her friend; Molly got right into bed and told me to get in with her. She looked wan, whether from fear or loss of blood I didn't know. The pallor and her helplessness had an appeal for me. I was ready to make love to her. This reassured her. Although she was very sleepy, she asked about the Group. I told her how impressed I was with Lee Strasberg and Harold Clurman, then tried to tell her the ideas behind the organization and how loyal the members were. I hadn't learned yet that any unqualified opinion, positive or negative, brought a doubting response from Molly.

"What keeps them all together?" she asked.

"The idea," I answered. "And the directors."

"Don't they get better offers? For other plays? Even movies?"

"Sure. Some of them. But they don't take them."

"Really? Why not?"

"Because they hero-worship Clurman and Strasberg."

"Hero-worship!"

"Yes. Wait until you hear them speak."

"You too?"

I ducked the question.

"Don't you do any hero-worshipping," she warned.

I told her how discouraged I was about the Group's opinion of me. "You won't be kicked out," she said. "Stop all that yammering. You're good. I know it. And they will shortly." Having delivered herself of this unqualified reassurance, she fell asleep. In repose, she looked like a saint. The next morning she gave me money to get back to camp.

She wrote me immediately. "This is just to reassure you if you need it. I feel very much at peace and glad we did it. I'm pleased with you and pleased with me and happy about us."

But I brought a contrary feeling back to camp. I was clenched in a ball like a porcupine, sharp quills protecting soft undersides. I'd had a narrow escape. Only by her goodness and generosity had I regained my freedom. She could have pressured me into marriage and I would have yielded. The abortion had saved me. I had to be careful now. Christ, I hadn't begun to live! Why tie myself down too early? I hadn't seen the world or "the field" yet.

I'd better think. I had no job, no prospects. I couldn't wait on table the rest of my life. I hadn't been taken into the Group and there was no indication that I might be. I had no money. Where would I go after the Group summer? Home? Hell, no! I recalled a visit my uncle A. E. ("Joe") Kazan had paid to my father's store. After watching me unfold a rug instead of rolling it up, he'd yelled, "Hey, George, you got a dead one here!" Father had not defended me. Even Mother seemed discouraged now about my future. What the hell did I suppose I'd ever get to be? An actor? With my looks? I'd better face the truth before something happened with Molly again. The truth was that we were completely different people. The truth was that she was brighter than I, an intellectual too. I had no shape as a person yet. The only faith I'd ever found was in the Group Theatre and its leaders. I resented her questioning the Group, but I had no confidence in my own future there. My experience in their camp had revived the feeling I used to have, that I was essentially a "good-for-nothing." I heard my father's voice and had, as always, an aftertremor of fear.

I determined not to gamble again. I'd break it off. Okay. Decided! But there was this: In all the world, Molly was my only loyal and understanding friend, the last and the most perceptive of a succession of women—my

mother, Lucy, my grandmother, Miss Anna B. Shank, and now Molly—
who'd supported me. Alone in my cot at night, I longed for her.

T H E O N E thing any ambitious outsider seeking recognition in an alien
society cannot tolerate is to be trapped in an enclosure where the gate is
locked and he doesn't have the key. The freedom to choose my next step is
what I live by. Anything that threatens this freedom throws me—still!—
into a fury. There've been times in my life when, feeling trapped in a relationship, a job, or a situation, even when everything seemed to be going
well, I've kept a valise packed and ready for an abrupt departure. I've
also—I still do this—kept complete sets of clothes, suits, shirts, hats,
shoes, underwear, in at least two places and sometimes three. Another confession: I maintain small bank accounts in Athens, Paris, and Zurich. Ready
in case. Of what? I don't know exactly. Ready. I once had more, in London,
Istanbul, and Los Angeles—small accounts of no consequence, carfare. I've
been obsessed all my life with the possibility that flight might suddenly be
necessary. I feel safer when I'm ready for it.

Twelve years after that summer at Dover Furnace, I directed a play on
Broadway by Franz Werfel and S. N. Behrman, entitled *Jacobowsky and
the Colonel*. The play had a most personal meaning for me, and perhaps for
this reason, I seem to have done it well. It concerned a little Jew, a mercantile man who, as the German armies bore down on Paris, was trying desperately to escape with his life by staying ahead of the advancing Nazis.
This man's whole life had been a series of wriggles out of danger.

From this chain of experience there came to be in the soul of Jacobowsky
a kind of enforced optimism, expressed in a speech I've never forgotten:

"My poor mother, wise woman that she was, always used to say that no
matter what happens in life, there are always two possibilities. For example, right now it is a dark moment, yet even now there are two possibilities. The Germans, either they will come to Paris or they'll jump to
England. If they don't come to Paris, that's good. But if they should come
to Paris, again there are two possibilities. The Germans, either they will
put us in a good concentration camp or in a bad concentration camp. If in a
good concentration camp, that's good, but if they put us in a bad concentration camp, there are still two . . ." And so on.

Perhaps Sam Behrman also made some connection between me and his
character, because he dedicated the play to me.

Jacobowsky, played by a forgotten genius, Oscar Karlweis, reminded me
of my father, even down to the splay-footed walk and the shuffle of his
trouser bottoms. My father had kept himself and his family just ahead of a
series of threats, massacres, and takeovers, going from Kayseri, in mid-
Anatolia, to Constantinople, from there to Berlin, then getting out of Ger-

many in 1913, back to Constantinople, and from there to New York, just before an event—the First World War—that would have ruined him and his family.

Any man who comes out of a climate of oppression has to learn to keep an eye on the back door and make sure it remains unlocked, to know the "right" people, to ease his way out of trouble before it becomes life-threatening, and to avoid all fights. Such a man lives by his wits—which are, because they've had to be, extra sharp. Cunning is his muscle and his bulletproof vest.

I'm such a man. I've always felt in danger. I've never felt totally secure, even when I was most successful and every author wanted me to direct his new play. I've thought affluence uncertain and praise temporary. I am obsessively aware that money in the bank leaks, that it shrinks. I don't trust the state—whichever state. Do you? Really? I fear authority. I don't believe that those who exercise it will continue to be friendly. I trust authority—to be unfriendly. I feel I will be apprehended as much for my thoughts as for past deeds and omissions. I've done nothing for which I might be arrested, but that doesn't seem to make any difference.

Even today, when I'm modestly affluent and recognized as a man of some achievement, I will be driving along or walking the streets or sitting at dinner, and suddenly I'll find myself in the grip of a fantasy in which I am defending myself—actually speaking the words, trying to wash myself of guilt. The police have me! I protest my innocence. I contest their accusations. The actors I'm working with are questioning my directions. I slam into them, challenging them with my reasons. My wife, the present one, who loves me entirely, or the one before her, who loved me less, is accusing me of some marital misdemeanor. True or false? Either way, I fight off the accusation. It seems I am constantly defending myself against an accusation of one kind or another. And I've been doing it all my life.

I feel like apologizing to the world. Can any of you readers understand that? I doubt it. "You think because you've been lying in a ditch for fifteen minutes," Jacobowsky says, "you know what it is to be me. It's not so simple. When I get up, the ditch follows me."

Yes, of course there are others like me, many. You have to admire men like this despite certain disagreeable qualities they have. The qualities you don't like are those that helped them escape and readapt and survive in new surroundings. I didn't like Kurt Weill personally—this after doing two shows with him, in which I found him always swinging to whoever had the most power—but I did admire his ability to make good in a new country, this one, and to adapt himself to the requirements of our musical theatre. If, when he left Germany, he'd landed in Java instead of the United States, within a year he'd have been writing Javanese temple music and receiving praise from their high priests. If he'd been dumped on an African savannah, he'd quickly have mastered the tribal drum!

Sam Spiegel survived many failures and endured to make some of the most adventurous and successful pictures in film history. He would go down but always rise again. His guiding principle—expediency, doing whatever was necessary—proved a great help in negotiations with Hollywood executives. He learned, for instance, to lie without a betraying tremor of his facial muscles; I've seen that. Hardships honed these men's cleverness; I've met none sharper.

During the production of a film, Sam sometimes seemed like a cheap bully, alert to whose ass it would benefit him to kiss and whose to kick for an advantage. At other times Sam came on as a most intelligent and cultured man, thoroughly gentled by civilization. Which was he? Both. He learned to make lightning-fast changes in protective skin coloring. He had to learn or not survive. I was never able to dislike Sam, despite the urging of some people close to me; in fact, I've always enjoyed his company.

I consider myself rigorously moral—moral enough, in fact, to admit this: There is one thing I've lied about consistently, and that is my relationships to women out of wedlock. I have again and again lied to my wives about this. I don't know how else to handle this problem, and I don't think you or anyone else does.

I've also occasionally lied to playwrights when they've offered me a play to direct that I've liked but with qualifications that were negative. I'd not mention those qualifications; I'd pretend I liked the play more than I did. I don't know how else to handle this problem either. Are you feeling morally superior to me? I've also often smiled at actors after run-throughs so that they'd believe they were making progress. If I'd shown them the concern I was feeling, they'd have had a serious setback. I know that all conditions in the term of a rehearsal are temporary. A director should not allow his feelings of doubt and despair to be seen; he's supposed to be a center of calm in a whirlwind of uncertainty. So why discourage actors? There's enough doubt in their bellies without a director adding to it.

I've met a few people in the theatre who've been absolutely truthful at all times. Just as I was an outsider by birth and by family history, Molly was an insider. She never doubted her place in life. For her there were never two possibilities; there was only one. As I was Jacobowsky's son, she was the daughter of a corporation lawyer who commuted on the same train every morning from South Orange, New Jersey, to a massive oak desk in Wall Street. Molly's great-grandfather was president of Yale University. I slipped around the edges of conflicts; Molly stood upright in the center of storms. I learned to compromise when I was young and so avoid confrontation. Molly's principles permitted no deviation from her obligation to what was right. She felt it was her business to speak out on anything she felt. I was born knowing that things could never be perfect. Perfection was Molly's standard for her life. She never wavered and she never changed, rather became more rigid as the years passed.

In time I was to develop an ardent admiration for her Yankee intransigence—in her and in her children. But it took time.

In our years together, she would read the plays I was offered to direct as they came to me and volunteer her judgment and criticism. She was often of great help to me. I knew what she'd give me was her truth regardless of what it cost her to say it. But it wasn't enough for her to state her opinion and offer her suggestions in great detail to the author of the play, to have him listen, nod, and reply, "Yes, yes, I'll certainly think about all that, thank you very much," and so on. He had to *do* something about her criticisms, or he'd hear from her again.

Looking back, I must believe that a compulsive demand for perfection in things can be neurotic and destructive, especially in the field where we worked. One must do one's best and at a certain point say, "I've done all I can; I'm not going to make this better." I've noticed that the best pieces of writing for the theatre I've known are complete at birth. The first draft had it—or didn't. In both *Streetcar Named Desire* and *Death of a Salesman*, I asked the author for no rewriting, and rehearsals didn't reveal the need for any. Those plays were born sound. The work, the struggle, the self-flagellation, had all taken place within the author before he touched his typewriter. Usually when there is a lot of tampering and fussing over a manuscript, there's something basically wrong to begin with.

W H E N I came back to the Group from New York City, I found that my experience with the abortion and my two-day absence made a disproportionate difference to how I saw the camp. I'd begun to have some doubts about what, only a few days before, I'd idealized. A boy sits on the floor at the feet of a master and writes down everything he says; a man does not. I have no notes inscribed after my return. I wore a shell rather than a skin, my protection against the negative judgment on my apprenticehood that I believed was coming.

I also saw signs of demoralization. The gloss of idealism had been partially rubbed off, replaced by practicality. There was much weekending in New York to get jobs by those who weren't in *Success Story*. "The Group is already talking," I wrote Molly, "about the good old days and the near-religious zeal they had last summer. There are factions and misunderstandings here now."

The attention of the directors was focused on preparing *Success Story* for presentation in New York City. The classes in acting, dance, speech, and so forth seemed side issues, even indulgences. *Success Story* had to work! The organization's future was at stake.

I looked at the members with a different eye when I got back. Yes, Molly had had an effect on me. I asked myself the question she'd asked: Why did

At right, on the fringe

they all stay together? I began to wonder. People not involved in the one production being intensively rehearsed were edgy with each other. At night I would hear shouts in the dark; nocturnal quarrels were reported in the morning.

Unbeknownst to all, a basic matter—the problem of a "permanent" theatre in our society—was being fought out. I break in here again, to point to Franchot Tone. He exemplified to me the problem of maintaining a permanent theatre company in our society. I wrote to Molly:

Everyone's talking about Franchot Tone's disappearance. He left camp the night before I came down to meet you; he still hasn't come back. The members are criticizing his faithlessness. He walked into the dance class, for instance, sized up Tamiris and what she was up to, and never went back. He's taken no part in the experimental work in Harold's classes. He read a mystery story all through the rehearsals of *Big Night* and Cheryl Crawford, who's directing that play, doesn't want him in her cast now. He has a car, a red roadster, and leaves camp every chance he gets. And he drinks. A lot. At the same time he's wonderful in his role in *Success Story*—as you'll see if you come up. I imagine that Lee Strasberg, who has someone else reading Tone's part now, will be very glad to see him back.

Where'd he go? All they know or say they know is that he had some drunken "tool" call Clurman and explain that Franchot had gone to see a doctor about his kidneys. Does he expect us to believe that?

Alan, who's close to Tone, told me the inside, that Tone is in New York talking to some Hollywood people about working in films.

The next day I wrote her again:

Strasberg made a big speech last night about Tone, said he was potentially the best actor in the country but Lee doesn't want him in the Group. His behavior, Lee said, was beginning to undermine the spirit of commitment and devotion that was necessary for the company's continuance. Strasberg was jumping up and down with emotion as he spoke and a couple of the Group actresses were crying. I think Tone takes pleasure in upsetting the chalice of high art here.

You can't help admiring him. He's better educated, just plain smarter, than most of the others and has greater curiosity about life and boldness in dealing with his desires. I like him. Perhaps some of the self-righteous members think of Tone as a sinner because he wakes the sinner in them. I've been wondering if they are, finally, jealous of his talent, his looks, his Hollywood offers and his money? As for his eccentric behavior, it may come out of what many here feel, uncertainty about the future. Me too. There's been more going to Pawling for drink after night rehearsals since Tone left, and the directors are worried about it. Clurman took Alan aside and asked him not to go on any more binges with Franchot. Alan thinks Harold was subtly threatening him.

A couple of days later, I wrote her:

Early in the morning, we heard a shotgun fired out the window of the room next to ours. Tone is back. He seems o.k., not hung over. He brought one of his old Cornell buddies with him and at lunch they got into a scrap. Tone's buddy threw water at him and when Clurman tried to quiet them, Tone stormed out, climbed into his red roadster and was gone. He came back at the end of the afternoon and asked for a talk with the directors.

I got what happened from Alan. Certain things were settled. Tone will be replaced in the role he hates in *Big Night* but he'll stay in *Success Story* through the New York opening—if there is one, no one knows yet—then go to California for the movies in November. They can't afford to lose him in *Success Story*. Meantime, he continues as the chink in their idealism. He does what he wants and isn't a bit docile. He believes in the Group idea but is not sure it's for him; he asks questions. Despite all, the directors admire him. He could burn the place down and still be the white-haired boy. He's the only really top-grade actor here—in my opinion—and that's the problem. I mean that's their problem, the directors: how to hold people of his talent and temperament while they get rid of three or four duds they've got here who believe! Oh, how those mediocrities believe! Oh, how they listen to Lee and nod and smile at his quips. Me too.

Two gallons of applejack came into the camp last night with a girl named Betty. She and the stuff are in Tone's room now. I love you.

Molly answered my letter, as ever, with a challenge. "This is a restless civilization," she wrote. "Do you really think it's possible to maintain in this country, where values go up and down so fast, the kind of permanent theatres they have in Europe?" She didn't think so. I did. I had to; I was there. Obdurate Molly said she thought the Group idea was possible only in a socialist state.

I'd thought Tone's excuse—taking five days to see a doctor about his kidneys—clumsy and unbelievable. It turned out to be true; he did have a problem there. And he did go to Hollywood after he left *Success Story*. But there his ego was not treated as gently by the studio heads as it had been by the Group directors. Drink became habitual for him. He hooked up with Joan Crawford, who ate him alive. I remember the day, some years later, when he brought her to the Group camp to meet his old buddies. At a party, I recall her sitting silently in a corner, knitting with two long white needles, hardly ever looking up. There was something predatory about her, I thought. But Tone said she was impressed. With what? I don't know. They returned to California. From there Tone continued to look back at the Group with nostalgia and with guilt at having left it as he had. When we needed money in later years, Harold played on this guilt and Tone would send a check. And, no doubt, feel better about himself.

In 1939, Tone, still trying to recapture what he'd lost, accepted a part, of equal size to five others, in a production of Irwin Shaw's *The Gentle People*. The reviewers rather slighted him; his return was less than a triumph. After the play closed, we lost track of each other. He went on drinking and, in time, did lose a kidney to a surgeon. He died before he should have and without fulfilling his promise or his hopes.

IN THE middle of a night, I called Molly in the Adirondacks and suggested she visit me. Molly had become my drug of reassurance. I reached for her when I was down.

I found a room for us "off campus." The bloom was back on the girl. She radiated good health, was brown all over and elegantly slim, wore sneakers, went bare-legged, and we loved each other all day. She'd brought a device with her—a pessary, so they were called then—and secure now, we enjoyed each other more than ever. My indelible memory is of how patrician her long, slim fingers were as they held the "tulip." In quiet moments, I

told her I knew how much she'd gone through for me—the best I could do
for thanks. In the morning, she spoke of marriage. I changed the subject.
By the second morning, I found myself so attached that life without her
seemed impossible.

I brought her to camp and introduced her to some of the actors, particularly to my best friend and fellow freak, Clifford Odets. No sparks were
struck. I introduced her to Lee Strasberg, who was short with her as he was
with everyone at first meeting. I explained in a whisper that Lee was carrying a great weight of worries about the future of *Success Story*. I took
Molly to Harold Clurman's class. He was in great form. I expected she'd be
impressed with his eloquence, but she backed off. "He sounds like one of
those healer-spielers," she said. In the Group, Molly spoke heresy. She
particularly detested Harold's phrase "ideologically cemented collective." "I
don't want to be cemented to anyone," she said.

Alan, her old lover, was there. Both were nervous at the encounter, both
smoked cigarette after cigarette. Tone passed by and Alan explained the
general disapproval of Franchot in the Group. Molly wanted to know if that
degree of condemnation was just. I assured her it was necessary; the Group
had to be kept together. Alan was less convinced. Molly scoffed, made a
face: doubt.

I found I was mad at her—as if my religion had been attacked. But to
listen without questioning was impossible for Molly. To be overwhelmed by
a force as strong as Harold's put her back up. Harold had become my particular hero by this time. "Let's go eat dinner," I said, cutting short the
conversation.

That night I took Molly to a general meeting, at which Lee announced
that Mr. Lee Shubert, the owner (with his brother, J. J. Shubert) of the
largest chain of legitimate theatres in New York City, was coming to a run-
through of *Success Story*, there to decide whether or not he'd give us a
theatre in New York to show our work. Lee Strasberg told a story for which
he was famous. The previous season, the authors of one of the plays the
Group was rehearsing had complained about Lee's methods of work, which
were improvisational and rather neglectful of the lines as written. Lee had
become angry with the authors and told them, in no uncertain language,
that the Group people were gathered not to do a production but to create
a theatre. I watched Molly's face as Lee told this story. A writer herself, she
was offended. Later, when we were alone, I told her I had read the play
and felt sure it would have been a failure no matter how it had been rehearsed.

"That's not the point," Molly said. She asked if Lee was always that imperious—that was the word she used. I said yes; it was necessary; Lee's
fierce conviction was what held the Group together. She nodded, seeming
to accept the necessity for Lee's "arrogance." But she didn't, and her attitude affected me. Despite my considerable admiration for Lee, I had to

recognize that I'd never been at ease with him. It was hero worship or nothing.

"You look worried," Molly said, as we were undressing for bed. "What's the matter?"

"Of course I'm worried," I said. "It would be a tragedy for me if I weren't made a member at the end of the summer. And I'm afraid I won't be."

"That's a big word, 'tragedy,'" Molly said.

"You mean you think they won't accept me?" I asked.

"What I mean is," she answered, "that they don't seem to have jobs for the actors who're already members."

"They have another play in rehearsal, with parts for a lot more people. What are you thinking—what?"

"I wouldn't attach all my hopes to the Group if I were you," she said. "They should take you, but—there are other people and plays and producers in the theatre, aren't there?"

I didn't answer.

"Tell me," she went on. "Isn't it inevitable that the talented ones will go and the ordinary talents remain? That seems to be already happening. The first thing they need here is someone to replace Tone, actors like him, some Irish faces, a Scotsman—"

I was disturbed in a way I didn't understand. She had a right, of course, to challenge me; why not? I'd often said to myself that I respected her for expressing her contrary opinions so openly and absolutely. But did I want that as a constant in my life, every morning at breakfast, every night before going to bed? What I didn't take into account to explain my annoyance is that I was an Anatolian, and the Anatolian wife is required, by tradition and under threat of a physical drubbing, to agree with her husband on all issues—or shut up.

"Turn off the light," I said.

"Docile people tend to be mediocrities—" she started.

"Okay, okay, turn off the light."

"Can't we disagree?" she asked. "Even a little?" Then she kissed me, and all was harmony again—for that night.

M R .   L E E   S H U B E R T   arrived in a chauffeur-driven limousine, and his visit was the professional climax of the summer. His judgment would determine whether or not the Group would have a theatre in New York City that fall. I realized what a precarious gamble the summer had been. Now it was all up to one man. Mr. Lee was escorted to a seat in the rehearsal hall, a large armchair that, when it was placed at the back of the space, resembled a throne. We, the underlings, were scattered around the floor, waiting for the judgment that was to affect us all.

I'd sneaked Molly in and we sat together in a corner at the side. I watched Mr. Lee more than I watched the performance. He looked, I thought, like a wooden Indian whose face had been so heavily varnished that, had it been alive, couldn't have moved. It didn't—not ever through the show. I saw no reaction even to the "big" moments of passion and *sturm*. In fact, I believe that at one moment Mr. Lee nodded off. This does not embarrass men with power. At the end of the performance, the three directors clustered around the throne to hear Mr. Lee's pleasure. There was a conversation, very brief considering the importance of what was being laid down. Our Lee was anything but imperious with Mr. Shubert; he and Harold behaved like anxious boys. Cheryl maintained her poise and walked Mr. Shubert to his limousine. Then he was gone.

Before his car was out of sight, we all learned that Mr. Shubert had promised the Group the Maxine Elliott Theatre, on the edge of the garment center. This theatre is now demolished, and it wasn't a favored location then, but the Group was delighted to have it.

Molly wasn't thrilled. "Glad you got the theatre," she said. "But what are they going to do about that girl?"

"What girl?" I said, ready for a fight. I knew what girl.

"The one who's supposed to be the oh-so-sexy kid. She was hopeless."

"Wait until Lee works with her," I said. "You know there's such a thing as the technique of acting, which they don't teach at Yale, so you don't know anything about it."

"I'll keep my fingers crossed," she allowed me. Then: "Let's not argue tonight, Sugar. Turn off the light."

The next morning Molly left. I was relieved to again be living unchallenged.

I T S O O N appeared, from a new surge of activity in the rehearsals, that Mr. Shubert had had the same reservations Molly had about the young actress who played the shiksa for whom the Jewish hero develops a throbbing passion. The wooden Indian who granted or withheld theatre bookings in New York City had found our girl insufficiently sexy. At first everyone resented the criticism and gathered around to protect the actress. Proper care was taken that she should not be demoralized; the extent of Mr. Shubert's criticism was kept from her. When she guessed the reason for what was happening in rehearsals, we all said to her, "Well, what the hell does he know?" That went on for a couple of days. Then came step two: "So we'll work!" It occurred to us only years later that she was what Molly had called her—hopeless. She should have been replaced immediately with someone from the "outside." Years later, when the reorganized Group put on Odets's *Golden Boy* and I had a voice in decisions, we brought in Frances Farmer. But this enlightenment took time; Cliff was the Golden Boy of Broadway in those years, and his good favor was not to be trifled with.

Lee went to work. The crisis called for individual attention; rehearsals were declared private. I know only what I was told by informants who'd had it from the problem girl herself. First Lee explained, in the vocabulary of intellect, what was missing. Then he directed her attention to certain advertisements in fashion magazines featuring models who possessed—the ad copy guaranteed it—infinite allure. Apparently not satisfied with the results of this technique, Lee took to his feet, desperation downing dogma, and did what is prohibited in the Method, played the part of the sexy shiksa himself, then asked to be imitated. I'd certainly like to have seen that.

You might suppose that the result of this desperate artistic struggle would have been to make our actress more aware of her deficiencies. Not at all. So great was Lee's hypnotic power that summer that she emerged from the privileged rehearsals glowing with confidence.

The next time I saw a run-through of the play, the effect of the glamour ads was evident in the artificial movements and absurd posturing of our "society girl." I came away from that rehearsal with my first doubts about the Group directors and their speeches against typecasting. Appearance isn't everything, right! But if the actor hasn't got the quality you want in her, you can't get it out of her. It wasn't an easy lesson to learn. It never occurred to Lee, as far as I know, to recast the part. That was the spirit of the Group that summer. Faith conquers all!

ALL THIS I watched from a great distance. I was less and less involved in the activities of the camp, increasingly ignored. By the end of the summer, I was a waiter in their dining hall and little more. Despite all, I went right on doing my voice exercises and shaving without a razor in the morning. "I seem to have caught the Group's eye at last," I wrote Molly. "At tennis. I believe I'm the fourth best player on the place." I was supporting myself typing. "I stayed up two nights of the last three typing *The Heavenly Express*, a new play by Albert Bein," I wrote her. "There's no part in it for me."

As I grew increasingly isolated, I missed Molly more. I was hungry for the reassurance only she'd provided me. Now she was writing me loving letters, beautiful letters. I still have them. It melted my heart that she made an effort to recognize the problems she'd created with her endlessly critical attitude. I wrote, confessing my side—the bad temper, the ever-ready suspicion—and asked her indulgence. Need reached out to need. It seemed we loved each other more when we were apart than when we were together.

The verdict on me was pronounced by Harold on the day before the camp broke up. Sitting by, silent, Lee looked at me only once. "You may have talent for the theatre," Harold said—I've never forgotten these words; I wrote them down directly afterward—"but it's certainly not for acting."

That's when Lee turned his face to me. He had a way of looking at a person without an expression. There was no sympathy there, not even curiosity. But what the hell did I expect? He had his own problems; he needed his mask too.

Later in life, when I had my confidence, I would admit that their judgment on me that day was correct. I was never much of an actor. Still there's this irony: Five years later, I was playing leading roles in Group productions under Harold's direction and getting excellent notices. What I could play successfully was a man-boy, angry at the world and turned to violence; I had great success as a gangster.

Harold gave me a crumb of kindness. He told me I could come to any classes the Group had after *Success Story* opened in New York. I didn't respond. Despite the fact that I'd anticipated the decision, it left me hollowed out. I was up against it now. Where would I turn next? How would I make a living? How could I avoid crawling home again and facing the "I told you so" look from my father? How could I continue to live by his forbearance?

I went out and Alan came in to receive his verdict. He wasn't taken in as a member either, but they did encourage him. Alan was already getting attention from film people—through Franchot, I supposed.

I didn't call Molly to tell her what had happened. She'd predicted it and that made me mad at her. The last thing I wanted was her pity. Jacobowsky's ditch followed me wherever I went that day.

Then came a miracle, a gift presented to me by Cheryl Crawford, offered with such casualness that it seemed doubly kind and valuable and served as a perfect reassuring counter to the hard decision Harold had laid on me. Theresa Helburn, on the Theatre Guild's board of directors, and a close friend of Cheryl's, came to camp to visit her friend. Cheryl brought me to where Terry lay on a hammock, reading a script, pencil in hand, and introduced us. When Cheryl dropped the suggestion that Terry might find something for me, a bit perhaps, an assistant stage manager's job, in the play she was about to direct, *The Pure in Heart*, by "that bowlegged Jew with the vivid face," John Howard Lawson, Terry grimaced prettily but turned businesslike. I imagine she didn't know what to make of me. Cheryl must have pitched for me later, because shortly after I returned to the city, I had a letter from the Guild's casting director, informing me that I had a job. It was to be a two-city tour before a New York opening, and I was to be paid fifty dollars a week.

I'd never done anything like this. I was highly excited. It was the big leagues now, not the Group. The real pros! I knew the Group people too well to consider them "big time." Now at last I had something substantial to tell my ever-doubting father and my long-patient mother. And Molly as well.

She was in New York, living in the apartment of her rich aunt and trying to "figure her life." After our first hour together, she began to talk about "getting something settled" between us. I felt I was being pushed into a corner, and slipped out from between the closing walls. I wasn't ready for any "settling," not of anything. When I faced Molly, the person herself, not the romantic creature created out of longing, when I looked at the facts of my own life and what I had in my pocket, when I contemplated my future and my character, the notion of marriage still seemed absurd and, on her side, quixotic. "Let's wait and see how this play turns out," I said, wriggling free. I must confess that the job made the difference. I simply wasn't as desperate for reassurance now.

All my life with her, even after we were married, Molly was to talk about "getting things settled." She would never accept that this was impossible, particularly with me but also in any life open to the pressures of the arts. I would never settle down except in spurts, preferred to swing back and forth, holding hard to opposites: security and the reassurance of being loved totally and, at the same time, the freedom to do what I wanted to do with whomever I wanted. This devotion to the creed of *both* became the pattern of my life. I was a bad risk for her. For anybody.

People have often accused me of being selfish and self-centered. They're quite right. All artists are. They protect like all hell what's most precious for them—the privilege to exploit the full range of their curiosity. On the other hand, in my case, brought up as I was, I also wanted a steady home, a good, strong roof over my head. I've tried all my life long to hold on to *both* ways of life, despite the fact that I know they are finally incompatible.

Or are they? Because of my cleverness and something slippery in my soul, I found that they need not be mutually exclusive. Later in life, I maintained a succession of girlfriends while, at the same time, "worshipping" in a middle-class home. Flaubert has said that an artist must be, *au fond*, a bourgeois. That is only half right, but it is half right.

On the one hand I took Molly's urging seriously; I didn't want to lose her. But I was, after all, barely into life. Why slam a lot of doors, close all windows, lock myself forever in an enclosure to which I didn't have the key? It was a dilemma I've never solved.

Molly enters the family

THE PURE IN HEART was a failure from the
first rehearsal. I was astonished at the cheery ineptitude of dear Terry Helburn. I realized only later that the Theatre Guild's success lay in recognizing sound and provocative scripts and engaging experienced actors who,
without much help beyond rudimentary "traffic cop" direction, would bring
the play off. I was also relieved of the illusions I had about professional
actors. These troupers were uninterested in anything beyond the immediate demands of their careers—how they'd do in this play, what notices
they'd get. There was no talk, as there had been in the Group, every day,
at every meal, about theatre or politics or art or society or even about what
might be wrong with the production they were in. After the final curtain
dropped, they took off their makeup and went their separate ways. There
was a class distinction too. The stars didn't mix with the small-part players;
they went to different bars. It was a cold, dreary experience. Poor Jack
Lawson struggled in vain; his play was much better than it appeared in
production. To my surprise, I found myself thinking: The Group should
have done this play; we—notice that "we"?—could have brought it to life.

There was one exception in the cast, Osgood Perkins. He was the definition of the word "professional." There was no "take a minute" technique with him; in fact, there was no emotion. Only skill. In every aspect of technical facility, he was peerless. Every night, fifteen minutes before the curtain went up, he'd come down to the set, ready to work, and check over his "props," those on stage and those off. This was my job, as the assistant stage manager. "I've checked them all. Don't worry, Mr. Perkins," I'd say to him. "Yes, thank you," he'd say, with his nifty smile. But next performance, there he'd be again, making sure that the tools of his craft were properly placed and in good working order. I've never forgotten Mr. Perkins. He stood for a whole other side of theatre art than the one I'd learned from Lee and Harold, and I thought it—and do now—immensely valuable.

Molly wrote to me—the play was in Cincinnati—and revealed what I couldn't have suspected, that in the week after the abortion, she'd thought seriously of killing herself. Which is what happens when a saint falls off the peak of the absolute. I was very tough with her. I wrote: "I'm a companion, not a solution. It gets me sore when you depend on me so. I'm no reason for you to commit suicide, no reason not to commit suicide. You've got to want yourself more than you want me. One of the few things you could do that I'd detest you for is kill yourself." I didn't get an answer to this.

The production closed on the road, without glory for anyone. The actors scattered like birds before a windstorm. I didn't want to return to my parents' home in New Rochelle, couldn't face the explanation I'd have to make to my father.

SUCCESS STORY had opened on the twenty-sixth of September, been admired by theatre people—Noël Coward saw it seven times!—and praised by most of the critics, but it hadn't attracted audiences, so the actors were living on cut salaries. Those not in the play were also being paid, which made it tougher still. Lee Strasberg and his new wife, Paula, as well as Clifford Odets and some of the other unmarried people, were living in a long railroad flat at 444 West 57th Street. They'd given the place a name: "Groupstroi" (we were all Russophiles by then). In a room with two other actors, I found an unused bed. This apartment was a convenient neutral zone where I could avoid the disappointment of my father and the persistent, anxious questioning of Molly, for neither of which I had a satisfactory answer.

We'd take turns cooking. On my day, I'd prepare my specialty, a great pot of bulgar flavored with tomatoes, onions, and lamb-kidney bits, in the Anatolian manner. Lee preferred boiled chicken; Paula boiled chickens. Cliff, also broke, was writing a play in a large kitchen closet, aptly called *I Got the Blues*. The atmosphere of the apartment was saturated with disappointment. People wouldn't greet one another when they entered. Bedroom doors remained closed all day, shutting everyone apart. We might as well have been living alone. Lee stayed in his room and read; when he came out he was silent, an owl by daylight. I got into a fight with another actor, kept slamming his head on the floor until I was pulled off. I've forgotten what the fight was about; it didn't matter. It had been a disappointing season and there was no new play for the coming season.

Molly would see me, but less frequently. She made it clear to me that she was not on call and had to know where she stood. I replied I had no money, I had no job, and she should lay off. She said money didn't matter; she had money enough for us both, and that would do for now. What was my disposition anyway? she wanted to know. She looked angry some days. Other times she was as loving as ever. Then she'd be silent and look at me strangely, be physically cold and unresponsive. I'd call and ask to see her, and she'd say, "I have other plans tonight." I don't think she was seeing anyone else, but she was preparing herself for the possibility that I might suddenly come out with: "Molly, let's call the whole thing off."

Clifford was my best friend; we lived by night. Sometimes with Harold, we'd walk the deserted, wintry streets and bellow our defiance. At whom? No one. Anyone. There were no listeners; it was only a way of releasing our anguish and easing our isolation.

I spoke to my fellow outsider Clifford about Molly, something I shouldn't have done. I knew he hadn't liked her when they'd met. Perhaps I wanted my hesitation to commit myself justified.

Clifford was a confirmed romantic, had bunked alone at camp in a tiny room in the cottage on the hill. People said he was writing a play there, but no one believed anything would come of it. He'd stride down the path to meals, swinging his elbow, a heroic strut that must have been modeled on some old-time leading man he'd seen. Some days he seemed in a continuous rage, would glare threateningly at people as he passed them by. No one thought much of him as an actor except Clifford himself, who couldn't understand why Luther Adler had been given the leading role in *Success Story* instead of him. He also thought of himself as potentially a great composer—the bust of his hero, Beethoven, was over his writing table. He'd improvise wildly and endlessly on the piano, usually in the middle of the night, driving everybody nuts. His emotions were intemperate, sometimes out of control. He'd create occasional scandals, perhaps because he felt a great romantic artist should. One night, heavy with drink, he entered the big room in the main house when everyone there was asleep, picked the balls off the billiard table, and hurled them at the door of an actress he desired—that week. He didn't understand how any woman could refuse him. He also had a gentle, tender side, was part Jewish mother. "Have three or four of these," he'd say to me, thrusting Hershey bars into my pocket. "There's nothing to eat in this damned place at night."

In their single encounter, Molly had affronted Clifford's masculinity. He'd found her competitive, aggressive, opinionated, a "college intellectual," and above all unwomanly. To save his inexperienced and naive young friend from a disastrous union, he spoke up boldly. "If you have to marry," he said, "find a peasant."

I nodded, thoughtfully. I agreed. Thoughtfully.

Clifford was convinced that an artist should never marry, but if he did, it should be to a woman who'd keep house for him, cook for him, bear his children, then nurse and tend them, at the same time protecting her genius from all distraction while he worked. In the company of the artist's peers, this perfect wife-creature would preserve a respectful silence. Clifford had noticed that Molly did not. Behaving "like a man," she'd join right in the conversation and as an equal. "Who is she?" Clifford roared. "What does she know about the theatre?" Molly had debated their every point of difference. Clearly she wasn't impressed with the Group and its reason for being. What Clifford didn't say was that she hadn't paid him the respect she would have given Beethoven.

But gradually I'd become defensive; everything he'd said against her turned me to her. I had a bad habit in those years of listening as if I were concurring with what was being said, while hiding my disagreement and often my resentment. Molly wasn't the creature he'd described. The more he criticized her, the more I remembered how she was with me, tender, generous, understanding, patient, supportive, and realized that I missed her terribly—even her contentiousness—when we were separated. I also found her bright, brighter than I, and as for Clifford, I'll grant him this: It was a standoff, a contest of equals. She'd been quite as outspoken about "that strange man" as he'd been about her, but kinder and curiously open.

Furthermore, to look ahead, Clifford didn't live by what he'd recommended so vehemently to me: "marry a peasant"; rather the contrary. The women I remember him loving were women of spirit; he particularly responded to talent and even to challenge. I recall an attractive young Jewish girl whose interest was science; I remember her for her independence and intellectual vigor, not for her housekeeping and cooking. Clifford pressed her again and again to marry him, despite the fact that she "behaved like a man."

Later, in Hollywood, Clifford fell in love with one of the reigning actresses of the film colony, a double Oscar winner, Luise Rainer. I visited the happy lovers soon after their wedding. They'd rented a Beverly Hills castle, and there, in an enormous, baronial room at night, Clifford was writing a play for the Group Theatre, to be called *The Silent Partner*. It was a serious play and, as was the style for serious plays by left-wing authors at that time, a strike play. I had the feeling Clifford had instructed Luise in the deportment proper for a wife with a husband of genius at work. I can recall him crouched over his typewriter, like a lion over prey, pounding away, accompanying himself with roars and grunts and snatches of dialogue—he spoke the actors' roles as he wrote them. At the opposite corner

of the room, on a chaise longue in her nightdress, was his lovely, nonpeas-
ant wife, Luise, looking at him as intently as a watchdog. She said nothing;
her posture said, "When will you be done? I'm waiting for you." How anyone could work under that pressure beats me. And a strike play! And in a
castle! With a theatre company anxiously waiting! As the representative of
those actors, I felt resentful and wished he had married a peasant. Finally,
feeling her sexual impatience as if she'd spoken it—Luise was a very good
actress—Clifford wrapped up what he was doing for the night. *The Silent
Partner* was never properly finished and never performed by the Group.

Perhaps the failure of this marriage reaffirmed his conviction that what
he should find for his days and nights was a woman with the attributes of
self-effacement and service that a "peasant" had. Years later, when he was
preparing a revival of his play *Golden Boy,* with John Garfield, a young
actress came to his apartment to be interviewed for the part that Frances
Farmer had played in the original production. She never left, not that day,
not the next. Clifford had found his "peasant," she'd found her ideal, a famous and passionate man. At last he had an uncomplicated, *real* woman.
For proof she bore him two children. Which Luise had not.

Now dissolve, as they say in films. One night, again years later, I'd arranged my personal life so I could spend an entire night with the girl I was
in love with at the time. Our lovemaking was to take place in the Central
Park South apartment of a rising young film lawyer named Arthur Krim,
which he'd generously made available to me. As it happened, Julie (John)
Garfield had talked to me that day, and I'd told him about my date. He said
he had a date too and didn't know where to take her. I invited him to share
Krim's hospitality, and he happily accepted. The place had two bedrooms.
My girl and I were just taking over one of them when Julie arrived. The
woman he brought with him was Mrs. Clifford Odets.

ONE FINAL note on this quest for a peasant. When we heard that
Clifford was dying, of cancer, in California, Harold Clurman and I went out
there. As we approached his room, we saw that he was raising his right
hand above the top of the curtain partition, wiggling his fingers as if he
were playing the piano or typing. Nearing his bed, we heard him say to
himself—or was it to the world?—"Clifford Odets, you have so much still
to do!" We spent some hours with him. Something was trying to carry him
off, he said, and he was pulling himself back "in." He didn't want to pass
out. "Death makes you horny," he said.

I remember Jean Renoir, another man who loved Clifford for what he
was and for what he wanted to be, arriving to pay his last respects. The
most impressive figure of all Clifford's visitors, he was truly and deeply
moved. He stood at Clifford's bedside, slightly stooped, a bulky man like a
big loaf of peasant bread. Clifford was going in and out of consciousness,

and Renoir didn't say a word to him but stood at the end of the bed, head bowed for several minutes, then went to Clifford, kissed his forehead, and left. He'd paid his tribute to his passing friend and, as Harold said, also paid tribute to death.

When Harold and I returned the next day, there was a woman sitting at Cliff's bedside. He was bent over toward her, as much as he could, talking to her intently, his face charged with energy and desire. It appeared that he was paying frantic court to this woman. This went on until he saw us. When he did, he raised one hand in a dismissing gesture and said, "I'll say goodbye to you fellows now." We said goodbye and left. His face had been fierce and not to be denied. His dismissal was curt and final, also not to be denied. The woman Clifford was supplicating was as far from a peasant as can be imagined—his own psychoanalyst. He was, two days before his death, asking her to marry him.

TERRY HELBURN offered me another job, a bit plus assistant stage manager, salary twenty-five dollars, in a play called *Chrysalis*. She liked me, thought I lived up to my nickname, "Gadget," being handy, useful, and able to cope with any minor emergency. She was to write in her memoirs that I was one of the kindest people she'd ever met and very loyal. I suppose I did give that impression, but as I said earlier, every artist has something of the spy in him; Terry wouldn't have considered my thoughts loyal. Molly read my copy of *Chrysalis* and described it as a play about a girl who wants something, she doesn't know what, and neither does the author. No effective rewriting was done; the Theatre Guild board members were around to grumble and bumble. As I watched her working, I thought: Oh, dear, Terry, you're lousing this one up too. It was rehearsed for three and a half weeks and was, when finished, a dreadful production. There were actors with big reputations in the cast, as well as less well known actors like Humphrey Bogart, who was playing a "patent-leather parlor sheik," but they didn't know what they were doing and Terry couldn't help them. I was no longer impressed with the "big time." The only real pro I'd met in two outings was Osgood Perkins. As for the rest, they were professionals in salary and billing but amateurs, some gifted yet still amateurs, in technique. I believe that after this effort, Terry Helburn quit trying to direct and began to write the book of her life in the theatre.

I'd come to see the point of the Group. Lee and Harold would have thought the same of this production and the acting in it as I had. But now, after the summer watching *Success Story* being rehearsed, after standing in the wings with my mask of anonymity on, "loyally" observing Terry Helburn wrestling hopelessly with *Chrysalis*, I had a newborn confidence in what I could do better than the Group directors and better than the people I'd once called the "big pros." I'd come to my own views on the art of directing and of acting, on where I was able and they were not. Behind my mask, I was the doubting "young stranger," waiting on the outside for his chance to push in. I was beginning to believe that it would happen.

About acting, I knew what none of them knew. I believed I could take the kind of art Osgood Perkins exemplified—externally clear action, controlled every minute at every turn, with gestures spare yet eloquent—and blend that with the kind of acting the Group was built on: intense and truly emotional, rooted in the subconscious, therefore often surprising and shocking in its revelations. I could bring these two opposite and often conflicting traditions together, as they should be brought together. Acting, I declared (to Molly, who was listening intently), is more than a parade of emotionalism, and it's more than gesturing appropriately and manipulating the voice. It is also more than a series of deft and clever bits of stage "business." It is—or should be—a human life on stage, that is to say, behavior: total, complex, and complete.

Nor is direction what the Group directors seemed to think it is, a matter of coaching actors. It is turning psychological events into behavior, inner events into visible, external patterns of life on stage. I could and I would, I vowed to Molly, apply what I'd learned about direction from Alexander Dean at Yale—the shaping of scenes and the manipulation of the positions and movements of actors so that the stage pictures revealed, at every moment, what was happening—to the Group's Method, which had found the way to create spontaneous, surprising, and true inner experiences. Only I—how arrogant I was in those years!—only I knew both sides of the problem of stage art, the external and the internal. A deaf man, I went on, should be able to tell from what he sees before him on stage the human event in all its complexities and subtleties. My work would be to turn the inner events of the psyche into a choreography of external life.

Besides all that, a director must direct the scenery, the costumes, the lights, the music; he must shape the course of a scene for rhythm, pace, and pause, and so arrange the stage pictures that they are at all times aesthetic and pleasing. It's a total job. I knew all this from an amalgam of all that I'd studied and seen. I also knew it as if it had been born in me.

I'd told it all to Molly—who else?—one day after work, told it as it had burst into my awareness of identity that very morning, told it with all the conviction—and cockiness—of first revelation. I hadn't allowed doubt, I hadn't accepted challenges, not yet. Molly was, in this moment of discovery and, I must suppose, growth, my best and only friend. I saw that she believed in me, believed that I could, in fact, do what I said I could do.

What is more winning than the light of faith in a young woman's eyes? I saw how beautiful she was.

With *Chrysalis* running, I felt I could go to New Rochelle and confront—fearfully, always fearfully—my father. And kiss my mother, who'd promised me my favorite Anatolian dish, minced lamb over puree of eggplant, if I came. I'd decided to take Molly with me and let them meet her. She was reluctant to go and I was too dumb to understand why. I got huffy. She had to explain to me that a visit of this kind has the same significance in all cultures. What the hell was I doing, she asked, auditioning her? Trying her out on the road? Finally she changed her mind. I picked her up at her aunt's, and we walked to Grand Central. It was a cold day in late fall, but she flashed open her coat and showed me what she was wearing: a Bavarian peasant costume, a dirndl. I'd told her the thought of Clifford Odets on the subject of the artist in marriage and the acceptable role of a woman in his domestic life. She'd scoffed. "See my pretty yellow ribbon?" she said now. "I borrowed it from my cousin's little girl. Think I'd get Mr. Odets's okay now? Do I look demure and yielding enough, do I look obedient? A peasant at last?"

What she looked was pretty. Where would I ever find another like this one? I thought. I knew I was losing her bit by bit; there was a new strange look in her eyes, and that's what it must mean. But did I want to lose her?

My childhood home embarrassed me; I'd just seen Molly's rich aunt's place. Our parlor furniture was bourgeois junk, joints glued, not mortised, a collection, now a bit wobbly here and there, that my father had claimed from bankrupt furniture stores to which he'd shipped carpets and not received checks. Molly saw only my parents; she smiled at them. My father said, "Very nice, very nice," which meant nothing or anything, and he gave her his "look." Molly said, "What smells so good?" and my mother took her into the kitchen. "Very high-class," my father said, "looks like society." Then, again, the look, meaning: Where are you getting money, girl like this, damn fool? I remembered that my father read the newspapers and must have seen the notices of *Chrysalis*, and it was unlikely he'd forgotten the quick death of *The Pure in Heart*.

To explain that look on my father's face, I must detour again, pull up another string from the tangle of twine and tell a little about the sorry record of the Kazan family in marriage, since that was the true genesis of the look that day.

Start with my father's older brother, A.E., who chose not to marry, rather provided himself with a mistress, named Bertha. In time A.E. became "Flat Tire Joe," a nickname he gave himself, and Bertha slipped into bed with the young man A.E. had assigned to watch over her when he went to Europe on business. This usurper happened to be A.E.'s favorite, his brother Frank. Frank was married, so the rumor went, but no one ever told me when or to whom or what happened. If such a wife did exist, I never saw her. I remember Frank later in life, his hair graying, but still a handsome man, hanging around the lobby of the old Waldorf-Astoria to pick up malcontent suburban wives in town for a day's sport.

My uncle Seraphim, a mild man, was married to a very nice woman long enough to produce two very nice kids. His marriage broke up for unspecified reasons and Seraphim died alone in a small toilet at the back of a rug store. My uncle Michael was married for precisely a week; his mother, my grandmother Evanthia, harshly criticized the bride's cooking and broke up the union. Michael returned to his mother's table. A preference for Evanthia's cooking was the most frequent cause given for marital breakups in that family. "She don't understand how to cook," the men would say about their wives.

My uncle John had a very grand church wedding to the daughter of the Greek archbishop Kourkoulis, a holy man with a heroic beard, who was accused, later, of dipping his hand into his church's till. This young woman, accustomed to greatness, found John disappointing. Watching her face in the mirror as it soured day by day, she became restless. John came home from work one day and found that his bride had departed, taking their infant son and the dog with her. My father conducted a delicate personal negotiation with His Eminence, in the course of which it was revealed that the reason she'd left her husband's bed was that John had refused to pay the phone bill of seventeen dollars. My father and her father brought them back together again (my father paid the phone bill), but not for long. John soon found another of his wife's phone bills excessive and refused to pay it. This time she left him for good. In partnership with a distant relative, a young man, she bought a bankrupt farm and went into the business of raising chinchillas, small, unattractive animals with dearly prized pelts. Father had a modest investment there. This enterprise into a luxury trade fell under an avalanche of high feed bills. So it went.

I haven't mentioned my uncle Berry. He went with whores, was the only completely happy one of the lot, and outlived the others.

That's the history of marriage for the men in the Kazan family. You've noticed that it was always my father who'd had to pick up the pieces and restore respectability to the family name. You can see why he might very sensibly be apprehensive about encouraging an addition to this unhappy record.

On Molly's side there was no such revolting history. Marriage with the Thachers and—her mother's family—the Erkenbrechers was still a sacrament, had to be because it was equally a property settlement. I would be invading, I learned in good time, the purlieu of the Social Register, where Molly's name, to her intense embarrassment, could be found. I didn't know what the Social Register was.

Not that my father was against marriage—as such. Over the last three years he and my uncles and aunts, charged with loving advice and undeterred by their own failures, had taken to parading nubile young Greek women, Anatolians like ourselves, and certified "home girls," under my nose, hoping to arouse my interest. I was not aroused. The more they pressed, the more I backed off. The maidens (all guaranteed virgins, all plump, back and front) came bearing sweets from their kitchens. Even this didn't lure me. The young ladies, soon aware of something fishy in my eyes, had the good sense not to smile beguilingly at me. All marital negotiations collapsed.

MY ARTISTIC confidence in the future endured, but my financial stability was short-lived, lasting only until *Chrysalis* closed, which it did abruptly, dumping us all on the sidewalk. I was back at my father's store— the last place I wanted to be; it was a constant humiliation.

His business had shrunk badly by 1932—Americans were not buying Oriental rugs—and he was often in a pessimistic and quarrelsome mood. Since the buyers were few and far between, he began to go to the track in the afternoon, often with his brother A.E. ("Joe"). When *Chrysalis* closed, he'd taken me back, but part-time and at ten dollars a week. It may have been all he thought he could afford; it was also a way of encouraging me— at twenty-three—to get serious about my future.

I spent my hours at George Kazan, Inc., Oriental Rugs and Carpets, in a kind of fog. The place was generally empty of customers. Father couldn't have blamed me for that, but he did look at me sometimes and voice an old Turkish expression: "The day of my ruination!" He'd stopped expecting good news from me.

I kept my mouth shut. I had no confidence except the one, that I had an outside chance to be good at my trade if I could only hold on, live on the fringes, duck the requirement of "bringing home the bacon" every week (marriage), and avoid the graveyard of creative people, the teaching profession. Yes, if I could continue to keep my needs minimal and my temper locked, smile in a pinch and disappear, live off a weekly visit to my mother (who was doing my laundry again) and Molly's occasional kindnesses and the off-the-cuff accidents of employment, if I could hang on tight, uncommitted and unobligated, slipping and sliding, as the black lyric goes, ducking and waiting and coming up only when I heard the "All clear!" making time until my break came, then, goddamn it, I would make my own life someday! Wouldn't I?

Late one afternoon, after a bad day at the track, my father cornered me for a talk. It was short and dead to the point. "Where's your money, boy?" he said. "How are you going to marry? Tell me that much." I wanted to reassure him that I wasn't, but he plunged on, telling the truth he knew, that I was a Greek, an Anatolian Greek, "not like these people over here," and that I should recognize my nature. "Hey, you listening me, damn fool? You understand what you are?"

"Pop," I said, "she don't want to marry me. Like you say, I have no money. Okay?"

"Only good news I hear all week," he said. "What you want with woman like that one? You crazy? How you going buy her stockings, tell me that much? Ten dollars a week! Even stockings! Look at your mother, boy, you ever hear her complain? Find one like that one. Hey, you listening to me?"

"Yes, Pop," I lied.

"We don't make divorce business, our people," he said, and went on: "You think you can make her proper-style wife, woman like that one? Hey, you! Woman like that one you bring home, she can kill you, boy. Ask your Uncle John! Marry archbishop daughter, then what happen? What's the matter with you? Don't you know what you are?"

I knew what he was talking about. When Anatolians stop fucking their wives regularly, their wives tend to get fat and stay at home. They don't dye their hair, they don't dress—frantically—to increase their allure. The black they wear is in mourning for their sexual death. But they keep the home going; that's what our men appreciate. They cook for their husbands and they produce more children, not as an act of passion but as family-building. The Anatolian man thinks this is the natural way for himself and his wife. Nature, he believes, intended it so. "When she's no longer young and pretty, how can I be expected to fuck her? On the other hand, she's a good wife, why should I give her up?"

Anatolians respect marriage; they don't divorce. This gives the wives a basis of confidence. They don't fear what so many American women fear, that they'll suddenly be abandoned. They don't see analysts for reassurance, which has to be reinforced every other day.

"It's in your blood like that," my father said. I knew it.

The Anatolian comes home for lunch, closing up his place of business, leaving his job. His wife feeds him his big meal of the day. This makes him sleepy and he gets into bed. His wife joins him. This is when most Anatolian children are conceived, a family duty. Refreshed physically, the man returns to his place of business, his male confidence at its peak. There is a sparkle in his eye, a spring to his step. If he is a salesman, he does especially well in the afternoon. At night he has supper with his men friends; they solve the outstanding political problems of the nation. Their mistresses may be there but never their wives. The mistresses don't join in the conversation; properly demure, they sit close up against their lords. But silent. The men don't worry where their wives may be. They are home, taking care of their children and, by now, happily asleep. They have received the physical assurance that their husbands still love them.

My father didn't tell me all this. He merely launched the subject's prow into my mind; I knew the rest very well. I'd grown up in the culture, seen it all my life, all around me—my uncles, my father's business associates, many of his customers. I needed no refresher course in Anatolian marital customs. Only Americans, I'd noticed, suffer from sexual guilt. All my father had to say was: "You think she's the kind of woman makes right wife for you?" and I'd understand what he meant. "Will she understand the way we live, our people? Will she understand you? Ishkabibble! Nothing doing! Guarantee. We are different people here!"

"I'm not getting married, Pop," I said. "Don't worry."

Having made his point, he reduced me to childhood. "You look terrible," he said. "Here's a dollar. Go get haircut and shine."

As a prognosis, what he'd said had a sound basis. Molly was a blue-blooded Yankee, forever rigid in her standards of morality and behavior. Even much later, when she'd yielded to mine, even then she had no "give" in her. In time I would come to admire her for her obduracy in many matters. But in personal affairs, her basic character—and my own—made for a conflict that had no solution. For her there were not ever two ways, only the right way. I had to admit that Clifford and my father were right. "Marry a peasant!" "Find a woman like your mother, an Anatolian girl!" Right! I had to admit it. Molly was not the woman for me to marry. It would be a mistake, a disaster.

On December 5, 1932, I packed my grandmother, dressed in her heaviest blacks, and my mother, wearing a cloth coat, into a taxi, and picked up Molly, in a dress with puffed sleeves, at her aunt's. I remember grumbling to myself on the way downtown, "What the hell did she wear that dress for?" It embarrassed me. In City Hall, we were married, with the two oddly contrasting Anatolian women as witnesses. My father expressed his regrets, saying I'd understand, he had to tend to business. Molly's mother was not there. I didn't ask why.

I don't know what changed my mind. Perhaps it was that Molly understood my hesitations. She said she'd get a job, and she did. She also said she'd contribute the furniture. She did. Her mother gave us silverware, pots, plates, towels, and fine linen sheets with her own mother's initials embroidered on them. Father gave us a carpet from the city of Hamadan in Persia, a barbaric design from an alien world.

More likely what had quieted my uncertainty was Molly's everlasting sweetness and goodness. I knew I was everything for her. I guess that is what people call love. I loved her too, my whole life long. I still do.

I hesitate to think what I might have become without her.

I didn't tell the Group actors or Odets or Clurman (with whom I'd become friendly). I let them find out, and when they spoke of it, I minimized its importance. I'm ashamed to say marriage was a social embarrassment to me; the less said about it the better.

The house joke: Molly's name had been immediately stricken from the Social Register; there was to be no loss in that organization's distinction.

She made good on her promise. The only person in the world who believed in me, she set up a life where I stayed home mornings and worked on a play or rehearsed scenes to show before the acting classes at the Maxine Elliott Theatre (where *Success Story* was floundering), while she commuted to work in Newark. Christmas was coming; she sold puppets for kids. Afternoons, I dragged myself to my father's store. She brought home thirty-five dollars a week; I brought in ten. Our apartment was over a stable for beer wagons; the rent: forty dollars a month. She had a small income left to her by her father, the Wall Street lawyer. I referred to it—snotty guy!—as our double-chin capital, but I was damned glad to have it.

She'd come home from Jersey at dusk or through the dark. I remember watching her from our window over Cornelia Street, walking slowly, in a haze of thought—as if she were narcotized. Later this was how I saw Stella in *Streetcar Named Desire*. Molly always brought home something sweet to pleasure me; I remember a "shadow cake," all chocolate, from Schrafft's, and tinned plum puddings from England. Then she'd make dinner. She made a life all my way. Her unwavering, one-way myopia raised my first flood of confidence.

Only later did I realize what a chance she was taking—she, not I. Only now do I wonder what she must have been thinking through those days and nights. Perhaps she was pretty damned scared—she'd held nothing back from me; everything she had, she gave me. Meanwhile I behaved as if I'd been trapped.

Looking back, I think of Molly's act—coming with me—as one of un-reasonable faith (which is why I call her a saint) and most complete gener-osity. Something inside told her what to do. When I think of what I looked like and what I was: a boy without train fare, with no visible talent, a reject as an apprentice with the Group Theatre, in character and culture com-pletely counter to everything acceptable in her society, disliked by her mother (at that time), himself the product of a freakish and possibly mis-placed family—call it disreputable, then laugh—a family in which there were traces of insanity . . . there was all that plus my continuous resistance, which she had to endure, understand, and overcome.

And, barely contained, my violence and anger.

But she bound herself to me. She became my partisan. Before her I had thought I was at the mercy of the world around me; with her I could not be. It was an act of purest daring, which I was too self-occupied at the time to appreciate but which I can now see for what it was, the will of a su-premely good heart. She, not I, clamped us together in a connection threat-ened by the profoundest differences—differences that we agreed, without daring to consult, could be overlooked but that, in the end, could not be overcome. Need met need: That was the story that year.

In the end, she gave me what I value most in the world, our four children.

L A V I D A *es un sueño y los sueños sueños son.*
Calderón cut a play's title out of that old Spanish proverb. *Life Is a Dream.*
The rest translates: "Dreams are dreams."

On the fifth of March, 1933, the banks of the nation closed. Led more by
a nose for drama than by the concern proper to a son, I hustled uptown to
see how the "old man" was weathering the crisis; my curiosity was not altogether sympathetic.

His business was located at 295 Fifth Avenue, the Textile Building, a
hive of importers, wholesalers like himself, dark-complected men, immigrants all, most of them Armenians but some Anatolian Greeks as well as a
few Persians, Syrians, and Egyptians. These men had come overseas from
the East, propelled by a dream: that here their throats would not be cut.
Working in the dust of carpets, living alone in dark back rooms, depriving
themselves of pleasures, they'd put the dollars together, year after year,

obeying the voice in the air of America: to accumulate money; that was safety, that was happiness. They married late, unromantically, going back to their native lands, as my father had, to find a proper woman out of their own tradition, ten, fifteen, twenty years younger, then made children as quickly as possible in half-paid-for homes while dutifully continuing to feed their accounts in banks whose doors, that morning, had remained locked.

Generally these men entered my father's store only when they had a customer whose needs they weren't able to meet from their own stock. They'd escort this buyer to Father's place and there pick up, in place of a profit, a commission. These encounters were rare since they were a last resort. My father's competitors paid each other no casual visits. But when I walked in that morning, there they were, a dozen or more, sitting cross-legged on piles of three-by-five Sarouk or Hamadan "mats," clumped together in static postures, like hens roosting. Motionless, inanimate, they seemed to be waiting—but for what? Occasionally a few mournful words would be mumbled, a puzzled complaint. No response was expected, none offered.

Skirting the motionless figures, I circled back to the small desk where I was supposed to tend the accounts-due books. With business as bad as it had been, there'd been little to do there that summer. I'd typed a few letters: "Your immediate check would be sincerely appreciated" or "We will regretfully be forced to place your account in the hands of our lawyers." But most of the time I'd tilted up the large stock book and hid *The Brothers Karamazov* behind it. This had been noticed, of course, and reinforced the general opinion that I was a young man without a future.

On this morning I sat idle, like the others, studying the assembly of merchants, men whose skins had once been a rich olive and were now pale from worry and the cold light that concrete walls shed. They're like ship-wrecked sailors, I thought, thrown up on a desert island and waiting for someone to rescue them.

Actually my father's business had gone "kaput"—his word—three years before, in 1929, when the market collapsed. He'd put the yield of a life's labor into a stock issued by the National City Bank. Bought at just over 300, climbing as millions cheered past 600, it then rumbled with all the others down the mountain of high finance, like the boulders of an avalanche, to 23. At that time, he'd thought of his disaster as something for which he was in some way responsible; he must have done something wrong, made some awful mistake. Had he been outsmarted? Had he been cheated?

But now, in 1933, on the day the banks closed, surrounded as he was by men who shared the catastrophe—no one smarter, no one luckier, he knew them all to be as ordinary as he was—Father must have begun to accept that what had happened was more serious than any mistake he could have made. The men around him were all bleeding from the same invisible le-sions. In a few years many of them would be out of business. They all shared a dread of what was coming.

That morning I saw my father—at last—not as a household bully but as Yiorgos Kazanjioglou, who'd come to America a young man from the backcountry of Turkey in Asia, to find a place in the world, a man who'd worked his life away. Now here he was, sitting in the debris of his days, puzzled, soul-weary, a gray fifty-six, he the browbeaten one, not I, with no place to rest except on the battlefield of his disaster.

Toward midafternoon, the rug men began to wander off, barely acknowledging each other's goodbyes. Father got up and walked to where his depleted staff, an Armenian repairman and a Greek porter, were sitting idle, and spoke to them in Turkish, the language they shared. He told them he wouldn't be able to pay their salaries that week. Then he asked them—not ordered—to unfold a large Sarouk, freshly arrived from washing, and spread it on the floor.

The process of washing an Oriental carpet makes the soft wool glisten. It also brings up the ends of the frame of cords on which it has been woven, and it was customary, on a dull day of trading or at the end of an afternoon when there was nothing else to do, for the hired help to sit down with sharp-pointed scissors and clip off these "white spots," the protruding ends of cotton string. On this day my father sat down with scissors, and after a bit, I found a pair and sat alongside, back bent like his, head bowed over the glowing Persian carpet.

We didn't look at each other, we didn't speak. There was only the clip, clip, clip of the sharp scissors. Once I heard him sigh. I remembered how our President before Roosevelt had tried to reassure American businessmen, asking them to trust their country and its leaders. Then he'd given up, said there was nothing more he could do. Perhaps my father was thinking something of the sort, that there was nothing more anyone could do, because he turned and gave me a bitter smile and put a Melachrino in his mouth. I looked away—there was such pain in his face. In a few minutes he got up. I remember how he was smoking the cigarette, untended, the ash falling on his lapel. "Closing up," he said, without removing the cigarette. "Best regards your wife," he said as we left the elevator and walked to the street. He turned north, up Fifth Avenue on his way to Grand Central Terminal. I turned south. At the curb of Thirtieth Street, I stopped and looked back to where he'd stopped at the corner of Thirty-first Street, waiting there, as I was, for a break in the traffic. Then he had it and went on through, slowly, splay-footed, a businessman who'd trusted his country and its leaders, on his way to the commuter train.

This was the first time I felt a pinch of love for him, a sting in the lining of my nostrils, familiar prelude to tears. "Well, anyway," I said to myself, "he's not going to ask me to go into his business now."

. . .

W I T H T H E system in collapse, I was on my own.

When the Group directors, after their financially unrewarding season, decided to set up another summer-long rehearsal period, it was at Green Mansions, a camp for adults who liked to pig out on kosher food, then chase each other into bed. The Group chose this place because they could get room and board for the entire company by providing entertainment, three times a week, for the camp's guests. The Group was broke.

This program would make necessary a great deal of backstage work and someone to do it. In this emergency, they turned to their hardworking "Gadget"—my faceless nickname—and offered to take me along if I'd do the job. I seemed to have energy without limit, and they'd been told by my old Yale teacher Phil Barber that I could build, paint, and light scenery, prepare the props and costumes as required, stage-manage the productions, and have everything ready in good working order and on time. I would not have been asked to come along, of course, except for my proficiency with inanimate objects. The directors had also detected a dog's devotion in my character, which they believed would help get them through what promised to be a difficult summer.

What made the summer in prospect difficult was that the play the directors had chosen to rehearse and produce on Broadway, *Men in White,* had raised only the dust of scorn from their actors; they'd trampled all over it. A good number of the company had been radicalized by then, and they declared that *Men in White* "said nothing." It was, they added, dramatically conventional. Nor did they conceal what they thought from the author, Sidney Kingsley; they patronized him too.

When I told Molly that I was going to spend the whole summer doing payless and probably thankless work for a collection of egos she considered maniacal, self-serving, and unappreciative of the devotion I'd already shown, she was not enthusiastic. When I let her read *Men in White,* she decided to spend the summer in Mexico, writing a play of her own. So we'd pass the summer apart. This was fine with me; I intended not to allow anything, personal or professional, to interfere with my work. Not even Molly's opinion. "All they want is a stagehand," she said. "Okay, I'll be a stagehand," I answered.

T H A T S P R I N G was when it began. I've found a notebook from that time, and it's full of a new passion. There are jottings about steelworkers walking off a job, tools held high (I'd read about that), about a job in a cement factory in the dead of winter and its hardships (I'd not suffered this cold), about construction workers on payday shooting craps in a half-finished building (I'd seen this but from a student's distance), about "hobo jungles" (I'd never seen one), and there's a long, ardent defense of the Bonus Army: "Those men came to Washington because they had nowhere else to go and were as willing to starve on the road as in the streets of the cities they call home." (I'd never been hungry.) Then: "You're breaking my heart, fellow, go starve somewhere else!"—dialogue to be attributed to the villains of the Hoover government or someone on General MacArthur's staff.

And there were several long notes I made after visits to the area of dye plants in Paterson, New Jersey (plants I'd not entered), telling how the acrid air stung my nostrils. All these excursions and imaginings were about "real people." (My father and his friends, no matter that they were crushed and forlorn, weren't "real.") No, I'd found the true drama of our time (not *Men in White*). I yearned to become part of the new world emerging to replace the one whose wake I'd attended in the Textile Building.

That notebook recalls what I was reading at the time. "Big Bill" Haywood (my hero that year) would lift his huge, powerful hand over the crowd, spread his fingers as far apart as possible. Then he'd seize one finger after another, bend it from side to side, saying to his audience, "Do you see that? Do you see that? Every finger by itself has no force. Now look!" And he would bring the fingers together into a bulky, powerful fist, lift the fist into the face of the crowd, and shout, "See that? That's the IWW!"

In this notebook I found a list of the films I must see, all Russian: Eisenstein's *Potemkin*, Pudovkin's *End of St. Petersburg*, Dovzhenko's *Aerograd*. I admire these films today, but in that year of quick growth, they inspired me. I didn't know films like these were being made, hadn't ever seen anything like them, not in theme, character, story, or technique.

Whereupon I made up my mind what I wanted to be: Everything! A film director as well as a theatre director as well as a playwright as well as an actor as well as a producer. Life's possibilities were spread open in front of me and, so I believed, not out of reach. I knew the kind of films and plays I wanted to make; I'd seen them, made by Russians, films about the one enduring drama of our time, the class struggle, the final conflict. I'd encased my scorn of Father's kind in a sentence, one with which I admonished myself: "The only people you should trust are members of the working class." It would be a while before I'd learn that workers were as "human" as the rest of us.

But that spring it was all romance. By the time I went to Green Mansions in June, I was ready for the Communist Party.

T H E   S A M E arousal had taken place in Hollywood. Albert Maltz, a Yale friend, wrote me from Paramount Pictures, where he and his collaborator on a successful play (*Merry Go Round*) had taken jobs. "It's really too bad," he wrote. "The medium is wonderful as we all agree. But I don't think it will be properly used in America until it is state-owned and its function is not profit making. Another reason for waving the red flag." Then: "Our ideas are always running up against censorship here. We don't dare leave the *Worker* lying around our office." Soon Maltz returned to New York. "Are you sure you won't be able to get a job with the Group?" he wrote me. Evidently I'd written him expressing doubts. "We may be able to help you with the Communist Theatre which is starting. They might have jobs at nominal salaries." Then he went on: "When we think of you, Gadget, we don't worry about your future because you'll obviously make one for yourself—if the revolution doesn't take your head off." And finally: "I hope to hell the Group directors are all that you say and that they pan out. Their heart is certainly in the right place and their goals are ours."

This last conviction didn't hold up.

I C H E C K E D into Green Mansions ahead of the actors, since I had to prepare the stage for the first entertainment to be offered the guests, an evening of Sean O'Casey's one-acts. I looked the camp over, then the accommodations offered me, a small room with two narrow beds whose mattresses were still dank from the winter's cold. I was to have a roommate. I decided not to, but to sleep instead in the wing on one side of the stage. It would be quiet there, except for show time, and I'd be alone with the neighborhood raccoons the rest of the day and night, to read, think, and write. There was another reason for this choice: The notion of a worker sleeping in his place of work appealed to me. I'd also developed a dread of chatter, talk to pass time, preferred silence and still do. Being alone was what I wanted. I decided to eat in a corner of the kitchen with the waiters— the workers again—and found an isolated table where I could spend the summer reading all of Lenin with my meals. I also preferred to keep a distance between me and the Group actors, whose conversation, since it would be about rehearsals I was not in, would make me feel excluded.

My goal that summer was simple: to make the Group feel they couldn't get along without me. So besides building, painting, and lighting all the sets, I snared every small part I could, from broad burlesque comedy—my specialty—to a one-line bit no one else wanted in Clifford Odets's play that was to be *Awake and Sing!* I wrote loving letters to my wife in Mexico, saying that I missed her but was glad she wasn't there. I assured her that I was an industrious celibate that summer (true), busy as a worker bee (they're neuter), learning everything about my profession on the job. I didn't want the distraction of a very bright girl taking exception—as Molly certainly would have—to a good deal of what was going on.

I've never been sure that I'm talented, even now, not compared with those for whom the word "gifted" is precise. But I was always able to work harder than anyone else, and my industry caught the eyes of the directors; toward the end of the summer, I was offered the assistant stage manager's job in *Men in White*. I jumped at the offer. Now I could watch rehearsals. Lee and the actors were doing a brilliant job, and I learned a great deal about the technique of improvisation, what and where its value is. Lee's production, at moments, seemed like a modern ballet; it relied not on words but on movement, activity, and behavior. In the theatre of the time, this was new. I expressed my admiration to Lee; he nodded, then looked at me without an expression. That warned me. I worked harder. My friend Clifford Odets touted me to Clurman. Cheryl Crawford had heard from Theresa Helburn that I did well backstage. Above all I was simply there, on the spot, behind every production, somewhere or other in every play, eager, energetic, ready for anything, slam-bang, jaunty, never down. Hell, by the end of the summer they had no choice. They made me a Group member.

So that dream was realized.

I W E N T back to our apartment on West Forty-fourth Street with a job, with purpose, and with confidence.

It was then that I found out Father had been sick most of the summer. My mother hadn't wanted to distract me while I was at camp, but now she wrote me: "He's worrying all the time. There seems to be nothing anyone can do to help business. Sometimes he's losing his nerve. I think it will do him a lot of good to have you around. [That surprised me.] Now that you're back, spare the time. He needs a little encouragement. That and some business and I know he'll be straight again."

I wrote in my diary: "I know the source of his sickness. The capitalist system. The fascism which keeps the gambler gambling long after he wants to or has the money—or blood—to pay with. [Certainly a lurid description of my father's modest trading.] The revolution I want is a society where everybody works to produce enough for everybody but not for profit." And then: "My father's neck is marked by the weasel teeth of Morgan and Mitchell. [Mitchell was president of the National City Bank, whose stock had given Father a big ride up, then plunged to the bottom.] He worked all his life for these men. Now he rattles in the wind, sick and miserable, walking up and down in his store, hoping something he cannot imagine will come to the rescue and save him."

Then this, which still astonishes me: "From now on I will be kind to him and—[I underlined the phrases italicized here] *I will revenge him*. Now is the time, as my strength is building. *I will make the revolution*. That is all I want."

Who the hell did I think I was?

That fall, after *Men in White* opened, I became a member of the Communist Party of America.

M E N I N W H I T E was a triumph and in time won the Pulitzer Prize. It gave the Group its first great success and the members a long flow of full salaries. With this sudden affluence, sixty dollars per, I made investments, not in stocks and bonds but in lessons for myself: speech to rid my tongue of its New York street slur, voice to enrich shallow resonators, singing in case I was called upon to hold an audience with a song (we were hearing about Brecht and Weill), fencing in case the role of Hamlet—or Laertes, more like it—was suddenly thrust upon me, ballet, which brought me to the barre three mornings a week to turn my toes out and strengthen my legs, and even tap dancing. I had to be ready for any role, believed I could do any part.

The members of the Group took the success of Kingsley's play in a characteristic way. It made them look down on the "bourgeois" critics, who'd praised the work, even more than they had before and provided them with even more intense reasons to scorn our "middle-class" audience. They didn't think more of the play because the theatre was packed eight times a week or of its author because he was wearing laurel. They believed that the style of Lee's production and their own ensemble playing had provided Sidney Kingsley's bone-bare text with what it didn't deserve, affluence for him and first place of honor in Burns Mantle's annual ten best list. All this reached Sidney, who resented it.

Certain elements in our company had other explanations for our success besides the debased Broadway scene and Lee's genius. We were, after all, pioneers of the left in our field; our time had come. This play, of course, was merely a way of tiding ourselves over into next season, when we'd begin to do plays that had "something to say." The Communist Party in the Group would be heard from.

When our stage manager, a large, impatient woman who spoke to actors and the backstage crew as if giving instructions to an unreliable staff of household servants, decided to give up her post, I was Johnny-on-the-spot, waiting to move in. Backstage of the Broadhurst Theatre, where *Men in White* was playing, became my turf. Who were my best friends at the time? The crew, of course. Moe, the property man, a canny old veteran too cynical to be impressed with actors, directors, or writers even in success, became my "professor" and gave me a postgraduate course to top Yale. We drank together after each matinee, his bottle belly up against an Eighth Avenue bar. I was prouder of this intimacy and the fact that I was surrounded at the brass rail by joshing but friendly members of the International Alliance of Theatrical and Stage Employees than I would have been at a college faculty party convened to celebrate an honorary degree being conferred on me.

It was time to celebrate, and sensible people would have, but we did not. The left had its duties. There was an exodus of Group actors downtown to the newborn "workers" theatres: the Theatre Collective, the Theatre Union (where Albert Maltz was), and the Theatre of Action. They truly were ideologically cemented collectives, modeled on what their founders had read about the Russian theatre. Many of us, while living on weekly salaries from Broadway, did our "real work" south of Fourteenth Street— the accepted dividing line between the bourgeoisie and the radicalized masses.

Leaving our old ground was an adventure, but it also had, for some of us, an element of retribution against our pasts. Many of us were ashamed of our families, our upbringing, our education, our class, our society, our traditions and values. Our rebellions were, as much as anything, against who we were, and I suppose the saturating color was guilt.

Molly leaped into an opening at the Theatre Union. It didn't disturb her that this theatre organization was dedicated to bringing down her father and his class; rather the opposite. Clifford Odets, the son of a promoter of mattresses (later of his son's career), taught acting at the same place. The Theatre Collective won over our cantankerous scene designer, Mordecai Gorelik, who believed that institution to be sound politically while the Group was "confused, because it was run by aesthetes, not workers." The Group was what Harold Clurman called it, a "middle-class theatre," but many of its members were on the road downtown to change that identity.

This kind of movement to the left by middle-class people in the perform- ing arts was general. The board of Frontier Films, where I worked for a time, held its meetings in the office of a wealthy tax lawyer, where the paneled walls were hung with expensive paintings. The board members were all men of culture and elite education. In this luxurious office, high above the troubled streets of Manhattan, they would plan films dramatizing the problems of the impoverished masses. One was *Pescados*, made by a fine photographer, Paul Strand, who had achieved eminence in the art world and whose prints sold for large sums of capitalist dollars. This film dealt with Mexican fishermen pulling a marginal living out of the sea, and it was shot in a style that was an *hommage* to Sergei Eisenstein. I helped make a documentary titled *People of the Cumberlands*, which dealt with the lives of strip miners and their families. It was directed by another fine photographer, Ralph Steiner, who'd earned a very good living in advertis- ing but was full of devout admiration for the working class. When I saw this film again recently, it filled me with nostalgia for those warmhearted but naive days.

It was a time of doubt and self-questioning for many middle-class in- tellectuals. Those were the years when parents were giving their sons

My first movie

working-class names: Nick, Pete, Steve, Chris, Joe, Ben—single-syllable "handles." I was called Gadg; no one attempted Elia, nor did I ask them to. To let everyone know where I stood, I wore a "working-class" cap, with a rabbit's foot tucked under the brim. I'd seen a taxi driver with that luck charm tucked under the visor of his cap; when the time came, a year later, for me to find a costume for *Waiting for Lefty*, I didn't have to look for it, I was wearing it. I jumped on stage, and people in the audience thought I was actually a cabbie. How proud I was of that!

So we went forth from the Group Theatre like the apostles of Jesus, teaching, instead of brotherly love and the Ten Commandments, the art of Stanislavski as filtered through Strasberg. South of Fourteenth Street was our Corinth and Antioch and Caesarea. We assumed it as our duty to enlighten the unenlightened. After my personal lessons in the morning and early afternoon, I would rush downtown to teach a course in directing at the New Theatre League, a Communist-front organization, preparing my notes for each talk on the twenty-minute subway ride. At the age of twenty-five, I carried on about the art of direction without the least doubt. Now I'd hesitate a long time before engaging to teach such a course and take months to prepare it. The more you know, the less you believe you know.

I T W A S during this time that I began to work with the Theatre of Action, a group of fifteen actors and actresses my age or younger; they seemed, men and women, to all be the same size and shape—about five feet six inches, thin, wiry, with lightning reflexes—Jewish, street-smart, many of them brought up by left-wing parents. A true collective, they lived in a Lower East Side five-story walk-up, took turns cooking, slept three or four to a room. I admired them because they went all the way with their idea— collective living, collective rule, collective bankroll. They had a proud spirit, each for all, and oh, how they worked, from nine in the morning until eleven at night, feeding on whatever they could buy cheap—apples, peanut butter, stale bread, cabbages—or pick up as compensation for their performances. When I first came to them they were preparing their own scripts and playing for whoever would watch, sometimes only four or five people. The thing was to keep working, to go on developing together. If a union or political club wouldn't get up the ten or fifteen dollars agreed upon, the actors would take what they could get, plus barter, once receiving from bakery workers twenty-seven pumpkin pies, on which they gorged. I was impressed; here was the collective idea in the theatre actually being carried out.

They became my personal acting company and I became, for a time, their hero. In improvisation, they'd do anything I asked. One of them said to me recently that if I'd asked any one of them to run from one end of the loft where we worked to the other, then on through the large, factory-size window, and continue down to—to whatever was there, the actor, so directed, would have carried out my instruction without hesitating. They did something more "professional" actors would not: go to the limit in improvisation. Scenes of anger had to be stopped short of bodily harm, love scenes cut off before they reached a final intimacy. When the material was within the range of their experience, their dialogue was absolutely true; they were the streets of New York incarnate. Still they moved like dancers.

I rehearsed a play with them, *The Young Go First*, a protest against the Civilian Conservation Corps. The script was incomplete—there was no third act—so I decided to create it by improvisation, placed a stenographer in the first row to take down what the actors said in the structure of scenes I'd arranged. I edited what she gave me into a satisfactory final act, and the play was realized. This impressed the actors, and I became even more admired. I was grateful for their flattery.

This harmony didn't last. I discovered that I was not a collective person or a bohemian; I was an elitist. I thought their collective apartment—after the first reaction of wonder at its novelty—rather squalid; it was not kept clean and orderly. The togetherness of the members often seemed rancorous. I discovered that while I liked the living together in theory, I did not in reality. Experiences later in life confirmed this trait of mine: I didn't like the kibbutz in Israel where I once stayed a week; I didn't like the permanent company I helped collect for Lincoln Center years later, even though many of its members were good friends. I don't like seeing the same people every day. I don't like collectives, communities, convivial neighbors, unannounced visits, groups, and clubs. Even though I may say that companionship in living is an ideal, I certainly would not have liked sleeping three in a room. Where did they fuck? I wondered. And there seemed to be a meeting every night. I hate meetings—hated them then, hate them now.

The worst of it was that the artistic decisions of the organizations were made collectively, at meetings of the entire membership. After rehearsals of a play had proceeded for a time, a meeting for "socialist criticism" would be convened, at which everyone's performance was assessed, not by the director, me, but by everybody. I attended one of these meetings and was shocked by the caustic comments the members made, an actor often criticizing the person with whom he or she played an important scene. No one could ever be in doubt as to what his partner thought of his performance— especially if it was bad. I didn't care for this, often didn't concur with their judgments. Even though they never turned on me, I was glad I wasn't a member, that I could, when I chose, walk away.

I slowly—oh, so slowly—became aware of another practice I didn't like. They had a successful and lively short play about La Guardia, the liberal mayor of New York City, whom they enthusiastically praised. Some time passed; I saw the piece again and there had been a complete turnaround; now La Guardia was being attacked by ridicule. I recall a line from the revised version: "What is Fusion, a snare and a delusion." Fusion was La Guardia's political ticket, which they'd previously backed. This switch had happened, as far as I knew, without a collective reconsideration. All political decisions were in the hands of three actors. Did they have the power to cause this complete ideological about-face? I wondered. I found out that the change was parallel to the new position of the Communist Party in relation to La Guardia, and the revised position had been ordered by Comrade V. J. Jerome, who guided the Party's activities in the arts from his office on Twelfth Street. The Theatre of Action had received orders, which they immediately obeyed, to toe the new line. I didn't think much of the intelligence of the actor members of this organization, but I had thought their spirits independent. I now began to cool and soon went my own way. Back uptown.

D E S P I T E the great success of *Men in White* and the fact that everyone in the company, working or not, was being paid each week, we had a dissatisfied member, Stella Adler. There'd been no part for her in *Men in White,* and the tension idleness produced in this actress became the persisting problem of her lover, our director, Harold Clurman. How Harold influenced Jack Lawson to accept Stella for the central role in *Gentle Woman,* his play about a WASP socialite widow, Gwen Ballantyne, is Harold's secret. A persuasive man, he had in this emergency the eloquence of desperation, for Stella never stopped flailing him with her conviction that the Group was not for her. But it didn't work, not the play, not the actress in the part, not the direction by Lee Strasberg. The play ran a dozen performances and was forgotten.

What I still remember is how anxious we were for the verdict of the left press. They jumped all over *Gentle Woman*, were particularly hard on Lawson. The essence of the criticism was that Jack had chosen the wrong hero, a bohemian off the open road, to contrast with his decadent socialite mistress. He should have chosen an honest working-class hero, he was instructed; perhaps a miner's son. This wasn't surprising, not that year. What did astonish me was Lawson's compliance. He quickly and publicly acknowledged the correctness of the attack on his play, writing his apology in *New Theatre*, a left-wing monthly, of which Molly was assistant editor. Lawson pledged himself to be less "confused" (the opposite of "correct") in the future. He proceeded to confirm his reconsidered revolutionary position in the best possible way: by being arrested in Alabama while gathering material for an article about a miners' strike. His next play, *Marching Song*, was not produced by the Group.

S O T H A T passed and we all hoped we'd learned a proper lesson from our pundit comrades. *Men in White*, scorned by them as a "Broadway" play, which the Group had put over because of Strasberg's genius and our Method, carried on so well that the Group decided everyone could have a two-week vacation—which would prove the worth of a permanent company; we had actors to replace actors on leave.

When Comrade Kazan's two weeks came up, I headed south to workers' America, first stop Washington. I was accompanied by a member of the Theatre of Action, Nick Ray (later a film director, variously respected in Hollywood, idolized in Europe), a man who was especially knowledgeable in American folkways and music. Our goal was the home of a man named Huddie Ledbetter, known as "Leadbelly," the rebel black who played the sixteen-string "Windjammer"—his ever-loving guitar. I was flattered when Leadbelly invited us to dinner for good workers' food, beans and rice. Afterward he "picked" and sang "Mary, Don't You Weep, Don't You Mourn," then a song about Tennessee water—it tasted like turpentine—and another, "Irene," which became a big fat bourgeois hit. I was in awe of Leadbelly. He was reputed to have killed a man in a "bottomland fracas." Had he? Another question not asked. Either way, they'd hung it on him and packed him off to a prison camp.

Real working-class heroes, I was to learn, often had reputations based on having been falsely accused of a crime, then sent off to prison. Looking at Leadbelly's permanently angry face (he clenched his eyes when he sang), hearing the sour, jailhouse tone of his voice—not pleasant by Broadway standards, but the "real thing"—I was glad he was on my side.

Next morning I was off in a hurry, heading south and west to Chattanooga. I'd made friends in New York with the Communist organizer for the state of Tennessee, a wiry little fellow named Ted Benson, aka Sid Wellman or Ted Wellman, aka Sid Benson, who looked as if he'd been beaten up many times. I believed he had been, and this made him glamorous to me. I urged him on, hungry for stories about this other, unfamiliar life. As he spoke, I studied his jaw, which was crooked. Had it been broken in a fight and not properly set? Ted-Sid took me to the CP headquarters in Chattanooga, and I enjoyed the whiff of danger that accompanied him wherever he went.

Oh, the glamour of peril; it ruled my feelings. I had always played it safe, been physically timid, in fact had been in only one fistfight after I was twelve years old. Now I wanted emersion in Danger. Since I had only ten days more, I headed south on the train to New Orleans, another fabled place of that world beyond the world of middle-class America. I had a letter to a Negro (they were still called that) musician named Bug-eye Nelson and dearly wanted to meet Sidney Bechet, a man who played blues on his soprano sax as if it were Mozart. I met them both and sat at their feet.

A few days later I was off for Texas, hitchhiking (how workers had to travel), going through the piney woods of East Texas, getting close to the "common man," talking to truckdrivers and waitresses in "bean wagons," beginning to imitate their country accents, finally ending up in the Panhandle of the Lone Star State. There I happened upon a poor rancher who was putting a well down into the arid land and needed help. I offered myself, was accepted, and for three days helped dig, pushing metal and pulling rope, until we struck water. One day, a large fitting riding a rod skimmed past my skull, and I was proud I'd come that close to being brained. I was really into life, "real" life.

SOON AFTER I got back, the directors announced to the members that the next Group production would be *Gold Eagle Guy*, a play by a left-winger named Melvin Levy—a critic who'd mercilessly roasted Jack Lawson for his political flabbiness the season before. This production would be prepared at Ellenville, a community in the Catskills, where we'd be housed in a cluster of buildings around a failed summer hotel. These structures were scattered over a hillside, the seat of frequent thick fogs that contributed to a plague of ringworms afflicting humans and animals alike.

Again Molly was not there. Clifford had had his play *I Got the Blues* (later *Awake and Sing!*) optioned, and he blew the five hundred dollars on records and wines, both of which I enjoyed. I remember we had distinguished visitors from the higher echelon of the Communist Party, now very much at home in our number. Alexander Kirkland, a movie star with no political background who'd been brought into the Group to play the lead in

Men in White, took me aside one day and confided that he was planning to write a play for me—I'd have the leading role. "But before I do," he said, "I have to read all of Marx."

As for the play in rehearsal, once again the actors were scornful of it. It was after a particularly dispiriting run-through that Luther Adler declared, "Boys, I think we're working on a stiff," a remark that was repeated at intervals through the rest of the summer. Luther was right.

To break in this new production, the directors had set up a three-play program in Boston: *Men in White, Success Story*, and the new one. Their plan did not work. The Majestic Theatre, an old movie "chair factory," was far too big, so the audience, even those interested, couldn't see the expressions on the faces of the actors. *Gold Eagle Guy* was coldly received. Levy, who'd written criticism for the *Daily Worker*, got his lumps from the left.

The play climaxed with the San Francisco earthquake. (Could that have been a piece of symbolism, the hoped-for collapse of the System?) This effect was set off by signals from me, which brought on a series of rope trips, light effects, and the release of "snow bags" containing "rubble" from overhead. It was a complicated series of cues for a stage manager to "throw," made more difficult because the director, Lee Strasberg, was never clear in what order he wanted these effects to occur.

One night, when the whole didn't work and the audience had obviously been bored by the show, Lee gave me hell in front of the company. He was not a man, then or later, able to take his share of the blame for any failure; he relieved himself of guilt by chastising those who couldn't fight back. That night, me.

When he laid the blame on his stage manager, I didn't say, "But, Lee, you've never told me clearly how you wanted the earthquake to work." Instead, I rushed down into the cellar, to the wardrobe mistress's room, and burst into tears. I hadn't cried since I was a little boy, and I resented Lee for causing this evidence of weakness. It's amazing how a humiliation so small, so passing, remained in my memory—"like a knife," Greeks say— when I've forgotten most everything else that happened in Boston that fall.

I am a normal man, which is to say I do not forget slight or injury; I am not forgiving. Although there were to be times in the years to come when I admired Lee and was impressed with his insights and observations, from then on I was always on guard with him. The next morning, going back to work, I tried to see his side, told myself that he must be exhausted and disappointed with the reaction to his production, that it had been a long, cruel stand in Boston and he had taken the full weight of it. But I could not feel charitable. I felt—and often felt again—that in order to be close to this tight knot of a man, one had to knuckle under. Others did; I did not.

Decades later, I noticed an ambivalence in him that I've noticed in many show people; when I was alone with him, he'd be gentle and open. I'd often be touched by a melancholy he'd reveal to me when we were in a quiet room, where there were no witnesses and no issues at stake. Then, at last, I'd feel sorry for him. But, as it happens with so many, the necessity of asserting authority transformed Lee into another man, and I'd move away.

That fall in Boston, I and some of the other actors began, for the first time, to doubt him as a director. I saw that his work on *Gold Eagle Guy* was heavy-handed, turgid, and clumsy, and lacked the spark of imagination. There were no surprises in the production; it was boring. I hated the play and the damned earthquake, but instead of attributing the disaster mostly to the playscript, which I should have, I blamed Lee, which was unfair.

Many of us now began to look elsewhere—to the left, of course—for an artistic path that was independent of Lee and the Group leadership. In that unhappy circumstance, a miracle occurred.

Representatives of the New Theatre League—I was on its board—came to our Communist cell in the Group and declared that they needed a play for one of their New Theatre Nights, to fill out a program of "revolutionary" ballets. Like good comrades, we immediately agreed to provide what was needed. We had a writers' collective in the Group; we called it SKKOB: the O was Odets, I was one of the K's. (Initials were the favorite designations in those years, and collectives were the approved way of doing anything, including script creation.) Three of the five SKKOBs were Communists, two were not. We called a meeting (was there ever a night those years without a meeting?), and Cliff proposed an overall scheme for the play. Naturally it was a strike story. When a play or a ballet was not about one of Hitler's monsters (the arsonist Van der Lubbe had been so honored) or a great Russian hero (another comrade and I had done a play about the Bulgarian leader Dimitroff), it had to be a strike play. Cliff's suggestion was that there be an overall dramatic frame, which he'd undertake, and five short, strong scenes ending in bursts of revolutionary fireworks. Each member of SKKOB would write one of these scenes.

We agreed. Then somehow none of us could get free enough of other work, or figure out how the scene assigned should go, or perhaps we were lazy and, despite our quick volunteering, actually indifferent. When the NTL (New Theatre League) began to press us for a date, Cliff holed up for three nights and wrote *Waiting for Lefty*.

Cliff read it to us and we liked it but had no inkling of what its effect on an audience would be. He'd written the play with specific members of the acting company in mind. We all had parts and were satisfied with them. Cliff was fond of saying that I looked like a hungry wolf, so I was perfect for the man who exposes his "own lousy [rat] brother."

We rehearsed *Lefty* without the supervision of an overlord; the performance was less directed than played. Over the years, in our acting classes, we'd all done scores of scenes like the ones Clifford had written. The production moved without the burden of analysis; it was energetic, light-hearted, bold, and sassy. And felt! The emotions were those in our hearts:

anger at what existed, demand for a change, and confidence that the change—you know which—would come. The lines didn't sound learned; they leaped out of the mouth at the moment. Still the total effect was sure-footed and confident. Which is how we felt: that artistic problems could be confronted and solved by group action, by us together. Now we decided that Lee inhibited actors and we should be wary of his influence. Without him, we knew we were relaxed and happy in our work.

When the play was running through, we invited him to a final rehearsal. When it was done—"Strike! Strike! Strike!"—he was asked what he thought. He shrugged. I don't remember hearing his opinion, not then, not later. I remember the shrug. This widened my alienation. And Clifford's; Lee had never shown the least enthusiasm for *Awake and Sing!*, the play Clifford had been working on for so many years.

I'm going to give you a brief summary of *Waiting for Lefty*, because when I reread it fifty years after playing in it, I was astonished by its naïveté and its power, and I believe you may be too. For reasons that must be partly unconscious, it thrilled me.

As the show starts, the head of a corrupt taxi driver's union, Harry Fatt, is addressing a meeting of union members. Behind him sit five men, a committee of cabdrivers. At the side of the stage are two thugs. "Stand up and show yourself, you damned Red." Fatt shouts his first line at someone in the audience. The man he has challenged does not reveal himself. "Yellow from the word go," Fatt sneers. "Red and yellow make a dirty color, fellows. Give those boys a chance and they'll have your sisters and wives in the whorehouses like they done in Russia."

One of the committee sitting behind Fatt asks to speak to the membership. "Sure," Fatt says, "let's hear what the Red boy's got to say." The "Red boy" says, "Don't call me Red! We're the black and blue boys. We've been kicked around so long that we're black and blue from head to toes. But I guess anyone who says straight out he doesn't like it, he's a Red boy to the leaders of this union." Then he goes on to tell how his wife talked him into calling for a strike. There follows the first of five scenes that dramatize the situation in the union.

We see this man's wife threatening to leave him because he doesn't bring home what they need to live on. "You're talking like a Red," he protests. "One man can't—" She interrupts. "I don't say one man! I say a hundred, a thousand, a whole million. Get those hack boys together and sweep out those racketeers like a pile of dirt. Stand up like men for your crying kids and wives."

The next committee member to speak is a young scientist who's been asked by his boss to spy on a fellow scientist. His reply is to "bust you and all your kind square in the mouth." Odets's following stage direction: *"Does exactly that."*

A young lover, who hasn't the money to marry his girl, tells of his brother, who enlisted in the Navy to find work and make a living. "Don't he come around and say to you, this millionaire with a jazz band, 'Sid, the whole world will know who you are! Get up on that ship and fight those bastards who're making the world a lousy place to live in. Take this gun and kill those slobs like a real hero, a real American!'" That took care of the antiwar theme.

Thus far, on opening night, I'd been sitting on the aisle, my cap with the rabbit's foot on my lap, and watching the show like the rest of the Fourteenth Street audience of progressives and left-wingers. I was totally unprepared for the bursts of passion from the people out front. It was the kind of reaction that sometimes occurs at the performance of a favorite opera sung by a favorite singer, where every aria is well known and eagerly waited for. No one there that night had ever heard or read this play, but the audience was onto it from the first line, as if they were speaking some of the lines with the actors. Bits of dialogue were cheered. The scene where the wife threatens to leave her husband unless he goes on strike brought forth a salvo of cheers. That is not an exaggerated figure of speech; it was like a roar from sixteen-inchers broadside, audience to players, a way of shouting: "More! More! More! Go on! Go on! Go on!"

Harry Fatt, to stem the tide that had been running against him, calls up a character named Clancy from the audience. Clancy (as played by my friend Bobby Lewis) was clearly a louse, just as Harry Fatt was a caricature figure from the propaganda theatre of the day. But is there anything more enjoyable than having a villain to hiss and wait to see foiled? Bobby addressed the meeting, his face wrinkled into a grimace of cunning and deception. The audience found him despicable; they wanted him torn apart. And I did it. I bolted out of my seat, ran up on stage, and exposed Bobby as a deceiver from way back. "He's my own lousy brother!" I cried. The audience exploded. Bobby sneaked off.

My appearance was a complete surprise to the audience. I was not a familiar figure in the theatre. I would not have been noticed or remembered from any of the Group productions. I looked like a man off the street outside, and a cabbie for sure. Oh, the balcony, the people in cheap seats, how they cheered! Their approval came down on me like Niagara Falls. I'd never heard anything like it in the theatre, and I've never heard anything like it since. History had been made.

That was the dream all of us in the Group had—to be embraced that way by a theatreful of people.

There followed a scene in a theatrical producer's office where an unemployed actor finds, once again, that he can't get work on Broadway. The producer's secretary takes pity on him, offers to lend him a dollar for lunch. "Want the dollar?" she asks as he's about to leave. "It won't help much," the actor says. "One dollar buys ten loaves of bread," the stenographer says. "Or one dollar buys nine loaves of bread and one copy of the *Communist*

Manifesto. Learn while you eat!" "Manifesto, what's that?" the dumb actor asks. "I'll give you a copy," the stenographer says. "From Genesis to Revelation, Comrade. 'And I saw a new earth and a new heaven because the first earth and the first heaven were passed away.' I'm saying that the meek shall not inherit the earth." "Who then?" the actor asks. "The MILITANT!" the stenographer says, and Odets capitalizes the word as I have. "Come out in the light, Comrade!"

A final scene concerns an old doctor out of a "real American revolutionary" background. "Yes, spirit of '76," he declares sadly. "Ancestors froze at Valley Forge. What's it all mean? Slops! The honest workers were sold out then too. The Constitution was for rich men, then and now. Slops!" This arouses the younger doctor, who's been passed over in his profession because he's a Jew. "Fight!" he vows at the end. "Maybe get killed. But goddamn it we'll go ahead!" Whereupon he stands with clenched fist raised, the Communist salute.

With that, Joe Bromberg came forward; he played Agate Keller, a man who'd lost one eye in an industrial accident. Clifford gave Agate a rousing summation. "Working class, unite and fight! Tear down the slaughterhouse of our lives. Let freedom really ring." Then on to attack the union's leadership: "These slick slobs stand here telling us about bogeymen, the Reds is bogeymen. But the man who got me food in 1932, he calls me COMRADE! The man who picked me up where I bled, he called me COMRADE too! What are we waiting for? Don't wait for LEFTY! He might never come—" Whereupon he's interrupted by a man—me—rushing down the theatre aisle and up on stage to announce: "They found Lefty—behind the car barns with a bullet in his head."

To my astonishment when I read this play recently, I responded as I had when I first read it. I was thrilled to the verge of tears. In the passing of that half century of time, I'd turned violently anti-Communist. But the yearning for meaning, for dignity, for security in life, stirred me now as it had then. The Communists got their influence and their power by speaking up for these universal human desires. It seemed that I hadn't changed; they had. How did they get their hold on the need for militancy? By being militant before the rest of our society knew it should. Something still alive in me reenlisted.

That night, the audience and the actors were simultaneously exhilarated and exhausted. At first the people out front stood and cheered on and on, as if they themselves were members of that union. "Strike! Strike! Strike!" they shouted. It was the most overwhelming reception I've ever heard in the theatre. The audience at *Death of a Salesman* may have been more deeply stirred; I believe they were. And *Streetcar Named Desire* may have stayed in the audience's memories more enduringly—it did. But *Lefty* "killed" them. When the audience were finally quiet, they did not leave the theatre. Dazed by what they'd seen and heard—which they judged correctly to be the voice of a new force in the theatre, one beyond praise or judgment—they sat in clumps and talked. Some climbed up on the stage, the place where the miracle had happened, walking, with dazed expressions, here and there, talking to friends, looking out front, then to the side, waiting for the actors to come out. Twenty minutes later, a hundred were still there. It was as if the experience would not have happened if they left.

And the actors? We couldn't sleep that night. We straggled north through the silent streets—Harold Clurman among us—found a Child's that was open all night, and lingered over our suppers, not talking too much, stunned by what had occurred. None of us was ever to be the same again, and I suppose we all knew it. But we had no idea how far and how fast this change would go. Cliff was to become a god. The next morning, I'd arrived. The review that would appear in the *New Masses* called me the "Proletariat Thunderbolt." (Who was ever less working class, more middle class, than I? But it never occurred to me to privately challenge this description. I was proud of it.) The company as a whole became a model for what a left theatre should and must be.

When we parted company, it was with the kind of sadness that the highest joy leaves behind. I walked through the predawn darkness from Twenty-third Street to West Forty-fourth Street. (Molly, exhausted by happiness, had gone on ahead.) I felt what I'd never felt before, that strange thing mystics talk about, a sudden enlargement of the space around them. Enormous space and power; I'd proved my power, at last.

Whereas up until so recently—three years before—I'd been out of things, hostile, secretive, frightened, uncertain, adrift, a boy without confidence and with no direction, anxious about my future and living outside the course of the rest of humankind, I now felt proud, positive, busy, certain, confident, not only "in" but in front, convinced of my worth, even a potential leader.

My hostility was no longer an alienation. The Party had justified it, taught me that it was correct, even reasonable. I could be proud of it; it made me the comrade of angry millions all over the earth. I'd reacted correctly to my upbringing, to my social position, to the society around me, to the state of the world. I was a member of what was sure to be the victorious army of the future. I had comrades. I could believe in my hopes; they'd be realized. I could openly declare my antagonisms; hadn't "Agate Keller"? They were worthy and correct; they'd been acclaimed—hadn't they?—that very night, by a thousand comrades. Hadn't their worth been proved in the Russian Revolution? And in the great Russian films I'd admired? I was on the right path. *Lefty* had proved that. I carried the roar of that audience's approval in my ears.

As for the theatre? My future? The Group had reassured me now. I was one of the leaders now. I could keep my head up, rabbit's foot and all—yes, the Proletariat Thunderbolt! I could walk with the best. I knew the secret.

I had the right technique. I'd proved my talent—as an actor and as a the-atre person. I wasn't someone to be bawled out publicly for fucking up a goddamn misplanned earthquake. Look at me now, Lee! I am admired, respected, needed, acclaimed! I felt that special gaiety only confident people can enjoy. I was a man who'd stood central in a glorious, historic theatre event.

All this—however foolish it may sound now—made me into another per-son. I felt reborn, or born for the first time. The days of pain were over. I was an honored leader of the only good class, the working class, and the only real theatre, the Group. And they—the workers and the theatre—were united; they saw things together. I was, finally, on top, every way. My dreams, the total dream, had come true. For the first time in my memory, I was thrilled to be alive. I was everything I wanted to be.

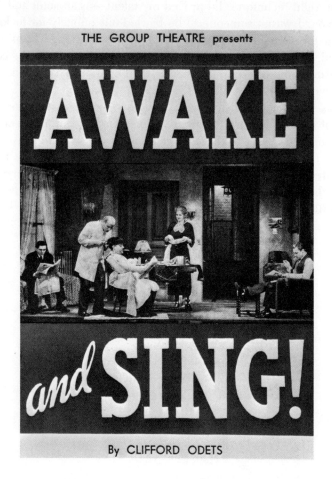

THE GROUP THEATRE presents

AWAKE and SING!

By CLIFFORD ODETS

L E F T Y was immediately performed in half a dozen theatres over the country. It was published, complete and thoroughly illustrated, in *New Theatre* magazine; copies were treasured. The critical review there had this comment: "The Group is emerging from its period of groping artistic introspection. The results of four years of collective work in a sound theatrical method are here (at last) applied to express their continually maturing revolutionary convictions."

Gold Eagle Guy and its lustreless production were forgotten, as was Lee's reaction to *Lefty*, a shrug. With *Lefty* taking the city and the critics by storm, the message was obvious to all—except the directors. They called a meeting in the cellar of the Belasco Theatre, where Melvin Levy's play was dying, and Harold, speaking for the three, announced that they'd decided to call it a season and turn their efforts to finding a play to rehearse during the coming summer.

Since it was January, this decision would throw the actors, still exhilarated from the triumph of *Lefty*, out into the cold streets, unemployed and without rent and food money. At this, Stella, the one member of the company who was not afraid of Lee's wrath, expressed what we all felt. "As long as we can find something to act," she said, "let's act." She looked at Clifford, who then suggested, rather timorously, that since his play, now called *Awake and Sing!*, was free—the man who'd optioned it hadn't renewed his hold—why not do what Stella urged: put it into rehearsal.

The answer of the directors was silence. Lee and Cheryl, who'd done the work on *Gold Eagle Guy*, were exhausted, but why, Stella demanded, did Harold, who had not worked and was not exhausted, feel obliged to concur with the other two? Why did he notify the actors of a decision with which he didn't agree?

Harold was on the spot. Stella knew, of course, what he really felt and would come down hard on him in private. Later Harold admitted that he was ashamed that he hadn't stood up for what he believed. The meeting was dissolved, but that evening, all through the performance of *Gold Eagle Guy* and afterward, there was a rage among the actors against the three directors. To throw thirty of us out on the street in midwinter without work or rent money when there was a play available—that was a cue for rebellion. The actors demanded another meeting with the directors.

Lee came to that second meeting with a reluctance he didn't conceal. Once again, his authority, which until *Lefty* had been unchallenged, was being defied. White-faced, tight-lipped, as the meeting gathered and got under way, he studied the sports page of a newspaper, giving the impression that since it was a meeting the actors, not the directors, had called, he was doing us a favor by attending.

It turned out to be a meeting that changed his life.

For a time he maintained his show of indifference; as far as he was concerned, the season was over. But the actors were no longer the docile, worshipful "children" he'd been training for more than five years. *Lefty* had changed them. One of their number had written it; they'd mounted it despite Lee's indifference and Harold's lassitude. Now, in a charged atmosphere, the actors were not to be denied.

They pressed Lee, forcing him into an unequivocal statement of his position. He spoke a single sentence, which, I believe, destroyed his power in the Group. Even more than what he said, it was his tone, his attitude, that did it. No one made allowances for his weariness and for the disappointments he'd suffered. Mouth clenched, all asperity, he said to a group of actors who'd made sacrifices year after year to keep the Group together, who'd been through deprivation and hardship and remained loyal to him summer and winter, who now wanted only what all actors want, to go on working, he said to Clifford and through him to the company, "You don't seem to understand, Clifford: We don't like your play!" These words were never forgotten or forgiven.

Silence! The actors looked at each other. Did that "we" include Harold? Harold didn't speak. Neither did Cheryl. I wondered if Clifford's sudden success and fame had shaken Lee up so that he was desperate to hold on to the power that he must have believed was slipping. For some reason, although everyone in the room had heard him, Lee now repeated what he'd said, again using the first person plural (a form he became increasingly fond of as he grew older): "Why don't you understand, Clifford? We don't like your play!" These words were spoken as if they would certainly conclude the discussion—and end the season. As far as Lee was concerned, the meeting was over.

The actors turned away; they no longer expected anything from Lee. Harold still said nothing, but the actors did. They decided what a number of us had already decided in a caucus that had preceded this meeting—that Clifford should read his rewritten play to the acting company.

Lee did not attend the reading; he said he knew the play. Harold came and by that act took the side of the actors. He had the benefit of hearing the play read again, to an ecstatic audience. The actors were completely won and confirmed in their determination. It was their play, charged with the spirit of their lives. The poetry of the dialogue reached them, and its humor broke them up. The decision was inevitable. Like it or not, directors, this play would be done! Now.

Harold convened a meeting on the closing night of *Gold Eagle Guy* and announced that the next production of the Group Theatre would be *Awake and Sing!* By doing this, Harold broke openly with Lee. No one knew how completely then; time would show. Harold also announced that he'd called our old colleague Franchot Tone in Hollywood, and Tone had promised to send the five thousand dollars needed to mount the production. (Yes, *five thousand dollars!*) Furthermore, Harold said that he would direct the production; it would be his first. In his account of these times, *The Fervent Years*, Harold reports Lee's comment when he heard that Harold was going to direct *Awake and Sing!*: "It will be very beneficial for him."

AS I NOTED, there'd been a caucus of certain actors preceding these meetings; this was the Communist cell. The idea of Clifford's reading the play to the actors—"going to the people," it was called, or, on a large scale, "going to the masses"—was not Clifford's alone. Since *Gold Eagle Guy* had opened in the Belasco Theatre, the Group cell had been meeting every Tuesday night after the performance in Joe Bromberg's dressing room, there because Joe was our leader (perhaps because he looked like Dimitroff;

had even played Dimitroff in the play another actor and I had written). Joe was an impressive man at this time and well schooled in dogma and its expression. In his dressing room the steps that led to the reading and ultimately to the production of *Awake and Sing!* were plotted; there we had determined that this play would be our next production whether Lee Strasberg liked it or not.

One member of the Group's cell was Lee's wife, Paula.

I was astonished years later, when I read Cheryl Crawford's account of her life, that she had no suspicion there were weekly meetings of the CP cell in the Belasco Theatre. Our conspiracy may have been of little importance, but it was successful. We achieved our goal—democratically.

HAROLD CLURMAN came out of the Lower East Side from a middle-class home and an affectionate, cultured family. Before Harold was ten, his father had taken him to see Chekhov performed by a Yiddish theatre company. Later Mr. Clurman was able to send young Harold to the Sorbonne. In Paris he met the intellectuals who shaped his thoughts and his values, among them Aaron Copland.

I was his stage manager in 1935, watched him as he directed *Awake and Sing!* He was the best first-week director of our time, as he was our best theatre critic. What he did during that marvelous first week's work was illuminate the play's theme, then sketch each role brilliantly, defining its place in building the final meaning of the production. Then he'd sit back and watch the actors struggle to achieve the goals he'd set.

I learned from Harold that a director's first task is to make his actors eager to play their parts. He had a unique way of talking to actors—I didn't have it and I never heard of another director who did; he turned them on with his intellect, his analyses, and his insights. But also by his high spirits. Harold's work was joyous. He didn't hector his actors from an authoritarian position; he was a partner, not an overlord, in the struggle of production. He'd reveal to each actor at the onset a concept of his or her performance, one the actor could not have anticipated and could not have found on his own. Harold's visions were brilliant; actors were eager to realize them. His character descriptions were full of details, of stage "business." They were also full of compassion for the characters' dilemmas, their failings and their aspirations. He was a man of broad sympathies; he blended perfectly with Odets's way of looking at life and people.

I used to read the notes he made in the margin of his text and to write down what he said to the actors after each rehearsal. I was with him every day and every evening, asking questions. (Stella was jealous of how close we were. "Is he queer?" she asked.) I marveled at the penetration and the humanity of the man's vision.

Harold's rehearsals were like parties, at which he was the guest of honor.

Most directors don't like people sitting in the auditorium behind them when they work; Harold encouraged it. After he'd unloaded a piece of instruction—or a joke with which he was particularly pleased—he'd look back over his shoulder, rubbing his palms together vigorously, to see if the people out front had appreciated what he'd said. Harold himself certainly had; his laughter was self-congratulatory.

Harold loved actors—to be with them, to goad them, to listen to them, to debate with them, to inspire them. He loved to fight with the Adlers, brother and sister; he valued contention. Those tiffs were great fun to watch. After they were over, one never felt that the actor had been cowed into obedience or forced to agree. In this respect his directorial style was essentially different from Lee's. He encouraged actors and admired them, instead of confronting them with their inadequacies. The atmosphere he created was of goodhearted fellowship. When there were quarrels, they were of the kind family members have. He enjoyed the life of the theatre, the companionship of writers, designers, and technicians as well as actors; relished their gossip and all the rumble and sport thrown off during work: the "irrelevant" arguments about art and politics, the sharing of problems about each other's love lives—in fact, everything related or seemingly unrelated to the play being worked on. It was all one to Harold, all part of the interchange of creation.

He had the culture to know that if you attempt difficult tasks you're bound to fail as often as not, and that it was no disgrace to fail. Defeat was temporary, never a defeat of the essence. In good fortune or catastrophe, I've never seen Harold humbled—weary, disappointed, hurt, yes, but not humbled. In failure, he did not sulk, grumble, or complain; he did not leave town. His pride was not vulnerable for others to tear down. In defeat, he was an example to me; he taught me to write my own notices.

And he taught me arrogance. I should inform you, reader, if you're not already aware of it, that I don't believe the meek will inherit the earth. The meek in the performing arts should change to another profession. Harold made me feel that artists are above all other humans, not only in our society but in all of history. I'm not impressed with any other elite, not of money, power, or fame. I got that from Harold.

After a glorious start came the second and third weeks. It quickly became evident that Harold had little stage facility. He had trouble turning the psychology he had so brilliantly detailed into behavior on the same level of penetration and originality. There was often something inept about his staging; he had trouble getting people in and out of doors. He relied on the actors to work this out, and occasionally, when he had a clumsy piece of stage movement to deal with, he'd ask me to work it out for him. I'd do what he asked, feeling not that Harold was incapable but only that he was above what he considered to be the mechanics of directing. An architect need not be carpenter, mason, electrician, and plumber.

Everyone has his limitations. But Harold's were of no consequence that year in that emergency. I believe he was perfect. There was no way *Awake and Sing!* could have been cast or directed or played better.

When the play opened, he sent me a telegram calling me his brother. We'd become close friends and would be so for as long as he lived. I did feel like his younger brother, looking up to him for insight and knowledge I didn't have. There were aspects of directing I knew that he did not and never would grasp, but the general spirit of how to approach a play and how to deal with actors, what the rehearsal of a play can and should be—a joyous process—I learned from him. I was ever after in his debt.

There was something I didn't realize until later: His artistic view and feeling were an antidote to the way Communists looked at life. He was a humanist, not a Marxist.

A W A K E A N D S I N G! opened on the nineteenth of February, 1935. Some of the critics carped, but none took exception to the essential worth of the play and its performance. Here was a new voice in the theatre! Critics on the left thought it "insufficiently revolutionary," but they forgave Clifford; after all, the play had been written before *Lefty*. They were sure he'd do better next time and dispatched comrades to advise him.

It was a professional triumph for the Group company; they also felt the triumph in another and more personal way: They'd been proved right. Lee's words about the play to Clifford in the basement of the Belasco Theatre were not forgotten; malicious souls repeated them.

But the company that had triumphed was the company Lee had worked so hard, for so many years, to gather and train. Harold had not made our actors a perfect ensemble; Lee had. For this he didn't get credit. He was, as we celebrated, a forlorn figure. Since his confidence, like that of all directors, was based on the readiness of others to believe and serve, Lee's own confidence took years to recover. In fact, it didn't—not in his time with the Group. He was never again revered, as he had been. Nor was he ever rewarded for what he'd contributed to the triumph of the company.

As for Clifford, he became the most sought-after celebrity in town. There was a media landslide—critical reviews, columns, radio chatter shows. The movie companies were all over him. Everyone wanted to meet him, look him over, ask him questions, listen to what he had to say—and fuck him. Women were especially curious; he was being sought by a different kind of woman now, more sophisticated, more experienced, and more aggressive. His dates overlapped. He suddenly found himself pursued by Tallulah Bankhead, a witty, entertaining bitch, impatient with the confinements society placed on her social life. Bea Lillie adored him. Ruth Gordon took him up, filling the space between Jed Harris and Garson Kanin with this other genius; they became close. A curious and experimental man himself,

Clifford

Clifford filled his pocket notebook with observations about them all. His life would never be the same again. He moved out of the modest apartment where he'd been living with Harold Clurman and took a place high over University Place, where his life would be unrestricted.

His name was dropped everywhere: "Cliff, Cliff, Cliff!" (But his old friends called him Clifford.) He was asked to speak, and his opinion was sought, on every subject. He was acclaimed—this naive and introspective man—for his political opinions. It's our way with artists that when they become famous for their work, they're made authorities in fields outside their ken—politics, for instance. Clifford was named head of a committee to be sent to Cuba to observe (and condemn) the rule of Batista. After a short stay in jail there, he and his committee were shipped back to the States. The newspapers reporting this misadventure made Clifford more famous than ever. He wrote a report on "conditions" there—although he'd spent most of his time in detention. Still it was front-page stuff.

I believe Clifford knew there was something fraudulent about his acclaim. Soon he no longer felt like a success. In the play he wrote two years later, *Golden Boy,* the woman he's pursuing says to the hero, who's moving to the top of his profession, "The thing I like best about you is you still feel like a flop." I can recall that at intervals all through this time of overblown adulation, Clifford privately doubted the praise showered on him. He felt increasingly morose and was frequently suspicious of and hostile to the sycophants around him. His time was being devoured—and his life—by activities he wasn't really concerned about. He longed for the simplicity of former days.

I remember the feeling I had in my own time of public prominence years later—and on occasion still have now. I asked myself, "Do I deserve that exaggerated respect?" I felt—and believe Clifford must have felt—the gap between what people said I was and what I knew myself to be. "I am not the person they're talking about!" I've asked and still ask who the hell they are talking about when they say that name. Am I Elia Kazan? Would they invite me to their parties if they knew who I really was? And what I thought of them?

I've learned what Clifford was to learn—how small the distance is between the top and the bottom in our field and how quick and sudden the fall can be. This has made me quirky and doubting.

Clifford clung to the Group desperately, to the friends he had there, the actors he used to play with, and to Harold, who was, for a time, his conscience. I think that is why I am now, decades later, so devoted to the Actors Studio and the actors there, especially the "unknowns." They remind me of my old self, the person I once was. I still wear the rabbit's foot in my cabbie's cap—but only I know it.

At the same time that his new fame distressed Clifford, he gobbled it up like a starved man who, when food is finally put before him, eats too much. He often seemed out of his own control and sometimes behaved like a damned fool. He was suddenly being asked to every party, mostly out of curiosity. Present at a certain gathering were Moss Hart and George S. Kaufman. Moss was especially curious about the young man with the burning eyes he'd been reading about, so he cornered Cliff for a talk. Moss used to take a gentle but perverse pleasure, as many sensitive people do, in self-deprecation; he told the "genius of the hour" about the trouble he and George were having fixing on a subject for their next collaboration. Clifford listened gravely, remarked that it was a trouble he did not have, since he had five plays in his files, "all laid out," plot-perfect, and that Moss and George were welcome to come to his apartment, look these outlines over, and take any one of them they wanted. "All they need is dialoguing," Clifford said (according to Moss). George, listening, looked owlish. Moss was aghast and repeated the conversation to others. It became part of Clifford's legend in the society of the time. But Clifford was less what Moss thought of him—insufferably arrogant—than naive and childlike.

The final bit of flattery came from the Party. They took Clifford's Party card away, erased his name from their lists, and pulled his record out of their membership file. Already alert that a repression was coming, they elevated him and some other notables to the supreme status: members without a card, also called members at large. If the Party offices were broken into by the "fascist cops," Clifford would be safe. I've always suspected that this was the honor accorded Lillian Hellman and some other glamour intellectuals.

So, in every way, Clifford's life was made simultaneously easier and more complicated. His pleasures were multiplied, while he had less and less time for himself. The flattery never stopped and he couldn't help eating it up, while at the same time he believed what was said about him less and less and finally not at all.

Here's the tragic heart of the problem—as I understood it. When the

irritations, the problems, and the conflicts that existed before the big success are eased and removed, when the struggle is (apparently) over and one
lives behind a permanent Don't Disturb sign, it soon becomes evident that
these troubles, now put behind, were the source and the genesis of the
talent that brought on the success. Fame and money were insulating Clifford from the discomforts and challenges of his earlier years but, at the
same time, "saving" him from those abrasions that were the source of his
"genius."

There's a price for everything.

Now came the classic questions: "Suddenly I can do anything I want, so
what do I do? I can go any which way; which way will I choose? What do I
ask of life? What do I want to do with my years and energy? If I do have
the talent they say I have, to what shall I turn it? Now that I have what
appear to be unlimited choices, which choices shall I make?"

We were all in the parade

THE TASTE of our triumph was most enjoyed in the Communist Party. Our cell was the pride of Twelfth Street. The men downtown were convinced that we were close to taking over the Group Theatre; now to go all the way! As we were being congratulated, we were being urged on. The Proletariat Thunderbolt was invited to sit across the desk from the cultural commissar of the American Party, Comrade V. J. Jerome, and have a talk.

After suitable congratulations, we came to the subject of future policy. V.J. (initials! initials!) knew how history had moved in other situations at other times. It was the classic revolutionary instant, he declared, and not to be allowed to slip by. The actors had forced this great success on the

Group's directors; they should now take command of the theatre. The slogan for the moment was the classic: "All power to the people."

It was my task to deliver Comrade Jerome's instructions (suggestions? no, instructions) to the cell. But before I did, I wanted to talk over my position with someone I trusted. I couldn't with Harold Clurman for obvious reasons, so I turned to the other person whose point of view and principles I respected, my wife, Molly. Despite being drama editor of *New Theatre* magazine, Molly was a person independent of dogma. Marx teaches: "Doubt everything." I'd never felt that the comrades doubted anything; they knew what they thought and what they thought was what they'd been told to think. Molly, a Yankee, was brought up, if not to doubt everything, to question everything. She sure as hell questioned the ability of the actors of the Group to run their organization. The thought made her hoot.

Molly had been an instructor at the Theatre Union and had experience with politically "correct" amateurs throwing their ideological weight around in an artistic organization. She'd been through the Theatre of Action experience with me. She'd been witness to the spanking the Party had given Jack Lawson and his humiliating retreat from his personal artistic intention. "Crawling to the feet of V. J. Jerome," she'd called it. "What the hell does Jerome know about the operation of a theatre?" she'd asked. Had he ever been backstage? Jack, having regretted his choice of the hero of *Gentle Woman* and expressed his contrition at length, moved to Hollywood, where, converted and rewarded, he was running the Party's show. Ranks marching left were not to be broken.

I carried Comrade Jerome's message back to our regular Tuesday night meeting in Joe Bromberg's dressing room, passed on his instruction that our cell should immediately work to transform the Group into a collective, a theatre run by its actors. It was a surprise to me when the members of our cell quickly and unanimously did what the Theatre of Action people had done in the matter of the La Guardia play—give in to the political directive from the man on Twelfth Street. Then it was my turn to speak. I was timid; despite my present reputation as a bullheaded man, up until that time breaking ranks was an act of boldness for me. I surprised everyone by my recalcitrance; I surprised myself. I believe I sounded apologetic for disagreeing. I could feel bewilderment and impatience around me. I suppose the position I took was a sign of disrespect for my fellow actors' political savvy. And possibly their courage. They voted me down.

Later I found out that they blamed Molly and the influence of Harold Clurman. They saw that I was on the side of the directors, not the "people." Therefore I was undemocratic. And therefore—how ironic!—not a good Communist. But what they blamed most was my character: I was an opportunist who'd do anything to get to the top. I've been accused of this many times by many people. The fact is that I do have—call it elitism—strong feelings that some people are smarter, more educated, more energetic, and altogether better qualified to lead than others. I also believed then and believe now that a person's agreeing with me politically is not a guarantee of his or her artistic talent. I was not impressed with the arguments of my cellmates.

Evidently there'd been more discussion after the meeting in Joe Bromberg's dressing room, because in time I was notified that another meeting was being called—but not by us. Apparently a decision had been made downtown, by someone higher up, that another gathering had to be convened to deal with our problem. This was not to be held in the Belasco Theatre dressing room but in the large, comfortable sitting room of one of our comrades, Mrs. Paula Strasberg. (Her husband, Lee, had agreed to take in a movie that night.) I was told where to go and I knew that what would take place there would be top-level, decisive, and final. I tried to prepare my position—but I wasn't prepared for the form the meeting took. Or who'd be there in charge.

Try to remember as you read what follows that this decisive meeting was held in an apartment above Sutter's Bakery, where they used to make the best cookies in Greenwich Village. They were baking that night, and all through the meeting the most delicious fragrances—caramel, cinnamon, and rich melting chocolate—rose from below and filled the room.

The morning after the meeting, I wrote a long note for myself, an account of the events of the night before. I knew it was a turning point for me, and I didn't want to forget the details of what had happened. I've edited what I wrote forty-eight years ago but not rewritten it. I gave it a title back then: "The Man from Detroit."

As soon as I walked into the Strasbergs' sitting room, I saw it was going to be a policy-setting meeting. The old flopping around in the minds of friends was not going to take place, not that night. True to the process of democratic centralism, the "line" was to be set not by the membership but by a "Leading Comrade." I was never introduced to the man, and I have no idea what his name is. There were a few other new faces in the room, who had about them a kind of "revolutionary" glamour [in those days, anyone who wasn't in the theatre seemed glamorous to us. They were "really in life," so we actors thought]. The principal speaker was an organizer in the Auto Workers Union, his headquarters Detroit. There was the strongest possible suggestion in the introduction that brought him on that we were damned lucky to have this man there with us; he'd set us straight. We'd gone slightly screwy—"the way artists have a tendency," the comrade said. (Everyone simpered at this.) So "we needed a little straightening out," he said.

Now Democratic Centralism got down to work. [Democratic Centralism is a process whereby one of the men from the "hard core," a

"Leading Comrade," lays down the true dope and everybody thinks it over and says, "I agree." Then they all go home and do what he said. Only people as full of self-doubt as actors could go for it quite the way our bunch did. The memory embarrasses me.]

The Man from Detroit spoke forcefully. And, surprisingly, all about me. He analyzed me. Although he'd never seen me before that meeting, he understood me perfectly. He'd met many others like me in his work, he said. I was the foreman type. I was trying to curry favor with the bosses; I wanted to join hands with the exploiters of the working class. (The "bosses" in the group were drawing fifty dollars that week.) He underscored my errors. If the man had met me on the street the next morning, he would not have recognized me, but that night he had, if no details, a wealth of theory. I was typical, he proclaimed. He had a very strong face.

I sniffed the smell of pastry from below and looked around. The rest of the boys and girls in the room were sitting there dutifully bewildered. There is an expression children get when they confront a problem too big for them, a problem that they are happy to leave to their elders—a look part dazed, part just plain waiting. There'd been an awful lot of very long meetings. Everybody was tired of them.

Suddenly the Man from Detroit got more direct. He spoke directly to me, urging me to straighten myself out. (Apparently all was not lost.) He heaped scorn on me in a nice, theoretical fashion. A door opened in the back and the husband of the comrade whose apartment this was (Lee) inserted a sleepy face past the edge of the door. Everybody sprang to life and shooed him away. The door closed on us and on me. I wished I were outside. My fellow members, shaken out of their fixed rapture, now looked at me for an instant, before turning their attention back to the speaker from Detroit. Their look now was kindly and forgiving. There are few pleasanter feelings to experience than granting forgiveness. I was going to be forgiven! I could rely on that. But first I had to eat a little more of the well-known black bird. The leading comrade was pouring it on. My God! I thought. This man never saw me before half an hour ago. He's got some damned nerve! And how can these people sit here and look at me that way? I began to hate that kindly look of tolerance for my errors that shone on everyone's face. I longed for the cold, clean winter air outside.

The Man from Detroit was coming to the end of his speech. I could tell because the end was the classic holding-the-door-open-for-the-return-of-the-transgressor. Yes, the door was being held wide open for me to walk back into favor, except that to judge by the cow eyes of my pitying friends, I was expected to make that walk back on my knees. I wasn't listening anymore. I wanted to get the hell out. [I was a sinewy young man and I was beginning to think about how many of these guys I could beat up. That, of course, was irrelevant.]

A vote was taken. I've forgotten exactly how the issue was put. I doubt that I heard it. It amounted to: How many against me? All except one. How many for me? My hand went up. I was for myself. A big step.

Outside, it was cold. The bakers, as I walked by, were working late. The streets of Greenwich Village were empty. At home, before going to bed, I wrote a letter, resigning from the Party.

I understood an awful lot about future events from that meeting, and all I needed to know about how the Communist Party of the United States worked. The Man from Detroit had been sent to stop the most dangerous thing the Party had to cope with: people thinking for themselves. There'd been some "discussion" after he got through. Comrades took the floor and competed as to who could say "Me too" best. They all did a grand job. The fact was that there was no appeal from the verdict of the Man from Detroit, so no discussion was necessary. I understood the police state from him; I know what I'm reading about when I see the words "authoritarian rule." The man was not only stopping people from thinking; he was setting up a ritual of submission for me to act out. He wasn't even operating out of a conviction of his own—he, too, was there on orders. He'd been sent to us with a hatchet, one he'd used before. Despite the grace of chocolate-covered cookies and sweet hot tea, the meeting was strictly strong-arm stuff. He'd come to make us all frightened, submissive, and unquestioning. The assumption of human cowardice on which he operated was so profoundly insulting that it didn't penetrate totally until years later. By then I was another man.

T H E N came a surprise. Despite my resignation, which was in no way equivocal, my relations with my old comrades did not change. The Theatre of Action people must have known of my withdrawal, they must have talked about me, but I continued as their training leader, without loss of respect or devotion. A few months later, on the first of May, I walked with my old Group comrades in that year's May Day demonstration. Look at the snapshot; there is the most congenial harmony among us. How happy and at ease I look! I was glad to be *out* and glad to still be *in*. For this year's parade, a united-front affair, we built a large triangular frame over which black cloth was stretched. At regular intervals holes were cut, through which we poked our heads. Each of us wore the headdress of a different worker—coal miner, steelworker, longshoreman, baker, cook, and I, of course, wore my taxi driver's cap. That May Day was a lively and happy celebration, and although I never again had anything to do with the Communist Party, I was as devoutly sympathetic as ever to the worldwide movement for the liberation of the oppressed and happy to march with the others to affirm this.

What did my former comrades think of me that spring? I was not told, but at a guess I'd say they considered me confused but useful. The harmony I enjoyed was a tactic; it was to pass.

I had an even bigger surprise. There is an old Greek myth of a demigod or human (I've forgotten which) who puts on a mask to disguise who he is, then after some time decides to take it off but isn't able to; the mask won't come off. So it was with me. It took me many years, as you will see, to pull that mask off.

In other words, I continued to think like a Communist. The theatre is a weapon. A play must teach a lesson. The third-act climax must send the audience home with hope and courage born of a sweeping revolutionary insight. Only I and those like me had the answers. I continued to regard the society around me as hostile and repressive, yes, corrupt beyond redemption by peaceful change. Why? Because it was run by moneymen. Change is necessary; in fact, inevitable. What kind of change? Complete. Final. A shift of power. Trust the working class. Only. Defend the U.S.S.R. With all its faults. (This did change.) My duty as a theatre artist was to teach others the right way and lead them down the right path.

All of us who came out of the "movement" and all those who remained in the "movement" were marked with this intellectual arrogance. We were sure of our "positions," and it was too damned bad for anyone who didn't agree with us. We were sure we were right. After I resigned, I did not think any differently than I did when I was a member. In fact, I still believe a good part of what I believed then.

The answer to why Party members didn't change toward me for a time is simple. These were the years when the Party's program was the Popular Front. The sole criterion in political matters was: What is most useful for the survival of the U.S.S.R.? More clearly than America's leaders, the Party saw the onrush of Hitler and World War II. Of course, they were much more threatened. Determined to make the broadest possible front of alliances to counter the coming threat, they wanted everyone in any way "useful," even someone as insignificant as I was, on their side. And they were determined that in the coming crisis the U.S.A. should be with them. The slogan they raised was: "Communism is twentieth-century Americanism."

Some people bought it. For a time I made that mistake, confusing the philosophy of this country with that of the CP. But against the Party's simulated democracy and tactical patriotism, there stood the man with the thrust chin and tilted cigarette holder. Behind FDR was the American tradition of individual independence. Behind that, the Constitution. What FDR said by every act and every posture, in every speech, was: "This society can be made to work. Our people are good. Our problems can be solved—our way. Democracy must be preserved. We'll overcome all obstacles." He didn't have to say any of this; he embodied it.

His presidency was the time in my years when, as a nation, we had unity, belief in the future, laughter, fearlessness, intelligence, energy, and even some love for each other. It was during his reign that I began to break my old Anatolian mold, through FDR and MDT—my wife Molly, another intrepid, stubborn individualist. It was during FDR's years that I began to see that I could be one of the people here, not against them. The spirit of the thirties rescued me from my roots.

T H E Y E A R after *Awake and Sing!* I was playing in Clifford's next play, *Paradise Lost*. It had not been enthusiastically reviewed, and we were all on cuts. One week I drew down eighteen dollars, another twelve dollars, and since Molly and I were having a child, I had to look around for supplementary income. I began to work as an actor on radio "hours," shows like *Gangbusters, Crime Doctor, The Ed Sullivan Show,* and, for Orson Welles, a thing called *The Shadow,* of which he was the star. I remember him arriving for rehearsal one morning; he'd been up all night carousing but looked little the worse for it and was full of a continuing excitement. A valet-secretary met him at the side of the stage with a small valise containing fresh linen and the toilet articles he needed. The rehearsal was never interrupted—Orson had unflagging energy and recuperative powers at that time—and he soon looked as good as new. There was no swagger of aesthetic guilt there; *The Shadow* was not patronized, only slightly kidded, and this affectionately. The cast were "his people"—many of them turned up in *Citizen Kane* later—and they knew their business, so that week's installment was soon done and well done. It was a way of making a good living in a bad time and no disgrace, especially in light of Orson's plans for the Mercury Theatre and the films he was preparing to make. Seldom have I been near a man so abundantly talented or one with a greater zest for life.

Half a century later, I'd left films and theatre and was writing novels. I'd never been close to Welles personally and lost track of where he was and what he'd been doing, informed only by the usual column rumors. One weekend I was in Beverly Hills to go on talk shows and help peddle my latest novel. My publisher had provided me with a limo to take me quickly—I had a tight schedule—from one show to the next. I was assigned a driver who turned out to be an aspiring writer. He'd once carried Welles from his hotel to the studio where he was making a commercial, had observed Orson carefully, and described him to me with a writer's appreciation of detail.

He said that Orson had become so heavy that he couldn't squeeze through the passenger door into the back of his limo but had to be wedged through the front door and set down next to the driver. Welles was holding a brown deli bag, and once they were on a thruway, he opened it, pulled out a roasted chicken, and began to tear the meat off a thighbone with his teeth. Piece by piece, he consumed the bird, breathing hard as he did, then he fell asleep. The driver had to wake him at the TV station and help him out of the car and into the studio where Welles was going to speak for a wine company. "Is he trying to kill himself?" the driver asked.

I made a point of catching the commercial. Orson offered the nation his assurance of the product's worth with a voice as resonant as ever—a beautiful instrument indeed—and his presence was, in some grotesque way, still imposing. I couldn't help wondering—as I do with any sponsoring of a product where an artist is paid to say what he's paid to say—did Orson, himself, believe what he professed? Of course, he must be broke, so he has to earn his living this way. What a tragedy, to put such a talent to this use.

I contrasted this puffy huckster with the dauntless, spirited fellow I'd worked with in the thirties. I remarked how he dressed now, entirely in black, a formless, unbound costume, the kind of garment old women choose to conceal the infirmities of an aging body. I thought of what he was wearing as a great tent inside which he was hiding. I also thought of him— remembering his glory years—as a great beached whale, driven onshore by a storm or, more likely, by some mysterious turbulence in its essence. Why this slow suicide among whales? No one has ever found out. Was there some compulsion of shame or spiritual defect here that made Orson "let himself go," then degrade his huge gifts by making commercials? Did he have an impulse, like the one that beached the whales, to rush to the end?

Some months later, when I heard him speak in Central Park at an antinuke rally, seated in a wheelchair on a platform to which he'd been raised by a forklift, he still said the old brave things and enjoyed the acclaim a favored celebrity receives. Yet I thought his defiant, antiestablishment declarations sounded hollow.

When I think of large talents that were beached by a crisis in their lives, I think first of Clifford Odets. There is one sorrow that must pain men so stranded most: that they were unable to live up to the image of themselves that once gave them their pride. Clifford was what Orson was not, a celebrated member of the Communist Party. In 1935, after his first two plays hit New York, he was the artist-revolutionary of the day, honored and respected by all good men. In 1952, he did what I'd done, named the Party members in the Group to the House Committee on Un-American Activities, and whereas that act, unhappy as it was, gave me an identity I could carry, naming his old comrades deprived Odets of the heroic identity he needed most. I don't believe he was ever again the same man.

I remember that a few weeks after his testimony, he, Molly, and I were walking down Lexington Avenue one evening, when we were accosted by a group of young people, decent and well educated they were, who began to jibe at Clifford, telling him how disappointed they were in him, how he wasn't what they'd believed him to be, and how badly he'd let them down. Clifford didn't defend himself; he was silent. The encounter did not last long, and we were soon continuing down the avenue. He still wasn't speaking, and there was nothing I could say or Molly wanted to say. I've been glad ever since that I did what I did, had regrets that some old friends had been hurt but none about hurting myself. Clifford, though, was distressed not because of hurting other people but because he'd killed the self he valued most.

Eighteen years later, during the decade when I could make any film I chose and Clifford was beached in Hollywood, I'd go west from time to time to speak with the studio heads who were providing me with production money, and the first personal friend I'd call was Clifford. "Come, I'll take you to dinner," I'd say. "Let's go to Chasen's." But he wouldn't, not ever, not once. Finally I stopped asking him out; I could see that the reasons that made him refuse were painful. He wouldn't go to the "in" restaurant in the film colony because he'd have to pass tables where people would ask, "What are you doing now?" and he'd have to either lie or say, "Nothing." Or he'd encounter liberals who'd look at him, then look away as he passed. The fact was that the only jobs he could get at that time were rewrites, patch-ups, and dialogue fresheners, which he'd have trouble admitting; but what would have pained him more were the snubs. So he'd answer me, "Let's stay here. I have some sirloin. I'll make us a pair of fine steaks, and we'll talk over old times." Which is what we did. His house was dark and quiet, and in an eerie way I saw that he was on an alien shore and that he was a beached whale.

There are others whom the waves of thought and art in the forties, when they retreated, left stranded. Brando, like Welles neurotically overweight, and by some mysterious choice out of things, respecting no one and least of all his own profession and his incomparable gifts, hides on a dirt hill over the film colony or in Tahiti. There are others too, many of whom make fat livings by boosting commercial enterprises—you've seen them on TV. These men in their private moments still present themselves as rebels— like old actors coming back again and again to play a favorite role, the one in which they scored their great successes. But in their hearts, I believe, they know the unhappy truth, that they are now deep in the system they once loathed and attacked. Many of them are affluent, with a Mercedes or the assurance of a stretch limo and an obedient chauffeur at their command. They are all good men, men of the "movement," as it was called, not the Communist movement but the surge of hope and confidence and determination that took over from the Great Depression, the anti-monopoly-capital movement, the common-man movement, the anti-colonialist movement of the thirties and forties. These were and are worthy causes, causes with which I am in sympathy, and, as much as the others, I hold on to the postures of those days and the dreams we once all had. But now, in the cold light of a cold morning, those dreams are troubled when they exist at all, and on the beach lie the remains of that other time.

There are a few out of that experience whom I've watched with less sympathy. I have a photograph of an ad Lillian Hellman made for a fur company. When she was asked how she came to give herself to a commercial display so crass, she replied that they'd "caught her on a bad afternoon." The interesting part of the photo is not the drape of the mink (her compensation), but the cock of her hand holding a cigarette in stock glamour-girl pose, and her face, which I read as saying, "I'm not so damned unattractive, am I now? I'm right in there with Mercouri and Streisand and even Bacall! Don't you think?"

I can sympathize with that but less with another recollection, one she does not record in her memoirs, of the days at the end of World War II when she'd bundle with Russia's ambassador, Maxim Litvinov, under his limousine's lap robe at the same time that her fellow Jews were dying by the hundreds of thousands in Maxim's master's labor camps. The story goes that during this time, Litvinov and his wife, Ivy, came home one night from a pro–United Front affair and as they prepared for bed, Max asked Ivy, "Don't these liberals here have any idea of what's going on in our country?" Lillian did know—hell, we all knew, and some even thought it justified—but Lillian was silent. She didn't remain beached, however, but spent her last days on the high seas, flapping her tail and spouting high!

All these people struggle to hold on to an integrity they feel does not exist now and a hope that died. Not having found a new life they were able to respect, they do their best, under circumstances that are difficult, to maintain what they once had and believed in. Above all, perhaps, they strive desperately to go down as themselves, to at least finish in their own style. Artists of talent, they fought and fight still to continue in their proudest identities. The talent they lack is a talent for facing certain painful truths. This is no shame. What they believed in, long ago, was not a fact, it was not substantial; it was a dream and no way less worthy because of that, but—

Los sueños sueños son.

Kewpie, in *Paradise Lost*

 I F I N D it difficult to believe now, but I was an actor for eight years. When I was admitted into the Group, rewarded for faithful services as a stage manager, I had no prospects as an actor.

 I have too high regard for the artistry of the great actors I've admired to place myself in their company. I had the energy of the era and the intensity of my neuroses. Someone wrote that I was supercharged. Thank you very much. My opinion is less flattering. On stage I could only be at ease riding a rage so violent—one I didn't dare show in life—that it overcame my self-consciousness. I could not play relaxed scenes. I had no variety. My speech was still poor, New York street stuff. The classics were beyond my reach. Despite all that, I was for a few years a cult favorite. I spoke for the times.

 Most of the parts I played were phases of the same human attitude. The

You see what I mean?

mood is invariably antagonistic. Also proud. "Fuck you all, big and small!"
I used to mutter during those years—to myself, of course, secretly. Offstage
I was known for being agreeable in any circumstance and under all pressure. Concordant. Sweet. "Gadget." On stage, I could be what I wished I
were, and during those eight years I became another fellow off. You might
have found it unattractive, the self that emerged, but it's the truer of
the two.

W H E N I was a boy of twelve, we lived in a small wooden house on the
upper half of Sickles Avenue in New Rochelle. A short distance from our
place, the street dipped into a steep hill, and when this slope was snow-
covered, it became a favorite sleigh ground for the area kids. At the side of
this incline and above it, there was a hump of rocks, jagged and unkempt,
where the young bucks settled differences. Those were the landmarks of
our neighborhood.

On this snow slope, the boys used to guide their Flexible Flyers alongside mine and flip me over. I'd go back up the hill without a protest, and
start down again. In warmer seasons, on the rocky hump, a sharp-fisted,
left-handed Jew kid named Dave beat me up three times. How come three
fights with the same result? Couldn't I have begged off? Did I prefer fighting to being left out? Could I handle a beating easier than an exclusion?

How to tell? Not a peep out of me. I remember going home at dusk, still silent, and reading my Tom Swift or O. Henry stories of fearless, adventure-seeking young men—quite unlike me.

My favorite burrow those days was the New Rochelle Public Library, three miles from home. I would run there—I was less vulnerable running—and read in the stacks all afternoon. Sometimes a wop kid who knew a patsy when he'd found one would wait for me in the street and, when I came out, accompany me home. It was not an honor guard; perhaps he was teaching me to respect the great Italian people and making sure I did. I remember peeping through the front window of the library, waiting for the street to darken, and when I saw him off guard, I'd sneak out a side door and run home by an alternate if longer route. Even on my own block I had to be spry, for across from us lived an Irish family, and one of their six mick kids used to punch up his status in our neighborhood. Those years, I never left home without checking out the window.

Yet when the years passed and the time came, I played nothing but tough guys.

Perhaps because of a solution I happened on. The last year we lived on Sickles Avenue, I made friends with a boy who lived at the bottom of our hill. His name was Greg Draddy, and he lived in the shadow of his brother Vin. For some reason he took to me—these attachments are mysterious among youngsters—and here is the scene I haven't forgotten: In a wolf's circle of teenagers, Greg and I are banging away at each other with our fists. The fight was staged, but no one would have guessed it from the murderous expressions on our faces and the purple of our curses. Our secret? We'd pledged beforehand never to hit each other in the face and to "pull" each punch a little. This made me bold. I could act out what I wished I was. Safely. It was the first acting I did, my first tough-guy role, and I must have done it well, because the following winter no one overturned my sled.

My intense life has always been the one within me. From the day I was aware of who I was and what my fate was to be (outside general society), I wished I were someone I was not—an American, for instance. What I did not dare do in my life I did in my daydreams. Even now, as I walk the street, I find myself involved in unspoken dialogue with someone who exists only in my mind. I live a twenty-four-hour movie, one in which I play many parts, some heroic, some defiant, some terrified, some amorous (X-rated). I'm not always the hero but always bolder than I am in life.

What happens "actually," in my waking hours, is rarely as interesting. I used to think this exceptional, but I've noticed that most people I pass on the street are playing out a drama written by themselves. The Stanislavski method was simple for me. I allowed myself to do on stage what I'd always done privately.

When I came into the theatre, the saying went: "You either have it or you don't." Acting couldn't be taught, it was said; stage deportment, speech, dialects, singing, dancing, fencing, gymnastics, yes, but not the central thing, not the art of acting. There were the gifted few and those less fortunate. The completely unfortunate carried spears. I, it was quickly judged, was of that hopeless fraternity. So I had to believe—did I not?— that talent grows unsuspected, underground, and may be found in the least likely places. And I had to believe that the essential art, the core thing, had a technique, one that could be learned, and I could learn it. Looking back, it seems to me that my outstanding asset was persistence in the face of rejection. No one had faith in me, but though I was turned back in every possible way, something irrational always kept me coming on. I was too desperate to be discouraged.

I remember, the winter before the Group took me to Green Mansions to build their scenery, standing in a long line outside the Plymouth Theatre, a line leading up to a small office off the balcony lounge. There, so I'd heard, Arthur Hopkins waited. The revered director of Barrymore's *Hamlet* was casting, and actors were presenting themselves for judgment. When I finally came close, I could see that this creature of legend was a short, plump man with a cherubic face over a bow tie and that he was seated behind a small table, looking down at its bare top. As each actor arrived before him, he raised his face, glanced quickly at the candidate, then, saying not a word, shook his head and dropped it again. That was what he did to me. I'd waited an hour, but considered myself fortunate to have seen the great man. Did I think it possible that, distracted from having seen too many anxious faces, one after the other, he'd made a mistake? I stood in line again and was rejected again.

Another humiliation I remember going through more than once was a "reading." Invariably this took place on a bare stage, and the person who read with me was the stage manager who'd just read with twenty other applicants and was understandably sated. The auditorium was usually dark or, if illuminated, lit by a naked thousand-watt bulb overhead, which caused people out front to slouch in what seemed to be attitudes of indifference, their hats down shielding their faces. The vocal response from out front, when its tone was friendly, tended to be "put on"; it isn't possible for anyone to be cordial hour after hour. When I was finished I might hear "Thank you," meaning "You're dismissed." Sometimes I heard whispering out front or low laughter; probably it had nothing to do with what I'd done or not done—but how could I be sure? I remember my cheeks burning. Often I had no idea who was out there. Was it the playwright (and his agent)? The director (and his girlfriend)? Or the director's assistant assigned to sort out candidates for the small parts? I never knew what he or they had thought. Or even if they'd paid attention. (A gofer had come down an aisle during my reading, with coffee and Danish.) I read, was rejected, and left. But it didn't take long before I was ready to try again.

Such was the life of the professional actor on Broadway when I came down from New Haven. Year after year they waited for an eventuality over which they had no control—a part, a play, a film, an interest, a friend in a high place (usually an older man with an itch for a young actress). How do they take the penury, the uncertainty, the scorn, and the rejection season after season without becoming cynics or drunkards or (now) cokeheads, or getting into terrible fights, or becoming some variety of criminal or a compulsive gambler? Pride would seem to demand a violent reaction. But they endure it all and, on the whole, maintain an extraordinary grace and generosity of spirit as well as a true love for the theatre while, with ever-increasing desperation, but with idealism undiminished, they try to shoulder their way into the work they want. There is no category of people in the theatre—or for that matter in our society—as gallant or as lovable. Year after year they continue to believe the illusion by which they live: that someday soon the part will come their way, the one that will "make" them, as a part "made" Brando (did it? a part?) or Dean or Julie Harris, Paul Newman, Bobby De Niro, Lee Remick, Jason Robards, Dustin Hoffman, Al Pacino—their heroes who "made it."

Of course, all this is a memory. But even now, when I'm not an actor or a director, when I'm not even in the theatre, I recall what I felt and put myself in their shoes. Actors are my favorite "children." I love them for their innocence and impracticality as well as for their tenacity. I find myself concerned for their welfare, grieving for their hopes unrealized, and delighting in their triumphs. I know that the hit play will close and life go on without them, but the actor will somehow survive.

Despite whatever dignity and confidence actors have managed to win for themselves over the years, they are still today the people in the theatre who have to please everyone—the producer and his partners, the playwright and his agent, the director and his agent, the star and his manager, the moneymen and their wives, as well as the audiences when they come and the TV commentators, the newspaper critics, the gossip columnists and mudslingers. No wonder that members of the theatre's first profession fill up with anxiety and, its opposite face, unreleased anger.

I did, fill up with both.

With everything else Harold and Lee accomplished, they also brought dignity to the actor. They restored him to a position of some standing and his art to a level shoulder-to-shoulder with the other crafts in the theatre. The honorable position of the actor—all of us, not just stars—was affirmed. Now an actor, even one who isn't anything near a star, will take the risk of being thought arrogant and ask what the character he's being asked to read for is all about. It is a question that embarrasses many directors. If the actor is nervy—and has other offers going—he may even refuse to read until he's had a script and a chance to read it through. The result is complaints from producers and directors about the arrogance of "our" actors. No wonder!

When the kicking shoe is on the foot of the man with the bruised ass, he's likely to use it. The actor has decided not to take any more shit. The star may punish the director or the producer for past indignities from another director or producer. Some call it arrogance.

Yes, I became arrogant.

THE GROUP THEATRE came apart in 1936, reassembled in an altered form in 1937, dissolved completely in 1940. It was then that the actors and directors out of that experience began to teach what they'd learned. Today, as I write this, there are schools of acting everywhere proclaiming variants of a central viewpoint, the Method. By a curious irony, the rebels of the thirties and forties have become the establishment of today. No one says, "You have it or you don't" now; they say, "Come to me. I'll make you a star."

Nearly every star today is claimed by one acting teacher or another; there are long lists of their "pupils" in the trade paper. It's difficult to have a conversation with Robert Lewis without hearing him mention Henry Winkler, an old pupil, or drop the name of Meryl Streep, a more recent one. It's a natural pride; architects point to their buildings. But now the thing is out of hand. Colonel Sanders of Kentucky Fried Chicken fame is dead; his place of business continues franchised, a syndication. Lee Strasberg is dead; his place of business continues. The right to speak his name is bought—at a fat price.

There are yards of books that will instruct the beginning student on how it's done, and how it has been done. Read all about it! The Stanislavski system made easy! I have a shelf of these manuals, but I've found that information rarely helps an actor; training does. Even those books written by close friends have bored me, although perhaps that was mostly because I've spent so many years listening to dogma on the subject. I cannot believe that an actor should be instructed while sitting in a comfortable chair listening to a "guru." The last class I taught (I mean the last, for I shan't teach again), I didn't let the actors sit down for two hours. They did the exercises I chose on their feet and found this exhilarating. The sight of actors perched row on row as magistrates passing verdicts on one another's work raises my hound hairs. When I hear the phrase "master class," I want to vomit.

Today when I'm consulted by an eager newcomer about whom to "go to for help," I generally answer that I can't offer advice unless and until I know more about him—which I make damned sure I don't have time to do. I shudder at the thought of giving quick counsel on the Art of the Theatre, on what will "get you there." Yes, the experience of other actors and directors can be communicated and does help, but on the whole it's better for a young actor, driven by a strong desire, to stumble, fall, pick up, come on again, so find his way. What I do sometimes say is that choosing a teacher is like settling on a lover; one size doesn't fit all. Strasberg, the most famous and financially successful teacher of our day, helped some people—Al Pacino and Ellen Burstyn swear by him. Other, equally excellent actors abominate him. Stella Adler, a spirited and flamboyant teacher who emphasizes characterization and role interpretation rather than emotional recall, came to her class the morning after Lee died and ordered them all to stand. "A man of the theatre died last night," she announced. For one minute, the members of her group, a large one, stood, some with heads bowed, all silent. Then Miss Adler ordered them to sit and said, "It will take a hundred years before the harm that man has done to the art of acting can be corrected."

This certainly seems excessive, and I don't know precisely what Stella was referring to. I think she might finally admit, with some nudging, that she learned a great deal from Lee in the Group's first years. I can speak for myself; despite the negative impressions I formed more recently, I owe Lee a great deal and owe to the movement Harold and he started, the Group Theatre, everything. Because I was an actor—and could not possibly have been one without their help or outside their theatre—I've learned never to be afraid of actors, so I've never treated them, when I was making films, as counters in a game to be moved about as I pleased. I've never wished them struck dumb, always opened myself to their imaginations and benefited by their suggestions. I've been able to remain undisturbed by the questioning that other directors resent. Even with the novels I've been writing—if they had one special quality, it's that the dialogue sounds as if it were spoken. I learned from having been an actor.

I do have differences with my old friends and associates. No one who came out of the Group and now teaches does it precisely the same way or with the same emphasis. Sanford Meisner, Robert Lewis, Stella Adler, and Paul Mann have all helped actors become artists. I know for the best of reasons; I've worked with "their" actors in films. But they are each extremely individual in their work and I've heard all four scorned by their own kind. Acting teachers tend to disparage each other's methods, and I've thought I detected here and there a hint of jealousy of Strasberg's financial success. As in other human endeavor in the arts, there is a fascinating variety. But despite that, the teachers I've mentioned make the same basic emphasis, which is fundamental: Experience on the stage must be actual, not suggested by external imitation; the actor must be going through what the character he's playing is going through; the emotion must be real, not pretended; it must be happening, not indicated.

That's our word for heresy: To *indicate* is the cardinal sin in acting. Yet even this is open to question. Some great actors imitate the outside and "work in" from there. Laurence Olivier, for one. Larry needs to know first of all how the person he's to play walks, stands, sits, dresses; he has to hear in his memory's ear the voice of the man whom he's going to imitate. I lived across the street from him at the time I was directing his wife, Vivien Leigh, in the film of A Streetcar Named Desire, and would often drop over to see him. Larry was working with Willy Wyler on Sister Carrie and, as ever, concentrating on what might seem to "us" to be insignificant aspects of his characterization. I remember pausing outside a window late one Sunday morning and, undetected, watching Larry go through the pantomime of offering a visitor a chair. He'd try it this way, then that, looking at the guest, then at the chair, doing it with a host's flourish, doing it with a graceless gesture, then thrusting it brusquely forward—more like Hurstwood that way?—never satisfied, always seeking the most revealing way to do what would be a quickly passing bit of stage business for any other actor.

Including for us, of the Group. We would work on the actor's disposition at the time of the visit, what Hurstwood feels toward his guest and what he wants to accomplish in the scene that's to follow. Having determined these—no, I'll put it correctly: Having experienced these, that is to say, having found them within ourselves, we'd trust that the detail of how the chair is offered would take care of itself.

Does it? Not always. Which way is better? As in all art, both. There is content and there is form. The artistry is in the passion; it is equally in the way the passion is expressed. Perhaps the problem we have to deal with is how to create an expressive form within which the spontaneous life, the one that yields the unexpected, the dazzling surprise, is free to work. The greatest actors are known for giving the same performance a little differently each night—but it is the same performance in all essentials. Both techniques are important: turning your emotional resources on and off, this way and that, while at the same time directing the cunning of your body to the most telling external behavior.

The technique of exhuming intense buried passions by arousing associations, what is known as "emotional recall," is no longer esoteric. We know all about Proust's madeleine and what it engendered. We are familiar with the glandular behavior of Pavlov's dog. To believe that true acting centers around that psychological trick—a teacher's delight in showing off, because it never fails to impress beginners—tends to make acting a competition as to which actor can produce the greatest emotional show. That is not important, nor is it the Method, which is concerned with the reason the character is on stage and what he wants to—and is able to—do there within the circumstances of the scene. The people of the Actors Studio are often criticized, as were the Group actors, for reducing acting to a display of emotional fireworks rather than playing the scene correctly within its true limits.

The problem of form is still the problem and applies as much to the insides as it does to the externals. Emotions differ; they have different qualities; they are part of a characterization; they are specific. We don't feel alike, nor do we all always feel at top pitch. "In life" most of us conceal our feelings, don't want them to be seen; many actors I know, especially Lee Strasberg's pupils, brandish these emotions as if they were the only true measure of talent. The basic problem of artistic control is the problem of having the emotion and giving it its most appropriate expression. This problem cannot be slighted in acting any more than it can be in painting or music. The great Russian directors of their classic period—before the Revolution fell to earth—Vakhtangov, Meyerhold, and even, at the end of his days, Stanislavski, were dealing with this problem: form.

I recently staged an adaptation of the *Oresteia* with a cast made up of actors from the Actors Studio, and although they were devoted and worked hard, although they were attractive people for whom I felt affection, they had, almost without exception, poor speech. It was, and still is, parochial and even ethnic, "off the streets," perfect for *On the Waterfront*. The unconscious premise of all too many of them was: If I have the emotion, that is all I need. They'd been trained by Lee Strasberg. I watched some who had very small parts, walk-ons, prepare in a daze for minutes before they entered, then do nothing original on stage. All the people who came out of the Group still have to answer the challenge put to them so often, with justice: Why have American actors not succeeded in the classics? Why have these plays, the greatest in our libraries, been left to the English for realization? There is much work for actors in this country.

Much work for directors too. I've twice tried to deal with a "classic" and both times failed disastrously. The plain fact is that I've had no training or experience to prepare me for such a task. There was no tradition here in this country from which I might have learned, not in my time. There surely must be some way of combining what the Group had with the glories of a stage devoted to the verse plays of the great dramatists.

One final word on this subject. There is a power the actual experience genuinely felt by an actor has that, when merely simulated or cleverly suggested, it does not have. You can see it in the greatest performances: Raimu, who, in *The Baker's Wife*, looked less like an actor than like a baker, but whose enacted humiliations, those an aging man will encounter when he's in love with a young woman, were so truly felt they shook me. Garbo in *Camille*, unsurpassable. What is her mystery? Her self. Judy Garland, at the end of her life, giving you flashes (by lightning, Hazlitt might have added, as he did of Kean) of her own life's pain when she sang the pop-blues. Caruso and Callas, he with that great theatric voice, hers with one often criticized, both offering depth that made you forget any flaw. Bessie Smith, who made a league of all the down-and-outers in our society, sang for them all and for her race as well. Brando, naked of soul in *On the Waterfront*, the best performance I've ever seen by a man in films because it had all the tenderness and delicacy in love scenes that you could not have expected. And all those others: Anton Chekhov's nephew Michael, Walter Huston in *The Treasure of the Sierra Madre*, Lee Cobb in *Death of a Salesman* before he "improved" his performance. And that great old Japanese actor Takashi Shimura in Kurosawa's *To Live*. Those are some of the treasures of my life. You would name others. Now ask yourself why these performances—or your own list—live on in your memory, and others, equally praised, equally famous, do not.

My own opinion is that they do because the actors—whether by technique or by accident—gave you pieces of their lives, which is certainly the ultimate generosity of the artist, and they did it unabashed. You were the witness to a final intimacy. These artists spoke to your secret self, the one you hide. They offered you more than cleverness or technique: they gave you the genuine thing, the thing that hurt you as it thrilled you.

What made these distilled experiences awesome and unforgettable is that in these cases, a kind of fear is aroused—not in them but in you as you watch—a fear that may be the ultimate respect you, the viewer, can give in return. You find yourself unsure of what is going to happen next—or in the end. Will they last it out, will they come through? As in life, there are likely to be surprises that discomfort you. All leading men and women should have something unpredictable and dangerous about them. You should be anxious about what they might do; it could get out of hand. Didn't Bogart have this? And Bette Davis? Will the leading man make love to his leading lady or will he strike her—Cagney. Who can plumb the mystery of Greta Garbo? She doesn't yield, she doesn't make friends; she's not after your approval, not ever. Yes, there should be a persisting menace, even in heroes. They should be the opposite of housebroken, only partly tamed, not quite civilized. Immoderate.

Sitting out front or before your screen, you realize you're witnessing a real event, one more real than life, for in "life" there are the limits of civilization—the police, for instance. In art there should be none. You should not know what the outcome will be. You watch apprehensively—as you did Martin Scorsese's *Raging Bull*, which Bobby De Niro played. In the company of those performers you should not feel safe, any more than you do walking through a Harlem slum street at night if you're white, or driving over an African savannah in an open jeep as the sun sets and the predators begin to stir. You feel the immediacy that you experience when you watch a terrible encounter in life or read the first act of *Richard III*. You wish for the best, but you're not sure it will come to pass. You hope, as you do when you enter *Lear*, that this greatest of the old men of the world will come out of his daze, even for a flash at the end—as Lear does—and for that instant see his life and the world clearly. When that happens, your own life has grown. What's happened to people on stage or on the screen has happened to you.

That is the kind of acting to which I aspired.

. . .

W A I T I N G   F O R   L E F T Y was a fall of the dice, but when I was cast in Clifford's *Paradise Lost* and another stage manager engaged to replace me, I knew I'd made it, I was a member of the acting company. Starting rehearsals from the beginning, I went through the full process of preparation for a wonderful part under the direction of a brilliant man, Harold Clurman. With him, I prospered. When the play opened—surprise! I was given a "hand" after each of my scenes.

Acting, I found, was the biggest charge I'd ever had. I knew the exuberance of playing before an admiring audience and hearing my secret voice: "It's happening! This is it! At last! They adore me. Listen to them laugh! Now how silent they are! What's that murmur? I think they find me sexy. No. Yes, I think so. I must look in the mirror as soon as I get back in the dressing room. The way they're listening, I must be important. Or is it what I'm saying that is? Of course, Clifford's words, you damned fool. But now, this instant, they're all mine. I think they love the son of a bitch I'm playing. Listen to that laugh, chuck, chuck, chuck. I love you, I love you, I love you. I know. Yes, I love you too. I'm great, you're great, we're great together."

So it went. Every night, I was being reassured by hundreds of beating hands. Who could ask for anything more? Oh, how that satisfied my soul! What other artist has it so good? Approval so quick? You think my reaction childish, don't you? You're right; it was primitive.

It didn't matter, with that going on every night, that the actors were all of a sudden on cut salaries and I was drawing a miserable eighteen and twelve dollars a week. Molly had a small income. Our month's rent was only fifty-five dollars. I loved my work. I loved her. She loved me. I loved the child stirring in her belly. Some women look less beautiful when pregnant. Molly more. Her face glowed. The child on the way seemed to be consummating her happiness. For the first time in my life, I had faith in my future.

Then to be praised by the newspaper critics, actually singled out, if you'll forgive me. And the "magazines of opinion"! Here is Mr. Stark Young's opinion from the *New Republic:* "Mr. Elia Kazan is a delight, a threat, a wag with fire. His address is sure. His, as it were, eye to the audience is both dramatic and twinkling!" "What's this guy?" I asked myself. "Queer?" Then the theatre people too. Jed Harris, that bastard, to whom I was going to be compared one day, said it in print: "A performance of genius!" I received a telegram from George S. Kaufman, asking me to be good enough to trot over to his office and see him for a part. What a pleasure to refuse a giant of the theatre in the name of my obligation to the Group!

There was a bigger event than any of these, and it happened inside me. I had a scene in which the author required me to burst into tears, despite

The original Group. At right, Clifford and I.

my character's take-on-anybody, tough-guy front. I hadn't been able to do this in rehearsal. But suddenly, before an audience, they came, the tears, in a rush. I couldn't stop them. I hadn't cried in my life—oh yes, once, when Lee scolded me about his damned earthquake. But my whole act in life had been not to let anyone see me hurt, never to admit humiliation, never ask for pity or even sympathy. Why now and in public? Was it because an audience was crowded close around me? Was that the greatest privacy?

I was showing feelings I'd always concealed. I knew this was the result of our work in the Group and of the ideal of complete emotional openness that Lee had held up. He used to say to his classes, "Don't deny your emotions, be proud of them!" Now, for the first time in my life, I was showing my emotions proudly—not *indicating* them; living them. I was offering the world everything I'd always masked, feelings I'd stored up for years and not let anyone know existed. I was singing my own "blues" at last and doing so without "male" embarrassment.

This experience on stage, night after night, broke down a reserve within me. The mask of the ever-compliant-good-kid fell clattering to the floor and I kicked it into a corner of the closet of my soul—just in case I might need it again sometime. Now I decided to enjoy being what I truly was, even if that proved to be a son of a bitch.

"So okay, let it fly," I said to myself. "Am I really that way? I don't mind. Why not? Let them see the truth. There! Look! All of you. Look!"

There was another change. When I was stage manager to this company of actors, my job had been to keep them orderly and comfortable so they could do their best work. Now I was in the bull pit, competing. They were experienced infighters, knew all the tricks of the profession. I had to learn to hold my own. When rehearsals started, I was treated as a beginner and given more advice than I wanted. This continued even after the play was running. Stella Adler, whom I came to like later in life, took it on herself to offer me her opinion of my performance plus certain recommendations for improving it. Our

Stella

director, Harold Clurman, did not show his strong side with this actress; I could guess what he'd said to her: "Sure, Stella, go ahead, talk to him, why not, he's a good boy." But that "good boy" was disappearing. What she was doing, I felt, was a kind of condescension, and I no longer forced myself to appear dutiful or attentive. I used a tactic I'd developed with my father: forgetting what I wanted to forget even as I was hearing it. A nod, a lift of the eyebrows, an ambivalent shrug, a distant smile, and soon Stella saw that she was not getting the attention she believed she deserved, and she fell silent. The other actors in the company would soon find out that I'd broken out of the nice-guy closet, that they were dealing with a proud—call it cocky—call it arrogant—young man.

And soon I found that I was able to do in life what I could now do on stage. My whole emotional self, the loving side and the angry side, began to show itself. I wasn't that compulsively agreeable kid anymore, the "gadget." I was someone new and, to my friends, a little startling. I strutted on the street. I walked by acquaintances without saying hello. I did look carefully in the mirror and found what I'd hoped for—my face was changing, and for the better. I believed in my potential; I had confidence in my talent. What was emerging was my true self.

P A R A D I S E   L O S T   closed after seventy-three performances, a commercial failure. We tried everything—statements of outrage, fervent testimonials from culture celebrities, and working without pay. Nothing sold tickets. We were out in the cold of disillusion and the winter season.

In the year that followed, the Group as it was first put together fell apart. There were many causes—very little survives failure in our theatre—but the main reason was that what had bound us together, the hero worship the actors felt for Lee and Harold, was no longer there. In the months after *Paradise Lost*, adulation was replaced by friendship. And equality.

We followed *Paradise Lost* with two productions that had little to recommend them; they revealed the flaws—common humanity, for one thing—of our leaders. And we began to encounter the difficulties of keeping a company of actors in a continuity of work. Can a permanent theatre be maintained in our country? It's a fine thing to attempt the impossible—so the song tells us—but it may remain the impossible. Where such companies exist and endure, don't they have state subsidies? In England, continuity of work is maintained by revivals of the classic plays of the country's past. We don't have a Shakespeare, and our actors were not and are not now prepared to play Shakespeare. Nor were they truly interested. The Group spirit was born in the thirties. We were gathered to do plays that "said something" about our lives. Our spirit was contemporary.

The resolve of the CP to lead the Group on had fizzled. Since I wasn't there, I don't know what was being said. With a company of restless actors on their hands, the directors felt that they had to find a play quickly and throw it into rehearsal. There was a further requirement—the play should have parts for all our actors. The Group was to be held together by work. What happened was inevitable: We did a play no one believed in, *The Case of Clyde Griffiths*, an adaptation by Irwin Piscator of Dreiser's *American Tragedy*, and we did it for the wrong reasons. Cold and schematic it was, theme-strangled and, for all the arrogance of its avant-garde form, quite obvious. Lee talked himself into directing it; he said there was a boy-girl story there as well as a formalistic challenge. Our directors rationalized expertly, but we—and they—knew better.

In the world of show business there is a virtue that is not a virtue. A director is praised in Hollywood, for instance, when it is said that "he can direct anything": westerns, musicals, love stories, social dramas, farce, whatever. This versatility only means that the man has no personality of his own, and what he does is likely to be synthetic, however professionally turned. I watched poor Lee struggle with Piscator's concoction, which was as far from Lee's own character and talent as he could go. Lee did have a personality; it was intimate and cloistered—not suited to many plays. But then a true artist, most often, has only one thing to say, one basic style, one theme. Look at them: Goya, Cézanne, Whitman, Mozart, Dante, Hopper, Eisenstein, Van Gogh, Renoir father, Renoir son, look at Tolstoi, Dostoevski, Stendhal, Kurosawa, Flaubert, Giotto (forget Picasso), Balzac, Proust, Dreiser himself, unadapted. Why should they want to be good at everything? (Forget Picasso.) That's for gossip columnists. Lee was not in the class of those I've listed, but he was an artist, and his faults—a narrow scope, a ghetto soul—were also his virtues. The measure of an artist's worth is his depth, not his breadth. The production of *The Case of Clyde Griffiths* got what it deserved: a short, unhappy life—nineteen performances—and an unmourned death. It left us exhausted, with a bitter aftertaste. And in need of rest.

R E A D this photograph with me. Here is a gathering
of old friends who've been through a lot together and earned a rest. We'd
just arrived at the Pinebrook Country Club, reassembled for another summer of work. Look closer: It's probably hindsight, but I'd say that the passion that had once made us so open to Harold's exhortations about what our
theatre might be if we willed it and worked for it, that fever had cooled.
We weren't "hungry" anymore. For the most part, we seem calmer, maybe
nicer, certainly more relaxed, ready to talk and laugh together, listen to
music, play tennis, and party, even work reasonably well without quarreling. But is that what's required to hold a group like this together? Isn't an
edge of fanaticism needed? Does that level of desperation and desire accrue
to none but the young? It would seem so. Only men of genius, once past a
certain age, look as if they'd kill for their work. As for the rest of mankind,
what more to ask of life than to gather on a sunny June day and enjoy the
company of good friends?

Leave it at that? No. I see a troubled look on the faces of the veteran
actors in the front rows, and I detect warnings of a breakup coming. Notice
that our two artistic directors are sitting on opposite sides of the frame. Lee

Strasberg, behind his glasses on the left, appears sullen and hurt. He rates my sympathy, having just carried a heavy load and failed. He's probably disappointed in himself but won't admit it. Lee could never admit weakness. To his left are Sanford Meisner, Robert Lewis, John Garfield, and, with Paula Strasberg looking over his shoulder, Harold Clurman. Does he look satisfied? He is not. The two men must have been aware that they'd failed in their primary responsibility: The company had no play ready to put into rehearsal. The actors would soon find this out and there'd be recriminations. Each director would blame the other for this and much more. Rancor would come out in the open. Meantime we actors had to earn our keep by performing for the camp's clientele. The first program: a bill of Chekhov one-acts.

Missing from the photo are three people. Stella Adler was a problem Harold had not been able to solve. There was no part for her in either of the two productions being contemplated, therefore no reason for her to come to our camp or even to continue in the Group. She distrusted Harold's avowals of concern for her career, felt he'd been conning her. We all resented the lady, believed she'd scattered Harold's concentration and corrupted his good sense. We thought the problem that had been distracting him—what to do about her professional life—irrelevant. We hadn't forgotten an incident during the run of *Awake and Sing!* Stella, at the curtain call, would pull off her gray wig to let the audience know she was doing the Group a favor—reluctantly—by playing an older woman. Harold got angry complaints from the other actors. He must have spoken to her, but she didn't stop taking off her wig at the call. We were convinced that she'd hurt the company's morale.

Joe Bromberg, who'd played Uncle Morty so brilliantly in that production, had left for California and settled there. He was not at the Pinebrook Country Club with us, said he'd become disillusioned.

Clifford Odets is missing from the photograph too. He'd taken a job in Hollywood to pay his bills, had rented a house for the summer on the periphery of our camp. And a few weeks after we first assembled, he brought Luise to meet the Group people. His hope was that she would link herself to the Group, which meant as much to him as ever. She arrived with a sore throat and seemed frightened. The actors had a chance to look her over and talk to her. Some of our women thought Luise was "acting all the time." She was certainly a hypersensitive person, accustomed to adulation and constant sympathetic concern. Luise felt hostility from all sides. She hated the house Clifford had rented and was jealous of his devotion to the Group people. Receiving an "urgent" call from MGM, she rushed west and the tension eased—temporarily.

Clifford had brought with him the manuscript of the play he'd been revising and now meant for us to do, *The Silent Partner*. Harold read the manuscript first and informed Clifford that while it could be his best play, it was not yet ready for rehearsal. I read it; it was not his best play and could never be. Among Harold's suggestions for revision was this: Clifford should write a good part for Stella, but please not an old woman like the part she'd played in *Awake and Sing!* I thought this outlandish; what the hell would Stella do in a strike play?

Clifford was affronted that the Group was planning to open its season with another author's play, one that was still being written. He decided that since his play was not going into rehearsal, he'd please his wife, go back to Beverly Hills, and do his revisions there. I observed that their love was most passionate when they separated.

In the weeks previous to the company's arrival in our camp, Cheryl Crawford, the practical one, had been working with Kurt Weill and Paul Green on a transplant of *The Good Soldier Schweik* to this country. (Weill's idea? Cheryl said it was hers. Harold implied it was his.) This was to be Total Theatre, with the influence of Bertolt Brecht. The actual writing was being done in Chapel Hill, North Carolina, where Paul was giving our musical play his unique American folk quality. Kurt could imitate the music of another culture better than anyone I've known, but the impulse to bring Schweik to America, while clever, was synthetic.

So we waited. We were past a point where we could take acting classes, though Stella, when she arrived, had the presumption to preside over some sessions that were expressions of her differences with Lee on the Method. There was mischief there: to shake the throne where Lee had sat for so long, so securely. Since Stella was Harold's lover, these classes deepened the rift between the two men. The summer was passing without rehearsals, and both men were on edge. We listened to Weill play the piano and reminisce about Berlin and Brecht, we listened to Lotte Lenya sing, we admired them both, but the drama was behind the scenes: Who would direct the musical?

Harold had a scheme. He'd been impressed, so he said, by my direction of the play for the Theatre of Action, thought me energetic and mechanically competent, just the person to provide Stella with the supplementary support she needed to function as a director. He suggested that she and I codirect. I knew Harold had made this suggestion only to solve his pressing personal problem. My ambition now was to become a director—and having watched the others, I believed that I could—but I didn't want to start as Stella's "caddy." I resented Harold's estimate of me—"mechanically competent"—and wondered why he didn't direct the Green-Weill musical himself.

Harold was clever enough to sidestep what he wasn't sure he could bring off. After some tense conversations behind the scenes, Harold, Kurt, and Cheryl, more in desperation than wisdom, jockeyed Lee into accepting the responsibility—"for the Group." Lee was no more suited for this material than he'd been for *The Case of Clyde Griffiths,* if for no other reason than that it was supposed to be funny. Lee directed wearing a psychological straitjacket, which is what gave his productions, when they were good, their intensity. Furthermore, it's one thing to talk about Brecht, which Lee did at great length, and another to be Brecht at work.

So we were waiting and wondering, when Molly called to tell me that her time was near. I rushed out of camp, but didn't get to the hospital by the time the baby arrived. I told myself that Molly "understood"—after all, she was a theatre person. But this priority of values was to be made evident again and would cause bad feelings between us. For the time being, Molly seemed generous about my "Group comes first" attitude, but how long could that last?

During the three days of my visit to see our newborn daughter, my life changed. The babe wrapped her hand around one of my fingers, held on tight, and I was lost. I was astonished to see how large Molly's breasts had become and how desperately the kid pulled at her nipples. She was going to have a strong character, we could see that, and began to argue what to name her. I realized that was quite a responsibility, to give someone a name for the rest of her life. (It took us months to decide: Judy.) I looked at Molly's face as she held the child and I saw fulfillment there, an emotion more passionate than any I was feeling. Something deeper and more important than playmaking was going on. When Molly fell asleep, the child in her arms, I sat and watched them. I was a father now; Molly had become not only a wife, companion, adviser, and roommate, but my kid's mother. Molly's devotion was now split, and I felt a surprising quirk of jealousy. When I clasped her, we were three in a bed.

When I got back to camp, my roommate, Bobby Lewis, threw a small party in recognition of my new state. I was glad to see my friends again, but there was something cool in the core of my heart. Judy's primitive hand clinging to my finger had asked something of me, I didn't know what: protection, support, warmth, love, constancy? Whatever it was, I'd give it to her. The grip of that hand had given a new firmness to my life. Like certain crustaceans born with a soft skin, I suddenly had a shell. I had to take charge of my own life and learn how to be tough about what was important for me. This was more of a revolution than I knew. I'd stopped being an obedient and faithful "Group" member; I'd begun to look out for myself.

Two weeks before we broke camp, we received a script of *Johnny John-son* to rehearse, and the parts were assigned by the directors. I was cast as one of a chorus of eight soldiers who were to sing Green and Weill's comments on war. High-level liberal stuff; I thought the songs and the play banal. I preferred the show about the boys in the Civilian Conservation Corps that I'd directed for the Theatre of Action—it had "more to say." I watched Lee's rehearsals, but not with my old intense interest. I followed direction, but without enthusiasm. "What are you thinking about all the time?" Harold asked me one day. I believe I shrugged. I was let down by the play and my role in it. I had other, disruptive thoughts, which I didn't know how to reveal to Harold. Or if I should.

I knew now that I must not take my bits of professional success as an actor seriously. *Lefty* and *Paradise Lost* were ancient history. I'd begun to believe, from watching Lee and Harold at work, that within the ranks of the men accepted as professional directors there must be a place for me. I should begin to look for this place. Was I justified in putting my life and my hopes in their hands, to do with as they thought best? I wasn't even sure they were able, and I knew they were no longer devoted to each other. I'd found out that along with Harold's considerable talents, he had a gift for rationalization—that is, lying to himself—and he had and would again use it for Stella's sake. Harold, I was discovering, would sacrifice a friend's best interests in behalf of his anxiety for Stella, then find words to justify it.

I also wanted a bigger piece of life than I had as a member of the Group, more air, more space, change, challenge, adventure, and more room for growth. I resented the insignificant part I had in that synthetic play and— this wasn't fair, but it was true—I resented little Kurt pattering back and forth along the orchestra rail, telling everybody how his songs should be sung. I was suddenly unfair, intolerant, and damned impatient.

I faced the fact that the summer had been badly organized by our direc- tors. I shouldn't expect a living from *Johnny Johnson*, because I wasn't going to get one. These directors, whom I'd hero-worshipped so recently, were not worth the trust I'd given them. I'd put my life in their hands, and I mustn't again. It was time to get tough in my own behalf.

The production ran for a few weeks and had more merit than I'd be- lieved. It was the only show in the city with a theme. But theatrically it was a goulash of European cleverness foisted on what its authors believed to be native material. In a word, it was a fake. When it closed, we were among the unemployed—with no regrets.

Now the tension between the directors was out in the open. Lee was blamed for the failures—uncharitably; he'd given the Group so much of himself for so long—and Harold was blamed for his bumbling inattention, and Stella was blamed for that. What went on behind the scenes when the three met, I don't know. Lee is quoted as saying that he didn't want to risk his sanity continuing as an administrative director of the Group Theatre. Certainly the brunt of the pressure had been on him, not Harold. Their relationship deteriorated further, then split apart. Cheryl made a sharp ob- servation in the book about her life: "Harold and Lee would never have stuck together without me. I had to constantly introduce them to each other." It wasn't long before Lee and Cheryl announced their resignations and, following that, plans for a production company of their own.

The actors had quickly grabbed what jobs they could find. I had to make a living, so I was back on radio. Only one actor among us had the good fortune, the personality, and the talent to land a good part in a successful play;

Her name was Judy.

he scored a hit in *Having Wonderful Time*, and the movies came after him. Julius Garfinkle was to become John Garfield. Cheryl, as usual, had done the simple practical thing; she'd helped a number of us get jobs in film-making. It was a goodbye gift, typical of her human concern for actors. My job would not make me rich; I was to get one hundred fifty dollars a week from Walter Wanger, the Hollywood producer, for "standby." I didn't know what that meant, but I had to take the chance and did need the change.

S O   I   W E N T west. Clifford was writing a screenplay for Lewis Milestone and promised he'd speak to "Milly" about a job for me. He invited me to stay with him and Luise again, and as much out of curiosity as friendship, I agreed. Their place was gloomy by day and night; Clifford liked his living spaces dark. Luise was not working, and I found her to be a warm, generous hostess who made sure I had everything I could possibly need. Several times we had breakfast together while Clifford slept on. I felt that she was lonely and in need of sympathy. They were having differences and each telling me his own side. I didn't enjoy the tension, so liberated myself by finding a small apartment in a rooming house, where I'd be alone.

Harold had been offered a job as assistant to Walter Wanger and came west to join Stella (now Ardler) in the sunland. Wanger was my boss too. I sent part of his hundred fifty home each week and lived like a mouse. "Standby," I found, meant making acting tests, with actors who had more serious prospects for fame. With luck I might attract the attention of a director who'd give me a job. I benefited by observing all the film production I could, soaking up everything done and said. I also studied Wanger. He was a Dartmouth man, a dashing figure at first view but with quite a naive side. I remember being impressed by his sports coats, his body perfume, and how far he'd gotten on how little. Tallulah Bankhead was to pay him this tribute when he died: "He had a good cock," the bitch said, "but he didn't know how to use it." I imagine she thought that suitable for his tombstone. Wanger didn't know how to use Harold either. Our sometime firebrand leader was nothing but an intellectual ornament for Wanger's office.

So there I was, exiled in Hollywood, and I determined to make the most of it. I acquired an agent, an affable fellow out of the William Morris stable. We had a meeting interrupted by the rat-a-tat-tat of his phone calls. If the people calling were "well known," he always dropped their names for me to pick up. Sandwiched between these conversations were avowals of interest; he said he was certain he'd be able to find me work. Still innocent about agents—I'd never had one—I believed what he said. I was to learn that agents con their clients, as I suppose they must. They may call it "encouraging" or "maintaining morale," but in the end it's lying. I had two days of hope. He told me I was up for *Dead End*, as Bogart's dumb sidekick. Maybe I was "up" for it, but I can't remember if I got into the office of the director, Willy Wyler, to be looked over, or was presented to Sam Goldwyn, the producer, and I imagine that if I had, I'd remember. When it doesn't "work out"—their phrase—agents don't feel obliged to explain or apologize or even to immediately notify their clients; the silence will tell it. They prefer to distance themselves from failure; it's you who've failed, not they. After a few expressions of lack of interest from directors and casting directors, the efforts of your agent collapse. If he believes that you might one day make a hit, he'll take you to lunch—a "write-off." I don't remember any lunches that summer. I got the score finally, expected nothing. In a desperate effort to fill my days, I even tried to write a "treatment" for a screenplay with another Group actor who was idle. The treatment disappeared into the maw of the William Morris office's literary department and was never heard from again.

I did do one test to "help out" Luther Adler, who was being considered for a part in the film Clifford was writing for Milestone. "They're trying Luther out for the leading role," I wrote Molly. "He had a nose operation this morning. They're trying to put a point on the thing. If he doesn't pan out, they'll use Henry Fonda." Fonda got the part. I remember the makeup artist's efforts to straighten out my nose and shorten it by shadowing its end. The hair department tried to arrange my hair so I wouldn't look so Anatolian. Nothing helped. I still "registered" as someone just off the boat—steerage. One look at the test and I knew I had no future, not as an actor, in Hollywood. I'd better be tough with myself, I thought, and face the facts.

I decided to go back east and work in radio, where they couldn't see me. I'd had loving letters from Molly, with tiny drawings of our little daughter in the margins. That was where I belonged.

Then it appeared that Clifford had indeed talked to Lewis Milestone about me. I was about to have six of the happiest weeks of my life. Milly had engaged Clifford to write a screenplay to be called *The River Is Red,* a love story set against the background of the Spanish Civil War. The thing then was to find new backgrounds for tried-and-true stories. At my first meeting with Milestone, I told him that what I wanted most was to be a film director, since I knew I had no future as an actor. Milly didn't contest that, and otherwise responded generously, saying that he was making a shooting script out of the dramatic material Clifford was providing him, and if I was interested, I could work with him as a secretary-assistant. It would be my schooling.

"I can type," I said, leaping at the offer. "No pay? It doesn't matter."

So after reporting at Wanger's every morning and being told there was nothing for me to do except stand by, I'd hurry to Milly's white colonial home in Beverly Hills, charge up to the study, where he was waiting for me in his bathrobe, and stay there until midafternoon. It was a beginner's course in directing. Milly had said to Clifford, "Write this just as if you were doing a play. Leave the rest to me." Clifford had done exactly that. Now, shot by shot, at Milly's instruction, I typed short, numbered paragraphs, the shots, substituting images and descriptions of action for Clifford's overload of words.

I was learning fast. "Don't describe it. Show it happening," Milly would say. I also observed that what he liked to do was center each scene around a significant object, one that he placed in the foreground of the shot, close to the camera. The action that followed consisted of the people in the scene moving toward this object into close-ups. Milly, to my surprise, thought of his film as a series of long scenes, rather like stage scenes. Where was Eisenstein's montage of short, quick cuts? I wondered. Milly had come out of Russia too. He also tried to bring each scene to a climax of meaning or a plot turn that would lead on to the next scene—again like the stage.

It was this experience, watching Milly make his shooting script and observing how different it was from the screenplay Clifford was writing, that gave me the idea—which offends members of the Screen Writers Guild— that the director is the true author of the shooting script. Milly—and I— made his screenplay, not Clifford.

But it was not creative work—no passion spent, no new insights, surprises, or ironies. It was a job, workmanlike, professional. Milly, a true veteran, had done it many times before and would do it again, always exactly as we were doing it, working methodically, adding shot to shot, making scenes that way, until we had a finished script less than half the length of Clifford's. Milly always knew exactly what he wanted to do; we were dealing in directorial mechanics. The man never doubted himself.

He also allowed no tension to disturb the pleasurable progress of each day. At about half-past twelve, a soft-spoken maid brought up two trays—

lunch. I remember fluffy omelets and sour rye bread, toasted. As we ate, Milly would answer my questions about the early days of moviemaking and particularly about *All Quiet on the Western Front*, his most famous film. He seemed to be a man completely satisfied with his life and in absolute command of its course. There was no discontent there, neurotic or divine. And somehow he had made our work seem simple. Day by day we'd piled up the shots of a screenplay, with Milly's explicit directions as to how they should be staged. I could certainly do that. I came away from our work every day a more confident man, determined now to become a director of films. Milly hadn't treated me as a student or as an inferior; he'd even accepted some of my suggestions. Yes, here was a solution for my future—but how to start, that was the mystery; how to get in?

Milly had a suggestion for that too: that I stay in California; he'd get me either a part or some other kind of work in whatever he did in the future. Although I wasn't to accept his offer, I was grateful for it. His confidence intensified my growing independence. But the movie was not being moved into production, and Milly couldn't say when it might be. (Actually it was never made.) So I would have to sit there and wait.

I'd come to detest the "Los Angeles area," as the airline people call it (I never got used to it). I hated the phony buildings, the fumes of heat rising from the macadam by day and the damp cold of the region at night. I hated the look of people; their suntans were like what a funeral director's assistant applies to the faces of the dead to make them look healthier than when they were alive. I hated the traffic and the trees, the restaurants and the stores, and I missed *The New York Times*. In years to come, although I was to work there several times for extended periods, I never found what there was about Hollywoodland to like.

What I missed most was the Group, the Group I'd been part of, and the people in it. This was astonishing to me, a complete turnaround. It came over me again how important it was to my sense of life and my sense of humor to be close to comrades in art, people who had the same hopes and the same values I had and aspired to the same goals. Yes, to my surprise, I missed the Group—not the organization, not all the personnel, not the leadership; simply the fact and the feeling of being together and united and living in harmony with people you liked, instead of the disharmony and indifference I felt around me in California.

I began to talk to Harold and to Luther Adler and above all to Clifford, who I knew needed the Group more than any of us. I proposed starting our theatre again. I found out, very quickly, that they all felt as I did, that southern California and its film industry was not for them or they for it, and there was no reason for them to stay there. It had needed the Group to break up for me to find out how important it was to me—and to them too, not as a theatre so much as a way of life. For the rest of my time, I'd continue to attach myself to a group, first the second coming of the original

Group and then the Actors Studio—where, at seventy-seven, I was still working.

So we began to make plans to save ourselves. Luther knew he hadn't impressed the front-office people. Harold was a clown in Wanger's office— they made fun of him behind his back—and he still had no plans for a film to direct. Clifford's dialogue, which sounded so good on a New York stage, sounded phony coming through a screen. And I? Nothing. No one of us had made a success in the film world, and this had intensified our feeling about the worth and importance of the Group. We all wanted to start again. And most of all, Clifford.

More than any writer I've known, Clifford needed to be needed to write. He was like a high-powered automobile with an uncertain self-starter; our need turned him on. Luther and I began to hound him to write us a play, and we jibed at Harold, who, despite his sorry state at Wanger's, seemed comfortable since he was close to Stella and eating in expensive restaurants where headwaiters greeted him by name. I remember observing with puritanical disapproval that Harold had grown plump and taken to flashy neckties. In prosperity, I concluded, this is not the same man. I recall another conclusion I reached, that idealism is possible only in conditions of penury; it is a unique man, I made up my mind, who can sustain the fever of his dreams when he has money to eat regularly. Perhaps this was a hangover from my old Communist-days motto: "Only trust the working class." The main objective I had during those weeks was to return Harold to hard times so he could again be his true self.

Clifford had told us about a play he'd been thinking of. It was about a young man who wanted to be a concert violinist and also a champion boxer. This theme, of course, was conceived out of Clifford's own conflict between two values, the Spartan devotion of the committed artist as against the free life of fame, fortune, adventure, and moral license. The Group was the violin; boxing was Hollywood, fame, and fortune.

The play's scheme also suggested my own conflict at that time. (It seems so simplistic now.) I hadn't been impressed with the operation of the studios or with most of their films. I was proud of what the Group had done—its plays, its level of production and acting. When it had been good, it had been uniquely good. I wanted our theatre back. Perhaps it influenced me that I had some position in the Group and I was nothing but an assistant without pay, "standing by," in California.

The play was biographically related not only to Clifford and me but to other Group members as well. I recall that Clifford had been sending samples of the handwriting of his friends to a graphologist, who returned detailed character analyses. Clifford was casting the play as he wrote it; into each part he put what he thought of the person he wanted to play it. For example, Clifford thought of me as a man with dreams who'd do anything to get what he wanted. The graphologist confirmed this. Clifford himself had been toughened in a hard world, so he rather admired my determination and even what he considered to be my ruthlessness. At the same time, he knew and responded to my easily hurt side. He built Fuseli, his gangster in the play, on this ambivalence and wrote it for me. I don't know exactly what he thought of the other Group actors personally, but I would guess that it might have been what he put into the parts he wanted them to play.

As for the part of the young woman with whom the young man falls in love, she was based on any one of a number of young women Clifford knew so well, who were "floating" in New York, vulnerable, unprotected, and used callously by men. Unable to take care of themselves, these women existed by attaching themselves to a man—the best one they could manage to hook—who'd support and protect them.

With this play nearing completion, we decided to go back to New York immediately. Gathering there, we rented a small suite of offices in the St. James Theatre building and set about the business of production. I became Harold's "exec." Molly, our play reader, looked for further prospects. (In time she "found" Tennessee Williams.) We sought out and engaged an able business manager to lift all business concerns out of Harold's hands. His name was Kermit Bloomgarden, and for some years he was one of my best friends. Ten years later, I was to bring him Arthur Miller's play *Death of a Salesman*. Five years after that, in 1952, we weren't talking.

My own hero worship of Harold had stopped, but both Clifford and I were convinced that he was the best man to lead a second coming of the Group. Harold agreed. We also believed that he had to be challenged, his judgments questioned. Clifford loved Harold "like a brother"; but he was particularly impatient with his weaknesses. I thought Harold's weaknesses corresponded to my strengths. For instance, since Harold's talent was not for the visual, I worked out the settings for the play with Max Gorelik.

What we were determined to get rid of forever was Strasberg's paternalism. Our new theatre was not going to be rebuilt on its old image, that of a Lower East Side—or my own immigrant family's—home where children were frightened into unquestioning obedience to their father. We would be a company of equals. We'd keep a daily watch on Harold, keep a finger of pressure on his back, energize him in his periods of sloth, let him feel our impatience when it was aroused. In this way we developed a somewhat eccentric but well-functioning organization.

We made one tough-minded decision immediately: We would cast the play with our most suitable and talented people and not feel obligated to find another play for the rest of the original members. So quite a number were left out in the cold, clamoring and complaining, and we didn't invite them in. Feelings were hurt; more would be. This is where I began to get some of my reputation for ruthlessness. We didn't burden ourselves with their fates—or yield to the guilt they asked for. Those excluded said we'd betrayed the Group ideal. Right! We were now veterans with hard experiences behind us, and we'd decided to accept certain realities even though they brought hard lots to old friends.

There was one difficulty, and it was a dangerous one. For months, Clifford had promised Julie Garfield the leading part—so Julie said. Clifford had also spoken to Luther Adler about it. Authors do this; it's one of their privileges. They conceive the character and, for the most part, know best what's required for its performance. Here a contest developed. Julie had, on the face of it, the perfect qualities for the part. But Harold didn't think so. Harold was the director of the play and the head of the theatre, as well as the intelligence Clifford most respected. Harold wanted Luther. He said the part was not primarily that of a fighter but that of a sensitive, virile young man, trying to find his way. Luther, Harold said, had more of the artist about him than Julie.

I didn't agree with either man. I thought I should play the part.

Harold won out; he convinced Clifford.

Julie, who'd been led by his big brother–pal, Clifford, to expect the part, was wounded. Although his loyalty to the Group held up and although he accepted Siggie, a good but smaller part, and scored a success in it, nevertheless he'd been led to expect the lead, and his wife had expected he'd get it. This sudden turnaround—or down—allowed friends and agents to move in and, by taking sides (Julie's), widen the rift and deepen the wound.

Julie believed, as I did, that Harold had chosen Luther so that Stella— his sister—would be pleased. They were separated now by a distance of 2,800 miles, and Harold was anxious to hold on to her. Although my admiration for Harold was revived by our working together, I was still convinced he could talk himself into anything he wanted to believe. Years later, however, I thought he'd made the right decision. I played Joe on the road, and looking back, I'd say Luther was the best of the three possibilities.

We brought in Frances Farmer as the leading woman. She was, that year, a perfect beauty. I've read that she was Clifford's lover at the time. If that is true, I was not aware of it. What I remember is that she had a special glow, a skin without flaw, lustrous eyes—a blonde you'd dream about. She also had a wry and, at times, rather disappointed manner, a twist of the mouth, which suited the part. She was a dramatic contrast to the dark up-from-under men she was going to play with.

As an actress, she was a beginner.

The rehearsals were the high point of my time as a performer, and they left me completely confident of my abilities on stage. I knew my trade, kowtowed to no one, not then, not ever again. This was not the same kind of performance as in *Lefty* or *Paradise Lost*, where I was playing a side of myself; this was a characterization. Harold put the problem to me in a phrase; he told me I was playing a predator and that my "spine"—that is, my essential activity—was to hunt for possessions. That is what I played, circling the young fighter I wanted "a piece of" like a hawk, then "stooping" to pick him up. I couldn't take my eyes off Luther; he was what I craved. I did research, studied photographs. I gave the part an elegance of manner and dress that I'd observed in top gangster figures.

I also made myself think like a homosexual. I once saw an assistant stage manager who was homosexual being given a small purse of money to hold by an actress as she was going on stage. He lifted the little sack, which had been hanging between the actress's breasts, to his nose, and on his face there was an expression of pure loathing. I recalled that fellow and what was on his face. When I looked at Frances Farmer on stage, I felt this disgust. I couldn't understand what the man I wanted saw in her.

The play opened, to great success. We were an SRO hit, in for a long run. I was besieged with offers for plays and for films. I had every reason to be completely happy—I'd achieved what I'd wanted to achieve. *Golden Boy* and the return of the Group would not have happened without me, I knew that. I'd prodded Harold and supported him where he was uncertain; I'd pushed Clifford on, which wasn't always easy. As we'd played handball at the Y, I'd eased Julie Garfield's resentments. I'd given our designer, Max Gorelik, ground plans for the physical production and brought young actors into our cast to replace the old Group members who were of no use now. I was the vigilante of the production team. As for my performance, everything written about it had been praise of the highest order, and I had no modesty about believing every word of it.

O N E   N I G H T early the next spring, an extraordinary thing happened during the performance. I was waiting offstage for my entrance cue to be spoken to play my first scene. When I heard the cue, I had the impression that it—the cue—was late. Then I realized that I'd heard it earlier—and had not moved. Now it was being repeated. I still stood where I was, just offstage, and began to wonder what was happening to me. I heard the words of the cue repeated more urgently from the stage. The other actors were covering for me. "They're improvising very well," I said to myself. I still didn't move. The stage manager looked around the back of the set and hissed. I entered.

Later, I offered no explanation. I didn't have one.

The others are Art Smith, Luther Adler, and Bobby Lewis.

I WALKED home from the Belasco Theatre, on Forty-fourth Street, to our apartment on Ninety-eighth; uptown the streets were darker. I told myself that what had happened was more than an absentminded episode. I hadn't wanted to go on stage, and there was a force within me powerful enough to prevent it. What was it? A message from my unconscious? Our Group training was to look for an underlying meaning in every act. Did what had happened mean that I didn't want to act anymore, even in a play as well received or a performance as warmly praised? Was it because I wanted to be a director and wanted it now? Or was it something mysterious, an unrest to which I wouldn't admit?

I'd been reading a book by Karen Horney, *The Neurotic Personality of Our Time*, and as I went through it, I'd jotted initials in the margins. C.O., Odets; H.C., Clurman; E.K.—we were all there. Horney treated success as a drug, which, once taken, "hooks" the "user," who behaves in ways he doesn't understand and does things he regrets, but having had the taste, he wants more and more and more. More of what? More of what he'd once been denied but which life could now provide him, more of everything pleasurable, reassuring, flattering, and thrilling. Of course, I'd begun to feel the effect of that "drug." I didn't need Horney to figure out that when success follows a period of humiliating failure, such as I'd had in California, the "user" will be willful and rash. Nothing was going to stop me now from getting everything I wanted out of life.

But that didn't explain what had happened during the performance.

As I approached our apartment house, I slowed down. I wanted to be quiet and alone. I knew Molly would be waiting up for me; she always was. I sat on the steps awhile. When I entered the apartment, I did it as quietly as I could, tiptoed down the hall to the bedroom. She was asleep, but she was waiting for me. "Hello, Sugar," she said, then fell asleep again, leaving her loving smile behind.

I walked into the kitchen to make tea. I felt terrible. It wasn't only that I was having an affair, the first serious one; it was how totally I'd given in to it. But what did that have to do with what had happened in the theatre? No relation that I could see.

I'd had casual boy-girl quick ones, easily forgotten, but this time I was not behaving like a sensible married man who loved his wife and his kid but still arranged an occasional, discreetly planned meeting with another woman, always keeping his emotions within reasonable bounds. I was running wild.

It had all happened, I believed, because I'd become a performer. Acting is a sexual act. An actor as much as an actress is presenting himself for desire. "I'm powerful," he's saying. "Look at me, listen to me. I'm important." He's also saying, "I'm potent." Acting had given me what I'd never had before, a sense of that kind of power. I felt I could have any woman I wanted. I enjoyed this potency on stage. My performance improved as I discovered I was open to sexual adventure. Soon after we opened, I was "looking around." This was strange, because I'd always been a cautious man.

Then it happened in a burst. Her name was Constance Dowling. She's dead, so I can name her.

That winter and spring, we'd been like animals in season or two criminals closely pursued, consorting everywhere—on cold nights up against the radiator that warmed the lobby of her apartment house; on the first miracle-warm day of spring, on the roof, back of the chimney stacks. Walking the dark city streets, we might suddenly turn into a narrow alley between tall buildings. Or, when the impulse insisted, we'd meet in a box in the Belasco Theatre before the audience had entered, our sounds muffled by the heavy weight of the drapes. Even during the performance (I wasn't in the first act of *Golden Boy*), we'd do it up against the rail at the back of the orchestra— just for the hell of it—or quickly in the lounge below. Afternoons we had more time and met in rooms borrowed from agreeable friends—I had a list—or, when I had money to spare, in an air-shaft single of a cheap hotel just off Eighth Avenue at Forty-sixth Street, sixteen dollars well spent. More than careless, I'd become reckless. Did it matter that the cabdriver was watching us in his rearview mirror? Was I trying to smash my well-ordered life so it couldn't be put back together?

Constance was nineteen and had every charm given to youth. She was a dancer, with those legs, had been in the chorus of a couple of musicals. She wanted to be a dramatic actress and was working as an usher at the Belasco, to watch our performances. Years later, when it was over between us, she became a film actress, rather a favorite in Europe, sort of a star.

There was a devil's battle going on in me. The moral code by which I'd been brought up made me feel guilty. But I found that what had been happening was thrilling, adventurous, and—the only word for it—educational. I'd never before yielded myself so entirely to my emotions. My life was no longer under control.

But what did all that have to do with what had happened in the theatre? Did I want out of that play? Did I still believe in the Group? Of course I did, even though it was a bit like life in a monastery. I'd never acted in a long-run play before, and perhaps what every actor wants and waits for, a great success followed by a long run, had turned out to be a restriction. Was I sick of my posture in the company, that faithful, obedient, good boy, always ready to jump in and help out, a veritable professional gadget with no uncontrollable impulses, always sure to do the right thing for our Group? Did I want to smash that too?

Molly came into the kitchen. Barefoot, she sat in a chair and tucked her feet under her. "Make me a cup too," she said. I remember how, still half asleep, she put her head down on the table but looked up at me, sideways, smiling tenderly. I looked at her a long time. I truly loved my wife and my young daughter. I loved my home. I loved coming in late and finding Molly in bed, warm and, even in sleep, waiting for me. She was the essential, decent, orderly world, my buffer against chaos. "Don't lose that," I said to myself. "Be careful. You need what she is. You're lucky to have her." I felt a chill of fear running through me. Recently I'd been coming home later and later after a meeting with—

"What is it?" Molly asked. "Nothing," I said. (The classic answer: "Nothing.") "Are you all right, Sugar?" "I'm fine," I said.

I made up my mind to break with Constance. I brought Molly her tea. We sat together in the quiet kitchen and she told me the extraordinary things my daughter had done that day. "That's remarkable!" I said, smiling and shaking my head in wonder—not only at what little Judy had done but at the light in Molly's eyes as she described it. I felt relieved by what I'd decided. We went to bed and made love.

The next morning I was no happier. Or just as happy; look at it either way. I still wanted both. As for the incident in the theatre, forget it! I simply hadn't wanted to work that night. Everything doesn't need a deep explanation. Leave that to Strasberg. Cabdrivers have been known to suddenly turn onto the Brooklyn Bridge, drive out to Far Rockaway, sit there and look at the sea. For no reason. Bricklayers must occasionally spend a long morning between their wives' legs and feel no call to explain why they're late for work. You don't have to be neurotic to behave eccentrically.

W E' D   A C Q U I R E D   *Casey Jones*, a new play by Robert Ardrey. Bob felt that Harold was too New York and urged him to let me direct the play. Harold agreed, and I was pleased. It was to be my first production for the Group, but it wasn't to be done with Group actors; they were busy with *Golden Boy*. That pleased me too, secretly, because the old-timers in the company could make it tough on the "new kid." So we cast from the open market. To find an actor to play the Casey Jones of legend, we thumbed through the Hollywood lists and found Charles Bickford. I hadn't met the man, didn't take the time or the trouble to go talk to him before rehearsals or to consult others about him. We were in a hurry; Ardrey was satisfied; his agent, Harold Freedman, was satisfied; Bickford was the right type and very available. We signed him.

I didn't know what I was getting into. Where I'd directed before, the Theatre of Action, there was no load of money at stake, no playwright's reputation at hazard, no author's agent standing guard over his client. I was about to get an education, not in the art of direction—what was about to happen had little to do with that—but in the problems of directing in a commercial situation. Directing on "Broadway" was, I found, a complete trial of a person's character. Every fault you have is revealed, every virtue needed. I also learned about the politics of directing, recognizing the tensions and the forces behind the scene, which is to say that I learned to protect myself. I learned that the director is altogether responsible for the success of the production; everything is his fault. Which is why successful directors get all that money: They stand on a mound, unprotected, and everyone who has a stake in the success of what's happening can take a shot at them. I stood on that mound and was shot down.

Bickford and I were not simpatico. I found him born hostile and invariably suspicious. I spent my energy straining to be nice to him, hoping that I could win his friendship by offering mine. But friendship wasn't the problem. I was afraid of the man, and he, like any beast, could smell my fear. This made him arrogant. I had still to learn that the only way to deal with a bully is to bully him. Charlie had the attitude of old-time Hollywood stars: Rehearsal was a trial to determine who was boss. Look at the photograph at the beginning of this chapter. I was embarrassed to include it, but it tells the story better than I could. Men like that will eat a director alive, if he allows it.

Something else that happened made me even more ashamed. Bob had written a fine role for a young woman, and I had an idea for casting it that I was proud of. Her name was Katharine Bard, and I considered her a "find." She had a purity and an innocence that were rare on our street. She, too, was overwhelmed by Bickford, believing (correctly) that he didn't approve of her being cast. This didn't help her with her work, or me with mine. Katharine's progress was slow, but I was convinced she could make it. Then the run-throughs started, and the people concerned sat out front to give judgment.

Among them was Harold Freedman, an Englishman with a highly visible discreet manner. There is a famous cartoon of Harold, which needed no caption. He is holding two phones, using both at the same time, the earpieces tight against his head and the mouthpieces close enough to pick up the most confidential whisper. My hearing is okay, but I always felt the man was talking below my range. When it became obvious in the first run-through that Katharine's scenes were not getting over, Harold Freedman, saying nothing to me, went off with his client, Bob Ardrey. This consultation after the first run-through is a critical one, and the result was that Freedman met with Harold Clurman and urged him to replace Katharine. When the people in the money seats see that a production is not working, their solution is always to replace someone—an actor, a director, whomever, but someone. Very rarely does this work; usually the play is at fault, but the author's agent can hardly say that, can he? Bob Ardrey, a good friend, behaved like a good friend, told me plainly that Katharine was my problem and I should concentrate on her. Harold Clurman was meeting with us. I told them both that while Katharine's progress was slow, I was convinced she'd get there. I was surprised to hear Clurman say that he wasn't at all sure, but that Ardrey shouldn't worry because what Katharine needed was special coaching and Harold knew the person to provide it. Whereupon he brought in Stella Adler.

The alternative I had was to quit. Or to raise hell and be fired. I did neither. What I did that I'm ashamed of was to tell Katharine that I thought Stella might help her, when I didn't believe she would or could. Two more disparate personalities than Katharine and Stella could not have been found. Stella was forceful and flamboyant, fully experienced in life and in the theatre. Katharine was delicately strung and experienced in neither. Part of the instruction a director transmits to a performer is nonverbal; any of this from Stella froze Katharine. Watching from the sidelines, I couldn't imagine what Stella had that Harold believed appropriate for the job. It was a piece of shameless miscasting—of the coach, not the actress—and an emasculation of me. Which I allowed. And deserved.

Of course, Katharine broke down. I saw that in her heart she'd given up. What I didn't observe was what was happening to me. Harold, by putting Stella over me for reasons I didn't believe were artistic, had deprived me of my confidence. Implicit (for all to see) was that Harold believed I couldn't direct a woman. The reason he wanted Stella was to advance her ambitions as a director and so keep her tied to him. He used me to achieve that. I should have spoken up; I didn't. Despite all that had happened in the preceding years, I still had too much respect for him.

As the final rehearsals foundered, the playwright's side came at Clurman hard and demanded that we make a quick casting change and bring in a "real pro." She was a goodhearted young woman named Peggy Conklin, whom I had to get up in the part within a few days. Stella had disappeared from the scene.

I'd had an education. I'd allowed myself to be bullied by Charles Bickford, all the time keeping up my nice-guy mask. I'd allowed myself to be used by my friend Harold Clurman, for his own purposes. I knew that I had to stick up for myself next time, even against a friend. I'd kept quiet, just as I had long ago on the snow slopes of Sickles Avenue when my sled was flipped over. I had no one to blame but myself. The shame I felt as I began to understand what I'd allowed to happen was hard to take but, in the end, helpful.

I left on the afternoon of opening night—which wasn't courageous of me. Alone in a Florida hotel, I received a telegram from our general manager, my friend Kermit Bloomgarden: "By this time you have no doubt heard the news that the play got bad notices simply because Mr. Bickford couldn't give a performance. He was scared stiff. . . ." And so on. Bickford was scared stiff!

But it didn't reassure me to blame another. I was exhausted, full of doubts about myself as well as anger at everybody. In the weeks that followed, I saw that directing was a trial of a man's character; I faced the facts about myself. We were sailing to London, where we had an engagement to show our production of *Golden Boy* to the British theatre world. I'd be playing my tough guy, Fuseli, again, and that would be a relief—and an irony. We crossed on a French boat; the sea was calm for all six days, and I played quoits and deck tennis. Molly, pregnant again, hadn't come along, so I was alone at night. Over and over in my dreams, I'd play the scenes I should have played with Bickford, and other scenes, in which I stood up to Harold Clurman and stood by Katharine. Why hadn't I fought Bickford? What in me prevented that? For a man whom I didn't respect and couldn't tolerate, I'd been frozen in a false front of respect. It was wrong to blame Stella or even to blame Harold for what had happened; only myself. I'd permitted it. I'd betrayed myself. My education in how to get tough was beginning.

.   .   .

L O N D O N was another world, with new sights, sounds, smells, and people. We opened at the St. James Theatre. With its red plush seats and drapes and its paneled dressing rooms, it was grander than anything I'd seen in America. Somehow the weight of tradition was reassuring. The English crew astonished me; they wore long smocks of ticking cloth over suit vests, stiff collars, and ties, and had the qualities of middle-class shopkeepers. They treated us with the greatest respect. Always "Mr." and "Miss." I was on the privileged side of the class gap.

British theatre people were astonished by our production and our acting. They and the audiences had never heard anything like our use of the colloquial. That level of talk has now become commonplace in their theatre, but in 1938 our speech startled them. The gangster I played impressed the audience not so much for threat as for theatre glamour. I was what they'd read about America: rumor and fantasy combining, heightened realism, the essential inner truth theatricalized and brought to life. British actors have told me that our appearance on stage influenced British production thereafter. Writers and directors began to look toward their "common" people for inspiration and source material.

My confidence in myself, which had crumbled as a result of *Casey Jones*, slowly revived. Generous applause every night and twice on matinee days helped. I bought my first made-to-order suit on Savile Row and a pair of "bespoke" shoes—which I later had to discard because, like all English shoes, they were designed for the narrow, pointed feet of aristocrats, not for my Anatolian paddles. The suit cost a lot but made me feel fine. I played a slickly dressed gangster on stage and continued with the character off, a "tough guy" and dangerous. I enjoyed that.

I soon had another girl, a Miss Diggins; I called her Diggie. She was not the blonde I'd always favored; she was not fashioned in the image of the girls I'd letched for in high school, the naughty blonde beauts our athletes were rumored to have enjoyed. Diggie's hair was short and black and slicked off her face, which was pale without a varying tint—for she was a creature of the night. Out of that white mask, her eyes glittered like bits of coal.

I was impressed with her. Without any formal education, she had the ability to interest me in anything she chose to talk about. Diggie was compulsively confessional, outspoken without restraint; there was no little censor sitting on top of her larynx. She was not trained to pretend to be proper. Or politically progressive. Or in any way an intellectual. I'm certain that the day after I left London, she had someone else. Fucking was as natural to her as eating, and she did it about as often. Had she ever known guilt? I wondered.

Several of the company members were married. Had they noticed? If so, did they disapprove of me? They knew Molly, of course, and I wondered what they'd say to her. But I didn't care. I was where I wanted to be, out in the open with the girl, as if I had no responsibility to anyone else. Besides, here was England in the prime of the year! So celebrate! When it was all over, I realized that because of knowing this girl, I'd learned more about English street and village life, the ways of the common man, of the "proletariat" we used to talk about in the Party, than I could have learned in any other way from any other source. Diggie, whom I never saw, wrote to, or spoke with again, is my keenest memory of that English engagement. Isn't it astonishing—I think so—that what I remember most keenly about my visit to London in 1938 is someone Molly would have called a tramp.

Was I trying again to break up my life?

TO PREPARE our next season, Harold and I returned to America before the company. We were waiting for another play by Clifford; our first job was to track the author down. He'd bought a Cadillac and was enjoying driving it here and there; it was his first car.

Molly met me at the dock. She was very pregnant and pink from the glow the sun brings, a heavenly vision in a straw hat and a summer frock; all mine. How can you want anything more? I asked myself. Are you crazy? We'd rented a house in the country and planned a quiet summer. I found that after my busy year, all I wanted was to be quiet. And alone. I played with my young daughter and loved her. I was trying to understand why I was always on the verge of messing up my life. I felt danger ahead. What the hell was eating me? What did I want?

September came, and we all went to Chicago and opened *Golden Boy* there. I would never again receive the kind of adulation I got there. It started a few days after the show opened, with a case of Scotch delivered to my dressing room. There was no card, and I couldn't guess who'd sent it. A couple of days later I had a visitor named Eddie Fried. He stopped me as I left the theatre and told me that a certain friend—of his? of mine? he didn't say—was inviting me to dinner. Would I come? He still didn't say who. Restless and intrigued, I said I would and would bring Frances Farmer.

A handsome Italian-American met us at the restaurant. I didn't get his name; it wasn't offered, nor did I press for it. He had graying hair and was fashionably dressed. He led us to the head of a table at the far end of the room and seated us on either side of him, our backs—and his—to the wall. I noticed there were no windows in the room. The entrance had been unimpressive and the stairs shabby, but once we were seated, the atmosphere was harmonious, the hospitality bighearted, the food savory, the wine fine on the tongue and plentiful. I was being accepted into a world I'd never been in before; I was privileged.

We ate in near silence, and when we were finished we thanked our host and left. If he'd had a reason for asking to see us, I didn't know what it was. He was genial and made sure we were served more than enough of everything we wanted, but he hardly spoke to me. Or to Frances.

A few days later, the doorman came to my dressing room after the show and told me a man was waiting for me below. "Who?" I said. "I don't know his name," the doorman said, "but you better come. He's waiting." I dressed and hur-

On the road I played the lead—
with Frances Farmer.

ried down. There was a man I'd not seen before. He was well dressed, with a certain threatening austerity, and he moved and spoke discreetly as he led me to a quiet place behind the dressing room stairs. You probably won't believe our conversation, but I remember it well, because I made notes later that night.

He asked me if there was anything he could do for me.

"No," I said. "But thanks. I'm fine."

I didn't know what he thought he might do for me.

"Anything at all," he said, "anything you want."

"No, really, thanks," I said.

"Is anybody bothering you?" he asked.

"No," I said. "Nobody's bothering me."

"Because if anybody's bothering you—" he said, making a slight gesture, "tell me. We'll take care of it."

"No; no, thanks; thanks very much," I said.

"If anybody's bothering you, you should tell me," he insisted.

"Well," I said, "if anybody does. But nobody is."

"Because we like you very much," he said.

I didn't ask him who "we" were.

"I'm glad," I said. I certainly was. I was relieved.

"We like the way you do the part in the play here," he said. "It's got class."

"Well," I said, "I thought he was a classy guy."

"We like the way you dress," he said. "You look good out there."

"Yeah, sure," I said, "I wanted him to look like—like class."

"We could see that," he said. "You make us look good."

"I'm sure glad of that," I said.

"So let me know if anybody bothers you," he said.

I reassured him once more that nobody was bothering me, and he left abruptly, but with a thoughtful look on his face. He didn't leave his name with me or a phone number where I could find him in case anybody began to bother me.

The next night he was back and asked me where I was living. "The Sherman," I said quickly, then wondered if I should have told him. He said would I mind if he saw my room? By now I was more intrigued than frightened, so after the show I led him to my hotel and showed him my small single. Obviously unimpressed, he gave the layout one brief look and left.

A night later Eddie Fried returned to inform me that "they" were moving me to a hotel on South Michigan Avenue. I didn't dare object; it was an invitation, as Eddie spoke it, with an edge of command. "How long will it take you to pack?" he asked.

I packed quickly, checked out of my room, and got into a car that was waiting for me at the curb. Eddie drove. As we moved down Michigan Avenue into the South Side, I realized that we were far exceeding the speed limit and that a car with a siren was following us. Eddie didn't slow down. I called his attention to the car closing in on us. He nodded. When the other car drew alongside, it was, as I'd anticipated, full of cops. The cop who was sitting in the seat by the driver—a sergeant, by his brass—leaned out the window and shouted, "Hello, Eddie!" Eddie responded with equal cordiality and drove on.

The man who'd asked if anybody was bothering me was waiting at the South Side hotel. I was shown a suite of generous size and informed that Al Capone had the suite directly above, the same layout and all. He wasn't there, they said, he was doing time, but they'd kept the suite for him. I gave indications that I was impressed and grateful. In the sitting room there were two girls, sitting on the edge of easy chairs. They sat like people at an employment agency, waiting for consideration. My protector greeted them as old friends, and I assumed they were with him. "Which one you want?" he asked me. I demurred, saying I had someone. "Well, case you change your mind," he said, "either or both, whichever." There were bottles of liquor on the sideboard. "No bills here," he said as he left. "Order what you want. The fellows want to show you their appreciation."

In the next weeks, I met a lot of the fellows. They took me up to Capone's apartment. It was very quiet; the shades were drawn. It was not only empty of him but empty of everything. Looking back now, I recall the homes of the dead in the suburb of Cairo I saw years later, completely furnished homes with no one in them except the spirits of the dead.

． ． ．

I HAD ANOTHER encounter that fall in Chicago, which I've thought back on many times. During those years, I was working on my voice, and, always an early riser, I'd go to our theatre to spend an hour on resonance, placement, diction, and so on. The theatre alongside ours had a play in which Laurette Taylor starred. This was before *Glass Menagerie*, and she was not being idolized, not yet. One morning when I arrived at our stage doors—they were side by side—there at the bottom of the fire stairs I found Miss Taylor, curled up on the concrete, fast asleep. She was sleeping off her "load." I understood why she was there by the stage door. For actors, the theatre where they're working is their true home. When lost or drunk, they search for it, want to get back to it while they still can, so they'll be ready for the performance and not oversleep somewhere else. I got her into her dressing room, where there was a sofa. I don't think she really woke up, because when I said hello to her a few days later, she didn't respond. That's how actors end up, I thought.

CLIFFORD had sent us a telegram from Canada, where he was "moving around." He informed us that he was "too discomfited to work" on *Rocket to the Moon*, the play we were anxiously waiting for. But he must have had a creative burst, because toward the last of our *Golden Boy* engagement he came through with the play, and Harold and he, along with Luther Adler and Morris Carnovsky, who were to play the leads, went back to New York to work on the production.

I took over Luther's role (Joe Bonaparte, at last) and Lee Cobb, Morris's part. I was billed as a star for the first time and learned what it was like to be the center of a production and get that kind of attention every night. If you like to scoff at actors and their self-favoring, try playing a leading role in a successful play sometime. It swells the head.

I was still living apart from the others and liking it. I had a girlfriend who would visit me from Joliet, a city known for its large jail. This young lady was exactly the same type—blond, slim, pouting lips, challenging walk— that I'd been attracted to all my life, the girls out of high school gossip tales. She also wanted to be an actress and, a few years later, would have a modest success in Hollywood. But I hadn't been able to forget Constance. I'd not had again what I'd had with her; she was literally the girl of my dreams. I'd cut the affair off when I went to England, felt it was endangering everything "solid" in my life.

I turned the light off, poured myself a slug of my host's Scotch, and sat facing the window over Michigan Avenue. That day I'd read an "item" linking Constance with Bob Capa, the war photographer. I was jealous as hell and angry at myself for letting Constance slip away. Capa was a man I envied for his way of life and the women he'd known. But I wanted—and needed—something he did not: a home. I was again resenting that I'd been carefully cloistered all my life—at home, at school, in college, at Yale, directly into the Group. When was I going to start to "live"? Acting the same part every night was the worst confinement of all. That's why I hadn't gone on stage that night in New York as I listened to my cue being thrown at me. I didn't want that restricted life anymore, and my unconscious was telling me so before I realized it. I didn't want to be confined. I was asking that dreadful question: "Is this all there is?"

The room was quiet; it was getting late. The lights from the avenue below created a kind of twilight where I sat. The place was featureless and I was alone as I wanted to be—not only there where I was, on South Michigan, but in Chicago, in Illinois, in the world. I was separated as I wished to be from everything and everybody. This was the first time that happened to me, but it was to happen again at various times in my life. I was on the verge again. I asked myself, "Do you really want to go back into what you had with Constance and what you broke off? Do you really want to lose Molly and what you have with her?"

L O O K I N G out the window of the room where I am writing this, I can see a building called a brownstone, even though it's presently painted a shell gray. When a building of this kind is owned and occupied by an affluent family, it's called a townhouse. This one, however, like most of the others on our block, has two small apartments for rent on each floor. I am familiar with one of those apartments.

My writing room has six old-fashioned wooden shutters, stained a mahogany brown and facing north. In order to concentrate the light from the sky on my typewriter—my eyes are more sensitive and not nearly as sharp as they once were—I keep all the shutters closed except one. The one I leave open faces the shell-gray brownstone across the street, and when I turn my head and look out this window, I can see, along the front of the house opposite, three windows in a row on the third floor. They have shutters like my own except for the color, white.

They are the windows of the room where some twenty-five years ago I used to meet a girl I shan't name. The past is across the street from the present; the distance between, slight. Directly under those three windows a sort of daybed was placed, and there—with the shutters closed—we used to come together. This young woman was unremarkable in every way except one. When she was making love, her face became an extraordinary high pink. That is what I remember about her most; she looked like one of Renoir's models. That pink was the evidence of a most loving and generous nature. If you had met her on the street, you'd certainly have thought she was a proper, even a prim girl. And she was—except in the exercises of love. Then she became another creature.

Do I regret all that happened across my street twenty-five years ago? How could I, when I remember with such tender feelings that young woman and how intent and pink her face became?

The city is full of ironies. My second wife found this house where I live and asked me to buy it and I did and we lived in it and she spent her last days in it. It strikes me as ironic that she would come upon and select a house directly across the street from those three windows whose mystery she knew nothing about. But that's the way this city is. As I write this, I live in the same house with my third wife.

The city is an album. I mean the whole city. When I walk it, and I do walk a great deal, it's like turning pages in a memory album. Wherever I pass I see apartment houses, brownstones, theatres, hotels, restaurants, bars, doorways, windows, park walks, and the edge of our great river where intimate and memorable events took place. These events are not recorded in our daily newspapers, but they mean a lot to me. I recall these events, I still wonder about them, puzzle over them, go over them in my memory like a legendary miser fingering his gold pieces. They are my wealth.

Do I regret any of that which happened? Do I regret what has made this city so rich for me? How could I? Yes, I did hurt some people, several who were dear to me, particularly my first wife when I was least controlled and most driven. But have you tried getting through life without hurting anyone? What did you answer to that question? It can't be done. Besides, how can you regret the memory of a human touch, a loving voice, a tender glance, a grateful body's embrace, a time of devotion, the help you received and the help you gave?

Sometimes I imagine that those three windows across the street are looking at me and asking, "Where did you disappear all of a sudden?" Or I ask myself, "What happened to that girl with the flaming cheeks? Where did she go?" I hope she's married and has kids and still blushes that surprise pink when she makes love to her husband. He has a treasure there. I wish I knew how she is. I wish I knew about them all.

That's another kind of wealth, the wealth I prize most, the wealth of my experiences. I wouldn't have missed any of it. Or the memories. What did the poet say? I loved them all in my own fashion—and I have no regrets. I wanted my album full.

Well, it is. How was I able to do it, and still live a "respectable" life?

The answer is—and here's the bad part—duplicity. That's the solution I arrived at in the suite below Al Capone's in that South Michigan Avenue hotel almost fifty years ago. What I decided in that season in Chicago was to cut myself loose from the plague of guilt, from society's approved restrictions and morality. Secretly, quietly, I scorned them and went my way, pulling out of life the pleasure and adventures I craved.

Has any society at any time solved the problem of the relation between the sexes honestly? Europeans tend to face the facts. French men and women take lovers and live happily with their legal mates. Mexicans have their *casa chicas*. No two people have the same desires or the same needs, and no single individual has the same ones at all periods of his or her life. Certainly novelty is part of it, why not admit that? An extensive sex life expands your knowledge. The album adds pages and each memory is a treasure. And a stimulus. Promiscuity for an artist is an education, a great source of confidence, and a spur to work. Ironically, it can also promote true marital fidelity. It's healthier than licentious dreams and unrealized yearnings. And guilt. These lead to secret resentment and hatred; they sour a life.

Marriage and sexual love are not the same. The requirements are mixed. Lovers often release the inhibited part of a person's life. Marriage is an opposite need. What you look for in a marriage partner is that he or she be a stable person, a homemaker, a mother or father candidate, that above all.

Boris Aronson, the scene designer, said when he met Marilyn Monroe for the first time that he understood why Arthur Miller wanted her. But, Boris added, with a heavy Jewish intonation and a most challenging lilt, "That's a wife?" I can still hear the way he sang that devastating question. The answer turned out to be: "Hell, no!"

There is another story about Aronson that I like. His wife entered their apartment early one afternoon and found him in bed with another, younger woman. Aronson told how he leaped out of bed, shouting, "It's not me! It's not me!" He was right. The person yelling "It's not me!" was not the person his wife had married but one she hadn't known was there. Or wished was not there. It was Aronson's other self, one he'd kept secret and now disclaimed. For the moment.

I didn't come to any conscious decisions that night in the suite just below Al Capone's—or on any other night of the four weeks I enjoyed the favors of the "boys" in Chicago's South Side. I didn't see Constance for many weeks, but when I returned to New York City I did call her. So, in effect, I had made a decision, though it was not a conscious decision. What I accepted was that my life was going to be in constant turmoil from then on. I was ready to allow whatever came to happen, rather than choking it down. I would not resist my desires and impulses, no matter what resulted. I would not confine myself further for practical, professional, emotional, or moral reasons.

I admitted what most people have to admit at some point in their lives— that life is insoluble, that there are problems one is never able to solve, that every question doesn't have an answer.

What I decided, without knowing it, was that I would live in conflict and confusion. I knew what that would mean; I'd have to sneak, cheat, lie, fake, dissemble—all shameful, all humiliating, all necessary if you want to have what I've called "both." I'd decided to take that step. But if I'd told this to myself in so many words that night in Chicago, I wouldn't have admitted it was true. I would have denied it. I'd have said, "Nothing happened. Life just goes on."

A schnook in love

M Y S O N Chris was born while I was rehearsing in
Irwin Shaw's *The Gentle People*. A run-through was interrupted to give me
the news. I received congratulations; rehearsals continued. I was playing
my first part that was not a tough guy, just a schnook like me. I even had a
love scene with Sylvia Sidney, one I didn't enjoy playing, possibly because
the lady did not interest me that way. Question: Is it helpful for the two
actors in a love scene to be attracted to each other? Answer: It doesn't hurt.
I remember hearing that Sylvia had been the beauty who'd broken up the
home of movie tycoon B. P. Schulberg. Even this didn't arouse my curiosity. She wasn't taken with me either; when we had to kiss, she'd leap at me
and bite me on the lips. I soon began to pull back when she came for me,
and this didn't endear me to her.

Again I worked with Harold on the production, and now was recognized as his right hand. On his behalf I presented our designer, Boris Aronson, with the layout we wanted. The ground plan is the first statement of the director's vision; it defines the style and the movement of the production he's conceiving, and he must give one to the designer for him to take off from. The cast in a drama (not a musical) is rehearsed to play the scenes *within* a setting, not in front of it. Boris, a delight to work with, was grateful for the help I could give him. You have to do more than hire a talented designer to do the visual side.

I knew that the company had not accepted me as a director, and when I came to direct again, I sensed doubt and in one case hostility. Irwin had written an experimental play, *Quiet City*, which, while it was incomplete and not well constructed, contained more of its author's genuine conviction than *The Gentle People*, which was conventional liberal stuff, assuring its middle-class audience that the goodhearted little man would win out over the bully—a thesis I'd not seen illustrated in life. I felt that *Quiet City*, if Irwin would work on it, could be a much better play, and the author would certainly benefit from seeing it "stood up." We decided to put it on for a series of six Sunday nights. Harold said I should direct it, so did Irwin, and I was prepared to try again. Our friend Aaron Copland wrote a beautiful score, and we were off.

The actors were playing *Rocket to the Moon* and *The Gentle People* eight performances a week; it was extra work for them. I sensed something wrong from the first day, but couldn't say what it was. Now I can. The actors were not on trial; the director was. I was still the intruder into their family; they might accept me, they might not. The one whose hostility became immediately evident was Morris Carnovsky, the oldest member of the company. Day after day, he was late for rehearsals, often as much as half an hour, sometimes longer. He'd apologize, but that didn't help; nor did I believe it sincerely meant. His tardiness was compulsive, beyond his control.

The image Morris liked for himself was as the company's elder statesman, setting an example of devotion and discipline for the others—the "Dean," Bobby Lewis called him. With me, Morris couldn't maintain that front. It would have been more honest of him to say, "I don't want to work with you." And more honest of me to have provoked an open quarrel. Carnovsky was Bickford behind a dutiful mask. My repeated reaches for his friendship and help were interpreted, as with Bickford, to be an evidence of weakness. Now, looking back, I believe I didn't have the capacity to turn Morris on to the importance of what we—and Irwin—were trying to do. That was my job and that my failing. The actors were accustomed to Clurman's razzle-dazzle, which I couldn't match. Boris would comfort me— privately he'd refer to Harold as Father "Diwine." But since I didn't have this capability, I envied it. *Quiet City* played its six Sunday performances and was forgotten by all, including the author.

. . .

I T 'S R A R E that a playwright-director relationship survives a failure. Mine with Bob Ardrey did. I believe he thought the membership of the Group in some way alien and thought me, perhaps for some quality of adaptability I had, more "American." He wanted me to direct his next play, *Thunder Rock*. Harold agreed. I was apprehensive; my experience with *Quiet City* festered. But something healthy was happening. I was beginning to resent the situation.

Thunder Rock was performed in London some years later, with Michael Redgrave in the leading role, and it was a success there. When we put on the play in New York, it was a failure. I believe that our casting had a lot to do with that. It would take some years before I'd come to a principle of directing I believe in: The cast of a play should have the same basic quality as the author. If Bob Ardrey justified the nickname some of the Group gave him, "Cornstalk," his play should have been performed by actors who had the qualities of people from mid-America—or by English actors; their emotion is understated and generally accompanied by a wry humor. Bob's play should not have been performed by our urban-bred and vividly posturing actors. The same goes for the director; I was out of place. Ardrey's play was "contained"; it was cool and intellectual. Its cast and its director were out of *Awake and Sing!* We went on playing Odets, and it didn't work.

But there was this irony: I felt more at home with Bob than I did with my fellow Group members. I realized I'd directed the company at arm's length, carefully avoiding any criticism, never quite expressing my true feelings, not saying anything that might be thought "personal." I was unspontaneous, cautious. I remember going home wearier than I should have been from a dress rehearsal and saying to Molly, "I'm not sure I belong with those people anymore. Why do I pretend that I do?" I was speaking of the Group, and it was the first time that had occurred to me.

A N Y E N T E R P R I S E binding humans may die before the members involved know it's happening. I played the leading role in *Night Music*, the last play Odets did with the Group, and our theatre died during that production, but none of us knew it while it was happening. The show closed after twenty-two performances, and when it was closed down, the knot of relationships that had made the Group work had come loose and the strands had fallen apart. We were to produce one more play, but that was a matter of the dead walking.

The ironic thing was that during the rehearsals of *Night Music*, I believed that everything was harmonious. Clifford, Harold, and I enjoyed many a lobster at Barbetta's restaurant, washing it down with Clifford's selection of wine, then sitting back in self-satisfaction with our Boch panatellas. Only after the play received an indifferent press and failed to attract an audience did Clifford make known that he'd been dissatisfied with Harold's direction and bitterly disappointed in my performance. "Every time he was being the most brilliant actor on the American stage," Clifford was to write in his journal, "my play went through the window."

What was being flung out the window, according to Clifford's biographer, Margaret Brennan-Gibson, was the "delicacy of his play." Perhaps delicacy was impossible for me, but why complain afterward, as Clifford did, that my characterization lacked "variety of approach"? "It's as if he walked out of his dressing room in his street clothes and shoes." Okay—but why never a word of this from either man during rehearsals? Why hadn't Clifford demanded that Harold direct me with a greater variety of approach? I might have done something about it.

There was a reason. "Harold and I never faced each other when I had to criticize some of his work," Clifford was to write in his journal. What were they protecting—their friendship? It didn't work. "He was a friend," Clifford was to say of me twenty-five years later to someone who hadn't been there, "so we couldn't replace him." What kind of friendship is it, I wondered after we'd closed and I'd begun to get wind of Clifford's rancor, when you work together and can't tell each other the truth?

I was to find out later that playwrights nearly always blame someone else for their failures—the cast or the leading actors or even the scenery, which Clifford here considered "ponderous." But in time I was also to learn the tough lesson that it's always the play. I've heard of A Streetcar Named Desire done by a dozen different directors with a dozen different Blanche Dubois, and it's invariably successful and often "better than the original." The same with Death of a Salesman. I've never heard of Night Music successfully mounted. Odets was to say later that he'd wanted Jimmy Stewart or someone like him. If he'd had Jimmy he'd have found a different flaw in the performance. It's the play that fails, first of all and finally.

I never worked with either Harold or Clifford again. But I was never to change my estimate of Harold: the greatest critic of our theatre, who knew everything about the problems of a play as dramatic literature but, after analyzing brilliantly, could do little about them on stage. I was envious of his knowledge and his insights and loved him to his last day on earth. I continued to love Clifford too, despite all; it's a difficult straddle, play or film production and friendship. When the play had closed and some years passed, Clifford and I made certain recognitions about each other and resumed as close friends. But I'd make sure, in the years to come, that my rehearsals were so conducted that the truth, if it had to be forced out, would be confronted early, when something could be done about it. As for that chumminess which makes frank talk impossible and prevents the kind of contention that is essential during a proper rehearsal, it should be kept in its place. It's friendship that killed *Night Music*, if anything beyond itself did.

When it was all over, I knew in my heart that our theatre was beyond reviving, and that I was far out on my way elsewhere and glad to be. I had an offer to act in a film.

T H E   F I L M director who wanted me was Anatole ("Tola") Litvak, a man of culture and considerable reputation, famous for his film *Mayerling*. A theatregoer, Tola wanted me to do in *City for Conquest* what I'd done in *Paradise Lost* for the first half of his film and in *Golden Boy* for the last half. My performance, in this sense, was a repeat and, for Tola, critically certified beforehand.

On the first day I came to the Warner lot, I was directed to the office of Jack Warner's assistant Steve Trilling, a sympathetic and decent man, who proceeded to read me a lesson in film acting. His point was that it was totally different from what would work on stage; I had to be careful not to overdo. I'd seen the test I'd made with Luther Adler, so I knew what Trilling was talking about. "There's a guy on this lot today," Steve said, "who's got acting for films down cold. Want to talk to him?" "Yes, sure, please," I said. He told me where to go. "Introduce yourself and tell him your problem," Trilling said.

At the edge of a working set, waiting at ease in a director's chair for the next scene to be prepared for photography, sat George Raft. I told him Trilling's concern about me and that he'd said that he, Raft, knew how to act for films better than anybody and particularly how it was different from stage acting. I must have played it pretty humble, because Raft spouted advice. "First of all," he said, "on the stage you have to talk, right?" "Yes," I said, "generally." "Here"—and Raft pointed to the camera—"it's pictures. The less you say the better. Get rid of as many lines as you can. Give them to the other guy. Let him tell the story and so on. You just look at him, like this"—he showed me—"sort of doubting, you understand? And find something like I have, this coin I flip up and down in my hand; it gives them something to photograph while you're saying nothing. Everybody in the audience will be wondering what you're thinking, which is not a damned thing, but they don't know that. In the picture business, wondering is better than knowing." I thanked him and backed off. When I watched him shoot, I couldn't hear what he said, but I did wonder what he was thinking.

I made up my mind to spend as much time behind the camera as in front of it and to visit every other stage on the lot. The Warner studios were very busy that year and crowded with stars. You could see them all, a parade going from their sets to lunch, the elite of the film community. Muni, Flynn, Cagney, Bogart, Davis, Cooper—they were all there. Ronald Reagan was there too, making *Knute Rockne, All American.* Watching directors at work, I noticed that they often relied on their cinematographers to tell them where to put the camera, which is something Litvak did not do. I wasn't impressed with some of the fellows I watched, despite their cordiality to a "New York stage actor." I felt that the most useful talent some of them had was the talent to have talked themselves into their jobs.

Tola had several reputations, and one particularly intrigued me—that of a Don Juan. He'd recently become notorious for crawling under a grand piano with a prominent actress of the day at one of "those Hollywood parties," there to enjoy a variety of lovemaking not shown in films. Perhaps, I thought, I might see something of the side of Hollywood I'd read about but not been in a position to study last time I was west.

The big lure for me, however, was Cagney, the star of the movie and one of my heroes. I'd have good scenes to play with him; it was going to be a fascinating experience. The first thing I noticed about him was that he had a strong antipathy to Litvak. It was deep and quite unexplained. I could see that Jimmy couldn't tolerate the man, but he never said a word out loud against Tola; it was more elemental than that. Was it racial? I wondered (until I knew Jimmy better). Cagney was Irish-Catholic, Litvak a Jew. The bad feeling had an intensity beyond reason. I tried to guess what there was about the director that his star detested so.

I must believe that he didn't like the way Tola was shooting the film and the kind of rehearsal this technique necessitated. Litvak's method was not straightforward, like that of Raoul Walsh or Jack Ford; it was showy and somehow "European." First thing in the morning, he'd ask that the camera be put on a dolly, a small platform rolling on a track. Then he'd sit on the camera seat and try to get as much of the scene as possible in one shot by moving in and out and panning right and left. The rehearsals this made necessary were longer and more complicated than the traditional long-shot, medium-shot, close-up techniques required, and those rehearsals were for the benefit of the camera crew, not the actors. The performers in each scene were required to hit marks chalked on the floor, not just one or two but a series, one after another, so that the movie camera's frame would contain the action neatly at all times. "Hitting your marks" became the main concern of the rehearsals, and Jimmy found this irksome and let us all see that he did.

The crew liked and respected Cagney—they were off the street too—but they didn't like the way Tola spoke to them, and Jimmy didn't either. Tola had an abrupt way of giving orders, was always dominating and impatient with objection and error. I was to hear the same bullying tone of voice in Europe when I worked there, particularly in Germany. Directors from there—certainly at that time—thought of their crews as laborers who didn't eat in the same cafés. American stars and directors tend to make a democratic show; they buddy-buddy with their crews.

I could also see that Jimmy didn't like Tola's reputation as a lady-killer. I've noticed that many "big" stars of that day, despite the glamour of their public images, were rather prudish sexually. Fonda was an exception, but he was reserved and private about his personal life; Errol Flynn was another, but he was British. I never saw a woman around Jimmy, never met his wife, even after months of working with him. Scenes with men came naturally to Jimmy; his love scenes with Ann Sheridan, a lovely girl, were perfunctory. I don't know if Jimmy had a problem with women. He called his wife "Bill," and I'm curious about men who give their wives boys' nicknames. Perhaps the famous scene in *The Public Enemy* where Jimmy mashes a grapefruit into Mae Clarke's face was not a completely uncharacteristic act for him.

More often it was the "big" directors who were the "lady-killers." It's almost impossible for an actress to resist the advances of a director she's working with or hopes to work with—unless he's physically as gross as Hitchcock. Every morning, when Cagney opened the *Hollywood Reporter* to the gossip column, he'd find the account of another date Tola had had the night before; a new conquest was suggested. Tola came to work not in sports clothes, like the rest of West Coast mankind, but dressed for the end of the day. I don't believe he had apparel suitable for golf, tennis, or horseback riding; only for seduction. When he left the set at night, he was correctly turned out for an engagement at an expensive restaurant. We'd all find out the next day who his companion of the evening had been.

Litvak tolerated Jimmy's scorn; he never "called" him on it. The reason for that was simple. What's pride worth when you have to beat a tough schedule? You eat the scorn and wag your tail. There is also this: that in the hierarchy of Hollywood, the person getting top money is boss. That was Jimmy.

In his quiet way, he made Tola eat dirt. In the last scene of the film, Jimmy had a heavy scar over one eyebrow, the kind prizefighters acquire. It was carefully put on by a makeup man in the morning. Toward the end of the afternoon, Cagney, whose contract specified that he was through at five-thirty, would look at his watch, and if, in his opinion—Cagney's, not Tola's, not the cameraman's—there wasn't time enough before five-thirty to get the shot the electricians were preparing, Jimmy would pull off the scar and so bring the day's work to a close. He'd walk off the set without a word to Litvak.

Jimmy was a completely honest actor. I imagine he'd have figured out each scene at home, what he'd do and how he'd do it, then come to work prepared. But what he did always seemed spontaneous. Not only didn't he need direction from Tola; he didn't want it. He had no schooling in the art of acting, although he had tremendous respect for good actors. If the Actors Studio had existed then, I'm sure he would have despised it. He didn't do an elaborate preparation for a scene before the camera rolled; I concealed

Back to my old ways

my own so he wouldn't think less of me. Jimmy didn't see scenes in great complexity; he saw them in a forthright fashion, played them with savage energy, enjoyed his work. He believed in himself and didn't need to be praised constantly. He was a complete actor. He raised many doubts in my mind about the artistic snobbery of some actors in the Group.

Seeing how much I admired him, he began to teach me tricks of the trade. I remember the day we had a scene together, one where we faced each other; he took my body and turned it slightly in the direction of the camera. He pointed to his face and said, "Let them see what you've got." Another time, when we had a scene together with the camera behind his shoulder, he said, "Talk to my camera-side eye." On the few occasions when Tola would try to give him direction that was more than mechanical, Jimmy didn't hear a thing. He was visibly disrespectful as he listened to Tola giving Arthur Kennedy and me—it was our first film—arbitrary and vigorous direction. "More, Getch, more!" Tola would say, mispronouncing my nickname. I finally got up enough nerve to ask him, "More what, Tola?" He had nothing to say to that, answering only with vigorous movements of his arms and body. I wasn't all that sure that "More, more!" was the best advice for me. I'd watched other actors working and saw how little they had to do externally to "register" on the screen—in the case of Gary Cooper, who was also on the lot, nothing at all. The camera, I concluded, is not a recording device, it's a microscope which reveals what the eye does not see. It also penetrates into a person, under the surface display, and records thoughts and feelings—whatever is going on. I would never forget this.

When *City for Conquest* opened, the review that generally passed as the industry's judgment on the movie and the people who'd made it appeared in the *Hollywood Reporter.* Arthur Kennedy and I, as newcomers, were praised, but a distinction was drawn. After predicting a great future for Arthur, the *Reporter's* critic had written: "However, Elia Kazan, having equally as much ability, because of his looks will present a casting problem."

I had a different final judgment; it was: "I sure as hell can direct better than Anatole Litvak."

I T W A S spring, the time of year Greeks call the "Opening," and Molly and I were driving along a blacktop road in Connecticut, talking about someday buying a place in the country. She'd been brought up in South Orange, New Jersey, a suburb where there were large, old-fashioned homes, the kind with servants' quarters on the top floor. She'd had a great yard to play in as a child, with trees that were monuments, a flower garden with brick walks, and a sundial, which actually told the time. She wanted our kids to have the same kind of advantage. So did I.

What happened is what you might read about in a novel you don't believe. Late that afternoon we'd climbed to a high spot in the road, and I stopped the car to get out and piss behind a tree. As I did, I looked down over a broad field and saw, through the trees that framed it, a body of water. I've always been drawn to water, be it a brook or the sea. What I was looking at was a sixteen-acre pond—some would call it a lake, but it was man-made; a brook had been dammed to provide the water for a corn and cider mill. Overlooking the field and the water was a farmer's home, painted white, with many windows facing west, now made golden by the setting sun. Behind the house was a saltbox barn, also white. The old sugar maples that guarded the place were beginning to show green, tinted with the red of their winged seeds. The house was not occupied. I called Molly to come look. I wanted it. Immediately.

We drove back the next morning. The place was for sale and—can you believe this?—113 acres, with the house, pond, and barn, as well as an old apple orchard, for $17,500. Impulse turned into good sense; we decided to buy it quickly. How we'd pay for it was another problem. We'd found our place, and it had already brought us closer. We talked about it all the way home.

I had a reason I was moved so forcibly, one I didn't reveal to Molly. Such a possession would be a token of enduring faith, a symbol of continuance to bind us together in the bad times I feared were coming. The money it would cost would be a penance for my sins. I was again behaving like a damned fool, as if I wished what was going on between Constance and me to be found out. Did I? Want that? The possibility frightened me. But the way I was behaving made it inevitable that I'd be discovered. More and more people were seeing us close together, sitting side against side in a movie theatre or slumped in the dark corner of a bar. I'd taken the final foolish step, rented a small room on a monthly basis in a Forty-eighth Street hotel, the Alpine, and we'd moved in some things. I now had two bedrooms. Sooner or later someone with a loose mouth was bound to come on us together in the lobby or leaving by the front door. Was I ready to face the consequences? Not when I thought about it.

Tola Litvak was offering me another job. Warners had bought a play I'd owned for a while, then given up on. It was about a jazz band and the conflicts among its members. I hadn't been able to get up the money for a production, so the author and I decided to sell it. Litvak, who knew nothing about this kind of music, was going to direct it. I suppose he was looking for another "real American" subject to shake off the label "European director." He'd offered me the part of the clarinet player, but I hadn't been anxious to work with him again, so had delayed my response. The house in the country decided me. The job would bring us the money we needed, and it would give me a chance, alone in California, to clear my head.

I said a passionate goodbye to Constance, then decided she should ride out to Chicago with me; we enjoyed a night in a lower berth, riding through the dark country with the shade up. Somewhere in the night, I'd said, "I love you, Constance." When she'd responded, "And then what?" I hadn't answered. I didn't want to lose her, but I knew no true way to hold her. Unable to handle my infatuation, I was, for the moment, doing the only thing I could do—putting distance between us, all three.

In California, I was immediately occupied with learning to play the clarinet well enough so I could be photographed doing it in close-up. I also had to learn to dance adequately, which was easier because no one in the cast could dance. Tola showed me nothing new; it was "More, Getch, more!" again. The only thing about the production that impressed me was the musical side. Jimmie Lunceford and his band were the best artists on the lot. Close at hand were Johnny Mercer, who wrote the lyrics, and with him the man who wrote the music, Harold Arlen, a genius. The blacks and the Jews, they had the talent. As for the rest of the cast—forgive me, fellows, if you read this—they were all second-raters. There was no Jimmy Cagney to make the days worthwhile.

I made sure that I was ready to drop, each afternoon when I got back to my room and pulled the bed out of the wall. I didn't go to parties on the hunt. I didn't want any other girlfriend than Constance. I didn't want another wife than Molly. What I did want was both. In my heart I didn't believe this irrational; it seemed perfectly normal and sensible, even though it was against the professed moral law of the society and that of my upbringing. I felt wrong, then defiant about feeling wrong. When I longed for someone, I longed for Constance. When I longed for home, it was for the home I had with Molly.

She was busy planning how we'd fix up the place in the country. There were unanticipated expenses; we'd bought the house without realizing that it was a summer place, without a heating system. Molly had engaged a "local" to install a furnace, radiators, pipes, and so on, and she was supervising the work. She wrote describing what was happening every step of the way, as well as providing sketches of the full cast of characters doing the work. She also sent me the first drawings in colored crayon by my daughter. Those damned drawings broke me up.

Constance kept me up on her life. She announced, joyously, that a representative of Samuel Goldwyn had shown interest in her and was going to introduce her to the big man next time he was in New York. At the end of each letter she told me how much I meant to her and how painfully she missed me. As I read these letters now, they seem to have been written by a passionate but circumspect girl, nothing like the ones we have running loose today. The ache her letters stirred in me didn't let up. I waited for these letters. I knew after a few weeks of this that the solution of running away wasn't working. Then I asked myself what would happen when the film was finished. I had no answer.

"A C T I N G," an old critic said, "is a lamp placed in the soul of man so we can see who we are and who we wish we are." Not that summer, not on the Litvak set. When *Blues in the Night* comes on the late-late show, I advise you to skip it. I'd decided, once the Group dissolved, that being an actor in our time and place was a humiliating profession. I didn't look forward to more of it. An actor floats in a vast stagnant pool, waiting for a tide that will carry him where he thinks he wants to go. The tide comes and he has the impression he's moving. Then the tide is still, the pool stagnant again, and the actor finds he is just where he was before. I have respected actors who stand by the theatre year after year. I feel for them. Producers gamble someone else's money, actors a piece of their lives. When the play is a flop, the author and the director, their wives and their agents, whisk off to the warm sea washing the shore of a Caribbean isle. Actors continue on stage, playing the role for which they've been roasted, in the play that's been rejected, often ridiculed. I decided that summer that I'd never act again. And I never did.

But no event or reflection had produced any such decision about my personal life. When I got back to New York City, I was not in the same situation as when I'd left; time's passing had made my problems worse, not better.

I C O M E from a family of voyagers; my uncle and my father were transients, less from disposition than from necessity. They were slippery, had to be. Raised in a world of memories, they grew up distrustful of fate. "Don't worry," my uncle used to say, "everything will turn out bad." He knew that no matter how well things appeared to be going, a fall was ahead. Neither man was analytical. The habit of years had become instinct. Like deer who crop the grasses and, as they raise their heads to chew, look one way then the other for predators, my people lived ready to run. This instinct was in me at birth.

Slippery men depend on luck. They play the numbers, shoot craps, work their way through college by studying poker. Lady Luck was my madonna. At this point I needed her, and she came with her bounty. Carly Wharton, the charming wife of a corporation lawyer, and Martin Gabel, a friend whose syrupy voice was frequently heard on the "soaps," asked me to direct *Café Crown*, a play about the Café Royale, a Second Avenue hangout for the Jewish theatre crowd. I read the play the way a starving man eats.

Being me, I was immediately suspicious. Why had they selected me? Of course, it was because I'd been with Jewish theatre people ever since I left Yale, played many times with Luther and Stella, the son and daughter of the legendary Jacob P. Adler. But then I began to find the less flattering reasons. This play was slight stuff, so every successful director in town must have turned it down. Since I was not an established director, they could pay me less, manage me more easily, and in case of trouble, dispose of me without damaging publicity. Martin Gabel had worked with Orson Welles and must have had ambitions as a director. With a fellow like me, he could run around my end and do some coaching behind the scenes. He certainly couldn't do that with George Abbott or Jed Harris. So I got the job.

Then I gave up the silly speculation. Did it matter why they'd offered me the job? I had what I wanted, another chance to direct. So I began to study the play—and the author. Hy Kraft, a Hollywood screenplay writer, had the thinnest talent of any playwright I've worked with—but he did have a talent. It was for the Jewish anecdote. I knew from my tours in the movie colony just where he was coming from: the back door of Stanley Rose's bookstore on Sunset Boulevard, a hangout for Sunbelt intellectuals and lefties, where they'd gather to drink and pass around high-level gossip about who was writing what for whom and boast about the "good things" they'd sneaked into their scripts that the studio heads were too stupid and too unpolitical to notice.

Planning how to direct the play, I resolved to stop trying to imitate Clurman's and Strasberg's flood of rhetoric; I didn't have that gift. The tension I had felt directing in the Group lifted. I decided that the main thing was to make sure I did very little. Sometimes it's smarter for a director to do less than he might and not attempt to pump the play up into something it's not. I would cast it colorfully, with vivid "ethnic" types, move them around in a way that would seem spontaneous and unstudied, and above all get the jokes "fed" correctly and the responses, where the laughs were, thrown at the audience clearly. This was a small folk piece, and it would be a bad mistake to try to make it into anything better. I would direct it from the outside, always having the focus in the right place and the people with the laugh lines facing out and well lit. It was a relief to have some "Broadway" actors to direct. I'd tell them plainly what I wanted, where to move, when and how to stress what needed to be stressed, and I'd expect them to carry out my instructions. I'd been too damned friendly with actors in the past; I was going to toughen up.

So I was not the old supercharged Group kid anymore, not at these rehearsals. There was nothing in the play to be intense about. Relaxed at last, I enjoyed myself, kept everyone in line while I laughed at the actors' shticks and readings. When a director laughs at his own show, it's usually a bad sign, but this time the audience enjoyed what I'd enjoyed and the play worked. I'd learned a number of lessons: Don't try to make a play what it isn't; in many cases less is more; a director's ease and relaxation are infectious and, therefore, of value; don't try to instruct an audience; if there is no theme, don't try to impose one; and finally, for me the most important, don't worry whether or not the actors like you. That is not essential. Carnovsky, who played one of the leading roles, and I got along without becoming friends. Friendship, I decided, is not necessary. It may be harmful.

The play was my first success as a director.

I W A S in Carly Wharton's office, going over our casting problems, when a secretary came in and said, "Turn on the radio." It was December 7, 1941, and that was how I heard about the attack on Pearl Harbor. A couple of weeks later, after I'd waited for some kind of call to arms, I went to my draft board and asked where I stood. I was eager to go, not because I was burning with patriotism but because entering the service would free me from the terrible tangle of my personal life. I believe many men who quickly entered the ranks had similar reasons. My draft board informed me that I was 3-A, by reason of my age, my marriage, and my two kids. I would have to deal with my personal problems personally.

I had a modest success with *Café Crown*, but because the theatre, owing to the war, was scarce of directors, my sudden rise seemed more noteworthy than it was. I was surprised when I was invited to visit a certain Mr. Michael Myerberg in the Hotel des Artistes and there told that he'd acquired the production rights to Thornton Wilder's new work, *The Skin of Our Teeth*, and that he wanted to talk to me about directing it. "Possibly," he added. He was a tall man, without the grace some tall men have, unnaturally thin, rickety, his complexion a washroom green. He went on and on, talking about his production ideas, which, since I hadn't read what he called "the text," sounded like gobbledygook to me. Was he trying to impress me with all that avant-garde drip? Why had Thornton, who—after *Our Town*—

could have had any producer in town, chosen this man? And since he could have had any director, why was I there? Was Myerberg on the level? I couldn't tell. He circled the subject like a figure skater on thin ice. I kept up a bright and agreeable front, just in case. Whatever accident of thought or purpose had decided him to call me in, I had to allow for the possibility that this might be a great opportunity. When I left, I asked for a copy to read. He made me swear not to show it to anyone. I agreed—but I had to have Molly's judgment on it; I relied on her for that.

In the next few days, while I was reading and rereading the play, egged on by my wife, who admired it extravagantly, I couldn't help wondering why Jed Harris, who'd done such an extraordinary job on *Our Town*, wasn't directing it. I asked my lawyer. He'd heard a rumor that Jed had demanded a share of the author's royalties—something for which Thornton had not forgiven him. A fellow in the cellar of Walgreen's drugstore, where actors congregated, told me that he'd heard Thornton had said to Jed, "You never understood the end of my play." If he meant the graveyard scene, in which the mourners carried open black umbrellas, I thought that brilliantly done. Who could ask for anything more from a director? I ran into an actor from the Mercury Theatre, who told me that Myerberg had been talking to Orson Welles. He would have been the perfect choice, I decided; he had more fantasy than I did and more style. I'd have picked Orson. Why suddenly so modest? Was I afraid to direct a play so boldly theatric?

At my next meeting with Myerberg, I asked him why he hadn't offered the play to Welles. Myerberg's answer? Gobbledygook. When I thought about it, I knew why he hadn't. Orson, at the peak of his reputation, would have insisted on his own cast, the actors with whom he'd worked at the Mercury, as well as his own designer. Myerberg had told me the kind of cast he wanted—stars, big ones!—and that he'd already engaged a designer, Albert Johnson, who'd made sketches.

Then Myerberg put it to me straight, and suddenly he was quite clear. Did I or did I not want to direct the play? "Yes," I said, and that was that. I sicced my lawyer on him, and protracted negotiations began. "Don't count on it," my lawyer advised. "I don't know what that man is saying half the time. Besides, he says he has to get an approval on you from his stars." "Who are . . . ?" I asked. "He either doesn't know or he won't say."

P A U L A S T R A S B E R G had been in the cast of *Café Crown* and enjoyed the benefits of the warm atmosphere—sisterhood and brotherhood—that exudes from even a moderately successful production. She'd become friendly with me and even friendlier with my wife, for whom she had a special admiration. Suddenly she became very concerned about the condition of our marriage. She'd got the idea that it was in trouble, and she wanted to help her friends.

She had good reason for concern. I'd done the most foolish in a series of foolish acts. Molly had urged me to direct a play she'd found by Paul Vincent Carroll, and although I didn't favor the play, in an effort to please her and make up for my recent neglect of her as a wife, as well as to deflect any possible suspicion before there was a suspicion, I'd agreed to take it on. Then I scooted off the end of the pier of good sense. The other reason I'd been moved to direct the play was that it had a part for Constance, the best part she was ever to play in the theatre.

It is customary, in our world, that when a man of some power in the performing arts attaches a young woman to himself, he will see to it that his darling is, in good time, offered certain professional benefits. Which is what I did. I gave her a part in the play, the play that my wife was still working on with the producer and the author. I was doing the play for Molly; I was doing it for Constance. In an act of personal and professional idiocy, I was trying to hold on to two women who were competing with each other, one of whom had no idea that she was competing, the other of whom was daily gaining confidence.

It was inevitable that people less innocent and pure in heart than Molly would soon realize what was happening, if for no other reason than by the look on my face when I was talking to Constance about her role. Gossip began to inundate rehearsals and leak through the theatre community. I knew that was happening and belatedly tried to control the manifestations of my fervor. But in our world, once "talk" starts there's no way to stop it. People are hungry for this kind of report about one another; it eases everyone else's conscience.

Paula had a great talent in this area. With all the sympathy of a wife past her best years, she dumped me into the soup. She wrote Molly in discreet and loving language to inform her that I seemed to be carrying on with Constance and offered her support in the crisis. I do believe she wanted to help us both, that she was undertaking a campaign to save our marriage. Her tactic was the classic one of the League of Bourgeois Wives: Get rid of the younger woman. Paula, I'm sure, was judging what Molly's reaction would be by what hers would have been—to eliminate the interloper, shame the husband, and, after a period of stress, forgive the foolish fellow.

But she misjudged my wife. Molly would not even talk to Paula about the problem, nor did she ask for more information. Molly was not the pliable show business type. She was a passionate absolutist. For her there was a right way and a wrong way and nothing in between. She loved her husband to the edge of the grave, but suddenly she wanted no part of him. She felt publicly humiliated. She'd been revealed to our small world as someone too naive or too blind to suspect what everyone else knew was going on. I'd opened her to the ridicule of the people around her. I'd delivered a blow to her vitals, which, in her case, was where her pride lived.

The result was a nightmare, one I'd brought on myself and deserved.

At Molly's request, I moved out of our bedroom and into my study, a small room wall-to-wall with the bedroom. Molly could control herself during the day, when the children were about, but at night, when they were asleep in their room, she couldn't stop crying. I can still recall the grate of her rasping sobs as they came through the thin wall between the bed where she was writhing and the cot where I lay sleepless. I told myself that the kids couldn't hear her, but I don't see how they could not have; the place shook. Molly's face in the morning looked like that of a drowned person fished from the sea.

In a few days she wanted a divorce. This was a relief, a kind of solution. Then she changed her mind, apparently after a conversation with a close friend, another wife, the gist of which, as I heard it later, was: "If you want him, you'll have to take him as he is. What's happened to you happens to us all; just wait a little." Molly called off the action. What she did was move out of our apartment. I came home one afternoon and found that she and our kids were gone—to my parents' home in New Rochelle. My mother loved Molly, and she was my mother.

We were now separated; Constance and Molly were in open, deadly conflict; and I was where I deserved to be, alone in the wreckage, shamefaced.

A few days after she'd gone, I moved to the Hotel Belvedere. I had a scruple about asking Constance to come to the apartment; I'd go there only to change clothes and see if there was a letter from Molly. I was still keeping the two camps apart.

Mother wrote me. Why the hell was everyone on Molly's side? What did anyone know of what went on between us? She said: "Many people come through small misunderstandings and bless the patience that kept them from making hasty decisions. Love will show the way to more understanding and forbearance." Where did she get that "forbearance"? She didn't know words like that.

The next day there was a letter from Molly, which enclosed her wedding ring. I wrote in my diary: "I know the pain it must have caused her to pull that ring off. She's worn it ten years without removing it for any reason; it had been on her finger through two childbirths. Even as I write this I feel a large pebble in my stomach which makes that organ clench." Molly's letter (which I cannot find) had two pages, one about how much she hated me and how much she'd turned against our marriage, the other about how much she loved me still. I didn't read the letter; I scanned it. It was too painful.

Constance came with comfort. Later I wrote: "She just left. I'm in love with two women. I don't know what I'm doing. She's so hungry for it! Always ready. I can see her standing in front of me still, her full little breasts, her perfect legs, her belly protruding sensually like the paintings of Italian Renaissance women we used to study in the art class at Williams. And her secret, fragrant bush. I love her eyes when she's being fucked. My pleasure is to see her pleasure. When she comes, she calls out, 'Oh, darling!' then she'd say, 'Oh, my God!' rather sadly and then, 'Don't stop. Don't stop,' her face a mixture of joy and pain. When I think of those moments, I never want to die. I feel, the hell with everything! Am I in love? I must be. I can't think of anything else. I don't want to work. I've become disconnected with any goal that I used to have. All I want is to see her every afternoon, every night. I've lost my ambition. Connie means cunt in old English. The delicate folded flower with its twin petals, that's my obsession! That's all I can think about."

I'd had a warm letter from Thornton ("Dear Gadget, stand up for the full compensation you deserve"), which was a relief; I'd feared he might not approve of the tangle in my personal life. Both Molly's family and his were Yankees from New Haven, Connecticut. I still felt that I was living on a narrow ledge over a deep precipice, one off which I could easily be pushed and so disqualified as an acceptable member of American society.

I'd go up to the Hotel des Artistes, on the way trying to arouse myself to a show of energy and eagerness. Mike Myerberg told me that I'd have to be presented to Fredric and Florence March (who'd agreed to play Mr. and Mrs. Antrobus), since their contract stipulated that they had to approve the director. He also dropped the news that Ruth Gordon, whom he was considering for Sabina, was saying she would play the part only if Jed Harris directed. Mike and my lawyer were still negotiating. Was I skating on thin ice? He left me with that impression. On purpose?

Then Mike arranged a meeting with the Marches. "We might as well get it over with," he said. "She'll give us a drink. Put on a nice suit and meet me at my place at four-thirty."

The Marches' expensive apartment hung over the East River. We were ushered in, asked to sit and wait. I envied them their view. On the walls were traditionally admired art; I liked our kids' crayon dabbings better. I'd never met this famous couple. This was a unique situation, I thought, a director auditioning for actors. Then they entered, Mrs. March first, followed by a cocktail cart pushed by a black servant, then Freddie. They were turned out in the manner of a wealthy couple interviewing a candidate for a top servant's position. Drinks were served. The advent of spring drew comment. Freddie made some jokes. Florence forced a laugh. I noticed that Freddie kept looking at Florence, rather like an anxious boy.

Then Florence took over. To my astonishment, what she wanted to talk about were certain social issues. I still knew all the phrases from back when and which side to stand up for. When Florence seemed to be approving my positions on a number of key questions, Mike asked if he could make a phone call and was shown out of the room. I continued "putting it on" for Florence, but Freddie and I understood each other immediately and without a word. He was an overgrown boy in a pin-striped blue suit and a banker's tie, but his smile promised mischief. I believe that this interview, which was an audition, embarrassed him. I'd find, as I came to know him, that one of his pleasures was to be naughty and have Florence—his surrogate mother—chide him. "Now, Freddie," she'd say, "now, Freddie!" He made me smile, as I still do when I remember him. He was, I'd find, one person when he was in the general vicinity of his wife and quite another out of her sight and hearing. Freddie seemed anxious to conclude the interview, she to prolong it.

I felt she was testing me—for what, I wasn't sure. I thought her attitude presumptuous and began to resent the position in which she was putting me. But my mask of the earnest, liberal-minded young man remained up; I was determined to do this play. However, I never quite got over the impression I formed of the lady that afternoon. When Freddie made jokes, she squelched them, keeping the séance solemn. I had to explain to her, at some length, how I saw the play and what it meant to me. It was fucking obvious what the play meant: that the human race would—in the author's opinion—persist by the skin of our teeth through any and all manner of disaster. But Florence had to hear me state this heartening message. And agree with it! Even Thornton hadn't asked for that. Perhaps what she was making sure of was that Freddie's new playmate was not a cutup. I refused a third cocktail. At the end, I found her to be a decent, honest, sincere, reliable woman, but how tedious those virtues can become when they're not leavened by doubt, self-deprecation, and openheartedness. She was, as I would find out, the perfect patsy for Miss Tallulah Bankhead.

B A C K at the Belvedere by midnight, I wrote in my diary:

Constance was not at the restaurant at eight when I said. I should have understood this because I'd given her only a few hours notice and she might have left home before my wire arrived. I then called her home; no one answered. I had another drink. I began walking the streets, midtown, in the unconscious activity of searching for her. I looked into the Faisan d'Or, the restaurant where, she told me, she used to meet Bob Capa. Did I really expect Constance to remain constant (Get that!) while I was in Hollywood making *Blues in the Night?* She told me she'd done it with someone else that summer. While I was celibate! In the back seat of a Pontiac, she said. I wondered which dress she was wearing that night. I couldn't stand the thought of anyone else fingering her. The image of Constance on her back eagerly taking someone else in, legs up! And there between her legs, the flower with two petals. I never tasted that before. It's always seemed gross. But not with her. Hers is delicate. Two pink petals and two hungry eyes. Now I understand jealousy. Don't forget how you feel now when you next direct a scene of jealousy.

I had another drink, then called her home again, this time raising her mother. When I hung up, more diary:

> Her mother hates me. I can hear it in her voice. She told me with some pleasure that Constance had gone for a weekend with Jack Houseman. Jack Houseman! For chrissakes! She'd once told me that Houseman was the nicest man she has ever met, but she said, in the next breath, that she loved me. I keep hearing the phone ringing when it is not. But if she's at his place, how can she call me? Where is his place? The hell with her. I don't trust her. The minute I turn my back, she's off for a weekend with another man. What the hell am I sacrificing my family for? I wish Molly would call me. She truly loves me. But that's a call I know I won't get. Ever again. No, not ever again. Molly's found out what you are.

In the morning, for no reason but that I didn't know where else to go, I walked to the apartment. The super's wife gave me a letter, which had arrived special delivery. It was from my mother, and if you could read the original, you'd see that she'd been distraught when she wrote it. I've not tried to fix the punctuation.

> Dear E. This is a sad letter and I am writing with a broken heart
>   Those things are hard to put in a letter and I understand how bad you must feel to talk about it   I have a sick girl here   You know Molly is very young yet but I do say she acts like a woman of 42 or 45 changing life as they call it. One thing I know she loves you very much and her heart is broken and unhappy   how long she can keep loving you and being hurt? You say everything will be allright by and by   What she says is different   She cannot bear it loving her one day, loving someone else the day after   nobody can   it cant be done   If you dont hurry you will have a sick wife on your hands the rest of your life   Love mother.

I called New Rochelle. My father picked up. "She go to Connecticut," he said, "to the headache place." (That's what Father had dubbed the place we'd bought, reminding me every time he mentioned it that he'd warned me it was going to give me money headaches.) Then he dropped his voice to a more intimate tone. "What's going on over here, God's sake?" he asked. "I don't know, Pop," I lied. I didn't want to get into a hassle with him. "Did she take the children with her?" I asked. "Yes, sure, what you think?" he answered. "She take good care those children. I tell you this much, that woman good mother." Rarely before had he spoken a kind word about Molly.

Diary:

Bridgeport and three hitches. I had to walk the last two miles up a green hill, then into the yard of the place, and there she was, hoeing the patch of garden I'd started to dig up and quit on. She ran into my arms as if my sudden appearance had answered a prayer. I saw that she was near a breakdown. I tell her I've come for good. "I'm not going away anymore," I said. I meant it then. My face and neck were burning up. While I'm getting a cold drink, she walks away and sits on the rock overhanging the bottom field. When I come back, she's not talking. I can see she's not ready to believe me, and I wish I hadn't said what I'd said. "It's not so easy," she says. Her face was stony, like the Yankee rock she was sitting on, the same stuff.

Then the kids came up like the marines. They led me around the place, the girl holding my hand and pulling me here and there. They showed me the changes they'd been making. I admired the clothes-line they'd all three put up. Coming back, I spot Molly through the trees, but when we get to where she was sitting, she'd disappeared again. She was hiding from us, but the kids think it's a game. "Let's find her," they say, laughing. We finally do, but she's not playing. She wanted time to pull herself together.

Supper. We were friendly. "Childhood stew" made from a big fat hen. Molly kept starting to open up, then catching herself, controlling herself. Later she put the children to bed. Then she showed me where to sleep. A prolonged good night during which everything is made clear. Molly's instinct tells her that I'm there on an impulse of pity—which she can't accept. It's not anything she can rely on, she says. I feel sorry for her now, she says, but I'll return to Constance. I stoutly deny everything, but I don't take her into my arms and force her to believe me. She wants me to leave in the morning. "It's not so easy," she says again. Across my mind flashes the thought: "Maybe Constance will be free tomorrow night."

I try to read *War and Peace*. Maybe the book will put me to sleep. Then she is standing in the doorway, wearing a nightgown. I'll never forget that nightgown. It was linen, with a cute girlish fringe of cutout stuff. It was short too, coming to above her knees, and in excellent taste: linen with just the least stiffness to it. As she stood in the door-way, you could see through it—just a little. This, for Molly, was the height of the seductress's art. I waited for her to speak, she for me. I didn't know what to say. "I'm tired," I said. "We've both had a long day," she said. "Did I ever tell you," I said, "how beautiful your face was even on that air warden's card?" She laughed, then said, "I should have known you were going through hell too." She seemed to be apol-ogizing. Or was she reaching toward me?

"If it had been anybody but that stupid, cheap, no-talent little blonde," she said. Silence. "That's what I can't forgive."

"Actually she's quite a nice person," I said. "I like her—as a person."

"Other ways too," she said.

"Yes, other ways too," I said. I was speaking the truth at last.

That did it. I tried to tell her that I loved her but I didn't want to come back because I couldn't come back until I was ready, that what she'd said was true, it wasn't all that easy. "Don't you think I'm right?" I said. "Don't you think that was wise?" And so on. In short, I cut her off, and in the middle of a sentence, she left the room.

I picked up *War and Peace*. I'd spent months trying to read that damned book. But it didn't serve. I put the light out and waited for sleep. It was beginning to come, when Molly rushed in, sobbing, and started to hit me—mostly about the head. "I hate you," she was screaming. "I hate you." "Shshsh," I said, covering my head. "The children will hear." "Let them hear," she shouted. "I hate you." She fell to the floor at the side of the bed and sobbed for ten minutes. "I'll always love you," I said. It was true. "Go away," she said. "Please go. And think a little who you are and what you want. Think!"

In the morning she asked me to put her car in the barn; it looked as if it was going to rain. Looking through her bag for the car keys, I found a little notebook. Across the cover, she'd written "Mr. and Mrs. Elia Kazan." It contained her plans for the decoration of the house we'd bought. On one page, the parlor curtains; on another, the furniture she intended to re-cover, and so on, even the dishes and towels, and opposite each, in the kids' watercolors, the colors she wanted.

Molly looked in pieces when I left. "Ask yourself if you meant anything of what you said," she said. Then: "Do you mind putting up a couple of towel racks before you go?" Right in the middle of breaking up her marriage, this girl thinks of towel racks! Is that what they call the "Eternal Feminine"?

The kids walked me to the place where I'd try to hitch a ride. They wanted to know why I was going, why I didn't stay. "There's a lot to do here," the girl said. The little boy looked at me sternly. I wasn't sure he wanted me to stay. "Business reasons," I said. I knew they'd spoken to her too, and I knew that if I had honestly, passionately wanted to get back with her then, I could have begged my way back.

In New York, I couldn't sleep. Diary: "Don't call her again, don't lead her up another blind alley. This is your last chance with her. If you want her ever again, you must . . ." Then there's a space. I didn't know what to say to myself. Then I went on: "You're trying to do something impossible, to hold both. It won't work. It's not human nature. Your mother is right. Give up."

. . .

I N T H E morning I had a call from Mike Myerberg. He told me that Ruth Gordon had given him his "out," and he'd been able to get the person he wanted for Sabina. Tallulah Bankhead.

I've hated only two people in my life. One was Tallulah Bankhead. In time I got over it. The other anger is still in me, and I'll come to that later.

The fact is that I owe Bankhead a gift; she made a director of me. When I'd directed the Ardrey plays, and at the rehearsals of *Café Crown*, I'd speak to the actors privately, apart from each other, in a whisper, never raise my voice, never show anger, not even irritation, disappointment, or impatience. I began to gain the reputation I have for reticence and self-control, and it cost me, because inside I'd be seething. Patience is a good virtue for a director to have if the threat of violence is waiting underneath. Bankhead taught me, without intending to, that there is nothing as necessary for a director as a tough-handed determination to get the result he wants, get it one way or another, preferably by patient kindness or gentle, subtle manipulation, but if not by these means, by any that the situation calls for—an intimidating voice or the force of rage, simulated or genuine.

Mike took me to the Élysée Hotel for my final interview-audition. We were shown up to the lady's suite and there invited by a pleasant black maid to sit and make ourselves comfortable. We were able to do only the first; even Mike seemed nervous. It was a quarter of an hour before the star sailed in; when she did, she was continuing a conversation with her maid and barely recognized our presence in the room. Then she was settled and turned to inspect me. I had the impression she'd never seen anything quite like me before. I smiled; no smile was returned. Her face looked as though she'd had a bad night. A few years later, I'd have said to myself, "She's been *on* something."

I can't remember what they talked about, Mike and she. I was left out of the conversation except for one crack from Bankhead about the Group Theatre. I swallowed my tongue, took it as a joke. As I sat there with that forced smile on my face, I considered quitting. I was fed up with all my crises; they were wearing me down. I had no idea whom Bankhead wanted to direct the play or even if she had a preference—but it certainly wasn't me. Mike talked his gobbledygook. Now I saw the purpose behind it. I thought him smart to avoid the subject we'd come there to discuss: Was I worthy? We left without any indication of her judgment; I got no approval or good wishes. The last thing she said to Mike—I was still not being addressed— was that she'd sworn off alcoholic drink until we'd won the war. I remember she dropped Churchill's name several times.

She had been auditioning me, but in a way contrary to Florence March's; Bankhead was auditioning me with her instincts, not her mind. "Don't worry—" Mike said in the elevator, but if that was the start of a sentence, it was to go uncompleted. Instead he coughed, didn't cover his mouth, and I saw that the inside was painted blue. What kind of a bunch had I hooked up with? "What did she say?" I asked. "What did she have to say when you hung back there with her?" "She'd call me," Mike answered, ducking my question.

So I was never to get Bankhead's verdict. But I knew where I was; I'd been there before. I was on trial. I'd have to win the job. Well, I would. I'd study the play and be ready to meet any uncertainty any of them had. I noticed the irony: I liked the play a lot better when I saw that I might lose it.

"Your lawyer is very difficult," Mike said as we parted. "Sometimes I don't understand what he's talking about." "That's what he says about you, Mike," I said. He ducked that one too. "He makes everything a contest between us," he went on. "But I believe I've managed to get an agreement out of him. So now—go to work! I've been worried about you. There've been days when you haven't looked like yourself—whatever that is." He laughed, and I saw the inside of his mouth again. Yes, indigo blue; a threatening color.

T H E N I woke one morning and my mind was made up and there was nothing to struggle over. I was hurting a lot of people who had no defenses and I had no solution. I'd been going over and over what had happened with Molly in the Connecticut home. I knew it must have been the biggest humiliation of her life, a wound that would never heal. I kept recalling how she'd stood in the doorway wearing that short nightgown. She is so discreet, so delicately made, that any offering of herself could only have come from the deepest feeling. It must have overridden formidable barriers of reserve. The next morning, when I left, I could see how hurt she was. I'd wounded a saint, a person who deserved nothing but good, who not only had no way of striking back—a weekend, however "innocent," with another man, for instance—but had no shell to shield her vitals. Each blow, with that girl, sinks into her soft center, as the face pales, the chin crumbles, and the eyes look at me, helpless. Each blow squeezes the life out of her, as I might squash a pillow.

Constance had one sure defense; she'd "see" (that all-purpose girl word) another man. Don't forget, I told myself, how quickly she found Capa when you were on the road with *Golden Boy.* And just now, a weekend with Jack Houseman. And some others for sure. The back seat of a Pontiac, for chrissake! If I left her now, she'd be out with another man tomorrow night. They all want to fuck her, and isn't that the ultimate compliment to a woman like Constance? Isn't it? One of her suitors will be attractive to her immediately. I'll have to be with her, guarding her, all the time. I don't trust her to be alone.

And our children—they'd pay for what I was doing in the years to come, perhaps for the rest of their lives. I recalled their faces when I'd left that morning and the little girl holding my hand. I remembered their question, "Why are you going now?" And how tense and solemn the little boy looked. Why hurt them further?

And my mother: Did she deserve the terrible pain that was in her letters?

I was killing everyone. I was a villain.

Was it really that important to have what Constance gave me? Was she the only source for that pleasure? Hadn't I simply got in too deep with her? Back off now. What was important was that I do a good job on Wilder's play and the hell with all those other tensions and troubles. They were wrecking my life.

I decided to blow the thing apart.

I wrote Constance. "My very dear Constance: This week in the country, I had what must be the worst week in my life. I've got to face it. I miss my wife and children terribly. I've said to myself, 'You'll get over it,' but it doesn't seem to work out that way. When I was in the kids' room it's as if a wild animal was in my stomach eating me. The signs of Molly's hand on that place—which are the signs of her hopes—kill me. Meantime she hates me and doesn't trust me to take the kids even for a weekend. All this is what's made me behave so strangely, have unexplained fits of depression and the blues, disappear suddenly without explanation. I do care for you, I do, but I've treated you abominably too and I'm sorry. That is why I haven't been able to work as I should. The new play is carrying me instead of the other way around. I'm just letting it happen to me, instead of being the core man, opinionated about it as I should be."

And so on. Finally: "There it is. An old, old story. I can't see you for a while. I've got to think all this out. I can't live without them but maybe I'll have to. Meantime I'll work. I've got plenty to do on this play—and to think about."

I received an immediate answer from Constance. "My heart is breaking. Don't write me or try to see me." That was all.

On the same day I'd written Constance, I'd mailed a letter to Molly, starting, "Dearest Molly," and continuing with a few housekeeping items about our place in the country. I'd gone there after they'd left and been overseeing the plumber as he put in the heating system. Then the last paragraph: "I broke with Constance today. I don't want any other girl but you. I stay by myself up here and work and have no other plans. I come into town only to see Mike Myerberg." That was it.

A few days later, I got this letter from Constance: "Darling: I don't know how to begin or what to say. Every once in a while I have to bite my knuckles to keep from crying. I do understand how you feel. I only wish I'd known sooner or, rather, faced it sooner. I've been kidding myself these past few months into believing you cared deeply for me but I knew you didn't. Not enough anyway. I'm grateful to you for what you've meant to me. Knowing you has been the happiest time of my life. The guy who said of love, 'All other pleasures are not worth its pain,' knew what he was talking about. You told me once you'd never be far away from me whatever happened. You were right. I shall always be proud that I was once your girl."

Constance's letter had its effect on me. I admired her. I thought her honest about facing contradictory feelings, while I wasn't. Absence also had its result; every day we were apart, I liked her better. I wrote in my diary: "I'm still crazy about that girl. I never felt more like writing her a love letter than I do tonight. I envy the man who gets her."

But I didn't write her. The diary goes right on: "Today the German H.Q. announced the capture of Rostov. The U.S. fleet seems to be losing the Battle of the Solomon Islands. Gandhi has been arrested and there is rioting all over India—which can only help Japan. . . ."

In a kind of desperation—for the separations were not working out as I'd hoped—I applied to the Office of War Information, asking to be taken in. It was the only solution I could think of to my problem. I was in bad shape; I needed help to get out of my dilemma. I received this answer from the OWI: "In reply to your letter, I am compelled to say that there is at present no opening in our organization for one of your experience—wide and diversified though it may be." I figured that they'd looked in their files and found I'd once been a member of the Communist Party. That was what they meant by "wide and diversified."

Molly had not responded to my letter. I couldn't blame her and didn't. Wanting both had ended with having nothing.

F R O M the instant Tallulah Bankhead strode on stage—"Marching as to war!" I said to myself—followed by her black maid, who was loaded down with more paraphernalia than was necessary for a first rehearsal, I guessed what she had in mind: to get me fired. Call me paranoid, but wait for the proof.

Four stars and Monty Clift, who was to become a star, were lined up before me. I introduced them to each other. The traditional show business embraces were not forthcoming; they nodded, smiled, waved hands, kept their distance. Monty was visibly impressed with the select company he was part of. Florence Reed, old Mother Goddam of *The Shanghai Gesture,* was visibly impressed with no one. Florence Eldridge March chattered, straining to be believed the cordial one—for the record, I suppose; I can't imagine she had any liking for Bankhead. Tallulah responded with her horse's laugh and nicotine cough. I'd anticipated that Mrs. March, with her rather artificial manners, "society" laugh, and inflated big-star posture, would be an irresistible target for Tallulah, and I could see from the glint in the bitch's eye that she smelled blood. As for Freddie March, he was on guard, anticipating that Miss Bankhead's purpose would be to make rehearsals so tense that she, not the play, would become the problem, and everyone would be spending his best energies satisfying her wishes. With these observations in mind, I'd seated Freddie between his wife and Miss Bankhead. My own concern was specific: I remembered the scene in the Hotel Élysée and expected that she was determined to make it evident that I was unable to control rehearsals, which would give her a cue for blackmail: "You want rehearsals to go well, Mr. Myerberg? Get rid of Kazan and bring in a real pro."

The author, Thornton Wilder, wasn't there through most of the preparations or the rehearsals. He was serving the air force (the 328th Fighter Group, Hamilton Field, California), so I saw him only on his occasional visits east. We communicated by letters; I'd ask questions and he'd answer, always telling me that he trusted me altogether—as he of course had to. "Here are some memos," he wrote me. "That's the way Jed and I worked and Reinhardt and I. It's especially useful when rehearsal time comes. There's nothing as draining and muddling as those endless post-rehearsal talks in a café." His general relationship to me was teacher to pupil, which was fine because I'd had no experience with a play like this one, nor had I read the literature—Joyce, I'd been told—that helped inspire the work.

This was the first play I directed that I found challenging beyond my talent and technique. I didn't immediately, as I had done with other plays, try to figure out how to cover its faults, but rather how to extend my own capabilities. I admired its theatrical imagination. There was a curious contrast here: The form of the play was novel and constantly surprising, but the author's values, on which it was built, were conventional and finally stuffy. Other plays I've liked were conceived out of the life experience of the dramatist; this play seemed to have been hatched in the library of a financially secure college campus. Wilder had a "clean" soul and a lively mind, but our country was in a nightmare of violence, a worldwide war. Thornton was telling us we'd survive this trial as we had others in our history. Nice to hear, but words of hope as simple as those in the play tend to sound hollow. Which is why, I suppose, the play is not revived as often as we, following its triumphant first reception, anticipated. Looking back, the plays and films that have shaken me most were those where no final reassurance was offered. Thornton, a "bookish" man, needed to do what college teachers must do at the end of a course—sum up and look forward to next year.

What Thornton detested most of all in the theatre was overemotionalism. His persistent instruction to Jed Harris about the direction of *Our Town* had been to "keep it sec." He wanted the sets of *The Skin of Our Teeth* to be like the backgrounds in comic strips—ours were not—and the behavior of the characters to correspond: I did well with that. But it's possible that all his plays lived best in his imagination. He did not communicate any enthusiasm to me about our production after it had opened.

When rehearsals started, two things were immediately apparent: The tensions between the Marches and Bankhead, which I'd anticipated, were really there; and it was my job daily to prevent fights between them. The prospect of having to play scenes with Tallulah terrified Florence March; she'd warned me again and again to be on my guard against "that bitch." Hardly a day passed that she didn't say to me, "When are you going to do something about Tallulah?" But I couldn't help liking what Bankhead was doing in rehearsal. She came to work every day steaming with some anxiety or grudge that overrode everything else within her, but there was a benefit from these tensions. She scorned Florence March for being so controlled and goody-good. She thought the tame way Florence approached life un- artistic. To my surprise, I found that I was often on her side, not Florence's. I also thought the antagonism between them valuable for the production and the character each of them was playing; I didn't want to hazard that.

Each of my actors wanted different things from me. Florence March wanted protection and endless explanations; I gave her these privately. Bankhead wanted unwavering attention and admiration; I had some trouble with that, but I managed it. Freddie said to me on the first day, "Don't let me ham it up." His need was the simplest to satisfy. Florence Reed wanted to be left alone; she had her performance and no other, and that was that. For a few days everything went well. I enjoyed my work, was having a picnic with the family scenes, the animals (especially the baby dinosaur), the children, and the bumptious roaring father. I found the play had been perfectly cast (by Myerberg, not me), and that it was going to come off. I worked fast because I had a premonition there'd be only so much time with things orderly and peaceful, then all hell would break loose.

One morning toward the end of the first week, Bankhead didn't come to rehearsal. I waited awhile, then called Myerberg and told him the news. "I know about it," he said. "We have a problem." I remember I appreciated his use of the word "we." "What's that?" I said. Obviously it had to do with Bankhead. "You better come over here," he said. "Now?" "Yes." "What'll I do, call off rehearsal?" "No," he said. "Put the understudy on." "But she's had no time to learn the moves." "Doesn't matter," Mike said. "Put her in; the stage manager will show her. Then get over here." "What's the score?" I asked. "She doesn't like the way you're directing her," Mike said.

As I left the theatre, Freddie came up to me—he'd sensed the situa- tion—and said he was with me all the way. That meant a lot to me. I knew this was the first big chance of my life and made up my mind to fight for it.

Bankhead's suite exuded the cordial atmosphere of a funeral parlor. The black maid, who greeted us at the door, spoke in a hushed voice, the tone employed in the anteroom of the dying. Again we had a long wait before the star entered. Bankhead looked drugged; she was wobbly on her feet. She fell on the sofa, throwing her head back as if she were the aggrieved person, and didn't look at me. I think now that she did feel mistreated, and perhaps she was embarrassed at what she'd determined to do—get me fired—but she was also determined to see it through. I'd made up my mind to have a total confrontation and drop my mask.

"What don't you like about the way I'm directing you?" I demanded to know. "He doesn't know how to direct a star," she said to Mike. "What don't I know about directing stars?" I said to her. "He's from the Group Theatre," she said to Mike, "where they're all equals or pretend they are. I'm not one of those actors. Why should I be treated as just another actress playing the servant of the Marches' household?" "I don't treat you that way," I said. "There are three other stars in that company," I went on. "They're not complaining." "Of course not," she said. "You're throwing it all to them." She'd turned to me for the first time, her eyes bleary and watery, and she looked hurt and victimized. "You let people cross in front of me," she said. Then, turning to Mike: "People are in front of me all the time. The audience is supposed to watch me, not a lot of old actors and animals and children crossing back and forth in front of me all the time. He doesn't know how to direct a star. He learned directing in the Group Theatre." "You mean nobody must cross in front of you ever?" I demanded to know. "Yes," she screamed, "yes, yes, yes, that's what I mean."

She appeared to be breaking down, then, as she became increasingly hysterical, fell off the sofa and onto the floor. The maid ran to her and helped her out of the room. I felt I'd failed, but Mike nodded approval to me. A few minutes later, the maid came back and told us Miss Bankhead couldn't consult any longer that day; she had to calm down and rest. "Tell her," Mike said, "that there's no hurry. We've got the understudy rehearsing, and everything is going along fine."

I knew I was doing okay, because Mike had had his chance to fire me and did not. The next day, Tallulah came back. We'd both digested the lesson of our meeting and were prepared for further struggle. I believe she felt that since I wasn't going to protect her privileges as a star, she'd protect herself. She did at every turn, but now the conflict was in the open. What a relief to be hostile! I felt easier. I enjoyed the Atlantic City scenes with peppery old Florence Reed; she was tough enough—and equally foulmouthed—to hold her own with Tallulah. The old-timers, actors and actresses we'd cast to play conveners, had seen stars come and go, and they weren't impressed with Bankhead's fireworks. If I looked melancholy in the morning, Freddie would take me aside and tell me his latest dirty joke, a laugh to start the day. I knew that if I could endure the resentment, the scorn, and the hostility our diva was spraying in every direction, if I could tough it out for a few more weeks, we might have an extraordinary show. But I also knew that at the next crisis, she'd try again to get rid of me.

When things didn't go quite the way she wished and I'd met stubbornness with inflexibility, she'd leave rehearsal, followed by her anxious maid. I'd pretend not to notice her departure and, having learned Mike's lesson, put in the understudy, continuing rehearsal as if nothing had gone wrong. I began to be proud of my ability to persist, even-keeled, in a continuous storm.

"D E A R E S T M O L L Y," I wrote her in the second week of rehearsal, "I was all set to go to New Rochelle last night [to see the children on Sunday] but Bankhead walked out on rehearsal after a day of squabbling and the evening ended again in a conference at Myerberg's. I should last out a few more weeks. I see nothing ahead except a series of daily fights with our feudal Baroness, every day fighting for every point. An atmosphere of terror, meanness, spite, jealousy, self-interest, all concealed under 'I only want the good of the show.' She tells everyone she's sworn off drink until the war is won. By our side, she means. Instead she sends the company manager to the drugstore for Spirits of Ammonia. What does that do? I don't know. She looks loaded up with something, her eyes staring wildly at me when I talk to her. I don't know whether she hears me or, if she does, whether she comprehends. Still she may steal the show. My friend in the cast is Freddie March." Then: "I miss you. I miss the kids. To wake alone in a hotel room in the middle of the night has a special terror."

That letter was not answered.

T H E F I R S T public performance was in the Shubert Theatre in Thornton's hometown, New Haven. He wasn't there, but we all had genial communications from him and words of gratitude. The company arrived about midday, piled into the Taft Hotel, alongside the theatre, then, without lunch, most of us hustled next door to see the scenery, which had been set up and was being lit.

No matter how often the designs for a play have been explained to a company of actors, no matter that they've seen models and sketches, the first time they actually have to work in a set is a shock. Albert Johnson's designs were unattached to the wings at the side; in the first act, the actors coming to the Antrobus home could be seen before they entered. This was a novelty at the time and appropriate for the play, but it outraged Tallulah. She was especially nervous under the strain of opening and was looking for something to rant about—I could understand that—but I wasn't ready for the fit she threw when she first saw what she had to work in. It was a frenzy near madness, which continued throughout the dress rehearsal and until after the opening night's performance. Even when she was offstage, she could be heard cursing the set, its designer, the management, and me. She demanded that "wings" be set up to shield her entrances. Myerberg refused to alter the sets. I refused to demand that the sets be altered. Meantime, I kept behaving as if she were a reasonable person making reasonable demands. Call it patience—but it cost me.

Mike was a very sick man, and he looked diseased. Now the outside of his throat was painted an electric blue, and he no longer tried to conceal the inside of his mouth. Whatever was wrong seemed so serious that we didn't dare ask what it was. He should have been in bed, but he had a cot placed at the foot of the right aisle, close to the stage, and, bolstering his head on pillows, watched the rehearsal lying down, an invalid desperately determined to bring his production through. I admired Mike.

The first dress rehearsal was a nightmare of hysteria. Bankhead was never quiet offstage, never on time for her entrances, never anything but hateful to the other actors. Florence March was wretched and, it seemed to me, frightened; Freddie furious; Florence Reed haughty and scornful of us all; and Monty Clift awed by the minefields of temperament exploding around him. We were all relieved when, because of the crew's union regulations, a dinner break was called and we were able to slink away from each other. In some way I didn't altogether understand, I'd failed—not the others; myself. I looked for a place to hide and rest.

I climbed narrow stairs to the second tier of box seats. Maroon velour curtains were drawn, closing off the auditorium. The soft dark was comforting. I fell to the floor, my sweater a pillow. Sleep—I hoped. I could still hear her rumbling. But less. "When are you going to do something about Bankhead?" How many times had Florence March asked me that? She had a point. Who had taught me that patience was such a virtue? It's a virtue in Turkey, where the Greeks are helpless, but no one respects it here. The Pride of Alabama doesn't like the set. Well, fuck her. I don't like the set much either, but it's our set and she's going to play in it. Do all Southern belles have such foul mouths? I don't know how much stamina I've got left, not of the kind I'm going to need. My famous patience! There's a tide of anger in me that a wall of tissue paper is holding back. I've had all I'm going to take of everybody feeling privileged to complain and wrangle, with me in the middle holding them apart. "When are you going to do something about Bankhead?" Miss Talloo happens to be confident, as everyone around me has always been, that I will not "do something about her," that I'll understand—or pretend to: nod and smile and assure them all that my sympathetic patience continues, that I can take whatever they throw at me and not hit back. Half asleep now. Give in. They'll wake you. My famous patience. That's what's killing me. It's gone on, to tell the truth at last, all my life. They can behave however they want to, say what they want to, do selfish and outrageous things; not to worry—I can take it. It isn't only Bankhead, although she's the limit. My best friends, even they, have treated me that way all my life. I let them. Which does raise the question, doesn't it, why have I gone on thinking of them as my friends? Harold Clurman, for instance, who's always patronized and used me. "Fix that little entrance for me, will you, Gadg? It's only mechanics." If it's only mechanics, why doesn't he fix it? But I don't say that. I say, "Sure, Harold, sure." When he'd thrown me to Stella to be humiliated, not a peep out of me. And my pal Clifford, sitting in Lindy's enjoying the cheesecake with Jed Harris and Billy Rose and telling them that I was the cause of his play's failure. It took me a year before I told him off, and when I did, it was by mail, not face to face. And Strasberg, my mentor, blaming me for his fucked-up earthquake. What do I do? Run down into the wardrobe lady's room in the cellar, to cry. And the goddamn Group actors who treated me like a lucky apprentice and Dean Morris Carnovsky, that self-righteous prig; I don't forgive him for coming to my rehearsals late, day after day. But I never said a word to him, not a sincere word. I can't blame them for treating me that way, when I have never shown them I had teeth. My wife too, with her "I hate you, I hate you!" then hitting me across the face, and her constant posture of moral disapproval. Why did I take all the blame for what happened between us? Doesn't it still take two to tango? Even my mother saw that. I don't exclude her either, my dear old lady. What does she know about the world as it is now—not 1906; now! What does she know of the joy I've had with Constance? Constance, now gone, now with someone else. With whom? Forget it. Dear Mother, I don't want to wait to enjoy the more mature joys of understanding and forbearance. Forbearance again! That's what's killing me, forbearance. Isn't that another name for patience? That's what's killing me. I'm talking to all of you, banked in my memory. I've stopped trying to win your tolerance and your approval. Because if I'm dirt, I'm dirt. I've known only one person who's not on some moral plane high above me—although she sure looks like an angel when we fuck. Constance is down in the dirt with me, an animal as I'm an animal, the animal I like. Now I've lost her, a sacrifice to "higher moral values," whatever the hell they are. Tell me the truth: Who's got them? I doubt everybody. So, Elia, stop hiding and whispering and hoping that they all approve of you. Take what you need. There's someone in the cast who's there for you, waiting. I don't really like her, but—why not? It'll do you good. For an hour. Tonight maybe? Then sleep is forgetfulness. Let it go, your true nature. Yes, if I'm dirt, I'm dirt, and I'll do what I want to do, even if it's not okay—perfect—approved. I'll live in the mutt world from now on, paint my face black and join the niggers, because I'm one of them and always have been outside "respectable society," just like they are. Let *them* practice forbearance, my moral superiors. I've had it with forbearance. Let them judge and be damned. If I'm dirt, I'm dirt. Okay? I'd better go down.

I T   C A M E   to an end at 3 a.m. the next morning. The crew was gathered on stage, waiting for Mike to decide what the coming day's call would be. The stage door had been locked—there'd been some pilfering—and the company was asked to leave by the front of the theatre. Freddie bundled his Florence off. I'll have another invalid in the morning, I thought. The old actors floated down the aisle and out of sight like ancient ghosts. At last Miss Bankhead, followed by her maid, was sufficiently together to go to her hotel room. As she crossed the stage, she saw me and was on me like a tiger, cursing me at the top of her voice for not standing by her on the matter of the settings. I said that I hadn't because I liked the sets, whereupon she lost all control and, looking half insane, began to scream at me, the climax of which *aria furiosa*, for reasons I didn't understand, was to call me a "Turk." This apparently had some sinister meaning for the Pride of Alabama, and she gave it her all.

It was then that I became a director. The dam broke. In the circle of the full crew, with Myerberg on his cot and the company manager, Bennie Stein, at my side, trying to restrain me, I lost my head. No one could stop me. I told Bankhead, at the top of my voice and in the crudest language, how shamefully she'd behaved. I told her that I despised her and that everybody else did too. I said, yes, I was a Turk and could yell louder than her—she was yelling back at me all this time, but I was louder. I told her I wasn't going to stand for any more shit from her, and when she continued to exit, down the steps into the audience (steps that she was to use in the second act and that she'd also complained about), I followed her to the lip of the stage and yelled after her all the way down the aisle until she disappeared at the back of the auditorium. "I know you've been trying for a month to have me fired," I shouted, "but I'm still here—see me? I'm still here!"

By then she'd gone, leaving the high ground to me. When she'd disappeared and I was quiet at last, the crew, seated in a circle around the stage, gave me a full round of applause. I walked into the center of that circle and looked at them all, acknowledging their endorsement. I'd made the grade. They considered me a director.

That occasion was the first time I'd permitted myself the anger that can save your life. When I got back to my hotel room, I found that my belly, which had been tightening every night after work and in the morning before rehearsals, was relaxed. And I stopped having headaches.

The next morning, I walked through the stage door and onto the stage, a hero to all. I owned the place. She didn't speak to me and I spoke to her only to deliver mechanical instructions. The memory of what had happened the night before was vivid, for her and for me and for everyone working on that production. I didn't apologize for cursing her. She was still complaining, but much more quietly, and only to poor Myerberg on his cot; this time it was about the steps leading to the audience, which she had to descend. I told Mike she was right—throwing her that bone—that those steps were rickety and should be shored up; then I didn't wait for Mike to give the order: I instructed the show's carpenter to immediately make the steps firm and safe. Myerberg was too weak to take charge, so I took over.

The opening went surprisingly well. I think the whole company, Bankhead included, was surprised at how smoothly the show went and how good the audience's reaction was. A full house was impressed, and they were amused. There's nothing as reassuring to an actor as laughter from an audience. Bankhead got more than her share; the audience adored her. She looked at me as she came out of her dressing room to leave the theatre, but she didn't say a word. If I expected a concession from her, I wasn't to get it; the expression on her face offered this contrary message: "Despite the obstacles you and Myerberg put in my way"—so I read her—"I came through, didn't I? You no-good Turk bastard!"

M A N Y   Y E A R S later, in 1983, looking through the papers that Molly left behind (she died in 1963), I found this letter from Florence March.

Dear Molly Thacher: I thought in forty years of living that I'd learned to mind my own business but I've had a compulsion to write you as another member of the "Wives Club." I hope you'll forgive me if I seem impertinent—it's just that if Freddie felt about me as Gadg does about you, I'd like to know it.

Last night we really had a triumph—a very difficult delicately balanced play came to life in an amazingly smooth performance and everyone felt that Gadg was largely responsible for it. We all gathered in Mr. Myerberg's suite and the room was filled with real enthusiasm from Phil Barry, Bob Ardrey, Harold Freedman, John O'Hara, etc. Gadg came over and sat on the couch and was very quiet. I asked him if anything troubled him and he said, "I didn't hear from Molly." He wanted to phone you but was afraid to wake you so late. But I had the feeling that only your approval would have been important to him.

Whenever in Mrs. Antrobus he wanted to point out to me some really fine quality—some moment of understanding or pride—he would explain it and smile so tenderly and say, "My wife, Molly, is like that."

Now after fifteen years of marriage, I know Freddie feels that way about me but there were so many times in the past when I was fighting through some feeling of hurt pride and the feeling that the battle wasn't worth the price. I would have been helped by knowing that I was basically his *raison d'être*.

Please forgive me if I've been bold but I know from the picture Gadg has unconsciously given me of you that I'd like you and so I wish you well. Sincerely, Florence March.

As far as I know, that letter was not answered.

You've realized by now that I had the gift of dissembling. The impression I'd made on Florence may have been seventy-five percent accurate; there were, however, concurrent and contradictory feelings. The opening had been a great success, and I felt elated and quite independent. As for Molly, I no longer knew where she was. I'd had a talk with Bob Ardrey (we were still close friends), and he'd told me that Jack Houseman—yes, that one again; he seemed to be on both sides of my street—had offered Bob and was about to offer Molly a job with the Voice of America, which Houseman was heading up. I could write her there, he said. Bob had also told me that Molly had found a small house in the East Nineties and had rented it.

That was a definite move away. I admired her for it—she was on her own. I wrote to her new address, a kind of acknowledgment that she—and I—was now independent. The new friend I'd taken up with didn't replace Constance. Or, in another way, Molly. I learned what "casual" meant. But even if it was a dead marriage, I was determined to preserve a link of friendship, at least that. In mid-October, from Baltimore, I sent her a couple of notices (not enthusiastic) and this note that stretched into a letter:

Ardrey told me where I could write you. Enclosed find two newspaper reactions; the third was somewhere in between; also befuddled. I'm very discouraged about everything and everybody tonight. The atmosphere of hatred between Myerberg and the cast is beginning to be felt in the performance and it was very hard to jack the cast up— feeling as they do—to any kind of rehearsal after those notices. Bankhead is sick or says she is. March is sick. Eldridge is personally discouraged. Reed got hit on the head with the curtain shortly following a heart attack. The Marches, when they get tired, give evidence that they're too rich and don't need the theatre and all this trouble. Bankhead resorts first to screaming and when she is shouted down—my privilege—resorts to hysteria, sniveling, weeping, threatening, and announcements to the company that she is quitting. Reed chimes in with her bombast, old-time stuff. The cast hates Myerberg, he despises them; he's firing three people to save money and the cast has appealed to Wilder who answered with evasive wires, putting his backing on Myerberg in a wire to him. Meantime the scenery falls, Myerberg raves at the crew who mutter threats to his life. Often it feels as if I'm the only one who holds everything together. The whole damned company and everyone connected with it tug at my arm around every corner. They whisper to me, complain to me, and ask me to interfere for them on this or the other particular.

Still we do business here, $2,500 opening night and that's good money. Wartime Baltimore is like a box office man with a hit. You have to beg a taxi to take you. The town is full of money, noisy, dirty, crowded with soldiers, sailors, and prostitutes spilling out of bars which pour out loud music. The crew in the theatre is composed entirely of old men, hard of sight and hearing and shaky of limbs. All the young men are in the service.

I live by myself and have no girl.

New Haven, when we left, seemed deserted and empty. I guess I spent the happiest six weeks of my life there. 1932.

I sent the kids some candy.

This letter is not totally candid. One thing I left out was Bankhead's effort to make up with me. I'd had a letter from her, which I couldn't then and can't now altogether decipher. She must have been "loaded" when she wrote it. It starts: "Gadget! It is 4 a.m. I have been awakened from my troubled sleep like from a nightmare. . . ." And then I can't decipher most of what follows except that she is showering Florence and Freddie with scorn, feels that they are "passionless" and "conventional" and "have given up the ghost." I was shocked for the first time into some kind of respect for Bankhead, saw that she did care, passionately, about the play. I remembered an old saying: "Anyone who cannot feel *passionate* love for women, flowers, or wine or for the work he is doing, anyone who is not in some way *un*reasonable and *un*balanced, will never, never have any talent for literature." This did not apply directly, but it did make me a little ashamed of what I'd thought about the woman.

Then one night, an hour or so after the show, there was an urgent knock on my hotel room door. I had no idea who it might be, but those days, with the constant crises and threats of violence, I could not ignore any knock as commanding as this one sounded. I jumped out of bed, unlocked the door, and leaped back under the sheets. Bankhead came in. Wasting no time, she dropped her short brown skirt. She never wore underpants. When she pulled off her beige sleeveless sweater, I remember noting that her breasts were pendulous. We hadn't talked in weeks except formally. If this was her way of breaking the ice, she'd gone clean through it. Now I believe it was as close as she could come to conceding victory to me. I'd outlasted her, at least that. She made a dash for my bed but stopped cold when she saw there was someone in it with me—also a member of the cast, but from a more modest salary level. Tallulah looked at me with a terrible fury, growled like an animal, pulled on her clothes, and left.

. . .

V A R I E T Y comes out on Wednesday of every week; it's our scorecard. The favorable review of our New Haven opening was written by a dour chap whose name was the one Ben Jonson might have given him: Mr. Bone. I thought maybe now my actors would feel better and stop griping, a hope that had no more foundation than a wish.

The day after *Variety* was on the stands, I received a surprise telephone call in the middle of the night: Constance. She'd read *Variety* and "just had to" congratulate me. I was so pleased to hear her voice that for a few seconds I didn't know what she was saying. Then I got it; she was telling me her news—which must have been the real reason she'd called, because it overflowed her lips. She'd met Sam Goldwyn, and he'd liked her, seen her again, and been "crazy about me." He'd told her that he was going to bring her to California to make some tests and hinted about the girl's part opposite Danny Kaye in the film he was preparing. I asked her when she was going out, trying not to sound anxious. She told me maybe mid-December—in seven weeks. Then, I said, we have two reasons to celebrate. It didn't take me more than another breath to invite her to come down to see my show, or for her to accept.

I'd given up on Molly—as she apparently had on me. The home she'd rented, the job she'd taken or would take with Houseman—the most sensible thing she could have done—quashed any absurd prospects I imagined I had. I was sated with the rancor everywhere around me and was hungry for the joy Constance could provide.

We had a night of continuous lovemaking, one time in my life when I never stopped. I found her as always clean and sweet, firm yet tender, nothing wrinkled, nothing extra, perfect. And altogether loving. It was a mild night, I remember; there was a waning moon. The windows of the hotel were wide, and we kept them thrown up. When we rested, we'd lean over the sills, side by side, and look out over the hushed city under its haze. Then back to bed. Perhaps our frantic intensity came to us because we knew that the new developments, on both sides, were a threat.

In the morning, we had breakfast in the room. "So I'll be going out west," she said. "Then what happens?" the man accustomed to being the center of his wife's life asked. "Then?" said the girl whose life was suddenly opening wide before her. "Then you'll come out too." She sounded confident and a little too commanding for my taste. "You've got to come out," she said, as if to close the subject. "When?" I said. "Soon," she said, "very soon. Don't leave me out there alone." Precisely my thought. "Okay," I said, "I'll do it. I'll come out."

Then we took a shower together and she was beautiful but suddenly quite pale. I realized that this life-hungry creature was not a wife, not even a steady girl, but a young woman with desperate ambitions and now with a way to satisfy them, a career person with good prospects ahead, ones that were—I should face it—sure to separate us. I decided not to talk about that, not to anticipate trouble but, leaving well enough alone, go on from day to day and enjoy each hour for what it provided. I'd raised this girl from a slightly shabby usher—I recalled the little black uniform with a shiny seat that she'd worn in the Belasco Theatre—to what she was that night, a sensitive, spirited young woman. Neither of us could possibly have imagined that what we'd resurrected that night would continue through many long separations over 2,800 miles for the next two years.

N O W, forty-five years after the production of *The Skin of Our Teeth* and my adventures with it, perhaps I see who and what I was—and am—more clearly. For instance, now I can freely acknowledge that I've always wanted a secure domestic life and, at the same time, the freedom of the bachelor's existence. But it never works. Somebody gets hurt. The curse of my life has been the illusion that I could have both. Still I've wanted it all, and in a way, gentled by the passing years, I still do. You know what I'm talking about. You're not altogether different, are you?

I'm not making reference to my sex life. I'm trying to deal with the whole thing.

For instance: I've preferred to believe that I'm an adventurous man, yet I remain bourgeois, even a bit stuffy, am now the head of a large, traditional family with nineteenth-century comforts in bed, bath, study, and at the dining table. My car is a Mercedes, not what I've sometimes envied, an Alfa Romeo.

I've dreamed of living, unencumbered by children, possessions, and pets, in a small apartment where I'd have only the essentials: my books, records, tapes, research, typewriter, paper in reams, razor-point pens by the box, and a full fridge. There, absolutely alone, I'd work every morning undisturbed by the emotional needs of others. At night I'd enjoy a flow of guests, never the same, no repeats.

But as I write this, I live happily and faithfully in a kind of zoo with an excellent young wife, her two children, a perfect secretary-assistant who runs my life, a devoted housekeeper, plus two dogs, two cats, and, at the other end of the phone line, five grown children and five grandchildren. Did I say unencumbered?

I value my young wife's old-fashioned morality and regular habits; she prefers to go to bed early and doesn't party. But even up until the last of my sixties, I'd found no way to resist adventures in other bedrooms. I was still learning that a dual devotion wouldn't work.

I have the reputation of being gregarious. In company I am happy; I laugh, tease, joke, challenge. In the summer, when friends come to play tennis on our court, I am overjoyed to see them. I am also overjoyed to see them leave.

I'm a neat man, but I'm a saver, a collector, a clipper, an accumulator. Wherever I've lived, there has piled up a mountain of notes, papers, letters, plans for projects I'd never do—to all of which I have now to pay attention. That's why it's taking me so long to write this damned book.

From time to time I make up my mind to spend the rest of my life in the country, wearing the same jeans and sweatshirt until they rot and fall off. I'd know the signs of the seasons coming and going and learn the technique of producing early tomatoes. Still I can't get away from this horrible metropolis; Manhattan's chaos attracts me, its dangers fascinate me. I've contrived, in this case, to have both, and I believe I always will.

I admire the U.S.A. more than any other country; it's given me everything I want and need. But from time to time, I make up my mind that where I'd really like to live is Paris. Oh, for the life of an old culture and rich food! I also want a home in Greece—which I will never have.

I want to live frugally; I am a Depression baby. But I want to travel everywhere—Japan, India, Mexico, Tanzania, and the full length of the Amazon. I want surprise and adventure. But when I do leave home, I carry an air travel card, an American Express card, a thick folder of traveler's checks, a small medicine kit, and a fully made out return ticket. I make damned sure I'll get home safely.

I want to be anonymous, to walk the streets of my city unrecognized. Yet I enjoy my modest fame, and when a stranger stops me and tells me she (preferably she) loves my books and films, I enjoy that. I leave her before she's through speaking, but that's to create the impression that, being a modest person, I am embarrassed by praise.

Politically, I consider myself left of center. I believe there won't be peace in the world until everyone has a dry, clean home and enough to eat. Socialism! Yes. Still I have a decent bundle in the bank and live off the interest. I own a stake in the capitalist system. I'm glad Ronnie brought inflation down, but I wouldn't vote for him.

I am an American, with a shameless drive for achievement and an aggressive stance in the world. I am also an Anatolian, with the cunning and indirection of my ancestors. I have their tenacity in trouble, their ability to absorb punishment without whimpering. Defeated, I back off, then return unobserved to where I was. I am my father, a modest mini-merchant; I am my uncle who lost forty thousand dollars in one day playing baccarat at Monte Carlo. My mother? I can't claim that. She was a saint.

I have at times put my feelings into a form that stirs others, but I turn away when I'm called an artist and don't enjoy the company of people who call themselves artists. I am proud of some of my work, but I doubt its final worth. I am more impressed with the films of other directors than with my own. But when critics make that judgment, I resent it.

I am proud of what I've been and done—my record, so to speak. With a few exceptions, which embarrass me to recall but which I am now fool enough to reveal, I respect myself. Writing about me offends my modesty, yet here is this long book, and you know what it's about. I believe what writers must believe: that when I tell about myself, I tell about you.

I want to be liked. I want to be feared.

I am cowardly. I am brave.

I am handsome. I am ugly.

I am vain. I am humble.

I am thin and wiry. I am bulky and big-boned.

I am slippery. I am reliable.

I am belligerent, but I don't fight, because I know I can't.

My present wife calls me "The Rock." I won't tell what my previous wife called me.

I am a determined and energetic man, and I don't stop working for any reason at any time; I work on Christmas morning—about that there is no contradiction. But in every other particular, what I've been describing holds. I've repeatedly astonished people by what seem to be total reversals of positions and attitudes. This has sometimes led to distrust of me. Again and again my conflicting desires have led to the surrender of one or the other.

That is where my life was at the time about which I've been writing. That, for the most part, is where it is still.

T H E S H O W opened in New York in mid-November, and Thornton had what he deserved, an enormous hit. *Skin* became the only thing to see, and we were set for a long run. Many of the audience were mystified—what did the play mean?—and there were walkouts. But those reactions were part of the talk that made the play immediately famous. I overheard one couple talking as they left the theatre. "What's it all about?" the man complained to his wife. "Why, George," she said, "it's about love and hate and passion and *everything*—ever since the world began." "Well," the man said, "there must be more to it than that." There were intellectuals who expressed disappointment in the "text," saying—to use one of Miss Bankhead's phrases—that there was less there than met the eye. My friend Boris Aronson came to see it, and as he walked up the aisle after the first act, I asked him how he liked the play. "Very good," he said. "It's so confused!" I caught him at the same place after the second act, expecting renewed praise. "How do you like it now, Boris?" I asked. "Less," he answered. "It's clearing up."

Each member of the cast was admired equally. Did I expect that the acclaim given to each of the performers would ease the tensions in the cast? Would they be more tolerant of one another's characters, wiser, more understanding people; would they be in time more generous to each other? Might all that have been reasonably expected?

Within ten days after the opening there was another crisis backstage, and to judge from the degree of Florence March's hysteria, a serious one. She summoned me to the theatre and delivered herself of a bitter complaint, the same one: I had to do something about Bankhead. "What now?" I asked. "Don't you see the show?" Florence wanted to know. (I am notorious for never going back to a production after it's opened and have been justly criticized for this.) "I haven't recently," I admitted. "Well, do," Florence said. "It's your show after all, and notice what that bitch is doing during my marriage speech in Act Two."

Grudgingly I went to the matinee and saw what Bankhead had thought up to do during the speech Florence believed in above all else in the play. ("I didn't marry you because you were perfect. I didn't even marry you because I loved you. I married you because you gave me a promise. That promise made up for your faults and the promise I gave you made up for mine." And so on. I'm certain Florence was thinking of Freddie and herself as she spoke it.) During this outburst, central to the meaning of Mrs. Antrobus's character, Tallulah was throwing her head back over a railing downstage, letting her blond hair fall free, then combing it out slowly and proudly. Florence was right, of course—this byplay distracted from the effect of her big moment, and Bankhead knew what she was doing and was doing it on purpose.

I had a problem dealing with this bit of mischief: Bankhead, since our scene in my hotel room in Baltimore, had refused notes from me. But I pushed my way into her dressing room, without knocking. When I entered, she covered her chest and went on making up her face, taking no further notice of me. I spoke my piece and perhaps my tone was peremptory, but patience was a virtue I'd run out of. I was sick and tired of my cast and their carryings on. Bankhead finally turned, looked at me hatefully, then, speaking in her grandest manner, told me I was never to enter her dressing room again and that she didn't want to hear another word from me about her performance.

It so happened that Thornton had come east on leave to enjoy his great success, and what do I chuck into his lap but this wrangle? I told him that Mike had gone for a vacation in the sun, that he looked already dead when he left, so he couldn't help. And since I'd been forbidden the lady's dressing room, perhaps he'd speak to Bankhead and curb the absurd behavior of the daughter of the senior senator from the state of Alabama. Thornton gave me a nervous giggle and a nod, which should have made me suspicious, because if they meant anything, they meant that this kind of temperamental behavior from actresses intrigued him.

I hung around to see what the result of their interview would be and get Thornton's report. I heard laughter in two keys and loud enough to come through the walls. Thornton emerged nearly an hour later, slipped out the door at the side of the stage, hustled through the empty auditorium and into the street—without seeking me out. He had kept Miss Bankhead's friendship.

I had no choice except to go backstage and confess my failure—and our author's—to Freddie before the show that night. Freddie had a severe sore throat, and I hated to load this on him, but since the lady wouldn't let me into her dressing room and would not take criticism from me, there was nothing to do except tell Myerberg when he got back and suggest that he call Actors' Equity. "Don't bother," Freddie said, and went on preparing for the performance.

I watched the show from the wings. Bankhead did it again. Then, in the next act, she had her own big moment, one that was her favorite because it was both serious and sentimental. It followed an exit by Freddie. I saw him walk into the wings, where his dresser was waiting with a small enamel bowl in which there stood a glass containing a medical solution. Freddie lifted the glass to his lips, tilted his head back—he was standing just off-stage, where some of the audience could see him—and he gargled. Then he emptied his mouth into the enamel bowl and, as Bankhead spoke, gargled again—I could hear it clear across stage—and again emptied his mouth. As he went on, his gargles were timed to coincide with the lady's lines. I saw her look in Freddie's direction and get the message. My stage manager told me that at the next performance, "Talloo" did not comb out her hair during Florence's speech.

There's more to the story, and Freddie told me about it weeks later. He knew she'd come back at him with something, and she did. In the scene where they kiss, she thrust her tongue deep into his mouth. "What did you do?" I asked Freddie. "I bit it," he said. That took care of that. For a while.

Is it ironical that a play of such philosophical pretensions was being per-formed by a cast that squabbled in this childish manner? That's the theatre. I decided not to wait around for further backstage incidents but to "disap-pear," leaving the actors in a state of war. I recognized that the quarreling would go on for the eternity that Wilder's play dealt with. Some problems, I decided, have no solution. I comforted myself with this: The fact that Tallulah and Florence detested each other was better for the production than anything I might have squeezed out of the two actresses by directing them for this antagonism.

I was receiving expressions of admiration in the press, but while I en-joyed reading them, I was too distracted by my personal problem to appreciate what they meant for me professionally. Constance had gone west to test for Goldwyn; Molly, it appeared, had made a new life for herself. Having denied myself the backstage of my production, I was alone night and day. Too befuddled to seek new companions, I moved to a hotel, alone, and although now that I'm an old man I enjoy solitude, when I was thirty-two I did not. Constance wrote me ardent letters pleading for me to come west and be with her. But that would formally and perhaps permanently separate me from my wife and kids, and I wasn't ready for that. So I was stymied.

I was rescued from this dilemma—temporarily—when I was called in for a talk with Gilbert Miller, who was producing and directing a play starring Helen Hayes titled *Harriet*. Miller was a famous and affluent producer, an elitist whom age was bringing down. His name stood for distinction and high living on both sides of the Atlantic. He himself was physically gross, blown up by heavy food and fine wine. The play he was producing was about Harriet Beecher Stowe and was about to go in Henry Miller's Theatre, which Gilbert owned and had named after his father, a renowned actor-manager of the last century. He took me to an expensive lunch at Le Pavillon and, during the lobster bisque, asked me to take over for him. I asked to hear the play read by the actors he had cast. He made a phone call, came back, and said we could go right over—as soon as I'd had a dessert and he a glass of port.

The actors were sitting in a row across the stage when we arrived, and they looked discouraged. I met the authors, a plump, gentle lady who'd gone past "discouraged" to "distressed," and her collaborator, distinguished-looking in the manner of a second lead in a British parlor comedy. I guessed correctly that she was the writer and he the escort-husband. Miss Hayes greeted me warmly and, with Miller alongside, expressed an urgent wish that I take over. He seemed undisturbed by her forthrightness.

I'd found the play replete with honorable intentions but light on drama. It sounded worse when the actors read it, which is the contrary of what generally occurs. Miller and I were sitting side by side, facing the cast. After about half an hour I heard heavy breathing and, turning my head, saw that Gilbert, who was sitting only seven or eight feet from the lineup of actors, had fallen asleep. The reading continued. He continued to sleep. Apparently this had occurred before; none of the cast seemed to think it out of the ordinary. I understood why Miss Hayes had been so frantic for me to come in.

Since the play had been in rehearsal for a week, I would have two weeks' work, for which I'd be paid $500 per week, and from then on, through the projected road tour, I'd be getting one percent of the gross until I'd been paid $2,500, at which point my compensation would stop. I was new to the trade, didn't realize this was not a suitable salary for a lifesaver. I was being cheated. Perhaps the lure of getting with a famous producer influenced me. Or the desperate gleam in Miss Hayes's eyes. But more likely I was eager for a focus of concentration away from my messed-up personal life. This job would keep me apart from both women and give me the time I needed to think things over.

I found the cast charged with the eagerness that arises from desperation. I worked to bring order to chaos and hope to despair. Which I did. Miss Hayes—Helen—was soon devoted to me and said, later, that what I'd done was bring my "extraordinary energy" to work on this play. To be more energetic than a sleeping director is no trick; no one fell asleep while I was there. As soon as the actors knew what they were coming on stage to do and why, they worked with zest. The morale of the company was restored with its energy. I actually enjoyed Gilbert's company. To my astonishment, he made an excellent suggestion. "Do you think that will work?" I asked him. "Think!" he exclaimed. "I know it will. I saw it work in Paris"—and he named the theatre, the play, and the year. "I am," he continued, "the triumph of memory over a third-rate imagination."

The play became a great hit, and I was acclaimed again. Two hits on Broadway at the same time! The story of what I'd done to save *Harriet*— "save," they said—was retold everywhere, with exaggerations. I was credited with turning a rather undistinguished play and a demoralized cast into a "brave evening in the theatre." On opening night, the authors sent me a note of thanks, which contained this jingle: "Kazan, Kazan/ The miracle man/ Call him in/ As soon as you can." "Miracle man" had started with *The Skin of Our Teeth*, a play observers considered a uniquely difficult job, especially with Tallulah Bankhead. Now I'd directed another big star and guided the performance that many critics considered her best.

When I first came in and had watched a couple of days' rehearsals, I believed that Helen was doing what she'd done many times before, giving us her special cliché image: a peppy little woman, energetic and determined yet ladylike, taking charge of a situation but never in a way that might prove humiliating to her man. She would make her miracles happen prudently, ever adorable, sugar and spice. We'd all seen this performance before; the image was totally familiar, her effects threadbare. As gently as I could, I brought this to her attention and appealed to her pride. "You don't want to do what you've done so many times before, do you?" I asked. "You can give a performance that will astonish everyone."

Who could refuse so flattering a prospect? She did not. "I see what you mean," she said. But it wasn't easy for her. After a week, she said that she wasn't comfortable doing what I was asking for. "You feel uncomfortable," I said with paternal sternness, "because you've never done it before. But that is precisely its merit. You're putting on a new artistic suit of clothes; you can't help feeling uncomfortable." Helen, a bright person, saw my point. We struggled along and I was pleased with the result—a homespun, gritty zealot energizing her way out of the nineteenth century, a person of fiber, one I admired.

Then we had our opening on the road, and as soon as she had an audience out front, responding to her, she reverted, gave them what they wanted, her repertory of adorable fandangos. I particularly remember a brisk little walk around and around in a circle, which made the audience—mostly women—gurgle with glee. Harriet Beecher Stowe had become the role model for every woman out front. When I, with uncharacteristic delicacy, called this reversion to her attention, she looked at me strangely. She'd received an ovation the night before. What the hell did I want?

The fact is the audience adored her. She had an awesome hold on their emotions; they were enchanted. The very elements that I'd been trying so hard to get rid of, her cute mannerisms, were what the audience devoured. Every time this bright little pony kicked up her heels, they quivered. When she gave her head an impertinent little toss, the women in the audience chortled with glee. The less I liked her performance—I thought she was playing J. M. Barrie's *What Every Woman Knows* all over again—the more enthusiastically the audience responded. If a miracle had been performed, it was by her alchemy. Suppose, I asked myself, she'd given the performance I'd asked for: Would the play have been a success? Might not the audience who'd come to see Helen (what else?) have been disappointed? It would not have been "their" Helen. The irony was that my reputation as a miracle man had been created not so much by anything I'd done as by Helen's performance, which I didn't like and which I'd tried to eliminate.

B U T   T H E irony did not occur to me—not at that time. My success had got to me. I have a photograph of myself with Gilbert Miller, which I will spare you. When I "read" it, I see an arrogant young man dominating an old Anglophile who stares at him in bewilderment (if not in terror), as if for the first and only time in his life he's been scolded. Whatever Bankhead had caused to be released in me had made me—and so quickly!—into a supremely confident stud.

Yes, I was certainly enjoying my success and the fact that my worth had finally been proven and recognized. I was enjoying the flattery I was receiving wherever I went—and now from some unexpected sources. My father had begun cutting bits out of *The New York Times*, and I enjoyed the change in his view of me. I was happy with my mother's pride in me; I'd paid her back for the support she'd given me over so many years. I enjoyed my triumphs on the streets that border our theatres. The headwaiter at Sardi's became a familiar. He always had a good table for me, and everyone looked up as he led me to it. I enjoyed the adulation of theatre people, who, it seemed, were all talking about me. Young directors would soon begin to imitate my personal style.

I took unnecessary walks up and down Broadway—walk? a modified swagger—enjoying the recognition and the glances of admiration. I answered questions about my technique of direction, asserting my positions and making pronouncements that dared challenge. I decided to write a book about directing; I'd kept my notes from my Theatre of Action days. I enjoyed the write-ups I got, cut them out (they're at Wesleyan University now), and savored the column squibs—even when I knew they were phony and exaggerated. I enjoyed being more successful than Harold Clurman and Lee Strasberg. I wondered what Molly thought of my productions. Had she read the newspapers? I'd become a theatre legend—what did she think of that?

Not a word from her. I was now the director everyone wanted and had a purse modestly plumped, so I sent Molly some money. She wrote me (at last) that she was "most grateful." It surprised me to find that she hadn't expected me to provide for her; my ethical standing there seemed to be very low. I knew I deserved that. I also knew that there was no comfort—or flattery—coming my way from that source. I sent her seats to *Harriet*.

My marriage, it seemed to me, was at an end. The hell with it! Reckless of consequences, hungry for relief, change, and pleasure, somewhat relieved of guilt, I decided to take what I wanted, whatever the cost. I bought a ticket to Los Angeles, arriving early in the morning. Constance met me in the lobby of the Hollywood Hotel, where I'd made a reservation. The room and bed had not been made up, but we hung a Do Not Disturb sign on the door handle and locked the door. I was a very needy male animal, she the prettiest and happiest I'd ever seen her. She put me at ease in a way I hadn't been since she'd left New York.

In that rabid community, I encountered the full extent of my success. No one knew about my failures; it was as if I'd directed only two plays, *The Skin of Our Teeth* and *Harriet*, both smash hits, both running on Broadway, both with difficult stars whom I'd handled skillfully and successfully. I was the kid with the halo, come in out of the blue. I was also—suddenly—in my own way—rather handsome. Women's eyes were telling me this, and I was ready to believe. "Who is he?" they asked. "Oh, don't you know? He's the one who—who—" "Who what?" Then they were informed who I was, in legend-sized exclamations, inaccurate so more flattering. "Who's he seeing?" they asked.

It seemed everyone knew I'd arrived in town. There were mini-interviews in the columns. The rumor that I was having "marital difficulties" added to my glamour. What genius doesn't have marital difficulties? The fact that I was new in the community, a novelty, added its luster. "What is he, Armenian?" "No, no. Jewish. Like us." I was invited to spiffy dinners and seated at the hostess's right (Constance mid-table), served the house specialties and the choice wines, all offered for my approval. The hostess watched as I sipped. I was credited with a New York sophistication I didn't have. I often asked: Could that be me they're talking and writing about? Still I ate it up.

Everyone had or pretended to have seen my productions. Thornton had won the Pulitzer Prize; in that big directors' world, I received much of the credit. "I don't see how you did it!" people said. I maintained a modest silence, the height of immodesty. The truth was that I'd come to believe I was better than other (or most other) directors in New York. Hadn't I seen their work? Hollywood, for that frenetic hour, agreed. Producers I didn't know were asking to meet me. Would I be interested in directing a film? "Of course; why not? What film?" A short man from the William Morris Agency took me to lunch and told me I had an unlimited future and would be very rich. A few days later, I had the final public endorsement: The head of that agency, Abe Lastfogel, famous for his honesty and cunning, took me to dinner at Romanoff's, where the great stars, directors, and actors ate. Over our "butterfly steaks" ("No butter," Abe's wife commanded; the waiter reassured her), Abe urged me to move west for good. I said I was considering it. He said he'd personally "handle" me—as if that would be an honor.

So it went. I'd become a show business myth.

Struggling—my first Hollywood film

        I I N T E R R U P T my narrative to tell about the character of Samuel Goldwyn (Goldfish), the producer; without his knowing it, he was to affect the course of my life. Goldwyn was one of the breed who swarmed into southern California during the twenties and thirties, the men who created what's called Hollywood. With one exception, I knew them all: Louis B. Mayer and his muscleman Eddie Mannix, B. P. Schulberg, the Warner brothers, Darryl Zanuck, Spyros Skouras, Harry Cohn, David Selznick, Samuel Goldwyn, and the lesser men who consorted with these marvelous monsters and used them for models. They were all men of unflagging energy of a size that's no longer about, with the possible exception of Rupert Murdoch, the Australian publisher. "Tycoon" is too tame a word to suggest the quality of the men I'm recalling; that is why I've left out the more cultured Irving Thalberg. I'm talking about a gold rush, about desperate men in a bare-knuckle scramble over rugged terrain, roughnecks thinly disguised, men out of a book by Frank Norris or Theodore Dreiser, alike in reach and taste, occasional companions in social intercourse but, when they felt they had to, ready to go for each other's throats.

        In the prime of their energy, these men were impatient to get to their offices every morning, rather like a champion fighter pushing down the aisle of a crowded sports arena, hungry to get to the ring and beat hell out of a challenger. Despite a few bad scenes, I admired them for their manic intensity and their vanity. Yes, vanity. With them it was a creative force. They competed with each other in the most wholehearted and uninhibited fashion to see who'd make the best picture of the year, who'd pile up the biggest grosses, who'd sign up the most important new star, director, writer. Making movies was their life; nothing else mattered.

Samuel Goldwyn was a proud man, proud of his productions with good reason, but also proud of himself: his figure, his bearing, his appearance, and his physical vitality. At sixty-three—when he had Constance under contract—he made a practice of walking from his home to his office every morning, followed closely by his chauffeur and car, ready to pick him up if he puffed. He must have been aware that people were observing and admiring him. "Oh, he does that every morning. Yes, he's quite a man, Mr. Goldwyn." Provided with the best suitings and haberdashery, carefully turned out by a devoted valet, he made an admirable figure. Sam wanted to look like Samuel Goldwyn.

Constance didn't know how lucky she was. Sam did not make a "program" of films every year, as did Harry Cohn and Darryl Zanuck, the Warners and Louis Mayer. He made films one at a time and was interested only in the best, employed the finest screenwriters, only the top stars, and, whenever he could, the man who was for him the best director of that day, Willy Wyler. As was the case with his contemporaries, the extraordinary energy of this man was sexually rooted, and he, no less than the others, had from time to time to assure himself of his continuing potency, but he did not scramble around his desk, chasing starlets over whom he had the hire/fire power. Here, too, he went only for the best.

They tell of Madeleine Carroll sitting on Sam's office sofa one day, cool, poised, and very British. For a onetime glove salesman out of New York City, she must have been an irresistible attraction. He managed to get on top of her, but this lady was out of a sophisticated culture and had considerable experience dealing with rampant males out of control. With a clever twist of her body, she dislodged Sam from her belly and threw him on the floor. As he "adjusted" his clothing, Sam drew himself up into his most dignified posture and, speaking in his characteristic sibilant purr, proclaimed, "I have never been so insulted in my life!"

Sam was proud, as was all this generation of producers, of the talent he discovered. Apparently he believed that Constance had what it took to make a star, for he was seriously considering testing her for the leading role opposite Danny Kaye in *Up in Arms*. The question is why he was so impressed with Constance, who had very little acting experience. Since all these men thought of every film they made, no matter how serious the theme, as a love story, they made a practice of casting by a simple rule:

Does the actress arouse me? Or will the actor awake desire in the women in an audience? When it came to judging a new actor's sex appeal, Darryl Zanuck would call in his wife, Virginia; he thought highly of her judgment and candor. Or he'd gather secretaries who were sure of their jobs and would speak their "truth." He might also be influenced by what was known as the actor's "track record." But when it came to actresses, not Darryl, not Harry Cohn, not Louis Mayer, not Sam Goldwyn needed consultation. They went by a simple rule and a useful one: Do I want to fuck her?

I believe this rule of casting is not only inevitable but correct, and quite the best method for the kind of films they made. The audience must be interested in a film's people in this elemental way. If not, something essential is missing. If the producer wasn't interested in an actress this way, he was convinced an audience wouldn't be and that this actress wouldn't "draw flies."

There was a more general aspect to this casting practice. Since many of these men who became the great producers evolved out of the very bottom of the middle class and were not blessed by birth with what might make them easily gain the favors of attractive women, and furthermore, since many of them were Jews and felt in some way "outside" the goyish upper-class society with which their films dealt, they were particularly drawn to blondes and to "proper" ladies (Grace Kelly). The unspoken, unwritten drama would consist of bringing these immaculate-appearing women (Deborah Kerr) down to earth (or the sea's surf), where the rest of us wallowed and sinned. Sam Spiegel preferred his leading ladies to be long-legged, small-breasted, "coltish" Anglos. *Gentleman's Agreement* had Dorothy McGuire, and Julie Garfield, a street kid in type, was given a scene telling her off. Hitchcock favored ladies who looked standoffish (Madeleine Carroll, Tippi Hedren, Grace Kelly) and pure (Ingrid Bergman), no matter what the facts of their personal lives. The film's action would consist of getting these women into trouble and bringing them down into the "muck" that is humanity.

There was another attractive image of women that these old fellows liked: the sassy girl, the ones advertising men today call "provocatives." Sam Goldwyn repeatedly told Constance that he was going to make her into another Carole Lombard, and she believed him. This kind of woman, by challenging the opposite sex, aroused in men a desire to subdue and dominate. Sam saw this possibility in Constance, and he believed it an elemental, basic quality she was born with. It certainly wasn't acting talent he saw, because adorable as Constance was, she had little acting talent. But she was a hoyden, and Sam saw it.

Sam would sit her on his knee, she told me, and give her instructions as to how she should behave. How? Like a star. Above the rest of womankind. He edged her away from certain friends, encouraged others. He advised secrecy in all personal matters. He introduced her to his confidential coterie, which social contacts were, in effect, auditions. Sam would call his friends the very next morning and ask what they'd thought of her. She was always on view and on trial. It happened that most of his friends found her charming, but some, wiser and more experienced, responded with: "I'd like to see some footage on her first."

Sam was telling her how to dress, walk, and make up. He was critical of her street makeup, favored as little as possible, wiped it off himself. He cautioned her not to say too much, ever. "They can't fault you for what you didn't say," was his idea. He believed mystery an important star element. Garbo! I didn't believe this was Constance's style, but he had her ear and her trust, worked to create an intimate and dependent relationship, made her feel free to come to him at any time for advice and think of him as a kind of daddy—a rather lecherous one, to be sure.

Constance

He'd instructed his press department to begin gathering material on her, photographs in all poses, dressed and undressed, as well as all kinds of stories, true or imagined, and have the material at hand so that when "it" happened, they were ready!

When it came to her tests, and there were several, he gave her "everything"—the best cameraman, the best wardrobe (he bought her four new outfits for the street, all a little overwhelming, I thought, but I was not in the business of making stars)—and assigned the man who was to direct the film, Elliott Nugent, to direct her tests. She was flattered to death by his interest and concern.

She told me that Goldwyn was eager to meet me and took me into his office herself; I suppose she was showing me how "in" she was with him. But it was so; they were very cozy. He told me he was going to make a star of her. I'd met Sam several years before, when I tested for his *Dead End*. I reminded him, but I don't think he even heard me. He couldn't think of anything except the film at hand. His energy and optimism got to me; he had me believing she was going to make it!

She would be at the studio all day, rehearsing with Danny Kaye, whose film debut it was also to be. I was free but didn't know what to do. As my interest in tennis wore out, I became restless and bored. There is nothing to do in southern California. At night she was edgy with hope and anxiety.

I sympathized but began to feel that she might prefer to be without distraction during the big moments ahead. I told her I'd go back to New York for a bit—to see my kids, I said. She didn't object. We'd been ecstatically happy.

I N N E W Y O R K , I found that Helen Hayes had been asking for me. She wanted some moments in the performance looked after. Nothing bores me more than picking up pieces, patching holes, and quieting backstage unrest. Without going to the Henry Miller, I went to our country place, to see how the new furnace was working. It was okay. I stayed on; it was my chance to be alone. When I got back to New York, I found that Helen, peeved by my show of indifference, had influenced Gilbert to stop paying me my fifty-dollar-a-week director's royalty. Perhaps she thought this would bring me rushing back to the theatre. It was an act that called for an answer, but after complaining to Miller and being told that Helen was his whole show and he didn't dare offend her, I said the hell with *Harriet* and didn't bother with it anymore. I recalled Helen's gratitude when I came in to take over rehearsals and the phrase "miracle man," all forgotten for fifty dollars. It was a lesson—mostly for my lawyer.

A C O N F E S S I O N . When the Soviets made their pact with Hitler, in August of 1939, my feelings were ambivalent. I understood the pact as an effort by the U.S.S.R. to protect its western border by turning Hitler in the other direction. This alliance, I told myself, is what a war of survival makes necessary. That was also the line of Communists everywhere. Despite resigning in disgust from the Party four years earlier, I still had protective feelings about Russia; the indoctrination endured. What I'd been against in 1935, I told myself, was specifically the American Party and its meddling in the theatre. The Soviet Union, after all, was the one place on earth where socialism was being attempted. A nation that had produced the films and theatre I admired had to have a sound core. And there was this: Since the Russian Revolution in 1917, the "Capitalist Camp" (there's a good old CP phrase!) had tried in every way to destroy the U.S.S.R.

That this loyalty had endured surprises me now. I do believe my reaction was more prevalent—secretly—than is generally supposed. What finally did turn me off was the flip-flop of the leading comrades two years later when Hitler turned his panzers east, invading Poland, then Russia itself. Many left-wing intellectuals vaulted shamelessly—in twenty-four hours— from considering the war imperialist to proclaiming it a war to save civilization, which it certainly was. I stood to the side of the great flood of pro-Soviet feeling that followed. That was the beginning of the end of my attachment to the U.S.S.R.

It was not until the Japanese attack on Pearl Harbor a few months later that I began to feel allegiance to our side in the war. I went to my draft board; they ruled me 4-F. When I wasn't drafted, I persevered with my work in the theatre. Later, in California, I observed with amusement the studio heads, producers, and directors becoming "instant colonels." They threw off their houndstooth sports coats, to be measured by expensive tailors for officers' uniforms. In London they moved into the Connaught and Claridge's, both hotels well behind the lines. But John Huston and Darryl Zanuck did court danger, and I admired those of my friends who enlisted as privates and went where they were ordered. I particularly admired Jimmy Stewart, who took risks over Germany beyond anyone else's. Meantime, I read the newspapers and followed the war from the sidelines, as I would a vast drama. In Hollywood the war was a great distance away; it was remote.

But when I returned to New York, I had contrary feelings. I felt ashamed and guilty as well as something else: I was missing out on the experience of my generation. As a filmmaker, could I afford that? Since I was still 4-F—I checked again—I tried to find another place for myself. I could speak Greek and Turkish, so it occurred to me I might have value in the Office of Strategic Services. I'd made a friend in California who was in the OSS, and I wrote asking that he propose me.

Meanwhile, I agreed to do a show in New York for the Department of Agriculture that would explain the importance of rationing to the public. I worked with Earl Robinson, an old associate from the left theatre, and with Arthur Arent, who'd been the main writer on the Living Newspaper. We cooked up lively direct-at-the-audience stunts, including one novelty where a woman on stage has an argument about rationing with her image on a motion picture screen. My old dance teacher, Helen Tamiris, represented a juicy steak in the movements of modern (aka revolutionary) dance. After we'd put it all together, the show was praised by Washington and, so I was told, played all over the country. I never heard of it again and have no idea if it was successful as a "Learning Play." I do remember that I felt less shame afterward; I'd done a bit of my duty.

I heard from Constance that she had the role with Danny Kaye; I should "hustle my parts" out there. She came to meet me, looking prettier than ever and suddenly more grown-up. Later she drew a very hot bath for us to share, and perfumed it. I wondered where she'd learned about perfuming a bath. We went to the Beachcomber's, our favorite haunt, to "recover," lifted three "golds." (A "gold" is a delicious, smooth, fragrant, sweet, tart, frothy rum drink.) The next day was Sunday, and we stayed in all day and talked, as she urgently wished, seriously. I represented no doubt to her about my divorce. Molly had asked for it, I said—which was true. I assured her that after one more stage show in New York, I intended to come west for good and make films—which was also the truth.

I was getting attractive offers to direct films; it was a matter of choosing. MGM wanted me on a term contract. Warner Brothers and their energetic, plump producer, Jerry Wald, had signed my friend Clifford Odets to prepare a screenplay from a story idea Jerry had; it was to be called *An Errand for Uncle*, a patriotic piece for wartime consumption. But it was an idea, not a script, and while I thought Jerry fun to be with, I also thought him a con artist; if I didn't like one idea, he had another, often quite contradictory, on the tip of his tongue. Despite Clifford, I backed away. Abe Lastfogel had taken me to Fox, the "goyish" studio, to meet Louis D. Lighton, a producer, who was going to make a film of Betty Smith's novel *A Tree Grows in Brooklyn*. I liked this man immediately. He spoke in a way I wasn't accustomed to, from far over on the right, but he also spoke of feeling and capturing an emotion, of humans in stress and the ambivalence within people. He reminded me of a New England Yankee, a farmer perhaps, a tall, proud man with a flat belly that contrasted with the chummy lard around Jerry Wald's middle. Actually, what Lighton did when he wasn't producing pictures was to "run" cattle in Arizona. He gave me a copy of Betty's book and told me I could take my time reading it.

With all this attention, I was living a delightful life—days of flattery, nights in "Arabia." There'd be spasms of guilt—why wasn't my mother writing me? how were the kids doing?—but when Constance urged me to move into an apartment she was taking on Sycamore Drive in anticipation of her success, I did. She was in a whirl—acting with Danny Kaye, enjoying constant attention, makeup, costumes, publicity! Everybody on the set loved her, I could see that. Whenever I could, I hung out in her dressing room, and she'd rush in between takes, looking for me. How cute she looked in her straw hat or, in another sequence, in her army fatigues! Bliss!

W H I L E all this happiness was being savored and all unhappiness suppressed, my old friend Cheryl Crawford asked me to direct a musical. Since I'd never done one, I was intrigued. This would be my last stage show, I told Constance, and once back east, I'd go into the details of the divorce. She was so busy and so happy, not only with her work but with the protestations of enduring love I'd made her, that one morning as she was taking off for work, I still in bed, she kissed me, so giving me her blessing, and was gone. I remember what I felt when I was alone: relief. I had another respite.

Back in New York, living in a borrowed apartment, I began meeting with Kurt Weill, whom I knew from *Johnny Johnson*, and with S. J. Perelman and Ogden Nash, whom I did not know. Weill and Perelman were preparing the "book" of the show, and Ogden was finishing his lyrics for the songs. Kurt, it soon became obvious, dominated this cabal of odd fellows. I asked him why they wanted me to direct the show. His response, spoken with the most persuasive conviction, was that they wanted the musical directed as if it was a drama, not in the old-fashioned, out-front staging tradition of our musical theatre. That style was dated now; *Oklahoma* had changed everything. After all, Kurt observed, songs were a continuation of the dialogue and should be so treated.

I'd read the "book" and heard most of the songs and told Kurt that although I'd liked the songs, I'd thought the book abysmal. (He must have told this to S. J. Perelman, which couldn't have endeared me to him.) That would be my job, Kurt said—to make the dialogue scenes carry their share of the load. That was why they wanted me.

But despite whatever I did and despite Mary Martin, who could make an audience believe anything, when we took *One Touch of Venus* on the road for its tryout, the book was still foolish and boring. Nothing we had going between the musical numbers entertained the audience. The "miracle man" had not performed a miracle. Dissatisfaction with my direction was expressed by Sid Perelman; he said I lacked a sense of humor. He was right—I didn't respond to the humor of his dialogue. Our audiences also lacked a sense of humor. His stuff may have read well in *The New Yorker*, but it didn't play on stage. We therefore resorted to the solution most musicals finally come to: We cut the dialogue scenes down to little more than "bridges," introductions to the songs and dances, so we could move as quickly as possible from one musical number to the next.

Kurt also had a complaint. He cornered me and, without referring to his earlier contrary instruction, said that his songs had to be sung down center, facing straight out front. He was as absolute about that as he'd previously been about his "continuation of the dialogue" concept. So I put Mary on a small, plain chair down center and told her to sing Kurt's best song straight to the audience, person to person. The effect was enchanting. But after I'd done something of that kind to the other songs, there was nothing more for me to do except bring the talent on and turn it loose, throw light cues, time blackouts, and take the curtain up and down.

I was soon reduced in rank. Conferences were being held without me. The scenery that I'd planned with Howard Bay was attacked and, without my concurrence, replaced. I found out who was boss. Not me. I'd become a sort of overpaid stage manager, subservient to everyone else. I decided that this kind of theatre was another species, one for which I had no talent. But that didn't save my pride.

Nevertheless the show, by the time we got to New York, was an enormous success—three in a row for me. Why? How had that happened? This time I faced the facts. The dialogue scenes didn't matter—even if they'd been better. The credit for our success belonged not to the "miracle man" but to three marvelous women Cheryl Crawford had brought together and to Kurt.

Mary Martin, our "Venus," was then, as she is now, an extraordinary girl—"girl" at any age—full of the love of being loved. She did everything asked of her better than any of us could have hoped. She was also a completely devoted worker. One reason was the good fortune of her talent, another her training, another her beauty, and another that she was married to a man who, it seemed to me, was almost more her manager than her husband. He was, I could see, precisely what she needed to function perfectly, looking after her every professional and personal need. I've seen this kind of choice of mate with many stars—Katharine Cornell, for instance, with Guthrie McClintic, as well as some others who are still living so I won't name them. This kind of arrangement enables these wholly devoted women to carry on their work freely. I cannot believe the sexual aspects of these unions are of great importance; that energy passes into their work.

The other two extraordinary women Cheryl had signed—the real miracle workers—were Agnes De Mille and her chief dancer, Sono Osato. Agnes is the most strong-minded stage artist I've known. She was absolutely sure of what she wanted to do and insisted that her wishes be precisely observed. She had choreographed the greatest success of those years, *Oklahoma!*; this had given her overwhelming confidence and the energy to overwhelm the rest of us. Kurt may have once wanted the show directed as if it were a drama, not a musical, but Agnes would not have tolerated any such nonsense. She immediately gave orders (to me) to have the stage totally cleared of all scenery for her dances. She wanted space! And she knew what to do with it. Her dances were superb set pieces, beginning, middle, and end, with what any true artist gives his work: a most personal theme. Her first dancer, Sono Osato, was a poem in movement. When she was on stage, I couldn't look at anything else.

I was deeply impressed by the devotion and discipline of Agnes's dancers. They never stopped working and had the commitment of fanatics. Few actors I've known have rehearsed with the continuous intensity of these "gypsies." They lived on the floor of their rehearsal space and stayed there from the beginning of work in the morning to the end of their day at night. They were as devoted to Agnes as to a cult messiah—which is what she was. I used to sneak away from my silly "book" rehearsals to watch Agnes's girls and boys work by the hour—hours I should have been trying to please poor Sid Perelman.

When the show was done, a question remained. I wondered whether, if I'd continued to direct the book and the numbers as Kurt had originally asked and if Agnes had gone along with his intention, the show would have worked. Just as I'd asked whether, if Helen Hayes had continued down the path my direction was pushing her, *Harriet* would have played 356 performances. It further occurred to me that somewhere along the line, every show needs a miracle from somebody, a performance or a gift that exceeds expectations. *Harriet* had Helen, this show had Mary, Agnes, and Sono— all four talents larger than life-size and more gifted than any of us had a right to expect. They'd made the shows. That's why they were stars! And that was theatre!

AN EXPERIENCED woodsman can read in a wilderness evidence that you and I would not notice. He can tell what animals and birds live in the area, which of them are dominant, and who caught and devoured a grouse. I've seen those little piles of soft feathers in the woods where I live, and I saw and read the evidence on the Goldwyn lot the first morning I got back to California.

I'd left New York a few days after the opening of *One Touch of Venus*, having stayed only long enough to enjoy the long lines at the box office. Constance had not met me at her apartment, because she was working on another film, *Knickerbocker Holiday*. I was curious, of course, to know if she'd succeeded with Danny Kaye and *Up in Arms*. That film hadn't opened yet; when it did, it would make or break her career.

When I walked through the front gate of the Goldwyn lot that morning, I ran into a pretty blond actress named Virginia Mayo. We'd met years before in Chicago, when she and Constance were in the "line" of a touring musical. Virginia was "going with" (that's how they say it) a popular singer named Dick Haymes. (Now dead. Alcohol. Cancer.) Both girls were staying at the same small North Side hotel and had become chums. One summer night, we had a get-together on the hotel roof, all four of us. No, no swapping—those were unsophisticated times, and Constance and I were an exclusive thing. Now Virginia remembered me and said she was glad to see me in California. I asked her if she'd seen Constance, who was working on the lot, and when she said she hadn't, I invited her to walk out with me and say hello, Constance would be glad to see her. Virginia said she was late for an engagement upstairs and hurried off. That's all there was to that.

I found out where *Knickerbocker Holiday* was being photographed. Goldwyn had loaned Constance out to play opposite Nelson Eddy. She'd written me this piece of news, and I hadn't responded. It was certainly what an Englishman might call an "awkward" combination; Constance didn't sing and Eddy didn't act.

I waited for the red light outside the stage door to go out, then sneaked up close to where the production was working. I saw a melancholy sight. There was my girl, rather overdressed in a costume of the Revolutionary War period—I'm talking about 1776—sitting in an isolated chair and reading a book. I don't know exactly why I thought this a bad sign, but I did— the reading, I mean. No one was interviewing her, no one running lines with her, no one fussing with her makeup and hair; no one was kneeling at her feet, begging for an autograph. There she was, the heavy dress pulled up over her knees, reading, all alone.

She was overjoyed to see me, playfully threatened that the next time I stayed away for so long, she'd get another fellow and so on—but the kidding didn't have the old bite. Or was I reading something into her calm? I pulled a chair up close. "I saw your old friend Virginia Mayo," I said. "Oh, great. Where?" "Here. On the lot. I told her I was coming to see you and asked her to come along, but she had somewhere to go." "We'll get together," Constance said, taking my hand, "next week. I'm so glad to see you. I missed you. I miss you even when you're here." I kissed her. She looked pleased. "How's your pal Sam feel about the film? *Up in Arms*, I mean." "Oh, fine," she said, "so they tell me. I don't see him so often now. He's awful busy—" She stopped, then she said, "What's she doing here?" "Who?" "Virginia?" "I don't know; she didn't say." Which was when they called her and the makeup man came to check her face. As she walked away, she said, "Don't watch now; you make me nervous."

I walked away and so ran into the little gimpy wardrobe man who'd dressed me a couple of years before for my *Dead End* test. He said hello, and when he turned to look at the rehearsal, I did too. He was always a taciturn fellow, but he said something to me then which I've not forgotten. I don't believe he knew I was "running around" (that's how they say it) with Constance, because he pointed to the actors working in their Revolutionary War wigs and he said, "See those costumes? There's never been a success in those costumes." I nodded and walked over to the cop at the door and said, "Tell Miss Dowling I'll be back."

I knew where to get the straight dope—from the cutter. (They call them film editors now, although the fact is that any good director does his own editing.) This one did all Goldwyn's work, an old acquaintance from the days when I was on the lot testing and trying to learn something about film direction. He was bent over his Moviola and had long strips of film on his racks, filling a great gray barrel and all over the floor. He did know of my interest in Constance. "How's it going?" I asked, after telling him a little about the success of *Venus*. "The Eddy film?" he said. "Pretty good." In Hollywood, great means pretty good, good means medium poor, and pretty good means lousy. "She photographs well," he said, and he tore a frame off a strip of film and gave it to me. I did a quick study, said, "Yeah, she's a pretty kid," and then said, "Actually I mean *Up in Arms*." "Pretty good," he said. "Who's this?" I asked. I'd noticed some strips hanging from a separate rack, and lifted one close. It was Virginia Mayo. "Somebody he's testing," the cutter said. "For what?" "I don't know," he said. "In general. For the future. Who knows? I read where you're going to be a director here. Smart boy." "Yeah, I didn't have much of a future as an actor, did I?" "You're not Gary Cooper," he said. "Speaking of the future," I said, "and since you're being frank, tell me this: Are there enough films on Mr. Sam Goldwyn's schedule for him to need two blond look-alikes?" "Saturday," he replied, "I'm going for albacore in the Catalina channel."

On the way to Connie's place, I added up the score. Just as high as Mr.

Sam had raised Constance, that's how far he was preparing to drop her. He'd encouraged the girl to believe she was a coming star. But if *Up in Arms* was disappointing—he must have had private screenings—the blame had to filter down. Kaye couldn't be blamed, because Goldwyn had him on a long-term contract. The director couldn't be blamed; he had a track record and was in demand elsewhere. That left—

I got to the apartment before Constance and found her sister, Doris, there. She boasted that she was seeing Billy Wilder, praised his fidelity, saying, "He's not a weasel like some other guys in this town." Then she told me Billy was giving her a part in a film about a drunk that he was making.

Later Constance told me that after I'd left, she'd run into Virginia Mayo in the makeup department and when she'd suggested that we might all get together over the weekend, Virginia said she had plans to go out to the desert. "She seem changed?" I asked. "She sure got nervous," Constance said.

I didn't know if Constance had caught on by then to what was happening to her. She was innocent as a child in bed that night and had to be gentled more than she used to need. I felt so sorry for her, felt that I'd taken advantage of her goodness and her innocence and her youth. She kept repeating the phony optimism her agent had pumped into her to hold his client. I had a terrible fear that in this place, where only the tough survive, this nice girl was about to be eaten alive and left in a little pile of feathers.

Also that because of my behavior, I was one of those responsible, perhaps the chief one of all. I thought it was time to stop deceiving her. Although I hadn't lied to her, I had stalled without telling her and was still stalling. "I'm going to accept her terms," I said. "My wife's. They're stiff, but I'm going to take them. She got herself a lawyer; you should see him: Wall Street walking. From her father's old firm. But I'm going to bow my head and take my licking." "When?" she asked. "Now. I'm going back in a few days and finish it off." And this time I meant it.

W H E N I got back to New York, I found that Molly had fixed up the small brownstone on Ninety-second Street beautifully. Here was all our old furniture, still standing by, as it were; waiting, it seemed. She'd arranged for the kids' schooling and apparently they were doing well; she showed me their report cards. I went upstairs. The swing that used to hang under the doorway of the kids' room in our old apartment was up again. Inside the room were sketches they'd made at school. I was relieved to see both kids looking so well. Molly was proud of what she'd accomplished on her own and had a right to be. She told me what she was doing at the OWI with Jack Houseman and Bob Ardrey—Nick Ray was there too—and I was jealous as well as admiring.

She was seeing an analyst, Bela Mittelmann. Her work with him had resulted in a greater firmness and confidence; now she didn't want a divorce. She said she didn't believe that, in the end, I'd continue with Constance, so she'd decided to wait me out. "You're smarter than that," she said in a tone I didn't altogether like. She also said that if I ever hoped to get together with her again, I'd have to go to an analyst myself. That sounded like what it was meant to sound like: a threat. She was convinced—in a way that only Molly of all the women I've known could become convinced— that it was the only way for me to save myself. She urged me to go to Mittelmann. I suspected that this development was his idea, and there was an aspect of it I didn't like—I was going to be policed by someone on her side. But I did go see Bela; I certainly needed help from someone.

Oddly enough, this doctor and I got along well. Why? He flattered me. He'd seen my plays and turned out to be a fan. After a couple of sessions, his basic attitude seemed to be that I was in better shape than Molly, that it was she who had the more severe problem. After all, I was doing successful work. This meant to Bela that there was nothing seriously wrong with me. But the result of this favorable conclusion was not what you'd expect or what he expected. I resented the man; I considered him treacherous to Molly. Obviously I was the one who'd made all the trouble. But Mittelmann, out of a mid-European male culture, was soon all on my side and, in a way, not taking my problems seriously enough. "If she continues as she is," he said to me one day, "you won't be able to live with her."

AS YOU know by now, I always had more than one reason for doing anything I did—for example, hurrying back east. Despite the fact that I'd told Constance *Venus* would be my last Broadway show, I now wanted to direct a play by Franz Werfel, *Jacobowsky and the Colonel*. It was owned by the Theatre Guild, and they'd offered it to me. Rumor had it that the play was also being considered by Jed Harris. A victory in a competition with him would be to my taste. So I accepted the job and was introduced to its adapter, S. N. Behrman, or, taking him back to his Worcester, Massachusetts, origin, Samuel Nathaniel Behrman. Sam was an Anglophile, a man who treasured his friendship with "Willie" Maugham and that generation of English writers. Perhaps "friendship" is too mild a word. He revered these men, their work, their wit, their worldliness, their unyielding wisdom, and their financial substantiality.

Sam was a delightful man, and we were, for a time, close friends. I'd admired him, thought his work an extraordinary combination of wit, sophistication, and a warm heart. Sam, who had several times supplied the Lunts with vehicles for the stage, believed in magic, the magic of the stars. He was right; his plays needed the miracles these dazzling creatures provided to put them over.

He was the best listener I've ever known. At the close of a conversation during which he'd made me feel that I was an excellent talker, even a wit—accomplishing this by the "transference" of his own wit—he'd suddenly flag and for no apparent reason release a deep sigh. There was some mysterious anguish in the man. He was married to an excellent woman, but what need he had of her or she of him, or what had initially brought them together, I never found out. He often had a craving to be absolutely alone, so he'd engage a room in the St. Regis Hotel, high above the street, summon room service, order all the newspapers and a supply of cigarettes, and hole up for a couple of days, enjoying the silence and not answering the phone. He was a chain smoker, and although he bought suits and overcoats from Knize, perhaps the most expensive men's tailor of that day, he soon had the lapels and fronts dusted with cigarette ash and the garment twisted out of shape so that it looked shabby. He loved to be seen in fashionable restaurants, and I can see him now, entering a gay room with a series of tiny, quick steps and beaming with the anticipation of pleasure—the conversation that was coming. Though he was a bit of a snob, and a name-dropper, I didn't find this objectionable because his reasons for admiring whom he admired were worthy. He quoted his heroes, successfully arousing my admiration for them too. I always looked forward to our meetings. When he died, he left behind a diary inscribed in a tiny hand on hundreds of sheets of notebook paper. I imagined that what I'd find there would be more candid than his talk and spoil the loving memory I have of this man, so I didn't read it.

Sam had been brought in to take over the adaptation of Werfel's play by the Guild and one of its two directors, Lawrence Langner. One of Lawrence's favorite theatre words was "comedic." An Englishman who'd once been—and I believe still was—a patent lawyer, Langner had a strange way of working with Behrman. Sam would bring in some pages, Lawrence would read them, I would read them. Then we'd meet, and Lawrence would observe that Sam was like a cow producing a great deal of milk, so what he, Lawrence, had to do was skim the cream off the top and throw the rest away. Which is, bit by bit, what he proceeded to do, accumulating Sam's "cream" slowly until he'd built an entire script. In the meantime, I was assigned a more difficult task.

The original play, which Clifford Odets had adapted—unsuccessfully, according to the Guild—was by Franz Werfel, the author of *The Forty Days of Musa Dagh*. Werfel had not yet agreed to S.N.B. as adapter, and Lawrence asked that I go to California, where Werfel was living among many other displaced German artists, and get his approval of Sam or at least a reluctant acquiescence. Long ago, Lawrence said, the Guild had done a Werfel play, *Goat Song*, and the production had not been to the author's satisfaction. "You may find him a bit difficult," Lawrence promised.

So I went to California and met with Werfel. I didn't find him difficult; I found his wife difficult. She was the widow of the composer Gustav Mahler, and in case anyone forgot that, she called herself Alma Mahler Werfel. She ushered me into a darkened room, where Werfel was sitting waiting for me, as if she were permitting me the privilege of seeing an extraordinary art object, one so delicate that it might be shattered by an abrupt rise in my voice level. Just before we went in, Alma Mahler acquainted me with Werfel's problem. "His heart," she said, tapping her own chest. She introduced us in a hushed tone, then moved behind her husband and placed her hands protectively on his shoulders. I was seated facing the great genius—rather like a suppliant before a judge—and after a few nothings, I launched into my pitch in Sam's behalf.

I didn't get very far. Werfel had no problem with his voice level. It was loud. Why, he wanted to know, was his play being adapted? What was wrong with presenting a simple, straightforward translation of his work? Who here was a better writer than himself? I said it was a matter of the American theatre audience. At this he began to yell at me. He said Americans had no dramatic literature worthy of the name—this at the top of his voice. I interrupted him in an equally loud voice, denying what he'd said. Then I noticed that Alma Mahler, behind her husband, had quickly and urgently indicated the place in her own chest where her heart would be. I became quiet. Not Werfel. In an even louder voice, he began to attack America's theatre, its films, its culture, and above all, the American character. "Savages!" he yelled. "You are savages here!" This was more than I could take, and I responded in a voice louder than his own. Immediately Alma Mahler waggled her finger at me and touched the place above her heart. I subdued myself, thinking of my mission. This byplay went on throughout the interview, and I got nowhere. All that happened was that I ate a great meal of abuse.

I told Lawrence on the phone that I'd failed. An experienced man with a lively legal mind, he observed that what couldn't be accomplished by debate might be achieved by the transfer of certain sums of money. "He wants a better deal," Lawrence said. Something of that kind must have happened behind the scenes, because Sam did indeed become the certified adapter of Werfel's play.

I W A S wavering. One day I'd think: Is this the family I want—a sister who attacks me and a mother who hates me? Suppose Constance should get pregnant, and I'm stuck with this—do I really want it? Do I, for instance, want to live permanently in Hollywood? I'd think of the place on East Ninety-second Street that Molly had fixed up and her steadfast determination about me—she knew what she wanted. Me. She must have faith in a side of me she thinks worthy and in hazard. I remembered our kids, their faces and how they moved, and how she'd never turned them against me. I longed for them.

One night when Constance and I were making love, I suddenly thought of that damned analyst. I'd told this man about our lovemaking to make him see how perfect and precious it was, told him that we would often raise the top sheet up and over our heads so we'd be in a world where there was no one else, a perfect world. His response to this intimate confession annoyed me. He said we were a pair of prime neurotics, and when we raised the sheet up and over our heads—our "tent," he called it—we were reaching for a perfection that did not and could not exist, a forgetfulness of all our problems through physical love. "You simply can't get rid of your problems that way," he'd said with that soft smile (which I thought patronizing), "because it's all over in a couple of minutes, isn't it, and there you are, right back where you started, in the same situation. Nothing's changed, except that you're tired and sleepy." I got mad at him. "Yes, we may be neurotic as all hell," I said, "and we may even be sick, but that is precisely what gives our physical relationship"—I used the plainer word—"its charge. You call it foolish and frantic; I call it wonderful!" I said this to him and he smiled that soft, patient smile as if he'd heard everything I'd said a thousand times from other equally foolish neurotics. But that night in California when I remembered what he'd said, I pulled the top sheet back down, and opened our "tent." It was she who pulled the sheet up over our heads again, and that is when she said, "I wish there were only two people in the world—you and me."

I'V E F O U N D in my files of that year a letter from the friend in the OSS I'd written to. It reads: "I'm sorry to report that we are not allowed to hire you. The security check was unfavorable, I don't know why but I assume for leftism. There is not a thing we can do and I'm truly sorry. If you're ever in Washington, drop by and say hello . . ." And so on. A few weeks later, as I was preparing to direct *Jacobowsky and the Colonel*, my draft board upgraded me. Lawrence Langner rushed in for the Theatre Guild and asked that I remain 4-F so that I could do their play. I didn't protest.

T H I S P L A Y was my fourth hit in a row, and I was now called the "boy genius of Broadway." But I didn't buy that. I'd had enough experience to take exception. There had been a miracle man on this show too, but it wasn't me. His name was Oscar Karlweis. I'd never heard of him before the Guild brought him to me; I was told only that he was well known in Europe as a light-comedy and operetta star. He gave one of the most deft and light-fingered performances I've ever seen. He had a magic that overwhelmed the audience—they gurgled—and deserved all those worn-out adjectives the critics use: "captivating" and "enchanting," for instance. He was both. He had charm, a quality the Group never mentioned—well, how can an actor be trained for charm? Oscar brought it in out of the blue. I didn't

Celebration after *Jacobowsky*

know what to expect when I began rehearsals, yet he "made" the show. I
had other good actors and many witty lines and a cute premise, but it was
as much Karlweis there as it had been Mary Martin in *One Touch of Venus*
and Helen Hayes in *Harriet*. I needed a miracle, and my madonna of luck
brought me one.

There is one thing I do commend myself for, a lesson I did learn. After a
week's rehearsal, I was disappointed in what I saw. I believed I'd got off on
the wrong foot, directed the play as if it was a realistic drama when in fact
it was a fairy tale. I was nervous about confessing this to the cast; would
they lose faith in me? But I called them together and told them I'd directed
the play as a Group Theatre drama instead of a light comedy, and we had
to make a fresh start, from the beginning. I said I hoped they'd understand.
Instead of losing faith in me, the contrary happened; the cast believed in
me more. I'd told them exactly what they, without being able to articulate
it, had felt about the way the show was developing, and they eagerly went
back to the "top." We started over again and I found that the important
thing in my profession is to tell yourself the truth, not to be defensive or to
rationalize, and to believe that your associates will appreciate being trusted
with the truth. The show, at least for two acts, did turn out to be what
Lawrence Langner called it, "comedic"; audiences were delighted. I realized how small the margin is for most plays between success and failure—
five, perhaps ten percent. I was sure that if I hadn't had Karlweis and if I
hadn't decided to trust the goodwill of my actors and start over, the production would have been a failure.

There is one sad note in my memory of that production, and it concerns
Joe (J. Edward) Bromberg, one of the Group company I most admired. I

thought he was an immensely talented actor when I joined that organization, a man who could play a great variety of character parts, but as we
rehearsed I saw that something had been crushed in him. Lou Calhern,
who was excellent in the part of the Colonel, was bullying both Joe and
Oscar, but while Oscar deftly dodged and kidded Lou out of his domineering "fun," Joe had no way, apparently, of defending himself. He behaved
like a wounded man. I finally told Lou to lay off, and he did. But Joe still
wasn't himself. Later this was attributed to the blacklist and the anti-
Communist pressure, but 1944 was early for that. Joe had traveled here
and there, playing parts that were not worthy of him; perhaps this had
wounded his spirit and his faith in his talent.

On opening night, he took me aside and thanked me for being patient
with him. I didn't realize I had been. I liked Joe and was glad to have done
him some good. He went on, "I feel better now, although the migraines are
still there." He touched his head and I realized he'd been rehearsing and
performing for weeks while suffering unrelenting headaches and had never
complained to me. He was indeed a victim of stress of some kind, and I
didn't know what that was due to, didn't ask, nor did he offer to tell me.
Seven years later, I was to name him as one of the people in the Group's
Communist cell; Joe had died by that time, and what had been bothering
him so deeply remained a mystery to me.

While we were still on the road with the play, in Boston, Constance used
a publicity tour for *Up in Arms* to come visit me. The idea, supposedly, was
to be photographed with Lou Calhern. She wore a rich fur coat—loaned by
the Goldwyn people—and looked very much the movie star, but when we
were alone, I could see that she was very dispirited. She revealed that her
agent had told her Goldwyn was not going to pick up her option; instead,
since she was still on salary, he'd sent her on the road to do publicity. She
wouldn't see me privately, but a few days later I had a call from her. Goldwyn's people had put her up at the Ambassador Hotel (now razed) in New
York, and she was there, sick in bed. She said she had a fever of one hundred and four, very sick for an adult. After that afternoon's rehearsal, I
rushed down by train. Arriving in New York about midnight, I went straight
to her room. I'd not told her I was coming. When I knocked on her door, I
could tell from her response that she'd been asleep. She had a candle in
the room, the only light—it was easier on her eyes, she said. I got into bed
with her and her body was burning. The fever made her passionate to the
point of desperation. She cried and cried as we were making love and when
she reached her climax, she shouted, "Goddamn you bastard!" Later in
the night, half asleep, she said, "Don't leave me. I'm so frightened. Don't
leave me."

About a week after she'd returned to California and I to New York, I
received a letter from a friend of hers, with a clipping from the gossip col-

umn of the *Hollywood Reporter*. It disclosed that Constance had been "seeing" (that's how they say it) Charles Boyer. I couldn't believe my eyes. Charles Boyer! When I read that clipped column item, sent anonymously in an envelope without a return address, I heard her sister's voice, I heard the word "weasel" as it had been spoken by her sister. I recalled the history of how high Sam Goldwyn had raised her, then how, putting her in a fur coat his wardrobe department had provided, he'd sent her on a publicity tour to certain minor cities to squeeze every bit of value he could from his contract with her—which he was tearing up. He didn't inform her of the bad news himself, had her agent tell the girl that he was dropping her like a hot rock; no, Sam didn't put her on his knee to inform her of the end. As for my part, yes, I'd weaseled. It wasn't an unfair word; it was the uncomfortable truth. I'd not told her the whole truth of my ambivalent feelings. Hers was a tragic story, and now I was eager to see her and comfort her and reassure her.

T H E   T R A I N west was no-man's-land between the warring powers. It was also what they call a "safe house" now; no one would find me there. I'd have an uninterrupted three days alone. I'd read *A Tree Grows in Brooklyn* again. Of course, I'd read it before I'd agreed to do the film, but that was once over, quick and light. I couldn't even remember if I'd liked it. No, I hadn't; not really. I'd thought it "soapy," a tearjerker, corny. Now I had the chance to read it slowly, as the director who was going to put it on the screen.

I was overwhelmed by it on that second reading, cried and had other emotions of a most personal kind. Perhaps it was because I'd just seen my children and felt my loss of them keenly. Perhaps it was because I saw no solution ahead for me, so was sympathetic to the man who was addicted to alcohol. Perhaps the figure of his ramrod wife reminded me of everything unyielding I admired about Molly. This, I saw, was the first piece of material offered me that made me think about my own life and my own dilemma. The dilemma of all the people in Betty Smith's novel was mine and Molly's. The little girl, who loved her father absolutely despite all, felt what my daughter, I believe, was now feeling about me.

I realized that I'd never directed a play that meant anything personal to me. My career up to then had been that of a mechanic, an able technician. Doing plays that meant very little to me, I'd gained the reputation of a myth. It was the triumph of the disconnected. I went over the four plays that had brought me to the eminence I occupied. Wonder boy of Broadway! Miracle man! Indeed! In each case there had been someone, not me, who was the cause of the triumph. I had had four smash hits and had accumulated this mystic reputation and—for a time—enjoyed it. But now it had suddenly gone sour and I was full of doubt. On that lonely train ride, the myth collapsed. When I arrived in southern California, I felt like a beginner again.

I'LL HAND her a surprise, I told myself. Was that my motive in not informing Constance I'd arrived? I wonder. I'd made a reservation at the Garden of Allah, a cluster of gloomy cabins around a swimming pool no one used. I'd heard that many famous writers had lived and drunk there. The name suggests romance, but my mattress was soggy and the wall behind the bed vibrated to the rhythm of the traffic on Sunset Boulevard. I was blue and did what people in the entertainment industry do when they're melancholy: I called my agent. He sent over one of his lieutenants with a bag of optimism. "Bud Lighton's wild about you," he said as he drove me to Fox.

I found Lighton reserved and quiet, not wild. I told him I liked the book. "She caught an emotion," he agreed. We were waiting for a call from our boss, Darryl F. Zanuck, to come and confer. Apparently Lighton was accustomed to waiting. How leisurely things moved there! When word came that our appointment would not be until after lunch, Lighton suggested that I spend the time settling into my office. He made a call and the executive in charge of office assignment, a special department, hurried up to show me my space and make sure I was pleased. Bud also called Transportation for me and arranged the loan of a studio car.

Offices, their location and size, the number of windows, private bathroom, yes or no, had the same meaning they have now: status. I'd never had my own office before and was both flattered and put off by its overstuffed comfort. The office-assignment executive, anxious that I should be pleased (in case I ever became a real big shot), kept waiting for me to ask for something more or point out a feature I didn't like. I made something up. "May I have a large bulletin board clean across that wall?" I said, with a sweeping gesture. "Of course, of course." He seemed relieved that was all I wanted. As he left, a young woman came in and introduced herself. My secretary. "I'll always have coffee ready," she vowed. Then I was alone, stretched out on the sofa.

Should I call Constance? No. I was in an unharmonious mood and valued the quiet. All my life, whenever I've committed myself to a job, I've immediately wondered how I could get out of it. What a giant step away from my family I'd taken! Did I really want to be exiled here for six months? Did I really want to make the film? Lighton called me back to his office. I had no way out of it now.

D.F.Z. had again postponed our meeting. "It'll be tomorrow for sure," Bud said. I was surprised at how patient he was. "In the meantime,"—he lifted a bound manuscript off his desk—"here's what I have. Two acts.

Working on the third." He nodded toward his desk in the other room, where I saw an elaborate apparatus of thick lenses and adjustable frames. I realized that Bud Lighton was near blind. Also that he was rewriting the script; I was never to meet the authors whose names were on the screenplay.

Back in my office, there was a message from the William Morris Agency: Mr. Lastfogel had invited me to dinner. During those years, dinner with Abe was either at Chasen's or at Romanoff's, both extensions of Lastfogel's work space. This night it was Chasen's, and there was an impressive parade of stars, moving from the establishment's entrance to their reserved tables. As they passed us, they left their salaams at Abe's feet. I met Spencer Tracy and was surprised at the respect he paid my agent.

Sitting at Abe's side was his wife, Frances. The Lastfogels appeared to be a down-home couple; they might have been the owners of a delicatessen on the Upper West Side of Manhattan. Frances had been a small-time singing comedienne up until recently—even though married to Abe, who certainly didn't need the money. I'd caught her act in Philadelphia, three comic songs in three ethnic accents. She was looking around the room threateningly, and as people passed our table, she seemed to be warning them not to show her husband less respect than he deserved, which was total. Abe was a king in the film world during those years, and Frances treated the biggest stars like kids around the block, giving them affection and, at the same time, a reprimand in advance. They'd better behave, for just as her husband was kindly, she was not; no, she wouldn't stand for any nonsense.

Sitting with us was Abe's partner, Johnny Hyde, an equally powerful agent because of the important stars who'd entrusted him with their careers. Johnny was famous for finding Lana Turner sitting on a drugstore stool. He was as short as Abe, both men five foot five. When I first met Johnny I thought he was Irish; he had a ruddy "Donegal" complexion. But it turned out that his parents had come from Russia and their name had been Haidebura. His florid flush was due to the overactive pumping of a straining heart. Seated at his side was his devoted companion, a fair-haired young woman, not blond, not straw, not platinum as she later would be, but a lovely natural light brown. She had the classic good looks of the all-American small-town girl, and when she looked at Johnny, she gave him that dazed starlet look of unqualified adoration and utter dependence. Clearly she lived by his protection and was sure of his devotion, for every so often he'd slip his hand under the table in her direction. The girl gave me a glance but was careful not to look too long at any male. I was introduced but didn't take the trouble to catch her name—I usually don't the first time around. Later I found out that with the advice of her agent-lover, she was changing her name. It had been Norma Jean Dougherty; it was to be Marilyn Monroe, a synthetic name as serviceable as most.

That union had a characteristically (for Marilyn) tragic ending. Johnny, although he maintained a hustling front like any good agent, was not to live much longer. When he died, it became clear how fierce his family's hatred for Marilyn had been. I believe her devotion to little Johnny was as pure as it was for anyone the rest of her life, not mercenary as the family chose to believe. She was at his side when he died, but the body was quickly taken away and she was forbidden to come near it. She learned that Johnny was "lying in state" in his home and that some of the family were staying there with the body. Late at night, she used her keys to enter the place. Whoever was guarding the corpse had gone to bed; the candles had burned low. Marilyn told me she climbed on Johnny and lay on him. In still, silent love she stayed there until she heard the first stirring of the family members in the morning. Then she slipped out of the house—alone in the world.

B Y   T H E   T I M E I got to Constance's place and was making up my excuses, it was past eleven, and when I rang the bell, there was no answer. I sat on the stoop, waiting, but decided that was an embarrassing position to be found in, so I walked across the street, sat on the curb against the wheel of a parked car, and kept watch down Sycamore Drive. In an hour, I saw her coming, prancing on those dancer's legs, and with her a man, older than I and bulky around the middle. He was doing the talking, she was listening diffidently, nodding her head as if to say, "Yes, yes, I see what you mean, of course, that's very interesting!" I figured that her companion was some species of intellectual and that he was directing his persuasion pressure to where she was weakest, her uncertain schooling. What powers these intellectuals have over first-blooming young women, I thought, as they passed into the dark courtyard, he clattering at her and she looking up at him with trust. Turn your back on a delicious girl in Hollywood, and before you know it, some high-dome is at her with the solution for her troubled life. It's not the good-looking young athletes you have to watch out for but these idea-peddlers, who get in there by filling the gaps where the young woman most needs reassurance.

I followed behind the bushes to where I could see her front door, arriving just in time to see her unlock it and see him, still talking, follow her in and the door close behind them. Inside, the overhead fixture went on, then off, leaving two discreet lamps lit at either end of the sofa—the same sofa where we'd made love so many times, my feet up against the end where his plump butt was now nestled. She came to the window, the light silhouetting her like the shot of a movie star setting the mood for a seduction scene, and slowly closed the curtains.

No, he didn't stay all night. I made sure of that—sat in the courtyard, lowering my head whenever anyone passed. About an hour later, the door opened and out he came, turning his back to receive the ritual good-night kiss. But it lacked the heat that whoever it was might have been hoping for; there was a troubled slump to his shoulders as he walked away. He was still talking—to himself. I waited a bit more so it wouldn't occur to her I'd been waiting outside a long time—I still had some pride—then rang the bell, and in time she opened the door a crack, the latch chain secured, and saw me.

After we'd made love, I told her what I'd been doing, and she asked, "Why didn't you come right in?"

"Was that Charles Boyer with you?"

"Are you kidding?"

"Well, who was it?"

"I won't tell you." And she didn't. "What did you think I was doing in here? Were you hoping he'd stay all night so you'd have something on me?"

I told her about the squib in the *Hollywood Reporter*. She said she didn't know anything about it. I didn't believe her but let the matter drop. Despite the mistrust, I was delighted to be with her again. She too? I think so. But a few nights later, she told me Capa had written again, asking her to marry him. She liked Bob Capa very much, she told me.

Her sister moved out—to be with Billy Wilder, I assumed—and I moved in. We were now recognized as a couple. I gave her address as my own (but not to Molly). Every time we made love, with the excitement and all, I'd say, "I love you, baby, I truly do love you." And she'd say—after she'd cooled off—"I don't believe you. If you did we'd be married by now." After which I'd back into silence or change the subject, and Constance would look at me, nod her head, show her teeth, and say, "All right then, all right then, all right!" I didn't know what that meant but did recognize the tone. Threatening.

W E   F I N A L L Y had our first meeting. I tried to look at Darryl without a preconception, freed of his media image. D.F.Z. was, I saw, a small, hyperactive man with beaver's teeth under a mustache filter. He shook my hand in a most unconvincing manner, then hurried back to his desk and picked up a polo mallet in the same way someone else might have lit a cigarette. As he talked, he swept back and forth through the open areas of his office, aimlessly it seemed to me, unless his purpose was to relieve himself of an excess of energy. A plump, motherly secretary was seated at the side of his desk, making notes of everything he said, lest any of us later had questions about Darryl's wishes. I've forgotten what he said and even what his concerns were; they must have had to do with *A Tree Grows in Brooklyn*, but I was too fascinated with the man and his behavior to pay attention. I thought, afterward, that a great deal of his spouting was self-hypnosis, as if the sound of his voice bolstered his confidence to the level necessary for his position and his work. If he was feeling a personal interest in me, I wasn't aware of it; I was to learn that his impression of me would depend entirely on the film footage I produced. Fair enough. I did notice that Bud Lighton was most respectful and, perhaps because he noticed I was silent, spoke bits of deference for me. I would nod, "pan" my eyes back and forth as the little man did his "turn," and stare in what must have been a ludicrously fixed manner. Then, suddenly, it was over, and we went back to Lighton's office. "What did he say?" I said. "It was a good meeting," Bud said.

I was in a new world now and in daily contact with two extraordinary men, both born in Nebraska, forty miles apart, but as different, one from the other, as men in the same trade can be. I came to respect both these men, neither of whom had come out of the theatre or the left, neither of whom could be called an intellectual. Both Darryl and Bud had started as writers of silent pictures, and both were to influence me. They represented opposite aspects of filmmaking in Hollywood, and together and in contrast, they stood for the best of a breed that has vanished.

Hollywood is now what it was then, an art organized as an industry. Since this is America, there is conflict. Darryl was hung up on both hooks. When it came to a choice, the manufacturer won. Darryl made a program of films, as many as twenty-five a year. Lighton was a craftsman, made one film at a time. Darryl ran a factory, ran it perfectly; he was the best executive I've ever known. Lighton ran his "one-film-at-a-time" unit. Darryl competed with the other tycoons of his day. Lighton competed with himself, strove to reach his own goals. Darryl lived only inside his studio; it was his whole world. Lighton kept a fine-worked western saddle in his office, "to remind me of my cows." He was, or behaved as if he was, eager to get back to his working ranch in northern Arizona.

Every day at shortly after one o'clock, Darryl swept out of his office, accompanied by the producer or director with whom he'd been conferring or a distinguished guest from "outside." Following him came staff people and those whose Darryl's departure from his office released from theirs. It was like the movement of a flotilla of warships, Darryl the command battle wagon. On the way to the executive dining room, where his chair was wait-ing for him at the head of the long table, he'd receive the salute of those he passed; everyone he acknowledged with a greeting was proud of it.

Bud Lighton walked to lunch alone. He didn't eat in the executive dining room; he had his regular table in a corner of the common cafeteria. If you saw him and he "looked through you," you recalled that he was near blind. People respected him but didn't talk to him.

As a manufacturer with the responsibility of turning out the yearly pro-gram of films required to fill the theatres his company owned, Darryl made what he felt the public would buy. He was to film the first popular drama about anti-Semitism in America, but I doubt he had strong feelings about the theme. The success of the Laura Hobson novel *Gentleman's Agreement* indicated that there was a large public ready for the subject. Nor did he show me a feeling for blacks when he made *Pinky*. Its theme was in the air, so it was economically feasible. Darryl was interested in whatever would make a good story. As for his politics, he made an expensive film about Woodrow Wilson, was pro-Roosevelt for a time, admired Wendell Willkie, later came out for Nixon. What was he for? Successful movies. Giving the public what they'd buy. He did have one genuine political conviction: patriotism.

Lighton made films one by one to satisfy himself. Each film he made contained the same themes, the same values. He had convictions, felt them strongly, talked about them constantly. They dealt with individual standards, never politics; with courage and decency, privileges and responsibility. He was against the New Deal of Roosevelt, believed that a real man would not accept relief, that it amounted to pity. He despised the East Coast, its ideology and the civilization there. He was for the frontiersman, who lived on a large tract of semiwilderness and asked no favors of his neighbor or of nature, the man who lived where he couldn't hear his neighbor's dog bark. Lighton despised communism but despised "liberals" even more.

This was the first time in my life that I disagreed with a man's politics and loved the man. Suddenly political choice seemed less important. Bud aroused something more fundamental in me. Call it pride and individualism, speaking out on your own, asking no favors, fearing no one, enjoying courage in the face of adversity. When I listened to him, my left-wing positions seemed provincial, my convictions shallow. He appealed to that other, more conservative side of my ambivalent self. What a shock it was for me to like this man as much as I did! Had I really believed what I'd said I believed? Did I really give a damn about politics? I did, yes! Maybe less, but still. Then how could I like this man as much as I did?

Zanuck's aesthetics were simple; they were out of the Warner Brothers product book: adventure and excitement, clash and drama, did he get her, did she him? He cared very little what the clash was about, as long as it could be made dramatically valid. When it came to casting, Darryl liked personalities, "stars" who could carry a picture, whose names on a marquee or in an advertisement would attract a large, loyal public. But with a few exceptions—Ty Power, Orson Welles, Clifton Webb—he didn't think of them as people. They were useful to help sell his product. Darryl was a captive of his corporate obligation, of a ravenous ego, and of his past. He had to succeed.

Lighton's work goal was to capture a single, strongly felt human emotion, one he believed in himself. His view of actors was that of all the old "tough" directors—Ford, Hawks, Raoul Walsh, William Wellman, Henry Hathaway, and his particular favorite, Victor Fleming. These large, intemperate men, dominating their sets with the threat of a violent temper at the end of a short fuse, were scornful of what they called "New York actors." They would say that if an actor knows he's heroic, noble, or good in a part, it wouldn't work so for the audience. Bud despised noble posturing above all else. "When a man gets angry in life," he'd say, "he'll walk away. If he's sad, he'll conceal it. Emotion is and should be private. Actors are proud of their emotions; they show them off. When they do, I don't believe the scene."

Darryl was a sensualist, so they say. Maybe so. A small city boy out of mid-America often has his ego hitched to his fucking. Many stories are told about Darryl: for instance, that a starlet was brought to his private office at the end of every afternoon and so on. It's probably true that a pretty young woman was a challenge to him—but that might mean that her proximity uncovered an uncertainty that he wanted to quiet. As for the rest, what do we know about what happens after a door is closed? When you look at his films, you must believe he was much more comfortable with men than with women.

Lighton, at six foot one and one hundred and ninety-five pounds, was married to a woman several years older, who, soaking wet, may have weighed eighty pounds. According to Henry Hathaway, a close friend, they had no sex life. Henry describes how Lighton relieved himself of unused energy by getting out in the morning sun and practicing with his bullwhip, as the perspiration ran down his face. An ascetic in every way, he romanticized women. He called Dorothy McGuire, whom we cast in A Tree Grows in Brooklyn, "Angel," which effectively robbed her of her sexuality. He disliked Constance the first time he met her and never again talked to her after they were introduced. He liked Molly a great deal, although he never met her. He thought her the right woman for me and admired in her the quality he most admired—devotion to the good.

Darryl's taste in glamour ran to French singer-actresses; they brought out all his cultural uncertainty. His idea of a glamorous residence was the George V in Paris, which was as close to a Beverly Hills hotel as a French hotel can be. He admired what he felt he lacked, international snob sophistication.

Lighton was not impressed with the society or the culture of the capital cities of Europe. He liked best the men he was working with on a film and the foreman who ran his ranch. He was most at home with his cowhands.

Despite all rumors about his private behavior, Darryl was a devoted family man. He did abandon his wife and home to live in Paris with a French singer-actress in 1956, but he didn't skip out and disappear. He made damned sure that each of his three children and his wife were protected with enough money so they'd be secure. Years later, when the company lost a fortune of money and the board of directors and the owners of the stock insisted on a change, he had the responsibility of relieving his son, Dick, of his position as vice-president in charge of production at Fox, a position into which Darryl had put him. People were shocked at Darryl's act, but my opinion is that he preferred to fire his son himself so it would be a protective paternal act, with as little pain for Dick as possible. At the very end of his life, when Darryl was sick and hurting, he returned to his wife and lived out his last years with her. She was the protection he valued most.

Bud Lighton, after the death of his wife, Hope, and a further deterioration in his eyesight, sold his beloved ranch, bought a house on the warm Mediterranean island of Majorca, and lived there until his death. He died alone. Perhaps because he had no children, his best films dealt with children, and the most touching scene in the film I did with him had to do with a ten-year-old girl. Bud conceived her scenes with genuine feeling.

People used to make fun of Darryl's vanity, but it was no greater than that of the other tycoons of his day. As contrasted to the products of the film businessmen today, each film these older fellows made had to be the best that came out of the colony that year. They had to beat their competitors— Darryl over Jack Warner, Sam Goldwyn, Harry Cohn, Louis Mayer, David Selznick—to the Oscar. Darryl spared no expense or effort, time or money, on the films he made that were his "personal productions." When, on *Gentleman's Agreement*, I thought a scene I'd done was not as good as it might have been and asked to be allowed to shoot it over, he didn't hesitate. "Sure, go ahead, tomorrow," he said. It was his film!

Bud had an equal passion, but it was quieter and revealed itself in a different way. He talked over each scene I was about to shoot, telling me the feeling he hoped he had put into it and now hoped I could get out of it. He talked of humanity, feeling, courage, pride, all the old-fashioned "American" values of the frontier society that he admired. Some people thought *A Tree Grows in Brooklyn* sentimental and corny, but I was sympathetic to what Bud stood for and did my best to help him realize his vision.

To all these men of that day, film was everything. They had to surpass all their own past creations, their dreams and hopes, each time they "went to bat." Beyond this quality of commitment there was something else Darryl created: zest, a passion about filmmaking, communicated to those working on a film together. Darryl had brought together the best cameramen, the best designers, the best actors, the best technicians, all of whom were there because he'd sought them out, he paid them well, and he'd been able to convey to them the importance he attached to his program of films. When this little man walked down the street from his office's side door to the executive dining room, everyone watched with admiration, noting who his guest was that day. It could be a politician, a famous author, the head of a rival studio. They believed D.F.Z. could hold his own with anybody. He'd go by, swinging his polo mallet or a cane, swaggering a little—who had a better right?—and he'd talk in a friendly way to whomever he passed. Yes, he was tough and he was able, but they also respected him for his fairness and for his affection for his own people. He made one unit out of that crowd of workers, technicians, and artists. All of them knew where they stood on that lot, whom they had to please, what they had to do. The old studios are gone today, but there was much about them I admired.

Finally there was another quality I, especially I, admired about Darryl: He wasn't afraid of anyone. When the other studio heads, Jewish men, had qualms about making *Gentleman's Agreement,* they asked Darryl to meet with them at Jack Warner's dining room. He replied that, unfortunately, he was too busy to go to Warner Brothers' studios at Burbank, but he'd send a distinguished guest in his place, Moss Hart. Moss, who was writing our shooting script, undertook the mission, went to Burbank, and sat down with these tycoons. They asked him to plead with Darryl not to make the film. Their point, as Moss later told Darryl and me, was that the Jews in this country were getting along fine now, so why stir things up—which this film might do. Moss reported that he was unable to persuade them that the film would not have a damaging effect.

Darryl ignored the frightened men and went right ahead with our project. The same thing happened when it was urged on Darryl by the Catholics who dominated the Breen Office that the heroine of our film must not be a divorced woman. Darryl was angrier this time. After all, the Breen Office was paid by the film companies; it was not its business to censor films but to see to it that they were made. There was no rule against having the heroine a divorced woman; those fellows were obeying another set of rules, from another authority. Nor, some years later, did the Mexicans get anywhere with Zanuck when they said that *Viva Zapata!* would be condemned in Mexico and cause a great wave of anger, one that might affect the reception there of all Fox product.

In all those cases, Darryl's belief was that the audience was ahead of the moralists and censors; he proved correct each time. The important thing for all of us who worked at Fox during those years was that the man heading our studio didn't back off when he was challenged.

A F I L M director does whatever is necessary to get what he needs from an actor. Sam Fuller would shoot off a pistol—without warning—to get a reaction of surprise and fear. Bill Wellman is said to have slugged an actor. I also—to his surprise—struck a boxer named Tami Mauriello, whom I had put in the foreground of a shot for *On the Waterfront* and wanted to show genuine rage. My directorial technique worked, but I made sure I had my bodyguard at my side.

Jack Ford, whom I admired as much as I did any American director, would be kind and brotherly, then suddenly hostile and even sadistic with actors. Although he might not have been aware of it, this is the technique used to break a man in what's called brainwashing. Both Dick Widmark and

Karl Malden, admirers of Ford, told me that sometimes in the morning, when they came to work, Jack would ask them how they thought a scene should be shot. They would give Jack their suggestions; he'd listen sympathetically, then shoot the scene in a completely contrary fashion, making fun of their suggestions at the same time. Ford got a value, he believed, by rattling his performers at the start of each day's work.

Henry Hathaway developed a style that earned him the nickname "Screaming Henry." He was a companionable fellow when he wasn't shooting but a bully when he worked. Karl Malden had the courage to ask him one day why he always screamed at everybody. Hathaway answered, "I don't know how to talk to actors, but I figure if I can create enormous tension on the set, it puts everybody on their toes."

Hitchcock told his screen stories as much as possible without help from his actors' performances. When Cary Grant, going into a film, asked him how he should play his part, Hitchcock answered, "Just do what you always do." Hitchcock relied on his camera angles and his montage (the juxtaposition of short lengths of film) to do what on stage we relied on the actors for.

An old-time director I knew once made an effort to tell me the difference between stage and screen acting. He said the best actor in Hollywood was Lassie, the dog. You could (her trainer could) get her to do whatever was needed by the most simple and direct means, and what Lassie did was always true. She didn't know how to fake, and she didn't ask for explanations.

What bugged old-time directors most were requests from actors for motivation. "Why do you do it?" Ford once roared at an actor. "Because I tell you to." Then he'd look at the performer in his most threatening way and the actor would not worry about motivation again. There are similar stories about Wellman and Vic Fleming. An introspective actor tends to be slow, which is a serious flaw in films, where it's beneficial to speak at least ten percent faster than on the stage. "Think *as* you speak," I've heard directors bark at actors, "not before. Don't eat up my footage for your damned thinking!" The only actor who got away with his pace in dialogue scenes was Marlon Brando, and that was because his silences were often more eloquent than the lines he had to say.

I was eager to have a long talk with Ford. I finally managed this and asked him how he got his ideas about how to stage a scene. "From the set," he said. I didn't understand what he meant. He was pretty grumpy that day, but I persisted. "Get out on the location early in the morning," Ford said, "before anyone else is there. Walk around and see what you've got." "Oh," I said, "then look at the script and fit the scene into the location?" "No," he growled, "don't look at the fucking script. That will confuse you. You know the story. Tell it with pictures. Forget the words." "What else?" I asked. "The actors," he said. "Don't let them act. Direct it like you were making a silent." Which I didn't understand then, but a few years later my ambition became to make a film the way Ford did, one that a deaf person could follow.

The prime example of this attitude toward the actor is that of Federico Fellini. He "dubs" in all the dialogue of his films after he has photographed the action. When he is casting, what he looks for is not a good reading but an eloquent face—*faccia* in Italian. A face, he believes, is a piece of sculpture that has taken a lifetime to mold, so it tells more than any actor's technique possibly could. I've watched Fellini work, and he did what would be intolerable for a stage director come to films (me). He talked through each take, in fact yelled at the actors. "Now, there, stop, turn, look at her, *look* at her! See how sad she is, see her tears? Oh, the poor wretch! You want to comfort her? Don't turn away, go to her. Ah, but she doesn't want you, does she? What? Go to her anyway!" And so on. I didn't hear him give these particular instructions, for I don't understand Italian, but it's how I saw him working one day, and that's why he's able, shooting his films at the Cinecittà studios near Rome, to use performers from many countries. He does part of the acting for the actors.

My own rule is: You can't get it out of them unless it's in them. That is why the practice of making an actor read the lines of a part has no value for me and can even be misleading. The best line-readers, I've found, are not the best actors for my films. Brando mumbled. Actors who are a great success in television have the ability to read a part impressively with a single look at their scripts, but after the first impression, it's unlikely that the director will be given anything that surprises him, which is why I take actors for a walk or for dinner and probe into their lives. That is especially easy to do with actresses. After a few moments of sympathetic attention, I've found that most people are more than ready, even eager, to tell you all about themselves. Women are easily led to reveal to anyone who seems to be a friend the secrets of their intimate lives; it is their most essential drama. A director has to know the materials he's going to be reaching for before he starts reaching.

Students have asked me if there's no difference between acting for the stage and for the screen. Before I directed my first film, I believed that a good actor was a good actor in either medium. Of course, there were exceptions: Jean Arthur was an exceptional screen actress but never did, could, or would make it on the stage. Some of my Group Theatre colleagues, as I'd seen, were too graphic—a nice way to put it—for the screen. A stage actor has to maintain a performance night after night, so a technique is necessary. He has to be both believable and highly visible, has to have a good voice and a way with words. Some intelligence helps.

But I soon saw that these requirements were not essential for the screen actor. What is required, I learned, besides an essential "animal" magnetism, is whatever's necessary to provide for the camera a true piece of experience. Whereas you can—and many effective actors do—get away with faking, posturing, and indicating emotions on stage, it's difficult if not impossible to get away with anything false before the camera. That instrument penetrates the husk of an actor; it reveals what's truly happening—if anything, if nothing. A close-up demands absolute truth; it's a severe and awesome trial. Acting for the screen is a more honest trade.

My producer, Bud Lighton, and I began to cast *A Tree Grows in Brooklyn*. Surprisingly we'd come from opposite directions to the same conclusions. Bud would quote Vic Fleming on acting: "A good actor is one who, when he's asked what he does for a living, will drop his head, kick a little shit, and speaking with a bit of shame, mumble, 'I'm an actor.'" This story offended me the first time I heard it, but when Bud and I began to work together, I saw that we looked for the same thing: a true emotion caught on film. In a phrase he would have abominated, Lighton, too, wanted an "agitation of the essence," the living experience, not "casting." This meant there had to be a difference in the casting philosophy for the screen and the stage director. An actor cleverly reading the lines of a part didn't impress me—or Bud. We had to find the thing itself, not a simulation.

Our story was based on a complex character, a man who was a drunk and a dissembler, a failure but still charming, able to hold the true and lasting love of his young daughter. It was a part that might have been acted on stage. For the screen, however, it seemed to Bud and to me that we had to look for and find a man who was a failure but still charming; a drunk, reformed or persisting; a dissembler who was nevertheless lovable. So we looked for such a man who happened to be an actor. And we did a piece of casting that seemed like a miracle: Jimmy Dunn. I knew what I had in Jimmy before I started photographing him, and so did Bud. Here was an actor who once had great promise. It was generally believed that nothing would prevent him from becoming a big star—except what did, his drinking. In casting files, he was marked: "Drinks!" That got around. He didn't get parts. This cracked his ego. He felt guilty of self-betrayal. I could see that on his face the first time I talked to him. That was what I would photograph—that face in stress. It was the evidence that he'd failed the test of life. Still he wanted dearly to be liked—it was all there, visible—and that made him touching, even charming. Jimmy Dunn was made for this part—by his life. I found all this out from hearsay and a single conversation. Jimmy promised he wouldn't drink while we were making the film, and he didn't—except on his days off.

The child in the film was played by a wonderful little girl named Peggy Ann Garner; she was another miracle. I found out immediately what was on her mind: She told me that she often dreamed of her father, who was overseas in the air force. When the day came in our schedule when she had to break down and cry, I talked to her about her father. Implicit in what I said was the suggestion that her father might not come back. (He did.)

Peggy cried the whole day through, and we caught that piece of feeling. We only got it once, but we only needed it once. Her outburst of pain and fear was essential to her performance; it was the real thing. I was proud of that scene, of its absolute truth. At the end of the day, her mother had to be summoned to take the child home. The next day, as children do, she'd forgotten all about it.

The only difference I had with Bud Lighton concerned this scene. I'd shot it with the little girl facing the camera, and there'd been tears rolling down her face. This affronted Bud; he abominated "overemotionalism." Tears made him turn away. Whenever an actor had a line to speak that could possibly sound sentimental, Bud suggested that I ask the actor to precede or follow the line with the phrase "For chrissake," spoken to himself. That would kill the mush. Try it. It works.

"But this girl wouldn't say that line, even to herself," I protested. "Then shoot the scene again," Bud said, "and keep her back to the camera." I did, and although the emotion wasn't as intense, the scene was better. A viewer could guess from the tension and quiver in her shoulders and the muffled sound what was going on. We imagined an even greater heartbreak than we'd seen before. What Bud was saying to me, in effect, was that it is better to arouse an audience to wonder than to show them the plain truth of what is happening. I recalled a bit of old theatre wisdom: When the actor cries, the audience won't. It is better for an audience to ask itself, "I wonder what she's feeling now. I wonder if she's crying." In this respect, too, less is more.

S O   I   W A S in a fascinating new world, thrilled with it and eager to learn everything I could about everything. The camera, for instance. Lighton provided me with a famous cameraman, Leon Shamroy, the winner of several Academy Awards. He was a man I would come to like a great deal, but not immediately. Leon arrived on the set in the morning, was provided with coffee and a *Hollywood Reporter* by a black attendant, then slumped in a canvas armchair. While he digested the news of the colony—who's fucking who—I rehearsed the actors, without gaining Leon's attention. Finally he'd look up and ask, "What's the garbage for today?" The "garbage" was the dialogue of the scene we were to photograph. "Didn't you read your script?" I'd ask. "Where's your script?" "I'd rather watch a rehearsal," he'd say. I doubt he ever read the script.

He soon saw that I didn't know beans about how to make a motion picture, knew only how to handle actors, so he suggested that I stage the scenes precisely as I might on a theatre's stage; he'd photograph the action for me and tell me what "cuts" and close-ups were needed after the "establishing shot" had been made. I told this to Lighton and he thought it a good idea, and that is how we started.

We went along fine until the day Leon said he thought he should receive screen credit as codirector, that the film should be presented as a directorial collaboration. Lighton didn't think that a good idea. I wasn't so sure. I had no idea about cutting or coverage or camera angles; I was totally dependent on Leon to tell me how the bits of film should fit together. Lighton said not to worry about that; he'd look at the stuff with Zanuck every afternoon, and they'd put it together for me, as well as tell me what more I needed in each sequence. I believe he spoke to Leon, because I didn't hear any more about codirection.

I hadn't yet heard how proud Zanuck was about his ability to edit a film, and both he and Bud probably preferred my innocence—I'd give them plenty of "coverage" on every scene, which they'd assemble into a sequence to their taste. Friends were warning me about Zanuck's tendency to "save" other people's films by taking all kinds of liberties with what was given him. There were stories about how he had put last reels first, then boasted that he'd rescued a botched job. Since film shot on the Fox lot was based on a script Darryl had approved and since he owned more shares of Fox than anyone else, he also owned every foot of stuff shot and could, in the end, do anything he wanted with it. I had no trouble with him on *A Tree Grows in Brooklyn*—Bud was there to protect me. Some years later, however, when Darryl turned a film of mine inside out and upside down in order to "save" it, and did this without consulting me, I resented what seemed to me to be his insufferable arrogance, and I never worked with him again. But that's another story.

DURING the filming of *A Tree Grows in Brooklyn*, a mysterious thing was happening that I understood only much later. The story I was making dramatized a child's struggle to hold her parents together; it spoke of the pain of separation, of a young girl caught between warring adults—a girl who reminded me, morning after morning, of my daughter, Judy. As I worked along and looked within my own experience for the emotion of a scene and tried to hold on to it all the day through, the film seemed to be standing up for one side of my life and Constance for the other. After a day's work, particularly with Peggy Ann Garner, I'd come home to Constance tense and resentful of her and wouldn't know why. She, too, didn't know what had happened during the day that had turned me cold and incapable of loving. I couldn't tell her because I didn't know—not yet. It would be long after our relationship had been broken off that I'd attribute some of the wrenching, destructive action of our separation to the process of making that film.

But Constance had an instinct. She felt unwanted on the set of *A Tree Grows in Brooklyn* and wouldn't visit me there. She knew better than I what was going on.

I REALIZE now that work was my drug. It held me together. It kept me high. When I wasn't working, I didn't know who I was or what I was supposed to do. This is general in the film world. You are so absorbed in making a film, you can't think of anything else. It's your identity, and when it's done you are nobody. When Darryl quit Fox and went to live in Paris, he found that there he was nothing but an aging "sugar daddy," sitting in an overpriced restaurant with a mistress whose respect for him was less than he was accustomed to. Darryl was D.F.Z. only when he was working on a film. When he wasn't, he drank and gambled and gave his fucking a more frantic importance than he should have.

I found that my own self-esteem had begun to depend on each day's "rushes." I needed the daily reassurance of a successful performance on a sound stage. Even now, so many years later, I am uncomfortable with myself when I haven't turned out a couple of passable pages for a book every day. I become depressed and angry at myself and at whoever's close enough to distract me. Work makes it impossible for me to dwell on my personal problems; I forget them. As soon as I stop work, my uncertainties swarm back—even now, with all the flattery I've received. I doubt the praise I've heard and believe my detractors. I wonder if I'm still capable. Molly used to say that whenever I became depressed, I'd sign a contract.

I believe work is what held Tennessee Williams together; he did it every morning, and nothing was allowed to interfere. He would get up, silent and remote from whoever happened to be with him, dress in a bathrobe, mix himself a double dry martini, put a cigarette into his long white holder, sit before his typewriter, grind in a blank sheet of paper, and so become Tennessee Williams. Up until then he'd been nothing but an aging faggot (his phrase, to me), alone in a world he had always believed and still believed hostile.

John Steinbeck was the same. A few years before his death, he told me he had nothing left. He seemed in good shape physically, and I didn't know what he meant. He explained that he had nothing more to write about. We'd once occupied adjoining offices over Broadway, and I remembered how he'd come downtown to work every morning, looking distracted and troubled. He'd sit at his table and spend ten minutes sharpening every pencil he had stacked in a Mexican cup, then begin writing on one of the legal tablets he preferred. When he'd filled the page, he crumpled it and threw it into the wastepaper basket. Observing that he did this every morning, wrote a page and threw it away, I asked him what it was that he wrote and discarded. He answered that it was nothing, just a warm-up and about anything but the novel he was working on (*The Winter of Our Discontent*). But I believe the warm-up reestablished who he was. He became the writer John Steinbeck again.

When my film was done and I was waiting for my cutter and Bud Lighton to put it together, I felt worthless. And angry at everyone around me. In desperation, I decided to make a trip to New York and see my family. I used that phrase, "my family," when I announced the trip to Constance, and she became upset. I'd promised her time and again that when the film was done, I'd go to Reno. I wasn't lying. I'd told Molly that I wanted the divorce still, and was determined about it. I told Constance that the purpose of my trip, beyond that of seeing my kids, was to argue out the terms of the separation agreement. "I thought you'd done that," she said. "I wasn't ever satisfied," I answered.

I had a more self-serving purpose. I believed then and always that my identity is partly geographical. In New York, I assured myself, I'd know again who I was supposed to be. The city and the memories it awakened would restore me to myself.

I found Molly, Judy, and Chris living in good order. Waiting for Molly to come home from work, I tried talking to the kids, but we no longer had anything in common, and the conversation was hard going. I admired what Molly had done; the house had a sweet, orderly tone. I couldn't think of this as my family, nor the house as my home. I told Molly that the kids looked in very good shape. She said she hoped they were, but the last time she'd talked on the phone to me in California, when she'd hung up she noticed Chris looking at her, and his face was purple. "With what?" I asked. "Is he angry at me?" "I don't know," she answered. "He didn't say."

We had dinner together, and I was part of them and admired what Molly had—call it dignity. Or "class"! She told me about what she and Jack House-man were doing at the OWI with the Voice of America. Nick Ray, who'd been my assistant as I was shooting *Tree*, had come back east to help them on the Voice. Molly said, "Nick knows more about what's going on in the back roads of this country than anyone." I remember wishing she'd been that impressed with me. She'd still not seen my plays. Nor did she ask me how the film had gone. A matter of what's important and what isn't, I thought.

Later that evening, a large, overweight man who'd been wooing her came around, and we talked. He was one of the editors of *Yank*, the magazine for GI's. That's all we talked about, the war. I decided to get my licks in, mentioned that everyone who'd worked on my film said that it had turned out well. No one picked up the topic. When I mentioned the character Peggy Ann Garner had played, I realized that Molly hadn't read the book I'd left behind for her. She was involved in more important matters, the kind of concerns, I thought, I should have been involved in. What he, Molly, and Jack were doing seemed so much more important than whether Peggy Ann Garner faced the camera or turned her back to it. I envied her and I admired what she'd done. She'd made herself the center of a family, and I was adrift.

At eleven o'clock I got up to go, and Dick Harrity, the suitor, said he'd go too, which I was glad to hear, not that I thought he might be staying with Molly, but I did want him out of the place. Dick seemed to be courting Molly by wooing the whole family; he said he didn't want to disrupt its "integrity," or something like that. We were walking slowly, and it was a cool night, but Dick, as he told me how impressed he was with my kids, was perspiring freely and couldn't stop. I suppose he felt guilty with me. I said I wished I was on *Yank* too, that I had to somehow or other get overseas and take some tiny part in the war. In self-defense, I told him I'd been turned down by the OSS because of supposed left leanings. Dick said nothing.

What the hell was there to say? I sat alone in my room in the Royalton Hotel, listened to the traffic below, and thought how worthless my life was. It wasn't so long ago that I'd been the boy wonder of Broadway and the envy of everybody. Now, watching Molly, hearing about Chris's anger, certainly directed at me, hearing about what she was contributing to the war effort, hearing about sweating Dick Harrity's work on *Yank*, I felt like nothing. It had all collapsed. And now I made it worse.

I'd met a girl down the hall, in room 506—I can still remember that number. I heard her door open and close, and feeling alone and isolated and also being mad at Constance because my passion for her had cost me my family, I knocked on door 506 and found this lone girl in a similar mood—an actress out of work, with bills piling up. We tried to comfort each other. But I was impotent; I couldn't. It seemed like the final wrong thing to do—my body was telling me that. My visit east ended on this sickening note. You're getting what you deserve, I said to myself.

I RETURNED, to hosannas. My film was "great." So I was informed. I was the boy wonder again. Nobody could guess that I was also in a hell of a mess. What this community saw was a young, energetic, aggressive man, a successful director. I ate with Abe Lastfogel, my proud agent, the very first night, at Romanoff's. Romanoff himself hung around our table—a compliment. Everybody who passed paid respects to Abe, and he introduced me to each one. They'd all heard about me and the "great" film I'd made. That night, when I was being lathered with compliments, I hadn't even seen the film. Lighton told me that our cutter was doing a few final things to it but that Zanuck thought it was "great." The next morning, in my office, there was a long note from D.F.Z., informing me that he'd shown the film privately to Spyros Skouras and a few privileged people from his distribution and sales departments, and they were "ecstatic" over it. "Virginia [his wife] cried," he wrote. After lunch I ran into Skouras, who embraced me and called me "*patrioti*," meaning that he was proud we were fellow Greeks. "Join me in the steam room later," he said, "*patrioti!*"

The steam room! Only for the privileged!

In a couple of days I saw the film. Perhaps my anticipation had been built up too high; it was all right, but Jesus Christ! It was just another movie. Despite all the unspoken "For chrissakes" and despite the turning of emoting backs to the camera, it was mushy. I did think Peggy was fine and Jimmy the real thing and Lloyd Nolan marvelous and Dorothy McGuire valiant, but the whole thing was poverty *all cleaned up*. Coming, as I had, off the New York streets, having shot *People of the Cumberlands*, a documentary, in the Tennessee shallow-mine country, having seen poverty down South when I visited there with the district head of the Communist Party and worked for a time on a ranch, I did know the difference between what was depicted in Zola's *Germinal*, the book I admired most in those years, and what I'd put on the screen. But in the condition I was in—thwarted, defeated at home, alone—how could I resist the flattery? By the next morning I wasn't resisting it. I accepted it, whatever the source. The affection of my crew touched me most. They were already on another film, for Henry Hathaway, but when I walked on the set all work stopped. They gathered around me and I felt loved—at least by someone. The next Monday they brought me smoked albacore and homemade bread and other kitchen presents. I felt like myself again—at least this self.

The next afternoon, Abe Lastfogel came to see me with that "cool" calm of his, and we sat in my office and he told me that Lew Schreiber had been after him. Lew was Darryl's executive, the man who made—and broke—deals. Fox—and Bud Lighton—wanted me to direct *Anna and the King of Siam*. "When?" I asked. "Immediately," he said. "Lighton would like to talk to you about it this afternoon." "But I've agreed to do a play by Sam Behrman in New York," I said. "What's that?" he asked. "*Dunnigan's Daughter*," I told him. "What's that?" he asked again. "A play," I said, "for the stage." "Oh, you can get out of that," he said. "You've got a great future in this town. Zanuck's crazy about you. Don't you like Lighton?" "More than any producer I've ever worked for," I said. "Remember," he said, "if you don't like that story, you can suggest another, by our contract. I think the way Zanuck feels about you, he'll let you do anything you want. It's up to you." That sank in. My ambition—to be a film director—could be satisfied now. "Think it over," he said. I nodded.

I was a success, it seemed, a great success. Or was I a failure, a great failure? Or was I both?

I M O V E D back into the Garden of Allah. Constance's mother had come west; the clan was gathering. Her sister was poisoning Constance against me by telling her the truth: that I was hesitating. Doris was the established girlfriend now of Billy Wilder, and I was waiting to see if she would prevail on him to marry her. Talk is cheap.

"I'm going to Reno," I said to Constance. "Stop bothering me about it."

"When?"

"As soon as I'm finished with the picture."

"Did you sign what you said you were going to?"

"No, but they're drawing up the papers, and I will."

"When?" Then she was silent. "Oh, God, I hate this. The way you've got me. And the way I have to talk to you. I hate it."

Later she said, "I wish we were alone in the world. That there was no one else on earth, anywhere. Anywhere."

We were in our "tent," of course, when she said that.

I didn't say anything about the "no one else" line. That would truly drive me nuts.

Here is the record of a day with Constance during this time. We were living in Hollywood, where a successful man, which I most certainly, most suddenly was, can have anything he wants and where life is lived for pleasure, which, by definition, must be perfect. We'd wake up midmorning in my cabin in the Garden of Allah, play around a little, staying half "under," so only half in ecstasy, then back into half a sleep. Shaking that off, we'd shower—Constance first, while I lay in bed. I enjoyed watching her dress, loved her in white underwear. We'd go somewhere for breakfast. Everyone else in the world was working by then, and the world belonged to us. We'd discover it was past noon when we saw the lunch crowd coming in. We had a long day ahead with nothing to do. I loved Constance, but she bored me during the day. I wished it were night. But it was high noon, and what I wanted was to sit quietly somewhere, alone, and read *The New York Times*. They weren't sending the *Times* out there by airplane in those days, but I had the baseball scores in the *Herald-Examiner* and I gave the accounts of the game in the East more study than they deserved. We had nothing to say to each other, which was okay when I was working, but when I wasn't I wondered what she was thinking. Was she going to pester me about that damned divorce again? No. "Let's go to a movie," she'd say. "There's nothing worth seeing," I'd say. "But let's do something! We can't sit around here all day, can we?" "Like what, do what?" Silence. "Let's take a drive." "Where? We've seen it all." Silence. "Tell you what," I said, "let's go to the Pickwick bookstore and buy some books." "You haven't read the books you bought the day before yesterday." "I will," I said. "Let's go."

We went to the Pickwick, which was on Hollywood Boulevard, wandered away from each other into opposite corners of the place, and took a long time looking over what was available. The books I bought there I'd mostly read standing up, by the time I'd paid for them. I made a sign to her and we went to the cash clerk with our selections. "I bought that book yesterday," I said to her when I saw what she'd picked up. "Put it back." "I want a copy," she said, "for *my* place." I felt I'd spoken to her in a mean voice. "All right, let's go to that movie you wanted," I said. "You changed your mind?" she said. "Yeah, let's go. Then we can go to the Beachcomber's and have some golds and some food." ("Golds" were my Lethe, my way to oblivion.) "It's too early for dinner," she said. "Let's go to the movie and see how we feel after." "No," I said, "I changed my mind. I don't want to see that movie. Let's go to bed." "Okay," she said. She was always ready for that.

Back in the "tent," everything was perfect—well, that is, near perfect. The tent quiets doubt and brings peace. Constance was a chicken with all white meat, and I devoured her. Here was a narcotic that succeeded just as surely as work, my other drug. We fucked ourselves to sleep. Last thing I took notice of was the traveling clock Molly had given me long ago. It said five o'clock, in the afternoon. When we woke, it was near seven, and the problem of the day was solved. The Beachcomber's! One gold, two golds, three golds. On the river Lethe! Oblivion! Dinner! Semi-Chinese food slides down easy. Sated? No. A last gold for the road. By eleven, back in the tent. The harmony of mutually induced exhaustion. We had no problems. Oh yes, one—her career. She was talking about that again. Since Goldwyn had not picked up her option, what should she do? He won't see her in his office now. "You'll get offers soon," I said. "That's what my agent keeps telling me," she said. "You're too pretty for them to pass by." She kissed me, loving me because I loved her, and I loved her because she loved me.

We'd succeeded in making our conscious day as short as possible. There were passages—minutes—when I didn't care if I ever worked again.

When I'd been in New York, that damned analyst had finally said something I agreed with. "How old are you?" he asked.

"I've told you. Don't you listen?" He gave me that soft smile. "Thirty-six."

"It has seemed to me," he purred through his soft Hungarian lips, "that you have been living your eighteenth year. But that will come to an end. We should just be careful you don't crack up first, right—what? What?"

He cracked up laughing.

I didn't go back to see him for a while.

Whereas I'd told Constance more or less the truth up until now, now I lied. That is, I was planning to do something I didn't tell her about. I'd made up my mind to see something of the war before it was over—if only as a spectator. Like any experienced Hollywood fellow who was a success, when I needed something I asked my agent. Abe Lastfogel would get it for me; he was the prexy of Camp Shows. He said I was right, I should go overseas like every other patriot, go before it was all over, and he would certainly arrange it for me. He talked as if it was a deal he had to negotiate.

My relationship with Constance began to have a desperate edge. Her impatience was becoming anger and expressed—in all kinds of company. Openly. The fact that she and her sister were right made no difference to me. I was under attack; I protected myself with distance. I began to ask myself a lot of questions you don't ask in the sublime condition of ecstasy. "Even when I'm divorced," I asked myself, "what the hell do I want to get married for? Constance needs it; I don't."

I believe women are smarter than men. I didn't say anything—silence was safe—but she knew what I was feeling. She stopped staying all night with me at the Garden of Allah apartment. Now I was there alone, and some terrifying things began to happen.

In the last hours of the night, I noticed that the sound of the cars rushing by on Sunset Boulevard outside was closer. No, it was the cars that were closer—that's what I thought. They were passing very close to my bed. They were racing, making the walls shake. The cars seemed to be attacking me. I'd wake and look out the back window. All was as usual.

I had a nightmare that I remember vividly because it was repeated several times. I dreamed that my son, Chris, had fallen off a subway platform and under a train. I heard the little boy cry out. I saw his mangled body. I screamed something. "Look out!" Too late!

On another night, I felt completely out of control and hysterical. It was on that night that I rushed out, naked, into the courtyard of the Garden of Allah and stood there sobbing until I realized where I was and what I'd done. I remember the intensity of my desire to get out of that bed, out of that room, out of that city, out of southern California—and out of my personal situation.

I knew I was in danger. A crack-up was near. I needed help. Whatever there was of worth in me—and I wasn't sure how much there was—had been thwarted. I was not becoming what I'd intended I should be. I was becoming nothing. The emotion I remember filling me when I was alone for those last nights in that apartment by the racing cars was that I had no home. I didn't want to continue living. I wanted out.

In a desperate mood, I went to see Abe Lastfogel and asked him whether his promise—that he'd get me overseas—could be counted on. He said it was "in the works," that the army moved at its own pace—which is slowly—but I should stay ready. And calm—for he'd noticed, I suppose, that I was living on a ledge. I told him that I might go back east to see my family again. (This was the first I'd thought that.) He said don't worry, he'd get to me wherever I was, arrange my transportation from wherever I was, see that all the papers were prepared, that, yes, I could count on it. Then he asked me whether or not I wanted to make *Anna and the King of Siam* for Lighton and Zanuck; had I made up my mind? I said I had not. He said Zanuck had to know one way or another pretty soon. What about it?

I must have had a visible, violent neurotic reaction to this. I had tears in my eyes. He saw them, because the tone of his voice changed. "Don't worry," he said, "they'll wait for you. But if they don't, you'll do something else. Everybody out here wants you now. You should plan to move out here. This is the place for you."

I left. Constance, for her own reasons, had been counting on my doing *Anna and the King of Siam*.

I began to avoid meeting her. The tent was empty more often than not. I didn't know what she was doing in the day, though I assumed she was meeting with her agent and trying to make a fresh start. For some irrational reason she blamed me for Goldwyn's dropping her, but I didn't feel it was my duty to worry about her career. I was in too much danger myself to worry about anyone else's problems. The success of *A Tree Grows in Brook-*

lyn did not ease the pain I carried around all day and slept with at night. For the first time in my life, I had no clear view ahead.

Lastfogel took me to dinner again. In a moment we had alone, he said, "I know what you're going through. Remember, you don't have to decide anything now. Go overseas. Take a break. See what happens." He was kind.

Then one night in desperation, I wrote Constance a note, left it in the apartment (to which she had a key), and disappeared. I took a cab downtown, got on the Chief going east, and lay in a roomette, watching the desert of southern California move slowly past my window and back out of sight. I pulled down the window shade and I slept. I slept through that afternoon as if sleep were my only refuge, and for the first time in weeks, continuously. When I woke, I examined myself. I was ashamed. It is a shame I still feel. I hadn't stopped loving Constance. What I'd done I did at a time when she most needed my support and help. But my love was of no use to her. Nor hers to me. Our life together was killing me. Love was not a solution now, not for either of us. "You've had a narrow escape," I said to myself.

I T O L D   H I M I'd left Constance.

"I'll never let myself get in so deep again," I said.

Mittelmann had taken humorously the crisis I'd heaved under for so many months. Which, reader, is probably the way you're taking it after all the ups and downs, ins and outs. But that's not the way it is when you're young. You're pulled apart. Mittelmann sat there, smiling that mysterious smile. "Why are you so anxious to get married again?" he asked. "Not that anxious," I said, and looked away. Why was I letting him put me on the spot? "Well, then, what's your hurry?" he asked, and waited for my answer.

I'd noticed before, in my other visits, that his consultation room was decorated with small wooden sculptures from another, more enigmatic civilization. Eastern, no doubt. Now I saw that these pieces had the same smile cut into their faces that he had. I resented them: Were they smiling at me? And I resented him. At the same time, I couldn't answer his question. "You don't have to decide anything now," he said. "Just live awhile, see what happens." I said nothing. "Your problem," he went on, "is that you're not selfish enough. You're always trying to please other people and so keep everything together. Don't worry about everyone's approval. You can't please everybody, ever." "I know that," I said, sounding huffy. "Well, then?" he said. "What does that mean—well, then?" I asked, ready for a quarrel. "Why do you try?" he said. "Her problem is not your problem, and the same goes for your wife. You can't please them both. Please yourself. Try to find out what you want." "That's why I'm going overseas," I said. "Good," he said. "Go." He gave me that twisted smile again, and even if he was right, I disliked him. "I'm ashamed of what I did," I said. "How?" he said. "I can't get her off my mind." "But here you are; you're here. Perhaps you weren't telling the truth." "Telling her the truth?" "No," he said impatiently, "yourself. Her too. But yourself. Think! Maybe you had a narrow escape. Maybe you saved yourself."

I walked uptown slowly; Molly had said she'd give me dinner. She fixed me a drink and one for herself, old-fashioneds, and told me again how wonderful Jack Houseman had been, how brilliant Nick Ray was, and what wonderful things they were doing at the Voice of America. "Remember when you went down South with Nick," she said, "how enthusiastic you were about what you saw and all the ideas you wrote me about?" "I remember," I said. She had her grandfather's clock in the house and it struck. "Kiss your father good night," she said to the kids. They did, and the three of them went upstairs.

Later I told Molly how grateful I was that she hadn't turned the children against me. She put her arms around me. The following Sunday we went to New Rochelle, all together, and had dinner with my parents. Nothing had to be said. My father and mother both urged me not to go overseas; they couldn't see any reason for that trip, and I couldn't explain it to them. Molly interceded for me, but she didn't win any favor from them for the effort. I went home with her.

I W I L L describe Molly.

In the city of Zurich, along the river that flows into the Zurich See, there are several substantial churches. They all toll the time, keeping the twenty-four hours of the day in order. One particularly impressed me, the Grossmünster. It is a Protestant church, built of great, square-cut stone blocks, its style established by round Romanesque arches, which settle, don't soar. When you push the heavy entrance door open, it closes quickly and of itself behind you. You see immediately that there is no altar, only a raised area at the end of the nave with stairs leading up to it, no barrier, no rail. All the windows at the sides of the church are of clear gray glass, and the impression of the body of the church is severe and old-fashioned, even rigid and cold, and so the totality would appear, except that in the depths, in the most intimate part, where in other times there may have been a holy place, there are three long high narrow windows of colored glass. These were designed and installed by a twentieth-century artist, and they are of the most intense and brilliant colors—blood red, night purple, deep sea blue, forest green—all richly saturated, passionate, and modern. Everything about the place is old-fashioned and uninviting, except when you look into the depths—there is the surprise! When you enter the depths—as I did—and see those passionate windows, they are the church.

Molly invited me to move into her house until I left for overseas.

THE FAVORITE plane of the men fighting that war was the C-47, a two-engine, all-purpose, prop-driven job that had the capability of landing anywhere and taking off on a short run. The least favorite was the B-24, the aircraft carrying me and the two fellows with me east to Hollandia, MacArthur's headquarters on the island of New Guinea. I was given this information when I walked up front, where there was a child—so he seemed; was he twenty-one, was he one hundred and thirty pounds?—at the controls. I got to talking with him. We were flying on automatic pilot—known as "George"—and the "boy" had been reading a movie magazine. During our conversation, he hardly bothered to look ahead through the white cloud cover. When I asked him why the B-24 was in such disfavor with the men who flew it, he answered that it was no airplane, it was a boxcar, and that it had a tendency to explode. "No one has figured out why," he said, "and if two of these four motors stop, or even one when we're fully loaded, we go down." This conversation didn't make me more comfortable; I returned to the cargo bay, where people were spread like the playing cards of a deck that had been flung on the floor, most of them in uniform, some not, all very young. They were sitting on the floor—

there were no seats—or lying down; the heavy rhythm of the motors had lulled many of them to sleep. I returned to *War and Peace*.

I'd read, before I went to visit the pilot, Tolstoi's comment on Nicholas Rostov's letter home: that it was impossible for a young man to write the truth; unconsciously he will always favor himself and reject events and details that do not fit into the way he preferred things to have happened. That's where I'd stopped reading; the observation had reminded me of the letter I'd sent Constance while we were waiting in San Francisco for our orders to go overseas. I'd written her how much she'd meant to me, how much I missed her, and that I thought of her all the time—which was true—and that I was ashamed of what I'd done. I suppose it was an attempt to cautiously make it up with her—at least a friendship. She'd answered, as I deserved, curtly; it was the last message I would ever receive from her. "Why don't you act like a man for a change," she wrote. "Forget about me. C." That was all. My letter had been foolish and self-favoring. Her answer, true to the situation.

During the weeks before this flight, when Molly had given me shelter, she'd noticed, "You were grinding your teeth all night. Twitching too." One thing I was concerned about in my sleep was that I might murmur Constance's name. Old friends I'd run into had noticed that I would lapse into sudden silences, was not responsive when they expected I would be, then would blurt out answers to questions put to me minutes before. I'd also noticed that when I was alone and therefore not on guard, I would from time to time be on the verge of tears.

Constance's letter finished me; she was right, of course. I was to have further evidence of her practical good sense. One of the fellows flying east with me, a Hollywood comedy writer, had brought along copies of the *Hollywood Reporter*, and on page two, the page to which everyone in that community turns first, the waiting world was informed that my Constance was going out with Helmut Dantine now and that they were, officially, an "item." That was quick, I thought—and good news for her friends. Constance was rebuilding her life; was it from another table at the Beachcomber's and in another "tent"?

Although I thought of Constance whenever I was alone, particularly and most often at night, still I believed that she'd been killing me. By contrast I recalled Molly's voice; the morning before we were put on this plane, she'd called me from New Rochelle, where she was visiting my parents again for Sunday dinner. My mother was all on Molly's side, and both she and my father got on the phone to wish me a safe journey. Only Chris, then five years old, would not come in off the porch to talk to me. Again Molly said that his face was flushed with repressed emotion. But Judy was right by the phone, and it was nice to hear them all, and Molly sounded, as she always did, wonderfully warm and well-bred, a person of quality.

Now, forty years later, I recall myself crouched on the floor of that lumbering plane flying away from the sun, my back against the metal sidewall, holding a book I couldn't concentrate on, a small anxious man in psychological as well as physical flight, bewildered and in some confused way reaching to recover his self-respect. What I see in my memory's eye is a man who has just made a narrow escape. I'd saved my life.

I'd done it by hurting someone—how badly I had no idea yet. I'd behaved shamefully, in a way that I'd never altogether get over. But I had not, when I look back, lied to Constance. The passion I expressed for her was genuine; it was only when I saw the life that this union would lead to, the day-to-day existence I'd have, and compared it with how Molly was living her days, that I became desperate enough to do what I did.

What a narrow escape! I might have ended up a Fox staff director. My first film had been a great success, and Zanuck was hot after me. My long-term contract would have been eagerly "adjusted," that is, enriched. I could have had a lovely, spacious home in Bel Air in any one of a number of styles—they were all there to pick from—or a beach house in Malibu, or both, and why not a ranch up north in the Ojai Valley (only an hour and a half away)? I could certainly have had a numbered bank account in Switzerland and a press agent to see to it that I was showered with praise often enough to quiet any and all doubts I had about myself. I could have had my name in the *Hollywood Reporter* once a week like so many others and, as a reward, have enjoyed any success-hungry young actress I wanted. I could have had every joy that a successful career in Hollywood could have given me. And here is the best of it: I was loved; not challenged, loved! The crews loved me, the designers loved me, the department heads loved me, the cameramen en masse loved me; they were all eager to work with me. "When? When?" they'd cried. "When are you going to do another picture?" The Fox lot, that year of '45, was the happiest place I'd ever enjoyed. If I wasn't a king—that was Darryl—I was a prince. Everybody greeted me whether they knew me or not; they couldn't afford not to, for who could predict how far up in the world I'd rise? As for missing the New York crowd, they were all there or on the way west, ready to drink with me evenings or, on Sundays, picnic around swimming pools of emerald water, clear and clean enough to drink. And as for my contract to direct Sam Behrman's *Dunnigan's Daughter*—well, it wasn't a contract, it was only a handshake; my agent would find a way to weasel me out of that. I didn't want to do that damned play anyway.

And if I still wanted her, what would have stopped me from getting Constance back? She needed a protector now, and who was more successful than I would be?

There it was, the prospect ahead. And except for Molly's good sense and her humanity, her respect for me when I didn't have respect for myself, I would have been that great guy in Successville, California, surrounded by friends who'd "made" it or were about to "make" it or looked to me to help them make it.

What stopped me?

Forty years is a long perspective, but perhaps it can afford a clear view. I look back at Clifford Odets—no one I've known was more talented. He couldn't resist the money, the flattery, the apparent safety and security in the movie community. And he lost himself. Harold Clurman, one of the men I've most admired, was lucky: The people who ran the big studios did not want him, and he had to come east again; that saved him, for he seemed lost in southern California. But I'm not praising the East over the West. New York was simply my habitat, where my sources were. In Hollywood I'd have had to rely on my cleverness and my facility, which are technical, not artistic, qualities. The one time I met William Faulkner, I remember he wore rubber boots and they were covered with the mud of his Mississippi winter. He never left his home in Oxford for very long. John Steinbeck left northern California and looked a fool in New York theatre society and on the right bank of Paris. Saul Bellow is wise; he stays in Chicago. As for Nick Ray, who knew more about the back roads and so on, I saw him give himself over and be lost among the moguls of the film world. And Orson Welles, the most talented and inventive theatre man of my day: What an ass he seemed in the posh restaurants and hotels of Europe's capitals, and how sad later, in financial desperation, making TV commercials. I was to watch with an awful pain how lost Tennessee Williams was as he shuttled around the bright spots of the world. The money his great success brought him allowed him to live in a way that squashed his talent. He would have been better off living in his native South, that part of the world where he was uncomfortable, even outraged, because he felt he was an outsider. Notice Picasso, how he stayed where his clay was, and Matisse and Renoir and Cézanne. It's difficult to get Fellini out of Italy for any reason, or Bergman out of Sweden or Satyajit Ray out of Bengal. They know where their artistic roots are. I was with Kurosawa in New York City and he seemed like a child eager to return home—which he soon did. Read the letters of Gustave Flaubert and notice how rarely he made the trip—an hour? two?—to Paris, where his mistress was eagerly waiting to see him. He knew his material was in the province of Normandy. And Proust: He lived in what he wrote about—a life no one else could tolerate.

I'm saying that the choice I had to make that year had less to do with two women—I had strong feelings about both—than with the way of life each of them would have brought me into. True, I would not have made the choices I made except for Molly and her recognition of what I now, forty years later, can see. I garden in Connecticut and I've learned how difficult it is to transplant a tree after its roots are down. But I almost tried it. From this distance of years, I look back and see that I was sick and that I was

saved by the concern and the respect that Molly gave me. It was her present to me, one she was able to give because she loved me.

As for sexual love, passion for the physical possession of a woman, it now
seems less relevant to me than self-preservation. We Americans have made
it into a kind of measure of worth. It is not. I dislike using the word "love"
now, it's been so soiled by our pop songs, although I do have the emotion I
call love for my present wife and my children and my grandchildren. I
notice that it is a far broader feeling than the competitive challenge of "Who
gets the girl?" I loved Constance, but being with her was wiping out my
life. Molly filled me with hope and some beginning of self-esteem, at least
a sense of who I was. Everything I saw and learned and knew on the trip
overseas that was to follow confirmed my belief as to what I should do with
what ability and gifts I had and what I was truly concerned about. If I was
sick, as I believe I was, that trip to the war zone was my cure. I would bring
back memories and impressions that have fed me the rest of my life. I
would return a rich man—not in money or fame but in materials for the
work I might do. Now, forty years later, I wish I had twice as long to live,
for I am just beginning to use the world I've seen.

A F E W words to finish her story. Constance never made it in Hollywood.
She went to Europe with her sister, Doris, and for years in Italy they were
admired and happy. There Constance became the lover of Cesare Pavese,
a fine poet who had sexual problems and no doubt others which were the
source of his sexual problems. Pavese committed suicide and Constance
returned to the States, married a film producer, and had two sons. She died
before she could fully enjoy her time of peace and her sons. When she was
forty-seven, a brain hemorrhage ended her life.

W E P U T down at Hollandia, on the north coast of New Guinea. I looked
for the place on the map today, couldn't find it; still I recall a settlement
there. No sooner had our plane landed than another followed; we were part
of an endless penetration. The first man we talked to said it was cool that
day on the "strip"; they'd known a temperature of 120 degrees. We rode
through the colony army engineers had thrown up on the coastal plain.
Here were the black soldiers, "service troops"; they'd not been given guns,
but drove trucks, unloaded supplies, tended to sanitation. I remembered
something Lighton had said about blacks; he regretted that they were being
educated, because they'd "lose their realest, childlike qualities." God, what
a fool!

We turned up the slope leading to the hill where MacArthur's headquarters had been; men from California had dubbed it Snob Hill. The general,
moving east, had already walked through the surf onto the island of Leyte.

"I have returned," he said. So had a lot of men with him. A heavy, wind-driven rain began to fall and would continue through most of the three weeks we'd be there. Our mission was to set up self-entertainment units for the soldiers, so keep the men from going nuts before they were shipped to other theatres of action or home. I found that the soldiers didn't think much of the USO shows. They enjoyed seeing pretty girls twisting and bumping, but afterward they called it cock-teasing. As for the jokemasters, the comics, the men felt most of them were third-rate cabaret entertainers, tasteless and corny. But there was nothing else to do except shoot craps and play cards.

Yes, there were the WACS to date. Someone described these women as the contemporary foreign legion; they all had some unhappy event in their past that had caused them to put on the uniform. In order to date one of these women, a soldier needed, besides a moderate show of desire, a jeep and a pistol. The jeep was to pick up the WAC and ride her to a dark place; the pistol, it was said, was to confront the blacks who, "as everyone knows, will rape a white girl quicker than you can say 'condom.'"

I felt our mission was absurd. Men out of combat didn't want to bother with anything but food and sleep. Their entertainment was gambling. Someone called the barracks where they lived rows of cots separated by crap games. I'd come for my own purpose. I would get up before the two fellows with me and hitch a ride to the hospital. There I saw the innocent faces of the wounded. They were no more than boys and remarkably open about their shattered fates. I saw some with the entire lower half of their bodies in casts. Others had had their faces remade, the noses realigned and large patches of new skin. What they wanted was not praise or sympathy but to be treated like normal people, which was of course impossible. Their great concern was whether they would ever be whole again.

It was there that I met a young actor, a pupil at the Juilliard School, a soft-faced kid with tender feelings. He was very handsome; that is, he used to be. He'd been in the first wave landing on Leyte, the next island we were going to; a grenade had shattered his leg and mutilated his face. He told me his story. His company had been ordered to take Hill 522. Intelligence had told their colonel in command that there was only a company of Japanese on the hill. Later it turned out to have been a regiment. The lieutenant in command of the boy's company was beloved by his men for his human concern. He protested the colonel's order to rush the hill; his men hadn't slept for four nights, he said. The colonel threatened to strip him down to buck private then and there if he didn't obey his orders. The lieutenant led the charge himself and was instantly killed. The company, when they found they were facing a regiment and were without a commanding officer, retreated, leaving their lieutenant's body on the field of battle. They watched the Japanese, high on drink ("They take sake before all battles," the Juilliard boy told me, "they fight drunk"), find the young lieutenant's body, hack it to pieces, and shoot into it again and again. Even after the lieutenant was hours dead, the Japanese took turns ripping it to shreds as the members of his company watched.

"I'm bored," Constance used to say. "Let's do something." "Let's go to a bookstore," I'd say, "and buy some books." "You haven't read the books you bought day before yesterday," she said. "Let's go to a movie. Let's buy some shoes for me, let's take a ride, let's do something!" "Let's have a gold and go to bed," I'd say.

I couldn't remember hearing Molly say that she was bored.

I heard endless stories of Japanese atrocities: how they'd hang a man up by his thumbs, slit his belly open and pour gasoline inside, then ignite it. Our men had their answer; they took forty-nine Japanese prisoners, tied them up in a tight ring, doused them with airplane fuel, and burned them all. Gasoline was in plentiful supply. When they flew Japanese prisoners back for questioning in a C-47, they kept the freight door at the side of the plane open, and when the questioning of each man was concluded, he'd be kicked overboard before they reached their destination. Neither side took prisoners.

I thought of the play I was supposed to do, *Dunnigan's Daughter.* How could I possibly make the problems of a wealthy middle-class woman important? I meant, to myself.

"If we leave one straw shithouse in Tokyo standing when we get there," an officer who'd lost a leg told me, "our children and our grandchildren should shoot us dead." This man, today, is probably watching a ball game on a Sony and driving a Toyota.

We had three weeks in Hollandia. The area had become a place for rest and recreation, but the recreation the boys wanted was not one we could provide. From time to time we went through the motions of planning what we'd been sent there to do, prepared reports and sheets of suggestions and so on, but I was indifferent to the plans I was urging and had secretly given up. I was there only to see something of this huge war operation before it was over and to escape a personal situation I couldn't handle. Now, with time on my hands, I was beginning to loosen the tensions I'd brought with me. I wrote notes on everything I saw and collected souvenirs. I took a long walk into the Papuan jungle with a soldier being rotated back to the States and picked up "jungle rot," which caused pieces of skin as big as quarters to peel off my underarms. I made notes on that too and would show the scabs as souvenirs.

Then the time came for us to be moved up closer to the fighting. We received orders to go on to Tacloban, on the island of Leyte, which had been the staging area for the assault on the main island, Luzon, and its capital, Manila. Where our C-47 put down, however, was not Tacloban but a very small island en route, Biak.

I could see as we came down that there'd been a great deal of fighting on Biak. In the surf along the ocean side of the runway were wrecks of planes in all stages of decomposition. Apparently some had crashed on land-ing or nosed over, and since, for a few days, planes were coming in at the rate of one every five minutes, the only efficient thing to do was bulldoze the wrecks into the surf. Our pilot, when he saw the mess, commented, "There are hot pilots and there are old pilots, but there are no old hot pilots." He put down carefully, for the strip was short and we came to it off the side of a hill. As we walked out of the plane it was raining, and the area smelled of fish rotting in a lagoon at the end of the strip. The island, essen-tial to General MacArthur's island-hopping program, had been stormed by the marines, and that had been costly. I recalled the words of a general—that he could never see a marine again without a feeling of reverence.

An artilleryman spoke of Japanese prisoners. "When they're taken," he said, "they have to be protected from our men, who'd as soon kill them as look at them; it only takes a second." But once the Japanese is made to feel safe, he may be as eager to revenge himself on his officers as our men are—for Japanese "brass" make a practice of slapping their underlings and hu-miliating them. One prisoner pointed out, for the benefit of our artillery, where his officer's command post was, directed the fire, jabbering all the time and jumping up and down for joy every time one of the pieces he'd directed had scored a hit. "What happened to him in the end?" I asked. "Oh, somebody got him," the soldier said.

I had a surprise that night; they were showing—believe it or not—*A Tree Grows in Brooklyn*. The theatre was a slope of rough turf; the soldiers sat on the ground, the officers and favored nurses on a low platform. The screen, with its projections of New York street scenes and the tenement of Jimmy Dunn and his family, was framed by palm trees, showing scars of the preinvasion bombing. It rained all through the show, but I had the impres-sion most everyone without a duty that night was there. Overhead the sky hung low. A plane was overdue and four great lights were sending up beams: beacons. P-61's, night fighters known as "Black Widows," circled on ceaseless patrol. The last alert had been three weeks before, but we were still very much on watch. Along the side of the theatre was the main road leading to the airstrip. Heavy equipment kept rolling by: "ducks," "cats," "six-by-sixes," the whole procession peppered with jeeps. The sound of all this movement never stopped during the projection. Neither did the rain.

With all this going on, it was difficult to be interested in the film. But when the reel broke at one point, there was a great groan from the crowd, and the final scenes were received with happy laughter. They liked our people. I heard a nurse say that at home she would have used four hand-kerchiefs. But I was impatient with the film; all I could think of was the contrast between the terrible intensity and cost of what was happening all around me and the sentimental fairy tale I'd made—so it seemed to me then. I left as soon as I could, went to my cot, and opened the can of sardines I'd brought with me. I didn't tell anyone that the film was mine. The next morning there was a rumor that a few of the Japanese still left on the island had sneaked to a place at the very top of the hill so they could watch the movie. No one had bothered them.

We remained in Biak another two days, then the weather improved and we left. On Leyte I ran into a couple of old friends, actors from New York, Salem Ludwig and Will Lee (Lubovsky). I knew Lee from the Theatre of Action and recalled the days, not long before, when Hitler and Stalin were in bed together and the whole left gang had been against taking part in this war. Now here he was, chipper as a grasshopper, the most cheerful man in camp. He would survive to once again, a few years later, indict "all capitalist wars" and make a living doing commercial announcements for Xerox. Despite this, I never stopped liking the lively little fellow.

When I was alone with Salem Ludwig, he told me he'd received a "Dear John" letter a few weeks before. It had come during a letup in Japanese artillery fire. In the sudden quiet, the men in foxholes had seen a jeep with the mail pulling up, and they'd jumped out of their holes and run for the home news. Salem had to stand in line for a while, and by the time he had his letter, the stuff was coming over again, so he rushed for his foxhole, crouched down into it, and opened his mail. The letter was from his wife and no way exceptional—five or six of his friends had been unloaded by their wives, fiancées, and sweethearts in the same "least painful" manner. They'd formed an informal club, calling themselves "The Betrayed," and kidded each other by quoting their letters. "The reason you haven't heard from me the last few weeks—*Dear!*—is that I've met someone—*Darling!*" (or in one case, that of a fiancée, "that I got married"). Then there'd generally be something like: "I wish you could meet him. I'm sure you'd like him very much." Which was the cue for the horse laughs and the pledge, "Yes, *Dear!* I'll look him up first thing I get home." A ranger who'd received such a letter wouldn't joke about it or even talk about it; the only way anyone knew what had happened was when he picked up a pail of paint at Supply and smeared a girl's name off the side of his jeep.

A few nights later I went to another USO show, *Girls on Parade*, and that's why we went, to be reminded girls exist. The day before, a C-47, credited by all as the safest plane in the air, had crashed at Hollandia. It was carrying eleven USO girls for another show, called *Mexican Hayride;* all had been killed. But nothing was said about that where we were sitting watching these other "kids" "strutting their stuff." The boys howled like wolves and yelled for more. They left aroused, dissatisfied, and ready for hell.

I'd heard that morning that the U.S. Army was running a whorehouse just outside Tacloban, and we walked over to have a look. It was being administered by MP's, and the boys who wanted to buy a piece lined up the same way they did for chow. It was a long line, and it led to six small huts. The tariff was ten pesos, about five dollars American, and my guess was that the army was making a profit. I don't know who the girls were, I didn't get to see any of them, but at those prices they couldn't have been imported from very far. The boys, hot out of *Girls on Parade*, were being hustled through the huts quickly, their stay inside averaging four or five minutes. From the huts, they were directed quickly to an army prophylactic station nearby. Down the road there was a pit, lit by the light from two old trucks, where the locals were fighting their game birds. Some of our men were there, betting; it made an evening of it.

A few days later, I was to enjoy a higher level of entertainment. I received an invitation to ride across water to the navy's installation on Subic Bay. "They have whiskey there," I was promised. And they did, with all the "fixings"—meaning ice—you could hope for. The navy brass lived on a plane above that of the army. Their officers ran a traffic by swift B-25's and torpedo boats to Australia. They brought back whiskey, green vegetables, and meat. "I mean proper steaks," the officer who was our host on shore said. As the whiskey worked, tongues were loosened. That day the subject was the savagery of our Philippine allies; admiration was mixed with scorn.

"When we broke the back of the Japanese fleet off Leyte south of here," one of them was telling, "thousands of Japanese sailors were pitched into the water and set out swimming for shore. A unit of U.S. Army was ordered to get down there and pick up a few prisoners for our G-2 to question. When they reached the point of land toward which the Japanese were swimming, they saw that the water was crowded with Philippine small craft—canoes, dugouts, and such. The Filipinos weren't killing the Japs. They had machetes and would lop off one arm, then the other, and leave the Nips, still alive, for the sharks."

When it was time to go, one of the officers, who'd been looking at me without speaking, offered his opinion—with a mocking smile—that the next war would be between New York and the rest of the country. Obviously he thought I was a Jew.

It was on the way back to the launch that I heard Roosevelt had died. He'd been my hero all through the Depression, still was, and is now as I write this. When I heard, the next day, that there was going to be a memorial service for him in Manila, I had to get up there quickly. This would require a change of plans, which, in the rhythm of the army, would take more time than I wanted to wait. So I broke the form and the rules. I went out to the strip and bluffed my way onto an Army Transport Command plane. It was easier than I'd thought possible.

THE CAPITAL city of Manila was a shocking sight from the sky. The airport hangars were demolished and the runways, except for the main strip, which had been immediately repaired, were pitted with bomb cra-

ters. Our plane had to pick its way around them as we taxied to our berth.
The city itself, it was said, compared for devastation with anything in Europe. I saw no whole buildings; everything standing had been gutted by
demolition bombs or burned out by the fires ignited by the departing foe.
Masonry walls had been reduced to rubble by our artillery. The enemy had
been left without a hole to hide in. Nevertheless the Japanese were stubborn fighters, and our men had to engage them house to house. Out of one
group of forty-five men dispatched into the city, seventeen came out.

How absurd our "self-entertainment" mission seemed compared with
what I saw around me. But there was nothing for me to do except stick up
for it. I went straight to the headquarters of the United States Armed
Forces–Far East and asked to see a Colonel Metcalf. By now I'd found the
army to be a mass of jealousies and intramural conflicts. Everybody pushed
and pulled for what he wanted. I'd decided that boldness would win out. I
wanted to stay on in Manila, then go on up north into the hills and get close
to some fighting.

In the letter I presented to Colonel Metcalf, I complained about the
indifferent treatment we'd received from Colonel Disston of the Service of
Supply in Tacloban, who clearly wanted us to give up our mission and go
home. I pointed out that Disston was a former cavalry officer from Fort
Riley, perhaps not the best person to pass judgment on the value of our
mission. I said that one of our fellows had already given up in disgust and
been returned to the States, that the composer who'd come with me was
on the verge of doing the same thing, and if I became convinced that we
weren't really wanted there, I'd go back immediately too. Colonel Metcalf
was surprisingly cordial. He said Disston was on his way north, and when
he arrived we'd consult together. Which was what I wanted—unsupervised
time in Manila. Colonel Metcalf said that the first thing to do was to get me
a place to sleep, and I was encouraged enough to say to him that my strongest desire was to attend the memorial service for Roosevelt. Colonel Metcalf shared my feeling for FDR; he said he'd let me know when it was going
to take place and would accompany me to the service. As I left, he shook
my hand and complimented me on A Tree Grows in Brooklyn. Now I
understood his cordiality; a celebrity is a celebrity.

I was still pretending, putting on an act of intense interest in our mission
when I didn't believe in it any more than Colonel Disston did. I was afraid
that if I didn't press this way, I'd be sent back to the States. I was now
completely involved in the drama everywhere around me; my way of life
had been challenged by what I'd seen.

I was billeted in what had been a wholesale dress house, now standing
with three walls; my cot was behind a trading counter of highly polished
wood. The place was packed with men; there were cots and mattresses in
every corner. As soon as I'd dropped my bag, I walked out into the street,
a main thoroughfare, which was littered with paper money, like the leaves

of autumn, printed by the Japanese for their occupation and marked in Japanese and English. A little Philippine boy, judging me to be what I was, a sightseer, pulled at my arm, saying, "Hey, Joe, hey, Joe, look! Dead Japanese, come, look!" He pointed to a row of trolleys, and I went along. They'd been used as barricades and were badly shot up. In one of them was a dead Japanese soldier. I smelled him before I saw him; he was decomposing. His arms, shrunken in decay, clutched his belly; evidently that's where he got hit. His lips were pulled back, revealing his teeth, a kind of smile; his hair had matted, as the perspiration dried, to a kind of felt. The little Filipino kid kept yelling at the dead soldier, "Son of a bitch, Japanese, goddamn Japanese!" Was he doing it for my benefit? I gave the kid a piece of their money, but he threw it away; he wanted U.S. money only. That's how fast history moves.

Nearby, off-duty soldiers, tourists for a day, were looking at a building. Inside there was a sign: "In this room, on this very wall, by these pegs, American officers and men were hung by their thumbs and beaten to death so you bastards could come to Manila and get drunk!"

So I passed that day and the next. Then there was a message from Metcalf, asking me to come by. He told me that the secretary of war, Stimson, and General Marshall, our chief of staff, had ordered memorials for Roosevelt to be conducted in every post and base where the conditions of war allowed. The service to which we went was thinly attended, and we had to wait some time for General MacArthur to arrive. Then there was a military bark and everyone, including me, jumped to his feet and to attention. MacArthur entered and gestured for the rest of us to sit. He took a place in the front row, and the service was under way. He seemed shorter than I'd expected; one reason he gave the impression of height was the arrogant—call it proud—carriage of his head. The ceremony was disgraceful, a mumbo-jumbo of traditional forms, banal gibberish rendered in a singsong, words about brotherhood and love offered up by men whose thoughts were only of killing. There was a hymn, "O God, Our Help in Ages Past," an invocation spoken in unison, and a psalm done in responses between the chaplain and the congregation, then a prayer, and we all sang "My Country, 'Tis of Thee." That was it. Not a single word of genuine regret was spoken; MacArthur said nothing. Three honest sentences spoken by the most ordinary person would have done Roosevelt more honor. Did MacArthur rely on those sterile forms to conceal the fact that he had no feeling of loss?

Two days later, Colonel Disston arrived, and we had our conference. What a back-and-forth purring went on between the two colonels. Apparently there was a conflict between two army organizations, and I was in the middle, but the truth was that they were both convinced that my mission was impractical. I said I insisted on writing a report in full detail before I left, and in order to do that, I would have to observe some units engaged in combat. Then I'd write my report, fly home, and deliver it to the authorities who'd sent me to the Far East theatre of war. That would bring my mission to a proper conclusion.

I'd discovered that writing a report is a threatening act to those who'll be mentioned. Metcalf and Disston were pleased to go along with my compromise suggestion, because the next day I was introduced to the public relations officer of the Thirty-second Division, which was engaged in an operation north of the capital, along something called the Villa Verde Trail. Promptly thereafter I had a radio transmission from the commanding officer of this the Red Arrow Division, a General Gill, two stars. It was addressed to an Alla Kaxon but was otherwise in order, in fact went beyond anything I expected. "I understand you are interested in obtaining information concerning the activities of the 32nd Division. I extend my invitation for you to visit our Division and examine its records of which we are proud. Transportation and quarters have been arranged for you and I wish to assure you . . ." And so on. Signed, Gill.

Concern was expressed that I might become a casualty item for the hungry media and that the military would catch hell for allowing me to go into a combat zone. I lied, assuring them my intention was to stay close to division headquarters, where I'd certainly be safe. Okay! A Piper Cub was being sent to take me north.

It dropped me on a strip so unmarked that I didn't see it until we were on it. I got out, the pilot followed, lifted the plane by its tail, turned it around—that's all it weighed—and he was off south again. A man stood by a jeep. "General Gill is expecting you, sir," he said.

"No, no questions, General Gill," I said, when I was taken to him. "I just want to tag along after you and see what I see." He smiled and made a hardly noticeable gesture with his head and one arm, a courtly gesture offered by a restrained man, which made me feel welcome. We were walking along the trail—it couldn't be called a road; it was exactly as wide as a jeep. On either side of us was a scattering of tents, not all the same size and shape and in no particular order. In the distance ahead of us, under a gray sky heavily loaded with clouds, was a row of round green hills, bare of trees, rolling off in waves until they disappeared under the clouds. The effect of this backdrop was melancholy, and there was a chill in the air. The breeze whined, accentuating the emptiness of the place. Despite General Gill's affirmation, in his radio transmission, of the Red Arrow Division's pride, the overall impression I had was not of pride but of gloom and exhaustion.

"Where's the front, sir?" I asked. He was preoccupied, even when he spoke to me; weary he was and had been for a long time. He had an inexpressive face, long drawn into a mask of pain and patience. He'd been striding along with his long legs, and I'd had to churn my short ones to stay alongside. My question broke his face a little—a sort of smile. "You can't call it a front," he said. "It's not that kind of war." He waved a long arm in a half circle. "He's all around us, the foe. The fighting is on every side of us and sometimes at our rear." Then he pointed directly ahead. "Hear that?" he asked. I didn't hear anything except the wind. "No, not the small-arms fire," he said, "the bulldozer. Hear it?" "Yes," I lied. "It's working this road so we can move up on it. Our assignment is to reach Santa Fe on Route 5 before the rains make this"—he pointed down to what we were walking on—"a quagmire. Then it would fall away, and all that we've been doing would be lost. We'd be isolated and cut off, and that"—another eloquent gesture—"that you could fairly call a disaster. That is our assignment, you see." Then for the first time he looked directly at me.

"Yes, sir," I said.

We passed a battery of cannon. "One-oh-fives," Gill said. "You'll hear them tonight. As for what you call the 'front,' they're also under us. The foe tunnels. Although what worries me most now is that our intelligence tells me there's a large body of them there." He pointed to a ridge of hills parallel to the trail at a distance of a few miles. "On my flank. My flank, it's thin. I don't know why they haven't come down yet, and that worries me. Maybe they're waiting for the rains to fall and wash away our road." He gave me a wry smile. "That would be terrible. I can't imagine it." Another faint smile.

"The foe," he went on, "is dogged and unyielding. He has to be pried out, cave by cave, or sealed in with dynamite inserted with long poles so we can smother him to death by blocking all entrances. These tunnels are elaborate; I saw one go three stories underground and with long arms. That's when we lose men, getting close enough to do what we have to do with the dynamite. We know when we have them, because as soon as the foe realizes he's trapped, he'll commit suicide with a grenade. Our boys hear a scream, then the sound of the grenade. The Nip, you know, doesn't surrender; he doesn't have the concept in his military vocabulary. They know we don't trust them. Too many have come up, hands in the air, but when taken they've blown themselves and whoever was at their side to hell and gone." He was silent again, and his stride lengthened; I had to hustle to keep up.

"How quiet it is," I said. It was just a comment; I didn't expect a response. I wanted to leave him in peace. He smiled and nodded. "Yes, it's a war of patrols. You'll hear small-arms fire all night." "Casualties heavy?" I asked. His face did not become more solemn; it had been drawn full length for a long time. "You mean ours?" he asked. I nodded. "A man in my position can't worry about casualties. If he did, he'd go out of his mind. Anyway, the foe is losing ten to our one." Then his face stiffened. "Which is no comfort."

He reminded me of Bud Lighton, a proud man full of pain he'd never relieve.

He was silent again, thinking of something that lengthened his stride, and he seemed to have forgotten me. I'd been told by his jeep driver, who'd picked me up from the plane, that Gill was from the South. "Virginia," he'd said, "a Virginia gentleman. He's someone you can die for, because he hasn't told us any lies. He doesn't like this campaign any more than the men do. But there it is, we don't have any choice. He fights for the men. Many of us have been combat weary for years, three years, and the rotation system doesn't work when it comes to us. They want the veterans here. But the veterans get tired, and that's when they begin to buy it; when you're tired you get careless. Gill fights for us, and he doesn't stay in the rear—you notice that? His tent is right up there with the rest of the men."

"How heavy *are* the casualties, General Gill?" I asked. He didn't hear me, and I didn't insist on the question. It had come out of me suddenly and I wished I hadn't asked it again. Then he answered—he had heard—saying, "About thirty a day. There, see." We'd come to the field hospital, a mound of sandbags, it looked like. On the ground was a line of bodies covered with blankets, except for their feet, which pointed straight up. Some of the shoes the dead wore looked almost new. There are families in the States, I thought, who don't know it, but they've lost a son.

The general ducked his head, hurried past the opening in the sandbags and on through a plywood door that a soldier was holding open. There he turned and made a sign to me and I did the same—but faster. I understood; the hospital had been or was still under fire. I stood just inside the entrance, flat against the wall, and watched while Gill spoke to the doctors—there were three—who looked well past a point that could be described as weary. I imagine he was asking if they needed anything he could give them. They shook their heads. There was an air of improvisation about the place: a row of cots at the entrance to receive the wounded when they were brought in, an ashcan for a scrub-up basin, empty bandage boxes for lampshades. I thought of the hospital in Hollandia, bustling with nurses; a rest home, compared with this. Gill was speaking to the wounded, laying a sympathetic hand on each of them, like a papa taking the responsibility for their lives. Then Gill was asking them about the placement and numbers of the Japanese they'd faced. The men answered soberly, pointing in the appropriate directions; they knew that their accounts were valued. Here was the infantry, the anonymous, dirty infantry, now learning to fight a war in the style of the Japanese, becoming night fighters, infiltrators, and dynamiters, as able with the silent knife as with the quick grenade. I imagined many of them were glad to be wounded; it meant they were on their way home. In a far corner, a pair was playing cards, blackjack. They didn't raise their heads when a soldier was carried out the door, laid at the end of the line on the ground, and covered with an old brown blanket.

"Yardage," Gill said; he'd walked past the hospital and on up the trail. "That's what they're screaming for. But this terrain, as you can see, is all up- and downhill, and our advances don't show on their maps, or they seem insignificant." Then he pointed. "There!" I detected pride in his voice. He was indicating a caterpillar-propelled bulldozer. "I finally got a cat that was armored," he said. "They'd killed two of my drivers and I had to raise hell, but they got it to me. Every once in a while, they take a shot at this boy or throw a grenade at him—you can see he makes a beautiful target sitting up there. But there he is, still cutting my road." When I asked where the Japanese were, Gill said, "Up ahead, maybe a hundred yards. But, as I told you, it's not a fixed line. Sometimes this kid"—he pointed to the cat— "penetrates past our farthest OP."

The driver of the cat, who'd been making a shoulder in the road, saw the general and turned across the road, stopped, and got out on our side, crouching behind his cat. Gill joined him, also sitting on his heels, and I sat on my heels, although it wasn't natural for a city boy. Gill was like a kid when he spoke to the driver; authority replaced by affection and admiration, he was like a fan with a ballplayer. "Quiet morning," the driver said. Then they talked about the road ahead. Since Gill's campaign depended upon this supply line being opened and kept open, he was grateful for the bravery of the "boy" in the cat; he hero-worshipped him.

I thought of the mass and wealth of the equipment that America's industries had supplied: the planes coming in, one every five minutes, and taking right off again; the fleet of ships I'd seen choking the harbor at Subic Bay, where I'd visited the navy and enjoyed their Scotch and their steaks; the PT boats and the huge supply ships and fuel tankers. I remembered Hollandia and the trucks making deliveries day and night, always driven by blacks, and I recalled the suburban comforts of MacArthur's hilltop headquarters. I remembered MacArthur, how he held his head, and his enormous staff, men with authority over lives of thousands of other men. I thought of the airfield in California, where there was a traffic of men and material so great that we had to wait a week for space going west even after we'd been put on alert. I thought of the men in Washington I'd watched when I'd put on that silly show about rationing: the "goddamn noncombatants," I'd heard them called, and included myself in their number—the swivel-chair generals and the chairborne commandos and Abe Lastfogel, who'd finagled this trip for me, and our comedy writer, who could always get a table at El Morocco. All that historic effort, America at war, ended up here with this single kid in a cat, pushing through a narrow road under sniper fire; he was the spearpoint! All of which told a truth: This war, the actual warfare, was being fought by a very few. All the rest were "support troops." They didn't risk their lives but ate breast of turkey and other delicacies stolen from Supply—moonlight requisitioning, it's called; they slept between sheets, laughed at Bob Hope's one-liners, and stretched their cocks watching—and dreaming about—the girls he'd brought over to do their bumps and grinds, and sat in the rain to see A Tree Grows in Brooklyn.

We walked along silently and I couldn't look at his face. I was there on a falsely presented cause, a fake. He, with his life in danger every instant of every day, was bearing up under the deaths of his soldiers, each day a heavy count and no end in sight, as he struggled to carry out orders that, I suspected, he thought unfair. I was in awe of the pain the man carried. I was abashed.

We decided (Gill decided) not to climb the hill ahead (I learned that fifteen minutes later it was well plastered). On the way back I asked him to drop me off at the field hospital. "Stay inside," Gill said. "We think it's covered by one of their mortars." I assured him I'd be careful, and he went off, a tall, gaunt man, shoulders stooped by pain and concern.

I watched the wounded come in, ordinary American boys, one after the other, the ones who had the job of beating the Japs for us. Some, twisted in wretched pain, were dropped on a cot, their last bit of strength gone. In the area near the door, there was that never-ending game of blackjack on the cot next to the one where the wounded were first laid out. The aides would carry in a man, put him down, then pick up their cards where they'd left off.

I edged closer. It seemed there was a major operation being performed every half hour—done in a miraculous style, deft, daring, quick. There was no time to lose; several of the men might have died if they'd been taken farther back in a jeep. At one table, a flashlight was being used for tight work. A boy who'd been given a local anesthetic impressed me. A doctor was working on his calf, digging out bits of shattered bone. On an adjoining cot, another man was reading a sheet of war news. The boy whose leg was being worked on raised his head and pointed out that the news was two days old and that the Russians were considerably closer to Berlin now. No one seemed interested in this development. The doctor, meantime, had been digging into the muscles of the boy's leg, and he now held up a jagged piece of metal. "Here's a piece of Stateside scrap iron for you," he said. The doctor dropped the metal fragment into a metal basin, and it made a sound I haven't forgotten.

Compared to all that I was witnessing, I was ashamed of the fuss I'd made about a "love" problem. Again I had the feeling that I didn't want to leave here, that I didn't want to go home—whatever and wherever that was.

Perhaps it was the kinship I felt so strongly with these men that made me, when I left the field hospital, turn the other way, not back to division headquarters but toward the cat. All was quiet ahead, all seemed peaceful. In the distance we heard planes at work, strafing. They must be ours, I figured; theirs would be closer to us, their targets. The sound of the cat working as I got closer to it was comforting. What was propelling me on? Gill had instructed me not to, and I respected his orders, but on I went. Pushed on by what? When I came to the cat, I made a sign, waving my hand out ahead, and the driver made a corresponding sign, informing me, I chose to believe, that all was clear ahead. I went on slowly, up what was now an overgrown footpath. Was this a manifestation of the bond I felt? Or was I just fed up with myself and didn't care what happened to me? Did I want to share what the wounded in the field hospital were suffering? The road, once I was past the cat, was no more than a trail, and there was some cover on it, a few scrubby trees. I was frightened now, but I didn't stop. The breeze was damp and it was fresh on my face, but the quiet, once I'd left the cat behind, was eerie. The only sound was that of the planes in the distance, across the valley. Again I felt that wish: that I would never leave here. I have rarely since felt this close to anything or anybody. Was that it, the closeness, that propelled me on? Or was it a manifestation of a crack-up, the one I'd been warned about? Did I want to end my life here, with people I admired without qualification?

As I was walking along, I kicked something soft—and hard. It felt peculiar to my toe. I stooped to see what it was. A Japanese head. The man was partly bald, and the top of his head looked like one of Luther Adler's old wigs, left over from his days at the Yiddish theatre. This fellow had been rotting awhile, for the odor was heavy. I walked on. You don't feel anything about their dead, I thought; ours break you up. I didn't approve of that thought, but there it was. Then I saw some men, ours, inside a crater made by a big shell. They were below the level of the edge, which is why I hadn't seen them as I approached.

"There's a dead Jap back there," I said.

"They're all through here," one of them answered. "Don't you smell them?"

"Better get down," another man said urgently.

I jumped into the crater.

"How do you know they're not ours?" I asked.

Then these men, so young, so hardened, spoke of smells. What they told me was that "theirs" (the smell of dead Japanese) was different from ours, that decaying bodies don't smell as bad as putrid, disintegrating blood, that there were areas all through where we were that were saturated with these smells; hadn't I noticed? One of them claimed he could tell a live Japanese by his smell, knew when they were close at night that way.

One of them didn't speak; he was observing something in the distance. I saw what it was, an air show. Our 47's were bombing and strafing the hillside opposite, the flank General Gill was worried about. Although the airplanes rarely reached the well-dug-in Japanese with what they dropped, they were, I could see, heartening to our men, reminding them of the power of our side. When the stuff was coming at us, going the other way, it was easy to forget this, and the morale of the men dropped. Another thing was that when they were being strafed, the Japanese artillery pulled in their horns. That's why it had been so quiet as I walked along the trail.

"Can anybody see what they're shooting at?" I asked.

"Shooting up their artillery, I hope," one of the boys said.

"What they're shooting up is my war bonds is what," the boy who'd been silent said.

There was a general grunt of agreement.

MY "QUARTERS" was a tent near the perimeter's edge, with barbed wire close up behind me. It had been suggested that I might prefer to go down to the village—five or six miles behind the fighting—to sleep, but I'd refused. Why? For the same reason that I'd walked in the wrong direction once I'd left the field hospital. I had two roommates. The division's PR man had come up, and with him was a fellow from *Yank* named Lew Gillenson (who later became well known in publishing), both of whom I'd met before. There was a full moon, and the view was enchanting, soft and glistening, truly beautiful. I asked whether a bright moon was favored by infiltrators; opinions differed. On the barbed wire behind our tent were strung, at regular intervals, either two empty ration tins close together or little horseshoe noisemakers; either would serve as a warning at night if a Nip was trying to get through. That's the terror time for the men, after dark. The Japanese army's special work was done then: knives and dynamite.

A fellow from Divarty (Division Artillery) who knew the man from *Yank* came by to visit. He talked about Santa Barbara, recalling all the romantic things about it. This boy was married and, like so many of the others, had a little boy back home whom he'd never seen. He said that when he got home, he wanted to put on a pair of light flannel trousers and a T-shirt and just sit on the porch. Do absolutely nothing, just sit there in the breeze. Maybe his wife would bring him a drink, maybe not; it didn't matter. The main thing was to sit there, coolly, comfortably, with no danger, no demands. I'd been to Santa Barbara with Constance not so long before, just to "get away from everybody," we'd said. This boy from Divarty recalled the waterfront and the restaurant at the end of the pier where we'd eaten too, and the hills covered with live oaks and the velvety air, and as he did, the 155's began to work, firing salvo after salvo. Sometimes before a salvo we could hear a distant voice calling out, "Fire!" Then the concussion, making the blankets flap where they hung over the edge of our cots. This was to go on all through the night.

The fellow from Divarty told us that the night before, three Japanese had infiltrated the perimeter around a 155 and placed a charge of dynamite under it, killing a sergeant and a private first class. "Where was this?" I asked. He pointed to a little cone-shaped hill just behind us. I decided to sleep in my clothes.

Then we broke up, and Lew and the PR man were soon asleep. But I lay awake. The moonlight and the fear had got to me. I thought the light was getting brighter, and the breeze had definitely picked up, making the bottom of the tent flutter. I kept looking at that. Then the 155's would speak, and I could feel the wave of the concussion strike my body and roll away.

I felt very sad and very happy. My trip was coming to an end, and I'd be going back. I looked at the moon-softened hills. "I wonder who's fucking her tonight?" I said to myself. My answer astonished me. "I don't care," I said.

It was over. All I wanted was to live through the night safely and for General Gill to get to Santa Fe on Route 5 and for no more of the boys I'd seen that day to get killed.

As for that other tent—it was a prison, and I was glad to be out of it.

Sundown Beach, the Actors Studio company

W H E N I'm interviewed now, I'm asked how the Actors Studio started. Here's the answer, not simple but true.

When I came back from the Villa Verde Trail, I decided to spend a few quiet days in Manila, writing my report. I knew that if I went straight back to the States, I would never do it, and it seemed important for me to conclude the experience there—not for the Special Services Command; for myself. I was assigned to a small hut in the Chinese section. It had a dirt floor and, since it was not airtight, had no need of windows. On my first night in "civilization," I went to see a film: Irving Berlin's *This Is the Army*. After Tacloban and the Villa Verde Trail, after the stories I'd heard, this glamorization made me angry. It exhausted me with entertainment, one song, one tableau following another. It made show business out of a complex and tragic event in which so many lives had been cut short or ruined. Empty, easy patriotism and corn, it was typical of the Hollywood and the Broadway I'd begun to reject.

I went back to my hut, determined to find a place where I could type, borrow a machine, and start working the next day. But with the morning, I found that my head was hot, then, an hour or so later, that my whole body ached; it was burning up and I was very weak. I fell on my cot in a corner, the fever raging—yes, it happened that quickly. I fell on all fours, and that was a relief. Crawling to a corner, I threw up, then I was shitting with diarrhea and puking too. A few hours later I was barely conscious, and my only relief was in crawling here and there on all fours; the movement and the posture helped. This went on all night, getting worse, so that by the next morning I didn't care if I lived or not. I was a dying animal without the will to continue.

"Well, now, how do you like it?" I kept asking myself. "How do you like it now?" What did that mean? During that year just behind me, when I was most in demand on Broadway, the boy genius with several hits running simultaneously, and a hit film all over the country, I'd been increasingly embarrassed by the acclaim I was receiving, believing that I didn't deserve it in some cases and in others that it was coming to me for work I didn't respect, not what I had in mind. Often I wanted to start all over again, a wish that I was to have repeatedly in my life—to be plowed under and come up again, to be brought down to my true level. I guess, despite the confusion of my mind due to the fever, I must have remembered this wish to be leveled, because it had happened—I was where I so often wanted to be, on the bottom again—and I was asking myself, "Well, now, how do you like it?"

My fever was the one called dengue, and it caused me for two days to lose the will to live. In that sense, I had the experience of dying. I "died." But then the relief I got two days later, when the fever had cooled and gone, revived both hope and desire. I came out of it feeling weak but clear-headed. As I wrote my report about the "mission," I made certain decisions about myself.

First I determined to take charge of my own life, to find a way to live professionally in which all artistic decisions would be mine to make: to do what I wanted, not what other people expected of me. I was not like anyone else, and I was not going to do what anyone else did. It would take time, but I'd find my own path.

I missed the Group Theatre, what it stood for and the life it made possible. I decided to someway create that kind of professional activity again. I had no idea how that might be done—it would be worked out a year later with Bobby Lewis—but my desire for my kind of theatre life and a determination to do something about setting it up: that was the start of what became the Actors Studio.

I also made another decision during those three or four bleak days in the cabin with the dirt floor, as my body cooled and my strength came back. That had to do with where I would live and how and with whom.

I suppose that even though the participants often don't realize it, every marriage stops from time to time. Often it is not revived, stops for good—and forever. If it continues, often it is in name only. But other times it is truly revived and the participants reengaged. In that sense it becomes a different union, on a new basis. This is true not only in the relationship between a man and a woman but in the relationship between two friends. From time to time relationships have to be reexamined from both sides and especially so in a marriage, for you are marrying not only a person but a way of life; in fact, a culture. People to be true to themselves have to ask: "Is this way of life, the one I'm entering now, how I want to live?" Then decide to marry or not.

As I saw how Molly had saved herself and gone on, she too reevaluating and in that same sense becoming a different person, I admired her and consequently loved her more. It particularly impressed me that she had not turned our kids against me—that would have been so easy to do. As the crisis between us intensified, I valued her more, respected her more as we separated further. But what I cherished above all else was the way of life she brought with her, her "baggage."

Then there was the matter of geography. In all the months I'd stayed in California, I'd never stopped longing for the East. It wasn't because of the houses in Los Angeles, which I found, row on row, abominable; it wasn't because I disliked the trees there and the not-green greenery; it wasn't because I longed for the seasonal changes and the promise of moisture coming in the cool eastern air; it was, again, the rest of the baggage: the California culture that went with it, the culture of the agency offices and of the restaurants, Chasen's and Romanoff's; and the atmosphere of the executive dining room and the steam room at Fox and what went with it all; the gossip columns in the crummy newspapers and the *Hollywood Reporter.* I determined to go back to New York and set myself up there permanently.

I didn't believe the report I was writing had value any more than I thought the mission that had brought me there had value. But the decisions I made about myself those last days in the Philippines determined the course of the rest of my life. Even though they were not entirely conscious, they stood up—God, how they stood up! Perhaps it had taken those two days when I was "dead," crawling on all fours, head down over a dirt floor, an animal voiding at both ends until there was nothing left of my body, when I was alive but without resolve, will, or desire—perhaps I needed to come out of that and be reborn a different person, with a determination to create the life I wanted for myself.

During those last days, I received two letters. One was from Abe Lastfogel, informing me that Zanuck had not been able to hold *Anna and the King of Siam* for me. "Don't worry," Abe said, "you'll have your choice of pictures here. Zanuck told me that he considers you the greatest directorial find of the last decade." I wanted to duck that bouquet; it wasn't what I thought of myself. As for "Don't worry," I wasn't worrying now, not about that.

The other letter was from Molly, a loving letter informing me that I was going to be a father again. I was so happy, I cried. It was what I wanted most to hear.

. . .

A P L A Y was waiting for me when I got home. Molly had read *Deep Are the Roots*, and she urged me to do it. We were healing; I'd returned the wedding ring she'd mailed to me in anger four years before, and she'd accepted it. She would give me another child, whom we'd name Nick. I was full of gratitude—like any good Greek—and eager to go along with anything she wished. The play dramatized the shameful status of blacks in the South, a theme that had my sympathy, of course. The authors were left-wing intellectuals like myself. All would be harmony. It was.

A black soldier returning home from the war is accused of stealing a watch, the heirloom of an old Southern planter. The mechanics of how the watch is "planted" on the boy, how a witness is terrorized to profess what she knows is false—all this would now seem, even to the authors, I'm sure, mechanical and manipulated. The old Southerner was—one of the authors later admitted—a villain drawn with a heavy hand. His blow-up speech to his daughter and her fiancé makes evident why this play is not revived today. "You'll be drowned in a murderous sea of black savagery," he warns. "The waves are already mounting high. They're lashing wildly at every citadel. This black horde will return from Europe, stinking with rebellion and ready to turn their weapons on us, their masters. Nothing will be safe, nothing will be inviolate. It is either them or us." It does sound like a speech from nineteenth-century melodrama, doesn't it? But it worked with the audience of the mid-forties, and I didn't ask that it be rewritten or that the character be altered.

After the play opened and became a hit, one of the authors, Arnaud d'Usseau, was asked to write about me. I quote because it describes the times and because of an unanticipated irony. "James Gow and I," he wrote, "believe in writing a play from theme; Kazan believes in directing a play in the same fashion. There have been many brilliant directors in our Theatre; some of them have made much more of a splash than Kazan. But these men have lacked a certain moral fibre, a certain ethical base. Their brilliance, after a short while, has been dimmed by a certain irresponsibility in their art. Kazan does not have any of this; in fact quite the contrary. He has a tough-minded seriousness that convinces me that everything he has done to date is but a beginning."

This was written in 1946. I can't help wondering what my friend d'Usseau thought six years later when I testified in the cooperative mode before the House Committee on Un-American Activities. You can see why the position I took then was such a shock to so many people. What d'Usseau said was true. I do work from theme, but I no longer believe that a play or a film need affirm a stand in a social struggle. But in those harmonious days we all thought alike—or seemed to. We crowded all over a political position like birds of transit flocking on a great sea rock. To use a word current at that time, we were "correct." In fact, we vied to see who could be the *most* correct. I believe that for a time it was I. After the play was a success, I became the "hope of the progressive theatre." A critic wrote: "There is nobody in the Theatre or Movies today who can raise more indignation about human misery, poverty and the like than Elia Kazan." Yes. Perhaps. Thanks for the good word.

But in my secret heart, I wasn't quite such a good boy. "Correct" is a word in the liberals' vocabulary that I shied away from. I didn't want anyone approving my artistic political position. It was why I'd quit the Communist Party eleven years before. Reading Churchill's speech at Fulton in 1946—an "iron curtain"!—I wondered if he was not right, in fact ahead of his time. The liberals called him a warmonger. But when Lithuania and Latvia had been gobbled up and disappeared, no one of my left friends protested. I was enthusiastic about the Truman Doctrine; I didn't want the same thing to happen to Greece. My friends didn't realize it, but we were drifting apart.

Gordon Heath and Barbara Bel Geddes,
Deep Are the Roots

Deep Are the Roots was part of a flow of plays built on the drama of the falsely accused. This mode had started ten years earlier with Lillian Hellman's *The Children's Hour*, in which two women who run a school for young girls are falsely accused of being lesbians. Lillian, a tougher bird than Gow or d'Usseau, pulled a switch and got to the real drama. In her third act, one of the women admits that she does have lesbian feelings about the other. With this turn, the play got down to a deeper issue: What if it was true, what then?

What if, in *Deep Are the Roots*, the returning black soldier coming back from an army that, as I'd seen, refused him weapons and further humiliated him by confining his services to driving trucks, digging ditches, cleaning latrines, and peeling potatoes, came back full of anger instead of being that fine, decent, patient, handsome black boy so purely in love with an equally pure white girl? What if he'd taken her to bed or to lie under a tree—she seemed willing enough, the way I'd directed the delectable Barbara Bel Geddes—instead of simply mooning over her? The real drama is revealed when the accusation is true. Black friends have said it to me plainly: We have a right to be sons of bitches too. As it was, all that remained for the authors to do was unravel the plot by proving the accusation was false.

The effect of treating a social problem in this way is that there is never any doubt in the audience's mind as to what they're expected to feel. They have the assurance from the beginning that they are on the side of the angels—the falsely accused. They have never been challenged to doubt. This, of course, does not prepare them for life as it's lived. They are also often masochists—so it has seemed to me—enjoying the middle-class white man's guilt about the black man. They've been told where to stand and what to think, and guaranteed safe passage to the final curtain. We are in a kind of conformity tide. That is a word liberals say they hate, and they do—except when it's their own conformity.

Such a play is not drama that informs life; it is liberal corn.

Some years later, when the blacks rose in anger, filling the streets not far from those Upper East Side blocks where many of the affluent liberals lived, when they no longer followed Martin Luther King but rather Malcolm X and were impatient for an equal measure of everything good, when it was revealed that the people they hated most were middle-class liberals—especially if they were Jews—where were we then? Where was I? Hiding. We stayed off the streets at night, relied on our doormen to keep the front doors of our apartment houses locked, appreciated the security guards brought in and the new locks and alarms we quickly installed. "I have a dream!" was replaced by "The fire next time." How had *Deep Are the Roots* prepared its audience for that day?

The most courageous man of all of us in that period was Budd Schulberg. He went into Watts while buildings were still smoking and stores being broken into. There he joined with the blacks, day to day, starting a class for their young writers. A few years later this group produced a book, *From the Ashes: Voices of Watts*. Budd's devotion was heroic; it was also correct.

A F T E R the success of *Deep Are the Roots*, Kermit Bloomgarden suggested that he and I form a production partnership. I gave his suggestion much consideration; he was an able producer and a close friend. But despite all that, I never looked forward to having dinner with him. Was that a reason? Yes. I knew what the talk would be; I'd heard it all. He, Gow, and d'Usseau were all fine fellows, but our relationship was cursed by the fact that we agreed on everything. I didn't propose to settle further into that. Besides, many of my views were changing. I wasn't where I'd been yesterday.

The only man in the theatre I knew who said anything that surprised me was Harold Clurman. He'd approached me also, suggesting that we form a theatrical partnership. I was attracted by his proposal. I was looking for a man smarter than I. I wanted brighter company. And challenge. I wanted to be close to someone who had more culture than I did. Harold had a subtler mind. He had a liveliness that made him an engaging companion. He also had something of the devil in him, so he understood human ambivalence.

I discussed Harold's proposal with Molly, as I did everything at this time. Her Yankee spine stiffened. I persisted, told her I'd learned a great deal from Harold and still could learn. "He was always interesting," I said, "always stimulating." (By now her backbone was a ramrod.) All right, he had faults, I admitted—selfishness, intellectual vanity, Boulevard St. Germain des Prés arrogance, yes, and his damned inertia—but he was able to convert these faults into virtues. "He thinks I should be lazier," I said to Molly. This didn't go down well with my Puritan wife.

By a mode of reasoning special to wives, Molly blamed Harold for my infidelities. She didn't mention this in our discussion, but I believe it was the reason she was so violently opposed to my entering a partnership with him. What she did say was that she didn't think so damned much of his intellectual abilities; they'd been corrupted by his devotion to his now-wife, Stella. He'd let Stella make a liar of him, she said; I should know all about that. Had I forgotten *Casey Jones?* Didn't I remember how he'd humiliated me?

I did remember. I let the matter drop. I had time to think—I'd contracted to do another play.

S A M   B E H R M A N , the author of *Dunnigan's Daughter,* was an endearing man, full of longing and pain, tremulous with uncertainty of every variety, and not a strong man in a crisis. He was a member of the Playwrights Company, dominated by Robert Sherwood. He was also dominated by his agent, Harold Freedman. And, for a time, he was dominated by me.

He had what the Japanese call a living soul. At sixty, he was still trying to grow and keep up with a rapidly changing world. He sensed that in the period after the war, the American businessman would try to take over the world. A new kind of imperialism was appearing, one not enforced by armies and garrisons, as were the colonial imperialisms of the previous century. The American businessman was going to make the whole world his colony, and the weapon with which he would gain his will was the sheer bulk of what he produced with the might of the dollar. In Mexico, a country that had attracted Sam's interest because of its painters, our foreign policy was called "gringo imperialism"; its goals were to devour that country while keeping a friendly face.

I'd underestimated the play when I'd thought about it overseas because I'd underestimated its author. Using his own palette, employing his own special style, "high comedy," Sam was making his statement about the world. American power affronted him because it frightened him. He felt for the tender gentlewoman who was the vortex of his play; she represented what he prized most in life, a warm heart and a civilized mind.

Sam and his plays needed a miracle man, someone who'd take over and fulfill his dream for him. Because of the success of *Jacobowsky and the Colonel*, I'd become Sam's hope. Opening night of that play, Sam sent me flowers with this note: "Dearest Gadg: Why should just girls get flowers? My feeling about you is first-love girlish, a tentative adoration. Tentative because I am unsure of your response; you are so masculine. But I feel deeply about our long trek together. It was good, it was very, very good. Call me tonight. Better still, come over." Sam's feeling for me I can only describe as the feeling a woman may have for the man who first brings her to orgasm, a temporary conviction that no one else can do it for her.

We'd been working on *Dunnigan's Daughter* together, to deepen its social content. The central male part was that of an American businessman who possessed his wives without either enjoying them or helping them realize whatever human capabilities they had. The story had a metaphoric relationship to the practice of our industrialists in the world. We were out to possess a world, Sam was saying, that we didn't understand or appreciate.

I'd cast the play uncertainly. It was a difficult cast to serve with actors because, while they had to be able to handle comedy lines, the performers had to be more passionate than those generally chosen for Sam's comedies. The woman at the core of the play had to be a model of feminine sensitivity—and humor. The businessman had to be something besides a villain. The audience must know without being told why the heroine had married him; they should feel potential unrealized in both people. Sam's tone was one of tenderness, compassion, and understanding.

The play was an abysmal failure when it opened on the road for its tryout. There was, however, one "rave" notice: "Mr. Behrman's new play is a good and fine play, a work with character and nobility of purpose, with courage, honesty, conviction, strength and optimism. It is not, however, a likeable play; on the contrary it is a little uncomfortable. If you feel you have to laugh loud and often, you'd better not look in on it. But if you feel inclined to listen carefully, you will have an evening of inspiring substance." This generous appreciation killed the play dead in Philadelphia; no one came to the box office.

When a road tryout is a failure in the commercial theatre, the forces of professionalism rush in. A play pleasing only to a limited audience is not acceptable. A serious play, particularly, must go "over the top"; it must, in some way, please everyone. Our two-week tryout stand proved not to be a tryout at all. We needed time and patience to work out our problems ourselves, but the old pros hustled in and took over. In the quiet way affluent men have, they were hysterical.

And I let them take over.

First among them was Sam's agent, Harold Freedman, a man with an air of culture overlying a most practical core. A failure for him meant loss of income. Also, possibly, of a client. Harold Freedman had to see to it that the play succeeded. I knew what he was saying to me but suspected that he was saying something different to Sam and giving still another message to Lawrence Langner of the Guild. I soon began to feel a cooler breeze in our production meetings.

Lawrence Langner was plainer; I wrote down what he said. "Sam has become discouraged about using Mexico as a background," he told me. "He's afraid of getting bogged down in political and social problems. After all, he just wants to get some comedy." Those were his words, and I translated them for myself: "Lay off Sam!" "Just get some comedy" must be one of the most cynical phrases in the theatre. The author's theme, the reason he wrote the play, is ignored. It's like summing up a love affair by saying, "All he really wanted was to get his end in." I soon found that while I was talking into one of Sam's ears, Lawrence was talking into another. Sam, in the middle, soon panicked. I lost face and power.

When producers don't know what to do in the theatre, they recast. I was told that I had to immediately find a more "professional" cast and one that could "handle comedy." Sam himself asked me, in the presence of the others, to recast four of the five parts. Since no one was buying tickets, something drastic had to be done, they said, or the play closed on the road. I saw how this threat frightened Sam. I felt for him. I did what they were asking.

What followed shamed me. Of course, the new cast didn't help. Nor did the "high comedy" readings. Our theme of innocence tyrannized by power was gone. The play lost its meaning. When it was all over, everyone thought I was a fine fellow, easy to get along with, always pleasant to talk to, and most cooperative. But the play died. The experience had a lasting effect on me. I began to ask: Shouldn't I protect myself as a director by becoming my own producer? Shouldn't I reconsider Harold Clurman's suggestion that we become partners and our own bosses? I thought about that, and the next stage play I did was billed "An Elia Kazan Production," so giving notice to the backers, the agents, and everyone else not responsible for the creative work that the production power was in my hands. People in the theatre, particularly producers, thought this billing arrogant. I want to say a word about that.

S O M E years ago, after a disagreement over a personal matter, I abruptly withdrew from a film that I was going to direct, whereupon the author of the book that was the source of the film, a man who was also the coproducer of the movie, wrote a letter breaking off our relationship from his side and offering as his reason that I was impossible to deal with because I was an "arrogant Anatolian."

The "Anatolian," of course, was accurate. The "arrogant"? I was elated by this characterization. "At last," I said to myself, "I've made it. It's what I've always wanted to be." I believe every artist is, as he has to be, arrogant. You may not go along with that; the word has unfortunate connotations. But whatever else an artist may be saying in his work, he is certainly saying, "I'm important!"

Arrogance, when it's depicted on the screen or stage, is usually projected by boisterous behavior. Not so in life. The most arrogant people I've known—people whom I admire for this quality as well as for the work they do—are often quiet with the special ease that comes from being sure of themselves.

Artists are different from other people, and they do behave differently. I've already expressed my opinion that vanity—one of the seven deadly sins—is often a spur to creation in a filmmaker. Now consider the seven deadly virtues for the artist. Here are seven: Agreeable. Accommodating. Fair-minded. Well balanced. Obliging. Generous. Democratic. You don't agree with my choices? How about these: Controlled. Kind. Unprejudiced. Yielding. Unassertive. Faithful. Self-effacing. And for good measure: Co-operative. They are all deadly—for the artist. They add up to what is suggested by "nice guy," "sweet," "pleasant," "lovable," "on the side of the angels." None of which any artist is, should be, or ever has been. If he seems that way, he is concealing his true nature. He should better be a disrupter, on the side of the devil. In the years ahead, every time I was a nice guy, cooperative, and yielding to the point of view of others, I had a disaster.

Arthur Miller has become, as he had to become, a stubborn, unyielding man. There have been times when, despite a fair-minded and democratic front, he has unmasked a truer self. When he has been dissatisfied with the rehearsal performance of one of his plays, for instance, he has stepped over the prone body of his director and lectured his cast. His theme was always the same: "My reputation is international, and it is at stake here. For the time being, it is in your hands, and you are failing me."

A contrasting instance is that of Bill Inge, but his gentleness on occasion amounted to self-betrayal. In a crisis, rather than protest, he'd leave town to avoid unpleasantness. The arrogance of Miller was truer and more effective and easier on the psyche. Inge died young. Miller is still going strong.

Did you see the photograph of Mike Nichols, a fine director, on the front page of a recent issue of *The New York Times Magazine?* Did you notice how he smiles, how charming and friendly he seems—at first glance? Then look again and notice the glint in the corner of his eyes, recognize the cunning and determination there, the hardness? Why not? It's what saves us.

Read the letters of Ernest Hemingway and ask yourself was anyone ever more intolerant of other people's views—more arrogant—than Ernest? Unless it was Ezra Pound. Unless it was Gertrude Stein.

Dick Rodgers had a genius for the melodies of love and tenderness. But you'd have been well advised not to try to buck him in a business transaction—or in a production. The same goes for Oscar Hammerstein. I know of no one more arrogant or more estimable than Agnes De Mille; she has always gone her way, and it was always the right way, because she, and no one else, was the choreographer. I watched Toscanini conduct a rehearsal. He was a terror and a bully—but he had to be to get his results. When a producer informed Boris Aronson that he didn't like the set Aronson had made for him, Boris's response was characteristic: "That's your problem," he said. "I like it." I played tennis with Chaplin years ago; what a monster of unrestrained egoism that man was on the court! Lee Strasberg sometimes wore a gentle mask; I did not trust it. "I don't teach the Stanislavski method," he proclaimed when backed into a corner. "I teach the Strasberg method." Why not? It was the truth.

I respected Harold Clurman most when he was bellowing. The restrained, agreeable, easy-to-get-along-with Clurman was sometimes devious and tricky. He had an astonishing posture when he shook hands with someone who had power over him; he bowed, jutting his head forward in a sycophantic, "Near Eastern bazaar" manner. When he bellowed he stood erect, arrogant and admirable. That was his worthy self and the Clurman I respected enough to enter into a partnership with in 1946.

THE FIRST offering of the Clurman-Kazan partnership was Max Anderson's *Truckline Café*, which Harold directed. I was disappointed in the production. The script when we opened was basically unchanged from what I'd first read; nothing had been done to improve it or make it more stageworthy. Although two small parts were brilliantly played by two unknown actors (Karl Malden and Marlon Brando), the central roles were limp, in both the writing and the performance.

I'd heard Harold's first talk to the cast; he was at his best. It was brilliant. I admired his analysis of the play and its meaning. The cast was dazzled, as were all Harold's casts, by the man's insights and his eloquence. But then— what had happened? Very little. The play had been an occasion for Harold to perform. When the actors, like the two I've mentioned, had exceptional talent, Harold turned them on to exceptional performances. But as for the rest of the show, it sunk into a slough and remained there. It was damned dull.

Despite—or along with—my disappointment, I took a perverse pleasure in the failure of the performance. That's not a pretty confession, but it's true. I couldn't talk like Harold, but I sure as hell would have done something about that playscript. I'd have kept after the author until he improved his play. I wouldn't have sat by, being brilliant and adored, while the play failed. I might even have interfered with the rights of the playwright given him by the Dramatists Guild and "fussed" with the text. Harold had said, when I'd indicated my impatience with the meager extent of Max's rewriting, "That's the play. You can't do anything about it. It will succeed or fail, but that's it." This fatalism I found intolerable.

Truckline Café, before he was famous

Later in my time, I was to be severely scored for moving in on playwrights, but if the accusation is true, I've never regretted it. Too many people's hopes hang on the outcome of a play's production to allow above-it-all behavior. When I've felt strongly, I've urged strongly. "You don't like it?" I've warned playwrights. "Then don't work with me." I simply couldn't stand by and wait to see how things would turn out. (There, incidentally, is the third quality necessary for a man working in the arts: vain, arrogant, and unyielding.) I have never regretted this way of mine. When the plays were right at first reading, like *Death of a Salesman*, *A Streetcar Named Desire*, and *Tea and Sympathy*, I've asked for no changes.

One thing was clear to me after *Truckline Café:* We needed our kind of actors to play the leading roles in our productions. The central parts in both Sam's and Max's plays had been inadequately performed. It was time to embark on the half-hope, half-plan I'd had in Manila the year before; it was time to try to produce the actors we needed for our theatre.

There have been foolish debates as to who first thought of the Actors Studio—as if there were some merit in conceiving the idea, when the merit consists in getting it going. Since the debate continues, I'll settle it. I thought of it first, that night in Manila. When I got back, I'd waited for the right moment. This was certainly that moment.

I spoke to Harold Clurman about it first, in general terms, saying that we certainly did need a better corps of actors for the plays we were likely to be doing and that I'd thought of starting a small studio for training young actors. His response was: "I'll speak to Stella about it." That concluded the discussion for me. I like Stella Adler now, but at that time her name recalled my humiliation during *Casey Jones* and the resentment I'd felt when Harold brought her in to "coach" the young actress I was directing. I didn't speak to Harold about my studio idea again.

I had another notion. All through my time in the Group, one of my close friends had been Bobby Lewis. Directly after the Group stopped work, Bobby and I had planned a theatre together. We hoped to make it a people's theatre and have a dollar top admission price (believe it or not). We even thought to call it the Dollar Top Theatre. Molly was involved, to find and prepare plays. Irwin Shaw responded to our enthusiasm by writing a play for us, its title burdened with a premonition: *Labor for the Wind*. Bobby had worked devotedly; I was impressed with how well organized he was. But even as we made our plans, the rising costs of production made a dollar admission price impossible.

This failure did not sour our relationship. Bobby, I believed, was the ideal man to start a studio for actors with me. It never occurred to me to involve Lee Strasberg. I had the same problem with him that I had with Harold: They'd both been my boss. Also, Bobby's teaching had characteristics Lee's did not have: simplicity, clarity, and a sense of humor. Bobby stressed the bolder, imaginative side of acting, rather than emphasizing the interior emotional event.

Walking with Bobby in Central Park, I told him what I had in mind. Without an instant's hesitation, he responded enthusiastically. We made our plans that very day: There'd be two classes, Bobby taking the more experienced players, I the beginners. In the days that followed, we went over the names of actors to invite, called some of them in and discussed our project with them. We decided there'd be no tuition charge and agreed to work without compensation ourselves. The only qualification for membership would be talent. No one would buy his way in. Our goals were modest, our principles clean. Over forty years, they have never been altered.

We needed an administrator who'd know what we were up to and not wish to convert a free studio into a money-making proposition. We both thought of the same person: Cheryl Crawford. She responded eagerly and was to do much more than administrate. Cheryl has never disappointed me.

Bobby did. He quit the Studio after the first year, for reasons I thought absurd. Cheryl and I replaced him with a series of teachers, all good people, but none of them wished—or were wanted by us—to be completely involved in what we were trying to do. During the three years we were looking for the right person, I kept my classes going. I knew if I dropped out the Studio would collapse. But it had become evident to me that I didn't really enjoy teaching and was no good when I forced myself to it. I remember the day I told Cheryl that it was not only a matter of finding a replacement for Bobby; we had to find someone I could "give the Studio to."

We came to believe that Lee Strasberg was our man—if we could seduce him to come with us. He'd resisted every reach, again and again, possibly because he resented that I hadn't turned to him first. After all, he'd been Bobby's teacher. Perhaps what finally brought Lee to us was the failure of his *Peer Gynt* with Julie Garfield, a production he'd been planning for many years. This disaster, capping a series of other setbacks for Lee in the commercial theatre, made him ready to come with us. Once he did, no one could have been more committed or more devoted. Or more valued by everyone there. Over the years, respect became hero worship, and hero worship idolatry.

IN THOSE good old days, the Super Chief would leave Chicago at a comfortable time in the late afternoon, allowing the hours before to be spent in the dining room of the Ambassador East and at the Art Institute. I was on my way west to direct Spencer Tracy and Katharine Hepburn in a film project I was keen about, *The Sea of Grass*. The two nights and a day that I'd spend on the train were, in effect, a vacation. I was glad to be away from the tensions of the theatre. I'd soon be making a real movie in the Great Plains, where the grass still grew from unbroken sod, not a photographed stage play like *A Tree Grows in Brooklyn*, set in a designer's cleaned-up slum tenement. This would be a step in growth for me, a "western" but with a story about a conflict in cultures, a theme I knew something about. I'd be working at the greatest film studio in the world, Metro-Goldwyn-Mayer, the home ground of "more stars than there are in the heavens." I'd be a director among many famous directors whom I admired. I'd made it.

I was met at the station in Los Angeles by a chauffeur-driven limo, naturally; this was MGM. I sat up front with the driver, naturally; I was a regular guy. The driver informed me that a fine oceanside house had been found for me in the exclusive Malibu colony; he was certain my wife and kids would love it. He also told me that as per the contract Abe Lastfogel had made, the studio's transportation department would provide us with two cars—one for Mrs. Kazan, one for me. What make did I want, what model? They had everything; I could have anything. A roadster? Sure. What color?

I was greeted in the office that was to be mine by a trim young secretary who was solicitous concerning the kind of pens and pencils I preferred. I told her I wanted a typewriter, a Royal if possible; twenty minutes later, I had a Royal. In the meantime, the director who shared my reception room came in to welcome me to the lot. I greeted him as Mr. Cukor and was proud that he'd heard of me, seen *The Skin of Our Teeth* and admired it. We talked of Tallulah; time and distance had gentled my rancor. Cukor impressed on me how lucky I was to be working with "Spence and Kate." There are no nicer people, he said; he seemed envious of me. I smiled, nodded, agreed. Yes, I certainly was lucky.

On my desk there were two brand-new copies of the shooting script of *The Sea of Grass*, marked FINAL in black block letters. The original book had been a favorite novel of Bud Lighton's and at one time a film project he'd worked on; this endorsement filled me with confidence. Apparently the script had been rewritten by a Marguerite Roberts. Well, I'd read it later.

At lunch, the studio "commissary" was a museum; all around me were the great stars that MGM and no other studio had: Lionel Barrymore, Robert Taylor, Walter Pidgeon, the head of the Hardy family, Lewis Stone, and my favorite comedian, Jimmy Durante. There was William Powell and Esther Williams, out of water, and with her, Lucille Ball. Claudette Colbert looked as "darling" as she did on the screen. And there, carefully shepherded by women in neutral-colored dresses, half nurses, half guards, were the great child stars Elizabeth Taylor and Margaret O'Brien, and, teasing Elizabeth, Mickey Rooney, and, laughing with him, Judy Garland, chattering like kids and laughing at silly jokes. What confidence they had, these kids!

The table that interested me most, of course, was the one where the directors had gathered. I knew who they were because Mr. Cukor was among them. He was telling a story and they all burst out laughing, then he laughed himself and, still laughing, looked in my direction. Then he leaned forward and whispered to the man next to him. By God, that was Clarence Brown! He'd done Garbo pictures! *Anna Karenina!* Mr. Brown turned and looked my way, and then he waved—was it to me? I wasn't sure, but I saw that it was, and I waved back. Oh yes, this was the big time, and I was part of it! Twentieth Century–Fox seemed like road company stuff compared with this. I was in Metroheaven!

A young woman who turned out to be Pandro Berman's secretary touched my shoulder; she brought a message from my producer. Mr. Pandro Berman regretted that he couldn't join me for lunch; he was running "rushes," but he asked that I come to his office afterward. Would I? Of course I would.

I hadn't met Berman before; my immediate impression was of a middle-class, middle-aged *gemütlich* fellow, compactly built, of middle height and possessed of a flow of friendly optimism, which is to say an optimism not necessarily based on the assumption that he was going to get the better of you. "We have," he boasted as we were shaking hands, "ten thousand feet of the greatest stuff I've ever seen." He seemed to be congratulating me. "I'm eager for you to see it; you'll be nuts about it, believe me. It's great!" He chuckled to himself.

I didn't know what Berman meant, what the "stuff" in "ten thousand feet of the greatest" referred to. "I'll have the film for you in projection room three at four o'clock." As he said this, he scribbled a "3" and a "4" on a slip of paper and handed it to me. "Here. Put this in your pocket," he said. "Hell, I'll be there with you. I want to see the look on your face when you've seen it." "What look?" I asked. "Gratitude! Happiness! Now, the first thing to do—" He turned and shouted to his secretary in the other room. "Get Plunkett on the phone!" He turned back to me and put his arm around my shoulder, and his voice dropped to a subtler level. "You have got to see Katharine's clothes and give them your okay. They're great!" The phone buzzed. He picked up and said, "Walter! Kazan is here! He's dying to see Katharine's clothes. What? Then let him see the sketches. I know, I know, but he should okay the sketches anyway. When? Now! He'll be waiting for you in his office. Get over there." He hung up. "Walter Plunkett," he said, "is the single greatest designer of women's period costumes in the world today! So recognized and so damn well paid! He's on his way to your office. His clothes for Katharine will knock your eyes out. Wait until you see them! You'll be nuts about them. They're already in the shop, of course, had to be; it's a big job." He'd led me to the door. "Another thing. You've got to look at Spencer's horses with him this afternoon. I'll arrange that. They're eager to meet you—not the horses: he and Kate. They want to take you to dinner. They're so pleased to be working with you. Did you know they're both from the New York stage? Did you know that, kid?" He opened the door. "I think we've got a real team here; it's going to be a great picture. I don't generally go in for that kind of prediction. Nominations we'll get! All down the line! Those stars, our script, which is great. You! Awards too; can't miss. See you at four. I'm not a bit worried." I was out by then, and he'd closed the door.

On the way to my office, I recalled this piece of irrelevant information:

I'd never met the authors of the screenplay of *A Tree Grows in Brooklyn*. I knew who they were, the novelist Tess Slesinger and her husband, Frank Davis, but I'd made the film without even saying hello to them. Had Bud Lighton arranged it that way on purpose? I sat behind my desk, waiting for Plunkett to arrive. I looked at the two copies of the shooting script. The letters in the stenciled word FINAL seemed bigger and blacker—and very FINAL. Were those letters telling me, "Don't fool around with this script"? Was I being told to stick to directing the actors and not fuss with the text?

When Plunkett came in, he seemed frazzled. "You look beat, Mr. Plunkett," I said, smiling sympathetically. "Beat?" he said, and laughed, a handsome man, carefully turned out in southern California leisure clothes, which he'd designed himself. "Do you have any idea how many costumes we're making for you?" he said. "No one has talked to me about them," I answered. "Well, for her alone, for Katharine, something like twenty-two. And she's helping us with them, full of ideas, some of them good. That girl has opinions on more than one subject, and she's not shy about offering them to a waiting world. Glad to meet you. Did I say that? No? Well, I am. Here, have a look." He'd been untying a large portfolio of carefully rendered costume sketches done in great detail, with bits of material attached to each. "This is about half. These clothes are finished. The rest are being worked on, so I couldn't bring the sketches. Go on." He'd noticed I wasn't looking at the sketches. "Excuse me for hurrying you, but I've got to get back to the shop."

I took a chance and let it out. "What exactly," I asked, "is the point of showing me these if the clothes have already been made?" "From Pandro's point of view," he answered, "the purpose is to have you initial them, which means you have approved my clothes. From your point of view, you should know what you have to play around with; you might decide to change what scenes they work in. From my point of view, I like compliments." He laughed, satisfied with his joke, then closed his eyes to rest them while he waited for my reaction to his sketches.

"Yes, they're very handsome," I said after I'd looked through the pile. "Thank you," he said, and began to reorder the pile. He was preparing to leave, it seemed. "But frankly," I went on quickly, "I did see the production more—er—homespun?" His eyes measured me as a threat. I was looking at the sketches a second time through. "This story," I went on, speaking carefully, "is supposed to take place, is it not, in the backcountry?" I looked at him. God, he did look tired! "I've read the script," he said. Now he was irked, a man on the edge of exhaustion, being put upon and having to control his temper. I wasn't going to be diverted. "Am I right?" I said. "No," he said. "Actually this picture takes place in Metro-Goldwyn-Mayer land, where you and I are sitting this minute. Excuse me, Mr.—how do you prefer your name to be pronounced?" I told him. Then he let out his peeve, and he was franker than I'd been. "I'll be equally plain with you," he said.

"This is one hell of a time to tell me you don't like my costumes. Don't you think?"

"But I haven't seen them before," I defended myself, then crawled a bit. "I like them very much, but my feeling about the film is—" Plunkett interrupted. "Pandro likes them," he said. "I'm sorry you're offended," I went on, "but my idea for the production is—" "I'm not offended," he interrupted again, "but I simply can't change them now. We've got a completion date in the shop. They're all going crazy there." He pointed in what I supposed was the direction of his shop. "It's going to be one hell of a rush as it is. Besides, everybody likes them. Except you. Katie loves them. She said so. Yesterday. Maybe you better talk to her about them. That's my suggestion." He began to bundle up his rejected sketches.

"It looks to me," I said, "that every time she goes in to take a piss, she'll come bouncing out of the can in a snazzy new outfit!" I didn't say that to him; I said it to myself. I was already choking down what I really thought. Perhaps, when I look back, that was the moment when I should have quit the job. But the fact was that it was already late; the Metromill was grinding, and I was between its teeth.

Plunkett was on his feet and turning to the door. "Besides, it's her honeymoon," he said. "I know that, Mr. Plunkett," I said. "I read the script." "She loves Spence, he's the love of her life, and she wants him to think that on any given day she's prettier than any other girl in the world." "I thought you meant in the movie," I said. "The movie!" he said, scornfully. "I'm talking about real life. Them! Is what matters!" He started toward the door. "Talk to Pandro," he said, "and let me know what you—I mean he—wants me to do. If anything."

My secretary came in. "The horses are waiting," she said. "Where?" I asked, feeling a little guilty. "Your assistant director is waiting outside in his car," she said. "Have you met him yet?" Plunkett asked. "He's the best on the lot. Mr. Berman said you were to have the best of everything, and we've been trying, we certainly have been trying." He turned and looked at me; I must have appeared bewildered, because he said, "Don't worry. There's one thing you can be sure of here: Every picture comes to an end." And this: "Everybody is a genius in Hollywood until they do something." Then he was gone; from outside I heard greetings and laughter. I was left with a crumb of dignity: I hadn't initialed the sketches. "Mr. Tracy is on his way out there," my secretary warned me.

My impression of Tracy from our brief meeting a year before at Chasen's was of a comfortable Irish burgher in the mercantile trade. When I knew I was going to make this film with him, I'd been anxious about the lard around his middle. He was supposed to be a man who lived in the weather, a contrast to city-bred, well-protected Katharine; someone like Bud Lighton, who got on his favorite horse every morning to help his "hands" with the cattle. I hoped Tracy had taken off some weight.

Waiting for me on the back lot were two bovine animals—large, beautifully groomed horses. They looked as if they ate regularly at the MGM
commissary. Strapped to their broad backs were western saddles, works of
art, with fine fretwork trim and horns of silver. I didn't know much about
horses—it would be another picture or two before I'd get to dislike them—
but I felt these beautiful beasts were wrong. I'd studied pictures of the old
West, Remingtons, read a shelf of books preparing for this film, and had a
definite idea what Tracy's mount should look like. These Metro animals
were unthinkable in the film I had in mind. The wranglers who were tending them were waiting, as Walter Plunkett had been, for expressions of
satisfaction and gratitude from me.

"Fellows," I started, "I was really thinking of leaner animals. You read
the script; you know what I mean." They looked at each other—no expression cracked the leather of their cheeks—and I had the impression they
hadn't read the script, that they'd seen no reason to. I also noticed that they
weren't in the least disturbed by my negative reaction, only puzzled; it
seemed erratic to them. "Your horses," I went on manfully, "are supposed
to be working cattle every day. This pair is very handsome, but they don't
look like working horses. Do you think? They're at least two hundred
pounds overweight. Wouldn't you say? What? No? And those saddles! They
look like—forgive me—like easy chairs in the parlor of an expensive dude
ranch." I stooped over and looked under the horses' bellies. "I mean look
at their bellies. Enormous. And look—" I made a gesture. "They've been
fixed," one of the wranglers said. "My man would be riding a stallion," I
said. "That's the kind of man he is. Read the script. He'd ride a fiery, high-
strung animal."

The wranglers looked at each other. "Have you seen Mr. Tracy ride?"
one of them asked. "No," I said. "You got to remember," the other wrangler
went on, "Tracy will be riding these horses. Because they've been fixed,
nothing bothers them. They hold still for a close-up. They're not camera-
shy. They won't rear up and throw your star." He took something out of his
pocket, sugar perhaps, and gave a bit to each animal. "I wonder where Mr.
Tracy is," my assistant said, relieving the silence, as he walked to a field
telephone.

Then a terrible thing happened, which I confess to now but which embarrasses me still. I decided to be friends—with everybody. Including the
horses. I decided to accept them. I also gave up on the costumes. I decided
not to fight for what I wanted. When did that happen? For sure at the
moment when Tracy was driven up—when he squeezed out of the studio
car, to be precise—and as we shook hands. He had not lost weight, he did
not look like a Remington, he was not tight-waisted like the wranglers or
even like Bud Lighton. Spencer looked . . . like the horses. And when I
gave up on the costumes and gave up on the horses and gave up on Tracy's
weight, I'd given up on the picture.

It got worse. Soon Spence had me laughing at stories he told, stories that made fun of Metro and the way they did things there; in fact, just what had been bothering me ever since I arrived. "At lunch," he said, "Mervyn LeRoy was raving about a book he'd bought. 'It's got everything,' he said. 'Surprise, great characters, an important theme, fine writing! But,' he said, 'I think I can lick it.' Honest. That's what he said!" We both laughed and we were buddies, he and I, I his admirer, he my star, and I had no fight left in me. Friendship had deflated me. About the animals? He had a sense of proportion, which is to say he was indifferent. Which one did he prefer? Neither. Either. Both. Did he want to climb on? What the hell for? Any riding he had to do, a double would do for him. I was assured there was a perfect double for Spencer under contract. All Spence had to do was sit on the animal's back for close-ups. That was that. "Goodbye, kid. We'll have dinner soon!" And he was gone.

At four o'clock I sat with Pandro Berman and saw ten thousand feet of the greatest stuff he'd ever seen. Even then I was too naive or too stupid to understand what was being conveyed to me. I was shown a dozen reels of the same scene, grass blowing in the wind under a clean sky and a bright sun—yes, seas of grass. The only variations were some scenes of horsemen riding across in the distance and some other scenes where a dozen men on horseback were photographed against the grass; they were arranged in an artificial composition, looking directly into the camera. I had no idea what this scene was for, but there were several sizes and some slight alterations in attitude by the men, so someone must have thought the shot important. "What are all these different ones for?" I asked Pandro, who'd kept looking at me to catch any enthusiasm I might show. "You take your pick," Pandro said. "Isn't it great stuff?" "Yes," I said, then: "Some of these men seem to be just sitting there staring into space. But we'll have a chance to get more scenes when we get out there." "Get out where?" Pandro asked. "Where the grass is," I said. "The grass?" Pandro said, looking at me as if I was kidding. "We're not going anywhere," he said. Then he explained to me that the film I'd been looking at was for rear projection, with our principals to be placed in front of it, Spencer looking masterful, Katharine looking out of her element. Our film, I finally realized, was to be made on the Metro lot with rear projection, not in natural locations. "Besides," Pandro concluded, "it isn't there anymore, the grass." "Where did they get these scenes?" I asked. "I don't know," he answered. "But at this time of year, wherever it was, it's dried up."

I must have looked as if the MGM Executive Building had fallen on my head. Which it had. Pandro explained to me how expert "our fellows" were at rear projection; "we" had a special large stage and a special staff just for that. "We do it better than the other studios," he said. "I thought you understood that." "No, I didn't," I said. "It's the only way we can make this picture at this time of year and for a price—and with this cast, don't forget that. We have to photograph Katharine right—it's not easy; Mr. Mayer is worried about that—and keep Spence together, if you know what I mean. You've heard the stories. Thank goodness Kate is with him now." He got to his feet. "Think about it," he said. "It's the best way. I've got a dinner guest waiting at home. Let's have that lunch tomorrow, and we'll talk."

I asked to see the stuff again and he said sure, but he really had to go, his wife would give him hell, he was already late, and so on. Then I was alone and the stuff was being run past me, but I wasn't seeing it. What had I got myself into? Even then I was too dazed to realize the full implications of my altered situation. I had to laugh. My dreams of doing a real western, a "Ford," were destroyed. The rough-and-ready country clothes I'd brought with me and the cowboy boots I was wearing to break them in, they were not to be used. Everything I'd been looking forward to was out of the question. I was a ludicrous figure, a fool.

Which is when I certainly should have quit. Here's a story Bud Lighton told me; I recalled it as I sat there in the flickering light. It's about Victor Fleming, the director whom Lighton held up to me as a model. He'd agreed, Fleming had, to direct a film to be made from the novel *The Yearling*. He approached the job as he did every job, intensely; he knew the emotion he wanted to capture for the audience. He searched all over the South for the right locations, selected a fine cast (including Spencer Tracy), got the best technicians, and prepared to give the project the kind of devotion for which he was known, the kind that made him worry so painfully that sometimes he'd throw up his lunch. He shot scenes of the film for three days on that far-off location, then suddenly left and went back to Culver City. "How can I make a picture," he explained to the outraged executives, "whose essence is that people love each other, when no one in the cast loves anyone or loves being down there or loves making the picture? They only love themselves. The kid wants to be a goddamn star and thinks of nothing except his vanity. Tracy is only thinking how he can get away for a few days to go up to New York and see Hepburn. And the mother part is always between a shit and a sweat about something, but never about the goddamn picture." So Fleming said the hell with it and quit. He was fighting what it seemed to me I was up against, organized indifference—but he had more experience and more guts than I had; he walked away.

I stopped unreeling the ten thousand feet of the greatest stuff Pandro had ever seen and sat in the dark. This was it, yes or no, on or off, stay or go, now or never. But it took more courage than I had at that time to walk away. Molly was coming out in a couple of weeks with the kids; they were all looking forward to it, California, Malibu, the house on the beach, and so on. And so on!

I decided to stay and take a licking. And perhaps learn a lesson. I did learn—a little. I had come out eager for a new adventure and been dumped into a perfectly structured organization that turned out product, so many films per year. MGM was what I knew it was, an industrial compound. That was the way it worked. At the studio, all decisions were made by men who made the machine run. Who were they? Pandro Berman? Hell, no. He did what he was told. Who from above him? One dominating power man was Cedric Gibbons, the head of the "Art Department," which saw to it that the backgrounds for the films were designed, built, painted, and put up. It was Mr. Gibbons who'd made the decision—long before I was hired—to shoot my film before a rear-projection screen, not out in the open country as I'd expected. He'd ordered the sets designed and built—I'd been walked through some of them, and they matched Katharine's costumes. He'd ordered them "tastefully" decorated and furnished by his department. He was the most influential person on the lot except for the owners, Nick Schenck in New York City and Louis B. Mayer in Culver City (the man who'd warned me, "We are in the business of making beautiful pictures of beautiful people, and anyone who doesn't go with that has no place here"). Those men were responsible for artistic decisions—not the artists. They were industrialists. I'd made a mistake, and now I'd have to pay for my mistake. Perhaps I wouldn't make it again.

Whenever an artist gets into the fix I was in, there's anger, resentment, and revenge. I understand why certain directors, when they've had some hits and the power that comes with having hits, not only have become defiant toward studio heads and their producers but have felt a need to humiliate and humble them. There is a famous story about when Jack Ford was making a picture at one of the big places and began receiving complaints from the front office that he was falling behind schedule. Ford wouldn't respond to any of this needling, written, spoken, or hinted. The head of the studio was too intimidated by Ford, who was known for his ferocious temper, to confront him personally, so he sent an assistant down to the set to notify the Irishman that he had to shoot faster. This emissary came nervously up to Ford where he was sitting—after all, he'd been asked to reprimand a legend—and spoke his piece. To his surprise, Ford responded amiably. He sent for the script clerk and asked for her copy of the shooting script, opened it, and began to tear out pages here and there and throw them on the ground. Then he closed the script, handed it back to the script clerk, looked at the producer's emissary, and said, "Now we're on schedule."

I developed my own method. A few years later, when I was a few years tougher, I was shooting the film of A Streetcar Named Desire and was told that I was falling behind schedule. I paid no attention, proceeding at my own pace. In a few days, Charlie Feldman, my producer, was sent down by the studio's head, Jack Warner, to remonstrate with me. He came into the stage—I'd been warned he was approaching—and found our set silent, not a sign of activity. When he inquired what was going on—obviously nothing—he was directed to me. He came up rather shyly to where I was sitting; Charlie was a sensitive man and really didn't care about anything except that the film be first-class and do him credit. He was just being Jack Warner's errand boy. "How are you?" he asked me, certainly a weak opening gambit for the mission he was on. "I have the most terrible headache," I said. "I don't think I can work anymore today. Perhaps I'll feel better tomorrow. I hope so. I feel this terrible tension all around me. I don't know what it is. What is it, Charlie, distrust? Is Warner dissatisfied?" "Oh, no, no," Charlie said. "There seems to be rancor everywhere, and I have a throbbing headache," I said. Charlie didn't know what to do, offered to get me aspirin, of course, but I said I'd taken aspirin twice and it hadn't helped. The problem was much deeper. Finally Charlie left; we didn't work much that afternoon. Charlie and Warner, of course, understood my game; they knew from the production reports that I'd slowed down, and they knew why. No one ever came down to reprimand me again.

But on *Sea of Grass* I decided to be cowardly, play tennis on weekends, and enjoy living in Malibu. I think the most humiliating as well as the funniest incident that occurred during this "shoot" was the day when Spencer had to enter the set that represented his home on the open range, supposedly after a night on horseback during a blizzard. Spence and I worked out the movement inside the house after he'd entered, then I knelt by the chair where my star was resting and in a whisper told him the kind of night it was and reminded him that he'd been working in a blizzard. He nodded. When the scene had been prepared by the cameraman and his electricians, I told Spence to get ready, this was it. He got up from his chair, heavily, rather unwillingly, I thought, and did what he always did to prepare himself, smoothed his forehead with an open palm. Then he did the scene. It was nothing. I went to where he was sitting, told him again that he'd been up all night on horseback tending cattle in a blizzard and so on—just what I'd said before. He silenced me with a gesture meaning that he understood perfectly and knew what to do.

When he'd taken his position outside the set, I sneaked around to where I could watch what was happening before Spence came on. As his wardrobe man was straightening his Norfolk jacket, a property man was flicking bits of artificial snow mixed with drops of water on his coat and shoulders, then on his neck and face. There is such a scene in a W. C. Fields comedy, and it's funny. Perhaps in response to my repeated instruction, Spence made a sign to the property man, who gave him a few more flicks of the artificial snow. "Roll 'em!" I shouted, then "Action!" and in came Spencer Tracy. He was perfectly believable as an actor, completely unbelievable in the scene. I printed the scene and walked away. I didn't know what else to do.

A few years later, when Jimmy Dean, a young man I didn't like (I did like Tracy), had to make a similar entrance, I ran his ass around the stage house until he was ready to drop before he made his entrance, and, truly exhausted, Dean gave me the real thing when he came in. But it never occurred to me to ask Spencer—portly, dignified, much-honored Tracy—to run around the stage house three times. I'm not sure he could have.

I liked both Spencer and Katharine. Katharine was like my wife, Molly, who knew no limit to what she'd do for a cause she believed in. The cause Hepburn believed in was Tracy. She'd watch him do a scene, and before I could comment on his work even favorably, she'd say, for my ears to hear, "Wasn't that wonderful? How does he do it? He's so true! He can't do anything false!" And so on. Which didn't leave much room for any criticism I might wish to offer. Was she protecting him from me? I don't think it was that. She truly adored him.

I couldn't help coddling Spencer. He was a man devoured by guilt—so he seemed and so I've been told—about the son who'd been born deaf. People said he blamed himself and his "sins" for that tragedy. From time to time, when the misery of his Catholic soul became unbearable, he'd lock himself in a hotel room with a case of Scotch and stay drunk for as long as the liquor would last. Katharine, so the story goes, slept on the floor across his doorway. If he needed help in the night, she was there. Spencer wouldn't let her into the room where he was, but occasionally she'd find a way to enter and wash his face and his body where he'd soiled himself, and see to it that he slept comfortably. He did need help, and when he would accept hers, she was proud. This is a story that's told—I wasn't there, of course—but I believe it because it's just like the lady. What it tells about her character is true. Devotion with her was total.

We came through our filmmaking as friends, but I'd offered nothing that deserved their admiration—only a friendly manner and what passed for patience. To be chummy, to enjoy Spencer's jokes, to be tolerant of his quirks, to not insist on what a scene needed because it might cost me their friendship—that doesn't make a good movie. Nor is it true friendship.

W H E N it was all over, Molly was pregnant again—she never looked more lovely than when she was bearing—and the kids, including Nick, the new one, were gloriously healthy from their summer on the beach. But we were glad to be going back east. I was a thoroughly discouraged man, but the warmth of my family made a great difference; it certainly was the natural way for me—to be surrounded by my own people. I'm a family man, European style.

The world and craft of the filmmaker, which had once seemed close and dear to me, was now, it appeared, beyond my reach. MGM and its organization had beaten down the beginning of confidence I'd acquired making *A Tree Grows in Brooklyn. Sea of Grass* was delayed; everybody in the great white hornet's nest of overpaid executives was consulting about it; Jane Loring, the head of the cutting department, was in with them, but I was not invited. The attitude seemed to be that I'd done my part and now was not

Life in the Kazan family

relevant. Just as well. We packed up and went back to New York. We were buying a house with Metrogold.

All this downgrading of myself was happening inside me. According to Abe Lastfogel, it was not the industry's evaluation. He said that they were "very high on me" at MGM, which I thought insulting since my activity there had consisted of submitting to their organization and doing what I was told. When the film finally opened, the industry press hailed it as "The Greatest Women's Picture in Years!"—which was not what I'd intended. Another critic in the industry's press wrote: "Hepburn has never looked more entrancing or more sexy than she does in Plunkett's gowns!" Good for him.

Smart friends, however, made smart appraisals. One of them said that my stars looked as if they were dressed for a Beverly Hills costume party: "Come as Mr. and Mrs. Cattle Baron." In New York, the *New Republic* critic wrote: "They wander through a lavish production like thoroughbred somnambulists." It's the only picture I've ever made that I'm ashamed of. Don't see it.

A P P A R E N T L Y Zanuck had heard good talk about me—or was I still riding the *Tree Grows in Brooklyn* wave?—because he sent me a script through Louis de Rochemont, a producer who was then making enacted documentaries (there's a cute contradiction!) for Fox. This film was to be titled *Boomerang*. When I read it, I thought it a routine little drama, and it had no interest for me. When Molly read it, she disagreed; she said something good could be made of it. Perhaps she understood that my deflated morale could benefit from activity, because she urged me to go ahead with it, and finally I did.

Molly was right; *Boomerang* was my cure. The author, Dick Murphy, and I became good friends. The producer, de Rochemont, a bright man who drank too much, offered the advantage of suddenly disappearing from time to time; he was an agreeable and intelligent man, agreeable enough and intelligent enough to leave the filmmaking to the filmmakers. He said nothing about anything we did. I cast the movie from my New York brood, many of whom were soon to come into the Actors Studio; plus Ed Begley, a reformed drunk and a fine man who had precisely the heavy load of guilt his part needed; plus Dana Andrews, who could learn seven pages of dialogue for a courtroom scene in an hour over black coffee, after he'd been up all night drinking something else; plus Jane Wyatt, who'd played opposite me in *Night Music*, as prim as ever and certainly not a drinker.

I selected all the locations, and not a single scene was shot in a studio set. We used the streets of Stamford, Connecticut, and the county courthouse in White Plains, New York. Dick Murphy was always at my elbow; if a scene didn't work, we made it work. We didn't have to consult anybody about anything. I had a cutter with me, Harmon Jones, who also became a friend and quickly convinced me that making films wasn't so difficult— "Look at the dodos who make them!" I'd soon master the technique of film editing, he said, and would be able to rely on myself; meantime, I should rely on him. We sent our stuff back to Zanuck, who responded with enthusiastic telegrams of inordinate length; they could have done with a cutter.

I enjoyed the crowds on the streets; one night we had five thousand people watching. I didn't keep them at arm's length but walked among them, talked and joked with them, became a neighborhood hero; when I asked the crowd to be quiet for a take, they were quiet. I gave parts to all the cops who'd accept them—there was a third-degree scene—and especially liked one formidable sergeant, who did surprisingly well. I brought my mother and father up from New Rochelle to watch me, and my father finally was convinced I might make a life of this strange occupation.

I also brought out my uncle—A. E. ("Joe") Kazan—to watch the shooting. An old eccentric, he'd been the subject of an amusing profile Sam Behrman wrote for *The New Yorker*. This old man was once the boy about whom I was to write (and later put on the screen) in *America America*, the first of our family to come to the new land from Anatolia. He was living at this time from some dollars I gave him each week plus what he could bully out of my father and whatever he could scrounge at the horse track by playing the tout and being rewarded with a couple of five-dollar tickets. So he endured. He had the family resilience, and his spirit never drooped. Despite the fact that his pockets were empty, he still wore the costume he wore when he was a millionaire—threadbare doesn't describe it—a black box coat, striped "ambassador" trousers, a wing collar, and a blue polka-dot bow tie, the whole topped with a derby hat. These items of apparel, even though they were worn and filthy, gave him a style and a kind of distinction. He sported a cane with an "ivory" handle, one he hadn't been able to hock.

He was impressed with my new incarnation; he'd only known me as the kid my father used to refer to as a "hopeless case." I gave him a part to enjoy his company. Although he had only an hour's work, we conspired to delay his scene so he'd hang around with us; also so that he'd draw two weeks' salary. His role consisted of escorting a middle-aged lady, presumably his wife, across a street; that was it. Since he'd never done anything like this before, I matched him up with an experienced actress, an Equity member. They did the scene a number of times, but Joe spoiled each take by starting late or jumping the gun or looking at me or the camera as he crossed the street. I'd do the scene again, asking the actress holding his arm to make sure they started across when they were supposed to and cautioning Joe again not to look at me or the camera until I shouted "Cut!" But the scene still didn't go well, and Joe, sensing my displeasure, took me aside and said, "This woman you give to me here, she can't act. You see she spoil it every time. . . ." I asked the "arrogant Anatolian" to please be

Uncle Joe

patient with her; after all, she was an elderly lady and could use the work. Joe was rather patronizing about it, but I finally convinced him to try it again. "Don't get her in trouble, Uncle Joe," I said. "She needs your help." I believe this appeal to his gallantry did it. He offered her his elbow, they tried it again, and this time the scene worked. Then I said, "Print!" triumphantly. Everyone on the street, watching—many hundreds were there—applauded. Joe waved an acknowledgment, and all the young girls in the cast surrounded him and hugged him, a tableau of adoration.

Joe died not long afterward. I was the first of the family to enter the hotel room. The body was sprawled on a sofa; Joe had never learned to sleep in a bed. On the table by an air-shaft window, I found a needle for the treatment of diabetes and two haberdasher's packages. One contained a brand-new black box coat to replace the one he'd worn out and soiled, the other a new derby hat. That is what he'd done with the money he'd earned acting. In the pocket of the trousers he was wearing when he died was an uncashed check from Twentieth Century–Fox—security against the future, which Joe had learned was pitiless.

I've called *Boomerang* my cure. It was. I walked the Stamford streets—they were my stage—as master of it all. Call it arrogance. I call it confidence, and it had come flooding back, filling the cavity that was emptied in Culver City. There was a lovely harmony in Stamford and in that White Plains county courthouse. Work was joy again. I'd found my way of making films.

W H I L E I was in Stamford shooting *Boomerang*, the following declaration appeared in *The New York Times:* "Harold Clurman, Elia Kazan and Walter Fried announce the formation of a new production company. . . . Scheduled for the first presentation of this new partnership is an untitled play by Arthur Miller, formerly known as *The Sign of the Archer.* It is reported that Franchot Tone will have an important interest in the new production."

Clearly, Harold had prepared this announcement; I'd not seen the copy, nor had we discussed Franchot Tone. Knowing Harold, I sensed his eagerness and his pride and, in the phrase "It is reported," his craftiness.

Harold had read Miller's play first and passed it on to me. I was impressed; it had a strength not found in the work of any dramatist of this time except Lillian Hellman, but Art's play was warmhearted instead of hateful, as hers were. Like other plays being written then, it concerned guilt, but not that of a person being falsely accused; the guilt in Art's play was real. By not setting up an accusation that was to be disproved in three acts, the play dramatized a true moral confrontation. I admired Art for dealing with his theme head-on. The guilt uncovered was that of the hero's father, whom he loved. This fact—a strong emotional attachment in hazard—deepened the theme. Since the guilt was that of a businessman, ergo that of our business community, the play made a social statement.

I immediately felt close to Art. He'd been inspired to write plays by the Group Theatre, we were both out of the Depression, both left-wingers, both had had problems with our fathers, considered their business worlds antihuman. We were soon exchanging every intimacy. I was to find that Art had many problems similar to my own in his home life; he was maritally unsteady, as I had been all my married life, but he'd been bound down by his inhibitions. He frequented our household. He liked Molly's intellectual feistiness, she his strength. Art was like a member of my family; I saw him almost daily and usually at my home.

Art was very interested in films, and I invited him to watch us working on Boomerang. He was impressed with the joyous spirit on the set and by the kind of actors I was using. They looked like his own characters, ordinary human beings, instead of Sardi's "Little Bar" hangers-on. He made friends with members of my cast. I put him in a lineup scene as a suspect, and he enjoyed that. He told me that he was interested in writing for films and about his experience during the war working in the Brooklyn Navy Yard. He said he thought there was exciting film material on the waterfront. We planned to work together—he to write, I to direct a waterfront film.

He wanted me to direct his play and use many of the actors in Boomerang—Ed Begley, Arthur Kennedy, and Karl Malden in particular. Art admired Harold but felt closer to me. I was eager to direct the play, which had been retitled All My Sons, but I was concerned that Harold would be hurt by Art's choice. And he was, but he wouldn't admit it; Harold believed it was a sign of strength not to admit a weakness; he never learned not to swallow anger or hurt. He had assumed—and with reason, since Art had given him the play to read first—that Art wanted him to direct it. The choice Art made, like all choices in the theatre, was public; people knew about Art's preference.

There was also this: The professional standing of a director depends on the plays he's able to attract. Harold had built his reputation on the plays Odets had written and given him to do. Then Odets had become alienated from Harold; in 1941 he'd asked Lee Strasberg to direct Tallulah Bankhead in his play *Clash by Night*. Harold's professional standing would have benefited if Art had given him his play to direct. It was not an unimportant loss.

He kept saying that it didn't matter, he wasn't upset; he went his cheery way, saying that I did indeed have certain useful qualifications for the job, among them the ones he always mentioned: energy, clarity, and mechanical dexterity. He, the implication remained, was the artist, with the extra-fine sensibilities and broad cultural outlook. Although there was some truth in this, it annoyed me. Oddly enough, he didn't grant me genuine praise for what I did until years later, when I'd begun to write novels. He told me one day that people thought more of me since I'd begun to write books. He was referring, of course, to himself, not to "people."

During the rehearsals of *All My Sons*, which started in December 1946, he behaved abominably; in fact, he seemed to be out of control. His discipline at rehearsals was that of a naughty child. He'd sit in the back of the theatre where I was working, our secretary at his side, presumably giving her notes. He'd talk to her audibly, laugh, and make comments. Working on stage, I heard him rumbling from the back seats and felt the stir of his restlessness behind my back. Sometimes he'd have another young lady at his side, one who gave him the privilege of warming his hand between her legs. He was always, one way or another, calling attention to his presence, would come on stage during the breaks and chatter about irrelevancies, laughing at his own quips, demanding Miller's ear when I needed it. Meantime, I'd be trying to gather my thoughts and solve problems I'd noticed in the rehearsal. Again and again, I went home wondering what the hell was eating him. Molly told me. "He's jealous."

There was one note he did give me, again and again—compulsively, I thought. It was that the wife of the guilty businessman should have some share of his guilt. It soon appeared that this had been one of Stella's reactions to the script. I disagreed with the suggestion, but Harold kept at it both to me and, when I'd turn away, to Arthur. I imagined that Stella was "bugging" him about it at home: "Well, did you tell Kazan what I said he should do?" I believe he even partly convinced Miller, who wasn't as strong then as he was to become, that Stella had a point. Art tried rewriting the woman, but it didn't work, and we had to return the play to order.

Our financial arrangement was that Harold and I would split the director's fee no matter who was directing—this to give us both the continuity of a small living wage. But I noticed that his main activity, along with that of our business manager, Fried, was to look for plays that Harold might direct independently—or that Stella might direct. He'd told me that he wanted Stella to direct a play for us; I, as usual, kept mum, but I was burning. I didn't respond as I should have: saying plainly that I would not produce a play that she directed. I supposed that all through this, Harold was catching hell from her at home. She always wanted him to prove his love by acts of preference.

There was another widening rift. Bobby Lewis and I had gone ahead setting up acting classes in the Studio, and as soon as *Boomerang* had "wrapped," these classes began. The message to Harold was clear: I'd preferred starting this program with Bobby; I hadn't waited for him to "talk to Stella." I'd rejected Harold's wishes and advice and gone my own way, leaving Stella out. But again he showed no reaction. If he was angry with me, he ate it.

Our work unit—*All My Sons* in rehearsal—functioned perfectly. Miller and I, the actors, and the designer, Mordecai Gorelik, jelled. We were a success during our out-of-town tryout; Art did a little more work before the New York opening, then we came in. Brooks Atkinson, the one fine man we had writing criticism in our daily papers, immediately saw the unusual worth of the play and that an important new playwright had come on the scene. Despite some lukewarm notices ("More indignation than craft," the man in the *Herald Tribune* wrote, and in the *Daily News*, Burns Mantle had his say: "Long before they'd stopped talking and Mr. Begley had shot himself, I was ready to go home"), we did excellent business. In time the play was to win the Drama Critics prize, beating out *The Iceman Cometh*.

The *Daily Worker* acclaimed the play: "Miller now comes forward as a leading figure among the rising generation of playwrights striving to restore and deepen social drama in America." And so on. We were the talk and, once again, I was the hope of left-wing theatre people. Harold was pleased and felt that his judgment of the play was vindicated. All that he says about the production in his memoirs is: "I produced *All My Sons*," and the play succeeded as he knew it would. He felt he had made all the important decisions, including that I should direct the play. I received an opening night telegram from him: "Dear Gadg. This is a wonderful beginning for us. You have done a magnificent job. But I want you to remember that this is only the beginning. Love, Harold."

If he was suspecting that I was reconsidering our partnership, he was right.

I was filled with confidence and a sense of my worth. I'd done a good job with Arthur and the actors on the play; I knew I was completely capable there. What was new was a hope that I might have something unique and personal to do in films. If I could bring fine writers like Miller into the movies—we'd gone on talking about a waterfront film—I might do work that no one else in this country had yet done. Up until then I'd relied on other people—on Harold, on Bud Lighton, on Zanuck, and on all the technicians in filmmaking: the cameramen, the art directors, and the cutters. But now I knew that to rely on others was not good for me. I had to get on my own.

This new resolve, along with my disappointment and anger at the way

Harold had behaved, began to bring on a wish to break up our partnership. I found myself looking for the reasons to do this, going over and over his behavior at rehearsals, his patronizing attitude toward me, his supercilious indulgence. I reread the slighting references to me in his articles. I recalled the evidence of his jealousy (Molly had it right). I reminded myself of the presence of Stella, always looking over his shoulder.

I opposed to this the joy I'd felt being on my own. In *Boomerang*. And during the production of *All My Sons*. I came to the conclusion that artists should not have partners. If they're any good at all, what they should produce is a piece of personal expression, theirs uniquely. The fact with Harold was that while we were partners in business, we were competitors in art— we would not ever agree about interpretation. The future proved this true.

Nor was the theatre, I decided, what I'd been taught by Lee and Harold that it was: a collective art. A fine artistic production expresses the vision, the conviction, and the insistent presence of one person. It is best when it is undiluted by artistic cooperation, when it is not characterized by any of the seven (or more) deadly virtues: fair-minded, well balanced, accommodating, unassertive, reasonable, cooperative, and so forth. An acting company is best when it's trained by its director (a benign tyrant) for a specific purpose: *his* production. In each case that revered acting companies became successful, from the Moscow Art Theatre to the famous works of Vakhtangov and Meyerhold, down to the ballets of Balanchine and the experimental productions of Grotowski and Peter Brook, they were trained by the director for his absolute purposes. The great theatre works I'd heard tell about and read about were finally the product of a single artist, an individual who was his own man, a visionary with a special vision and a dominating ego. It had always been thus and always would be. I knew that very well now. I knew that dependence on, or collaboration with, even a man I respected as much as I did Harold was not good. Actually it was becoming increasingly difficult for me to collaborate with anyone. Harold would be the last dependency of my life, and I would have to break it.

But I still hesitated making the cut. I kept wondering if Harold's feelings would be hurt. How badly? I didn't want to do him harm. For several weeks, I was on the verge of rejecting, publicly, a man whom I still—despite all the contrary reasons I'd found—loved. For a few weeks, I couldn't bring myself to do what I knew I had to do.

It was at that time that Darryl Zanuck sent me Laura Hobson's novel *Gentleman's Agreement*. He said it was going to be his "personal production," which meant it would be Fox's picture of the year and have everything in the way of production help. Would I direct it? I jumped at the offer. I'd get out of New York City, away from the Clurman-Kazan tangle, have a chance to think things over and find out what I wanted most. I also decided that from now on I would play both coasts—do plays in New York, do films wherever it was best, but preferably, as I'd done with *Boomerang*, on location. I'd give up nothing, have it all.

When we were trying out *All My Sons* on the road, I'd received a letter from my son Chris, aged nine, which had to be his own idea even though typed for him by his mother. "Dear Daddy," Chris said, "I wish you would quit your job so you could see us more often. The whole thing, the theatre and everything." I made up my mind, with that letter, that I'd take the whole family west with me. Fox would get us a home with a swimming pool, provide us with cars, and keep us handsomely in food, a cook, and a housekeeper. That might please and satisfy Chris as well as his amanuensis, Molly. I'd go to work every morning like a regular father, come home at night, play around the yard weekends, and the kids would learn to swim. I told this plan to everyone at home, and they were delighted.

Just before I departed for the West with my family, there came the incident that made up my mind about the partnership. Brecht was in New York then, and Harold had been working on him for the rights to *Galileo*, which Harold wanted us to produce, with him directing. I am not an admirer of this play, and it was not to my taste to produce it. What I wanted to do was a series of contemporary American dramas, in either film or theatre. Harold was pushing me to agree to something I didn't want to agree to. We met with Brecht, his son, and Audrey Wood, his agent. They would agree to an arrangement with our production company only if I, not Harold, directed the play. I said I couldn't because I was going to make a film now. I was embarrassed for Harold as he went on and on, trying to get Brecht to agree to him as the director. "I don't want mood," Brecht said. "You'll give me mood. Bring me here a circus director. You are a Stanislavski man." "My name is Clurman," Harold shouted. All to no avail. Brecht would not have him.

Harold notes in his book that I was silent through this discussion, that I didn't try to convince Brecht that Harold should direct the play. Harold is right; I was silent, and naturally this disappointed him. He wrote that he supposed I was worried because "Brecht's reputation as a Communist might render him [me] similarly suspect." He also believed that was the reason I wouldn't agree to direct the play. This reason never occurred to me; it was 1947, and I didn't testify to the House Committee on Un-American Activities until five years later. In 1947, I would have testified in an opposite mode. The reason I didn't urge Brecht to give us the play for Harold to direct was that it was then, sitting there during this wrangle, that I became certain I didn't want to continue with the partnership. That was the day.

My family and I went to California and settled into the house Fox had rented. From my office on the Fox lot, I wrote Harold a letter, breaking off. I gave reasons and tried to be gentle, but the reasons were irrelevant, and I was gentle only because I was sure of myself. It was finished!

I believe that Harold never quite forgave me for that letter. I believe that, being no more than human, he had to find ways of hitting back at me, not by attacking me openly but by slurs disguised so that only I got them. He never wrote anything genuinely enthusiastic about anything I did in the theatre.

In 1978, two years before his death, I made a joke of this. I was the final speaker at a tribute in his honor. I said that if he'd been asked to speak about me that night, after all our years of friendship and all I'd accomplished, I believed "the final word he'd say about me, even now, would be, 'Kazan? Oh yes, he was my stage manager.'" Harold laughed uproariously at this. So did I.

H O W   Q U I E T   things were in California after New York! Zanuck was at his best; it would not ever be this good again with him. The staff people at Fox were all behind me. At home, the swimming pool was clear and clean and just the right temperature. Molly and the kids were in it twice daily and I jumped into it as soon as I came home every night. Weekends, I played with my kids. Molly was proud and especially happy that I'd broken off with Harold.

He didn't answer my letter; there was nothing to say. Now I had no one to turn to for challenge and inspiration. I realized how dependent I'd been all my professional life on others. At last, I was on my own.

T H I S   M O R N I N G   I read the obituary of Lillian Hellman in *The New York Times*. It was not signed; obits of important people are usually credited. Did this mean that the newspaper had taken particular pains with Lillian's? Had they found and assigned someone special, who wished to remain anonymous? The copy glowed with the adoration once accorded saints. Lillian was a person I did not like, but since this is being written on the occasion of her death, *de mortuis nil nisi bonum*. She did, sometime after the period with which I've been dealing, tell an ugly lie about me, but I'll come to that when her body has cooled.

Surprisingly, the first thing that came to mind when I read the news was the memory of a drawing Lillian had made of herself. Some years ago, a bookseller asked a number of people who'd distinguished themselves in the arts to draw, no matter how crudely, self-portraits. A collection of these sketches was later published. Lillian chose to present us with "What I wanted to look like and don't." She produced a line drawing of a starlet; "blond curls, natural," she specified in a note at the side of the page, with "deep blue eyes, natural." There is, of course, a short nose, turned up at the end, and, indicated by two dots, her nostrils. When I found this book on my shelf and looked at her drawing—her self-representation was that of a high school prom queen—I was restored to some sympathy for the lady by her humor about herself. The book, of course, is adult play, but since all play is on the level, I had to believe that a wish, until now unsuspected, was being expressed. Was this frustrated longing, I wondered, one source of her famous anger?

In time Lillian enjoyed what few of us do: Her fondest wish came true. She was portrayed on the screen not by a look-alike but by darling Jane Fonda, a choice Lillian of course approved. She had the resources to certify her attractiveness for the world to see.

Another way she was able to ease what she seemed to have considered her misfortune of birth was by gathering men around her, living testimonials to her allure. Once, it is said, she kept a house in which she provided hospitality for a cadre of vigorous intellectuals, the chosen. They were: a discarded but still devoted husband, her ever-reliable and most capable director, the lively editor of the liveliest liberal newspaper of the day, and, leader of the pack, Dashiell Hammett, of whose love the lady boasted so frequently and so ardently that one couldn't help doubting it. Lillian, I'm sure, loved them all. Her friends, if any such read this book, mustn't imagine I'm kidding when I say I admire the lady for providing herself with this mini-harem. It's something that I, even at the peak of my powers, would not have attempted. It is also the kind of setup that, to reverse the sexes, many males have secretly yearned for. But she did it.

What went on in that charmed house no one has said. Did the sultana summon her choice to her side, a different one at different times? Or is that malicious fantasy? Since the queen bee kept the workings inside her hive secret, I will respect her privacy and not speculate. My point here is only that this arrangement testified to a need that is not part of the image Lillian has, in other ways, created. It testifies, I believe, to her common humanity. And with that, for the moment, R.I.P.

Irene, Tennessee, and I

IN APRIL of 1947, I received a letter from the author of *The Glass Menagerie;* Tennessee Williams wrote me from New York City.

Dear Gadg: In town for a few days, my first chance to see *All My Sons*. This tops any direction I have seen on Broadway. Incidentally the play is dynamite. It ought to take both prizes easy. The sort of eloquence this country needs very badly now. I will write Miller my congratulations (though tinged with envy).

Irene Selznick is going to send you a script of mine. It may not be the sort of play that interests you but I hope so. Tenn.

I received the script from Mrs. Selznick's office but didn't rush to read it. I wasn't sure Williams and I were the same kind of theatre animal—Miller seemed more my kind; I was also put off because I'd heard that the script had been given to Josh Logan. People in the theatre were talking about Logan's enthusiasm for the play; he'd expressed it openly and often. I didn't want to compete with him; he was a friend and a man I liked.

But Molly, who'd once caused the Group Theatre to give a prize to Tennessee for three one-act plays, read his new play immediately. It was titled A Streetcar Named Desire. Tennessee was impatient to know my reaction and called the next morning. Molly knew a masterpiece when she had it in her hands and told Williams on the phone how much she thought of his play. He was still worried what my reaction would be. "Gadg likes a thesis, I know," he told my wife, "and I haven't made up my mind what the thesis of this play is."

W H E N Irene Selznick acquired A Streetcar Named Desire for production, there was a hysteria of snobbery along Broadway's inner circles. I'm embarrassed to say that I was part of it; snobbery comes quickly to the successful on our street. My close friend Kermit Bloomgarden was "shocked." A man who enjoyed assuming moral postures publicly, Kermit was frequently shocked. Other producers scolded Audrey Wood, Tennessee's agent. They'd spent years of their lives, they complained, working faithfully to keep the "fabulous invalid" alive; how dared she give the new play of a prize-winning author to an outsider? An intruder from Hollywood! A beginner. What the hell did Mrs. Selznick know about the theatre? At Sardi's, the fact that she was Louis B. Mayer's daughter and David O. Selznick's wife was chewed over with the cannelloni. How did she get the play? the faithful demanded to know. A rumor spread that Mrs. Selznick had loaned (given?) Audrey and her husband enough West Coast gold to acquire a home in a fashionable Connecticut suburb; a favor of this kind to a powerful motion picture agent, one who could lead (or mislead) a client in the direction an even more powerful studio head wished, was not unknown. Mrs. Selznick had been brought up by Mr. Louis B. Mayer, hadn't she?

I've known Irene forty years and never known her to do anything dishonest. She, not her father, produced Streetcar.

In the process of becoming acquainted with a new field, Mrs. Selznick arranged to meet a number of the fixtures on our street. Not all of them were welcoming. She would question these veterans, freely confessing her ignorance and inexperience. At her invitation, superior knowledge was brandished. Irene played it cool, compared opinions, nosed out contradictions, weighed the answers. Among others she asked to see was Bill Fitelson, the lawyer of many theatre people, including Josh Logan, including me. She invited Bill to come to her office. He found time for an interview but, according to Irene, resented being asked to come to *her* office. There is a canon in the world of show business about who goes to whose office. Irene reports that Bill was rude, that he swore none of his clients would ever work for her. I didn't hear their conversation, but Bill Fitelson did live with a chip on his shoulder. The fact is that he didn't have that kind of power over his clients; was it swagger or, more likely, a first step in negotiation?

It was perfectly natural for Irene Selznick to think of Logan; he was Broadway's most successful director. Now, following an instinct, something irrational, Williams was asking Irene to tell Logan that he would only have me. I had still not read the play, but my wife, overwhelmed by it, kept after me. When I read it, I must confess, I had reservations. I met the author. His modesty took me by surprise. We had a plain talk and liked each other immediately. I told Bill Fitelson I wanted to do the play but must have absolute artistic powers over all production decisions and a billing that would ensure me these rights.

Williams and I met again, shook hands, embraced. As far as we were concerned, the matter was settled. He "removed himself" to Cape Cod; I prepared to caravan my family to California, where I was to direct *Gentleman's Agreement*. Irene Selznick and Bill Fitelson entered the same room and closed the door. There was a union not made in heaven. Unrecorded conversations took place. "I have just heard," Williams wrote me, "from Mrs. Selznick and she says that Mr. Fitelson told her you felt a great deal of work had to be done on the script. Is that correct?" I'd not said that to Bill and, having read the play again, didn't believe it. The meetings about contract, it seemed, were going down a familiar path where it was hard to tell what was true from what was bargaining pressure. Williams invited me to come to the Cape before I went west and spend a weekend going over the script; he said he was eager for my ideas. "There are some weak passages and some corny touches," he went on. "I'm sure a lot of good will come out of consultation between us. The cloudy dream type, which I admit to being, needs the complementary eye of the more objective and dynamic worker. I believe you are also a dreamer. There are dreamy touches in your direction which are vastly provocative but you have the dynamism my work needs."

After this letter (I gobbled up the compliments), I belonged to him. About to leave for the West Coast, I called Fitelson and demanded to know where we stood in the negotiations. He suggested I leave the dealing to him. The process was delicate, he explained, because our demands had hurt Irene's self-esteem. But he felt confident that since the author wanted me, she had no choice except to meet our terms. He asked me to stonewall.

I was, by this time, so anxious to do the play that I wrote Tennessee a letter undercutting my lawyer. "Thanks for your wonderful letter," I wrote. "I read the play again last night with no phones ringing and I felt close to you. I'll do everything possible to do your play. But I work best in single collaboration with the author. I'll never go back to working for a producer when it means consulting with him (her) on every point as well as with administrators, executives, production committees, agents, backers and various and sundry personal associates. All meetings on *All My Sons* were between two people, Miller and me; that is the best way. I've talked this out with Fitelson and we've come to a proposal which Mrs. Selznick may find acceptable. I hope so. It will depend somewhat on how much you want me. I'll be very happy if it does work out. This will sound corny but I might as well say it; I'll be honored. The play calls for me to grow, to do more than I've done before and . . ." And so on.

Dear reader, can you see that I was continuing the negotiation in my own, subtle way?

In return I received a letter from Williams that is so revealing and so beautiful that I will pass on some of it:

I am bitterly disappointed that you and Mrs. Selznick have still not come to an agreement. I am wondering what has been the primary trouble, the script itself or your unwillingness to tie up with another producer. . . . I am sure that you must have had reservations about the script. I will try to clarify my intentions in this play. I think its best quality is its authenticity or its fidelity to life. There are no "good" or "bad" people. Some are a little better or a little worse but all are activated more by misunderstanding than malice. A blindness to what is going on in each other's hearts. Stanley sees Blanche not as a desperate, driven creature backed into a last corner to make a last desperate stand—but as a calculating bitch with "round heels." . . . Nobody sees anybody truly but all through the flaws of their own egos. That is the way we all see each other in life. Vanity, fear, desire, competition—all such distortions within our own egos—condition our vision of those in relation to us. Add to those distortions in our *own* egos, the corresponding distortions in the egos of *others*, and you see how cloudy the glass must become through which we look at each other. That's how it is in all living relationships except when there is that rare case of two people who love intensely enough to burn through all those layers of opacity and see each other's naked hearts. Such cases seem purely theoretical to me.

However in creative fiction and drama, if the aim is fidelity, people are shown as we never *see* them in life but as they *are*. Quite impartially without any ego flaws in the eye of the beholder. We see from the *outside* what could not be seen *within* and the truth of the tragic dilemma becomes apparent. It was not that one person was bad or good, one right or wrong but that all judged falsely concerning each other. What seemed black to me and white to the other is actually gray—a perception that could occur only through the detached eye of art. As if a ghost sat over the affairs of men and made a true record of them.

Naturally a play of this kind does not present a theme or score a point unless it is the point or theme of human understanding. When you begin to arrange the action of a play to score a certain point, the fidelity to life may suffer. I don't say it always does. Things may be selected to score a point clearly without any contrivance toward that end but I'm afraid that happens rarely.

I remember you asked me what should an audience feel for Blanche. Certainly pity. It is a tragedy with the classic aim of producing a catharsis of pity and terror and in order to do that, Blanche must finally have the understanding and compassion of the audience. This without creating a black-dyed villain in Stanley. It is a thing (Misunderstanding) not a person (Stanley) that destroys her in the end. In the end you should feel—"If only they all had known about each other."

I have written all this out in case you were primarily troubled over my intention in the play. Please don't regard this as "pressure." A wire from Irene and a letter from Audrey indicate that both of them feel you have definitely withdrawn yourself from association with us and that we must find someone else. I don't want to accept this necessity without exploring the nature and degree of the differences between us. Especially as they are now talking about someone I have never heard of, an Englishman named Tyrone Guthrie. Finding a director aside from yourself who can bring this play to life exactly as if it were happening in life is going to be a problem. But that is the kind of direction it has to have. I don't necessarily mean "realism"; sometimes a living quality is caught better by expressionism than what is supposed to be realistic treatment.

This letter became the key to the production for me. For one thing, it was the reason I cast Brando as Stanley. I have never, in all the years since, seen another production of this play, but every photograph I've seen of Stanley and Blanche together as they were in other productions shows an arrogant bully abusing a creature whose faults, whatever they might be, were totally concealed by her spirituality. Blanche was always a heroine without a blemish and Stanley what Williams feared he might become in our production, a "black-dyed villain."

What was distressing Irene and Audrey was not any rewriting I might seek but that Fitelson was asking (and we would finally obtain) twenty percent of the profits of the production, which meant that Irene's investors would get less than they might feel they had a right to expect and that Tennessee himself (and so Audrey) would get less than he would have taken with another director. As for the matter of billing (*Irene Selznick* presents ELIA KAZAN'S PRODUCTION of), considering that I felt our producer was a beginner, for whom I would have to do much of the work of production, I thought (and do now think) this protective billing fair enough. But as the terms that concluded the negotiations became known, I was judged to be arrogant. Very soon, however, every director who could swing it was demanding this same billing and enjoying the same powers. Our negotiations had altered the position of the director on Broadway.

I H A D reached no such eminence in films; in Hollywood it was still a producer's game.

I've been wondering why the store of my memory on *Gentleman's Agreement* is so bare. Although Darryl carried off the Oscar for best picture and I for direction, there is very little I have to say about how it was made. A model of big-studio production, it was perfect of its kind, which means it had no face, only *faces*, those in a group photograph: the faces of Darryl Zanuck and Twentieth Century–Fox's department heads. The production was perfectly managed by Zanuck, with an energy that never relaxed and a determination that on every shooting day he'd get the best out of everyone working. Some few years later, when he was gone, that way of making films was never again in hands as capable. It is not my way, it's the opposite way, but Darryl did the job he believed in with passionate devotion. Everyone who worked for him respected him. So did I.

Before I left for the West, I'd had a succession of long telegrams from him concerning casting (Gregory Peck and Dorothy McGuire: okay? Okay) and asking who I thought might do a good job on the screenplay. Notice that he'd chosen the director first and was consulting with him; MGM had not. I urged that we do the film as I'd done *Boomerang*, in real locations. When he agreed to this, I suggested he engage Paul Osborn, who would, a few years later, write the screenplay of *East of Eden*. Darryl wired that Paul was busy, that every writer under contract to Fox wanted the assignment, but that he preferred going "outside" and finding someone exceptional. He did. Moss Hart. Once Moss was engaged, he had to be turned loose to write the screenplay in a series of dialogue scenes rather than action scenes. The idea of flinging the story into the streets, offices, and apartments of New York City had to be relinquished.

When I arrived in California, Moss had been working with Darryl and they had two acts ready for me to read. It went like this: Dorothy McGuire, a young divorcée out of polite New York society, has become involved with Gregory Peck, a writer engaged in writing a magazine piece exposing anti-Semitism in the United States. He finds it in unsuspected places and on the most "liberal" levels. Finally, during a conversation with his fiancée, he detects evidence of the prejudice in her. When he accuses her, they quarrel and break up. That's what we had; now where do we go? Moss asked for my ideas. I always have ideas; this time they were worthless. Moss had his own way of telling a dramatic story, through private talk between people of some culture who observed certain standards of well-bred behavior. This conflict would break the mold. He knew what he needed but didn't know how to get it. He decided to disappear for a few days, be alone, and see if he could find the solution.

There is often just one element that makes the difference in a film. It may be the stars or the production numbers, the novelty of the backgrounds, some extreme of violence or some sexual boldness in the action. Whatever. In the case of this film, it was what Moss brought back from his days apart, a short, delicate scene in the last third of the story. I believe it was the critical find, the one that made this film work. Here it is: Dorothy McGuire, anguished about the separation from her fiancé and believing his opinion of her unfair, asks Peck's best friend (John Garfield would play this part) to come and talk to her. Anxiously she tells him how unjust Peck's accusation against her is and offers as evidence her feelings at a big dinner party she'd attended that evening, where one of the guests, a powerful and wealthy man, had dropped anti-Semitic slurs. She tells Garfield how outraged and angry she felt. "And what did you do?" Garfield asks. Dorothy continues even more eloquently, describing her feeling of moral fury. "I despised him," she says. "Everybody at the table despised him." The Garfield character interrupts again: "And when he had finished, what did you say?" "Oh, I wanted to yell at him," McGuire says. "I wanted to get up and leave. I wanted to say to everybody at the table, 'Why do we sit here and take this?'" "And then what did you do?" Garfield asks. McGuire begins to get the point. "I sat there," she says, "we all just sat there, and when dinner was over, I said I was ill and left. It's true. I still feel sick all through me." "I wonder," Garfield says, "if you'd feel so sick now if you'd nailed him? There's a kind of elation about socking back." He stares at her. For a moment, avoiding his gaze, she's unable to speak. Then she puts her hands over her eyes and the scene is over. Through this confrontation, the issue between the lovers is resolved, she contrite, he forgiving. Hero and heroine are reunited, more in love than ever.

This kind of story solution was the essence of Darryl's theory of how social issues had to be handled for the American film audience, always through a love story in which the lovers are involved in the issue under

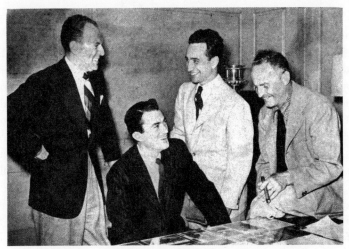

Moss Hart, Darryl Zanuck, and I with our star, Gregory Peck

conflict. Any less personal treatment, Zanuck believed, would not hold his audience's interest. Our film was the perfect example of that day's "liberal" films. And it worked. Chosen by the critics, hailed by opinionmakers, a box office winner, it provoked many statements about the movies' finally coming of age. It was repeatedly pointed out that here the word "Jew" was used for the first time in a major Hollywood film. Well, good!

But now the film is rarely revived and is generally considered to have skated over the surface of an issue that needed a more penetrating treatment. It doesn't have what would have made it lasting in its effect: the intimate experience of someone who had been through the bitter and humiliating experience. Now we have to ask whom did it truly affect, who felt guilty after seeing it, who might have been against what it was saying, who was altered, who converted? In fact, audiences were flattered to find that they were, after all, on "the side of the angels" with three distinguished men. But so much, so horrible, has been recognized about the attack on the Jew since the film was made that it now seems inadequate to the issue. Its success was its limitation.

As for the men who collaborated to make it, here were three unchallengeably successful men in their prime saying what they were certain would be applauded by their friends, making a film they were clever enough to plan so as to win even those who might consider it "propaganda." In the light-footed way the issue was offered, the film was beyond challenge. And we all three had, as did Peck in the story, an out. Our lives were not in hazard any more than Peck's character was a Jew. He was only pretending to be a Jew, for a magazine assignment. As I see it now, the film is patronizing. We seem to have been doing a favor to people who we considered needed a favor of understanding. Noblesse oblige. In relation to the depths of the issue, it also seems not quite true. Like Peck, it has an out. Made in Hollywood, 1947!

Once the screenplay had been prepared, Darryl and I satisfied, Moss pleased, as he had every reason to be, once FINAL FINAL had been stenciled on the script cover in heavy black letters and the designers and back lot people been put to work, any one of thirty directors available could have done it as well as I. As for the performances, they were decent enough but not exceptional. Peck was Peck, sober, worthy, no way intriguing or mysterious, completely "straight," no surprises. He was running the summer theatre at La Jolla while we were making the film, and when I looked for him to give him a note or to rehearse, he was often on long distance. Dorothy McGuire was perfect for the part—not the nicest thing to say about a fine girl. Again "straight," no surprises. Garfield, the best of the lot, had his New York street energy, along with a maturity he hadn't shown before. When he finally appeared on the screen, halfway through the action, it was a relief. The other performance I can recall is that of Anne Revere; she had bite and was at the same time caustic and affectionate.

The bulk of the profession's credit should have gone to Moss, who didn't get an Oscar (his work wasn't showy enough), and to Darryl, for running the production so perfectly. Peck didn't get an Oscar, not because he was constantly on the phone to La Jolla but because his role wasn't showy either. It's the role that gets the Oscar, not the actor. Celeste Holm did well, but she got an Oscar because she had Moss Hart's wittiest lines.

Those were my Hollywood glamour days. No sweat! I came to work wearing a white sports coat and took tennis lessons weekends. In restaurants I was led to the elite tables without asking for them. Journalists hunted me down. After work, I might or might not look at the rushes from the previous day. Darryl had already seen them and for the most part was enthusiastic. I trusted his judgment—particularly when it was favorable. Sometimes I enjoyed the hospitality of the big shots' steam room at Fox and let the "Turk," Darryl's masseur, do me. But mostly I'd drive home and jump into our pool. Molly and I would have old-fashioneds and I'd play with the kids on the lawn. This was as near as I ever came to being happy in southern California. I slept with the windows open to a pepper tree in the backyard, without a blanket and without worry. And I was faithful.

W E E K E N D S I worked on *Streetcar*. Irene had brought Tennessee west so we could confer. With him came Pancho, his companion at the time, a rambunctious young Mexican. Tennessee and I took to each other like a shot and without any of the usual gab about mutual friends, tastes, experiences, and so on to bridge the gap. It was a mysterious harmony; by all visible signs we were as different as two humans could be. Our union, immediate on first encounter, was close but unarticulated; it endured for the rest of his life. How did it happen? Possibly because we were both freaks. Behavior is the mystery that explains character. For instance, he was, as I was, a disappearer.

When I was young, a shorthorn buck, my favorite quick line was "I've got to go." I'd arrive at a party, immediately feel ill at ease, then, with an "I've got to go," disappear. Often I'd not even give that nonexplanation, and I'd never hint at where I had to go or why so suddenly. I'd just vanish. Some years later, when I'd become a middle-aged goat, I'd go to parties with one purpose in mind, and if I saw there was no one in the traffic for me, I'd leave abruptly. I'm afraid I still do that. People ask me why I drop out that way and where I go so suddenly. "We missed you," they say. "We had a lot of fun after you left," they say. But that doesn't prevent me, the next time I'm in tight company, from disappearing just as abruptly. It seems that when I'm in the society of my fellowman, I feel trapped, soon need to get away and do.

Williams would show up for a conference at Irene's beautiful home in Beverly Hills, a place where there was every symbol of easeful pleasure: a limpid pool, a tennis court without a scratch, a projection room where long, deep sofas invited viewers to relax (even doze), a park behind the house (not a backyard) where there were trees as gracious as those in an English preserve (what the hell are gracious trees?) and manicured lawns (manicured? by Japanese gardeners). But soon I'd catch a shifty quiver in our author's eyes, and it would turn out that he had another date closely following the one with us; I can't remember that we ever had an open-ended get-together. Which was fine with me, because I had to go too—for the same unreasonable reasons. Did he also feel trapped in the company of others, no matter that they were friends? So it would seem.

Or was he concerned, as I often was, that somewhere unspecified and mysterious, something more interesting, more pleasurable, more rewarding was taking place that he (I) was missing, and that he had to move quickly not to miss any more of that special pleasure than he'd already missed? Something like that must have been the case, because if I walked back into Irene's house (from the garden where we were talking) to use one of her "conveniences," when I came out he'd as often as not have slipped away, the Mexican jungle cat with him. Tennessee loathed conferences as I did, never accustomed himself to them any more than I did, never learned their worth—if they do indeed have worth.

When he left, I had the impression he was leaving for another country, or planet—the gay world, where I could not follow him or find him later if I suddenly needed him to question or consult. I had never come close to a homosexual before, even though there were two fine such fellows in the Group Theatre, good friends of mine. But I was so square that I would still ask myself who does what to whom when faggots bed together. A year later I made up my mind to find out, so I double-dated with Tennessee in the company of a young lady, one couple to each of his twin beds, and my curiosity was satisfied. But that summer, their way of life was a mystery to me.

Even in this respect, however, there was a bond between Williams and me: What the gay world—then still largely closeted—was to him, my foreignness was to me. We were both outsiders in the straight (or native) society we lived in. Life in America made us both quirky rebels.

I had thought, since Tennessee had written me those fine letters, that as soon as we came face to face we'd talk and I'd unload my ideas about his play's production. But when I made a couple of passes at this kind of chatter, his eyes would waver and glaze—he was thinking of something we weren't discussing—and he'd slip my reach for his attention with a little dip to one side, rather like a boxer when he slips a punch, then smile as if to say, "Why do we bother? We don't need to talk." He was a writer, not a talker.

Irene was a talker; it was her pleasure. She'd gather us for an in-depth discussion, but Tennessee, joking and jiving, enjoying his drink, would change the subject and I, very happily, would give up my plan to lay my directorial intentions at his feet. He'd chosen me by instinct, the voice within he trusted most, and that was that. I didn't need to prove myself. Perhaps if I had pushed any theoretical generalizations, he might have been perplexed or even thrown into doubt. It was just as well, that silence. What was unsaid was heard, plainly, by us both. He was content to trust me and to wait results.

There was another unspoken sympathy that bound us. Just as I was, and have been all my life long, Tennessee seemed to be waiting all the day through for the morning to come, that time when he'd be safely alone. The first hours of the day were the dearest ones for this man, his openhearted time. Mornings were when he worked, the only time he could, it seemed, and work was why he lived. He was to write in his *Memoirs:* "Mornings! It sometimes appears to me that I have lived a life of morning after morning, since it is and has always been the mornings in which I've worked." And then: "Work, the loveliest of all four letter words, surpassing even the importance of love—most times." He also wrote of his most persisting and terrible fear. "An artist dies two deaths," he wrote, "not only his own as a physical being but that of his creative powers which die before his body does." Did he seek to prove to himself every morning that he was still alive? That other death would happen to him, and I'd be a witness to his pain, but in our first days together, he still waited for the first light of each day, when he'd be not alone but alone with himself.

Mornings were when I was exposing negative on the Fox lot—I'd get there by seven-thirty—so at our conferences on *Streetcar,* when Tennessee would disappear I'd say to Irene, "I have to go," and be off to pump up strength and clear my mind for the next day's filming. He and I meshed in that respect too. We respected each other's special needs.

The one thing we did manage to talk about was casting, but even that briefly. Irene's suggestion for Blanche, Margaret Sullavan, had been conned into reading for the author, an event I did not attend because it took place on the East Coast. Tennessee's reaction, according to Mrs. Selznick, was that Miss Sullavan seemed to be holding a tennis racket as she spoke his lines; Tennessee doubted that Blanche would have been a tennis enthusiast. My suggestion of Mary Martin was a reach in the dark toward a woman I admired, but it struck no chord of affirmative response from either Irene or Williams—and not really from me. Tennessee spoke of Pamela Brown, and my reaction was: "Oh, please, not an Englishwoman." I was to direct the play and then the film, and, wouldn't you know it, both with English actresses playing Blanche.

So for the time being we were stuck on the part. John Garfield was interested in playing Stanley, but although he was one of my oldest friends and for years my companion on the handball court, I wasn't truly enthusiastic about him. I thought: Garfield and Sullavan! I'll be right back in the star system! So when Irene began to negotiate for Julie, I was satisfied with the slow grind of the Selznick gears and didn't run around her end to urge Mr. Garfield to be more responsible with his terms or show impatience to Irene about her pace, which was that of a Swiss interurban train entering a long, dark tunnel under one of that country's mountains. I mean it was slow and it was dark and you couldn't mark its progress. I preferred to wait for what luck might bring.

I N T I M E I would get over the feeling I had that summer in Beverly Hills, and during the autumn of work which followed, that Irene Selznick was a complete novice. Actually I was wrong; she was a beginner with a desperate will to learn to excel. This I should have seen and respected. She'd had an education in production from an exceptional man, the husband from whom she was separated, David O. Selznick. It was this training and the tradition this man embodied that caused the difficulties between us; those difficulties were not personal or temperamental, for Irene was and is a warmhearted woman who'd made a courageous decision to leave her husband and their *grand luxe* home in Beverly Hills and set up in New York.

I have just read a speech David Selznick delivered at Columbia University in 1937, an excellent speech with which I totally disagree. It tells more clearly than I could what Irene came out of, so I will quote a few sentences. David is talking about filmmaking, but the reference to theatre is easy to make. "A producer today," he said, "in order to produce properly, must be able, when it's necessary, to sit down and rewrite a scene he does not like and, if he is criticizing the director, must be able, not merely to say, 'I don't like it,' but to tell him how he would direct it himself. He must be able to go into a cutting room and if he doesn't like the cutting of the sequence, which is more often true than not, he must be able to recut the sequence." And so on.

I, on the other hand, was in the forefront of another movement, equally absolute. I believed that those same powers over all aspects of a production should belong to the director, that he, not the producer, should be the overlord of a production. I and those like me were the "Young Turks" who took over the theatre of the forties and fifties. (One phrase used now to attack such an assumption of power is "concept-happy director.") This movement not only continued, it progresses. All the best directors of the sixties, seventies, and eighties, from Tyrone Guthrie to Peter Brook to Peter Hall, from Bob Fosse and Hal Prince to Michael Bennett and Mike Nichols, have demanded the right to shape all production elements to their vision. It is all directing; they direct the whole.

Many of these men respect a text no more than it deserves and sometimes less than it deserves. Irene was to have an experience with this kind of theatre director when Larry Olivier did his production of *Streetcar* in London. If she'd thought me domineering and absolute in my demands, what could she have thought of Larry when he forbade her coming to his rehearsals and would not show her the cuts he'd made in Tennessee's play?

In my view, the producer should be the director's executive, serving and supporting him so he can carry out his vision of how the play should look, move, and feel. That was the relationship I would have with Kermit Bloomgarden and Walter Fried on *Death of a Salesman*, the play I'd do the next season, and that was the relationship I established on *Streetcar*. Irene was unprepared to accept the director as artistic tyrant, but in time she would, because she had to. On *Streetcar* I established a concept in support of which all other craftsmen working on the show had to shape their contributions. The producer was reduced to the status of an owner who observed the production process but had little part in it. This outraged the Selznick tradition in which Irene had been brought up. Such was the conflict that caused tensions between us; it is a credit to us both that we survived as friends.

Actually she'd engaged the scene designer I would have chosen—"buying the best," as David would have done. He was Jo Mielziner, an excellent man and a close friend, who was relieved when I came on the show. We had many meetings (without Irene) and planned the setting together. I'd given him a rough ground plan, as I always did, a ground plan being the director's avowal of intention in concrete terms. I discussed every aspect of the show with him: the colors, the materials, the transparency, the effects, and the lighting—which Jo, wisely, was to do for himself. When we knew what we wanted, Jo made a number of small sketches, and we presented our scheme to Irene and to Tennessee; they were glad to have it, for it was good.

I did the same thing with our talented costume designer, Lucinda Ballard, had separate meetings with her and worked out what I wanted. When she became annoyed at some of Irene's overanxious supervision, I defended Irene. Lucinda was a true artist, with a volatile temperament. I didn't want a civil war backstage. I also selected Alex North, the composer, a good family friend (until I gave my testimony to the House Committee on Un-American Activities five years later, after which he became a less good family friend). Alex knew jazz, which was—New Orleans!—what I wanted. The score may have surprised Irene, but I believe she was pleased with it.

So I took over the facets of the production. All the people working on the show knew what was required of them and how what they were to contribute fitted into the overall scheme. Was my takeover arrogant? Yes, but done as gently as I could manage it and just the way things should be done, the correct artistic "table of organization" for theatrical production.

In time I was to feel a softening and a shift in Irene's attitude, whereby an allegiance to me replaced her devotion to David's way. Perhaps she saw that the only thing I wanted was to fulfill Tennessee's vision—complex, subtle, and contradictory—which is all he wanted and all she wanted. But in the heat and tension of rehearsals, I sometimes handled the lady with unnecessary crudeness; I was rude, but I'm not sure I could or would behave differently now. A director is constantly threatened by the possibility of an erosion in the goal he's set for himself. Since art is the product of a single vision, the director must, at all costs, maintain his grip on what he wants. Compromise is a trap, always ready to spring. I had to gather all the artistic contributions—Tennessee's, Jo's, Lucinda's, Alex North's, and that of each member of the cast—into one intention. Since they were all talented people of decided opinions, this was not always an easy task. Williams's play was to undergo the great change, become a production, no longer what Thornton Wilder called a "text"—a word I loathe in the theatre. It now had to be transformed into a living thing, and I had the responsibility of supervising the metamorphosis.

T H E D O O R was wide open and the goddess Luck pranced through in the astonishing guise of my good friend Hume Cronyn. He and Molly had been the first New York theatre people to appreciate the size of Tennessee's talent; Hume had promoted him as had Molly at a time when Williams needed the recognition most. Now Hume had mounted in L.A. a one-act play of Tennessee's, *Portrait of a Madonna*, at the Actors Lab, a workplace refugees from the Group Theatre had organized to prevent them from going nuts when they weren't working in a film—which was most of the

time. The play was Tennessee's sketch for *Streetcar* and its central figure a
first drawing of Blanche. Had Hume put the play on knowing that the author, presently in California, might get to see it and perhaps be struck with
the talent of Hume's wife, Jessica Tandy? People thought this Hume's design; the timing was perfect and Hume was an enterprising theatre man
with the most practical devotion to his actress wife. We all went to the show
and we were, as Hume had hoped, completely taken with Jessie. She'd
solved our most difficult problem in a flash. The task of finding a Blanche
could have meant weeks after boring weeks of reading actresses in New
York, might even have sent us looking to England, but here she was, we all
agreed, in a leap of relief and gratitude. Irene plunged into negotiations
that, by contrast to Garfield's, were a lark. Jessica wanted the part, we
wanted her, we had her. Irene and Tennessee (and his Mexican boy) packed
their gear and were off to New York.

s o i finished *Gentleman's Agreement*, or to be more accurate, I dropped
it, two thirds done, in Darryl Zanuck's lap. Although I'd directed four films,
I wasn't a filmmaker yet, because I didn't respect the work to the end. It
was the classic director George Stevens who declared that one third of making a movie is script preparation and casting, another third directing and
photographing the scenes, and a final third editing and scoring. I might
give more emphasis to script preparation, but otherwise I would agree.
That is, now. But as that summer almost forty years ago was coming to an
end, I was glad to leave the editing to Zanuck and he was glad to take over,
for that was the work he enjoyed most and where he considered himself the
best in the business. His personal cutter, Barbara McLean, had assembled
my rushes into sequences as I shot them, but there's a lot more to editing,
as I was to learn, than assembling a film in the order a script indicates.
Zanuck gently suggested I not see the film put together until he'd put it
together properly. As for scoring, I don't remember taking any part in that.
A few years later I would have thought this proposal of Zanuck's outrageous;
I clashed with him when he assumed such privileges on another of my
films. But by then filmmaking had become my major interest. At the time
I shot *Gentleman's Agreement*, the theatre was what concerned me most. I
was also fed up with southern California and happy to be relieved of whatever final responsibilities might keep me there. Molly was eager to get our
kids into school on time, so I accepted Darryl's great thanks, did some quick
interviews—the Academy Award buildup had already begun—piled the
family on the Super Chief going east, and opened the script of *Streetcar.*

a t t h i s period, every actor who had gained some prominence on
Broadway, then gone west to become a movie star, would be heard declar-

ing that he had the most passionate intention to return to the "New York
stage." He bathed this phrase in a cathedral light as if the theatre was, by
definition, a great deal more worthy than films. This may have been true at
times and at times not, and when it was, it was by the accident of talent.
These avowals of resolve coming from poolside actors in happy-happy land
were so absurd and so dubious that even columnists ridiculed them; they
knew that nothing of the sort would happen because it never did. The reasons were simple: The actors were human. Julie Garfield was as goodhearted a kid as you'll find in the annals of show business; he half meant
what he said. What better opportunity could he have had than the Williams
play, with a close friend to direct and protect him from anything that might
go wrong? But still, when it came down to terms, the deal collapsed. Garfield asked his agent to say he could only appear in the play for four
months—"appear" is the West Coast synonym for "act"!—and furthermore
would require that he be guaranteed the role in the film version. Clearly
he was saying no to our offer by asking what was not possible. My guess is
that when his wife, Roberta, considered the necessity of closing her home
in California and taking everybody (they had two kids) to New York, or the
alternative—separating from her husband and allowing him to freewheel in
the gamiest part of New York City—it was something she, understandably,
would rather not do. So Garfield's agent gave us Julie's final terms, which
he, being an experienced agent, could not imagine we'd accept. We didn't,
and it was over.

F I N D I N G a Stanley proved almost as simple—once we forgot about
movie stars (the natural place for Irene to look)—as finding Blanche. Again
the goddess of good fortune played a part. The first place I went to when I
returned to New York was the Actors Studio. Bobby Lewis's class was already well organized and I began to get my "beginners" together. Among
them was the boy who'd scored such a hit in a five-minute bit in *Truckline
Café*. I'd always thought of Stella and Stanley as a young couple in their
early twenties, Blanche as a good deal older, mid-thirties perhaps, the
shady side of the street. I thought that if Williams could see the casting that
young, it might work, so I went looking for Marlon Brando. It seemed that
this "Arab" threw himself down to sleep in a different tent every night and
perhaps with a different bed partner. Finally, with the help of spies, I found
him, gave him twenty bucks, told him where to go—Provincetown on the
Cape—and whom to ask for when he got there. I called Williams to tell
him to expect this young actor and consider him for Stanley. That's all I
said. I waited. No return call. After three days I called Tennessee and asked
him what he'd thought of the actor I'd sent him. "What actor?" he asked.
No one had showed up, so I figured I'd lost twenty bucks and began to look
elsewhere. A day later I received an ecstatic call from our author, in a voice

near hysteria. Brando had overwhelmed him. Why the delay? Marlon had needed the twenty dollars to eat; he'd hitchhiked his way to the Cape.

There was no denying Williams or me on the casting, and although Marlon did not represent the picture of the part Irene had in mind—she'd immediately turned from Garfield to Burt Lancaster—she accepted our suggestion. The more I thought of it myself—Brando had been a shot in the dark—the more I liked it. Tennessee liked it so much that he told me he wasn't going to bother with the rest of the casting; he'd leave the other roles to me. Karl Malden had come to me when he first arrived in New York from Chicago. I'd cast him in a bit in *Golden Boy* and, later, in *Truckline Café*, where he gave a brilliant comedy performance; Irene thought he was a natural for Mitch. We had trouble with Stella because I enjoy looking at girls, so it always takes longer. But Irene had seen Kim Hunter somewhere and brought her in. The minute I saw her I was attracted to her, which is the best possible reaction for a director when casting young women. As for the rest of the cast, they came out of the Actors Studio, old friends. The job was done.

T H E   R E H E A R S A L S   of *Streetcar* were a joy—which wasn't what I expected. With Jessie a graduate of the Ben Greet Academy in London, the rest of the cast my strange ducks out of the Studio, I'd anticipated there might be tensions—particularly with Marlon. He had mannerisms that would have annoyed hell out of me if I'd been playing with him. He'd not respond directly when spoken to, make his own time lapses, sometimes leaving the other actors hung up. I believed this might drive Jessie up the wall, or send her running to me for help. But she never complained, even about his mumbling—which didn't mean she liked it; it means that she didn't complain. My secretary has dug up research in which Jessie is quoted saying Brando was "an impossible, psychopathic bastard." There may have been days when she felt that, but there were more days when she felt what everyone else in the cast felt, admiration for the scorching power of this man-boy. Jessie was show-smart; she knew that actors give better performances when they work with partners whose talents challenge their own, and that she had to be very good indeed to hold stage with Marlon.

The most touching scene in my memory of that rehearsal has to do with Jessie's husband. Early in the third week—we were running through by that time, and the production was coming to life—I let Hume watch. I was very fond of this man and glad to have his opinion. I don't know whether he thought I was favoring Brando in the staging, which was not true, or that Brando and not his wife was going to be the discovery of the occasion— which anyone could see might happen. For either reason I couldn't fault Hume for his concern. Jessie was playing the central character of the play, and I realized as well as Hume that she must not be overshadowed by anyone. What I did not tell Hume was that I wanted Blanche to be a "difficult" heroine, not one easy to pity, and for the audience to be with Brando at first, as they were closer in their values to Stanley than to Blanche. Then, slowly, Jessie and I and the play would turn the audience's sympathies around so that they'd find that their final concerns were for her and that perhaps, as in life, they'd been prejudiced and insensitive.

Hume spoke to me after the run-through and gave me his reaction, which was: "She can do better." I didn't know quite what he meant, how Jessie could do better. He persisted. "Don't give up on her," he said. "Keep after her. She can do it." Perhaps Hume meant that by contrast with Marlon, whose every word seemed not something memorized but the spontaneous expression of an intense inner experience—which is the level of work all actors strive to reach—Jessie was what? Expert? Professional? Was that enough for this play? Not for Hume. Hers seemed to be a performance; Marlon was living on stage. Jessie had every moment worked out, carefully, with sensitivity and intelligence, and it was all coming together, just as Williams and I had expected and wanted. Marlon, working "from the inside," rode his emotion wherever it took him; his performance was full of surprises and exceeded what Williams and I had expected. A performance miracle was in the making. What was there to do but be grateful?

Jessie's size was in her generosity; she told me during the third week that she thought Marlon was marvelous, where another actress would (and later did) complain, "You never know what he's going to do next, where he's going to be or what he's going to say." (Vivien Leigh made that complaint at the beginning of the rehearsals for the film, but she got over it.) Marlon was a challenge to the other actors, and Jessie, after Hume had seen the run-through, took the challenge as a stimulus. I didn't "quit on her," kept after her, but I'm not certain I ever satisfied Hume. He hung around the back of the auditorium, looking at me with both encouragement and impatience. He'd brought us Jessie and couldn't allow me to be disappointed. I was not. The contrast in acting styles helped create the contrast between the cultured woman from Belle Reve and the New Orleans "Quarter" redneck. There was one door in Jessie's performance I could never unlock, but I wasn't sure I wanted to. The character of Blanche should have certain inhibitions, no? She was, wasn't she, bound by her tradition?

But then I began to worry. Was I rationalizing? Was Marlon overwhelming Jessie theatrically? Was Hume right that something essential in the balance of the performance had gone wrong? I looked toward my authority, Tennessee. He was no help; he seemed enraptured by the boy. "The son of a bitch is riding a crush," I said to myself. He'd work on his next play in the morning, have lunch with Pancho, then drop in on us, respond audibly to what pleased him, then adjourn to a neighborhood bar to celebrate. When he was worried ("Kim is jumping around like a coed in a benzy kick"), he'd adjourn to the same bar for contrary reasons. There was no work for him to do. We cut five pages out of the last scene and that was it. He did insist on rewriting the throwaway lines the actors spoke to cover activities like carrying Brando to the cold shower. Tenn called them "dummy lines," wanted even these bits to have some quality of writing, so he'd give me scraps of hotel stationery with what he wished the actors to say instead of the improvisations I'd allowed. He wanted everything to be as worth hearing as watching.

Irene Selznick was full of enthusiasm and devotion, and I was beginning to like her. And she me. At last. She was one hundred percent with what the actors were doing—if she could only hear Brando. I'd reassure her about this ("Give him an audience, and he'll be heard"), and she'd be relieved, but the next day when she couldn't hear him again or when he mumbled, Irene would be on me again, gently. Her attitude, a mélange of anxiety and admiration, became a nuisance at times. She'd sit directly behind me and, as I watched rehearsal, lean forward to whisper her reactions deep into my ear. Inexperienced as she was, she had no sense of process. As I was building the framework of the house, she'd be asking me when I was going to paint the kitchen. One day, fed up with her buzzing, I turned on her and barked, "For chrissake, Irene, will you stay the hell out of my ear?" I certainly could have found a nice way to ask this. She forgave me— but never trusted me to be "civilized."

I thought the rehearsals had gone well, that we were making a performance of one piece, an ensemble, but the people who came to the last run-throughs before we left town for the road, while they were enthusiastic, worried me. They raved about Brando. Many of them were actors, I said to myself, and perhaps it was inevitable that they'd be especially aware of a performance by a new, hot talent. But why didn't they speak of Jessie? When I asked about her, they'd say she was fine, but I had to ask.

We arrived in New Haven and set up at the old Shubert Theatre, where Bankhead and I had had our row, checked into the Taft Hotel, where Thornton Wilder had held court after *Skin of Our Teeth* opened. We were in uncertain shape technically, because Jo Mielziner and I had planned an elaborate series of light cues, which we weren't having an opportunity to rehearse. With one thing and another—first time on the set, first time in costume, only four days to work everything out, particularly the lighting of a transparency background—we simply didn't get our work completed in time. When the technical aspects of a production remain erratic, the concentration of the actors remains uncertain. But despite this, the play enthused its audience, particularly the theatre people who'd come up from New York and the Yale boys who'd got wind of it. There were expressions of admiration from all sides.

But what had been intimated in our final rehearsals in New York was happening. The audiences adored Brando. When he derided Blanche, they responded with approving laughter. Was the play becoming the Marlon Brando Show? I didn't bring up the problem, because I didn't know the solution. I especially didn't want the actors to know that I was concerned. What would I say to Brando? Be less good? Or to Jessie? Get better? Raising the subject might have a destructive effect, especially on Jessica.

Exuding enthusiasm and relief after the opening was a visitor from another planet, Louis B. Mayer. He sought me out to congratulate me and to assure me that we'd all make a fortune. Irene was glad to see us talking cordially, but I never told her what her "old man" had said. He urged me to make the author do one critically important bit of rewriting to make sure that once that "awful woman" who'd come to break up that "fine young couple's happy home" was packed off to an institution, the audience would believe that the young couple would live happily ever after. It never occurred to him that Tennessee's primary sympathy was with Blanche, nor did I enlighten him. After his years of command, with not a day of self-doubt, it was useless to argue with him. He brought all his rhetorical power, which was considerable, to bear on me, but I slid out of his grip like an eel. "You must tell all that to Irene," I said. But his misguided reaction added to my concern. I had to ask myself: Was I satisfied to have the performance belong to Marlon Brando? Was that what I'd intended? What *did* I intend? I looked to the author; he seemed satisfied. Only I—and perhaps Hume—knew that something was going wrong.

We worked hard on our technical problems during the four performances in New Haven so we'd have a smooth show in Boston. As we left town, Irene sent me what I remember as ten pages of single-spaced notes. (This

must be an exaggerated recollection.) Hume was in my room when I received the notes, and I showed them to him. Then I made a drama of
dropping them into the wastepaper basket. They were all small worries,
and I was concerned about something fundamental. I was weary, knew what
I had to solve, at least for myself, and wanted to be alone. But after Hume
left me, I lifted Irene's notes out of the basket and began to read them,
went on with them at breakfast the next morning, finished them on the
train north to Boston, marking what I'd do after I'd got everything I believed important done. I wasn't gallant about the lady's opinions.

What astonished me was that the author wasn't concerned about the
audience's favoring Marlon. That puzzled me because Tennessee was my
final authority, the person I had to please. I still hadn't brought up the
problem; I was waiting for him to do it. I got my answer not on a Boston
stage, not by an artistic discussion with him, but because of something that
happened in the Ritz-Carlton Hotel, across the hall from my suite, where
Tennessee and Pancho were staying. One night I heard a fearsome commotion from across the hall, curses in Spanish, threats to kill, the sound of
breaking china (a large vase smashed), and a crash (the ornamental light
fixture in the center of the room torn down). Pancho was having his innings.
As I rushed out into the corridor, Tennessee burst through his door, looking
terrified, and dashed into my room. Pancho followed, but when I blocked
my door, he turned to the elevator, still cursing, and was gone. Tennessee
slept on the twin bed in my room that night. The next morning, Pancho
had not returned.

I noticed that Williams wasn't angry at Pancho, not even disapproving—
in fact, when he spoke about the incident, he admired Pancho for his outburst. At breakfast, I brought up my worry about Jessie and Marlon. "She'll
get better," Tennessee said, and then we had our only discussion about the
direction of his play. "Blanche is not an angel without a flaw," he said, "and
Stanley's not evil. I know you're used to clearly stated themes, but this play
should not be loaded one way or the other. Don't try to simplify things."
Then he added, "I was making fun of Pancho, and he blew up." He laughed.
I remembered the letter he'd written me before we started rehearsals, remembered how, in that letter, he'd cautioned me against tipping the moral
scales against Stanley, that in the interests of fidelity I must not present
Stanley as a "black-dyed villain." "What should I do?" I asked. "Sometimes
the audience laughs when Brando makes fun of her." "Nothing," he said.
"Don't take sides or try to present a moral. When you begin to arrange the
action to make a thematic point, the fidelity to life will suffer. Go on working as you are. Marlon is a genius, but she's a worker and she will get better.
And better."

A little later we heard Pancho returning, and Williams went back into
his suite. He didn't look frightened, dismayed, or disapproving, but happy
that Pancho was back and eager to see the man who'd made such a terrible

scene the night before. The violence had thrilled him. If Tennessee was Blanche, Pancho was Stanley.

We were a great hit in Boston, and Jessie improved every day we were there. In the end, the play was the event; not the cast, not the director. The play carried us all. In years to come, this masterful work, written out of Tennessee's most personal experience, asking no favors, no pity, no special allegiance, always moved its audience. There was no way to spoil *Streetcar.* No matter who directed it, with what concept, what cast, in what language, it was always hailed, often as "better than the original production." What could I say to that? Bravo, Tennessee!

My mother and father came to the opening night in New York, heard the cries of "Author! Author!" saw Tennessee hustle on stage with his campy shuffle. I was in the darkest upstage corner of the stage house and had tears in my eyes: exhaustion and relief. I listened to it all as if it were happening to other people. I was told that after many curtain calls for Williams, a few people called for me. I didn't respond, but I did wonder if my father had heard.

There followed a long run, and I disappeared as usual, had to be dragged back from time to time, once by a letter from Jessie, speaking for the cast. "It's your show," Jessie wrote. "You should keep it up." By that time my thoughts and feelings were far away, and even when I did go back, I wasn't helpful. Once she had her success, Irene came into her own, mothering the production and the performers. But there was no use pretending; shows don't keep up in a long run, they deteriorate, even when the actors work hard to improve their performances. There is a famous story about George S. Kaufman. He went for an overseas vacation after one of his most successful openings and came back a few months later to have a look at his hit. He didn't like what he saw and sent the cast a telegram, calling for a rehearsal "to take out the improvements." This cast of mine did better than any I've had, but soon its prime became a memory. What endured, however, was always a credit to us all, and for that I give thanks to Irene.

THE PRODUCTION of Tennessee's play became a legend. But there is no such thing as a definitive production of a play like this one any more than there can be a final *Hamlet,* a *Mother Courage* that makes it impossible for another actress to play the role, or a Willy Loman that concludes the history. I claim nothing exceptional for the way I put *Streetcar* on the stage except that it's not the way anyone else would have done it.

Long after I'd done *Streetcar,* I kept puzzling over the play—which must be a measure of its size—and about the author. The more I thought about it, the more mysterious the play appeared. It was certainly not what it seemed to be, a moral fable of the brutalization of a sensitive soul by a sadistic bully. Then what was it? Something far more ambivalent and far more personal. I began to ask myself questions about the author and investigate the play as a piece of autobiography. Tennessee was far too guarded to be tricked into revelations he would not like to be known. I hung out with him, as much as he'd let me—with him and his rambunctious lover, Pancho—and I noticed that when my mind returned to the play after I'd spent an evening with them, it "read" differently.

Tennessee was not what I'd expected. Sometimes he gave the impression of a man recently released from a "protective confinement" or a sailor on a long-delayed shore leave in a foreign country. I found a curious combination of a foolhardy boldness—he and Pancho "cruised" certain streets together, picked up sailors and "rough trade," took them home, endangering themselves, I thought—and a rather prim, well-brought-up boy of the gentlest sensibilities. His mother was the source for the mother in *The Glass Menagerie;* in the traditional Southern manner, Tennessee called her Miss Edwina. He might describe the lady today as a failed Southern Princess. His father was of coarser stuff, a drummer and, according to Williams, a whoremaster, who was constantly away from home and, like the character in *Menagerie*, loved "Long Distance" and finally disappeared for good. I could see both parents in our boy. What could such a father have thought of a "faggot" son? What a struggle it must have been for Tennessee to face his homosexuality in a society where it was thought shameful. There had to have been an early anguish in his way of life and a separation from the "normal" society around him. There was no gay movement then, and his sexual orientation must have made him feel what I felt all through my teens, an outsider. Was that why we understood each other so well?

Was there something of the Puritan guilt there, that he'd betrayed the moral standards of his people, that the way he behaved when he was most "himself" was sinful? In years to come, when he finally began to talk about himself to me, I learned that his two favorite people were not lovers or friends of his own bent but his grandfather, the gentle Reverend Dakin, an Episcopal minister, and his sister, Rose, who'd had severe psychic problems and was believed permanently "touched." He spoke lovingly of them but of no one else. I wondered if the inner conflict I was scratching for was that of the gentleness of his true heart against the violent calls of his erotic nature? Was that clash the source of his gift? The play was certainly as autobiographical as I'd guessed. But I couldn't think of him as a Puritan fighting a "baser" nature. I'd had considerable experience with the Puritan character—my beloved wife—and its outstanding characteristic was the compulsion to pressure others to do right. "Stop trying to straighten me out!" I used to warn Molly. There was none of this in Williams; he went his own way and gave others the same space. His effort seemed simply to live life to the fullest, his own life in his own way. He was more D. H. Lawrence than Calvin. He was not Arthur Miller; he had no need to teach. "The only unforgivable thing," Blanche says in *Streetcar,* "is deliberate cruelty to others—of which I have never been guilty." Art would never have written that.

There is in the play another ambivalence I puzzled over long after I was done with the production, the scene with Mitch just before the end, Mitch whom she wanted so desperately because she believed that in him she'd found the "only safe place." But then why that terrible outburst to Mitch, so defiant and so reckless: "Not far from Belle Reve, before we lost Belle Reve, was a camp where they trained young soldiers. On Saturday night they would go into town and get drunk and on the way back, they would stagger onto my lawn and call 'Blanche! Blanche!' The deaf old woman remaining suspected nothing. But sometimes I'd slip outside to answer their calls. Later the paddy wagon would gather them up like daisies, the long way home!" Was that reckless revelation from pride—hers, and the author's—to deny nothing? And there was that futile reach for Mitch's understanding: "I lived in a home where dying old women remembered their dead men. Death used to sit here and she would sit over there and death was as close as you are." And then again: "Death. The opposite is desire." Of course, this finished Mitch's interest in her. And her own hopes. Did Tennessee feel what Blanche felt, that she (he) needed someone like Mitch and what he represented, someone who'd someday give him (her) "a cleft in the rock of the world" that she could hide in?

A few years later, Williams would find such a lover, a young Italian-American, Frank Merlo, and they continued together for eighteen years, like a married couple, closer than most and, to their astonishment, happy with the arrangement. I recall them now, going shopping for groceries like French bourgeoisie, their plump pet bulldog on a leash waddling at their side; they'd return home carrying large brown paper bags full of household supplies. It was, I thought, the happiest time of Tennessee's life; he never again had anyone as loving, as loyal, and as honest as Frank Merlo. But it wasn't to last, happiness doesn't, not that which depends on another person—so said Tennessee afterward. Finally they did break up, and Frank died of cancer. Williams never learned to trust life.

Was the play an affirmation of spiritual values over the brutish ones? Certainly. But that simple? No. When Stanley says, just before the rape, "We've had this date from the beginning," is there not some truth in that? Irene Selznick thought so. She suggested to the author that after resisting Stanley, Blanche might, unexpectedly, "begin to respond." Williams was intrigued by the suggestion, gave it serious consideration. He knew all about the anarchy in sex and its lawlessness. I talked him out of the idea; I thought Irene had seen too many movies. But still wasn't there something basically flirtatious about Blanche's character and about all women brought up in that tradition? Weren't they trained to flirt? Politely. Didn't they, as a matter of course, lead men on? Was it because on the frontier they had to rely on men for protection? Men assured their safety. "So I came here," Blanche says, speaking of what happened when she was run out of her

hometown. "There was nowhere else I could go." She didn't go looking for a job. She moved into Stanley and Stella's home—uninvited. As soon as she did, she saw Mitch, sized him up, and set about winning him for her safety. It was automatic.

What about what I'd noticed about Williams? Wasn't he attracted to the Stanleys of the world? Sailors? Rough trade? Danger itself? Wasn't Pancho a Stanley? Yes, and wilder. The violence in that boy, always on trigger edge, attracted Williams at the very time it frightened him. When Stanley's wife reprimands him for his table manners, he teaches her a lesson in how to talk to a man by smashing all the plates on their dining room table. I doubt that Williams found that act vulgar; he'd have found it thrilling. I can recall his cackling over the way Brando did it in rehearsal. It was kind of a release for Tennessee; perhaps they were his mother's plates.

And when Stanley says to his wife: "When we first met, you and me, you thought I was common. How right you was, baby. I was common as dirt. You showed me the snapshot of the place with the columns. I pulled you down off those columns and how you loved it, having them colored lights going! And weren't we happy together, wasn't it all okay till she showed up? Weren't we happy together? Wasn't it all okay?" I can hear Tennessee talking, telling about his own experience as a young man properly brought up by Miss Edwina, his Southern Princess mother, then abruptly awakened to the life of desire and his own erotic possibilities.

I've noticed as I write this that I've come to the same thing I came to when I first studied the play. As I write "him (her)" or "she (he)," I keep linking Blanche and Tennessee. Another director, Luchino Visconti, when he directed the play in Italy, called the author "Blanche." I came to another conclusion: Blanche is attracted by the man who is going to destroy her. I understood the play by this formula of ambivalence. Only then, it seemed to me, would I think of it as Tennessee meant it to be understood: with fidelity to life as he—not all us groundlings, but he—had experienced it.

The reference to the kind of life Tennessee was leading at the time was clear. Williams was aware of the dangers he was inviting when he cruised; he knew that sooner or later he'd be beaten up. And he was. Still, I felt, even this promise of violence exhilarated him. Possibly he did feel guilt about his way of life. Later he would report nightmares in which he "walked very slowly down a corridor . . . toward a lighted room . . . in the mincing exaggeration of the walk of a drag queen, chanting, 'Redemption! Redemption!'" But that was much later. At the time I first knew him, he was devouring life; he wanted it all.

I also noticed that at the end of the play—always an author's essential statement—Stella, having witnessed her sister's being destroyed by her husband, then taken away to an institution with her mind split, felt grief and remorse but not an enduring alienation from her husband. Stanley was the father of her child. Stanley had turned on the "colored lights" for her. Above all, Stanley was there. As he'd declared, they'd been perfectly happy until Blanche moved in. The implication at the end of the play is that Stella will very soon return to Stanley's arms—and to his bed. That night, in fact. Indifference? Callousness? No. Fidelity to life. Williams's goal. We go on with life, he was saying, the best way we can. People get hurt, but you can't get through life without hurting people. The animal survives—at all costs.

Molly and I were going on with our lives: a beautiful daughter, whom we named Katharine.

HAROLD CLURMAN, who was then the theatre critic of the *New Republic*, referred (in a brilliantly written review) to my production and particularly to the effect of casting Marlon Brando (an actor whom he admired) as Stanley Kowalski. After praising the staging of the scene where Stanley, from his knees at the bottom of the stairs, calls for Stella, Harold goes on: "This, as I have noted, is done beautifully. Yet Brando's innate quality and something unresolved in the director's concept makes the scene moving in a way that is thematically disruptive; it is not integrated with that attribute of the play which requires that Kowalski at all times be somewhat vile." Elsewhere in the same review, he says: "The play (with Brando playing the role) becomes the triumph of Stanley Kowalski; with the collusion of the audience which is no longer on the side of the angels . . . Mr. Brando is tough without being irremediably coarse."

When I read this I became angry, but as I'd always respected Harold and still did, I wondered if there wasn't something in the point he was making. When it came time for us to put out a road company, I found that I no longer had the energy or the will to deal with that excellent, strong-minded actress Uta Hagen, so—whether out of curiosity or perversity or both—I prevailed on Irene to offer Harold the job. He eagerly accepted. I'd already cast Tony Quinn as Stanley, and he is an actor amenable to being led; he listens like a child. So I thought: There you go, Harold; come on, get it on, do it your way, let's see.

The production—I saw a rehearsal—turned out to be what I expected. Tennessee in this version became a poet of frustration and his play said that "aspiration, sensitivity, departure from the norm are battered, bruised and disgraced in our world today." Those are Harold's words and his belief, and they accurately describe the effect of what I saw on stage. Since all of us in the Group Theatre thought of ourselves, at the time we were banded together, as aspiring, sensitive, and departing from society's norm, wasn't this mode of thinking self-favoring, even self-pitying? What I saw recalled our old wishful way of thinking in the thirties, the belief that the good and the true in our time were inevitably taken advantage of by the villains of capitalism and money corruption—an idea I now believe to be sentimental malarkey. The play, with Harold, had become a moral fable, presenting the people we believed ourselves to be, with ethical values so clear and so simple that the audience could not doubt where their sympathies and allegiances should be placed.

Oh, I thought, if life were only that simple! The difficulties and ambivalences the author had found in living had been ignored. Clarity prevailed. *Streetcar* had been turned into a play of the thirties, when we in the Group blamed everything on the System and never on anything in ourselves. We would bemoan our alienation rather than accept what Williams accepted, that there was a tragic element in life itself. "Life should not be printed on dollar bills," Odets wrote. Agreed! Odets also wrote: "There are no third acts in America." But that did not prevent him from feeling obliged to conclude each of his plays with a trumpet solo of romantic hope, however falsely based.

Tennessee had told Molly that this play had no theme; it had a deeper meaning because it described a universal struggle in the soul of its author. What can be worse than false hope, falsely promised? The human race progresses and does so through the vision of artists, yes, but slowly, not in lurches. The Group Theatre was an extraordinary theatre adventure. But when it came to teaching (which we took as our obligation), it taught very little. What happened to our dreams of revolution? They were as shredded paper. And the gains we made? Yes, there've been gains but small ones, grimly won. The first step in creating a new world is to look truthfully at this one—and at ourselves.

The people we've met like Stanley may very well be attractive and the Blanches we've run into pests. What the audience should feel for Blanche in the play should not be an immediate sympathy. But as the play progresses, and especially in the scenes where Blanche fearlessly declares herself and tells her history, the onlookers should admire her courage. It was my hope that they should then slowly reappraise her and perhaps even be dismayed at their original prejudices. Only in the end and with difficulty should the audience find the special worth in this difficult person. But it must not be done at the cost of making Stanley "at all times . . . somewhat vile." That simplification of the moral counterpoint would be unreal and worthless. As for the "side of the angels," doesn't the presence of the "devil" in all of us have to be acknowledged?

Was my conception of *Streetcar* what Harold declared it to be—"unresolved"? The answer is yes. Life is a puzzle, unresolved, and as we enter it, no one is there to hand us a book of instructions, the kind you get when you buy a new car. And "thematically disruptive"? Yes to that too, Harold. I wanted to thwart an audience, not flatter them by too quickly and too easily admitting them to the company of "angels." That elevation they should have to struggle to reach. While the arduous journey through Purgatorio was being made, perhaps the wayfarer would hear Williams cry, "Fidelity! Fidelity!" and be heartened.

W H E N I finished work on his play, I was full of admiration for Tennessee, especially because he'd found his story in his own life's struggles; the man had used his personal contradictions and the memory of his pain to make it. When I considered him, I saw that the true artist must have the courage to reveal what the rest of mankind conceals. I'd not forgotten and would never forget his word "fidelity," and that he thought it an artist's duty to deny nothing and avoid self-favoring. He should not apologize for anything, never beg for pity, be pitiless with himself. After this experience, I saw every play and every film that I worked on as a confession, veiled or partly exposed, but always its author's self-revelation.

I'd never thought of becoming a writer, believing (as I still do) that I have no gift for prose. But I did believe that I have an ear for dialogue, for speech under stress, and it was because of Williams that I thought I might someday dramatize the history of the people in my family. I didn't write *America America* until many years later, but it was because of Tennessee that I came to believe that, in time, I might. I began to recall the events of my earliest days in Turkey and in the enclave of Anatolian Greeks on Manhattan's 136th Street, to remember the stories my grandmother told me, and to value as dramatic material my parents and that most eccentric lot, my uncles and aunts. It was because of Williams that I began to look at my life, see it as drama, and think that I might someday become some kind of dramatist myself.

A few months ago I met Eddie Kook on the street. "Kookie" was head of the firm that provided productions I'd done with lighting equipment; he'd worked on all of Tennessee's plays. Now a man of eighty-two years, benign and cleanhearted, he brought me a message from the grave. He said that the last time he'd run into Williams—only a few weeks before his death— Tennessee had said to him, "When you see Kazan again, tell him to keep on writing." I have rarely received encouragement from my fellow writers; most of them haven't bothered to read my books; but Williams was always ready with encouragement and most generous with praise.

OF ALL THE PLAYS I've directed, *Death of a Salesman* is my favorite. When I read it again recently, it hit me as hard as it had when I read it the first time, thirty-eight years ago—just as hard and in the same place, immediately, on page two! I am a man who has trained himself to let no pain show, but I felt tears coming as I turned that page. I suppose the play revives the memory, long at rest, of my father, a salesman of another product, of his hopes for his sons in this new country and the gently twisted Anatolian smile on his face when he'd ask me, a muddle-headed kid of sixteen, "Who going support me my old age? Hey, you Elia, what you saying to that?" When I had nothing to say to that, but looked away, feeling threatened, he'd shrug and mutter—I'd hear it— "Hopeh-less case." That and more from those years of my life, as well as other memories, without words or faces, lying in wait with their burden of sadness, swarmed up when I read that damned disturbing play last week, just as they had when Art Miller, the day after he finished it in 1948, gave it to me.

After I'd read it that first time, I didn't wait for the next morning to see if I'd have a more "balanced" judgment, didn't delay as I generally did in those years to hear what Molly might say about it, but called Art as I turned the back cover and told him his play had "killed" me. "I wrote it in eight weeks," he replied.

When I say this was my favorite play, I don't mean it was the best play. I am not a critic, and I do believe Williams wrote better. They were both Puritans, they were both concerned with morality—Tennessee more open about his "sins" and his problems, Miller more guarded. Still *Salesman* is the play that got to me most deeply. It's as if a brother was speaking of our common experience, a man who'd been through precisely the same life with his family that I had with mine. Art does an extraordinary thing there; he shows us a man who represents everything Art believes to be misguided about the system we live in, then goes on to make us feel affection and concern, pity and even love for this man. Then he goes deeper and we are aware of a tragic weight. Is it for the Salesman? Is it for ourselves? And along with arousing this sympathetic pain, his horrendous hero is able to make us laugh. He is ridiculous and he is tragic all at once. How is that accomplished? I don't know any other play in any other language that does all these things at the same time. But Arthur Miller did them all—that one time and never again.

I believe the reason he was able to do this was not that he was more understanding than anyone else about his fellow Americans and the system we live in, or knew better than the rest of us what was wrong with our civilization. It was because of his uncle. I remember—and I hope I remember correctly—that he derived Willy Loman from his uncle, "a very small man," the original stage direction reads, "who wears little shoes and little vests . . ." and "His emotions, in a word, are mercurial." Which is the way Art expected the part would be cast, not with Lee Cobb, certainly not great lumbering Leo Jacob Cobb. Art had this most ambivalent feeling about an actual person, thought him completely wrongheaded, believed he'd misguided his family and that everything he said that was meant to be serious was rubbish, but he still felt great affection for him and enjoyed his company and relished his passionate, nonsensical talk. The man made Art laugh, and Art likes to laugh. In short, he had the living model with that impossible combination of qualities in his own family, and he was smart enough, Art was, and talented enough to recognize that he had a character who could arouse affection and pity at the same time he evoked total condemnation and that both these reactions were significant separately, but together, in the same person, they were much more meaningful; together they could be tragic; together they were all of us.

Studying the play, as I was preparing to direct it, I began to see my father differently; I stopped being angry at him. I was ready at last to forget what I'd considered tyrannical and appreciate what he'd done for me. To gain an understanding of the play, one of the first things I did was sum up the similarities of my father to Willy Loman. George Kazan was a man full of violence that he dared release only at home, where it was safe to be angry. But the possibility that he might blow up at any time kept us all in terrible fear.

He also had about him, my father along with Willy, the euphoria of a salesman. When it came time to seduce a customer, he was expressive to a theatrical degree. "Feel it!" I remember him shouting at a buyer, as he lifted the end of a large Kashan carpet and thrust it into the man's hand. "Go on, take it in your hand. Give yourself the pleasure. No charge. Like butter, right? Eh? What you say? Like sweet butter! Tell me where you find piece goods like this piece goods, tell me that much." And so on. People in the trade said he was a great salesman. But when I watched these mercantile revels, they embarrassed me.

"Baba" dressed as a salesman and had his shoes shined every day. Even when he went to my aunt's apple farm in the Catskills for a weekend's vacation, he'd bring along other rug merchants, to talk about prices and the market and the sources "on the other side," then to play poker or pinochle most of the night. Sundays, when he would supervise the shish-ke-bab, bending over the hot wood coals and carefully turning the spits thrust through the cubes of well-marinated lamb leg, he wore a hard collar and a bow tie. Sometimes he even wore the jacket of his business suit and a flat-brimmed straw hat. In the Catskills on a Sunday, he was a merchant waiting for Monday.

It's the essence of the salesman's philosophy that your success or failure depends on your impressing others not only with the goods you have for sale but with yourself. You must gain their approval of your personality, make them believe that anything you say is true, even when you know it's grossly exaggerated or even totally false. That is how my father lived, by saying with the passion of unqualified conviction what was useful in winning a customer. Come to think of it, it was not different from what actors do on stage; they must make an audience believe the poetry and the nonsense, even when they don't believe it themselves. They are rewarded not with a sale but with applause.

Like Willy, my father considered his eldest son a special failure and oh, God, this hurt him! And me! But how could I blame him for what he expected of me and didn't get? Obviously what his wife had produced for him, this silent, secretive, mysteriously sullen son, was not going to rally to his side and sell rugs, not any to anyone, ever. Father preferred his next two boys: one was bound to study medicine—Father already called him "the doctor"—and the other actually did show, for a time, an interest in the business that had been my father's life. But he was afraid to tell himself the truth about his eldest son, the truth being that I didn't give a damn about the Oriental rug trade and, despite his persisting hopes, would never go into it; and if I did, would soon defect; and if I stayed, be no damn good. But just as Willy did, George Kazan kept pumping up hope, and the burden of that hope was on my back.

Willy had Linda, ever-faithful, fiercely devoted Linda; my father had my mother, Athena. She'd stand behind him every night as he gulped the dinner she'd spent the day preparing, would sit to eat her own meal only after he'd moved to the sofa; typically Anatolian that, taking a quick nap after his *yehmek*. Old lions sleep after eating what the lioness provides.

There is an unarticulated tragedy when a woman discovers that the man she married is not what she hoped he was when she married him. Both Linda and Willy's best friend, Charley, saw through him but still loved him. Like Linda, my mother would not tolerate any criticism of my father from me; not while he was alive. If I indicated some disaffection, she'd turn on me and tell me he was a good man; "he never goes to other woman," she'd say, and someday I'd come to appreciate what he'd done for us all. He'd brought her to America, you see, not found her here, and she appreciated this. She protected him until the day he died; but when he was finally quiet in the grave, she surprised me one day by saying, "Your father was a stupid man." And soon afterward she said, "These years"—those following his death—"are best years of my life."

Art's play had such deep value for me because it forced me to understand my parents better. Even recently, when I read the play again, it made me wonder about the way I was treating my youngest son, ask myself if I was being as understanding of him as I should be. It disturbed me that I'd discovered my father's traits—even his facial expressions!—in myself. It disturbed me greatly when my youngest son told me that for years he'd lived in terror of my anger. I was repeating the pressure patterns of my father, and I was ashamed when I read Art's play and realized this. That damned play cut me where I was most vulnerable: Was I a good father? No? Why hadn't I done better?

I know it did this for many men; it was the only play I ever directed where men in the audience cried. I recall hearing sobs at the end of a performance, and they were mostly from men.

All the critics rushed to nail down the theme of the play, and Miller helped them with what's in the dialogue: "The man didn't know who he was," spoken over the grave, and a line even closer to the meaning, "He had the wrong dream," which is stated and restated. But it seemed to me that I, as the director, had to take another step and ask what that "wrong dream" was. I came to believe that the point was far more lethal than anything Art put into words. It's in the very fabric of the work, in the legend itself, which is where a theme should be. The Christian faith of this God-fearing civilization says we should love our brother as ourselves. Miller's story tells us that actually—as we have to live—we live by an opposite law, by which the purpose of life is to get the better of your brother, destroying him if necessary, yes, by in effect killing him. Even sex becomes a kind of aggression—to best your boss by taking his woman! That contrast between the ideal and the practice specific to our time is the sense in which the play is a "social drama," and this theme, so shameful and so final, permeates the work's fabric and is projected through the example of human behavior so there can be no avoiding it. Here is an antisystem play that is not "agit-prop." We are out of the thirties at last—the audience does not have to suffer instruction or correction. The essence of our society, the capitalist system, is being destroyed not by rhetoric but by that unchallengeable vocabulary, action between people, which makes you believe that the terrible things that happen are true, are inevitable, and concern us all. Furthermore, the conflict we watch is between people who have every traditional reason to love each other. Miller makes us reach out for the lesson; it is not thrust down our throats. The question remains: Why do we live by that law when we know—and Art shows us this—that the result is so humanly destructive?

Art was trained first of all by Henrik Ibsen. The play has a strong structure. The viewer is immediately made aware, first by the title, then by Willy's revealing that he found himself driving off the road, that we are gathered together to watch the course of a suicide. That promise of terror and tragedy lies under every scene in the action that follows and makes the tension continuous. You wait in anxiety as you watch this ridiculous, tragic, misguided, frantically obsessed man—whether Cobb plays him, or the actor is a smaller man like Miller's uncle, doesn't matter. What you watch is yourself, struggling against the fate you've made for yourself.

THIS PRODUCTION became the other half (with *Streetcar*) of a theatre legend. The fascinating game of what is fact and what is public relations buildup began to be played. In the accounts of the production and in the remeasuring of the people involved, what had actually happened was replaced by what a hungry press needed—good copy!—and what the imaginations of the people who saw the production were prepared to believe. Furthermore, within each of the people involved there was a swell of confidence. We became convinced of our ability to do anything we chose to do. Success seemed the natural course for us all, the inevitable reward of our efforts. The great success of the play certified our worth. Truth was soon out of sight; we all puffed up. Our producers, Bloomgarden and Fried; Lee Cobb, Arthur Miller, and Elia Kazan were never the same again.

The play became, to the surprise of many theatre people, including its producers, a great success, selling out immediately. Kermit Bloomgarden, an excellent "line" producer, who had the ability to see to it that everything necessary for mounting a show arrived on time and in good working order, was now offered to the public as something more, the leading producer of "class" plays that no one else dared produce on Broadway. His pressman immediately set about creating an enlarged reputation. But how Kermit was able to acquire *Death of a Salesman* and what he thought of it is more interesting than this "puff." Daring is not a feature of the true story; luck is.

At the end of the triumphant opening night performance, Eddie Kook, who'd provided the equipment for lighting the show, was sitting behind Cheryl Crawford, listening to the applause storm. Eddie noticed tears in Cheryl's eyes and commented on the play's power. "That's not why I'm crying," she said. "I had this play and let it get away." This was true. When Art and I weren't sure which producer to entrust it to, I suggested we give it to Cheryl. To my surprise, the force it would have with an audience did not strike her. She hesitated; the time allowed for hesitation in the theatre is brief. Cheryl seemed especially dubious about the play's commercial potential. She'd given it to friends to read; they hadn't been sure either. Since a lively enthusiasm is a necessity for a successful ride through the obstacle course of a Broadway production, and Cheryl didn't show any, I told her to forget the play.

Now luck was loose. Art and I decided to pass the script on to another good friend, Kermit, and his associate, Walter Fried. They'd accepted the play for production, but, as had been the case with Cheryl, they were not sure of its box office strength. Kermit told me he'd consulted theatre owners and box office treasurers, and everyone had cautioned him that the word "Death" in a title invited death to the ticket window; this had been proven time and again, so they maintained.

One morning when I was in Kermit's side office, working on casting, he burst in and declared that he was convinced the title of the play had to be changed. He said there was an "upbeat" phrase in the play that would make a fine title, commercial as well as meaningful. Fried and he were determined that *Free and Clear* should be our title. When my reaction was negative, then obdurate, then—when they persisted—scornful, they asked if I'd mind if they talked to Miller without me there. I don't know why I was so damned gracious, because my emotions were violently hostile, but I did say, "Go ahead," and they summoned the author quickly for consultation. Art had to pass the small office where I was waiting with the door open. When he came by, I pulled him in, and without telling him what their proposal was, I said, "They want to talk to you about something I'm dead against. Don't you dare say yes." Art went in, they talked without me; our title was not changed.

But Kermit was a man who made it a matter of pride that he never changed his mind. Perhaps he thought that I, along with others who knew his original concerns about Miller's title, might think him weak if he altered his stand. Kermit had a horror of appearing weak. On opening night, he was cornered by Irving Hoffman, who wrote theatre reviews for the *Hollywood Reporter,* and although Irving didn't ask him what he thought of the title, Kermit volunteered, "I still don't like the title, but it's Arthur Miller's play and he wants the title we have and that's all right with me." Perhaps Kermit was throwing up a defense for himself in case Hoffman didn't like the title either. His anxiety about what Hoffman might think was not altogether unfounded. The "head" of the review in the *Hollywood Reporter* read: "Tragically We Roll Along."

THE IMAGINATIVE qualities of Art's play, the nonrealistic aspects, worked successfully on stage and added a great deal to the force of the theme. They were indeed innovative, and Art deserved all the praise he's been given. How they came to be in the production, however, is a story that brings credit to the theatre as an institution, as well as confirming a string of influences. As Tennessee Williams admired and was stirred by *All My Sons* ("It has the kind of eloquence we need now," he'd written me), so did Art benefit from *A Streetcar Named Desire.* I remember the night he came to see *Streetcar.* After the performance he appeared to be full of wonder at the theatre's expressive possibilities. He told me he was amazed at how simply and successfully the nonrealistic elements in the play—"*Flores! Flores para los muertos!*"—blended with the realistic ones. These two men, completely different humans who never mixed socially, influenced each other's work and owed each other a debt.

After *Death of a Salesman* had made theatre history, it was published, and the sentence that follows "The Curtain rises" on the first printed pages is: "Before us is the Salesman's home . . . an air of a dream clings to the place, a dream rising out of reality." However, the stage direction in the original manuscript that Art gave me to read directly he'd finished it does not mention a home as a scenic element. It reads: "A pinpoint travelling spot lights a small area on stage left. The Salesman is revealed. He takes out his keys and opens an invisible door." It was a play waiting for a directorial solution.

The concept of a house standing like a specter behind all the scenes of the play, always present as it might be always present in Willy's mind, wherever his travels take him, even behind the office he visits, even behind the Boston hotel room and above his grave plot, is not even suggested in the original script. Although the spectral home is a directorial vision, it was not my idea any more than it was Art's. It was urged on us by the scenic designer, Jo Mielziner. I went for it—it solved many problems for me—and when we took it to Miller, he approved of it. In this production, it was the single most critically important contribution and the key to the way I directed the play. Both Miller and I were praised for what Jo had conceived;

he never got the credit he deserved. Art rewrote his stage direction for the book based on Jo's design. A published play is often the record of a collaboration: The director's stage directions are incorporated, as are some of the contributions of others working on the show—actors' "business," designer's solutions, and so on. The theatre is not an exclusively literary form. Although the playscript is the essentially important element, after that is finished, actors, designers, directors, technicians "write" the play together.

L E E J. C O B B became the great star of that season; people marveled at his power and his brilliance. This adulation may have done him more harm than good. When I recommended that we cast Cobb as Willy, I knew him well from our days in the Group and a road tour we'd played of *Golden Boy*. Our friendship had started close, but like many actors' friendships, it thinned out. I knew him for a mass of contradictions: loving and hateful, anxious yet still supremely pleased with himself, smug but full of doubt, guilty and arrogant, fiercely competitive but very withdrawn, publicly private, suspicious but always reaching for trust, boastful with a modest air, begging for total acceptance no matter what he did to others. In other words, the part was him; I knew that Willy was in Cobb, there to be pulled out.

When he received his fabulous notices, Lee awarded himself a status even higher than any the theatre world gave him. He was great as Willy Loman until he was told he was great and believed it—then he was less great. He was at his best during the last week of the tryout in Philadelphia, before his New York triumph. After we opened on Broadway, he began to share the audience's admiration for his performance and their pity for the character he played. Life on Broadway would not, because it could not, satisfy this man's hunger for unqualified recognition. He withdrew from our play before he should have, claiming that he was dangerously exhausted— which we might have appreciated except that we all saw he was dramatizing it beyond its measure. He said he was on the verge of a breakdown and demanded that I consult with his analyst. I did; we had a bad scene. I still don't know how serious Lee's trouble was; he was a very good actor and determined to prove that he had to leave the show.

Once he was "available" again, no more parts like Willy came his way. He began to masquerade as a martyr to an unappreciative theatre. Something pouting in his character waited for "justice," meaning that a role of great worth was his due and had to come soon. He'd certainly be the Lear of our time, he boasted. Friends agreed. But the theatre is no more just than life, and nothing came along that he found acceptable. Today, Cobb is remembered for Willy Loman and that is all; it became the story of his life.

Many actors are remembered because of a single great performance, but this comfort from history did not satisfy Cobb. When another season's crop of new plays came along with nothing for him, he decided to return west and to films. I brought him back east to my "location" in Hoboken, to play the corrupt labor boss in *Waterfront,* and he did well, even had an Academy Award nomination. But after that the roles offered him in films were beneath his talent. He felt aggrieved and insulted, and found that the people who dominated the film community were no less arrogant than I. To save his pride, he responded with arrogance. To release his tensions, he gambled more frequently and more seriously. I know only what I heard, the outside of the story. He disappeared from my view. Then suddenly he was dead, too young and—I agree—insufficiently rewarded. What a waste!

T H I N K E R S who think about the theatre have said that success is a problem more difficult than failure—an astonishing thought to anyone who'd been hungry for recognition as long as I'd been. I didn't find success a problem; I was not uncomfortable sitting on a peak. I was credited with all kinds of magic and became the coy object of artistic temptation and commercial seduction. Every play of worth intended for Broadway was offered me first. I had to shrug them off. In films it was only a matter of what I wanted to do, name it. I could see no limit to what I might accomplish. I began to make notes on ambitious future projects, those I'd once only dreamed of. Now they were within reach; all I had to do was extend my hand. And work! That was easy; I had perfect health and boundless energy. I enjoyed the devotion and the intimate friendship of the two best playwrights of the day; one was writing a play, the other a film, both intended for me. I didn't have an enemy, not that I knew of; no, nothing but admiring followers. I was so successful there was no reason for anyone to be jealous of me: I was too far ahead of the pack. I was certain all this would endure—why would it not?—sure that my success would swell, my friendships deepen, my creative associations become richer. No longer suffering from self-doubt, I quit my analyst.

In time I had to confront some facts. I am a mediocre director except when a play or a film touches a part of my life's experience. Other times my cleverness and facility will not overcome my inadequacies. When I rely on mechanics, I do only what a good stage manager should be able to do. I am not catholic in my tastes. I dislike

Reading the notices, my father and I

Beckett—his work. I am not an intellectual. I don't have great range. I am no good with music or with spectacles. The classics are beyond me. I enjoy humor and the great clowns, but I can't make up jokes or amusing bits of byplay and visual humor. What I need I steal. I have no ear for poetry. I have a pretty good eye but not a great eye. I do have courage, even some daring. I am able to talk to actors; I don't fear them and their questions. I've been able to arouse them to better work. I have strong, even violent, feelings, and they are assets. I am not shy about ripping the cover-guard off my own experiences; this encourages actors to overcome their inhibitions. I enjoy working with performers; they sense this and have been happy as well as successful with me. This is useful.

Molly used to say that I was too hard on myself. But I don't feel the above is inaccurate. I prefer this measure to the pumped-up state of fame I had after *Death of a Salesman* and *A Streetcar Named Desire*. It took me some years to face what I was as a director; in fact, it took a painful defeat at the Lincoln Center Repertory Theatre. At the time I'm writing about, I was mired in media mud; I'm afraid that for a time I believed what I read. When I see my photographs from that period, I don't like what I see. For three years I was on the very top, then life twisted, as it will; by surviving a great deal of pain and trouble, I became a different person. But that's looking too far ahead.

A F I N A L word about directing. The present period in the theatre is occasionally referred to as the Time of the Director, or something of the sort. I've been held partly responsible for this development. The critic Eric Bentley went so far as to name me as coauthor of the two plays I've been discussing. This is nonsense, of course. The question remains: Is directing a creative art or is it merely the technique of an interpreter? The old answer will stand: Like music, painting, and architecture, it's an art when it's made an art. But something special has happened in the theatre; movies and television have taken over most of the traditional ground. What we see today on the screen, large or small, cannot be matched on a stage by any realistic production. Naturalism has been made irrelevant. This is not a setback; it's an invitation to the imagination. The theatre now has to be theatre. The great productions I've seen and those by directors whose work I've read about and seen photographed have ventured far past anything literal. They've taken a piece of material—an old play, a novel, a folk story—and transmuted it into another form. Call it Pure Theatre. "Show" is a good word. The only Shakespeare I've truly enjoyed was Peter Brook's *Midsummer Night's Dream*, done as a kind of circus play and precisely in the spirit of the text. Most Shakespeare productions I've found lumbersome and boring; I prefer reading the plays. Our most imaginative theatre work today is in dance and in our musicals. When Bob Fosse cut loose, what realistic play could keep up with him? Facts no longer interest us. See the *Today* show if you want facts; wait for the seven o'clock news. But theatre as an event of the free fancy, one that involves its audience totally in a flight of the imagination, will exist always and I believe become less "realistic," and so, like painting and dance, more of an art. Wonder is our need today, not information.

T H E   P E R S O N most affected by the success of *Death of a Salesman* was the author. It did fine things for him, altering his life in more ways than

he realized then or perhaps—excuse the presumption—knows now. Nothing was the same for him after that play opened in New York. It even made Art reckless— albeit in a cautious way—with certain constraints on his personal life and curious about experiences that lay outside the bounds of his behavior up until that time. His eyes, to speak of externals, acquired a new flash and his carriage and movement a hint of something swashbuckling. He was at his best during this time, still searching, still unsure of himself, not yet Lincolnesque. Always an amusing man, with a lively sense of humor and a "country" gift for storytelling, he released these talents broadside and enjoyed their effect—which was seductive. It was

at this time that I had a first premonition of danger coming, that particularly domestic peril which results when certain ties of restraint that a middle-class man has always lived within are snapped. Art was entering a period of personal drama, and my secret opinion was that it could do him nothing but good. I watched and waited. A writer is a spy.

He and I were best friends that year and for the next two; the success of the production had brought us closer. We were in daily contact, one of those rare theatre partnerships, so recognized throughout Broadway. I didn't admire Art more than I did Tennessee—or less. Williams lived in another world, the homosexual enclaves of certain places he considered romantic: Key West, the North African shore, Rome, especially these. I didn't see much of him; his daily life didn't relate to my own. Art and I were consanguineous; except for our appearance—he looked nobler—we could have been blood relatives. By all distinctive features of behavior, we were the same fellow, or so it seemed. I don't remember that during the production of *Salesman* we differed in our tastes, our convictions, our pleasures, or our politics. We were strictly lower-middle-class neighborhood kids with a college education who'd swung to the left and were new to money and to pleasure. When the play was a great success trying out in Philadelphia and we felt affluence moving our way, we celebrated not by throwing a party and getting high but by going out together one afternoon and each buying himself a pair of new shoes.

During the first year we were friends, Art got the idea, from the piece of land and the old house Molly and I had bought, of acquiring a place in the country. He purchased a modest home near Roxbury, Connecticut, carefully chosen not to burst his budget. It had a rather run-down appearance, but he went to work to improve the place himself, puttering about, with his tools, like Willy Loman. I thought him extremely careful about money; I'm rather "cheap" myself, but he outdid me. When we went out to dinner together, I can't remember him picking up the check. Art once explained the reason for his tight fist. He said he didn't know when he'd have an idea for another play or if he ever would, and if he did, could he write it, and if he wrote it, would it be produced, and if it was produced, would it bring in enough to pay his bills. This is a fear many authors have. Writing is a hazardous life. Art spoke of that challenging white sheet, sitting blank in his typewriter. As I write this, he's making something like sixty thousand dollars a week from a revival of *Death of a Salesman*. Security at last!

In the days when I first knew Art, during the production of *All My Sons*, I thought him rigid with inhibition. When he embraced a young woman in friendship—not in any way a "come-on"—he did it turned sideways, with the side of his body against the front of hers, and usually he'd look in another direction, not at her. I'd noticed that he liked someone in one of our casts, but I doubt that he ever expressed his interest to her in either words or touch.

But after *Salesman*, now world-famous and the recipient of unending praise from every side, Art began to look around and to be—cautiously— curious. He had to recognize that there was a hell of a lot more to see, do, feel, and enjoy than he'd permitted himself to enjoy, feel, or even see within the confines of the ultraconservative pattern of careful living he and his wife had established. Have you noticed how many "progressives" and "liberals" have extremely bourgeois home lives? Art's success opened his eyes and woke his appetites. He told himself, I must suppose, that he had more choices than he'd taken advantage of, and that the world around him was bigger and more interesting than he'd known. It was inevitable that there'd soon be a crisis.

One weekend during a gathering of intellectuals for political deliberation, Art did something his wife Mary thought he should not have done. Considering the boredom that hangs like a fog over these events, perhaps his wife might have excused his "sin." But he told me Mary was unyielding. What astonished me was that Art appeared to agree with his wife. He paid for his "lapse" without resentment strong enough to cause a rebellion. If we are to judge solely from his next play, *The Crucible,* we would have to say that Art did think of himself as a sinner; the central character in it expresses contrition for a single act of infidelity. I had to guess that Art was publicly apologizing to his wife for what he'd done.

But I believe that within Art there was a serious conflict, even if he wasn't totally aware of it. On the one hand, I assume he must have felt he deserved punishment because he had hurt his wife—every time he looked at her he could see that. On the other hand, memory of pleasure is not easily forgotten. He respected the moral law, but he also must have found it constricting to a suddenly reawakened side of his nature: the life of the senses. His side trip into new territory had made him feel great!

As with so many artists, Art must have had feelings that he was not ready to admit to in the courtroom of his home. In contrast to his uxorious guilt, there was a lively if secret yen to explore once again the lovely fields outside the walls of the life he'd led with his wife. What lay ahead? Art was in that old quagmire of ambivalence, the natural home for an artist; he had a roving eye but a bleeding heart. He wanted to stay safe and secure inside his home, wanted to roam freely outside. Another man with that conflict to which there is no solution. Mary waited. She entered Vassar to take some courses and to reconstitute herself. Art admired her for this. In time—for a time—they reconciled.

The avalanche of praise and the absolute nature of the respect Art received everywhere had another result. He's still a companionable and amusing man when you're alone with him, but it began to develop and to be noticed that when he was in his public-behavior, on-view phase, he sounded a bit pompous. I can only guess that like so many other "left of center" heroes, he'd been invited to stand on too many platforms of honor and asked to answer too many reverential questions. Perhaps, like many others, he began to try to live up to what people were saying about him, trying to be the "Arthur Miller" they were writing about, an ideologue to be trusted, a trailblazer, and so on. That kind of reverence and praise is hard to resist, a danger for us all. Art began to relish the joys of being right. A supposed rebel, he lived the life of an establishment god, and he liked it. There is a danger for an artist of becoming a man who sees his role to be teaching others and pronouncing judgment on one and all.

Art had not judged Willy Loman; he'd permitted Willy's acts to pronounce final judgment. He loved the Salesman he was condemning. He didn't offer a final answer except the one life gives to a sensitive man: "How bewildering! How funny! How terrible! How noble! How tragic!" Art was not a writer who made up stories. His material had to be experienced; he reported on his inner condition. Art had to go through a crisis; that would provide him with material for a play. He had to have that living connection with a subject before he could make drama of it. He is not a clever man any more than I am, nor is he an intellectual, although he often stands as one. At his best he is true to what has happened to him. Out of experience came his good work, conceived in ambivalence and his own confusion and resolved in pity and a recognition of terror. When he attempts a final clarity he is less convincing, and, in the end, he's smart enough to know this. The question remained—and it wasn't his uniquely, of course—would he ever again go through the kind of experience in life that might result in another play as good as this one? How many really good plays does a writer have in him? How many lives can he live? Art was to have a second life. And then a third. And I was to be a witness to them.

He didn't write *Death of a Salesman;* he *released* it. It was there inside him, stored up waiting to be turned loose. That's the measure of its merit.

I BELIEVE Mary Miller blamed her husband's moral "deterioration" on me. I suppose I did give him a gentle shove down the slope into the jungle of turpitude. She said to me one day—and this is exact, because I quickly wrote it down—"Art is acquiring all of your bad habits and none of your good ones." I wondered what she thought my good qualities were that Art was failing to acquire. I knew what she meant by my bad qualities.

I believe Mary looked on me as a "womanizer." It is a word I dislike, a prim, stuffy, frightened, middle-class word, and it demeans women. What it means to the people who use it is inaccurate in my case. I have been with a number of women outside my marriages. That number has been exaggerated. Was I "promiscuous"? Hell, no! The relationships I remember have been mostly with actresses with whom I had a strong bond of interest—the production of a film or a play. It was in most cases, believe it or not, a natural part of the work—so it seemed to me—happening as the problems of the production brought us closer. I became emotionally, then physically, involved with an actress because, for the span of a production, we had the same concerns and hopes. We relied on each other: I depended on her, she on me; that bond is as close as any imaginable. I became, for the time of that production, her all-powerful father figure, believing in her, supporting her through her bad hours, adoring her for her gifts. She was to depend on me for her security—who else is as close during those days?

I believe it is inevitable for a director and his actresses to connect in this way, the affairs arising out of interdependence and a need for each other. These "affairs" are not casual; they often amount to a kind of temporary marriage. They rarely endure past the course of the production, and in this sense, they don't endanger other, more lasting, human bonds.

I began to measure these passing relationships accurately. I became cautious about romantic excesses. Granting their emotional intensity, I also recognized that these unions were essentially temporary. I preserved a careful secrecy. This was harmful to me, because I became an expert dissembler. Each time, I deceived more easily. I became adept at covering my tracks. This is a severe price to pay, but I paid it. I did everything I had to do to preserve my marriage and my home while I preserved myself. There were many narrow escapes. I made what will seem an absurd concession to decency; it consisted of not saying the word "love" to anyone I was with. But that was false too. I don't know how to grade these experiences, but there was love there, certainly. Call it intense devotion, an exchange of human gifts and human rewards.

As the years pass—and I'm braving the wrath of my women friends— men always begin to look elsewhere for rejuvenation, poor things. Their penises, barometers of their continuing vitality, become less cooperative. This awakes anxiety. Men also search elsewhere for fresh entertainment— we have our geishas too. And for spiritual reassurance—remember wife number one, the oldest queen, in *Anna and the King of Siam*? But perhaps what they come to need most of all is hope. Desire, Tennessee Williams said, is the opposite of death. In desperation we do what we can.

It's more difficult for women. They have the same needs—rejuvenation, entertainment, reassurance, hope—that men have. Most women have not been able to find relief and help as readily or as easily. I've noticed the faces of wives who, impelled by their notion of duty and even more by their fear of being abandoned (so many middle-class wives have confessed to me that they fear their husbands will find out what they really think—an unguarded mumble in their sleep—and quit them), do their duty all their lives through, preserving their real thoughts in silence and their deepest desires unfulfilled. The faces of these good creatures acquire a wistful aspect, a dreamy look, as they fade back permanently from life and the hope of solution. They live in a fog of neglect and longing. An experienced hunter can always tell when women like that are on the slippery edge and ready to tumble off. They are equally ambivalent with men. In time their children become more important to them than their husbands, but the day comes when the children leave home too. Then they face the final fact: They are alone.

Now women have claimed their independence and asserted their equality. Perhaps they do this more completely in my profession than in any other. Why? A successful actress has power equal to that of any actor, as well as—more important—her own money. Something else that's interesting is going on. I've observed incidents of compensatory revenge, in payment, perhaps, for years of demeaning relationships. Long-bottled-up resentments are being released. Long-silent anger is being expressed at last.

The man I've watched treating women in the most arrogant way of all is Jed Harris. I particularly noticed this when I played opposite his wife, Louise Platt, in a play titled *Five Alarm Waltz*. Jed was abominable to her and didn't conceal what he thought of her talent as an actress—which was very little indeed. There was nothing for her to do at the time except take the punishment; he had her, at least at that time, completely beaten down. I then began to keep track of Jed, talk to people about him, make notes on his character, dig up stories about him, and so on. When I read about the suicide of Rosamund Pinchot, one of Jed's longtime companions, I wondered if it wasn't an act of revenge against Jed. Perhaps, I thought, Miss Pinchot wanted to make him feel guilty for the way he'd treated her, something she'd never been able to do when she was alive. Years later, I heard from my friend Paul Osborn something Jed had told him after Miss Pinchot's death. "After Rosie died," Jed told Osborn, "they found an entry in her diary which read: 'Why do I get into bed with that dirty little Jew every night?'" Did she know Jed would, sooner or later, read this? I must believe she did—or hoped so. Jed had his own revenge; it consisted of telling Paul what the woman had written, proof of her anti-Semitism. A mystery remains: not why Jed wanted her, because he always needed to subjugate the daughter of the goyim, but why she wanted him so desperately that she stayed with him that long.

THE AFFAIRS I've had were sources of knowledge; they were my education. For many years, in this area and only in this area, I've used the lie, and I'm not proud of that. But I must add this: My "womanizing" saved my life. It kept the juices pumping and saved me from drying up, turning to dust, and blowing away, like some of my friends. The life-in-hazard that I lived kept me curious, interested, eager, searching, and in excellent health. I struggled with the impossible: how to make it all work together without shaming myself. I failed. But I did not settle for a solution that would have choked me to death.

As always, there was a price. I led a double life and became a double person. It marked me. This took—as one analyst pointed out to me repeatedly—an enormous amount of my vital energy. But I didn't know and don't now know the solution. Even though my mendacity was confined to one area, it made me a different kind of man than I'd like to have been. It also hurt someone else, which resulted in the guilt I've carried all my days. It was finally inevitable that, despite what seemed to be her acquiescent silence, I hurt the person who was closest to me and meant the most to me, my wife Molly.

.   .   .

A LAST word about Miller: I was to watch that man struggle through a terrible personal ordeal. He survived. I admired him for what he was going through, that he'd allowed himself to be that vulnerable. I admired him less as the unassailable hero of progressive culture. He shared, for a long time, the common lot of humanity. Although we're no longer "tight" friends, I still feel some closeness to and sympathy for him. I was there at his awakening. I watched the rest of his life with empathic interest. Here was true ambivalence: a desire to be the most esteemed, the most honored, the most secure, the most correct public figure, while he wrestled with the temptations the rest of us face—vanity, pride, lust, greed, and so on. This conflict is his humanity.

MY FATHER'S favorite expression was *bot-tuh-muz-gune*, Turkish for "the day of my ruination." He'd give that expression many readings, including ironic ones, for he was not a self-pitying man. He was, on the contrary, resilient (as am I), and when he'd find himself suddenly far back of where he'd hoped to be, he'd pick up and try again—for instance, at the horse track. He handled reverses by expecting them. When he got a phone call from one of his six half-brothers, who were, at regular intervals, indigent, instead of saying "How are you?" he'd say, "How much money you asking this time?" If the call was from his sister, a woman whose social pleasure consisted of going to the funerals of close friends, he'd ask, "Who died?"

So it happened that his son always expected bad news rather than good. I've lived much of my life on the edge of a crumbling cliff, alert to detect the first rattle of pebbles announcing the avalanche. You American-borns expect the good times to continue, but they won't; take it from an Anatolian. Disaster hurts less when you expect it. Don't cry; shrug.

I've never been higher in my profession than I was after I'd directed *Salesman* and *Gentleman's Agreement*, both the same year, and won all the prizes on both coasts. That was the top; I knew it. The only place I could go was down. Meantime, I lived like a Gypsy king, commuting back and forth on the 20th Century Limited and the Super Chief, to be met at Pasadena, the favorite disembarkation point for big shots, by a studio limo and, coming the other way, by my agent's messenger with a script for me to reject. But I'd been brought up right; I didn't trust this affluence, fame, and privilege. The lesson I'd learned from my father was not to expect the good to continue and, consequently, not to be crushed when it didn't. Anatolians have always believed in the classic Greek concept of Fate, but not as it was thought of in the fifth century B.C. Our Fate was a Turk waiting in a shadow, with an unsheathed scimitar.

There I was in 1950—I'd never be that high again—but in the next two years I was to know every kind of reversal: condemned by the right, damned by the left, and constantly having my plans and my hopes destroyed by malignant forces I could not place or describe. I knew that the higher you get, the more visible you are, and targets that are most visible draw the most fire. As a great cultural hero in 1950, the only man who then excelled in both theatre and film, I was, for a short time, beyond criticism. Or so I thought. Two years later, I ended up beat (you might say "punchy") and disrespected by all decent liberals—the people among whom I'd been living my life. But perhaps because I'd not trusted my eminence, I survived my defeats. I tried to keep my balance and stay on my feet, because I knew that if I fell to the ground I'd be an easy mark for malice and revenge. I kept my footing, and I found that the middle ground, between the extremes, was my place, the middle "held" for me; it was where I could live and work. It was what I liked about this country and what made it mine.

I didn't expect a fall, oh no; I had high hopes. Art Miller was writing his screenplay for us to film, a story of the Brooklyn waterfront, where Art had worked during the war as a steamfitter on British warships in for repair. It would certainly be the best film material I'd ever had, and I was waiting for it eagerly. Tennessee Williams was writing a play he expected me to direct, *The Rose Tattoo*. Wherever he moved in the world, he kept in touch with me. John Steinbeck, whom I'd tracked down in northern California the year before, was marrying Elaine Scott and moving to New York. He was working on a film for me about Emiliano Zapata, the Mexican revolutionist, a subject he'd fussed over for many years; we'd quickly become close friends. No one else was preparing ventures like these. They would amplify my image as the leading progressive in the performing arts.

I was now of a rank so secure that I could afford to do Darryl Zanuck a favor. He called me in New York to tell me that Jack Ford had come down with a case of shingles (I looked it up for you: "an eruptive nervous disorder of the skin") and had to drop out of the film he was making. Darryl asked me as urgently as he was able to ask anyone to rush out west and take over. Ford was the American director I most admired; I thought it would be an honor to stand in his shoes on his set. What a romantic I was! I made up my mind to do the favor, but in the manner of a grand gesture. Darryl had offered to rush me the script by transcontinental messenger. I told him that wasn't necessary, I'd do the job sight unseen; read the script when I arrived and be ready to shoot the next morning. What a fool! The movie was *Pinky*.

I even thought of doing the job without compensation but recovered my good sense in time. I did ask, even though I'd be working only a fraction of the usual schedule's time, that I be paid my whole picture salary and be allowed to leave the day after I made the last shot. Agreed. Agreed. Honor preserved! I also insisted that I not use any of Jack's stuff, no matter how good it was. This was also not a problem; Darryl was happy to junk Jack's film, and when I saw it I understood why. Something must have been bothering the old man besides shingles.

I soon found out what. Arriving on the lot before Darryl in the morning, I talked to the crew, many of them old friends and all realists; they told me the score. Then I went in to see Darryl. "Jack's not sick," I said, "is he? He just wanted out." Darryl answered, unabashed, "He hated that old nigger woman"—he was speaking of Ethel Waters—"and she sure as hell hated him. He scared her next to death." I discovered that the whole cast was jittery. They'd come expecting to work with the great John Ford, and he'd walked away. They'd not had the time to get to like him—which did require time. I gathered he hadn't taken to this cast, particularly Miss Waters, who had a leading role. Jack didn't know what to do with her. He couldn't curse her, as he did "Duke" Wayne. When he indicated the least disfavor with what she was doing, her reaction was not fear but resentment and retreat. Handling Ethel would be half my battle.

I'd learned to be patient and work the long road. I gentled Ethel and treated her as if she was intelligent—which she was, in a rather paranoid way—and pretty soon the old girl knew I liked her and settled down to good work. She was a unique combination of old-time religiosity ("His Eye Is on the Sparrow") and free-floating hatred, always ready to overflow. I'd never been this close to an old-line black before, but pretty soon she was kissing me every morning when she arrived on the set, doing whatever I asked, and at the end of the afternoon, when I told her she'd done well, asking the Lord to pour down His blessing on me.

My problem was not Ethel, who was a talent, but my leading lady. She was a good soul, a pretty girl, obedient, gentle, yielding, and, I suspected, catechism schooled. She defined the word "ingenue," yet had four children, was to have two more—conceived I wasn't sure how, for she gave the impression of being forever fifteen and intact. She seemed what many veteran producers liked their young women to be: docile victims for the aging male with money to take advantage of and, afterward, so inexperienced they'd not question his performance or complain when dropped. Perhaps it was not Ethel but this actress with her goodness who'd brought on Jack's "shingles." There would be days when I'd long for a bitch!

As we began to work, I noticed that her face under all dramatic circumstances remained inexpressive; she floated through her role without reacting. I had to find a way to make an asset of this emotional passivity. She was surrounded by a cast of colorful, highly charged personalities, and the contrast with them, I saw, might make a point: that she'd been permanently frozen by her situation. Instead of being impatient with her, which would have been disastrous, I required very little except her own submissive vacuity. She perfectly represented a victim of an unfortunate trick of the genes, her light complexion, and was, in the end, effective in the role.

My favorite in that cast was Ethel Barrymore, a grand old battlewagon, all flags still flying. I used to hang around her just to hear that ripe voice croak out anecdotes about the brothers Barrymore. She had a way of kidding me I enjoyed; she mocked my seriousness. Like many old-timers, she had patience for only one take of a scene. And no heavy Actors Studio–type directorial analyses beforehand, please. When I'd ask her for another take, she'd say, "Why? I can't do it better, boy." And if I still pushed her, she'd come out with: "What do you want it for, your collection?" But she blew in ready to work every morning, and I loved her.

In one sense I was a veteran now, knew just what I wanted from the actors and how to get it. This was reassuring to everyone; I wasn't complicating the job or prolonging it. I'd learned not to pretend something was deeper than it was. We all knew we were not making a masterpiece, so no one pretended we were. The crew liked it that way, quick and professional. I was that season's hero on the Fox lot; I'd saved a filmful of jobs.

But about halfway through, it hit me: I didn't know how to make a film, only how to talk actors into doing what I wanted them to do, which is another racket. "You should have started like the other fellows did," I said to myself, "making two-reel comedies." I had a jolly, capable cameraman, who'd suggest where to put the camera; I'd agree because I didn't know better or different. I'd asked for a cutter to be on the set with me, and Darryl had given me an experienced man who had directorial aspirations. He'd tell me what close shots I should make after I'd done the "master." Since I had no firm suggestions of my own, I accepted his. He quickly settled into a routine.

But then it became evident to me that after making four films and picking up an Academy Award for directing, I was still a stage director and no way prepared to do Art's *The Hook* or John's *Zapata*, subjects that called for bold pictorial treatment. I was inept at my profession. Sometime during the middle of the schedule, I resolved to use all the time I had before the two films that meant so much to me, and learn the proper techniques of filmmaking. I wanted not to continue leaning on other men but to be able to make my own directorial choices stand up. Otherwise, when I got to Brooklyn's Red Hook waterfront and to Zapata's province, rocky Morelos, I'd be incapable of achieving what I was determined to achieve. I had to replace the stage director in me and become a filmmaker.

At night, I began to plan the next day's scenes visually, the camera positions and moves, then, on the set, I'd match wits and cunning, design and content, with my cameraman and cutter. I encouraged them to debate my choices, make me defend my ideas as I was making them defend theirs. So what had started as a routine job began to be fun; I was a student again and perhaps learning what I should have learned a long time before. Having nothing better to do at night, I began to look at films and tried to learn what I could from the masters and the veterans. Each morning I'd come on the set with an idea, which often slowed things down, and perhaps—so they believed—led us into some mistakes. Still I knew that no matter what I did, Darryl, when I'd left, would take the film I'd given him and do what he wished with it.

Now I was eager to get back east and check on the progress of the scripts Art and John were writing. They knew even less about filmmaking than I did, so I wanted to get together with them early and work on their screenplays. I said goodbye to *Pinky* without regret. My most vivid memory is the end-of-the-schedule party. The cast and crew gave me their affection, and I returned it. I had a ticket in my pocket for the next day's Chief, and I was celebrating; so I got awful drunk. Ethel Waters and I were especially cozy until she put down one drink too many. I saw this was my chance to ask her what I'd been meaning to ask for weeks. "You don't really like any white people, do you, Ethel?" I said. "No, I don't," she answered, her religious mask clattering to the floor. "Not even me?" I asked. "Not even you," she said. "I don't like any fucking white man. I don't trust any of you." The next morning the mask was back on, and she kissed me and thanked me and once again called down the Lord's blessing on me. She was sorry to leave. There weren't many parts waiting for an old black woman. I was happy that she was friendly again, but I knew that when she'd been high, she'd spoken the truth.

B A C K   E A S T, I told Molly I'd decided to forget about the theatre for a while and concentrate on films, Art's and John's. She gave me excellent advice—"Wait until you've read their screenplays"—which I decided to ignore. I also told her I wanted to take a vacation by myself. "You've just been by yourself," she said, sounding at the end of her patience. "No, I've been with a lot of other people," I said. "I'm going off for a bit." She was suspicious. "Who're you going with?" she asked. "With myself," I said. "I'm the one I've lost touch with." I suppose I figured that since we'd both been to the same shrink, she would understand and possibly be sympathetic, but she didn't and wasn't.

What I did was eccentric. I hitchhiked into the Southwest, into open country. It was not the same as a sound stage. I saw the people who lived there; they were not like actors. I'm good at stirring up conversations; I listen well. I carried a notebook and wrote down whatever struck me. I particularly remember the harbor of Galveston, Texas, and its fishing fleet. It was a breezy day, and the wind could be heard flapping the sails and rustling through the trees. "There's no wind on a stage," I said to myself. The harbor's water rippled, catching the light and throwing it back. How could an art director's construction of plywood, canvas, and paint catch that? A boat was unloading fish. The salt of the sea was in the air and I could smell its creatures. The sounds were poetry, the scale enormous, the effect exotic. This is what movies are, I thought: environment, scope, size. Out of doors!

Here, in the open country, life stretched out and there was the promise of adventure everywhere. I was no bigger than anyone else, but I was no smaller. I was not a Hollywood big shot, but I didn't want to be. At the same time I was not insignificant. No one there was huddling together for safety. I was not part of any group except the biggest one; I was an ordinary American. I began to have some idea of what that was. Like the rest of the country's men, I was independent and needn't fear anyone. I didn't have a cellmaster or a *führer.* All around me were my fellow citizens, people, not stars with their plump, soft-skinned, indoor faces. I was in the land of the free and I was free and could do whatever I wished. It was time for a switch in my life.

I knew that what I was feeling there, at the edge of that harbor with the wind off the water and the sharp smell in my nostrils, was not something that could be captured on a theatre's stage or inside a Hollywood film studio. The "exteriors" of *Pinky* had been shot indoors against a "sky drop," and they were disgraceful. As for *The Sea of Grass*, "MGM!" said it all. No words that I had or was able to use could describe the exhilaration I felt looking out over Galveston harbor that day. Only the language of film could tell what I was feeling. I knew the pictures that could convey my feeling; the sounds were there to be recorded; I even knew how to suggest the smells. I knew how important the atmosphere of a dockfront would be for *The Hook* and I was confident I could capture it. As for *Zapata*, I'd better get down to rocky Morelos again and learn what pictures and sounds would tell the story of that very different country and its people.

That was how this director might become a filmmaker.

I had another deficiency, which I felt less hopeful about. Sooner or later I'd have to learn to write or at least to collaborate on the screenplays of my movies. I knew from studying the films I admired that they were finally the vision of one man and that the first step to making an exceptional film was to be involved in the script, and I promised myself that someday I would be. For a reason I wasn't sure of, Molly still discouraged me about this, and I wasn't confident enough to contest her judgment. But I said to myself (not to her), movies are not literature, they're sequences of photographed action arranged to tell a story; they are images and movement, not sentences and words. They're another medium. Quite possibly I'd never be able to write acceptably, but I could learn to conceive and construct my own shooting scripts; I had to learn to do that! Who else could write the films I'd promised myself I'd make, those about my family and its history, those about my own life, except me?

Back in New York, luck was waiting for me. It was a movie being offered me to direct, one written by my friend Dick Murphy, who'd written *Boomerang*. This one took place in New Orleans, where the Mississippi drains, and concerned a search to apprehend and quarantine a man who was carrying the plague and so prevent a pestilence. I wasn't stirred by the script as I was by the prospect of making *The Hook* or *Zapata*, but I knew Dick well and felt sure we could make a lively picture together. At the same time I could exercise the techniques I'd decided I lacked. I'd make a "silent," a film that a deaf man could follow, make it with people or with "my own" actors, who looked like people. I called Darryl to make sure I could shoot it entirely, every shot, on location, and he agreed. I told him I didn't want the producer around either, and Darryl said he wouldn't be. I didn't want a big old-time star, I went on, and we agreed on my pal Dick Widmark. Now I began to be excited about the film. New Orleans would be my true star, that wonderful city where you can smell the river, the coffee, and the Creole cooking everywhere you go. I took the job.

THE TITLE, *Panic in the Streets*, was the contribution of Fox's sales department; it suggested that they were nervous about the popular appeal of the film. What I was going to do was not a novelty in filmmaking but in our oldest tradition, the way the first great action pictures were shot. When Chaplin was making two-reelers and heard that a night's heavy rain had flooded Griffith Park, he'd quickly call his crew together, plus a couple of his comics, then rush down to use the flooded areas for laughs. The script? He "winged" it. The massive, overornamental sets came with the development of lights and particularly with the wish of certain studios, such as MGM, to make their stars look like gods and goddesses. My intention was the opposite.

This "shoot" was a lark, the first film I purely enjoyed making. There was no tension anywhere, perhaps because there was no producer present, but mostly because I was so clearly enjoying myself; a crew and a cast take their mood from the director. The author was with me every minute, and we

Here's Dick Murphy.

reconceived each scene according to my directorial notions. I'd get to the location each morning before anyone and figure out the sequence of shots that would keep the story's excitement going. Then Dick would show up, and we'd drop the tailgate of a truck, ask the property man to set up our typewriter, and, together, adjust the script for that day to fit my ideas. We rewrote every scene every day, and I was at the typewriter as much as Dick. But it wasn't writing; it was filmmaking.

I ran free all over the city. The mayor was a fan, his police part of my staff; the great restaurants' doors were wide open. I'd brought my family down; we had a large house with a great backyard. For a time I had the use of a tugboat and took my kids for a ride on the Mississippi. Sundays, some of my people would gather for brunch, after which we'd play horseshoes. Sometimes I'd box with one of my assistants, who put me in my place. On Christmas Day we feasted on ostrich eggs, scrambled like any others—two eggs feeding thirty of us—then told stories and laughed the afternoon away.

We used the city's people as our extras, and their homes, shops, and streets for scenery. We were welcomed everywhere by everyone, and they had as good a time as we did. I went wild. There were all kinds of girls on our set, visitors and extras. It was a "carny" atmosphere or like that around a second-class rock band on tour today. All this was a fantastic liberation for me; I'd been such a disciplined, serious, and dutiful boy before. Now I lived and worked by impulse. I got everything I wanted. In one sequence, for extras we emptied a whorehouse of its girls; that was a jolly day! A room at the biggest hotel in town was at my disposal. After my family returned to New York to get the kids back in school, I bunked with a gentle, generous young woman who'd recently given birth; when we made love, her milk was all over my chest. Living irregularly, I was in heaven.

Meantime, I was learning how much more there was to directing than getting performances from actors. For the first time, I didn't have a cutter at my elbow, so I had to make all decisions myself: which shots, where they'd fit, how they'd go together, what close-ups I needed.

Following *Panic in the Streets*, with the exception of *A Streetcar Named Desire*, which was written by Tennessee Williams and altogether too good to touch, and my last film, *The Last Tycoon*, made when I was sick at heart for family reasons, I collaborated happily and boldly with a writer on every film. You won't find my name on the credit sheets, but all those other movies were either launched by me or conceived in collaboration with their writers; in every case, the authors and I worked harmoniously on the structure. A filmscript is more architecture than literature.

This will get my friends who are writers mad, but it's the truth: The director tells the movie story more than the man who writes the dialogue. The director is the final author, which is the reason so many writers now want to become directors. It's all one piece. Many of the best films ever made can be seen without dialogue and be perfectly understood. The director tells the essential story with pictures. Dialogue, in most cases, is the gravy on the meat. It can be a tremendous "plus," but it rarely is. Acting, the art, helps; that too is the director's work. He finds the experience within the actor that makes his or her face and body come alive and so creates the photographs he needs. Pictures, shots, angles, images, "cuts," poetic long shots—these are his vocabulary. Not talk. What speaks to the eye is the director's vocabulary, his "tools," just as words are the author's. Until *Panic in the Streets*, I'd directed actors moving in and out of dramatic arrangements just as I might have done on stage, with the camera photographing them mostly in medium shot. My stage experience, which I'd thought of as an asset, I now regarded as a handicap. I had to learn a new art.

I learned, for instance, that film time is different from stage time. One of the most important techniques a film director has is the ability to stretch a moment for emphasis. On a theatre stage, true time goes its normal course; it's the same on stage as it is in the audience. But in a film we have movie time, a false time. Climaxes in life go clickety-click and they're over. When a film director comes to a crucially important moment, he can stretch it, go from one close-up to another, then to people who are dramatically involved or concerned watching the action, so back and forth to everyone connected with what is happening. In this way time is stretched for dramatic emphasis. Other parts of the film can be slipped over swiftly so that they are given no more time on the screen than their dramatic value justifies. Film time then becomes faster than real time. A film director can choose to leap into the "meat" of a scene or from high moment to high moment, leaving out what, in his opinion, is not worth the attention of the audience. Entrances and exits—unless they're freighted with dramatic substance—mean nothing. It doesn't matter how the character got there. He's there! Cut to the heart of the scene.

I also learned, at last, that the camera is not only a recording device but a penetrating instrument. It looks *into* a face, not *at* a face. Can this kind of effect be achieved on stage? Not nearly! A camera can even be a microscope. Linger, enlarge, analyze, study. It is a very subtle instrument, can make any face heavier, leaner, drawn, flushed, pale, jolly, depraved, saintly. I was so late finding all this out. I'd always place the camera at eye level— the equivalent of the stage view—instead of all the other places it could be. I'd not known there was a valuable choice in lenses. I was a successful director who was technically an ignoramus.

I also discovered that a camera can set a mood or capture a great commotion, and that this is the use of the long shot, of which D. W. Griffith and John Ford and George Stevens and Howard Hawks and others of the thirties and forties in this country, as well as the great Russian directors of the twenties, were masters. After my trip to Texas I was alert to what could be done this way. Certainly *The Hook* and *Viva Zapata!* would require excellent long shots, and I'd find them. I began to look forward to those films even more than I had.

I hope you're interested in all this, because you look at film constantly— it's now the language of mankind. Speaking of the close-up and its uses, a familiar instance for some of you might be the way directors of professional sports shows use them. Watch a professional game. See how, after each play, the director will cut to the person who's just won or lost, to the athlete most affected by what has just happened, or to the winner and the loser in alternation, or to the coaches, even to someone in the stands who's excited by what's happening. The close-up underlines the emotional content. There is no technique on stage to match it except an exaggerated hot light or bringing an actor downstage and turning him or her straight out to the audience. But this is crude by comparison and not as effective.

Of course, the close-up has simpler uses—to show off the beauty of a lady, for instance. But above all it keeps the story's progress clear. We see in close-up that a person is undecided; the "tight shot" shows the indecision on the person's face, we can read it as clearly as if it were spelled out in words—but with all the values of ambivalence. Then we see the decision being made and the new course taken. Except for that close-up, the change of intent or direction would be inexplicable. Because of it, the progression of the story, the "inner line," is kept clear.

New Orleans was full of the music I love. In my nocturnal wanderings, I got to meet a number of the jazz musicians, chief among them Sidney Bechet, who was a master and a poet. I also met cruder artists; I enjoyed them too. After dark that city was full of pulsing sound. I'd walk down a street lined with "joints" out of which jazz flooded into the soft night air. I tried to fill the sound track of the film with this music, but I didn't do as well as I should have. Next time! I said. And on *Zapata* I did better. In New Orleans, on *Panic in the Streets*, I learned the importance of music in film, and I would never again leave my sound track to a producer and his musical director. Often it's as important as anything except the sequence of pictures that will tell the basic story.

I found during the four months that I worked in New Orleans that I was fed up with the stodgy "cause" movies and plays I'd been doing. The first film that uses the word "Jew," the first film where "nigger" is said! So what! They were still conventional. As for the kudos of using big stars like Tracy and Hepburn, Peck, McGuire, and Garfield—the hell with that. It felt fine to be surrounded with the knockabout gang I'd assembled and to be doing a script that wasn't loaded down with "significance" and "depth." I can't imagine anything more "leather-bound" than *The Sea of Grass* or more boring, more "worthy," than *Pinky,* so predictable and tedious.

I learned why Jack Ford surrounded himself with roughnecks when he made a film. You can ask them to do anything or to cause anything you might dream of to be done. It uninhibits you; you stop worrying about the actors' comfort or even their safety. Remember in *The Sea of Grass* how the property man, awed by his star, flicked a little water on the fine-cut coat of the "lord of the prairie" who was supposed to have just come in out of a blizzard? In *Panic in the Streets*, we had to fish a man out of the river for a scene, a dead man, presumably, who'd been in the water overnight. How did we do it? There was only one way: throw someone in. You can't throw Spencer Tracy into a river. "Who'll do the bit in the 'drink' for me?" I asked. I had volunteers. When our man was good and wet, his clothes soaked through, and when the camera was ready, we photographed him floating in the garbage and the dead fish along the edge of the dock, and he looked dead. The actor got an extra check. I got my shot.

I had a visitor on the set: Lillian Hellman. I enjoyed the visit; it was flattering, a signal to me that I'd made the grade with the intellectuals of the left. She was crowning me the director most desired. Don't be misled by that choice of words. Playwrights are always looking for directors who'll do justice to their plays; Lillian herself had said so in an article printed at the time, rating me *numero uno* on her list. She may have had a less professional purpose in mind on this occasion, but nothing of the sort came of her visit, even though she extended it into a second day. If it had been anyone less formidable, I might have thought she was offering herself to me. But even as it turned out, I thought her intrepid; that lady had balls! She went after what she wanted the way a man does. The shameful truth, however, is that my tastes are more ordinary. I would have preferred someone like the little darling Lillian drew for that bookseller's book, the kid with the upturned nose and the blond hair in true curls, the artist's image of what she'd have wanted to look like. I had the same ideal of beauty, it seemed, that Lillian had.

Each director has a favorite in his cast, and with me it's usually been the traditional and most conventional one, a young lady. Some directors—Otto Preminger, for example—have had a favorite to bully; early in their schedule they select an actor or actress (Jean Seberg was one) on whom they can unload their frustrations. My favorite this time was Zero Mostel—but not to bully. I thought him an extraordinary artist and a delightful companion, one of the funniest and most original men I'd ever met; I never knew what he was going to say next. I constantly sought his company. He liked me too—one reason being that he was one of three people whom I rescued from the "industry"'s blacklist, which was already in effect. For a long time, Zero had not been able to get work in films, but I got him in my film—and so earned increased admiration from "our side." I was a political hero as well.

After the film was done and forgotten, I didn't see Zero again for several years. In the meantime I'd changed my mind about many things, including my feelings about the investigation into communism in this country. To the horror of a few of my best friends, I testified friendly to the House Committee on Un-American Activities.

One winter's night, on Seventy-second Street near Columbus Avenue, I ran into Zero. By that time I'd hardened myself against the disapproval some old friends were giving me and didn't much care what people a good deal closer to me than Zero thought. But for some reason I did care what he thought. He stopped me and put an arm around my neck—a little too tight—and said in one of the most dolorous voices I've ever heard, "Why did you do that? You shouldn't have done that." He took me into a bar and we had a drink and then another, but he didn't say much and I didn't say much. All he did was look at me once in a while, and his eyes were saying what his lips were not: "Why did you do that?" I never saw him again.

W H E N I came back from New Orleans, Miller was still working on *The Hook*, and *Zapata* wasn't near ready, but Tennessee was back from Europe and I went to see him. He hadn't finished *The Rose Tattoo*, but he told me that Charlie Feldman was going ahead with a film of *Streetcar* and that he—and Tenn—wanted me to do it. "Oh, God, Tenn," I said, "it would be like marrying the same woman twice. I don't think I can get it up for *Streetcar* again." He persisted, and I saw that it meant a lot to him, so I said the usual: "I'll think it over." It would be easier to refuse by letter than to tell him face to face. I owed him a lot.

But later, alone, I began to see the offer as an opportunity. With the confidence I'd gained using the locations of *Panic in the Streets*, I saw how

I could "open up" *Streetcar*, make the play into a proper film by putting on screen everything that Blanche describes in dialogue about Belle Reve and her last days there. The scenes were all described in her speeches. I'd get out of that tight little stage setting, those two miserable rooms. I'd photograph the old family place and the dying deaf woman within, the night scene with the young drunken trainees on the lawn calling "Blanche! Blanche!" and how she'd go out to them, what happened then, and show the paddy wagon the next morning picking up the young soldiers. I'd photograph the day Blanche was run out of town and the unyielding faces of the townspeople, glad to be quit of her. I'd film all this somewhere in the delta country of southern Mississippi, get on film something truer and more telling than what we had on stage. I would shoot Blanche's arrival at the old train station in New Orleans, materializing out of the cloud of smoke from the old locomotive (I'd steal that from *Anna Karenina*). I would also dramatize Stanley's world, do scenes in his favorite bowling alley, the bars he frequented and the streets where he hung out with Mitch and the others. I'd make the old city's presence a force, create a veritable redneck Kowalski world. What a contrast to Blanche that would be! And a great lesson in filmmaking. I took the job.

I worked hard with a sympathetic writer; we completed a screenplay and I was pleased with it. In a mood of self-congratulation, I decided I deserved a vacation—Mexico! Zapata! Morelos! Was that a vacation?—then I'd come back to hurry on with the production problems, especially finding the right "Belle Reve" place in Mississippi. But when I reread the "opened-up" screenplay, I found it was a fizzle. The force of the play had come precisely from its compression, from the fact that Blanche was trapped in those two small rooms, where she'd be constantly aware that she was dangerously irritating Stanley and couldn't escape if she needed to. Everything we'd done to "open up" the play diluted its power. I threw our screenplay into File and Forget, decided to photograph what we'd had on stage, simply that.

I chose an excellent designer for the film and was able to get a cameraman who understood what I wanted. Together we worked out three things that would help. We had the walls of Stanley and Stella's home built in small sections that could be removed, so making the set grow smaller as time passed, more constricting and more threatening to Blanche. This is an eerie effect, and it worked. We also decided to take an image Williams had given us, a moth beating its wings against a wall, literally. We asked Lucinda Ballard, our costume designer, to make Blanche's dress for the rape scene of a light, diaphanous material, the same color as the very light window curtains of the bedroom where Stanley corners her. This also worked; it created a sense of mortal panic. I also asked our designer to make the walls "sweat" to suggest the humid heat of the place. I'm afraid this sounds more effective than it was. We did surpass the effect of the play with certain close-

ups. I particularly remember the one of the naked light bulb from which
Stanley has stripped the ornamental shade. In the close-up where Mitch
turns on the light bulb, we thrust Blanche's face under its harsh light. She
looks pathologically drawn and aged. This was more telling on film than on
the stage.

Charlie Feldman had said I could use my New York cast except for Jessie;
Warners, who were putting up the money, insisted we get them a film star
in the part of Blanche, so said Charlie. He was a charming man, with an
excellent collection of nineteenth-century French paintings (good investments all), but he was a yielder. I'm not sure now that if I'd stood my
ground and insisted on Jessie, Warners might not have come around. But
at the time I didn't know Charlie well, and he convinced me that Warners
were not to be moved. I told Jessie the deal; she took it as well as anyone
possibly could. She said she'd expected the rejection, had resigned herself
to the probability she would not make the film. So I let it go. To confess the
hard truth, I'm not certain, looking back, that I didn't want a different actress for Blanche. Feeling stale on the play, I needed a high-voltage shock
to get my motor going again.

We decided on Vivien Leigh to replace Jessie, and I confess I entered
that relationship with misgivings—concealed, I hope, but I'm not sure.
Molly and I invited her and her husband, Larry Olivier, to come to our new
studio in Connecticut for a get-acquainted visit. We had a cordial time; I
took to him more than I did to her. In California, Charlie had arranged
accommodations for us, giving Vivien and Larry his lovely home on Cold-

Vivien and Kim

water Canyon and providing for my family a smaller and less luxurious place across the side street. Brando moved in with me until Molly and my kids arrived, but his presence was not reliable. We were all to be neighbors for the duration. Things simply had to work out.

Our single setting was erected on a great Warner Brothers sound stage. I asked that a "mock-up" of the setting be provided at one side, with the same dimensions and with furniture as close to the pieces we'd be photographing as could be found so I could rehearse the actors while the cameraman and his crew lit the production set. On the first day, as I directed the first interior scene on my mock-up, the whole production nearly went blooey. I requested that Vivien do something we'd done with Jessie in New York, and she came out with: "When Larry and I did the play in London . . ." and went on to tell us all what she and Larry had done, which she clearly preferred to what I was asking her to do. Irene had told me about the London production, which she considered misconceived. As Vivien spoke, I became aware of the other actors looking at me. They knew what I knew, that this was a moment not to be allowed to pass unchallenged. "But you're not making the film with Larry in London now, Vivien," I said. "You're making it here with us." Then, as gently as I could, I insisted on my way. It took a full two weeks before she was at ease with me, and the scenes

shot in those weeks, if you'll forgive the conceit, are the ones where she appears most artificial, most of the theatre, and most strained. Slowly we began to like each other, then suddenly we became close friends. In the end I was full of admiration for the lady. She had a small talent, but the greatest determination to excel of any actress I've known. She'd have crawled over broken glass if she thought it would help her performance. In the scenes that counted, she is excellent.

W H I L E I was directing *A Streetcar Named Desire*, all hell broke loose at the Screen Directors Guild of America, my guild. I'd kept myself at the far edge of that organization for two reasons, the simplest being that meetings bore me. But an issue had come up that would involve me, like it or not. Cecil B. De Mille was going for throats, including mine. He'd gathered the most conservative directors on the guild's national board to work with him to uncover and discredit left-wingers in the membership and make their continuing to work as directors impossible. He would do this by drawing up a list of those who refused to sign a loyalty oath, then delivering this list of undesirables, inside a guild-franked envelope, to the head of every studio in town. On this list would also appear the names of those about to be called to Washington for testimony before the House Committee on Un-American Activities. I suspected I'd be one of the chosen, but I wasn't sure.

This concern was the other reason I'd been trying to stay out of the industry's politics. Even though I'd quit the Party more than sixteen years before, the men in Washington wanted names and they wanted publicity. For these purposes I might be thought useful. Those organizing the right-wing movement in the guild suspected anyone who was reported to have left the Party but continued to make the same kind of movies and had never, as evidence of patriotic good faith, spoken up against communism in their work. These men believed that the films I'd made and the plays I'd directed after I'd quit the Party in 1935 were "Communistic," if not in literal content, by reason of their influence. Among these films were *Pinky* and *Gentleman's Agreement,* but Zanuck was not vulnerable; I was. I knew what they'd think of *The Hook* and *Zapata,* and I prepared to fight them; no one was going to tell me what films or plays I could or could not do. I still felt safe in New York, but I knew I'd be an undefendable target in any investigation that "C.B." and his posse of patriots made in California. (Darryl Zanuck, in a burst of friendly candor, had told me there was a general suspicion—and I couldn't tell if he shared it—that I'd resigned from the Party only to throw people off my track, that I was in fact still a Communist.) If I was cornered, I decided, I would take a defiant position; I'd never bow to De Mille—or to the House Committee on Un-American Activities.

The president of the guild at this time was Joseph L. Mankiewicz. In successive years he'd walked away with double Oscars, writing and directing, for *A Letter to Three Wives* and *All About Eve*. After he'd been knighted with his third and fourth Oscar, Joe had sailed for the European vacation he'd earned. While he was gone, De Mille's group, in the name of the guild's national board, which it dominated, put the question of a loyalty oath up to the membership and asked for a vote. The vote was to be by open ballot—every ballot would carry the name of the person whose response it was. In this way, De Mille and his fellow conspirators would know who stood where.

Joe Mankiewicz, at that time, was a handsome man in that nonmuscular way many women prefer; he enjoyed the gift of his sexuality and an abundant scoffing humor. To scoff in that society was to demonstrate good sense. How he came to be president of the guild, Joe, a classic nonjoiner, cannot now explain. He was not an easy man to stir up for a cause or from whom to expect political action; he was an artist, and artists are never where they're supposed to be. Still, on the night of October 22, 1950, Joe presided over a meeting of his guild brothers, routed the opposition, silenced Cecil B. De Mille, and saved the guild by confirming its identity as a democratic organization.

What happens to old directors who'd once known fame as rich and power as absolute as Joe's had once been? Now, at age seventy-eight, his hair thin above a face plumped by ease, he lives, on money he made long ago, in a handsome home in the elite backcountry of New York's Westchester County, looked after by a gracious and understanding wife and guarded by his four Oscars. Unsympathetic to the present trend in filmmaking, Joe no longer makes movies. He moved east more than twenty years ago, having decided to spend the rest of his life writing. But for some reason he can't explain, he suffers from writer's block. It's not a matter of memory, for last summer he sat with this old director (who's also unsympathetic to the "industry"'s present course) and talked with perfect recall about the night of October 22, remembered the events of that night, as well as the week that led up to it, with gleaming clarity and spoke of it with passion.

"It was not really an important moment in your life," he said to me, "was it? That moment when you stopped at the door and would not go in to our meeting?"

Actually it had been, but I didn't correct him; I wanted him to go on.

His wife, Rosemary, brought us coffee, and after she left, I prompted Joe. "The door?" I said, although I knew very well the door he meant.

Joe was up to speed now, and he plunged on. "As you know," he said, "I've never joined anything, never belonged to any anti-Nazi or any anti-Communist outfits. But when I got back to New York from Europe, I heard for the first time that the Screen Directors Guild membership had voted by open ballot to adopt the loyalty oath, meaning that in order to direct a film in America, you had to sign a pledge of patriotism. This knocked me off my feet; suddenly I wasn't so indifferent. I'd never heard of this vote—

and I was the guild's president. And I didn't like it. Others were outraged too. I must have had twenty-five telegrams waiting for me at my New York hotel. And phone calls! Jules Dassin got me on the phone. He said, 'Go down to the lobby and call me back at this number from a public phone.' I said, 'I'm very comfortable up where I'm talking. Go ahead.' He said, 'Your line is being tapped, believe me.' I said, 'Come on, Julie, cut it out.' He said, 'All right, I'll talk to you later.' But I never heard from him again. Next thing I knew, he'd fled to France and begun to work as a director there.

"When I got back to California I called a meeting of our national board and found out that according to our bylaws I had no vote, only the privilege of calling general meetings and presiding over them. The board had the right to pass that thing without even consulting me! Which is what they'd done."

"This national board," I asked, "were they all old-timers?"

"You know the bunch. De Mille, Clarence Brown, George Marshall—the old-timers. De Mille informed me that the vote had been eight hundred ninety-seven to fourteen, something like that. 'Are you going to be on the side of the fourteen?' he asked me. 'I'm on the side of all the members,' I said. 'They didn't have a chance to discuss this.' 'Now is the time,' De Mille said, 'for good Americans to stand up and be counted.' 'Very true,' I said, 'but who appointed you to do the counting?' That was when I found out that along with the list of members who were not in good standing because they'd failed to pay their dues, the board was also planning to send to the producers a list of members who wouldn't sign the loyalty oath. 'But that's a blacklist,' I said, 'by anyone's definition. And your open ballot,' I went on, 'that's not right. It's un-American.'

"Then the meeting got savage. Jack Ford was there, for a change, and he said, 'My closest friend is Merian Cooper'—remember Merian Cooper: he made the original *King Kong?*—'and he happens to be a brigadier general in the United States Army, and last night, as we were having dinner, Coop said he wouldn't sign any goddamn loyalty oath and he said what we were making was a blacklist, and if a brigadier general in the army tells me it's a blacklist, then it's a goddamn blacklist!' And George Stevens came down to De Mille's chair and he said, 'By the way, C.B., when I was up to my ass in mud at Bastogne, how were the capital gains doing back home?' It went on in that spirit, and after a while I'd made up my mind, and I went ahead and ordered Herbert Leeds, our secretary, to call a general meeting of our members for the very next Sunday night. Whereupon De Mille walked out of the place, slamming the door behind him.

"Next day I was watching a movie, and my brother, Herman, gets me on the phone and says, 'What do you and Andrew Johnson have in common?' I said, 'How drunk are you?' And he said, 'You are, this instant, being impeached. John Farrow just came over and he gave me a whole bunch of totems and amulets, all blessed by various popes, and John wants you to wear them close to your balls because that's where they're going to cut you.' It seems that George Marshall, one of the old-timers, had shown up at Farrow's house in the sidecar of a motorcycle and he walked into John's house and said, 'Here. Sign this.' And John said, 'I will not sign it.'" Farrow, Joe reminded me, "was a prime reactionary, you know."

"I remember," I said.

"Well, it got like a Pete Smith comedy—remember them? Old-timers on motorcycles dashing all over Beverly Hills, getting signatures on a paper demanding my recall."

"What for?"

"To impeach me. So I wouldn't have the right to call this meeting—the one I'd called. Well, the next day I got a request, would I come over to De Mille's office at Paramount—from where the whole thing was being run— and when I got there, they were waiting for me, most of the national board. De Mille said they were willing to resubmit the loyalty oath on a closed ballot for another vote. 'But,' he said, 'of course we'd want a statement from you, Joe, before we did that.' 'What kind of a statement?' I said. Now these are De Mille's exact words: 'You might call it an act of contrition,' he said. Then I cursed them all and left, and the next morning it's in the *Daily Variety:* 'Mankiewicz Refused to Perform an Act of Contrition That De Mille Demanded'—the whole story. Meantime, all that day a dozen motor- cycles were charging all over the area, getting signatures to recall me so I wouldn't have the power to call the meeting that I'd called."

"They were trying to impeach you before the meeting?"

"Yes. Then some of the fellows on my side decided we ought to have a lawyer. So we got Martin Gang—he's Sinatra's lawyer now—and he got a quick injunction from a judge so we could have our meeting, and the next day, Sunday, the day of the meeting, you and John Huston came to a bed- room I'd taken at the Beverly Hills Hotel, remember? The meeting that night was to be downstairs in the ballroom, and the two of you worked over the speech I'd written just as if it was a screenplay, making cuts and sugges- tions for changes. I still have a copy with your pencil marks on it. You worked on it all afternoon, and then somebody comes up and says, 'It's eight o'clock and the place is absolutely packed,' so we go downstairs, Hus- ton and you and George Seaton and a couple of others with me, and as we pushed toward the entrance door, guys were saying, 'Good luck, Joe,' and others were silent, so you could tell where they stood. Then suddenly, just as we got to the door, you pulled me to one side and said, 'Good luck, kid; this is as far as I go.' I was absolutely stunned. I didn't know what you meant. 'I'm not going in with you,' you said. 'But that's impossible,' I said. 'I need you desperately. You're a jungle fighter. I need your help.' Then you said, 'De Mille will be looking for me.' Remember you said that?"

"I remember."

"'Why should he be looking for you?' I asked. And you said, 'Joe, he's going to use me to kill you.' I didn't know what you meant by that. 'I think De Mille knows,' you said. 'Knows what?' I said. 'I believe he knows,' you said, 'that I'm going to be asked to come to Washington.' 'Is that true?' I asked. 'I believe so,' you said. 'So long. See you later.' Then you gave me a hug and a kiss and walked away."

"Did you understand why I was not going into that meeting?"

"Not completely."

"I didn't tell you I'd once been a Communist?"

"No. All you said was: 'De Mille knows I'm going to be asked to come to Washington.' Later I figured it out."

"I was guessing that De Mille might know something I did not know. It turned out that way, didn't it? He knew all about it."

"Well, yes. When I got in there," Joe went on, "George Seaton comes up to me and says, 'Where's Kazan?' And I said, 'I don't know.' And George said, 'Al Rogell, De Mille's right hand, is asking where he is.' And I said, 'You mean Rogell is looking for Kazan?' And George said, 'Four or five of De Mille's fellows are all over the place, looking for him.' And it was true. De Mille and Rogell and Vernon Keys and—"

"So I guessed right?"

"On the nose. And this I remember vividly: Willy Wyler came up to me and said, 'Why are they looking for Kazan?' I said, 'I don't know.' But I knew that De Mille wanted you spotted and he had some intention with reference to you. Seaton even sent me a note, up on the platform, saying, 'Why is Rogell looking for Kazan?' And I could see Rogell still walking around the auditorium looking for somebody. There was no doubt in my mind by then whom he was looking for. You."

"That's why I didn't go in. What would have happened if I . . . ?"

"If you'd been there and they'd spotted you, you'd have been the star attraction of the Cecil B. De Mille Show."

"Then what happened?"

"Then I read my speech and it was well received, and after a lot of back and forth, De Mille made his mistake. He gets up and says, 'Let me just read the names of those who are Mr. Mankiewicz's champions.' And he begins to read the names of the twenty-five guys on the petition to get an injunction against my recall."

"The one I didn't sign."

"Yes; I was glad that your name wasn't on there. And he reads, 'Mr. Villy Vyler'—that's the way he read all the names."

"Made them German?"

"No, Jews. Yiddish. Villy Vyler. Like that."

"But all those guys were clean."

"Not for De Mille. 'Mr. Fred S-s-s-ini-mon'—you know, sort of hissing the s's. And so on down the list, and suddenly six hundred men in that ballroom began to boo. 'Boo! Boo!' They booed him until he sat down. I didn't say anything. I didn't have to. When De Mille heard those boos, he knew the meeting had turned against him. He was beat."

"Was I mentioned at all?"

"Not a word. But if your name had been on the injunction or if they'd spotted you in the audience or if they hadn't booed De Mille the way they did . . . Those boos saved you."

"What could he have said? I wasn't there."

"Don't kid yourself. He'd have said something like: 'Mr. Kazan's strange absence leads me to believe,' and so on. Or 'Mr. Kazan's not here tonight because he's probably preparing his testimony before the So-and-so Committee' or 'I'm in possession of certain information about our guild brother that—'"

"That was McCarthy's technique."

"Or 'It is alleged in certain quarters . . . ' or 'I happen to know, although I can't reveal my sources, that . . . ' and so on."

"McCarthy's techniques."

"Exactly. Well, I finally stopped the booing, and then Jack Ford got up and he said, 'My name is John Ford. I make westerns.' Everybody laughed, and he went on, 'I don't agree with De Mille. I admire him, but I don't like him.'"

"That sounds like Jack."

"'And I think Joe's been vilified and that he needs an apology.' Then Mamoulian got up and said, 'Mr. De Mille, you were lucky to be born in America. I was over twenty-one before I became a citizen. But I think I'm a better American than you are, Mr. De Mille.' And then Fritz Lang got up—I never thought this would happen, that Nazi bastard—and he said, 'Mr. De Mille, I want you to know that for the first time since I am in America, I am frightened—because I have an accent. You've made me frightened, Mr. De Mille.'"

"Wonderful."

"And Delmer Daves got up and began to say something like: 'How dare you?' then: 'How dare you?' But he was crying with anger or whatever, and he couldn't continue and sat down. Then Willy Wyler—Villy, you know—he said, 'I heard my name before spoken with a certain intonation. The reason I'm sitting in the front row is because I'm deaf in one ear. It got blown out over Berlin in a bombing mission for the air force, and I'm tired of being called a Communist because I'm left-wing or because at one time I belonged to a leftist organization. I want it to be clear that the next man who calls me a Communist or suggests that I am not an American, no matter how important he is or how old, I'm going to kick—' And he stopped because he was sitting next to Ida Lupino, our only woman member at the time, and she said, 'Say it, Willy!' And he did, he finished the sentence, and there was applause which went on and on, seemed like everybody was relieved and approving now, and there was a lot of commotion after that, and the meeting was ours."

"And De Mille?"

"He had nothing more to say, and the fellows on his side didn't dare buck that tide. The meeting ended with Jack Ford saying it was the will of the membership that the whole national board resign and a new one be elected. Next morning I read it in the paper: 'Mankiewicz in Overwhelming Victory,' and in another part of the paper, I read that at Seattle University, half the faculty had been forced to resign. Those were the days; it was like a disease in the country. But we saved the guild that night."

I NEVER got to explain to Joe why the meeting I hadn't attended meant so much to me. It was because I saw that what my guild brothers were defending was the middle road. The men who beat De Mille, an extremist of the right, were not from the left. Many were "reactionaries" like John Farrow or Jack Ford. But all were for the way of fairness and decency. What they were defending was classic Americanism, our basic way of living with each other in this country. And they'd succeeded.

But if part of me believed that forces of good had won a lasting victory, some Old World instinct warned me that despite the guild's triumph, I should now be especially wary, that my enemies were not scattered in defeat but regrouping in the shadows, and that their next show of strength might come from a totally different direction. It was not over; it was beginning.

So when John Steinbeck wrote me that he had a script of *Zapata* ready to read, I finished the film of *Streetcar* as quickly as I could, cut it, scored it, and hurried back to New York. I knew I was in for a fight, and I did have certain doubts. They were about my character. Joe Mankiewicz had called me a "jungle fighter." Jungle fighter, my dimpled Greek ass! My way of survival had been to avoid a conflict and come back when the smoke had cleared. What I admired about my guild brothers was how they'd stood up to De Mille. Nothing he'd said or implied had made them back off. I admired Joe Mank and Jack Ford, George Stevens and "Villy" and all the rest and how they'd behaved. I was proud to be a member of the guild, and I esteemed my profession. A director cannot avoid an issue; he must meet it head-on to do good work. Courage and a gift for swift, direct confrontation are professional requisites in our trade. A crisis was certainly coming.

Steinbeck

A T   T W O   O ' C L O C K one morning in the spring
of 1950, a number of women in their middle years clustered at the side of a
croquet court by a sumptuous house in Palm Springs, California. The court,
as smooth as a billiard table and as green, was brilliantly lit by two rows of
floodlights up high. It was chilly in the night air—spring nights in the
southern California desert are cold and surprisingly damp. The women kept
looking at their jeweled wristwatches and pulling their cashmere sweaters
tighter around their chests and shoulders. They were waiting for the game
to come to an end. They did not speak, having earlier exhausted all subjects
of mutual interest. All of them wanted to be thought loyal to their husbands—the players. That's why they'd waited. However fed up and irritated they might be, they'd made the accommodation of silence. The only
sound was that of heavy wooden balls kissing.

The players—all film producers and directors—were either employees of their host, the short, vigorous man who was the most enthusiastic competitor, or hoped they soon might be, "when the right script comes along." They'd all had more than enough croquet for the night but didn't dare leave the game until the man who was the source of their family's income would declare it concluded. But he, with his great stogie in his mouth, seemed prepared to play until the morning light. He was winning, and when Darryl Zanuck was riding an enthusiasm and winning, he didn't stop.

Two guests, however, were already asleep in their beds, John and Elaine Steinbeck. John and I had been brought to the Springs to confer with Darryl on the script for *Viva Zapata!* If this was an incongruous setting for a conference on the story of a Mexican revolutionist, it hadn't occurred to Darryl. "It's just a big western," he was to say to me later, "*The Scarlet Pimpernel* with a dignified motif!" Darryl had made an awful lot of pictures, and they were categorized in his mind by type.

That evening we'd been Darryl's guests at dinner, along with the men who were to play at croquet and their wives. As we pushed back from the long table, Darryl said to John, "We'll talk tomorrow. Get some sleep." Ten minutes later, he was on the croquet green, setting up the game. John felt he'd been dismissed and was fit to be tied. He threw down another fast Scotch, then marched off to bed with Elaine.

Still on New York time, they were up early the next morning. I got up with them; I was anxious. I sensed that John was getting fed up. Zanuck had treated him like an employee, although I don't believe he knew it, because he treated everyone that way; he didn't have the time or the patience for the ordinary courtesies. I was apprehensive that John might simply pick up and leave, and if he did, I doubted that Darryl would try to restrain him. Not on this story. I was working without compensation—"on spec," as it's called. I was used to that; it's the way I always worked in the theatre until production time. I wanted to make this film, and I was sure that no other producer in the industry would even consider the subject. Darryl had indicated a modest interest when I'd first told him I wanted to make it, but I wasn't sure how secure this interest was. Perhaps his concurrence came from the fact that all the films I'd made for his company had been profitable. But I knew that he'd quickly drop the project if crossed; I was walking a tightrope.

John was working on spec too; novelists are accustomed to that. John had made a policy of never taking an advance from his publishers, feeling that would give them an excuse to crowd him. John did question how genuine Darryl's interest was; I had to reassure him constantly. "Don't forget," I'd say, "he's the guy who made *The Grapes of Wrath.*" Zanuck had assigned one of his assistants to work with John and prepare the script we were there to consider. I didn't think much of what they'd done, but I hadn't said so to either John or Darryl. I wanted to do nothing that might discourage either of them. I could see, as we sat around the swimming pool that morning, drinking coffee and waiting for Zanuck to join us, that John was feeling rebellious. He had a characteristic expression when he was reaching the "fed-up" point, his teeth clenched, cutting edge to cutting edge, his brow furled, one eye drooping, and his voice a rumble impossible to understand. I, on the other hand, was used to waiting for Darryl or for anyone else when I needed to. Anatolians feel what it's expedient to feel—in this case, patience.

Finally we gathered in a corner of the common room to talk story. There was an immediate male competition between our host and Steinbeck. Darryl offered us cigars and I accepted mine, but John held his for an instant, observing that Zanuck had reached into another humidor for his. "I'll have one of those," John said, pointing to the Zanuck special. Darryl gave him one, then began to talk. He had many criticisms of the script, but I fended them off, like a hockey goalie keeping the puck in play, saying things like: "That's interesting, Darryl, we'll certainly work on that," and so on. Zanuck spotted the weaknesses accurately; the problem was in the solutions he offered. He wanted to solve every difficulty then and there, that noon in Palm Springs. He worked on so many scripts, bringing them into shape to shoot, that he was a grab bag of quick suggestions. He had a solution for everything, all of which he offered as if they were inspirations of the moment. The fact was that they were routine devices to move the action forward, threadbare movie clichés. I knew enough about him now to believe that if we could slip past his suggestions, stall him, pretend to be impressed—I'd advised John about this—he wouldn't be surprised by any changes we'd made next time he read the script. He would have forgotten what it was that he'd suggested, since he'd have performed the same service for a dozen other scripts in between.

When John went to the toilet, Darryl said to me, "I know this guy's a great novelist, but he doesn't know how to put a screenplay together. You better get on this with him." I indicated I'd had the same idea and said, "Wait until the next script before you make any decision." He agreed, and the meeting adjourned. I felt lucky that we were leaving Palm Springs without the project breaking down.

Darryl made only one suggestion that he was insistent on. He'd stolen it, no doubt, from an old Warner western, but he offered it as if it were pristine stuff. "Zapata must have a white horse," he said, "and after they shoot him, we should show the horse running free in the mountains—get the idea? A great fade-out." We got the idea, all right. Darryl was innocent about the symbol in his suggestion, but so enthusiastic about the emotion of it that he practically foamed at the mouth. John's face was without expression. Actually, while I thought it corny, the idea worked out well in the end.

John and I went back to New York and worked on the script until May, I sitting at the typewriter, John close by, either whittling or working on a leather pouch to hold his cigarette lighter around his neck. I had worked up a frame of action for the whole script, and I would ask for lines of dialogue from John, which he'd provide one at a time. I'd type, then go on to the next line we needed.

There was one thing that John and I discussed, but not with Darryl. I was determined to shoot the film in Mexico, precisely where its events had taken place. John agreed; he knew the area well and had spent many months nearby. He'd also had a short story, "The Pearl," filmed in Mexico and told me that their crews were the best in the world. They didn't have the divisions into trade departments that our crews in California have; everybody did everything in a Mexican crew. John was also a close friend of the famous Mexican cinematographer Gabriel Figueroa. "Gabby," John said, "is *el presidente* of the Syndicate of Film Technicians and Workers and will be eager to help us." So we decided to head south and talk with Figueroa, look over the land one last time, decide where we'd want to photograph our action, and, when we'd obtained an assurance of the cooperation we needed, inform Darryl of what we'd been up to.

We took rooms in the Hotel Marik in Cuernavaca and, as we'd arranged, met with Figueroa. Gabby and John embraced like revolutionary *compadres* and discussed old friends and alcoholic adventures. Maleness was a cult in that country; who was the most macho? Who could drink the most? We had tequila, then beer, then tequila, then more beer with our enchiladas Suizas, hot peppers calling for cold drink. Afterward we stretched out side by side on the grass, like brothers come together after a long separation. John told Figueroa we wanted to consult him and ask for his help. Gabby's response was overwhelming. "As you know," he said, "I am the president of our Syndicate of Film Technicians. For you, anything you want. *A sus órdenes!*"

But when John said the word "Zapata," Figueroa's face altered. "Yes," John went on, "we propose to make a film about the life of your great hero Zapata." "Emiliano Zapata?" Figueroa asked, as if there were another. Then he looked at me, and his expression was incredulous. "And you, Señor Kazan?" he said, and I felt the hostility. Then he seemed to recover, was affable again, and I thought he was getting over the shock. When he spoke, it was hard to tell precisely what his feelings were. "Of course," he said, "we should have made such a film ourselves a long time ago. He was a great hero of our country. Perhaps the purest. Next to a saint!" "But since you haven't," John said, achieving a perfect Latin shrug, "we thought perhaps . . . The truth is that we want to make it ourselves because we are the greatest admirers of your hero and we propose to make it here, in his own state, Morelos, you understand, precisely in Cuautla, his own village, there in the country of many stones, where it happened, which is the only proper way, no?"

"How no?" Figueroa said. Then he was silent.

I finally spoke—and lied. "And we eagerly want you to do it with us, you as the cameraman I esteem highly." This was not true. His work was full of filtered clouds and peasant madonnas, their heads covered with *rebozos*. There was sure to be a scene in each of his films where fifty of these creatures would be standing in a clump, holding burning candles. How would I prevent such a scene? I'd wondered. I probably could not. And the Marxism would be there nevertheless, that peculiarly romantic Marxism which sentimentalizes the working class and which I no longer believed in. "Yes, we will be very happy working together," I went on. "You mean," he said, "with an American actor"—his expression said "gringo," not "American"— "and a director from Hollywood?" "No," I said, "from New York; my home is in that city." "No one"—John came to my defense—"could be more devoted to this subject than my friend Kazan." "We have a script," I said, "which John wrote. It's in English." "You think I don't read English?" Figueroa said. "I will read it tonight. I will be most eager. Yes, tonight." So I gave it to him and he stood up and John and he embraced like *compadres* again—it reminded me of the embraces between comrades in the Russian films of the twenties. And he left.

The next morning, he called John and said he'd like another day or two, perhaps the weekend, to think it over. It was not a simple issue, he said— John passed all this on to me—in fact, it was a very complex problem. He must make sure that he understood our intentions for the film precisely. Of course, he'd do all he could to help us, but there were difficulties. "What difficulties in particular?" I heard John say. Then he listened for a while. Then he chuckled. Then he laughed. "That's a good idea!" he said. "Why don't you?" Then he listened again and said, "Monday. So we'll hear from you Monday." And hung up.

"What was so funny?" I asked. "I've forgotten how Mexicans are," John said. "Well, what did he say?" I asked. "'On any other subject,' he said, 'there would be no limit to what we could do to help you here. But Emiliano is the hero of every forward-looking patriot here. For instance, imagine if we went to your state of Illinois with a Mexican actor and director and made the story of Abraham Lincoln, what would you think?' That was when I said, 'That's a good idea! Why don't you?' That was when I laughed! Well, I guess all we can do now," John went on, "is have a beer. I like their beer, maybe a couple, no?" "How no?" I said.

So we relaxed, swam in the pool, and drank a good deal, especially John. He fell asleep on the lawn, but I was remembering a number of things, because I thought I recognized what was going on. When John woke, I asked him, "Isn't the Syndicate of Film Technicians and Workers here Communist-dominated?" "You know you're getting obsessed with that subject?" John said. "All right," I said, "I'll lay off. Or maybe I won't, and you'll have to take it. Because something in what's called instinct tells me that there are other people reading our script—at this very moment. That's why he wanted more time. What do you think of that?" John replied with his Latin shrug. "I'm familiar with how these things work," I said.

Then I told him the story of Albert Maltz. "In the year 1930 and up until 1932, I had a good friend at the Yale Drama School; his name was Albert Maltz. In the spirit of that time, we both became members of the Communist Party. I was in the Group Theatre and he was with a theatre closer to the Party line, the Theatre Union. Maltz was an honorable man with an honest heart; I liked him and I respected him. By the time I left the Party, in February of 1935, I'd lost touch with him and even forgotten about him, until the year 1946, when he did something I considered heroic. He wrote an article in the *New Masses*, the Party's magazine, the gist of which was that he'd come to believe that the accepted understanding of what 'revolutionary art' is—a weapon in the class struggle—was not a useful guide for writers on the left but a—and I remember the phrase—a 'straitjacket.' Maltz felt this about his own work and he'd felt it about the work of other 'comrades.' Then he said something that was bold and, in the context of his continuing membership, even foolhardy. 'It has become necessary for me to repudiate that idea and abandon it,' he declared."

John still didn't understand my point. "There are other people reading our script," I said, "believe me. And some consultations too." "What's all that got to do with Maltz?" John asked. "Albert's statements in the *Masses* gave hope to many artists in the left movement," I went on. "Even though I was out of the Party by then, I still considered myself of the left, and I thought what Albert had written was the truest thing I'd ever read about literature from any comrade and a kind of liberation for so many writers. I believed fine things would now come from Maltz and from others, who'd been heartened by his challenge to the old laws of the Party. But what happened was not that at all. Party leaders arrived in California from New York to reeducate Maltz and straighten him out. There were many ideological meetings, kangaroo courts, as it were, to persuade him to recant, then to demand it. And he did. He took it all back. Later, I believe, he made a trip to Europe, one *they'd* suggested, to 'clear his mind.'"

"Aren't there people reading our script in California and criticizing it to Zanuck?" John asked. "Sure," I said, "but we don't have to do what they say. Only what Zanuck says." "Is that better?" John asked. "I prefer it," I said, "for the simple reason that Darryl is geared to company profits." "You may regret that expression of choice," John said.

I stuck to the subject. "There was another such case," I said, "concerning a writer named Budd Schulberg and his novel *What Makes Sammy Run?* His comrades in California thought the book anti-Semitic, and again there were many meetings behind the scenes, with Schulberg. John Howard Lawson was the point man in that attack. He demanded that Budd rewrite his book according to a schedule of changes he gave Schulberg. But Schulberg was not Maltz, and he had the courage to refuse. The pressure on him was just as heavy; it even extended to his wife and to the man who was his closest friend. When Budd didn't yield, this fellow, a college classmate, didn't speak to him for years. But Schulberg held fast; he resigned from the Party.

"So you see," I continued, "I'm a veteran of these wars and I recognize what's happening now. Figueroa needed the time not to formulate what he thought—he knew straight off: 'Gringo, keep off our soil!'—but to consult his comrades and make sure he'd thought correct. 'Correct!' There's the word I hate. I don't think we're going to get any help from anyone here." John shrugged. "You're getting all wound up on that subject," he said again. "If it isn't the right, it's the left," I said. "They're coming at me from both sides!"

Monday, Figueroa came by, and with him was another man—Mexican, of course—dressed, it seemed, so as not to attract attention. Four *cervezas* were brought, then Gabby spoke. He said our script was impossible in its present form and that he wanted to tell his *compadre* Steinbeck what was wrong with it. He'd studied it with the greatest care; no, it was not hopeless; yes, he'd be glad to help us, but no, the script in its present form . . . And so on and so on. I knew damned well since he was so sure of his position that it was now the official position. I looked toward the other man; he nursed his beer in silence. Gabby looked at him. He shook his head and didn't speak. Then Figueroa said again that he'd be glad to help us with the story and proceeded to tell us how the story should go and particularly what the figure of Zapata should represent. That was where I stopped listening to his words—English and Spanish mixed; John understood both—but listened to the tone of his voice instead, and that was a familiar tone. I'd heard it years before on Twelfth Street in Comrade Jerome's office and from others in the Party, and I knew what we were up against. They were going to tell us how our story should be rewritten to suit them. We'd run into a stone wall. When Gabby stopped to draw a breath, I turned to the man he'd brought with him. "Your opinion is the same as Señor Figueroa's," I said, a statement, not a question. He responded with what I felt sure was their prepared position. "We'd be proud to have you make a film in Mexico, Señor Kazan. We know your work. But on this"—he indicated the manuscript, which he had read, just as I'd anticipated—"no."

I didn't offer to shake hands with Figueroa when he left.

After he'd gone, John and I talked. Figueroa had suggested that after we made certain changes, we should send our "corrected" script to the official government censor. John had said we would do that. Now he proposed that we prepare a script precisely for this purpose. He said we shouldn't give up. Shooting the movie in Mexico, in real surroundings, meant everything to us both, and we should hold on tight. John also introduced me to a magic word. In a sort of singsong, he said, *"Mordida, mordida."* "What does that mean?" I asked. "It means you don't understand Mexicans, so never take their first position as their final position. Even when they're Communists, they're Mexicans first." "And the word you said—what is that?" "*Mordida!* Bribe." Then he explained that based on his previous experience, making *The Pearl,* he believed that everybody in Mexico up to the president himself could be bought, and who depended on how much gringo gold you had to spend. Fox had a lot, he said, and the next step was to get a Mexican producer to work with us, somebody who knew the channels of influence and what everyone's price was and where to parcel out Fox's money. John knew just the man for us, a Señor Dancigars, who'd produced *The Pearl.* "I think he is a refugee from Germany, with all the cunning a refugee has had to acquire in order to survive. He's the man we need, a master of the *mordida.*"

So we decided to prepare a partially "corrected" script for Mexican consumption, and John would write to Dancigars. We heard back from him, promptly. He said he'd be honored to help us and even to involve himself with us if we cared to invite him in. "Please send script pronto." Which, a few weeks later, we did.

O N T H E eighth of January, 1951, I wired Darryl from New York: "Arriving Monday. Will bring with me original screenplay by Arthur Miller that I want to do immediately. You will get first crack. Regards." I also wired Abe Lastfogel: "Arthur Miller and I will arrive Monday on the Super Chief. Will bring re-written Miller script, ready to go. I want to do it immediately. Give Zanuck first crack, but doubt he'll do it. If he doesn't, I will move quickly in the direction you choose. This is the big push. Affectionately."

Neither telegram reflected my true feelings. Arthur believed it was impossible that anyone in California would want to do his screenplay. I felt Art had done a half-ass job finishing the script, that it was not "ready to go" and would require considerably more work. But I was determined to do it next and was convinced that if we could set up a production and if Art and I could work together for a few weeks, we'd have a good screenplay. The first thing we did was meet with Abe Lastfogel and Lew Wasserman, our agents. I noticed that both men were demonstrating more affection to me than in the past. My conclusion was that the word was out on *Streetcar,* and that once certain Breen Office "code" problems were settled, it was sure to be a great success. This gave Art and me power with *The Hook.*

Art was encouraged in a rather tentative way by the warmth of our reception. But he was really not himself. Of course, he never was, not the self that the world of show business had fastened in front of him like the paper garments that are fastened by tabs to the cutout doll figures in children's scissors games. At this time, a psychoanalysis Art was undergoing had him on edge; he was distraught and ill. The worst of it was that he was unable to write. He was longing for something nameless, a condition I recognized from my own life. What did he want? It was not complicated: Call it fun, a new experience, ease of mind and heart, relief from criticism, happiness. His life, he told me, seemed to be all conflict and tension, thwarted desires, stymied impulses, bewildering but unexpressed conflicts. "What a waste!" he cried one day on the train, referring to the devastating result of tensions in his friends—and of course meaning himself. Above all, he had sex on his mind, constantly. He was starved for sexual release.

I felt sorry for him, and determined that as soon as I settled in, I would get him a date. There was no good reason why Art should not have been happy, especially after the enormous success of *Death of a Salesman*. He was self-crippled. Everyone invents his own reasons to explain why he is miserable, but Art was still in the dark. The result was thinly covered, undirected anger, released after he'd had a couple of drinks and to be found even in his jokes. Art meant his jokes, and at this time they were full of hostility. As I watched him now, I felt sorry for his wife. It's the terrible fate of wives, I thought, to be helpless in a situation like this one. Art was on the verge of something disruptive, and Mary could only wait and prepare to apply moral sanctions when the inevitable happened.

It appeared that I still had censorship, preview, and length problems with the film of *Streetcar*, which I'd considered finished. When Charlie Feldman, my producer, offered to put me up at his house, I accepted, even though I recognized his offer of hospitality as a tactic to soften me to his will in the issues we had to settle. His home was tastefully furnished and had a heated swimming pool, and the bedroom Charlie offered me had a separate entrance to the street.

In the next weeks, I had a fascinating time observing my producer and through him the men in this community. Charlie was exceptionally well dressed—he bought his ties by half-dozen lots of each color or design— and rather handsome in a soft, yielding way, his body suited to bed and armchair. He ran a successful agency, and this gave him prestige in the community and power over young actresses. Still he was full of complaints about his love life—if you can call it that. "Now it's Uncle Charlie," he griped, referring to the response young women were increasingly giving him. "I say, 'How about me?' and they laugh. There just aren't any real women anymore. High school girls!" He would spend long hours on the telephone, holding a little black book in his hand, trying number after number. I remember a scene in the "game room" late one afternoon, when three men of recognized glamour, Pat De Cicco, Raoul Hakim, and Charlie, all constant presences in gossip columns that celebrated their successes with women, each with a telephone and each with his little black book, were calling girls one after another, razzing the ones who wouldn't or couldn't and razzing the ones who did accept. Either way, the frequent response as they hung up was: "Why do I bother?"

Often Charlie would have a date, and they were quite pretty girls, usually recent arrivals in the community. Charlie would ask them to come to his house in their own cars, so he wouldn't have to drive them home later, and they'd go out together to Romanoff's or Chasen's, always one or the other, and when they came back I had to assume they went into Charlie's bedroom. The next morning I'd say to my host at breakfast, "How was she, Charlie?" And his answer was invariably one word: "Nothing." He once had taken out Greta Garbo; he dropped this to me one day, and of course I asked him, "How was she, Charlie?" "Nothing," he said. "Nothing!" And he shrugged. I couldn't imagine what the hell he was used to, and I never heard him take any responsibility for his sexual partners' lack of ardor. It didn't occur to him that the fault might be his. On the other hand, as an admirer of Miss Garbo's genius, I had to face the possibility that one night, for a few hours, she'd desired Charlie Feldman; I must say this upset me.

It was at Charlie's that I heard that Johnny Hyde had died a few weeks before. Charlie said that Johnny's girl was now on the loose, and she was a knockout. All girls were more attractive to these men before they made it with them. He hadn't succeeded in getting into her yet, he said, but he would: "It shouldn't be a problem." The men around Charlie considered Marilyn Monroe a kid to pass around and someone now available. They said even Johnny Hyde had referred to her as a "chump." But apparently she'd been true to Johnny and was now completely broken up by his death. The tribal report had been confirmed: No one had scored there yet. She hadn't even gone out with anyone, which puzzled these men. Lasting grief was not a normal emotion in that community. I was alone nights now and would be for some weeks, so I wondered if I shouldn't look the girl up; less lechery than curiosity. She'd sat at Johnny Hyde's side, the night when I'd seen her, like a frozen image. Why had she been so devoted to him? What was the story there?

One afternoon I was summoned by Darryl; he'd read *The Hook*. Lastfogel, of course, drove me out to the studio. I was a director in the rank of "true creator" at this time, so wherever I went I was protected by a top agent. Zanuck was brief and plain; he "passed" on Miller's script—"subject matter," he said—but was keen on *Zapata* and demanded to know where the script was. I promised it would be in his hands very soon, then Lastfogel and I left. I suggested to Abe that he give *The Hook* to Warner Brothers; it was more their kind of project. He agreed, said he had to drive there now, did I want to go with him and say hello to Jack Warner? I said I'd decided to pay a few calls on the Fox lot.

The man I called on was my former cutter Harmon Jones, who'd achieved his ambition: He'd been given a film to direct. The script, *As Young as You Feel*, was by Paddy Chayevsky, and in the cast were Monty Woolley, Jean Peters, and David Wayne. I congratulated Harmon, then chatted with him while the crew was lighting his next setup. When that was done, the assistant director called for the actors, and I heard her name: "Marilyn!" Then, in a tone less patient: "Marilyn!" No response. "That girl drives me nuts," Harmon said. "What's the matter with her?" I asked. "She can't stop crying. All right, the man who was keeping her died, but that was three weeks ago. Every time I need her, she's in the next stage, crying. It puffs up her eyes!"

They finally got her to work and I watched the scene and she certainly wasn't star material. When Harmon said "Print!" and began lining up the next shot, she disappeared again and I followed her into the adjoining sound stage and found her in a dark corner of a large, empty office setting. She was crying; I could hear her as I approached. I told her I'd been a friend of Johnny's, in fact a client, and had liked him very much, and I'd just heard about his death. She didn't respond, but turned her head away. I sat there with her, not saying a word until she was called to go to work again. Then I followed her and after the next take asked Harmon to introduce us. I thought I'd skip the in-betweens and asked her to have dinner with me. "I wouldn't say a word," I said, "just be with you, then take you home." She refused, but this time she looked at me. I decided to give it some time, and went to the cafeteria where I used to eat with Bud Lighton. There she came up to me, looking sad, and said, "Thanks," and I said, "What for?" She shook her head and seemed to be about to cry again. At this I asked her again to have dinner with me, and she accepted. I'd supposed that she'd heard from Jones that I was a Big Director. Later I found out that what changed her mind was the way I'd sat next to her in the dark and not spoken. I had a kind face, she said.

Relieve your mind now of the images you have of this person. When I met her, she was a simple, eager young woman who rode a bike to the classes she was taking, a decent-hearted kid whom Hollywood brought down, legs parted. She had a thin skin and a soul that hungered for acceptance by people she might look up to. Like many girls out of that kind of experience, she sought her self-respect through the men she was able to attract. Johnny Hyde had been, at least for the time, perfect protection.

People talk of the technique of seduction as if it's an art. In my experience it consisted of listening, paying attention, affording true sympathy, and letting some time pass; that is to say, being human and not pressing. All young actresses in that time and place were thought of as prey, to be overwhelmed and topped by the male. A genuine interest, which I did have, would produce results. I'm still surprised at how quickly women will empty the most intimate secrets of their lives into a sympathetic ear. I was good at listening, and the stories she told me, with neither malice nor regret, were amazing.

She'd married Jim, her first husband, so that she wouldn't have to go back to the orphanage where she'd been put after the dissolution of her parents' home. She was sixteen. She didn't like "anything Jim did to me—

except when he kissed me here" (she touched her breasts). After he was finished, Jim would fall asleep, leaving her awake and unsatisfied. She remembered taking long walks at night along the tracks where they lived in Sawtelle. A lover found her available. Fred was a musician, scrawny but able in love. She came as many as three times with him in one go. He was vulgar and coarse and scornful with her. He said she was no good for anything except fucking. He found her dress "cheap." He told her her breasts were too big. He didn't like to sleep in the same bed with her. He thought her beneath conversation, said she was stupid and only good for one thing, which he didn't regard too highly. He boasted that he never had to make a pass at a woman—they all came after him.

In those days, she said, she used to be prepared all the time. That was her word, "prepared." She'd sit in a chair, and when she got up there'd be a little mark on the back of her dress. "It was embarrassing," she said, so she went to a doctor, and he said, "You have too much of that particular thing," so he gave her a shot, "and now I'm not ready all the time."

Somehow she came to the attention of a big Hollywood talent agent, Johnny Hyde. By the time he met Marilyn, he was "older than my father—wherever he was." Johnny wooed her a year before she "went" with him. He got her entirely by being kind and defending her, talking to her openly about his intimate life and listening to her stories about hers. But above all because she felt he really needed her.

When she left Fred for Johnny, Fred became frantic, and his attitude changed completely. He begged Marilyn to marry him. When she refused, he would visit her at night—after she'd come home from Johnny's house—pound on her door until she let him in. Then he'd abuse Johnny to her, calling him a wrinkled old man and—scornfully—an agent. But he began to suffer so much that his mother came to see Marilyn, begging her to marry her son. Marilyn said she liked the old lady, but she didn't go back to Fred.

I asked her if she was attracted to men who abused her; when Freddie stopped being mean to her, was she no longer attracted? I asked her if she respected men who were scornful of her because their estimate coincided with her own. "I don't know," she said.

She said Johnny had the body of a young man but a small penis. Nevertheless—it seemed—his life was built around his conquests and on his knowledge of "love" Hollywood style. He prided himself above all on the girls he'd had and subtly let everyone know about his famous successes. His small penis was a symbol of his anxiety, and his whole life was spent laying that anxiety to rest. Marilyn on his arm at Chasen's or Romanoff's did that.

The last thing he asked of Marilyn before he died, the last thing he wanted to hear from her, was that she loved him. She'd said it, but Johnny knew there was a reservation. Toward the end of his life, he got so desperate that he begged her to marry him. Marilyn wouldn't. The more he begged her, the less she loved him in the way he wished. Johnny wanted to have intercourse every night. He had a heart "condition," and before he made love he would take a pill. Marilyn knew what it was for—one of the main arteries from his heart was defective or blocked.

As he continued to press her, ever more frantically, told her she meant more to him than anything in the world, she would respond by telling him that she did love him, but—that girlish distinction—she was not in love with him. This was attacking him where he was most vulnerable. But the evidence that she was not in love with him was there: She wasn't "coming." She felt his disappointment when she didn't respond totally, and not wanting to hurt him more, she'd try hard to "come." Of course, the harder she'd try . . . Nothing happened. The girlish distinction she'd made was true. He used to say to Marilyn—who was violent in love—that he had trouble holding on to her when they did it. "You need good strong hands for that," he'd say. "Look at my hands, how small they are." Of course, this intensified his anxiety. Inevitably she began to avoid meeting him. This would make him furious, but he would always follow fits of rage by begging her to marry him.

Just before he died, feeling that he was going soon and hadn't really "been in there" enough, he made his last plea that she marry him. When Marilyn refused him again, he told her he didn't want to see her anymore. Perhaps he needed to end up on top somehow. He told her she'd "fall on her ass like all the others." "You're not an expert, baby," he told her, "so don't try to get by on your fucking. Take it from me, I know. I've had experts." The next day she called him up. Brusquely he asked, "Why are you calling me?" She answered, "Because I'm unhappy when you're hurt, Johnny." She went to see him and he melted. Again he begged her and finally became so desperate, felt he'd lost so much face in the community because of her refusals, that he pleaded that she let him say they were going to be married, even if they weren't. She said no.

The scorn these men have for women is total! Marilyn knew that. Johnny used to refer to all girls as tramps, near tramps, and pushovers. But mostly he called them—including Marilyn—chumps. At a nightclub once, when they were watching some black entertainers, Johnny said to her, "You have a behind like a nigger." She didn't like this, didn't respond then but didn't forget it. One day during his last illness, when he was being scornful of her, she suddenly came out with: "Johnny, I never told you, but I have colored blood." She stuck with this feeble lie until Johnny, by God, believed it and accepted it. He loved her more than ever then. He never loved any woman like he loved her, he'd say, she meant more to him than any living soul, he'd say. But when he died, in his estate of $600,000 there was not one cent for her. When she was alone again, the only things she had that he'd bought her were six bath towels, six sheets, and three pillowcases.

When I first knew her, after Johnny's death, she was being courted by

Joe Schenck. He hadn't moved in as quickly as I—he'd allowed a "decent interval" to pass—but soon he was trying to see her regularly. Mr. Schenck was one of the richest as well as the most respected men in the "Hollywood" community, especially honored for having gone to jail for bribing an officer of the International Alliance of Theatrical and Stage Employees, to prevent a strike in the industry. She told me about the night when Schenck had taken her dancing and asked her to marry him. Mr. Schenck was then seventy-one years old, had at least fifteen million dollars (a lot more money than now), and had had his first cerebral hemorrhage. He was a pretty good dancer for an old man, she told me, and as they moved around the floor, he suggested that they fly to Las Vegas right then and "get spliced." "Every night you'd be right here in my arms," he said. Later he took her to his home and showed her a large, expensively decorated room that would be hers anytime she wanted. But he didn't make a pass at her. Then he gave her some paternal advice. "Don't be a scalp in some man's belt," he said, "don't be a cuspidor, don't be an ashcan." Again and again he told her his age, that he was not long for this world and his widow would be "fixed" with millions. Marilyn got the suggestion, but she didn't respond; then Joe Schenck made his final appeal. "I'm seventy-one," he said. "I know I'm a man of limited powers. But you'll find that I'm understanding. If my wife feels she must go with other men, I'll understand. But only so long as it's not the same man twice in a row." This did not appeal to Marilyn, who was a romantic. She was very touched by Joe's offer, but the fact was that he had nothing but the money with which to try to buy his happiness at the end. A few nights later, she gave him her answer. I wondered about the women who had watched Darryl's croquet game. Might not some of them have been tempted? In that culture, it seemed to me, Marilyn was the pure in heart.

The girl had little education and no knowledge except the knowledge of her own experience; of that she had a great deal, and for an actor, that is the important kind of knowledge. For her, I found, everything was either completely meaningless or completely personal. She had no interest in abstract, formal, or impersonal concepts but was passionately devoted to her own life's experiences. What she needed above all was to have her sense of worth affirmed. Born out of wedlock, abandoned by her parents, kicked around, scorned by the men she'd been with until Johnny, she wanted more than anything else approval from men she could respect. Comparing her with many of the wives I got to know in that community, I thought her the honest one, them the "chumps." But there was a fatal contradiction in Marilyn. She deeply wanted reassurance of her worth, yet she respected the men who scorned her, because their estimate of her was her own.

When I began seeing her, she had a tiny apartment near that of her drama coach, who was giving her lessons "on the cuff." Her place had a large room, empty except for a white concert piano. I never heard her play

it, but this large instrument meant something special to her. When she moved to a place where there was no space for it, she'd have it carefully stored. Who'd given her the piano? I never found out. I saw her frequently at Charlie Feldman's house, and we'd stay together until the morning light and I'd listen to her stories. Sometimes she'd weep. I gave her comfort. She had a bomb inside her. Ignite her and she exploded. Her lover was her savior. At dawn, morning after morning, I'd put on one of Charlie's white terry-cloth robes and drive her home. She often wore white. I'd put the top of my convertible down and we'd drive through the empty streets and boulevards, two "mad monks," singing and laughing. She told me Johnny used to send her home in a taxi.

One night Charlie Feldman gave a party for Arthur Miller, who'd won the Pulitzer Prize and was a celebrity now. Art had been having a doleful time. Warners had refused *The Hook*, Abe Lastfogel had taken it to Columbia, and we were waiting for Harry Cohn's decision. We'd worked on the script, but we couldn't go at the job eagerly until we had some practical interest. I'd promised to take Marilyn to Charlie's party, but I'd also made a date that night with an actress Darryl was urging me to consider for *Zapata*. Again, curiosity, not lechery; she was attached to Howard Hughes, and I'd often wondered how his "girls" carried on and what they thought of him. So I asked Art to cover for me with Marilyn.

When he called to tell her he'd pick her up, she said she'd come in a taxi and meet us, him and me, at Feldman's. Art wouldn't allow this; no, he'd come and pick her up. Again she demurred, said not to worry, she was used to that. But Art insisted, and the first thing that impressed Marilyn about her future husband was that he refused to let her come to a party in a taxi. How little these glamour girls expect of life, I thought.

So I went first to the closing party of Harmon Jones's picture, in which Darryl's candidate had been performing, and danced with her. We both got high, and she asked me to drive her to her car, which was parked down one of the boulevards. We stopped by a bar, had another drink, went on to her car, parked directly behind it, and got to know each other for half an hour or so. Then she seemed to be reminded of something and suddenly ran out of my car, into hers, and drove off. And I drove to Charlie's.

When I arrived, I could see that need had met need and the lovely light of desire was in their eyes. I watched them dance; Art was a good dancer. And how happy she was in his arms! Not only was he tall and handsome in a Lincolnesque way, but he was a Pulitzer Prize playwright. All her doubts about her worth were being satisfied in one package. The party thinned out and the three of us sat on a sofa, and if my memory is correct, I did the decent thing, said I was awfully tired and would Art take her home. Marilyn glowed. I don't know what happened later that night, but Marilyn, without going into specifics, said that Art was shy and this pleased her too after all the mauling she'd taken. She also said that Art was terribly unhappy in his home life. She'd certainly opened him up.

For the next days, those before Art suddenly returned to New York, Marilyn was our "mascot," and we involved her as a passionate spectator at all our dealings on *The Hook*. I was still seeing her at night from time to time, but she had a violent crush on Arthur and couldn't talk about much else. He was also stuck on her, and I believed the time was coming for me to gallantly step aside. But I wasn't sure how much time Art was making with her. He was not an aggressive man in this area. Marilyn had stars in her eyes when she talked about him, but they were the stars of romance. We were essentially a threesome, and there was fun of various kinds for all of us.

M R. H A R R Y C O H N , president of Columbia Pictures, was a bully; that is how he ran his studio. He'd given orders that he be informed every morning when the first shot of each production was in the can. He was also suspected of having wired the offices of the producers on his lot so he'd know what was going on. He'd indicated to Lastfogel a willingness to produce *The Hook* if it could be "brought in for a price." The first day I met with him, I asked what he thought of Miller's script. "Burn it!" he said. "Throw it in the ashcan!" Then why did he want to do it? Because of my absurd reputation, which was never to be as mythic again. He told me this as a way of putting me on the spot. He said to me one day, "You're a bit of a whore, you know. You want us to gamble on this picture, but you won't." To call his bluff, I offered to do the picture for nothing "up front" and twenty-five percent of the profits. He agreed. But it was all macho talk. We both knew that my agent would not stand for it.

I was playful and bold in those days, and Harry amused me rather than terrified me. I once took our "mascot" into Harry's office, dressed severely as a secretary. It was the day when Harry proposed to tell me what was wrong with Art's script. I introduced her as my personal secretary and said I'd brought her so I'd have a precise record of every one of his objections. Marilyn was at that time a contract player at that very studio, getting seventy-five dollars a week for playing bits. I wanted to prove to Harry that he didn't even know whom he had under contract. Marilyn sat in a corner, wearing large horn-rimmed glasses, pad on her knee, pencil poised, ready to write down what Harry said. "Did you get that exactly, Miss Bauer?" I'd say. "Yes, Mr. Kazan," she'd answer. Cohn kept looking at her; something about her appearance puzzled him. Why did he think he knew her? But Marilyn pulled it off, and she walked out undetected. The next day I asked Cohn how the hell he was able to run his business when he didn't even know whom he had under contract. Cohn was not embarrassed. Marilyn was known thereafter to Art and me as Miss Bauer.

I didn't let up on Cohn, had a crazy actor friend go into Jerry Wald's office at Columbia and fire a pistol—blank cartridge—which turned the whole studio upside down. Cops were running everywhere; Jerry was under his desk. I was found out in time, but Harry had trouble getting angry with me, seemed to like me better after every such escapade. The climax came when he invited me to his personal projection room one night to see a film he'd just produced. I arrived in the company of another young lady, an actress I knew, who had the manner and the air of a demure virgin. I introduced her to Harry as the best friend of my young daughter and asked Harry to kindly refrain from using off-color language in her presence. We sat down directly in front of him and, once the film was rolling, began to neck and embrace more and more violently, until we fell on the floor. We rose to our feet, made our apologies, but were soon at it again. Finally Harry was roaring, and I led the young lady out of the projection room. Those were the days! Harry liked me so much that he invited me to stay at his home, and later, during the time I was putting the last touches on *On the Waterfront*, I did.

S U D D E N L Y we were being warned that we—and *The Hook*—were in danger of being attacked. Politically. I'd begun to have the feeling I used to have in the Communist Party: that there were secret meetings going on about me to which I hadn't been invited. It was at this time that there appeared on the scene of the film capital a new phenomenon—the political go-between or "fixer," who specialized in guiding those in trouble of this kind through the danger zones and seeing to it that they were "cleared." Although ostensibly little more than advisers—they so represented themselves—in fact the fixers had some kind of ill-defined power. They became important, were sought after and courted.

One day Harry Cohn informed us that there was danger cooking for our film, and since this was serious, he'd arranged for a meeting with a man named Roy Brewer, who was the head of the International Alliance of Theatrical and Stage Employees, the men who, in the theatre, go by a simpler name: stagehands. Since it was an important meeting, Harry himself would be present and participate in the discussion. Art and I appeared in answer to what amounted to a summons. Brewer, a muscular man gone plump, was a veteran of the labor movement in New York and in California; his "Alliance" was a member of the American Federation of Labor. Cohn made sure we understood the man's importance before we went into the meeting; Brewer had the respect, even the deference, of the studio heads. Harry restrained his bumptious side that day; his role was mediator.

Roy Brewer came to the meeting confident of his power—given him by his superiors in the labor movement. Since this power was being challenged it had become ferocious and ruthless, but you wouldn't know it from Roy's modest and seemingly reasonable tone of voice. His concern was not Miller or me; we were disposable. What he wanted was to win Harry Cohn. Cohn, the most practical and hard-fisted of all the studio heads, saw immediately that his bank balance was being threatened—which is why he was nicer than necessary to Roy. Brewer wanted to walk away from that conference leaving me behind, thoroughly deflated, Miller exposed for whatever Brewer thought he was, and Cohn on his side!

"Roy feels the narrator is not given enough to say," Harry said to Miller and me once we'd sat down together. "Perhaps a foreword would take care of it." Brewer joined in: "I think it would help to have a foreword." I quickly agreed to this. Forewords are inevitably cut out of the final film, and if by any chance they're retained, no one reads them. As far as I was concerned, Roy could have any kind of foreword at any length he wanted.

Then he got down to business. "Have you thought of anything," he asked us, "for the anti-Communist gimmick?" Neither Miller nor I answered him immediately, so Brewer went on. "As a suggestion, why couldn't we have a reporter from the *People's Worker* approach Marty [the central figure in *The Hook,* a longshoreman] and ask him for his support? Marty could say, 'We don't want any Commie sheets around here.'" Brewer stopped, looked at us, and waited.

Harry Cohn was studying Miller.

Art responded that we could try to get that in some way. Brewer noticed the lack of enthusiasm in Miller's voice. "You don't want to give the impression that your picture is a plea for the support of Bridges, do you?"

Harry Bridges, president of the International Longshoremen, was a man we admired.

"You should show in the strongest way you can," Brewer went on, "that Marty does not represent the so-called progressives. The great problem in the unions is the Communist. The racketeers are much less a menace to labor than the Communists."

Miller volunteered that we'd show that we were correcting our social evils in the American way, by the technique of democracy. This didn't satisfy Brewer. "Have a guy come in from the *People's Worker,*" he urged, "and try to tie up with Marty and his gang. Marty could say"—and Brewer's voice dropped dramatically—"'Nothing doing! We don't want anything to do with a Commie sheet.' That would be a real way of showing he is not a Commie, because a Commie would say he is not a Commie, he'd lie about that, but he'd never disavow an official Communist paper. It's very important that you do this." I looked at Art, waiting for his response. There was none; he looked as if he was thinking.

Then there was an interval during which less important points were brought up and solved. We found ourselves trying to please Brewer and didn't like that. Suddenly he reverted to: "Have you made up your mind on the *People's Worker*?" "Art said he'd work it in some way," I replied, putting off discussion on this until Art and I had talked. We all knew there'd been a near confrontation and that we were evading it.

The discussion was continuing on small points concerning safety provisions for longshoremen and so on, when suddenly Harry Cohn stood up and cut through the baloney. He said he had to get back to his office, then turned to Brewer and asked, "How do you think we stand on this, Roy?" Brewer answered cautiously. "There is a certain amount of danger doing a picture of this particular type at this particular time," he said, an answer that did not satisfy Cohn. "Do you mean," he asked Brewer, "unless the changes you brought up are made?" To which Brewer gave an answer even less satisfying: "Even with the changes, there is still a certain amount of danger doing this film at this time. However, Harry, if you have a commitment to do it, perhaps we've done as much as we can to make it acceptable." Which was a totally unsatisfactory answer to Harry Cohn; he waited for more from Brewer, who said, "Before I give you a definite answer, Harry, I want to talk to my boss [the president of the American Federation of Labor, which Art and I considered a highly conservative organization], because he will know the answer." Then he looked at Miller, and there was a challenge in his manner and his voice. "If you plan to make the picture, make it." Which is a statement open to more than one interpretation.

As we left the meeting, Art and I didn't know if we had an agreement or not. I wondered about Cohn's reaction. It had been a dreadful scene. A man we'd never met, who had nothing to do with the artistic values of our script, seemed to believe he had the power to decide whether or not we could go ahead with the film. We felt humiliated, so much so that we couldn't discuss the problem. We told our secretary, Miss Bauer, only the bare facts.

The next day, Art suddenly left California and went back east.

But I found that the budget meeting remained as scheduled, which meant that Harry Cohn and his studio were going ahead with *The Hook*. Quickly I planned my positions on costs—where I'd yield, where stand firm. My tactic was one familiar to directors who make films off the common path: to get the work rolling, involve actors contractually, build sets, collect props and costumes, expose negative, and so get the studio in deep. Once money in some significant amount had been spent, it would be difficult for

Harry to do anything except scream and holler. If he suspended a film that had been shooting for a few weeks, he'd be in for an irretrievable loss, not only of money but of "face." The thing to do was get the film going.

Meantime, Art had to solve the problem of Roy Brewer. I felt nervous about Art. Before his abrupt departure, he hadn't said anything. What had he thought of the meeting? I didn't know. What was his plan?

But I got an encouraging letter from him, and enclosed were some pages of script revisions. He'd been working on our problem but didn't say too much about it, because almost immediately he switched off *The Hook* and was going on in the most rapturous tone about certain feelings he'd been having, awake and asleep, dreams of longing. Marilyn had sent him a cleverly worded telegram, presumably from Harry Cohn's secretary, urging him to get his revisions done and get back out there. Her wire had done more than anything I could have to get him working on the problem we had with Brewer. Only at the end of the letter did he get back to that; he said he was looking for a way to solve the "red thing."

I reread his letter for the overtones. Some of it was written in a kind of brotherly code, telling me about his situation at home, which was worse, and how, nevertheless, he felt extra fine and had been thinking joyous thoughts. There was something jaunty about this letter that I'd never found in anything else Art had written. He was a young man again, in the grip of a first love, which was—happily—carrying him out of control. He didn't read like the constricted man I'd known. I remembered the lovely light of lechery in his eyes as he was dancing with Marilyn in Charlie Feldman's softly lit living room. I hadn't known he had it in him, that light in his eyes. I'd really done something for my friend, something he could not have done for himself. He asked me to look at her once more for him, and he asked me for her address; he needed to write her.

I felt very affectionate toward Art after that letter, grateful that he was ready to continue work on the revisions we needed but especially sympathetic with his turbulent feelings. He was in trouble, the kind of trouble we should all be in once or twice or three times in our lives. I felt more devoted than ever to our project; it bound us together. Goddamn it, we'd do that picture and do it right! I could now go into the coming budget meeting with confidence—and a tactic that I would make work.

I've kept the multipage big-studio form for our budget meeting. It's only partly filled out. The meeting was going along well enough, until it was suddenly interrupted by the entrance of a secretary to tell me that I had a call from New York. "Somebody must have died," I said to myself as I went to the phone. I was right. Our project had died. It was Art on the wire. He said he couldn't talk at length but would write me, the point being that he'd decided to "withdraw" *The Hook.* I was too shocked to ask questions, and he was too nervous to answer them. It was the collapse of a huge edifice of hope for me. Past disappointment, I was sick at heart. I crawled back to the budget meeting, sat down with the head of production and his staff, and coughed up the news.

Then I went to see Harry Cohn, a man who didn't live in doubt. "I knew it," he said. "Miller is a Communist." I protested that I didn't think so. Cohn said, "Then tell me what other explanation there could be for what he did. First, he can't face any more questions. Second, he sees that the movie will not say what he hoped it would say. It all figures." I told him I didn't agree. "I could tell just by looking at him," Cohn said. "He's still one of them." "What about me?" I said. "You're just a goodhearted whore like me," he said. "We'll find something else to do together."

Later I went to see Abe Lastfogel. He was busy, so I had to sit in a car with him and tell him the news while we drove to his next date. Abe said he wasn't surprised; he'd never liked Art. "Obviously," he said, "Miller doesn't have the intestinal fortitude to face the fight that would come up." "Harry Cohn thinks," I said, "that Art isn't in a position to fight." "Perhaps," he said, then: "Forget about it. What's next?"

I couldn't help comparing what had happened to what had taken place in Mexico with Figueroa. Art had allowed himself time to reconsider the situation. What was his complete turnaround due to? Whom might he have consulted? Mary? He must have talked it over with Mary. Anyone else? Possibly. Who?

Sometime later, Mary and he were reconciled; when he wrote his next play, he dedicated it to her.

I forced myself to keep working on the script, thinking I might still persuade Art to pick up and go on. Then I had a telegram from him, declaring that he was sick about it, but in the light of what was happening in the country he was convinced that we'd have no way of defending ourselves, and that there had been inquiries launched by Roy Brewer about him and about me. Art spoke of certain evil men who'd gone on the attack because of Roy. He said he didn't believe that anything we had or could decently agree to would protect us or our project.

The Hook was dead. It had suddenly been jerked out of my hands. I didn't mind being beaten in a fight, but I didn't like running from a fight. What had made Art do that? The tone of his wire was an utter contradiction to that of his "jaunty" letter. I was puzzled and I was angry. I'd given up Tennessee's *The Rose Tattoo* to do *The Hook*. We shouldn't have stopped our effort to get the film made; we should have forced them—Brewer and whoever—to stop us if they could. Harry Cohn hadn't backed out. Why had Miller quit without a fight? Depressed and very blue, I didn't answer his wire.

Art had made his decision unilaterally. He wanted to get off the hot spot; I could understand that. But he wasn't writing about a Communist in *The Hook*. Marty, the central figure, is a unionist, who becomes militant for reasons Art and I could sufficiently dramatize. A militant unionist is different from a Communist. There was nothing sly about Art's script or secretive about his hero. Marty didn't take orders from higher-ups. He was an independent, cocky fellow, not conspiratorial. He wanted only what any good union man wants: to improve the working conditions of himself and his fellow union members. The essence of a Communist, as I well knew, was to go to meetings that were secret, take orders from above, carry them out without questioning, and operate underground. Who could disagree, in the end, with good unionism, even militant unionism? Not the majority in this country, not even at that time. We should have continued to fight for our project.

What was Art protecting—his script or himself? I recalled his telegram. He'd been panicked—it had to be called that—by an investigation that Roy Brewer had launched at me and at him. Art had said that the alternative to postponing our film until things got quiet was to leave ourselves open to an attack we wouldn't survive.

Was that really the only alternative?

What was Art afraid of that would be uncovered by an investigation? I didn't believe he'd been a Communist; he knew I had. Even though we were close friends, we'd never discussed the matter. I'd given up worrying about the threats to me; I'd accepted that before too long I'd be hauled up before the committee in Washington. The thing I wanted to do soon was warn Darryl; tell him the facts about me. But I was sure all the big studio heads knew much more than they were letting on about me and others like me. There was an underground stream of information flowing through their offices. I'd made up my mind that when the time came, I'd simply say yes, I had a carried a card for a year and a half. I wouldn't hide anything that concerned me, I wouldn't "take the Fifth," but I would not, under any pressure, name others. That would be shameful; it wasn't an alternative worth considering.

Why couldn't Art do the same thing—if he had reason to? Then—and perhaps here I was naive—we could continue our project. Maybe Art had been rattled by his marital situation and the distress it was causing him. But how could he be that deeply involved in a passion for Marilyn? (How quickly I'd forgotten Constance and how much I'd been on the verge of giving up for her!) He wasn't a teenager, after all. It had to be because of his inexperience. I mean he couldn't be thinking of marrying her! Marilyn simply wasn't a wife. Anyone could see that. Even with all his inexperience, he was smart enough to know that. The wife he had (how patronizing I was!) suited him. He certainly wasn't going to upset his whole life, divorce Mary, leave his children; it was too absurd to even imagine. I had the European viewpoint: Everything in its place. Marilyn was what she was, a delightful companion. A delightful companion is a delightful companion, not a wife.

Now that he'd left California and I was alone, I had a caretaker's relationship with Miss Bauer. I knew she was in love with Art despite any feeling she had for me. His letters to me showed how much he cared for her. He needed what he got from her. After what had happened with *The Hook,* she was a blessing to me; she lifted my spirits. But I was not desperate about her—or she about me. We were good fellows. If Miller came back, I'd yield, and wait and see what happened.

I H A D work on *Streetcar* to keep me occupied. There was to be a preview to test the film, particularly for its length, in Santa Barbara, which was supposed to be a community superior in intellect and sensitivity to Los Angeles. Driving up there with Alex North, our composer, and my traveling secretary, I purchased a quart of vodka to ease my melancholy. We'd take swigs of the stuff from time to time, and the more she drank, the more Marilyn would talk about Art—and the less, I believed, realistically. Even the night before, while we were making love, she'd talked about him. She had Art's photograph on a shelf behind her bed, next to the copies of his plays, and after I'd finished, I'd raised up and looked into his eyes. There he was, looking as if he'd just won the Nobel Prize. He was the romance of her life. His love for her excused her past. I believe one thing that especially got her was his constant complaining about how unhappy he was at home. That's an open invitation for a woman to move in and make a man happy.

By the time we got to Santa Barbara, we'd drunk a lot of vodka, and Alex, who didn't hold his liquor even as well as I did, wanted to sleep before the show. We parked on a dark street and I told him I'd wake him in time. Then Marilyn and I got in the back. She clung to me as if I were her whole life—or perhaps as if I were her only bond to someone she loved even more, who was beyond reach. I doubted they'd ever see each other again. It never occurred to me that she might go to New York after him.

T H E N we went in to see the show, and I had a shock: The audience laughed at Blanche. We were in trouble. Charlie Feldman called for the marines, and they were all named Jack Warner. I saw what I thought was the cause for the laughter and told Jack not to worry, to leave it to me. He said okay, he would. I could see that Feldman had been talking to him, and as I came up to them, Charlie avoided my eye. I began to despise him. As soon as I got back to the Warner Brothers studios, I went into my cutting room with David Weisbart, my film editor, and fussed with the place where the audience had laughed. It was, for those of you who may recall the film, the scene where the Young Collector comes to her door and Blanche speaks to him in a bold and yearning way. I saw that what caused the laughter was the young boy's reaction to her "reach" for him. I eliminated the shots of this reaction, making him almost a creature of her imagination, and also made some other trims, amounting to about four minutes. I showed what I'd done to Charlie; he thought I hadn't done nearly enough. At this stage of a film's production, a nervous producer is not a help. Charlie wanted me to slash the film, and I could have ruined it if I'd been obedient or in his power. I decided to pay no further attention to him and went to Jack Warner. I told him that I thought I'd fixed our problem places and asked if he'd come see what I'd done. In the projection room, without Charlie, he liked the changes.

Then I said to him, "Jack, I want your word that this picture goes out as it is now. It's two hours and fourteen minutes, which is not long for a picture of this caliber. I want to go back to New York and see my family, and I don't want to be worried what Charlie will do behind my back when I'm gone." Jack answered, "The picture will go to the theatres as it is now." I said, "Tell David"—Weisbart, our cutter, was with us—"that no one, and I do mean Charlie, will be allowed to fuss with it while I'm gone. Tell David that." And Jack did. Then I said, "Charlie, to be plain about it, is worried about the film and has become nervous. Remember how he got nervous about *The Glass Menagerie*, and how he ruined it? You'll watch him for me while I'm gone, won't you, Jack?" And Jack said, "Don't worry about Charlie. He's put every cent he has in this picture, buying the property and so on, and he's scared to death. That's why he's so rattled. But don't pay any attention to him. You go on home. You made a hit of it before, and I trust you'll make a hit of it again." So I said, "Okay, Jack," and we shook hands and I left.

I went to see Darryl at Fox, told him I'd finished with *Streetcar* and was ready to move into *Zapata*. He asked me if we'd had any censorship problems on *Streetcar*. I didn't know what he'd heard. I said I didn't think so; we had the Breen Office's okay now. Darryl's response might have worried me if I hadn't had Jack Warner's word. "The Breen Office is not a problem," he said. "We pay those guys. They're there to help us get pictures done, not prevent us. But what about the Catholic Church, what about the Legion of Decency?" I said I didn't know anything about that outfit, but I had Jack Warner's word that the picture would go out as it was. This didn't impress Darryl. "Jack and I shook hands on it," I insisted. He nodded in a rather peculiar way; I was going to remember the look on his face later.

Now Darryl came back to our film and told me a few more things he wished John and I would do. They were good ideas, and I promised that the second thing I'd do in New York, after seeing my family, would be to sit down with John and work on Darryl's suggestions. The outstanding problem for me, I said, was where we'd make the picture; Mexico, I hoped. "That's what I want to talk to you about," Darryl said. Then he called three men I'd noticed in his reception room into his office. They were Ray Klune, the head of production; Jason Joy, a sort of high-level public relations man on Darryl's staff and the best-dressed man on the lot; and Lew Schreiber, Darryl's exec, a man created by God to take orders. We were gathered to discuss the fate of *Zapata*.

Klune, the outstanding production head in the industry, was a tall, thin man who brought one word to mind: control. After the greetings, he handed out copies of a transcript of a recent phone conversation he'd had with a man named DeFuentes in Mexico City, an agent of Klune's whose assignment had been to report on the attitude of the Mexican national censor board to our picture. DeFuentes had had a conversation with the official censor, and this man had asserted that he knew the true historical events and John Steinbeck did not. DeFuentes told the man, "We're not trying to make history; we're trying to make a picture." This did not impress the censor. John's "*mordida, mordida*" approach had not worked either.

Then Klune said to us, "Turn to page three of the transcript, please," and he read from his copy. "DeFuentes. Quote. 'Once we get by the national censor, we will have to deal with the Defense Department. They will want to read the script too, and then there will be somebody else trying to change the thing.' Notice my answer." Klune read it to us at a deliberate pace so that it would sink in. "Mr. Klune. Quote. 'In other words, you feel that even if we are able to satisfy the censor board, we will still have to make further changes to satisfy the Defense Department?' Here is De-Fuentes's answer. Quote. 'Yes. Because it is a completely different department. One is political, the other soldiers.'"

Now Klune looked at me. "So I asked DeFuentes," he said, "would we almost have to rewrite the story to satisfy these people? 'Absolutely,' De-Fuentes said. 'They would not object to the picture if they had a hand in what to write. A fellow came over from the Defense Department, claimed he'd fought with Zapata, and said, "Tell your people to send Mr. Steinbeck to us and we will give him our ideas and then he will make a fine story."' There is even a brother of Zapata alive, a half-brother, actually, and he said, 'The Indians there know me, and I can handle them. But if you don't take me in, you're going to have a tough time there.'"

Everyone was looking at me as if it was up to me to defend the notion of making the picture in Mexico—which it was. "I know those Indians," I said. "I've been there. I'm not worried about them." "Bottom page six," Klune said. He turned the pages, and read: "DeFuentes. Quote. 'Those Indians in that part of the country have a reputation of being very, very bad. They can be dangerous. You might run into serious trouble there.'" Klune looked at me again. Darryl, who'd been pacing back and forth, swinging his mini-ature polo mallet, stopped and looked at me to make sure that what Klune had been saying had sunk in. It certainly had. "First *The Hook*," I was saying to myself, "now *Zapata*. It's going to be a bad year."

"What about Dancigars?" I asked, fighting for my life.

Klune turned to Jason Joy, a tall, white-haired man who looked like a candidate for an opening on the Supreme Court. "I have," he said, "a 107-page report from our State Department proving Oscar Dancigars to be a Communist; in fact, an active collaborator." He offered a sheaf of papers to Darryl. "Give it to him," Darryl said, pointing to me. I was saying to myself, "Guess I'll go back to the theatre." Jason Joy held out the 107 pages to me. "I'll take the word of the State Department," I said.

Then Klune read what he believed to be the clincher. "Mr. Klune. Quote. 'Señor DeFuentes, I want to ask you a very plain question. Would the people you talked to in the Mexican government like to see Zapata presented as a man with Communist leanings?' DeFuentes. Quote. 'Something like that. Yes.'" Klune folded his file.

At this point Jason Joy asked to be excused and left, but Klune and Schreiber, the men at the studio closest to Darryl, remained. They spoke urgently to him for more than half an hour to influence him to give up on *Zapata*. Darryl listened closely to their arguments; even I thought they were convincing. Occasionally Darryl would look at me and nod. When the men of his staff were finished, he didn't respond either as they must have wished or as I—despite all—was still hoping. He sounded very gentle and kind when he said, "Thank you, fellows," to dismiss them and quite brusque when he said, "I'll see you tomorrow, Kazan." I'd noticed many times in the past that when Darryl liked something I'd done, he called me "Gaydge," and when he didn't, "Kazan."

It was a low point for me. I returned to my big office and asked not to be disturbed for any reason. I'd counted on these two films for more than a year and a half. Now, suddenly . . .

My secretary came in, with a message written on a small slip of paper: "Mr. Zanuck will see you at noon tomorrow." He's made up his mind, I thought; he's going to wash it up. Tomorrow, the ax!

I thought back to Klune's attack on the project and how well armed he'd been with facts and figures, dollars and cents; that was what had finished me. That and the political climate. Klune hadn't said anything about the political climate in southern California, but everyone knew what was going on in the industry. Fear. People were taking no chances that their political position might be misjudged. Klune had killed my picture, without an apology, while I sat there. As for Darryl, what could I expect from him? He was running a business, had to show a profit or he'd be gone. That's why they call it the "industry." So that was that. I'd go back to the theatre. Left-wingers were still safe in New York.

Since I was desperate, I thought of a desperate measure. When I walked into Darryl's office the next day, I didn't waste a minute. Determined to speak before he said anything, I told him I knew that this was a tough picture for him to do commercially and that I wanted to voluntarily cut my salary from $162,000 to $100,000 ($100,000 was still a lot of money in New York City). Darryl didn't seem impressed by my offer, a disturbing non-reaction. Then I was foolhardy and went all the way. I told him that in 1934 I'd been a member of the Communist Party for a little over a year. "So I can appreciate," I said, "that you have to protect yourself on our script in every way you can, because it—and I—might be subject to attack from certain sources which you know all about." He didn't respond to this; I had the impression that he already knew about me. What he did was call Ray Klune and Molly Mandaville, his trusted secretary, into his office, and he put a question to them and asked for a yes or a no. "Do people around the lot think this picture Communistic?" he asked. Both Klune and Molly said no. That's all Darryl wanted to know from Klune, but he kept Molly there, and we began to go over the script, cutting out about four pages that might incite the far right—but nothing that I thought hurt the screenplay.

At the end of this conference, still not having heard from Darryl whether or not he was going to do the film, I asked him, "Do you feel all right about our picture now, Darryl?" To which he answered, "Oh, I've crossed that bridge already." I had a rush of emotion to my head, like a kind of stroke. I felt such admiration for the little bastard that I wanted to embrace him, but he wasn't that kind of fellow; I couldn't even shake his hand. All I could say was: "Good!" and then: "I'm all yours." To which he answered, "About your offer to cut your salary: We accept it. Now the next thing you have to do is take a unit manager, an art director, and a driver and go along our border with Mexico and find a location you can use." "Sure," I said. "That's right, Darryl! Thanks. See you tomorrow." And I was out of there with my future restored.

Here is what I was saying to myself as I walked to my office: It wasn't Harry Cohn, generally thought of as a son of a bitch, who'd walked away from *The Hook;* it was my pal Art Miller, and I still didn't really know his reasons. It wasn't Darryl Zanuck who'd opposed making *Zapata;* it was the Mexican "patriots" on the left. Darryl had told the rich Jews who'd tried to prevent *Gentleman's Agreement* from being filmed to go boil their bagels. He'd told the Catholics who'd insisted that the leading lady of that same film not be a divorced woman to stay the hell out of his business. Now he was telling the Mexicans, their official state censor and their Department of Defense, their generals and their politicos, to make their own films; he'd make his. And even though he now knew I'd once been a Communist and undoubtedly suspected I'd sooner or later be called up before the House Committee on Un-American Activities (he must have been told this again and again by the superpatriots of our community), he'd stood by me. He was giving me everything I needed to make John's film, including his personal support, where the sensible thing would have been to follow Ray Klune's advice and walk away.

There was no doubt where I stood—with the business boys, with the movie moguls, with the "gonifs," with the old, unfeeling, insensitive, crass, vulgar industry barbarians. I trusted them most because I could rely on one thing: If in an open competition I could make an exciting film that people would want to see, they'd go with me. If they thought they could make a bundle, they wouldn't knuckle under to censorship—at least not yet. There'd be no mysterious withdrawal for reasons not clearly defined; there'd be no underground actions that would take me by surprise. I'd rather have their hard-boiled supervision, I'd rather contest them in open conflict, than deal with the men, consulting in secret, who'd made my old friend Albert Maltz crawl in public and tried to make a man I didn't yet know, Budd Schulberg, rewrite his novel. I'd rather deal with tycoons than with the men of the Legion of Decency, who were still, so rumor had it, conspiring to castrate the film of my friend Tennessee Williams's *A Streetcar Named Desire*.

That's what I thought. Of course, I was wrong. I was to find out that there were many conspiracies a filmmaker in our country had to deal with—that of the right, that of the left, that of the self-appointed moralists of the Catholic Church, and that of the men who tend the springs of gold. But for the time being, for that season and that crisis, I preferred to trust Darryl and even Harry Cohn and Jack Warner. I'd find out only much later that two years before, Jack Warner had confidentially offered this astonishing statement to the House Committee: "Arthur Miller and Elia Kazan worked on Broadway where they practiced some sort of subversion."

Back in my office, while my secretary was fixing me a drink, I got Steinbeck on the phone, and he was pleased and surprised; he'd been sure Zanuck would drop our film. Then I got Molly. Days before, I'd told her *The Hook* had died. Her response had been: "It's a lousy script anyway." Now I told her the news about *Zapata*, and she was overjoyed and relieved for me. I thanked her, for it was Molly who'd urged me to work with John. She laughed and said to hurry home. I remember I thought what a beautiful voice she had, how I'd never noticed before how gentle and fine her voice was. I told her that the film was going to be shot in the United States, probably on the Mexican border, and I wanted to take our whole family along; it would be an experience for the kids. She was delighted with this and told me she loved me. I told her the truth, that I loved her too.

Brando on location

I HAD a nickname for her, "Noble Day." Noble is
noble, which she was. Day was her middle name. She came from an old
New England family, the Days. If you saw *Life with Father*, the obdurate
fellow presiding over the dining room table was a Day. Molly's great-
grandfather had been president of Yale University, and he'd kept the students in line. The other half of her father's family chart showed a succession
of Thachers. They were from New Haven too, didn't live in doubt, and
were known for going their own way. Mix the two together and you have
Alfred Beaumont Thacher, her father, and you have her: granite. Her maternal grandfather was of unrelieved German stock, the head of the herd,
an industrious man who made more money than he needed and gave the
city of Cincinnati its zoo. It's still there, carrying his name, Erkenbrecher,
which means what you think it means, earth-breaker.

Quite a load for a gentle girl to carry.

The Days and the Thachers had a family motto, although they didn't know it. I gave it to them. "There's a right way and a wrong way and nothing in between." The Days and the Thachers prided themselves on their plain talk. They had no reason not to be plain, since their parents and uncles and cousins ran the community; they were its judges and its public authorities. The Erkenbrechers were known for their pertinacity. Like the Days and the Thachers, the Erkenbrechers had ramrods up their asses—although their backbones didn't need stiffening. Molly never learned to compromise. Why should she have? She had it all, from the first day. I envied her firmness; other times it drove me nuts.

I assume you're making the inevitable comparisons with my people.

Of course, Molly should not have married me. Her mother knew it. But that ill mating had a meaning for Molly. Among the other people she disapproved of were her own. In the end, I liked her mother more than she did. Molly was determined to break from her family and its tradition. Enter Elia. That did it. She also wanted to tear down the culture into which she'd been born. She became associate editor of *New Theatre*, a Communist-front magazine, taught playwriting at the Theatre Union, closed ranks with Odets and Albert Maltz. Marrying me was an act of defiance, directed at her own kind.

I should not have married at all. At twenty-four, I wasn't ready for it. It would be almost half a century after we married before I was ready. By then Molly was dead.

I married her because I was anxious about my worth—I suppose that was it—and she was elected to reassure me. I also married her because I loved her. I've always loved her. I still do. But our life together was, among other things, impossible. I couldn't even work with her on how to arrange the furniture in our apartment. There was a right way to do this, and she knew what it was. I got into a bad habit; I'd say, "You arrange it, I'll accommodate myself." When she did that, I resented it. And her. The only room I'd insist on fixing for myself was my study, but when we had enough money to build a studio in the country, she planned my workroom with an architect. It was on a rather grandiose scale, and I saw what she wished I was. She was ambitious for me; that is to say, I was part of her ambition.

But I was not what she liked to think me. I'm not a powerman, to sit behind a desk, defended by a brace of secretaries, or to stride down a corridor, assistants at my elbows, dictating orders. I am not an office animal. Molly liked to run things. At Vassar she ran the college newspaper and did it well. She transferred her inclinations to me, wanted me to be a "top guy." But I didn't want to be obligated to lay down the law for a gang of theatre or film people. The older I got, the less I liked groups. Every time a film closed down, I was relieved—I could go my own way again. If I'd had a choice during my "big days," I believe I'd have chosen to disappear. As I have now. I've vanished, people tell me. Where? Into myself. Into this book, for instance.

Then why did I marry? And why Molly? It's a long story, but I'll simplify it. Everything in my early life gave me a sense of worthlessness. (Relax, reader, I don't want your pity.) My foreignness. My looks—or what I thought of them. The mumps at fourteen and what resulted. My father's opinion of me and his disappointment, the boys in school pushing me outside their society, the girls whom everyone else was "taking out" and their indifference to me. At Williams I was not invited to join a fraternity, at the Yale Drama School I showed no talent, and none as an actor to the directors of the Group during that first unsuccessful summer. I finally had to believe what Harold Clurman believed: that I had no gift except an excess of energy, therefore no future with the Group or anywhere else.

On all these particulars Molly set out to reassure me. She was the first person who saw artistic potential in me; she not only stood behind me, she pushed me forward. She was sure I had a great talent; when events proved that I did have some, she became my talisman of success. She made me feel I could get to the top of a profession in the performing arts. With her help! And along with all that, she couldn't wait to get in bed with me.

This was a blessing and a miracle. But when you admit another to that position in your life, you give that person power over you and, naturally, resent her. The sympathy itself is humiliating. Oh, pity the sweet, earnest, compliant, hard-working little Greek boy (with the beautiful brown eyes!). "Help me, help me!" he cries. So she did; she guided me and told me what was right and what was wrong. I began to resent that she was so positive about what I should be and do. And too often right. In time I wearied of arguing with her, let her have her way, then got mad at her for taking it. Anger was the genesis of revenge, the kind of revenge men take on their wives.

So at home I had a guide, a critic, a mentor, a constant adviser, as well as a wife. It was something I'd encouraged at the beginning, but I hadn't anticipated how far it would go. I began to feel her guidelines as constraints. "Will you stop telling me what to do!" Those angry words, hurled at her in a loud voice, were heard often in our home. Then I began to let her criticisms pass in silence, and silence is dangerous; it's a threat. But she didn't see that. She kept right on doing what was "right."

She wanted a regular, well-controlled domestic life. She'd revolted against her parents' way of life, but in the end, that was precisely how she tried to organize our life. Dinner at seven, properly served by a "domestic" to a discriminating bourgeois couple and their four properly brought up children. I noticed that our eldest boy began to slip out of the house before dinner. He was loosening bonds too. Molly could never accept the proposition that some disorder is inevitable in life, even preferable. She wanted a firmly controlled existence; perhaps it quieted her own uncertainties, so she insisted on it.

Increasingly I wanted a less ordered life. She feared what she could not prepare for; it threw her into a panic. But I'd hardly lived yet; all I'd done was work. I longed for what I'd not experienced—which was most everything! Domesticity was her reassurance; she wanted uniform silverware with our initials on it. Nothing I'd seen of the world told me that relationships endure except by slow, gentle dissolution. They endure by shrinking; then there's no conflict.

· Still we loved each other; two fucked-up people clung together and produced four excellent children. There's a piece of her in each of the four, and in each it's the better piece. Our bond endured through hell's fire, the one I lit.

I wanted everything I could get and went after it. When she withheld her approval—or when I thought she did or might or would—I resented her. After a time even her esteem alienated me; I didn't want to have the qualities she praised me for possessing. Anger fired revenge, and the revenge was always a woman who liked me for what Molly disapproved of. I would seem perfect to the newcomer and I'd enjoy that and contrast it to the critical stance of my wife. But since I was the same man, the others soon developed the same reservations about me that Molly had. For a time they'd be reticent about expressing their criticism; there's always a mini-honeymoon in these affairs. Then the same relationship would recur—with a different person.

All that sounds sick, and it was. But there was a true side to the struggle, which I cannot discount. People make fun of the male crisis at forty-five. I had that crisis all my life. I knew there was more to life than I was getting, and I didn't want to miss out on anything. People forget that we only live once; I knew it from the day I was born. Every new girl was an adventure and an education, a friend in need, someone from whom I benefited in many ways. I even believed that my infidelities were an effort to continue with my wife, to "save the marriage." It was the only way I could go on with her. As I say, I should not have married. But I wanted that too.

Did she know about these other relationships? Some of them, yes. There were violent scenes, and sometimes I'd break off with whoever it was and sometimes pretend to. Molly started divorce proceedings twice, calling in an expensive "Wall Street" lawyer from her father's old firm. Then suddenly she jerked the legal rug out from under her counselor and called the whole thing off. I believe she finally came to accept me as I was—that is, as I'd become. We recognized certain limitations in each other. One thing she knew for sure, I do believe, was that I'd never leave her. And I didn't, not ever. Perhaps that is the most we can hope to be sure of from one another.

Have I explained what I set out to explain? I doubt it. I shouldn't have tried.

. . .

W H A T brought our conflicts into the open was Molly's compulsion to tell the authors whose plays I was directing what was wrong with their work and how they should fix it. She did this carefully, earnestly, and with the greatest sympathy, but I could see that these men, increasingly, pulled away from her, resented her advice, and rejected her suggestions. The bad word, of course, is "should"; "should" is the word that would kill her. Again and again I had to remind people: Molly speaks for Molly; I speak for myself.

I can recall her sitting behind a long table with Irwin Shaw, working over *Bury the Dead*. Irwin was a boy then and had a boy's devotion to her. Molly would "mother" playwrights—if they'd let her—in my behalf. But Irwin didn't show her his next play. Tennessee Williams's talent had an element of mystery for Molly: How did he get to be that brilliant? So she handled him gingerly. But Arthur Miller was within reach, or so it seemed. Molly fed Art, listened to him, argued with him. Art respected her candor and her frankness—for a time. She was overjoyed when *All My Sons* won the prize it deserved, and she recognized the stature of *Death of a Salesman* immediately. When Art and I made a cut in the play script, she objected, and what we saw in rehearsal proved her right. After that success, Art sent her a copy of the printed play with this inscription: "To Molly, for in effect saving it."

When I returned home after the scuttling of *The Hook*, Molly told me about certain frantic (her word) phone calls from Miller, three of them at least, she said, ones he'd made to her before he called me out of the budget meeting to notify me he was withdrawing his screenplay. She said he sounded like a very nervous man when he described the encounter with Roy Brewer. Art felt sure, he told her, that they would stop *The Hook* from being made, do it by hauling him up for questioning. "They will ask me," he told Molly, "if I was a member of—" Then he stopped short, Molly said, and there was a pause before he completed the sentence. "A member of the Waldorf Peace Conference," Art continued, "and I would have to say, 'Yes, I was,' and that would finish me." He sounded panicked, Molly said. Art had explained his concern to her, and she'd agreed with him that *The Hook* was dangerous to do at that time. "Better not expose yourself," she said. Perhaps if she'd liked the script, she might have felt differently.

Molly wondered why Art had been quite that shaky. She was curious about his life at home and bugged me with questions. I kept mum, never mentioned Marilyn, didn't tell Molly that I'd introduced them and how Art had fallen for the girl and she for him. I didn't want to open that area to inquiry. But Molly knew there was something wrong. She saw before I did that Art and Mary were going to break up.

.   .   .

I R E T U R N E D to California on a weekend from my scouting along the Texas-Mexico border, having decided on the locations I wanted. I had an empty Sunday—a disaster in Los Angeles—and dropped in on Marilyn to say goodbye, for I was about to leave that part of the world for many months. We vowed we'd always be good friends, a pledge that didn't hold up after she married Miller and became Lee Strasberg's household pet. Among other things, she told me she was pregnant and seemed rather pleased about it. "Don't you worry," she said. I guess she meant that she'd had abortions before and knew where to go. But I did worry; it scared hell out of me. I knew she dearly wanted a child and women were becoming single parents. Like any other louse, I decided to call a halt to my carrying on, a resolve that didn't last long.

Again that night I looked at Miller's publicity photograph that Marilyn had placed on the shelf behind her bed. Next to it was a neat pile of letters; Art had been writing to her. She told me he was unhappy and asked me to do all I could to help him. "He needs friends now," she said. I wondered what the hell he was writing her. I didn't feel as friendly to him after his escape from *The Hook*, but I told her that of course I'd be his friend. She was so obsessed with her passion for him that she couldn't talk about anything else. He must have been sorely tempted to remain there with her; perhaps this was another reason he'd departed so abruptly after the Roy Brewer meeting.

After I left, she wrote me letters. From Miss Bauer. One of them informed me she'd had a miscarriage. In every letter, concern about Art was expressed. "Try to cheer him up," she wrote. "Make him believe everything isn't hopeless."

Art saw what was coming more clearly than I did.

I'D S T A R T E D making notes on a film about Emiliano Zapata in 1944. It's the first film I made from an idea that attracted me—a revolutionist fights a bloody war, gains power, then walks away—one I started and saw through to the end. I'd made three trips to Mexico, knew every stone in the province of Morelos, done years of research and study, followed by bursts of frustration and doubt. (What the hell did I really know about Mexico and Mexicans?) But I'd gone on with it for seven years. Was it worth it? The answer, if you think of the years and the work and if you insist on having it, is: "Of course not. You think I'm crazy?" On the days when the work had gone well, the answer was: "Of course it's worth it. What else is there?"

Shooting film on a distant location is a refuge and a relief. You are in an insulated world, where everything is organized around your enthusiasms and wishes. You are protected from all challenge—at this time, from political challenge. You're in hiding; no one can reach you. Furthermore, I was living the life I liked best, working with a crew that followed me wherever I went and, with the ease of magic and with great good nature, did whatever I dreamed up. When they found a rattlesnake coiled under a rock I'd asked them to move, they thought it funny and let it go. Overhead, vultures circled, waiting for us to leave the remains of our lunch behind. Great rainstorms rode over the flatlands; you could see them born, burst, and die. This city boy learned that if you have the gear, rain won't harm you; you work in it. Other times the sun poured down heat until it hit the one hundreds—which made the after-work beer taste that much better. At night I had Molly and my kids waiting for me in air-conditioned motel rooms in the small, civilized city of McAllen, Texas. We dined on Mexican food, tickled our palates with hot peppers. I narcotized myself, didn't worry about the political threat I'd left behind. I was safe out there.

The work on *Panic in the Streets* paid off; I'd told myself in New Orleans to pretend I was shooting a silent. Now I was able to combine the psychological technique I'd brought from the stage with clear and vivid pictures. I used many more long shots, didn't "wing" the setups this time, carefully studied the photographs in six volumes of Archivo Casasola's book, *Historia Gráfica de la Revolución*, and tried to bring them to life. I was delighted when I could create a picture that told the story without a word. I was becoming a filmmaker. As I was making this film I turned my head to the future, filled with hope and belief in myself. And I was blessed by the help of two superbly gifted actors, Marlon Brando and Tony Quinn.

Marlon delighted me. In *Streetcar* he'd been playing a version of himself, but in *Viva Zapata!* he had to create a characterization. He was playing a peasant, a man out of another world. I don't know how he did, but he did it; his gifts go beyond his knowledge. It was more than makeup and costuming—that was easy despite Zanuck's quibbling about his mustache. (Should it turn up or down? Was it too long or too short?) I spoke a few words of help: "A peasant does not reveal what he thinks. Things happen to him and he shows no reaction. He knows if he shows certain reactions, he'll be marked 'bad' and may be killed." And so on. But no one altogether directs Brando; you release his instinct and give it a shove in the right direction. I told him the goal we had to reach, and before I'd done talking, he'd nod and walk away. He had the idea, knew what he had to do, and was, as usual, ahead of me. His talent in those days used to fly.

It was simple for Marlon to understand that Zapata's relationship to women was not what men in our society feel—or are supposed to feel. "Don't be misled by all that shit in the script about how he loves his wife," I said to him. "He has no need for a special woman. Women are to be used, knocked up, and left. The men fighting the revolution were constantly leaving them behind for months at a time. The woman he woos, Josefa, is middle-class; perhaps she represents a secret aspiration of his. She may also be some sort of idealization. There are plenty of other women available to satisfy his simpler needs. Don't mix it up with love, as we use the word. He loves his *compadres*. They are ready to die for him, and he would do anything for them." I was telling him not to play the scenes with his wife in the kind of romantic love stupor American actors pretend. For these peasants, I told Marlon, fucking is not a big deal; it's become a big deal for us in America. But our kind of romantic love (if it is romantic, if you can call it love) is a product of our middle class. Zapata's social concerns are his real concerns.

This wasn't hard for Marlon to understand. He was that way in life. I've watched several white women (he preferred women of color) make it known to him that they were interested and available. I've rarely seen him respond. Perhaps this was discretion or shyness, but the warmest relations I've seen him involved in have been with men. What I described for the peasant Zapata was very close to the way Marlon lived his life. For both of them there were deeper needs than "romance."

Once I saw that Marlon had found the man in himself, I gave him less and less direction. In certain scenes, I didn't say a word. When you start giving too much direction to an actor like Brando, you are likely to throw him off the track he's instinctively found and harm the scene. "If it isn't broke, don't fix it," the saying goes. I learned from working with this man that when a director deals with a really talented actor, he has to know when to stop talking. The first thing for a director is to see what a talent does on its own. It may be, as it frequently was with Marlon, better than anything you can describe. I also learned with him to try to capture the first flight of his instinct; I "shot the rehearsal." If you don't get what you want, then start directing—but not until then. Above all, don't show off how smart you are and what a brilliant director. Sometimes the best direction consists of reading an actor's face and, when you see the right thing there, simply nodding. A few words, a touch, and a smile will do it. Then wait for a miracle. With Marlon it often happened.

I believe Marlon got a lot from his contact with Tony Quinn. It took time, but a true friendship developed out of an intense competition: Who was most macho? I didn't discourage this competition. Marlon had turned out to be a fine rider, but Quinn dominated a horse, *caballero* style; he overwhelmed the animal. He was not sitting up there hoping the horse would forgive him for taking him away from his feed box. The animal Quinn saddled respected him. Tony damned well saw to that! The horse was macho, but Tony was more macho. I think Marlon noticed this and admired it.

Tony was half-Mexican, and Mexicans, even half-Mexicans, are a suspicious and jealous people. He said to me one day, "You son of a bitch, why

do you give Brando more direction than you give me?" "I hardly talk to him," I answered. "You're always talking to him," Tony said. "You don't talk to me!" I knew I had to take charge right there; it was early in our schedule, and Tony had to know who was boss. "Tony," I said, "that's a lot of shit! So you eat it!" His face went white, and he was furious, dangerously so. For a day, he remained in an intense sulk. Then I said to him, "Tony, haven't you yet noticed I hardly talk to Marlon?" "I see that," Tony said, "but he's still your favorite." "I don't have favorites, Tony," I said. "I think a lot of you too." But he remained sulky and I worried.

So I went to Marlon and told him that Tony was resentful of me and why, and asked him to do something about it. He did. He chummed up to Quinn and they began to hang out together and go swimming in the river after we were through work. I waited up for them like a mother, watching the clock, anxious that they shouldn't turn an ankle on an underwater branch. Only when I'd heard them come back to their quarters did I sleep easy. Soon they were close friends, as I became theirs.

The most memorable piece of directorial "business" in the film was suggested by Tony. It is the scene where he wants to call the people together to rescue his brother, whom the police are taking to detention. Tony picked up two small stones and began to beat them together. Then others near him did the same, and soon everybody in the area was doing it. Tony had heard about this peasant telegraph when he was a boy growing up in that country. The people, called together, gathered and rescued their leader. It was a specific for Zapata's country.

During our time in Roma, Texas, I came to love the Mexican people who'd settled there, and forgot all about their country's official censor and Department of Defense. I put many of them, particularly the women, to work in the film. As I got to know these *muchachas*, I realized they were like the photographs I'd seen of Greek peasant women, and I began to think of making a film in Greece. I compared them to the women in Giotto's paintings tending the body of Christ. My favorite scene in the film is one without either of my stars. It takes place at the end of the story, in the town square on a hot day, with the sun beating straight down. The women are hardly visible, because they sit against the side of the buildings that bind the square, in the strip of shade. They are not seen clearly because they wear black, and the shadow they sit in is black. A troop of horsemen rides up and dumps the body of the murdered Zapata on a cistern top in the middle of the square. It is hollow underneath, and the corpse makes a heavy, thudding sound. One feels the weight of the body from that sound and remembers how much potency was once there. The horsemen ride off. The women don't move from where they are, almost invisible in the black shadows. The impression is that they've many times before seen one of their best men dead. Their memories are full of the death of heroes who, having protested unjust conditions, have paid with their lives. Slowly, the women move out of the black to the body of their hero. They wash and compose it as they might have the body of their Lord. I kept the camera respectfully back. Since it is not close and since what it shows is not altogether explicit, the imagination of the viewer is free. The reason I tell about this scene here is that it meant to me that I'd at last moved past the stage and its techniques, to become a filmmaker.

Molly was happy all through the time I was making this picture, despite the heat that kept her in the air-conditioned motel room most of the day. This was because I came home every night needing her, and we were together. The children were rather bored, because it was too hot during the day for them to go out and play.

Molly did a beautiful thing for me. Zanuck would send me wires almost

Nick and Katie

daily. In the beginning they were laudatory and appreciative, but soon there were hints that I was falling behind schedule, then more than hints: complaints and bitter ones. Abruptly the telegrams stopped. It was a relief not to read a scolding after a long day spent broiling under the sun. When I'd finished my work on location, Molly handed me a sheaf of yellow paper, telegrams Darryl had sent. She'd kept them back so I wouldn't be troubled.

F A R   F R O M what is thought of as civilization, I'd heard nothing about the Communist hunt or what my own prospects were. Nor did I have a word from either Jack Warner or Charlie Feldman to inform me what was delaying the release of A Streetcar Named Desire. Having finished what I had to do on location, I came back to California to make some final scenes at Fox's Malibu ranch. It was on the very first morning I was in my office that I heard about the death of Joe Bromberg.

It's been said that the House Committee on Un-American Activities (HUAC) killed Joe. Certainly the pressure he was subjected to shoved him over the brink. I'd also heard, upon my return to California, of the death of a fine actress, Mady Christians. After a succession of rejections "for mysterious reasons," she died of a cerebral hemorrhage. It was beginning to happen. A terrible threat was in the air and moving closer—as it does before a great thunderstorm when, with the day darkening, the clouds not gray but black, lightning bolts thrust through the heavy overcast and no one can be sure where they will strike next. I was eager to be in New York, not California. Let it come, I felt; I can't stop it anyway. One thing that did help me was my determination that, while I would tell the whole truth about myself, I would refuse to name any of my old friends.

It was at this time that I became aware of the similarity of the Catholic Church to the Communist Party, particularly in the "underground" nature of their operation. I had just returned to California, was having my first lunch in the Fox commissary, and found myself sitting next to Jason Joy, Darryl's liaison with the Breen Office. With him was one of Breen's lieutenants, and at that luncheon I learned for the first time that Streetcar was having trouble, as Darryl had warned me it would, with the Legion of Decency, the censorship agency of the Roman Catholic Church. Warners' New York sales manager, who'd booked the film into Radio City Music Hall, had put in a frantic call to Jack Warner, asking that someone be rushed east to deal with the Legion's people. Warner had then consulted with the industry's own censorship board, and in due course, Jack Vizzard, one of Breen's best, had been dispatched to New York. I knew Vizzard well, having dealt with him on another film.

I wanted to put myself on the record, so I wrote Jack Warner, stating my concerns accurately and in a calm manner. "I recall," I wrote, "that Vizzard was trained for the priesthood: he is certainly the most conservative and squeamish of Joe Breen's people. The person representing us with the Legion of Decency should have a hearty respect for our picture. In personal conversation with me, Vizzard characterized *Streetcar* as 'sordid and morbid.' I would say that he was not the best person to defend it.'"

My impulse was to rush to New York and defend the film myself, but there was no way I could, since I was still shooting the last scenes of *Zapata*. Anxiously, I made further inquiries. Feldman was in New York, and I finally got him on the phone. He said yes, there was a threat of a "C" rating, but their objections were not serious and to leave it to him. This was not reassuring. A few days later I heard that the Radio City booking had been canceled. Clearly this was because of the Legion of Decency's threat of a "C"—"Condemned." None of this information was forwarded to me; I had to dig it up by penetrating the institutionalized silence of everyone at Warners.

The composer for *Zapata* was Alex North, who'd written the music for *Streetcar*. He'd become very friendly with my cutter, David Weisbart, and was living in his home. He came to me and revealed that David had been dispatched to New York by Jack Warner, and the last instruction David had had from Warner was, "Above all, don't tell Kazan you're going to New York City." Possibly to make David's trip seem innocent, his wife, Gladys, had been sent with him. "They're at the Sherry," Alex North told me.

I immediately called Weisbart in New York. He told me he was not there on *Streetcar* business. Of course, this was a lie. Then he added, "Although it might develop into that." He then stumbled about and finally said that nothing had happened so far, but something might. . . . And so on. I was embarrassed for him; I was making him lie to me, I knew. I was angry at Warner for having put this decent if weak man into that position. The conversation continued, full of innuendos and evasions; clearly David had been instructed not to tell me anything. Did he expect me to believe that he didn't know what the hell he was doing in New York?

I called Feldman again. He said he was sick of the whole matter and was leaving for Europe, so dumping the problem in Jack Warner's lap. I tried to get Warner on the phone, couldn't, but did talk to his right-hand man, Steve Trilling. Steve was a man I'd always found honest in a position where it was almost impossible to be honest. He confessed to me that the Legion had seen the film and was going to condemn it. What changes did they want? Steve wouldn't specify, quoting Charlie Feldman that there was "nothing to worry about." I told him that I was furious that all this had happened behind my back, that any changes were plenty to worry about, and that I didn't want any meddling by the Legion into the body of my film. I said I should have been told about it all immediately, and what might seem minor to Jack and Charlie would not seem minor to me or to Williams. Perhaps in response to my anger, he finally confessed that the Legion had asked for another showing, that this was serious, and what they wanted was this: "We must make the audience believe that Stella and Stanley will never again be happy together." Which was contrary to Tennessee's intention and his goal of "fidelity."

My patience was undone. I'd finished all the scenes of *Zapata*, so I asked Darryl if I could go to New York and see if I could prevent this disaster. I told him again that Warner had promised me that the film would open in New York as I'd left it, and that we'd shaken hands on it. Darryl's answer was a smirk; I promised I'd come back as soon as I could. My absence didn't bother Darryl, who enjoyed editing more than any other part of the work— especially if the director was not present. I left my *Zapata* with him.

In New York I went straight to the Sherry Netherland Hotel, where David was staying, and demanded to know what had happened. He told me with the greatest embarrassment that cuts had already been made in the film, by order of Jack Warner and following a schedule of changes drawn up by Martin Quigley. Quigley was the publisher of several motion picture trade papers. He was a Roman Catholic, a "Knight of the Church," and an honored personal friend of Cardinal Spellman of New York. I happened to know that Quigley had written the code for the industry's Breen Office, which was, presumably, a nondenominational agency, serving the industry as a whole. Now Jack Warner had brought Quigley in to suggest what would enable *Streetcar* to avoid a "C" rating. I asked to see the film as Quigley had "fixed" it. It would take a few days to get the film ready to show me, David said. In other words, Jack Warner had instructed him to delay showing me my film.

I asked Quigley for a meeting. He was a large man with a fleshy face and a conference-room complexion. He stood when he talked, arms hanging loose, fingers entwined in front of his abdomen. He had complete confidence in his position and power, so had no need for overstress. He spoke proudly of having had lunch with Cardinal Spellman, whose devotion he was honored to have. Could one topic of their luncheon conversation have been *Streetcar*? Could it not have been? I told Quigley that his involvement in the matter of my film must not have been comfortable for him since it was secretive and, in fact, conspiratorial. He agreed to the first characterization but not the second. He told me that his presence in the issue was at the invitation of Warner Brothers, who'd found themselves with a picture that was headed for a "Condemned" classification by the Legion of Decency and—he stressed this—a mutilation or a refusal of a permit for exhibition by several censor boards operating under legal statutes in the various states. "I sought to indicate," he said, "the minimum alterations I considered necessary to avoid the gravely undesirable consequences I have noted and to plan the proposed changes in a manner which sought the least possible invasion of the artistic integrity of the picture." Then he said something that shocked me. "From this [what he'd said] you will see that you are really not in a position to ask anything from me. I simply made an honest and careful recommendation." How clever, I thought.

I said I'd see the film—and, finally, I did. There seemed to be a dozen trims, whose general intent was to change the story of Stella, Blanche's sister and Stanley's wife, so that it was now—again quoting Quigley— "about a decent girl who is attracted to her husband the way any 'decent' girl might be." There was a brilliant close-up—I'm speaking of Kim Hunter's performance, not my direction—of her coming down the stairs to her husband when he's called desperately for her to come back. This close-up had been cut short and with it the piece of music Alex North had written. The shot and the music were both considered "too carnal." Other lines that were cut hurt the film, but what was hurting me was the arrogance of what had been done, as well as this: The Church people felt unembarrassed about it. There seemed to be nothing I could do. Who owned the film? Warner Brothers owned the film. Money was talking.

But I had to do something. I asked to meet with Quigley again. "Don't you think, Mr. Quigley," I said, "that I should have been asked to consult on this?" I knew his answer before he gave it to me. "Do you really believe that in our situation that would have helped?" The plain fact was—and I had to recognize it—the picture had been taken away from me, secretly, skillfully, without a raised voice. I discovered I had no rights. I was out. Now congenial, Quigley pleaded with me to be sympathetic to the "complicated position of your friend David Weisbart. He was strictly enjoined by his superiors to secrecy. He frequently expressed himself as devoted to you personally and as an ardent admirer of your professional talent. He contributed painstaking and skillful effort to the technical job that seemed necessary to be done." And so on. Quigley was out to make peace.

I wouldn't go for it. I said I resented the secrecy with which the whole matter had been masked and resented the cuts, which came from the superimposition of one set of moral values over another, that of the author and me. How can you seek to enforce, I asked, an ethical position which is that of your Church on the entire population of this country? His answer amazed me; I've never forgotten it as an expression of pride in power. "The American constitutional guarantees of freedom of expression are not a one-way street," he said. "I have the same right to say that moral considerations have a precedence over artistic considerations as you have to deny it." "But whose moral standards are you talking about?" I asked. His answer was: "I refer to the long-prevailing standards of morality of the Western world, based on the Ten Commandments—nothing, you see, that I can boast of inventing or dreaming up."

The absolute confidence of the man amazed me. He had no doubts about what he'd done. He felt he'd saved *Streetcar* for Warner Brothers. He told me that originally Father Masterson, the priest who was head of the Legion, had said that Quigley's task was impossible and that when he'd shown Masterson what he'd done, the priest had asked for more eliminations. Quigley boasted that he'd succeeded in gentling Father Masterson away from these requests. All the while, behind the scenes, a possible action by the Catholic War Veterans was being hinted at, as well as the possibility of boycotts—of the theatres that showed the film and of all Warner Brothers product.

The phrase Quigley repeated over and over was: "the preeminence of the moral order over artistic considerations." When I said that Williams had his own morality, that he was and his film was an example of art serving a strong personal morality, Quigley smiled faintly. I saw that he felt sorry for me.

In desperation, I made two requests of Jack Warner—who was now posing as a victim of the Catholic hierarchy. One suggestion was that two films be exhibited in New York. Since the Catholic population of the country amounted to about twenty percent, the film as "corrected" by Quigley and the Legion should be shown in a theatre twenty percent the size of the big "chair factories," and that the film as I had left it, and as the author wanted it, be shown in a large theatre, one to which Catholics would be forbidden admission by their Church. Priests, I suggested, could be stationed in the lobby to write down the names of parishioners who defied the Church's interdiction. Of course, this suggestion was rejected as foolish and uncommercial—as I knew it would be.

Then I made another suggestion, and I saw no reason why it could not be granted both by Warners and by the Legion of Decency. I asked that since the film was being sent to the Venice Film Festival, the version shown there should be the film Williams and I had made. This was also refused. The response was that if the film was ever shown anywhere, even once, it would immediately be given a Condemned rating. The Church wanted its moral standards to be those of the world.

That was, I thought, the limit of my power. I was the victim of a hostile conspiracy. I don't know what else to call it. I had no recourse except—I recalled our struggle inside the Directors Guild—to throw light on the matter. Possibly anticipating that I might make myself heard, Warner sent word to me through Steve Trilling. Quote: "Tell Kazan not to be vindictive." Well, I *would* be vindictive. I'd be heard. I'd raise my voice. I'd throw the issue out to the people—as Joe Mankiewicz, on a smaller scale, had done. The least it could do was give me satisfaction. I was choking to death with this requirement of silence. The thing I could least tolerate was all the gentility and friendship from the men who were mauling my film.

I told Darryl that I was going to write an article for *The New York Times* and expose everything that had happened, so that people who loved movies would know what went on behind their backs. Darryl shrugged. "It may help your business," he said. "But those people don't change. You cannot persuade them to change. And if you don't have them, you'll have someone else." He didn't encourage me.

I believe that it was Darryl who let Charlie Feldman, just back from Europe, know what I was thinking of. Charlie waited until the film had opened, then he sent me the following wire, a perfect self-portrait. "Dear Gadg: In view of the wonderful press on Streetcar and everyone's belief you will win award, I sincerely feel you are hurting yourself by issuing statements regarding cutting, etc. But in any case, as personal favor to me, would you please not make any additional criticisms for they only hurt prestige of picture as public will feel they are getting mutilated version and probably stay away. Bear in mind that everyone who has seen the picture including critics love it as it is and have attested to its artistry. In last analysis, I repeat, you are hurting yourself and, of course, hurting me immeasurably. Would appreciate your consideration this wise but if you decide to do otherwise, I guess I will try to understand. Best always. Charlie." Charlie was such a nice guy!

The *New York Times* film critic, Bosley Crowther, a Catholic who'd liked the film and said so, asked me for my comments. I told him I'd prefer to write an article for his paper. I wrote what I had to say and showed it to Molly for her reaction. "Do you mind," she said, "if I work this over a little?" I said, "Of course not" (a lie). But she was proud of me for deciding to speak up. She showed me her revised version; I admitted it was probably better. The Sunday *Times* printed it, and everyone in town was talking about it. I'd really thrown a floodlight on the matter; I was pleased with myself.

But I didn't see the implications of what had happened. The Legion of Decency had acted with a boldness and an openness that were unusual for them. What it meant—and I didn't immediately recognize this—was that the strength and confidence of the right in the entertainment world was growing stronger. Jack Warner had been deathly afraid of the Church; they could kill his business. After Charlie Feldman read the piece in the *Times*, he wired me again, again at excessive length, to warn me to accept what had happened with grace, since Jack Warner was powerful and could turn against me. I ignored Feldman's warning. The next time I ran into Jack, he was as friendly as ever. I realized you can't insult these people: There's no concern with morality there; only business. *Streetcar* made a bundle—that defined me to Jack. Not long afterward, Jack and I made a deal, highly favorable to me, to produce another film at his studio. And that was that.

I W A S glad Molly approved of what I'd done; I couldn't take any more disapproval from her. We weren't leading a regular domestic life; I wasn't coming home from work every afternoon, so she was frequently in a dither of nerves and attacking me for one reason or another, any reason would do. The nights were worse than the days; our bedroom was a prison. Molly's anger at me contested with her ingrained sense of fairness, which prevented her from expressing all that she felt. A tense silence prevailed. Of course, I had no one to blame but myself. Unless it was her. I was fed up with the strains between us and longed for another mood in my life: carelessness, relaxation, pleasure, joy, a haphazard life with no responsibilities.

Bone-tired, I was an easy mark for depression. Those unspoken accusations coming at me from all sides, were they real or imagined? It seemed that I'd been under general attack for as long as I could remember. One night I had a nightmare: More cuts were being made in *Streetcar* behind my back, and I was struggling to save my film. I heard hoarse shouting in my sleep; it was my own. I was suddenly short of breath, then stopped breathing altogether. I understood how a person could die in his sleep from a failure of the heart. In the morning I wanted to get off the battleground and let others do the fighting. But of course they were my battles, and no one cared about them but me. Besides, I had to stay where I was and prepare myself for the political confrontation I knew was coming.

The article Molly had rewritten for *The New York Times* had made me a cultural hero again, but I felt dissatisfied with what she'd done. I thought it temperate and reasonable and balanced, whereas my feelings were intemperate, unreasonable, and probably unbalanced. I'd made the film, worked like a demon and a slave, only to be forced to submit it to the will of a proud conspiracy, led by the gluttonous Pope of Fiftieth Street and the men who worked under his guidance to win his approval—"The Powerhouse," it was justly called. I'd had no defense or even opportunity of resistance. One thing I was sure of: There was a large and effective organization conducting its business and seeking its goals in secrecy, and it had beaten me. Despite the piece in the *Times*, I'd been humiliated. And it wasn't over yet.

Now an air of dissolution settled everywhere around me. From sources I didn't know, mysterious pressures were attacking the professional lives and, as a consequence, so it seemed, the personal relations of many of my friends, dissolving friendships, breaking marriages, voiding good resolutions once made in full faith. Chaos was in the air; all kinds of human connections were coming apart. I remembered how many of these human bonds had started with high hopes, now defiled.

During the time of my meetings with Quigley, I'd had a long talk with Art Miller. He and Mary were breaking up. What pain on both sides! Month after month he'd begged Mary to take him back, but she couldn't bring herself to forgive her husband. Her confidence in the worth of their union had been undermined permanently, it seemed; she didn't believe anything Art told her. He'd been doing his best, he said, to hold their marriage together, but according to him, his wife was behaving in a bitterly vengeful manner. He said their home had no warmth of love or generosity. She didn't make the least effort to please him or make his friends welcome. Brought up Catholic, she'd renounced that faith, turned to the left, taken to psychoanalysis. Again I realized how indelibly, once the knee touches the floor, a Catholic upbringing stamps the concept of sin on its people. Art simply had to be punished—despite the fact that I believe Mary felt she'd failed in the marriage too. It was obvious to me that another woman could now take Art away.

Marilyn had from time to time been writing to me at the Actors Studio, telling me how bleak life had been since we'd left California, then going on to passionate declarations of her persisting love for Art. To my astonishment, she was becoming quite a star and was very much in demand. One day a letter informed me that she was coming to New York and Art was planning to meet her. She said she hoped I'd at least drop by her hotel, say hello, and wish her well in her quest. She did arrive, and I did drop by her room to have a few words with her. I found her obsessed with her passion for Miller, rushing down to have her hair done so that when he called, she could ask him to come right up. She hadn't heard from him yet, and I had an uneasy feeling that she was going to be stood up. I told her I'd telephone later and did so at the end of the afternoon. She sounded desolate. Art had called, she said, and with the greatest regret canceled their date. She begged me to come up and comfort her, so I did. Her hair, which had been all trussed up by a hairdresser, was in disarray. Humiliation had torn it down. The next day she returned to California.

I knew how wounded she'd been because I'd seen how high her hopes were that morning. But my feelings, if not my sense of justice, were with Art. There is nothing more painful than pulling down a home where your children live. I'd seen our own furniture carried out the front door by moving men. I could appreciate why Art had behaved as he did.

W H I L E I'd been making films, Lee had made the Actors Studio his place. He had an artistic home now, and it became his power base. He was not being paid for his work there any more than anyone else was. For his living expenses, he relied on his private classes, which were becoming famous and brought him a good living. The sessions at the Studio brought him something more: the adulation he hungered for, as well as a unique power. Lee controlled who was admitted to the Actors Studio, which, largely because of the films I was making, became known as the birthplace of stars. An actor, it was believed, could step from there directly into one of my films.

Now came Lee's glory years. Every Tuesday and Friday at eleven in the morning, he entered a place where an eager crowd of actors was waiting for him. He sat in the front row before the acting space, with his wife, Paula, at his side. A secretary handed him a card, and Lee read off the title of the scene to be played and the actors who were to play it. His face was solemn; his intensity made everyone feel the importance of our profession. When the scene was finished, Lee questioned the performers. "What were you trying to do?" This question lifted the discussion that followed to a craft level. The actors had been made aware earlier what their special problems were and had been working to deal with them. We'd been watching an exercise in technique, not an entertainment. Having heard what the intention of the players was, Lee turned to those sitting behind him and asked, "Well, what would you say?"

Now there was great hesitation; opinions were offered fearfully. Suppose Lee didn't agree? Suppose he took offense? We'd all been made aware of his temper. Sometimes responses were offered in a tremulous voice. An actor might preface his statement with: "As you said last time, Lee," or "Like you always say, Lee," followed by an observation he had reason to believe Lee would agree with. I'm not sure Lee liked this crawling, but he didn't stop it.

After he'd heard what "the people" had to say, Lee turned his back to them, and the microphone at his side was switched on. Notebooks were opened as young actors and actresses prepared to do what I'd done a quarter of a century before: make notes of whatever Lee had to say. Every comment he made about every aspect of our craft was preserved for posterity. He was a stern and devoted father and, equally, a loving mother who assumed a near total responsibility for the welfare of her family. He was also a tribal chief leading a movement that was to change the art of acting in our theatre. His sessions had the intimacy of a family gathering but also the intimacy of a cabal. Nowhere and for no one have I seen the honor given Lee during those years. Everybody loved him then. So did I.

Responding to her need to find something somewhere that she could respect and from which she could learn, I arranged for Marilyn, when she was in New York, to be admitted to Lee's sessions as an observer.

M Y   W O R L D of friends was now in political as well as personal turmoil. I hadn't seen most of my friends for months; when I did again, I found great changes, a sign, I believed, of the swelling power of the right. Its particular type of terror was about to be imposed on our little world. My old friend Kermit Bloomgarden took me aside one day and, in dire tones, gave me his advice. "You'd better come back to the theatre now," he said, "and stay on the East Coast." That's all he would say. Did he know something I didn't about what was going to happen? Or was an instinct talking? I noticed that with his pressman, Kermit was hastily building a strong public image for himself in the city. Would this protect him?

Months before, Julie Garfield had testified as I intended to, not offering names, defying the committee. Immediately well-wishers, whose number included his agents and others who had a financial stake in his well-being, were at his side to advise him that if he maintained the position he'd taken, his career in films was over. The studio heads already were afraid to employ him, and a star was becoming an unemployed actor. When I saw Julie, the impression I had was that he'd begun to look seedy and to wonder what was most important in his life. He turned to a lawyer, Louis Nizer, for advice, and I suspected that Julie's feelings were shifting to a more "reasonable" position. His wife, Roberta, had hints of Julie's evolving change of heart and disapproved of it. Julie told me that he was now uncomfortable in his own home, that his living room was always full of people who were scornful of him—friends of his wife. He said that when he came home he didn't feel welcomed. He hadn't done anything overt, but the left was alert and quick to condemn.

We had Mr. and Mrs. Fredric March to dinner one night, and drink loosened Florence's tongue. She told us how badly Freddie had treated her—and Molly looked at me. She also spoke of how she'd constantly been forced to hold Freddie up politically. "How hard it is," she said, "to be a mother to someone your own age!" Freddie said not a word. They'd both been under assault by a watchdog newsletter, *Counterattack*, which was sent to studio heads. For six months, she told us, the calls for Freddie's services could be "counted on the fingers of one hand, with a finger or two left over." Finally they sued *Counterattack*. Her husband, Florence maintained, had not been staunch in the crisis. "He was ready to take anything he could get and run," she said. The case was finally settled out of court; one of the provisions was that the Marches file an anti-Communist statement in the newsletter. It amounted to a public humiliation. They did it, but despite the clearance, the smudge remained, and it was a while before Freddie worked again. It was a demeaning time and put a bitter barrier between the couple.

I also spent an evening with Clifford Odets, who was preparing what he would say to the committee. It would be defiant. At this time, when he needed support at home, he was breaking up with his wife, Betty. He told me the story of their relationship from the beginning and of her adventures. He said he'd been forced to tend their children as a mother. Made distraught by all this, he couldn't write. Meantime, his funds were running low. I thought perhaps personal desperation might make him write plays again, but this proved not to be true.

I had a message at the Actors Studio: Would I please call Lillian Hellman. She told me over the phone how much she'd enjoyed her visit to my set (*Panic in the Streets*) and that she'd like to entertain me at dinner. A Louisiana lady, her specialty was gumbo. She was all spiffed up for my arrival, wearing not a dress but the garment known as a housecoat, zipper front. From the point of view of allure, it was unfortunate. She informed me her cook was out for the night. She'd made the gumbo herself, and it was the real thing, delicious, and there was plenty of garlic bread to mop up with and bottles of rich red wine. I felt like a young girl cornered by a rich old man who expected the reward she could afford to pay for the fine meal he was providing. I became acquainted once again with her chronic cigarette cough, which was racking-coarse, and her wit, which was the same. She made fun of the cowards who'd already buckled before the House Committee and of those who certainly would, and invited me to join in her laughter. I did, for a while. Then she scoffed at some people I liked, and I saw that her general attitude toward the world around her was derisive. She made fun of everyone she talked about, and I wearied of her. Despite all, I could detect a nervousness there, a reaching for allies. Even her laughter was nervous. I suppose what she hoped would happen with me might have some way reassured her. But I said I had to get up early for a rehearsal, thanked her for the delicious gumbo, and left. Perhaps I was abrupt, because she seemed offended. Whatever her needs were that were not satisfied that night, they were met later through the attendance of Jed Harris. Jed outdid Lillian; his entire conversation consisted of putting down everyone. What a clatter of derision there must have been when those two coupled.

I H A D a unique letter from Tennessee Williams, containing a rather desperate request. I was very close to him now, and he was asking me, in the greatest confidence, if I could arrange for a lady friend of his to be artificially inseminated. He didn't say who the lady was, and perhaps, in this case, it didn't matter. The point was that Tennessee, still with Frank Merlo, very happy and likely to remain so, wanted offspring. He wasn't sure he could achieve the physical arousal necessary for him to penetrate a woman, this not from impotence but from whatever it was that had blocked him all his life. He'd had one affair with a girl, he'd told me, before he'd ever been with a man; that had been his last. The result was that he didn't have the confidence that he could create his own child. I told him I'd look around, but when I didn't hear any more about this from him, I forgot about it. He would die childless.

N O W , S I N C E I wasn't working, I should have had ease and time for reflection, but this proved impossible. Everything was making me anxious—the future, the past, my marriage, my character, my work, and the fates of my friends, which undoubtedly anticipated my own. I believed I'd soon be required to testify before HUAC. I also believed that after my article in *The New York Times*, Cardinal Spellman would press the full weight of his influence against me. I suspected then and I believe now that this church—in its upper cadre—was hand in hand with McCarthy. Spellman was to stand up for McCarthy later, even after he'd been discredited.

I could not call what had happened around *A Streetcar Named Desire* anything but a well-organized conspiracy.

I still felt safe in New York and in the theatre. Having convinced Tennessee that we could enlarge his short work *Ten Blocks on the Camino Real* into a full-length evening, I planned to do the play with actors from the Studio and with my friend Anna Sokolow doing choreography inspired by the Mexican primitive artist Posada. I set up my production office where the Studio had its quarters and engaged a secretary, Mae Reis. Tennessee came north and we began to hold readings for the cast.

Early one afternoon, Mae Reis informed me that there was a "Negro" waiting to see me. At that instant, I was on my way into our rehearsal space to hear Lili Darvas read for a part. Tennessee had preceded me, so I was in a hurry. "About casting?" I asked. "I don't think so," Mae replied.

He was a fine-looking black man with a kindly face and a decent smile. I said, "You want to talk to me?" He stood up and said, "Can we go somewhere?" This puzzled me, but I led him a few steps toward the entrance door, a hint that I was in a hurry. There he showed me his identification, which I didn't read, then he took a double-folded pink sheet out of an envelope and gave it to me. "This will be a secret session," he said, lowering the level of his voice. "You don't tell anyone, we don't tell anyone. We expect you to be a cooperative witness." I said, "Thank you" (I don't know why), took the subpoena, and hurried in to hear Miss Darvas try out for the part of Marguerite Gautier. During that afternoon, I forgot about the subpoena. I didn't feel nervous after we stopped work. How casually, I thought, and how quickly critical events in life happen. I'd been "called"; it was over. I had a drink with Williams—a double martini for him, an old-fashioned for me—and we chatted about our casting problems.

But that night, I couldn't sleep.

      I N 1934, when I was a loyal and energetic member
of the Party, I met many of the "leading comrades" off duty, and of them all,
the one I liked best was Andy Overgaard, a man of Swedish or Norwegian
stock, whom all of us in the Group were so fond of that in the summer of
'35, we invited him to the Group's rehearsal camp in the Catskills. He was
delighted to come and was a most enjoyable guest, as interested in our

theatre work as we were in his experience in the "movement." What I admired most about Andy was his independence of spirit; there was nothing secretive about him. He was up-front about his Party membership no matter who the company, proud to be what he was, and not ready to conceal what he thought about any subject. I would hold Andy's example up to others in our cell for admiration. Why couldn't we all be as open about our membership as he was? I asked. Andy's attitude was an inspiring contrast to the secretive behavior of other comrades and the sometime timidity in my own heart. Wouldn't it be better for us if we were all altogether plain about who we were and what we believed? Stealth, I declared, is un-American. When the Party offered the nation the motto "Communism Is Twentieth Century Americanism," I thought: If they mean Andy, I believe it.

AT TEN-THIRTY on the morning of January 14, 1952, I arrived a half hour early in the chambers of the House Committee on Un-American Activities in Washington. I'd made up my mind what I was going to say: that I'd been a member for a year and a half, that I'd quit in disgust, that the plan of the Party to take over the Group Theatre had failed, that we'd never really influenced the course of our theatre. I knew they'd ask me to name the others in our "cell" and I'd refuse.

Exactly on time, the committee's counsel, Frank Tavenner, came in and led me to a waiting room. I was alone there for fifteen minutes, then Raphael Nixon, the director of research for the committee, entered and took me to his office. There was some pressure drilling outside, so some of our conversation had to be shouted. Nixon seemed friendly and relaxed. At one point he hinted that the committee's main interest was John Garfield, but I didn't pick up on that. Perhaps his casual manner made me more anxious, because suddenly I blurted out, without being quizzed, that I'd been a member for a year and a half and then told under what circumstances I'd gotten out. I was relieved to get all that off my chest.

He didn't respond as I'd anticipated, didn't try to persuade me to reveal more. Our conversation became "chatty." He seemed anxious to have me believe that the committee was not out to destroy individuals. He said the members were particularly sensitive to the criticism that they smeared people and ruined lives. A subpoena, Nixon said, was merely an invitation to come down; no opprobrium was attached. In the course of this "casual" conversation, he asked about Clifford Odets. Was he one? I responded as I'd planned, informing Nixon that I'd cooperate in every way about myself but would not discuss others. He reacted indifferently to this, but at the end of our talk he advised me, again in the friendliest manner, to reconsider, whether I wanted to withhold names from the committee. He gave me three Government Printing Office pamphlets to read during lunch, the testimony of Budd Schulberg, Eddie Dmytryk, and Richard Collins, all of whom had been "cooperative." He suggested a place where I could have a decent meal and asked me to be back at two, when there'd be an "executive session" of the committee, one that was private, not public. Whatever I said there, he assured me, would be kept confidential.

Over a minute steak at the Hotel Congressional, I looked through the pamphlets but couldn't concentrate on them. My mind kept switching back to my conversation with Nixon. I realized how nervous I'd been; that was why I'd kept blurting out what I hadn't been asked.

At a quarter of two, I reappeared, again early and anxious. Raphael Nixon strolled in, and I followed him into the hearing room. I found myself in the hold of a raised, open-end rectangle with chairs along the rim above, and in the pit a long table with a chair at either end. Four of the eight committee members entered and took their seats above me. I was introduced to them. I can recall only two names, Velde of Illinois and Kearney of New York; I remember them for good reason. Nixon, who was to question me, sat at one end of the long table, I at the other. The members looked down at me. A film director could not have devised a more humiliating setting for a suppliant.

Nixon repeated that this was an "executive session" and that what I said would be kept confidential, then he proceeded to his questions. During what followed, various members of the committee would go out, then come back in; it seemed they were conducting several courses of business at a time and that of them all, mine was not the most pressing—which was fine with me. Maybe the questioning would come to an end quickly.

First, birthplace, citizenship, how obtained; then education, what and where. Next queries about the Group Theatre. Was it a "front" organization, as the Tenney Committee had decided? The Group, I said, was not a front, and its three directors were not Party members. (Why the hell did I offer that? They hadn't asked me that.) Had I been a member? Nixon wanted to know. I'll be Andy Overgaard, I said to myself, profess everything about myself without guilt, then tell about the Man from Detroit; they'd eat that up, and maybe that would conclude the questioning. Nixon interrupted: "Who recruited you?" I refused to answer. Nixon went right on. "How about Garfield?" (So that's what they were after, scandal about celebrities!) I volunteered that to the best of my knowledge, he was not. "What about Odets?" (Another celebrity. Yes, what they wanted was a big public score to justify their existence.) I said I would not answer questions about Odets. (But didn't my refusal to answer about Clifford as I had about Julie Garfield suggest that he was a member?) Did I know the risks of contempt? Nixon asked in a soft voice. "Yes," I said. Then silence. The pit I was in seemed deeper than before. I said I was not asking for immunity of any kind. One of the committee members walked out.

Now Nixon was thumbing through a stack of index cards, reading off the names of organizations I'd belonged to or spoken up for. I stopped listening when I heard him mention *New Theatre* magazine. That reminded me of a quarrel I'd had with Molly the night before. I'd expressed anger at being hauled down to Washington to answer questions to which I was sure they knew the answers. "All they want is to make a spectacle of me," I said, and my scrupulous and ornery wife, who didn't admire the tactics of the committee or its members, burst out with one of her contrary opinions. "I can't say much for their procedures," she'd said, "but it's the duty of this Congress to find out all there is to find out about the Party and what they're up to and to ask people like you what you know. I hope you tell them the truth."

Nixon was still reading off the names of the organizations to which I'd had some attachment. I admitted connection with some, didn't remember others. No one seemed interested; they'd heard it all before. Then abruptly, after thirty-five minutes of this, Nixon put his cards away, and I prepared to get up from my chair.

But Bernard Kearney of New York wanted to say something. He urged me to give the committee the names of the other Party members in the Group Theatre. I said I would not, that even though he would claim the committee was not deliberately trying to harm people, nevertheless any person I named would find his career in jeopardy, and any person known to have been at a meeting with them and not cooperated fully would have his employment in TV, radio, and films cut off. Kearney challenged me to name one film director who'd freely confessed and recanted and whose employment had stopped—which was not at all my point. I said that if Jack Warner knew I was in that room and had refused to identify the people who'd been members with me, any film I might be preparing for his company would be canceled. Kearney didn't respond, but from his hostile expression I knew he was placing me in another category, one with which he had no patience. I concluded that what these fellows were conducting was a degradation ceremony, in which the acts of informing were more important than the information conveyed. I didn't doubt they knew all the names they were asking for!

Nixon had a cordial chat with me after the committee left the hearing room. Again I volunteered I'd be glad to help them any way I could but would not name old friends. He said he understood, then helped me fill out my expense account and per diem form. He told me that after our morning session, he'd spoken to the members, and several had been for not bothering me further but others feared that if they passed me by, they'd be open to criticism: Why so easy on him? This way they could always say they'd questioned me under oath. In other words, I was going to be called back.

.   .   .

I'M N O T a hypochondriac; I don't think I'm sick when I'm not, and when
I have been, I've rarely imagined it more serious than it was. But I see by
a diary I kept that when I came back from Washington, I went to see our
family doctor. The symptoms I reported were pains in the heart area, trem-
bling in my hands, particularly the thumbs, that I got out of bed in the
morning dead tired, and, for the first time in my life, woke again and again
at night. There was something that worried me even more: I often felt I
was going to fly apart. "Physically?" he asked. No. Then how? Well, for
instance, I felt myself rushing when I didn't have to and performing the
most everyday activity in a frenzy. The doctor scoffed, said I was okay by
every measure he knew, but gave me some iron pills for the hell of it and
pronounced the cause of my symptoms psychological; not his department.

I turned to my analyst. Bela knew the causes of my tension. Since he
was my wife's counselor as well as mine, he knew our marriage was on thin
ice. If she learned about my ongoing sexual duplicity, the union would be
broken. Bela would have to advise her to save herself by leaving me.

I described what happened in Washington, told him that I was sure from
a reaction on Kearney's face that I'd soon be called back for a public session.
What did I intend to do then? Bela asked. When I told him, he said,
"Wouldn't that make you unacceptable to the film industry?" "Probably," I
said. "Wouldn't that be a terrible loss for you?" I said I'd thought it over
carefully and decided I could get along okay without film work. I had the
theatre and even a play to do immediately. And some money saved. "I can
take the loss," I said. He seemed dubious. "I'm wondering," he said, "if your
fellow members would do the same for you if they were called upon to
protect you by endangering their careers." It was obvious what he thought.
I recalled that Bela was a refugee from . . . I'd never asked him exactly
from where, but to judge from his accent, it was east of Vienna. "That's not
the point," I said, and changed the subject.

I told him I had a sudden oppressive sense of my limitations. I'd seen
Viva Zapata! and been disappointed. I thought it another "almost"; I had to
do better. I'd looked back at my work and compared myself with the playwrights I'd served, and I shrunk by comparison. Perhaps I was a service
person, not a creative person. Sooner or later, I'd have to find a way to turn
to my own stories and themes and pay respect to my own emotions. Bela
had warned me again and again that I was preparing too many projects. I
should concentrate, he'd said, on the one dearest to me. Go to the country,
he urged, rest and be quiet and find out what you want to do most. "I wish
I could write," I said. "But you're a filmmaker," Bela replied.

I did go to our place in Connecticut, but I couldn't relax. I kept going
over my experience in Washington. When I'd sat in that investigator's pit
being judged, I'd felt humiliated. I'd sensed vainglory in the men looking

down at me. They seemed pleased with their power, and I'd detected a sadistic streak in their command over me. Kearney and the others were making the most of their political opportunity, scoring points for their careers because of the publicity their investigative position brought them—all at the cost of people's lives and careers. I bitterly resented them.

At the same time, when I thought about it, I agreed with Molly. I believed it was the duty of the government to investigate the Communist movement in our country. I couldn't behave as if my old "comrades" didn't exist and didn't have an active political program. There was no way I could go along with their crap that the CP was nothing but another political party, like the Republicans and the Democrats. I knew very well what it was, a thoroughly organized, worldwide conspiracy. This conviction separated me from many of my old friends.

So I was in the clutch of a dilemma, between two emotions, swaying one way, then the other, and the squeeze was just beginning. I didn't want to cooperate with this committee. On the other hand, I didn't want to defend the Party by a silence on critical points of their inquiry.

I T   W A S   at this time that Art Miller came to our house with a book. "It's all here," he said, holding it up, "every scene." The book was *The Devil in Massachusetts*, by Marion Starkey, and the play Miller saw in that book was to be *The Crucible*. He was excited by the prospect this book offered and urged that I read it immediately. It was taken for granted—although Miller later denied it to HUAC—that he wanted me to direct it; we were the perfect team. I couldn't read it just then, but Molly, a Miller-watcher from their first day, grabbed it, and the next thing I knew, she was criticizing the parallel Art had seen in the story of the Massachusetts witch trials and becoming indignant. "What's going on here and now is not to be compared with the witch trials of that time," she said to me and, first chance she got, to Miller. "Those witches did not exist. Communists do. Here, and everywhere in the world. It's a false parallel. Witch hunt! The phrase would indicate that there are no Communists in the government, none in the big trade unions, none in the press, none in the arts, none sending money from Hollywood to Twelfth Street. No one who was in the Party and left uses that phrase. They know better." Molly wanted Art not to write this play. Which didn't endear her to Miller. In a way Miller admired my wife, but not so much as he resented her. Now there was a serious gap between them, a political one.

Molly knew what she was talking about; she'd been in the trenches. She'd been assistant editor of *New Theatre* magazine when it had published *Waiting for Lefty* and Irwin Shaw's *Bury the Dead*, as well as many fine pieces of criticism. Herb Klein, the editor in chief, with Molly's day-in, day-out help, had raised the circulation to 35,000 copies a month and survived with hardly any advertising. But the Party "Fraction" inside the magazine began to meet with V. J. Jerome, their political "commissar," and they decided together that the magazine was too "liberal." Jack Lawson was dispatched with a Party delegation to "sit down" with Herb Klein. Why publish excerpts from Archibald MacLeish's *Panic?* Lawson demanded. Archie was a "Wall Street boy" and worked for *Fortune* magazine. The Fraction members had opposed Molly's presence on Herb's staff and now demanded that she be replaced. Herb stood firm.

Whereupon V. J. Jerome was brought in to find a solution. He recommended that the magazine be closed down for a month or two, during which it would be "reappraised" by the Party. This was a classic Party tactic; death by delay. Herb responded that if the magazine was closed down, it wouldn't last more than three months when it was reopened. But the pressure was strong, and much to his disgust and Molly's, *New Theatre* did close down for "reappraisal." Herb went to Russia, where he encountered further difficulties when he said that Meyerhold was the best director whose work he'd seen there. The Party in the U.S.S.R. was getting ready to "terminate" Meyerhold. He was a director whose work I'd studied and admired. They did terminate him—that is, do away with him, kill him—and this fed my anger at the Party.

Coming back to reissue the magazine, Herb was again confronted with Jack Lawson. Herb's patience was growing short; he said he didn't like a man who was making a salary in four figures a week (Jack Lawson, in Hollywood) telling him how he should run the magazine, where Herb was making fifteen dollars a week. But the criticism from the Fraction members intensified. They began to bully Herb and threaten him; it seemed, they said, that he didn't want their aid in distributing the magazine. This was a threat, since they controlled many of the newsstands where it was sold. Finally they got what they wanted. Herb quit and went to Spain. Molly quit, came home, and told me the story in detail, confirming everything I already felt about the Party's role in the arts. The magazine? Reopened and closed after two issues.

I thought Molly was right in her dispute with Miller. It sounds childish now, but witches do not exist, and I knew very well that the comrades did. In that sense I thought Art's bright idea questionable and his claim later that his play should not be read for "contemporary significance" seemed dishonest to me. But more cautious—and more devious—than Molly, I was content to wait and see what Miller would do with the play when he actually wrote it. He wanted me to direct it, and we were close; the old bond of many-colored twine was still there.

O N   T H E sixteenth of February, 1952, the House Committee on Un-American Activities hit front pages with a demand that Congress enact a law to punish espionage against the United States, in peacetime as well as in war, by execution or a life sentence. With equal urgency, they criticized the motion picture industry for failing to do more with "sufficient firmness to weed out Communists" and pointed to Hollywood as "the Communists' greatest financial angels," with contributions totaling a million dollars made by show people who'd joined "front groups." Since Hollywood lives by the favor of the general public, its ticket buyers, this public complaint from a high source panicked the industry's leaders.

I received a call from Spyros Skouras, the president of Twentieth Century–Fox, asking that I come to his office for a talk. Spyros, a bulky, flamboyant man, who always wore a good boy's blue Sunday suit, was one of three brothers who'd made it to this country from a small village in the Peloponnesus of Greece. The village was named Skourahori—that is, the village of the Skourases; the family had a history of dominance there, and the boys were born to power. Energetic adventurers, they'd immigrated to this country and gone to Saint Louis, where, in time, they'd found a way through the back door of the business of exhibiting motion pictures, then clambered up, all three, to positions of power and influence.

In their guts, however, they remained newcomers to America, with all the uncertainties immigrants have. Anxious to be everyone's friend, they would head up charities, dish out favors, seek the company of men who had larger influence, make frequent optimistic statements to certify their good hearts, and take popular positions as often and as publicly as possible to reaffirm their civic and national loyalty—which no one had questioned. A crisis revealed their insecurity. Like most immigrants then, they would defend themselves by flaunting their patriotism.

I do not altogether exclude myself from this characterization.

Spyros had just seen the final print of *Viva Zapata!* and it worried him. He was the man responsible for exhibiting and selling the picture, and he didn't like it. He anticipated great resistance to the film at this time, even a boycott. He was particularly concerned because I was a Greek. He believed first-generation Greeks had a responsibility to remain "cleaner" than other people. "We love this country more than the Americans love it," he said. With this in mind, he'd prepared a letter from me to Twentieth Century–Fox, which he wanted me to sign. It would, he hoped, scotch a very possible hostile criticism to the film and to its director, and be in effect an apology in advance. I should then, he urged, go on to reveal and explain my past "involvement" and, as a manifestation of my good heart, offer his company the right to drop me if public exposure of my past caused difficulties in the release of the film. His presentation was larded with professions of affectionate concern for my wife, whom he called "beloved Mary" in Greek, and for my "wonderful children," whom he'd never seen.

I refused to sign the letter. Skouras went on as if I'd not spoken. He reminded me of how much Fox had done for me, cited my "genius" when I made films like *A Tree Grows in Brooklyn*, which had no political concerns, and urged me to feel free to consult him on all my problems, personal, marital, and financial. These generous words gushed out of his mouth like water from an open hydrant. Suddenly he was suggesting that I go to Washington—he would go with me, yes, it would be his privilege!—and meet with J. Edgar Hoover and his trusted right hand, Louis Nichols. "He's Greek too," Spyros said. "A good boy! I arrange everything, don't worry. We go down in the afternoon, have nice dinner in the Occidental, and next morning you will take proper steps to clear yourself."

"They'll ask me to name my old friends in the Party," I said. "I won't do that."

Apparently Skouras didn't hear that either. He went right on about our holiday in Washington. "In the second place, I don't feel guilty," I said. I couldn't tell if he'd heard that, because now he was urging that I voluntarily go before HUAC and present a revised testimony. But even this didn't seem to satisfy him. He said I must make another film right away, something definitely anti-Communist. "I have the right book for you," he said. "Don't worry." I said *Viva Zapata!* was anti-Communist; that was the political point of the story. However, this was not the impression he'd had from the film. He shook his head dolefully and was about to go on, when we were interrupted by another call for his executive attention. "I will send you the book you must make now," he called as he hustled out of the room. "Don't worry."

I waited five minutes for him to come back, passing the time by looking at what was on his desktop. There I found an advance copy of the Sunday *Times* drama section, which contained a favorable notice for *Viva Zapata!* from Bosley Crowther. I propped it up on Spyros's desk and left.

At the end of the afternoon, I received from Skouras a copy of Herbert Philbrick's *I Led Three Lives*. I read the book swiftly—that is, carelessly. Then I wrote Spyros and referred to the Sunday piece in *The New York Times*, which I hoped he'd read. "Bosley Crowther understood the politics of the film very well," I said. "The point of Communist activity is to gain power, then use it. No Communist in history has ever given it up once he'd gained it. Zapata does precisely that. I suggest you send copies of Crowther's piece to anyone who questions the picture's theme—for instance, your friends in Washington."

I didn't hear from Spyros, but I did hear that business at the Rivoli Theatre had started well, then fallen off drastically—which would cause my Greek boss to have even greater doubt about the politics of the film. I decided to call Zanuck for the details. He asked if Skouras had mentioned a letter to me. I said he had. Darryl said to sign it or not sign it; either way, it was all right with him. Obviously he thought Skouras a bumbling fool.

. . .

A P L A Y I'd been directing for Irene Selznick—*Flight into Egypt*—opened, to mixed notices; "mixed" is theatre talk for failure. Living in apprehension, guarding my secret situation from everyone except Molly, I hadn't been able to keep my mind on my work, and it showed. The day after the opening I escaped. Tennessee Williams was waiting for me in California. We'd been conned into going west by Charlie Feldman and the Warner Brothers press, sales, and promotion people. They were convinced—or said they were—that *Streetcar* would sweep the Academy Awards. "Can't miss!" Feldman asserted over the phone, in the overwrought voice he used to convince himself of what he wanted someone else to believe. He said a poll indicated that all four of our actors were lengths ahead of the competition and the film neck and neck and gaining. It would be the first time in Hollywood history, Charlie told me, that all four acting awards would go to the same film.

But I had other problems, as I was to be reminded five minutes after my train dropped me off in Pasadena. The driver of the car Charlie had sent to pick me up handed me a copy of that morning's *Hollywood Reporter*, where the lead item in the gossip column read: "Elia Kazan, subpoenaed for the Un-American Activities Committee session, confessed Commie membership but refused to supply any new evidence on his old pals from the Group Theatre days, among them, John Garfield." How did they get that piece of news? My Washington meeting had been before a confidential "executive" session. But there it was, out in a floodlight, no dodging it now. The press would be hounding me. And what a splendid irony ahead! I'd have to sit in the auditorium of the Chinese Theatre, placed prominently for the cameras to pick up, waiting to applaud the actors, my friends, as they carried off their awards, while my film career went up in the flames of newspaper cuttings.

When I checked into the Bel Air Hotel, where Williams was waiting for me, I was given three call back messages, all from New York. Molly, Abe Lastfogel, and Bill Fitelson, my lawyer, had all called to inform me that George Sokolsky's public affairs column in the *New York Journal-American* was about to break into print with the story of my past. Sokolsky, I was told, had also been given the minutes of my "executive" meeting with the House Committee on Un-American Activities by one of its members, Bernard Kearney of New York. So much for their confidentiality.

My people in the East said I was being threatened by public exposure, a trial by publicity; they were very worked up about it. I, on the other hand, wanted to lie down in tall grass and let the world turn without me. Sokolsky had appointed himself the scourge of the left and made a good thing of it. The judgments he offered to the public on this issue were a call to action, to which various patriotic groups responded at a gallop.

I decided to look the other way until forced to pay attention. This is a trick animals have, going under a rock or under a bed to hide until the heat cools, but one that sincere, responsible, decent, concerned men abhor. It's evasive, it's cowardly! But to hell with what sincere, responsible, decent, concerned men would do. I went to the bar and had a drink. I called Williams; he was no help. He'd started drinking early, and his mind fluttered. I could tell that he very much wanted *Streetcar* to win, but like me, he lived ready for rejection. I don't know if he'd read the item in the *Reporter.* He must have heard about it, but politics was not his game. I told him I was exhausted and went back to my room.

I decided to live by New York time, ordered another old-fashioned and a menu. I would eat dinner, courtesy of room service, and go to bed. I turned off the phone; "Only New York calls," I said. Then I decided to turn them off too. I ate heavily but couldn't sleep. Just for someone to talk to, I called Marilyn. She lived in another world, the one I preferred to inhabit at the moment. I had lost touch with the girl, but with her first words, she bridged the time between. "I have wonderful news—oh, wait till you hear," she said. "Tell me, tell me!" I said, desperate for a new subject. "I can't over the phone," she said. "But I have a dinner date with him, and as soon as I can get away, I'll come to your hotel and tell you all about it. What's your room number?"

"What the hell is Art Miller doing out here?" I said to myself.

Then I was in a thin sleep and the quiet enveloped me and I was alone and at ease in a kind of emotional truce, unchallenged for a few hours. The Bel Air Hotel is situated in a damp hollow of ground, what the Romantic poets of long ago would have called a "dell." All around the scatter of bungalows are great trees, the sweet-smelling eucalyptus, but other trees too that we don't have in the East, live oaks that keep their leaves in winter, and still others, of a tropical variety, with leaves like green leather. At night the dew is heavy in this hollow, the air cool, and I could hear the breeze. It brought on brief sweet dreams, flashes from the first years Molly and I had been together and loved each other without reserve or concern for the future. I dreamed of the happy days and nights we'd spent in the country, when the only problem in life was to preserve what we had, to continue to work and to love.

Now something had happened, and I didn't know what. How had things become so complicated between us? What had altered? Well, for one thing, twenty years had passed, and we were different people. Would we have married if we had met now, she as she is, I as I am? I woke and looked at the clock. It said one-thirty. I got out of bed and walked out of the bungalow into the night, naked. My body felt cool, and it was young again. She's not coming, I thought. Just as well. But when I went back in, I left the door unlatched just in case. I knew her to keep eccentric hours.

She was getting into bed, and that woke me. All excited and very happy, she announced her engagement. "I'm going to get married," she said. "I made up my mind tonight." "A hell of a time to tell me," I said. "It's three-thirty in the morning." "I wanted to tell you first," she said, "because now I'm not going to see you again." "Sounds real this time," I said. "He comes all the way down from San Francisco just to have dinner with me," she said, "and we haven't even done it yet!" She sounded astonished. "Who?" I said. "Who are you talking about?" "Joe," she said. "He wants to marry me, and I really like him. He's not like these movie people. He's dignified." Then she went on about Joe DiMaggio, and I could tell she really did like him. It was nice to see someone so happy and so hopeful. We made love; congratulations and farewell.

Then it was morning, and the tensions were back. Zanuck had invited me to have lunch in the producers' dining room at Fox. There were some twenty men there, dressed in the sunland's bright sports attire, Zanuck presiding at the head of the table and I, that day's chief guest, at his right in my New York clothes. The item in the *Reporter* was the first topic of conversation, but no one seemed really interested, and the men passed on to their own, more immediate problems and to trading the latest stories and jokes. After lunch Darryl took me to his office and told me that when he'd read the item in the *Reporter*, he'd called Wilkerson, the paper's publisher, and protested. Wilkerson told him that he'd had the minutes of my "secret" hearing from Representative Harold Velde of Illinois, who'd told Wilkerson that I was going to be called to an open meeting soon, and my testimony there would be public. Wilkerson also informed Darryl that Sokolsky was going to make me the subject of a column, whereupon Darryl called Skouras, and Spyros had stopped or at least postponed the Sokolsky piece.

Then Darryl urged me to "Name the names, for chrissake. Who the hell are you going to jail for? You'll be sitting there and someone else will sure as hell name those people. Who are you saving?" He said he could understand it if I was trying to save someone, Garfield for instance, from perjury. I said that wasn't it, that I believed Julie Garfield had told the truth. To which Darryl responded, "You never know about this thing." Then he told me that he'd had a good deal of experience in Washington during the war, and "the idea there is not to be right but to win." I had nothing to say to that, and Darryl had other problems waiting, so I left.

Bud Lighton, a man I respected, had been at the luncheon and not said a word. I went to his office to talk to him. Like any man sure of himself, he was brief. "There's nothing else you can do," he said to me. "Would you let someone go to jail for you? If they would, the hell with them." "The men they're waiting for me to name were once good friends," I said. "I don't care how good friends they were; there is nothing else you can do now." This was all he had to say, and he offered it as a fact beyond debate.

That night, at the Academy Awards ceremony, *Streetcar* lost to *An*

American in Paris, I to George Stevens, Brando to Bogart. My other three actors won awards, and I was happy for them. I thought *Streetcar* was what it turned out to be over the years, a classic, and should have won. I wondered if I'd lost votes, especially from people on the right, because of what De Mille knew, what had happened at the meeting Mankiewicz had called, and the gossip about my politics that followed. I don't believe that now.

I decided to go back east the next day and face the music. There was no point in staying on. I believed my days in that town and in that industry were over.

T H R O U G H the last ten years of her life, my mother was quite deaf. Since I was the eldest son, it became my obligation to keep her hearing aid in good working order. She enjoyed my chatter and "news breaks," and whenever I got her onto her past, her people, her youth, her marriage, on how we came to this country and our first years here, I was fascinated and couldn't get enough. She followed each of my ventures from beginning to end. She was sixty-five, I forty-three; still we became closer than we'd ever been. I reaped her stories for the books I was hoping to write, and she listened carefully and thoughtfully to whatever I said; she lived partly through me during those last years.

But I noticed that not everyone had the privilege of her undivided attention. When a person who'd proved tedious persisted in unloading nonsense or malice on her, I would see my mother's fingers steal to the place in the clothing at her chest under which there was the tiny control box of her hearing aid. I'd see my mother's eyes fix on the person boring or offending her, and when the speaker's eyes wavered, even for an instant, I'd see a twinkle of my mother's fingers and know that her antagonist had been tuned out and that Mother was no longer being burdened by what she didn't choose to hear. I became fascinated by this tactic and how skillfully she performed it, and I often wished I had something like this little control box under my shirt.

Then—it was at the time I'm writing about—I realized I did have such a device, built in, had had it for years, and that it was still operating. For instance, there are certain opinions to which Party members were not supposed to offer respectful attention. My little device would automatically turn these off and put them out of my mind. But now I was being forced to look at issues and take stands. Memories I'd pushed aside now thrust themselves forward for attention. I recalled the scene on the lawn of the Hotel Marik in Cuernavaca, where John Steinbeck and I had been instructed how to rewrite our Zapata screenplay by Figueroa and the man whose name I'd not been given. I felt anger at what had happened there and the quiet arrogance of the Party man. The stories about Budd Schulberg and his *What Makes Sammy Run?* and my old friend Albert Maltz and his *New*

Masses self-denial ran through my mind again. I recalled how the Party's literary police had bullied the two writers and how Budd had stood firm and Albert had not. I couldn't clean out of my mind the voice of V. J. Jerome and its tone of absolute authority as he passed on the Party's instructions for our Group Theatre cell and his expectation of unquestioning docility from me and the others. I heard again in my memory the voice, arrogant and absolute, of the Man from Detroit as he humiliated me before my "comrades" in Lee Strasberg's apartment over Sutter's bakery. I recalled the smell of the sweet chocolate topping and the cinnamon from below and how silent my fellow members had been, unresponsive until they'd voted against me.

If I truly wanted to fight the CP's influence in the arts, didn't I have to listen to everything? And when I disagreed with a Party program that was being enforced secretly, didn't I have to break into the stealth, instead of tolerating it by my posture of goodhearted, liberal indifference? I'd been letting the Party fellows get away with what I hated most, by not being ready to question and doubt and then forcefully express my contrary convictions. I'd had every good reason to believe the Party should be driven out of its many hiding places and into the light of scrutiny, but I'd never said anything because it would be called "red-baiting." I knew that "comrades" were working secretly all around us, and I wondered if they shouldn't be forced out into the general light.

Forced out? Yes, even that.

I'd never dared think anything like that before. Perhaps that was the worst of it: I'd censored my thinking. And my curiosity. For instance, I had an energetic and devoted lawyer, the man I've mentioned, Bill Fitelson, who'd done me and my family many services. I would almost always accept Bill's recommendations on business matters. But politics? That was something else. He was intensely caught up by the political infighting of that day and was the first person I knew who was left and also anti-Stalinist. He was called a Trotskyist. I didn't know what that meant, but the way it was said by my friends confirmed my untutored suspicion that it was something I didn't want to be. It was either a left-leaning divergent of a left Party or a right-leaning divergent, and either way, it was somehow unsavory and to be detested by all proper radicals. Bill was—and now I understand it—a premature anti-Stalinist. I was not interested in the political factions of the left. To the extent I thought at all, I was a softheaded hard-liner. The reason I'd resigned from the Party was not their politics but their determination to control artists by working behind the scenes.

When Bill would talk about Sidney Hook, a man who combined progressive convictions with an anti-Stalinist position, I'd stop listening. When he asserted that Stalin was a criminal equal to Hitler, my imaginary hearing aid turned off. Bill gave me a subscription to his favorite magazine. When I read: "No one can call himself a liberal who is not anti-Communist," I'd thrown the magazine down. But when I came back from that last unhappy trip to southern California, I wouldn't allow my imaginary hearing aid to shut off. I would listen and read and even think a little. For the first time I understood what they were saying, the men Bill Fitelson had been urging me to listen to, and I discovered a shocking thing: Despite the fact that I'd been "out" for seventeen years, my basic opinions were still the "correct" ones, those held by my "comrades" and mutually approved. I'd thought what I was supposed to think. I'd forbidden myself doubt.

I made another discovery that shocked me. I'd successfully impressed whoever had cause to care that I was still a true "progressive," a man who, in this emergency, would be a staunch defender of all "right-thinking" people against the attacks of the House Un-American Activities Committee—despite the fact that I had little sympathy for the Party's program or upholders and had not had for seventeen years.

If you're asking if I believed that the social programs of the "progressives" in the arts were influenced by those of the Party, my answer is yes. If you're asking did I believe that everyone who defended himself by calling on the Fifth Amendment—constitutional right though it is—was a Communist, I must confess I did believe that. Why else would they resort to the Fifth? I'd known them all too long and too well, been scornful of their disguises, and often thought their public postures hypocritical. That doesn't mean I didn't share some of their objections to what was going on in the world. But never with their secrecy, never with their tactics, never with their goals.

But if I'd believed their public postures false, why had I posed as a left-oriented liberal for so long? I'm embarrassed to confess that it was for no real reason. It was only because, in that position, I was "in." In what? Damn if I knew. But in. "On the side of the angels." Why had I tried so hard and for so long to stay in good with my old comrades when I no longer believed in anything they stood for? Answer: I'd been trying to stay in good with all sides, to be liked by everyone, to have it all, left, right, and center, just as I'd managed to have both Broadway and Hollywood, commercial success and artistic eminence. I'd been successfully multifaced. My old friends in the Party should not have liked me. But they did. I should have long before alienated them. But I had not. I didn't like what they stood for, but I'd successfully masked my true beliefs.

It was then that I began to allow myself certain questions that I'd squelched before. To start at home base, how could I deny the conspiratorial nature of our conduct in the Group Theatre when, in that tight family organization, at least one of its three directors, Cheryl Crawford, a close friend, had no idea that there was a Party cell meeting every Tuesday night after the show in Joe Bromberg's dressing room? Was she stupid or were we clever?

Hadn't I played the same game of conspiracy in Actors' Equity meetings?

The secret caucuses before, the clever tactics during, the calculated positioning of our "comrades" in the meeting hall to create the effect of a majority when the fact was that we were a small minority?

If that kind of thing had gone on in our insect society, how could it not have gone on in the State Department and the foreign office—something I'd routinely denied? The people who contested that, were they ignorant or liars?

Was I really a leftist? Had I ever been? Did I really want to change the social system I was living under? Apparently that was what I'd stood for at one time. But what shit! Everything I had of value I'd gained under that system. After seventeen years of watching the Soviet Union turn into an imperialist power, was that truly what I wanted here? Hadn't I been clinging to once-held loyalties that were no longer valid?

Wasn't what I'd been defending up until now by my silence a conspiracy working for another country? Hadn't I watched my "comrades" staggering through political switch after political switch by instructions not written in this country?

Was the question really what the "comrades" said it was, the right to think what you will and say what you believe? Or did it have to do with acts, allegiances, and secret programs?

For a start, why didn't all of us in the Group now name each other? Wouldn't that clear the air, if everyone admitted to everything? If we were open about our membership at last, wouldn't that reduce the issue of Communists in the Group Theatre to its proper scale? Why had no one suggested that?

I knew very well why not. Party discipline.

Why were my old softhearted "progressive" friends—if they were progressive and if they were softhearted and if they were my friends—stonewalling? Answer: They were protecting the Party. Did I really believe in the noble motives they professed? Weren't they also protecting, as I had for so many years, their own pasts? Why, except for that, didn't they now step out of the dark and do what I was beginning to consider doing?

"You can't give that committee names!" I said to myself. But why should I be alone out in the cold? I hadn't heard from any of the others in our cell, although they all knew what had happened. A certain paranoia was developing in me. Cornered and angry, I wanted to name everybody, break open the secrecy, not only of those in our cell but of everyone else I knew to be "in," at any time; anywhere and everywhere, starting with those who'd given Molly a bad time at *New Theatre* magazine and everyone who'd continued after I'd quit in '35 and snake-danced their way through the political postures that followed and who still believed. I was against them all. I wanted to hit the Party's elite especially hard; pull them down into the muck with me. I knew damned well they weren't good for the country.

Why had I taken so long to even consider telling the country—that's what it amounted to—everything I knew? Was it because of the moral injunction against "informing," which was respected only depending on which side you were on? Wasn't Bela right about one thing? If the situation were reversed, wouldn't the "comrades" protect themselves without hesitation and by any means? Including naming me.

Alone in New York City now, with no work to occupy me, and feeling the strain of being directionless—*Camino Real* had been postponed—I began to measure the weight and the worth of what I was giving up, my career in films, which I was surrendering for a cause I didn't believe in. It seemed insane. What was I if not a filmmaker?

Reader, I don't seek your favor. I've been telling you only some of the things I was asking myself on the way "down." But if you expect an apology now because I would later name names to the House Committee, you've misjudged my character. The "horrible, immoral thing" I would do, I did out of my true self. Everything before was seventeen years of posturing. The people who owe you an explanation (no apology expected) are those who, year after year, held the Soviets blameless for all their crimes.

Quote: "There are plenty of sins [in Stalinist communism] and plenty that for a long time I mistakenly denied." That was Lillian Hellman's disclaimer in 1976. It was too little, too late, and I doubted its sincerity.

I W A S drifting. So I decided to consult some friends who I was certain were "on the side of the angels" and would want to talk me out of wrongdoing.

I wrote down what follows early in the spring of 1952, before I'd testified "cooperatively." It is from a diary.

A conversation with Art Miller, in the woods back of my home. I mentioned that Skouras had implied I couldn't work in pictures anymore if I didn't name the other lefties in the Group, then told Art I'd prepared myself for a period of no movie work or money, that I was prepared to face this if it was worthwhile. But that I didn't feel altogether good about such a decision. That I'd say (to myself) what the hell am I giving all this up for? To defend a secrecy I didn't think right and to defend people who'd already been named or soon would be by someone else? I said I'd hated the Communists for many years and didn't feel right about giving up my career to defend them. That I would give up my film career if it was in the interests of defending something I believed in but not this.

Art said that it would be a personal disaster for him if I was "run out of pictures." He hoped that would not happen. He could see that it would concern me deeply. After all, he could write in jail, whereas I couldn't make movies except with financing and an organization of some kind. I said I wasn't contemplating doing it to save my job. But since this was going to happen, I couldn't pretend it wasn't. I only had to consider this: was I sacrificing for something I believed in? I didn't believe in the secret membership of the Communists, had fought it when I was a member. I then told Art how I'd been pushed to resign from the Party.

Art and I had never been frank about the Communist business. This was as much my fault as his and as much his as mine. But mainly it was that no one asked if his friend was a Communist in these days. Art never offered to tell me. He knew I was anti-Communist, but I'd always refrained from what I considered to be "red-baiting." Art went on about the political situation. He was against the Marshall Plan [which I was for; it rescued Greece] and against what we were doing in Korea. He said I was naive. We talked for three-quarters of an hour. He looked terribly worried. Walking back to the house, just before we came into the view of the other people, he stopped and put his arm around me in his awkward way—the side of his body against mine— and said, "Don't worry about what I'll think. Whatever you do will be okay with me. Because I know your heart is in the right place." I was surprised by the phrase and, as soon as I could, wrote it down. "Your heart is in the right place." It was like the truth in a pop song title. There was no doubt that Art meant it and that he was anxious to say this to me before we separated. We parted on affectionate terms.

Some months later, I was leaving the Victoria Theatre building, where my office and Kermit Bloomgarden's office were located, and ran into Art and Kermit entering the building. They saw me but didn't acknowledge that they had, either by sound or by gesture. Although I was to work with Art again ten years later, I never really forgave him for that snub.

I A S K E D Lillian Hellman to meet me at the Oak Room. I laid every- thing on the table, told her I wouldn't be able to work in films if I didn't testify to everything I knew. Then I told her what I'd told Miller, that while it would be a blow, I'd prepared for it and could get along okay without film work. But whereas Art, when we'd talked, had shown understanding and his own worry and pain, Lillian was silent as a coiled snake. I didn't realize until later how threatened she felt in the same emergency. She said nothing to turn me away from where I seemed to be moving. Immediately after eating, she excused herself. (Later I was to find out where she'd gone—not to the ladies' room but to a telephone booth, where she reached Kermit Bloomgarden and consulted with him on what to do about me. "Walk out!" he must have said, because when she came out she said she had to leave and did.) Going out of the Plaza, I felt the shame a fool feels. What the hell

had I expected from her? I believe now that she wanted me to become the
"villain" I became. Life was easier for Lillian to understand when she had
someone to hate, just as her plays were easier for her to construct when she
had a "heavy" to nail. It simplified the issues. Later I heard her reaction to
me, the old familiar one: He sold out! He did it for the money! It was not
the reason. In the end, when I did what I did, it was for my own good
reasons and after much thought about my own experiences. I did what I
did because it was the more tolerable of two alternatives that were, either
way, painful, even disastrous, and either way wrong for me. That's what a
difficult decision means: Either way you go, you lose.

L A T E R she was so pleased with her testimony to the committee, and
especially the reaction to it, that she made a pressbook to hand out to reporters. She kept on a table by her front door, for visitors to see, a book of
congratulatory letters and telephone messages.

Lillian spent her last fifteen years canonizing herself.

I S T I L L hadn't made up my mind what to do. I was edging toward
cooperating with the committee, but of all the people I might name, the
one for whom I felt the most concern and affection was Clifford. I certainly
couldn't name him—if I chose that way—without his permission. I made
up my mind, as I asked him to have dinner with me, that if I found him in
accord with my old "loyal leftist" position, which is what I expected, I'd not
name him, not name anyone.

We ate at Clifford's favorite restaurant, The Lobster, just off Broadway,
where the environment was down to earth, the seafood fresh, and the waiters familiar. Then we walked slowly uptown, and I told him that I was of
two minds, but seemed to be veering toward telling the committee everything I knew about the Party in the Group. Yes, I'd name the others in the
cell with us, all seven of them, and name him too. Then I told him that if
he did not agree to my naming him, I'd do as others had done, refuse to
cooperate with the committee. I'd give up filmmaking and work in the theatre; I was prepared for that. "But," I said, "both you and I know what the
Party is. I remember you explaining the Stalin-Hitler pact to Frances
Farmer sympathetically, but those days are long gone, aren't they? You
wouldn't do that now, would you? Not sympathetically. I don't have any
respect for the Party's secrecy and won't mind breaking it, and I don't have
any respect for their program. I do have respect for the truth and the effect
that it would have if it was spoken. I believe we should all of us name all of
us, establish the truth of what went on. That would make clear how small
the scale was, and this thing would be off our backs. But you are one of my
best friends, and I won't even consider that without your permission."

He was silent. Naturally he'd given the issue a great deal of thought. To my surprise, I found that what he needed from me was what I'd needed from him, permission to name the other. We were, it turned out, in agreement, and when his time came he did the same thing I did, he named names.

The sad fact is that what was possible for me hurt Clifford mortally. He was never the same after he testified. He gave away his identity when he did that; he was no longer the hero-rebel, the fearless prophet of a new world. It choked off the voice he'd had. The ringing tone, the burst of passion, were no longer there. What in the end gave me strength drained him of his. I realize now that my action in the matter had influenced him strongly. I wish it had not. I believe he should have remained defiant, maintained his treasured identity, and survived as his best self. He was to die before he died.

When I told Molly how Clifford had reacted, I asked her at last for her advice. "I've asked everyone else on the island of Manhattan," I said. "Now you." She didn't give me the answer I expected, but said, "I want you to do whatever will make you happy in the end." That is all she said. But later that night she couldn't sleep, and she said, "I don't worry about you; you'll survive anything. But I do worry about Clifford."

A couple of years later, New York not having solved his problems as he'd hoped, Clifford, needing money, returned to Hollywood, where there was work rewriting the scripts of other men. Meantime, I'd survived the scorn of a large part of New York's intellectual left, had done well in the theatre and even better in Hollywood. After *East of Eden* had its flashy New York opening and received an excellent press, Cliff sent me a telegram: "Hurrah for the notices of *East of Eden*. My heart swelled with happiness and pride just like at last I was getting some fine notices of my own. That must really be friendship. I don't go around swelling for many others in my forty-eighth year. But I confess to a little corner of jealousy. Here I am in Hollywood, trying to bring a concrete slab to life, consoling myself with only one thought, to wit, 'At least you won't have to direct this!'"

It was then that I saw that it had been a terrible mistake for Clifford to testify as he did. I saw the awful damage HUAC had done to a man I loved, and I regretted my influence on what had happened. But by that time— two years later—I had no regrets about my own actions.

A F T E R our talk that night, having found that Clifford felt as I did, I walked home through the dark streets. I felt like a pariah in my city, and I knew I'd made up my mind.

I had one more chore. I called Paula Strasberg and asked to see her. The next afternoon, she, Lee, and I sat over tea-in-a-glass. Of course, it was Lee's opinion that concerned me, not Paula's—although she was the one I would name. I told the whole story and said that I'd decided to do it. It was the first time I'd said that.

Lee didn't take long to deliberate; he spoke before Paula did, saying, "There's nothing else you can do."

"What would you do?" I asked.

"No one knows what he'd do," Lee replied, "until he's in it."

I turned to Paula and put it to her. Her response was that although she couldn't do what I said I was going to, "I don't mind if you name me."

We drank our tea and that was that. I returned home, feeling like someone carrying a dangerous secret. I told Molly what had happened and that I was going to write out the whole story, everything, in full detail, naming the other eight in the Group. Which is what I did, the complete truth. Then I asked to appear before the committee again and was given a time. I went to Washington and turned in my statement.

C O N C E R N E D friends have asked why I didn't take the "decent alternative," tell everything about myself and not name the others in the Group. But in the end that was not what I wanted. Perhaps ex-Communists are particularly unrelenting against the Party. I believed that this committee, which everyone scorned—I had plenty against them too—had a proper duty. I wanted to help break open the secrecy.

Now came a storm of anger against me and, among close friends, sick-hearted disappointment. Molly thought I was being unfairly reviled. She urged me to write a statement explaining myself to the public. I said that was not my way, that I didn't feel I owed anyone an explanation, my act explained itself; nor did I feel compelled to share my experience with friend or foe. She persisted, asked if she could write something in my name, only for me to consider. I said, Sure, why not.

So she locked herself in her study and I heard the typewriter, pages being ripped out impatiently, the carriage slammed back to its start position, then more typing. It wasn't easy, what she was trying to do, and she didn't stop for food. When she came out, it was the end of the afternoon, and she had a single page for me to read. She'd described the circumstances and the issues that led up to my testimony, what she considered to be the social necessities, what my own intentions had been, and finally she'd given an assurance to the reader I didn't anticipate, that despite what anyone might think and what some were already saying, I would be doing the same kinds of films and plays I'd always done, with the same themes and from the same point of view.

I thought what she wrote was true and fair in its tone. She watched me read it, and I could see how much it—and I—meant to her. We bought space in *The New York Times* and ran it as an ad. But it didn't change anyone's view of what I'd done. Instead of understanding, it brought me scorn and hardened the antagonism. I soon became the target of a well-organized campaign branding my act as shameful. That was to continue for many months and, in certain quarters, still persists.

I had my childhood answer: distance. I withdrew. I was silent. Never as firm as Molly, I always saw two sides to every issue and every judgment. And so, in the body of my conviction, there appeared the worm of doubt. I still believed what I'd done was correct, but no matter that my reasons had been sincerely founded and carefully thought out, there was something indecent—that's how I felt it, as shame—in what I'd done and something murky in my motivations. What I'd done was correct, but was it right? What self-concerns were hidden in the fine talk, how powerful a role had my love of filmmaking, which I'd been discounting, played in what I'd done? I felt unresolved, alternately humiliated then resentful of those who criticized me. Which is why I remained reserved and silent for so long. My refuge was what it had always been, to drown unhappy feelings in work.

No one who did what I did, whatever his reasons, came out of it undamaged. I did not. Here I am, thirty-five years later, still worrying over it. I knew what it would cost me. Do I now feel ashamed of what I did? When a friend who read the manuscript for this book recently asked if I had met with the others I would name as I had with Clifford and Paula and Lee Strasberg, I answered I had not. For a moment I wished I had. But to wish that now, after all these years, is meaningless. The truth is that within a year I stopped feeling guilty or even embarrassed about what I'd done, and the reason for that is a series of events in the year that followed, which I will now come to.

Bavaria

THE HOUSE COMMITTEE on Un-Ameri-
can Activities was not publicity shy. They rushed my statement to *The New
York Times* the day after I'd given it and, suddenly, there it was on the front
page of the world's greatest newspaper. I started to read it but couldn't. I
felt embarrassed and ashamed. The statement didn't represent my true
feelings, which were not that clear but confused and contradictory. Here is
a piece of diary, written the next day: "Stayed home all day. Miserably depressed. Can't get my mind off it. I know I've done something wrong. Still
convinced I would have done something worse if I'd done the opposite. I
spend every minute making rationalizations for my act. Only one thing in
my life before filled me with such shame and guilt: leaving Constance the
way I did. This now seems sneaky too because no one had reason from my
past conduct to anticipate I would do what I did. I couldn't go to the Actors
Studio or anywhere else. Molly keeps looking at me. Why?"

I stayed home the next day too. Then I decided to return to the normal
routine of my life and walked to the Actors Studio. We were situated high

in a building on Broadway. My office was there and my secretary, Mae Reis. When I entered, she was waiting for me. She announced in her small, prim voice that she couldn't work for me any longer. I didn't ask why—I could see the reason on her face—but she told me, quietly and plainly. I'm sure she believed she was performing a heroic act. It was a shock. Mae gave me the mail and left. She would soon be working for Mike Nichols. And answering questions about me.

I decided to walk through the place. Actors were waiting for a class. Was there a tension toward me? Was I imagining it? I went back to my office and closed the door, picked up the mail, found I was nervous about opening it. I listened to the actors buzzing outside; there were perhaps thirty in that class. No one came in to see me. I'd always been the hero there.

I recalled that as I'd walked down Seventh Avenue toward our building, an actor whom I was preparing to greet suddenly crossed the street away from me. I hadn't thought anything of it at the time, since he'd entered a smokeshop and must have gone in for cigarettes. The actor was Curt Conway, who'd been in my acting class at the Theatre of Action years before. Was he still one of *them?* I cautioned myself not to ask that question. I also told myself not to imagine rejection; I thought I'd got over that. But I knew that Curt had avoided me.

The class was in session. I could now get out of the place without encountering anyone. I went home.

Any doubts I had about the reaction within my world were soon settled. I received two letters, both handwritten.

Dear Gadg: I saw you today for the first time since you appeared before the Un-American Committee. I think you will soon understand that the majority of the people at the Studio were thoroughly sickened and upset at your testimony and felt sure you would not show your face there for a long time.

Perhaps you thought that mentioning some of the names that had been mentioned before wouldn't do any harm but only yesterday Art Smith was barred from playing two dates in Summer Stock for Mr. Paul Crabtree because his name came up in your testimony. You opened the door to the Un-American Committee here on Broadway. You slammed the door on some innocent people whose only crime is that they think differently from you. Dr. Frank Kingdom said in the N.Y. Post about the deaths of Bromberg and Miss Christian—"If America has become a land in which sincere and decent people can be hounded to death for political hearsay it is no longer the America of Franklin [then three words I couldn't make out]. Any American who has any share in hastening another American to torture for a political difference is no true American."

I cannot sign my name because you hold an economic whip over those of us who are only actors—but I want you to know that many, many people, both in the Studio and on Broadway, feel this way.

Another letter, one I didn't believe was from an actor:

Elia. Shame! I shall continue to greet you in the course of our associations but only on the basis of formal courtesy. If it remains uncontested that you refused to pay public tribute to JEB [Bromberg] and to denounce those filthy politicians who hastened his breakdown, I shall one day lose my composure and publicly castigate you, preferably at one dinner or another.

Never have I agreed with past so-called progressive ideas you have expressed; but my respect for your opinion is shattered by your cowardice in the face of the McCarthyism which even my conservatism cannot stomach.

You have funds and fame beyond your need; use them to revive your once strong promise to discredit the revolver-kultur of your poisoned profession.

This letter was also unsigned.

I thought it would let up, but it became a dogfight and I was the bone of contention. There were many phone calls, "unsigned" and hateful. I changed my phone number. When I began to move among people again, I found I was notorious, an "informer," a "squealer," a "rat." I'd become the star villain for "progressives"; just as they'd expected me to be the staunchest defender of their position, they now labeled me the most treacherous of traitors. Others who'd done what I did, perhaps because less was expected of them, were not attacked as I was—not Burl Ives, not Jerry Robbins, not even Budd Schulberg. What made people especially furious with me was that I'd bought space in *The New York Times* for a statement (written by Molly) that urged others in my position to do what I'd done. Very soon I heard of meetings organized by the Communist Party ("Called by all Right-Thinking people") to isolate me for attack. I'd become the primary target.

Since I'd lived most of my youth under a cloud of disapproval—real or imagined—my situation was not new to me. Being an immigrant and an outsider had prepared me to "take" it. I was the accused in a gigantic public trial before unidentified judges, where the verdict, determined in advance, is known. I really didn't understand the intensity of my guilt—everything rational told me that I'd done right—but I seemed to have crossed some fundamental and incontrovertible line of tolerance for human error and sin.

The mail from people against me came with the bills, every day. One person recalled Jack Ford's film *The Informer;* on a penny postcard he'd written: "Congratulations Brother Rat. Sincerely, Gyppo Nolan." A letter referred to Odets's *Waiting for Lefty,* quoted my speech at the moment after

I'd rushed on stage to identify an informer: "The son of a bitch is my own lousy brother!" It was now thrown back at me. The *Daily Worker* used its imagination: "One can imagine the chairman of HUAC putting his arms around him and saying, 'This is the greatest moment of your life!' It is the lowest moment of Kazan's life, one which will haunt him forever." In other space, the paper predicted the loss of my manhood. Actually I'd heard of a fellow film director, Bob Rossen, who'd confessed that for a year after he'd testified cooperatively he'd been unable to maintain a satisfactory erection. There were many people who asserted that now I'd certainly lose what talent I had and my work would go downhill.

I received a long, rather doleful letter from an aging filmmaker, Leo Hurwitz, who'd been on the board of Frontier Films with me. He concluded with this bit of condolence: "I do not envy you your sleep or any quiet in which you might remember people or things past." To which I replied: "Dear Leo, yours was the third hostile reaction I received in the mail [today]. It had something over the first two. It was signed. You're not a stupid man so why don't you take a chance. For half an hour leave the door to your mind open. Consider: maybe I meant what I said. Maybe I am for all the facts being known by all the people. I might have even *meant* that it is the duty of a citizen in a democracy to respect the organs of his government. All crises are a strain, Leo, and this was a crisis for me. But I'm sleeping all right. I'm sleeping fine. How are you?"

That letter sounded more confident than I was. I wasn't sleeping well.

One thing that distressed me was how many lies were abroad about my action and how they were swelling. The most self-righteous one was told by Tony Kraber, a man who'd been an actor with me in the early thirties. When he testified, Tavenner, the committee's counsel, asked him, "Was any part of Mr. Kazan's testimony erroneous?" Tony, ducking the question, answered, "Is this the Kazan who signed a contract for $500,000 the day after he gave names to this committee?" This lie surprised me by its boldness; it was the "big lie" technique of Hitler, which appealed so deeply to prejudices already awakened. Tony, a man I used to play tennis with, went on with his lie. "Would you sell your brother," he said, "for $500,000?" It was a lesson to me about how tenaciously a falsehood can persist and be believed. As for my being his brother, that was another whopper! I was his "brother" from 1933 to 1935. I quit the Party then, and from that time on I was less his "brother." After 1937, when the Group was reorganized and he was not part of the new company, I didn't see him at all. During the war years, I imagine, he would have justified the Stalin-Hitler pact. During the years of the Korean War, I could not have been his "brother." As for his being fired by CBS, I believed then and do now that Communists should not be in positions of control in communications. His testimony reminded me to be proud of myself because I'd always told the precise truth while being attacked by manufactured falsehoods.

Murray Kempton shamed his profession. "There is a piece of Theatre gossip," he wrote some time after I'd testified, "about *A View from the Bridge*, his [Miller's] new waterfront play. When he had finished it, the story goes, he sent it to Elia Kazan. Kazan is supposed to have sent it back with an enthusiastic assumption that he would be the director; and Miller is supposed to have answered that he sent it because he wanted Kazan to know what he thought of men who informed on former Communists." All that was untrue. Isn't there something disreputable about a journalist passing on gossip that way? ". . . is supposed to have . . . is supposed to have . . . the story goes . . ." Kempton had not bothered to check the facts with Miller; a phone call would have done it. He drew Miller's own scorn in a letter Art wrote to the New York *Post*.

The Nation also slurred me, with the lie that I'd done it to preserve a fat Fox contract. The truth was that Darryl had called me into his office and explained that since I was now a controversial figure, he couldn't pay me my salary or anything like it on the last picture remaining on my contract.

I had become the target of opportunity for people seeking to promote themselves at my expense and an easy mark for every self-righteous prick in New York and Hollywood. I was especially scornful of the wealthy "liberals" in southern California who'd never lived without servants, never been involved in any action except a divorce action, and only seen the life of the streets through the windows of an expensive car.

The favorable reactions didn't hearten me. The *World-Telegram*, an afternoon paper, ran an editorial commending me. This I found embarrassing because I knew it for a rigidly right-wing paper, one I'd always disliked. The only commentator I respected who offered support publicly was Arthur Schlesinger. "After searching his conscience," he wrote, "Kazan published an explanation in the form of a newspaper advertisement which to my depraved sensibilities seemed a reasonable and dignified document. But to *The Nation*, Kazan's whole performance seemed beneath contempt; as *The Nation* suggested, *The Informer* had been filmed once and there was no need for Kazan to do it again. But if Kazan had been an ex-Nazi or even an ex-Klansman, telling the same story, would not *The Nation*'s reaction have been completely different?"

I especially valued those letters from old friends who I knew had disapproved of what I'd done but still wished to express the loyalty of friendship.

Karl Malden, in an act of reassurance, gave me a pair of seats to the opening night of *The Desperate Hours*, a play in which he was starring. He also gave seats to his friend the actor Sam Jaffe, intending that Sam should take Karl's wife to the show. But when Karl told Sam that he'd be sitting in the same row with me, Sam refused to go.

Joe Mankiewicz reported the following conversation with Marlon Brando while they were rehearsing *Julius Caesar* at MGM. The news of what I'd done had just reached them, and Marlon's eyes filled with tears. "What am

I going to do when I see the man next?" Marlon asked. "Punch him in the nose? Because I loved that man." Joe said, "When you come across him next, put your arms around him. He's your friend. He did what he had to do. Don't side with the crazies on this."

Clifford also had a talk with Marlon, before Odets testified. "That was a terrible thing Gadg did in Washington," Marlon said. "I'm not going to work with him anymore. But he's good for me. Maybe I'll work with him a couple of times more. At least once." Which is what happened. Marlon's alienation was not so final that he wouldn't make *On the Waterfront*.

I was often embarrassed by those "on my side." For instance, the columnist George Sokolsky. He called me up after I'd testified and wanted some information about Frank Silvera, an actor I'd worked with in *Viva Zapata!* Sokolsky said he'd been "talking to the Coast and Frank Silvera's name came up. He's a bad one, I know. What about him?" I told Sokolsky I had objections to furnishing that kind of information to him, that I'd done it only for the government. "A blacklist," I went on, "is not what will win theatre people away from the influence of the Stalinists. It will have the opposite effect." Sokolsky's response was: "Okay. Everyone must do what he sees fit to do in this matter." I wasn't sure there wasn't the hint of a threat in his response. Was I becoming paranoid?

I was comforted by something Budd Schulberg wrote me; his experience paralleled my own. "The person in my difficulty," he said, "since he cannot please all his old friends, must settle for pleasing himself."

Bela quoted Nietzsche: "What doesn't kill you will make you strong."

I H A D N ' T heard from the man I respected most in the theatre, Harold Clurman. And I hadn't heard from Art Miller.

One day I was told that Harold had sworn he'd never work with me again. I didn't believe he'd said this, until the day he snubbed me on the street. His snub had less *brio* than Bloomgarden's. (Kermit's face got flaming red; he was to die of high blood pressure.) Harold managed his simply by looking preoccupied as he passed me—an expression not unlike his habitual one. But Harold was not as morally rigid as he enjoyed pretending, and some years later, when it was to his advantage, he worked with me without hesitation. By then, while I was still fond of him, he was no longer the man I respected most in the theatre.

About Miller. I heard talk that he, too, was saying I'd done it for money. At first, recalling our conversation in my country place, I didn't believe it. Then I received his public dismissal through the newspaper. The *Post's* headline: KAZAN SLAP AT REDS COST HIM MILLER PLAY. And following that: ". . . since then, Mr. Miller has expressed strong disapproval of that stand to Broadway intimates and cut off all communications with his theatrical teammate." It would have been nice if Art, at this moment, while express-

ing the strong disapproval he felt, had acknowledged some past friendship—or even written me a few words, however condemnatory. But he
didn't, not a word. The only reaction I got from him came indirectly,
through Arthur Kennedy, who played the lead in *The Crucible*. Kennedy
told me that at the opening night party for that play, Art raised a glass of
spirits and, in a tone of vindication, said, "This one's for Gadg!" And so we
separated. Although many years later I would enjoy Art's company when
we met—he's an excellent storyteller—and would even direct another play
of his, I would never really feel toward him quite what a friend should. Nor,
I imagine, he toward me.

More and more often, I suspected resentment and malice where they
were not and found bad opinions not intended. A look would do it, a drop
in the voice level, or the cutoff of a conversation as I came near. I got into
the practice of hurriedly opening newspapers to the gossip columns and
editorials, to discover if there was something hostile directed at me that
day. When I encountered people on the street, I would study their faces to
find out only one thing: for me or against me. I began to snub people myself, to "beat them to the punch." I would bond people together, friends or
foes, nothing in between—which was certainly stupid, and I knew it. But I
couldn't help it; I was on a great social griddle and frying.

There were also days when I'd long to be forgiven, when I yearned to
return to my old innocence, those harmonious times of long ago. Other
days I became rambunctious, and what I longed for was a fight. I felt myself
toughening. I enjoyed the apartness, had to. If I was a wolf, I'd be a lone
wolf, not a herd animal. I thought about it and believed then—and I'm
afraid I do still—that what's best is to be half liked, half disliked. It's a more
trustworthy relationship for an artist. Why should he expect everyone to
like him? He can't have much that's truthful to say, I concluded, when
everyone likes him.

And then the dreams! I dreamed one night that I took Lillian Hellman
to dinner and we were on good terms again. What the hell did I want—
that bitch with balls to forgive me? I dreamed I was having a chummy
conversation with Albert Maltz; he laughed at my jokes. I dreamed that
Tony Kraber and I were tennis-playing buddies again; he'd made dinner
for me, and I kissed his wife, Wilhelmina, when I arrived at his place.
I dreamed of Zanuck. He was swinging his miniature polo mallet and
shouting, in his half-loyal, half-combative way, "It's un-American, it's un-
American!" I didn't understand this until I remembered there was a clause
in the letter Skouras had urged me to sign that permitted a motion picture
company to break a deal with an artist-employee on the basis of bad taste
or political embarrassment.

The sorrow that ate me most concerned my children, how in years to
come they'd have to carry the burden of my "informing" and be ashamed.
This worry never eased.

.   .   .

I N   1 9 3 4,   when I was "in the Party," we helped start a left-wing movement in a very conservative Actors' Equity association. Our prime goal was
to secure rehearsal pay for the working actor and to limit the period when
a producer could decide to replace an actor in rehearsal without further
financial obligation. Up until then it was possible for an actor to rehearse
four weeks without pay, open in the play, and if it was unsuccessful, have it
close in a few weeks or a few days, leaving him without enough money to
pay for his carfare. Actors' Equity was, at this time, a hidebound organization under the presidency of a decent but dusty old actor, Frank Gilmore.

I was working on reforming Equity with a fine man named Phil Loeb,
who, bedeviled by the Communist-hunters, was to commit suicide a few
years later. Our cause was so just that now, looking back, it's hard to believe
there was any opposition to what we were proposing. Still it wasn't an easy
fight to win; we had to score with a majority vote at the annual meeting of
Equity. We planned our tactics cleverly, scattering our forces (a decided
minority) all over the ballroom of the Astor Hotel, where the meeting was
held. This was so that when the reform motion was proposed, there would
be actors speaking for the motion from every side, creating the impression
that there were more of us than there were. We also planned who would
say what, so there would be a swelling tide with no repeats until the vote
was taken.

Our other tactic was to wait until a time close to the end of the meeting,
when "new business" was called for from the "chair," because at that time
all the working actors, those more affluent and because of this more conservative, had left for a quick meal before hustling into their dressing rooms
to make up for the night's performance. Until that exodus, no hint was to
be given of what we would be up to. Then, with the ballroom half empty,
we went into action. Only the old professionals were present by then, and
we Young Turks, waiting in ambush. At a signal, one of us jumped up and
proposed our motion, reading a carefully prepared statement. Quickly it
was seconded, and then came a fire storm of support from all sides of the
ballroom. Our demands were heard and acceded to, and before long actors
had their simple right, pay for rehearsal.

Now skip twenty years to a moment just months after my testimony,
when I received the following letter from an actor I didn't know:

You may or may not know what happened at the annual Equity meeting. When practically all business had been concluded and many
members had left, it presented an opportunity that a goodly sized
"pinko" platoon of members had waited for. The order for new business had come up and one Michael Lewin went to the microphone
and read from a prepared motion that he presented to the meeting. It

attacked you for your frankness before the HUAC and the motion moved that you should be reprehended for doing so and expelled from Actors' Equity Association.

At this point an old actor, David Perkins, rose to his feet crying, "I protest, I protest!" and strode to the front and seized the "mike" from Lewin's hand. Mr. Perkins stated that you had frankly admitted that you'd been taken in and were a loyal American, that as a loyal American you were right in giving whatever information you had to the House Committee. He then made a motion to adjourn the meeting which was promptly seconded from the floor and when the question was put, the motion to adjourn won by fifteen votes.

Mr. Perkins told me at the end of the meeting that he did not know you but he believed in fair play and was more than repaid when Margalo Gilmore came to him at the close of the meeting, kissed him and said that her father, Frank Gilmore, would have been proud of him.

I didn't enjoy the irony. I knew Michael Lewin, who'd made the motion, and I recognized the tactics of taking over a meeting. I think we invented them. I was happy that an old-timer had stood up for me. But the episode made me sad; Equity was my first union.

I was still to learn how widespread the campaign against me was. On my forty-third birthday, the following item appeared in the New York *Herald Tribune*. The heading was THE RED UNDERGROUND and the subhead, "Party Preparing a Blacklist of Cultural Anti-Communists." It then went on: "The Communist Party has ordered a blacklist of its enemies. At a secret meeting in New York last week, subversive Reds in the 'cultural' field were given orders and instructions for the blacklisting of anti-Communist authors, actors, playwrights and sinners who have offended the Party. A list of those in Communist disfavor was prepared with the promise that it would be kept up to date. A list of 'actions' to be taken against an enemy was also given to the comrades. They were told to exert subtle pressure on publishers, advertising agencies and other outlets of talent. They were also instructed to start rumors and whispering campaigns against their enemies, charging moral degradation, personal abasement, intellectual dissipation, and anti-Semitism and to imply that the blacklisted anti-Communist never had any talent or had lost whatever talent he may once have had. Unfavorable reviews and criticisms were to be applied. Among those slated for blacklisting because of asserted damage to the 'progressive movement' are . . ." And there was my name.

There was an equally feral attack from another source, the "newsletter" *Counterattack*, which was sent by its publishers to all producers in the public entertainment field. Not long after my testimony, this appeared:

Kazan has a contract for over $2,000,000 with 20th Century–Fox [a bigger "big lie" than Tony Kraber's!]. His reported CP front connections have been publicized in several places, including this newsletter since he first testified. He would have brought more unfavorable publicity to Hollywood and 20th Century–Fox when his testimony was made public if he had remained uncooperative. It might have developed that his employers would have had to release him—and then face a suit by Kazan to collect the huge unpaid portion of his contract salary.

How much pressure was exerted on Kazan to change his mind? And as long as pressure was exerted, how heartfelt is his change?

Kazan's statement comes very late. And in spite of the fact that he has had "an abiding hatred" of Communism since 1936, he has helped Communists and never joined any organization formed specifically to combat Communism.

What attitude should you take toward Kazan? His case can be regarded pro and con. You can't read his mind but you are justified in judging men by their ACTIONS and ASSOCIATIONS. It's up to Kazan to show definitely where he stands by more than words. Until he does that, who can be sure? Yours faithfully, COUNTERATTACK.

Counterattack had been started by three men, one of whom quit after the newsletter had been made successful. He sold out his share and received a handsome capital gain. Now he was in the best possible position to go into a new business, that of clearing those whom he'd smeared. So he opened a "clearing service," which he offered around the industry. His first job, as part of the staff of Columbia Pictures, was to clear Judy Holliday, a girl he'd smeared.

Counterattack was not altogether wrong. For weeks after my testimony, I'd have days when I felt guilty and sometimes regretful. As for the CP's blacklist, I hadn't forgotten the scene with Clifford in the street. Neither had Molly. Many of the more vicious attacks were aimed at her. At first I showed them to Molly, but I saw they were getting under her skin and I stopped. Whenever I was out at night and a few minutes late getting home, I'd find her wretched with worry. She was convinced they'd strike back either at me or at the children. Our four kids were perfect targets. Molly decided we must never leave them alone in the house at night. I told her that the fellows she was worried about were talkers, not fighters; I should take debating lessons, not karate. She didn't think this funny. Molly was especially on edge because I was leaving for Bavaria soon to research a new film; she didn't want herself and the kids left in the house unguarded, so I engaged a young man to live in while I was away. He was gutter-smart, able with his fists; Molly trusted him. It would be many months before she lived without fear. She knew that most of my "comrades" blamed her for my testimony.

Darryl had been trying to help me. He'd told me that people didn't believe my testimony was sincere and that I was sure to be attacked again unless . . . "Unless what?" I asked. Whereupon he suggested I make a film, *Man on a Tightrope*, about a small, seedy circus that had escaped across the heavily guarded border between Communist Czechoslovakia and free Austria, performers, animals, and all. I read the script; it was by Robert Sherwood, a man whose *Roosevelt and Hopkins* I'd admired, but this was not worthy of him. "Why not?" Darryl demanded. "Because it's badly written, all-black or all-white characters, typical propaganda stuff, and I'd only be doing it to satisfy a pack of red-baiters who want my ass." "It's not propaganda," Darryl said. "It's true. It happened exactly that way. Didn't you read those newspaper clippings I sent you?" "I can't read German," I said. "They were illustrated!" He was shouting now. "You can read pictures, can't you?" "Don't you consider it degrading," I asked, "to knuckle under to *Counterattack*, George Sokolsky, Victor Lasky, and whatever other—" "It's not only them," Darryl interrupted. "A lot of other people still have questions about where you stand." Then he said it: "Including me." "I don't care," I said. "I've done all the crawling I'm going to do." "It's by Bob Sherwood!" Darryl shouted. "He wrote *The Best Years of Our Lives*, for chrissake! Won every goddamn award!" He was on the verge of giving up on me. "To hell with the writing," he said, waving his arms and pacing up and down. "It's the action that counts. We can make one hell of a picture out of that material. Go think somewhere. Let me know tomorrow, yes or no. There are plenty of guys waiting to take it away from you."

Alone, I put Darryl's question to myself. Why had I rejected that story so absolutely? Was I still blocked by my own iron curtain against saying anything unfavorable about the Soviet Union? I ought to find that out. The next day, I asked Darryl to let me go to Bavaria and meet the circus that had jumped the border, talk to their people. If I found out that what I'd read in Sherwood's script was true and not pumped-up propaganda, I'd make the film; if not, not. Darryl said sure, go ahead. Then he did a clever thing; he got Bob Sherwood to go with me. Bob needed details of geography and circus personnel to finish the job, Darryl said. I suppose he figured I couldn't say no to Robert Sherwood.

T H E R E were still great areas of rubble in Munich, some close to the classic buildings, like the opera house, in the heart of the city. At night, the street illumination was uncertain. People passed without looking at each other. The distrust of the war years was still there. Bob hadn't arrived yet, so I walked the streets alone. I've often been told that I look Jewish, and many Bavarians I passed must have been Nazis and thinking: How did that one get away? Or was I paranoid? For three days I was at the bottom, a demoralized man in a ruined city.

Then Bob came and we went to see the Cirkus Brumbach. They were just what the newspaper clippings had shown—an impoverished group of humans, grinding out a living at an old trade. As for their history, it was what Bob had described in his script: They'd broken across the border, they'd risked their lives. I was not dealing with a faulty scenario; I was dealing with an event in history. There was only one conclusion I could come to: I had to make this film to convince myself—not others—that I was not afraid to say true things about the Communists or anyone else, that I was still capable of free inquiry, that I was no longer a Party regular in my head.

Bob was disappointing. I liked him a great deal personally, but he was much too distracted to consider further rewriting. I had the impression his marriage was breaking up. I was also beginning to see Darryl's point: The words meant very little this time; it was the action that counted. Bob left, and I went on observing the circus, but since I had no German, it was as a stranger, from the outside. A week later, I flew over the pole to southern California, did the essential casting there, did the rest in New York, then left for Europe. Alone.

W E   S E T   up our production offices in Munich. Darryl had assigned an "associate producer" to the film, a quick thinker named Gerd Oswald, who could explain what I wanted, when I knew what I wanted, to the German crew we were assembling. The "producer," Bobby Jacks, was not in evidence, nor was he ever during our work; an affable fellow, he was Darryl's son-in-law.

This was to be the first film made by a large American company with an all-German crew, a decision I'd enthusiastically endorsed but that created difficulties. Our first task was to engage a cameraman. We looked at films and interviewed some men, but I found I had little basis for judgment. Gerd made the decision, assuring me that we had the best man available. The conversation I'd usually have with a cameraman before the start of production, to explain my slant and goals, was futile; the man nodded, smiled, looked at Gerd, who responded in their language. I gave up. I met the department heads—carpenter, lights, props, costumes—but since we couldn't converse, I had no impression of them or they of me. Most of them looked as if they'd just got out of Hitler's Wehrmacht.

The first helpful decision Gerd and I made was to use the circus that had actually made the break across the border to free Austria. This choice reinforced my style. It became necessary for me to become thoroughly acquainted with the circus people, and that was my talent. The Cirkus Brumbach was a one-ring affair, a second-rate attraction. Each act had its own equipment and artists, and both the people and their material were a bit run-down. But as I got to know them, I found them endearing. I soon picked up a buddy, the dwarf who worked in the comedy routines. He broke the ice by asking me to have a cognac with him. Then it was my turn, then his turn again. *"Zwei freund, zwei cognac!"* the dwarf would command a servitor; that became our hailing cry. He came up to my belt buckle, but was broad of girth and fearless, a survivor who could dodge and hide but also, when cornered, fight like a badger. He was my entrée into the comradeship of the others in the circus world and was at my side every day that followed. Through him I came to see that circus people were outsiders in any society—freaks, in fact—and since we were so compatible, I must be the same. That identity suited me that year, and I made the circus my home, hung out there all day long, day after day, and was accepted as a member.

Then the actors began to arrive, and when I got to know them, I saw that they were freaks too. They all had something eccentric about them; I'd assembled a marvelous supporting cast of second-raters. That sounds like a slur, but I don't mean to insult these gallant professionals. There are very few first-rate actors, and I've known only one genius among them. To be a second-rank professional is a good rating. Beneath them are the third-raters, the incompetents, and the phonies. My cast was enthusiastic and "hungry," and we were to have a good time together. I was delighted not to have to put up with temperamental superstars on a location less comfortable than what they were accustomed to in the States. Alone with me in a strange land, they made me their father.

Freddie March was as warmhearted and genuine a man as ever lived. I believe that sitting on the blacklist for those mean months had diminished his spirit. This role—and our friendship—revived him. The first thing he said to me was what he'd said before rehearsals of *Skin of Our Teeth:* "Watch out for me. I overdo everything." Few actors have ever been as plain about their faults.

He and I would have a *schnapps* together, the dwarf at my side, and Freddie would tell me his latest dirty jokes—an endless supply. When we got back to Munich for the interior shots, he turned into a boy; he played. Living with me in the magnificent Vier Jahreszeiten Hotel, Freddie got into trouble with a chambermaid, and late one night I had to rush to the police station and intercede for him. He was being threatened by the chambermaid's husband; this unreasonable man was out to become famous by killing a movie star. Freddie was a child who couldn't keep his fingers out of the cookie jar.

When his wife came to visit, Freddie became another person. One of the damned fool women in our group warned Florence March that she'd arrived just in time. But Mrs. March was used to Mr. March being "naughty." She didn't like it, but she wasn't unaccustomed to it. Florence was the intellectual leader of that household. Poor, blacklisted Freddie was no more a Communist than my cat, while Florence was a rather rigid liberal who believed it her duty to straighten out whoever wasn't thinking right and supported organizations she thought deserved the family name on their letterhead. When I directed her in *Skin of Our Teeth*, I found her a conscientious professional, but I'd never heard her say a sentence that surprised me, either as an opinion or as an observation. She thought in a straight line and brought Freddie along with her. He altered miraculously when she left to return to the States.

The others in the cast were also "freaks." Gloria Grahame, who played Freddie's unfaithful wife, was a slightly over-the-hill siren, intent on reinforcing her career. She arrived with many pieces of luggage, one of which was heavy enough to break a back. When I asked her what was in it, she confided that it contained dumbbells and other gymnastic equipment. Gloria's breasts were not as large as she'd have liked; she was determined to get all the professional advantage she could from them by exercising her pectoral muscles.

Terry Moore, who played Freddie's daughter, was a gutsy little thing who let it be understood immediately on arrival that she was the mistress (later, as she claimed, the wife) of Howard Hughes. This plutocrat and scientific "génius," who made such a notable industrial contribution to our war effort as well as designing and building the great six-motored plywood seaplane the "Spruce Goose," had been paying Terry's household bills so she'd be available to him whenever he needed her. He was doing the same for several other young women he'd stashed away here and there in hotel rooms and apartment houses, so he'd always have an ample and varied supply. Particularly concerned about Terry's fidelity—an anxiety she'd probably aroused; it's always a good tactic for a mistress—Hughes had assigned Terry's mother to go along on the trip to Germany and commanded her to be with Terry every instant. Literally so. To augment this supervision, he would call Terry every night from California. How he got through to Bad Tolz and the obscure guesthouse in which she was staying, I never found out. No one else got through; I never received a call, even from Zanuck. When I asked Terry what Hughes had to say to her that was so urgent, she whispered, "He makes the alligator's love call." Of course, you don't believe that, and neither did I until one night I heard Terry responding with the subtler cry of the female alligator.

I was intrigued by this relationship and made a play for Terry, out of curiosity more than desire. I did succeed one night to the extent of getting into bed with her, but I found her mother sliding in one side as I did the other. My research into this fascinating relationship was terminated, but I continued to enjoy her company. "Tell me," she said, pointing to a hill one day, "is that an Alp or a mountain?" Terry was a fearless girl, and when we came to the scene where she had to swim downriver through rapids, to the music of *The Moldau,* she insisted on doing it all, long shot and close-ups; another actress would have demanded a double. I admired the girl, alligator love cry and all. Years later she was to sue for her share of the great man's pie, and it made me happy when she got her slice.

Adolphe Menjou, who was on the left-sponsored blacklist as Freddie was on the right wing's list, was a fine pro who came to work every day prepared and eager and most "democratic." Darryl had suggested him and I'd resisted; but it turned out that Menjou was no more a Fascist threat than

Freddie was a Communist, and since I'd reaffirmed Freddie's position in his profession, I decided to do the same for Menjou. Casting him as I did was one of my private jokes; he was playing a member of the Soviet secret police, and he did it perfectly. Left and right circled and met.

I was to find out that I was a second-rater too—most of the time. In our business, extravagant praise is cheaply won. Only rarely have I been genuinely good. As far as this film went, I was less than second-rate, for as Darryl had anticipated, I didn't have the vaguest idea about how to direct an action movie. I knew only the techniques of directing psychological stuff, close-ups of people staring meaningfully at each other and jawing away. It would be a few years before the lessons I thought I'd learned on *Viva Zapata!* and *Panic in the Streets* would sink in, and even then I'd never be another Jack Ford. This production still from *Man on a Tightrope* tells it all. Gerd Oswald and our cameraman are walking down a country road, side by side, and Gerd is pointing authoritatively to something ahead and the cameraman is listening intently to the instruction in German. Some feet behind that pair walks the bemused director of the film; he looks "out of it" and happily so. The truth is that although my name was to be splashed all over the opening publicity, Gerd Oswald directed more of this film than I did. My main purpose was to prevent Freddie from being hammy and to give some semblance of truth to the intimate scenes, which, in hindsight, are the poorest in the film.

Here is how I came to respect—and like—my crew: A few days before we started work, the cameraman we'd chosen suddenly walked out. Since we hadn't been able to talk, I had no idea what ailed him. Gerd told me that the man had "some personal problems"—which is saying nothing—then quickly found a replacement. On the first day of production, I found out what had happened to the original cameraman. It took a long time for our caravan of production equipment and circus wagons to get to the place Gerd and I had selected for our opening shot. Gerd was getting impatient and driving the men, when, all of a sudden, everything stopped. The crew was gathered around a small radio, listening to a broadcast. It was in German, but I could tell that it was a list of names, pronounced in a manner that reminded me of broadcasts from Radio Leipzig, the official East German station, and that it was a warning. The list of names was the roll call of our crew, and they were being ordered to quit our film. Then came the names of the circus members, warning them of revenge without limit if they went on working with me. Gerd told me that the members of the circus and some of the crew had relatives in East Germany. When the broadcast was over, the crew and the circus people all went back to work; they did not heed the warning, they did not respond to the threat. Gerd then explained what had happened to our first cameraman; he'd quit because he had property in East Germany and was sure it would be confiscated if he worked for us. His replacement also had property in East Germany. Glad to be working for us, he'd given up on his home there.

This incident changed my attitude toward our crew. Perhaps they, too, were second-raters; our Hollywood technicians were more proficient. But my Germans had escaped from the hardships of a disastrous war with their lives, and it had left them tough. One of them had been smuggled across the border under the hood of a car. He showed me the burn marks on his body. Another had lived close to the border and told how at night he heard the mines go off. Rabbits? Humans?

The weather in those Bavarian hills where we worked was never good, and the roads got worse under the rains. A break in the clouds was a surprise, and it didn't last. When it wasn't raining we were blanketed in a heavy fog. The areas where we parked our equipment trucks were generally hub-deep in mud, nor were the vehicles in the best of shape, but we were never late, never behind time. The solution was for the crew to get up in the dark and get the rolling stock rolling. These crew members were the toughest I'd ever seen; they made many of our Hollywood set technicians look soft-handed and spoiled. The Germans were rough of manner and quarrelsome, and sometimes I could see violence boiling up to the brim of the pot and about to spill over. But a few sharp words from Gerd or their own leaders would stop the quarrel. They did drink, but so did I; we all needed to cut the cold of those dark mornings and relieve the heavy weariness of the work. I came to admire my men—they became "my men." They did anything they were called on to do, crossed trade lines, never backed off work, never looked at their watches. I contrasted the crews I'd worked with in California, who came to work in their gas-guzzlers, never crossed trade lines, and quit promptly at quitting time.

A few weeks into the film, a sort of miracle happened: I found myself suddenly relieved of all tension. I liked getting up in the dark with the crew, I enjoyed the harsh weather, I was proud to be hardy. I wanted to be as tough as the crew and made up my mind I would be. Instead of seeking shelter and warmth, I stayed out in the weather with them, the dwarf at my side, as they prepared the next shot. I learned the morale value of a director staying with his men no matter what the weather. If they could take it, I could. It's the best way of winning a crew to your purposes. But I was really doing it for myself. I found myself becoming less sensitive to cold and wet and discomfort; the hardship restored my health. I got over my headaches. I never had a cold. My eyelids stopped twitching. I enjoyed listening to the men squabble and wrangle. I even began to understand a little German. And I believe they appreciated the fact that I was always standing by. I wanted to be like them—Nazis though many of them had been. We were soon communicating without talking. By this interchange of good feeling, *Man on a Tightrope* became a time of joy for me.

When I asked these men what it was like in the east, where many of them had come from, there was no mumble-mouthing. Many had relatives there. They'd accepted the loss; it had become every man for himself. What with the work and the fun and the example of the resilience of these defeated people who were rebuilding their lives and their city, Munich, with such desperate energy, I became unburdened of self-pity. It was such a relief to be out from under the heavy issues, to be up against the simplest one, survival, and to enjoy the rough comradeship of my crew. I determined to accept what they had accepted, that one part of my life was over, and not to look for support or friendship where I'd once had it. I determined to look everyone in the eye when I got back home and tough it out, as my crew was toughing it out.

The example of the escaped circus was another lesson to me; they were simply going ahead with their professional lives. Although the official Communist radio would warn them repeatedly and threaten them with loss of property and the abuse of relatives in the east, they carried on. My questions as to where they stood on the issue that had split me in half seemed ridiculous to them. How could anyone ask such questions? The Communist regime had been ugly and harsh enough to make them gamble their lives to escape it. How could I question where to stand? They laughed at my doubts.

When we finished with the location shooting, I returned to Munich. There I had an opportunity to learn something about the more "ordinary" people of that place and time. I learned about survival and about courage from the women. It was simple to meet them. I was an American film director, and for an actress, Hollywood was still the big chance.

I immediately observed that the young women of Bavaria had developed the ability and the technique of taking care of their needs and their futures at a time when there were far fewer men than women in the country and before the great tide of West Germany's postwar prosperity had rolled in. Just underneath their obligatory romantic postures, these girls were what they had to be, hardheaded and tough-hearted. They were dramatically different, physically and mentally, from the young middle-class women of our Eisenhower era. These fräuleins, like the men, were making sure they survived in this bad time and had what they needed.

One, having sought my acquaintance, offered to take me to the opera. We enjoyed the evening. I was not surprised that she knew a great deal more about Wagner than I did. Then she drove me home in her old-style VW. She didn't stop in front of the hotel to let me off but pulled up on a dark side street. There she showed me how the seat I was occupying could be pushed back to make a love bed. We then performed the farewell ritual. Following which she told me her story. She'd been married twice; both husbands had been soldiers, one killed in France in the first days of the war, the other in Russia at the end. She had a child by each.

Still another young woman, an actress, came all the way from Vienna to see me. She was an exquisite girl, with perfect white skin. A great deal of her conversation had to do with her fiancé, a medical student, younger than herself, whose tuition she was paying from her salary at the Burgtheater. She was a bold lover, which astonished me because the roles she played in Vienna were operetta ingenues, a special type of young maiden with the unearthly charm of a fairy princess and a voice like a bird's chirp. But while she was the soul of innocence professionally, she was looking out for herself and for her husband-to-be. There was no future in playing operetta in Vienna, so having once made my acquaintance, she wrote me, on and off, for the next twenty years, asking if there wasn't something, anything, coming up in one of my films that she might play. I never found the chance to help her.

I admired these women. Once their primary desires and curiosity were satisfied, our conversation was far more interesting than I'd anticipated. They made me realize that we Americans had never known the hardship of a war, never known its costs. We'd always been able to maintain our middle-class comforts and security. These women all had harrowing tales of their parents' experiences in the war. When they told me of their deprivations and the fear they'd known, I felt for them. They all had to find a way to secure their future and did it the best way they knew how.

This time of lechery had a special importance for me; I recalled Bob Rossen and his failing. I was determined that my struggle with the testimony, the loss of some friends, and the guilt that I no longer felt were not going to have any such effect on me. "Wilt, scoundrel!" so old friends had said to me. "Turn over and die; you never had any talent anyway," their ideological leaders had said. This exercise in lechery was one part of my answer.

W H E N the filmmaking in Bavaria was over, I was told that I was to be given a present by the crew at the closing party. They were all there that night, dressed up in the best they had and drinking heartily, as I was and Freddie was. (Florence had gone back to their Firefly Farm in Connecticut, so Freddie had reverted to his "lesser self.") Adolphe Menjou made a speech, which the crew applauded, more for his startling try at German than for the sentiments he was trying to express. Then one of the crew, who looked a little like a George Grosz drawing, announced the present for Herr Kazan. In walked eight musicians in concert clothing, carrying their string instruments. They sat in a semicircle of chairs arranged by the crew and played Mozart's *Eine Kleine Nachtmusik*. That was the crew's present to me. It destroyed me. I did my best with a speech, but it wasn't up to the occasion; I hugged some, shook hands with them all, even kissed a few, then went back to my hotel, choked up with affection and admiration. The next day I heard that after I'd left, there'd been a fight between two members of the crew, and one of them had stabbed the other with a knife. They'd all carried long folding knives, and that fight had been a long time coming. But it didn't spoil my memory of the occasion.

I A M not a forgiving man. I do not ask for the forgiveness of my enemies, nor do I forgive them. Damn them and the company they keep. Not forgotten are those actors who joined with one another against me and who—many of them—still sought my help. Not forgotten are those newspapermen who'd fitted me for a noose—or a cross—who, day after day, held me up to shame in their papers.

When I got back to New York City, something mysterious had happened. I found I was the possessor of a new degree of energy, one that would send me spinning through ten years of unremitting work. I would make nine films, all of which, to some extent, I initiated, and stage six plays, which were received with gratitude by an ailing theatre.

I was also another person to the casual eye, silent but in some way unsettling. I prided myself on being able to conceal my feelings of hostility from everyone. I just worked harder than anyone else, never asking for sympathy or for understanding, never giving myself the relief of expressing how I felt, just a silent human motor pushing its load. No one could figure out what the hell made me go so hard. I had an impenetrable front. Only the discerning few could see what I was saying by my behavior: "You can't hurt me; you haven't penetrated my guard; I can beat you at any game you choose to play, because I may not be smarter than you or more talented,

but I never get tired and you do. You will also be forced to admit publicly
that despite all that you're thinking, my work is better than yours."

Not a word of this was articulated. It couldn't be, because I didn't understand it; I only rode it. There was no cry from the interior, no roar of anger
or whimper of pain. I prided myself on my control and my silence and my
ability to take punishment.

Once back in the big city, I decided to cut off certain friends, those who'd
wavered in their allegiance. I decided to stand alone in what would be a
strange environment for me—one where not everyone liked me—and say
nothing. I'd not seek to be taken back into destroyed friendships or to be
"accepted" again by those who were "kindly disposed." I'd been defeated,
yes, but only so I could come back stronger. Just as my circus had, I'd
survived all threats, spoken and implied, and was going on. The thing was
to be hardy, no matter what the "weather," not to expect the comforts of
position, the constant flattery of praise or the false assurances of comradeship. I would be what I had to be—tougher than my enemies—and work
harder.

The only genuinely good and original films I've made, I made after my
testimony. The ones before were professionally adept, not sufficient
praise—that word "adept"—for a man as hungry for excellence in achievement as I was. The films after April 1, 1952, were personal, they came out
of me, fired by what I've been describing. They're films I still respect.

So came the mark of anger on my face, that cast of countenance which
has made all three of my wives ask again and again, "Are you angry?" "Are
you mad at me?" "No," I've answered, "it's just my face." But now you know
the truth. What happened during the time I've been describing and how I
dealt with it—that choked silence—made my face what it is today.

The day after I arrived in New York, I walked to the Actors Studio, and
here is what I thought: *Warning to certain old friends.* When we pass on
the street and I nod and you pass me by without responding and, after
you've gone on, you look back and see that I'm smiling, that smile doesn't
mean what smiles generally mean. It's a different smile and not a "nice"
smile but a sign that I'm pleased with myself. "Ah!" I'm thinking. "I've lost
another false friend."

I went into my office, leaving the door open. Tennessee joined me there
and we started once again to interview actors for his new play, *Camino Real.*
A member of the cast who was glad to have me back and somewhat surprised to see how I was, asked me, "What keeps you looking so young?" I
answered, "My enemies."

D I R E C T L Y on finishing writing what you've just read, I came down with shingles, a painful and only partly understood disorder of the body's network of nerves. My clever wife fingered it: "Must have been a tough chapter to write," she said. I had to laugh, because when Jack Ford quit *Pinky* and claimed shingles for an excuse, I'd scoffed. Pain made me a believer. Had some inner tension been reawakened to cause me to suffer this—whatever it was? Doctors didn't help. One of them assured me it would be over in a matter of weeks, another warned me I might have the pain for the rest of my life. "You'd better hurry and finish this book," I said to myself.

B E F O R E I'd left for Bavaria to make *Tightrope*, finding myself alienated from Miller—our friendship, once so close, now cold—I became aware of a hole in my professional life. At Molly's prompting, I wrote Budd Schulberg, suggesting we meet before I left the country. He responded generously, invited me to visit him in New Hope, Pennsylvania, and stay overnight so we could have a good long talk.

On the theory that misery loves company or that men in a fight should seek allies, Molly and I drove down to spend the weekend with Budd and his wife, Vicki. We quickly discovered that we'd been through the same experiences, he in southern California, I on the East Coast. With his book *What Makes Sammy Run?* he'd experienced what I had when the Party's "leading comrades" tried to influence the course of the Group Theatre. The scene I described to him featuring the Man from Detroit corresponded to one he'd had with comrades Jack Lawson and V. J. Jerome concerning his novel. He'd refused to be disciplined, had been discredited by the Party, then left the ranks rebellious. Following which, Budd had testified as I had, been reviled by many of his old companions as I'd been. His closest friend had stopped talking to him as Miller had shunned me. Now the "progressives" had us both on their shit list. As we talked that first night in New Hope, there was an immediate warm sympathy between us. We became brothers.

There was a difference, however. Ever since his release from the army, Budd had been living in the Pennsylvania countryside. The people around him there either were indifferent to the issues that had twisted our lives or agreed with Budd's position. I lived in New York, had an office in the same building I'd had before my testimony, encountered people every day in the elevator or on the sidewalk who'd turned against me and felt it their obligation to let me feel their scorn. I was in essence the head of the Actors Studio, the man who'd determined its basic policies, and I'd been made to feel the condemnation of the actors there or at least their disappointment in me, which hurt more. I'd also been selected as the number one blacklist target of "all right-thinking people," and was the frequent object of attacks by liberal columnists in newspapers I read every day. Up until this time I'd made it a policy not to respond to these attacks, thought it the only way I could gain some peace. The result was the contrary, of course: The attacks had grown in venom and frequency. Budd's life was easier than mine.

We found a surprising coincidence in the dramatic material we were looking for to work on. I'd declared after my testimony that I would continue to make the same kind of films I'd made before. I proposed to Budd that we make a film together; he responded enthusiastically. I suggested the story of the Trenton Six, black youths caught in a miscarriage of justice. He knew the story. Then I told him about my experience with *The Hook* and what had happened in the budget meeting at Columbia Pictures. Whereupon he revealed that some years before, he'd bought the rights to Malcolm Johnson's Pulitzer Prize series "Crime on the Waterfront," and written a screenplay based on the material. It had not been made. He found the screenplay for me and, lying on the floor, I eagerly read it.

Budd's script was titled *The Bottom of the River,* and it started with a scene of dredging for the body of a murdered rank-and-file longshoreman leader. It was strong, true stuff but, as they say in our line, needed work. When we parted I told him that either that material or the story of the Trenton Six would interest me very much, and he should decide which he preferred and let me know. I called him before I left the country and he told me he preferred the waterfront and would work on it while I was away.

Months later, when I came back from Bavaria, I'd undergone an essential change. I was no longer defensive but was determined to reclaim my self-esteem and fear no cabal of old friends turned to enemies. I landed in New York, and the first person I sought was Budd. Despite the fact that Molly had sent me in Munich Bob Anderson's beautiful new play, *Tea and Sympathy,* which he wanted me to direct, a stroke of good fortune indeed; despite the fact that I had long since agreed to direct Tennessee's *Camino Real,* a lovely dramatic poem which I could immediately and most happily put on the stage, the project with Budd on the waterfront answered a need that was deeper. It was my reply to the beating I'd taken. The emotion I brought back from Bavaria was not a pretty one; it was a desire for revenge. I would turn the tables on those who'd said I'd lost whatever talent I had, that I would never again do anything bold and worthy, that I would now turn conventional and cautious. I was more determined than ever to make a film about the New York harbor and what went on there, thus to show everyone, including myself, that I hadn't backed away from my convictions and wasn't to be insulted or bullied again. I was also determined to show my old "comrades," those who'd attacked me so viciously, that there was an anti-Communist left, and that we were the true progressives as they were not. I'd come back to fight.

Budd was wildly excited about the waterfront and was eager to take me across the river and show me the scene. He'd practically lived in Hoboken, had walked the dockside streets, made friends with the dockers, hung out in their bars, drinking even-up with them, amassing an intimate knowledge of their homes, their families, their lingo, and their humor, and of how those who'd defied the rackets responded to the threats on their lives. He told me the details of the struggle within their corrupt union, who the longshoremen's enemies were, about the pilfering and the payoffs, where the spoils went, and the secret links to the politicians. He'd uncovered a dramatic gold mine and, more committed to working on the story than I could have hoped, had written an outline of the possible course of action for the film, which he offered for my response. It was an excellent start, and I responded to it and he to my criticism of it. Now he wanted me to go to Hoboken and spend some time there with him. I was eager to, but told him I hadn't cut *Tightrope* yet, it might take a couple of months in California, but as soon as I had, I'd immerse myself as he had in our material. What

Budd had given me when I returned from Bavaria was the most heartening gift anyone could have made me.

After seeing Budd, I met with Bob Anderson, another man who became a dearly valued friend, to talk about *Tea and Sympathy*. I thought the play beautiful and perfectly constructed, but felt that it needed the most delicate handling and casting. I told Bob I'd committed myself to do Tennessee's *Camino Real* immediately on my return to New York, and if Bob wanted his play done straight off, perhaps he should get another director. "How about Harold Clurman?" I said—under the circumstances, a mischievous generosity! Bob preferred to wait. This delay turned out to be a blessing; it enabled us to work more carefully on the physical production and to involve the help of my friend Karl Malden, who (pre–American Express) hoped to be a director and wanted the learning experience of casting a Broadway play.

Next I met with Cheryl Crawford to get the production of *Camino Real* set up, conferred with lawyers to work out contracts, and began the search for actors. I'd made up my mind to cast the play entirely from the Actors Studio, offering the parts to the actors I wanted, and so forcing their attitudes about me into the open. In casting interviews, I was head-on—that was a relief—prepared to be belligerent if necessary, otherwise professionally friendly. No one backed away from me. About this I didn't deceive myself. I knew a director's influence exists when he has a play actors want to work in and the backers to give the play a ride. I had both.

Then I flew west. Before I'd left Munich, I'd written Darryl, asking if I could remain in New York for a few weeks to see my family and tend to my future plans before coming west to edit the film. Darryl had graciously granted me the favor. "He must really like my film," I told Molly.

Here is how you receive news of your downfall in a big Hollywood studio:

When I landed at the Los Angeles airport, there was no studio car and driver waiting for me, even though my agent had informed Fox of my arrival. I rented a car and drove straight to the auto gate of the Fox lot. The policeman in the booth informed me, "You're in the Old Writers Building now." Which is something of a misnomer. What he was referring to was an old building where Fox housed young writers whose tenure was of uncertain duration.

I drove past the spiffy Executive Building, where my office had been ever since *Gentleman's Agreement*. The lot seemed to lack the excitement of its good days—or was that my heart speaking? I passed between the great sound stages where I'd shot so many scenes; they did seem unused now. Then I turned down into a hollow; here was my building, a shapeless structure of crumbling red stone, surrounded by ragged eucalyptus trees. I had difficulty finding my office. My name was not on the door. I had a roommate; the reception room had two desks and two secretaries, idle and gossiping. Mine informed me she was there on "loan-out, just to fill in for a week." Then added, "There's a letter from Mr. Zanuck on your desk." My space, small and sunless, looked directly into the slope of the hill above. On my desk was an envelope, which contained a two-page letter:

> Dear Gadg: I have asked Dorothy to work over the weekend making the last group of changes we have done in the editing of *Tightrope*. We will have the picture ready to show you Tuesday night and I have asked Dorothy not to tell you anything in advance as I prefer that you see it for yourself without any preconceived idea of my "butchering." You will be infuriated at some of the things I've done and you will be delighted with others. In each instance, I will try to convince you after you've seen the picture as to why we made some of the more or less major adjustments. I feel we have a wonderful picture but it needed radical editing.

I'd believed that I, not Darryl, would edit my film, had come to California to do that. His letter finished with: "Virginia saw the picture and she was crazy about it. The same is true of Darrylin. They both cried and said the suspense is terrific. Even the Frenchman, Jacques, cried."

The ultimate praise Darryl could pay any film was: "Virginia cried." Virginia was Mrs. Zanuck, Darrylin one of their two daughters. Jacques was a Frenchman whom Darryl had engaged to stay at his side and talk French, a language that would be useful in days to come when he took on a series of French mistresses. Jacques was now a regular in Darryl's screening room, along with the Turk, a masseur, Sam, the master of the commissary, and various directors agreeable to playing croquet all night. They liked what Darryl liked. Jacques had even learned to cry.

What's the first thing a "big" director does when he feels outraged at how he's been treated by the head of production? Right. He calls his agent. What happened then illustrates the role of the great agents of that day. They mediate. They lower tensions. They keep things going, prolong the pay dates, make sure their ten percent keeps coming in. One of Abe Lastfogel's favorite bits of advice to a client about to blow his cork was: "Don't prejudge!" Abe had great faith in the healing powers of time. He told me precisely how to answer Darryl: "Received your letter. Look forward to seeing the picture with you Tuesday night." Not another word. No offensive "How dare you!" Abe gentled me, and for a day I went along. My next diary entry tells me: "I had a wonderful talk with Abe and he agrees that it was now time for me to step out and do my own films—where I could make all the cutting decisions . . ." And so forth. Of course, Abe was conning me, gently, like a father with a troubled son.

He invited me to have dinner with him and his wife, Frances, at Chasen's, where the atmosphere of success and compliance permeates the air and friendship as soothing as Muzak lulls the guests. My complaints suddenly seemed unimportant as I enjoyed a perfectly made Caesar salad. Afterward Abe took me to my hotel in his long black limo, and as we parted, he said, "About Darryl. Remember when you needed a friend, not so long ago, remember? Darryl was for you then, wasn't he? You have a bond of friendship there. Don't forget that."

I chewed that remark over all the next day. It was true, but after a night's sleep I saw it otherwise. Wasn't Abe telling me that professionally I was in a weakened position because of my testimony? That I had little ground for a violent protest, no matter what I thought of what Zanuck had done with my film? I read Darryl's letter over, now between the lines. I was not being consulted; I was being told the final score, how it would have to be. He was being polite to me, but it wasn't necessary for him to be polite. I had to eat what he put on my plate. The testimony crisis had made me a contractual cripple.

So I decided not to whine—not to Abe, not to anyone—but to learn my lesson. That was when I resolved to forget about friendship and all that muck and face the facts of life: Darryl owned the negative. He'd decided he had a commercial failure in *Tightrope*. About that he proved to be right. He believed he could "save" it as he had "saved" other films, by juggling a director's work. About that he proved to be wrong.

I saw the film with him and found that in the process of "saving" it, he had trampled over my intentions and those of Bob Sherwood. I also saw that I could hold no brief for either Bob's writing or my own work in the "personal scenes." Both were poor. Maybe the picture deserved Darryl's "saving." Even so, I didn't want to work that way, not even if he'd turned the film into a commercial success. Darryl had squeezed and tightened it into a conventional action melodrama, with its heavies and its trouble-beset hero, plus the inevitable bit of romance. Only the costumes and props were different. Thinking the film a failure, he'd done his best to get Fox its money back. So "Virginia cried"! Could Fox bank that?

Now I was professionally at the bottom. I'd directed a film that would be seen all over the world by film financiers. It didn't represent the talent I had. It would make it difficult for me to get backing for future films. I told Darryl I didn't like what he'd done. He responded, calmly, that he'd had no other course with the film I'd given him. Beneath everything he said lay the confidence that accrues to a man from ownership. But there was also the hint of an opposite feeling, some disappointment that I hadn't responded positively to what he'd done and even the slightest anxiety that I might be right: Perhaps the film was still a dud, despite his laying on of hands. This apprehension, I'm sure, didn't last long. Darryl would have an eager corps of studio faithfuls in to see the film the next night and reassure him as to how great it was. I told him I recognized I had no power in the issue, so I'd go back east immediately. He didn't urge me to stay. I left California the next day.

Ironically, when the film opened in New York, it drew quite a favorable press. Darryl was vindicated. But no one bought tickets to see it. I was disgraced.

I'd thought of Darryl as a friend, but he'd run over me ruthlessly. What the hell did I expect—that an industry head, for friendship's sake, would allow a film to be exhibited in a form he was sure would lose his company money? How naive of me! His job was on the line too. The bosses, his and mine, are your friends when you bring in the cash; the rest is for show. I mustn't kid myself again.

There was another irony. I'd heard during this visit to California a few hints about my "controversial political image." These slurs undercut my position at the studio. Were they so intended? I thought it over and came to the conclusion that if *Tightrope* had been commercially successful, I'd have been much less controversial politically. As it was, with the film a failure, people would think I'd made it only to get on the safe side of the McCarthyites. There was enough truth in that so that I felt shame.

Some shame. But not a hell of a lot. Those days were gone; that was another fellow. In New York, Budd was waiting for me. And Bob Anderson. And Tennessee Williams. Who had better prospects? The hell with Darryl and Fox and my controversial political image. A new day was coming. My time of working for others was over. Now I'd work for my self-respect. And gritty, formidable, quarrelsome, sour, bitter, harsh New York, my home city, was waiting for me.

I W I L L not forget Budd Schulberg on the streets of Hoboken and in its dockside bars. And I will never forget "Brownie." Budd was doing research, but not as I'd done research. He was immersing himself in the subject as he would a cause; he'd become a partisan of a rotten union's rebels. By the time I got to the waterfront, the longshoremen we encountered and to whom we talked had accepted Budd as a champion of their side. These men who lived by their muscle and were suspicious of strangers and particularly leery of men wearing the mark of money—for them, all privilege had to be corrupt—trusted Budd and spoke openly to him. The most hard-domed of them all was Arthur Brown, "Brownie." He'd become Budd's constant companion, a walking certificate of acceptance, for all his fellows to see.

Budd was an upper-middle-class kid, raised in a California sun-country "mansion," where servants tended to his every need and he had every domestic luxury, to the point where he took them for granted. His father, B. P. Schulberg, was head of production at Paramount Pictures, and Budd was a prince of that realm. Brownie was the epitome of the men with the hard hands and the hard faces who walked the west shore of the Hudson

River with cargo hooks around their necks, professional tools and weapons of defense as well. In Hoboken these men were Irish or Italian, Catholic, and many of them anti-Semitic from the cradle. How had Budd won this man's perfect acceptance, and his affection?

Brownie, at five foot five, was a formidable battler and defiant of the "mob," which crawled all over the edge of the river like flies on a rotting carcass. An outspoken "insoigent," he'd once been brutalized by thugs until senseless, then dumped into the winter's water and left for dead. Somehow he had done the dead man's crawl out of the cold and filthy North River to live again—perhaps the cold revived his senses in time—and was found on the streets the next day by his murderers, as defiant as ever. Along with his fearless swagger, he had a mocking humor, which made "dem hoods" his favorite target. I was sure Brownie had come out of the water laughing, for of all the laughter I've heard in my life, Brownie's was the most irreverent. He became for Budd, and later for me, the symbol of the longshoremen's defiant spirit. His photo is in a place of honor at the head of this chapter.

The more serious and concerned men of the waterfront's work gangs had read what Budd had been writing about their struggle, particularly his pieces in *Commonweal*, the liberal Catholic magazine. Surprised that they knew the writer who'd done the articles, they were grateful for Budd's honoring of the "waterfront priest," Father John Corridan, a man who'd made it his parochial duty to support the reform element in the corrupt union. I would come to know and admire Father John as Budd did, and trust him as the longshoremen did. But my friend Schulberg had simpler bridges to the feelings of the men who worked the docks. For one thing, he was what I am not, a "good drinking man." One drink inebriates me, two drinks put me to sleep. Budd could stand up to a bar and match Hoboken's finest, drink for drink, all night. He called them his "creative drunks"; he would throw down a few, then a few more, so get the fire going, and then his inhibitions would be lifted and his stutter stop. Strong drink brought his deepest sympathies to the surface, and suspicious, often short-tempered longshoremen spoke plainly to him, for they saw that he had genuine concern for every sorry twist of their lives. I envied how Budd ate up detail, and I envied his remarkable memory. He could recall whole speeches and every article of apparel his subjects wore. He penetrated into every aspect of this other world of hardship and corruption.

Budd was also a true authority on the longshoremen's favorite sport, the fight game. Bar birds were fascinated to hear the inside dope Budd fed them. He'd even owned a piece of a fighter once and had surprising stories to tell about him. Men would bunch around Budd to hear what he had to say, closer and closer, less and less guarded; they all respected him for what he knew and who he was, a writer who was with them in every way. In time I was there too, gathered in that group and accepted.

I would always remember that this was the way to prepare a screenplay—not to observe at arm's length and scribble notes, but to make yourself one of the people in whom you're interested and to make the essential story of that place and time your cause. My first impression had been that Budd was working cleverly as an investigative reporter, but then I saw that his interest was not a tactic of the trade but passionate and true, and that he saw the grim tragedies and grotesque humor of that place as great stories are seen, with compassion for the victims and devotion to the just. Budd had made himself more than a writer engaged to prepare a screenplay. He'd made himself a champion of the humanity on that strip of shore. It was a great lesson for me, one I would not forget.

So that when Budd said he was ready to sit down and write out a screenplay, I knew that he was ready and knew that what he produced would be worthy of its subject. I then took a recess from Hoboken; it was time to put Tennessee's *Camino Real* on the stage.

I P A S S E D from a film that dealt with the broadest possible scene, a panorama of human suffering, to a play that penetrated into the most intimate area of all, the soul of an artist. *Camino Real* is as private as a nightmare. No playwright except Eugene O'Neill in his last plays was as personal as Tennessee Williams. His collected dramatic works might be read as a massive autobiography, one far more truthful than the book he wrote and titled *Memoirs*. The plays, with a little discernment, prove to be as naked as the best confessions. They—and this play perhaps more than the others—are about great fears of the author, of distrust and betrayal: distrust of his own fate and of other humans and the betrayal he was certain would come, both from other men, even those close to him, and, because of its anarchy and cataclysmic speed, from time itself.

Already world famous in 1953, Tennessee lived like a fugitive from justice, always changing his whereabouts, ever moving. He traveled along an archipelago of culture islands that were congenial to him, places where he might feel, for a time, at liberty to be unobserved and totally himself— London, Paris, Rome, Sicily, North Africa, Key West. Only a few people knew where to find him. Their communications frequently reached him after he'd departed for a "destination unknown." I was one of the privileged; we were in continuous touch by mail. The centers of civilization that he found agreeable were, of course, those populated by his own kind: artists, romantics, freaks of one kind or another, castoffs, those rejected by respectable society. He settled into these nests of outsiders to feel at ease. But it was never for long; he'd soon be off again. "I usually work best," he explained, "when I've just come to a new place."

Williams, a homosexual before the existence and support of a gay movement, was the complete outsider. The presence of his name and often his photograph on the front page of a newspaper in each new encampment did not quiet his unhappy conviction that he was not liked, not wanted there, and scorned for his sexual preference. Fame and money did not solve his problem. He still expected to be betrayed socially and personally, even by his closest friends and, as he grew older, by his lovers. But above all and most painfully, by his "public."

About this he wasn't mistaken. The last years of his life were pitted with public failures, one disaster following hard on another. But he never stopped writing—and offering his chin for the knockout. Bob Anderson tells a story of the night when he attended a preview of *The Seven Descents of Myrtle*, written late in Williams's life and certainly not one of his better plays. Just before the curtain was raised, the author slid into a side box. Yes, *slid;* his movements in public had become stealthy. He slumped deep into his seat, but some members of the audience noticed him, then others, and applause began. The lady seated next to Anderson turned to him and asked, "What are they clapping for?" Bob pointed and said, "That's Tennessee Williams, the author of this play." "Well," said the lady, "shouldn't we wait and see whether or not we like this play before we start applauding?"

Is it a mystery why he and I, so different in every apparent respect, remained so congenial? The year before I directed *Camino Real*, I'd performed the act that had separated me from the company and respect of many of my peers. The big shot had become an "outsider." Williams was always that. We both felt vulnerable to the depredations of an unsympathetic world, distrustful of the success we'd had, suspicious of those in favor, anticipating put-downs, expecting insufficient appreciation and reward. The most loyal and understanding friend I had through those black months was Tennessee Williams.

There was another way in which we were similar. When we were mounting *Camino Real*, Tennessee was living with Frank Merlo. In effect they were married and enjoying the steadfastness of that way of life. Tennessee described the satisfactions he was gaining, but with a qualification. "The heart should have a permanent harbor but one it sails out of now and again. I doubt that anything did me more good as a writer than the many years of loneliness, of cruising around, making sudden and deep acquaintances, one after another, each leaving a new and fresh print on me. Thank God, Frank understands that and I can still do it sometimes."

I came back to New York from my encounter with Zanuck, having been flung to the bottom of the darkest pit of Hollywood, where the undesirables wait for employment. I understood Tennessee's play *Camino Real* very well; I was its unfortunate hero.

Camino Real is an imperfect play, but it is beautiful, a love letter to the people Williams loved most, the romantics, those innocents who become victims in our business civilization. The central character, Kilroy, is a homeless mid-American boy who, wandering without direction over the earth, has arrived at the final, mysterious place where Death waits. Here also,

waiting for the end, are the high fliers Tennessee cherished, all now "over the hill": Jacques Casanova, Don Quixote, Marguerite, La Dame aux Camélias, the Baron du Charlus. They are all doomed, but Kilroy has a quality the others have lost: He can still struggle to get up when he's knocked down.

The favorite word of one of Tennessee's romantics is "brother." Williams calls it the forbidden word on the Camino Real; its use there is punishable. Williams sometimes addressed me in his letters as "Fratello Mio." But with reference to most people, when he was in one of his black moods, Williams had this to say: "What is brother to them but someone to get ahead of, to cheat, to lie, to undersell in the market. Brother, you say to a man whose wife you sleep with." In a line from *Camino Real*, he went further: "We have to distrust one another, it's the only defense we have against betrayal." Did I have to learn to distrust the film producers, for instance? Otherwise would I, like Kilroy, continue to be cheated, slugged, and knocked about? Tennessee's play described the perilous and uncertain condition I was in at that time; I was Zanuck's Kilroy, bullied and rejected despite his cordial "Dear Gadg" letters. I'd just been knocked down and was flat on the canvas, with Darryl counting to ten. I had to do what Kilroy—and Williams—did: get up off the mat and come back fighting.

The artist has his solution; Tennessee exemplified it. It was his way of self-restoration. In a letter I received from Williams, there was this: "For the past five years I have been haunted by a fear which has made it necessary for me to work like somebody running out of a house on fire." Once when I asked him what his play was about, he answered, "It's the story of everyone's life after he has gone through the razzle-dazzle of his youth. Time is short, baby, it betrays us as we betray each other. Work, that's all there is!" Then he went on: "There is terror and mystery on one side, honor and tenderness on the other." Once, in a fruity mood, he described the play as "an encomium, despite all else, to the enduring gallantry of the human spirit." I didn't think it necessarily described the play, but it did the author.

These words, this spirit of his, had their effect on me. Here was a man in many respects less fortunate than I was, more permanently an outsider in the society where he'd been born and brought up. But he'd persevered and continued to believe in the human virtues. I admired the man; our friendship had a restorative effect on me. After we'd opened, I wrote him: "To tell you how much your companionship has meant to me is impossible. In the deepest possible way, I'm indebted to the experience of working with you. I've come out of the production feeling healed. And reinstated. What we've done together has made me feel in the forefront again."

Well, yes, but not quite.

It's better not to look back at what you've done and particularly, in my case, not to reread the plays you've directed. Last week, I did read this play again, and I know that I didn't touch its potential. I wanted a production that had the bizarre fantasy of the Mexican primitive artist Posada. It was an idea to which my choreographer, Anna Sokolow, responded; she knew Mexico well. But the play didn't take place in Mexico or in any other land that can be found in an atlas. It happens in the topography inside the author's head. What it needed was the vision of the right artistic collaborators. I talked about Posada, yes, but it is not sufficient to have "brilliant" ideas and enthuse everyone concerned. Posada! Sounds great, doesn't it? Especially if you haven't seen his work. Candied skulls and skeletons! Great! But something beyond talk is required, in this case the right help from the right designer.

I wrote the designer we'd chosen a long note explaining what I hoped for in the set. I didn't get it; what I got was a lugubrious realistic setting that was, in a word, heavy-handed. And too real. It made the fantasies that took place inside it seem silly. I should have ordered a new setting, but I didn't. I betrayed myself by not sticking to my guns. I'd buried my original—and I believe correct—intention in talk. And good fellowship. The designer was a friend.

A young director, about to start his first film in Hollywood, asked the veteran director William Wyler for advice. Willy responded, "Resist the temptation to be a nice guy."

The other thing that went wrong was the casting—and for the same reason. What had encouraged Williams to rewrite and expand his original short play was the work I'd done at the Actors Studio with three of our actors, experimenting on the grotesque comic ritual when, at the rise of the full moon, the Gypsy's daughter's virginity is restored. Williams was pleased with what the actors and I had done, and I cast the whole play from our number. They responded generously, with spirit, loyalty, devotion, and all the talent they had. But I knew when I read the play again that many of them, dear and good people, were—with the exception of Eli Wallach— not up to the needs of their parts. They were trained in a more realistic technique. So was I.

The idea of a permanent company working in repertory was planted in my theatre generation as an ideal and a goal by the Group Theatre, specifically by Harold Clurman and by our reading in the thirties about the Russian theatre. It does have substantial advantages; the theatre is a group art. But in this country, where success is so sudden, so lucrative, so irresistible, it does seem impossible to hold actors of rank who are devoted to such an effort for very long. I've tried and failed. Our government does not help. Furthermore, how can a permanent company bring off all its plays? I was "forcing" the casting of *Camino Real* and distorting my own requirements to declare that the plays must be played by members of the Actors Studio; it was artistically false. I did develop, and very soon, a loosely gathered company of favored actors who played in a series of my films and plays, and many of them were from the Studio. But those productions were in a realistic vein. I did not stick to a hard-and-fast rule that I had to fill every role from the ranks of the membership.

I believe that the reason for this insistence in the case of *Camino Real* had little to do with an artistic purpose. It came from a desire to again be accepted as their hero by the actors of that organization, to demonstrate my courage and my steadfast loyalty to them and to live up to an ideal to which I'd pledged support again and again and for which I'd demanded theirs. By demonstrating that I had the power to force things to happen our way, I would make the Actors Studio mine again. In plainer language, I wanted to be liked. An unworthy end, and one I achieved at some cost to the Williams play.

A D I R E C T O R commits himself to a production more than once. When things go well and luck is on his side, there may take place an event that brings about a final enlistment, one that is irrevocable. The negotiation of a contract, the ceremony of signing your name where lawyers have marked their little *X*'s, the handclasps and words of fealty spoken to the author, the expressions of assurance and happy anticipation offered to actors—all these don't do it. What the director hopes for is a moment, later, when something will happen to make the great effort ahead totally his, to make the story he is about to put on the screen or on a stage speak of something that is his own. He is enlisted then, finally and totally, and that is the great moment in the preparation of a production. I've several times experienced such a moment of commitment and several times waited for it and been disappointed and subsequently realized that something was missing that I should have had in the work that followed. When it did occur, that final enlistment, it was generally when I found that I was in some way the subject of the drama, however disguised, and what was about to be shown an audience was a critical moment in my own life. This did happen as we prepared *On the Waterfront*, and here is when and how.

After I'd finished staging *Camino Real*, there was a wait, one Bob Anderson and I had planned, before we began to put his play *Tea and Sympathy* on stage. At this time, I'd taken to returning once more to Hoboken and spending hours there with Budd. It was then that we heard the legend of Tony Mike. Tony Mike deVincenzo had had his own pier once, been the hiring boss there. His friends and relatives had been and some still were part of the "mob," exploiting the longshoremen. Tony Mike had not only seen the corruption, not only known all about the rackets, but had probably, at one time, benefited from them. Then apparently the injustice got too much for him. He began to feel himself the victim, not the benefiter. He also began to be threatened when he did not do what the racket bosses asked him to do. He resented being bullied as much as he scorned the dishonesty. He started to balk. Suddenly he was on the other side, and the racket life he'd once accepted as inevitable on the waterfronts was beginning to threaten his family. That he would lose his job as pier boss was certain. He was blacklisted by the mob. The best he could do was a job as a supervisor of the Hoboken sewer system, at $3,500 a year. He quit that and was reduced to selling newspapers at a street stand. He still dressed as a hiring boss, wore his snap-brim felt hat and topcoat, but he was making a humiliating living.

Then came the big step, one that may even have surprised Tony Mike. When he was subpoenaed to testify before the Waterfront Crime Commission about the corruption he'd seen and how it worked, who "took" and how much, Tony Mike told the full truth as no one had before. He named names. When he did that, he broke the hoodlum law of silence: If you want to live, don't talk. He was called a rat, a squealer and stoolie. He was ostracized, then threatened. Friends he'd had for years didn't talk to him. Along with this isolation in shame, which had become his life, he was the object of threats to himself and his family. Everyone in Hoboken was certain he'd pick up a newspaper soon and read that Tony Mike had "disappeared." Then another paper, a few days later, would break the news that Tony Mike's body had been dredged up from the bottom of the river. That was the classic story of the labor informer, squealer, rat.

Budd knew when he had a live one; he sought the friendship of deVincenzo. When Tony Mike invited us to dinner at his house, we jumped at the chance. It was a heavy, pungent Italian meal that was served us, pasta and peppers and meat-loaded sauces and red wine. Tony Mike told us about his experiences. If you want to live, the mob had warned him, don't talk. He'd talked. He was still alive, but he knew that the last man who'd opened New York's waterfront rackets to view was found dead in a lime pit. At a certain point, I remember well, he told us he'd so feared for his safety and his family's that he decided to carry a pistol, and when he saw on our faces the suspicion that he was overdramatizing himself, he reached into his clothing and pulled out a handgun and laid it on the table, where it remained as we finished our meal.

I doubt that Budd was affected as personally as I was by the parallel of Tony Mike's story. His reaction to the loss of certain friends was not as bitter as my own; he had not experienced their blackballing as frequently and intensely as I had in the neighborhood known as Broadway. I believe Budd regarded our waterfront story with greater objectivity, an objectivity I appreciated. But I did see Tony Mike's story as my own, and that connection did lend the tone of irrefutable anger to the scenes I photographed and to my work with actors. When Brando, at the end, yells at Lee Cobb, the mob boss, "I'm glad what I done—you hear me?—glad what I done!" that was me saying, with identical heat, that I was glad I'd testified as I had. I'd been snubbed by friends each and every day for many months in my old show business haunts, and I'd not forgotten nor would I forgive the men, old friends some of them, who'd snubbed me, so the scene in the film where Brando goes back to the waterfront to "shape up" again for employment and is rejected by men with whom he'd worked day after day—that, too, was my story, now told to all the world. So when critics say that I put my story and my feelings on the screen, to justify my informing, they are right. That transference of emotion from my own experience to the screen is the merit of those scenes.

When I ate the garlic- and tomato-spiced dinner at Tony Mike's, heard from their own lips what he and his wife had been through, and looked at the faces of his children, then at the handgun where it was on the table, I remembered Molly and her fear and how I'd felt compelled to arrange for her protection while I was away. This hour at Tony Mike's was the instant of final commitment, when I saw that, in the mysterious way of art, I was preparing a film about myself. It was then that I amassed the weight of determination that made it possible later for me to endure every kind of discouragement and rejection and, when so many people tried to kill the film, never to let it be canceled, and even when our producer didn't back me with the help he should have given me, not to waver, not on this film, because it would mean I was wavering on myself.

It was soon after this dinner at Tony Mike's that Budd informed me that he was going to retire from the process of artistic investigation, that he knew enough about the people, the story, and the "color" of the Hoboken scene to write his screenplay. This timed out well, because Bob Anderson and Karl Malden and I had been working on casting *Tea and Sympathy,* and we were soon to go into production.

S U C C E S S deserves study; it is not easily come by. I do not believe that Bob Anderson's play can be produced better than we did it. But we didn't fall into our success; every element had to be chosen just right. After it was all put together, only then did it look simple. In the production of a play, one bad mistake may abort the whole; I believe every choice Bob and I made was correct. Once we came out on the sunny side, we forgot how ticklish our choices had been; all were embedded in the final result and seemed inevitable. They were not.

The first important thing was an act of faith and holding to it, not mine but Bob's and that of his wife, Phyllis, and, as important in this case, Molly's. She'd been watching over Bob's plays from the time he started writing for the theatre. When he was in the navy during the war, he would send her his plays from the Pacific. Sometimes she was encouraging, sometimes not, but her interest was constant and kept him working. Molly was a person of absolute opinions; if *Hamlet* had been sent her by Shakespeare, she would have had some astute reservations and put them in a four-page, single-spaced, carefully reasoned letter to the author. She truly liked Bob's play and assured him it would be produced. She also believed that I would like it and told Bob she'd send it to me in Bavaria. And did.

The other person in whom Anderson had great faith was his agent, Audrey Wood, who was widely esteemed for encouraging young playwrights. Bob gave her the play and she, in the routine of agents, had six copies made and sent them to six producers, with a cautious word. Time passed. Then Audrey took Bob to lunch and gave him back five rather tattered copies, with an I-told-you-so expression on her face. The play had been turned down by everyone she'd sent it to. The sixth copy, she explained, was with the Playwrights' Company, and "as soon as that comes back," she said, "I'll send it to you. Now get on with your next play."

Clearly Bob's agent had no faith in his play, and at this moment, the whole project might have collapsed. But Bob did not lose faith, and one reason was that Molly and Phyllis had assured him the play was worthy. Their tenacity was rewarded. The script Audrey had sent to the Playwrights' Company—number six—did not come back. Bob Sherwood liked it and kept it. I liked it; I thought it small in scale but deep of content— and the truth about Bob as a young man. I said I'd do it, and when I came back from Bavaria, I met with the Playwrights' Company; we reached an agreement and the work began.

Audrey didn't change her mind, not even later, when the play had opened on the road and received a favorable press. She ran into me backstage one night after our first public performance and said, "So you've performed one of your miracles again." Nonsense. No miracle was involved. The play was and is a truly felt work and it is faultlessly constructed. Molly saw that first.

Since I was involved in *Camino Real*, the rehearsals of Bob's play had to be postponed until fall. The delay gave us a chance to go over and over the manuscript, scrutinize each page and every line, discussing every value. A complete understanding between playwright and director was reached. In the rehearsals that followed, Bob and I never had a disagreement about ends and rarely about means. The delay was our great good fortune.

I've hated the crapshoot nature of our Broadway theatre, but it does have one merit. In the desperate pressure, every effort possible has to be exerted by everyone involved. Nothing can be neglected or slighted; it's all or nothing, a time of frenzy near hysteria. The production of even the simplest play becomes a life-and-death struggle, and this often brings out the best efforts of all the people involved.

In preparing our script for production, we found two main problems. A famous film director, when he was asked for advice by a beginning director, said, "Work on the heavies." We had two of them: the father of the boy who was suspected of homosexual tendencies in a prep school, and the husband of the woman who, at last, chooses to perform the act of sympathy that saves the boy. The father had been so insensitive to his son's problem and pain that the young man had grown to be self-doubting and isolated. The husband was so insensitive to what his wife needed from him, he was so macho, so conventional, so doggedly old-fashioned, that his wife was starved for human warmth. The result? She could be deeply aroused by the need of the boy and respond to it totally. Both men were characters whom Bob and I could not have liked in life. But the audience had to believe them, not reject them as people, and the fact remained that our woman had married her husband and must have once found him attractive and worthy. The father's flaw was not in wishing ill for his son but in lack of insight and understanding. Here again the delay was a blessing. These two characterizations got the benefit of Bob's careful rewriting before we went into rehearsal, and what he did in both cases was crucial to our success. We were eventually to show the husband trying to save his marriage the best way he knew how—and failing. We were to see the father, on a visit to his troubled son, trying to understand the boy—and failing. In both cases, what was salutary was the effort both men made to overcome the limitations of their characters; this made them believable and, while "wrong," sympathetic. Without this dramatic correction, the play might have seemed mechanical and melodramatic.·

When we began work on the production, I decided that the scale of the show must be small, that Bob Anderson was a miniaturist. The play was not a symphony (*Death of a Salesman*) or a concerto (*A Streetcar Named Desire*) but a string quartet. In contrast to the other plays I'd done, I decided not to overload this one with my characteristic heavy-handed dramatics. I'd tone down my professional ego, curb my tendency to violent physical action and strong unequivocal events. No voice was to be raised here, there was to be no shouting. The strings of the production were to be muted, the action always controlled and discreet, with hesitant inflections and half-realized gestures. In the end I was especially proud of the production's delicacy. This was new for me, an advance. The play and its production were as full of good heart and tenderness as Bob himself.

The climactic scene showed a lovely young married woman and a young man of seventeen, still adolescent, sitting close together in a small room warmed by a setting sun. The final action was a "close-up," the slim fingers of this gentlewoman touching the buttons of her pink blouse as the lights faded. We were to guess what followed. It was at this moment that she spoke the line: "Years from now . . . when you talk about this . . . and you will . . . be kind."

The series of intimate scenes—of two people, of three people—that led up to this climax determined the scale of the physical production. Having failed in the setting design for *Camino Real*, I was determined not to be backward about what I needed here. I made our designer, Jo Mielziner, a ground plan of just how I wished the set to be, indicated the dimensions of each wall to make damned sure that what he would give me was as intimate as I knew it must be. I'd come to believe that it's the obligation of a director to give his designer a careful sketch of the ground plans he wants and to be precise about the dimensions and scale of the whole. I wanted a setting for "close-ups," and Jo understood me. He was grateful for the guidance; he accepted my ground plan, then went on to raise a beautiful setting on it. He also lit the show himself, making the lighting sympathetic and evocative of the various moods of the action. The result was a triumph for Jo.

The leading performer in the production was Deborah Kerr, and she was urged on me by Bob Anderson, who'd worked with her in a TV adaptation and found her enchanting. I resisted the choice, so we considered many other women. But Bob kept coming back to Deborah. My refusal to consider her had less weight with Anderson than it might have had, because I'd never met the lady. I confess to a prejudice against working with movie stars in the theatre, one I still have. They're sure to get a sore throat on the seventh day of rehearsal, and you have to bring in a doctor, who insists they go home and to bed—which is where you conduct the rest of your rehearsals, in bed: that is, they in bed and you, straining to conceal your resentment, in a chair at their side.

Finally, our failure to find what we each thought we needed led Bob to ask me to make a trip to California, where Deborah was shooting a film, and meet her. I did, and that was that. I came back and told Bob he was right, I was wrong, Deborah was perfect, let's sign her! Now, looking back, I am convinced that without Deborah, it's quite possible the play would not

have been a success. We were to have the services of another successful
and famous movie star later in the "run," and she came off well enough in
the press, but with her the play seemed mediocre and slightly sordid. This
actress, excellent in many movies, did not have Deborah's immaculate delicacy, and there was no way I could direct that into her. No matter what
Deborah was doing—in this case, being unfaithful to her husband in behalf
of a troubled young student—it was impossible to believe it was for any
reason except the most decent and honorable. She was everything good in
a woman: kind, understanding, sensitive, wise, gentle, considerate, helpful, funny, upholding—and very bright. I'm talking about Deborah herself
as well as Deborah in the part. No one could help falling in love with her; I
did and the audience did from their very first look. Bob wrote the play;
Deborah made the production.

How did we know when we had a "hit"? It happened during the last
We had one crisis with Deborah, and it happened on the third day of
rehearsal. When our stage manager called for the actors, Deborah didn't
emerge from her dressing room. I asked the stage manager where she was,
and he informed me, in a whisper, that Miss Kerr would not come out on
stage. I waited a little longer, then went into her dressing room. I could see
that the girl was frozen with fear. My Anatolian cunning, as it's been described, began to work. I said to her that I didn't feel like working either,
and perhaps an afternoon off would do us all good. I also told her that I was
worried, because Bob's confidence in his play had begun to waver. Would
she have a drink with us?

Huddled in the corner of a bar, I didn't make the least reference to
Deborah's refusal to come on stage. I behaved as if my problem was Bob
and only Bob. As Deborah listened, I reassured Bob at great length and
with complete conviction that he'd written a wonderful play, finely
wrought, deeply human, funny as well as sad. I laid the praise on with a
shovel. Then we went back to the theatre, and I called rehearsal. Deborah
rehearsed. I never had another problem with her.

How did we know when we had a "hit"? It happened during the last
scene, at the moment when Deborah's hand goes to the top button of her
blouse. During our first engagement on the road, there would be some
giggles at this moment. This worried us terribly. We made some adjustments in the lighting, starting the "dim down" sooner, and I directed the
scene as quietly as I could and have the actors heard. This helped, but
there was still a restlessness in the audience and an occasional giggle, followed by "Shshsh!" The actors were worried, despite anything I'd say, and
it began to show. Bob and I held firm; after all, it was the right ending for
the play and we had to make it work somehow. We didn't; the newspapers
did. We began to get good notices, and our audiences were told before they
took their seats that they were about to see a hit. The giggles stopped.
Miraculously. What we had instead was a great silence. The most satisfying
thing in the theatre at the climax of a serious play is not applause but that

awed silence that comes when the audience is deeply moved. There is nothing so eloquent and so heartening. When we had that, I knew we were going to run a long time.

One final incident—again about my Anatolian cunning. After we'd played for nine months and were scheduled to continue on the road, I went to see the play at the urging of the author, so that what we were about to send to the other cities would be as good as it could be. As I watched the performance I saw that something had gone wrong. No cast could have been more devoted or sincere—oh, God, they'd worked hard!—but the play had taken on a rigidly professional and machinelike quality. The actors knew where the effects were, the laughs and the tears, and they were going for them. I assembled the cast the following afternoon, redirected the first act: every scene, every move. I worked them hard and I saw that they were trying their best to do what I wanted even though it was contrary to what they'd been doing for months. They wanted to please me, even though they were bewildered by what I was trying to do. When the rehearsal was over, the cast stood before me, looking bewildered. Deborah spoke. "Do you expect us to put all that in tonight?" she asked. "No," I said. "Do it just as you've always done it." And I walked out. Smiling. That night's performance, I was told, was the best in many months.

It was with this play that I began to learn not to try to pin a play's meaning down to a didactic theme. We used to do that in the Group; it was the essence of our work as directors. We were "teaching" the audience with each play. Clifford Odets felt it necessary in his third acts to grab the audience by their shoulders, shake them, and say, "Don't you see what all this means? No? Well, I'll tell you." And he did. Now I preferred an opposite effort: to tell a story that was as human and, therefore, as ambivalent and as unresolved as life itself, so that the audience would leave the theatre asking, "I wonder what the hell all that means." Which is the same experience one has in life, isn't it? Or when reading a great novel. You can't boil either down to a homily, motto, or slogan. Life is a puzzle, and you are generally left feeling: "How do people get through it?" and "If they're both right, then who's right?" and "God almighty, isn't life awesome!" The emotion of wonder is better in the theatre than the emotion of recognition. Even Brecht in his so-called learning plays preserved an element of doubt unresolved. The audience should keep puzzling about a play long after they've left the theatre; when the play is worthy and the performance fine, an audience will ponder it for days. But if you sum it all up for them, they won't. It's precisely what happens after a dramatic experience in life—it unsettles you for a long time. You keep trying to puzzle it out.

So it was here that I realized that the theme should not be insisted on, in fact should be constantly and repeatedly contradicted. The viewer should not be bullied into agreeing with what a character says about the theme. He should be sent out of the theatre marveling at the richness and com-

plexity of life, the mystery of it, and the contradictions that defy understanding. Any theme that can be stated in a single simple sentence is
inevitably a simplification of life—and meaningless. Don't tell me your play
is about responsibility or loyalty or truth. Tell me it's about mankind.

There was a personal event during this production as important as any
public one. I acquired two good and close friends, Deborah and Bob. I
needed good friends in the spring of 1953. Deborah's opening night wire
was: "May you always remember Deborah." I have. Bob is still one of my
closest friends.

I C A M E out of that production reestablished professionally and with a
full tank of gas; my energy was back. I was eager to return to the battlefield
where, a year before, I'd been humiliated. Earlier, in midwinter, as we
were about to begin rehearsals on Bob's play, Budd gave me his first draft
of the waterfront screenplay, titled *The Golden Warriors*. I convinced him
that we should send the script to Darryl Zanuck. I assured Budd that it was
the kind of material Darryl couldn't resist. Budd was less sure; having
grown up in the betray-your-brother society of the film world, the author
of *What Makes Sammy Run?* seemed to distrust the whole movie colony.
"But Darryl made *The Grapes of Wrath*," I said to him. Then I had to
convince myself. Except for the editing of *Man on a Tightrope*, I'd had good
experiences with the man. So the script went off, and we waited.

It was four weeks before we had a response from California. I believed
Zanuck was in Europe, or perhaps that's only what I told Budd. I was always defending Darryl to him. On the fourth of February we heard. "I have
struggled with the problem of the waterfront story as this means a decision
of great importance to the company." (Business at Fox had been bad. It was
hoped that CinemaScope would save them.) He went on: "I like the basic
material enormously, as I told you when I read the treatment" (we'd earlier
sent him a thirty-five-page story summary) "but I continue to be worried
about the labor support." (He wanted us to secure the backing of George
Meany, the president of the American Federation of Labor.) "We must not
hit everything on the nose and get up on a soap box. If we do that, we will
certainly have a failure. We must stick to the personal story and permit the
picture to speak for itself as far as theme goes." (By personal story, he meant
what he'd meant in *Gentleman's Agreement*—the love story.) "I am certain
that the picture as a whole, by what it shows not by words, will reveal the
corruption on the waterfront. We don't have to make speeches about it. I
believe that the evil of the waterfront situation should be the background
as it was in *Pinky* and that the personal story must predominate. There is
no use in making a wonderful picture like *Zapata* which nobody comes to
see except the intelligentsia. I recommend that Budd and you come out
here next week for one or two days. I believe I have some valuable story

contributions which will help the girl from looking like an amateur detective who is out to right the wrongs of the world. This is an important undertaking and if we are to go ahead with courage, we have got to know conclusively that we understand each other."

I answered that if I were not in rehearsal with a difficult play I would fly out, even for a few hours' conference. "I feel the best alternative," I wrote, "is for Budd to come out alone as soon as it's convenient for you both. He will be talking for me as well as for himself and whatever you two agree on will have my backing."

Darryl accepted this proposal, and Budd went west and conferred with Darryl twice. The meetings were successful, according to Darryl: "The last day I saw him he [Budd] shook my hand and told me that no matter how it turned out he had received valuable assistance and that working with me had been a unique and exhilarating experience." Budd doesn't recall saying any such thing—but he did come back satisfied, said he'd reached a basic understanding with Darryl. Now he could get back to work on the screenplay. Budd seemed more confident than ever that the film was going to go through; I was certain of it. While I was putting on *Tea and Sympathy*, Budd worked on the new draft, and in April, with the play opened, I began to go to Hoboken again and to work with him. We found that some of Darryl's suggestions, when put to the test, helped our story; others did not, and we didn't use them. At the end of April, we sent our completed work to Darryl and waited for his reaction.

Again four weeks passed, and Budd became impatient and more than a little suspicious; I was worried too. Budd thought we should now have some contractual assurance from Fox; we'd worked up until this point "on spec." Was it yes, was it no, were we in, were we out? I suggested we see Spyros Skouras, the president of Twentieth Century–Fox, and ask him. Skouras was in an ebullient mood. He invited us to lunch with him—all Greeks feel a visit deserves a meal. We settled for a drink, some cheese and olives. Then I came to the point: We hadn't heard from Darryl, so we were there to find out if Fox was going to make our film or not, because if Darryl was not going to make it, we'd turn elsewhere. This last was one of those negotiation threats. I was absolutely sure that Darryl, the man I'd worked with so many times and whom I knew so well, would not "pass" on this picture. Spyros heartily confirmed this. With all his vigor, he assured us Fox would definitely make the film. I was sure the man meant every word. We shook hands, Budd with Spyros, Spyros and I. Then, as a tray of cheese and olives appeared, we drank ouzo to commemorate our union.

Budd was satisfied, and so was I. When Darryl asked us to come out together and meet with him on the script, we didn't hesitate. If Darryl had been going to turn away our picture, he would have done it quickly, with a telegram. The talk he was asking for had to be about casting, production, location, staff. We'd gone too far; to turn back now was inconceivable.

Just before we left New York, there was an incident that fired up my hunger for revenge again. While I was working on *Tea and Sympathy*, Molly was seeing something of our old Yale Drama School classmate, Phyllis Anderson, Bob's wife. Phyllis revealed to Molly that John Wharton, the distinguished theatrical lawyer whom Art Miller trusted with his contractual concerns, had said to Kay Brown, Phyllis's colleague at MCA, "Gadg isn't going ahead with that waterfront picture, is he?" And when Kay asked why, Wharton said, "Because if he does he'll never again get one of Miller's plays to do." Wharton, I had to believe, was telling Kay Brown so that Kay Brown would tell Phyllis so that Phyllis would tell Molly so it would finally be passed on to me that if I still hoped for Art's plays, it would be wiser if I abandoned my film. Wharton was a man I came to like, but not that season; he was the classiest possible lawyer, and this was certainly a classy threat. I've often wondered if Art knew about that call.

O N M A Y 2 5, guarded by my agent, Abe Lastfogel, we entered Zanuck's office and were seated around his deskfront. This time Darryl did not walk around the room swinging his polo mallet. He stood in place behind his desk and laid it on the line. "I'm not going to make this picture," he said. "I don't like it. In fact, I don't like anything about it." Then he stopped and looked at us. He'd made the leap he'd wanted to make, and there was nothing more he could say—although he did—that would modify this absolute rejection.

We were in shock, Budd and I, so stunned that we didn't even look at each other. Finally I spoke. "You mean, Darryl," I said, "that you don't like anything about it? Anything?" "It's exactly what audiences don't want to see now," Darryl said. "Who gives a shit about longshoremen?" He told us about his struggles with our script, how he'd tried unsuccessfully to heighten its drama. "I even tried making Terry [our hero, the part Brando was to play] a member of the FBI," he said, "but it didn't work." Then he told us how bad business was and that Fox was going to commit its whole program to CinemaScope, and it would save the company. Didn't he see that we weren't listening, that we didn't give a damn about CinemaScope or his company's fate? No, he didn't. He was suddenly talking about his plans for *Prince Valiant*, a film to be based on a comic strip—a perfect CinemaScope subject, he said.

I got up abruptly. I couldn't sit still for any more of this. I was in such a turmoil of feelings that I can't describe them. I looked at my agent and "protector," Abe Lastfogel. He'd said nothing, not a word. Paranoid by now, I was convinced that he was happy Darryl had killed our project. My heart was pounding too fast; I had to get out of there.

Darryl was saying that he felt Fox owed Budd some money for his work—he'd worked long and hard; Zanuck acknowledged that—but he felt the company owed me nothing: "because you're rich." Which was news to me. This is the man, I thought, who begged me to rush out to Hollywood and, on twenty-four-hour notice, as a favor to a friend, take over *Pinky*. It was all a one-way street for Mr. Zanuck! Obviously he felt I was someone he could kick around as he pleased and get away with it. Why had I ever thought otherwise? Again I turned and looked at Abe Lastfogel. He stayed silent.

"I'm going with Abe," I said to Budd as we left the office. Budd wasn't speaking to me. I knew what he felt. Outside, we drifted apart, he toward the car that Fox had given us for transportation and I with Lastfogel. Abe led me to his Cadillac limousine; the chauffeur, when he saw us coming, held the door open. We got in, the car took off. "Well," Abe said, "what are you going to do now?" The question shocked me, and I can still recall the way he said it. It was obvious he believed the waterfront film stone dead. He hadn't made a move to protect me, to protest Zanuck's summary dismissal of what we'd worked months on, or to claim any obligation Zanuck had to me for the time and work I'd put in. Isn't that what an agent is for?

"I'm going to make this picture," I said, "if I have to make it in sixteen millimeter and with the cheapest producer in town. Who are the King brothers?" Abe looked at me as if I were crazy. Then he invited me to have dinner with him and Frances. "I have to talk to Budd," I said. "Let me off at the Beverly Hills Hotel."

Budd was furious, and it was at me. He felt I'd led him into a trap where all his work had come to nothing. "I told you he was no good," he said. I had no answer. I didn't say, "He made *The Grapes of Wrath*, didn't he?" "Why bring us all the way out here for this?" Budd said.

We had some drinks—we were still living by the hospitality of Twentieth Century–Fox—then we sat looking at each other. We didn't say much, but we did recall Spyros Skouras's handshake. Now, years later, I think it's possible that there was a behind-the-scenes conflict between the two men; Darryl may have resented Spyros's assuring us the film would be made. That was Darryl's privilege—to say yes or to say no. So he'd said no. Spyros's ouzo, olives, and feta cheese didn't mean a thing. Darryl had not only put us down, but he'd put Spyros, whom he considered a bumbler and a showboat, in his place.

Then a strange thing happened. We began to talk about our script again. We still liked it. Some measure of confidence in it began to reemerge. I called Lastfogel and told him Budd and I had talked and that we were absolutely determined to make this film, that I would take nothing else until it was done, and that I wanted him to send copies to the other major studios. He said he already had sneaked one to Harry Cohn, president of Columbia Pictures, and Cohn had not responded to it. Apparently Abe had done this while we were waiting for our meeting with Zanuck. Had he anticipated that Darryl wouldn't go ahead with it? "Send it to the others," I said. "It's a Warner Brothers–type picture; they're sure to like it."

But they didn't; by late the next afternoon, the news was in. Abe told me that Warners had had a quick look at it—been eager to see it beforehand—but when they'd read it, they "passed." On the next day, Paramount and MGM saw the script—or had it described to them by Lastfogel; I can't imagine they could have read it that quickly. They passed on it too. One way or another, we were turned down by every last studio in town. And by Columbia twice. We were dead, so it seemed—beyond recall. Still we kept making small revisions in the script. We couldn't stop; it was like the reflexes of a dead animal that keeps kicking and twitching. I remember we'd carried off a typewriter from Fox and a great stack of blue paper; the floor of our suite in the Beverly Hills Hotel was littered with crumpled balls of blue paper.

At the end of the afternoon, I went to see Lastfogel in his office. He gently reminded me that *Zapata* had been a failure, even *Panic in the Streets* had been a failure, and—so Zanuck had informed him—*Man on a Tightrope* was fast becoming the lowest-grossing picture in the history of Twentieth Century–Fox. "I think," Abe said, "you ought to take whatever picture Darryl will offer you. You need a success. I wish you'd accepted *Anna and the King of Siam*, but since you didn't, let's see what he has for you." "I'm going to make this film," I said. Then we looked at each other, and he told me that every studio had now passed on the picture and—this was implied but not stated—passed on me. "I advise you to forget that waterfront project," Abe said, "and not keep stewing about it."

I took one of the William Morris secretaries back to the hotel with me. Budd and I needed company, because talk between us was now rather strained. When Budd drinks, a cantankerous side of his character appears; he seems to crave a fight. Since we were still Fox's guests there—Abe had told me we had another day of this privilege—we ordered a hell of a meal for three with plenty of drink and kept the door unlatched for room service. We were both courting the secretary from William Morris, more because there was nothing else to do than from desire; soon we were competing for her favors.

The room across the hall from us was also the scene of lively social life. Standing in the doorway was George Stevens, one of the industry's great directors, saying goodbye to the man he'd come to see, S. P. Eagle, whom I recognized because during the days when everyone was courting the director of the Academy Award film *Gentleman's Agreement*, I'd been a guest at his house many times.

Both Budd and I had a bellyful now. The booze had eased constraint between us and made us eager for play. Sam was someone to play with. I shouted a greeting across the hall, and he came over to visit us. We told Sam our story—and then we found ourselves telling him how great our script was. He said he'd like to hear all about it—the story itself—and Budd said he'd be glad to tell it to him. They made a date for the next morning, when Budd would be sober and Sam serious. That's when the miracle happened. Budd did go across the hall directly after coffee, and Sam stayed in bed—with the covers up to his nose—and heard Budd tell our story. We expected nothing to come of this; we simply didn't know what else to do.

I remember that Budd came back to our suite, where I was having breakfast with the William Morris secretary, and he said, with the greatest astonishment I was ever to hear him express, "He likes it!" S. P. Eagle liked our story. "He says he will do it," Budd said. Luck had turned her other face to us.

Why not? S. P. Eagle had come to Hollywood with a failure as complete as my *Man on a Tightrope*; it was a musical medley of film clips called *Melba*. It was—as they say—"doing nothing" at the box office. He needed a project, if for no other reason than to milk it for a producer's salary. In this case, I knew better than Budd that Sam's reputation was that of a clown. He had made—or John Huston had been induced to make for him—one good and successful picture, *The African Queen*. But despite that, people laughed when they said S. P. Eagle. Lastfogel laughed too; then he said, "Watch out for him! He has moves you've never seen before." "What choice have we?" I asked. "I told you what choice you have," Abe said, pressing me yet again to forget about the waterfront.

One thing about Mr. S. P. Eagle did impress us; he wanted to get right to work. He was booked to go back to New York, where he was quartered in the St. Regis Hotel (I'm not sure Sam had an office at that time), and he wanted us to go back with him. It was like a godsend; the Beverly Hills Hotel was asking for our suite to be released and room service was about to be cut off. But we did have the other half of our ticket to New York. So we packed up and went home.

A week later, the publicity department of Twentieth Century–Fox put this item into the hands of the press of the nation, including *The New York Times*. "Twentieth Century–Fox has dropped plans to make *Waterfront*, with Elia Kazan directing from a script by Budd Schulberg dealing with the gangster influence along the New York and New Jersey piers. The subject was taken off the July shooting schedule last week by Darryl Zanuck, studio production chief, because he does not believe it adaptable to the widescreen CinemaScope technique to which Fox has committed its entire output. Only last April, the Studio announced that it would depart from its new policy to make this particular picture."

Was this announcement necessary? Certainly it would not help our efforts or Sam's to get the financing we needed. Did Zanuck know that? Was he trying to kill our project? If not, why did he allow that release? I couldn't help imagining the satisfaction this squib would give some people, for instance John Wharton.

So ended my story with Darryl Francis Zanuck. I never entered his office again.

WE WERE NOW in a mythological country, the land of S. P. Eagle, the man we called Sam. I made two films with him and had innumerable chats, dinners, and trips, including one on his yacht, but still I can't tell you anything about his past. For instance, how had he escaped the ovens? Was it Sam or was it Otto Preminger who'd been smuggled over a border in the trunk of a car? Once free, where did Sam get the money to live? Someone was to say of him that if he were dropped, stark naked and without funds, into the heart of a capital city, by the next morning he'd be fashionably dressed and living at ease in a *grand luxe* hotel. Yet I noticed on his bureau top at the St. Regis two fat rolls of American Express checks. This suggested that he was ready to make a quick getaway at a moment's warning.

There were all kind of stories about his chicanery and trickery; I never knew what to believe about him and what not to believe. But I've never been sure that it was important to believe anything definite about him; just take him as a mythological figure. Certainly he had the courage of the desperate. For instance, how did this plump little Jew win the cooperation of King Hussein, or whoever ruled Jordan at that time, so that David Lean could shoot his great *Lawrence of Arabia* scenes in the desert known as Jebel Tubeiq, on the border of Saudi Arabia? Were Jewish people welcomed there? No? Sam was. Before that he had made it possible for John Huston to film up and down the Ruiki River in the Belgian Congo and saw to it that his company—actors and crew—had clean water, edible food, and reasonably good spirits. The English technicians he'd brought there took sick with everything from malaria to the African trots, but Sam stayed perfectly healthy and vigorous throughout, and got the film made, and made it a success as well.

That's when I knew Sam first, when he was preparing *The African Queen* and, for the most practical reasons, wooing John Huston. Sam would throw large, elaborate parties for John and his lady at the time, Olivia De Havilland, and invite anyone they wanted as well as anyone who might, at some later date, prove useful to him. Everything Sam did was tactical. I sported an Academy Award and some hits at that time, so I was invited. He had a tennis court at the back of his house, and it was mine to use. After the game, sweating, I would swing open his fridge door and there were stacks of champagne splits. No Pepsis or Cokes for Sam; only the best! At the same time, despite the parties where nothing was spared and the food and drink were superb, I had the impression that Sam didn't have a cent. This guess of mine proved to be on the nose. Shortly after *On the Waterfront* opened, the *Los Angeles Times* reported Sam's financial landslide rewards, which, the paper said, would enable him to regain possession of his home in Beverly Hills, a residence the tax department had taken away from him. These IRS people had deceived themselves if they thought their action would depress Sam's spirit, curtail his social life, or crimp the parties he threw.

He did everything in the world to make directors and writers beholden to him and would in time end up many times richer than any of us. When I was a big success in Hollywood, he placed an upstairs bedroom in his house at my disposal any afternoon when I had no other accommodation to take advantage of a sudden piece of social good fortune. I appreciated this, and I did feel beholden to him for his favors; in fact, everything was cool between me and S.P. until I began to work with him. Then I got to see his other side, and I alternately wanted to kill him and embrace him. I have often asked if he was worth the grief and the trouble he was to cause me. In the case of *On the Waterfront*, he certainly was!

Sam was by far the canniest negotiator I've ever known. On every issue we negotiated on this picture and the other I did for him, he got the better of me—and my lawyers. Like all good negotiators, Sam kept everything secret. I never knew what the hell he was doing with *Waterfront*—despite the fact that I owned twenty-five percent of the film. He was making some kind of deal with someone, but I didn't know what the deal was or with whom. It seemed to be with United Artists and seemed to involve Frank Sinatra. Sam did call me on the phone one day and say that I might have a chat with Frank.

That was one of Sam's favorite words: chat. He never asked for a business conference; rather he suggested we might have "a little chat." Even his vocabulary was disarming—that is, tricky. I was alternately on guard against him and admiring of his savoir faire, his insistence on the best food and the most "in" restaurants. The best was none too good for Sam. I admired the deftness with which he tipped headwaiters. I would come to see that everything he did had a purpose. I'd warn myself, "Don't let him fool you!" But he did, again and again. To lie, for Sam, was as effortless as to tell the truth. I used to study him, as puzzled as a child.

One day Sam told me he'd "set" Frank Sinatra and that I might have a chat with him about his costumes. I knew—and believe now—that I could make the picture with Frank and that he'd be fine in the role. So I did talk to him; we both knew what the man should wear. Frank had grown up in Hoboken, where I was going to shoot the film, and spoke perfect Hobokenese. He'd be simple to work with.

Next thing I knew, I heard that Sam was talking with Marlon Brando and with his friend Leo Jaffe at Columbia Pictures. But it was all secret, and neither Budd nor I knew just what he was doing. I believe that Sam regarded Budd and me as children when it came to negotiations, and in my case, time would prove him right. Compared with Sam's life experience, I was indeed a foolish innocent. Sam could smell a victim immediately, and he had the affection of a predator for his prey. Make no mistake about it: Sam was charming; he charmed you as he cheated you.

One day, Sam asked me how I'd like to have Brando in the film. I said it was impossible, since I'd already met with Frank Sinatra and talked to him about his costume. This moral consideration, of course, did not deter Sam. He went right on as if I'd been affirmative in answer to his question about Brando. He revealed to me that Marlon had told him he wouldn't work with me because of my testimony to HUAC. I bridled and said I didn't want the son of a bitch in the film, he wasn't right for the part anyway, and I was perfectly happy with Frank. Again Sam went right on as if he hadn't heard me. He didn't regard all that political squabbling as important, unless it might stand him in good stead with some lefty writer he was courting to say that he totally disapproved of what I'd done. Probably what he told Marlon was that he, too, thought what I'd done was regrettable, but after all, I was a good director as well as a fool, that Terry was a good part, and "let me talk to your agent." Which he did.

I went right on planning how I would direct Frank in the part and where and how I'd make the film, and Sam went right on along his route. He had eyes only for what he thought best for the film. Budd Schulberg believes that the reason Sam was so intent on dumping Frank and acquiring Marlon was that he could get only $500,000 to make the film with Frank but twice that with Brando. Frank was not a great star yet; Brando had made *Streetcar*. Sam would have more money to play with.

Then the Eagle informed me that Brando and he had had a chat, and Brando would do the picture, despite what he'd thought of my testimony, if he could get off every afternoon at four to drive across the river to meet with his analyst. This was my old friend Bela; I'd thrown Brando to him and I suspect that the compromise suggestion that brought Brando into the film was Bela's work. He always had a yen for show biz—and for more clients. About a year earlier, before my testimony, Brando had told me that he needed psychological help and I'd recommended Bela. Now they were—apparently—devoted. What a tightrope Bela must have been walking! But he was good at that. Brando had only his conscience to deal with, and he solved this problem by telling me again, and again, while we were making the film, that the only reason he'd agreed to work with me was so he could continue his psychoanalysis in New York.

I confess I ate shit. Sam had conned Marlon into making the film, and I let him do the dirty work and said nothing. I wouldn't have done what Sam did, but I was glad he did it; it was what I really wanted. I turned my face the other way as S. P. Eagle informed Sinatra's agency, William Morris, that Frank was out. I was silent because, although I liked Frank and was sure I could make the picture with him, I always preferred Brando to anybody.

Sam had a rationale to give William Morris for his switch. Frank and Lastfogel had asked for a cutoff date for Frank's services, since he'd agreed to do a concert somewhere on a certain day. Sam had said we could no way guarantee to release Frank on that date—he'd suddenly discovered this problem when it was useful. I was then a witness to a meeting between Sam and Abe. I've never heard so much screaming from a pair of short, fat men. Lastfogel attacked Sam directly where it hurt and without mercy. He called him many things, most of them true. I sat as an onlooker. Just as Lastfogel had said nothing when Zanuck had pulled out of our picture in California, I was silent now. I had no use for either man that day. I knew Lastfogel was fighting to retain his client—who might (and did) go to another agent if he lost this picture because Abe hadn't made an ironclad contract early enough. Abe had the Eagle flushing crimson, floundering and perspiring and flapping his wings. I was sure he'd have a heart attack. Lastfogel was insulting as only a man who has right on his side can be. On the other hand, putting myself in Lastfogel's shoes—and remembering my experience with him in Zanuck's office—I wasn't sure that he wanted Frank to be in the film. That was Frank's wish, but I knew that Lastfogel thought nothing of the film and had been relieved when Zanuck dropped it—and me—thereby, he hoped, turning me to a more lucrative prospect. All Abe had to do was put on a great show so he wouldn't lose a valuable client, and he did that, put on a stupendous show—and lost his client anyway. I believe Sinatra was the most honest man in that circus. I wasn't. Although I could say I disliked what Lastfogel was doing and distrusted him—he hadn't fought that fiercely for me in Zanuck's office, had he?—I didn't come out and say, "I'm satisfied with Frank and I think what Sam is doing is wrong."

Sam's trickery—and you might call it dishonesty—was more honest than my own stance: silence, accepting anything that would bring me the actor I wanted. I did write Sinatra, telling him how sorry I was and how fine he would have been. It was months before I heard back. "For me to tell you that I was not deeply hurt would not be telling you my true feelings. However with the passing of time and after re-reading your letter, how could I do or say anything other than I, too, want to be friends with you. I hope it's going well." Frank had let me off easy.

IN THE DAYS that followed, whenever Sam did something Budd or I didn't like—and there were many such days—we'd remind each other that it was the ninth inning, this was our last time at bat, and he'd saved our ass. Now I know for sure that except for Sam and his cunning, not only with casting but with his persistence over restructuring and rewriting the screenplay, our film would have been a failure. Both Budd and I owe Sam a lot, and we know it.

There were four reasons why *On the Waterfront* was such a success. Brando was one of them. If there is a better performance by a man in the history of film in America, I don't know what it is. Then there was Budd's devotion and tenacity and his talent. He never backed off. I was tough and good on the streets and persisted through all difficulties. But finally there was Sam. After the casting of the main part had been settled, the rewriting process began, and it was here, above all, that Sam showed his worth.

I still can't say how or why Sam knew so much about screenplay construction. But he did have an instinctive story sense; he knew it had to be unrelenting as it unfolded, that it should never let up tension and always aim for the end. Perhaps it was natural for a man who'd spent a good deal of his early life fleeing from one place where he was oppressed to another place, where he was perhaps less oppressed. Movement had been the essence of Sam's life. Keep moving in order to survive—that's a pretty good law for screenplay writing. With it came a certain tough-mindedness: We were never to believe we'd solved a problem until we had.

Sam had a saying that used to infuriate Budd. "Let's open it up again," he'd say at a time when Budd was convinced the script work had been completed and we were ready to shoot. There was a night in Budd's country house when his wife, Vicki, woke to see the bathroom light on and Budd

shaving. It was three-thirty in the morning. She asked Budd what the hell
he was doing, shaving at that hour. "I'm driving to New York," Budd said.
"What for?" "To kill Sam Spiegel," Budd said. He went to New York, but he
didn't kill Sam. If Hitler's men hadn't succeeded in doing it, how could a
goodhearted, reasonable man like Budd? So we went on working, week
after week, and the script kept improving—growing shorter and tighter
until what we had was pretty close to what we shot, a script I consider a
model screenplay, a near perfect piece of work. All Sam's infuriating insistence paid off, just as did his tricky work with Brando and Sinatra. Suddenly
we were ready to shoot. A date was set. We were all three satisfied.

My wife, Molly, was not. My Puritan had disliked Sam from the first time
she met him. "How can you stomach that man?" she'd say. "I wouldn't have
him in the house." I'd reply that I liked Sam, rather; that he was smart,
rather—hedging all my affirmatives, because all bets involving Sam had to
be hedged. One day he called and said he wanted to come up and chat with
me in our apartment—this was years later—and Molly had to be agreeable
because there was no way she could not be. He was announced from the
lobby, and ten minutes after he arrived, Sam had his arm around her waist
and she was laughing shamelessly at the wit of his perceptions. He had
charmed her. Again!

But when I let her read the script, the FINAL *On the Waterfront*, she
told me it was not right. "For God's sake don't do it," she begged me. "The
script isn't ready to go." I said it was as ready as it was going to be, because
we were shooting in three days and that was it. Unbeknownst to me, Molly
called Sam and begged him to prevent me from plunging ahead. I don't
know what answer Sam gave her, because everything was engaged—the
crew, the first location, the equipment, the cameraman—and there was no
way to hold off the production. But Molly was awfully strong and awfully
determined, and she kept at Sam until he had all he could take and told her
that the die was cast and that was it. Sam then told Budd and me what
Molly had done.

I was used to that kind of interference at home. I knew, even when it
infuriated me, that it always came from the best possible motives—my welfare as she saw it to be—even if there was a gentle arrogance there. But it
took some time for Budd to forgive her. Molly was a damned good woman
and a most loyal wife; she believed Sam had talked me into believing the
script was ready to shoot when it was not. In the cause of what was right,
she could brave my displeasure anytime; she had causes greater than pleasing me. Budd, however, took what she'd done as inexcusable interference;
he was outraged. We'd both had enough of other people chewing up our
script. After all, we'd worked terribly hard and long—first alone, then with
Zanuck, then alone again, and finally with S. P. Eagle. Now we were more
than ready to go from fighting in an office to fighting the story out on the
tough turf where we'd imagined it taking place. We'd had enough of eye-

ball-to-eyeball arguments, even with each other. The only eye I wanted to look at was the eyepiece of a camera. On my feet with my cameraman and my crew, with the actors I'd chosen, many of whom were friends, I'd be in a position of power and authority; I'd take over not only from any and all critics but from my producer. I had no more patience than Budd had for hearing what was wrong with our script. We'd both had enough of "Let's open it up again." Let's shoot!

O U R   F I R S T day's work was on rooftops from which the camera could look down the slope of the city of Hoboken to the Hudson River and across to the other side, New York City. It was a misty day, and the New York skyline in the distance was visible but gray, frosty and indistinct. I was very disappointed. But what appeared to be our misfortune that morning was a truer value; our view of the famous New York skyline throughout the movie was always gray and indistinct—the opposite of a picture postcard. This created the correct mood for the film, and I wasn't smart enough to realize it immediately. But in time I did, and I suppose by the old rule that luck evens out, every time we turned our cameras east, the sky was gray and threatening and the way I wanted it to be.

But that morning, arriving in a quarrelsome mood and climbing to the rooftop before anyone except my assistant and good friend to be Charlie Maguire, I looked at the gray skyline and thought: How much more bad luck will I get on this fucking film? Here we were, with the coldest and the grayest and the shortest days coming, up on a damned rooftop facing toward a skyline I'd counted on to be, again and again, a dramatic contrast to the degradations we'd show on the waterfront—and you could hardly see the damned skyline. I felt the rage again. I knew that morning that I was fighting for my professional life. But I'm not sure now if, had I been well balanced, cheerful, agreeable, friendly, companionable, decent, forgiving, charitable, and all those other fine virtues, I'd have survived the cold and the hardship of the work that was to come on the icy shore of the Hudson River. I believe my anger kept me warm. It's not pretty, but that rage carried me over insurmountable obstacles. It was a once-in-a-lifetime anger, and I've never felt it that hot again.

I didn't think much of my crew either. The cameraman, Boris Kaufman, whom I would come to admire enormously, seemed on first view awfully soft for the job ahead of us and the place where the job was to be done. As for the crew, who'd been haphazardly gathered, they already seemed uncertain and uncomfortable on the location, as well as shorthanded and perhaps the least bit timorous. All that and more made me angry before I had reason to be.

Then I had reason to be. Charlie Maguire told me that our producer was chiseling. We were supposed to work on three adjoining roofs, and Sam's production manager had obtained permission for us to set up on one of the roofs and on the roof two away, but the roof in between had not been cleared. Evidently, Charlie said, they'd asked more money than our side was willing to pay. When he'd protested, Charlie had been told that when we wanted to go from one roof to another, we'd have to go down the stairs of the building we were on, proceed along the street, and go up the stairs of the third building. This would apply not only to human traffic but also to equipment; it had to be carried down five flights, then up five flights. Such had been the front office dictum; it was penny wise and pound foolish, of course. That day's work took much longer and I shot far less than I might have.

But there he was that first morning, our leader, there to commemorate the start of the film with the mayor of Hoboken and the chief of police, still photographers all around them. When these stills were made and done with, Charlie came to me and said, "Mr. Kazan, we're ready to shoot." And I said, "Not until you clear the roof." So he said okay and went to ask everyone to get off, then he came back and said, "Okay, we're ready." And I said, "Not until you clear the roof." And Charlie looked around, and there were the mayor and the chief of police, so Charlie went over and told them they had to leave because we were getting ready to shoot and the director didn't want anyone there. And they left. Then Charlie came back and said, "Okay, we're ready." And I said, "I told you to clear the roof." Charlie looked around, and the only person he saw who was still there was our producer, S. P. Eagle. Charlie looked at me, but I didn't let up, and he went over and told Sam that I wasn't going to get a shot until he'd left. So Sam left.

That's how I felt about his chiseling and his character that first day, and things didn't improve much during the shooting of the film, because he chiseled on every cost and took it out of our hides and legs and patience. But he got what he wanted and what he'd been working for, a film that cost $880,000, which was remarkable because Brando got $100,000 and I got $100,000 (plus twenty-five percent). Where Sam chiseled was on the crew costs and every little insignificant thing he could cut out or cut down. But the film cost $880,000, not $1,880,000, which it easily might have. And in the end I'd be grateful for that.

The cold was our hardship. The crew had great metal barrels burning away and every kind of wood they could rip off, so that the flames were bursting out of the barrels and the metal rims were red hot. I'd learned on *Man on a Tightrope* that a crew has better morale and works better if the director stays out in the weather with them and sets the example. My assistant, Charlie, a great guy, obeyed the old First Assistant's Rule: Get yourself two pieces of string ten feet long. Tie one piece to the camera, the other piece to the director, and hold both free ends in your hand. I never had to look for Charlie or he for me. And we never came in out of the weather.

The actors, understandably, stayed in the hotel—the Grand, it was called (a name it certainly didn't deserve)—and they'd be called out to face the ice-fanged wind off the Hudson just before we rehearsed and just before we shot. They suffered from the cold more than Charlie or Boris Kaufman or I, because we were soon used to it. The bite of the wind and the temperature did a great thing for the actors' faces: It made them look like people, not actors—in fact, like people who lived in Hoboken and suffered the cold because they had no choice. In some scenes their breath was visible as they spoke, which made the scenes completely believable. Brando was occasionally difficult to bring out into the cold; I remember a few times going into the Hotel Grand and dragging him out. He remarked later that it was "so cold out there that you couldn't overact." But once he began to work, he was great, prompt, loaded with talent, full of surprises that improved scenes, a marvelous artist. Charlie says now that the crew especially admired Marlon and that he was the most professional actor Charlie has ever worked with.

Budd Schulberg came to Hoboken rarely, and since I stuck very close to the script there was no reason for him to come up from Bucks County and suffer with us. When I wanted to change bits of dialogue or drop them entirely, I would call him at home and get permission; I was careful about this. When he did come up, he was soon in a bar with Brownie or some other longshoreman, drinking and laughing.

Despite the cold and the wind and the snow, no one got sick. I suppose they all became accustomed to the weather, but perhaps a more important reason was that they believed in the worth of what we were doing. And none of them ever dared cross me, because I seemed so intense and suffered the hardships longer and better than anyone. There were more-real problems. The "mob" was around, watching what we were doing, and perhaps in the beginning there was danger. I decided I'd be easier and work better if I had a bodyguard; he was a fine fellow named Joe Marotta, the brother of the chief of police. Joe carried a pistol and was never more than six feet away from me throughout the picture. One day some hoods pushed me up against a wall and, holding me there, began to berate me, their point being that I was making the people of Hoboken look bad—yes, they were that civic-minded. But Joe walked up and they walked away. I also had my prizefighters, who played mob figures: Two-Ton Tony Galento, Abe Simon, and Tami Mauriello, heavyweights, and a middleweight named Roger Donohue, who'd once killed a man in the ring but who was soft-spoken and rather cultured. I kept these fellows as close as I could and became friendly with them. To make them act reasonably well was a more difficult job. Once during a very tense scene, I had Tami Mauriello close to the camera, prominently featured, and no matter what happened, his face never fixed on anything, his eyes would always wander here and there, so that he gave the impression of indifference. I finally became desperate. Telling the camera operator to be ready, hand on switch, to roll the camera, I went over to

Directing the extras. Brownie is at lower left, Charlie Maguire at my left.

Tami and suddenly whacked him as hard as I could with my open palm across the face, then, shouting "Roll!" I leaped back to the safe area behind the camera, close to Charlie and Joe. Tami was okay in that scene.

The nearest any of us came to bad trouble happened to Charlie Maguire. We'd made a deal with the longshoremen to play extras in the picture, which is one of the reasons the film looks real. They were to get the same pay as longshoremen, with a four-hour minimum guarantee, and would be paid the next day at noon. Once we used a whole bunch of them, and the next day, at noon, the money was not there. Charlie was setting up some background action on a pier when two big gorillas, over six feet they were and loaded down with muscle and arrogance, came over to him, grabbed him, and held him over the water off the side of the pier. "Where's our money?" they demanded. Charlie said, "It will be here." Then they put him against a wall and said, "We don't see any payroll table here. Where's the money?" At just that moment, Spiegel rolled up in his limousine with his paymaster. They'd stopped somewhere en route for coffee. The gorillas followed Charlie all the way to the pay table to make sure the money rolled.

So it went; there was always some crisis, and you never knew who was standing on the outskirts of the crowd, watching intently. Both Boris Kaufman and Charlie Maguire felt the tension, but they behaved magnificently; they knew that the rough circumstances within which we were making the film gave it the look it needed. I think Charlie minded the cold and whatever harassment he encountered on the set from the hoodlums less than what he had to take from our producer. Sam would call Charlie's home, sometimes as late as two in the morning, most of the time from "21" or whatever other "in" place he patronized. Charlie felt that Sam must have had a girl with him, because he was trying to impress someone close by with the authoritative tone of his voice. (Sam's young ladies were always kids—nineteen, twenty, twenty-one—and easily impressed.) Sam would bawl Charlie out, demanding to know why he'd "let Kazan in scene number eight-four go for nine takes." And why had Charlie let Kazan print three? This was Charlie's first big picture, but he was learning fast; he'd say, "Well, if you don't want him to do it, why don't you call him and tell him yourself?"

After a time, Sam did get up the courage to call me directly at home, but Molly would never let him wake me; she didn't give a damn about the man. The next day I'd tell Charlie how Molly had behaved, and soon Charlie's wife, Jessie, was refusing to put Charlie on; the Eagle began to shriek, but both our wives held fast. One night something slipped up in Jessie Maguire's security system, and Sam did get Charlie on the phone and talked to him for forty-five minutes, frantically, urgently, begging him to do his best to stick to the schedule. "Keep Kazan to the schedule," he screamed at Charlie, "I don't care how. Do anything. Yell at him! Insult him. Apologize later."

Sam hardly ever came out to Hoboken. When he did, it was always in a limousine and usually with a girl. He'd be wearing a tan camel's-hair coat and expensive alligator-skin shoes, which certainly seemed out of place there. The girl would stay in the car while Sam pattered around the puddles, complaining to anyone whose attention he could get, most of all to Charlie and to Boris, then go back to New York. I was in such a state of temper that he generally stayed away from me. His most famous visit was late one night toward the end of the film. We were shooting the scene where a truck tries to run down Marlon and Eva Marie Saint in an alley, and it had started to snow. Boris asked our crew to hang a tarp over this alleyway, because we'd shot some of the scene the previous night, before the snowfall, and it wouldn't have matched. God, it was cold that night, and the snow didn't help, and the crew was awfully tired after a long, tough schedule.

That was the night our producer decided to come out about one in the morning and give the crew a boost—not by praising them but by scolding and threatening them. It was freezing cold, and the snow was half sleet but thickening, and the tarpaulin over the alley was filling up with the stuff and threatening to collapse. The crew had just put the canvas cover up and one of their number had fallen off a ladder and broken his leg and been driven to the hospital. The crew had taken a break, ducking out of the arctic wind into a little factory off the alley to get warm again. And up comes Sam, fresh from the Stork Club, and he had on his camel's-hair coat and those one-hundred-and-twenty-five-dollar alligator shoes—so Charlie Maguire re-members it—and everybody was getting ready to go outside again and finish the job, when Sam orders Charlie to get the crew together, and as soon as they were there, staring at him resentfully—again according to Charlie, because I wasn't allowed in—Sam launches into his speech of com-plaint and outrage. "You're killing me," he said, "you're absolutely killing me with your incompetence and your laziness." Mind you, they'd been out all night in ten degrees of temperature (no one measured wind chill in those days), and they'd had enough. But Sam didn't sense it. "Apologize later" was his motto.

There was a little propman on that crew, Eddie Barr was his name, and he'd been around working props for a million years, and he stood up and he said, "You Jew cocksucker!" Barr was a Jewish guy, and he could get away with that. "You Jew cocksucker, if it weren't for Charlie Maguire and that little guy outside"—me—"we'd all be home. Nobody wants to be out here tonight. This is blood money tonight. We don't need this kind of money. Now you better get your ass out of here if you want us to make this picture." So Sam left; you couldn't blame him for that, only for not having the hu-manity to thank the men for the work they were doing on that very hard night. The only discomfort Sam could ever appreciate was that of the wealthy and of the established snobs whose friendship he valued.

The most famous scene in the film, the one played over and over on TV until I got sick of it but never so often that I didn't marvel at Brando's and Steiger's performances, was the scene in the taxicab. It is the perfect ex-ample of how this picture was made by a series of accidents and misfortunes that turned out well in the end. When we started on it in the morning, everything seemed wrong, because everything *was* wrong. My original in-tention had been to shoot the scene in a real taxi, an actual cab in traffic. I was lucky I didn't, of course, because if I had, I never would have got the performances I did. Then this seemed too difficult and too expensive for Sam, so he procured for us a shabby old taxicab shell, which he had placed in a small, shabby studio. I asked to have a projection of traffic seen through the rear window. When we got to the studio that morning, Boris and I found that Sam, to save a big bill, had not arranged for the rear-projection equipment. Boris was upset and I was upset. There wasn't time before Brando's departure at four o'clock to do a hell of a lot, so Boris solved the problem in the simplest way possible, by putting a small venetian blind across the window at the back of the cab shell and shooting straight in to avoid the side windows, except for an edge that he caught with a flickering light to suggest traffic going by. We had some of the crew shake the taxi shell to suggest movement, and that was it; we thought it a crude, primitive solution, but we got by with it. The audience watches the actors, not the taxi, not the traffic outside.

I've been highly praised for the direction of this scene, but the truth is I didn't direct it. By the time Boris and I had figured out what to do with the set, the morning was gone and Brando was leaving at four; there was nothing to do except put the actors in their places—who on which side of the seat? did it matter?—and photograph them. By that time in the schedule, Brando and Steiger knew who they were and what the scene was about— they knew all that better than I did by then—so I didn't say anything to them. Sometimes it's important for a director to withdraw a little. If the characters are going right, to begin to talk about who they are and motivation and so forth may result in the actors' becoming concerned with satisfying you instead of playing the scene. You can spoil a scene by being too much of a genuine director—call it showing off. Here the scene had been set in motion long before; I knew that and was smart enough that day or troubled enough by my technical problems not to do anything more.

By the time Brando had to leave, I hadn't photographed Steiger's close-up, and it was the last thing I did, reading Marlon's lines myself from off camera. Rod had reason to be annoyed; in fact, I doubt that he ever quite forgave me for slighting his "side" of the scene. He said I treated Marlon better than I did him. He was right, I did, but in this case it didn't hurt the scene; Rod was excellent. I believe that what happened hurt his self-esteem but not his performance. If Steiger has played any scene better than that one, I have not seen it.

But of course the extraordinary element in that scene and in the whole picture was Brando, and what was extraordinary about his performance, I feel, is the contrast of the tough-guy front and the extreme delicacy and gentle cast of his behavior. What other actor, when his brother draws a pistol to force him to do something shameful, would put his hand on the gun and push it away with the gentleness of a caress? Who else could read "Oh, Charlie!" in a tone of reproach that is so loving and so melancholy and suggests that terrific depth of pain? I didn't direct that; Marlon showed me, as he often did, how the scene should be performed. I could never have told him how to do that scene as well as he did it. The same kind of surprising delicacy appears in his performance at the other most unlikely moment, when he finds his dead brother hanging from a meat hook in an alley. The first thing Brando does when he sees the body is not touch it. The body is hanging there and Marlon simply comes up alongside, putting his hand on the wall and leaning against it. He doesn't look at the body, but you know very well what he's feeling.

My favorite scenes in the film are the love scenes between Marlon and Eva Marie Saint. I've been praised for the scene in which, as they walk, Edie drops her glove and Terry picks it up and, when she reaches for it, doesn't give it to her but draws it on his hand. I didn't direct that; it hap-

pened, just as it might have in an improvisation at the Actors Studio. Later, in the bar, when Edie starts quizzing Terry about her brother's death, the depth of guilt as well as tenderness on Brando's face is overwhelming. Marlon was always presenting me with these small miracles; he was more often than not better than I, and I could only be grateful for him. And still am.

So we finished the film in the cold, which was numbing on many days, and through all kinds of difficulties that again and again proved to be of benefit to us. We would feel less that we'd completed the film than that we'd survived it. But the cold, and the danger—there were always some members of the "mob" standing behind the rest of the crowd watching us work—were stimulants. And even the spying. Marlon suspected that the chauffeur whom Sam had assigned to drive him to New York would report on his conversations with whoever rode with him—on the non-Bela days, me. A year later, I had a letter from Darryl Zanuck, who was then bitter about losing the film and anxious that I should do another for him; in that letter there is this: "When I see you personally, I will tell you what I was told by our New York lawyers regarding an affidavit they obtained from a chauffeur who overheard a conversation between Marlon and you. It was, at the time, very disturbing to me and since it was in the form of a 'voluntary affidavit' I had to accept it as being at least half true."

Then we were through shooting, and everything shut down except for what happened in my cutting room, where I was working with Gene Milford, my film editor. Neither he nor I nor Sam suspected we had a film that was going to be a classic. Actually Sam was concerned that the film would be a box office failure and further lower his standing in the industry. Anxious to get another prominent name on the advertising copy, Sam invited

Leonard Bernstein to see our rough cut. It was down to length but clumsy and uneven in details. This was also to be the first time Marlon would see the film; he sat directly in front of me at the screening. As soon as the last shot was over and we "went to black," Marlon got up and, without turning his head to me, left the screening room. Not a word, not even a goodbye. Yet I owe a debt to Brando; I know what my film would have been without him.

Sam had been talking to Lenny Bernstein, and something about his apologetic tone angered me further. He was so humble and uncertain about the film that I got furious enough to yell at him the conviction I'd just come to at that screening. "This is a great picture," I shouted—the first time this had occurred to me. Bernstein agreed with me and we had a composer.

I don't know how it reflected my annoyance with Sam's mealy-mouthed pandering to Bernstein, but it must have, because I suddenly, irrationally, turned on him and said, "Sam, you've finally made a good picture. Now why don't you drop that phony S. P. Eagle and bill yourself as Sam Spiegel. That would be honest." And it wasn't long before he did.

Sam was often embarrassed by my crudeness and my hostility toward him, and he was right to be. But I always esteemed him as the man who produced this film when no one else would and the man who persevered against Budd's and

Budd

my inertia until we had an excellent shooting script. I believe we would have had a failure without Sam, and a fiasco with Zanuck. That is the reason why, no matter what Sam did, I never turned totally against him. I suppose he had some such feeling about me.

When the film had been scored and was in its final form, Sam asked me to take it out west and show it to the president of the company that had financed it, Harry Cohn of Columbia Pictures. Harry had a projection room in the cellar of his mansion near the Beverly Hills Hotel. I was supposed to sit with him while he saw the film, take notes about any reservations he had and whatever suggestions he might make. It was a formality, of course; the picture was finished. The only thing Harry asked before the projection started was: "How much did it cost?" I told him under $900,000. He nodded and made a signal to the projectionist. He had a girl with him, of course: they always do. They'd had drinks and dinner upstairs and probably some other pleasure, because about a third of the way through the film, I heard a familiar sound and turned and saw Harry fast asleep and snoring. The girl stayed awake throughout and liked the film. I didn't tell Harry that he'd slept, because he might have asked to see the picture again.

W H E N it comes down, it comes down like an avalanche. I don't know how they find it out, the people who buy tickets. It's like an animal smelling blood. Even before the newspapers have taken notice of the "entertainment," there is a long line at the box office. They can't explain why they're there, so don't ask them. The Astor Theatre, now replaced by a let's-have-fun hotel, was in its glory that morning in April of 1954 when the film opened. There were three hundred people in line at 9 a.m., before the box office opened. I went downtown, I saw the line. What brought them there? I noticed that many of those waiting were men and many of them "tough guys," the kind that generally don't rush to the movies. Somebody quipped that if the three hundred people in line that first morning had been booked and taken to police headquarters, the crime rate would have plummeted. But that's a foolish exaggeration; the audience we drew weren't all criminals. So what's the answer? Yes, the story is strong and well put together, and there is a lot of violence and a love story, and there are even a few laughs, and sure everyone likes to see the underdog come out on top of the hoods—but three hundred people before the box office has opened? What is it they smelled?

My guess is that it's the theme, that of a man who has sinned and is redeemed. But how can that be? After all, Terry's act of self-redemption breaks the great childhood taboo: Don't snitch on your friends. Don't call for the cop! Our hero is a "rat," or for intellectuals, an informer. But that didn't seem to bother anyone in the audience, not given our villains, those whom Terry was fingering. Which is proof that Budd Schulberg struck a deep human craving there: redemption for a sinner, rescue from damnation. Redemption, isn't that the promise of the Catholic Church? That a man can turn his fate around and by an act of good heart be saved at last? There are gut reasons like that for the success of the great hits. They touch a fundamental hunger in people. Yes, that a man can, no matter what he's done, be redeemed—particularly if he has a sympathetic young woman as his confessor. She's better than a priest, but does the same job. That is why Budd's insistence on the prominence of the love story was so instinctively correct. It was during those most tender moments that Marlon enlisted the audience in his favor. Is it possible that many more people than we imagine have a feeling that they've done wrong and yearn for forgiveness and rescue? Wasn't Brando playing out the hopes of the audience? Something like that must have gone on, because people have told me that they've seen this film a dozen times; every night it's on TV, they make sure to see it. Apparently it's more than entertainment. Something central has been touched. And it's bigger than anything Budd and I had devised. We didn't know what we had or what we'd done. For instance, try and repeat a great success, and you'll surely fail.

W I T H that first morning's line at the Astor Theatre, I was back on top in the film world. The line was the news, not the reviews. The fellows who wrote film criticism would have had to write poetry to measure our success. I'd been up and I'd been down, I knew the way stations and the end of the line at both ends. I knew where I was now, on top, and why. The "notices" were good, but what told me I was *in* were the offers. Abe Lastfogel now assured me I could make any picture I wanted to make. Poor old Darryl began to come on to me, full of regret and self-justification. Quote: "The advent and debut of CinemaScope was responsible, more than anything else, for my final decision against the property." Oh, yeah? He'd let an Academy Award picture slip through his fingers, and everyone knew it. Actually Darryl was right. If he had done the film it would have been a dud. I turned away from him and went to Warner Brothers with *East of Eden*, the novel by my friend John Steinbeck. Jack Warner promised me what Zanuck could not: final cut. Which means that if you get an approval from the industry's self-censoring board and if you "bring the film in" at or near an agreed budget figure, no one can tell you how to put your picture together or how to score its drama. Final cut is the prize of success for a director.

Brando was glad to get the Oscar he deserved; he didn't send an Indian maiden on stage to pick it up for him, as he would later. Budd and I accepted our trophies in New York City—which was just. Going back over the old newspapers, I found a page with our photographs as we received the honor. My face has a look no one else's has. It wasn't pretty. I wasn't proud of it. But you can understand that I was tasting vengeance that night and enjoying it. *On the Waterfront* was my own story; every day I worked on that film, I was telling the world where I stood and my critics to go and fuck themselves. As for Art Miller, the film spoke to him and to Mr. John Wharton. I would in time forgive them both—but not that year.

W H I L E writing the chapter you've just read, I was invited to a party at Sam Spiegel's penthouse on Park Avenue, and I accepted. The big brains in the entertainment field were there, and Sam lived up to his reputation as a great host. He made everyone feel wonderful, including me. I also felt guilty. I was shocked at the fact that I'd just been writing about Sam and at how two-faced I was to come to his party and hug him when we greeted each other and appreciate how he flattered my pretty wife ("Once seen, never forgotten"). Still everything I've written about his conduct on *On the Waterfront* is precisely true—in fact, understated.

So what is one to do? Life slips by in a pleasant concord of days, while the truth is buried under time's passing, good food and drink and convivial chatter. The truth is that socially I couldn't help responding to Sam with pleasure and friendship; I liked Sam. The truth is also that I can't forget how badly he behaved on the two films we made together.

Some months later, I went to a symposium, one of a series conducted by the Dramatists Guild, this one about *Death of a Salesman*. There at hand were Art Miller and a great lady, the actress Milly Dunnock. I greeted Art cordially and he me and we spoke well of each other to the gathering. I don't know what he thought about what I said, and as for me, I didn't think he was nearly as pompous as he has sometimes been in public. (There I go again!) But a witness would have thought we were the best of old fast friends. And we were and are; that's the astonishing part of it. I've been perplexed and angry at him, as he, I must believe, has been disgusted and mad at me. But still we greet each other cordially and even warmly as becomes old campaign comrades, and we part saying, "Let's see each other soon again," which of course we don't. But I like Miller; I wouldn't even mind being cast away on a desert island with him.

Here's a question: Am I two-faced? The answer has to be: "Certainly, sometimes." I've made a great practice of getting along, just as most of you have, by concealing negative feelings about people. But if I were to go back and relive some of the scenes where I felt the pinch of a relationship, I doubt that I'd know how to behave differently. And I ask myself, haven't I had enough of choking down memories that make *me* uncomfortable? Isn't discretion a false solution? If I write about my life at all, I have to write as I feel about Sam and Art and the actors I've worked with.

Particularly with actors, a director has to be two-faced. They're up there, those tremulous souls with their pleading peepers, waiting for a good word or two that will send them home believing that they are going to make it. They feed on your approval; they quiver, anticipating your disapproval. The beautiful and the terrible thing about actors is that when they work they are completely exposed; you have to appreciate that if you direct them. They are being critically observed not only for their emotions, their technique, and their intelligence, but for their legs, their breasts, their carriage, their double chins, and so on. Their whole being is opened to scrutiny, waiting for your praise, concern, and help. Sometimes a gentle kiss will mean more to an actress, her confidence and her performance, than whatever you can say. How can you feel anything but gratitude for creatures so vulnerable and so naked?

Acting is the only art where you can't judge your own work, even in films. So the director tends to say what will get the result he needs. It may even be necessary to say something negative or doubting—just a little; you mustn't destroy the actor. Perhaps to leave rehearsal without a word of any kind, and so give him a hint of doubt. Perhaps to praise the other person in a scene and not praise him. That can work. Whatever it is, it's a tactic. It's like what you tell your wife when she asks for the hundredth time, "Do you still love me? Are you going off me?" (English expression: cooling.) Maybe you question everything in the world that day, including yourself in marriage, but why bother her with your existential doubts? If you say, "I'd just as soon be dead today!" she'd be certain to take it as a discredit to her. "I haven't made him happy," she'll say to herself. "I guess I never will." Then she'll funk out, and you won't get a decent meal for the next three days.

Yes, I believe all directors tend to be a little two-faced, just as I believe all writers are spies. Notice one of those bastards sometime, how they shift gears in the middle of the conversation. You go along talking to one of them, and suddenly they're not gabbing with you, not spontaneously, not exchanging views freely. They've pulled back; they're listening and recording what you're saying, to use later. You can hear the clickety-click in their skulls where nature's tape recorder spins. Probably what you've just said fitted into a scene they're writing. That's what I mean by spying. They may even encourage you to go on, despite the fact that they totally disagree with what you've said and resent it. I've seen writers sit still at a party, listening to a discussion that I know offends them, but they don't respond or counter or demonstrate what they feel. Later they will report that conversation to home base, their notebook.

I don't know what the answer is. Only the result, which will certainly be that everyone who feels hurt, exposed, or shamed by what I've written about him or her will be furious. So what can they do—punch me in the nose? I'm too small and too old for anyone to go after me that way. Am I sorry to have hurt the memory of men I've just said I liked? A little—or else I wouldn't be writing all this, would I? But mainly I'm glad I have the power, the time, and the memory to tell the truth about my own life. That is what this experience means to me; let the chips fall where they may. I don't know why I've lived through all that I've lived through, except for the privilege of telling it all as I believe it to have happened. People have been complaining for years that I've remained silent in the face of intolerable provocation. Now that I'm speaking up, I must say it feels good.

E K K E H A R D   S C H A L L , the great actor from the Berliner Ensemble, was in New York; some of us spoke to him about the philosophy and methods of that extraordinary theatre. Their stage is in East Berlin, and Ekkehard spoke of their firm Marxist orientation. "What is that in play production?" he was asked. "What in terms of acting technique?" He answered in a number of ways, using the word "dialectics" many times, of course. I didn't always follow. But there was one phrase he repeated again and again that I found stimulating. He said the point of their work was to present "contradiction as unity," that is, to combine in the same piece of behavior opposing and conflicting impulses and goals.

That meant a good deal to me. I am preparing to write about that time in my life when I was squeezed between conflicting tendencies which tightened around me, pulling and pushing me in opposite directions at the same time. For instance, I wanted to be an independent producer and director of films, going my own way without restriction or reservations, but I also wanted the power, equipment, and prestige of a Major Studio behind me.

With the huge success of *On the Waterfront,* this seemed possible then. I also wanted to write my own screenplays, while I still valued and heeded the insights and talents of better writers. I wanted to write my own story and that of my family, but I also wanted to write about the social history that I'd witnessed in my time. I wanted to be in with the big shots of the entertainment world, but I also wanted to lead a quiet, reflective life. I wanted money, plenty of it, but I certainly didn't want to pay for that money with onerous services. I wanted to be a bourgeois with a townhouse and a country home, a cook and a housekeeper, two cars, a regular winter vacation in the Caribbean; but I also wanted to keep my expenses down so I would never feel compelled to do a film or a play about which I was not enthusiastic. I wanted to be a member of the rough gang, the street people, like those I'd gotten to know in Hoboken, plain old "Gadg." I wanted to be a lefty, a radical, certainly a socialist—at least that—but I also wanted to be a Democrat, sitting squarely mid-America, loyal and loving to the U.S.A. I wanted to lead an irregular life, wandering here and there around the earth as the impulse moved me, keeping my own hours; I also wanted to be the head of a nuclear family, a firmly established and respected Anatolian paterfamilias, with all household events on time, clean sheets every third day, heavy "Turkish" towels, linen napkins, and a good dinner served each night at seven. I loved Molly, my smart, immaculate, completely honest and absolutely trustworthy wife, but I also wanted adventures and to be, every so often, irresponsible and out of control. I wanted it all. But how did I shape these contradictions into the unit of contradiction that the actor from the Berliner Ensemble spoke of? The answer is, I didn't. I wasn't able to. What I did was give in to them all, and when they warred with each other, I yielded alternately but completely to conflicting devotions. I swayed back and forth, all the way at each end; I was unresolved.

A terrible personal drama was approaching, and a terror that would last for many years. Each opposite course had its champion, a woman who exemplified its virtues and its attractions, each urging me her own way. They never really met, the two women, never studied each other in close-up, but they fought fiercely for my allegiance and for my person, until it was inevitable that one of them would win, and the winner would win nothing except a man who longed for what he'd given up, who went on yearning for what he was missing. Either victor would be a loser; the struggle ended tragically for both. Only I survived.

D O N'T you get tired of hearing people who live with their mouths pressed to the tit of the film and TV industry complaining about their lack of artistic freedom? What did they think the rules of the game were? Money is magic; very simple. When *On the Waterfront* was filling theatres, my "artistic position," as it's called, changed overnight, as if by magic. I could even have had my offices at the Warner Brothers studio in Burbank repainted any color I chose.

Here's how the deal for *East of Eden* was made. I went into Jack Warner's office alone—which is to say, without Lastfogel—sat down, laughed at a couple·of Jack's old-time one-liners, then told him I wanted to make a film based on John Steinbeck's new novel. He hadn't read the book, didn't propose to, didn't even ask what it was about, and didn't ask whom I was going to cast. What he did ask was: "What'll it cost?" "About one six," I said. "You've got it," he said. I doubt Warner ever read our screenplay; he was a hunch-bettor. I was his hunch that year. I told him that since it was about young people, I might use "newcomers." He stood up. "Come have lunch with me," he said. "Cast who you want." I was on my own.

Being an Anatolian, I knew that all this beneficence was as temporary as anything else in life, including life itself. It would last as long as I brought in the money. A few years later, after two box office busts in a row, I no longer had final cut. After another losing effort, I couldn't get backing at all.

Paul Osborn, who was writing the screenplay, said I should have a look at the young man playing the bit part of an Arab in a play at the John Golden Theatre. I wasn't impressed with James Dean—I'd begun to think about Brando again—but to please Osborn I called Jimmy into Warners' New York offices, for a closer look. When I walked in he was slouched at the end of a leather sofa in the waiting room, a heap of twisted legs and denim rags, looking resentful for no particular reason. I didn't like the expression on his face, so I kept him waiting. I also wanted to see how he'd react to that. It seemed that I'd outtoughed him, because when I called him into my office, he'd dropped the belligerent pose. We tried to talk, but conversation was not his gift, so we sat looking at each other. He asked me if I wanted to ride on the back of his motorbike; I didn't enjoy the ride. He was showing off—a country boy not impressed with big-city traffic. When I got back to the office, I called Paul and told him this kid actually *was* Cal in *East of Eden;* no sense looking further or "reading" him. I sent Dean to see Steinbeck, who was living near me, on Seventy-second Street. John thought Dean a snotty kid. I said that was irrelevant; wasn't he Cal? John said he sure as hell was, and that was it.

Now I was into studying Dean, so I decided to take him to California and make some screen tests disguised as wardrobe tests. I was being pampered with a long black limo in New York; after it picked me up to take me to the airport, I had it drive to the obscure address where Dean was holed up. He came out—believe it or not—carrying two packages wrapped in paper and tied with lengths of string. He looked like an immigrant sitting in the back of that luxury limo. He told me he'd never been in an airplane before. Airborne, he sat with his nose pressed to the window, looking at the beautiful country below. Warners' transportation had the limo's California cousin waiting for me in the airport. When Jimmy asked if we could pause on the way into town at the place where his father, a sort of lab technician, worked, I was delighted. Dean dashed into one of those very temporary-looking buildings that flank highways there, and came out with a man he said was his father. The man had no definition and made no impression except that he had no definition. Obviously there was a strong tension between the two, and it was not friendly. I sensed the father disliked his son. They stood side by side, but talk soon collapsed, and we drove on.

I believe the encounter shocked Dean. I saw that the story of the movie was his story—just as it was, in a way, my own. My father used to complain to his assistant at George Kazan, Oriental Rugs and Carpets, about me. "That boy never be man," he'd say. "What am I going to do with him?" Jimmy's father didn't seem to think his son's future very promising either.

When I shot Jimmy's tests—it was his first time before a movie camera, though he'd been on TV—he wasn't nervous. He seemed to take to it. The crew—directors always watch the reaction of a crew to a newcomer—were not impressed. They thought Jimmy was the stand-in, that the real star was still to appear. When I told them Jimmy was it, they thought I was nuts. Warner must have seen Jimmy's tests, but he said nothing. I don't know what he thought; he was used to Errol Flynn, Jimmy Cagney, and Gary Cooper. Now comes this twisted, fidgety kid from New York. But my magic held; Warner said nothing. I was still on my own.

What has always fascinated me is the response of newcomers to success. I watch for it and don't expect it to be honorable. A couple of weeks before the end of our shooting schedule, it was getting around that the kid on the *East of Eden* set was going to make it big. Jimmy heard the news too, and the first thing I noticed was that he was being rude to our little wardrobe man. I stopped that quickly. Then he began to complain that he couldn't do a certain scene that had to be played standing on a slanting roof outside a second-story window. He was right; he did the scene poorly; but it was an important scene, so I took him and Julie Harris, the "love interest," to an Italian restaurant and loaded Jimmy up with Chianti. That did it—it's a technique I've used on occasion to supersede Stanislavski.

Ray Massey, the old-timer who'd played Lincoln enough times to establish a franchise and was now playing Jimmy's father, anticipated that Jimmy would quickly spoil rotten. He simply couldn't stand the sight of the kid, dreaded every day he worked with him. "You never know what he's going to say or do!" Ray said. "Make him read the lines the way they're written." Jimmy knew that Ray was scornful of him, and he responded with a sullenness he didn't cover. This was an antagonism I didn't try to heal; I aggravated it. I'm ashamed to say—well, not ashamed; everything goes in directing movies—I didn't conceal from Jimmy or from Ray what they thought of each other, made it plain to each of them. The screen was alive

Ray Massey and Jimmy, at right

with precisely what I wanted; they detested each other. Casting should tell the story of a film without words; this casting did. It was a problem that went on to the end, and I made use of it to the end.

The first thing Jimmy did with his suddenly augmented flow of money was to buy a palomino. Raised on an Indiana farm, he'd always wanted a horse of his own, and a palomino is the most beautiful of animals. For a time I arranged for him to keep the beast on the lot, but the corral was far from the sound stage where we were shooting, and Jimmy was always running off to feed or curry or just look at his gorgeous animal. I finally had the horse exiled to a farm in the San Fernando Valley. Then Jimmy bought a motorbike, but I stopped that too. I told him I didn't want to chance an accident, and that he absolutely couldn't ride the bike until the film was over. Next Jimmy bought himself an expensive camera, and he was flaunting it everywhere, taking rolls of pictures that he had the studio lab develop for him. I wasn't crazy about this either, so I told him not to bring it on the stage where we were shooting anymore. That made him sullen for a day.

I noticed that a couple of mornings he came to work late, looking pooped; whatever he'd been doing the night before seemed to have worn him out. Well, I thought, isn't it natural for a kid that age to get laid once in a while? Nevertheless it didn't help his performance, nor did whatever else he was doing at night—was he drinking or fighting? I didn't know. I began to worry that something would happen to him and delay my work or make him less able to carry out what I wanted, so I moved myself into one of those great star dressing rooms on the lot and Jimmy into the one across from me. My front door opened to his front door, and I could hear what went on in his quarters through the walls. What went on was Pier Angeli. But clearly that didn't go well for Dean either; I could hear them boffing but more often arguing through the walls. I was glad when she "found" Vic Damone. Now I had Jimmy as I wanted him, alone and miserable. All he had was his camera. Narcissism took over. He used to stand in front of the mirror in his room and take roll after roll of close-up photographs of his face, with only the slightest variation of expression. He'd show me the goddamn contact sheets and ask which one I liked best. I thought they were all the same picture, but I said nothing. As a hobby they were better than his unsuccessful devotion to Pier Angeli, so I encouraged them.

Brando was Dean's hero; everyone knew that, because he dropped his voice to a cathedral hush when he talked about Marlon. I invited Brando to come to the set and enjoy some hero worship. Marlon did and was very gracious to Jimmy, who was so adoring that he seemed shrunken and twisted in misery. People were to compare them, but they weren't alike. Marlon, well trained by Stella Adler, had excellent technique. He was proficient in every aspect of acting, including characterization and makeup. He was also a great mimic. Dean had no technique to speak of. When he tried to play an older man in the last reels of *Giant*, he looked like what he was: a beginner. On my film, Jimmy would either get the scene right immediately, without any detailed direction—that was ninety-five percent of the time—or he couldn't get it at all. Then I had to use some extraordinary means—the Chianti, for instance.

I was totally unprepared for his success. We had a first preview at a theatre in the Los Angeles area, and the instant he appeared on the screen, hundreds of girls began to scream. They'd been waiting for him, it seemed—how come or why, I don't know. The response of the balcony reminded me of what we'd got from the balcony when we played *Waiting for Lefty* for the first time—Niagara Falls spilling over. The goddamn kid became a legend overnight and the legend grew more intense with every showing. When my friend Nick Ray cast him in *Rebel Without a Cause*, he intensified Dean's spell over the youth of the nation. It was a legend I didn't approve of. Its essence was that all parents were insensitive idiots, who didn't understand or appreciate their kids and weren't able to help them. Parents were the enemy. I didn't like the way Nick Ray showed the parents in *Rebel Without a Cause*, but I'd contributed by the way Ray Massey was shown in my film. In contrast to these parent figures, all youngsters were supposed to be sensitive and full of "soul." This didn't seem true to me. I thought them—Dean, "Cal," and the kid he played in Nick Ray's film— self-pitying, self-dramatizing, and good-for-nothing. I became very impatient with the Dean legend, especially when I received letter after letter thanking me for what I'd done for him and asking me to be a sponsor of a nationwide network of Jimmy Dean clubs. I didn't respond to those letters.

I doubt that Jimmy would ever have got through *East of Eden* except for an angel on our set. Her name was Julie Harris, and she was goodness itself with Dean, kind and patient and everlastingly sympathetic. She would adjust her performance to whatever the new kid did. Despite the fact that it had early on been made clear to me that Warner, when he saw her first wardrobe test, wished I'd taken a "prettier" girl, I thought Julie beautiful; as a performer she found in each moment what was dearest and most moving. She also had the most affecting voice I've ever heard in an actress; it

conveyed tenderness and humor simultaneously. She helped Jimmy more than I did with any direction I gave him. The breakup of a film company when the schedule concludes is often a sad event; none was sadder for me than when I saw this young woman for the last time.

I N   1 9 5 5 the Actors Studio organized a benefit performance of *East of Eden* at the Victoria Theatre. It was a highly publicized affair; everyone of prominence in our theatre world and in the New York film world was there. John Steinbeck came with me, our wives at our sides. Marilyn and Marlon did publicity spots together. Our actresses ushered. Politicians felt it would be useful for them to attend. With the proceeds we bought the old church at 432 West 44th Street that became our permanent home. There Lee was enshrined.

Even before the Group Theatre existed, Lee had noticed that actors would humble themselves before his rhetoric and the intensity of his emotion. The more naive and self-doubting the actors, the more total was Lee's power over them. The more famous and the more successful these actors, the headier the taste of power for Lee. He found his perfect victim-devotee in Marilyn Monroe, who'd been attending his sessions as an observer.

Marilyn had married Joe DiMaggio in 1954, which made her more famous, and then divorced him and, in 1956, married Art Miller. In sex, persistence wins. We've all seen the photographs of Art, his happy bride, and, at their side, Art's parents. Marilyn at last had everything she'd ever

wanted, including in-laws. Dutifully, she studied Mrs. Miller's home cooking. Art and Marilyn were always seen clasped together. Their marriage
appeared to be ecstatic. Art gave her a rose-tinted view of her future, that
of an elite actress, doing serious work. He promised to write a film for her,
and in time he did; it was titled *The Misfits*. But before that, I'd begun to
hear of conflicts, harsh ones. In time Miller would be wounded too. Marilyn went for the drug reassurance, from Art to Lee Strasberg.

Quickly Lee took her over, giving her special attention, private lessons
and passionate encouragement. It could reasonably be said that he captured
her; when he told her she had "real tragic power," she believed him because she needed to. He became the living certification of her worth, encouraging her beyond her gifts in the direction of goals she was not
equipped to reach. Although she was a charming light comedienne—certainly a respectable talent—Lee convinced her that she could play roles of
greater weight. He pointed to Eugene O'Neill and *Anna Christie*. He
worked privately with her on Lady Macbeth's great scenes, assuring her
that one day (if she continued to work with him) she could play that part.
He soon had her spellbound, feeding her the reassurance of worth she most
craved. He made himself indispensable to her, turning her against all other
authority figures and influences—other teachers, other directors; even her
husband. Marilyn was Lee's ticket to the big time, and he was hers to the
station in life she most desperately needed. It became a question of vanity:
not hers—his.

I W A S N'T aware of it at the time, but something serious was beginning
to happen: I was shedding playwrights. Looking back, I can see that I was
managing to lose the very playwrights I'd worked so hard to secure for
myself, the playwrights every producer and director in the theatre wanted
for his own. This behavior, which would end by severing valued relationships, was unconscious. It started with nothing more than a kind of impatience, but it grew into a resentment that I choked down for many years; in
fact, until now.

One afternoon early in the rehearsal period of *Cat on a Hot Tin Roof*,
Tennessee Williams, fresh from a lunch where he'd treated himself to a
bottle of cool white wine, wandered into the theatre where I was rehearsing
his play and plumped himself down in the middle of the theatre's orchestra
section. On stage, Barbara Bel Geddes and Ben Gazzara were working on
the first act of the play. Suddenly I heard my author call out, "More melody
in your voice, Barbara; Southern girls have melody in their—" I cut him
off. I didn't get mad at him then, because I knew how anxious he was. He
hadn't wanted Barbara in the role of the Cat; I'd rather forced her on him.
She was not the kind of actress he liked; she was the kind of actress I liked.
I'd known her when she was a plump young girl, and I had a theory—which

you are free to ignore—that when a girl is fat in her early and middle teens and slims down later, she is left with an uncertainty about her appeal to boys, and what often results is a strong sexual appetite, intensified by the continuing anxiety of believing herself undesirable. Laugh at that if you will, but it is my impression and it did apply to Miss Bel Geddes. I knew how much a working sexual relationship meant to this young woman and that in every basic way she resembled Maggie the Cat. I trusted my knowledge of her own nature and life and therefore cast her.

In general, actors or actresses must have the part in the accumulation of their past. Their life's experience is the director's material. They can have all the training, all the techniques their teachers have taught them—private moments, improvisations, substitutions, associative memories, and so on—but if the precious material is not within them, the director cannot get it out. That is why it's so important for the director to have an intimate acquaintance with the people he casts in his plays. If it's "there," he has a chance of putting it on the screen or on the stage. If not, not. Readings tell you very little. They can be, on the contrary, misleading.

I knew that Tennessee Williams, that afternoon, had imbibed a good deal of wine and that I should, of course, forgive his disruptive behavior. But I had to prevent a repetition of this outbreak at my rehearsals and let the actors know I would protect them from any such recurrence. If I didn't immediately do this, I would lose authority with my actors—take the chance, for instance, that Barbara's feelings would be hurt and her confidence undermined. Since Williams had never said sweet words to her—he couldn't—she had doubts about his approval, which I didn't want inflamed. So I slid down the aisle and sat next to Tennessee and whispered to him that if he did that again, I'd quit. The cast was watching; they couldn't hear, but they knew what I was saying. Tennessee responded generously, said he understood me; in a few minutes he quietly left the theatre, and he didn't come back that day or the next. When he did, I suppose he'd decided to contain his reactions in the future. He even told Barbara that she'd improved.

Something similar happened with Burl Ives in the part of Big Daddy. "Burl Ives?" Tennessee had said when I suggested him for the part. "He's a singer. Do you really believe he can carry off the part?" "He's certainly a singer," I said, "but he's also real 'country,' and as far as singing goes, I'm going to walk him down to the edge of the forestage before the beginning of that long uninterrupted speech you've given him, have him look the audience right in the eye, and speak it directly to them. Straight out, as if it were a concert." Williams, I could see, didn't appreciate my proposal, it puzzled him, but in those days I was known as a magician with actors, so he held back his reaction—a little. "But it's a realistic play," he protested. "Do you mean," I said, "that in the Mississippi delta country, old cotton planters talk that eloquently and that long without interruption?" "Yes," he

Big Daddy Burl

said. "Who'd dare interrupt him?" "Wait and see how it works out," I said, "then say what you think." So I went against the grain, for I knew it was the only way Burl could play the part, straight out; that was where he had the confidence born of his concert experience, that was the style of performing that he—and I—enjoyed.

Which brings me to the setting: Tennessee didn't like that either, but I was determined to have it as I wanted it. Jo Mielziner and I had read the play in the same way; we saw its great merit was its brilliant rhetoric and its theatricality. Jo didn't see the play as realistic any more than I did. If it was to be done realistically, I would have to contrive stage business to keep the old man talking those great second-act speeches turned out front and pretend that it was just another day in the life of the Pollitt family. This would, it seemed to me, amount to an apology to the audience for the glory of the author's language. It didn't seem like just another day in the life of a cotton planter's family to Jo or to me; it seemed like the best kind of theatre, the kind we were interested in encouraging, the theatre theatrical, not pretending any longer that an audience wasn't out there to be addressed but having a performer as great as Burl Ives acknowledge their presence at all times and even make eye contact with individuals. Wasn't that the style of Shakespeare's theatre, weren't his long speeches done that way? So I caused Jo to design our setting as I wished, a large, triangular platform, tipped toward the audience and holding only one piece of furniture, an ornate bed. This brought the play down to its essentials and made it impossible for it to be played any way except as I preferred.

Williams used the word "beautiful" a great deal; I used the word "theatrical." He liked poetry in the theatre; he knew what he'd written and how he would like it staged. I took liberties with his work to yield to my own taste and my overriding tendencies. I didn't miss "melody" in Barbara's voice; I heard exactly the tone of anxiety, fear, and loneliness that I believed should be in Maggie's voice. As for Burl, I'd directed him long ago in Jean and Walter Kerr's musical *Sing Out, Sweet Land!* and spent a lot of time with him offstage because he was my favorite in that cast. I'd seen him drunk one night, macho and rampant, aroused to a point where he was looking for a fight, anywhere and with anybody. He was a formidable man, with a frightening temper; he evoked respect for his violence. Late one night, soused again, he reversed his emotion and I was afraid that he was about to throw himself out a window. Some of us had to tackle him and hold him to the floor. I remembered that violence and thought it, plus his intolerance of parlor-bred manners, more important than an ability to sashay around a realistic setting and speak the lines as they'd be spoken in a normal, realistic way by a well-behaved man.

At any rate, I had the setting I'd asked for; Jo had given me what I wanted. Tennessee had approved of it earlier, when he was ready to approve of damn near anything I asked for, because I was the director he wanted. Now the setting was up on stage, too late to change, and on that setting there was only one way for any human to conduct himself: "out front" it's called. Dear Tennessee was stuck with my vision, like it or not.

All this was background to the struggle Williams and I had over the third act. I believed Big Daddy could not be left out of the third act. I felt that his final disposition in the story had to be conveyed to an audience. I also thought that the third act was by far the weakest of the three—one and two were brilliant and as good as anything Tennessee ever wrote. I suggested that Big Daddy be brought back into Act Three, a suggestion that had nothing to do with making the play more commercial. Tennessee said he'd think about my suggestion, and a few days later he brought me a short scene in which Big Daddy did appear and told a dirty joke. It wasn't this author's best work, but perhaps it was better than nothing. I asked him if he wanted me to use it, and he said he did, so I directed Burl and the others in the new scene and put it in.

I saw immediately that Tennessee wasn't sure he liked it—and I wasn't sure I liked it. I asked him if he was certain he wanted it in; again he answered that he did. But I continued to have the feeling that he was not happy with the way his third act had evolved, and I was anxious that my influence over him should not be taken advantage of. Ten days before the play was to open in New York, I brought it up again. I told Tennessee I could see he wasn't happy about the third act, wasn't sure about bringing Big Daddy back; did he want the play performed as he'd originally written it? I said I could change it back in one day, for the actors had already played it that way, and I could take care of any unhappiness Burl Ives might feel. It was up to Tennessee, I said. He answered, "Leave it as it is." So I did. We opened and the play received acclaim almost equal to that for *Streetcar;* it was what Tennessee deserved.

Months later, the published play appeared, and it had two third acts, plus an explanation by the author. He'd published the third act he said he preferred to the one I'd influenced him to write. I thought his book made me out to be something of a villain corrupting a "pure artist." I especially resented Tennessee's calling "my" third act—which I didn't write, plan, or edit—the "commercial" third act. I'd had no such purpose in mind. It was Williams who wanted the commercial success, and he wanted it passionately. All he'd had to say was: "Put it back the way I had it first," and I would have. Apart from friendship and devotion, I'd have had to restore his original by the mandate of the Dramatists Guild. His complaining about me in print hurt me, even though I appreciated the anxiety he felt. I noted he was often surrounded by sycophants, who stirred up his discontent with the so-called Broadway corrupter of his most poetic side. But I decided to swallow the indignity; it was his play and his reputation and his life. Besides, I truly loved the man and always would.

A couple of years later, Williams and I had a comparable incident when we produced *Sweet Bird of Youth.* The play had an obvious weakness: The second act had very little relation to what had happened in the first and introduced a whole new set of characters, who'd been barely mentioned before but now took over. The first act, brilliantly written, centered on the Princess Kosmonopolis. She didn't appear in the second act, then reappeared in the third. Perhaps I was overly anxious about this failure of unity, but I determined to reinforce the second act and carry it off by a theatrical device; I asked Jo Mielziner to mount a vast TV screen at the back of the setting, and on it I projected the image of Boss Finlay speaking at the same time the audience saw the man himself speaking from the forestage. This was not only to indicate that he was being listened to throughout the area, but also to suggest the power he had in the community and the danger in his threats of violence against the character Paul Newman played. I'm not sure my production idea was organic, and it certainly made Tennessee nervous, but I enjoyed the stunt, as directors will, and when we came to play before an audience, the device of the huge TV screen worked effectively and made its point.

However, it necessitated a setting that was even less realistic than the setting of *Cat on a Hot Tin Roof*, and again I had the feeling that I was violating the author and that there was a gap between us, on one side of which I was satisfied, while he, on the other, was not. I was again determined, however, to go my own way and produce the play as I saw it, and I was fortunate again that the play was a great hit, because if it hadn't been, Williams and his agent, Audrey Wood, would certainly have blamed the failure on me.

Here, too, we had a casting problem. In the plays and films Williams wrote after my time with him, he'd have great stars like Tallulah Bankhead and Elizabeth Taylor and Richard Burton. But with *Sweet Bird of Youth* I again went for the inner qualities I knew were in Geraldine Page, an actress I greatly admired. At the first reading of the play by its cast, everything fell apart. Tennessee left before it was over. Gerry Page quickly returned to her dressing room. As with Deborah Kerr, I went in to see her, and again I found an actress in despair. She was convinced that she couldn't do the part. I told her she could and would, that it was a stretch for her, true, but that she had to be courageous, and if she was, she would play the part precisely as I wished it played and no one else could or would play it as I wished. I knew I had to use some extreme measures—like making her "camp" the part for a few rehearsals, to break down the inhibitions that the truth-seeking of the Method often causes in our actors. I knew I could rely on her talent and her courage, and that very soon she would give an absolutely brilliant performance in the role. It only needed me to hold her hand for a few days, then spur her on.

After dealing with Gerry's fears that first afternoon, I went to see Williams. He knew Gerry's work—she'd appeared in *Summer and Smoke* in a beautifully written part and done a brilliant job. But her fearful and hesitant reading that first day convinced Tennessee that she didn't have the bravura for the role and that this time I was wrong. More seriously, he doubted his own play; he wanted it withdrawn. I believe that only the rather mystical faith he had in me persuaded him to go ahead. I had never seen him so timorous after a first reading, had only seen him in such a panic once before. It was after the opening night performance of *Camino Real*, when I'd brought John Steinbeck, a great admirer of the play and of the author, to Tenn's place so he could offer his congratulations. Tennessee had crept into his bedroom and would not come out to greet John. We'd had to leave without a peek at him. Now I had to convince Tennessee to trust me a little longer, which he did. We went ahead with Gerry, and she gave the performance that carried the play, as my stunt with the TV screen carried it when Gerry wasn't on stage. I say all that I do about Williams with the greatest sympathy, for the panic he was experiencing is the same one that didn't allow me to attend the opening of the films I made. I, too, hid and waited for someone to come and assure me they'd got by okay. How much worse for an author who'd entrusted his play to a cocky director determined to put his own imprint on the work!

Having read what you have, you must believe I was pretty arrogant at this time, and, yes, it was then that I began to win this reputation. Perhaps the need to assert myself at all costs was a bounce-back from the beating I'd taken the several previous years. Whatever it came from, in my wish to make them "mine," I did overpower these two plays. But although both were great successes, I kept reading and hearing that I was in some way displacing the author's unique intentions and drowning his more sensitive gifts under my crude effects. I remember I was resentful of this criticism, and defensive, believed I was right to take the plays over and that the plays needed what I did to them. But I can see now that there was some truth in what was being written and said about my impact: A sort of distortion was going on. I remember I'd felt an irritable impatience as I'd worked on those plays and, with it, a need to speak for myself at last. Here was born, I must suppose, the resolve to stop forcing myself into another person's skin but rather to look for my own subjects and find, however inferior it must be to Tennessee's, my own voice.

I'd also behaved willfully with John's *East of Eden*, happily accepting Paul Osborn's suggestion to discard the first two thirds of the book—certainly not one of John's best—and tell only the story of the two sons of Adam Trask. In this way, I related it to my story with my father, how he'd preferred (so I believed) my younger brother, "Sweet Abie," and never quite got over (so I believed) his disappointment in me. I'd made *East of Eden* part of an autobiography, and for this I had and have no regret. The film reached people not only as I hoped but—so he said—as John wished. It was also a successful attraction, nationwide, an Academy Award nominee, and *Cat on a Hot Tin Roof,* running at the same time, a Pulitzer Prize winner.

But despite these successes, I felt disconnected from the world of the theatre and films and even from the country that had provided me shelter for more than forty years. The vacation I took with my wife in 1955 was not a rest but a search for a new path.

F O R   Y E A R S I'd been thinking there might be a fine film, and one I had to make, in the story of my uncle Avraam Elia Kazanjioglou, known in the rug trade as A. E. ("Joe") Kazan, who managed to come to this country at the age of twenty, put together some dollars, and in time brought his brother, my father, across the water, then, one after the other, the rest of the family—his sister, his half-brothers, and his stepmother, Evanthia, my favorite of them all. When I was five or six, my parents would leave me with this old woman when they went visiting or took a trip out of the city. An Anatolian Greek of near-peasant stock, she spoke no Greek, only Turkish, the language of the oppressor; even her Bible was written in Turkish. She used to take me into her bed and tell me stories of life in Turkey and how we'd managed to escape and come to America. I'd never forgotten that old woman's stories.

I'd discussed the idea for this film with my wife, whose opinion in these matters I respected. Molly thought it a fine idea and urged me to find a good screenwriter to write it for me. When I hinted that I was flirting with the idea of writing it myself, she said what a number of close friends said, before and since: "You're a good director. Why the hell must you also be a writer?"

But who could know as well as I did the story of how my uncle was able to get to this country? In someone else's hands, it would lose its flavor. I'd grown up in that environment, remembered every sight, sound, smell, and taste, how the men in my family behaved—I can still hear their voices in argument—and how the women were, bold in the kitchen, cautious on the streets. I knew the idioms of the people, their rhythms of speech, their daily living habits, their fears and their aspirations, their food and their drink. I had to write that screenplay myself.

The thing to do was go there. I'd left Turkey when I was four, been back once when I was twelve, remembered nothing except the Hôtel des Étrangers on the largest of the Princess Islands and how soft and warm the bathing water was. Now I had a purpose, to study the country and its people, penetrate into the heart of the place and follow the course of my uncle's journey from Kayseri in the interior to Istanbul, where he boarded the *Kaiser Wilhelm* to America. I was out to secure the material for a film: story, locations, people, theme.

I have many memories of that trip, but the most important one was my encounter with my cousin Stellio Yeremia, and the recognition I had that this man, almost precisely my age, was the self I would have been if I'd not been brought to America by my father. I found my discarded self.

M O L L Y and I sailed out of New York harbor on the *Cristoforo Columbo*, seen off by our kids. We lolled over the summer sea for a week, passed Gibraltar, then crossed the Mediterranean to Napoli, where we boarded a ship to Piraeus, the port of Athens. There we were swamped by newspaper people, who were impressed because a Greek who'd gone to the States and made it there still spoke a fluent Greek. We visited awesome Delphi, exquisite Nauplia, and the sea at Marathon, then, sated and impatient—for I had a purpose—we passed on by way of the Turkish airline ("Roads Across the Sky") to the land where I was born. There we were hugged and kissed

by relatives I'd not seen in forty years, people who had the same complexions, the same noses and eyes, manners and memories.

Molly and I both needed sleep, but the next morning I was eager to get out in the streets of Istanbul, and while Molly rested in the Parc Oteli, I wandered here and there, without direction or goal. Everything I passed stirred up memories I didn't know I had, as a long stick might stir up mud at the bottom of a pond. I felt at home, but I also felt fear, fear that I was never to lose in Turkey. At the time agreed upon, I walked to the Taksim, the crowded uptown traffic hub, the arena since our visit of many demonstrations and much violence. There I was to meet Stellio, the man grown from the boy I'd played with when we were three and four years old. For the two weeks I remained in that country, we were constant companions.

The first thing I noticed as he came walking toward me was that he walked very quickly, a kind of hustle or slither along the walls of the buildings that lined the streets, and as far from the curb as he could get. In the days that followed, I noticed that Stellio hurried this way even when he had no reason to. He reminded me of those small ground animals, easy prey for predators, that come out of their holes, rush to gather what food they're able to find as quickly as they can, then dart back into their holes.

He had the morning papers with him but preferred not to show them to me until we were back in the hotel room with Molly. There we looked at the photos taken at the airport, and Stellio translated the Turkish into his school English. The interviews were friendly; I was heralded as the famous man from Anatolia who denied absolutely that he was Armenian. I was heralded as the local boy who'd gone to America and come back rich and famous. There was no mention in the stories that I was a Greek. This publicity worried Stellio. His reaction was that it would have been better to say nothing. "Don't trust them here," he said. "Tomorrow you'll see, they'll write bad about you." He said what my father used to say: "When they ask you something, it's better to say you know nothing. Don't give them anything to criticize."

I told Stellio a little of why I'd come, that I wanted to go where my father was born and where my mother's people had lived for generations before they'd left the interior for Istanbul. Would he come with us? It would take a week, perhaps. "I have to," he replied. "I have to keep you out of trouble." Then he took us to lunch at the best restaurant in the city, where the food was heavy and rich. A big belly is not an embarrassment in this culture but a mark of affluence. Everyone takes a nap after a midday meal—they're so loaded up they have to. Molly thought it a good idea, but I wanted to see the sights.

We headed down the main street of the city, the Istiklal Caddesi, toward the waterfront and the harbor, passing the Pera Palace hotel, where the rich Armenian and Greek merchants used to stay (my uncle among them when he was doing well), then on, down the grade. The street, narrow and cobbled, curved erratically around buildings that might better have been torn down. Animals and machines struggled to get past each other in both directions at once. Horses were beaten without mercy, donkeys prodded with short, sharp sticks until blood was drawn for flies to feast on. There was thick grime on the buildings. We passed tiny open-front factories in side alleys and had to walk around peddlers who'd spread their wares on the street. Hawkers walked with full baskets on each arm or pushed carts loaded with fruit, baked goods, nuts, and sweets. Cool water was offered for sale by the glass. Cries, rhythmic and beguiling, sang out the excellence of wares in a kind of street poetry. Here, too, were desperate people, the sick and the diseased, everywhere. As much as they dispirited me, for a filmmaker it was a vast dramatic panorama, something stirring and profound. I must make my film here, I resolved, in the environment out of which my uncle and my father had escaped and where, apparently, it was still as it had been. I must put on film what I was seeing and hearing and feeling that day.

Then we began to hear the sounds of the boats that zig and zag across the bay into which the Bosporus empties, carrying suburban traffic to the city mornings and back home at night. We were descending rapidly, turning sharp curves in the uneven streets, when suddenly there was the harbor, the core of the city, spread out below us; Istanbul was filthy at that time, but it sits on one of the most beautiful locations of any city in the world. And in its heart, the Galata bridge, carrying the rich and the poor, the powerful and the pitiful, men and beasts; I saw it as a great democratic thoroughfare. But this was an impression quickly corrected by Stellio, who told me that in Turkey there was no democracy, no equality, or if there was, it was only at the very top: the politicians then in power, the top officers of the army, the handful of very rich merchants; or at the bottom that other equality: the poor who live without hope, the scavengers who would do anything or sell anything to stay alive. In between, Stellio said, were a great mass of Turkish people, living in fear and uncertainty.

When Molly heard this, she did something that surprised me—she kissed me on the cheek, why I don't know. Perhaps it was simply in recognition that I'd made it out and that she was glad I had.

We crossed the Galata bridge to where the wholesale markets were, and there we found the hamals, the human beasts of burden. Their burdens, when they were of lighter stuff, could rise to a height of six feet, but sometimes the hamals carried loads too heavy for them to hoist, which had to be dropped on their backs by others. When they walked, they moved forward in a quick trot of short steps, just as the donkeys did who passed the same way, equally loaded and competing for the same work. When the hamals responded to an encounter, an order, a traffic snarl, they did so harshly but without facial expression. Their eyes had "died." Their way of life and their history made them expect no good for any man. Some of them appeared to be in their sixties—did anyone survive that long at that work? There were also young men—couldn't they find better employment? Apparently not. These creatures were neither friendly nor unfriendly—again not different from the donkeys. They gave little warning cries to get us out of their way, since they didn't propose to stop the forward momentum of their bodies and their loads. That cry did not sound like any other human call. They were at the bottom level of this society and of humanity.

I didn't realize it immediately, but I'd found the hero of my film *America America*.

A few days later, Molly, Stellio, and I were on the road to Ankara, the capital city, driving east over broad plains, the Anatolian plateau, where women, on their hands and knees, were working the fields, and through villages where men were clustered around tables before coffeehouses. Seeing us, they would stop whatever they were doing, bickering or playing backgammon. "Why aren't they out there with the women, working?" Molly asked. "What are they doing, sitting there like that?" "They're solving our political problems," Stellio said. I thought this funny, but Molly didn't. "This looks like very rich land," she said. "It could be their Iowa, if the men would only get to work."

A little later I said to Stellio, "Tell Molly what happened at your store." From his place of business, Stellio supplied cotton goods, wholesale, to small merchants in the interior. He'd told me about the last great riot that had taken place in the cotton goods wholesale market and had been, so Stellio believed, subsidized by the government. "They brought several hundred criminals from the interior, gave them plenty raki, the cheap kind, a bottle to each man, put them on the boat to Istanbul, and told them, 'Go 'head, the city is yours. Take what you want, so long it's Greek or Armenian.'"

"Did they break into your store?" Molly asked. She'd been nervous ever since we'd reached Turkey. For some reason that was not scientific, she believed Turkey was darker than other countries. She distrusted the food and loathed the toilets.

"No," Stellio said. "My place they don't touch." Then he told how that had happened. He had a neighbor in the same center of wholesale cotton goods stores, a Turkish merchant but still a friend. This man knew what Stellio did not, that a riot was being stirred up, a ritual warning to the minorities in that society to be content to stay in their proper places. These holidays for criminals were celebrated regularly in that city, Stellio said.

"Where were the authorities?" Molly asked. A law-respecting Yankee, she was indignant.

"The authorities?" Stellio said. "They buy the raki. All the Greek stores in the middle part of Istanbul would be hit, my friend told me; there'd be enough raki for maybe three days, and food too, lambs to slaughter and roast at night, whole herds. So my friend, he came to me one day and he put a little mark over my door, where no one could notice it unless they were looking for it, something like a crescent. 'What's that?' I asked. 'Leave it,' he said. So I did. The trouble lasted three days, and I stayed at home, blocking our windows as we used to when we lived in the interior and there was trouble. Suddenly all was quiet again; maybe they were sleeping from the raki, I thought, and I went down to the city, and every Greek store in our area except mine had had its windows smashed and there were cotton goods all over the street, in the mud and the puddles of water, and the donkeys had left their little presents on top. All that wealth—such hard work to make money here—gone. Finished! No doubt there was also plenty cotton goods going to the interior to put on the *golos* of their wives— excuse the expression, Molly—here." He hit his behind. "That night," Stellio said, "I took my friend to dinner."

Molly tried to joke. "Is this trip absolutely necessary?" she said to me. "That's why I told Elia," Stellio said, "better less in the papers where we're going." He turned to me. "When we get there, don't be big American hero, criticizing everything to the journalists. The less you say the better." He turned to Molly. "Tell him to be careful," he said. "Why do you live here?" Molly asked. She was outraged by the situation. "It's not easy to move," Stellio said. "Especially if you have a little money. You can't take it out."

I studied my cousin's face; it was uncreased. Although he lived in continuous worry—the shortest walk had the possibility of danger, which is why he always hurried on the street—he still managed to be affable. He made his way by pleasing his enemies as well as his friends. He was the most circumspect man I've ever known, neat and clean and well-ordered. Which came from a lifetime of concern for the consequences of any out-of-the-way behavior. He had lived all his life under the eye of authority he knew to be hostile. Fear had ordered his life. I compared myself: I was not altogether different. I am, for instance, neurotically prompt—in fact, always ahead of time for appointments. Why? So as not to allow the least opening for criticism. I recognized myself in him.

THE FIRST thing that impressed me about Ankara was the coal dust in the air, a kind of black fog, and how grimy even the state buildings were. An audience had been arranged for us with the great political figure of the day, Celal Bayar, the last of Mustafa Kemal's strongmen. When we entered his office, I was shocked to see Stellio sidle up to Bayar, kneel before him, and kiss his hand. It was an Oriental gesture, which the old man seemed to accept as his due. I didn't follow suit; my father had made it unnecessary for me. Later Molly asked Stellio, "Why did you kiss Bayar's hand? He took no notice of it." "If I had not," Stellio answered, "he would have." As we talked I noticed that the corridors behind both door openings were filled with police in plain clothes, big men with the special confidence secret police have. Bayar was perfectly assured; he lounged back in his chair and studied me, and again I felt fear. Something about the whole setup made me nervous. Not Molly; she asked the only intelligent questions. I was as circumspect as Stellio, careful to say what would not possibly sound like a challenge. I was happy to leave the office and the building it was in.

A dinner had been arranged by the local theatre people and intellectuals. The streets we drove through to get to the party were dark, and again I felt the irrational sense that I was in danger. The guests were more like members of a cabal than people invited to a social get-together. Was there something wrong with our banding together to eat? Strong drink relieved the tension. They asked about New York and Hollywood—that was America for them—the plays I'd done and their authors. I was an object of wonder. How had I gotten out? How had I managed to be working in a free theatre in the most affluent society in the world? They regarded the passage of my family to New York City as a miracle, and I was having feelings about my father I'd never had before—gratitude, for instance. The questions about the theatre and Hollywood were mostly answered by Molly.

Back in the hotel, safe, I raised the windows before going to bed. The next morning, the coal dust was piled on the windowsills like black snow. I looked out and saw that the hotel was surrounded by factories burning soft coal. Molly was suffering from the soot in the air and had a cough. She hadn't liked anything about Turkey and suggested she might do better to go back to New York. This was at breakfast. I influenced her to stay, since we'd come all this way to see the place where my families had come from. "Next year, Hotel Hilton will be finished in Istanbul," Stellio said. "You'll enjoy it here better, Molly." But later, privately, he encouraged me to "send" Molly back. "The toilets in Kayseri," he said, "you remember?"

A word about those toilets. They were the first I knew and they consisted of a small closet with a floor of stone, possibly marble, pierced with a round hole possibly six inches across. There is a handle at each side of this cabin's wall, to which the person using the facility holds on as he or she does his or her business. It is the job of whatever servant is on duty to throw a pail of water down the hole from time to time. This does not solve the problem of the foul smell rising from the accumulation below; rather it aggravates it for a time. The toilet is no easier on men than on women, because the women there—before your day, reader—wore floor-length dresses or skirts and did not always wear underdrawers. So they simply stood or squatted with their legs parted and held on to the handles at the sides. A man, for one of his functions, had to drop his trousers to the stone floor, which was always wet and unsanitary. For an American girl brought up in a substantial middle-class home in South Orange, New Jersey, and graduated from Vassar College, the whole facility would be revolting.

By midday, her cough heavier, Molly decided to go home, and I didn't try to dissuade her. We drove her to the airport.

The next day, Stellio and I motored east on roads of gravel through open country, and the wind over the plains was clean. Four hours later, we drove into the central square of Kayseri, the city where my father was born and raised. It was a large, open, half-paved area, bounded by the vilayet (the office and residence of the provincial governor), by a dun-colored mosque with its thin minarets, by the post office–telephone central, and by a four-story hotel, with its front of time-blackened concrete. We were half a century behind Istanbul. A few automobiles moved slowly past horse-drawn wagons. There were donkeys everywhere, under loads that seemed much too heavy for them. By the front of a shop, a pair of these animals, unburdened, stood at ease, with heavy hanging penises. Crouched against the side of a building, their heads cloth-bound, hamals waited for employment like cabs in a taxi line. Women, their faces covered except for their eyes, hurried past, looking straight ahead. A couple, the man a few paces ahead of his woman, passed close by, with large flat metal pans on their heads. "Baklava," our driver told us. No confection or pastry, Stellio observed, is too sweet for a Turk. Sugar is believed to add to a man's sexual power. A wagon in front of the vilayet was piled high with melons for sale. There was a cloud of flies where some of the ripe fruit had fallen and broken. From the back of an open wagon, two men were selling rough-cut chunks of ice. Kids scrambled for the chips.

Our car drew up in front of the vilayet, and we got out. Beggars covered the steps of the building; some stretched out their hands. Escorted through a passage guarded by armed men, we were shown into the reception room of the province's governor. As we entered his office, through one door, he burst out a door down the hall. He'd been waiting for us: a small man, almost a dwarf, one leg shorter than the other, walking with a cane but making brisk speed. "Osman Kavundju," he said, introducing himself. Kavundju means "melon man," which must have been the occupation of one of his forefathers. I could feel the man's bright energy and was soon engulfed in his cordiality. When he sat in the chair behind the desk, Stellio rushed up and kissed his hand. Kavundju Effendi was not impressed; he was looking at his American guest. I smiled back.

The first question asked of any visitor in Turkey is how he prefers his coffee—sweet, medium, or without sugar. Kavundju ordered an assistant to obtain this refreshment for us, immediately! No matter how slowly things move in Turkey, every order, every compliance, is qualified with the word "immediately." That does not, however, affect the speed of what follows. During the last "great" war, our correspondents' nickname for Ankara was "Yavashington," *yavash* being the Turkish word for slow.

The little mayor showed me his city

As we waited—there is always a silence to be broken—the wali passed around a small silver plate containing cloves, to sweeten our mouths after the long, dusty journey. Then he went back to his large official chair, a kind of provincial throne. I noticed that his feet did not touch the floor. Behind this twisted little man hung a huge colored photograph: a martial pose of the national hero, Mustafa Kemal, the general who'd routed the invading Greek army in 1922, so making Turkey all Turk for the first time in its history.

Kavundju broke the silence. He declared that he personally was going to show me his city; it would be a great honor for him to do so. And over the next three days he did just that, with an energy and enthusiasm that reminded me of New York's Mayor La Guardia. What he showed us was not parks, monuments, libraries, and schools but new factories for sugar, textiles, and rugs (where we were given tiny tabletop rugs as presents). These establishments were going to change the life of the people, he said. His pride was infectious; I liked him immediately; I didn't feel fear in his company. Soon I was calling him Osman, he calling me Elia.

The next day I asked to see the less impressive sights, particularly what had once been the Greek neighborhood where Father's family lived. Here I saw long rows of walls without windows, facing the streets. We went into one of the places. It had a large courtyard, the only source of light. Four people slept in one bedroom. There were no Greeks in Kayseri now, Osman told me; they'd moved out of the city at the end of the 1922 war. "Moved or made to move?" I asked. I trusted him enough now to ask that. He made a little gesture with his hands; it was Oriental, a sort of acceptance that history moves in ways not to be questioned. I imagined my father, his parents, his half-sister and half-brothers living in one of those faceless streets and how they must have felt, outnumbered and powerless. What instinct had told my uncle and my father that it was time to get out, that they'd better move on when they did? Osman was completely friendly, even affectionate, but when I thought back and imagined the past, I felt guilty about liking him.

The next day, I asked to be taken to the neighboring town of Germeer, the original home of my mother's family. It was about nine miles away and lay at the foot of a great cliff. We went there as we did everywhere, whether in cars or on foot: in a procession. On both sides of the cobbled principal street there were houses, now in bad repair, that must once have been handsome, better built and better appointed than the homes we'd seen in Kayseri. These had been the homes of Greeks, men of substance, many of them merchants with places of business in Kayseri. When the exchange of population had taken place in 1922, the emptied homes had been taken over by Turks, who had allowed them to deteriorate. Handsome stone carvings framed the doorways, and the windows above were shaded by "harem screens" of beautifully worked wood strips. My mother's family had been more affluent than my father's.

The residents had no idea who I was, but to welcome a stranger, particularly one accompanied by the governor of the province, women came out of their homes offering flat bread, still warm from their ovens. They showed no fear, but when they noticed me looking at them, they quickly lifted a corner of their shawls over their faces.

On a level above this street there was a small plaza, and around it there had been a number of houses, now fallen to ruin. Bits of the walls along the ground indicated where the rooms had been. Osman asked some of the old men who'd been trailing us about my mother's family, the Shishmanoglous. No one was sure where their home had been. "Yes, yes, here, of course," one patriarch said, "one of these here, certainly." Another old-timer said, "No, no, it was just there, opposite to where we are." "We'll find it," Osman told me, "don't worry. When you come back you will kiss the ground at the threshold."

"Are you really coming back?" Stellio whispered to me in Greek.

In a corner of the plaza, the Orthodox church was also down, except for a few bits of plastered wall, on which traces of religious paintings could be made out. While I was inspecting them, old Turkish men were assuring me of how much they missed the Greeks and how well the two races used to get along. Observing the ruined condition of the place—nothing had been kept up—I understood how much the Greeks were missed. As we walked down, other old fellows were telling me they admired the "cleverness" of the Greeks who'd lived there. "A Greek," one of them said, "can make money without working. He sits playing backgammon all day, and when the sun sets, he's richer. We work all day and hardly make enough to feed our families." What he envied was the skill of the Greek merchants in buying and selling at a profit. I wondered about the relationship between envy and hatred. The fact was that my father's father was not rich. He simply "worked without working." "Turks use their backs," my father used to say. "We Greeks use our brains."

On my last night, there was a farewell banquet in a grove hung with lanterns. I was happy and never stopped drinking. How dark and mysterious it was in that grove. How much darker it must have been in my father's day. But for the first time, I didn't feel fear. I knew these people as my friends now. Osman and I sat side by side at the head of a long table. I could see many faces watching the event from behind trees and bushes. "We lived by the mercy of the Turk," my father used to say. I didn't feel that way now. The toasts, filled with emotion, spoke of our mutual longing for harmony. Osman and I pledged a lifelong friendship. I felt sorry for Stellio, who still looked tense and guarded; he said, "Don't trust them—even when they smile." But I kissed Osman as we parted. He called me "my brother in America," and gave me still another gift, a rug—this one, he said, for my wife's feet when she got out of bed. I vowed to come back soon.

I HAD reason for my feeling of elation. I'd found my true material! As we drove back to Istanbul, I made up my mind. I would make a film about my uncle's journey from Kayseri to America. I jotted down notes about the terrain and details of the villages we passed, as well as the people, who they were, what they wore, and what they were doing. I took photographs. I'd begun to work.

In Istanbul, I spent two days following hamals from job to job around the waterfront, ate what they ate, listened to what I could understand of their talk. Many of them were from the interior, some Kurds among them speaking another language. I took notes secretly so that hamals and stevedores wouldn't feel spied on; I was afraid of them, and I knew that was a good sign. The hero of a drama should arouse some of the respect that comes from fear.

Whenever I needed to relax or rest, I'd go to Stellio's place of business or meet him for lunch at a waterside restaurant. He spoke of my father and had a special admiration for him because he'd succeeded in getting our family out of Turkey. "He was a clever man," Stellio said. I noticed that the word my relatives used for "intelligent" was "clever." The Anatolian Greek is famous for getting along by his cunning. Father had been clever enough to bring his family to America before the whole area blew up in a great war. His cleverness had ensured the safety of his children. "You owe him a great debt," Stellio said. "You should kiss his feet when you see him next."

Stellio and Vili

A farewell dinner was arranged at Stellio's house, where I'd meet my other cousins as well as Stellio's wife and their children. We sat around a table that was heavily loaded with savory food; they inspected me and I them. I found them all excellent people, well educated, discreet, and kindly. I noticed that whereas my father had been a terror in our home and ruled his wife and four sons with the threat of a temper about to explode, Stellio's wife, Vili, was boss in their home, sat at the head of their dinner table, cut the meat (always the male prerogative), served the food, and dominated the conversation. Stellio's posture could only be described as conciliatory; he seemed to be anxious that we should all get along, especially that everyone should like me and that certain doubts and concerns—I didn't know exactly which—should be kept under cover. I noticed that his two sons didn't respect him as Greek children should their father, and I believed this hurt him. My guess was correct; some years later, he said to a friend that he doubted his sons would come to his funeral.

Wine made me contentious. Perhaps I was feeling the Greek male's resentment at a woman who dominated a home. In a confident and exuberant mood, I described the events of our stay in Kayseri, spoke of the friendly feeling everyone there had for me and for Stellio and of ours for Kavundju, how much I admired Osman and what he was doing in Kayseri. "I wish you could see what's happening there now," I said, "the new factories and buildings, the atmosphere of progress." I told them about the old men in Germeer and how often they'd said they missed the Greeks who were no longer there and how generous everyone had been to me, accepting me as one of theirs. Perhaps, I said, the tensions and hatreds of the past could finally be set aside. I said that no matter what the military men who ruled the country felt, the Turkish people themselves were good people and ready, I believed, for a new era of friendship. I said I'd decided to make a film, would make it all in Turkey, using the people as extras, and that my purpose, beyond making an exciting film, would be to make some contribution toward bringing about better relations between the Turks and the Greeks. That had to happen, I said.

I got a sour reception. I'd noticed that Vili was becoming furious with me, so I'd aimed my talk particularly at her. The wine unlocked her tongue too, and I soon had a "report from the interior." When she began to talk, she looked away from me and directly at her husband. She seemed to be speaking primarily for his benefit; was she blaming him for what I'd said?

"It's easy for you, Elia," she said, looking at her husband, "to go where you want and say what you think and be so brave, then come here and instruct us on how we must understand the Turk when we've lived all our lives under his foot. You come and tell us how friendly and kind and generous the Turkish people are, that they are not bad people and so on, but friendly and so on." Then she turned, facing her husband and speaking directly to him. "Yes, it's easy for him to talk big and play the hero. But, Stellio, you don't have an American passport in your pocket, do you?" She turned back to me. "When he was younger, my dear husband, he used to talk big out of his mouth too. So I told him, be brave in the house, keep your mouth shut on the streets. You have a wife and two sons now, and you're not risking only your neck but ours. Still he was brave, until they broke into his store the first time and threw everything into the mud outside, and except for a friend, they would have done it again. Did he tell you?"

"Yes," I said, "he told me that he had a friend, a Turk who put a crescent over his door, which saved him, and that shows there are good Turkish people and we must not think of them as our enemies forever—"

"*Had* a friend!" Vili said. "He *made* a friend. My husband is very clever. Did he tell you the whole story?"

Stellio interrupted. "I told him, Vili."

But she went right on. "Did he tell you how many of his own good customers he sent to this Turk and how, when I was baking, he'd say, 'Bake for him too,' and I would? Did he tell you how often we made our vacation shorter on the island and gave our place there to him and his families? Yes, the man had two wives. And how Stellio always paid for the lunch when they ate together and how—"

"Vili, enough," Stellio said.

"Oh, yes, my husband is very clever. He knew what to do. But you think that way of life is a good example for his sons? Does it teach them strength? Must we be so clever all our lives to survive here?"

"Vili, Vili, shshsh," Stellio said.

"Never mind that shshsh," she said, turning away from me altogether. "I don't want him here encouraging you with how nice they are and how human, when the truth is that they are animals, who tasted our blood many times and want more, like animals." She turned to me. "Did he tell you how for three days and three nights we stayed here, inside, with the shutters closed and heard those beasts running wild through the streets and saw the flames near us and the shouts of the people whose homes they were looting and how the next day, even though it was quiet, we didn't dare go out for bread and meat or milk for the boys? We know it's going to happen again and we know that the government wants it, they provide money for the ouzo they drink, so don't tell me about your governor in Kayseri who gives banquets for you, the big American with his name in the newspapers. He's not innocent either, your Kavundju Effendi. Is he, Stellio? Is he? Say!"

Stellio didn't answer, and nobody else spoke. Then Vili turned to me, and she was calmer but more hateful than before. "Elia, we're living well here now. He does a good business, and we have money enough for food and most everything else we need; not trips to America but a month on the island, and we have our donkey there too. Our boys go to a good school and wear decent clothes and so—so—so leave him alone! Leave us alone! This is not America, and we are not Americans. Remember that. Anger is a luxury we can't afford! We live as we must and—and I'm satisfied. Just leave him *alone!* I'm satisfied. Excuse me."

She got up and left the room. A door closed.

The dinner party broke up soon afterward. The boys went to their room to do their homework and Vili didn't come back. Stellio and I had a few moments alone. He apologized for his wife. "She's a good woman," he said, "and makes a good home for me here. She's had some frights in the street, and to tell you the truth, although I wish she hadn't said what she said, I agree with it. That is our situation here. At least for now."

Then he reached into his pocket and pulled out a small, well-sealed packet and gave it to me. "Some jewelry," he said, "and some British pounds." He was whispering now—in his own home! "I have a sister in Athens, you know. When you go there, give this to her. They won't open your bags, not yours. Perhaps better put it in your pocket. Her address is written here, see? She knows what to do with it."

As I walked back to my hotel, I wondered: Was Stellio planning to escape from here? Was he planning to start over again in Athens? And if he was, would he be able to do it? I doubted it. I thought of my father, who'd made the journey to America, started over again there, and made good. Wasn't he of tougher stuff than Stellio? I thought so. Understanding Stellio, I understood my father better. I appreciated him more, for I'd seen what he'd come out of and a little of the fact of it—not just the romance. For the first time in my life, I had respect for my father and what he'd done. I understood him.

Sailing back to the States, I made notes, a diary of our days in the interior and about Stellio and Vili and about Osman Kavundju, for whom I had tender feelings. I put down everything I'd seen and heard before it faded; I knew I'd use it one day. And I began to have a feeling that surprised me: that it was my "calling" to speak for my father and my uncle and for the people I'd sat at the table with that night.

.   .   .

B A C K home, I was fired up. I'd decided I'd no longer wait for authors to send me their plays or for film producers to propose movies I might direct. I'd initiate my own projects. I determined that with each project, I'd take an active role in organizing it and, in time, even in the writing. This would save me the humiliation of waiting for the favor of authors and producers. I began immediately, putting together a screenplay from three one-act plays by Tennessee Williams. I picked up on Budd Schulberg's suggestion that we make a film based on his short story "Your Arkansas Traveller"; we agreed to do the research together and explore as equals the form, the structure, and the characters. I decided that by then I should be ready to write a screenplay myself, so I talked Fox into buying a novel about a proud old woman who was about to be put off her bottomland by the Tennessee Valley Authority as part of their program of flooding valleys to provide inexpensive electricity for the people of the region. I resolved to make these three films one after another, and so start on a new course.

Easier resolved than accomplished.

The family on the *Baby Doll* location

B A B Y   D O L L was a lark from beginning to end. I never enjoyed making a film more. I even enjoyed Francis Cardinal Spellman's attack on it.

The story is primitive and not to be taken seriously. A penny-ante entrepreneur (Eli Wallach) bulls his way into a community of the Deep South and sets up a more modern gin to process cotton. One night the gin burns down. Eli suspects arson and has a hunch that the man whose business he's taken away (Karl Malden) did it. To make sure, he drives his pickup to Karl's home, a crumbling white mansion, and begins to question Karl's wife (Carroll Baker). She is a nineteen-year-old infant who still sleeps in her childhood crib. Eli finds that the marriage, arranged by her father on his deathbed to ensure his daughter's protection, has not been consummated. Carroll, as she regularly informs her impatient husband, is not ready for marriage. She is also very ready—but not for him. Eli's revenge is to begin to seduce the girl, whereupon she blurts out a confession that her husband did burn the gin down. The film never makes clear whether the seduction is consummated. Waiting for Karl to come home, Eli naps in Baby Doll's crib. When Karl arrives, after a hard day's work ginning out Eli's cotton in his own gin, he finds Eli waiting for him. Eli leads him to believe that he's had Carroll. That is his revenge.

When I proposed this film to Tennessee Williams, he wasn't interested. I went ahead anyway, put a script together, and sent him what I'd done; he gave me an unenthusiastic "go ahead." He was working on another play—or two; Williams always wrote on more than one project at a time. He said he'd work on *Baby Doll*, but what he did he did with half a heart. He'd mail me a page or two on the stationery of whatever hotel he was at, with the instruction: "Insert somewhere." In places these scraps helped; often they did not.

The first sign of his genuine interest came when I brought him to the Actors Studio to see a scene from the script I'd put together, played by a young actress I was eager to have in the central role. In his one-act *27 Wagons Full of Cotton*, Baby Doll Meighan is a great lump of a girl. I don't favor heavy legs on a woman and wanted Carroll Baker, then a new actress at the Studio, to play the part. Williams interrupted the scene almost as soon as it started. "That's it!" he sang out. "She's it!" He embraced Carroll. I seized on this flare of enthusiasm to wring a promise from him that he'd come south with me and work seriously on the script. For instance, we had no ending.

"But I must have a swimming pool," he said; it was his way of consenting. I flew to Greenville, Mississippi, where we were going to be put up, found that there was a swimming pool in the city, presently inoperative. Our production manager, again Charlie Maguire, impressed the civic authorities with the honor Williams would pay the community by his visit. They restored the pool to service. Williams came down, tried the pool, and seemed happy. Then he told me he was going back to New York. The reason? He didn't like the way people looked at him on the streets. Of course, this was imagined, but I couldn't convince him; he must have had other reasons for leaving and needed this justification. I reminded him we still had no ending. He said he'd send me something, which he did. His "something" contained the lovely fade-out line Carroll says to Milly Dunnock when they discover that both men have disappeared. "We'll have to wait and see if we're remembered or forgotten."

Now I was without an author, but I didn't mind. I was what I'd wanted to be, the source of everything. I had my New York crew, all old friends. My actors were from the Studio and would mix convincingly with the townspeople who played extras. Working with me again was the great cameraman Boris Kaufman; we decided to give the film a faded white-on-white style. The people of the area were suspicious at first, but soon their generosity took over. The town of Benoit reminded me of a community in a Chekhov play. Its citizens were warmhearted and curious and had a talent for soul talk. I brought my family down and they were adopted, entertained, and fed; ponies were provided for our kids. For a dozen years, I would

receive Christmas presents from the residents, mostly pecans from their own trees.

There was another side to this culture. One weekend I went along on a deer-hunting party. Some thirty animals were slaughtered and hung, head down, on a long rack, blood dripping from their mouths. I watched hounds tearing one animal down and a man, hunting with bow and arrow, disable, then kill, his trophy. I'd never eat venison again. Another day, a black man who'd fallen into difficulty with some of the locals appealed to us. We hid him in one of our trailers for two nights and a day, then got him out of the region by car.

I thought we made a nice film. Many people said it seemed like a European movie, an artistic cousin to the films of Pagnol, a director I admired. I didn't think *Baby Doll* was a masterpiece, but it was an original.

It took Cardinal Spellman to make it famous. The darned old fool came back from Korea, where he'd been conducting mass for the boys at Christmas, stood in the pulpit of St. Pat's cathedral to tell about his experiences and how self-sacrificing our soldiers were, then said, quote, "What did I find when I came home? *Baby Doll!*" He went on: "I was anguished by the news that *Baby Doll* was about to be seen in theatres everywhere. The revolting theme of this picture is a contemptuous defiance of the natural law." And so on. He forbade Catholics to see the film, "under pain of sin."

He said it was everyone's patriotic duty—yes, he actually said patriotic!—to boycott the film.

All this from a power broker who played the market, consorted with politicians, promoters, and real estate speculators, a wheeler-dealer priest, a drinker, a bully who wore a mask of kindliness and who was called by Catholics who were ashamed of him "the Sammy Glick of the Catholic Church." But he did have power, as I would find out. Although the New York *Post,* then a liberal daily, did stick up for Williams and me with strong editorials, no other newspaper in our city carried even a news item about Spellman's absurd outburst.

I suddenly had the suspicion that this bag of sanctified wind had not seen the film he was condemning. Calling a journalist friend on the conservative New York *Herald Tribune,* I suggested he ring up the "Powerhouse" (the cardinal's residence, at Fiftieth Street and Madison Avenue) and ask point-blank if Spellman had seen *Baby Doll.* Which my friend did, getting an evasive answer. Finally the *Herald Tribune* printed a confirmation that the old priest had not seen the film. A day passed before Spellman came out with his defense. "Must you have a disease to know what it is?" He relied, he added, on people whose judgment he respected about such matters. Did he mean Martin Quigley?

Williams spoke up for our side, matching the cardinal's syrupy eloquence. "I cannot believe," he said, "that an ancient and august branch of the Christian faith is not larger in heart and mind than those who set themselves up as censors of a medium of expression that reaches all sections and parts of our country and extends the world over."

The cardinal wasn't shamed; he didn't lift his injunction against the film. In many theatres, priests, stationed in the lobbies, notebooks in hand, wrote the names of parishioners who defied their spiritual leader. People were reading that the film was breaking box office records. This was not true; the cardinal's attack hurt us. There'd be one good week, then a quick slide down. I never made a profit.

A big fuss was made about the sexual scenes in *Baby Doll.* French film historians who put out books on erotica included stills from the film. Today these stills seem tame. If you were to look at the film now, you'd see a rather amusing comedy and wonder what all the fuss was about. I still have a considerable affection for *Baby Doll.* But oh, God, were the critics who wrote about it pompous!

I H A D reports of further developments in the Strasberg-Monroe story. He'd influenced her to demand that his wife, Paula, be on every film set (at $2,500 per week) to help Marilyn with her performance. Paula would station herself directly behind the director, and after each take, when Marilyn looked in her direction, Paula would either nod or shake her head. If she shook her head, Marilyn would demand that the scene be shot again. At night, there would be conferences about the next day's work; the director of the film would not be present. Didn't Lee realize how insulting this was to the director? Why esteemed and independent filmmakers tolerated Paula behind them giving signals was beyond me. To complain later was undignified; they should have thrown Paula off their set the first day she appeared.

Why didn't they? It isn't easy to deal with a mesmerized actress. When they protested, Marilyn would use her girl-girl weapons. She'd come to work late. Or she'd not appear. Sick! For a day or two. Or longer. It would depend. On what? On when the director had learned where the power was located. This is a very effective weapon, attacking, as it does, the most vulnerable part of a producer's organism, his budget.

Lee soon found himself urgently called upon for help. He was never far away; it was a role from which he didn't shy. What kudos to have the great public's greatest movie star depend on you for advice that would supersede that of the filmmaker for whom she was working. Now Lee had power over producers like those who, twenty years before, had hired him to make tests of actors, then fired him. A failure as a director himself, he was now directing directors of the first rank. He would appear for a conference, wearing his solemn-owl expression. In time a solution would be reached through his good offices. He'd promise to have a talk with Marilyn. The next day she'd appear, eager for work, more or less on time. With Paula behind her. To do this to a man like George Cukor, who'd made high-comedy masterpieces, was a public indignity. Was Lee aware that this humiliated the director? Did he care? I was puzzled.

Nothing went as they hoped. Paula went to England to be on hand when Marilyn did a film for Olivier. Larry despised Paula. Soon things weren't going Marilyn's way, and she needed a lift when she woke in the morning. She began to drink. Perhaps she felt the straining gap between her ability and the goals she'd been promised. And for other reasons, I'm sure; personal ones. Billy Wilder, a director of the first rank, had said of her, "She started to drink at eleven in the morning. She and Miller had awful fights on the set. At last I've found someone who hates her worse than me." What the hell were Miller and Paula Strasberg doing on Wilder's set? If there was anyone in Hollywood who didn't need help writing a scene or getting a performance, it was Billy Wilder.

Andy and Patricia

A FACE IN THE CROWD was ahead of its time; Budd Schulberg, its author, anticipated Ronald Reagan.

The film received a good press and one extraordinarily good notice:

When two stool pigeon witnesses before the Un-American Committee conspire to produce one of the finest progressive films we have seen in years, something more than oversimplification of motives is needed to explain it. Both Budd Schulberg, who wrote the screenplay, and Elia Kazan, who directed it, did not hesitate to betray what both believed in before the witch-hunting House Committee. But they must have learned something during their days in the progressive movement and motion picture audiences will be the beneficiaries. *A Face in the Crowd* is a hard-hitting exposé of the television industry and the way a hillbilly guitar plucker can be built up to be a national menace. The film will help educate the film audience into an understanding of how public opinion is manipulated in the U.S. and for what purpose. Whether it is the residual understanding Schulberg and Kazan retain from their days in the progressive movement, or whether it is a guilty conscience (or both) that has prompted them to give us this picture, we should be grateful for what they have done.

This review appeared in the Communist Party's West Coast *People's World*. *Counterattack*, the news militia of the right wing, fell on its author.

Counterattack feels that even a fictional motion picture must make some concessions to reality, or truth. If the author is projecting a fearful picture of a possible future, then that's one thing. But that isn't the case here. The use of current terms and incidents clearly indicate their purpose is a present one. This is partisan propaganda. But we doubt that it is the result of a hang-over from the Communist pasts of Budd Schulberg and Elia Kazan. This is exactly what these gentlemen would be writing and thinking today even if they had never been near the Communist Party. This is the stuff that goes to make up the credo of commercial liberalism. It is beginning to sound strange because it is now a very long way from the world of reality. The commercial liberal has to keep on raving about conformity and thought-control because he doesn't have anything else. A few symbols and a handful of slogans are about all he has ever had in the way of a faith or a cause. Still commercial liberalism rules the communications roost today, as it has for a long time. All that effort to beat a straw man into the dust— a straw man of a theory that isolationists, reactionaries and anti-communists are ready to seize power in the United States and throw everybody who voted for Henry Wallace into a concentration camp. It's bunk but it's very profitable bunk and Messrs. Schulberg and Kazan are masters of the art of dispensing it.

Although I thought both reviews stupid, I did think *Counterattack's* description of the "commercial liberal" fitted some of my old friends.

The CP never let up on me. During the trip Molly and I had taken together, wherever I was interviewed the questions would commence about the films I'd made and the actors I'd worked with, then somebody who'd been silent, usually at the back of the room, would pop up and challenge my HUAC testimony. Quickly he'd be joined by others in the room. It happened in Paris, but with some grace and a bit of cynicism. In Athens, however, the Communist daily, *Avghi*, saluted our arrival with a full-spread attack. I must say, at the risk of sounding paranoid, that all these questions and comments, even the way they were phrased, seemed much alike. I thought them coordinated.

My response was silence. I knew that I was the official target of a well-organized campaign that had marshaled lefties everywhere and provided their dialogue. I knew their tactics well, and many of their people. So I went my way, didn't worry about lost friends, and lived it out. Was there some guilt in my silence, as many of my critics alleged? Yes; at first; some. But there was also a growing belief in what I'd done. I could take it now and damn well did.

I was particularly proud of *A Face in the Crowd* and still am. Of course, it's exaggerated—all satires are—to make a point. But until its very last moments, when the satire falls to earth, it is successful and great fun. Budd and I were a perfect team, and I was in on this one from the beginning. I dug up research with Budd and helped plan the story structure. Budd rented a place near me in Connecticut, and we spent the summer working together. It was a valuable experience for what I intended in the future. I was a co-storyteller, even though not a word of the dialogue was mine. By contrast to *On the Waterfront*, where Budd was rarely near the camera, I'd insisted that on this film he should be with me every day we shot. This sounded fine, but as it turned out, sometimes he was too close and I caught myself trying to please him, not myself. There are few surprises in my direction, perhaps for that reason, but to balance this I benefited by many excellent suggestions Budd made. We came out of the job better friends. The thing that drove us was our belief in the theme, our anticipation of the power TV would have in the political life of the nation. "Listen to what the candidate says," we urged, "don't be taken in by his charm or his trust-inspiring personality. Don't buy the advertisement; buy what's in the package." I've always regretted the preaching of the "liberal" writer at the end; certainly everything he says is obvious in what went before. But I had no better idea, and at least we had Walter Matthau delivering the summation.

The film has an external story, but there is also a secondary story, running concurrently and hiding, as it were, behind the objective one. This "hidden" story has an intimate reference to the emotional life of the author and the director. It is the story of women as conscience. The film can be told this way: A bright and idealistic young woman who comes down from Sarah Lawrence College to build a career for herself in radio discovers someone she considers a "find." He is a country boy with country horse sense and a gift for storytelling. There is an intolerance of fraud in this fellow's intelligence. Believing she's found a personality with great potential for good, she helps him achieve a prominence she feels he deserves. As she guides him on and up, she falls in love with him, as much for his potential as for his person. He becomes her voice. Then she notices that he's going bad and tries to restore him to the self she loves. But things have gone too far; she sees that success has corrupted his honesty. Since he is her creation, what he has become, a corrupting influence, is her responsibility. And, figuratively, she kills him.

This story, as you can see, has little to do with American politics or even with life behind the scenes of the television industry. It is both more fundamental and more intimate. It takes place within the woman and her conscience. Its elements consist of choices Budd made as he dramatized the "human" side of the tale. He drew on what he had to draw on: his own life. This other story applies equally to me. There is a two-way autobiographical note here.

Both Budd and I have chosen strongly influential women in our lives. Budd has often responded to a woman who would represent, at least for a time, the "right" way or the "best" life. He's also needed—and now I'm being presumptuous—someone he could sin against like an errant boy, whom she would then scold, make to feel guilty, and straighten out. I've even believed that he enjoyed this guilt—so long as he was taken back. This was especially true of his third wife, Geraldine Brooks Schulberg, who was very strong. She ran Budd's life, and he was grateful to her for what she did. This would correspond to what Pat Neal represents in A Face in the Crowd, rectitude and concern for her man's best self and strongest aspirations. Budd has, from time to time, experienced temptation. While these temptations might have been strong enough to shake his marriage, they never got strong enough to break it. What he must have told his wife—and himself—was that it was only a kind of male play.

If the intimate drama of our film had some reference to Budd, it had equal reference to me. For many years, I'd clung to Molly because she was my talisman of success and my measure of merit. She was the reassuring symbol that the very heart of America, which my family had come here to find, had accepted me. That is why we never divorced, never could or would or did. Behind my bluster, I was still a person uncertain of his final worth. If there was anyone who represented conventional, decent, historic America, it was Molly Day of the New Haven Thachers. Other women I might take up with were all—so I saw them—temporary flings. They made Molly more important, not less. I was as sure as she was that I would "straighten myself out" sooner or later. This proved to be only partly true.

And she? Why me? Because I was her creation—as Lonesome Rhodes was the creation of Marcia in our film. And that's the realest story in A Face in the Crowd.

S O L I T A I R E is an effort to create order in a disordered pack of playing cards. Year after year, as Molly planned the creative work she hoped to do—playwriting—she'd sit on the floor of her study with the door closed and a deck of cards arranged before her; there'd be no sound from within. Then I'd hear a burst from her typewriter, and I'd know that an idea had come to her. Silence again, solitaire again, another interval, another burst of typing. The play was progressing. Finally, in the spring of 1957, she had a completed work. It was titled The Egghead, and like solitaire, it was an attempt by the author to create order out of chaos—that is, out of a civilization, ours, that Molly considered incorrectly ordered. Goodhearted Molly was the self-appointed Spokesperson of the Truth.

A close friend, Karl Malden, agreed to play the leading role, representing the liberals Molly considered softheaded. Another close friend, Hume Cronyn, agreed to direct the play; he had strength equal to hers and was in

sympathy with her viewpoint. The play tried out in Cleveland, and Molly, our eldest child, Judy, and I made a family holiday of our trip out; it was a most harmonious excursion. Loyal and determined, we went to stand up for Molly in her time of public trial. At last she'd achieved her goal: She was the author of a play that was to receive a fine professional production and publicly articulate her stand on a basic moral issue. At the Hanna Theatre, the play received respectable notices: Who could not respect a person so earnest, so decent, and so fair? The production was brought to New York. Again it received respectful attention, but intemperate New York had less patience with being instructed. The play was on the boards for nine performances.

Molly's work had a fault that is fatal in the theatre, one so deep in her character that it could not be corrected. There was no moment in that evening's entertainment when it appeared that both sides might be right; only Molly, the author, was right. In the theatre, order, clarity, and goodness are not enough; to be correct is not a sufficient virtue. An audience wants to be shaken and for a time kept in doubt. That's the fun of it. Molly, being absolute about her opinions, had no inner conflicts herself; she could therefore create conflicts only within a perimeter she'd set. The audience felt that she knew the solution to everything happening on stage and that she'd uncover these solutions when she chose to. This produced the one unforgivable dramatic fault: The conclusion was predictable. The conflicts were not genuine because they did not exist in the author, so were not felt as genuine conflicts by her. Her audience, good-natured and kind, may have agreed with her "positions," but they were not interested in the confrontation—more like a school debate or a "fixed" fight—that she set up. In the theatre, there has to be a belly of chaos under the event. The audiences should be uncertain of the outcome until the end. Only then may a resolution be of dramatic interest.

The experience—and failure—of her production had two strong effects on me. One was sympathy and a kind of sorrow for this good woman who'd struggled so long and so hard with her play and who was so firmly bound by good sense and the conviction that her position on how to deal with left-wing radicalism in a democracy was unchallengeable. I felt that Molly's critical faculty had choked her creative impulses.

The other reaction I had was disruptive. Despite the sympathy I felt for Molly, I was personally alienated from her. I would resent any future effort from her to "straighten me out," to instill "order" in my life or in my thought. Her positions, I felt, were "stuffy," those of someone who doesn't welcome further challenge. I thought this was not the way of the artist. I preferred chaos; in fact, I sought it.

For the first time I became aware that she was older than I—which she'd always been, of course, but now she seemed considerably older. There was some sort of calcification of viewpoint there, the opposite of quest and growth. I became convinced that an artist needs an anarchist's heart and has to be pulled more than one way at a time. I had to be open to the unexpected. I hungered for other voices, with sympathy for what I was feeling—no matter where they came from. All doors and windows open, all escape hatches closed.

I'd come to that point in life—I was forty-eight, that critical age—when I was asking myself, "Is that all there's going to be? Is this, what I have now, it?" I set out to destroy what I found stifling and replace the predictable with the unpredictable. I courted what would be disruptive. I was more determined than ever to concentrate on my own projects and prepare my own scripts. For this program, I found an ally. When you want to hear something very much, you'll soon find someone to tell it to you. In the last stages of work preparing *A Face in the Crowd*, I'd met a young actress who, many years later, was to be my second wife. I was immediately taken with her. At first our affair was nothing more than dog and bitch. There were others at the same time; neither of us expected the relationship to be anything beyond a temporary lusting. But I'd never encountered anyone like this girl, anyone who'd uncover what is generally kept discreet with such complete candor. Conceived in a field of daisies, Barbara Loden was born antirespectable; she observed none of the conventional middle-class boundaries, the perimeter walls within which Molly lived. A roulette wheel that didn't stop turning, Barbara would keep me wondering when it would, and where. Life with Molly, to continue the figure, was a safe-deposit vault.

It impressed me that Barbara was not in awe of my reputation; that avalanche of nonsense about my magic directorial touch had not swept her away. This indifference to my professional eminence reinforced my own uncertainty about the worth of my work. Because I was now trying to write a film about a country girl and a big-city intellectual, I was enlightened by her. (Even in romance, I didn't waste time.) Barbara was feisty with men, fearless on the streets, dubious of all ethical principles, and capable at the household trades a country girl must know. She was rebuilding everything inside the shell of an old brownstone, wearing a tool apron, using hammer, saw, and crowbar, working long hours with an old nonunion carpenter named George, and asking for nothing more than to know that when she had the children she so much wanted, they'd have decent shelter.

There was something improper about her and something of the prig about me, so I kept her in the dark—literally so. I'd rent a hotel room, arrive there first, get into bed, turn off the lights, and leave the door ajar. She'd come in wearing work clothes. I'd leave before she did, because I always had to hurry to a rehearsal or to an "important conference." She'd go back to work on her house. We'd hardly talked, but I became accustomed to having her near me.

Meantime, I was not doing well with my TVA screenplay, which, in my program of work, I'd decided to write myself. This rattled my confidence. The screenwriter's craft was more difficult than I'd believed. I'd done three versions, and I was not satisfied. Ready to admit that I needed help, I turned to my friend Paul Osborn, who'd done the screenplay for *East of Eden*. He wasn't enthusiastic about my proposal or the basic material. Like many playwrights who'd done a number of adaptations of other men's material, he believed he should be doing his own work. I said I'd wait for him. Perhaps this fetched him. Having already spent many months on this story, I didn't care how long he needed. I figured I'd learn a lot about why I'd failed when he succeeded.

In those days I had no tolerance for idleness. I always had to be doing something or else I'd begin to rattle. I was also becoming increasingly reckless with Barbara and with others, so that my carrying on was being noticed. I had to siphon off my excess energy into some stable activity. I undertook the production of a new play that Molly strongly recommended to me, William Inge's *The Dark at the Top of the Stairs*. I can't say I was wildly excited about this work. I went into it partly because I wished to please Molly, which, translated to the truth, means that I wanted to mislead her into believing that we were still close in this essential respect and that she could continue to guide me, because, just as I had in the past, I totally respected her judgment. This professional respect was of prime importance to her. It was the strongest bond we had at this time, and I was determined to keep it strong. Our relationship had become more a partnership than a marriage.

For the hell of it, I showed Barbara the Inge play. I thought there might be a part in it for her, but didn't say so, rather waited to see what she thought. I wasn't surprised that she found it boring; this ratified my own first reaction. However, I was to learn a lesson as I went on with the play, which is that all Bill's work—his other plays and the film that I would do with him a couple of years later—seemed on first view to be conventional mid-America stuff, with nothing that hadn't been seen and said before. But all of it suddenly, to the audience's surprise as well as my own, would produce scenes of exceptional poignancy—not thunder and lightning, but insight and tenderness, Inge's own gifts. And always a quiet terror—which is what Bill had lived through and survived. His work, furthermore, provided actors with exceptional opportunities for good performances, climaxing in moments that revealed their best gifts. This was not because of what they'd been given to say by the author but because of the underlying emotions, the ones Bill had felt when he wrote the scenes. Someone like Barbara would call the play "tame," but a wiser woman, Molly, saw that what started as conventional and unchallenging would, as the play progressed, produce moments that were surprisingly affecting. Molly predicted this about *The Dark at the Top of the Stairs*. Theatre pieces are not for reading, she said, but for performing.

The Dark at the Top of the Stairs was Bill's fourth smash hit in a row. We opened for a tryout in Philadelphia, and the reaction was "mixed"—that is, disappointing. Next morning Bill had disappeared, was nowhere to be found. I needed him to do some work, even though most of what had to be done was my job and the actors'. A couple of days later Bill reappeared, looking just the least bit shamefaced. I said nothing; no one said anything; we didn't have to. Bill had years of experience in forgiving himself and going on. We set to work together, and when the play opened in New York, it deserved the acclaim it received.

During this time, I developed a great fondness for Bill and, I believe, he for me. In New York, I began to see him and enjoy his temperate goodness, so different from the overheated emotional lives of other authors I'd worked with. His telephone calls to me were quiet but, in fact, ardent reaches for companionship—a meal, a stroll, a talk. It took some time before I began to detect what was desperate there. I sensed some mystery in his past, began to believe he might have been damaged psychically at some time. I found out that he'd been a patient at the Austen Riggs institute in Stockbridge, Massachusetts. I noticed that his apartment in New York was on the second floor, just one floor above the concrete backyard of the apartment building, and had no other view. One day I asked why he didn't change it for another apartment, one with an attractive view, high above the dirt and noise. We were good friends by then, and he told me that it was because where he was now, no matter how depressed he became, he would not ever be tempted to suicide. Years later I'd remember that conversation.

I noticed things that were childlike about him. Sometimes he spoke like a mother's darling boy. He'd use phrases that had to be hangovers from the table talk of his youth. "I think I'll have my supper now," he'd say; not "supper," but "my supper," just as his mother, standing at the foot of the stairs, might have called up to where he waited above in the dark: "William, your supper is ready." Bill became very fond of Molly, particularly for that side of her which had appealed to Montgomery Clift, another sexual borderline case. They both valued Molly's motherliness. Bill, later in life, was to live with his sister. He never made an enduring intimate connection, and the years after his youth's big vigor were sad ones. Not surprisingly, his best subjects were small events within the confines of a family fold and rarely broke loose outside. Nor did he.

A S I ' V E passed through the episodes of my life, I've tried to understand my behavior and explain it to you and so to myself. But at this point in my history, I cannot account for what I was doing. The explanation, if one can be found, is beyond my reach. From the time I found that *Waterfront* and *East of Eden* had made me one of the most respected men in my profession and that I could choose among unlimited opportunities, I began to behave in a manner I can only describe by saying that I was two men alternately within the same man, with two needs, two "souls"—one black, the other "normal."

I was enjoying a double life, seemed to want respectability and general esteem while, sometimes on the same day, even within an hour, I was being driven by irrational emotional needs to behavior that was shameful. No, that isn't true. The remarkable fact is that I felt no shame, did not believe that what I was doing was out of the ordinary or in any final sense reprehensible. I was not burdened with a sense of mortal sin, and what I was doing, since it defied understanding, needed no justification. Being determined at this time to deny myself nothing, I plunged on. I was lawless.

I appeared to be, and was, a well-controlled member of our culture-oriented theatre, with many admirers and devoted friends among the "progressive" intellectuals. (Still? No, again.) At home, after a day devoted to good work, I'd sit at the head of our table and take part with confident charm in the dinners Molly threw for our brighter friends; I guided the conversation skillfully, kept it going over bumps and stalls, saw to it that everyone was included in the talk. With Lee Strasberg and Cheryl Crawford, I'd appear at the yearly judging of young actors applying for membership in the Actors Studio as a sober authority figure, a position of great power at that time. I'd also begun frequently to attend meetings being conducted in the effort to set up a repertory theatre at Lincoln Center. I was invited everywhere, submitted only to important interviews, where I told wise stories, answered questions seriously, offered principles and conclusions, and generally behaved like a member of our elite establishment.

At the same time, I had a secret life, which I can best reveal by including an excerpt from my diary of that year. The hour and a quarter I describe followed a meeting with John D. Rockefeller III and his blue-ribbon staff, where I, in my capacity as "consultant" being considered for a permanent involvement in the creation of a repertory theatre, had spoken and impressed the company around the long table. I then excused myself from the planned luncheon and hurried to the theatre where one of my plays was running, to apply my quietly spoken but unchallengeable discipline to a certain young actress, our ingenue, about whom there had been complaints from the leading actors in the company. There was a further crisis: Another of our leading performers had come down with measles. What you will now read is in the how-it-really-happens vein and might carry the title "The Director Makes Everybody Happy."

Diary: The measles! As he hurried to the theatre, the director hoped to God she hadn't infected the rest of the cast. It was half past noon on a matinee day, and the stage manager was sitting in the middle of the auditorium, where the director had sat weeks before, conducting the understudy rehearsal. The replacement was going on that afternoon. From what the director could judge at a glance, she was determined to preserve her artistic integrity by avoiding the very best bits of the performance of the woman down with the measles. Whatever was effective in the other actress's work, the understudy would not use; she was "developing her own performance." The stage manager was overtly kind and patient (but out of the side of her mouth, disdainful); she'd decided to imitate the more "Christ-like" aspects of the director, spoke, when she did, in an excessively kind voice. The director sat next to her and turned his face to the stage. That morning, he hated the theatre and had had it with this play. The assistant stage manager brought him a cigar and some tea. The director enjoyed the cigar and thought of other things. Once he interrupted just to let the understudy know that he'd arrived and was watching. Then he retreated behind the smoke and waited, taking pains to look attentive, which was a strain. He was saved by the bell; the rehearsal was over.

Just as it finished, the ingenue whom he'd been called in to discipline showed up, late and looking guilty, for the stage manager had asked her to take part in the rehearsal. It was common knowledge that she'd been having some personal problems; had played the comedy first act the night before in tears. The director knew what the others did not, that she was late with her period, and perhaps it was this that had upset her.

The director walked slowly up on the stage, his eyes on the ingenue. Then he walked past her without a greeting, a kind of reprimand. Now he encountered the leading lady, who was hurrying to her dressing room. She gave the director a quick kiss and asked if she could see him; it was important. The director replied that he had a few notes to give the understudy, after which he would come to her dressing room. Then he took the understudy, who was going on that afternoon, into the back of the set. "Let's sit here in the love seat," he said. As she sat, she looked at him, humbled and anxious. "Will I be all right?" she asked. "Will I be funny?" The director couldn't help thinking: Christ, you might be moderately amusing if you would do the goddamn part as directed. But since she was going on in an hour, it was late to go into all that. He said she only needed one thing, told her what that was, and promptly forgot it. But he spoke with a good show of concern, and the understudy felt relieved. There was moisture in a corner of one eye, gratitude. She looked at him and said, "You are so sweet," and kissed him and said she had to run up and fix her hair. The director said he'd come by her dressing room later, look at her hair, and wish her luck. She trotted off feeling happier than he'd found her. After all, what more could he do? Miracles?

Now he went in to see the leading lady. She said she wanted a long, long talk with the director soon. "This is no longer a happy company," she said. Everyone was always threatening the director with a long, long talk. If there was anything that would make him leave town in a hurry, it was the threat of a long, long talk. Wearing a dressing gown, carelessly gathered, she sat there putting on her base, and she looked very concerned. The producer of the show had told the director the day before that they would have their first empty seats at that matinee. His star was a good actress, earnest and sincere, altogether decent, but there were empty seats at his hit show. Better someone less altogether decent. The director forced himself to attention. She was telling him again that she had to have a long, long talk with him. The director had long since come to the conviction that anything human beings had to say to each other, no matter how important, could be said in the time it takes to soft-boil an egg. Maybe her long, long talk could be had right then and there, in the form of a few words. Ah, at last! She was getting to the subject. The ingenue! The fucking ingenue had played the first act in tears. Backstage discipline was shot to hell. It was beyond the stage manager. The director should talk to the ingenue. He put on his most concerned face. The behavior of the ingenue (that little cunt!) was intolerable. He would certainly talk to her. The leading lady plowed on. The ingenue, she said, kept having

phone calls between the acts and even during the performance, ones
that upset her and brought tears to her eyes during a comedy scene.
Did the director believe, the leading lady wanted to know, that actors
should have phone calls during the performance? "Certainly not," he
said. The director noted that the leading lady had a phone on her
dressing room table. The "kids" in the cast had to stand by the stage
door and use the wall phone there. The leading lady went on developing her theme until the director had had enough and cut her short
with the announcement that he would go up to the ingenue's dressing
room immediately, now, and settle the ingenue problem once and for
all. There is nothing like settling these things quickly, he told the
leading lady, as she took his hand. He'd go up now! He freed his hand
to scratch his neck (which did not itch) and kissed her on the forehead,
leaving her happy. He always left everybody happy; that was his job.

Upstairs, the ingenue was sitting with her feet on the dressing
room table, eating the chicken out of a chicken sandwich. The director
closed the door. "Anything happen?" he asked. "Not a sign of it," she
said. Of course, that was what had upset her during the week. Was
the director expected to do something about menstrual flow, for chrissake? But she had a more serious problem. She told him she had a
new boyfriend, "but I don't know whether he really likes me." The
director asked if she liked him. She said she wasn't sure. The announcement from the girl that she had a new boyfriend reawakened
his interest in her. He told her that he'd called her last week. She
said, her voice slipping just a little out of control, that she was going
to get a service so he could leave messages. They were soon involved,
she on his lap, his hand between her legs. He didn't mention what
the leading lady had talked about and what he'd said he'd take care of.
He told her to raise her leg a little. After another moment of play, he
asked what time it was. This was not a question about the time. It
meant who'd be upstairs in their dressing rooms on this floor by this
time. She suggested he visit the fellow two doors down the hall and
find out what time it was—and so give her a moment. Which he did,
after standing a few seconds and shaking it off.

He found the young character actor making up. He was a boy, born
queer, and always a little guilty, so that his conversation went as
quickly as possible into affirming his dutifulness. He told the director
how well he'd been living, what good care he'd taken of himself, how
much he'd been sleeping. The director wondered what had brought
all this on. Had the boy had a bad night of drinking and now felt
obligated to go into this display of virtue? The boy must have read his
mind, because he blurted, "I haven't had a drink in three weeks!" The
director smiled and told him how well he looked because of that, and
was then about to ask what time it was, when the second assistant

stage manager went by, calling half hour. The director thought: If I'm going to get it, I better get it now, and he left the young actor's dressing room. He could see that he'd left the boy happy.

His hand found that the ingenue was now protected. "A little late for that, isn't it?" he said. She chuckled. My God, he thought, she carries the fucking thing around with her. Always ready! Why not! She either spent the night with her new boyfriend or she spent the night with her new boyfriend. He dropped his trousers. When she saw it, the ingenue acted greedy. A little of this was enough. How much time did they have anyway? The director put her on the floor of the dressing room, where there was a rug he'd given her two months before. The problem was the dressing room door. "The lock doesn't work," she said. The director put his boots (purchased in Arkansas) up against the door. That would serve. She said she loved him. He said isn't this wonderful. She forgot her problems. Their relationship was good— that way. The director thought: Downstairs, the leading lady is completing her makeup. Somewhere, John D., the Baptist banker, and his elite staff are eating their lunch. He heard the actor in the next dressing room come by and pass on. The ingenue, her mouth open and her eyes closed, said, "Oh, my God!" Then she came. He muffled her sound. Then he came. They lay there. Someone hurried down the hall and stopped by their door, talking to the person across the way. The ingenue said, "It would look kinda funny if . . ." The director said, "Wouldn't it though!" He stood up. "You guard the door," he said. Her soap was covered with makeup, so he didn't use it. He washed in water and dried it with Kleenex. The ingenue, leaning against the dressing room door, kept watching what he was doing. The director said he loved danger. She said she did too. He pulled off a bit of Kleenex and flicked it at her image in the mirror. She laughed and kissed it before he put it away. She fluffed her skirts around, laughing. It had been very quick and a little nerve-racking, but they both laughed.

Then, thoroughly composed for the casual eye, he opened the door a little, so it would not appear to be locked. The fellow across the hall was the leading male understudy, who had a yen for this girl. Was he her new lover? the director wondered. But now he didn't care. He sat down opposite the ingenue and gave her a little talk, his manner suddenly stern. He reminded her that a dressing room was not only a place to put on makeup; it was a place to compose oneself for the performance. He said no matter how upset she felt because of her problem and the events of her day, it was her obligation to come into her dressing room early, retreat into it—that's a good word, he said, retreat—and pull herself together for the show. She should now say to herself, "For the next two hours I'm going to think of nothing but my performance." The director told her she was pretty good in the part but could be better, and reminded her that a thousand people at each performance would have paid to see her at her best. The ingenue looked very earnest and a little frightened, not at all as she'd looked five minutes before. She looked like a schoolgirl being scolded by a principal for whom she had the greatest respect, and no little fear. She looked at the director, with her eyes fixed wide open. Why, wondered the director, are all actors so grateful for a bawling out? He finished with an extra bit of sternness. She was in the big time now, he reminded her, this was her first professional job, and she should behave like a professional. When he left, he saw that he'd made the ingenue very, very happy.

He checked the woman understudy's hairdo as he'd promised, gave her a chaste kiss on her forehead, then walked across stage, called the stage manager, and asked her to tell the leading lady that he'd taken care of the ingenue. "I'm so glad you came around," the stage manager said. "We all miss you here." As she said this, the director was wondering if his fingertips still carried the scent. He told the stage manager to put an announcement up over his name, asking the company not to receive or answer phone calls after half hour and during the performance. The stage manager respectfully suggested that she'd rather notify the doorman not to call actors to the phone during the show, take messages instead. The stage manager's suggestion was made in the most deferential manner, and the director accepted it, making her happy too.

On the way out, the director gave the doorman a dollar. Outside, the streets were filled with eager theatregoers. He walked numbly through the taxi traffic. He was meeting his wife and two of his kids at another theatre, getting them into the matinee, then would hurry back to the meeting about the proposed repertory theatre at Lincoln Center. The clock on top of the Paramount Theatre building came into view; it was two-thirty. He was late. He began to run.

T O   B R E A K the bind of meaningless escapades and that of a somnolent marriage, I flew to Athens alone. There was a reason more urgent: It was my last chance to withdraw from Lincoln Center—if I was going to. The voice of instinct kept warning me: "Don't go on with it; it's not what you really want to do now. Or should do." Still, whenever I was asked to come to a planning meeting, I wouldn't refuse. I was now accepted as a participant by everyone except myself. What the hell was holding me there? The flattery of the position offered me? I was not immune to flattery. The prestige of being publicly sought? The adventure of sitting at a long table and consorting with John D. Rockefeller III and his elite staff? Or was it because

more than twenty years of my training had been devoted to preparing myself to guide a company of actors in playing repertory, so it would be a
shame not to?

Real reasons are simpler. Molly was urging me to do it, not hard but
without remission. She especially liked the man who'd be my codirector,
Bob Whitehead. "You're not accustomed to working with anyone as nice as
Bob," she said. I liked Bob too, but every time I sat around Lincoln Center's
board table, I had the feeling I was with strangers. Giving Molly her wish—
she did want it badly—would serve to reassure her, in a situation that was
deteriorating steadily, that we were still, at least in this essential respect, as
close as ever. It would make up, I hoped, for my neglect, my edging away
from her, and my betraying her.

The voice from within would not stop. I truly did not want to be the
leader of a group. What fulfilled Harold Clurman did not fulfill me. Increasingly I'd sought my own voice and my own way. I knew that in the immi-
gration of my family to this country, I had a subject as close to me as my
skin. I decided to stop everything else, drop out, shun Molly's influence for
a spell, relieve myself of the pressures of prestige and flattery, and make a
trip alone, back in time as well as in geography. I'd do what I'd so often
dreamed of doing: charter a forty-footer that relied mostly on cloth and,
giving myself time and privacy, sail the Greek islands, those which had not
caught up with the world. I'd lie on the deck in the sun and by the light of
the moon, and I'd see if I could plan a film about my family; more than that,
a series of films, our history dramatized. I believed that if I pulled back
from all things contemporary and all influences pushing me toward Lincoln
Center, if I immersed myself in the culture and the language of my family's
life before they made the thrust west, the structural solution I needed
would come to me. With the reassurance of a viable plan, I could return to
New York, gracefully resign from what I'd been slipping into, and devote
myself to myself.

I said very little to Molly about the purpose of my trip—she would have
tried to talk me out of it. All I told her was that I needed a vacation alone.
In Athens I found what I wanted and rented it, the *Stormie Seas*, a forty-
foot caïque, flying the Union Jack. It had a crew of two social rebels, a
young married couple—navigator and captain, mate and cook. I told them
the kind of islands I wanted to see and they understood. We cleared Piraeus's channel on our five-horse motor, then shut it off and, relying on
cloth, turned south toward those islands of the Cyclades that tourists don't
trample. Quiet at last, my load of tensions eased, I asked myself a question
I'd asked before, but now in earnest: Could I disappear from the world
where I'd trafficked all my life and become someone else? Could I start
over again? You will certainly say that is the most foolish of questions, but
in time—it did take time—that is what I did: disappear from the world I'd
inhabited all my adult life, to become someone else.

We passed from one neglected island to another, climbing to the citadel of each, pausing at the small whitewashed chapel to light a candle, then sitting in the plaza under great trees. There I studied the old men, who still wore bloomers and carried curved-handle knives in their belts, and the women, in black, nothing showing except gleaming eyes, doing their errands, and the donkeys, inactive except for the play of their long penises. We drank our ouzo, nibbled olives and cheese, and observed Greek life, which hadn't changed for a hundred years. I'd talk to myself. "Why do you direct plays you don't really like? Why films with stories not your own? Why did you ever agree to become a consultant to the repertory company that the Rockefellers and their rich friends propose to set up at Lincoln Center? Is that really you, what you want to do? Get out of it. Now! Start on your own track before it's too late."

At sunset we'd put in at a deserted cove, and the captain's wife, a plump blonde out of the British middle class, would cook us a decent enough meal, which we'd wash down with resinated wine. Then I'd sleep on deck. The sea was beautiful at night, even more beautiful at the sun's rise. I thought of Homer's adjective for the ocean water, "purple." I was satisfied to be alone and to have nothing pressing me. With the day, I began to make notes of what I remembered of the tales my grandmother had told me, a boy of six, in her bed at night, the old lady dredging up memories long forgotten. They were good stories, simple and modest and human.

But no sense of how they might be put together came to me. I could see what I had to do. I had to go back to Turkey—not these glistening isles— back to where my family had come from, and this time in dead earnest, meaning it this time, really look and listen and stay put whenever I found something that aroused me. The more I thought about the early history of my family, the more complex it seemed and the less I found I actually knew about it. I was a kind of tourist in my family's history. I had not experienced the events or the pressures I proposed to film or write about. I hadn't been through the crisis of persecution and want, never knew the desperate thrust for liberty that I wished to dramatize. I was a middle-class American boy, a stranger to my own history. I wasn't ready, if I ever would be, to conceive and write screenplays for my own films, especially on a subject in which I had no experience.

One day, as if to emphasize my failure, a wind of near hurricane force came out of a perfect blue sky, the *melteme*, driving us straight toward the rocky shore of the island of Poros. Our captain did manage to turn the back of his craft to the shore and rev up his motor until it rattled. But its 5 HP was not effective in the face of the storm. Soon the *Stormie Seas* was butting the rocks, and we were lucky to get to shore, well soaked. On the island it was quiet, a land with no one in sight. There was a serious repair to be made, for which a new part was needed. The captain dispatched his mate across the island to take the boat for Piraeus, there to pick up the part he needed and send it back to him. I went with her, an eighteen-mile hike to the opposite shore. The land between was barren, the wind the only sound.

In Athens, the captain's mate found the part her husband was waiting for and sent it off. He hadn't seemed anxious about being left alone, and his wife didn't fret. The British, I thought, possess an enviable inner contentment. It became evident that her life on the *Stormie Seas* was driving her upon rocks sharper than those on the eastern shore of Poros. She was, as most wives seem to be for longer or shorter periods, on the verge of leaving her husband, suspecting him of indifference to her appeal, a heavier sin by far than infidelity. She was eager to entertain an abrupt change of course in her own life. In a hotel opposite a small church whose bells never stopped ringing, we came to know each other. "It's nice to have my heart beating again," she said.

Then I made a mistake. I went to American Express. Three cables and a pocketful of letters informed me that I hadn't properly prepared the production of the play I'd contracted to do next, *J.B.*, by Archibald MacLeish. There were pressing decisions to be made that only the director could make. With great reluctance, I booked passage west. The captain's mate gave me her London address as she saw me off on the plane. I'd grown a beard, looked like a native.

J . B . won the Pulitzer Prize and I was happy for Archie MacLeish. I must confess that the merits of that play eluded me. I must also confess that I have no ear. Poetry makes me impatient, even Shakespeare, although when I stop and consider his speeches line by line, I see what a surpassing genius he was. But to read through some of those plays! I can't keep my mind on them. Be scornful of me, but how about you? When was the last time you read one of the man's lesser plays all through? As for *J.B.*, I am not convinced that it is poetry. It looks like poetry on a page, but it doesn't "rise." I didn't believe it was poetry when I directed it. I staged *J.B.*, which is different from "direct," and did it with my eye, which is pretty good, not my ear. I read it all the way through only twice. After that I let the actors speak it and I moved them around, choreographed it like a ballet. If a speech was longer than three sentences, I got bored and moved someone this way or that. I let the stage pictures do the talking.

I'd worked out an excellent setting with Boris Aronson, and he'd designed it brilliantly. It was, at all times, the most artistic thing on the stage. I admired the actors, especially Chris Plummer, but more for their persistence and seeming faith in what they were saying. Oh, God, how they believed that stuff! But they didn't suspend my disbelief. I'd been assigned Jimmy Baldwin by the Dramatists Guild, the idea being that he would watch the progress of the production and be better prepared to write his own plays. He sat at my side all through, pad and pencil ready, and he full of charm. But if I was uninterested in the play's content and writhed under the weight of the lines, Jimmy was poisonous. I thought Archie was awfully cordial to Baldwin and Jimmy successfully slippery in avoiding telling Archie what was going on in his mind. It was a case of two different cultures, Harvard and Harlem.

You mustn't scorn me for my aversion for poetry. It's another time, isn't it? We talk by pictures now, and a well-chosen photograph often tells it all, faster and better. We simply listen less and suspect words because they've been used so treacherously. We are drowning in advertisements and claims for products, mostly lies. But we know that an unposed picture, a simple snapshot, tells the truth. Remember Joe McCarthy whispering in Roy Cohn's ear? Take any picture of Richard Nixon trying to win votes. Can you beat it for conveying information? Nothing need be said. Dickens and Flaubert wrote long descriptions of places, costumes, character behavior, body posture, artifacts, conveyances, meals, the weather, and so on. The great Russian film directors of the twenties—Eisenstein in particular—had great admiration for Dickens because his detailed descriptions could, sentence by sentence, shot by shot, be photographed for film montage, to build a mood or establish an environment. But now it's sixty years later, and we've seen so many pictures in the newspapers, on the tube, and in every magazine from W to the National Geographic, that what Dickens and Flaubert and the other great novelists of the nineteenth century used to do seems unnecessary. We get the idea, catch on quickly. A few words, a hint, and we have the picture.

The walls of my office in New York are covered with photographs—snapshots, mostly—of my family and my close friends. If someone were to offer to replace them with corner-to-corner Picassos, I wouldn't make the swap. The photographs of the people in my life fill me with memory and emotion. So do many news photographs. I clip them and collect them. I am part of the picture era.

I certainly don't mean to convey that I was indifferent to my responsibilities to Archie; I worked like a digger. He never knew what I felt about his stuff—although I am not sure of that, because when he wrote another play, despite all his professions of affection and gratitude to me, he offered the new work to another director. I believe I put his play over, as they say. I think that except for what happened during our Washington tryout, it would have been a failure. Our reception by audiences there was indifferent. I sat down with Archie and talked straight to him, treating the work as if it were a plot play with the structural faults of a failed plot. We analyzed what he had to do and he stayed up much later than was good for his health and by the time we opened in New York City he was on the edge of exhaustion, but the play worked and earned the praise of Mr. Brooks Atkinson, who called it a great work of the theatre, so helped get it the Pulitzer Prize. I do believe that if we hadn't stopped to do a structural repair, the play would have been a dud shell, propelled by a lively production to fall deep in the mud that was our opening night audience, there not to explode. If the basic legend has power—and here it did, modern man as Job—it's the last part of the work that may make the difference. What we did in Washington reversed the score.

I D E C I D E D to try again; I went to an analyst. He was a close associate of Karen Horney, whose book *The Neurotic Personality of Our Time* had impressed me. This "shrink," Harold Kelman, was a tall, powerfully built man in his sixties, who looked as if he'd rowed stroke on his college crew. His consultation room was illuminated with a filtered light, and he sat there in the massive posture of a judge. I remember that his bald head glowed— but that could not have been.

I decided not to lie down on the professional settee with its Oriental cover but to sit facing him and looking at him squarely. I felt challenged by his magisterial posture and was determined not to back off. Beginning arrogantly, I told him why I was there and what I expected. I told him I'd been analyzed before, sort of, that the late Dr. Bela Mittelmann had reassured me, which was not what I wanted, that Bela had told me I should be happy with who I was and what I'd accomplished, stop worrying, and pay his bills. If this was a joke, it fell flat with Dr. Kelman. Analysts don't have a sense of humor about money. I went on saying I was not happy with who I was and what I'd accomplished. I was coming to him because I wanted to live a different life and do different work. He didn't respond, even with a nod. I continued. He had the ability to look at me for fifty minutes and not blink, not shift his attention, not feel compelled to respond. The only other man I'd known who didn't blink was Spencer Tracy. I noticed that on the corner of Dr. Kelman's desk and on a shelf at one side there were small Oriental heads sculptured in stone. Burma? Cambodia? Their expressions were profoundly enigmatic, but no more so than that of my new analyst. "I want to start over again," I repeated, an effort to sum up what I'd been saying and jolt him into a response. No response. "I want to become another man," I said to a face of stone. We came to the end of the session and he hadn't said a word. Now he spoke. "All right. We'll continue." He gave me a time and watched me as I left the room.

The elders and dignitaries of Kayseri welcome me. P.S. I don't play the Turkish guitar.

WHEN THEY heard that a great complex of buildings to house the New York Philharmonic, the Metropolitan Opera, the New York City Ballet, and a repertory company was being planned, it was inevitable that the actors at the Studio would believe what Lee did, that since we were now recognized all over the world as the innovators of a new style of acting (see Kazan's films), it was only just that this repertory theatre should be given to us. The actors believed this and Lee believed it.

Only I didn't believe it.

Cheryl and I were invited by the Rockefeller people to serve on a committee of advisers, and I went to the meetings. We were listened to carefully, thanked, and dismissed. Lee was troubled; why hadn't he been asked? He was eager to talk to John Rockefeller, and I told him I'd arrange a meeting. Lee felt that the trio in charge of the activities at the church on Forty-fourth Street, he, Cheryl, and I, should be given the task of organizing the repertory theatre. Bob Whitehead had informed me that he'd been given the responsibility of setting up and operating a repertory company, and he wanted me to work with him as an equal partner.

Soon I was being asked regularly to the planning conferences for the building that would serve the theatre. I sat in on fascinating discussions between Eero Saarinen, the architect, and John Rockefeller and his staff. Eero and John were concerned about the exterior, and Bob and I helped plan the stage with Jo Mielziner. Years later this interior came under attack from more practical men, and there was much talk of redesigning what we'd worked out. This was the desire of management, of course, whose interest was to have a place they could rent out for "Broadway" productions—which had not been our intent. We'd planned a stage that would not only allow but, by its concept, compel productions of imagination.

I kept going to the meetings. I've often wondered why I accepted an executive post, responsible not only for the creation of a company of actors but also for administering a kind of theatre that was new to me and to us all in New York. Although I'd often proclaimed that repertory was the only kind of theatre I believed in, I doubt very much if I was enthusiastic about fathering the day-to-day life of a company of actors. That job would require a total devotion, near fanaticism. I didn't have that. What I was passionately devoted to now were the dreams I'd invoked lying on the deck of the *Stormie Seas*. It was those yearnings I was determined to make come true. I knew what I wanted, and it was nothing as grandiose as a post at Lincoln Center, but rather something small, intimate, and selfish. As I'd told Dr. Kelman, I didn't want to be Elia Kazan anymore; I wanted to be another man, leading a totally different life. The dream of repertory was part of my past. Did it relate to my future? I believed not.

Nevertheless I continued meeting with the Rockefeller people and with Bob Whitehead, whom I liked. Why did I keep going on with it? A repertory theatre was, after all, what I'd trained all my life to achieve, the very post that was being offered to me now. It couldn't possibly be that when I finally had it, I wouldn't take it.

There was another, unexpected influence that made me go on with the meetings: Art Miller. He wanted to be part of this effort and promised us his plays to produce. A reconciliation happened through Bob; it could not have happened through me, not yet. But once brought together, Art and I got along well—even though I was somewhat tense in his company, because we'd never discussed (and never did discuss) the reasons for our "break." I believed he was the playwright closest in character to me and that I was the natural director for him. I admired the effort he made to come together with me again, an effort that could not have had the endorsement of a number of his closest friends. I responded equally—against the inclination of some of my closest friends.

And there was pressure from actors everywhere, not only from the Studio. I believe that if the professionals in our theatre had been polled that year to determine whom they'd choose to head up such a theatre in New York, they would have voted for Bob and for me. Just then I was the "best." I wasn't "Broadway"; still I was Broadway. This support from my old profession stirred me. I felt it whenever I met an actor on the streets of our theatrical district. I'd also been successful with the best playwrights, and many of them were hoping I'd take the post. Except—there was an exception—Tennessee Williams; he tried to talk me out of it. Be a creator, he said, not an executive.

Of course, there was Lee. He was certain I must accept the position, and that I'd include him as an equal in my plans. But when I began to think about it, I wasn't sure that I wanted to be involved with Lee as a producing partner in a permanent theatre. A leader is a leader; the word is not plural. It had worked out okay at the Actors Studio because I'd "given him the place." I'd found, however, that whenever there was an issue, he was not able to operate on a basis of equality but became despotic and tolerated no contradiction. The devotion near idolatry from the actors in his classes had swollen his pride to where he believed he and only he knew the solutions to the problems we would face.

Nor did I feel the pressing need for an adviser ever present at my side. I already had one: Molly. She was more than enough.

I did make one effort for Lee. "Dear Lee," I wrote, "I want to make an official offer from Lincoln Center to the Actors Studio. As you know the small Theatre in our building will be running concurrently with the larger Theatre above. Bob and I would like the Studio to do two productions there each year. The idea is Bob's and I am enthusiastic about it. It means that the Studio will have a realistic and living tie with the activity at Lincoln Center, while, at the same time, preserving its own identity completely. I urge you and Cheryl to give this proposal favorable consideration. I'm all for it."

Receiving no response, I asked John Rockefeller to meet with Lee and listen to him. Then I arranged my ticket for Turkey, to pursue goals that meant more to me.

T H E D A Y before I left, I had a session with Dr. Kelman. He was talking at last. That was the first I heard about the lump.

"How did you know I had it?" I asked. I touched a place under the rib cage on my left side. "It's been there for a year. Something like a dull ache or a—a presence. Sometimes it actually hurts, and sometimes—"

"That's not what I mean," he said. "Although it may be related. What you have in you is a great lump of unreleased anger."

"Of what?"

"Of unexpressed resentment and rage that you've stifled and—"

"But my wife says I'm angry all the time."

"It's safe to let her see it. But how is it that you never get angry at the people who've been publicly trying to kill you?"

"Who?"

"I understand from what you've told me that certain old friends of yours have been kicking hell out of you for years, and you've responded with silence. Not a word of protest or perfectly justified anger or even an assertion of your own position—which is a correct one, by the way."

"I've got a grip on my temper."

"That grip you have will give you a real lump someday, unless you—"

"I can take it."

"No you can't. Why are you so ready to forgive your murderers?"

"I don't forgive them."

"How would anyone know? You're silent. You swallow your rage. Talk about betrayal! The worst betrayal is self-betrayal. That's what you're paying for."

Then I was silent and after a while I dropped my head. I didn't want him to see that I was crying.

"Think about it when you're gone," he said. "This is the first time you've shown any emotion here, despite the fact that we've been talking about your life and your death—"

"The lump? Why do you call it that?"

"Because down where there was once quick life, there is now a lump, which can't be awakened or quickened to anything. Or angered. It's as if something had died of neglect. It sits, this lump, in the middle of your being like an enormous lump of fat, without muscle or nerve, getting bigger and heavier. You're even ashamed to let me see you cry, although it's the first sign of real life you've shown here."

I didn't speak.

"That's why I told you it would be better if you weren't going on a trip now. What's happening in this room is more important. But—"

I didn't speak.

"All right," he said, looking at his wristwatch. "Have a good trip."

T H O U G H T S flying east over the Atlantic: Her picture had been in the paper—not the *Times*, the tabloids. She'd physically attacked a film casting director on an open street of the theatre district, slapped him around until, to save himself further punishment, he'd stopped denying what he'd said that got Barbara so mad (slurs on her character as well as her talent), stopped trying to explain and excuse himself, but simply, soft-gutted, hauled his ass down the street. That was what I admired about the girl. She hadn't called on patience, hadn't written a polite note of reproval on monogrammed letter paper, but had gone after the fellow herself. What would

I have done? Swallowed the slight and forgotten. Barbara had no lump. I didn't know anyone like her, not even Sylvia Miles, who would later dump a plate of well-spiced linguine on the dome of a certain pundit who'd called his public's attention to defects in her figure.

I envied Barbara; she made me understand what Kelman meant.

OSMAN KAVUNDJU was waiting for me at the Ankara train station. He was now a member of parliament and had changed in ways I didn't immediately appreciate. Cane and all, he'd always walked with a rolling, confident gait; now there was something added: a strut, a defiant swagger. He hustled me to the airport in an old Mercedes, chauffeur-driven. An army plane, one of our old DC-3's, was waiting for us. One hour later we were in Kayseri. On the way out, I'd explained to Osman that my intention was now practical, not sentimental. I wanted to carefully inspect Germeer, the town where my mother's family had lived, especially the part on the cliff's face. He told me he'd read my letter and assured me everything had been arranged as I wished.

I was quickly installed, this time in an enormous sugar factory collective, my quarters *grand luxe* for this part of the world. "I'm ready," I said, throwing my bags in a corner. "Let's go." On the way to Germeer, Osman and the new *Wali Bey* (Mr. Mayor), who'd replaced Osman when he moved up to Ankara, proudly showed me every change they'd brought about in the city. By the time we got to the dried-up riverbed, the boundary of Germeer, it was late afternoon, and the light had begun to fade, so I didn't immediately notice the crowd waiting for us. Every able-bodied man in Germeer must have been there. When our jeep reached a point one hundred yards from where they were waiting, they began to clap their hands, and when we stopped they swarmed around us. I got out of the jeep, and someone gave me a bunch of roses, then man after man came up in a semiservile crouch; some gave my right hand a short, intense downward wrench, others kissed it. They all looked at me with intense admiration; I was a creature from a higher world. I had to remind myself that my people had lived here in terror and were lucky to have escaped alive.

Suddenly we were walking, two or three hundred of us, crossing the river bottom, then going up a path that had once been a road that had once been a street. The new *Wali Bey,* Osman, and I were in the heart of this procession. The men ahead of us kept shooing children out of our way as if they were sheep, cuffing those they could reach. "*Ayeep! Ayeep!*" they shouted, which is "Shame on you, shame!" But the kids didn't mind; they'd still weasel through the ranks of their elders to get a closer look at me.

There were no women in the procession, but now, here and there, I got glimpses of the *kadin,* well back in the doorways of the Turkish homes that were still standing, their hands holding shawls up to their faces. There were some on the rooftops, too, and others under and behind trees, and always in the proper *kadin* posture, their head shawls held over their mouths, their chins, and the bottom of their noses. Only their eyes showed. They behaved as if they were naked, starting back as they caught me looking at them, as if it was a shame for them to be seen. *Ayeep! Ayeep!*

Then the procession stopped; we'd arrived where we were going. In a poplar grove, a table to accommodate forty diners had been set. It was altogether covered with heavily flavored foods. At the side were three musicians, who'd begun to play. I was seated in the place of honor. Oh, Isaak-pappou, from your seat at Jesus' right hand, look down and see your grandson now! The waiters were the town's leading citizens; they were dressed in woolen suits, and some wore felt hats. They were bowing, scraping, watching solicitously, ever putting more food on our plates unasked, as we began to eat. All around the table, held back by police and some young strong men, the crowd watched in silence, as if they were observing a ritual. Intensely curious, they were absolutely still except when they were smacking the kids away.

Then, well back in the dark, under the trees, like deer that suddenly appear when you're not looking, I saw the women, perhaps thirty of them in a cluster. Their eyes showed over their raised shawls. They never came closer—only the men waited on us—but it had been the women who'd prepared the food.

Later some of the men danced, snapping their fingers to the music and swinging their hips, inadequate imitations of women. This drew responses at last from the huddle of *kadin*, who whispered and snickered, but when they laughed they quickly covered their mouths and were silent. No one of them responded to the rhythm of the music. That would have been *ayeep!*

As we left, there was more applause. I thanked Osman for a wonderful evening but said that now I wanted to go back to Germeer alone and take pictures and not be followed or hurried. He smiled and said, "Of course, of course, don't worry," as he kissed me on both cheeks. But I knew it would be difficult for him to allow me to go anywhere alone.

T H A T night I dreamed of my father; he was smiling at me. What was he saying? "Now maybe you know something, eh, boy? What? How you like it here? What?" Then his face changed into my own, and I saw that I had the same smile he did, the smile of the outsider, pleading for favor, assuring everyone, "I'm not dangerous," placating, saying, "Don't be mad at me" and "I can take it!" covering all my own anger, choking it down, down, where it had gathered into the lump. Now that I was awake, I remembered that my father had a terrible temper in our house, often directed at me, but in other places, at other times, nothing. I'd never seen him angry outside the house or at Americans. Now that I was here and had some idea what it must have been like for the Greeks, I asked myself if I'd lived here seventy-five years ago, under the Turk, could I have afforded to be angry? Isn't it inevitable that he never displayed that gift outside his own house? Wouldn't I have squelched it too? Of course. Silence is safer for an outsider. "Come on, I buy you lunch!" I remembered how he used to say that to the cocky American buyers who came to his store, as he flashed his refugee smile. But what did he feel beneath? Did he have the lump inside him too?

THE TOWN of Germeer is backed up against a cliff perhaps two hundred feet high. Into this rock face caves had been cut, and there is a footpath leading to the plateau above. Long ago, this cliff with its caves was all there was of Germeer. People lived there for safety when land pirates roamed the countryside. Then, as some kind of order was established in the area, homes were built on the land below the cliff—the place where I'd been the night before.

I'd jumped out of bed with the first light of the sun and prevailed on someone to drive me out. I was alone now—as I wanted to be—walking up the path mounting the cliff. As I passed by the caves, I would look into them. I saw that some were still occupied by the poor, the underprivileged, and the old. I am not a religious man, but I was touched by finding some relics of my people's faith painted on the walls, faded religious figures. Churches too? Yes, this cliff had once been the whole town. I could guess that even more recently, in time of terror, the Greeks had come up here to hide from their Turkish oppressors. It was said that their Turkish neighbors had not harmed the resident Greeks, but bands of roaming "outside" Turks had done their duty by their God. Which meant bloodletting. You enter heaven and enjoy a beautiful houri according to how many nonbelievers you've killed.

The higher I got, the more intense was the silence. Only the wind—which was a breeze that day—made a sound. Otherwise there was an August calm. This silence, I thought, and those caves are the equivalent of my own silence and the privacy into which I've crawled for safety. Except it hadn't worked, not for me. It had resulted in the inner death that Kelman had called the lump. I began to go over what he'd told me, began to taste the anger I should have felt at the reaction of certain "friends" to my testimony, feeling at last my proper response to being snubbed on the street and insulted in every way during those bad years. I began to talk to myself, broke the silence, responding at last to the organized effort to make me a nonperson and to frighten people into not working with me. Kelman was right: I'd never allowed myself to feel that anger. But now the lump he'd talked about was stirring.

I was feeling the anger I should have felt when I'd heard that my friend Harold Clurman was telling people he would never work or talk with me again (he certainly had when he needed to); feeling at last the anger with which I should have responded to Kermit Bloomgarden, that venal, self-righteous sycophant, for snubbing me in the entrance to my office building; he'd blushed beet red as his ailing heart pumped. Silence! That had been my response. I'd trained myself to silence under any and all provocation. Silence is the safest condition for a refugee. Like these caves—I was in one now. How quiet it was in there. And how safe!

I understood the lump now. I'd let Marlon Brando off when he proclaimed that he was working with me only because he wanted to stay in New York and see his goddamn analyst. What condescension! I'd let him off scot-free. And Miss Hellman, the person Kelman had mentioned—she had the sharpest knife of all for me. Still I would tell people that I rather liked her, when the fact was that I knew damned well what she was: a liar for one thing and my enemy for sure.

And all those people at the Actors Studio, which I'd started and kept going, defended and preserved: all those nothings giving me "ice." No wonder the lump grew bigger. It would pass, I'd told myself as I stopped myself from feeling. That's what a refugee knows. Crawl into your cave, way in the back, where there isn't a sound. Outside they'll knife and kill for a few days, then it will pass. My forefathers, living by the mercy of the Turk, hid in these very caves, and when it was quiet they went down to the valley again. So you wear the mask of affability, wait out the trouble, eat the insults, shrug and flash that good-natured, ever-ready smile. A refugee can't afford pride. He must save his life. He can't afford to be angry at anyone, because he isn't provided with the weapons he would need in a fight and has lost the habit of courage.

I went out into the sunlight and sat with my legs over the side of the ledge. The cliffside air, I saw, was full of plump pigeons. They flew frantically from one sheltered place to another. Then I looked up and saw why. Circling overhead were two hawks, of good size, a dark, rich brown, circling without wasting a move. The air below was their larder. Whenever the hawks needed a meal, they'd stoop and take one. The pigeons were like refugees: They didn't fight back because they were underarmed; heavy and plump, they didn't have the speed or the habit of courage.

Kelman had said that I'd trained myself not to feel. I knew the rest of that story. When you train yourself to choke down your feelings, you get so you no longer can feel. When someone who works in the arts can't feel, he works from craft, not emotion. He stops being an artist and becomes a technician. But that was not what I wanted to be. That was not the best of me. Come to think of it, I wasn't such a good technician; I couldn't get away with being just that. The best work I'd ever done had come out of an emotion of some kind. I'd solved *J.B.* technically, but my true voice was never heard. I'd done play after play that I had no true feeling for, and I'd again and again suppressed the feelings I did have, choked them off, my hands pressing at my throat, stifling the scream that, if it could be heard, would be my true voice.

Speak now, I said to myself, release your true feelings before it's too late. Be yourself. Take your place in the world. You are not a cosmic orphan. You have no reason to be timid. Respond as you feel. Awkwardly, crudely, vulgarly—but respond. Leave your throat open. You can have anything the world has to offer, but the thing you need most and perhaps want most is to be yourself. Stop being anonymous. The anonymity you believed would protect you from pain and humiliation, shame and rejection, doesn't work. Admit rejection, admit pain, admit frustration, admit pettiness, even that; admit shame, admit outrage, admit anything and everything that happens to you, respond with your true, uncalculated response, your emotions. The best and most human parts of you are those that you have inhibited and hidden from the world.

Work on it. Stir up the lump whenever you can. Raise your voice. Embarrass yourself. Humiliate your dear, beloved, polite wife if you must. Don't let that huge, inert lump congeal further. Cut it into small pieces, chop it into bits that can pass out of your system. Court every chance to feel.

Notice how—in your past—every time you were angry you were frightened. You have a right to anger. You don't have to earn it. Take it. Anger saves.

O N T H E way home I went to England, to spend a few days in Somerset with my friend John Steinbeck. I found him in bad shape, and I didn't know why. "I'm not sure we love each other anymore," his wife, Elaine, an honest woman, said to me. I knew that if what she said was true, it had to do not with Elaine but with John.

He wanted to go to London. On New Bond Street we went window-shopping. John was tight as a drum. He said to me, in a soft voice, as if he were dropping an unimportant piece of information, that he often thought of killing himself. He was bitter about his children, said they were shallow and selfish, that it was too late for him to help. "They're not trained as my children," he said, "and I'm not trained as their father." His work was not going well, so his life was meaningless. He was loaded with an explosive substance, self-disgust.

The next day we went shopping in earnest. John knew the best place to buy shoes. I bought a pair I didn't need and boots I have never worn. He bought a knife he didn't need. Then he told me about his life. He would have lunch with Douglas Fairbanks, Jr., say, whom he didn't really want to see; would go to a matinee, barely listening, hardly making contact with those he was with, then to tea, eating a pile of cucumber and butter sandwiches; would take a bath, fuming and tossing and scowling, then go to dinner with his publisher or agent or someone or other to whom he was indifferent, be bad-tempered all through the meal, "looking for a fight," he said; then he'd drink a quantity that would make him sleep as if drugged, the sleep being precious to him because it was the closest thing he could get to the peace of death. He knew he was not John Steinbeck anymore.

Occasionally he would take out whatever was eating him on Elaine, but she was able to defend herself, and he was too decent for this to work. I told him a little about my psychoanalysis, and he began to attack psychoanalysis violently. He said it excuses a man's actions for him instead of making him responsible for them. He told of a girl whose parents were sending her to a psychoanalyst when what she needed was a good spanking. Then he told the story of an old con. A new prisoner came up to him in the jail yard, and they fell into a conversation. The new man was elaborating on the various unfortunate incidents that led to his incarceration—the unfairness, the bad luck, the double-crossing he'd endured. The old con interrupted. "Listen, fellow," he said, "you do your time and I'll do mine." John said how gallant that was, this assumption of responsibility, this facing up to facts and debts and the truth. I don't want to hear excuses, the old con meant; I did it and I'll do my time. I knew the rules of the game and the penalties involved. I lost. I'll pay.

Then John turned to me. He said that I had to get back to myself; that was my problem, finding myself again. He said I'd become a lot of other things, including the worst thing of all, a nice guy! He said I was so busy getting people to like me and approve of me that I'd lost myself, who I was, what I wanted to be, my true identity. I'd become careless with my own desires and wishes and positions; I'd become so used to sacrificing them that I no longer knew it was happening.

Then he got onto my nickname. "That goddamn name is not you," he said. "That is not what you're like. You're not—or weren't—a handy, friendly, adaptable little gadget. You made yourself that way to get along with people, to be accepted, to become invisible—a Gadget! What a neuter nickname! Useful for everyone, except yourself!"

John's solution was: "Get mean. Get selfish. Be yourself. Find out who you are—it's the only creative source you have. Determine what you want and don't stand still for anything else. Find out what your place in the world is and claim it for your own and don't let anyone take it away. That goddamn nickname is a piece of self-effacement."

When he got through with me, he felt a lot better, and I thought him a real friend.

"IN EVERY man's life," Thomas Mann has written, "there are things which he does not reveal to everyone but only to his friends. There are also things which he does not reveal to his friends but at best to himself and only under a pledge of secrecy. And finally there are things which a man hesitates to reveal even to himself. Every decent person accumulates a considerable quantity of such things. In fact you might say that the more decent a person is, the greater the number of such things that he carries around with him."

When I started this book, I wasn't sure how far I should go in exposing what is traditionally masked. But soon I forgot that anyone but my editor was going to read what I wrote. My only inhibition has been concern about what my children would think, since I dread losing their love. There is this small comfort: I've noticed that everything in life seems to be more quickly digested and forgotten than I anticipate. Of course, my children have wondered what took place at certain well-shaded periods of our lives; they will be unpleasantly surprised at my successful duplicity in one area. Now they have to put these new, explicit revelations alongside what they know about me. The good and the bad will be seen together as one life.

I've long since relieved myself of shame about any of it. I feel that the truth is rarely told about how most of us live—not until some terrible disorder breaks out and, in the case of public figures, newspapers uncover secrets. Until then a glossy front of hypocrisy prevails; the public face is the only face. We devour gossip about others and say, "Certainly all that carrying on must be the behavior of more impeachable characters." What's told about our own lives doesn't correspond to what we prefer to believe. I have no special shame in revealing more about my life than a biographer could. I offer the first words of Rousseau's *Confessions:* "I desire to set before my fellows the likeness of a man in all the truth of his nature."

Now come the sixties, a time of the reassessment of moral values, of the alienation of friends, of the dissolution of marriages once believed "perfect," of crack-ups and the death, willed or inevitable, of so many of my friends, men and women who seemed to have no reason to kill themselves or surrender to collapse. But for me, those years, more than any others, were a time of self-confrontation.

I T W I L L read like an incident of no great moment: A theatre director is sent a play for production; he declines it, and the playwright's agent takes his client elsewhere. This happened in 1960 between Tennessee and me on his comedy *Period of Adjustment.* But the event, which should have been routine, took place when Williams was feeling competition with William Inge, who'd had four hits in a row, and at a time when I was about to do a film based on something Inge had written. Tennessee saw the incident as a rejection, a signal that I preferred working with Inge. He made me aware of his feeling that he couldn't trust anyone, not even a director to whom he'd given several great hits.

It took a struggle for me to say no to Williams. Why had it been so difficult? Did I owe him my services? Did I feel that I was once again treacherously betraying a friend? Why had it been so hard for me to walk away with an easy conscience? I'd almost been sucked into a production that I didn't want to do. I'd even felt it my duty to help him find another director, a good man, "better for the play than I would have been with my heavy hand." Why did I aspire to be such a model of trust in the New York theatre, especially now that I was less and less interested in it?

I'd now acknowledged to myself that I wished I'd never gone into the Lincoln Center Repertory Theatre project. I knew I had to see that through; I'd led too many people into it. But if I could have found an honorable way out, I would have taken it. There was also my resolve, when I came back from Europe, not to work for anyone or with anyone again.

When directing the plays of the authors whom I'd now begun to shed, I'd been their servant, and that was as it should have been. These plays had been written at the cost of a year or two of the playwrights' lives and guarded by anxious producers and jealous agents. Now I told myself that they—Tennessee with this play, for instance—needed me but that I didn't need them. I no longer gave a damn about the themes of other men; I didn't give a damn about the problems of the people in *Period of Adjustment*. How good it felt, despite the cold wind of Tennessee's disappointment, to be free. I'd felt the same way about other authors, but now I was admitting it. I no longer had to pretend to be the concerned champion of their view of life. I no longer wanted to handle the phalanx of backers and agents protecting each new play, deal with their anxieties and their hysteria, find the right actors, scenery, and costumes, and, while keeping everyone reassured, push the whole through to commercial success.

As for films, I had to make a break there too. I simply couldn't again work for Darryl or Jack Warner. If John Steinbeck had dried up, I had not. I'd come back from my travels with a strengthened conviction of what my true material was. No matter if I was a lesser talent than the men for whom I'd been working. I would go on my own now.

So I resigned—my announcement to myself—from the elite club of sought-after Broadway directors, walked away at the peak of my success. By refusing the Williams play, I was, in effect, refusing all other plays by authors of similar stature. I was abdicating from the successful career I'd made. I vowed not to look back.

PAUL OSBORN had finally agreed to write the screenplay for my Tennessee Valley Authority story, *Wild River.* It is difficult for a temporarily unemployed author to refuse a friend; working together is the best fun.

In talking to him, I discovered an astonishing thing; I'd switched sides. I'd conceived of this film years before as homage to the spirit of FDR; my hero was to be a resolute New Dealer engaged in the difficult task of convincing "reactionary" country people that it was necessary, in the name of the public good, for them to move off their land and allow themselves to be relocated. Now I found my sympathies were with the obdurate old lady who lived on the island that was to be inundated and who refused to be patriotic, or whatever it took to allow herself to be moved. I was all for her. Something more than the shreds of my liberal ideology was at work now, something truer, perhaps, and certainly stronger. While my man from Washington had the "social" right on his side, the picture I made was in sympathy with the old woman obstructing progress.

Perhaps I was beginning to feel humanly, not think ideologically. The people in my life for whom I'd felt the deepest devotions were three old-fashioned old women: my grandmother, my mother, and my schoolteacher Anna B. Shank. I no longer had a taste for liberal intellectuals. I always knew what they were going to say about any subject. I simply didn't like the reformers I'd been with since 1933, whether they were Communists or progressives or whoever else was out to change the world. I'd only believed I *should* like them. I'd followed the crowd, which during those years was going that way.

The way the reversal in the film's central emotion was carried out illustrates how drastically a director can change the meaning of a story he's chosen to tell. For instance: I had cast Montgomery Clift as the man from Washington. Spyros Skouras had urged Monty on me, and I'd resisted being influenced by the moneyman. Then I began to see how the part could be played as a rather uncertain and inept social-working intellectual from the big city, dealing with people who were stronger and more confirmed in their beliefs than he was. I'd known Monty for many years, directed him sixteen years before in *The Skin of Our Teeth*, remembered him even before that as an insecure boy who'd curl up on the floor at the foot of the chair where Molly was sitting and confide his problems to her. Molly was, for a time, his surrogate mother. Monty's sexuality was that of a child waiting for his mother to put her arms around him.

Monty had had a terrible car accident one night when he came down the hill from Elizabeth Taylor's home in Beverly Hills loaded with warm rosé wine and "steadied" by two "downers." He'd slid off the side of the narrow, winding blacktop and crashed into some concrete pillars. His head was knocked out of shape and he didn't look like Monty Clift anymore. He was no longer handsome, and there was strain everywhere in him—even, it seemed, in his effort to stand erect. As far as my story went, he'd be no match for the country people whom he'd have to convince of the "greater good," and certainly no physical match for any of them if it came to violence. Pictorially, the story would be the weak against the strong—in reverse. I accepted that readily, and reinforced the pattern with every bit of my casting.

The old lady of the island about to be covered by the man-made lake was played by one of the great character actresses of that day, Jo Van Fleet, aged thirty-seven, as difficult and dear a woman as a director in need of a performance could hope for. I'd worked with Jo in *Camino Real* and in *East of Eden*, knew her strong will and knew its purpose: to excel. Full of unconstrained violence, she'd eat Clift alive, and I was prepared to let her. No lump there. And what a professional Jo was! Whereas Clift, sleepy and shaky, had something wobbly about his appearance in the morning, Jo would barge into the makeup room at 4 a.m. and give five hours to transforming herself into an indomitable backriver matriarch. Even on days when I told her we wouldn't be coming close to her with the camera, she'd spend an hour applying the liver spots of an old woman on the backs of her hands. "Jo," I'd say, "we're not going to photograph your hands today. Get another hour's sleep." "This is not for the camera," she'd answer. "It's for me." Clift was a tenderhearted shell of a man, Jo as formidable and unyielding as the rock-ribbed country where we were working.

She was the proof of the advantage of having a fine character actress much younger than the role she plays. Jo's emotion had the intensity that generally passes as youth passes. Her makeup was a triumph, because it etched the power, rather than the literal fact, of age on her face. One of my favorite scenes in any film I made is the silent one at the end, where Jo, having been taken off her island against her will, is sitting on the front porch of the small house in town provided for her. On her lap is a bundle of her possessions, still bound by a cord. In her very small front yard, nibbling at grass, is her cow, brought from the island in a flat-bottom rowboat by a loyal black man. The audience didn't need to be informed by dialogue that the old lady would be dead within days. Jo did it without a word.

What followed in Jo's career was unhappy. She waited for roles worthy of her, but our theatre lacks opportunities for gifted older women. There is little production here of plays that might exercise their larger talents. Jo stagnated and, since she knew it, became bitter. She waited, wrote letters to producers and directors, pleaded with agents to help her, year after year to no avail. As she became more bitter, she became more difficult. Impatience soured her. This is a typical experience for many actresses of size. Mildred Dunnock was another superb actress who didn't find nearly the roles she deserved. Both these women suffered the deprivations more keenly than less sensitive artists would have. The destruction of talent in an artist destroys the person; such people are torn apart and their health is destroyed. What waste!

As for the "love interest," I cast one of the finest younger actresses I knew, Lee Remick, then at the top of her strength and confidence—but not without some official opposition. On one of my trips to the Fox studios in southern California, I'd had an absurd casting conference with the new head of production, Buddy Adler. He urged me to cast Marilyn Monroe in the role. Had he read the script? I knew Lee from *A Face in the Crowd*, and she was now an even more ravishing beauty—as well as an exceptional person. I thought her confident sense of her own worth was in part due to her marriage to a handsome and successful man, the TV producer Bill Colleran, a union generally spoken of as perfect. The contrast between her sureness and Monty's insecurity was what I wanted. In their love scenes she was dominant and Monty seemed sexually uncertain. He was. She was playing a war widow who, remembering her relationship with her dead husband gratefully, had reason to be sexually confident. And aggressive. This contrast was so strong that at first I was frustrated and disappointed. Then I decided to go with it. In one scene Monty, at the instant of arousal, slumped to the floor. I cursed him under my breath as a limp lover. Then I decided to play the scene as it happened, on the floor and at the very back of the room. I didn't move the camera closer. At twenty feet, the lovemaking seemed spontaneous and heated. Still, Lee was taking him, not vice versa. Again the accident of personality turned out to my advantage.

I'd also come to particularly respect country people because of my friendship with Barbara Loden. A "hillbilly" from the backcountry of North Carolina, Barbara had a side to her character—to go with her great sensitivity—that

Lee

Monty

Jo

was defiantly tough. She feared no man—feared only what she might, in some instant of desperation, do to herself. Barbara was as wild as the river I was making a film about.

I thought she had precisely the spirit that I was trying to capture on film, so I brought her down to Cleveland, Tennessee, where we had our production headquarters. I gave her a small part in the film—a clerk in Monty Clift's office—to justify her presence there. I noticed the first day she worked that she'd not made the slightest effort with makeup to look prettier; rather the opposite. Her hair was up tight in curlers, country style, and there was a rag of a scarf over her head. When she stood next to Monty, the contrast I was reaching for, that reverse balance of strength between him and the natives of the region, was plain to see. The picture itself told the story—as it always should.

I also had to cope with the problem about which everyone had warned me, Monty's drinking. Before agreeing to take him for the part, I'd extracted a solemn promise that he would not take a drink from the first day of work until the last. He kept his promise, surviving days of stress and physical discomfort without the help of a bottle until the very last day, when he arrived on the set swaying on his feet, then keeled over. When I got to him on the ground, he was asleep. I forgave him the lapse; I thought he'd done well by me. I knew I was handling a sick man, who was goodhearted and in no way evil. I can still recall the pathetic happy laugh that would burst out of him, then subside just as suddenly. I knew that each morning he underwent the humiliation of covering the transparent areas in his thinning hair with black makeup. As we went along, his confidence grew, and I believe he was easier to work with in films that followed. Despite all, I felt tender toward him. He was just a boy.

The worst problem I had with Monty was his dramatic coach, Mira Rostova, a dark young woman who'd been a pupil of Bobby Lewis, in whose acting class they'd met. Mira appeared on my set the first morning and took a stand behind the camera. "Ah," I said to myself, "I have a codirector." I couldn't check on what signals of approval or disapproval she was conveying to my hero, but I knew that a glance at the wrong time could make trouble for me, so I told Monty I didn't want her there and she disappeared.

Mira was a pocket Paula Strasberg. When she'd been excluded from my set, she continued, I was sure, to work with Monty at night. At least she kept him distracted until dawn, so I never inquired into what they did between "It's a wrap!" and "Makeup!" He always showed up in the morning, quivering but ready and willing, and perhaps I have her to thank.

The film that resulted from all this is one of my favorites, possibly because of its social ambivalence. Jean Renoir's famous phrase, "Everyone has his reasons," was true here. Both sides were "right." *Wild River* is also a favorite of certain French film critics; one prominent fellow went so far as to name it as one of the twenty best films of all time—which it certainly is not. Skouras and his sales force had an opposite view and treated the film deplorably, jerking it out of theatres before it had any chance to take hold and booking it thinly across the country. It was not exhibited in Europe until I staged a stormy scene in Spyros's office and shamed him. I hope the negative is safe in one of Fox's vaults, although I've heard a rumor that it was destroyed to make space for more successful films. This would not surprise me. Money makes the rules of the market, and by this rule, the film was a disaster.

N O W duplicity had become my way of life. My efforts to conceal my infidelity were minimal; I felt no guilt. My days on the set of my next film, *Splendor in the Grass*, were a revel. Out of control, I didn't care if I was found out. During every lunch break, I enjoyed my lover in her dressing room. At the end of filming the New York scenes, I was driven home in a company car and dropped off at my doorstep, and I entered 212 East 72nd Street, where Molly kept an orderly home. Dinner was at seven; a maid served it. Molly disliked her mother, but the dinner ritual she established in our home was not different from that of her mother's home. After the meal Molly read Mark Twain to the two younger children. It was a life without excess or indiscretion. I'd become accustomed to this two-faced existence and didn't think it out of the ordinary; in fact, it seemed "normal" to me. I'd climb upstairs to our double bed and, exhausted by my long day, fall asleep.

These weeks were exhilarating both because I enjoyed the work and because of the pitch of desire I was riding by day. My evenings were restorative, restful and secure. I did truly love my wife. That a part of our initial relationship was no longer there did not mean that I should leave her—not for anybody. The best part of it—for me at least—was still there. If I had not schooled with people who believed in puritanical principles of correct behavior, if I'd been living in another country at another time, I wouldn't have questioned my way of life, not for a minute.

I have a friend, a filmmaker, who, when he learned that his wife had taken a lover, did not leave her; he congratulated her and bought the happy couple a house, where they could see each other privately. When the lovers cooled, husband and wife were reunited, and are making films together again.

Here's how making the film *Splendor in the Grass* came about. During the production of *The Dark at the Top of the Stairs*, when Inge and I had grown to like each other, I dropped a casual remark that we might someday make a film together and asked if he had any material for a good screenplay. He told me a story of a couple of high school kids in Independence, Kansas, where he'd lived, and I said let's do it. He produced a novelette and I made it into the screenplay for which he was to win an Academy Award. He'd

done some fussing with the scenes, and some of the dialogue he added was good and some not necessary; photographed action would tell most of it. His story had the one essential, an excellent flow of incident to a true conclusion. Bill was an accomplished storyteller; it's a special talent. But I also knew how much I'd contributed, and this gave me the confidence in writing that I'd lacked until then. I was ready to try my own story.

There was another perfect marriage on this set. Natalie Wood and Robert Wagner were often billed as Hollywood's most loving couple, and in their case that tabloid headline was based on truth. Possibly the fever I'd stirred up on my stage got to Natalie; the atmosphere was intoxicating. She had love scenes with Warren Beatty. Natalie had been declared "washed up" by the sages of the film community; now she saw an exciting future opening for her, partly through an association with Warren Beatty. Sexual notoriety is one of the most attractive colors a movie star can wear. It was clear to Natalie, as it was to me, that Warren was bound for the top; this perception was an aphrodisiac.

When Natalie was first suggested to me, I backed off. I didn't want a "washed-up child star." But when I saw her, I detected behind the well-mannered "young wife" front a desperate twinkle in her eyes. I knew there was an unsatisfied hunger there. I became interested—professionally. But I didn't immediately reveal my interest to her bosses at Warner Brothers, who had her under contract. They pressed me to take her, told me they had no parts "penciled in" for her and that she could be had "cheap." I saw that they'd be glad to have someone else take over part of her salary and possibly "bring her back" as an asset to the company. I talked with her more quietly then and more personally. I wanted to find out what human material was there, what her inner life was. I saw that she was a restless "chick" who reminded me of the "bad" girls in high school who looked like "good" girls. I remembered that kind and how they'd have nothing to do with me, only with the big "letter men," like Warren Beatty. My memory assured me she was perfect for the part. I could see that the crisis in her career was preparing her for a crisis in her personal life. Then she told me she was being psychoanalyzed. That did it. Poor R.J., I said to myself. I liked Bob Wagner. I still do.

I doubt if movie stars can truly experience what they sing songs about and what they act out on the screen, true love and so on. I've rarely observed this feeling lasting for any time in a star—certainly not with the intensity they devote to their careers. It's probably inevitable that the careers are more important to them. Why not? They *are* more important. In most cases, the advent of children causes an irksome problem of finding nurses, au pair girls, baby-sitters, tutors, and a corps of doctors, each for a different part of the body. Then there's the business of furnishing a nursery and showing it off to their friends and to the press. Well, an interior decorator can take care of that. But the protestations of love and concern that these parents make to interviewers is bullshit. Their affairs of passion are trains that rush along parallel tracks for a time, then bifork. Warren? To be in love with Warren Beatty! What girl can run that fast? And why use the word "love?" Warren—it was obvious the first time I saw him—wanted it all and wanted it his way. Why not? He had the energy, a very keen intelligence, and more chutzpah than any Jew I've ever known. Even more than me. Bright as they come, intrepid, and with that thing all women secretly respect: complete confidence in his sexual powers, confidence so great that he never had to advertise himself, even by hints.

All of a sudden, he and Natalie became lovers. When did it happen? When I wasn't looking. I wasn't sorry; it helped their love scenes. My only regret was the pain it was causing R.J. His sexual humiliation was public. A goodhearted man, always decent, he stood by for a time, being patient, as love experts advise; then he disappeared. Where? To wherever rejected husbands go. In time they were to remarry and again become the perfect couple.

The film rushed on—its momentum uninterrupted, but rather spurred on by what was happening in the wings. My friend Barbara, who played Warren Beatty's sister, was a little bitchy and occasionally a pain in the ass—as well as a pleasure there. Warren was a little "snotty"—I don't know a better word for how he behaved and can't find one in my thesaurus—but he was to grow into a formidable man. They were both more edgy and less placable, because they were more talented. I enjoyed them. The film itself was easy to direct; the scenes Bill wrote were the simplest I'd ever done.

Warren and Barbara

People came together, spoke to each other, a point was made, an issue decided, quietly and meaningfully. Then they parted and the story went on. That was Bill's talent.

THERE is a scene in this film where the character Natalie played tries, in her desperation, to drown herself in a lake. Some days before this scene was scheduled, Natalie took me aside and explained to me that she had a terror of water, particularly dark water, and of being helpless in it. Of course, I thought how perfect for the scene she had to play, but I reassured her. The next day she told me that the fear would paralyze her in the water of the small lake I'd chosen, and she wasn't sure she could play the scene. Couldn't we do it in a studio tank? I assured her it was a very shallow lake and that her feet would always be close to the bottom. She said that even if her feet were *on* the bottom, she'd be in a panic of fear about it. So I asked my assistant, Charlie Maguire, to get into the water with her, just out of camera range, while she played the scene of struggling to save herself. This didn't entirely reassure her, but she did the scene and did it well—then clutched Charlie. "Cut!" I cried. On dry land she continued to shake with fear, then laughed hysterically, with relief.

Years later I was to remember Natalie's problem with that scene when I read the newspaper accounts of her death. "The actress may have been panicked, missed a step and slipped into the water while trying to board the yacht's dinghy. . . . About midnight, a woman in a boat anchored nearby heard someone calling from the darkness, 'Help me! Somebody help me!'"

The name of the yacht from which she'd stepped into the dark water was *The Splendour.*

THE FILM was a typical Bill Inge work, a soap opera until suddenly it appears there is a little more depth and humanity there, as well as a balanced view of life. That "little more" was what gave our film its distinction. Along with *Wild River*, it is a favorite film of certain French critics and admired there more than my other films. I suppose the reason is that the French are the most middle-class of all people—even the working class there are bourgeois—and enjoy those substantial benefits of home, table, and bank account. Inge's story is about a simple struggle of right, wrong, and social disgrace, of what is practical in life and what is best for property and family. It is not my favorite of my films, but the last reel is my favorite last reel, at once the saddest and the happiest. Natalie, just released from an institution and declared sound again, visits her old love—Warren—in the hope that their relationship might be revived. She discovers that he is married, leading a life that's far reduced from the station his father had envisioned for him, with a rather plain wife who is beginning to raise a family.

What I like about this ending is its bittersweet ambivalence, full of what Bill had learned from his own life: that you have to accept limited happiness, because all happiness is limited, and that to expect perfection is the most neurotic thing of all; you must live with the sadness as well as with the joy. Perhaps this theme rings so true because Bill himself had come to a point where he had settled for less, a place not in the first rank of playwrights along with O'Neill, Williams, and Miller but on an honorable sub-platform where—damn the praise, damn their prizes—the work would be its own reward; he realized that he'd find peace only if he sought goals within the reach of what talent he had and didn't hope for miracles.

Or am I talking about myself?

I'V E acquired contradictory reputations over the years: aloof and social, secretive but open-faced, agreeable or cantankerous, concerned, indifferent, generous, cheap, given to unannounced appearances and to sudden disappearances. The reputation I'd rather not have picked up is for being a betrayer of trust. I haven't liked that. I believe it unjust.

But there are reasons for it. Like many of you, I've worn the friendship mask; I often look friendlier than I feel. But then, when I have what I sought, the mask would clatter to the ground, and what I truly am would be revealed. From time to time, I do what no one is prepared for; then someone is hurt or insulted or abandoned or simply puzzled. I let people come skin-close, until they trust me entirely and feel sure that I like them. But when the need is eased, the production opened, the seduction completed, I back away, suddenly become cool and remote, and those I've lured close don't know what happened. For years I declared myself an ardent liberal in politics, made all the popular declarations of faith, but the truth was—and is—that I am, like most of you, a bourgeois. I go along disarming people, but when it gets to a crunch, I am revealed to be a person interested only in what most artists are interested in, himself. I come on as a guy you can trust, but I'm just an ordinary, searching-surviving get-alongnik, who doesn't like to be crossed, never forgives an insult, and, despite the ready smile, is angry a lot of the time—or at least looks angry, for reasons that are never quite clear. So I can't blame people for what they think of me.

Now I'm out to do a little housecleaning.

As you've noticed, I save everything. Be careful what you write me! Among the items I've rediscovered while working on this book was a recording of a talk Lee Strasberg gave at the year's-end get-together of the Actors Studio in June 1961. Although I wasn't in the room that day, the entire speech was aimed at me. Lee, who'd known me for thirty years, invariably referred to me as "Mr. Kazan," which was both a put-down and a compliment, since it raised me to the same platform if not financial level as John Rockefeller III. Lee said I'd betrayed his best hopes and those of the loyal actors in the room by accepting the post of coproducing director of the repertory theatre at Lincoln Center despite the fact that he and the body of the Studio's personnel had not been invited to be part of that venture. Lee spoke with strong but contained emotion that day, and what he said to the actors—us against the world!—reminded me of his talks to the Group Theatre thirty years before and awoke feelings in me that had been long asleep. There were Lee's familiar tribalisms—he called the actors "the people," as though they were en masse crossing the desert to escape from Egypt—and he began a section of his talk with a line Yogi Berra might have spoken: "In the first place there are two things." But the hurt behind the words was genuine and, since it was covered with pride, affecting. He was wildly applauded by the actors when he said that the Lincoln Center people had made a serious mistake by not accepting the Studio as its production arm and expressed disappointment that I had not sufficiently insisted that it must. I'd let the Studio down—that was his text. I'd betrayed his trust. When I listened to the recording of this speech twenty-five years later, I realized what a terrible disappointment it must have been for this man to be insufficiently supported by someone he'd trained and trusted, myself, and then to be muscled out, no matter how gently, from a plan to set up the kind of theatre he'd worked all his life training actors for. When I heard his speech, I felt for him.

Here's another souvenir I uncovered from that time, a letter I wrote to George Woods, the watchdog of the corporate arm of the Repertory Theatre and a man close to and trusted by the Rockefellers. "Dear George," I wrote, "we feel a mistake was made when the school [for actors] was given to the Juilliard." Then I gave my reasons and concluded with: "We ask that the school of Drama be taken away from the Juilliard and given to the Repertory Theatre."

It was there that I believed I could succeed in involving Lee and the program of work we had at the Studio. What I did not know when I wrote that letter was that the top committee of Lincoln Center had long before decided on the Juilliard for their acting school and was not looking for leadership personnel, because they'd decided on Michel Saint-Denis. He was to determine the nature of the training and organize a school for it. Michel was touring the country to familiarize himself with the training being done in various theatre centers.

George Woods never answered my letter.

But even if the Rockefeller people had heeded my request, the post I was asking for was not what Lee wanted or even—for some reason—expected. He believed himself the most qualified person in this country to guide the course of a repertory theatre. He thought of me as the best functionary under him, the energy source to do the heavy work. That's the way Lee saw it, and that was the hope that was being frustrated when he made his speech to the actors.

In this situation Lee was right; I hadn't tried as hard as I might have to get him the post he thought he should have had, and the reason I didn't was that I didn't believe Lee was qualified to be a producing director. A teacher, yes, although there were at least two other teachers whom I esteemed as highly. When Lee suggested that the Studio should be the practicing arm of the Lincoln Center complex, it meant that he and Cheryl Crawford should be the producers and I Vulcan to their Jupiter and Juno. But we were far past that possibility. The man the Rockefeller group had selected for producing director was not me but Robert Whitehead. I was there because Bob wanted me. Given that, what Lee must have expected from me was to resign from the Repertory Theatre in moral and artistic indignation, thereby giving the Rockefellers an ultimatum: They couldn't have me unless they took Lee. That was an arm twist I didn't choose to make.

I'd arranged a meeting with John Rockefeller and a few of his lieutenants, so that Lee could offer his point of view directly. I was out of the country at the time, but I heard about the discussion. Lee was in the glory of his pride, instructing Rockefeller that if he hoped to have a theatre in his Center, the first person he should have consulted was Lee Strasberg, because Lee and no one else grasped the artistic problems and their solutions. To do five plays with a company of twenty-five actors, he declared, was an absurd idea. This was true, but then he offered his alternative, a "floating company," drawing actors as they were needed from the Actors Studio. There was a vast reservoir of talent there, he said, that didn't need contracts. "And they're all stars on the outside."

"The outside" is a phrase he used frequently. In the thirties it referred to anyone not in the Group Theatre, afterward to anyone not from the Actors Studio. Lee was to test his theory of organization—the "floating company"—later.

Whatever John Rockefeller thought of Lee's contentions—and his passion—he was too polite to respond plainly. I can see Rockefeller concluding the meeting with his gentle smile and his missionary-among-the-natives manner, so that Lee would not realize until later that this was the end of his hope that the Repertory Theatre would include him or his "floating company" of Actors Studio stars. What seemed like truth and pride to Lee came over as arrogance and bumptiousness to the Baptist banker. He allowed Lee's fiery speech to die of its own weight. Silence was John's answer.

Perhaps the main alienating factor was the simplest: John and his people and Lee and his were from different animal tribes. Bob Whitehead could get along with the Lincoln Center brass—for a time—and I am adaptable or seem so. But in the end we didn't fit, either of us—not Bob, not I. At least Bob was a man who dressed like the men around John, behaved like them, and talked with the same controlled and modest-seeming manner. And I'd had four years at Williams and learned how to tie a tie. Lee was immediately marked as a man given to excessive statements, and the committee members around John found this offensive and in some way alien. They felt bullied by a foreigner. Lee sensed their reaction—but vaguely; when no response was offered him following this meeting, he was surprised and shocked.

So the truth was the one Lee stated in the recorded speech I've quoted. I didn't try to get Lee the post he believed he deserved, but sought only a post I believed he was suited for. I didn't resign, as he doubtless would have wished. I didn't believe in him as an equal partner or as a producer, or want him as a standby adviser or as an overlord, however benign. Nor did I feel that Cheryl Crawford had the "guns" to match those of George Woods. It turned out that neither Bob nor I had guns of that caliber.

So the "betrayal," as Lee saw it, did take place, and he was left out in the cold. But it was because I made a hardheaded judgment—one that I know was correct.

Lee had a criticism of Bob and me, which proved to be valid. He said that a true theatre has to have a unified approach set by its artistic leaders— clear goals and a basic theme. He was to say that Bob and I didn't have one, and looking back, I believe he was right. It was a critical issue on which I failed from the beginning. We had no face. We hadn't made up our minds who we were going to be, rather tried to be everything for everybody. Nor did our production program grow out of our personalities. The result was that we wobbled from side to side, and nobody knew who we were. Neither of us was firm, clear, and final about the kind of theatre we were planning to be, and so there was a general fuzzy air to what we were doing. No more than a person can a theatre be everything to everybody. When it tries, it becomes nothing.

Bob made a serious mistake at the very beginning, and that was when he chose me to be his coproducing director. Not because I had less talent than other available directors; I had more; but because my training had been entirely in the psychological realism of the Group Theatre. That is all I'd learned, all I truly understood, and until then, all I really cared about. I was perfectly suited to "realize" the works of Miller and Inge, Williams and Anderson, and could even stretch a bit for MacLeish. But I had no training or capability to do what the Lincoln Center people had a right to expect of me or what Bob Whitehead himself hoped for. The attempts I made at putting on an Elizabethan play or, years later, my own dramatization of a Greek tragedy were disasters. I am not catholic in my tastes, and my talent's range is not wide. It has, on occasion, been deep—within my limitations. I like only what I like. I believe Bob chose me because I'd been of help to some contemporary playwrights, because actors generally liked working with me and responded to my direction, and because I'd had a long string of hits—rather those reasons than my suitability for the Repertory Theatre job. The only kinds of plays I was expert at directing were— to borrow a phrase from the Russians—plays of social realism. Perhaps given time and the opportunity, perhaps if I'd wanted to make the effort, I might have learned to extend my range. Also, perhaps not. In the meantime, audiences, sponsors, and actors had a right to expect more of the coproducing director of a theatre aspiring to be our national theatre than I was able to provide. Furthermore, as an administrator I was hopeless. In offices, I get headaches.

To complete the unhappy story, the actors I chose from my personal preferences were not the best ones to make possible a great variety of productions. Some of our very talented actresses had difficulty carrying a speech longer than two sentences; they were suited to films, in which a roaming microphone would pick up whispers. Still I plunged ahead with Bob and cast Miller's *After the Fall*. But by choosing actors because they suited this work, we immediately limited our program to the contemporary. Possibly we should have accepted that limitation—made that our "face"— rather than attempting plays like *The Changeling*. At the least we should have allowed time for training our actors—and myself—and not tried to produce in a style other than contemporary realism without adding a different kind of actor to our company to carry most of the load.

British actors seem able to bridge this gap; our actors, particularly those I like, cannot. Lee would talk about the wonderful Shakespeare scenes he'd seen in his classes, but what I saw there did not impress me. We never really succeeded in wedding the necessary vocal force, clarity of speech,

dexterity with words, and love of the language to the emotional techniques
of the Stanislavski-Strasberg method. The only solution I could think of is
the one Joe Papp found: He based his program on contemporary American
authors and, when he moved beyond that range, engaged actors who had
the necessary qualifications. But he was not trying to create a permanent
company; we were. When I worked with Actors Studio members in the
kind of play that was outside their habitude, I found them terribly limited.
Let me say it before you do: This may have been my limitation at least as
much as it was theirs. We all needed to be trained—I as much as anyone—
in the techniques of what's called "style."

In any case, Bob's choice of me did not help the Repertory Theatre. I
was not the man to solve this problem. We were to be heavily criticized,
Bob and I, and neither of us, in the end, thought we did too well; but both
of us believe—we still do—that if we'd been given the time and the support, we might have found our genuine identity and created an acting company to suit. Time is what we needed, and this kind of leeway we never
got; so whatever it was that we learned, we never put to use.

I'VE just come back from a short vacation in Paris, where a friend suggested we pay a visit to the theatre of Patrice Chereau in Nanterre. This
town is a bedroom community for the middle class and close enough to
Paris so theatre lovers can make the trip after their workday. The theatre
building there is large and low and without a clear shape; it contains two
theatres, several rehearsal rooms, a workshop for building scenery, another
for costumes, and it was put up, box by box, as the money became available. The roof of the structure is flat; the theatre has no "flies," since it
wasn't intended as a theatre where scenery would be "flown," as it is in
traditional houses. The interior has a pleasant spread, contains a modest
restaurant and a sizable bookstore. There is an air of ease about the place,
a lack of pretentiousness; Lincoln Center, by contrast, is all pretension.
Work comes first at Nanterre. When I saw it I immediately said to myself,
"This is what we should have had."

But the fact is we did. We did have it. It was called the ANTA Washington Square Theatre.

Bob and I took on our jobs at a time when Rockefeller's committee had
just approved Eero Saarinen's final plans for the theatre to be named after
its wealthy patron, Mrs. Vivian Beaumont, and we were told that it would
be two years, at least, before we could begin to work there. Bob thought
this delay would be harmful, so rather than wait for the Beaumont, he
planned and caused to be put up a temporary theatre in Washington
Square, financed independently, on land that New York University loaned
us. I believe that what Bob did was the greatest achievement of our two

years with Lincoln Center. It was also the cause of persisting resentment of Bob by George Woods, the strong boy of the Lincoln Center committee, since Bob had it put up and financed it over Woods's objections.

Bob's theatre consisted of a geodesic dome pitched over a hole in the ground, the auditorium slanting in a gentle slope to the open stage. The roof was sustained by prefitted support pieces of light steel. The building was utterly functional. It was not our intention to have "flats," which had to be flown up and down to provide background for the action; instead we wanted environment within which the action would take place. That theatre was a perfect expression of what we intended to do uptown at Lincoln Center, and of course we should have stayed there and persevered in our intention. And since we couldn't do that, because of New York University's building program, we should have sought other quarters in the same style, as unpretentious and as inexpensive to operate—and above all, in the same spirit.

But we didn't. As we were preparing to produce Art Miller's play downtown, we helped plan the Vivian Beaumont Theatre uptown—its interior and its stage.

A building of any kind expresses not only the requirements and perhaps the character of a client but also the architect's feelings about the culture of his day. We can see in the pyramids, the complex of buildings at Delphi, the cathedral at Chartres, St. Peter's in Rome, a Mayan temple in Guatemala, and the twin towers of our World Trade Center how different those cultures are and what are their basic values. Lincoln Center with its opulence reflects the tastes and ideals of the kind of upper-middle-class person who goes to the opening of the opera each fall dressed in the costume head-

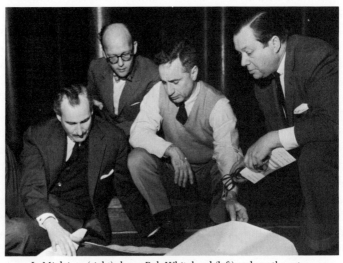

Jo Mielziner (right) shows Bob Whitehead (left) and me the set.

waiters wear. The two Chagalls hang like trophies in the opera house, their details out of all scale with the place. "America can buy the best!" might be the motto there. "Culture is good business!" is also being promoted. We hoped there would be a contrast between the pretentiousness of the outside of our building and what was offered within. The stage we planned with our designer, Jo Mielziner, was a demand we were making on ourselves for a more imaginative program of production. We wanted a stage that would help impel us to braver work by its design and its placement in relation to the audience. Determined to change our production habits, we planned to make more traditional productions impossible.

In Nanterre I saw Patrice Chereau's rendering of a Marivaux play, *La Fausse Suivante*. It was performed on a "space stage," where the movements of actors were not confined by realistic decor. We in the audience were as far from the movies as we could be taken. Theatre here was a different art. It regained its preeminence and made ninety percent of films seem boring and banal. This kind of nonrealistic set, a sweeping ramp on one side, a few set pieces on the other, permitted the actors eloquent and free movement, movement that came from their emotional impulses. Perhaps the theatre at its best is not realistic. With the Greeks, with Molière, with Shakespeare, with Vakhtangov and Meyerhold and Brecht, it has never been. At Nanterre, everything that is lovely and imaginative and surprising in theatre existed. The scenes were danced as well as played. Barriers of wood and canvas did not exist to confine extravagant and expressive direction of actors. Ballet and theatre were married. Leave realism to documentary films.

When I saw this production I knew that Bob and I should have tried to move our efforts to a neighborhood of people like ourselves, our natural audience; and that we should have kept the scale of our costs and consequently the price of tickets at the level that Chereau was able to maintain at Nanterre. What kind of theatre can there be where the price of good seats is forty-five or fifty-five dollars per? Answer: an expense account theatre.

But we went on planning the Beaumont, watched it rise. By the time it was up, my own life's course had changed, and much of Bob's energy had been expended in his defending himself against the attacks of George Woods. My own work as a director had been miserable, and within two years both Bob and I had been boxed out. What we'd planned so carefully and worked on for so long was passed on to others, who couldn't help being bewildered by what we'd handed down. Now Jo Mielziner is dead, Eero Saarinen is dead, John Rockefeller and George Woods are dead, and Bob and I rarely see each other. The story of our building is the story of Lincoln Center, an art administrated by real estate operators and bankers who demand, not effort in a new direction, but reliable returns on an investment and proof against costs, and who have neither the patience nor the money to give to people who might be trying to create a new kind of theatre, nor the time they need to find their way.

The exterior of the Vivian Beaumont when I walk past it now reminds me of the tomb of a Japanese emperor.

Y O U'V E noticed that I'm obsessed with death, the subject. I'm typing these words in the middle of my seventy-eighth year, so my interest is a natural one. Have you found my going on and on about it neurotic? Or merely laughable? I, too. Both. An old friend, now dead, once said, "I open *The New York Times* to the obituary page every morning to see if I died during the night." Death tells a secret: At the moment of death a person learns the bad news about his life. Or comes to see what was most important to him that he ignored.

Have you read Tolstoi's *The Death of Ivan Ilyich?* If you have, you'll remember the question that is the story's theme. Ivan Ilyich, as he dies, begins to believe that "he had not spent his life as he should have." It occurred to him that his scarcely perceptible attempts to struggle against what was considered good by the most highly placed people, those scarcely noticeable impulses within that he had immediately suppressed, might have been the real thing and all the rest false. "All you have lived for," he says to himself, "and still live for is falsehood and deception, hiding life and death from you."

How a person dies may be the most characteristic thing in his or her life.

I'V E had some distressing news about myself, the first hints of what lies ahead, the erosion of certain common powers, particularly my memory. I pass an actor on the street, one I know I directed in a production, and I can't remember his name. Sometimes I remember the name of the part he played but not his name. Or pass an old lover—this is humiliating—and not know how to address her. Is that simply a matter of indifference at the end of life? I prefer that explanation.

I've been having throbbing headaches too, frightening because I don't know what brings them on. So I've been beginning to feel the cold wind Time makes as it rushes by. Heeding those warnings, I've determined to live what is left of my life on the precipice—that is, recklessly. The word "reckless" can be defined as "without concern for the consequences." I believe writing this book this way is reckless. Since I don't ask for your forgiveness or even your understanding, I will not try to explain or excuse certain features of my conduct that are coming up. Here are only the facts.

I've had several times in my life, usually in the spring of the year, that I recall as perfect. One was the night in May of 1932 when I first came together with Molly. It was in a field along the edge of a lake, under a lopsided moon, and it was close to midnight. I can never forget that night and how, in a few minutes, it changed my life. Another such time was in the coldest weeks of winter, when I was first with my present wife, Frances; I used to walk from my house on West Sixty-eighth Street near the park to her apartment on Ninetieth Street and Riverside Drive. The wind off the North River cut me like a knife, but I didn't mind. In the morning I'd walk back—it was even colder—and I remember saying to myself as I returned home from our hours together, "I'm in heaven!" If "heaven" has a meaning, that is it.

But I can't say that I've ever had a happier spring, altogether, than that of 1960. I'd rented his Sixty-fifth Street apartment from Budd Schulberg, and I'd get there early in the morning and write. I was working on the script about my uncle's journey from Kayseri to America; it would be the basis for the film *America America*. I'd work all morning, then Barbara would bring me some lunch. I'd tell her how the work had gone that day, which was usually well, and how pleased I was with the change I was beginning to make in my profession, and that I'd experienced for the first time pride in something I'd written. I was actually beginning to believe that I might one day become a writer—at least a screenwriter—because I could feel this screenplay growing under my hand. Then I'd tell her again how grateful I was for the encouragement she'd given me when I needed it most. We'd make love and I'd usually nap afterward—Anatolians always do this; after dinner too. Usually when I woke she'd be gone, and I'd wash and dress like a good middle-class boy. And I'd become my other self.

About three, when the Lincoln Center heavyweights had returned from their "working lunches," I'd return to my involvement there. John the Baptist and his good souls would be debating dollars in dulcet tones. Oh, God, they were a polite bunch! They were dressed in the best possible taste, traditional Ivy, as they planned what was to be the Beaumont. I sat through those meetings only half present; they seemed irrelevant to my genuine interest, which was my screenplay. Something kept telling me, "Walk away and don't look back," but I was a dutiful boy and I didn't. I tried to make everything work together.

Late that spring, at the same time that Lee was expressing his outrage against me for defecting—that's what he called it—to Lincoln Center, and at the very time that I was being called a traitor by some of the actors in the Studio, I was having one hell of a good time, and I don't mean only because of Barbara and the lovemaking, but because I could see that I might someday really get to be what I most wanted to be. I was becoming an independent artist, and this was in contrast to my previous life, when I'd wait for some playwright or producer to offer me a play or a film to direct. You see the difference?

That was the happiest spring of my life.

When the screenplay was finished, I showed it to Molly, with some trepidation. She liked it! "This could be published," she said. I remember her voice saying that. Months later, when I was in Greece and Turkey, photographing the screenplay, she and Sol Stein got together; he was starting his publishing house at that time, and the first book he published was *America America*, which he and Molly, by some deft additions and a few explanations, had made into a book to be read.

B A R B A R A told me she was pregnant.

There are certain common rules of human behavior I believe in and others I don't. Barbara had been with me, devoted and loving, for a long time. She'd been the only one who'd encouraged me in my screenplay writing. She wanted a child desperately, had tried for years without success. She wanted the child that she'd begun to carry. Perhaps I could have stopped her, but I didn't. I didn't see whose business it finally was except ours, and I've never regretted having that "love" child. Having endured difficulties more trying than those of the ordinary boy, he's now becoming an exceptional man.

Some people close to me have believed that Barbara "trapped" me. For what? A meal ticket? So what? Didn't I owe something to the person who'd encouraged me and stood by me? What greater gift can we give each other than encouragement when it's most needed? And support? If you truly examine your own life, you'll doubtless find that the most enduring bonds are those of ties stronger than the legalities. I've never regretted telling Barbara that if she wanted the child it was all right with me. Knowing my nature, wouldn't you say she was taking a riskier chance than I was? The difficulties we were to encounter, all three of us—were they more difficult than the usual difficulties of marriage and of life? Of childbirth and of rearing offspring?

But the morality of the matter? Don't talk to me about that. I've seen too much not to doubt conventional standards of morality. I'm aware of the general hypocrisy in our society: one face, another reality.

S O I went all the way and opted for chaos and for pleasure. I took Barbara to Turkey. I felt she'd earned the trip. I knew I'd be photographed the instant I stepped off the plane at the Istanbul airport, but I seemed to be insensible to caution. Did I want to tear my life apart, reorder my world? Wasn't I concerned about consequences?

It started as comedy. Driving into the *kentron* of Kayseri, where blocks of ice cut from the summit of Mount Argaeus were still being sold from the back of a wagon, we were met by a policeman, who insisted on driving us to the office of the new mayor. There I introduced Barbara as a friend and professional colleague, but he took her to be a movie star, because she wore dark glasses and covered blond curls with a silk scarf. At the moment she wanted a bathroom, but we had to act at ease through a prolonged visit with His Honor, during which several prominent citizens came visiting, whether summoned or not I couldn't tell. At regular intervals, small cups of muddy black coffee were hustled to us, pistachios dyed red were passed, and the mayor offered us a silver saucer containing cloves. "For the breath," he said.

No one knew what to talk about, so I asked about my old friend Osman Kavundju, the former mayor of Kayseri, the person I was·most anxious to see. Everyone was vague about where Osman was—probably in Ankara, one man said; no, more like Istanbul, said another, although Osman often went to Izmir, even though his favorite city was Antalya, "because he liked the girls there best."

The memory of this feisty superfly made me laugh. I felt brotherly toward him, and oddly connected.

When I laughed, others joined in, but not the mayor. He made a sound "Shhutt!" and a signal with his hand to get off that subject. His face was stern, even threatening. And I felt threatened.

No one spoke. In the silence I got an urgent look from Barbara, and breaking the rules of Oriental hospitality, I stood up and, speaking in Turkish, informed the mayor that Barbara had need of the facilities of our hotel's bathroom. I thought we might shake him off with this, but he assured me he'd accompany us to the hotel, inspect our room to make sure it was "correct" in all details, and if it was not, find us another accommodation, suitable for our station. I said that I was honored by his solicitude—what else could I say?—then, smiling, said, "Haydeh gedek," which means "Let's go!" and is a call used to spur on a recalcitrant donkey.

We went to the hotel in two cars followed by two more, containing newspapermen and cameramen. Again speaking privately to the mayor, I asked him whether for reasons of personal preference we could be relieved of the flattering attention of photographers. I intimated that guzel Barbara (guzel is "beautiful"; he'd repeatedly called her that) was not legally tied to me, which gave him the cue to behave like a man of the world. She would feel much more at home, I said, if her companionship with me was not publicly proclaimed. With this the mayor stopped our caravan of four, leaped out of our car, and bustled back to the one containing the photographers. I heard a great deal of shouting and saw that a crowd was gathering. His scolding was effective, and we proceeded without our tail, but of course this was about as foolish a move as I could have made, because it was sure to turn what I wanted hidden into prime public gossip.

Once shown our hotel room, which was one flight up from the street, the mayor seemed about to linger, but guzel Barbara came out from behind her dark glasses and said that the room, which the mayor had said was unworthy of us, was satisfactory to her, and what she'd appreciate most now was a hot bath and a long sleep. He looked at her, smiled knowingly, expressed a hope that there was hot water, and kissed her hand. I accompanied him to his car. As we said goodbye, he put his arm around me, dropped his voice a bit, and said, "My grandfather was also an old-fashioned man. He also had two wives."

The Japanese, the Mexicans, and the Turks are alike; they alternate between an elaborate docility and uncontrolled violence. They humble themselves before authority, then break loose in demonstrations of anger beyond bounds. Watch a Mexican in a bar, see him greet a pal with a huge *abrazo*, two arms tight around his back, then not long afterward you may notice that he is close to killing this same friend. Why? A careless word, an imagined insult. When are the Turks going to respect human rights? When will they give up police rule? I doubt whether this will happen for many years. They are a dangerous people, and the honor of their males always seems to be on trial; their courage has to be publicly reestablished again and again. They need to show the world that they cannot be intimidated; still they fear their authority figures, and they damned well should, not because they elect them but because those with power will suddenly and unexpectedly use ultimate force over their subjects. When a Turk bends his head in obedience, that is the time to watch out.

That night, one of the photographers who'd been ordered off our tails put a ladder against the side of our building. Barbara, who slept lightly, heard a sound, woke, and pointed. There outside our window was a man with a camera, preparing to get a "news shot." As she pointed she ducked under the sheet—just in time. A flash went off, and I rushed out of bed. The man dropped from the ladder and was gone. The next morning I went to see the mayor and made a complaint in a form a Turk would understand. "I am going back to Ankara this afternoon," I said, "and tell the newspapers that you don't seem to have the necessary force to control your own people." And so on, all rendered in a hysterical tone of voice that I would not have used in our country. Within the time needed to bring us another coffee, that photographer had been dragged into the mayor's office, terrified, and been humbled until, in the most pitiful way, he was begging for my pardon. "It's only because you're such a great man," he said. "How often do we see you here?" The mayor promised me absolute protection from then on and sent flowers to *guzel* Barbara. "Oh, what a garden of beauty your country must be," he said. "Paradise!"

W A S she that *guzel?* It was years ago, and I can't remember. They all look beautiful when their eyes light up. When she looked at me during those first years, hers did. The first time I saw her, something bold and out of the ordinary about her struck me. She showed up at a re-recording session for my film *A Face in the Crowd.* I didn't know what her purpose was, hanging around there; I was her purpose. I was to find out that Barbara would hunt just the way a man does. At Reeves, the audio studio where I was finishing the film, I got restless and reckless at the end of the afternoon and followed her into the lounge of the ladies' room. Everybody was going home, and the place was empty. I pressed her hard. She said no decent woman does it the first time she meets a man—an estimable moral principle—but to ask her next time I saw her. I said I would and did.

Was she that irresistible? A film director, after all, is surrounded by nubile girls. They all have short noses that turn up a little at the end, firmly held breasts, and tight little asses. That's not the point, though; that's standard equipment. What's described and illustrated in *Vogue* magazine and *Harper's Bazaar* quickly wears thin; as a lure, it lasts about two weeks. There was something mysterious about Barbara's appeal, and it had to do with memories, the reappearance, in the person of this young woman, of those taunting girls I'd served spiked punch to at Williams College house parties, dreamed about later, and seen again the next morning, flung out on the floor, asleep, a sight at which my flesh tingled as if ants were walking across my body. Constance had been such a reincarnation, and here it was again, giving me certain signs and signals that I recognized, for they are the signs and signals that all girls know how to give without tutoring. When I followed her into the ladies' lounge and she said, "Not so quick," I took it as a promissory note—which it was. With her I broke all the rules of decent behavior. I'd decided by then that the worst thing was to live in regret.

But there was something else about her, something that kept me more than casually interested. It was what I found out about her when I worked with her: the special intensity of the girl, the tough hide—I'm talking about her spirit—the ability to rebound off a setback and come back to try harder, to suffer any and all rejection. There was a hardness there—she made her own rules—and with it, an honesty. I liked her less than I was intrigued with her, but I also liked her. Yes, she was being aggressive with me, she was offering herself for my interest, and her directness about this shocked me, but I thought it honest that year of my life. I was in a devil-may-care mood that year.

When the new mayor of Kayseri had put his protection around us—and offered us a jeep—we proceeded immediately to Germeer, the town that had started in the side of a cliff and come down to the plain below. I had my camera and Barbara held pad and pen; and she proved to be a great assistant. Once she had put aside the dark glasses of glamour and pulled her hair straight back and bound it, she looked quite ordinary, and the people who lived in the ruins of my family's old hometown didn't know anything about the Hollywood look and paid attention only to me. Barbara wrote down everything I thought useful. She'd read the screenplay and knew what I was looking for; I was glad I'd brought her along. She seemed comfortable in conditions that were not perfectly sanitary (to understate) and had a way with country people. She carried her three-month load up and down the hills without complaining. I was proud of her. For this side of my life, she seemed to be the perfect companion.

But in a few days, the blues came over her and she began to withdraw and be silent. I let it pass for a while, then spoke up. She told me we might as well face the facts: It was time for her to go home and prepare for the child that was coming. It was best, she said, if we cut off completely and went on, I one way, she another. I knew she was right; we'd come to the end.

I went to the mayor's office to say goodbye. This time we were alone. "Tell me," I said after a sip of coffee, "what happened to my friend Osman Kavundju?" "I don't know where he is or what's happened to him," he replied, then walked to the door, shut it, and in a scoffing voice asked if "that little hunchback with the twisted legs" had asked me for money to buy himself an automobile. I said no, he'd asked for money, but it was to make certain improvements in his city. "How much did he ask?" the mayor wanted to know. "Was it four thousand dollars?" "I can't remember," I said. "Well, some people do remember; maybe you too. Because he bought a four-thousand-dollar Cadillac car and rode everywhere like an *agha* in the back seat; we all saw that."

I still felt compelled to defend Osman, said that I liked him very much and thought him a credit to the city. To which the mayor did not respond. I was surprised by my intensity; it was as if I were defending myself. The mayor was staring at me without speaking when the sound of an auto horn from outside told us Barbara was becoming impatient and that it was time to go. I thanked the mayor for his courtesy, said I'd be coming back to Kayseri with my staff to show them what the film should look like, and he said welcome. Then, of course, he ordered a last coffee and passed the silver dish of cloves. "For the breath," he said.

In Istanbul's airport, I said goodbye to Barbara. She'd slumped; the long ride had tired her, and now anyone could see that she was pregnant. What had started as a foolhardy act was now a cause for anxiety both for her and for me. And we both had to break a habit.

I had a lot of photography to do in Istanbul and some walking the streets with a notebook in my pocket. More of my story took place in the rotting alleys behind the Galata waterfront than in Kayseri; it was in Istanbul that I had to show my hero's life as a hamal, a human pack animal, and the whole series of incidents that led up to his passage to America. So I stayed for another ten days, making notes and photographing everything and everybody. I also got to know some dissident newspapermen, discreet and slippery—call it careful—until they'd downed a couple. Then they'd speak up plainly. One of the things they told me was that if I really wanted to know what Turkey was like, I should come with them to an island just offshore and see the great political trial of Adnan Menderes, the prime minister who'd recently been deposed, and of the grand old man of Turkish politics, Celal Bayar. They were to be tried for violating the constitution—that is, for corruption in office—and with them most of those prominent in the previous government, which amounted to an entire political party. The opposition was being liquidated. I decided to go along; their newspapers had provided them with a motor launch.

When we landed we were directed to a long hall, before which soldiers had been posted. Inside there were bleachers, ten rows of seats on each side, flanking a long rectangular area; the space reminded me of a jai alai fronton. Between the bleachers it was empty, and there was a hush in the place. The men on trial for their lives, I was told, would have to stand. Political defeat in Turkey ends not in a best-seller memoir, not in a comfortable exile in Paris, not in a trip back to home ground, but on the gallows or in prison. I was particularly astonished that Celal Bayar was on trial, since he had been a close associate of Mustafa Kemal Pasha and, as such, the man most respected in Turkey. The last time I'd seen him, my cousin Stellio was kneeling and kissing his hand.

Doors opened at one end of the hall and the judges entered, to take their places on a raised platform. Then the doors at the other end opened and the defendants entered, several hundred of them, well guarded in a ceremonial sort of way. They came forward in long lines, ten abreast, all dressed in business suits, and stood facing their judges. In the front row was the deposed prime minister, Menderes, and at his side the old man Bayar, walking with difficulty. Menderes looked terribly frightened, Bayar not. Directly behind them were the politicians who'd attained prominent positions in an earlier administration, and among them was Osman, my "melon man," who'd called me his brother. Using his cane, he walked without his old swagger. He looked like the others and had the same prison pallor. I sat through that day's trial but could understand little of what was said; most of it seemed to be directed against Menderes. I had the impression a decision had already been reached in his case by the victorious political party. But my interest was in observing my "brother" with the hunchback, remembering how proudly he'd shown me his city and another time, when we'd enjoyed an adventure in another place.

At the end of the trip I'd taken to Kayseri alone, when I'd sat on a ledge of the cliff over Germeer and did what I could to dissolve the lump, I'd felt in need of a rest and a vacation and said to Osman that I wanted to go south to the coast, swim in the Mediterranean, and see the city of Antalya. I'd begun to think of locations for my film and had heard of that city's beauty and the possibilities for pleasure there. Osman jumped at the chance to go with me, got a car and a driver from the army, and we were off. I noticed that the man behind the wheel had a sidearm and the man in the seat next to him a rifle, standing ready between his legs. We were to go through the mountain passes, I was told, where bandits would tumble down the hillsides to plunder the unprotected. Osman liked to be driven at high speeds and encouraged our driver to keep a heavy foot on the accelerator. "*Koosh! Koosh! Koosh!*" he'd call out when the car slowed down. *Koosh* is Turkish for "bird." It is also, by the simple logic of that tongue, the word for "fly" and "hurry" and "rush." Only when the car went as fast as the road would permit was Osman satisfied.

I recall that the car stopped once in a wild part of the country for no reason that I could see. The driver explained by pulling out his handgun and pointing it at a large hawk on a post nearby, then shooting the bird. "*Koosh! Koosh! Koosh!*" Osman shouted as the hawk fell like a broken kite. There was a burst of laughter as the beautiful raptor flapped on the ground, where the insects would consume it. Then we drove off.

Antalya was a place of perfect beauty, with a harbor that, when seen from the approach above, is shaped like a crown. The encircling hills gleamed with white buildings. That night it proved to be the gayest city I'd seen in Turkey. Osman knew where to find good company. Dinner was a party. Young women of adjustable morality appeared—Osman's eyes gleamed when he saw them coming in. Oh, how he laughed that night, scampering and capering, kissing the women, ordering them to kiss me, and vowing eternal friendship to his "brother" from America. He ordered strong drink for the entire company, which kept growing larger and larger. He was drinking too much, but it was inspiring him to sing ballads he remembered from his father. And how the women adored him! Rising to his full four feet seven, thrusting his cane into the air, he boasted about his sexual powers. This threw the women into fits of laughter. He told us all how many women he'd enjoyed in one night and vowed to provide me with female companionship. "Take anyone you want," he said, and the women cocked their heads. I responded squeamishly, saying that I was grateful for my brother's offer, but I would not deprive him. He drove me to my hotel, where all hugged me in an explosion of high spirits. "Kiss him, kiss him," Osman ordered the girls. "He's rich man, drives Cadillac car. Maybe he take you to America!" He kissed me too before they drove off, God knows where.

The next morning, seated at a small table in the hotel dining room, I had a visit. Osman, in a grave mood now, spoke with some bitterness about his life. He told me that the restrictions a mayor suffered did not permit him a side of life that he needed: "*Kef,*" he called it, pleasure, joy, adventure. In Kayseri he had to watch every move, behave in a "proper" way that was not his true nature. I'd noticed this surprising puritanism in Turkey and in other authoritarian societies (Iran now, for instance), a puritanism that denies the joyous side of man and throttles women, confining them to the status of household servants. The wife in a typical Turkish home was a drudge; the men had it all. Women would sometimes become prostitutes in preference to marrying. Osman, it was clear, had two totally different lives: as a public servant in Kayseri, constantly under scrutiny, he kept his conduct carefully above reproach; he sought relief by occasional outbursts of high feeling in another city, where he could find several days of uninhibited pleasure.

It was in this alternation of modes of living that he reminded me of myself.

He was drinking, and soon the alcohol had made him bold. Could I, he asked, as he drank still another raki, since I was a native son and forever a friend of Turkey, as I'd repeatedly declared myself to be, as well as a famous and therefore a supremely rich man, give him a contribution for the city where my father was born and raised? He reminded me, and his face and voice were strained, that I'd said I had nothing but friendship for both races. One purpose for which he'd use the money, he said, was to save my maternal grandfather's well in Germeer, restore it to good working order. A plaque would be placed there, he promised me, with the name Shismanoglou on it. Tearing off a corner of the menu, he asked me to print the name as I wanted it to appear. He seemed eager and most sincere and mentioned a sum, four thousand dollars. I replied that I was not as rich as he imagined, but I would certainly make a contribution to the causes he'd spoken of. Three hundred dollars, how would that be? He seemed disappointed, hesitated, then accepted the traveler's checks that I signed. He left rather hurriedly, seeming exhausted and vaguely dispirited by the pleasures of his days away from duty, and when he kissed me his breath was stale. He looked like a poker player at dawn after a disastrous all-night session. Of course, that is what he was—a gambler, gambling desperately, it would turn out, with his life.

Now, five years later, by the end of the day on that island in the Sea of Marmara, all defiance had gone from the face of Osman Kavundju, and he looked like what he was, a jailbird frightened for his life. After the judges had retired to one end of the long hall and those on trial had been marched out the other end, I went back to my hotel and, saddened by what I'd seen, wrote a long letter to the newspaper *Hurriyet* (Freedom), saying that Osman had indeed asked me for money, and I'd given him three hundred dollars. Then I wrote what by then I knew was not true, that the money he had asked for had been intended not to help purchase a car for himself but to repair a wellhead in the village where my mother's people had once made their home. I said that Osman reminded me of our greatest mayor of New York City, Fiorello La Guardia, had an equal love for his city and concern for its people, and that Turkey should be proud of him. And so on.

I showed my letter to a newspaperman. This man was a patriot and he didn't like my letter. A foreigner, he said, did not have the privilege of criticizing Turkish justice; it would be resented and do Osman harm. If I ever hoped to film in Turkey, he suggested, I'd better be quiet. "Besides," he said, "justice was done. Wasn't it?" I didn't answer. "I know," he said, "you Greeks believe that there is no rule of justice anywhere east of Athens." "We've read about justice east of Athens," I answered. "He steals a loaf of bread, you cut off his hands." Our conversation stopped abruptly. As I walked back to my hotel, I remembered my happy hours with Osman and how he'd brought light into a dark city. So I sent the letter. It was an act of defiance. It was also, in an oblique way, an act of self-defense.

That night I received a telegram at the Parc Oteli, informing me that my father was back in the hospital and urging that I come home. I left Istanbul the next morning.

I'D FEARED my father most of my life. I remember the day my fear of him stopped. It was late in his life, and I'd taken the train from New York to New Rochelle to pay him and Mother a visit. As I walked down the slope of the avenue toward the old house where I'd grown up, I saw him sitting on the porch, staring into space. Although he wasn't going anywhere, certainly not to business, he wore a business suit, a hard collar, a tie, and a commuter's felt hat. A cigarette was in his mouth, but he hadn't flicked off the ashes, and they were all over the lapels of his suit. As I turned in to our front yard, passing between the evergreens he'd put in forty years before, he saw me approaching and quickly moved his quivering hand from the arm of his chair to his coat pocket. Father had Parkinson's disease, and his hand shook uncontrollably; he didn't want me to see it shaking. "Bad for business."

In the last years of his life, my mother found the task of taking care of a four-story house beyond what was left of her strength, and she plotted with one of her sons to move elsewhere. Father resented the move, particularly because she had made the decision, not he. "She don't talk to me on that subject," he said. But they sold the old house at a price he thought much too low, gave away most of the furniture, and relocated to a small condo in Rye. He resented what she'd done so intensely that he couldn't speak to her. "Your mother giving orders around here now," he said to me bitterly. Becoming delusional and hateful, he began to suspect her, a woman of seventy-three, not in the best health herself, of infidelity. He'd imagine her lover at the other end of the room and point him out to me. "They waiting minute I don't watch," Father said, "then *tak!* They go upstairs." He'd imagine he heard the noises of their lovemaking coming from her bedroom above. "I can't hold her anymore," he confided to me one day. "I only have eight hundred dollars in the bank now."

He never forgave her for moving him. He'd sit in the parlor of their new place—two small rooms, a kitchen, and a bathroom—his hand shaking; he no longer tried to hide it. When she inquired if he was hungry, he wouldn't answer her or comment about what she placed before him. He ate less and less, seemed to be reflecting on things far back in his past. He always seemed to be angry at something or other. One night he had to go to the bathroom; he'd been warned that whenever this was necessary, she had to go with him to make sure he wouldn't fall. He'd found her presence at this function humiliating, so one night he got out of bed, headed for the bathroom alone, which he'd promised not to do, fell, and broke his hip. He had to be taken to the hospital for his hip joint to be repaired. He needed constant care. My mother had to undo his trousers and free his shrinking member so he could urinate; that was a final humiliation. He didn't object to the suggestion that he be taken to an old people's home.

He had a roommate, an old Jewish gentleman who could hold his own when it came to grumbling. Father found life there insufferable, and his spirit sickened. When I got back from Turkey, I heard the news: He'd contracted pneumonia, called "the old man's friend," because it's the least painful way to die. The instant I saw him, I knew the end was coming in a matter of days. I stayed at his side and heard his last words. They came out of a coma. I'd been sitting by the side of his bed all afternoon, evening, and into the night. There was nothing anyone could do but wait. Mother was asleep in her condo when Father died at three that morning. The gurgle in his throat which revealed that he was still breathing began to grow irregular. Just before it stopped, I saw that his lips were moving and leaned close to catch, if I could, what he was saying. What I heard was: "Pappou! Pappou!" the Greek word for grandfather. His voice was low but surprisingly clear, considering that he was never again to regain consciousness. Father was particularly fond of Jennifer, the daughter of his youngest son; when she called him "Pappou," it had a loving sound. I thought he might be reliving a visit from this young woman and hearing her voice again. If so, was the emotion he was experiencing at the last moment of his life the one expressing what he wanted most and perhaps most valued—some loving tenderness? Which he'd never had enough of?

O N E evening when I was having dinner in the hospital's cafeteria and reading my *New York Times*, I happened on the results of the trial. The prime minister, Adnan Menderes, had been hanged; immediately. I remembered how piteously he'd trembled as he stood facing his judges. Out of respect for the past, Celal Bayar had been given a life sentence. He'd seemed more self-possessed than the men judging him. It was reported that nine of the others, all provincial governors, had been hanged, but no names were given. Although I went back to Turkey the following year and talked to newspapermen, I did not learn Osman's fate. But I was told that he'd been accused of using public funds to lead a dissolute life, one that cost— they had proof of this—four thousand American dollars. Where did he get such a sum of American money? The authorities had a pretty good idea where he got some of it, and they were sure that the reasons for Osman's conviction were valid. There'd been a great housecleaning, I was told. Turkey was clean again.

"The American-born don't appreciate their country," I said to myself as I ate my diet dessert. "At least here the punishment may fit the crime and rascals can become presidents."

I never saw Osman Kavundju again—except in my imagination. Several times I dreamed of my little friend with the short twisted legs, dancing at the end of a rope and still brandishing his cane.

O S M A N's fate, more intensely felt because imag-
ined, had an effect on me. Like the reprobate of legend, I determined to
transgress what seemed to be my nature and behave. With the Repertory
Theatre becoming a reality, with so many people looking to me, I was
obliged to be the "pappou," providing moral example, clearheaded decisions, and even some inspiration, while surrendering myself to respectability. I had an impressive-sounding title, new stationery with my name in a
position of command, an office with a second secretary, and I was expected
to attend meetings of the Lincoln Center board at regular intervals, properly dressed.

At the same time, I had a task dearer to me, the production of a difficult
film, my own. I no longer spent my days writing in the morning, then
seeing Barbara, but was organizing the production of *America America*.
The most difficult problem was getting the money I needed to make the
film. Friends in the business seemed to admire the script, but none of the

major companies would risk capital for its production. We were even turned down by Warner Brothers, who were to be our eventual sponsors. I was bitter about this; I remembered how much money my films had made for Warners and Fox and Columbia Pictures. Finally a firm that was just beginning—Elliot Hyman and Ray Stark—indicated interest, and a deal, not favorable to me, was agreed to. One thing that made all this difficult was my determination, in the interest of realism, to cast the film with actors industry people call "unknowns." There was also something "grubby"— someone used that word—about my story. Skouras, when he turned me down, said, "This isn't Kazan!" What the hell did he think it was? I had believed that he, as an immigrant boy, would appreciate the drama of what I'd written. Perhaps it embarrassed him.

I proceeded with casting, but had no one in mind for the leading role, an Anatolian boy who makes the journey from Kayseri to New York. It was, I believed, a fine part for an actor to play, but the character was not distinguished by nobility of motive or grandeur of vision; he was not a hero. Quite the contrary: He was an ordinary kid whose outstanding quality was tenacity. He made his way west, as so many had, in the best way he could and not always honorably. I had the image of my uncle in mind, a colorful rascal who, after he'd prospered in business here, betrayed his partner, my father. I didn't scrub the character clean; I was looking for a ferret, not a lion, someone who had what was my boy's single redeeming quality, devotion to his father and family.

Finding the right actor for the central role of a film is critical; the total effort hangs on your choice. The main thrust of the character as imagined by the director must truly be in the actor he chooses; when it's faked, it will seem fake. The director should also hope to find an element of danger in the actor himself; if he or she is a person the director would hesitate to cross in life, this amounts to a kind of respect. There should also be something inscrutable about the actor, a mystery, so that as you watch him, you wonder what he's thinking. The actor the director chooses must be a person who, for any of these or for other reasons, you would like to see more of, as you would in life; someone the director will not get bored with over a long shooting schedule and the audience will not tire of watching for two hours on a screen; someone the camera "loves," makes more, not less interesting. In short, a person impossible to find.

I looked everywhere; took trips to England—no luck—then to France; brought a French actor back to America to test and found him much too good-looking. Handsome men, I decided, lack desperation. I looked in California, but there was mush in the hearts of the actors I saw there. Of course, I looked in the Actors Studio; no luck. Finally I did the obvious, went to Athens, and in the office a film director found an apprentice sweeping the floor so he could be near production work. I liked the kid and his looks, but he had little acting experience or English. Still I talked to him and was won over by his stories. His father had been in the civil war on the Communist side, was beaten around the kidneys by the rightists until he began to hemorrhage internally, then bled to death in his son's arms. When he told me about his father's death, detail by detail, I saw the material I needed for the part in the boy's face. I believe that if I'd found a De Niro, a Hoffman, or a Pacino, the film might have been more effective and certainly more successful commercially, but this boy had one merit superior actors did not have: He was the real thing. *America America* is my favorite film both despite the performance in its central role and because of it.

I brought the boy to America, made him speak English all day, encouraged him to find an American girlfriend—the best way to learn a new language. I found him devoted, honest, and loyal; all you had to do was look at him and you believed the story; he was too amateurish to contrive. It was to be not a characterization but a fact; this young man was it. His performance can be compared to that of the man in De Sica's *Bicycle Thief.* Like that nonactor, Stathis Giallelis may have been hurt by his sudden importance; after my film, he went on trying to be an actor in America but never learned to speak English without a noticeable accent and didn't have the patience to train himself. He was a good boy, but he was also what Greek mothers call sons they're proud of: a rooster. The only son in a family of four daughters, he'd been spoiled in every way; his women made him believe that all he had to do was speak and he'd be obeyed. Served at the head of the table by his women, fed, clothed, and supported, praised for virtues he possessed and those he didn't possess, he was that wonderful thing, a male. Most Greek men are mother spoiled.

T H E R E continued to be an unspoken tension between Art Miller and me, but also a little of the affection that had once been there. The problem was that the discord between us was unarticulated; we were both determined to get along for the sake of the Repertory Theatre, and we did. I admired Art for his unwavering devotion to our cause. We were together on a raft in the middle of the ocean, and there was nothing for us to do but paddle; to save my life, I had to save his.

There was one subtle problem, and it's difficult to explain. I did tell him everything I thought about the scenes he read to us as he was writing his new play, but in one fundamental respect I backed away from the truth. Bob Whitehead and I found ourselves in the desperate circumstances of needing the play to be ready on time; we'd begun to feel the pressure of dates. We wanted to open the Washington Square Theatre as soon as it was ready for an audience. We knew that enthusiasm drains away. So while I plainly criticized the details of Art's play, I didn't tell him what I thought of the overall pseudoconfessional concept and particularly that of the first half of the play, which I didn't like then and like less in retrospect, or of the central figure, based, I had to believe, on Art himself. I found him a bore.

The first act concerned Art's crisis under the pressure of HUAC and deals with his ambivalence. There is a character based on me and my testimony, and although that character is not how I thought of myself, Art must have considered it reasonable, even generous, and I was ready to accept it as how, looking back, he saw the events. He had a right to his version of that bit of history. However, I thought that the self-dramatization, the turgid introspection, and a kind of self-favoring in Art's Quentin were heavy going and not interesting. Art's historical viewpoint on Arthur Miller, the hero of the McCarthy crisis, made for dull drama—and that was the first act.

I did truly admire the second act—the one so many people resented. It was about Art's obsessive romance with Marilyn Monroe. He had denied, foolishly, that the story of that relationship in the play was based on his personal history, denied that his character, Maggie, was based on Marilyn. But he put into the mouth of Maggie precisely what Marilyn had thought of him, and particularly her scorn for him at the end of their marriage. This character is true and has an interesting dramatic development from adoration to contempt. Art is rough on himself, giving us all that Marilyn said in her disappointment and resentment. The play's summation—summations are by definition boring—is insufferably self-favoring and "noble." Audiences should be able to make up their own minds what the events shown have meant, but Art knew what he wanted the audience to think, and he told them.

As an independent director I might not have done the play, but as a responsible producer, I did.

B O B and I were putting together our company, and the essential requirement was that the actors would be well cast in Art's play. Quickly we found actresses who suited all the women in the play except the central role of Maggie. The men were easy to find; some of them were members of the Actors Studio. No one I invited to join the company from the Studio refused, this despite the constant rat-tat-tat of anger from that temple of self-righteousness, and the prompting that came from Lee Strasberg in a jet stream. Liska March, probably the oldest and one of the most devoted members of the Studio, not an actress but an administrator, was there throughout this time. She reported the boiling of anger that went on as Lee fed the flames. "He was a god then," she said to me, "and you didn't say no to him when he berated anyone. Instead the actors got on the bandwagon and added their two cents, spoke up saying how awful what you'd done was and how disloyal, how could you do such a thing, and so on." Liska felt that

Lee incited them to say what he wanted to hear. Some of the actors who came with me were also the objects of revilement—but soon they didn't care, and I certainly didn't.

Then I got a surprise. Rumor spread that there was an Actors Studio Theatre being formed. Liska March said that this was in order to prove that they could get along without me; but it had a more serious purpose. The theory behind the theatre was to be Lee's concept of a "floating company," in which one actor would replace another so that productions could be maintained by the presence of a strong constellation of "stars" or near stars. Lee and Cheryl had sent a pledge form to all members. The form read: "I understand and am fully in sympathy with the Actors Studio's plans to extend its activities to include a production organization. I am aware of the principle of the Floating Company on which this theatre will be based and as a member of the Actors Studio, I would like to participate in this program. I will make myself available to the Actors Studio Production Unit for a period of at least four months during the year 1963 . . . 1964 . . . 1965. Signed . . ."

I received one of these pledge forms and thought I should respond. "Dear Lee," I wrote, "I've thought about your plan for a Floating Company and I can't go along with it." I didn't explain my reasons.

Then I thought that the cleanest thing for me to do was resign, not as a member but as one of the directors, since my onetime associates were pursuing a policy I disapproved of. I was never in favor of the Studio's becoming a theatre and had resisted that at every turn. A studio is a studio—a place to experiment, to work without tensions, where actors can be free of the stresses of commercial production. To make a theatre of the Studio would require a fundamental change in its purpose, its organization, and its leadership. Since I didn't believe that Lee would be a capable leader for a production theatre, I decided that a complete break would be best for both sides and composed the following letter:

Dear Cheryl: Life is tough enough without making it tougher. When I read the announcement that you and Lee were forming an Actors Studio Theatre, I could only think, "Well, God bless them both." Why do any of us do anything except make things easier for each other? You and Lee want to go ahead as you and the actors there see fit and I certainly don't want to do the least thing to impede you. Nor do I want to sit here and look disapproving. Not my role in life, is it? Or to be off in Turkey this summer, the absent dissident. The hell with that. I'll simply resign from the Board of Directors, which is clean and quick, and give you all my blessing and fervent good wishes, as a member of the Actors Studio—which I will always be.

Then I went on more formally:

I am sending a short announcement to the hungry press as follows: "The time is now coming for active production in the Lincoln Center Repertory Theatre of which I am co-producing director. At the same time, the Actors Studio, of which I was a founder and on whose Board of Directors I sit, has embarked upon its own program of production. This activity overlaps and competes with some of the activity for which I am responsible at the Repertory Theatre. It seems right to me that I now resign from the Board of Directors of the Actors Studio in order to be able to give my undivided attention and effort to my job at the Repertory Theatre. That resignation I have effected today and am no longer a Director of the Actors Studio. ELIA KAZAN."

I also wished to communicate clearly and directly with the actor members, and I sent them this telegram: "To all: I resigned as a director only. That was necessary. But I'm still with you and for any and all efforts you make. I'm sure whatever you do will bring credit to our years of work and to Lee's teaching." It was signed: "The First Member."

I am not proud of that telegram. It doesn't sound like what I was feeling but like what I thought was "right" for me to say.

Liska March told me that the telegram was several times torn down from the bulletin board where she'd pinned it but that she kept putting it back. She also told me that some members felt my loss, wished me luck, and missed me a great deal. I believe Lee did too—miss me, not wish me luck. Most of the actors were for him and, since they felt abandoned and rejected, resented my departure. Lee did nothing to discourage this resentment, but instead encouraged a hero worship that created a Khomeini-like terror. The powerful man as a martyr is a great force.

I then decided to make the emotional and artistic break complete. I wrote an article for *The New York Times*, summing up my true feelings. "The Actors Studio," I wrote, "has made a historic contribution to the American Theatre. It is now no longer a group of young insurgents. It is itself an orthodoxy and takes particular pride in its roster of stars. It deserves the acclaim it has received. My great disappointment with the work there has been that it always stopped at the same point, a preoccupation with the purely psychological side of acting. I am speaking of my own failure as well as that of others."

That was a true resignation. After that I became comfortable with Lee's anger and stopped worrying about it. The long theatrical civil war that followed was not fought in the dark but in a blaze of newsprint. Most everything said, each stand taken, was printed and became gossip. STUDIO DIVORCE, a headline in the New York *Post* announced, and it continued: WILL KAZAN GET THE KIDS? The *World-Telegram & Sun* predicted in a headline: TALENT RAID FORESEEN AS KAZAN SHIFTS JOBS. Paul Newman was quoted, saying that my leaving the Studio was as great a disappointment as if his wife had walked out on him. "I'll stay with the Studio," he concluded. And the most official theatrical column, that of Sam Zolotow in *The New York Times,* gave the schism feature space beneath the headline: KAZAN QUITS POST. We hadn't realized until this outburst of interest that we were quite that important. "Not since Leon Trotsky left Josef Stalin," wrote one columnist, "has any rift caused as much rancor as Elia Kazan's departure from the Actors Studio to head, with Robert Whitehead, the Lincoln Center Theatre."

Even now, a quarter of a century later, some of the bitterness endures, and if some people can't find anything else for which to criticize me, they recall this old "treachery." I recently asked certain actors to record their memories of that time on tape. Some of those most prominently involved refused to return my phone calls, even though, had we met on the street, they'd have been quite civil and given me the smile of concord. I particularly wanted to hear Cheryl Crawford's side of the issue, because she was at Lee's side throughout the split and on into the formation of the Actors Studio Theatre. Cheryl told my secretary, whom she knew well and who has done some work for her, that she couldn't recall the events in question because she wasn't involved in them. But photographs prove she was there, arm linked with Lee's. I appreciate her tender concern for Lee; he was badly hurt and was to be hurt even more in the next two years.

T H E R E is a corny joke about three "men of God" being asked to respond to the fundamental question When does life begin? The Catholic priest answered, "At the instant the sperm joins with the egg in the womb." The Presbyterian minister's answer was: "At the instant when the mother feels the first movement in her belly." The rabbi's answer was: "When the last child leaves home." This was happening to Molly and me. Our daughter Katharine was about to go away to the George School, and Molly and I would be left alone together. We had a servant to prepare dinner, make the bed, and keep the place clean, so all Molly had to do, at last, was write. It was the moment for which she'd been waiting all her adult life.

When I thought of what Molly had done for me and for our family of children, I felt guilty, and I completely enlisted in her coming struggle. The guilt I dealt with by vowing to her that I'd support her in every way, be home every night for dinner and thereafter. I was glad that we were still married, glad that Anatolian men don't divorce. I was grateful to her and knew it was time for her to be rewarded. She'd given me four fine children who, whatever else they thought, loved me—not always easy to do. She'd kept our family together despite my chaotic behavior, remained loyal to me through painful times, and tried to understand a nature as different from her own as it was possible to be. She'd set up a series of homes for the family in apartments and brownstones here and there around the city. She'd fixed up a country home for us and for the kids and then, on the same piece of land, built a studio for us, in which she would write, I work on my projects. It was a beautiful building, plain and sturdy, with no false ornament, perfectly functional; it was like Molly. I am typing in it now.

She'd also seen four children through four schools, selected the schools carefully—with no help from me—and, on the whole, with good sense. She'd made sure that the children were properly and appropriately dressed, sewn name tapes on their summer clothes. She'd also seen them through psychological difficulties, been attentive to their problems, day after day, again without much help from me. On three occasions she'd brought the entire family to the location where I was shooting a film and set up a home for us, making my work on location more comfortable and more stable. She'd always been every way loving.

She herself had been through a long psychoanalysis, which was painful; for a time I thought it would never come to an end, but it did and not happily. The analyst to whom she'd been going several times a week for three years, and to whom she'd been devoted, announced one day that he didn't think he could help her further. It was a shocking dismissal. This depressed her terribly and made me furious with the analyst. Molly had to believe that the man thought her hopeless. Seeing what it had meant to her, I determined to provide her with the support she'd lost from him. I would pay reparations for my own past behavior.

Now the time had come for her finally to put other people's needs behind her and devote herself to herself. The first thing she wanted to do was move us into a small apartment, one that would be simple for her to take care of. I told her she could have anything she wished for and to spare no cost. She found and we bought an apartment on the sixteenth floor of 115 Central Park West. She set about planning alterations and choosing the furnishings for what she called our "final, perfect apartment." She meant those words, but I didn't believe anything was final or perfect or that happiness and good intentions last. However, I kept my doubts to myself. I was determined to do my best to see her effort succeed.

There was a room facing east and, adjoining it, a balcony over the park. It was a beautiful room, and choosing it for her study was the first time she'd treated herself generously. Every detail of that writing room was pleasing to her eye and appropriate to her work pattern, and at last she was going to have what she wanted, her final, perfect place. She also bought two pretty housecoats to work in, one pink, one green. Her rapture—that's what it was—moved me deeply. I sought her out now, became truly devoted to her, and paid her the admiration she deserved. I found her beautiful again, distinguished, patrician. Years of alienation and virtual separation were put behind us. I wasn't seeing Barbara or anyone else. Molly's cheeks regained their high color and she bought herself new clothes that were more frivolous as well as choosing a new, trimmer hairstyle. Observing the change in me, Molly was pleased and she was made confident. We were going to start another life, in an apartment where we'd be secure and happy forever.

W H E N we had cast Art's play totally, except for the crucial part of Maggie, I had an inspiration: Barbara. I'd seen her with a blond wig when I was making *Splendor in the Grass* and had then and have now great admiration for her work as an actress. I believed that her scope was limited, but within that range she was as good as anyone working in the theatre. At this time she was monumentally pregnant, but one day I said to Art that I had an idea that might solve our problem. With considerable difficulty, I convinced Barbara that she should come, pregnant as she was, and read for Art. I got her a blond wig and did the best I could with her belly, keeping her seated before the reading. She read the part brilliantly. It was obvious she'd be the right choice, because she understood the role in ways totally experiential; she'd been there! Art was immediately taken with her—Marilyn-lookalike wig and all. Later he was to say that she hurt his play because she made the audience believe it was Marilyn he was writing about. Whom did he think he was kidding? But at the time he was vastly relieved that our casting problem was solved.

I talked with Barbara after the reading to tell her how well she'd done. Then I asked how she was getting along. She gave me a nonanswer. "I'm all right. Don't worry about me." Was I guilty about Barbara's coming child? I have not noticed that children brought up in an orderly and traditional manner are invariably sounder and smarter than those brought up in difficult circumstances.

Now, with the play fully cast and I believed well cast, the theatre at Washington Square almost finished, the "perfect and forever" apartment progressing, and Molly about to start writing her own plays at last, with the Actors Studio problem settled—at least for me, if only by indifference—I left for Europe to embark on what was, despite all else, my major interest: making the film of my screenplay *America America*. On the way to Turkey, where the crew would meet me, we stopped off at Stockholm to do some advance publicity for *Splendor in the Grass*. There I received the telegram from New York, phrased in a prearranged code, informing me that a son had been born.

I N A N K A R A, the capital city of Turkey, sitting on one side of a table that could have supported a small tank, Charlie Maguire and I confronted the Turkish censorship board, five men, two of them in uniforms of the Turkish army, whose permission we had to obtain to film there. They'd read the script I'd presented, but apparently they weren't certain what their opinions were. No one of them wanted to be that member of the board who'd allowed a scene to slip through that might outrage men of higher rank. The safest thing for them to have done was deny us permission. But then they'd face another charge: that they'd let pass a chance to bring at least half a million American dollars into their country.

They kept glancing at one of their number, the officer with the most citation stripes, the only one of them who'd not spoken—although he'd frequently cleared his throat. He'd studied me as I made my presentation, didn't smile back when I smiled at him. It was obvious that what the others were waiting for was this man's judgment. I was waiting for it too, especially anxious because I'd omitted two scenes from the Turkish script I'd given them, ones I knew would cause them to reject my application. Silence makes you imagine many things.

He stood up. He had, I now noticed, a more Asiatic cast to the bones of his face and to his eyes. He spoke in a voice of command to a translator, who said to me, in a tone even more imperious, "You will have a person from our government at your side every day and he will tell you what you can show and what you cannot show. That is our requirement."

I had it! I'd won their permission!

"Do you accept?" the officer said in Turkish to the interpreter. It was immediately translated into English, even though I'd assured them all to begin with that I understood Turkish.

"Of course," I replied in Turkish, "I understand the colonel's concern."

"General," the interpreter corrected. Then more Turkish was given to him to pass on to me. "Our pasha hopes you are sincere. But as they say in your country, talk is cheap. What we must expect of you is a film master-piece that will show our people not as they are shamefully portrayed in American films but as they are in truth, honest and hard-working, with great love for their soil and for Allah."

"That is precisely my intention," I lied.

The pasha smiled at me in a curious way. Being a politician as well as an army man, perhaps he appreciated cunning. We shook hands American style when I left. "I've been to Pittsburgh," he said, in English. "And Akron, Ohio."

"s o we'll be watched every minute we're here," I wrote Molly as soon as I got to the hotel, then described the entire interview.

I'd received a disturbing letter from her. She'd decided to move earlier than planned out of the brownstone we were selling into the apartment we'd bought. That way, she could supervise every change, as it was being altered to her specifications. She was determined to "settle everything," so she could get down to work on her plays. Molly had a passion for order in the details of her life, as people do who feel their inner lives are disordered.

While all the building activity was going on, she found time to brood over our life together, overseeing the past and peering into the future. "You have much reason for pride," she wrote me, "but I've been off my center of gravity. Now here I am, free of many old burdens, with our last one off to school, and this is my chance. Now if ever. I've got to get firm with myself. And forget much of what happened between us. I don't think 'fault' means much—your fault, my fault. We did what we couldn't help doing, being the way we were." She wrote about her loneliness. "It's been twenty-five years since I've not had a kid to look after and with you gone too, the house feels empty. But for a time that's what I need, isn't it? There's nothing to distract me now. No one to blame . . ." Then she wondered: "How'll we do in our new place? You'll work, I know. I? That's my problem."

I had to linger in Ankara a few days to get the official certificate of approval. During this time I had another letter. I could tell she was frightened but, being what she was, concealed her fears from herself and so from me. Morally fastidious, she was careful not to write what might upset me in my work. I read her letters with admiration but with mounting anxiety. I had the impression she was now challenging herself, do or die.

"Things have improved," she wrote. "I have a table that will hold a type-writer, and one scaffold is out of the living room. When the carpenters give me my study, I'll be able to think about working. At last. I have to. Soon. All I do now is work on the house. It's hard to concentrate because of the tile man and the plumber, the damned phone calls and spending all afternoons scouting wallpaper. So I fall into bed exhausted at a foolishly early hour, rise with the sun and sit at the typewriter. But NOTHING HAPPENS."

She'd go on and on about the children, with whom she kept in touch constantly. She was discovering what it would take me longer to realize: that parenthood doesn't stop, that a mother continues sewing on name tapes for the rest of her days. Otherwise she'd committed her mind totally,

blocked off all escape routes. As she said, it was now or never. What frightened me was that perhaps it was a gamble taken too late, a bet placed on
herself after the race was past winning.

Then it occurred to me that a great part of her problem was my fault. I
saw that my lies about our intimate life, since they'd been successful, had
prevented her from confronting the conflicts in her own life. The shield I'd
put around my behavior, and so hers, was so perfect that it had not permitted her to face her dilemmas. By concealing from her our true situation, I'd
harmed her, that way more than any other. It was as if I'd prevented her
life from happening to her.

I defended myself. After all, there'd been painful conflicts in our life
together, of which she'd been made aware. The Defense League of Central
Park West Wives, Paula Strasberg, president, had informed her about my
affectionate relationship with two of my close friends. Molly had felt publicly shamed—and I was guilty of that. Twice she'd moved to divorce me,
employing powerful lawyers in her father's old Wall Street firm. They'd
leaped to horse and presented me with terms that were devastating, trying
to break me. But I'd agreed to those terms, since she was "in the right." At
which she'd called off the legal brigade. But here's the question: Would she
have written this drama as it had happened? She was completely attached
to me while, at the same time, altogether condemning my behavior. If she'd
written the part of an unfaithful husband in a play, would she have been
true to the contradictions of her own experience? Would she have given her
"villain" the qualities that made her persevere with me? I doubted it.

That's why I doubted her gamble and didn't dare think what she'd feel
and what she'd do if she failed. Her total worth was at stake—not for me,
not for the rest of the world; only for herself. So I worried terribly, woke in
the middle of the night believing that harm had already come to her or soon
would. I waited anxiously for each letter from America, asking the reception desk and our office two or three times a day if anything had arrived
from home.

Then I was blessed with a cheerful letter. It contained the news that one
of her short plays, which had been performed in a small New York theatre
to quite a good press, was about to be done at the Spoleto Festival, and
she'd been invited there as a guest by the festival's organizer, Gian-Carlo
Menotti. Could I, she asked, possibly come over and be with her, even for
a day? I knew how much a performance at Spoleto would mean to her now;
my presence would make the celebration complete. But there was no way
I could, not at the time she indicated, nor ever until my film was "in the
can." Difficulties and the demands on me were becoming heavier every day.
I wrote her this, sandwiched in between the most ardent congratulations.
Then, the next day, wrote her the same letter again.

· · ·

F R O M the Istanbul airport I went straight to the Hilton, where our crew was being put up. I found them in the bar, vacationing. They were a new bunch to me, so I socialized with them and with my cameraman, Haskell Wexler. I noticed he was signing bar checks not in his name but in that of my company. I recalled that he came from a wealthy Chicago family. My experience is that those born to wealth tend to be the most careful with their money and the most spendthrift with others'. That's how they stay rich.

The crew were talking about the city, how dirty it was and how mean the people on the streets looked. Our apple-assed script girl had discovered that the flush toilets in the Istanbul Hilton were not up to strict U.S. standards. Advice was being swapped about how to spot pickpockets, how to avoid disease, what not to eat, and what to do about the water. They were all particularly horrified by the hamals, the human beasts of burden. "They're hardly human," one of them said. In our story, my "hero" becomes one for a while. I refrained from making a comparison of the humanity on Istanbul's streets with that of our American crew, who seemed thoroughly spoiled by our affluent civilization. We had some Italians—our head electrician and carpenter were from Rome—and they seemed at ease and not at all frightened.

While I was drinking and becoming less and less amiable, I was informed that I had an overseas call, New York. Afraid of bad news coming from Molly or about one of the children, I rushed to the nearest phone. The man on the line was my lawyer, Bill Fitelson, who loved real-life drama. "He's out!" he said, not bothering with the usual prologue about the weather. "Who's out?" I asked. "Stark's out," he said. Bill had written my deal with Ray Stark and Elliot Hyman, and he was telling me they'd withdrawn from my project. "How could they?" I asked. As he told me, I thought of the crew running up a fat bill at the bar; the check we'd been counting on to pay this and the room charges was not going to be coming from Stark-Hyman. "What are we going to do?" I asked. "You keep your mouth shut. Let me work on it." Bill's aggressive tone was reassuring. "I'll get back to you," he said, "as soon as I know something," and abruptly hung up.

As I walked away, I gave in to the useless exercise of cursing Stark and Hyman, but remembering Bill's admonition about not looking disturbed, I walked into the bar and ordered an ouzo. After a few minutes, I found an opportunity to take Charlie Maguire aside and, having warned him to show no anxiety, told him the news. "We don't have money to pay the hotel bill," he said. "Do the bar bill first," I said. "That will maintain our credit." "I don't have the money for that either," Charlie said. Later I gathered all my trusted people—Anna Hill Johnstone, Gene Callahan, and Charlie—in my hotel room and we dug into our pockets, brought out our cash and American Express checks, and managed to pay the bar bill.

The next morning, heeding Fitelson's instruction and behaving as if nothing had gone wrong, I walked with Wexler around the city, showing him what I hoped to photograph and from what angles. He didn't respond favorably to my suggestions—or point of view. He was to tell me a few weeks later that I had no "eye." I'd always thought it was an "ear" I lacked. Now it seemed I was without the two essentials for a director.

The prime relationship in filmmaking is that between a director and his cameraman. I was to discover two things about "Pete" Wexler: He was a man of considerable talent, and he was a considerable pain in the ass. This is often the case with people of talent in show business. I realized early on that I'd made a mistake engaging him. But there we were, in Turkey, and how would I go about changing a cameraman, where would I interview alternate choices, and what would I do about the crew? They'd come with Wexler, they'd go with Wexler. So I decided to suffer it through, to treat Pete as a challenge, one I might learn from. And it happened that I did learn from him. He gave me my first experience with the hand-held camera. Pete could, with the smoothest motion, dip and turn, move in and out like a perfectly operated small crane, all the time making his focus-length adjustments. He was damned good, I had to admit. I admired him even as I begrudged him the respect I felt.

Later I was told that he'd held my anti-Communist testimony against me. That would explain what went on between us, but why, then, had he accepted the job with me? On the last day of shooting, I accosted him. "Tell me, Pete," I said. "Now that we're through, what did you think of my script?" "I thought it was a piece of shit," he said. "Then why did you take the job?" I asked. His answer was: "I knew what a Kazan picture would do for my career." Years after the film had opened and been awarded some praise, Wexler volunteered, "Now I begin to see what you were getting at." A halfhearted apology makes you like a man less.

Whatever I felt about Pete, there was nothing to do about it. And two days after he'd given me the bad news, my gallant, hustling lawyer called; he'd rescued me. "Warner Brothers!" Bill said. That was a puzzle, because they'd turned down the project months before. Why they'd changed their position didn't matter to me; I didn't even ask for the details of the deal. Money was on its way east. We could pay our hotel bill, load cameras, and begin to expose negative before the mosques, streets, and waterfront of Istanbul.

H E   W A S   a little fellow in his early thirties, and there was nothing about him that suggested the censor. He was pear-shaped, most of his weight bundled below his belt. He wore a neatly pressed suit and a thin mustache, was well groomed and well mannered. I woke my Anatolian guile, which is never totally asleep, and had a stool placed under the camera's lens, telling him that was the position traditionally occupied by the director, because from there he'd see precisely what would be on film. He demurred at this welcome—after all, it was my place, he said. But I insisted and finally he acquiesced and sat where I'd indicated, back straight, knees primly together. All around him the camera operator and the man who "pulled" focus hustled; my censor had to scrunch up tight to stay out of their way. I saw to it that he had a copy of the script—as edited for the Turkish authorities— placed open on his lap so he'd know where what we were photographing would appear in the film, and I gave him the silver American ballpoint out of my pocket. This gift particularly affected him, and his face warmed. I explained what I was doing and why—which was not difficult on our first day, because we were photographing my "little *gevur* boy from Kayseri" walking past the great *camis,* the mosques of Mohammed. At the break, I had a box lunch brought to him so he could eat with our leading actor and feel one with us. Food is a great seducer.

By the end of that day, Ankara's little watchdog and I were getting along like old friends, so well that I began to feel embarrassed at my trickiness. I knew I had scenes ahead that would reveal less attractive aspects of Istanbul and its society, but I felt confident that by that time I'd have him totally on my side, or to put it otherwise, I would have completely corrupted him from his duty.

O N   T H E   third day, we organized ourselves to shoot the scene we most needed, a main reason we'd come to Istanbul. A line of hamals carrying ship's cargo file across an open dockside to load an American merchant ship. They walk slowly; their burdens are crushing and the heat is in the nineties. Many of the hamals are young and able, but there are others whose strength has been drained by years of this work, their backs permanently humped. Watching at one side is a crowd of idlers, and among them is my little *gevur.* On his journey west, he's been robbed of the goods and money his father entrusted to him. His pockets are empty, but he's too ashamed to turn home for help. Desperate, he must find employment or go hungry.

Suddenly one of the older hamals mounting the ship's stairs with his load collapses. An officer turns him over; the man is dead. The hamals loading the ship go on walking past his body. Stavros, seeing his chance, dashes to the fallen man, picks up his load, and takes his place in the line. He has a job—at the bottom of the social ladder.

That day there must have been at least five thousand people watching us work, those who had nothing to do or chose to have nothing to do. The crowd was lively; there was a constant taunting murmur of curiosity, sparked by laughter, jibes, caustic comment, calls, and shouts. Hawkers of nuts, sweets, and bread rings, as well as vendors who sell cool water by the cup, passed among the bystanders as they would work a holiday crowd. Every so often there'd be a wave of unruliness, which made me feel that the crowd was somehow hostile and potentially dangerous. I was still afraid of Turks and would never get over it. There had been mention of me in one of the morning newspapers, objecting to my presence there; I'd come to shame the Turkish people, an editorial declared. The effect of this accusation was intensified by my fearful imagination. Besides, it was close to the truth.

My little censor, on the other hand, in the spirit of the occasion, was growing livelier by the hour. He seemed to be enjoying his prominence, sitting under the camera or sometimes rising to lean on it with his elbow— a member of the "shoot." I noticed that he was carrying his copy of the script in a new binder and that he held it proudly.

It was then that I noticed my cousin Stellio. Far back in the crowd, he was gliding along the wall of the buildings like a shadow, looking our way but never slowing his pace or stopping so he might better observe what we were doing. I waved to him to come stand beside me, but he didn't respond, rather scuttled off like a crab and disappeared from sight. Ten minutes later, he hurried by again, moving in the opposite direction. I waved and was sure he'd seen me, because I was standing on an electrician's box behind the camera. But he slithered off and disappeared. Clearly he didn't want to be publicly identified with me, and it didn't take much thought to figure out why. If the film turned out badly from the Turkish government's point of view, which was bound to happen when I included the scenes I'd not shown their censors, he didn't want to be connected with me. I was actually putting his life in hazard. Ten minutes later, when he scooted by again, I didn't wave; I understood why I shouldn't.

Despite the heat, he was dressed neatly in a vested suit, collar, and tie. I thought about this "business suit," saw it for what it was—a kind of uniform. It identified him as a merchant and a *gevur*. The *gevur* had for many years won a traditional place in Turkish society. He was the educated man, the clever one who could read, write, keep accounts, and speak several languages. He was the office manager, the treasurer, the diplomat, the administrator of the sultan's staff, and highly regarded as such. His Western clothes and manners affirmed his identity.

My father had been one of this number. I have old photographs of him wearing a business suit and vest, a high, hard collar and a tie, cuffs stiffened and held together with links. This costume, while it was evidence of a higher capability than that of the native Turk who "worked with his back," also marked him and other Anatolian Greeks as targets in times of riot, so it became essential for these Greeks to behave circumspectly on the streets, be above criticism at all times, self-effacing, and as near invisible as possible. That is how my cousin was acting and why he made me think of my father.

If George Kazan had not brought his wife and two sons to America in 1913, I could have been there now, dressed as my cousin was dressed, hustling everywhere as he hustled everywhere, "invisible." If it hadn't been for my father's courage—a quality I had not until that day associated with him—I'd now be what my cousin was.

Perhaps it was this feeling of gratitude and reconciliation that brought on an extraordinary feeling late that afternoon. There comes a moment on a production, usually toward the end of the first week of work, when a crew will notice that their director's tensions have eased, that he's no longer edgy and anxious but confident and even playful, enjoying both the power that's rightfully his and the work itself. Such a moment took place that afternoon—a flash of assurance and swelling confidence. It was on that afternoon, as the crew was breaking for the day, that I believed I had it all, that nothing could or would stop me, that I had something special here, that it was all going to work!

The next morning, we set up our camera at the end of an alley in an impoverished part of the city. It was littered with rubbish—a perfect set-ting—and I instructed my crew not to alter what was there in any way, not how the refuse was piled on the pavement or how the vegetable trimmings rotted in a corner. The shot was background and mood, and it would tell what I wanted it to tell. It would not, however, attract tourists to Turkey.

My censor had not objected to anything I'd done; he'd watched with admiration and deference, particularly appreciating the differences be-tween what was in the script he held and what I was photographing. He was becoming a student of cinema, not a censor protecting the touristic hopes of his country. I was treating him as I might a nephew of whom I was fond. That morning he'd brought me some sugar-dusted pastries from his mother's oven.

I'd asked Haskell to pan his camera at the end of the shot to include a close-up of the large pile of rubbish and rotting vegetation. As the camera wheeled, I walked behind my "nephew" and put my hand on his head. I didn't expect him to object to what I was doing, but I thought I might make things easier for him if I didn't permit him to see where the shot was to end. So I held his head, affectionately but firmly, to prevent it from turning. We got the shot I wanted; I made a joke; he laughed. He belonged to me!

We moved on to our next location, a bazaar where rugs were being traded—again, background and mood to be part of an opening montage depicting my little *gevur*'s first impression of Istanbul. He was to walk through this scene at a moment when the bargaining over price was heated. Four men were engaged in this *bazaarlik,* and I encouraged the actors to make the bargaining graphic and lively, since the scene was in a language no Western audience would understand. The censor watched with interest, laughing, looking back at me, nodding his head. It was a familiar sight to him.

Suddenly, from out of the crowd behind the camera, there burst a man of about forty-five, dressed in a gray suit that reminded me of the men standing by outside the censor's office in Ankara. I immediately placed him: secret police. He was confident as only police are in that society, and his face was ferocious. Turkish men, like Japanese and Mexicans, have no gradations of anger; it's friendship or frenzy. This man rushed up to my little censor, screaming murder. As near as I could make out, what he was demanding to know at the top of his voice was why my censor permitted that kind of overemphatic bargaining in a scene; audiences, he said, would laugh at the Turkish people. I tried to intercede, but the secret policeman ignored me and went on shouting at the censor. "Why everybody waving both hands like crazy people? Why eight hands waving like that? The world will think Turkey insane asylum. Speak! Say! What! What?"

The little censor, silenced by panic, had no defense. His new world of friends collapsed. I guessed that this secret policeman had either been watching us earlier or been tipped off that our censor was becoming too friendly with the Americans. The cop in gray kept illustrating what he didn't like by gesticulating in the same fashion he was objecting to, waving his hands in the censor's face. Then he ordered my "nephew" to get up and led him off. I never saw the little censor again.

A half hour later, this same secret policeman came back and, to establish his authority, objected violently to a scene I was making around a waterspout. Did he want the world to believe, I asked, that poor Turkish people in the first decade of this century had running water in their homes? That they didn't have to stand in line at a public spigot to wash their clothes? I myself had witnessed what I was putting on film, I said; it was true. He demanded that it be changed. We folded our equipment and stopped work.

Charlie and I went to my hotel room, I stretching out on the bed as usual, Charlie alert. I was very depressed. I found the prospect of unrelenting surveillance intolerable. I ordered a drink—a Scotch, not raki. "Let's get out of here," Charlie said. "You think the room is bugged?" "I know it's bugged." I had a little balcony, and I followed Charlie out and closed the door. "I didn't mean out of the room," he whispered. "I meant out of Turkey." He was looking at me hard, and I could see he meant it. "How the hell are we going to move?" I said. "All our equipment—camera and sound and clothes and film—and what'll we do with our exposed film? I don't mean to lose that. We're trapped. We have no choice except to stay and make the best of it." "You'll go crazy here," Charlie said. "That fellow who broke in on us today, I noticed him in the background before. They got cops on their cops here. I've had to spread some loot around to get us as far as we've gotten." "What would we do about the film we've shot?" I said. "Let me worry about that," Charlie said. "And you let me think about the whole idea," I said. "But think fast," Charlie said. "If we move, we've got to do it before they catch on. And don't talk about what we've talked about, not to anyone. I'm going to get some expert Turkish advice." "You know a Turk here you trust?" I said. "I know no one here I trust," Charlie said. "But there are men who value the dollar, especially when it's deposited for them in a Swiss bank. I'm going to squander some Warner Brothers gold, and when I come back, I'll tell you if it can be done, and if it can, what it'll cost. If you spend enough dollars, you can do anything here, including have the prime minister shot."

He left me and I thought about it. To move was a disaster for me. In that extraordinary city, I had before my camera the rotting hulk of the civilization from which my hero was to escape and from which my father had freed me. We'd never find its like again—not the harbor, not the streets, not the mosques, not the people's faces. Where would I find extras like these again? And quite as important was the effect of the place upon me; as it was a source of fear, it was a source of inspiration. The very force that drove my hero west was the one I experienced every day as I walked the streets; I was a foreigner who feared his surroundings. I still felt what my hero felt: I've got to get out of here alive. Didn't Charlie know how important this place—even its inconveniences and its corruption—was to me? He was thinking like a unit manager, not a director. Besides, we'd lose the film we'd shot; they'd certainly confiscate it, and what we had that would accredit my film as real, make my story a true story, not just a "movie," would be lost. Where the hell could we get stuff like what we'd shot again? Where else were there hamals? Nowhere!

By the time Charlie returned, I'd decided to stay there and do the best I could under the circumstances. But Charlie came back with a practical plan to pull our unit out of Istanbul and move it to Athens. "It will take some time to make the move," Charlie told me, "so there'll be a delay." I was against it until he told me he guaranteed to get the film we'd exposed out of the country. This changed my mind. And he made good. Some days later, when I got to Athens, where our people were already finding new locations and building sets, Charlie told me how he'd saved the scenes I'd shot. The exposed film had been put into boxes marked "raw stock," passed through Turkish customs, and arrived safely in Athens. On the film the Turkish government had confiscated, unexposed negative placed in "used" boxes, there were no images.

So it turned out that I would have five or six days off before the transfer of equipment, camera, sound, and crew could be made. It was my chance to get to Spoleto and be with Molly.

THE INTERVIEWER, a grave, gray-haired man, was asking Molly questions she'd never been asked before. A serious student of the theatre—more than kindly, genuinely concerned—he wanted to know what she'd meant to say in this work. European commentators treat plays and films as pieces of personal expression; in New York we grade openings: moneymaker or flop. Molly was answering the man thoughtfully and at some length; he noted her responses carefully on a fold of graph paper. How happy she was! I didn't want to cut short so satisfying a conversation, so I interrupted only to kiss my wife and walked out on a small balcony. Below me the city of Spoleto floated in space. Here was gathered, so Molly had written me, the greatest collection of Roman remains in any Italian city. For this Festival of Two Worlds, the streets had been further enlivened with pieces of contemporary sculpture. I'd also read somewhere that one of the main industries there was the collection and preparation of truffles; yes, it was called an industry.

Then the interview was over and we were alone. On the way to lunch, she proudly showed me the theatre where her play was being performed. The sides of the interior were of fine old paneling. "It is one of the most beautiful theatres in the world," she said, "and could only have been built by an aristocrat. Democrats don't build theatres like this." Along the twisted cobbled streets, people greeted her, and in the restaurant that she'd selected, the waiters smiled at her. "In Europe," she commented, "taxi drivers and waiters know more about plays and films on view in their area than some of our critics know. And their interest is more heartfelt. Our critics use words like 'Devastating!' and 'Overwhelming!' but if they'd been overwhelmed and devastated as often as they say, they'd hardly be alive now. That interviewer truly cared." Molly was in heaven.

We had linguine primavera, which a rich red wine eased down, then a rum-soaked pastry and black espresso. I was delighted to be in her company and listen to her talk. Even now—and she's been dead twenty-five years—often when I have a problem I wish I could consult her. It was a role—adviser and truth teller—that she fell into easily and enjoyed. I'd never known her to shade the truth, and she helped me on this day too.

There was a moment in my film story that several of my advisers and backers had talked me out of. They said it was old-fashioned theatre for my little Anatolian, when he finally arrives in New York, to fall on his knees and kiss the ground. "You're not going to use that corny old bit, are you?" one of them had said, and in the end I'd been influenced to eliminate it. "After all," I'd reasoned, "the whole film demonstrates how grateful he is to be in America at last. Why do I have to punch it home with a cliché?" I told Molly I'd decided to cut it. Her face was stony. Then I told her about my experience in Istanbul and my belated appreciation of what my father had done for me. "I doubt that anyone born in the United States has or can have a true appreciation of what America is," I said. "Then how can you even consider making that cut?" she asked. "Don't listen to other people; you've been there, you've been through it. You're a fool"—and now she was violent—"for listening to other people's opinions!" (Except yours, I whispered to myself.) "That is an instant of genuine emotion in your story. They're precious and not to be slighted or to feel embarrassed about." Our talk accomplished just what I knew it would and what I wanted it to. I felt clear about my course.

I suppose she saw the love and sympathy on my face, because now she told about herself, and how something was happening that worried her. She said that she'd start to consider a subject or a scene, then her mind would wander. She sometimes couldn't remember the next morning what she'd been writing the day before. Something uncontrollable seemed to be wrong with her concentration. "What were those old exercises for concentration Lee Strasberg used to give?" she asked. "I get my mind on a subject I want to explore, but it won't stay there. This never happened to me before.

Maybe it's because no one is waiting for my copy. Or that I have to finally shed a lot of concerns I've always had and—"

"And be selfish," I said.

Something childlike came over her face. "Yes, the way a child is," she said. "I'm also starting over in life. A child has no problems with a wandering mind, does she? Sometimes I even fall asleep when I'm working. Do you know what I'm talking about? No, you wouldn't."

I asked her where her mind went when it wandered. She said, "Sometimes to the children. I wonder how they are and plan what to write them or have imaginary conversations with them and consider advice I want to give one or the other of them. That's all right; it's inevitable I should think of them. But often—for instance, I'm suddenly having an argument with a traffic cop or advising an author in the playwrights' group at the Actors Studio. But I'm afraid I'm the one who needs advice. Then silly things. My nails! I'm going along, then suddenly my nails worry me. So I fuss with them for a while, then play another game of solitaire. Can you believe that suddenly I'm solitaire-crazy? I despise that game, but I never stop playing."

I told her that this was the first time in her life she'd been alone with the whole weight of each day's worth on her back and that her puritanism required that she improve each day with some accomplishment. She got mad at that word. "I'm not so damned puritanical," she said. "I merely wanted to tell you," I said, "that I don't know anyone with a better mind. You and Harold Clurman are the two best critics writing about the theatre today—" "I don't want to be a critic!" she said, and her face showed a fury I'd never seen there before. I'd insulted her. But I laughed—or tried to—then poured some more of the red wine and asked her to take me around town and show me the sights.

I stayed three days, and maybe I helped her and maybe I didn't. "There's something too neat about my stories," she said to me over our breakfast on our last day. "They're too predictable. What do you think? Something's wrong, isn't there? Do I have any talent really? Really? Tell me. Answer what I've asked you." She looked at me anxiously and waited, but I didn't answer as I should have, because I wasn't sure how far I should go and whether I was right in what I thought. But I knew what would have happened if the positions had been reversed. She would have told me exactly what she thought, and it would have been the truth. Here's how I ducked the issue: "People who see your play here, how do they react?" I asked. "Oh, they laugh," she said. "They seem to like it. They respond. Sort of. That's what I'm worried about. That 'sort of.'"

We flew to Rome together, she to catch a plane for the States, I for Athens. The night before, I'd seen the performance of her play and its companion piece by Ed Albee. Watching them, any fool would know that Molly was a nice person and Ed perhaps less nice, but his play had heat and punch, and hers did not. After the show, I saw that everybody in and around the theatre—the actors, the stagehands, and the management—loved Molly, recognizing that she was a person of rare class. I also saw that this wasn't what she wanted. When we kissed goodbye, I told her that she, along with my mother, was the best person I'd ever known, but I'm afraid that wasn't what she wanted to hear either. During our three days together, we'd not made love.

T H A T night, in Athens, I wrote her a letter:

Dear Day [her nickname]: I want to tell you what a good time I had with you. It seems silly after all these years to say this. I'd gone along supposing it would—somehow—be taken for granted despite all personal miseries and inner troubles. But you always seem to doubt it so I want to say it to you plainly. I enjoyed being with you. I enjoyed getting you things and having you look good when you were cared for and flattered and fed and listened to. You are a nice looking woman, an exceptionally fine looking woman, an unusually beautiful woman, with both rectitude and softness, gentleness and the bearing of worth. In Rome, your plane to America was right next to my plane to Athens and I watched you walk on and I thought: that girl doesn't have enough confidence in what she has and is. And I thought, it's your fault, i.e., my fault. Then I thought, no it isn't your fault, then it is, then it isn't and so on, back and forth. But I guess all that makes no diff. The only point of this letter is that you are an unusually fine looking person who doesn't know it, mixed up with a very mixed-up person, me, who does know it (about you). Perhaps he'll be able to do something about it. I don't know if anybody, repeat, anybody, is worth the amount of concern you've spent on me. But I'm now trying to— well, what? I don't always know. Perhaps to find out what got all twisted up between us and what we might still become in the time that's left.

She answered:

It's true, I'm shaky. And I guess it's true that if somebody I cared about had been propping me up all the while, I might be firmer. But then you (in yr. mix-up) got me attached to you (in mine) and just how you could have coped with it, I can't imagine. So you acquired one very shaky girl—who always sounded positive—about everything except herself.

Then she got going:

Tell me. Write me sometime. Not all that shit—"Rectitude!" I hated that! But tell me, do you really still like me? I feel as though I'm a very neglected, very undernourished item which has to be given sunshine and vitamins and a reason to live. Then maybe—slowly—it can change—a little.

And then:

The trip was great. Kay Brown [her agent] tells me I look better than I ever did in my life. She must mean the new coat and hat. Well, I still like hearing it. Now I'm back in this terrible city where, in the immortal words of Arthur Miller, "There's too many people!"

And finally:

Strasberg had a long, boring but fascinating interview in the *Trib* which I will save for you. One quote: "I always hoped the Studio would become a Theatre; I assumed or hoped or expected that it would be part of Lincoln Center." Who gave him this hope or expectation or assumption? Did you? I don't remember that you did. There isn't a session at the Studio that he conducts without rapping you. And Cheryl with her big soft heart supports him. I can't help wondering what she really thinks.

I'VE TRIED to tell the truth in this account of my life. There must be inaccuracies of dates, places, and what people did or failed to do; that's inevitable in a narration of what happened so many years before. But I have told the truth as far as I know it—except for one sentence a page back. The truth, which I know very well but avoided saying, was that I hadn't made love to my wife in three years—not only over those three days in Spoleto. We weren't intimate that way through the last years of her life. In a Western civilization, with a "Western" woman, I was making the grand experiment of the Oriental male, to separate love and sex. In every other essential, I was faithful to Molly; I'd devoted my energies without reserve to supporting and, when she needed it, protecting her. I was her husband truly, and my thoughts and my energies were always with her. Friendship, at the end, was our truest bond. Was this enough? For her? For me? Could it be? Not by American standards. And perhaps not in fact.

. . .

IN ATHENS, Charlie and our production designer, Gene Callahan, had performed a miracle. Everything was humming. New locations had been found to replace those we'd lost in Istanbul; they weren't as telling, but they would do. Some settings to match those we'd lost were already being built. And the film I'd shot, so precious to me, had been processed in Rome and the lab report was okay. We were set up to work at the Alfa Studios, at the edge of Athens—a perfectly adequate facility, it seemed to me, if poor compared with our great industrial plants in California. As for the people Charlie had engaged to support the core of technicians we'd brought from America and Italy, it was all conviviality and chaos. I was to find these Greeks lovable and quarrelsome, sycophantic and arrogant, devoted and unpredictable. Gene Callahan got the best work out of them by bullying them at the top of his voice. The Greek extras demonstrated the poverty in which they lived by stealing toilet paper rolls and cloth towels; these had to be resupplied daily.

For my personal needs, I was provided with a "service flat"—four rooms and a housekeeper, who had dinner waiting for me when I came back at night. To attend to other needs, I acquired a mini-harem built around two actresses whom I could call on whenever I chose. They were good girls, lovely as well, who wanted to get ahead in their profession and made the mistake of believing I would help; one was exceptionally bright in the ways of the theatre and the other a beauty-prize winner, "Miss Greece." Both of them introduced me to their fathers, who apparently accepted the relationship for what it was and thought nothing wrong with it for their daughters. But for me there was one drawback: None of the girls had anything difficult about them. Or challenging. After I came, I would wonder how quickly I could clear them out of the place so I could sleep in peace. I remember the farewell words of one of them. Looking particularly flushed and pretty, she said as she left, "Did I please you?" Can you imagine an American girl asking that before going home alone?

In Athens I spent my full store of patience and energy each day at work, then, exhausted and often harassed by difficulties, didn't want to talk and was glad to be alone. There were times, however, particularly weekends, when I did feel lonely and thought of Molly. I'd been writing her three or four times a week, and she'd responded with the details of her daily life, of her psychological unrest, but above all of her hopes for our future. I found that I missed matching wits with her, even of getting mad at her for her unqualified stands and her moral rigidity. So I asked her to come spend some time with me in Athens. I had to talk her into this, because she didn't want to let up on supervising the preparation of our "perfect and forever" apartment, and also because—I must suppose—she had suspicions I'd made other sexual arrangements for myself in Athens and that she would, despite my cleverness, be made aware of them when she came there. How-ever, she did finally agree, as I'd hoped. "Got your good letter about com-ing over. I will!" Then a sure sign that she was coming: "Will Athena Productions pay for my trip?" she wrote. "I think it should. I'm valuable. I think I can help, I mean just being there to sound off to because you can't tell your worries to the people you're pepping up. And we could sleep together—eat a little—gas a little—all that stuff—and I like to share the makings—be around. Well, I will be at the end anyway."

If there is anything I don't like to do, can't do, and won't do, it is to "share the makings" of a film or anything else with anybody, especially someone as clever and critical as my wife Molly was. But the rest of her letter was so loving and so perceptive that I was delighted to read it again and the next morning again. I'd complained about the heat and she'd re-sponded: "I wish I could send you a cool, green drooping tree to stand under." Her letters were the best things I received, and because of them our bond never loosened.

Then came a telegram informing me that she was in Doctors Hospital, that it wasn't serious, and, chasing this wire, another, which she'd dictated to my secretary: "Don't worry, it's not serious. I am awfully disappointed about not coming." Then a letter from my brother, Avraam, a doctor him-self. "It's a cut and dried diagnostic and therapeutic situation. Phlebitis, as you must know by now, is a common ailment—the pleurisy associated with it being the only complication." And another from Molly, scribbled with a pencil on typewriter paper: "This is some drama that Jim Leland [our doc-tor] is having with an unseen and unlocated blood clot! All I had was some-thing that felt like a pulled muscle but Jim shifted into his crisis tempo and here I am under orders. Bed rest! I feel dopey but in a pleasant way." I got the impression she'd needed the rest and was enjoying it thoroughly. "But I feel bad not to get there. This means I won't."

Then for three weeks came loving letters about all the attention she was getting from our friends. And one from our daughter Judy:

Each day she looks better than the last time I saw her. She sits on a high bed, surrounded by flowers and thick, intellectually titillating books, the kind you want to read but never do, and sweets, all kinds of sweets. She wears a pale green bed jacket to match her eyes and a soft pink flower to match her cheeks. Your business cronies send her extravagant presents and call her with news and ask for news of you, as well as for advice and for reassurance. Standing on her table are pictures of old friends, Ralph Steiner and Clifford Odets, along with folders and clippings of possible dresses; she is still too cheap with her own clothes. Also ready is the French edition of her two plays, which she inscribes proudly. Her husband has called from Greece and she quotes the latest *word* from the Front. Apparently that is the cure. She looks lovely and rested and happy—except for missing the trip there. And it was probably (in light of what happened) a very good thing.

There followed a flood of letters—as she dropped declotting pills—letters full of love and longing as well as of news about the newly formed Actors Studio Theatre. Lee Strasberg had come to visit her with Paula, and he'd told her that he wished I hadn't resigned, that I couldn't be replaced. (But Gerry Page and her husband, Rip Torn, had replaced me on the board of the new venture, and I was relieved.) I wrote to Molly and called her, trying to tell her how sorry I was, particularly that I was not there to be a comfort. But the truth is that, while I was concerned about the phlebitis, I was relieved that she hadn't come over. Things had become increasingly difficult on the set. It was not an easy picture to make, and I didn't want to talk to anyone after each day's work, not to Molly, not to anyone else. I'd go home alone, go to bed after my supper, and get up early in the morning to think of how to perform that day's work. Molly's presence there, despite all the love and good sense she'd have brought, would have been one complication too many.

A T   T H E   same time, and often in the same mail, there came a cascade of letters from another source. Barbara praised our son, kept me up with every change in his appearance—his eyes were turning brown at last—and told me how everyone who saw him, when she wheeled him through the park in his carriage, marveled at the little boy. "He has a whole fan club," she wrote, "and holds court every day." She'd named him Leo. Whereas Molly wrote wisely about my professional problems and sympathetically about each of my friends, Barbara was jealous of attention I gave others, held my friends in dubious esteem, and was suspicious of those she believed did not approve of my interest in her. Molly wrote me at great length about the Repertory Theatre and how hard Bob Whitehead was working on our "tent" theatre in Washington Square. Barbara wrote me that she'd been interviewed by Bob and by Bobby Lewis, who was in charge of our training program—I was pressing to have her included—and that Whitehead had "kissed me and flirted with me." Barbara often felt this about men she encountered; did she ask for it? Bobby Lewis visited Molly in the hospital and told her stories to make her laugh. Barbara despised Bobby and his "superficial" teaching. "He shows off and camps all the time," she wrote, "and he doesn't like me. Natch!" Molly had high hopes for our theatre; Barbara, who doubted everything in the world, expected little good to come of the venture. Molly's letters were full of broad concerns, family interests and, at the same time, political events. Barbara's letters were pitched on a single key, our sexual relationship and how she missed it and hungered for me. Her letters were filled with intimate memories and expressions of desire; she hoped I wouldn't forget her.

"W E'R E having childhood stew for dinner," Molly said.

"Wonderful. Now I know I'm home."

"I bought a fig pudding too and made the brandy butter. Oh, I'm so glad you're back in one piece, it's over, all the waiting. Well, there are your big windows. Aren't they magnificent?"

"God, how dramatic!" The whole two-story wall over Central Park had been filled with a pair of windows sixteen feet tall. The light, pouring through, hurt my eyes.

She knew my every expression. "There'll be curtains to filter the light," she said. "Going up next week. It's hard to get good men to come to work, the men you want. Wait until you see the view at night: the whole city at your feet."

"I can imagine. You've really done a job here. Aren't you proud?" She smiled, nodded. I was trying to remember how much she'd told me the windows cost. "And here"—she turned, pointing to the right—"is my study."

"Oh, wonderful!" I said. "Your dream come true."

"Nakashima made the table for me. The man's an artist. And the chair." She read some concern on my face. "I'm paying for all the new furniture," she said.

On the Swedish rug, a game of solitaire was spread; it hadn't come out. "How's the work going?" I asked.

"So far so good, but slow. Too many irrelevant things on my mind." She pulled me away. "Come look at the kitchen. I know it will be your favorite place."

It was large enough to hold a table and two chairs. "We'll have breakfast here," she said. "Like it?"

"It'll be my favorite place. Oh, there's a phone," I said, starting for it. "I'll call Bob Whitehead."

"Couldn't that wait until morning? He knows you're here."

"How? He's waiting for my call."

"I told him when you were coming in, that you'd be all wound up, and that you'd call in the morning. Really, darling, you should start to unwind. There's nothing that can't wait a day, is there?"

"No, of course not; you're right."

"I do hope. Oh, I do hope."

"What?"

"That you can unwind here. It may seem strange to you now, you're not used to it, but it's all here to make us both comfortable and— Come look at your study."

We walked through the room under the giant windows again. They were a force. Then she turned into a side room with a long table and two chairs. My familiar desk litter was there—arranged and waiting.

"Look in that closet," she said. "Go on. Open the door."

I did, revealing a fully equipped photographic printer.

"Ralph Steiner put it in for me," she said, "so it would be perfect in every detail. I told him to make it all the best but on a small scale. My welcome-home present. Welcome home."

I kissed her. "And the developer?"

"Ralph said there isn't room for a developer, and he knew you wouldn't have the time or the patience for that."

"He was right. I don't. But this—it's wonderful. Thanks."

"I got it so you would spend more time at home. Unwind. Relax. I'm so glad you're back. Do you like the place? Tell me. Really. The truth. Come see the bedroom. Do you really like it?"

"Oh, yes. You've done an extraordinary job."

"I have worked hard. There's an architect's drawing for everything. But it's for the rest of our lives, so— I've got some unwinding to do myself."

"Oh," I said, "there's our old bed."

"I wouldn't change that," she said. "After all, four children were con-ceived there."

I'd fallen onto it, closed my eyes, thrown my forearm over them. I was tired.

"Good," she said, "relax. Give in. I'm going to make us an old-fashioned."

She was gone. I heard the apartment house's elevator through the walls. I recalled our brownstone on Seventy-second Street and its porch directly off the bedroom, where I used to sleep nights under the summer sky. Then I found I was controlling myself. May my children forgive me, I didn't like the place. I hated those big windows; they were bullies. The room under them looked cavernous. I like softly illuminated rooms. I knew I'd never print any pictures. Who has time for that in my line of work? As for un-winding, how the hell was I going to unwind when I had a long, unevenly shot film of dubious worth to edit, a most uncertain leading man to make look good, a composer, Manos Hadjidakis, whom I didn't know well, on his way to New York to score the film, and—and the whole damned Repertory Theatre program, with its mess of unanswered questions and the choices I'd have to make with Bob.

Unconsciously, I'd picked up the phone. Then I put it back on the bed-side table. "Unwind, for chrissake," I said to myself.

So commenced what she'd planned to be the final phase of our life to-gether. I would hit out in the morning between nine and ten, and she'd sit in her office, on her Swedish rug, and spread a solitaire game. "Helps me think," she'd say. When the game wouldn't come out, as most of them did not, she'd deal again. If, for some reason, I'd come home during the day, she'd be on the floor with solitaire still spread before her. Success or failure, she'd have no reaction except to continue.

To make up for lost time, I'd try to come home to dinner every night—after all, she'd been alone all day. Radiantly glad to see me, she'd say, "Darling, would you fix me an old-fashioned?" I'd do so, then sit by her side and hold her hand. Nothing satisfied her so much as talk. It was what she missed most in her home life: not physical attention, which I suppose she did miss but never spoke of; the exchange of ideas, that was what she wanted. But I was usually so tired when I came home that I had no talk. Even in the morning, thoroughly rested, I didn't speak; I was constantly preoccupied, planning the day to come. She'd wait for me, delay dinner, so we could talk. I'd come home and she'd be reading one of the plays Bob and I were considering. "Do fix me an old-fashioned," she'd say, "and sit with me." But I wouldn't talk about that either—the play, I mean. I felt her loneliness, but I was too tired for discussion that might turn into an argument.

It hurt her that I didn't include her in the life of the Repertory Theatre. Partly I felt that if I did, I would have to include Bob Whitehead's wife, who was also a pleasant woman to be with but not as clever about such things as Molly. "I fail to see why we can't talk about what's happening at Lincoln Center, or why we couldn't have a chat about the plays you're planning. After all, you left this play on the table for me to read. Surely you want to hear something more meaningful than I like it or I don't like it, do it or don't do it. There really are problems with this play, for instance, and you should listen to me before it's too late. Miller too. You mustn't believe what you read in the papers about him. Art's not that good. We don't want that proven at your expense, do we?" But I would never discuss my professional problems, and she felt that I was excluding her from my professional life.

When she had a gathering of guests, it was my opportunity to come home a little later, for then she'd have friends to fill out her life for an evening. She was hungry for what they gave her that I did not: talk. I'd apologize for my tardiness, lest it be seen as indifference to their presence, then try to enter the conversation. But with me there, the talk inevitably changed to questions concerning the Repertory Theatre. I had to respond to the doubts that gossip had stirred up, all in anticipation of what we might or might not do, and to defend Bob and myself against the latest attacks while still trying to be fair and understanding. How easy it is, I thought, to sit on the sidelines and take potshots at those who are exposing themselves. I strained to be modest and pleasant—that was Molly's favorite word of the hour: "pleasant"—to not be arrogant, to show that my judgment was balanced, for inevitably I'd be quoted. Then I'd catch myself on the brink of sleep and, as I pulled myself back, wished, with that pleasant smile still on my face, that they'd all go home to their beds so I could get into mine and prepare for an early rise and a long day.

In all that talk, I heard Molly's gentle, cultured voice, more confident than the others—or so it seemed—more certain she was right. Was this confidence a show, was it a sign of uncertainty? She would insist on her point again and past all reason, so that by the time the evening came to an end, she was wrung dry and more exhausted than anyone. What I did particularly admire was her ability to make a negative comment to a man she knew would be hurt, speak the truth in a kind voice but without hedging or shaving her point, and, having done so, having caused a wound and killed a favorite position, increase that person's respect for her. How did she do this? The pure in heart!

Sometimes, having come home on edge and short of patience, I'd deliver myself of a hurtful or cynical quip to one of the guests, and Molly would scold me after the visitors had gone. "That wasn't really very funny, you know," she'd say. "I know," I'd say, impatiently. "But then you're tired," she'd say. "When are you really going to unwind?" Then she'd propose a trip to the Caribbean or a cruise on a luxury liner. "Some of those boats, I'm told, are very pleasant. Or we could go to London and sit in a hotel. You should see some of their productions." "I'll talk to Bob about it," I'd say. "Maybe we could all—" Which is when she came close to breaking. "No," she'd say, "no! Why are you always pushing me away? I want to go somewhere alone with you." "Yes, of course; as soon as I see an opening of time," I'd say.

I knew those trips would never happen, not tired as I was. I also remember that inevitably, after her guests had gone and the weariness was on her face, plain to be seen, she'd say, "Let's stay up a little longer and have a talk, just you and I for a change. We never really talk anymore. I won't go on about Lincoln Center, since you don't want to. Let's talk about anything. The children. I got the most beautiful letter from Judy yesterday. I left it out for you to read; did you read it?" "No," I'd say. "You haven't any idea what a lucky man you are," she'd say. "Four wonderful kids!" Then she'd tell me about Judy, the news being that she was pregnant and happy about that but determined not to have more than two because she was an aide at her local Planned Parenthood. But soon it would come out: "How are things going with you and Bob? Really? He's such a fine man. So you be good. But tell me. Tell me!" "Darling," I'd say, "I've just got to get some sleep."

Sometimes I'd come home very late from a meeting with Jo Mielziner and Eero Saarinen or the Repertory Theatre board or from looking at an actor we were considering for the company. When I got home, she'd be asleep on the bed, not in it, the bed light burning and an open book by her head. She looked like a child, all pink innocence. I would wake her just enough so I could get her into bed. I recall her voice now. "Hello, Sugar," she'd say, then fall asleep again, smiling.

AMERICA AMERICA is now my favorite of the films I've made, but early in 1963, when I was editing it with Dede Allen, I had doubts about its worth. Then, when I needed luck, I got it. Manos Hadjidakis came my way from Athens and bolstered me, first by his help in finishing the film—the last five percent of the work on a movie is often the difference between success and failure—but even more by his confidence in the worth of what I showed him. Manos was a king that year; he was also a man perhaps excessively devoted to his mother, who'd lost his four front teeth and never bothered to replace them. He was plump—I don't mean gross—and when the occasion called for it, given to releases of a terrible temper during which his whole bulk shook. He was also a genius.

Most composers who work on films, when a director doesn't like what they propose, become contentious and, one way or another, hold on to what they've already put forward. Some will sulk. If I didn't like a tune Manos offered me, he'd make a quick gesture of dismissal with his plump hand, discarding what he'd suggested. If we were conferring in a bar, he'd ask me what kind of thing I wanted, spread out a paper napkin, draw five quick parallel lines, and scribble a melody. Quickly he'd have a solution for me, so I became bolder about making my contrary wishes known. Manos believed that it was the treatment, not the melody, that mattered. At his orchestra rehearsals, sitting at a piano, he'd sketch the basic melody for the musicians he'd brought together, then walk from one to another, telling each instrument where to come in with what, and in a short time, standing on his feet, he made his arrangement. This method of work has its advantages; it allows the composer and his instrumentalists to exchange reactions and make suggestions. It is built on one talent's faith in another. As a director, I understood. I called it improvisation.

Manos was not only a composer, he was a dramatist, and his sense of where the drama was, how to reinforce it, how to join various episodes so they'd have the most effect, surpassed my own. He also had the most overwhelming joy in working and in his work; it was easy for him, and once he started, he was like all the other geniuses I've known, a compulsive hard worker. He'd earned his success the hard way. The old saying that genius is ten percent inspiration and ninety percent perspiration underestimates the importance of relentless effort. But work doesn't describe what these men do. There is a blacking out of everything else in their lives; it's all secondary—love, greed, pleasure, family. The work experience is what they want from life. They don't know how to "unwind," nor do they want to.

Necessarily there is an intense selfishness and arrogance about the men called geniuses, and there was about Manos. I've been called arrogant and selfish and self-centered, and I'm not, by any stretch of the imagination, a genius, but I've borne the accusation—if that's what it is—and my answer is: "Why not?" What's more important, who's worth more among us? Let the common man put up and suffer. A person of talent who can function with that talent is the finest thing on earth and the only answer to the old question: Who is man and why is man and what is man supposed to be? Manos did not tolerate any interference with how he wanted what he'd composed to sound. His musicians were terrified of him, and again, why not? So were Toscanini's. It helped the end result.

Men called geniuses have been the joy of my existence—but I didn't know them as geniuses. All those I've known and worked with—Aaron Copland, Clifford Odets, Tennessee Williams, Harold Clurman, Orson Welles, Marlon Brando—have a joyous intensity in work and have passed it on to me. They are blessed. Along with all the other sparks, they all have great laughs. Laughing comes easy for them because life is what they want it to be; they are what they want to be, doing what they want to do. They don't question their worth. They no longer respond to disapproval. Manos never, not once, showed any hesitation about what he wanted or what I'd think of it. He did wonderful things for my film at a time when the film most needed that contribution.

All the above is skipping over the essential question: Are these people born with the divine gift or do they acquire it? Granted they work harder than others, granted that their lives have usually been richer and, therefore, better soil for growth, granted that there is some special eagerness about them and usually an especially strong energy—granted all this, how does the phenomenon called a genius come to be?

I don't know. But this I have noticed about people with mysterious gifts: In many cases, a wound has been inflicted early in life, which impels the person to strive harder or makes him or her extrasensitive. The talent, the genius, is the scab on the wound, there to protect a weak place, an opening to death; that's how it came to be. These are our heroes, those who have overcome what the rest of the race yields to with self-pity and many excuses. When I've worked with men and women who came successfully out of misfortune, I've found that they have strength that is extraordinary, and their strength is a gift to me. So it's been, not only with Manos, but with other talented composers and with the actors and particularly the actresses I've worked with. Their precious gifts, for which they paid in pain, have made me successful when I was successful. I've relied on their talent; it's the essence of what I've needed most from the rest of the race.

A L L that summer, Bob and I worked with Art Miller on his new play, which he was calling *After the Fall*. We'd drive to his home in Roxbury, stop a moment for refreshment, then adjourn to his work cabin and hear him read what he'd written since our last visit. Invariably we praised and encouraged him, for he had worked hard. I admired his devotion and was grateful for it. What did I truly think of the play? What I thought was: It has to work. This reaction, while heartening for Art, was not really fair to him. I don't think I was much help to him that summer. I was so anxious to see him finish that my judgments were not true. Did we have a choice except to encourage him consistently? Our theatre was hanging from a rope that we were braiding together. By now all my conscious reservations had been put aside. We were all three veterans, determined to make the future come out our way. The Repertory Theatre's fate was being decided in that cabin back of Miller's home in Roxbury, and we knew it.

Later, waking in the middle of the night or at idle moments of distraction in my cutting room, I knew the truth: that during my experience with *America America*, particularly in those months when I was overseas directing it and making all decisions every day, I'd felt totally myself in a way I never had before. In the making of that film, all activity had started from a directive I gave, and each day's program was based on my wishes. That was what I wanted to be, the unchallenged source. I recognized that from now on I'd only be able to work that way. I'd achieved the goal I'd always sought: to be on my own. I could no longer cooperate with others as I'd once been able to; up against the obligations of the Repertory Theatre, I felt threatened, overwhelmed by issues and demands in which I wasn't truly interested and sharing the power of decision with other men. *America America* had spoiled me. I'd become intemperate and quick to resent encroachments on my time and my authority; I found it increasingly difficult to control these reactions; I also found that I didn't want to.

But I was in the clutch of a situation I'd invited, so I shoved my dissatisfaction back into the darkness and the future. I was a good boy at our board meetings, I was a good boy at our program-planning sessions, I was a good boy in the company of the actors we'd selected, and I was one hell of a good boy, compliant and respectful, with Art Miller.

However, the main reason for my devotion to the cause was my concern for Molly. She'd invested her soul, nothing less, in her hopes for a pleasant life of work together, side by side, in the "perfect" home she'd made. Pleasant! I grew to hate that word. I don't know exactly why; perhaps she used it too often. By the end of that summer, I'd begun to feel that her hopes were doomed. I was behaving "badly" again; after controlling myself all day, I came home frazzled and on edge and not at all pleasant. I was edgy too, "antsy," for implicit in her "perfect" life was the condition of celibacy for me. I could see that wasn't going to work, and it didn't.

I'd finally pumped up the courage to show her the rough cut of the film. Her reaction was crushing. She detailed it in a five-page single-spaced letter of judgment that might have come from the Supreme Court, and it destroyed what I'd done. She said she couldn't follow the film, that I should use a narrator's voice all through, explaining to the audience what they were seeing. She'd written this letter carefully and very well—no one wrote a better letter—and with a lordly sympathy. What she was saying on every page was that I'd loused up an excellent script, one she knew well, for she and Sol Stein had made it into a book, which attracted praise I'd enjoyed; she did have a proprietary interest. I was so upset that I did no more than scan the letter, have read it carefully only now, and although I knew that what she'd written came out of an anxious concern and a good heart, it was unrelated to anything I could do. I'd used every scene I'd shot and had no material to make the changes she suggested, even if I'd wanted to. I thought her critical powers had run wild and become destructive. My response was that most hostile one: "I'll think about it." I'd admired her critical candor when it was directed at others, but when I was the target, it made me furious and alienated. I wasn't allowed to forget her points, however; she constantly worried me about them—she loved the book that much, she said. So I crawled into my cave of silence and never again showed her the film.

I C O U L D N'T help wondering if she had a reason of the soul for wishing my film to be a failure. In time I got up the gumption to ask her this, and she had the gumption to answer truthfully.

"It separated us," she said.

Perhaps at last she was responding to my "neglect" of her.

O N   T H E   24th of October, in a hall over a kosher
restaurant, we started work on Art's play. Brought together for the first time
was the company of actors we'd selected. At their side were our two stage
managers and our designers, Jo Mielziner and Anna Hill Johnstone. Seated
at a table far to my right was Molly, who wanted to see our cast. With me
on the producer's side of a long table were Bob, Art, and Harold Clurman,
whom we were still trying to involve with us and who still hesitated. Perhaps he felt slighted—felt he should have been in my place, making the
traditional opening remarks of a rehearsal.

I came to my theme from an unexpected direction. Twelve weeks earlier
I'd had a call from California informing me that Clifford Odets was down
with cancer and dying, and I'd flown west with Harold to see him before
he went. I'd thought a great deal about Cliff in the weeks that followed, and
at the first meeting of our acting company, I spoke of what his premature
death had meant to me:

The tragedy of our time in the theatre is the tragedy of Clifford Odets. Not that I share the sentiment expressed in his obituaries that he'd failed in his career. Clifford influenced a generation of playwrights— Art Miller, who's sitting here; Tennessee Williams, who told me that his first arousing experience in the New York theatre was *Awake and Sing!*; and a roomful of other writers. Like all true creators, he influenced men who'll never know it.

Cliff spent the last dozen years of his life writing films to pay bills that were too large for a man who hoped to continue working in the theatre. He made his home in a Beverly Hills "Spanish mansion." He drove a Lincoln Continental and had what he claimed to be the outstanding collection of Paul Klee in the country. He worked frequently and was well paid by New York theatre standards. But he was always broke or near it, and I believe he died broke or near it.

In his last years, he'd stopped turning out original film scripts. Rewriting big-budget films that had a pressing start date and were in script trouble paid better. And by sticking to "polish" jobs, Cliff avoided the artistic responsibility for the final film, so he didn't soil his reputation. He would juggle a few scenes, throw in some colorful dialogue, and drive away. He wanted no screen credit; perhaps he was ashamed.

Odets was the first man I called on when I made a trip to California. We always had dinner alone and always in his house. He would welcome me as if I was a lifeline to the shore where he longed to be and the sea stormy between. He had five plays all laid out, he'd tell me, and waiting for the day. His plan, he said, was to spend only nine months more in southern California, then come back to New York and get these plays on. They'd be, he assured me, the best plays of his life, even told me the story of three of them in considerable detail, and I believe they would have been fine plays, for they were deeply conceived and personally felt. Cliff wasn't "shot." Something was wrong, but the mind and talent were alive in the man. He'd had terrible difficulties, marital and political, and gone west to find the strength to again affirm the purpose of his life.

The last time I saw him outside a hospital was in February of this year. I was full of Lincoln Center, and I reminded him that he'd always said that if a theatre existed, he would write for it, that he could not and would not write for "Broadway." I told him that we were trying to do what he'd been waiting for, and he must write his plays now and write them for us, that we wanted to produce them all at the Repertory Theatre. Again he answered that he intended to spend only nine months more in California—it was the Dick Boone show this time, not a movie rewrite—and once that job was done, he'd be through there. Then he went on again about the five plays that he had all laid out—a phrase that by then had come to have an ominous connotation.

I paused for breath. I found Molly. Her eyes were glistening. At the end of Cliff's life, she'd come close to him and he to her. She knew the rest of the story.

He died on the fourteenth of August, but on that day in February, there wasn't a sign of illness on his face, and his eyes flashed with fire as they had when he was twenty-five and writing *Waiting for Lefty*. His skin had the velvety look of a healthy man in his mid-fifties. Did he believe that he was going to remain in Hollywood only nine months more? Did he believe that the TV shows he was writing for Dick Boone and the residuals therefrom would solve his financial problems, that there'd be no more polish jobs, scavenger jobs, dialogue jobs, save-the-show jobs, that all these humiliations would come to an end and he'd be back speaking for the human spirit again from a free stage and giving forth his special incandescence?

He had to believe that. So he did.

I looked at Barbara. She was studying Molly, then noticed I was observing her and dropped her head.

I said, "Clifford, what frightens me is the possibility that you will finally not write those five plays, that they will be found as notes in your files at the end. I fear there's very little time left. For any of us. You say the date on your plane ticket east is nine months from now. Do you really believe that? Tell yourself the truth before it's too late. Because suddenly the race will be run, the victors posted, and it's part of history. Here we are sitting calmly on a warm evening, enjoying the exceptional wine you're pouring, but time is running by at the same headlong pace and— Cliff, are you listening? I mean don't count on its mercy. Hurry!"

He was hurt. He shook me off. And I gave up. Despite what I'd said, neither of us knew how late it was. In six months, the disease that eats you had eaten him. He lay on a bed on the sixth floor of the Cedars of Lebanon Hospital when I saw him for the last time. At one moment during that long day, he raised his fist for the last time in his characteristic, self-dramatizing way and said, "Clifford Odets, you have so much still to do!" Then he looked at me, slyly, and said, "You know, I may fool you, Gadg. I may not die." He contemplated that for an instant, then he was elsewhere, thinking of something unspoken. His mind was wandering. He gave me his hand to hold and looked around as if he wasn't really where he was. Then, again changing abruptly, he glowered at his nurse, a fine, patient woman, and declared, "I want to shout, I want to sing. I want to yell!" The nurse, who'd heard it all before, said, "Go on, shout, yell, sing if you want to!" Then he tried, I remember he did try. But his shouting days were over. He was a mighty sick rooster. So he lay there and glowered angrily at the world in general and whatever it was that was cornering him now. No longer able to avoid the tragedy he'd lived or the tragedy that he was or the thought of what he might have been, he beckoned to me to lean closer, and he whispered—I remember the words well—"Gadg! Imagine! Clifford Odets dying!"

What I'm saying to you through this true story is that the chance we have here won't happen again. The series of accidents and aspirations, along with real estate deals, civic concern, and guilt feelings, and the desire of rich men to have their names remembered after they die, all those piled together produced this surprising opportunity for us. It won't happen again. Not for many years! So let's not lose it.

The tragedy of the American theatre and of our lives is what could have been. Forces dispersed instead of gathered. Talents unused or used at a fraction of their worth. Potential unrealized. We all know our problems. We are not kids, we are not students. We know we are here on short leases. It is now time to stand up for ourselves before we disappear from the scene.

The man who, in the forties, promised to be the Hamlet of our time has yet to play Hamlet, or anything like. The man who could have been the Lear of this generation is playing a sheriff on a TV series. I don't think he plays sheriffs very well. He could have been a great Lear. The man who could have been the greatest actor in the history of American theatre is sulking on a grubby hilltop over Beverly Hills or on a beach on the island of Tahiti. What happened to them? They don't know. Don't look down on them. They are not weaklings. They were idealists too. Nor are they corrupt, confused, or sicker than most. They are your brothers.

What is so terrible in our society is that people like ourselves are only rarely in control of their own lives and destinies. We don't do what we want to do. We do what we think we have to do. Or what's worse, what other people want us to do, what "they"—whoever "they" are—want us to do. We settle for costarring roles on a TV series we despise, for the approval of our agents and a better contract this year than last. When we go from flop to flop we are terrified. When we find ourselves in a hit, we are bored to death.

Now we are going to try to do something we respect for a change. It is hazardous. When you say something is difficult, you are saying it might not work. We are here to attempt a birth. All births are difficult. Look at a baby's head. Don't you wonder how it managed to get through? Like everything else worth doing, it is impossible.

I had dinner with my film agent the other night. He has other clients in this room. After we'd ordered, he opened the conversation with: "Well, tell me, Gadg, what are you going to do now?" Which is exactly what he said years ago as we left the Fox studio after Darryl had backed out of *On the Waterfront*. I'd told him many times what I am doing now, but his mind wouldn't take it in. He thinks of this as a temporary aberration. So I told him again. He asked how much I was making here. I said I hadn't been paid anything yet, but when we got started I'd get so-and-so much. You should have seen his face! "Well," he said, "do a couple of plays, then get the hell out." He didn't say what I should get out into.

For you to be here makes no sense by the philosophy which thinks of life as an escalator of richer deals. Common sense does not advise you to take this step. The people who warn you that it's impossible are right. Imagine building a theatre building to be occupied for two years only! That's my crazy partner's idea.

I smiled at Bob Whitehead. I was proud of him.

Yet in a long and lively life, I haven't found anything worth doing except the impossible. Theatre historians have often called the Group Theatre a failure. By what standards? I just made a movie that every wise producer in the film industry believes must be a failure. It probably will be, in their books, but I'm especially proud of it. All I gave was time, and all I'll probably get is pleasure. But what could I ask for that's dearer? We are here at the first meeting of a group of theatre people who are, as I see it, attempting the impossible. In a money-oriented, marketplace society, we are embarking on something because we believe in its goals and because we anticipate being exhilarated by its challenges. Don't look for common sense here or for practicality. You won't get rich here; go elsewhere for that. Only remember that this day I said the word "impossible."

THE NEXT morning we began rehearsing. Art had suggested he might start things off by reading his play to the cast. He said he hoped that hearing the play read by its author would convince the actors that it would flow successfully from present to past and back. He sat facing his cast, and as he opened his script, he said, "This is a happy play, the happiest work I've ever written." Then he read the scenes in a rabbinical voice. By this time

Art had been the object of so much flattery because of *Death of a Salesman* and his response to HUAC that he must have expected all reactions to whatever he did to be favorable. But some of the actors, experienced backstage birds, didn't respond to his play as he'd hoped. They were bored by it, which Art didn't immediately notice but I did, and it worried me. It wasn't a good start for a difficult production.

The next day the actors read, and again the response worried me. I should have anticipated one reaction. Jason Robards's part consisted of Miller speaking to the audience what he might have said to himself. Jason knew immediately that his role was a dud. Many of the scenes were played *around* Quentin, not with him; for him to observe and comment on but not take part in. In theatrical parlance, he was frequently "feeding" other actors lines that they would "top." Jason saw this and resented it. It was at this reading that I began to suspect that Jason wished he'd never come into the play or our theatre. In time my suspicions proved to be true.

And in time Miller became aware of the disappointed reaction of his cast, and he responded correctly. He is a courageous man, and very soon he faced the fact that not only were there problems but he, not I, had to do something about them. I told him we could get through the first act okay and bring the audience back to their seats, but our problem was Act Two. I told him it was serious, but I knew for sure that he could fix it. For this opinion I had good reasons.

Although Arthur denied it and still does—why I can't understand—the second act of this play is about one thing: his marriage to Marilyn. I knew a bit about this relationship because of something that happened in 1960. She was making a film titled *Let's Make Love*, and her leading man was Yves Montand, a French actor whom Fox was trying to make an "international star." They failed in this, but he didn't fail with Marilyn. When I heard about this infidelity, flagrantly conducted, I wondered, as did many others, whether Miller could take the punishment. What I didn't wonder about was Marilyn's boldness. I knew how audacious she could be when she wanted something. This defiance of custom can be astonishing in women, but they are often impelled by a desperation men don't know. Art, by comparison, was an innocent, and out of his depth. I felt for him.

I was in California at the time and called him. He seemed grateful for the attention and the sympathy. Hearing the emotion in his voice, I suggested we have a meal together. Over the food, I didn't bring up what was going on, but I saw the pain on his face and some anger too, manfully controlled. Three years later, remembering the way he was that night, I knew there was more to the second act of *After the Fall* than he'd allowed himself to reveal. If he would dig into those bad times, to which I'd been an arm's-length witness, if he'd go all the way and tell the truth of what Marilyn had done and what he'd felt, we might have a strong second act.

I'd also spoken to Marilyn, once, after their divorce, and she'd revealed her anger at Art and a degree of scorn (which I'd thought unfair). She'd expressed revulsion at his moral superiority toward her and to much of the rest of the world. I knew that there were scenes between her and Miller that were a lot more dramatic than those he'd let us see.

I didn't remind Art of any of this during those first days of rehearsal; I only said that the second act could be much better, then let him hear what he then had, read by the actors again. I urged him to go home to Roxbury and give me a chance to get the first act "on its feet" while he concentrated on the text of the second act. I'd need at least a week to do my part, I told him, so giving him uninterrupted time to make Act Two what I hoped it would be. I was playing a hunch that if he went home, troubled by the knowledge that his cast and director thought his second act disappointing, he would dig into his memory and produce something that was intimate and bold, overcoming his play's shortcomings by the strength of its climaxes.

THE OTHER reason I was sure that the second act could be powerful was Barbara. I hadn't needed anyone to tell me she fitted the role. I knew her past in detail and knew Marilyn's personal history as well. They'd both been "floaters" and come out of almost identical childhood experiences, which had left them neurotic, often desperate, and in passion difficult to control. It was obvious to everyone at the first cast reading, even to those actresses who hadn't understood why I'd given her the role, that she could be brilliant. I turned to my authority: Molly had been watching Barbara as she read the scenes. "What do you think of my cast?" I asked her, gambling that she'd say something about Barbara without my asking directly. "The girl is excellent," Molly said. "Perfect for the part. Where did you find her?" "She's in our training program," I said. "Bobby Lewis told me about her."

True and not true. Bobby had indeed commented on Barbara, not only to me but to several others. "She's only in the training program because she's Kazan's girl," he'd said. Of course, this got back to me, as Bobby knew it would. Not one of the teachers in our program had given Barbara good marks. My old friend Anna Sokolow, who conducted the dancing classes, made this judgment: "She may be talented as an actress, but her movements are tense and she's too lazy to improve." Our voice teacher's judgment was that Barbara's voice had not improved and never would. He was right; her voice had not improved and never would. The general impression was that her means were limited and what range she had was narrow. Again true.

But in the arts, versatility is an overvalued asset. Barbara could range from A to B, but within that range she went deep. Every value the great British academies of acting value—and correctly value—she lacked. Her voice was squeaky, her body without notable grace, she had very little variety and less brains than cunning. What she did have was passion, and in the right role, there was no one like her. Anger liberated her body and brought unexpected shades to her voice. She was able to go from the kind of innocence we used to believe fifteen-year-old girls possessed to a pitch of rage that actually frightened Jason Robards, her partner in their scenes.

Molly's "Perfect for the part" was not altogether a compliment. In the wig she was going to wear in the production, Barbara did look like Marilyn. Molly had found Marilyn, quite apart from any connection I may have had with her, distasteful, thought of her as a corrupted neurotic and one who'd cost Art grief and humiliation. To Molly, this Marilyn Monroe part was a villainess; I must suppose that Barbara projected that to Molly.

Later, when I saw Barbara alone, I asked her what she'd thought of Molly. "She's a very handsome woman," she said. Clearly implied was: "What are you bothering with me for when you've got her?" That reaction was a common one in the Repertory Theatre. I don't really know what the two women thought of each other. What women say in that situation is not what they think.

As Barbara began to work on Miller's revised second act, she won everyone's respect. There was a naked truth in her acting that we rarely see. I knew I'd made this possible by giving her confidence in her talent, encouraging her boldness, bringing her to Miller and urging him to accept her. So I was pleased.

I'D I N S I S T E D on an extra-long rehearsal period; the play needed it. Toward the end of the fourth week, we got the news from Dallas. Rehearsal stopped dead; the cast was immobilized; the actors closed their scripts and sat where they were, stunned. I remember Faye Dunaway, Barbara's understudy, sobbing. Many others cried. Not since Roosevelt's death had there been so catastrophic a blow to show people. They'd believed in this President, as they had in Roosevelt, not because he was devoted to them or had supported them; I doubt that Jack Kennedy really liked the theatre. It was because of his "air," how he carried everything off. One look had told me that he was an actor too and understood our way of life, shared our values and our morality. He was one of us. He had that old leading-man quality, *dash*.

The Bay of Pigs? Forgotten. Khrushchev and Vienna? So what? The gossip about his backstairs escapades in the White House made him more, not less, attractive. Our actresses were flattered by proxy. More power to him! Actors admired him; he was making it with the same girls our show business glamour figures enjoyed. I'd been invited to the White House twice during his term and I'd stayed close to him, watching everything he did. He reminded me of a certain kind of star who could do light comedy—*The Voice of the Turtle*, for instance, not all that heavy Group Theatre stuff. I won-

dered who could play him on the screen and decided on Warren Beatty.
Warren had everything Jack had: looks, intelligence, cunning, and a commanding eye with the girls. Not many escaped either man. Warren also
suffered from lower back trouble. I once asked him if this hampered his
lovemaking. "It doesn't hurt them," he answered. Our President had the
poise that a leading man needs to carry a play. Like those fellows who walk
into Sardi's and make every head turn, he enjoyed the adulation that was
showered on him. He enjoyed being who he was.

A miserable, jealous, excluded little extra had killed our leading man.

Kennedy was hardly a statesman; he was a politician of the new breed,
media made, as Roosevelt had been, but with more clout because the
equipment he used was better. Like all the great show business personalities of his time, he had fine writers to meet every occasion, whether a
speech or a quip. One never knew how much of what he said was his. This
technique became the politics for our day. Sock it to them! Jack was in a
line that would go on to Ronald Reagan. Like Reagan, he made what he
said seem his own. (Compare Mondale. Who didn't) Kennedy was riding
the wave of the future. "Jack," as someone said, "gave off light instead of
heat." His writers lived and wrote by the light he shed.

It was clear that rehearsals could not go on that day, so I told everyone
to go home. Many of them didn't; they clung to each other for comfort. I
went to see how Molly was taking it; Jack Kennedy was her hero. She stayed
in front of the tube all day, watching the tragedy develop, and all through
the evening too. When she finally went to bed, I could see she was furious,
particularly at the observations of one commentator, who'd said that the
country would have to wait for history to judge this President's worth. She
was determined to challenge that. In the morning, when I went for coffee,
I saw her writing with the greatest concentration of purpose I'd ever seen
her show. There was no solitaire game on the Swedish rug that morning.

What she wrote, a poem, was read by an actor at a requiem service for
show people at St. Clement's Protestant Episcopal Church. Sitting in the
audience were the people of our world, and among them the theatre reporter of the *Herald Tribune*, Stuart Little. He was very moved by the
poem and took it to his newspaper, where it was passed around. Molly got
a call: The poem had made a deep impression on everyone at the paper;
could they print it? Molly was thrilled. The next morning her work was on
the front page of the paper's second section. Featured.

The public response was overwhelming. There were so many requests
for copies that the *Herald Tribune* prepared reprints and made them available to whoever called at their office on Forty-first Street. The managing
editor of the paper wrote Molly: "This newspaper is proud to have published your poem. We salute you for the heart and sensitivity that shone
through every line." Channel 13 used the poem as part of their Kennedy
tribute. Molly herself received several hundred requests for copies. "I'm

still hoping to get a few extra copies," she wrote Stuart Little, "as I'm cleaned out and more people have asked for it today."

    This note was written on December 8, six days before she died. At last she had the triumph she wanted. The qualities that made her plays seem didactic fitted this form: a woman's tribute to her hero, written with love and softened by Molly's gentleness. It describes Molly as much as it does Kennedy.

        I think that what he gave us most was pride.
        It felt good to have a President like that;
        bright, brave and funny and good-looking.

        I saw him once drive down East Seventy-second
        Street in an open car, in the autumn sun
        (as he drove yesterday, in Dallas).
        His thatch of brown hair looked as though it had
        grown extra thick the way our wood animals in
            Connecticut
        grow extra fur for winter.
        And he looked as though it was fun to be alive,
        to be a politician,
        to be President,
        to be a Kennedy,
        to be a man.

        He revived our pride.
        It felt good to have a President
        who read his mail,
        who read the papers,
        who read books and played touch football.
        It was a pleasure and a cause for pride
        to watch him take the quizzing of the press
        with cameras grinding—
        take it in his stride,
        with zest.
        He'd parry, thrust, answer or duck,
        and fire a verbal shot on target,
        hitting, with the same answer,
            the segregationists in a Louisiana hamlet
            and a government in Southeast Asia.
        He made you feel that he knew
            what was going on in both places.
        He would come out of the quiz with an "A"

in Economics, Military Science,
   Constitutional Law, Farm Problems, and
   the moonshot program,
and still take time to appreciate Miss May Craig.

It felt good to have a President
who looked well in Vienna, Paris, Rome, Berlin,
and at the podium of the United Nations
—and who would go to Dublin,
put a wreath where it did the most good,
and leave unspoken
the satisfaction of an Irishman
en route to 10 Downing Street
as head of the U.S. Government.

Our children cried when the news came.
   They phoned and we
phoned and we cried and
   we were not ashamed of crying but we were
   ashamed of what had happened.
The youngest could not remember
   any other President, not clearly.
She felt as if the world had stopped.

We said, It is a shame, a very deep shame,
But this country will go on
more proudly
and with a clearer sense of who we are
and what we have it in us to become
because we had a President like that.
He revived our pride.
We are lucky that we had him for three years.

I was proud of her.

I T   S E E M E D to me that during those last weeks we'd finally found a way of living together, one that made us both content. It was not conventional in this society and time, but not unusual either, and apparently it was what we both wanted, since we settled into it easily and it did work. I had lived on an either/or basis and had been constantly on edge. Now I'd come to another solution, one with which I felt satisfied because I had both relationships I wanted. My "experiment" seemed to have worked; a stable work life, a wife I loved, a mistress I found stimulating, each offering me different benefits. Wasn't this the way many men lived, though they didn't admit it? Even if it was in their imagination? I didn't know what else would work for me, not after all that Molly and I had been through together. Or work for Molly either. She didn't require of me now what I could not give her, and apparently what she did get from me was enough. She seemed to have finally come to some sort of resolution of her feelings, an acceptance of my nature, that I had different needs from hers, just as she had different needs from mine. So I was careful and she was contented.

I wondered why people make such a fuss about infidelity; sometimes it's the only thing that keeps a marriage together.

I still saw Barbara, but less frequently, irregularly. Neither of us looked to the other for any further development. She didn't totally trust me or totally admire me. She wanted to do her own kind of work, not mine. Later in her life, she did. We'd come to a solution that worked, or seemed to. The strain of it all was easing, our situation was gentling down to an agreeable routine. It was the best we could do.

I am speaking, of course, only for myself; I can only surmise what the others felt. That was a mystery.

REHEARSALS had resumed. I came home late every afternoon, directly from Washington Square. Molly would be waiting for me. "Make me an old-fashioned, would you, darling?" she'd say. I'd fix a pair and sit with her to hear the events of the day, who'd called to praise the poem, who'd written to express thanks. A friend of hers had decided to send it out as a Christmas greeting and asked permission to do so; Molly had been flattered. Senator Jack Javits had read it aloud to his children. There'd been scores of letters full of gratitude for having put into words what so many people were feeling; she'd articulated the consciousness of the moment. The thanks she'd valued most came in a warm note from Bobby Kennedy, written in his squiggly hand. Molly knew that she had made many people feel better.

The poem, not the play, was the subject of our conversations at this time. When she'd ask about rehearsals, I'd be evasive. "We're in the set now," I'd say, and drop it there. She frowned and lit a cigarette, her signal to be prepared for a long conversation. "How does this setting work?" she asked. "Does it help the play? Tell me." "I hope so," I said. Nothing more. "How's Art?" she asked. "Is he behaving himself?" I didn't know what she meant; I'd forgotten all about our "political" differences, but Molly had not. "Art's fine." "Did he say anything about my poem?" "Nothing," I said.

Art was fine. He'd brought in a new second act, which was strong and true. I did not believe, as many people did after the play opened, that he was unfair to Marilyn. I'd seen how she'd humiliated him with the Frenchman, and I was sympathetic to Art, not to her. I knew how unprepared he was for that kind of tension. I also knew the degree of anger and vengeance she'd felt; it had been unremitting and without pity, and now it was all in the play. I admired Art for being so candid about their relationship, and I did not think him, as some people in our circle did, self-serving. I believed Marilyn came off better in the play than he did. Maggie was exciting and true; Quentin was a bore.

Now that Barbara had the scenes and the lines, now that she knew the reach and the depth of the part, we could all see that however dull Jason's part and his uncommitted performance would be, Barbara would be superb and perhaps unforgettable—if there is such a thing in the theatre; I mean she'd "carry" the play.

O N E   M O R N I N G   I left for rehearsal at a quarter to ten. Molly was affectionate as I went out, yet I left her happy to be alone to work. She said that because of the poem and the fuss about it—which was thrilling—she was having trouble getting down to work on her play. "I'm not a poet!" she said. "I'm a playwright." I reassured her; yes, she was a playwright, so go ahead and write her play. Then I kissed her and left.

Her birthday was two days away and, on the way downtown, I bought her a present, a ceramic statue from Peru, perhaps ten inches high and pregnant. On the card that was to be delivered with it, I wrote: "Patience, I guess. Love, December 1963."

I came home at seven. Our maid, Becky, was sitting alone in the silent living room under the great windows. The TV was not on, and Becky loved the TV. "Mr. Kazan," she said, "you'd better look into the bathroom. Mrs. Kazan has been in there for hours."

I knocked on the door. No answer. I tried the door. It was locked. I called again. No response. "She had a headache all morning," Becky said, "had it bad," she said. Now I hammered on the door. "Molly!" I called. "Molly!" I decided to break the door down. I ran at it and threw my full weight against it, again and again. Finally the lock splintered the jamb.

Molly was on the floor, at the foot of the bowl, her clothing pulled down. I turned her face to me, covered her body, flushed the toilet. Her eyes were open. I spoke to her; perhaps she'd fainted. No response. I carried her into the bedroom and stretched her out on the bed. Nothing I did caused a reaction. Her eyes did not see, her ears did not hear, her reflexes did not respond.

I called Jim Leland, our family doctor, and told him what had happened. He said not to move her again, he'd be right over, and that he'd send an ambulance for her and arrange for a room at a hospital. Before the ambulance arrived, Jim did. He didn't name what had happened, but it was obvious from his face how serious he thought it. His silence was the diagnosis. "She had a bad headache all morning," I told him. Jim nodded as if he'd expected that. "Cerebral hemorrhage," he said. Then he tempered his flash diagnosis. "That's what it looks like."

Her eyes remained blank as we waited for the ambulance. Jim tested her heart; it was beating normally. But there was no other sign of life. "Molly! Molly!" I kept whispering in her ear, but there was no response. She still didn't hear, she didn't see. So we sat there helpless. Jim said he'd go ahead to the hospital and make sure her room and bed were ready.

Becky left too. On the rug in Molly's study, a solitaire game was spread; unsolved.

The ambulance staff had encountered scenes like this one every day. Molly became part of a routine. I remember the trip through the lobby of our building. The staff watched the procession—Molly, the ambulance attendants, and me—with a look of fear on their faces. The presence of death frightened them, but they'd get over it in an instant; they'd also seen this kind of thing before. Then we were in the ambulance. I didn't know why they drove so fast or why they needed to sound the siren so often. Was there that much reason to hurry? Apparently they'd been told there was.

Jim was waiting for us at the hospital. A nurse and I put Molly into the bed. She was still. Jim told me not to expect a recovery. I asked him what the word he was using, "aneurism," meant. He told me that it was a weak spot in the wall of a blood vessel in the brain, usually congenital, made weaker by the rush of blood past it over the years, until it bursts. "What makes it burst?" I asked. Guilt was rising in me. "It's the blood rushing past, usually past a curved place, finally wearing the wall down. No one can anticipate that it will burst. The breaks are always like this one, sudden and past helping. Then the flow of blood destroys the brain. I'm sorry," he said. "But the truth is you shouldn't hope." "What can we do?" I asked. "Nothing," he said.

After a while he left. Molly and I were alone. I held her hand. The pulse was still there and seemed strong. No one came into the room. I stretched out at her side and held her in my arms. And waited.

Later I noticed that her feet were becoming cold. I held one in each hand, to keep them warm. But I knew that wouldn't help.

It occurred to me that I had to tell the children. I found a phone booth and called Judy, our eldest, and told her what had happened. "Oh," she said, "oh!" I asked her to call her brothers and her sister. Then I hurried back to Molly. I held her feet again. They were colder than before. There is a pulse just by the ankle, and it was still there but seemed weaker.

Her face was beautiful. Relieved of life's tensions, it had eased; the lines and wrinkles were disappearing. She looked years younger.

At three in the morning, the pulse stopped. "The heart goes last," Jim had told me.

. . .

T H E   T R O U B L E with being a film director is that you rarely see your children as they're growing, and when you do, you're under stress and a bit irrational. You can go through the years, as I did, without being really close to them. If you're shooting, you're trying to decide in the morning where to put the camera, and in the evening you wonder why you hadn't approached the scene from another angle. Weekends you're working with the author, trying to get the scenes for the next week right, or with the casting director, trying to fill in for a sudden defection or to cast the parts you haven't cast yet. Then the film is finished and you're asked to help promote it in the big cities, and you have to travel through a jungle of humans, telling half lies that you hope will be believed and listening to other half lies.

The sorry result, in my case, was that although there was much love between my children and me, there was very little practice of love. Add to this my upbringing: My father was an Anatolian role model, and I maintained, or felt I had to, an authoritarian posture, head of the family, which, carried to extremes, confined the children to chores, supporting and obeying their male parent at all times. So you can understand why there was a gap between my children and me.

It took their mother's death to bring my family close, for me to really appreciate how fine the children she'd given me were and finally surrender any posture of command over them. A wonderful relationship started at that time, and despite its tardy start, it has continued until now. They take care of me; I, when I can, of them. We became, in the small things that make a true union, a family.

The first thing we did together as equals was plan a requiem service for Molly and plan where her body should lie. We agreed to stage this service, open to everyone who wanted to attend, in St. Clement's Church, where Molly's poem about the fallen President was first read. We decided that I was to speak. We decided that I was to take her body and bury it in the quiet field below the studio she'd planned and had built in Connecticut. When I wrote what I intended to say, I offered it to them for their comments and corrections.

Our family conference was frequently interrupted by phone calls, most of which I didn't take, and by visits, which I tried to cut short. I was too stunned to communicate with anyone except my children, so I stayed in my room with the door shut. All the old Group Theatre crowd came and sat with the kids, whom they hadn't seen in years. They were impressed and gave Molly the credit she deserved. Harold Clurman, Lee Strasberg, Cheryl Crawford were all there, as well as the members of Molly's playwriting group, as well as actors from her productions and mine. Soon the apartment had a lively, convivial air, not at all funereal. There were calls from California, among them one from Karl Malden, informing me that he was coming east for the service. There was a call from Washington to offer admiration and sympathy; it was from Bobby Kennedy, who'd not forgotten Molly's poem. I wrote him: "One of the things that would have meant the most to Molly would have been your phone call. I'll never forget it." Bobby was the only politician I've ever liked.

I don't know how events of this kind are announced in theatre circles, but they get around with a speed that's amazing. When I got to the church, the place was standing room only. Molly's memorial service had become a civic event. I made a good speech, a compression of regret, love, longing, and admiration. When I'd thought about what to say, I'd lived over part of her life with me, and I was steeped in regret. I said, "This immaculate girl was struck down without warning, cause or reason, lived without hope of survival for twenty hours, after which her heart stopped. She was not a member of any church. If she had a religion, it was the truth, telling it at any cost. She mothered four fine children, helped playwrights, who are here to acknowledge her support, helped me in everything I did for thirty-one years. She leaves her own monument."

Then I said, "When I was looking over the papers she left behind, I found this note: 'Our writers have all been crying shame, shame! They say that dark pools of misery and injustice exist in our country, cultural deserts and racial discrimination. All true. But where is the pride? The pride because we do attack these flaws? We do make headway? Our goals are high and we achieve much. Where is that balance which says we're only human? Let us esteem what we have done. Let us continue to attack our failings but let us not put on sackcloth. The human condition is not perfect, but the sense of shame can become a paralysis. Let's give thanks that we have high standards and, being human, we have done as well as we have. We have a damned fine country, yes, in trouble, but show me a better!'"

The atmosphere at the memorial service was the kind that often results when a hero is taken before his time. What I saw on people's faces as I spoke reminded me of what I'd seen on people's faces when the news came that Kennedy had been assassinated—but it was warmer for Molly. What surprised me was that there were people present who I knew had differed violently with Molly many times but now came to present their sincere sympathy. There had been widespread criticism of Molly among those leaning left; many of them had blamed her for my testimony, said that she'd influenced me, which was unfair and inaccurate. All she'd ever said to me was: "Do what will make you feel best in the long run." Now, as I spoke, I recognized the faces of some of the people who'd reviled her eleven years before. If they still felt hostility toward her, it was not evident. The atmosphere was one of healing.

Later, at home, we sat around, ate, drank, told anecdotes, laughed, and renewed friendships. Actors came in after the final curtain of their shows.

We stayed up all night, family and friends, and loved each other. And so
her life ended.

THE NIGHT after she died, while the body was being prepared for
the funeral, I walked alone toward the Paris Theatre on Fifty-eighth Street.
I stopped at a distance from the crowd in front of where *America America*
was opening that night. I didn't want to be seen or to talk to anyone. An
opening night party had been planned, then canceled. I waited a block
away until all the audience had entered. As I waited I recalled Molly's reaction to the film, how negative it was, even hostile, and I wondered about
the intensity of that reaction. What had caused it to be so violent? I'd been
shocked at the time and been resentful. Now I tried to understand it. Making the film had separated us at a time when her last child was leaving
forever and she was being thrown totally on her own, with only me to be a
support and a companion. Wasn't that reason enough to resent the film?
She'd put it plainly one night. "I hate that picture," she said to me.

I turned away and walked home. I wanted to relive part of my life with
her. In my imagination, I went over it from the first time I saw her. I was
behind a counter, serving food to a line of students at the Yale Drama
School cafeteria. I could recall the suit-dress she wore, a pepper-and-salt
tweed. Then I went on through the years, and I saw that nothing could
have been different. Our characters are our fates, and hers was strong and
mine was—what it was. It would have all come out the same.

Perhaps, failing every other emotional and physical bridge, our artistic
connection was the only one she could count on, and when that was taken
away she felt bereft and, even worse, resentful. My film had made her feel
more alone than ever. Had she become tense with anger and hatred of the
film and of me in the film, and had this final tension precipitated the break
in the blood vessel in her brain, the aneurism?

I walked into the empty apartment. There was a pile of telegrams I'd not
opened and mail, some delivered by hand. I was astonished, in fact dazed,
by the number of people commiserating with me. I had no idea that people
cared that much, if not for me, for her. There had been so much criticism
of us both during the time of my testimony that I didn't expect this avalanche of affection, concern, and esteem. I believe her unalloyed goodness
had finally reached people. One could disagree with Molly but never doubt
her sincerity. It seemed now that everyone in the theatre felt the loss of
this woman; even people she'd never met wired their sympathy. What had
happened?

The poem had opened Molly to our world; they saw her now for what
she was. By what she'd written, we'd all been joined together over Jack
Kennedy's shattered body. The telegrams and the letters served their purpose too. When the children were there and reading the messages with

me, our grief became stronger for being mixed with pride. The surge of pride was her last gift to us.

I T O O K her body to our place in Connecticut, driving my car behind the long black hearse. It was an exceptionally cold December day. There was a powder of light snow on the ground. I knew just where I wanted to lay her body. A man with a backhoe was waiting for my instruction. I showed him the place to dig, then went up to the home she'd built.

There I found Karl Malden and Bill Fitelson. I built a small fire outside, invited them to go into the house but said I wasn't ready for that yet. We all three crowded around the fire.

The man operating the backhoe walked up the rise in the land and told me that he'd come across a great boulder, some seven feet long, where I'd told him to dig. "Get it up," I said. "Lay it across the back of where the grave is going to be."

I looked at the body a last time. She still wore her thin silver wedding ring. I didn't take it off. It's buried with her. She lies where the boulder had been.

T H E   N E X T day, the four children, no longer children, went back to their own lives. I spent a day alone in the "perfect and forever" apartment. At the end of the afternoon, I pulled up the long curtains and watched the light of the setting sun on the apartment houses across the park. Then night came.

I began to hear noises. And voices. In bed, I couldn't sleep. The elevator's whine came through the wall. I was frightened of the dark. I felt very uncertain of my bearings and of what I'd do next with my life.

I decided to go back to rehearsal. That would divert me.

But it didn't. I returned to the apartment alone at night. It was still haunted. There was more mail. I decided to read it all—I'd avoided this until then because it would make me feel bad. And it did. A lot of the condolence notes remarked on how happy she must have been with my film. An insensitive newspaperman called my attention to "What a classic irony! Triumph and tragedy on the same day!" And a note from Barbara: "I'm sorry, I'm sorry, I'm sorry. Please *forgive* me for my stupidity and all the worst things about me that may have upset you."

The letter that affected me most was from one of the men I'd named in my testimony, Tony Kraber. I'd been closer to him than to the others, closer in the simplest ways; we'd played tennis together and eaten at each other's tables. Then I'd begun to direct movies, spend time in California, so we grew apart. I didn't hear from him during the decade between 1942 and 1952, then after I testified there came a postcard that I'd believed was his, quoting the line I'd spoken in *Waiting for Lefty* when I'd exposed the labor spy: "This son of a bitch is my own lousy brother!" After that, silence. It had been Tony, responding to an interviewer, who'd said that I'd been able to sign a half-million-dollar contract with Hollywood because of my testimony. This was a complete fabrication, but once expressed, it became common, spiteful gossip. I hadn't answered that slur, just as I hadn't answered others that were false.

Now this letter:

"Dear Gadget. I can't help but write you a word of sympathy and grief at Molly's death. We always loved her and thought of her fondly (both of you, if you can believe it). It seems such a pity that such a beautiful person won't be with you for the next twenty or thirty years of your life. Our hearts go out to you. Tony."

After I'd read this letter, it didn't matter that he'd told the lie he'd told about my imaginary Hollywood contract. That he'd written me surprised me, that he'd had that much courage. My response couldn't match his.

"Dear Tony: I was very touched by your note of sympathy. I know it wasn't easy for you to write me and that made me value what you did write more. Thank you."

It was the best I could do.

T I M E'S passing did not cure me. I was afraid in that damned apartment. I heard sounds that weren't there. I'd wake from a dream, saying, "I can't let her die, I can't let her die!" Then go back to sleep. Sort of. But even in the daylight, I'd speak to her, sometimes with longing, other times scolding. I'd walk out into the high-ceilinged living room and say irrational things: "Molly where are you? Molly! Where are you, dear? Where did you go? Where the hell did you go? Goddamn it, where the hell did you go? Why did you leave me like this? Damn you! Molly!" My voice was angry, not sorrowful. I wondered if she could hear me. Or who could. Who was listening? I feared the dark room and kept the lights on. I couldn't sleep. I felt I was sinking.

I knew that something had happened which had completely changed my life, required that I start all over again. Well, I'd brought it on myself. Wait! Why did I say that? How much of it was my fault? Was I being paid back for everything bad I'd ever done? Okay, I could take that. I deserved it.

Then I'd resent that yielding. Like hell I deserved it! I didn't deserve it.

I decided to lift my guilt. In the morning, I called Jim Leland, told him I blamed myself for creating the tensions that had caused the blood vessels in Molly's brain to burst. I quoted *The Merck Manual* to him: "Rupture may follow trauma, fear, exercise, coitus, straining at stool or any other condition which elevates blood pressure." In other words, I could have brought on her death. Possibly because he heard the irrational tone in my voice, Jim said he'd send me the autopsy report, also write me exactly what had happened. His voice was gentle. He was trying to calm me.

I received a letter from him the next morning:

I can't give you the autopsy report, because the Medical Examiner's office does not send them out. As you know, I saw the autopsy and the sole finding was a large blood clot in the brain and over the surface of the brain due to a ruptured congenital aneurism of the middle cerebral artery. These are congenital weaknesses (with a little saccular expansion) of the arterial wall and may rupture at any time in life, usually in middle life. They are not hereditary. If you wish, I can write Dr. Milton Helpern, Chief Medical Examiner, and ask him.

I called Jim to thank him for his letter, but he could tell I was not satisfied. His letter had explained everything except what I was concerned about, why the aneurism had ruptured when it did. Perhaps he saw that I was still uneasy, because he said he'd ask the chief medical examiner to write me.

Two weeks later I had this letter from Dr. Milton Helpern:

Dear Mr. Kazan: Dr. James Leland, whom I know personally and hold in high esteem, has asked me to write you to explain the nature of the illness which caused the sudden unexpected death of your wife, Molly Kazan. The deceased's sudden illness resulted from the unforeseeable rupture of a small, previously unsuspected silent aneurism of the left middle cerebral artery with progressive bleeding into the substance of the brain and the subdural space. Although designated as congenital, these aneurisms are usually not present at birth but develop during the lifetime of the individual—

There! There, I thought: "develop during the lifetime of the individual." Now we're getting somewhere. I returned to the letter.

—develop during the lifetime of the individual on the basis of a structural weakness in the artery wall where branching occurs and because of the repeated pulsations of the blood within the artery. Many aneurisms which give rise to fatal hemorrhages are of very small size and rupture before there is any suspicion of their presence. Some aneurisms reach a size large enough to produce symptoms of pressure and headaches before rupture; in others, the initial bleeding is slight and subsides with subsequent episodes until a fatal hemorrhage may be the first manifestation. I hope this letter of explanation of the cause of your wife's unexpected death will clear up any doubts you may have concerning it. The death was entirely natural.

I wrote Dr. Helpern, thanking him. Jim Leland must have told him what was concerning me, because that last sentence, "The death was entirely natural," sounded as if it had been suggested by Jim; the whole letter seemed to be a kindly put-up job. But Helpern hadn't told me and couldn't tell me what I wanted to know. Nobody could—except myself. And I could only guess.

Jason Robards and Barbara in *After the Fall*

I DECIDED to get out from under. I rented two rooms in an apartment complex a couple of blocks from the ANTA Washington Square Theatre. No ghosts there, no sounds in the night except distant traffic. I worked on Art's play as best I could—that is, "professionally." I did my job. But the play needed more from its director than expert techniques.

I was alone whenever I could be, lying on the new bed downtown, an animal in a thicket, or walking here and there in the Village at night, trying to figure out what I truly wanted from what was left of my life. I could go anyplace now, live anywhere, do anything I wished. This was a shocking realization; it was also the first cheering thought I'd had. Barbara would visit me from time to time, but she found me inert and listless. "How long is this going to go on?" she'd ask. "I don't know," I'd answer. "This could be the new me."

Mornings, before rehearsal, I'd sneak uptown to the apartment, pull open Molly's filing cabinet, and look through her papers. What I found shocked me—a series of false starts on plays, aborted first acts: pages 1–9; another, pages 1–12; another, pages 1–8. On top of the cabinet were two decks of playing cards. What frustration and pain were there, what waste of a fine intelligence! Living in my memory was the spectacle of constant striving after achievement, people losing themselves, faltering, stopping, and disintegrating. Might that be my fate too? Something malignant was gripping me, which I didn't understand but had to shake loose. I determined I would not be one of this number; I'd find a new life.

That thought—to find a new way—kept coming to me. Here I was, deeply involved in Lincoln Center and its Repertory Theatre; a good part of the fate of that effort was on my shoulders. But after Molly's death, whenever I allowed my mind to move freely, it asked for a drastic change in my style of living. My daydreams told the truth: I must get rid of that haunted perfect apartment and live somewhere else, alone, quietly; not necessarily in this country, perhaps in Greece, where I knew the language and the people; perhaps in Paris, the city I loved best after New York. It embarrassed me to confess, but despite the impassioned speech I'd made before the first rehearsal of Art's play, now, only five weeks later, Molly's death had jarred something loose and I didn't give a damn about anything happening at the Repertory Theatre or in its future. It wasn't right, it was shameful, but obviously it was heartfelt or it wouldn't keep coming back.

It was then, during that time of "going through the motions" at the Repertory Theatre—passing whole days without talking except when my professional duties required that I must—it was then that I decided to quit. I didn't know it; I wouldn't admit it, because it was disloyal to so many good people; I would have denied it vigorously if anyone—a psychoanalyst, for instance—had suggested it. But it was during those days, in my silences, that I decided to become another man, ply another trade, and live in a totally different way. It would be almost a year before this actually happened, but during those weeks after Molly's death something pulled my old self loose from what was binding it to what it didn't want.

A S I W A S thinking about this chapter and looking over notes and letters, I happened on Tony Kraber's letter again, the one I've quoted. When I'd copied it into this manuscript and then my answer, I thought I'd finished with it. But I read it again before turning it face down on top of the pile of matérial for that year.

Then, a short week ago, I had a dream that surprised me. I was visiting Tony in his apartment, and all was peaceful and friendly. Tony was glad to see me and I was happy to be with him, but no special fuss was made about it; it was an everyday thing. There was nothing about this dream that made my being there and his welcome surprising. Nothing was said about my naming him to the House Committee on Un-American Activities. We were in the simplest harmony, and it felt fine.

His wife, Wilhelmina, whom I used to like, for she was a stalwart girl, was not in the room, but there was a boy there: his son, I supposed. He wore metal-rimmed glasses and looked rather frail. I don't know what children Tony has or, if he has a son, whether the boy is anything like the person I imagined; he couldn't be, because such an offspring would be well into his middle years now. But I saw the boy young, frail, and withdrawn— hurt. "Where's Willy?" I asked suddenly. "She'll be out," Tony said. I listened for resentment in his voice, but there was none, and I was relieved. "But his wife," I said to myself in my dream, "she must still be angry at me. And this boy, their son, he's not well." Then Wilhelmina came in, greeted me in a casual and friendly manner, then said a sparky "Goodbye, see you later" to her son and her husband and was gone. She'd seemed cordial to me, and I was overjoyed.

Then I half woke and knew it was the middle of the night, because my wife was sleeping beside me. I rolled her to me and she put her head on my shoulder and I thought what a terrible thing I'd done: not the political aspect of it, because maybe that was correct; but it didn't matter now, correct or not; all that mattered was the human side of the thing. I said to myself, "You hurt another human being, a friend of yours and his family, and no 'political aspect' matters two shits."

I wanted to apologize to Tony. "It's not necessary," he said, guessing my thought and speaking again out of my dream. That's generous of him, I thought, just as his letter had been generous. I felt ashamed. I knew my dream was expressing a regret and a wish. What did those old politics or any politics matter to me now? "Political aspect" indeed! Did it even matter that Tony had told a lie about me? He was human and I'd hurt him, and perhaps I'd made it harder for the son whom I'd imagined and kept at that young age. I felt that no political cause was worth hurting any other human for. What good deeds were stimulated by what I'd done? What villains exposed? How is the world better for what I did? It had just been a game of power and influence, and I'd been taken in and twisted from my true self. I'd fallen for something I shouldn't have, no matter how hard the pressure and no matter how sound my reasons. The simple fact was that I wasn't political—not then, not now. I only wished that I could have been as generous and as decent as Tony had been with me.

As for why I'd done it, I couldn't look at that anymore.

Then I woke all the way and had breakfast. I knew the past was past and there was nothing to do about it.

A M E R I C A   A M E R I C A was given a mixed welcome in our press. International critics liked the movie. France coddled it with honors. But here, at home—mixed. My friend Walter Kerr took exception to the dubbing. Had he gone to the showing blindfolded? My pompous pal on *The New York Times* stammered for a few paragraphs, then said it was too long. When they don't know what to say, they say, "Too long!" Financially it proved a disaster. I felt sorry for Ben Kalmenson at Warners, who'd "taken a bath" for me. Otherwise I didn't care. It's my favorite picture. Full of faults, it has virtues that are rare.

Only one reaction truly concerned me—my mother's. I found I was surprisingly anxious about what she'd feel. There were scenes out of her girlhood nightmares, and she'd see them, not read about them. Words can be a buffer. She would see the "savages" she feared most, behaving as the Anatolian Greeks who'd lived in Turkey remembered them. Mother might fear that because of what I'd put on film, they'd revenge themselves on me. I'd never before been so wound up about what she'd think of anything I'd done. But she was the person in the world I loved most in those years; age and her recent widowhood had rendered her more vulnerable. If I hurt her, I'd wish I'd never made the film.

So I proceeded cautiously, surrounding her with the claptrap of security. I hired a limo to take her and a friend to the building in New York where people from Warner Brothers would escort her to a projection room. Then I waited. After I was sure she was back in her apartment, I called. She said very little, but seemed to be pleased. I was so relieved that I chided myself for having been so nervous. After all, art is all, I said to myself. If the film had upset her, she'd simply have had to get over it. Whatever she'd thought would not have caused her physical harm; she'd recover. Why had I worried so, why was I so relieved now? Still I rushed out to Rye to make sure she was okay.

Now, twenty-five years later, the same anxiety has surfaced again, raising the same question with reference to this autobiography: How far does a writer who uses the material of his own experience go when he knows he might cause embarrassment or humiliation to someone dear to him? I am referring to my present wife, Frances. When we were "courting," she didn't even know I'd been a film director. It didn't take her long to find that out, as well as a great deal more "background" that concerned friends provided. I worry that when she reads what you've read, no matter what warnings she's been given, it might upset a relationship that is now happy. I don't know what to do. It's another me that she'd learn about; the portrait of her husband and his past in this book is not altogether flattering.

Eileen, my secretary, after typing one of these chapters a few months ago, advised me that when the book was out I wouldn't have a friend left in the world. That doesn't worry me. What does is the possibility that I won't have a family left. What I've written might offend some of my children. "You must remember it all happened a long time ago," Eileen says to them. But what can I do about that? I make judgments, say what I think, expose things that other autobiographies may mask. Rousseau is my model. I wouldn't write this book any other way. Still I know I'm taking a fearful chance. My family, my children, my grandchildren, my closest friends, mean more to me than anything else in the world.

Except what I'm writing.

s o   n o w   Lincoln Center. I've never sounded off, not a peep, about my experience there with Bob Whitehead and Art Miller or with John Rockefeller and his board. But I failed there, and I was "separated" from it, fired, or would have been, and it was a public humiliation. Although I've been silent about what happened, I've not forgotten. Bob and Art and I worked like patriots, with fanatical devotion, and for long stretches without compensation, then were treated shamefully. Especially Bob Whitehead. I haven't forgotten what I felt. I swallowed it, but it went down hard and doesn't lie easy. Both Bob and Art were and are exceptional men; they were not properly respected, and despite all Lincoln Center's searching for replacements, their equals were never found. Bob and Art were kicked around by their lessers. They tolerated it for a cause. Bob, throughout the years since he was relieved of his position, has maintained a silence, which may be the only dignified way to deal with what was done to him. Now I'll break it.

To start with, we were naive. We never faced the fact that we were not partners but employees, in a vulnerable position, without tenure. Employees have no power in a conflict. The boss has it all. Whom did we work for? Not villains, not bad men, but men out of another world, who were not capable of handling the responsibilities they were given by the men who owned the real estate and had the money. I offer as evidence George Woods, the president of the board of the Repertory Theatre.

George was the most interesting man I met at Lincoln Center. It follows that he was not what he appeared to be. I'm embarrassed to say that I liked him—I'm perverse that way—despite the fact that he became the mortal enemy of my partner, Bob Whitehead, and in time of our effort at Lincoln Center. From behind the scenes he was to supervise our removal from the Repertory Theatre.

Who was he? The chairman of the board of the First Boston Corporation, a director of the Campbell Soup Company, the Chase International Investment Corporation, the Commonwealth Oil Refining Company, Inc. (Puerto Rico), the Industrial Credit and Investment Corporation of India (Bombay), the Kaiser Steel Corporation, the New York Times Company, and the Pittsburgh Plate Glass Company. Does that convince you that he was equipped by his experience to oversee the creation of a repertory theatre? No? It didn't me either. Well, then, add this: He was a close friend of John Ringling North for many years, and a director, treasurer, and financial adviser to the "Greatest Show on Earth." Does that help?

There was a good reason why he held positions on all those boards. He was the essential board member, one tough *hombre,* dressed in the WASP corporate manager's uniform, the three-piece suit of no particular color. I'm not sure he wore the same suit every day, but I'm not sure he didn't. His clothing was designed, chosen, and worn by him and others of his trade so as not to give warning of danger brewing as they took seats around a board table. Men of excessive wealth, like the Rockefellers, who cultivate a culture-loving and public-spirited image—"service" was their ideal, the Asia Society their hobby—need people like George to do their cutting up and paring down. George's presence with his hatchet kept their hands clean. The man, his manners, his actions, his ultimate mystery, fascinated me even as he was "killing" us.

I understood George best by comparing him with my partner. Bob Whitehead's family is Canadian, clean and secure, solid old-time stuff, well educated and well heeled. They own, along with other considerable interests, a good hunk of Labatt's, a pretty good beer. They vacation on cold northern lakes and are expert light tackle fishermen, a talent only the affluent can cultivate. Bob has about him a charming air of gentility.

George Woods was charming too, but not because of gentility; he had, despite his cultivated corporate board manner, the soul of a street kid. Not everybody liked him; he was an acquired taste. I couldn't help believing that the way George behaved was not natural to him; it had to be learned. He must have studied to dress as he did and to conduct himself in a manner that reassured the Rockefellers and their brothers-in-money because it was professionally useful. But oh, God, was he ever tough! He soon found the soft spot in Bob's decency, his sensitivity, his basic kindness, his ultimate good nature—and perhaps his somewhat vague way with the figures on a balance sheet. Bob became George's pet victim. The board table was George's killing field; his eyes would tighten to focus as soon as Bob and he sat across from each other. He hounded Bob down, meeting after meeting.

It seemed that he couldn't stand the sight of Bob and his distinguished good looks. A clash of what's called "chemistry"? That too, of course. But there was in particular a certain "fudging" Bob would retreat to when George came after him with his long knives at a board meeting. Bob would be discomfited just a little, would stumble and lose the rhythm of truth, when George thrust a direct question of costs at him. Then the smell of first blood flowing would stimulate a feeding frenzy in George, and not disguising his scorn, he'd persist until he'd finished Bob off.

But that was in the room where the board met. There was a bigger arena. It started with the incident of the ANTA Washington Square Theatre, which George had tried to block every way he could. When we went ahead with it anyway, Bob deciding here, I agreeing from somewhere behind the camera in Greece, that did it for George. I'm not sure he needed an excuse to hate anyone he chose to hate, but if he did, he had it. He would certainly never forgive the person who'd publicly, openly, and without apology defied his authority and gotten away with it. Perhaps, to see it from his side, Bob's decision to go ahead and put up his "steel tent" seemed to George to be the kind of reckless behavior with corporate cash that only those born to wealth would indulge in. It wasn't Rockefeller's money, actually, but it was certainly Rockefeller's principle of the thing. There it was, defiance! The "tent" went up, the public liked it, patronized it, and it housed one considerable hit. Everyone around town knew what George had said—"You can't!"—and Bob, in his genteel way, had put it up anyway, for Miller and me to produce our show in. And it didn't look half bad. It wouldn't have done uptown, but down there, with all the scholastic freaks, it seemed appropriate. There was a gleam of triumph in Bob Whitehead's eye, and George saw it. People don't take oaths of vengeance anymore, but if they did, George would have, and its point would have been to destroy this gentleman from Montreal who had to be taught that you can't be so cavalier with corporate wealth and, even more important, that you don't fool around with George Woods, who was president of the board and the corporate watchdog over that pile of cash.

I don't know what George thought after the popular success of *After the Fall*. He was quiet. People were paying good money to get in and see the show. I felt he should have been happier than he appeared to be. But no. He was waiting; he knew whom he wanted to "get," and like any jungle animal, he knew better than to strike too soon. But I saw it coming. From the incident of the ANTA Washington Square Theatre, the issue became Who's boss? Who has the authority, the men with the money or the men with the theatre savvy to do the job? We made a mistake. We thought it was an equal contest, one we might win. What we forgot was that we were hirelings. Money was boss. The success of *After the Fall* postponed an outcome that was inevitable.

· · ·

THE critical response to *After the Fall* puzzled me. And still does. I found, when I looked back through the newspaper clippings, that Miller's play was, on the whole, well received. The critics who tore it down were mostly the campus-based academicians who make their way by writing about other writers, making books out of other books and grading artists when they're not grading students.

Some seemed outraged by the fact that the play dealt with the intimate history of a woman who'd become, for reasons I can't understand, their house martyr. They berated the play and the production in defense of a certain Marilyn, whom they'd never met and wouldn't have understood if they had. They found Miller's portrait of Marilyn self-serving, scolded him for using her to make himself look good. If you read the play now, I believe you'd find what I did, that its "hero," Quentin, is a bit priggish and rather pompous, while Marilyn-Maggie, despite her vengeful hysteria in the last scene, is pitiable and tragic. But suddenly she became a cause, and bright boys from every side rushed to her defense by attacking Miller. Norman Mailer wrote about her without having met her—easier to do that way— relying on the illustrations to market the book.

I was amazed, and favorably so, that after his dull first act, Art could write something as *un*-self-favoring, as powerful, as his portrait of this desperate girl and so unflattering to himself. On the whole the audience responded to what certain critics did not. Ticket buyers had never seen anything quite like this play and its production, and everyone without exception cheered Barbara's performance.

We followed *After the Fall* with a production of *Marco Millions*, a minor play by Eugene O'Neill, which confirmed the critical opinion that our sights were aimed too low. Mild and undistinguished, the play offered neither new insight nor theatrical art that could not have been found in a community theatre.

Then it was my turn again, and I made our first "fatal" mistake. Sam Behrman's *But for Whom Charlie* not only could have been done on Broadway but should have been done there. It desperately needed the services of stars, personalities who could carry a play because of what they were, intriguing theatrical "camps" who lived only on stage and had all the mannerisms and cunning of entertainers, not people. Our company had been populated with actors who'd served Art's play and who were to my own taste of realistic psychological drama. To put them in Sam's play was unfair to him—and to them. His play had to be performed as an intellectual vaudeville of quips and bright sayings; our actors wore heavy shoes. The production revealed my limitations as a director, who was clearly working outside of his range, and as the artistic leader of a theatre. I added nothing to the play of wit or charm, of the spry and the sly—nothing that was un-expected or delightful. It should have been directed by another man.

The worst of it for me was that the failure hurt Sam, a dear old man of whom I was fond, in effect demonstrating publicly that he had nothing more to say to a contemporary audience. Sam, understandably, blamed me and never spoke to me again. He retreated into a dark back room of his apartment on Park Avenue and rarely came out of it.

We followed this disastrous production with one that was worse. *The Changeling* might have been worth doing if we'd had the actors to bring it off and the right director. The basic fault, again, was mine. I'd chosen it, I'd asked to do it. But in the face of its problems, I was incapable. Didn't I know who I was? Did I really believe I could do anything? Why would I want to? Did I want to be everybody except myself? Surely, whatever worth I had as a director emerged only when I had material to which I related or in which I had a strong emotional interest. As for our audience, what meaning did the play or its performance have for them? None. There was no reason for them to come to it. The critics who'd informed me again and again that I wasn't suited to the job I held were right.

Although I tried with all my might, was as conscientious and devoted as I could be, I felt little pain when I failed so miserably. My heart had left the Repertory Theatre. After Molly's death, I continued because it was my duty and because I felt loyal to Bob and to Art. My loyalty, however, had a negative effect. I should have admitted my alienation and urged Bob to engage another director. I was still too unsettled emotionally to work well, and I told Bob to be prepared, I was leaving my position there, but that I wouldn't do it or talk about it until a time that was agreeable to him. Per-haps he believed I'd get over this feeling; he certainly didn't want to be left alone on the hot seat. So I did what I've done often in the past, put my head down and took a beating.

There was a bitter irony to all this. I'd trained all my life to be a member of a permanent acting company. From my beginnings in the theatre, I'd made this the goal of my professional life. But when I finally won the posi-tion for which I'd prepared myself with so much reading, training, and hard work, I found that I didn't like it. I didn't like being in the same place every day, didn't enjoy dealing with the same problems every day, didn't like being the father to thirty and more actors who looked to me for guidance and leadership. With some of the actors, I found, I stood as a sort of villain; Jason Robards, for instance. I'd somehow trapped him into an effort that was "no fun," as well as "too much work." The very essence of a repertory theatre, rehearsing one play while performing another, then alternating in roles, wasn't for a few of our actors what it was supposed to be. Nor was it for me.

For Barbara Loden, life with us was one unrelenting contradiction. She'd scored an immense success in *After the Fall*, which made her happy, but then, following her triumph, she saw me as a roadblock preventing her from reaching the stardom her talent deserved. Friends told her that after her success in the Miller play I was depriving her of an even greater success, the kind other, less talented, actresses enjoyed. Barbara would repeat this opinion to me, half giving it her support, testing me, waiting to see how I'd respond. I'd shrug.

She had her photograph as Maggie on the cover of the *Saturday Evening Post*. But even while that issue was being read and she was enjoying compliments, the following week's issue came out, with someone else on the cover, and Barbara felt that she was letting her main chance slip by. The next part in which I cast her was a "bit" in Behrman's play, three lines. Sam was delighted to have her in this tiny role; it affirmed what I'd promised him would be the value of giving his play to the Repertory Theatre. But Barbara resented the role. It diminished her. She believed she'd earned the rewards of having put over a great hit, one that had brought lines of people to the theatre every night. But I was denying her those rewards. She felt trapped.

At the same time, Barbara, like all the other actors there, was an idealist, believing that what an actress should aspire to was to be a complete theatre artist playing many roles, to be a member of a continuing artistic institution doing plays that "said" something. She'd voice these ideals frequently, throwing them back at me and pointing, as we all did, to the theatres in Russia and England. But the pride of being part of a great acting company didn't count in this country as it did in England and Russia, partly because we were not yet a great acting company but more significantly because of what was in the American air, that speedy upward mobility, those sudden dramatic rewards for success. Barbara wanted desperately to be a movie star, at the same time that she despised Hollywood and the films it turned out.

While she believed passionately, or said she did, in the ideal that our theatre was dedicated to, the vry passion of her belief made her more disappointed and so more vehement in her criticisms of our work, especially my own, when we failed. "This is a fake," she'd say to me. "It isn't what you said it was going to be. I'd be better off in the movies. At least that would be honest." "Go ahead," I'd say, "leave. Goodbye." But she didn't go. "I'm a lot better than those actresses in films you used to sleep with," she'd say. "Why shouldn't I have what they have—a decent home, a nice car, and servants and comforts and security? I'll never get those here, will I?" "No," I'd say, "not what you're talking about. Not here." "Well, then, I'm quitting," she'd say. But she didn't quit.

Jason was an idealist too, but without the contradictions. He criticized us from an eminence of what a theatre should have been and could have been, but his behavior was less lofty. He hated the role in Miller's play and said so to whoever would listen. He said I'd given him no help; in fact, according to *Newsweek*, he threatened publicly to "kill Kazan for putting him on stage in *After the Fall* and leaving him without a shred of direction." He made similar comments to gossip columnists. My own impression was that he thought I'd given him too much direction. And also that Barbara had stolen the show and he knew it.

But he wasn't all wrong in what he felt. Since I didn't like the part myself, I didn't know how to make it interesting. But, I thought, isn't it inevitable in a repertory theatre that actors are assigned some parts that are less gratifying than those they'd like? An actor and a director had to do what they could with those parts, while continuing to behave well at all times. Jason did not. I believed his behavior shameful. He'd look at the audience while other actors, farther upstage or at his side, were playing scenes that he was supposed to be reacting to. He'd grumble openly or stare at the people out front with an expression on his face that said, more clearly than words, "Did you ever hear such shit?" Then he began to go further and bitch under his breath to the actors with whom he was playing, whispering irrelevancies, carrying on far outside the play's dialogue, so releasing his scorn of the play, its direction, and the theatre, of everything he felt trapped in and he wished he'd never agreed to. He also encouraged some unrest backstage, nurtured a rebellious little cell based in his dressing room and dedicated to doubt and to what naughty behavior they could get away with. The thing to have done, of course, was to fire him, which he was clearly asking for, but I believed, mistakenly, that there was no one else in the company to play his role. There is always someone else. So I took the punishment. Besides, I was the fellow famous for handling actors, wasn't I?

The irony of it all was that I understood Jason's behavior, even had moments when I secretly sympathized with it. I wanted out, too, but concealed it. I did tell Bob, after *The Changeling*, that the ideal man to have held my position was Harold Clurman. Harold liked being father to a group of actors and dealing with their everyday problems; he'd had years handling Stella Adler's tantrums. Family quarrels in the Jewish theatre were a natural thing, and for Harold they were part of the fun of it all. Furthermore, Harold had no "outside" ambitions, as I did—that is, filmmaking. So to an extent I was feeling something of what Jason felt while, at the same time, I was resentful of his behavior and trying not to make it possible for him to leave the company.

There was one encouraging development. On the male side, we had the beginning of a good acting company, perhaps ten men of talent who didn't have the movie itch and knew they could fulfill their capabilities only in a repertory company. They were a staunch group and remained my good friends. Our next production, a worthy if not exceptional play by Miller, directed by Harold Clurman, was well played by this group of men. For the first time, we presented what was an excellent ensemble of actors playing together in an exceptional way. Watching them, I saw that there could be a repertory company in this country; given patience and time, it could work, could succeed as an artistic unit.

Our final production was *Tartuffe*, directed by Bill Ball, a director we "brought in" from outside our original "family." He was Bob's idea and recommendation, a good choice who did a good job. It was a first step toward bringing additions into our acting company, actors with the capability of performing in plays outside the contemporary realistic mode. These actors and Ball promised to add variety and depth to our company. This step also showed that Bob Whitehead, who was making the fundamental decisions by then, had taken notice of our company's limitations and of mine and was beginning to overcome them. The production was given a good reception by the press. It should certainly have indicated that we were open to criticism, including self-criticism, and were determined and able to adjust our policies to make possible a broader program.

What we needed was what we never got: time—time to discover and analyze our mistakes and to correct them by releasing certain actors and replacing them with others more suited to what we were trying to do. This, I felt sure, could be accomplished. More difficult to arrive at was a proper program of plays and projects, but we'd learned a great deal from our mistakes there too. Perhaps most difficult of all was for me to deal ruthlessly with my own artistic and personal limitations, determine and define what use I could and could not be. In light of this, I wrote Bob a letter to be shown to the board, suggesting that we reorganize our leadership, include Art and Harold in all decisionmaking, and reconstitute ourselves as a foursome rather than a two-man partnership. This we did toward the end of our time there, and it was an effective first step. But our early mistakes and my limitations overtook us and it was, before we knew it, too late to save our theatre.

The disaster of *The Changeling* had destroyed our defenses, and we were now vulnerable both to our corporate bosses—George Woods and his augmented board—and to critics who were seeking to destroy us and never let up. Most of these men, Robert Brustein and Richard Gilman leading the pack, were now being attended to by the board. What they'd predicted appeared to be true, that we were mistaken choices who could not bring off what we'd undertaken. No one noted the adaptations we were beginning to make and the significance of these changes. A living sacrifice was being called for to pay for our failures.

N O W a new figure came on the scene. William Schuman, chosen to be the new president of Lincoln Center, was and is a famous composer; he'd written nine symphonies, the same number as Ludwig van Beethoven. He was very bright, wore his clothes well, and gave off the air proper to this post: Culture can be good business. He had a quick wit and knew how to arouse confidence. With some of the qualities of a hypnotist, he could influence people and solve problems. Having run the Juilliard School of Music for nine years, and there proved his competence as an administrator, he was clearly the man for the job. The top people at Lincoln Center were confident Bill Schuman could solve the crisis at the Repertory Theatre, and he shared their opinion. He saw himself as the Repertory Theatre's artistic savior.

George Woods was educated enough to read the periodicals that carried the attacks by cultural kibitzers on Bob and me, but I doubt if he bothered. What he read were balance sheets, read them quickly—a glance at the bottom line would do—and he came to conclusions that led to action. During the period of my two disasters, George had accepted a job in Washington as head of the World Bank. But John Rockefeller, for all his soft-spoken ways, knew what he needed and went for it. He asked George to remain in a position of power with the Repertory Theatre and, particularly in this crisis, help out in the difficult days ahead. George agreed to continue as chairman of our board, and I believe his was a dominant influence behind the scenes in what followed. He chose a new president of the Repertory Theatre, a man who was the executive vice-president of the First National Bank. Robert Hoguet didn't seem to me to be as bright as the other two men, but he was perhaps more pliable and readier to listen. If he had an opinion of his own about what he saw on stage and what would make more sense backstage, he didn't allow his ideas to influence his behavior. He would consult George Woods; everyone consulted George Woods.

All three men were to react to the pressures brought on them from two directions—the box office failure of certain plays we'd produced, particularly my work, and what they'd read or were told about the attacks written by certain critics. Instead of putting the blame where it belonged, on me and my choices, these three men chose Bob Whitehead as the lamb to be sacrificed. The balance sheets spread on their desks spoke like Ouija boards and said, in the language they understood, that the root problem was the operating budget. From the beginning, Bob had warned George Woods that our deficit would be large. He'd made a startling and courageous statement, saying that a repertory theatre would always be a deficit operation, and that as we got better, our deficit would be larger, not smaller. This statement was intolerable to our bosses. It violated every principle on which their lives were built. They were also not prepared to pay for what they said they wanted. Instead they decided to get rid of Bob.

Now came the final episode in the life of our Repertory Theatre. The grotesque character of the events that followed cannot be appreciated unless the reader remembers that the men involved graduated from our best colleges, had read the best-sellers, dressed correctly, spoke convincingly on a variety of subjects and in the moderate tones of the well-bred, were perfectly at ease at a formal dinner, could tie a black tie and escort a lady to the opera, then gracefully to bed. These men were our elite. But in our final crisis they behaved like characters out of a cinema caper whose subject is a CIA-inspired plot and whose dramatis personae, bungling criminal conspirators, are all played by Peter Sellers.

I T   I S   Bill Schuman's character to recognize a crisis and do something about it; according to *Variety*, he promised that he himself would provide the necessary artistic "input" in the future. What the Repertory Theatre needed now, he said, was a new administrator to replace Bob. He had a candidate to recommend, Herman Krawitz, an assistant manager of the Metropolitan Opera, the man who'd been in charge of setting up that operation in its new home at Lincoln Center and done it well.

Mr. Krawitz was under contract to the Metropolitan Opera and a favorite of the fiery autocrat who presided there, Rudolf Bing. Everyone knew how short and volatile Bing's temper was, so knew they had to tread carefully as they approached Krawitz. Obviously, if anything of this kind was to be done, it had to be done with discretion and a delicate touch. Bill Schuman was the man for that, they all agreed. And Bill agreed.

Having received the approval of George Woods, which meant that Hoguet approved, Schuman decided he would feel Krawitz out secretly to ascertain his interest in replacing Bob—if the obstacles to the transfer could be removed.

What was being considered now reached John Rockefeller, a man superior in the ways of gentility. He urged Schuman to be sure to make his reach for Krawitz "through the front door," which, translated, meant that any conversation Schuman wished to have with Krawitz should be discussed beforehand with Anthony A. Bliss, the president of the Metropolitan Opera, who was a gentleman, not a raging lion like Bing.

But Bliss was out of town at the time and Schuman thought it important to move without delay and feel Krawitz out before he spoke to Bliss; there was no reason to go through all this if, in the end, Krawitz was not interested. So he decided to find out discreetly, which is to say, secretly. All big shots, from time immemorial, have had lieutenants to whom they give assignments that they consider inappropriate for themselves. In this way they can disclaim responsibility if anything goes wrong. Instead of speaking to Krawitz himself, Schuman instructed Schuyler Chapin, a hell of a nice guy from academia, to sound out Krawitz and report back.

In the meantime, Anthony A. Bliss returned to the city, and Schuman met with him. Mr. Bliss opposed the suggestion. But Bill Schuman had not climbed to where he was in our world by being deterred so easily from reaching a goal. He still wanted to know if Krawitz would be interested if the way could be cleared of obstacles.

So Schuyler Chapin met with Krawitz, who was flattered, of course, but said no. He had a contract with Rudolf Bing and was concerned about Bing's temper.

Schuman was still not deterred. He instructed Chapin to go back to Krawitz, hold another confidential talk, and offer a "sweetened" proposal. Krawitz would be both artistic and administrative head of the Repertory Theatre, replacing Bob and me, with an appropriate increment in salary.

This was indeed a tempting offer. Krawitz was tempted.

Bob Whitehead, who'd worked six years—four without pay—at Lincoln Center, whose sole interest during those years was the Repertory Theatre, and who was now to be replaced, was not informed of what Schuman was up to. Nor was I.

Rudolf Bing, for whom Krawitz worked and who held a contract with Krawitz, had not been informed or consulted by Schuman.

Now came the inevitable leaks. When I heard about what was happening behind our backs, I was certain, appreciating George Woods's character, that he was calling the plays. I knew the intensity of the antagonism George felt toward Bob, and I believed that the force of this spite would overcome any tendency in George to caution, discretion, or kindness. The Repertory Theatre had to be saved, and the way to do it was to cut Bob Whitehead loose and replace him.

It was at this point that the fire-eating head of the opera heard what was going on behind his back and, bang, Bing blew up! "If our sister constituents are going to be free to raid each other, we're back in the jungle," he proclaimed, "and I don't want to be in Lincoln Center." With which, a man of his word, he resigned from the Lincoln Center top board.

John Rockefeller was distressed. I wondered what he said to Schuman.

Now all this could not be kept out of the newspapers.

Bill Schuman was publicly embarrassed, but I doubt George Woods gave a damn. He still wanted Bob out, one way or another. I suspect that he knew that what had happened would result in Bob's walking away without another push, which was a hell of a lot easier—and cheaper—then firing him.

Bob and I were now hearing full details of what had been going on behind our backs and of our humiliation by the bankers. Bob was furious, I, disgusted.

Had we forgotten whom we were dealing with? It would have required more understanding and courage than these men possessed for them to have taken a stand at this point and replied to our critics, "Whitehead, Miller, and Kazan are good, devoted men. They haven't had sufficient time to do the extremely difficult job we've asked for. That might need five years to accomplish. They are, however, already adjusting their policies so as not to make the same mistakes again. We believe they should go on."

Nothing like that was considered. Woods, I imagine, had tasted the blood he wanted. In these situations, there's always a victim.

Schuman was concerned about redressing himself in the public eye. He'd felt free to humiliate Bob, but didn't favor humiliation for himself. So he sent another nice guy, Mike Burke, someone I might have considered a good friend except that he was the man George Woods had brought in to tip the balance of the board and defeat our proposal for the ANTA Washington Square Theatre, the proposal we'd made good on over George's opposition.

Mike met with Bob "for a week." I can't imagine what they talked about for a week, because the proposal Mike conveyed from Schuman was simple—and insulting. How many different ways can a man pronounce "Quit"? They were asking Bob to continue for the rest of the season, knowing that he'd then be replaced.

Bob immediately "resigned to *The New York Times*." In his statement, he asked how a man would work efficiently when he knew that, behind his back, he was being replaced, secretly at first, then openly. Had this question occurred to the board? It was never answered, nor did Bob need an answer.

Robert Hoguet, the new president of our board, did give his own statement to the *Times*. "We could not deter Mr. Whitehead," he said, "from quitting." And so on. All that when everyone who'd been following the chain of events knew that Schuman and Woods had been exerting every effort to make Bob quit. Hoguet also said that they'd "just been looking for someone to go along with Bob." Which, it seemed to me, was simply a falsehood spoken falsely to save face. This astonishing statement was further soiled by an expression of regret.

When Bob resigned, Art and I resigned. It was then that George Woods took me aside and asked if I'd continue without Bob. I've heard that another member of the board asked Miller (who'd written the two plays that paid their way) the same question and got the same answer I'd given George.

So the effort to set up a repertory theatre in New York's Lincoln Center, which had started with a burst of energy and hope, ended with falsehoods and the crunch of disgrace. After it was all over, Bill Schuman retreated into what he called a "dignified silence." Which he nevertheless broke to make one astonishing public complaint. He said he'd been dismayed at the lack of brotherly feeling in the Repertory Theatre.

Whatever feelings of "dismay" Bill was feeling in his dignified silence did not deter him from bringing on our replacements. These men, the products of a highly publicized talent search, were Herbert Blau and Jules Irving, who had been urgently touted by the culture kibitzers who'd worked so hard and so long to displace Bob and me.

Blau and Irving, at the time of their first production, made the statement that they were going to offer "revolutionary" plays at Lincoln Center. Whom were they kidding? Themselves. They were to find out soon enough whom they were working for, and that any promises of independence they'd received could not be relied upon. For the playbill of their first production, Blau wrote copy linking President Johnson with certain international social despots. He was influenced—if that's the word—to withdraw this slur *tout de suite*. If they really meant that their wish was to do plays espousing social revolution, Lincoln Center hardly seemed the platform from which to launch such a program.

I can't help believing that their choice of plays had been made with a degree of consultation with our campus-based critics. Their choices were what could have been expected—another kind of standard fare. I doubt that *Danton's Death* meant or could mean something very arousing to the audience who sat in the red plush seats of Lincoln Center's Beaumont Theatre. On opening night, Jules Irving did something out of his naive good heart; he went from dressing room to dressing room before the performance, told actors that the future of the American theatre was in their hands. The actors they'd brought in from San Francisco may have believed this, but the actors they'd retained from our original company had another reaction: that the men who'd been directing them were fools and amateurs.

On the morning after the opening of *Danton's Death*, Robert Brustein, our kibitzer with the sharpest teeth, wrote: "I cannot conceal my disappointment . . ." And so on. Clearly he would have wished to. He'd heralded the program of plays that Blau and Irving had announced. Now he didn't try to conceal his disappointment at their production. Blau and Irving found they were building a theatre on a quicksand of opinion, and no one, not even their friends, was ready to give them even as much time as we'd been given to accomplish what they wanted.

A year later, I was told that Blau was on his way out and was offered his post. But I'd had more than enough of Lincoln Center and the men who ran it. I'd decided to follow my own bent and write novels. Then I wouldn't be at the mercy of a board of real estate operators and bankers.

There was one surprise in all this history. Whereas there had always been some reservation within me about working at the Repertory Theatre—especially after I'd written and produced my own film—or in any theatre of any kind, a doubt that this was really what I wanted to do and what I was good at, I found that when I was edged out with Bob and became the butt of critical target practice, I was mad as hell. During the years I'd devoted to the Repertory Theatre, I'd often felt that I was not doing what I truly wanted to do. But when it was all over, I was furious. I didn't like failing, not at anything I undertook; I didn't like leaving as a loser and I didn't like the way we'd been manipulated out. I didn't like the way Bob had been treated and I resented that Art had been insufficiently appreciated. I knew how good these men were, how hard they'd worked, and that Lincoln Center would never find their like again.

When it was done, friends could see on my face what I was feeling, and some thought I was cracking up. Deciding to remain apart from everyone, I'd disappeared from view. Whereupon several actors, old friends, worried about my health, sought me out to see what was eating me and could they help. I told them no, thanks, I felt fine, which worried them more. Didn't I even know that I needed help?

What was "eating" me made me turn my back on the theatre and never go back to it. I'd made up my mind that I'd not direct anyone else's work again, that now I'd write my own screenplays, as I had with *America America*, and possibly try myself on a novel.

Before I put these memories behind me, I must say something about the Actors Studio Theatre and what happened there.

THE VIOLENCE of Lee's feelings when he learned I'd committed myself to the Repertory Theatre without insisting that he and the Actors Studio be included must be understood with sympathy. For more than a dozen years, this man had devoted his best efforts to making actors better artists. Together, he and I had brought into prominence another kind of performer. Authors, producers, and directors often saw this new breed as the bane of the profession, because while "reliable" actors did as they were told, our actors had the effrontery to ask questions. The phrase "He's studied with Strasberg" became a curse in some Broadway offices, just as "He's one of Kazan's people" made some producers uneasy. Both phrases were used to identify a curiously ambitious and restlessly searching kind of actor—"You never know what the son of a bitch is going to do next!"—who never wallowed in admiration for stars and took no guff from directors he considered incompetent. Our actors were proud, and that made them difficult. They couldn't be intimidated, but neither could they be condemned out of hand, because they might suddenly brighten a moment that was dull or save a performance that was failing. What they "did next" often had an exceptional ring of truth.

Lee's lifework had been directed to the day when, with the actors we'd trained, he would be in command of a repertory theatre. But I'd gone ahead with Bob Whitehead and resigned from the Studio's governing board. When Lee promoted Rip Torn and Gerry Page to my position at his side, he explained to another member, "I put them on the board to make sure Kazan didn't take over the Studio." This, of course, was the farthest thing from my intentions, but it was an indication of how Lee was thinking. It disturbed me. I decided I should let the actors know just where I stood, instead of disappearing from their number without an explanation. Hearing there was going to be a meeting of some Studio members, I asked if I might attend. I was certain that whatever I said would be transmitted to the members at large. And to Lee.

Pleased to find that the atmosphere at this gathering was cordial, I explained my position calmly, saying that the Studio had been conceived as a place for training and that it should continue as such, free of the stresses that would come out of production involvement. It should not have been at Lincoln Center, I said, I hadn't wanted it there, and in this respect my position was opposed to Lee's. As the meeting progressed, I believed that the actors present understood my point of view; I bid them a friendly farewell and left.

I was told later that the instant I walked out the door, a flood of vituperation was released. "Everything was fine while you were there," my informant told me, "we made jokes and so on, but when you'd left, the room went wild. I don't know what got into those people."

I knew what got into them: the hysteria of resentment and revenge that Lee had stirred up. Some of them might have felt professionally rejected by what I'd done, but the extraordinary intensity of anger against me was Lee's, not theirs.

T O   T E L L the story of the Actors Studio Theatre, I move to Paris in the early eighties. One pleasant evening, I was walking along the Boulevard Saint-Germain-des-Prés, very much at home in the City of Light. I always felt happy in Paris, because no matter how indifferently my films did in New York, they were generously received in France. *America America* had been screened there that summer in nine small theatres, which is nine more than it had played in New York that summer. So I was jaunty and full of the dreams that rise on a warm autumn evening, as I passed the Café de Flore and Jimmy Baldwin came galloping out. I saw him older, as plain as I am, bug-eyed to boot, and as adorable as ever. Years earlier I had suggested that he write a play about a black teenager named Emmett Till, who, having been north for a spell, came back south possessing the kind of independence that would get him in trouble there. In time he was lynched, and his murderer was exonerated. I suggested a basic structure for the play. Jimmy liked it and began to work.

I was eager, as I prepared to launch our repertory theatre's program, to have a play about blacks, written by a black. The whole Lincoln Center institution and its program was altogether too lily-white (and still is). Jimmy and I reached an understanding; then I went to Greece to make my film. I didn't feel I had to hold Jimmy's hand as he wrote the Emmett Till play. But acquiring a play from a playwright is like a love affair: If you allow a vacuum to persist, someone else will get in. Rip Torn did. He and Jimmy picked up with each other, and Rip influenced Jimmy to give the play I'd suggested to the Actors Studio Theatre. I was mad as hell, but didn't ask Jimmy for an explanation. He casually offered two: first, that I was too much like his father and he wanted to be on his own, not under my influence; second, that Lincoln Center had no blacks on its board. The second reason was my own for wanting that play; the first I could do nothing about. Rip taking that play away from me was an entrepreneurial triumph for the Actors Studio Theatre and for Lee; it was sweet revenge. I swallowed my anger, decided to still be Jimmy's friend, and went about my business.

Alongside us in time, the Actors Studio Theatre did very well. Starting with an all-star production of O'Neill's *Strange Interlude*, played by eminent actors and well received, they'd done *Marathon '33* with Julie Harris, then a play called *Baby Want a Kiss* with Paul Newman and Joanne Woodward. These productions were cordially received by both the critics and the audiences while I was struggling with *But for Whom Charlie* and *The Changeling*, which were hooted at by critics and refused by audiences. Lee's idea had turned out to be more practical than ours, because it ensured the public what it wanted, guaranteed classics or easy-to-take new plays carried by established stars. Lee had asked actors to pledge four months a year, which would permit them to work in films and maintain the level of living to which they'd become accustomed. Bob and I had asked our actors to sign up for two years at modest salaries. Lee called his troupe a "revolving" or "floating" company, we called ours a permanent company playing repertory. His theatre showed no intention of becoming a repertory theatre, and that raised questions: Was repertory relevant on Broadway, was it possible, was it useful, was it of value?

What I couldn't help gathering from every announcement of productions to come was the boast a competitor makes, that the Actors Studio Theatre would win its war with the Lincoln Center Repertory Theatre. To judge what was written by the drama critics about their productions, it did: "a brilliant production of a gargantuan drama," about *Strange Interlude*, and a most generous welcome for Miss Harris and for the Newmans. Lee had successfully bridged the Actors Studio and Broadway. While my prestige was crumbling, his was growing. His idea of a revolving company seemed to be working out. Wasn't it more practical in our culture? Never before had such outstanding actors been gathered for a series of productions. Now to come were Jimmy's play and Lee's lifelong dream, a production of Chekhov's *The Three Sisters*.

I was asking myself, had Bob and I bitten off more than we should have? Were we on the wrong track?

Years passed and I was still curious to know what had happened behind the scenes at the Actors Studio Theatre. Now, in Paris, with both organizations long dead, the questions remained. I invited Jimmy to come to Lipp's with me, have some drink and eat a meal. After we'd ordered, I told him I'd read Cheryl Crawford's autobiography and remembered a scene she describes in which Jimmy climbed thirty feet up an electrician's "A" ladder to tell Cheryl and Lee how disappointed he was in their production of his Emmett Till play, *Blues for Mr. Charlie*. I wanted to know why he'd climbed thirty feet in the air to voice an author's objections to the work of a company, a director, and two producers. "What the hell were you doing up on a ladder, yelling at Strasberg?" I asked. Then Jimmy, time having replaced rancor with humor, told me the story of *Blues for Mr. Charlie*, the play I'd suggested he write and that he'd given to Rip Torn, and how it had turned out.

He told me he'd been dissatisfied with the rehearsals of his play, and for several reasons he blamed Rip Torn, who was in the cast. Rip, Jimmy told me, not only thought he was directing the play—Burgess Meredith was the "billed" director—but thought he'd written it. Since Lee and Cheryl couldn't or wouldn't fire Rip, Jimmy fired him. Having done this, he went to Washington to see Hubert Humphrey and demand to know why he'd been refused a visa to go to Europe. "Because every time you go to Europe, you besmirch America," Humphrey had explained. Jimmy answered, "When I read that a black meeting place in Alabama has been bombed, tell me what to say, Mr. Humphrey." Jimmy got his visa and, returning to New York, had a couple of drinks on the train to celebrate, then went immediately to the theatre where his play was being rehearsed.

As he approached the theatre, he saw Rip Torn walking toward the stage door. (Remember, the story of what followed is Jimmy's; Rip may not remember it this way.) Jimmy says he stopped Rip and asked him where he was going. Rip answered, "To rehearsal." Jimmy reminded Rip that he was no longer in the cast, but Rip continued on toward the stage door. Jimmy, in high spirits because of his triumph over the visa agency—and the drinks—needed little firing up. He acknowledged that Rip was bigger and very likely stronger, so he wouldn't fight him, but if Rip went into the theatre, Jimmy would kill him. Rip hesitated, then seeing that Jimmy meant what he'd said, literally, he turned around and didn't go through the stage door. Jimmy did.

He was asking himself who the hell had invited Rip to come back to the cast after Jimmy had fired him? It had to be Lee Strasberg, the theatre's artistic director. Now Jimmy was in a fury. When he bolted through the stage door, he knew that, inspired by alcohol and justified anger, he might do something excessive, so in order not to choke Lee, who was on stage, or physically attack Cheryl, who was in the audience, he climbed thirty feet to the top of a tall electrician's "A" ladder, and there, swaying, as the cast watched with what I'd been told was considerable admiration, he unloaded his rage. The actors, Jimmy said, were not too happy with how rehearsals were going either; they were ready to applaud him.

So there was my fellow nigger, thirty feet in the air on the single ladder length that comes out of the top of the "A," which was swaying from the violence of his emotion, and shouting at Lee Strasberg that he thought him incompetent "to the point of sabotage" and so on. Lee's lips tightened to a white line. High up on the swinging ladder, finally done, Jimmy waited for Lee's response. There was none. Everybody waited. From the seat at the side of the stage where Lee had been watching the rehearsal came a silence to impress Jehovah, a calm that was, of itself, a threat—which was Lee's way. When he finally started to respond, it was too late. Jimmy had scrambled down the ladder and streaked out the stage door like a bolt of black lightning, and from there to his favorite bar.

Those who'd waited for a show of strength from the producers were denied it for the moment. But Jimmy didn't tell me the whole story in Lipp's, because Rip did return to the cast and did open in the play. How this was permitted by the dissatisfied author he didn't say, but it probably happened like many things in the theatre, by waiting the trouble out. There is strength a director or a producer gets from merely being on the ground. The play was quite well received by the New York critics, always with respect, at times with kind concern. I don't believe that the script—which, I've been told, was five hours long to begin with—was ever properly prepared for rehearsals.

What I did ask Jimmy that night in Lipp's was: "Did Lee ever forgive you for what you did? You humiliated him in front of his cast and you knew that incident would be, for a time, the talk of Broadway, not to Lee's credit, but to yours. Did Lee ever hit back at you?" "He never said anything about it," Jimmy said. "Forgot all about it." I knew Lee better, and I knew that Lee did not forgive him, but that is another part of the story; it happened later, in another country.

N O W   C A M E the production everyone had waited for, the work of the master. It had been Lee's dream, often publicly affirmed, that one day he would mount *The Three Sisters* of Chekhov, do it when he had a cast that was up to the play. Now he had such a cast, all stars or near stars, and eager to work with him: Geraldine Page, Kim Stanley, Shirley Knight, and Barbara Baxley—who could ask for anything more? It was only a matter of supporting them with a staunch group of men and turning them loose. Lee did that. And it all came together for him. To cap the event, he dedicated the production to Marilyn Monroe.

At last he had the personal triumph he wanted and deserved. The next morning he read this: "Under Lee Strasberg's direction, the company's production deserves the word 'masterpiece.'" The *Daily News* made it plainer: "The Actors Studio Theatre's production of *The Three Sisters* is a stunning achievement and Lee Strasberg is the true hero of the occasion." And *The New York Times:* "Under Lee Strasberg's direction, the Actors Studio Theatre is doing the best work of its youthful career." The New York *Post* gave him what I believe he wanted most: "It's difficult to believe that there has ever been a more organic and total production of *The Three Sisters* anywhere, whether in Russia or in the United States." Lee was now where years of work and devotion had placed him, on top of the heap. He was to become a mythical figure.

There were some carping notices, and I'll admit I was fractious enough to be on the side of the "refuseniks." At this time I was struggling with *The Changeling,* so my reaction will be suspect. Still I must take exception to what Lee and his actors were doing. What I saw on stage put my back up. I left the Morosco Theatre that night with my lips buttoned tight; I didn't visit backstage. But now twenty years have passed and more, so I'll say what I thought, and you think what you will.

An exaggeration will make my point: I am reminded of a psychoanalyst named Wilhelm Reich, who believed that the universe was alive with its special energy and that this energy could be captured and contained for the benefit of an individual in what Reich called an orgone box or, at other times, an accumulator. This was nothing but a box of a size to contain a human body but not much larger, and it was lined with wood and metal. The person who was to be exposed to the force of the accumulation of the energy of the universe would take his place in this box. There would ensue a communion between the energy of this person and that which charges the spheres, and this would fill the orgone box—and so the person inside would benefit. I hope I've got that right.

What I certainly have right is the instruction in acting that Lee and Harold Clurman gave the actors they'd brought together in 1929 to form a "group" theatre. To simplify the essence of this technique: The actor would be asked to recall the details of an occasion in his past when he was experiencing a particular emotion, and by the act of recalling these details he would exhume the energy of the long-buried emotion and so be aroused to the pitch the scene he was about to play required. I was Lee's stage manager in 1934 and 1935, and I remember that it was recommended, even insisted upon, that before entering a scene, an actor of our company was to "take a minute" to recall what would arouse him emotionally to the pitch

Lee believed was proper for the scene, and only then to play it. Did it work? Yes. In good ways and in bad. The actor was more concentrated— not on whoever else happened to be on stage with him but on his memories. I would play bit parts and, launching myself this way, I'd certainly feel the tremor of a feeling. As stage manager, I was required by Lee to call out "Take a minute!" before the start of a scene, whereupon all the actors would.

This technical requirement was a continuation of the classroom work that Lee was conducting in those years. There the actors would compete to demonstrate to Lee the intensity potential of their emotions and so win his approval. I remember that he would sit before his rehearsals as in front of his classes, a judge, not an artistic collaborator. This put him in an invulnerable position; his own creativity was never up for judgment. He maintained his domination—and so his safety—by this distancing.

But increasingly it became evident in his productions that the actors and actresses would perform on stage as if they were moving in a miasma of self-devotion. When we see a person on the street behaving in that way, we call it "sleepwalking." When we see it on stage, we may say, "That's Method acting." This kind of performance became characteristic of the early Group Theatre in the plays Lee directed. It was certainly better than the "hammy" acting, the posturing and the gesticulating that passed for the evidence of emotion, in the old theatre against which Lee and Harold had turned. Every revolution seems to have its positive and negative sides. We began to see the negative.

I, among others, turned against Lee's kind of instruction and sought simpler and more "present" methods of arousing emotions, ones that were less self-hypnotic, which would, for those reasons, present a more lifelike performance on stage. We sought techniques that would not result in behavior that seemed to be happening in a fog of self-devotion. For these rebels, the key was not the emotion, but what the character wanted to do, what his objective in the scene was. Precisely as in life. Lee, however, continued his methods. He no longer commanded, "Take a minute!" but, it seemed to me, his actors still tended to play their scenes with themselves, not with the other actors on stage.

I remember what I thought when I watched him directing love scenes: that they were the expressions of the pain of love for an inhibited man; in other words, how Lee himself might be in love. He'd often direct his actors in scenes of passion to look in contrary directions—that is, away from each other. Sometimes he'd place a post or the edge of a door between the lovers, so separating them. Perhaps the hand of one lover might reach around, fumbling for the hand of the other, but the faces would not turn. I can't remember a face-to-face confrontation of lovers in his work. This was, of course, an expression of Lee's own nature in those years. It was impossible for him to express even an affectionate feeling openly and directly, with an outpouring of emotion or at the least enthusiasm. I'm sure he must have in his private life—he had four children—but on stage, it was always "Take a minute!" and the pain of it all. I could see on the faces of the actors, playing their passion for each other, that they were not thinking of each other as much as of an occasion in their past when they'd experienced the emotion of the scene as Lee wanted it. This separated them as much as the post or the door's edge between them.

Now back to *The Three Sisters*. Imagine a stage full of Reich's orgone boxes waiting to be charged with their separate fervor, in this case drawing their energy not from the universe but from something equally remote— their own buried pasts, the long-ago memory experiences of each per- former. It is inevitable that there would be a quality of what I've called sleepwalking and certainly a great deal of self-love. You might believe that this kind of inner life is precisely Chekhovian; I would not agree. Weren't Chekhov's people always reaching out to each other? That's my impression. They were not an assembly of separate "boxes" but a community of souls with deeply related problems. However indirectly, they were reaching out to each other for understanding and for sympathy. Chekhov instructed Stanislavski, his director, to avoid the lachrymose and the self-indulgent. The play is a comedy, he said. Nor should an actor behave on stage as if he knows his character is pathetic or tragic. He must not be constantly nudging the audience to observe how pitiful he is and how deep his pain. The great thing in life, when you detect that a person is in a tragic situation, is watch- ing what he does to conceal his pain and to contain it. Often what people do is surprising and characteristic. Then the audience will see sorrow and courage, humor and honor, simultaneously. That is the essence of the life in the plays of Chekhov. In the production I'm discussing, I thought some of the actors were behaving as if they were still doing classroom exercises, competing with each other to give "great performances" and win Lee's ap- proval. The sorry fact is that I've come to dislike the acting of some of my Actors Studio people—even though I like them all personally. I would pre- fer more humor and verve and less self-indulgence, self-pity, and self- awareness. I detest emotional stripteases.

B U T   J U D G E by the notices: This production was a great success. Lee was interviewed repeatedly and asked the questions put only to celebrities. He boasted that even if *The Three Sisters* did not become a long-run suc- cess, it didn't matter because he'd proved his point. When Cheryl Craw- ford reported to him that their organization was growing short of money, his answer was: "Something will come along." Something did: an offer from a TV producer to make a film of *The Three Sisters* and put up an advance of fifty thousand dollars. Lee's private classes had swelled with his reputa- tion, and this income kept him going. But the TV film, done quickly to minimize expenses, like many films made directly from stage productions, was not a success because it was not cinema. In the wake of this failure, a Ford Foundation grant was abruptly discontinued. The day came when the Actors Studio Theatre was out of funds. Actors looked for work elsewhere. But Lee held firm, and again luck came to his rescue.

An offer was received from Peter Daubney, an English producer, who'd organized a World Theatre Festival to take place in London each spring; he wanted the Actors Studio Theatre to come over and participate. This would place Lee's theatre among the most esteemed in the world. Daubney wanted the Baldwin play, as well as the Chekhov. Jimmy's play would appeal to the English intellectual left. There was great excitement on Forty-fourth Street.

Only Cheryl hesitated. There would have to be a great deal of recasting and further rehearsing. Gerry Page was pregnant, so she could not go. Kim Stanley refused to go if she had to play with Kevin McCarthy again. She demanded that George Scott be engaged even if he was not a member of the Studio. As for *Blues for Mr. Charlie*, Rip Torn, it seemed, had had disagreements with Burgess Meredith, the director, so he had to be counted out. And Diana Sands, who'd given the outstanding performance in the production, was in a hit play and couldn't or wouldn't leave it.

Here now was the test for Lee's revolving company. If Cheryl believed the trip was ill-considered, Lee knew it would work out. The light of the prophet shone in his eyes. He vowed he'd gather replacements as good as the originals, and he'd rehearse the plays again. When Paul Newman, out of his quirky goodness, arranged free air transportation to London for the actors and the scenery, Lee took it as an omen. He had absolute power and, at the moment, little patience. He decided: We go! Cheryl was silenced, and was soon caught up in the spin of activity. Secretly she still felt there was something irrational in Lee's rush across the ocean, but she didn't have the strength to stand up to him. Few people did. She even recognized that Lee, within himself, had no choice, that the decision was compulsive, that he was being impelled by an irrational and mysterious force.

He plunged on. To replace Shirley Knight, he cast Sandy Dennis, an actress I have trouble watching in any role. I can't imagine that Lee chose her with an easy heart. He went on recasting, plunging deep like a gambler who is losing but keeps doubling the stakes. The setbacks and defections did not deter him. Like the blind prophet, he rushed off the edge of a cliff. He had to have more. More of what? Proof of his venture's validity, praise both personal and professional for his theatre. Especially personal approbation; he was ravenous for that. He'd tasted the elixir of success and found it, as so many have, a potent drug. But in my opinion, what he wanted most of all was revenge. In London he'd finally show the world that he'd gotten the better of me, while proving to the Lincoln Center board, who had passed him by, that they'd made the wrong choice. I believe this was the dominant drive impelling the man at this time. No other reasons could explain the demonic force that was to push him to make so many reckless choices.

The plan was to rehearse a week and a half in New York and a week and a half in London. In the middle of the first week, Kim Stanley announced that she would not fly to England with the rest of the company but take a transatlantic steamer. Perhaps Kim wanted to get away from the formal rehearsals and work on the part by herself. Perhaps she'd found that George Scott's personal reasons for going to London had to do with Ava Gardner. Lee did nothing effective to prevent Kim's willful choice, although it ruined his rehearsals. I can't imagine what reasons she gave him. I'd cite Kim as especially given to the orgone box kind of acting, and I'd suspect that in the end she preferred not to be influenced in what she did by what the other actors in a scene were doing. This was certainly the moment to bring in an actress from the floating company and save the rehearsals in London.

Lee and Paula

A director never knows what happens in the personal lives of actors between his rehearsals. When Kim disappeared, George became upset or fed up. I've been told he went to Harlem that night and got himself a fight—and a black eye—then called Lee the next morning and offered to resign from the company because, he said, he was obviously being destructive in the production. This considerate offer was not accepted, of course, and George continued in the cast but did not show up for any more rehearsals in New York. The most direction Lee was able to give him was during the flight to London, when he sat next to him and talked—hardly the way to get the best performance from any actor.

When Lee got his cast to London, with only a few days left to rehearse, he found there was no rehearsal space available. People were sent out scouting, turning up lofts, armories, tennis courts, any kind of space; the company had to gather in new places every day. Available props and furniture were haphazard. This had to be the fault of the executive producer, Cheryl Crawford. Always a careful and devoted theatre worker, she'd not been able to make facilities available for Lee to do the work he needed more than ever to do. Perhaps she'd been partially demoralized, since she'd had no part in making decisions but been ordered by Lee to carry out those he'd already made.

On opening night Jimmy Baldwin waited in the pub nearest the Aldwych Theatre for London's verdict on his play. Runners brought him the audience's reaction. Everyone complained about the lighting; the play was being performed in a murky twilight. Half the audience, according to Jimmy's friends, liked the play, the other half was outraged. There were angry shouts from the balcony, including "Go back to Africa!" from an extreme right-wing group. The write-ups the next morning could not have been much worse. "What one had hoped," the *Times* critic wrote, "was that if there was any company in the world equipped to dig through Mr. Baldwin's rhetoric to a core of true human feeling, it was the Actors Studio of New York. Nothing of the sort took place in last night's performance and it was with astonishment that one realized that the company, far from deepening the play, were broadening and coarsening it." The battle for the play's worth was lost not that night in London, of course, but long before, in the script preparation, the recasting, the chaotic rehearsals, and the technical supervision.

The next day Lee did something that no one involved forgave. In the face of the bad notices, he called a press conference and told reporters and drama critics that they must not judge the Actors Studio Theatre from the performance of Jimmy's play, that this production was not representative of the work at the Studio, that they must wait to see his production of *The Three Sisters*. This desperate statement was a betrayal of a performance, a company, and an author.

The night of the opening of *The Three Sisters*, Jimmy was back drinking in his pub, with Michael Redgrave and Groucho Marx. As they enjoyed each other's company, a black actress from the cast of *Blues for Mr. Charlie* charged in. "They booed it," she announced to Jimmy. "They booed it between acts and booed it at the end." The next morning the papers had a picnic. "A cluster of celebrated names rendered a death blow to the 'method' school of acting last night. No less a figure than Lee Strasberg directed this slow, sleepwalking production of Chekhov's wondrous play. . . . Kim Stanley played Masha as though she were acting to her own reflection in the bathroom mirror. Miss Sandy Dennis distinguished herself as the most self-conscious actress to have visited these shores within the span of memory. . . . a director who can achieve that must have a genius for destruction." Another paper carried this: "The saddest event of the week was the last, the booing at the end of the Actors Studio's version of *The*

Three Sisters. . . . this production accomplishes the supposedly impossible task of making Chekhov a bore." Penelope Gilliatt, long an admirer of the Studio, wrote: "The World Theatre Festival's dismal task has been to mount the suicide of the Actors Studio."

Paula Strasberg told Sidney Kingsley that when Lee read the notices he burst into tears. His dream had collapsed.

I've never known Lee to say, "I was wrong; it was my fault." The day after the opening, he called a company meeting and there criticized the actors for their performances. George Scott became furious; he looked at Lee with the full George Scott menacing look and said, "Are you blaming the actors for last night's catastrophe?" At which Lee backed off, explaining that what he really meant was . . . and so forth and so on, as Scott left the theatre. The one thing Lee should have done he could not do: tell the truth about what had happened. The company, after all, had been gathered in a haphazard way, had not had the time or the space to rehearse the delicate play properly, and the fault was his. Lee would have gained respect by admitting the truth. But he never allowed himself to be held accountable for anything, always stood on the very treacherous ground of a man who was never wrong. What a burden to shoulder!

The result of this catastrophe was far-reaching, and it was tragic. Cheryl and Lee, who'd worked together since 1928, were never close again. She has written that this experience was the greatest disappointment of her professional life. The truth is that it was partly her fault. She didn't stand up to Lee. Consequently the entire expedition to London had been badly conceived and mistakenly undertaken. Why had Cheryl gone along with Lee's compulsive behavior? Why had she not brought her very good sense to bear? Why had she yielded to the demon in Strasberg? Because Lee had always made it impossible for anyone to contest anything he said or did; he'd always made that kind of concession the only possible basis for working with him. In the face of a fanatic, Cheryl was weak, where he was erratic, pompous, and hysterical. She didn't challenge him; she surrendered everywhere.

I'd had the same difficulty with Lee. I saved myself by leaving his side.

NOW THERE began to be disillusion and resentment among the members of the Studio in London and especially in New York. Our actors, hundreds of devoted people, read the London notices, heard the stories that I've repeated here, and talked among themselves. It was noted that many of the cast representing the Studio in London were not members, had never appeared in Lee's Tuesday and Friday classes. It became apparent to the people in New York that Lee might have destroyed the Actors Studio Theatre by his decisions and choices. Certainly the production that was reviled and laughed at in London was not better than it would have been if the play had been produced on Broadway; it was worse. Lee had gone back to the kind of rehearsal procedure that forty years before he'd revolted against.

The New York members, once loyal without question, now felt they'd been falsely represented and that the production did not merit the billing "An Actors Studio Theatre Production." They'd been humiliated for false reasons. Great questioning and doubt was expressed in the old church on Forty-fourth Street. Was this production anything but an assembly of stars and quasi stars brought together for a short run to swell Lee's ego? Our name, a name of which they'd been proud, had been shamed.

The feeling began to grow that Lee was overly devoted to stars, that he gave them favored treatment and other considerations that he didn't accord to members who'd been faithful to him for so many years. The presence of Marilyn Monroe in Lee's classes had added to this resentment. The older members had seen that their leader held this movie star, a surprisingly modest girl of modest talent, in awe. They'd believed that he had praised her far beyond her due and no matter how uncertain her work. And that he'd enjoyed his power over her. His raves about her talent they'd considered to be mistaken and in some way related to what happened later in London. Some hardheads began to refer to Lee as a "star-fucker." They weren't talking about his sex life; in the years that followed, the broader implication was that Lee was impressed with anyone who'd made a success in films or on Broadway, no matter what the actor's talent or character, experience or technique. Lee told Ellen Burstyn that only celebrities should be on the board of the Actors Studio. Our members couldn't help seeing that Lee added "names" to the membership lists of the Studio, not because they'd tried out before our talent judges—which had once been the only way to become a member—but merely because they were heralded in the press and professionally powerful. In this way he betrayed the original spirit of the Studio, which had always held the members together. "Talent is all!" was replaced by some kind of media standard. Slowly many of our best talents saw what was happening and drifted away.

A F T E R the catastrophe in London, Lee reoriented himself, resumed the private classes that gave him a good living, then married a handsome and energetic woman who helped him realize the full commercial potential of his talent. With the help of a devoted lawyer and the prodding of this ambitious wife, he went into the business of making stars. There came the Lee Strasberg Institute on both coasts: New York is the fertile ground for talent, California where the stars and the money are. Entrance, of course, was not by talent alone; the philosophy of the Actors Studio was superseded. Tuition charges were high, but actors and actresses clawing their way up the ladder of fame were ready to do most anything to meet Lee's price. He'd made many great stars: he could make many more.

Lee became the most famous teacher of acting in the world. Students from everywhere clamored at his door. He'd learned a lesson: This kind of involvement in the theatre did not expose him to the dangers to his reputation that directing plays did. He enjoyed his position of preeminence— and his wealth. To drive him to work at the Institute's building in New York, a chauffeur-driven Mercedes waited at the entrance of his apartment house; its license plate read METHOD. Students at the Institute wore sweatshirts carrying the legend ACTOR BY LEE STRASBERG, or LEE STRASBERG SUPER-STARS around the image of the master. At play in his apartment were two "mutts," one named Method One, the other Method Two. Lee himself could not have dreamed up the sweatshirts or the license plate. On the other hand, he'd not prohibited them. America had given the Stanislavski method its commercial realization.

People laughed at these grotesqueries. But Lee had paid his dues and there was a genuine tragic element in the man's life. I've never forgotten his face during the early years of the Group Theatre, how rapturous it was when he described the work of directors he admired and whom he hoped to emulate. Or how much knowledge of acting he'd given us all during those first years. He'd not only raised the self-esteem and standing of actors at the Studio but brought a new dignity to actors all over the world. There are fine performers who owe him their careers. In this respect, he succeeded and deserves to be honored. What is tragic is the residue of dreams unfulfilled—but most of us have that in our guts. Was the success he'd won the success he'd wanted? Of course not. In the end, you do the best you can. When I saw him in his last years, sitting in the back of the Mercedes, his handsome wife at his side, there seemed to be something puzzled about him and, despite the presence of his devoted spouse, isolated. He had, it seemed to me, the look and feel of a captive. Captive of what? Of whatever it was in his character that had sent him charging off the edge of the cliff in London. Was it the drug vanity cries for? You'd think, considering the fame he'd achieved, he would have satisfied that hunger.

The last time I saw Lee was on a TV screen. Alexander Cohen had devised a great gaudy show to celebrate the hundredth anniversary of the Actors Fund, a glamorous spectacle called *Night of 100 Stars*. Instead of one hundred stars, Alex, true to his nature, had gathered two hundred. The final contingent of perhaps forty luminaries strutted past the TV camera to the theme of *A Chorus Line*, a Rockette on each celebrity's left arm, each right arm free to doff the top hat with which they'd all been provided. Each greeted a nationwide audience with a smile, a prank, or whatever characteristic gesture had helped make him or her famous. All were numbered, their numbers superimposed across their TV images. Number 167 was Milton Berle, 182 Al Pacino, 183 Bobby De Niro, 195 Rocky Graziano, 196 Lee Strasberg. At 200, the parade was over.

I was so curious about Lee's feelings when he'd doffed his top hat to the TV audience that I watched the tape twice. Although Alex told me that Lee's wife, Anna, had declared that this day had been one of the happiest in Lee's life, that was not my impression. Where every other numbered star had pranced by the camera in the spirit of the occasion, Lee had doffed his top hat, as he'd been directed to, but his face was somber and tense, as well as gray and weary. My impression was that he was simultaneously trying to be part of the occasion and maintaining a distance apart. It was as if he was saying by his conduct, "I don't really approve of all this, but I decided, for reasons of publicity, to go ahead with it." Or, more simply interpreted, Lee was saying, "I'm here, but I'm not here."

He died in his sleep two days later. "It tired him," Anna said of the rehearsals for *Night of 100 Stars*. It could reasonably be said that other things had previously tired him more. What had happened since those years long ago when Lee had been able to inspire a group of actors with the hope of a great cause? Year after year, with defeats and regrets and insurmountable obstacles, those dreams had thinned out, faded, then altered, until, at the end, Lee was another celebrity out of the celebrity machine, clicking past the camera with a number across his chest. Or a legendary "guru" for aspiring students of acting who could manage to beg, borrow, or steal the cost of instruction that would allow them to boast, "I've studied with Lee Strasberg."

The advertisement for the Institute now features Lee's photograph in the posture of a saint and under it the caption: "Artistic Director in Perpetuity." At the Institute in New York, a space has been named the Marilyn Monroe Theatre, a come-on for female students. There is also a Marilyn Monroe museum there, under the surveillance of Anna Strasberg.

On safari

I DON'T understand Catholics. I have a friend who upholds the faith of Rome and follows his good wife to mass at St. Pat's every morning before going to work. Yet he is a hardheaded realist and quite cynical about many things in our time and place. I've never heard him say a favorable word about the late Cardinal Spellman, a distinction I value, nor does he have a kindly tolerance for most of our political officers. Recently, when he heard that someone close to me had died, he consoled me by saying, "When God takes away, He will give back." I'm not any kind of believer, and I'm certainly not waiting for a gift from a mysterious source. Nevertheless, one day when I was blue, I heard myself saying (to myself), "Now He owes me one."

Gamblers streak through my family, right down to the present generation. One of my sons, a Harvard graduate, studies the *Racing Form* every morning, grades the entries, and when he finds a nag going that he likes, phones his bookie and lays his money down. He doesn't seem upset when he loses or exultant when he wins. I believe his philosophy of life must be the same as that of my Catholic friend. Gamblers say, "Luck evens out." I suppose my son, when he loses, feels that the bangtails owe him one.

It's a helpful philosophy. I've often been pronounced "dead." "Now Kazan is at the nadir of his critical standing" is how a wise scholar recently put it. I anticipate that another terrible fall from favor will follow the publication of this book. But I come from a resilient race, and we know that even without the help of the gods, time heals, and at worst, the human animal will become sufficiently indifferent to pain so that disaster will be tempered. That's our faith: Survive and wait. Things will turn around.

Of course, it's not true. You don't get over the death of someone close to you. I haven't gotten over the death of my wife Molly. The closest I've come to being "at the nadir" was during the year after she died. Characteristically, the final "low" didn't come over me until two months after I'd buried her. I didn't know what was hitting me that afternoon when I held her feet and felt them growing cold. It took time for me to see that much beside her body had died—including something within me—and that nothing afterward would be the same.

How could it be? Whatever differences I'd had with Molly, our bond—a partnership as much as a marriage—was the strongest tie I've had in my life. Because of the feelings of shame and guilt it brought me, I'd asked myself whether I had contributed to her death. And I still didn't know, so I did what an animal does when it's wounded; I crawled into a hole, the small apartment near Washington Square I'd taken after her death had made it impossible for me to live in the "perfect and forever" apartment. That home was haunted by the dead woman. I heard voices there.

I have a lively memory; I don't say a "good" memory because I believe that like most people's memories, it tends to retain what's amiable and dismiss what's painful. But even at that, I believe it works well enough and when sparked by some old jottings and letters can even be considered reliable. But of the year 1964 I remember almost nothing. I've occasionally recorded the events of my life in a diary, but I've found no such record of 1964—only some notes of the sessions I was having with a psychoanalyst. One reason was that I didn't want to look back at anything that had happened. Or ask questions like: Had I brought on her death by intensifying the tensions under which she'd lived? Of course I had. I'd spent years of our life together deceiving her about my private behavior. Had her apparent acceptance of our "arrangement" cost her? Of course it had. So leave it at that, I advised myself. But do answer one thing: Had it been wrong for us to stay together when we were no longer sexual partners? I had no answer to that. We'd been so bound together, she'd helped me so much, that it never occurred to me to leave her, and when she'd considered it, she'd backed off.

So for a very long time I didn't look closely at what had happened. We were responsible for each other's lives, of course, I for hers, she for mine. If I'd increased her tensions, hadn't she mine? Or was that just a desperate defense, a question I could not answer except by silence—which was no answer? So I avoided asking myself these questions; they'd only result in deepened shame and unresolved bewilderment and couldn't be answered. Gradually the defense mechanism we all have, by which we stay alive, was working again, and for the first time in my life I lived without self-scrutiny. I'd made self-awareness, the investigation of the processes of mind and feeling, the techniques of my professional life. Now I was mute and unresponsive.

How did I live through that year of 1964? At a distance from myself and from everyone. I watched Bob Whitehead continue despite the attacks by his board, go on with the Repertory Theatre's program, correcting some of our mistakes in program and in personnel. I watched Art Miller come up with another play for our theatre, a production in which he was much better served by Harold Clurman as director than he would have been by me. I admired Bob and Art; I thought them gallant. I was happy that Harold was finally with us. I watched the scenes behind the scenes at Lincoln Center, a scornful observer. I kept up a good front, heartened by the knowledge that my time there was limited. I stayed on, I did my best. I didn't want to let Bob and Art down. I didn't want to go out a loser.

But if I'd come into the Repertory Theatre in good measure because I wanted to give Molly, at last, the reliable life she wanted—a demonstration of my constancy—once that cause didn't exist, there was no reason except loyalty to my associates and responsibility to my actors to continue service there. In the end, I was glad I had persisted, because when Bob resigned, it was simple for me to walk away too. In my feelings, I didn't have to go; I was already gone.

Now, alone, unoccupied, I had a new "disease": indifference. I had no fight left in me. How did I spend that winter? I don't remember anything after *The Changeling*. I "lay about," as the British put it. In my small apartment on Third Street, I would curl up on my bed like a man with a painless but debilitating disease, one that made me sleepy all the time but woke me soon after I fell asleep. I'd do the best I could with my final duties at the theatre, then hurry back to my place, where I'd be alone. I found other ways of using this city, went to a film almost every day, alone, to the library and the museums, strolled in the park, stopped by the zoo at feeding time. Occasionally I'd have a visit from Barbara, but the zest had gone out of that union. I wondered, ironically, whether Molly had had to be there to make the relationship "work."

At night, alone in bed, I'd no longer experience the usual sexual yearnings. I was limp. As any woman would, Barbara understood this for what it was: I was "off" her. But the true fact, which she found it difficult to believe—any woman would—was that I wasn't "on" anyone else. I didn't have the desire or the energy to behave as I had all my adult life. Something in me had given up.

As for my professional self, I knew I was at my "nadir." The disaster of my last two productions at the Repertory Theatre had their cost. I wasn't the "miracle man" anymore; my professional confidence had been deflated. As for films: my favorite, *America America,* when all the addition and subtraction had been done, had resulted in red ink on the bottom line. It was a financial disaster. I knew this would make it impossible for me to attract financial backing for a continuation of that story—and possibly for any other film.

The one reassuring element in my life was my psychoanalyst. Dr. Kelman told me not to be disheartened by the sudden slackness I felt about everything. An austere man, he offered me no pity but told me that what I was going through was natural, that a death of someone close always changes everything, and it would be months before I would be "myself" again. He told me that the wound Molly's death had left would not heal, not to hope for that. Rather it would be absorbed as part of an altered self. He minimized my feelings of guilt, reduced them to their true size and slowly began to reestablish the self-esteem that the culpability I'd felt after her death had shattered.

Then he said he'd heard something new in the way I'd talked with him after Molly's death and thought it was hopeful. All my life, he said, I'd choked down my true feelings because if they were known—that much anger, that much hatred!—it would make me unacceptable to the authority figures around me whose favor I wanted, and in the theatre, it would alienate an audience. I was able to do *Tea and Sympathy* and the "poor, sensitive soul" plays of Williams and Inge, but they did not represent the way I felt about anything. Pity and self-pity, he said, are not tragic emotions and not native to me. He said I'd become so accustomed to presenting myself as a compliant, ever-sympathetic, one-hundred-percent nice guy that in time I came not to have a true voice or even my own face. I'd become a character I'd made up—"Gadget"—because it was expedient for me and acceptable to others, who might have some power over me.

Then he said that in the first months after Molly's death, I'd begun to display a truer self and to sound a truer voice. That emerging self, he said, wasn't the prettiest thing in the world, but "it is who and what you are and it's good that you're insisting at last that it be seen and heard. It's becoming apparent to you that you are not really interested in pleasing anyone else—as you've always pretended." He said that the new sounds he'd been hearing were not like the sounds I used to make, "those shrewdly-calculated-to-please-others voices of expediency." The recent sounds of distemper were my true voice. Anger, he said, was a gift, a talent. I'd lost it and was now recovering it.

As for Lincoln Center, he said they'd made a contract with a man who no longer existed. "Whom I killed" is what he actually said, whereupon he repeated something he'd quoted before: "In every psychoanalysis there is a murder." The fellow Rockefeller's people had at the end did not suit the taste of their audiences, who had little tolerance for ugly subject matter. They wanted even their tragedies pleasant.

As I walked home that day, I said to myself, "Baloney! He's just coddling me." But I kept thinking about what he'd said. He'd used "pleasant," the word Molly had used so often and I'd come to hate. He'd related the Lincoln Center audience to Molly. He'd also told me, as my friend Steinbeck had, "I don't believe it's possible for you to direct other people's work any longer," and that the best material for me to work on now was what was happening within. "You're the body inside which a tremendous drama is now being played out," he said. "Why don't you look at that." This advice I did believe and did think about, allowing that thought to lead me on.

And in time I began to change in a way I hadn't anticipated. I didn't know what was happening, knew only that I felt a flood of new emotions charging me. Why? Why so suddenly? Now, looking back over a twenty-five-year gap, I can confess what is painful and even shameful to admit: Molly's death had liberated me. I know now that's what had happened. I felt unbound. But even if what I've now admitted had occurred to me then, I wouldn't have admitted what I just have. I wouldn't have allowed myself to think it. Not until I'd begun to work on this book and forced myself to try to understand what happened in my life at that time could I see that the person I'd loved so deeply for so many years, who'd given me four children to whom I'm bound more than to any other living beings, that woman had had me tied up in ways I didn't understand, and her death had released me. So while her death was a tragedy for me, it was also a blessing. I'll try to explain.

Arriving in this country from a land where his people had existed in terror, an immigrant boy without the language and accompanied by a family of adults, foreigners who lived here in suspicion and fear and never gained secure positions in this society—such a boy became convinced that to survive on the streets and in the schools, to be accepted, he must do whatever was necessary to gain the favor of the powerful people around him, be they adults or kids his own age. This became my technique in life, doing whatever I had to do to gain the tolerance, the friendship, and the protection of the authority figures in my life. I developed into a child-person and, inevitably, into an adult who, I'm embarrassed to confess, did whatever it was necessary to do and became whoever it was expeditious to become to get by. I created a nonself. I wasn't anybody definite; I was many different people, depending on the circumstances. I was an adapter, taking on any color, yielding to any pressure, so long as I was accepted by those stronger than I and was thereby safe. That is what, decades later, I had to try to throw off by great effort, at great cost, and with considerable pain.

This need, to get along by pleasing the authority figures in my life—the ruling class of Anglo-Saxons, for instance—to show appropriate signs of liking and respect for them no matter what I truly felt, had an inevitable concomitant: resentment. As I tried to please those I thought had power over me, I resented them. As I yielded to pressures, some imagined, some real, I would be planning how, when the day came, I'd turn the tables and have my revenge. I'd play up to those strong ones, reassuring them of my fidelity and admiration while, in a curious simultaneous way, I hated them because they had power over me. I'd play all sides, be all things; join a Boy Scout troop and, not too many years later, the Communist Party, neither of which I gave a damn about. All my moves came from the same need, to be in good with the power people, whether the kids on my block or the actors in the Group who were already Party members. I had only to find who and what it was most useful for me to serve.

The ultimate authority figure, the person who could always tell me when I was going right or going wrong, was my wife, Molly. Her approval became my reassurance that I was on the right track. For many years, I lost sight of what I might have wanted for myself, as I tried to find what she wanted for me. The completely "in" person who never doubted her opinion and never wavered, Molly was both softly human and rigidly moral, taking positions that I would now call intolerant. Toward the end, I used to say to her, "You'd better learn to bend a little or you'll break." She never did learn to bend and finally did break. In the years when we were close, at least the first twenty years of our marriage, it was a confirmed truth for me that if Molly believed a course of action, a play, a friend, a choice, was good, it was right for me; if she approved, I went along.

However, in time, her rigidity began to suffocate me. Despite whatever respect I still had for her moral imperatives, the truth of my character emerged. My genes asserted themselves. My needs, from initial deprivation and from growing up "outside" this society, spoke up. My appetites and my yearnings demanded to be satisfied, and most of them were counter to what Molly stood for. These urges, easily satisfied through the power that success in my profession had brought me, became disruptive of our marriage. Once I'd tasted life outside the "yard" she'd fenced, I liked it and found it necessary. My actions were then beyond any approval I might win from her.

But I still didn't want to give her up. So I developed the art of dissembling, the ability to successfully conceal certain acts—where I'd been, when, why, and with whom. I became expert at the craft. This resulted in some unfortunate personal characteristics: "He's tricky." "You never know where you stand with him," and so on. But these experiences also resulted in a broad education. I learned a great deal about an awful lot of people. Having no sisters, I'd been cut off from the particular world of the other sex's experience. When it was opened up, I found it dramatic. Soon I didn't give a damn whether Molly approved or didn't, because after all, the life she chose to live, the one she thought "pleasant," was, so I saw, killing me. My infidelities saved my life.

For many years I lived this life of dissembling, and the one I deceived was a person who had a brilliant mind, who'd made me a family, who'd been unfailingly loyal, and whose actions were never anything but in my interests. She was my champion, with devotion beyond measure. She never spoke anything but the truth, her truth! Even when I was most against her, when I believed her narrow, rigid, intolerant, destructive, and above all restrictive of the full possibilities of life, I was devoted to her.

Then she died, and I found myself in a situation I'd never known. I didn't have to explain anything to anyone. I didn't need Molly's approval for anything I wanted to do. I found myself standing on a mound of years from which I could survey without shame everything that had happened, and from this vantage point of time and space I could try to understand myself. With this new curiosity, I looked at myself hard and found myself wishing a wish that mankind has had from the beginning, a hope that, as I was becoming a different person, I might start over again and live another life. I began to see that this was possible. Molly's death had unlocked the door. My old life—personal, professional, and emotional—had died; it was done with; it was gone. I'd discredited all the needs I'd once thought vital, those over which Molly had dominion. Now, as I grew free and became myself, I developed new needs and new goals, which were my own. I was liberated.

What I've attempted to explain I can see only now, twenty-five years after her death. At that time, I understood none of this, only felt a determination and a need to destroy what I had been and, if I could, start again on a new course, whatever it might be.

"I W A N T to break off from Barbara," I said.

"Well, what stops you?"

"I don't know, Dr. Kelman. Nothing. Everything. What do you think?"

He stared at me without answering; a habit or a technique—which was it? It made me damned uncomfortable, and I suspected he knew it.

"Since the play opened," I picked up, "she's been asking to know where she stands with me."

He stared at me, waiting.

"Dr. Kelman, have you been listening?"

"Don't you have a son there?"

"Yes. But Barbara's all wrapped up in her career now, and I can't help her with that anymore. I have my own problems." Silence. He stared at me. "I didn't hear what you said."

"I didn't speak."

"Your lips moved." Now I made an effort to be absolutely calm and analytical. "She seems to have some extraordinary hold on me. What is it? If you know, tell me: What does she represent? The girls I didn't have but every jock in high school did? Is that it? Tell me why I've always and only liked young blond women of that size. Like an eighteen-year-old girl. And preferably just a little bitchy. Why does that always get me?

"What color was Molly's hair?"

"Light brown. She was an Anglo—but not bitchy. More educated than Barbara but not necessarily smarter. What's their hold on me?"

"You said it yourself. 'They'll crawl,' you said. In other words, revenge. Molly? You married the enemy. Which perhaps is why you were so mean to her. Didn't you tell me once that you especially enjoyed taking the wives of other men, particularly of Anglo-Saxon, upper-middle-class, college-educated men?"

"But Barbara's not upper class or middle class. She's working class. Her father and brothers carry pistols when they go out to drink at night. She's self-educated—and smart. Had to be to survive. She says the same thing, that bitch, that you do about me, that I'm an emotional cripple, by which she means that I don't release my true emotions, that it's all cover-up, what I show the world. Isn't that what you said about me?"

He stared at me, shrugged; unimpressed.

"I get mad at her, but I respect her because she hides nothing. Imagine telling me every goddamn boyfriend she ever had. All the ones who—you know—in detail—every one!"

"Maybe she wanted to make you feel bad."

"She succeeded! But this time she went too far. The things she told me were intimate things, the very things I hide from everybody, even you. I admire her for that. But I don't like it. Anyway, I don't want to be tied to a damned actress, do I?"

He chuckled.

"What are you laughing at? I'm going to break it off with her, no matter what you say. When I'm with her I grind my teeth at night. I admire her for telling me all that she did, but it's been on my mind ever since, every detail, I didn't believe anyone would do that, tell it all. I wouldn't. She said she wanted to clear the air once and for all between us so I wouldn't be always wondering and worrying and have doubts eating at me. So she spills the whole pot in my lap, and if that was intended to make me stop worrying, it didn't work. It made me feel worse!"

I heard him sigh, which was his signal that our time had run out.

"One more minute. Please. Tell me. Why do I keep going back to her?"

He seemed irritated with me.

"Well, what do you want me to do? Tell me!" Now I was angry too. "Stay with her?"

"I don't give a damn what you do," he said. "That's not the point, whom you're with. Haven't you understood anything that's happened here? The way you are, you'll do the same thing with the next woman. They all have histories. What do you expect? They're human."

"Tell me why I stay with her," I insisted. "I know you know. Tell me."

He stood up, ready to leave the room. "You stay with her because she's like you," he said, "the victim who victimizes. She gets back at those who hurt her by hurting them whenever she has the power and the chance. That's what you do. Revenge. Poor Molly."

"Bullshit," I said.

He stood still for a moment, then said, "Poor Barbara," turned, and left the room. I sat there for a moment, exhausted. Then I got up and went home, where I wrote her a letter telling her I wasn't going to see her anymore. Then I tore up the letter and decided to meet with her and talk face to face. I wrote another letter, this one to Dr. Kelman, informing him I wasn't going to see him anymore and asking him to please send me his bill.

A C T U A L L Y I hadn't told Kelman the entire truth. The fact was that I'd been working myself loose from Barbara for some months on my own, and those who'd taken part in this process had not always been blonds. As Barbara rehearsed and performed at Lincoln Center, busy in the afternoons and at night, I'd experimented.

There was a girl I'd met in Tennessee, a member of a religious choir there, second row, third from the left, wearing an old-fashioned white frock, brought up a strict Baptist: she was so full of guilt at her pleasure that she'd kept her eyes closed tight throughout the act. I saw that two warring emotions, mortification and desire, can be experienced simultaneously—a lesson in directing actors. And she wasn't blond. There was a Greek girl who asked if I would provide her with a child if she'd promise never to ask for support or any other paternal duty—or even to see me again. I refused, but I did pass some time with her, and she certainly wasn't blond. There was a black girl, from whom I learned another lesson. She was middle class and had been brought up strictly. In bed she behaved very much like some of my white lady friends, and I discovered that class seems to mean more than race when it comes down to it. All these experiences having been highly educational and of value to a director, I decided that the only sin in my trade is to avoid encounters. I was surprised to find how many famous beauties considered themselves worthless and how many had flirted with suicide.

Nor had I told Dr. Kelman that on a late September afternoon, while Barbara was being fitted for her costume in *The Changeling*, I'd walked to the park to kill time and tension by watching a softball game, and on the way through the entrance I came upon a charming girl with gleaming dark eyes and a baseball cap over her dark brown hair. We watched the game together, then I walked her home and learned her history. Her husband had died not long before and she'd fallen to pieces but was now recovering. We exchanged reminiscences and we pleased each other. She was Jewish and extremely well educated; I enjoyed her company and she brightened my life that afternoon. She was at that ecstatic time in a pretty girl's life before she becomes weighted down with children and responsibilities, worries about her husband's career, and fears that she's losing her looks. She was a pure hedonist. I continued to see her, and one day she rewarded me with her dead husband's favorite sweater, which I was happy to wear.

What did this add up to? At the least, an instruction to look around and not be bound, to learn new lessons, to be open to life. Allow surprise. See the sights. I'd been with Barbara for over seven years. No one can tell me that novelty is not a great charge in sex.

Furthermore, these episodes resulted in an insight, one I came to without the help of a psychoanalyst. I saw that if I found the "right" woman, I had a chance now to live a life without lying; I wouldn't have to be devious or evasive, depend on any kind of counterfeit behavior or daily quackery. What a load would be lifted! I wouldn't have to pretend, deceive, misrepresent, or betray. Perhaps the young widow I'd met in the park was the one.

I called Barbara and told her I'd pick her up in a cab and take her downtown. I was about to hurt her, but there was no other way.

As we rode downtown, she got onto the subject we'd been discussing the day before, the audio recording the company was going to make of *After the Fall*. I'd agreed with the producers that she should get less than Jason for her services; he was an established star, she was just beginning to come on. She told me that even though she'd originally agreed, everybody else was "getting his," so why shouldn't she get all she could? When I refused to go along with this, she began to attack the Repertory Theatre, saying that it hadn't been what she'd hoped for when she got into it, that there had been no "idealism" connected with it, that all the Lincoln Center people were interested in was money, that, furthermore, my rehearsals had not been creative, that I'd "blocked" scenes mechanically, not truly worked with the actors—and so on and on, until I got fed up with it all and turned on her.

Of course, all this got me into the right mood to tell her what I'd decided to. When she saw that she'd angered me, she put her arm around my neck and as soon as we got into the room, took off all her clothes. Our practice had become to make love first, ready or not, as soon as we were alone and the door shut. And so we did now. I suppose she knew from experience that I'd be more malleable afterward. But this time less. We did it once and the results were okay, but something was hanging in the air, unexpressed, and we both knew it. I wanted to lie still on the bed and hold her. But I noticed she didn't like this the way she once had, and although her head was on my upper arm and her leg over mine, she seemed tensed, like a runner before a race.

Then she said, with a casualness I thought feigned, "Daddy, I wish you'd tell me what you want me to do." This question was a bull's-eye; there was only one target, and we both knew what was coming.

I decided to skip all intermediate stages and all reconnoitering. Actually I'd practiced the speech. "I dread it," I said. "I'm deadly afraid of it. I don't want to get married. I don't think it will last two months—"

"How do you know?" she said. "We'll never know unless we try it."

"I know," I said.

There was a stunned silence. I'd come out with it. I was relieved.

"I dread it," I repeated.

There was a long pause. Her head was still on my arm and her leg over my leg.

"Tell me the truth," I said. "Don't you look forward to it with trepidation?" Suddenly that word out of left field, "trepidation." But there it was.

"How do you know," she said, "what it'll be?"

To which I answered, "I don't believe it will work and I don't want to do anything anymore unless I'm enthusiastic about it. I want to start a new life, not go back to something that's all—" I stopped.

That hit her hard. Her face, on my arm, clenched.

"It's either we marry or break up for good," she said.

I didn't answer. I'd said whatever I had to say, and I remained in my usual defensive silence.

She got up, got dressed. In the cab, she didn't speak; she didn't have to. I knew where she was—back on her old hunting grounds, where I'd found her: "Trust no man! All you have is your body. Make them pay for it. Never give in totally. If someone hurts you, revenge yourself by 'seeing' someone else." And so on.

The cab stopped in front of her place, and I told the hackie to keep his meter going. Without looking at me, she said, "I should never have put all my eggs in one basket." And then: "I'm not as worn out and tired as you think I am."

I told her I thought she was beautiful.

She still didn't look at me. "I feel sorry for you," she said. "Because I don't think you'll be able to start a new life." Then she looked at me. "But I will."

"What does that mean?"

"You'll see," she said. "I'm never going to see you again. I don't get anything from you now anyway, only a warm body up against me once in a while. That's all. So now you're free, okay? Absolutely free. So am I. You don't owe me anything, anything at all." And in a very bright, very final voice, she said, "Thanks for everything you did for me. I don't want you to ever say that I wasn't grateful." Then, sarcastically, "I hope you find some-one worthy of you."

She got out of the cab and walked to her front door.

I told the cabbie to pull away. At home, I had a drink and remembered the words of a close friend: "You marry her and you'll end up with a quick divorce and a fat alimony. That's what she's after." I'd defended Barbara. I thought then and I think now that she'd been very patient with me and generous with herself and her time.

That night I saw the young widow I'd met in Central Park, made love, slept great, and didn't grind my teeth.

But after she'd gone in the morning, I thought of Barbara, that she was an extraordinary girl. I'd taken some of her best years and given her very little. I'd built her hopes to the skies, and when it came time to fulfill my promises, those in words and those implied, above all those that love-making affirmed, I had not. She had a right to be furious with me.

I knew that her hold on me was still strong. When she looked sad, I wanted to help her; when she was defeated, I wanted to lift her up. But I'd done that too often, led her on and on and on, then backed out at the end. I'd made up my mind, and I wasn't going to be diverted by other people's wants and emotions. Now I was free for the first time in my life, had the opportunity for a new life, in which I wouldn't have to lie, deceive, or connive. I'd never had that chance before, and I wasn't going to lose it.

A few days later, I got Kelman's bill—psychoanalysts are exceptionally prompt about dispatching their bills. I'd made up my mind to leave the country; go to Europe with a folder of traveler's checks and an air travel card; land in England without definite plans beyond that point. I thought it proper to see Kelman, tell him the news, and say a decent goodbye.

He nodded, looking simultaneously magisterial and ambivalent, which is quite a stunt. Then we shook hands, and I turned for the door. He stopped me there. "Have you told Barbara?" he asked. That surprised me. "No," I said. "You'll feel better later if you do," he said.

I was afraid to talk to her. I knew I'd disappointed her terribly and, despite everything she'd said, knew that I'd hurt her. But I'd succeeded in resolving matters and I didn't want to open them up again. So I didn't call her.

On the last day of '64, having given up the apartment on Third Street, I went downtown on the subway, carrying a couple of empty suitcases for my belongings. There was a spook in the place: Barbara. There'd always been something unearthly about the girl; her arrivals and departures were be-yond simple explanation. She had a large "D'Ag" shopping bag, which she'd filled with what was hers. Then apparently she'd sat on the edge of the bed to rest and lifted the package onto her lap, clasping it with both arms. She looked like an immigrant on Ellis Island holding a bundled child and wait-ing for an order to move. "Been getting my junk," she said.

I sat down. I'd often thought she had ESP. Something had told her I was coming down, and she'd been waiting for me. I never knew for sure what she was thinking, but this time she told me. "You've got the wrong idea about me," she said. "I understand all that you said about marriage. I remember your friend John Steinbeck, that time you took me there, how he looked like an animal in a cage." (John had warned me, after that meeting, to stay away from Barbara.) "I wasn't trying to trap you into something like that."

"I like John's wife," I said. "He's lucky to have her."

She went on. "I wanted to help you live the kind of life you wanted—if you knew what it was, which I doubt. For instance, you wanted to be free, but me not to be. That was all right with me. Everybody's different, right? If you'd only explained what you wanted, I'd have understood. But you never explained anything to me."

"I know," I said.

She stood up, still holding the bag. "No use talking about it now." She turned her head away. "I've been so ashamed of you. There were times—I can't imagine what you thought of yourself. You used to say, 'I'm not for hire!' But you took Rockefeller's money and gave them what they'd paid for. You thought I was trying to demoralize you when I was critical, but it turned out like I said, didn't it? You just put on plays. There wasn't anything of you in those shows. You didn't get anything more out of the actors than any other director might have."

"Only out of you in the Miller play," I said.

"I did that myself. What I'm trying to say is that you're not their kind of man. You should have known that with one look. Not Bob Whitehead's kind either, even though he's a nice enough fellow. You look funny behind a desk and he doesn't. You put your feet up on it like you want to dirty it. Anybody could see that you didn't fit there. I never understood why you went into it. Where was your pride? But that's not my business anymore, so—"

"I had hopes that someday I could—"

"You're just saying that. I watched you there three years and I didn't see where you were hoping for anything except to get those plays opened and running. Where you had hopes was when you were sitting in Schulberg's apartment and writing your movie. That was you. I used to tell you you were better than the writers whose plays you were directing. Remember? But you didn't believe me. Hopes! You could have done so much. But what you did was work like a regular Broadway 'get it on, get it done' director. There were times I could see that you knew that what you were doing was disgraceful: not for anyone else—you were always better than the rest—but to what you could have been."

She hitched up the bag of her belongings. "Believe it or not," she went on, "I'm glad you're going away, even though it means we're finished.

Maybe you're still alive and not satisfied, and looking for something out of you, not like everybody else in show business. I hope you find it, no matter where it takes you. I hope you don't ever again settle for less than you're capable of, because then you become like the others. And you're not. I can't help it—I still believe you're not!"

She was silent, and there were tears in her eyes. "Aren't you going to see Leo before you go?" she said. "You haven't seen him since he grew up."

"Grew up?"

"He'll be three years old any minute."

"When do you take him to the park?" I asked.

Leo was a beautiful boy with luminous eyes. When he looked at me, he had the same effect Barbara had: I wondered what he was thinking.

"Talk to him," Barbara said. We were sitting on a bench, all three silent. Leo was watching two old Italian men who were—very gravely—playing boccie. We could hear the wooden balls kiss.

I didn't know what to talk to Leo about.

"This is Eeek," Barbara said to him. "He's an old friend."

Leo didn't respond.

"I'll send him something from wherever I'm going," I said. "What would he like?"

"Ask him."

"Comics," the little boy said without turning his head. It was as if he was offering me the solution to a riddle.

"I'll get you a mess of them when I get back," I said. I was speaking to my son for the first time.

"Where you going?" His eyes were still on the old Italians at their game.

"You know what bears do in the winter, Leo? They find a deep, dark cave, crawl into it, and stay there through the stormy weather."

"What do they do there?"

"They sleep or think or something. That's what I'm going to do."

He looked at me and smiled. "You look like a bear," he said. The players of boccie got into an argument and Leo wandered over to watch.

The boy's smile had enchanted me, but his eyes had never lost the doubting look that stirred up my guilt. "He's a beautiful kid," I said to Barbara.

"The other women here, when they see him, they die of jealousy. He makes their kids look like little dressed-up monkeys."

"I can see why," I said. "Well . . ." I stood up to go.

"Hope you find your cave," she said.

"Oh, that? It's portable. I carry it with me."

As I left, I passed Leo to say goodbye, but he looked away as if we hadn't met.

· · ·

I DIDN'T tell her I was taking someone with me. On an impulse, I'd asked the girl I'd met in the park if she'd go to Europe, destination un-known. She answered she'd go anywhere with me. When? I left mid-January in a snowstorm, British Air for London. She followed three days later. When I met her at Heathrow Airport, she was tingling with excite-ment and hungry for pleasure. The widow had come back to life.

Sam Spiegel, wintering in a warmer, drier place, had offered me his apartment at the Grosvenor House, a hotel. There was a bed with a lace-edged canopy (not exactly Sam's style in love), an extravagantly stocked bar, and an ever-ready, nimble-footed room service waiter. It never stopped raining that week in London, and when the weather improved, it drizzled, but the peat moss was kept burning in the fireplace all day. Sam, a most generous host, had instructed the hall porter to get us theatre tickets, but I didn't want to go. What I might see would aggravate my sense of failure. We had everything we needed indoors—at least for a week. Then I decided that Sam's apartment wasn't really what I wanted, and I told my friend I was taking her to Paris. She'd been hoping I would.

I reserved a room at the Relais Bisson, a small hotel on the Grand Quai des Augustins, whose kitchen was famous for its seafood. I'd stayed there before and knew the room I wanted, one without a view, a dark, soft cave in the bowels of the place. The wallpaper was of cloth, and no sound pene-trated from the world outside.

During the next days nothing happened—so it seemed to a man accus-tomed to vigorous and decisive physical activity. We woke early, had break-fast in bed: croissant, *confiture d'orange,* and dark, bitter coffee softened with hot milk. Then she'd go off, as I'd asked her to go off every day, and not come back until three in the afternoon. This suited her fine; she had those hours to go to museums and shop, while I had precious hours to look into the mirror that only I knew was in the room, where I could see my face and the faces of everyone I'd ever known.

I'd never written anything longer than a few pages before, and certainly had no intention of writing the novel that would be titled *The Arrangement.* What I wrote had one merit: Since it never occurred to me that anyone would see it, I set down what I thought and felt without self-censoring. A true expression of anger, love, and bewilderment, it consisted of letters to myself and long explorative notes, moving ever closer to the bone. There followed, usually later in the day, when I'd cooled, descriptions of various characters I'd encountered in my various professions; my affection for, fol-lowed by my alienation from, the big studio heads; along with a circus of show business friends and enemies, who no longer seemed to be enemies as I tried to understand them. I wrote about my life in the New York theatre and in the radical movement, in the theatre of the thirties and in California, where Molly and I had rented homes when I'd gone west to work—all this with good humor, because I was no longer a captive of either the theatre, the "movement," or the film industry. Then I moved on to the people close to me, my intimate recollections of the women I'd known and their private lives as they'd revealed them to me; and I began to consider the wives of certain friends, women I'd not liked, as well as their husbands, and what I thought went on between them. Finally I wrote of my brothers and their wives, my father and my mother, whom I'd never thought about objectively. With all this I found that I'd had a rich and tumultuous life, one that had loaded me with a wealth of human material.

An astonishing thing happened as I wrote these scattered pieces. They began to come together in a kind of form; there appeared a shape and a movement—call it story. The story had to be—with this launching—about me, about my experience. There were factors that impelled these scattered pieces in a definite direction. One was the recent defeat in my own life. Another was the challenges I'd thrown at myself about my work and accomplishments, which weren't different from those Barbara had thrown at me as we parted. I recalled her tart and rebellious spirit toward what was established and generally praised in my world and particularly how she doubted so much that others had accepted and honored. The combination of this challenging spirit and that of a man leaving one mooring, adrift for a time, going here and there with the tides, looking for a new anchorage, began to give shape to my story. It seemed, as I examined myself, that the male character with whom I was dealing would have been content to allow things to remain as they were—except for the scorn and the thrust he received from this woman. I began to write about the disintegration in myself, the overwhelming self-doubt I'd felt, the chaos underneath, my disrespect for the success I'd had, and with this sense of failure, my determination, now rising and increasingly felt, to change my life and find a new course.

All this I wrote straight out of my feelings and in candor—no one would read it, I was sure—and sometimes extraordinary things happened that I'd never experienced before. As I wrote, I discovered feelings I'd never suspected were there. I began to surmise characteristics and then events about other people and violent emotions within myself—of anger, particularly that. What I wrote began to be more than a collection of memories and impressions; it began to be a penetration into that unknown part of myself that I'd never before delivered from the dark.

The one person I could not write about was Molly. I could not, at this time, conceive that someone so good could play a negative part in my life, and if I'd thought of it, I'd have been ashamed to admit it, both because I knew her to have been so goodhearted and because it would portray me as weak. Since I couldn't identify her as the "villain" from whom the hero had to break away, I invented another character, taken from the wives of friends I'd known, who I believed had tied their husbands down with a dog's leash and restrained all that was most exceptional, lively and rebellious, questioning and scoffing, about their men, had nailed them to that uxorious cross which was the center support of their home. Later a couple of these ladies were to guess that I'd been inspired—if you can call it that—by their characters and their ways of manipulating and controlling their husbands, and although I vigorously denied it when I was accused, they were right. Many people who read the book and knew me and knew Molly believed the character of Florence was derived from her, and this disturbed me because I thought Molly miles ahead of that character, both in intellectual worth and in spirit. The fact that the character was often identified with my wife worried me, but I passed it off as a mistake that people would inevitably make. No doubt some of the rancor and resentment I'd felt, consciously or unconsciously, about her showed through, and the home as "fortress" in the book couldn't help but recall the "perfect and forever" apartment that Molly had made for me and in which—so it seemed to me not long before her death—she'd incarcerated me.

One true feeling I did express plainly, and I marshaled evidence to support it: my conviction that infidelity had saved my life, or that part of my life I most valued. This was drawn not only from my own experience but from that of other men and women I'd known. It accounts, I believe, for the extraordinary popularity the book was to have—most surprisingly—among women. The fact that so many women identified with my male hero, felt as he did, and even walked out on their marriages, which they'd found restrictive as he had found his, can't be explained any other way. My hero spoke for them.

When it came to my father, I could for the first time—now that he was dead and I was ready to tell the truth about anything and everything—reveal what I'd felt about him all my life long. Here a great change took place. Whereas the first part of the book started out as a work of memory dramatized by imagination, as I progressed what I wrote got closer to what had really happened and how it had happened. I began to see that what I was writing could not be anything but a dramatization of my own life and often amounted to autobiography; my own life had been my material, and the nearer I got to it, the better the work was.

When people would ask me later if what I'd written was autobiographical, I'd deny it vigorously, but it was as close as I dared to get at the time. At first I had feared that people would recognize themselves and be embarrassed, even hurt. Then I took a bold step: I decided not to care about hurting others. At this time, with Molly dead, my father dead, Barbara elsewhere, and everyone who'd been close to me in the past now at arm's length, there was no one I felt I should protect by silence except my mother, and I had nothing but adoration to express about her. I couldn't give up the link with my true emotions; I knew that whatever worth the book had would come from my feelings of desperation and bewilderment and from my searching for a new way for myself. Truth was the best basis for fiction.

I T O L D my friend we were going to Athens. I wanted to sit in the middle of the place, hear my natal tongue and be a Greek again. I'd come to know a great number of people there when I was making *America America* two years before, and I wanted time and talk with them. I went to a hotel with a terrace over Stadiou Street, where the political demonstrations march, and where, as we lay in bed, we'd have a view of the Acropolis. I'd been there many times; the manager and the chambermaids were friends and we were greeted like newlyweds.

In the morning I telephoned my relatives and got a wonderful surprise. My cousin Stellio had succeeded in moving his family to Athens, had even set up a business, manufacturing inexpensive shoes and exporting them to America. We met immediately, and on the days when I was in Athens, I tried to spend as much time with him as I could. I noticed a miraculous change in his character. In Greece, he'd become bold, outspoken, argued with me freely and confidently, saying what it pleased him to say in an unmuffled voice. He had lost that circumspect and timid manner I'd remarked on in Istanbul; he wheeled boldly and freely around the streets. He was another man. I was thrilled by what had happened to him. This one man exemplified for me the two different kinds of Greeks, those from Greece itself and those from Turkey, who'd lived under the Turk and learned what it was necessary to do to survive. The native Greeks were less sensitive, on the whole, less intelligent, but independent, fearless, and outspoken. Those who'd escaped from the Turk, particularly those who'd fled from Smyrna in 1922, when the Turks had burned the Greek and Armenian neighborhoods of the city, considered themselves lucky to be alive and were quite in contrast to the natives; they'd become anxious and manipulative, sometimes to the point of being craven and tricky. They got along by pleasing others and by making themselves, as my cousin Stellio had been, as nearly invisible as possible. My father had been one of this number. I recalled how he'd say "I know nothing" when confronted with a difficult choice or when someone—other than his wife—expected him to take a stand. If he was asked his opinion and believed he might be held to it, he'd shrug and say, "It's not my business." Compare the Yankee who, when challenged, says, "Mind your business!" How admirable that blunt response is!

I'd observed all this before, but now I saw the connection to my own life. I did not separate myself from my cousin Stellio, who'd once walked close to the edge of buildings and was now free. I was made of the same stuff. I saw that my background had made me ideal for show business, where the basic interest is to please others—the audience, the critics, the moneymen, the playwrights, and the producers. It was perfectly natural for me to obey these cardinal laws: Please those who pay. Don't say what will offend those in power. The native Greeks were not as shrewd as those of us who'd come from Anatolia; we were the clever ones, and our cunning taught us to be servile to the strong. Those born in Greece, particularly those who'd been there for generations, had a fearlessness close to arrogance, which I envied.

I was a man who'd spent his entire adult life working in the theatre and in films—that is, Hollywood—pleasing those with the power to give me jobs. Now, having sat for some time in a "cave" in the Quai des Augustins in Paris, and being presently in a room with a view of the Acropolis, which still spoke of the public liberties of the fifth century B.C., I suddenly found that the change in my cousin reflected a corresponding change in me. In that year of 1965, I'd found joy, not from a good notice on Broadway or a new conquest who "responds," but from a more central thing: I was now my own boss, doing what I wanted, saying what it pleased me to say. I'd finally paid myself the respect that came from believing that my own material was worth investing the time of my life in, and possibly that what I felt and what I'd gone through were important and that people would listen.

This had never happened before. I had always lured people to pay attention to other men. Implicit in what I was now doing was this: that I considered myself, at least for myself, more worthy of attention than anyone else. It was the most confident thing I'd done in my life, this writing, and it would change the course of my life. I was never to be the same person again. It didn't matter if the book—if it became a book—was good, bad, or indifferent. It was mine, my book, and I would be telling people, if I went on with it, to listen to my voice and consider my experiences.

I knew then that I had to go on with what I was doing and make a book of it if I could, a book about myself and what I had been through and what I felt now.

What a joy I was experiencing and what a load was lifted! And when I'd lifted that load, I felt: My God, I have power! No one has to fill my tank; I've got all the fuel I need. I have an enormous supply of energy—and more coming every day—as well as of desire and of meaning and of material. What a joy not to work for someone else, not to lead someone else on, not to scold, cajole, trick, inspire someone else, which was the terrible burden I used to carry with actors, but to deal only with myself.

This triumph went all through my being. Suddenly, where, so recently, I'd stopped caring about making love, I was unceasingly potent. I discovered what I never again forgot, that my sexual potency is related to my success or failure in more central matters.

Now I would wake in the middle of the night, not out of worry or grief or doubt, but because I couldn't wait to get to work again, needing to let loose my own voice, speaking of my own concerns. I knew I could sit at my table, before my portable typewriter, and change anything, add anything, cut out anything, plumb anything I wanted, without asking permission or worrying about the effect on others. I had complete power over each page. My mornings were spent in heaven. "I am *axios!*" the young priest says when he is taken into his church and affirmed as "worthy." I'd done it, finally, for myself.

This time of elation followed the deepest dip in my professional and personal fortunes, and the pain I'd known gave scale to the exhilaration. I had to be down that far to come up that far. I had to have lost my voice to have found it those weeks in Paris and Athens.

Since that day the question has never been whether or not I am a brilliant writer. I know I'm not. But that has not been the point of what I am doing. I carry my own measuring rod with me, and by that I am a success. In a world where everyone is trying—as I had for so many years—to please someone else—a boss, an ideology, a mate, a leader, a critic, a backer—I had finally found a way of living by pleasing only myself.

I could feel the change. I began to laugh a lot and listen to others without feeling a need to judge them or, the opposite, to impress them. For the first time I loved other people, whatever they were, instead of competing with them or manipulating them, impressing them or selling myself to them. Up until that time I'd believed myself arrogant and conceited—only a cover for a feeling of worthlessness—when the opposite was true: I was working to please people who were not worthy of me. The truth was not that I was a selfish person but that I hadn't been selfish enough, that I didn't respect myself enough, that I had no true self-esteem but rather a big bravado show of too much. As I left Athens and remembered Paris, I knew that I could do my own work now, direct my own films, write my own books, be myself forever.

Feeling these spurs to self-respect, I would connect them with Barbara. It was what she'd hoped I would think and feel—and do. So I wrote to her, told her I'd been thinking of her and how much she'd meant to me and where I was going—to Calcutta, then Thailand, and finally Japan—and where she should write me. And so a correspondence was started.

S T E L L I O ' S story has an unhappy ending. One day, some years later, careless in his new freedom, he was struck by a taxi that climbed up over the curb where he was standing off guard, talking to a friend. Stellio was thrown against a lamppost, then taken to a hospital, where he died ten days later. His new freedom had cost him his life; he'd never been off guard in a street in Istanbul.

W E   L E F T Athens for Bombay. I'd not been to India. We found a modest, clean hotel and settled in. It was to be our last week together. I can't recall whether it was she who wanted to return to the States or whether I wanted her to go; perhaps both. Either way, it was agreed that she would go on with me as far as New Delhi and take a plane home from there. I believe that if I'd pressed her to continue, she would have, but I didn't press her. Barbara had written me that she could meet me in Japan if I was going there. I'd answered that I'd be glad to see her and would write or cable when I was arriving in Tokyo. The basic premise was to be the same: No enduring relationship was to be formed. But as I went on planning the structure of my book, I'd found that the character of the woman who stirred up the discontent of the hero was inspired by Barbara. She'd had some such effect on me, one that I'd now dramatized in fiction. I felt a continuing interest in her and I also felt gratitude that the relationship was still meaningful for me. The further I progressed with the story, the more I needed her to stand as model. I especially wanted an ending that I'd believe honest and in scale with the rest of the book, an unhappy/happy ending. I had a hope that her sour, doubting stance in the world would help me to get something that I'd consider true, not contrived.

Meantime, in Bombay, I enjoyed what was there, what I had, while I could. We were at the peak of desire and spent part of our afternoons where we spent our nights. I watched her sleep after love and wondered if this person, with whom I continued to find the easiest and most natural pleasure, would not make a good permanent companion. We were still without the accumulation of old disappointments and tensions, of doubts and rancor, that more "permanent" relationships inevitably accumulate.

On our second night we decided to take in an Indian movie. We were told where we could find a typical "hit," decided to walk through the late afternoon light, stop somewhere to eat, and catch the late show. We had dinner at a highly recommended restaurant, where the food was expensive and excellent. Before the tables, set outside, was a plaza, and as we ate dinner we watched lepers, "regulars" in front of that restaurant, who lay on the paving with their arms stretched up to display the ends of their fingers, devoured by the disease. We sent our waiter with a donation but skirted them when we left.

Walking through the streets, now dark, we made our way along sidewalks, past doorways and storefronts, packed with people bedded down for the night's sleep, whole families in clumps, children with their heads on their mothers' laps, the adults hushed and watchful, waiting for sleep with open eyes. These silent streets were the bedroom of the city. I couldn't guess how many people passed their nights this way; it must have been in the thousands. The theatre's entrance was jammed tight with people too, eager to get in. They reminded me of a crowd who'd been without food, waiting for the handout that would save their lives. The film was a "period" love story of a syrupy kind, one that had no relationship to the lives of the

people in the audience. This feature offering contrasted to the strong odor
of unwashed bodies, as well as of certain heavy perfumes new to me.

Sitting there, holding my friend's hand, I realized I'd allowed myself to
be separated from the impoverished of the world. It was thirty years since
I'd been a member of the Communist Party and believed—or said I did—
that the struggles of the poor would be my central concern for life. Success
had separated me from the great mass of people struggling for nourishment,
security, and dignity. My emotional problems had become the main concern of my life. I'd become a competitive man, not a devoted man. My days
and nights had been eaten up by the special travails of show business, and
my constant companions were those who lived in the world of film and
theatre. All I'd seen that night—this hardship, this struggle—would continue when I'd departed and was elsewhere, safe, well fed, and indifferent.
Money, ambition, and rivalry had deprived me of brotherliness.

In Delhi I said a fond farewell to my friend, thanked her for the pleasure
of her company, and promised I'd see her in New York. It was a foolish
promise. I had no idea what condition I'd be in in New York or what I'd
want for myself. I was glad to have been with her and now equally glad to
be alone. I looked forward to meeting Barbara—a more complex and interesting person—in Tokyo, both with eagerness and with its opposite, uneasiness. I didn't know what to do about Barbara or about my departed friend.

Was it possible I wanted them both and needed a way of life in which I'd
have the complicated one *and* the agreeable other? Could that kind of arrangement be set up? I'd find out.

A R R I V I N G at Tokyo a week before I'd told Barbara I'd be there, I was
met at the airport by a Japanese lady friend I'd known in New York. She
took me to a traditional inn, where guests sleep on futons on the floor and
expressionless maidens slip silently through sliding screens to wake them
in the morning with an offering of hot tea. A theatre star I'd not met before
left an invitation for me, and a few days later he entertained me at dinner.
There were four of us, all men of the theatre, and at the side of each was a
geisha in traditional costume, not a sexual companion for the evening but
there to make sure each dish was prepared properly and offered in the most
pleasing manner. Between courses, the geishas entertained us with discor-
dant songs and musical instruments that screeched. The dinner had a rather
severe atmosphere, almost puritanical, and despite the presence of the
geishas, no sexual overtones: another stereotype reduced to its true
meaning.

I regretted encouraging Barbara to come to Japan. I didn't know what to
propose to her and what to exclude, whether to warn her again of the limited nature of my involvement or to simply go where the tide took me.

When she arrived, I noticed a striking difference in her manner. A female wise in the ways of her sex might have tipped me off that this change was a manipulation, chosen to achieve an end. I would never exclude craft from a place in Barbara's bag of techniques, nor would I deny that any dog could wag its tail and I'd be charmed. Still I truly believed in her altered personality, even if it was an effort to reassure me that she could make good in a more permanent connection, one in which different personal qualities are required. I was delighted with how we were together for the next two weeks. She was always interesting, frequently surprising, ever loving, and would listen when I talked, without her mind wandering as it often had in the past. Talking with her gave me ideas for Gwen, the woman in my book. Barbara enriched my work. I was happy traveling with her by day, two outcasts from an inhospitable world we seemed, and so pleased with her companionship by night that I prolonged my stay in Japan.

At the end of the second week, possibly because she had been so agreeable and understanding, I confessed to her that I'd had a companion on the earlier part of my trip, a confession both foolish and wise. She took it without visible reaction. I knew her well, so I suspected that there had been a violent reaction but far underground, one that would be revealed later, in a way and at a time I could not anticipate.

W H E N I got home to New York, I broke into the haunted apartment over Central Park West, not perfect now or permanent, and took over Molly's study and table for my workplace. I was riding high. Early chapters were finished, and I was enjoying a mania of devotion to work that I'd never known as a director. The stuff poured out of me, and my outline stood up. I'm not sure I'm a writer, but I may be a storyteller; my film work helped with that. The planning and the structuring are more important for me than the words. I hadn't realized how much I knew, not in a philosophical way, but in the wealth of detail and of incident to illustrate character and flesh out the tale I was telling.

As for my personal life—so miscalled, because nothing could have been more personal than what I was writing—I'd come back to New York determined not to give up either woman, not to be forced into a solution by the rules of a middle-class society I didn't favor. How I would go about that I didn't know. It would be a problem, but not the main problem of my life; the book was that. So I tried for a time to keep both relationships going, but lacked sufficient devotion to either. My hope that I could now lead an open and undeceitful life was scuttled. There were, for a time, a series of awkward encounters and narrow escapes. I became tired of all that; these incidents made my days and my nights too complicated, melodramatic, and distracting. I found that nights of passion didn't mean as much to me as working with energy and concentration the following morning and without interruptions. My analyst, whom I was seeing again, contributed this: "Do you realize how much energy you squander on all that?" I soon did. Perhaps it was my age, although I was to have periods of resurgence in years to come. The fact was that I simply didn't care as much as I used to and now shrugged off what I used to wait for all day.

I remember I met Marcello Mastroianni at a party one night. Both "loaded," we compared lives of turmoil that were surprisingly alike. He said he'd come to the decision that no woman was worth upsetting your life for. If it was not one woman, he said, it was another; finally they were the same. I thought this very Italian. But I was soon to see that, at least for the time, I didn't need anything vital from either of my women. The only important thing was the work I was doing. I told my dark friend, in the services of truth (at least half truth), that I was "seeing" Barbara and that Barbara meant a lot to me. I also told her that Barbara had once said that if I wanted to see others but would mainly stay with her (Barbara had indeed said this), it would be okay with her.

The problem was mine, not theirs. Not yet. Not according to what they each said. So I worked all day in my cavernous apartment with its sixteen-foot windows and sometimes saw one, sometimes the other, and sometimes neither. There were many nights when I couldn't wait for morning, rose before the sun so I could go on with what I'd been doing the day before.

Then, one night, the shit hit the fan. And Barbara's cool heated up. She'd been growing suspicious and was questioning me about where I'd spent the day. I resented being policed. I was losing my cool too. I'd had a bad dream one night that shocked me. I was slashing Barbara's face with the serrated knife I'd used to gut fish. Her response should have warned me. "I don't mind if you hit me," she said in the dream, "or even if you kill me. Just don't leave me." But during the day she'd respond to my evasiveness by becoming devious. She would not tell me how she'd spent her own day. I told her that intrigue and jealousy were not necessary to hold my interest; they had the opposite result, I claimed—they alienated me. The height of arrogance, that! "But I feel I'm losing you," she said. "How *will* I hold your interest?" I had no answer to that. Well, actually I did. "I have to get back to work," I'd say. Or I'd say, "I'm thinking about my book now," and we'd quarrel.

So the tension grew. One night we were lying on the bed in the Central Park West apartment, no longer quarreling but not made up, preparing to sleep, an intermission with tension, when the phone rang. I'd told my dark-haired friend never to call me there, but she'd been drinking and was happy and sounded very cheery. I quickly said, "I'm sleeping," which I wasn't. She said, "Oh, okay," and hung up. That took care of that—I thought.

But Barbara asked me who'd called, and I was still feeling quarrelsome, so I said, "That was the girl I took to Europe." Barbara then got terribly upset and asked me why I hadn't told that girl not to call me anymore, and "Is it still going on?" I said that I'd told her not to call, and as for Barbara's other question, yes, I did see her, but infrequently. Barbara's anger charged the room; anyone could see why she was such a fine actress. She began to strike my chest with her fists, and I had to finally hit her back to make her stop. Not the least satisfied, she was determined to call the other girl on the phone. "What's her number?" she demanded. "I don't know her number," I lied. Whereupon Barbara rushed for my pocket phone book on the table, but I beat her to it. Barbara dressed and left the apartment.

The next afternoon, after I'd finished writing, I called my onetime traveling companion to warn her that Barbara might be trying to see her. "She can be pretty rough," I said, "so look out." "She's right here," the girl said. This set me back; I didn't know what to say, other than: "How are you getting along?" "I like her very much," the girl said.

So I decided to turn the drama over to the women. I was vicious enough to be interested in seeing how they'd work it out. I bet on Barbara; I knew both women well and considered Barbara the tougher. She'd done what experienced and smart wives do, consorted with the competition, and to judge from the tone in my other friend's voice, they'd had a sisterly visit. I wasn't there, so I can't report on the specifics, but they'd compared notes on me thoroughly and I'd not come out as well as I might have wished. The conversation had started out with the dark girl saying things like "What makes you think he's all yours?" But Barbara knew you catch more flies with honey than with vinegar, and soon the conversation took a sororal tone. It seemed they were both tied by a strong bond, my two victims; that had caused the dominant sympathetic note. Apparently, at the end, the conversation got into jolly girl talk, and I was the butt of the humor. Then Barbara had said something charming, like: "He says you've got a big ass," and the girl was offended, not at Barbara but at me. Barbara was clever; this brought them closer, and finally—so I gather—Barbara said, in a very sweet but firm tone, "Please don't call him anymore now. Because he's with me—" and then: "that bastard." With which they both could agree. I had, after all, led them both on.

A few days later, Barbara came to see me. Obviously she was the victor and knew it and now was very much at peace. She informed me in dulcet tones not to worry, because my traveling companion had found a readier lover, one less treacherous; in fact, if she could believe her—yes, they had gone on talking as good friends—she'd had two others on the very night after Barbara had seen her.

The result of all this was that I had once again established myself in a cave of quiet and could continue work on my book without further sexual intrigue. It would be months before I emerged from that cave. Barbara did sound her war cry of triumph, however. "Don't ever underestimate me again, boy," she said. "You thought I was promiscuous. I've never been

unfaithful to you for seven years. I've thought of it. I wish I could have been, but I never could. That girl did it with two men the day after you left her." Then she said something I had trouble believing: "I love you more after what happened; I can't tell you why." That both puzzled me and impressed me.

D U R I N G that year, Barbara moved in with me. This made my life more settled. No more girl-hunting, no more courtship, no more wasting time. I had many plans ahead now for writing, and I was eager to get on with them. Barbara respected my need for quiet and saw to it that I was relieved of interruption and turmoil. The first thing she did when she moved in was lead Leo by the hand to where I was behind the fortification of my typewriter, and put him on my lap. He was a remarkable-looking boy, and again I felt from him that extraordinary questing behind his eyes. They were dark brown now, the same color as mine.

I N T H E spring of 1966, *The Arrangement* was finished. I'm prouder of this book than I am of any film or play I directed—for the simplest reason: It came out of me. When I reread it recently, I found it entertaining, true, and penetrating. If you haven't read it, I recommend it to you. It says all I had to say at that time about our way of life.

When I had a completed manuscript, I took a copy to Dr. Kelman, put it on his desk, and told him that if it hadn't been for him, the book would not have existed. His expression did not change, which doesn't mean that he was not pleased. At the same time I gave the book to Sol Stein, the publisher who, with Molly's help, had made a book out of my screenplay, *America America*. I was prepared to hear him say that it was unpublishable.

Anxious about this, I took Barbara and went on safari in East Africa, together with Hume and Jessie Cronyn, old good friends. I'd earned a vacation.

I've asked my secretary, Eileen Shanahan, to look up the date when Barbara and I were married. Before I learn from her what it was, I'll describe when I believe we were married and how it happened. It had nothing to do with a ceremony, a license, or solemn words spoken and later regretted, with any kind of civic confirmation or personal celebration, or any definite date. It had to do with lions and sharks. And it wasn't a decisive step as much as a process. We first started to be married when we were on safari in Kenya, along the Mara Masai reserve. The Cronyns didn't know that this union took place, and Barbara didn't know it, but I had a pretty good notion that something of that kind was happening. Up until then I'd been the older one, the more powerful one, the more successful one, the smarter one, the richer one, the tougher one, the more respected one, and even the braver one. Anything I did for her was a favor from above, bestowed sometimes generously, sometimes in a patronizing way, on a lesser being. The moment we began to be "hitched" was the moment when I felt, and I believe she felt, that in some essential human way we were equals. That started to take place on this safari.

What we'd come to Africa looking for we found, with the help of an excellent white hunter: all manner of wildlife running wild. We even saw leopards, which we'd been told we might not see, one guarding the crotch of a tree where she'd dragged a Thomson's gazelle kill, and another flashing out of a wall of green, seeing us, and flashing back out of sight, a most startling five-second encounter. We saw all the rest of that area's citizens, cheetahs and rhinos and wild dogs, hippos, hyenas, and a long parade of wildebeest, giraffes, and eagles, all close up, all going about their business. Apparently they knew we carried cameras, not guns. But what we wanted most of all to see were lions, and we did. They weren't afraid of us; nor were we afraid of them—that is, not our white hunter, not Hume, not Jessie, not Barbara. But I—I was afraid of them. Most of all at night. They felt privileged to stroll through our encampment when the great fire cooled, and no one denied them that privilege. They wandered here and there, looking for what they might eat, for despite the majesty we've bestowed on them, they are, like those other kings the eagles, scavengers as well as killers.

Barbara and I were in our tent, deep in a double bed, under a heavy comforter and encased in canvas. Barbara was sleeping, I was not. I was listening. I could hear their breathing and their heavy pads stealing closer. "You hear them?" I whispered. "Barbara, listen!" She didn't answer. Then I heard something heavy brushing against a side of our tent. "They're right outside," I whispered. "Barbara! They're touching the tent side. What'll I do?" "Go to sleep," she said. "Hume promised we're safe in here." "Barbara—listen!" "Shut up. You're keeping me awake. You're also telling them where we are." That point I got. I was quiet. Then something at the entrance of our tent was knocked over; I heard a metallic ring and I recalled that was where our washstand had stood. Fear silenced me.

The next morning, I peeked out and found the washstand on the ground. The blacks had a big fire blazing, which was reassuring. One of them saw me and hustled over with a cup of hot tea. "The master has had his shower," he said. (He meant Hume.) "Yours is ready, sir." He pointed to where a barrel they'd filled with hot water had been pulled into the air by a rope over a tree limb. It hung about forty feet away from our fire, at the end of a path through thornbushes. "We just filled it again. You'll find the water quite warm. Merely pull the rope at the side. It will refresh you, sir." "I don't require a shower this morning," I said, as Barbara appeared through the tent flap. "There's a shower," I said to her. "See the barrel hanging there?" "Oh, great!" She popped into the tent and came out dressed in a robe and holding a heavy towel and a bar of lavender soap. "You going out there?" I asked. She trotted the distance to the shower, there hung her robe on a bush, and standing quite naked, pulled the rope that released the water. I heard sounds of pleasure. "Come on in," she called. "It's nice and warm!" "Maybe tomorrow," I answered as I went back into the tent to dress.

That day I realized I had something special in that girl. She was a lot tougher than I, and in a crisis of lions—or any other kind of animal, as three muggings on the streets of New York would later verify—she could hold her own. I was the chicken-hearted one, she the lioness-hearted. I was glad it was Barbara I'd brought with me. Along with her several other attractions, this one, courage, particularly struck me—perhaps because physical courage is a virtue I lack. At breakfast I looked at her with fresh admiration and spoke to her with new respect. In the jungle called Manhattan, perhaps something of this kind was what I needed. That was when it started. That was the day—excuse, if you can, my patronizing tone—when I began to yield to her. "Watch out," I said to myself. "You may be getting into something permanent."

Later Hume was to introduce us to another jungle, the one beneath the surface of the Caribbean Sea. Here were other predators, equally dangerous—the ever-patrolling sharks and the chomping barracuda. It was fascinating to watch them, and I did—with just a bit of my masked head underwater and my hand never relinquishing its grip on the side of our boat. Jessica would dive twenty feet to a pit where the local langouste congregated, grab one by its feelers, and wrestle it to the surface, then dump the creature into the boat where I sat. I jumped out of the furious crustacean's reach. Barbara was not in the boat with me; she was under the surface of the sea, following Hume wherever he went. When they encoun-

tered what the "master" called a "business shark," she did not rush to the surface of the sea and seek the safety of the boat, but seemed as unimpressed by the danger as Hume was. I saw one of these encounters—from a safe distance—and admired her again. There must have been occasions when I've been courageous, but not in the Caribbean, not on that trip.

Equality is never a feature of an Anatolian marriage; dominance by the male is. The husband, always older, does the young woman he "takes" a favor, and refers to her thereafter as "my wife, poor thing." Barbara, first in Africa, then in the Caribbean, scrambled this old-time relationship; she established an equality between us, certainly in the more essential human virtues. Ours was a union confirmed in stages and consummated without our awareness. The ceremony commenced in Kenya, finished months later in the Caribbean. I cannot recall when the legal prose was read over us, but our bond was sealed when and as I've told it.

A F R E N C H sportsman, who'd just shot and skinned a leopard, crossed our path. Having been informed where we'd be by the white hunter's underground, he handed me a cable. It was from Sol Stein and contained the news that, in Sol's opinion, my grammar was lousy, but I'd written "a lion of a book." Unbelieving, I wanted confirmation. In Nairobi, I had a second cable from Sol, more formally phrased, announcing that he proposed to publish *The Arrangement.*

I WAS now in a new profession. My publisher Sol Stein was my producer, and my editor Sol Stein was my director. I was the author and the product to be sold.

At the beginning of the editing process, I told Sol how inexperienced I was, an unnecessary confession. He saw quickly enough that my grammar is wretched, my spelling uncertain, that I delighted in saying the same thing over and over, thereby minimizing its impact ("One plus one equals a half," Sol would say), and that anything I'd learned about editing films didn't help me edit a book, particularly if it was my own. Stein took charge of me; he had to. He would ask, then suggest, later insist, and finally proceed ruthlessly (so I thought) to cut out chunks of the book, scarcely asking my permission. He seemed to relish looping paragraphs in red ink, then transferring them, by the continuation of the red line, to another location in my text. My pages became a battleground after the battle; he'd violated them with lines, scratches, arrows, circles and curves and great wasted gaps.

So we had squabbles, but usually I saw that he had a point and that I tended to be foolishly proud. Sol was overwhelming me in the same way and for the same reason that I'd overwhelmed actors who'd never before been in films: for my own good. Furthermore, since he was determined that the book come out at a time when it would be most advantageous commercially, he pressured me to rush, which, as a former big shot in another profession, I did not enjoy. Voices were raised. But in the end we improved the book by cutting out about a quarter of its length. I'm especially grateful to Sol for a suggestion he made about the ending, where I'd reached for a certain uncertain tone and failed to get what I wanted. He changed a declarative sentence to a question, and we had it! I learned a lot from him; he handled an occasionally cantankerous and quick-to-be-offended author with skill and persistence. He never gave up on his suggestions for alterations. I would pay respect to his recommendations, examine them carefully, then fight for myself.

Sol rushed the finished book into the stores weeks before the publication date and shipped me out across the country's TV circuit. I found myself caught in a production machine, rushing to a finish line. I was to be my own PR man. Sol gave me this advice before I went out: No matter what questions the interviewer asks—about your film career, for instance—quickly bring the subject back to the book. Jacqueline Susann was expert at this, Sol said, and he suggested I study her technique. For a time I enjoyed being a traveling salesman and playing the promotion game. I was even good at it. But then there were some humiliations. Many of my interviewers had not read the book, and some had got through it twenty pages at a time. This was understandable, because the next day they'd be interviewing another author about another book. A few fellows were out to needle me; it would make livelier listening if I got angry. My worst day was in Chicago, where I followed an act featuring two large white performing poodles with teeth of gold.

The promotion party I enjoyed most took place in Brentano's bookstore. The other guests, interviewed and photographed with me, were "my authors": Tennessee Williams, Art Miller, Budd Schulberg, and Robert Anderson. The most generous of them, as ever, was Tennessee. I doubt that Miller ever read the book; if he has, he's never mentioned it to me. But he was affable and cordial, if a bit bewildered. He'd never thought of me as an author.

To my great surprise, the book was an immediate best-seller. The people of the trade called it a "page-turner." They said the book "ran" out of the stores. And so on, all "trade talk." Readers everywhere took to it, and it was obvious why. I was describing their own experiences and problems. Still the speed with which the success came amazed me. I didn't know how this underground swell of opinion developed. I had only one "selling" review, written by Eleanor Perry, and it appeared in a perfect place, *Life* magazine. My publisher—twenty years later—still quotes her review: "This is a novel to change your life by," which I'd believed excessive, except that so many people told me the book played a part in changing their lives.

Of everybody who wrote about the book, I thought Jimmy Baldwin got it best. "The tone of the book," he wrote in the *New York Review of Books*, "does not seem to depend on anything that we think of as a literary tradition but on something older than that: the tale told by a member of the tribe to the tribe. It has the urgency of a confession and the stammering authority of a plea. Kazan is talking, trying to tell us something and not only for his sake . . . but also for ours. 'I don't like my life! How have I become what I have become? . . . These men who cried, America America!, as the century died, had come here looking for freedom and all they found was the freedom to make as much money as possible.' This is not the official version of American history but that it very nearly sums it up can scarcely be doubted by anyone with the courage to look into the faces one encounters all over this land, who listens to the voices, hearing the buried uneasiness, translating itself hourly into a hatred of all that is strange or vivid, into a hatred, at last, of life."

The rest of the write-ups were a bit patronizing. Again I smelled prejudice—for the usual reason. But nothing slowed sales of the book, and I confess that a certain appetite for revenge was being satisfied in me. Could there have been a sweeter taste, after my highly public failures and the scorn and mauling I'd taken from critics, than to suddenly turn things around? Even though I was still not accepted by the literary fellows—nor have I been since—I felt proud and satisfied. I'd found my own material and it was all there, stacked in my memory and my experience. I'd found my new profession.

Proudly I gave the book to my mother. When I'd given her *America America*, she'd told my brother, "Now I have something to show my friends." *The Arrangement* was established as a great success now, the Literary Guild had accepted it as a main selection, and people everywhere were talking about it. My mother had certainly heard some of this talk. I didn't expect her to read it quickly, for it was a long book, but weeks passed before I heard a comment from her, and it was made not to me but to Barbara. "Elia, he is clean boy, isn't he?" she asked Barbara—of all people! I'd left the apartment to buy us some ice cream. "Oh, yes, of course, dear," Barbara had responded. When I returned, my mother, trained not to offend, still said nothing about the book.

It was a month before I had her true reaction. I got a message that she'd been taken to the hospital for an operation and that it was serious. She hadn't called me for help; she'd called my brother George. The surgeon who was to do the job told me that her stomach had ulcerated extensively and he would have to cut two thirds of it away. He assured me she'd live and that her body would in time adapt itself to a stomach the size of a small pear.

I sat in the waiting room as the operation was being performed. I blamed myself and the book for what had happened. I'd hurt the person I loved most in the world, the person who, when I needed it desperately, had supported me and stuck up for me against my father. Hadn't I known she might be hurt? That she might find the book a personal disgrace and a public humiliation? She was a creature out of another time and civilization and, as was the tradition, depended on her eldest son, on his strength and on his goodness. She'd idealized me. She'd had no experience with the kind of life and behavior I described in *The Arrangement*, with the episodes and personal adventures I'd been through. Naturally she'd find them "not clean." I wished I'd never written the damned book.

After the operation she was brought to the recovery room and sedated to sleep. There was nothing to do but wait. I went back to her apartment, and there was my book on her bed table. I read what I'd written about her and particularly about the mother's reaction to her husband's death. She'd complained about the old house where they'd lived, the house the hero of the book burns down. "That old house ate my life," the mother says, whereupon the narrator observes, "I knew who had eaten her life but she was too well brought up to say his name. What she did say was, 'God forgive me, now I'm going to live!'" Which was an accurate insight into how my mother had felt when my father died. She was truly relieved, but she didn't know it and would have been shocked—as she was—to be told it was so. The narrator goes on: "At the funeral my mother didn't weep. There was no escaping it, she was secretly rejoicing that her husband was gone."

Now, too late, I realized how this would shame my mother and offend her image of herself. She'd not have been aware of her relationship to her husband as I'd observed it. She was a "good wife." How could I have exposed her to guilt and shame that way? Had I stopped to think of what might happen? Hadn't I cared if she felt disgraced in the eyes of the world and her other children? Hadn't I known that my words might wound her? Are authors so heartless? Was I?

Apparently I was.

Mother recovered. Although she remained thin and pale, it became evident that a surprising amount of energy was restored to her and even a new appetite for living. After so many decades of wifely servitude, she now cut housework to the minimum, didn't eat much, preparing just enough to get by. She went back and forth to the local library, returning books, bringing home others. She read *The New York Times* every morning and got the events of the day from Chet Huntley and David Brinkley in the evening. I sent her books and magazines I'd enjoyed, and others did the same. She became a cause. She kept up a regular correspondence with all her children, grandchildren, and in-laws, earning the title "Mission Control," which meant that she, of all of us, knew where everyone in the family was and what they were up to. We'd all gather in her little apartment on holidays and she'd do what she'd always done in the big house, roast a large turkey and bake a juicy apple pie, then preside over the feast.

Now there was a fresh candor in the woman. "Your father," she said to me one day, "was a stupid man." I realized we'd never talked plainly, not in all our time before. "And he was not a nice man." "Why not, Mom?" "Because he didn't like anybody. He had such fine children. But he didn't care for them." "Whom did he like, Mom?" "Joe Kruskal," she said. Mr. Kruskal was one of Father's bridge and pinochle regulars.

I asked her if she'd translate some old Greek aphorisms for me and paid her fifty dollars for the work. It was the first money she'd earned in her life. She framed the check; I still have it. I felt she was trying to make up for what she'd missed in the years of her marriage and get all she could out of the last of her life. This burst of activity enlivened her soul; it also produced an eccentric daring. Several times, when I went out to Rye, I'd encounter her striding headlong, face locked straight forward, disregarding the traffic as she crossed the street. The cars would have to stop for her. There was a challenging independence about her that, considering her age and fragility, could only be called gallant. I could see the potential that had been there and not used.

T H E   F I L M I contracted to make from my book *The Arrangement* meant more to me than any film I'd made, for the simplest reason: It was the most personal. The book had continued at the top of the *New York Times* bestseller list, and it was anticipated by Warners, who'd bought the film rights, that I'd make a film that was equally successful. With my own confidence high, I'd broken an old personal rule and taken money in advance. I'd always given labor before taking dollars, but I'd bought a dunetop cabin on the south shore of Long Island, and the hundred thousand I took in advance would pay for that and the IRS as well.

There's an old Jewish saying: If you take with one hand, you have to give something with the other. As I drove through Warner Brothers' gates, I had a reaction I couldn't understand: I felt trapped. My office, I found, had been redecorated in my honor and still smelled of paint, a smell I can't tolerate. On my desk, there was an expensive present from the new head of production, a decent young man who was counting on me to make his debut a profitable one. Fresh paint and presents are signals: I was on top. They've also been—at times—auguries of disappointment ahead.

I determined to contest big-studio production banality and front-office wisdom. I would cast Marlon Brando, bring him back from some bad outings, and opposite him, not the latest California sex symbol, but my wife,

Barbara, who'd bring out the realest values of the part. As for the rest, I'd cast all "New York actors," and they'd give the film truth—and my look.

I was convinced that Marlon was the perfect person for the film. He could project the conflicting sides of the character, the office salesman who was selling himself to his bosses as he was planning how to sell their product to the public. Marlon was not only (at that time) the best actor in the country but the actor with whom I once had the closest relationship. He'd alienated himself from me after my testimony, but consented to work with me in *On the Waterfront*—and given the best performance of the year. I saw him rarely after that; it was obvious he felt reluctant about any friendly connection because of what he heard from friends: that I was a reactionary bastard. But when I did see him, he seemed cordial.

Then something began to happen to him that dismayed me. I'll report a little of what he said one night in January 1963, at the home of Clifford Odets. Clifford had cancer by that time, and perhaps the presence of death approaching made Brando more outspoken about his own condition. I wrote it down. "Here I am, a balding middle-aged failure. . . . I feel a fraud when I act. . . . I've tried everything . . . fucking, drinking, work. None of them mean anything. Why can't we just be like—like the Tahitians?" And so on.

A letter I wrote him three years later, when I was making every effort to get him into *The Arrangement*, will tell the rest of the story.

Dear Marlon: I want to talk to you at length but I think it's better if you read this letter first. I went to Warner Brothers with my novel because I've had good experiences with them. They didn't try to supervise my work and I've always had complete say on casting. They wouldn't give me that authority on this picture and it was because of you. They anticipated, correctly, that I'd turn to you first. They had resistance to this and to a degree that shocked me. But I'm not going to make this picture, or any other, with a cast not of my choosing. I want you. I think when you've been in form, you've been our best actor.

But then a conversation we'd had at the St. Regis bar came to mind. You said there that you'd lost your feeling for acting, that there were other things you preferred doing now. Nevertheless I asked you to read my book. You did, quickly, called me and said some warm things. I asked if you might be interested in doing that part with me and you hesitated, then said you weren't sure you were right for the role but that you might "take a stab" at it. This reaction upset me.

I remembered *On the Waterfront*, where you told me repeatedly that you were only making the film because your psychoanalyst was in New York and you wanted to make enough to pay his bills while remaining in the city. Then I read a bit in a newspaper and—I differ from more rational men, I believe what's in the gossip columns. You or your press man or your agent must have said something that made this columnist write that Mr. Brando didn't think he was really right for the part in my book.

I was meeting with Warners at this time and they urged me to see *Countess from Hong Kong* and *Reflections in a Golden Eye*. Their point was not about your talent but two other things, first that you'd become terribly heavy and second that you were just "going through the motions" now. The new head of Warners kept saying, "He's not the same fellow you're thinking of. He's another man." I saw the Chaplin film and they were right, you were overweight to the point where you did not seem to be the same fellow. And they were right about your indifference—that's the only word to describe your performance in that film. You'd told me the story behind the Chaplin film, so I was prepared for what I saw. But it affected me anyway. I began to wonder who else could do the part and I did see another actor who responded enthusiastically. We talked many hours; his interest matched my own.

I'd found at the Lincoln Center Repertory Theatre how corrosive the lack of genuine enthusiasm and devotion in the people with whom I'm working can be. You said to me on the phone, "Well, I might take a stab at it." And I thought, "Fuck him!" I'm too old now to pump up an actor I'm working with. I need all that energy for the real problems, which are enormous here. Of course I know that enthusiasm is more often professed than felt and I am by nature suspicious of euphoric gargle, but still—I thought that on this one, which is so difficult and so close to me, I'm damned well going to give myself an actor who comes to work each morning like a young man coming up, not someone tired of his trade or wishing he was not an actor. I promised myself someone who, as they say in the fight game, comes to fight.

Then I saw *Reflections in a Golden Eye*. And I admired you. Without any real help from Huston (he directs to make everyone a "character," thus, in a subtle way, patronizing them) you were bold and daring and made a difficult part moving and human. I admired you. But what I said about your looks in *Countess from Hong Kong* was even more true here. You did look like a "different person." Some people, when they're anxious and full of self-disgust, eat a lot. Others get thin. My character, Eddie, is of the second group. I don't know whether you want to go back to the weight you once were. It's very tough after forty—as I know from my own experience. And except for vanity, there isn't much point to it. It means cutting out a lot of the more enjoyable things in life. I won't urge it on you but—

I don't want Eddie plump.

I'm not trifling with this picture. That's why there's a chance it might be a good one. But just as I'm not kidding in this letter, don't kid me now. If you tell me, "I don't really want to bust my balls acting any more," I'll admire you for telling the truth. I want you to do this film but I only want you if you're genuinely enthusiastic about it and only if you will come to me ten months from now at the weight you were at during *On the Waterfront.* Be a true friend and don't kid me. If you really want to, you can be a blazing actor again. The wanting to is the hard part. Much love.   E. K.

I didn't hear from Marlon immediately and never in the plain language I was asking for. But in time I got an actor's answer: His agent began negotiating for him. Then Marlon asked to see me, and I drove up the hill to where he lived. What he wanted was to talk about hairpieces and to ask me to order them for him from a man in Rome. I quickly agreed, delighted because he was going to do the film.

I proceeded with the work, sending him changes and informing him who was going to be in the film with him. No comment from the hilltop. Then came the bad day when Martin Luther King was shot. Marlon, whom I hadn't heard from for a while, called me. He sounded distressed and asked me to come up the hill again to see him.

He was waiting for me in the parking area in front of his house. When I got out of my rental, he fell all over me and began to tell me what a terrible state the country was in. King had been shot, and this had made Marlon fear for our future. I agreed that it was a terrible tragedy. We went on talking, standing in the parking area. He was so intense and so convincing that I didn't realize he'd walked me back to my car and opened the door to help me in. Before I got behind the wheel, he informed me that he simply couldn't do the part in my movie. At which he kissed me and looked so sorry I didn't ask any questions but drove away, planning to call him in a few days. I saw the man in the rearview mirror, walking to his house and going in; he looked desolate. I never saw Marlon again, haven't seen him to this day.

It was a few hours before I remembered that he was one hell of an actor, and although his feeling about King was certainly sincere, the depth of emotion he projected came as much from his talent as from his sense of tragedy. Then I began to get mad. We were already making the man's hairpieces, for chrissake!

That is when I should have quit the picture. I was beat and didn't know it. But it's my nature to persist. And there was another reason, less noble: I'd taken money and spent it, and I was obligated. Now, years later, I feel certain that if Marlon had played the part, the film would have worked. But I was on a treadmill, and a frantic kind of activity gripped me. An agent recommended that I talk to Kirk Douglas. I found him to be terribly bright, very eager, and genuinely enthusiastic. What a relief that was! We con-

ferred for a week, and he told me his problems with the script. Most of them were valid. I also saw that he was my character, Eddie—up to a point.

There was one problem with Kirk. Eddie has to start defeated in every personal way; the film rests on how basic and painful his initial despair is. Kirk has developed a professional front: a man who can overcome any obstacle. He radiates indomitability. Marlon, on the other hand—with all his success and fame—was still unsure of his worth and of himself. Acting had little to do with it. It was a matter of personality. Kirk, a bright man who devoted himself to the work we were doing and tried everything I told him to, was wrong. All Marlon would have had to do was come and be photographed; you could have read the part on his face. Talk about typecasting! Kirk without knowing it gave the lie to the part throughout—even in the way his clothes sat on him, even in the way he tied his ties; certainly in the way he walked. I wished I had Marlon, fat as he was.

Two anecdotes may make my point. On another film, Kirk had been bawling out a young actor working with him, doing it repeatedly in front of the cast and the crew. Finally the cameraman couldn't take it anymore and spoke up. "Kirk," he said, "I remember you when you came up. You were a nice kid. Now you've become a complete prick." "You're wrong," Kirk said. "I was always a prick. Now I've got money and can afford to let it show." Give him an "A" for telling the truth.

Not too long ago, a friend of mine influenced Marlon to do something I thought impossible: come to a rock concert and make an appearance before a large audience. Marlon at this time was only being offered parts for a lot of money, which, when he accepted them, further reduced people's respect for him. He'd become very suspicious of adulation, having had so much of it and seen it fade like yesterday's rainbow; on the other hand, his self-esteem was starved. When he was introduced by the lead singer, the audience gave him a tremendous round of applause, and he could hardly get off the stage. Finally he did and went to my friend who'd brought him there and, in a whisper, boasted, "You know, them's not extras out there!"

Once I had Kirk in the part, Barbara didn't fit, and I asked Faye Dunaway to play it. Barbara never forgave me. I would pay for what I did many times in the years to come.

After Kirk and I had shot ten days, I knew I'd made a dreadful mistake. But there is no exit in a production of this kind. I was in for nine weeks, during which there'd be a gnawing at my stomach every morning. I survived. The cameraman and the crew, as ever, saved me. I was always glad to see them. Together we did the work and finished the job.

A F T E R this experience, I decided not ever to make another film in Hollywood. But I didn't want to give up filmmaking. I would show myself and the men who controlled the industry that films could be made inexpensively, that the process was essentially simple and didn't need the pumped-up costs, the services of coddled stars, and the pressure by the men who bring the money. I gave my son Chris, who's one of the best screen dramatists I know, something I'd cut out of a newspaper, the story of an ex-GI who'd brought evidence of a war crime—the rape and murder of a Vietnamese girl—against two former buddies, and how these two men came looking for him at the end of the war to hold him to account. Chris responded to the idea and took only a few weeks to write a screenplay. I was pleased with what he gave me and set about producing it, determined to make it in the East, on location, with a cast of what are called—most patronizingly—unknowns.

It quickly became clear that there was no money available for this subject, not even as I wanted to make it, on a very modest budget. I'd had several flops in a row, and my credit was not high. I decided to borrow the money from a bank, putting up my own collateral, and make the film for "nothing," which meant with a small, nonunion crew and a cast of actors who'd work without contracts. This would be breaking all the rules that we'd all worked hard setting up to protect ourselves against producers: the bylaws of the Screen Directors Guild, the Screen Actors Guild, and the International Alliance of Theatrical and Stage Employees. But it was the only way to make this film, and rather than be thwarted, I decided to go the illegal route. Chris and I cast the film with a girl "Yalie," a Puerto Rican cabdriver who aspired to be an actor, two actors who were totally new, plus an old-time SAG member who had a good heart but wasn't getting work. Chris had written the script to be shot on the piece of land in Connecticut where both of us have homes and to take advantage of the season, the dead of winter, when the ground was covered with snow and our pond frozen. For reasons of cost, we decided to put up the actors in our homes. We enlisted a cameraman, Nick Proferes, who was ready to work with nonunion help. We hired a crew of four: a soundman, a man to place the lights and adjust them, a camera assistant to load the camera and care

for the exposed negative, and a fourth man to do everything else. They were all nonunion. We made the film at a gentle, unhurried pace, but it came together quickly and easily. The total cost was $175,000, which was considerably less than the salary we'd paid Faye Dunaway for appearing in *The Arrangement*.

I'd found the joy of filmmaking again. There was no pressure on any of us. We worked hard, but it was because we wanted to work hard. We enjoyed each other's company and were glad to see each other every morning. All suggestions were listened to and many used. Nobody rode a high horse. Chris cooked the meals for the actors and the crew. I was the property man, discovered it was a tough job but manageable, and I directed the actors. The whole thing was shockingly simple; I mean it was so simple that I was shocked. I realized this was the way films used to be made. I recalled Ingmar Bergman's answer to the interviewer who'd asked how he made his films. "I make them," Bergman had replied, "with eighteen friends." My "friends" were four in number. But if you ever get to see the film—United Artists keeps it in a dark vault, out of circulation—you'll notice that it moves around for locations freely, it is mostly well photographed, and the scenes are technically creditable. When *The Visitors* was done and edited—by the cameraman—I was proud of it. It had been an exhilarating experience; I came out of it refreshed, not exhausted. We'd made the first film to deal with the effect of the Vietnam war on the people at home.

We opened at the Little Carnegie Theatre in New York. Chris and I had no idea what the audience reaction would be. We were both shocked when the film was booed at the end by part of the audience. I didn't know why, and I still don't know why. I immediately suspected the usual reason; I'd watched the audience coming into the theatre and recognized a few old "lefties." Was I becoming paranoid about this? The subject—the GI who'd informed on two old friends—certainly related to my testimony. Was my "inglorious" past paying me back? Again? Or was it because some of the audience resented our rather scoffing attitude toward the girl "peacenik." But that wouldn't account for the intensity of the hostile reaction. As the audience moved out, I stood in the back of the theatre, waiting for someone to come up and explain why the film had been received so hatefully. No one did.

Then the reviews came out. They were all negative except Vincent Canby's. He qualified his praise, but he wrote: "It is an extremely moving film, partly I think because everything—from the physical production to the melodrama—is kept in small scale, as if not to get in the way of, or to confuse, its very legitimate expression of a major American sorrow. . . . I find *The Visitors* moving because I happen to share the Kazans' political and moral concerns." This would have pleased me even more than it did, except for the fact that Canby blamed Chris for the film's faults, which was unfair because I was there, behind the camera, judging every rehearsal and absolutely responsible, as any director should be, for everything on the screen. Chris was hurt by Canby. He wasn't accustomed, as I was, to the slings and arrows of journalistic critics. We both felt even worse the next day, when only a few people came to the theatre. They did not boo the film, but they weren't enthusiastic either. In this country, the critics, I'm sorry to say, tell the audience what it's right for them to like.

I was protected from the hurt Chris felt by thick scabs over old wounds. I mind very little what film critics write, because I've seen the stuff they like. There were also people who'd either called me or spoken to me on the street to tell me they thought it a film of value. I knew it was. I was also happy because I'd found my way of making films—simply, at minimum cost, with a few "friends." I was proud that no pressure had stopped me from making the movie. I liked it and no one could change my mind about that.

When the French reactions came, they were nearly all positive. I decided to take the film to France, enter it in the competition at Cannes, go there myself as public relations man, and see if I could pump up interest in Europe—and some business too. When I told the United Artists people— they were distributing the film—what I wanted to do, they did not respond

Defiant in Cannes

with enthusiasm. They'd quit; having "taken care of" my bank loan of $175,000, they didn't propose to lose any more money by sending me to Cannes. I reminded them that I'd lost $10,000 of my own on the film. They weren't impressed with my financial sacrifice but finally agreed to send me to the festival and even help me a little there.

As soon as I arrived at the Carlton Hotel in Cannes, I was met in the lobby by a very nervous man: Jean Nachbaur, the head of publicity for United Artists in Europe, who informed me that Joe Losey was chairman of the jury that year and that I had a problem with Losey. He said all the journalists were talking about it, were sure to bring "the whole thing up" at the press conference I would hold after the showing, trying to egg me on to say something hateful about Losey for their headlines. I'd known Joe when we were both young radicals in New York, working for the WPA Theatre. He had gone one way, I another. I answered Mr. Nachbaur that I had no problem with Losey, but he had one with me, because if he said anything or did anything as a judge that was against me, he would have to defend himself against a charge of prejudice. I added that I didn't consider Losey a small man and certainly if he felt prejudiced against me—or any other filmmaker—he would disqualify himself. I thought this pretty clever, but Mr. Nachbaur wasn't impressed.

Nothing that might have made my United Artists man more nervous happened. The film was well received; I didn't hear a single boo. A good part of the audience stood up and applauded me when I appeared—but then in Cannes they do this for everybody. I had several close friends among the French critics, and they gathered around me. I'd forgotten that I was a legend in France, one of a dozen American directors they considered worth remembering. The people at the press conference were extremely respectful, almost reverential. Mr. Nachbaur went back to Paris relieved—and a little puzzled.

What Joe Losey did, he did behind the scenes in the jury room. This action, of course, was not reported in the press—only the gossip wranglers in the Carlton lobby learned of it. Newspapers announced throughout the world that *The Mattei Affair* had won first prize. Then came the small talk. I heard there'd been considerable sentiment for *The Visitors*, but had no facts until I met Bibi Andersson, the Swedish film star, who'd sat on the jury. She'd voted for our film, she said, along with a couple of other jurors, and we'd lost primarily because the chairman of the jury was violently, persistently, and most absolutely against it and never let up attacking it. (Later Losey admitted to a friend of mine, a French critic, that he thought it a very good film.) Apparently his influence was the critical one in the voting. I had to laugh. Some friends said I shouldn't have bothered taking the film to Cannes when I heard that Joe was chairman of the jury, and so on, but actually I'd enjoyed the experience, the jockeying and the gossip, the nervousness of my United Artists executive, and the flattery I received at the press conference. I didn't expect a left intellectual to forget in 1972 what had happened in 1952, because I hadn't forgotten either. I shed no tears, ate the most tender part of the greatest fish in the Mediterranean, the *loup de mer*, breached bottles of my favorite wine, Château de Sancerre, laughed at French jokes I only half understood, and never saw Joe Losey.

Some time later, an article appeared in *Variety*, headlined: FURIOUS AT KAZAN'S CUFFO JOB FOR SON, SCREEN ACTORS CALL "THE VISITORS" UNFAIR. Here's a bit from the body of the piece: "*The Visitors* has been placed on the Screen Actors Guild 'unfair' list. The Board of Directors took action because the film was shot without a Guild or IATSE contract. The Guild has also filed a complaint against Kazan with the Dramatists Guild of America . . . saying Kazan's sense of values in describing his work on the production as 'exhilarating' reaches a new height in non-professionalism when it was achieved at the expense of his colleagues in the industry who have contributed so much to his earlier successes. . . . What apparently vexed the actors and other coast unionists is the prominence of Kazan. Most unknown features are directed by unknown or ambitious film course graduates." "Ah!" I said to myself. "That's what I want—to be an unknown again."

I was summoned to stand before the board of the Directors Guild. I found them fair, understanding, and cordial. As brothers, they were forced to impose a fine on me—the bylaws had to be honored. But all was conducted with good humor. Mel Brooks was especially funny about the case. I said I'd be happy to pay the fine. I understood the importance of the bylaws, but I confessed that if I again came up against a situation where a film I wanted to make could be made only this way, I'd do the same thing in the same way. I reminded them that we were a guild, not a union, and urged them to alter our bylaws so as to make it possible for filmmakers, especially young ones, to make films cheaply if they could not be financed more generously. In time our guild did loosen the restriction of the bylaws, for the benefit of all. Soon afterward I was elected to the national board, and I've served there ever since.

When I was back in Connecticut and told my son Chris what had happened in Cannes and how craven the United Artists man there had been, my feeling was: To hell with film. I'll stick to the novel.

O N E blustery day in March, when winter had gone on too long, I went out to visit Mother. Driving north on the New England Thruway, I'd caught glints of yellow, the promise of forsythia. Around her condominium the sap had begun to rise in the maples, breaking the grip of the buds. Climbing the slope off her parking lot, I saw that her windowsill flowerbed had begun to bloom. It was her custom to spend the first part of each morning sitting at her window, reading. She was not there. Then I saw her through the kitchen window. She was peering out. Was she looking for help? Although she was staring in my direction, she gave no sign that she recognized me. Always a perfectly ordered woman, she had her hair undone, damp curls drooping in front of her eyes. Her face was the color of wood ash. She looked like a witch.

Inside, I found her leaning on the back of a straight chair. She moved toward me, pushing the chair before her, a few inches at a time. On her small drop-leaf table, last night's supper was on its plate, the spinach separated from its water, the poached egg congealed into a kind of plastic, the slice of salt-free bread curled at the edges. Close to her, I heard the sounds she was making. But even listening carefully, I had to guess. "I can't walk"? Was that it? Or "I can't talk"?

She could do neither. In the bedroom, the bed had not been used. Apparently whatever had happened had happened just as she was sitting to supper. Which meant she'd been up all night, waiting for morning—and for help. I sat her down, kissed her, went to the phone. "I think it's a stroke," I said to her doctor. "I'll have an ambulance there right away," he answered. "She's afraid of hospitals," I said. "Her husband died in that hospital. Can't you come see her at home?" "If it's what you're describing," he said, "the quicker we get her into a hospital bed the better."

After a few days, it became evident she would never again care for herself. The doctor, an honest man, made no reassuring promises; he suggested with some reluctance that the best thing for her would be a nursing home. One of my brothers, the sensible one, agreed. But the old lady remembered how miserable her husband had been in a "home," and although she couldn't talk, she shook her head savagely every time that recommendation was made. I thought she was right; I considered nursing homes to be disposal plants for the elderly no one wanted to care for. My mother loved her solitary life in her apartment. The walls were lined with framed photographs of everyone she loved. She was not going to be moved. She also feared what Greek people fear more than most: that she might be "put to die with strangers."

Her sons conferred. We had some money from our father's insurance. Adding what we could each contribute would enable us to engage a twenty-four-hour live-in nurse and keep her on for three years. How long would Mother live?

We were lucky. We found a fine woman named Ruby, and for a time things worked out perfectly. There was very little Mother needed. No longer able to read, she would pretend, turning the pages, then turning them again, and that was sad. But she was improving. At first she'd lean on Ruby to walk, but each day she'd go a little farther. Luckily, spring was coming. There was a rustic bench under a tree, where she and Ruby would sit in silence for hours at a time. Slowly the old lady began to regain some speech. Curiosity reappeared in her eyes. Once in a while she'd laugh. I could see that she wanted to improve, and I became obsessed with her struggle. As the eldest son, I made regular visits, three times a week. When Ruby saw me approaching, she'd tell Mother, and the two would retreat to the bedroom and "fix up." I'd sit waiting and in a few minutes the old lady would come chugging out, her arms and fists pumping, a radiant smile on her face. She was showing off. I believed she was going to make it, all the way.

Then I noticed changes in the other direction. She'd complain about Ruby, who was a saint in her duty. "I don't like strangers here," she'd whisper in Greek, looking straight at Ruby. Privately I'd tell her how lucky we were to have Ruby. Mother would shrug, look doubting and cynical and even a little suspicious of me; that was an expression I'd never seen before. "I don't want her here," she said one day—then forgot she'd said it. Once she made a reference to Ruby's color, and I was shocked. I was used to hearing "nigger" from Father, but never anything of that kind from her.

Perhaps Ruby's presence embarrassed her, for a terrible humiliation had come to Mother: incontinence. I noticed it one afternoon when I was leading her to the bench under the tree. There was a trail of drops behind us, and instead of ignoring it, I looked at her and saw a shamefaced smile on her face, like that of a child caught in the act. I knew that she might be ashamed and, therefore, resent Ruby, who had to constantly clean up after her and wash her underthings. Ruby "had something" on her.

Then came another crisis. Winter was approaching, and this frightened Mother. Her circulation had lost its force; she frequently felt chilly. Her hands were always cold, and she began to keep them on the radiator under the window where she sat. I brought a large electric blanket for her bed; she asked Ruby to wrap it around her during the day. I brought in two electric heaters; in their orange radiance, she looked pale. The weeks passed. I began to wonder if she'd get through the coming winter. To enliven her life, I arranged visits from my children or from friends of mine whom she knew. But I saw that she couldn't follow the conversation, so I allowed the silence to prevail. Day after day she'd sit by the window with the electric blanket around her, her hands on the radiator and, when she asked for it, a radiant heater aimed at her feet. Was that to be the end of the story? I didn't know what to do.

One day, I made her a solemn promise that she'd never again pass the winter in Rye.

The very next day—that's how it happened—Sam Spiegel asked if I'd go to California with him to direct a film he was making from F. Scott Fitzgerald's *The Last Tycoon;* Harold Pinter had written the screenplay, Sam boasted. "Is that the film Mike Nichols was going to direct?" I asked. "He's out of it now," Sam said quickly. His face was a mask; I couldn't tell if he was disappointed or relieved. I'd heard that Sam had offered the job to still another director, who'd walked away from it. Did that matter? Why should it? I asked Sam a few questions and got up to go. As he gave me Pinter's screenplay, he said, "You'll get back to me soon, won't you?" "Tomorrow," I said. Which was a mistake. Sam had looked so sincere and affectionate that I'd been accommodating and not given myself time to think carefully. I'd forgotten that even sincerity and affection can be tactics with Sam. Did that matter? No—I wasn't marrying the man! But I wasn't eager to work with him. I'd enjoyed his company socially—his parties had it all, and he gave many kinds of parties—but I hadn't enjoyed working with him when we'd made *On the Waterfront*. On the other hand, he'd been good on script, and that did matter. Furthermore, this film was going to be made entirely in southern California, where it was warm in the winter. That was the point. He'd provide me with a comfortable house in the sun, high above the smogline, and Barbara would look after Mother during the day and— No! I'd take Ruby! I'd ask Sam to pay for Ruby. I'd have breakfast and supper with Mother and Ruby every day. But wait! What about the script? Read the damned script, read it carefully, for chrissake! Hell, I didn't have to read the script. I'd read the book. Twice. With Pinter, it had to be good! Sam had promised we'd go to London together and work with Harold, who was having marital problems and couldn't come to the U.S.

When I got home, I asked myself what was important. Mother's health, of course. But hadn't I sworn, after two unhappy experiences, one of which was *The Arrangement,* that I would stick to the novel now and never make another film? "Stop," I said to myself. "Hesitate! Consider! Why are you plunging into this? Give yourself time to think. Remember *The Arrangement*. It was a catastrophe. You're talking about a year of your life. Rent Mother a house in Florida, maybe in Tarpon Springs, which is full of Greeks. You can afford that." But it would be difficult to visit her and watch over her in Florida. That wouldn't work. Stop. Think!

It's easier not to think. The next afternoon—I still hadn't studied Pinter's script—I waltzed into Sam's office and said, "Let's talk." Sam slid open the bottom drawer of his desk, extracted a box, and opened the lid. An aroma announced that the finest cigars in the civilized world were available. "We're going to get along this time," I said to myself. Then I thought: What a whore you are! For a two-buck cigar! And I laughed. An hour later I'd agreed to take my mother to California—and make a film of *The Last Tycoon*, which should have remained on the bookshelves like my own novel, *The Arrangement*.

So in October, when a cold wind was beginning to strip the red and brown leaves off the oak trees, I picked up Mother and Ruby in a heated limo and we drove to Kennedy. A wheelchair and an attendant were waiting to take her to the gate. Her eyes were shining as, holding Ruby's arm, she walked down the aisle of the great Boeing. Wonder had turned on that light. The old lady looked like a child entering Disneyland. She'd never been in a plane before; her reaction made me notice how very big a 747 is. We'd reserved seats in the front row of the cabin, right under the movie screen. She looked around at the passengers—were they as excited as she was? The stewardess bent down to ask if she could get her anything to drink. "Too much trouble, too much trouble," Mother said. "No trouble at all," the stewardess said. "It would be a privilege." "She likes orange juice," Ruby said. Then a notice about seat belts was flashed on the screen in front of Mother, and Ruby found Mother's glasses and put them on her. I'd placed her in the middle of the plane, so she couldn't look out the window and see how far above the ground she was; I thought the view might frighten her, but it wouldn't have. She was taking everything in stride, thanking the stewardess and lifting her eyebrows to me, holding up the glass and saying, as if she'd never tasted it before, "Orange juice!"

Not too long before, I'd been where Mother was born, on the shore of the Sea of Marmara, and I'd also been inland, where her family had come from. I knew how far west she'd come and what that distance meant in terms of civilization. So did she; that was the reason she was smiling at me. When our plane touched down in California, she whispered to me, "Now I made this journey too." Perhaps she knew it might be her last; if she did, I doubt that it bothered her, not that day. I'd asked her many times to come to Greece with me and see her sister, who was old and not well, and whom she hadn't seen since 1913. Mother had always refused; she only traveled west. East would be going back where she'd come from, and the Turk might not let her return.

A wheelchair and an attendant were waiting at the Los Angeles terminal, and Mother and Ruby were rushed to the ladies' room. She'd only "gone" once during the trip, and that must have been quite an operation, with Ruby and the old woman and their big all-purpose black bag in a tiny space. But in Los Angeles, when they came out, Mother nodded her head, so everything must have gone all right. Now we entered another limo, arranged for by Mr. Spiegel's office. I thought she'd be interested in the bizarre city, but she'd had enough novelty for the day and fell asleep.

The home Sam's office had rented for us was a ranch-style single-story structure—I'd specified "no stairs"—one of a tier of such homes thrust into a dirt hillside. It was blazing with flowers, all in different variations of red. The sun was out; we were above the smogline. Barbara had come west earlier, and she was waiting to greet Mother. My wife didn't like me much anymore, but she was devoted to Athena. She showed her her room and sat with her while Ruby unpacked. Barbara was working on a film script with Nick Proferes, the man who'd photographed *The Visitors*. Ruby cleared everyone out and told Mother to lie down until supper.

She came out to watch the sun set, and I led her to a comfortable garden chair to see the last of the light. The instant the sun disappeared behind the dark hills to our west, a chill filled the space, and Mother began rubbing her hands. "Tomorrow the sun will be very hot, don't worry," I said. She nodded, said, "I hope so," and I took her hand and held it. I was sure—one of my brothers was not—that I'd done the right thing to bring her west. I only wished the sun hadn't disappeared so quickly.

Barbara called out that dinner was ready. The dining table was large and round and had a glass top covered with food that was easy to chew—meat loaf, mashed potatoes, and creamed spinach. Barbara knew what to do. Next to Mother she'd seated Leo, with Ruby on her other side. We were the perfect picture of a happy family.

But the true spirit of the scene was a contrary one. Barbara and I were finished, had been ever since I'd dropped her from *The Arrangement*. That wasn't the only reason, but it was the final one. Barbara, like most actresses, always looked for a supporter, a savior. I'd been that for many years. Then, as she saw it, I'd betrayed her, and she'd found Nick, discovered that his taste in film was close to her own and, since he was ready to work with her, his usefulness was much greater than mine. I'd noticed that they'd become close, and I didn't blame her. Aside from everything else, she had the same old cause for bitterness: I hadn't behaved well. But when I suggested breaking up, she seemed determined not to allow a divorce. "I can get more out of you when we're married," was her explanation. She was talking about money.

She'd been a generous mistress, year after year, caring, devoted, always ready in love, but once she became a wife she'd changed. She hadn't liked *The Arrangement*, believed I'd exposed her private behavior patterns in the book. When it became number one, she didn't celebrate with me. She liked the film even less, and deeply resented that I'd replaced her with Faye Dunaway. "You have more faith in Faye than you do in me," was how she put it. Faye had been Barbara's understudy in *After the Fall* and watched her performance night after night from the wings. "She's just a lousy imitation of me," Barbara said. When I explained to her that it had nothing to do with faith, that Faye went better with Kirk just as Barbara would have been better with Marlon, her response was: "Shit!" Then she began to make open fun of the film with one of her pals, and although I may have failed in every way, I didn't need it rubbed in so often. She never let up. "You know that old song 'Everybody Needs Someone to Love,'" I said to her one day. "Your version is 'Everybody Needs Someone to Hate.'" At which—I can still see it—she awarded me her little vengeful smile.

So we'd been married legally but no other way for several years, and I'd just let the whole thing hang. Divorce really was "too much trouble" and being married a convenient excuse for not prolonging other relationships. Barbara, a wise old cat, knew what I was doing on the side—and perhaps the final insult from me was that I didn't ask her how she got along and with whom. So my days were filled with a kind of convenient chaos and that's the way it was in that lovely ranch-style abode high above the smogline in Beverly Hills.

Still she loved my mother and took heartfelt care of her, night and day. I believe she wanted Athena to love her as much as she'd loved Molly, but it never happened. Perhaps Mother felt the coldness between Barbara and me. I used to look at Barbara sometimes, realize that what I was thinking (how had we ever been close?) might show and Mother might pick it up— so I quickly raised the mask. I knew that if she had the means, she would have left me long before. I also knew I could obtain a divorce if I really wanted to, but I was too lazy to turn things upside down. So the relationship we had was my doing. Furthermore, I'd already found a young woman in California who was also in a marriage she didn't want to tear up. We played at part-time love at the end of every afternoon, before I went home. Then I'd jump into our heated pool, put on a robe, kiss my mother, and sit to supper. A much simpler solution, wasn't it? Did it serve? It had to.

Nicholson, De Niro, and Russell

IT BEGAN as a conveniently timed job, one I'd
not have undertaken except for Mother's debility. When I accepted it, I
immediately urged Sam to forget any notion of using Dustin Hoffman (Mike
Nichols's preference) or Jack Nicholson (Sam's) for the role of Irving Thalberg, and that we make the film with Robert De Niro. I knew little about
Bobby; I was playing a hunch. For one of the women's roles, I disliked
Sam's recommendation of Ingrid Boulting, thought it personally engendered. He kept saying, "She's coltish," a quality especially attractive to a
pudgy man. Sam requested that I work with her; I did and began to like
her and feel she might be able to do the part. My nature is to see potential,
not linger over faults. I urged Ingrid on Harold Pinter, who was immediately and violently opposed to her. Sam was then able to retreat to the
position he preferred, in the middle, with me as Ingrid's sponsor while he
maintained a posture of artistic uncertainty which would protect him from
blame in case she didn't do well.

The same thing happened with Theresa Russell, the actress who played
Cecilia. Sam suggested her; I had strong reservations, saw some values but
more drawbacks. It was obvious to me, and later conversations with Theresa verified this, that Sam had, for a long time, tried to gentle her into his
bed. I say this without prejudice, because the truth is that most men of

imagination and passion in the arts tend to use their power over young women—and young men—to this end. It's life-loving and it's inevitable. Sam, according to Miss Russell, had pursued her for many months unsuccessfully, and apparently he'd not given up. When I worked with her, as he requested, I liked her too, came to believe she was certainly the best of a poor field and would bring something unanticipated to the role. I urged Sam that she be cast and he yielded to me, which is the way he liked this kind of decision to be made. Now he was able to remain doubtful of all three actors I'd recommended (as he saw it), which kept him free of responsibility and put that weight on me. If they worked out, the two women would be to his credit; if not, the black mark would be on my scorecard. Bobby De Niro was altogether my responsibility. I found myself the champion for all three, with the obligation of defending them on any day that Sam thought their work less than he'd wished for—or chose to say so. Pinter persisted in his opposition to Ingrid; Sam's response was that he had strong reservations too, but depended on me to bring her through.

The result was that I could no longer behave in a detached manner. Having taken on the load, I had to make the picture "work." At several points in our schedule, Sam spoke of changing all three performers. But since this would be very costly, I knew it was a Spiegel bluff to make me anxious, work harder, and keep me vulnerable to any criticism he might have of any day's work. It was a tactic. I soon rediscovered what I'd learned in Hoboken when I shot *On the Waterfront:* that the only way to deal with the man was to throw a fury fit every few days and make it uncomfortable for him to come on the set. He found my behavior vulgar and he wasn't wrong; desperation doesn't recognize the laws of polite deportment.

Were Sam to read this, he would act very hurt—a tactic of friendship—and ask, "How could you say those terrible things about me? I thought we were good friends." To which I would answer, "We certainly were good friends, but my feelings of friendship for you, just like yours for me, depended on a true understanding of our characters." His hurt would vanish overnight. It would be untactical for him to remain angry with me.

B O B B Y   D E   N I R O is one of a select number of actors I've directed who work hard at their trade, and the only one who asked to rehearse on Sundays. Most of the others play tennis. Bobby and I would go over the scenes to be shot in the week coming up, and since the two women in the cast were new and eager to make good, they came to work on Sundays too. I did improvisations with them for three weeks before principal photography began. My problem with De Niro was to transform a New York Italian kid into "Hollywood royalty," a thin, somewhat sickly Jew with erudition and culture. That wasn't easy. I didn't know much about Bobby—our coming together had been on instinct, his and mine—but we immediately understood each other. Bobby, a tough kid, was capable, like Marlon, of extraordinary sensitivity in a performance. Like me, he would do almost anything to succeed, in this case cutting down his weight from about 170 to 128 pounds. By the time we began to photograph him in the scenes, he actually looked frail.

That was the external aspect; the internal was the problem. He had to play a person who succeeded because he had a better mind than those around him. There was one acting exercise I gave him that we worked on again and again, its purpose being to complicate his thinking and give him the necessary quality of thoughtfulness and reserve. I wanted an observer to feel: You never know what that man is thinking. The improvisation, which we called the "double think," consisted of Bobby's retaining some supplementary or contradictory thought when he spoke. Again and again I asked him to actually think one thing as he was saying something quite opposite. I suggested he practice doing this in life, and it began to change the way Bobby "came on." An intellectual, I told him, can seem friendly and generous but is never altogether trustworthy. We are all spies, I told him, rarely offering to those we're with what we truly think of them. There should always be something that people call "fishy" about you, I said; call it ambivalent.

Directing of this kind should only be undertaken with a specific actor playing a specific part. With Bobby it worked well. The problem he had in the part was the problem I had with the script: an underdeveloped love story. There was nothing he could do about that, and in the end, there was nothing I could do.

I'd gone to England with Sam three times for the purpose of consulting with Harold Pinter, once in a desperate search for an actress to play Kathleen and satisfy Harold as well as me, but twice to talk about the script. I'd written to him what I believed was missing in the love story and given these letters to Sam. I thought my observations carefully reasoned and convincing, but they apparently didn't convince Harold. Pinter never commented on them and absolutely nothing was done to strengthen the love story and make it interesting. I had not realized how "tight" these two men were. I believe that Sam was impressed by Harold's eminence in the British literary world and thought his job was to protect Harold from a dominating director. They'd worked long and hard on the screenplay, alone and with Mike Nichols, and by the time I came in, the concrete had set and hardened. Perhaps Harold had run out of gas on the script. Sam won points with Harold by treating his work as holy writ. Our script conferences, long and tedious, were on the level of deciding which was correct in a certain spot, a comma or a semicolon.

Harold was also distracted by a personal problem, and perhaps this was why he wasn't thinking straight about his story. One day he asked my opinion on whether or not he should leave (i.e., divorce) his wife, Vivien Merchant. It was the most intense conversation I had with him on any subject. How could I blame the man for not wanting to get into a mess of rewrites? This was a real question, with real values at stake. My advice was stupid. I told him Greeks don't divorce, and said it as if it were a practice Jehovah had recommended to us. I told Harold that there wasn't a whole lot of difference between women—which is nonsense. And "sexist." Harold paid no attention to me; he was just worrying out loud.

I finally got weary of waiting for Sam to discuss the content of my letters with Harold, so I cornered him and told him that while I liked the script very much, I truly did, it had a great hole in its center, the love story, and went on about how vague and skimpy the action between the lovers was. "It's like it's all happening under water," I said. Harold's response was: "Isn't that where it always happens?" What the hell could I say to that? I shut off my objections, dived in, and did the best I could.

P A G E S from my diary while making *The Last Tycoon:*

I knew how serious it was with Mother when, at a time she couldn't go to the bathroom without Ruby's support, she said she wanted to go back to Rye. Did I do right to bring her west? I believe so. I told her we'd go back east as soon as spring came, and went to work.

When I woke this morning, Barbara said, "Sam called last night." "What did he say?" "I don't know. He was raving. I just left the phone off the hook." What Sam's worried about is Bobby De Niro. He thinks Bobby is "common," a judgment made not on the basis of film he's seen because we're not shooting yet nor on any of the improvisations I've been doing with Bobby where he's growing every day—I haven't let Sam see those—but on discussions he and Bobby had had about Bobby's personal expenses: would Sam pay for this, that, and the other? Sam kept on and on about how tricky Bobby is. "A petty-larceny little punk," he called him. Does Sam think that making me believe this will result in a better performance of Monroe Stahr? I had to remind myself that there are two Spiegels, one cultured, generous, and intelligent, as charming a dinner companion as you'd want to have. Then there's "Big Sam" (the crew's nickname, spoken mockingly), the Spiegel a director rubs against in the stress of production. I'd forgotten about him.

Mother keeps falling asleep, wakes, falls off again. She can't get up out of a deep chair without help from Ruby. Leo and Barbara have colds. I tell them to stay away from the old woman and Ruby to see to it that they do. A bad cold might carry her off. I fear I might wake up some morning and hear from Ruby that Mother died in her sleep.

Sam is hurt because Sue Mengers is having a party and he wasn't invited. To ease his life, I let him see a rehearsal of a scene. He said I'd done wonders with Bobby. (Later) I took Barbara to Sue's house. "Everyone" was there. Mme. Tussaud's waxworks come to life. "Swifty" Lazar and I talked. He told me that Irwin Shaw, despite the immense sales of his books, is constantly worried about money. Shaw, according to Lazar, talks as if he's living from hand to mouth. "Whenever he gets hold of a victim, he tells him his hard luck story and cries like a baby." Writers do worry more about money. They have nothing tangible to hold on to but can only wait and hope that another idea for a book will come to them.

She hasn't eaten in three days and is weakening fast. Perhaps she really is homesick. Should I take her back? Who the hell would look after her? When she sits, she seems to have a small soccer ball in her belly. Her doctor in Rye said, before we left, that if there was anything serious wrong (he meant cancer), there was nothing he could do about it. She is too weak, he said, to survive an operation.

We started shooting. Sam came to the stage to wish us luck. His girlfriend, eighteen years old and "coltish," is in the scene. A bit. I did him the favor. Later I suggested to Sam that he influence her to give up acting. That would be a favor too.

People edge away from the dying. Like the old-time fears of magic and transference. I felt that kind of protective aloofness in Barbara last night. As if she knew Death is approaching Mother and the dreadful thing might snatch her away too. The Middle Ages continue.

Sam doesn't like Bobby on film either. He says Bobby has no nobility and that he has a "petty larceny look," particularly when he smiles. I tell Sam I'm not going to let Bobby smile often, then remind him of what he said three days earlier, that I'd "done wonders with Bobby." Sam replied that he was trying to keep my spirits up. That man always has an answer.

This afternoon Ruby took Mother to see Dr. Herbert Gold. I was looking at some stuff in the cutting room when I got a call from Gold. They'd taken Mother to a hospital. I rushed to my office, shut the door, and asked, "What's up?" He said, "Her heart seems to be strong, but as you guessed, the trouble is elsewhere. The abdomen. I can feel a mass there. It seems to be in or near the liver and that is especially bad. Judging from what my hand tells me, it's a malignancy under the liver, pressing up, which is why she can't eat or drink and why she experiences trouble breathing." "What's the prognosis?" I asked. "I only know what my hands tell me," he said. "She says she wants to return to her home in Rye, New York. Would you recommend that?" "If she is happier there, I'd take her back now," he said, "while you still can."

Sam says he has five and a half million dollars of his own money invested in this film. I never know whether to believe Sam. "It's riding," he says, "on this boy who's spoiling fast and is so willful and arrogant." Then Sam reminds me that Bobby was my recommendation but does it by a half-ass compliment. "There is no director in the world except you," he says, "who could have influenced me to take a chance on Bobby." Later, at the end of the afternoon, while we were having a drink in his office, he said that despite this overriding faith in me, he is thinking of replacing Bobby. He's bluffing.

Dr. Gold has been making tests to find out what the large hardness in her abdomen might be and what organ it is affecting. I went to the hospital this morning before going to work and she was mad. "There is nothing the matter with me," she said. "I am not sick. That Dr. Gold gave me a lot of trouble yesterday." Mother hates him.

I think Sam is afraid of Harold Pinter. If I make the slightest change in the script, he comes after me. So today I let him have it; I was furious and let him know it. Whereupon he hung up on me. Every time I become angry with Sam, I remind myself that this is the man who made *Lawrence of Arabia*—that took courage!—and *The Bridge on the River Kwai* and how, except for him, *Waterfront* might not have been made, and of his great parties and—oh, the hell with all that. I'm finding him impossible again.

Now I'm having my lunch in a studio car on the way to the hospital. I sit with Mother half an hour, then go back to work. She is very weak and almost unresponsive; refuses to put in her hearing aid. She keeps making the Anatolian gesture of helplessness, parting then opening her hands in her lap. She keeps saying in a weak voice, "I want to go home." She waits for me to say I'll take her, but I don't.

Sam hates the costumes Anna Hill Johnstone has made for Theresa Russell. I defend Anna Hill, but she herself saw Sam's point. Very

Sam, Jeanne, and I

cleverly, very gently, Sam brings in another designer to do Theresa's clothes.

My brother George has come west; reinforcements for the coming emergency. After he saw Mother, he said she reminded him of an orange that's been in a bowl too long. She is shriveling and the skin has begun to bunch and wrinkle. Terrible but true.

Jeanne Moreau is here from Paris. She doesn't like the song Pinter and Jarre wrote for her to sing. Pinter says he does, so Sam says he does. I agree with Moreau and don't like the song, but I wish she did. This kind of trouble I don't need now.

I had a call from Dr. Gold on the set. I told him I'd see him in the hospital during my lunch hour. "We're walking on thin ice," I said to him when he arrived. "We're walking on water," he replied. "What would you do if it was your mother?" I asked. "I'd let her die graciously," he said. Did he mean gracefully? Can a person die gracefully? "Her heart," Gold went on, "is held together by spit."

Sam was right. The new costumes for Theresa are much better. We got them just in time; she starts working tomorrow. This is her first professional job. A big gamble. Sam thinks she's my girl.

The nurse couldn't find a vein this morning into which to insert the IV needle. Dr. Gold told me that every time you use a vein for IV, you destroy it. How many veins has she available?

In re Sam's criticism of De Niro (which never lets up), here are mine: His voice is rather inexpressive. He never stops fussing with props. But he's a damned true actor and is going to be excellent in the role. I must think in terms of his possibilities, not his drawbacks. So with all actors.

This morning, she walked to the wheelchair despite the fact that she was walking into a mystery. They're taking her downstairs to probe her colon with a metal "snake" which has a knife and a light in its head, and try to slice off a bit of what's up there. An indignity? It sure is. Her head reminds me of certain fifth-century Greek marble heads. They shouldn't do that to the goddess Athena. She still says she wants to go home, but she has another, more existential question: "What it's all about?" she asks, parting her hands in her lap, a question for which I have no more answer than she does.

Sam said after seeing Theresa's first day's work that she would steal the film from everybody. Is this another way of putting Bobby down? Sam reminded me that he recommended her to me. He says that anybody who doesn't like Theresa has something wrong with them.

The diagnosis is in. The cancer, as it swells, presses against her kidney on one side, so preventing it from functioning. This results in an increase of uric acid in her urine. "What does that mean?" I ask Gold. "It means," he says, "that it's going in the wrong direction." He seems positive, but I can't get rid of the impression that he, no less than all doctors, is guessing.

Now Sam has turned on Theresa. He says she is hopeless, even embarrassing, and that he wants to replace her. Then he gets on the personal level, says she is completely spoiled and arrogant. I try to stay calm, knowing he'll cool down. Erratic and contradictory as Sam's opinions are, they are always worth hearing. Acting is like quicksilver: What you're sure about one day, you doubt the next. And face it, Theresa is a beginner.

Suddenly Mother is very hostile to George and particularly to me. When we offer her affection, she rejects it. I kissed her yesterday and she shook her head violently. She rejects food. When Ruby forces it into her mouth, she spits it out. All she'll say is: "Go home. I want to go." Is she angry at me because I took her out of her condo in Rye? I don't know what to do.

Sam asked me to meet him in his office after my last shot of the day. I told him I had to go to the hospital. "Only for a few minutes," he said. It was the same old thing, De Niro. He finds him monotonous, with very little variety. "Who saw the rushes with you?" I asked. Which was insulting, but the cutter had told me that Sam had watched the rushes during the afternoon with a girl named Cynthia. Sam has his own opinions. Also those of whoever watches with him. Bobby lacks authority, Sam says. Authority! I don't want him to sound like a fucking English actor. "The character," I told Sam, "should have a thoughtful and gentle side. The big scenes will come later in the schedule." This reassured him—for an hour. "Give my regards to your mother," he said. And gave me a cigar.

Death, I find, is not a single event. A person dies in stages. It is a series of small setbacks. First one organ goes, then another. Now her teeth are out of her mouth and her face has collapsed.

I went to dinner at Irving and Mary Lazar's. They have "priceless" paintings all over their walls, sometimes hung shoulder to shoulder. Sam has the same overcrowded walls of paintings in his New York apartment, shouting "Look how rich I am!" Sam was very hurt because he wasn't invited to this dinner. Every big *macher* was there and his "bride." It was like a comic show because I knew what they all think of each other.

I had a terrible scene with Dr. Gold today. I noticed that the IV was out of Mother's arm and asked why. "Because I didn't write the order for it," Gold said. "Why not?" I asked. "She isn't eating or drinking anything, and she's losing strength every day." Then I put it to him hard. "You think it's hopeless, don't you?" I said. He had the strangest expression on his face. "It would be the kindest thing," he said. It took me a while before I recognized how arrogant, presumptuous, and unfeeling that was.

I meet with my girlfriend after we finished work. I believe the warmth of this young woman is keeping me going. There is a great, icy barrier between Barbara and me. My new friend and I embrace in a dressing room on the lot, and oh, do I feel better! It's the warmth I need. Then I go to the hospital. On the way I ask myself, Why am I keeping this old woman alive? For whose sake? She can't hear, can't see, can't hold her urine, can't eat, can't drink, can't talk—or won't—refuses to recognize anyone and, at the moment, is full of anger at me. So why? The answer is simple. Because it's what she wants.

There is one thing that surprises me about De Niro. Even though this part is quite a reach for him, he's going to be excellent. I know that now and I tell him so, but still he often seems anxious. Is he riding some deep worry of inadequacy that he doesn't dare show me? Is there always some uncertainty in all actors that they hide for professional reasons? Of course.

Dr. Gold gave me a lecture on the subject of coma. It's nature's way, he said, of carrying someone off gently. They gradually become numb, feel less and less. You ease into death with very little pain. Gold is preparing me for what's coming. Graciously and gracefully too.

Now Sam believes I'm too nice to the crew, too much their friend, too much one of them, not authoritative enough. He is accustomed to sterner stuff from a director. David Lean, I suppose, or Franklin Schaffner. Then he says—how contradictory he is!—that everyone on the set is scared to death of me. Which is it? And what does he want?

Do the dying resent the living? How could it be otherwise? Mother hates everyone at the moment—an indication that she is still ferociously asserting her will to live. Whom else can she blame? I brought her to California. I put her in the hospital. I brought in Dr. Gold, whom she hates. Long ago I promised her that when her time came, she would die at home—but what is home for her? My family? I doubt it. She wants to go back to the home she made for herself in Rye after her husband died.

The scenes with Ingrid Boulting don't come off. It's not her fault. The scenes, as written, are lousy. Or is tension distorting my judgment? Sam didn't listen to me when I told him there was a big hole in the love story. I still don't know if he gave my letters to Pinter. I doubt it, because Harold never commented on them to me. But if something is wrong with those scenes on the screen, it is not Ingrid's fault, it is Sam's and it is Harold's. But who will be blamed? Ingrid.

At the end of the afternoon's work, I went to the hospital, found Ruby there, and we brought Mother home. The first thing Ruby did when we got there was get the nail scissors and nip off the hairs which had grown on the old lady's chin. Clip, clip, clip! Before she left the hospital, they took bone marrow from her spine. This will show if there are cancer cells there too. Something essential is manufactured in the bone marrow. The white cells? Later. Gold says we must bring her immediately to another hospital. I don't fight him. I yield.

Sunday I play tennis so I won't go nuts, but I can't concentrate on the game. After I shower I make a list of shots the way they teach you in film school. This is not my usual practice. I like to "swing," make things up as I go along in a scene. But the resilience has gone out of me. And the fun. I show Sam the list. He seems reassured by it. He feels for me. He also feels for his film. It's not an ideal situation.

Katharine is here, a wonderful young woman. She and George moved Mother to the new hospital in Beverly Hills. The IV fluid has given her strength so she feels the pain more. Irony on top of irony. Katharine saw that her grandmother was in pain, so she demanded to know from Dr. Gold why he hadn't given the old woman a sedative. He answered that it would slow down her respiratory system and this would make her more vulnerable to pneumonia. Now they are not hoping that she'll come out of this, only to keep her alive as long as possible. Why?

I did the ballroom scene as if it was a classroom exercise, followed my list of shots, invented nothing. A "good professional job" doesn't make a good film. I can't keep my mind on the scene. I look forward to lunch in the studio car on the way to the hospital and even on what I'll find when I get there . . . it's a kind of relief.

She doesn't respond now when she sees me. Her face has collapsed into an expression of bitterness and anger. It seems mean, even hateful. Still it is my saintly mother. Had she always had that resentment in her, did this illness allow it to be seen? Like the story about Kirk Douglas? A new problem. One leg is swollen much larger than the other. When she toddled from the bathroom to her bed, leaning on Ruby, her gown opened in back and I saw her poor shriveled body, all welts and creases. There is a huge spreading rash all over her back.

I make a list of another sequence and show it to Sam. I can't judge anymore; I actually want his opinion. "Have I laid it out properly?" I ask. He says I have. Type comforts him. I don't know if it's bad, but it sure as hell ain't good or original or startling or funny. Just routine. I'm worn down to a stub. One good thing: Sam thinks Ingrid is beautiful in the ballroom scene, says he called Pinter in London to tell him so. That's a relief. Sort of. He'll change his mind tomorrow.

George and I decided (on the phone; he flew back to Delaware) to bring her home again, even if it's not the home she's been asking for. But she knew she was leaving the hospital and she was glad to leave. I believe she's accepted that she's dying.

We're doing a scene where a huge Siva head, shaken free from its foundation by the earthquake, comes floating down a flooded studio street. I suppose it's believable in the book, and I can't complain about Gene Callahan's design, but as I watched it happen, I didn't believe it, not for a minute. Ingrid is supposed to be clinging to the top of the head. Bullshit! I used to call home between shots to ask about Mother. Now I don't. Have I given up too?

Last night she began to groan on the outgoing breath, every one. She could be heard all through the house, a terrible sound. But I didn't know how much pain she was actually experiencing. She didn't look as if she was experiencing anything. Quote from Dr. Gold: A coma is nature's way of easing a person into death. Ruby says she's getting close.

Ruby woke Barbara and me at 3:15. "You better come in now," she said. I sat next to the bed, held her hand, stroked her head. I remembered how angry she'd been at me, a few days before. As she moved toward death, she became a different person. What happened? Was she resenting her wasted years? Was she angry that the men of the family had had such control of her life, even up to the end? The marks of anger were still on her face. I told Barbara and Ruby to go out of the room. I wanted to be alone with my mother. I waited. The heart stopped. There was no pulse in the hand I held, but she continued to breathe a little. Breathing is a reflex. She looked at me once. There was a cough and a press of the hand and she was gone. I stroked her hair. She stopped breathing.

I telephoned my three brothers and all my children. Nobody was surprised. I told them that, speaking for myself, I didn't want a ceremony. She hated priests. I'd learned what R.I.P. means. Yes, she should rest and be in peace. Then it was day. Time to send for an undertaker.

She was at ease, her head on the pillow, her hair spread over the pillow like that of a young girl in a breeze. Or after love. She was both a girl and a matriarch. Her face, as it cooled, relaxed. The tension and the anger left it. But her belly, home of the cancer, was very large and her legs swollen. I sat with the body, waiting for the undertaker people to come, watching over the slight, wan figure on the ochre-colored sheet. Alone in the room with her, I cried, then and never again.

Two nimble little Chicanos wearing black suits came from the funeral home. They wrapped the corpse in crushed purple velvet and took it away. I never saw her body again.

Nothing to do but go back to work. I thought I should try to reawaken some sort of interest in the picture. Then I said, The hell with it! I'll just finish the job. (Later) There were some expressions of sympathy on the set, but I slipped away from them. Some of the crew seemed to care, others not. What did I expect? After all, it happens to every-one. On Monday mornings there is always a new joke someone has picked up over the weekend. This Monday it was: "How do you make a Jewish woman stop screwing?" Answer: "By marrying her."

I decided not to fly east for the funeral. I'd had my own service with her and didn't need another. One of my brothers was urging that a minister be present. I didn't like that. I told my brother George, who'd been through the whole thing with me, that I wish he'd talk. He promised he would. "She wasn't really religious," I reminded him.

There was a letter for me at the studio. Why then I couldn't under-stand. Here it is: "Elia. You are a piece of shit. Read the enclosed transcript and be ashamed of yourself. An animal like you should be cleaning toilets not making movies." It was unsigned. Enclosed was the official transcript of the House Committee on Un-American Activ-ities, from January 14, 1952.

Ruby is leaving. I've become very fond of her. "You better take care of yourself now," she said. "You don't look good."

Yesterday I yelled at Sam over the phone like a madman. I didn't like his manner when he asked me to have a certain line spoken precisely as written. I was shocked at myself. I seemed totally out of control, insane. I immediately wrote Sam a note of apology. But apologies and explanations are without point. He's under tension too, and he is what he is and he'll be impossible again tomorrow, and I am what I am and I'll blow my cork again tomorrow. I wish the film was over. In the meantime, it doesn't hurt for Sam to believe I have a short fuse.

The house is quiet. There is a final irony. I am relieved. A great stress has been lifted.

Tony Curtis, having finished his part, came on the set to offer me a present in appreciation of the direction I'd given him. Taking me aside, he asked me to hold out my thumb, nail up. I thanked him for the thought but refused the gift. Then he told me a joke: "Any man who would fuck his wife is an animal." I was back on the picture again.

T H E question that disturbed me for weeks and is still there concerns the antagonism Mother had shown me at the end. True, I'd taken her out of her home and brought her west. But hadn't she wanted that? Barbara had been wonderful with her, and so had Leo. Still, as she began to face the fact that she was dying, another, less loving side of her showed itself, deep, violent, and from her center. I looked back at her life. It had been spent serving her husband and their four sons. Had she secretly resented that? Had she felt that I'd again chosen to control her life as I wished by bringing her west? Had she always had rebellious thoughts and impulses that she'd squashed down? To judge by her final disposition toward me, she must have. Of course, I'd like to think that she'd died happy, praising me as a good son. But when I tried to tell myself the truth, it was that she'd died in bitterness, alone and far from home. If I had to plot her secret life, the one she'd never articulated, I'd have come to the conclusion that her attitude toward me at the end and even toward George, whom she loved more than me, had its roots in previously hidden feelings. Those years after Father's death, when she was living alone and suddenly aware of how precious and independent life is and what she'd squandered for her five men, must have pumped up a head of anger. The final feelings of antagonism against me had to be the bent twigs which traced her path back through the forest of despair. She'd died, as we all must, alone at the end, but her disposition had been created on the way by events that left no objective evidence but still must have been there. I wondered if this unexpected antagonism didn't speak the deepest truth.

I H A D a letter from my son Nick, who'd seen her just before the end. "It was extraordinary," he wrote, "that a woman who couldn't control her bowel movements, and whose urine collected in a plastic bag at her side, could look so majestic on the day she died." That was not what I'd seen.

O N F E B R U A R Y 3, before leaving for the East, I asked Sam what he thought we had in *The Last Tycoon*. He smiled confidently and said he thought we had something very good. "So do I," I said.

Back in New York, I worked with our cutter to make an "assembly." On the first of March, we had a rough cut ready and showed it to Sam. Who was ecstatic; I was pleased too. "The picture hangs together," I wrote in my diary, "the performances are good, outstanding in the case of Ingrid and Bobby De Niro, and the film has class, beauty, humanity, subtlety, and even emotional power." It was the only supremely favorable notice we were to receive. Sam, euphoric, called Harold to give him the good news.

On the morning of the 27th of April, Pinter arrived in New York and saw the film at three in the afternoon. When the lights came up, he crossed to me and shook my hand. He also congratulated Sam. He seemed very sincere and spoke of the picture with great feeling. I enjoyed hearing him so much that I stayed with him until ten-thirty that evening. He especially liked De Niro. He thought I'd done a miracle with Ingrid. He'd been prepared to hate her but was completely surprised; she'd even moved him. He also liked Theresa, said she was not what he'd written but worked well in the film and made her quite different interpretation stick. I was relieved.

On the first of June, Sam showed the film to Barry Diller, the operating head of Paramount—because, he said, he didn't want Barry to lose faith in Bobby De Niro, who'd just given a poor performance in Bertolucci's film *1900*. Everybody in the motion picture business is either losing faith in someone or having his faith restored in someone. Barry telephoned me the next day and said, "It's a wonderful picture," speaking in a deep, sincere-type voice, and "Ingrid is wonderful." "Tell Sam," I said. Sam was very happy about Barry's reaction and said to me, "I never had any doubts about this film."

Now came the first uncertain reaction. Our cameraman, Vic Kemper, saw the film and didn't call me. I told Sam about Kemper's silence and what it must mean. Sam said he didn't give a damn what anyone said or didn't say now; he was, he said, completely confident about the film, completely satisfied that it was good. In my diary, I wrote: "Remember that!" Which must indicate that I was beginning to feel some doubts.

On June 29, we had our first small audience, made up of some of Sam's close friends, like George and Liz Stevens; Barry Diller's lady friend; my wife and her collaborator, Nick Proferes; the sound crew, who'd never seen the film together; Kemper, his wife, and their daughter. After the film was over, people were silent. George Stevens came to me, and what he said was: "Bob Mitchum gives an excellent performance." Mitchum plays a small part on the fringe of the story. I didn't need anyone to explain the significance of what George had chosen to say. By the time everyone had left the projection room, it was clear to Sam and to me that we had a dubious commercial product, and it was clear to me if not to Sam that the reason was that we had fudged on the basic dramatic situation. The film had not gripped anyone; no one was concerned about Monroe Stahr's fate. Barbara was especially impatient with the film's love story and with my direction. "Why the hell doesn't he take her?" she demanded. "She's waiting for him.

What kind of a man is that? He's so limp!" Which is another way of express-ing the objection I'd had when I'd read the script the first time and said to Harold that I felt like kicking his hero in the ass. Everything I'd thought wrong with the story the first time I'd read it was wrong with it now. Scene by scene the film flowed, but no one could be concerned about De Niro's troubles or respect his pain. Some of the individual scenes were good, it did have tender moments and some amusing ones, but there was nothing to compel an audience to see it.

Now a dark cloud descended on the film. It was eerie the way this hap-pened, how quickly, how subtly, yet with what finality. Someone from Par-amount said that he doubted that the "kids," on whom the industry depended, would go to the film. I didn't give a damn about these kids, but that kind of reaction was bad news to Sam. He began to have changes of heart, small at first but, like an avalanche, beginning with a distant rumble, ending with a roar. He began to second-guess his choices and regret those he should have made and didn't. For the first time he said he should have been "freer" with Harold and asked to have more dramatic situations. The whole story should have had more conflict, he said, more violence, and been "in the idiom of present-day moviemaking." Sam was in trouble, and he looked it.

We had another showing, and this confirmed our situation: We had a dud. Many people, including some of Sam's good friends, got up and left without a word. A close friend of mine came to me, kissed me, and walked off without comment. Bobby De Niro was there; he didn't respond to the film. David Lean seemed to rather like it—how could anyone tell?—but he did not like De Niro. He said Bobby wasn't a leading man, that he played the individual scenes acceptably but was not interesting overall, the way a star should be. Which is all that Sam needed—a good push down the slippery chute. Only Jeanne Moreau sincerely and passionately extolled the film. Which was a sign of what was coming: that the French would again like a film of mine that audiences in the United States did not. Should I go live in France?

On the fifteenth of July, Sam took the film to London, to show to the European distributors who'd helped finance it. Days passed, and I didn't hear from him. In show business, silence can mean only one thing. By now I was working on a novel and thinking of Sam's film in the past tense as a failure. When Sam did call me, he had made up his mind what was wrong with the film. "I told you," he said, "that he was nothing but an East Side punk. David Lean was right. Our trouble is our leading man." "I like Bobby in the film," I said. "No one could have done the part better." By the time he'd returned to New York, Sam had begun to blame himself. After all, he'd been the producer. There has to be a scapegoat in every failure, and if you can't find one, you are reduced to blaming yourself. That's what Sam had come to.

He did tell me that Harold and his new wife, Antonia, had been to a showing. Pinter was still enthusiastic and Antonia as well, except for Ingrid; she didn't like Ingrid. Nine years later, I ran into Harold at a party Sam gave for him and told him that the problem with our film had been the love story—in other words, his script. He disagreed, absolutely; he said the film had only one flaw, Ingrid Boulting. That night, Sam agreed.

L O N G before this, I'd made up my mind never to work in films again, that *The Last Tycoon* would be it. I'd come to that conclusion on the last day of our schedule. I had one final scene to do. Harold and Sam, despite their convivial script conferences in London, had provided me with nothing to shoot for an ending. This is the worst possible situation, because it means that something is very wrong earlier in the story. I had to make something up on that day and I did. I also had a hunch that it would be the last shot I'd make in my life, and perhaps for that reason the ending I devised said more about me and my feelings than it did about the film's hero.

I asked Bobby to walk slowly down a deserted studio street. Perhaps it was Sunday—no one was in sight—perhaps it was a scene in his imagination. He came to a stop at the side of a sound stage whose great rolling door was wide open. One could not see far into the interior of the sound stage because it was dark, but there was an impression that it was empty and not being used. Then a close shot revealed that my man was holding back some private despair and regret. Bobby hesitated for a moment, then he walked slowly into the dark of the unused stage. The gloom enveloped him and he disappeared. Forever—it seemed. It was the end, the fade-out of the film I was making and the end for me and my time as a director. I walked away from the shot and the crew and entered my office. As I began to pack my books, my records, and my diaries to send back east, it hit me that this was indeed my last film and that it was a kind of death for me, the end of a life in the art where I'd worked for so long. It was all over, and I knew it.

THIS IS as far as I'm going. From that time on, there's nothing to tell that I believe would interest you. I didn't make any more films, nor have I, except for a training production at the Actors Studio, directed another play. I lived a quiet life, sat before my Royal every morning and typed pages of a book. The novels, six of them, tell whatever there is to tell. I believe they have merit, though many critics thought not. This didn't bother me. To the extent an aging man can, I enjoy my days and nights. I've had regrets and feelings of guilt, but I have tried to resolve them and succeeded.

There is an event coming, of course, that does concern me and might interest you. Since this is an autobiography, I cannot write about my death. But I do wonder how it will happen and when, and have an eerie feeling that I should have some control over the event, and even delay it if I'm not ready for it.

Some men I've known have had formidable and quite unrealistic images of themselves. That's not necessarily bad—most artists require a pumped-up opinion of their importance. But as these men grow older, they often find they've fallen short of their self-image. With their minds dulled, their physical strength deteriorated, and their sexuality atrophied, some choose not to continue as diminished people but terminate their lives. That's everyone's right and choice but not mine. Wishing to live at sixty-five and seventy-five as at twenty-five and thirty-five is not gallant or brave. The admirable thing is to recognize what you've become. I hate old age; I don't believe it's the "best of times." I am seventy-seven as I write these words, and there are days when I feel the final chill approaching, rub my hands together as my mother used to, and laugh at the recognition. But I have to accept it, even make something of it. So I write this book.

I've studied friends at the end of their lives. Who that I've known has shown me something of how to die? On the other hand, who claimed my sympathy but not my admiration? I can still hear Clifford's operatic out-cry—this at fifty-seven—"Clifford Odets, you have so much still to do!" And, his last, "Imagine! Clifford Odets dying!" I can recall the laughter of Orson Welles, like an explosion of impatience and pain, a laugh that seemed to be mocking everyone, above all himself. What could the genius who'd made *Citizen Kane* have thought as he studied his bloated image on a studio relay monitor, assuring the nation of what he had no way of knowing himself? How had he maintained the dignity he deserved in Paris as he strained to amuse Darryl Zanuck at dinner so Darryl would pick up the check, then loan Orson enough dollars to travel to wherever it was he wished to go next? What had Orson felt then? Perhaps Tennessee Williams, who knew that feeling, had a name for it, something like self-disgust.

So it happened that when I read that Orson had died of a heart attack, I wondered if that death, like the others I've observed, was less a single event than the last of a series of small "deaths," none of them visible to the eye but all demoralizing something essential within him and leading to the final collapse. I didn't know Welles intimately enough to provide details for this speculation, so I looked at the lives of people I knew better, privileged and gifted people all, now dead, who'd gone through a series of crises in which something essential to them had been defeated and so filled them with disappointment and anger at themselves that they had "died" again and again before they died. I tried to recall or imagine what these small deaths on the way to the final one were and, also, what had been wounded. The nervous system? The soul? I even consulted friends in the medical profession, doctors who broke with custom and confessed their uncertainties. I asked them if a person might be so badly hit in his self-esteem and his pride, and so repeatedly, that his natural defenses—those given him at birth—against the killer diseases were weakened to the point where they

became ineffective and surrendered their host body. Can there be a biological wound from a psychic blow? Where is it experienced? What does it do
to the body?

I N   A N apartment high above Third Avenue at Seventy-second Street in
New York City, Elaine Steinbeck, the devoted wife of John Steinbeck, lay
at his side on top of their bed and waited for what she knew was coming. It
was five-thirty in the afternoon of the shortest day of the year, and through
their bedroom window Elaine could see a great sweep of the city glowing
in the dark. She'd posted herself close at hand in case her husband, whose
coronary arteries were clogged and choking, required oxygen, which he
could not get for himself. She raised her head and checked him, as she had
every few minutes all that day. The face of that great-chested bear of a man
had wasted, but there was still a belligerent pride there. Elaine saw that
for the moment he was okay. The nurse they'd engaged had noticed an
improvement and suggested that, weather permitting, Elaine might take
John for a drive the next day. Elaine thought the nurse naive. Exhausted
from her long vigil, she fell into a light sleep. Some minutes later, she
opened her eyes and saw that John had died. He was sixty-six years old.

I'd met John at the lowest point of his life. At Molly's suggestion, I'd
gone west to ask him if he might be interested in writing a film about
Emiliano Zapata. He said he'd thought about Zapata for many years, had a
stack of notes, and had thrown several passes at the subject. Although neither of us made friends quickly, we soon became—as Elaine was to say—
"brothers." He told me everything; I told him everything. He said Gwyn,
his second wife, had humiliated him during their marriage. Now they were
separated. In anger and shame, he'd moved out of their home and into a
hotel; he was still hoping that Gwyn and he might make up. But there'd
been no such indication from her. So he'd retreated to his old home in
northern California, which was where I met with him. Then, becoming
anxious about his two sons by Gwyn, he'd made another trip east, again
hoping that she'd relented. She had not; she insisted on a divorce.

John was drinking heavily. He'd called me as soon as he'd arrived in the
East, and several nights when we were together I'd had to help him to his
hotel and put him to bed. Finally he'd given up hope for a reconciliation
and gone back to California and settled in. Bitterly lonely and in need of
money, he tried to get on with the script about Zapata. But he wasn't thinking clearly, and nothing went well for him. When John didn't sharpen
twenty wooden pencils every morning and sit to write on his yellow legal
pad, he didn't know why he was living. He was constantly in turmoil, a
violent man with tender sensibilities, part pride, part self-doubt. He was
rocketing around without purpose or direction, when he had a piece of
luck.

He met Ann Sothern and through her met Elaine Anderson Scott. Elaine took to him. She raised his spirits, restored some of his confidence, made him feel like what he was, an exceptional man with an exceptional talent. She was a strong woman who'd been working in the New York theatre as a stage manager, a job that requires a firm and, when necessary, a hard hand. Born and raised in Texas, she'd made New York her scene. This may have been part of her attraction for John; he'd always been stagestruck. They went back east together and, in time, freed themselves to marry.

Through Elaine he met the lords of Broadway. They and John were flattered by each other's interest. John determined to write plays for the theatre; he had no idea how difficult this is—no one who hasn't worked as a playwright on Broadway does. We finished the work on *Zapata* together, got a "go" from Zanuck, and John, at last, had some money and was free to write his own plays. I remained in the West, making that long, complicated film, so I didn't see him for almost a year.

When I got back to the city, I saw him immediately. He was happy with Elaine. Through her he'd become a familiar of Richard Rodgers and Oscar Hammerstein, the most successful producing firm on Broadway. They were planning to make a musical of John's book *Sweet Thursday,* and Harold Clurman was to direct it. John was living in a different world now. He'd pulled up his roots and replanted them in other soil. Riding high, he was dressing like a man of the big city, had a smarter wardrobe, even sported a cane on the street, and he was spending weekends with men of equal importance at their country homes in Connecticut and Bucks County.

Still a part of him remained untouched. They say you can take the man out of the country, but you can't take the country out of the man. John was a native son, a dirt-road boy, and still a surprisingly naive person. He was intensely emotional—you could see it on his face—and especially protective of his wife, possibly because of how Gwyn had deceived him. The story goes that when an old friend of Elaine's at a party kept his hand on her shoulder after John had asked him to take it off, John took a knife out of his pocket, pulled up the blade, and thrust it through the man's hand. True or not, accept it as evidence not only of how entirely John was attached to Elaine but of the unreleased violence in the man.

I don't think John Steinbeck should have been living in New York, I don't think he should have been writing plays, I don't think he should have hung out with show people. He was a prose writer, at home in the West, with land, with horses, or on a boat; in the big city, he was a dupe. If you don't believe me, take the word of his beloved editor, Pat Covici, who said to John, late in his life, "There are two places which proved poisonous for you, Hollywood and New York. As far as you're concerned, they are good to visit but not to take to heart." That's what John did, perhaps for too long; he took New York to his heart.

But in time he learned. It was more than the fact that his musical had been a foolish flop, that the play he wrote, *Burning Bright*, had died of a cold heart; it was that the books he'd been writing were not up to his mark or his talent. He knew it. He'd lost himself.

I heard that he'd been hospitalized and was being prepared for an operation on his spine, so I went to see him. It's a shock to an artist especially to have surgery on a vital part; he realizes that the work time he has left is limited. I sat by John's bed that day, and he looked old and full of anger. At himself. We had a long conversation, like "brothers," and he said, "I have nothing to write about anymore." It was a collision with the truth, and he said it with scorn. At first I thought it might be a passing depression, but as he went on, I knew he was speaking from the heart. What else could he believe after what had happened to him on Broadway? "The job of a writer is to tell about his time," he said. "I've been too concerned with what's past." I saw that John was not playing a game of postures. He'd found out something about himself that he didn't like. "I've also lost touch with the country," he said. "I don't know what's happening out there anymore."

What I admired about him is that after he'd come to this conclusion, he tried to do something about it. The operation on his spine was successful, and everyone rejoiced. John was told to give himself a long recuperation, to do nothing, to rest. He resented this advice and the frightened concern he was getting from his friends and even from his wife. He thought they were trying to make an invalid of him, and he wasn't going to go for that. The operation had been a warning. Did he want a chance at another life? He had every reason to lie back and be cared for—no one could have loved him more than Elaine. But he felt that his situation was desperate, and he had to keep alive that part of himself he valued more than his body.

He started a novel, not about the past or about another country but about his time and his place. He and Elaine had acquired a country place on a finger of land toward the end of Long Island, and John had had the opportunity to make friends with the people of Sag Harbor. Out of this and the disappointments he felt about so much that was going on in the country, he wrote a book that said what he thought of our condition. This book was his hope for regaining his true self. The title tells the mood of the author: *The Winter of Our Discontent*. It was not well received. For the book readers of the country John was a has-been, and for the literati, an exhausted voice. But he could take it; he didn't respect the critics. He'd said what he believed. He was—or said he was—satisfied.

He was soon heartened by the Nobel Prize in Literature, given to him with the greatest respect. John was reassured. Then *The New York Times*, in an editorial, asked whether the Nobel Prize committee might not have made a better choice. The editorial writer thought so. So did many others in the intellectual community. John took this public humiliation hard. It was a painful setback for a man who'd been trying to make himself worthy

in his own eyes. I found no way of convincing him to ignore the *Times* and its despicable editorial.

He was withdrawn, he quit for a while, then he told me he was buying a truck large enough to hold his essentials—a bed, a small stove, a refrigerator, a table and chair and chest of drawers, and a lamp. He was planning to drive slowly across the northern reach of this country, then ride back along a southern arc. He would see the people again, listen to their concerns, find out what he used to know without having to go looking. He asked me to go with him, but I was involved getting out *The Arrangement*. Instead of me, he took his poodle, Charley. I understood his trip as the effort of this man to save the most precious part of himself; I was touched by it and encouraged him on. He was like a young man responding to a dare.

So he drove off in his truck. Elaine had not wanted him to go. I believe there'd been some hint of the trouble he was to have at the end—he'd blacked out once. Was it a premonitory stroke? This worried Elaine every day he was gone. He missed her terribly, invited her to join him at several points, but through a great deal of the trip he was alone with Charley. He did find it more difficult to talk to people than he'd imagined, even when he'd invite them into his truck for a cup of coffee or a beer. He was reminded of many affectionate and colorful things he'd once known, but there was also something that worried him about what he saw, a change. He got a successful book out of it, *Travels with Charley*, but I believe his experience on the trip was deeper than the one reflected in the book.

Still he drove himself. One of his sons was a soldier in Vietnam, and John was receiving letters from him. He got the idea that the most important thing he could do was get an assignment as war correspondent and send home dispatches about what he saw at close hand, report the experiences of the men in the war. He got the job from *Newsday*. He also got encouragement from his friend President Johnson, who saw to it that everything

John wanted was made available to him. This time Elaine, concerned more than ever about his health and stamina, went along, not to where the shooting was but close enough so she could be near at hand—just in case. John drove himself, as Elaine knew he would. He had to show the world that he was still John Steinbeck. He did what his pal Bob Capa, the photographer, had done, immersed himself in the thick of the action. But what had been a romantic adventure in 1944, behind the lines of the western front of that other war, was now a desperate drain on an elderly man's constitution. Only his pride drove him on; he would not back off. He interviewed the common soldiers and the commanding officers, liked them both. He sat in on helicopter raids under fire, went on foot patrols behind the lines. A photograph shows him walking on the edge of exhaustion. Was he testing himself? Punishing himself? He sent his copy back regularly and faithfully. It was true to what he saw and how he saw what he saw. He was especially impressed by the caliber of the American fighting man, praised the army and what it was up to.

It was, of course, a period of disgust with the war and what we were doing there. With American deaths now measured by the ten thousands, there was no patience in the country for John's point of view. He said the American soldier was excellent. But weren't many of them on dope? Weren't they selling army fuel to the corrupt South Vietnamese? And so on. John's dispatches seemed—were?—loyal to the war effort at a time when most everyone had come to the conclusion that we shouldn't have been in that part of the world with our arms and our men, and certainly not on the side of Saigon.

The New York *Post*, a left-of-center paper at that time, attacked John for betraying his liberal past; a self-betrayal, they called it. *Newsday* canceled his dispatches. It was another public humiliation, another blow at the most sensitive part of this man. He stayed on in the Far East, still writing what he believed but now in letters to the President, telling Johnson his suggestions for conducting the war and his concerns about our policy there.

When he got home, he was exhausted in his body, in his spirit. His effort to resurrect what was best in him had not failed, but it had cost him. Still he'd seen it through. I admired his courage and his devotion to what a writer should do: tell his own truth. But it was too late. The nation was riding another emotion, to pull out of Vietnam. John's truth wasn't a popular truth, and he paid for it.

He'd also been driving himself beyond his capacity to endure hardship. It wasn't long before he had a heart attack, then another, then a final one as his wife dropped off for an instant of sleep in their apartment far above Third Avenue on Seventy-second Street.

. . .

W H E N I heard that film director Nick Ray was in Sloan-Kettering, a hospital specializing in cancer cases, I paid him a visit. We greeted each other affectionately; we were old friends. I was shocked at his appearance; it was evident that his time was running out. I sat at the side of his bed, and we talked about old times. He had no illusions about his condition, told me straight out that the cancer was spreading rapidly through his body. When I left, I told him I'd be back, and I remember how he nodded. His mind, I thought, had fluttered here and there, and he was altogether uncertain.

I returned two days later, feeling that I might be seeing him for the last time. He wasn't in his room, so I went to the nurses' station and asked about him. The nurse told me that Nick had been taken for radiation treatment and pointed down a long hall. On the last of several trips into the hall, I saw a nurse pushing a wheelchair, thought it might be Nick, and walked to meet it. I didn't recognize him immediately; then I thought: He'll look better in his coffin. His head had been shaved clean on one side, and there was a target mark indicating where the X-ray should be aimed. I made the only possible assumption, that the cancer had moved to his brain.

I said, "Hello, Nick," and he looked up to greet me, but it was less cordial than usual, not unfriendly but distracted. I walked along at the side of the chair, asking a few questions, getting uncertain and brief answers. He seemed to be in a hurry, as if he was late for an appointment. When we got to his room, Nick greeted someone, calling him "Wim." I saw two men assembling a motion picture camera and some other filmmaking equipment; sound, I supposed. I got the idea. Nick was being photographed for a film—as he was dying. Just like him, I thought. I'd never met the director, but had heard his name—Wim Wenders, a German. Clearly they wanted me to leave so they could get on with their work. Nick threw me a hurried goodbye. As I left, I said to myself, "Nick is like an actor preparing to play his most important scene." I thought about what was going on and found it grotesque: a man cooperating in putting his own death on film.

Walking home, I thought more about what I'd seen. I thought Wenders ghoulish, but I also thought that this might be what Nick himself would most wish to do: dramatize himself as he was dying, make that his last act on earth. What kind of man would do that? Nick was, if the opprobrium could be lifted from the word, a poseur. He had never been just one man, but had been many different men at different times, matching where he was and whom he was with and what the scene needed. His way of being was characteristic of a certain kind of actor and director—to be a tough guy when you're with tough guys, a poet when you're with poets, a bar fighter when you're with bar fighters, a lover who believes a life well lost for love when you're with a woman. It was an aspect of the Stanislavski system, in which Nick, long ago, had been trained: to get "inside" all characters; to be able to be them all and all at the same time—that was the complete actor. I knew this from myself. Nick was several contradictory things—a bourgeois and a veteran of the class war, a master of the technique of acting, with his differences from Lee Strasberg, an aristocrat in his tastes and a peasant in his soul, a faithful husband and resolute father nevertheless out to top every girl who aroused his fancy, to have it all, be disciplined and dissolute, saint and sinner, modest and arrogant, a partisan of the left yet submissive to the right, always rebellious, finally uncontrollable. I asked myself, "Don't most artists want to be everything, to miss out on nothing, to experience every experience, even death, to know it intimately, to taste it all and enjoy it all and respect no limits?"

Nick and I were much alike. We'd both started as actors and become directors. But he went "all the way," and I did not. I was more disciplined, more in control, more cautious, more bourgeois. Perhaps, I thought, he's been more of an artist, more of a gambler. But hadn't it been man's deepest desire all through history to have it all, heaven and hell? Faust sells his soul for that. Is this hunger applicable only to actors and directors? Hell, no. Is it specifically American? No. It is the question that life asks: How much do you want and how much will you give up for what you want? I recalled that Nick had always created an image of what he wanted to be perceived as— but it was always a different image.

We'd once been very close. When I'd directed my first play for the Theatre of Action, he'd been a member of the cast. As the war was closing down, I went to Hollywood to make *A Tree Grows in Brooklyn* and got Nick a job as my assistant. He was studying filmmaking techniques and learning fast. Jack Houseman gave him his first job of direction in Hollywood, *They Live by Night*. It was immediately evident that Nick had a unique talent for directing actors.

His career went forward with a rush. He became a glamour figure, especially in France, where the men of the "New Wave" discovered him. In Hollywood he made *Rebel Without a Cause* with Jimmy Dean right after I'd made *East of Eden*. His film became a monument to the "misunderstood" youth of the time. I didn't like this, but we didn't discuss what he thought, and I was glad to see him so successful. He went on to make other films in Hollywood that were highly praised, and he was idolized in Europe.

But few careers in Hollywood are smooth sailing, and very few can survive a period of no financial returns—as I knew very well. Not getting the work or the respect he needed in California, he began to spend more and more time in Europe. So I stopped seeing him, knew about him only through gossip. I heard he was doing drugs. I heard he'd lost one eye in a bar fight in Madrid. I heard that he was back in California but was not doing well. I knew he'd taken to borrowing money from his friends, had run up a phone bill—so I was told—for thirty thousand dollars and had exhausted the patience even of people close to him. I loaned him money, which I'd not see again. I recall a phone call I had in 1975 from a man named Bob Greenberg. "I've got to get him out of my house," Greenberg said. "He's driving me up the wall. Or else move out myself and leave my place and my roommate to him. He's going to parties now where there will be coke, so he can get some free. Gene Kelly bought him a suit, while Nick plays the role of martyr of the system which destroyed a generation." And so on and on.

But nothing disturbed the affection I felt for Nick. I even wondered, when my films began to not quite come off, was my life too even-keeled, while he'd been living as an artist should?

The very first time I heard that he was in a hospital and that the trouble was cancer, I went to see him. He was on his feet, dressed in pajamas, and was walking around, seeming perfectly well. There was another man in the room, but he remained quiet as Nick and I talked. We embraced and kissed as we always had, then sat and caught up with each other. When he told me about his medical condition, he peeled off his pajama top, turned his back, and exhibited a long red scar diagonally across his back. He seemed proud of it. They'd opened him up, seen that the cancer was beyond control, encircling the aorta and invading a lung, so they'd closed him up again. Nick put his pajama top back on, sat in an armchair, found a cigarette, and lit it. I wondered if he was doing that for my benefit—or for his own. I figured that it was his way: He was challenging death. The other fellow in the room explained why he was there. He was from a college and offering Nick a job lecturing on film. Nick had to take what he could get to pay his bills. But he behaved as if he was doing the man a favor to even consider his offer. Which I suppose he was.

He took a job at the State University of New York at Binghamton. Wearing a black patch over the socket where his eye had been, he was a glamorous example of the go-it-all-the-way artist to the students there, a hero. He made a film with them rather than lecturing for them to take notes. The film referred to his own work with the students, and both they and he played roles. Much of it was improvisational, and the students found they were making artistic contributions. I later saw some of the footage, and Nick looked bad, but his spirit was fed by the adoration of the students. They were never to forget the man.

A week after I saw the student film, at the time when I was thinking about this part of the book, I obtained a copy of the film Wim Wenders made of Nick's death—which I'd vowed not to see—and I looked at it. I thought much of it clumsy and tedious. But then came an extraordinary long close-up of Nick near the end. The dying director, who knows he's dying, looks straight into the camera's lens and directs his last scene, which is his death. Nick looked unbelievably exhausted. There could be no doubt that he had only a few days to live. But there was also no doubt that, with those last hours of his life, this was precisely what he wanted to do. And to my surprise, the same belligerence I remembered on John Steinbeck's face at the end I saw on Nick's.

A director when he watches a scene and has what he wants calls out, "Cut!" But sometimes, when the scene is going surprisingly well and is providing some astonishing things, he will whisper to his cameraman, "Don't cut," and allow the scene to continue past where he'd rehearsed it. Nick Ray was directing his own last close-up. Toward the end of the shot and of what he had to say in the shot, he called out, "Cut!" Then, "Don't cut!" Then a pause and again, "Cut!" then "Don't cut!" What Nick was calling out was something more than an instruction to a cameraman. He was prolonging his life where he'd most lived his life—on film.

Nick didn't want to die. He wanted to go on. He didn't give in, not a minute, not on an inch of film. Even in his last terrible misery, he clung to every "foot" of life, the film on which his living was being preserved. You may call it phony, and I will understand why. But I call it heroic. In a way, I thought, he was speaking for all artists. I'd first thought what Wenders was doing was one step this side of grave-robbing. Wenders was concerned about this too, and possibly to save himself from such an accusation, he put himself in a scene expressing this concern. But he went on with it, and when I finally saw the film, I thought his decision to continue was justified. I admired him. With all its brandishing of Nick's physical deterioration, the film came over to me as a tribute to a friend, and beyond that, to a human being's dogged determination to die as himself.

O N   T H E   seventh floor of Mount Sinai Hospital in New York City, a woman was getting desperate attention from a nurse who had wheeled to her bed one of those machines brought on at the end of an illness, more as an experiment than with any genuine hope that it may save the life past saving.

Suddenly something broke down within the patient's body; the nurse knew it, turned the machine off, and withdrew its mouthpiece. An instant later, what looked like coffee grounds flooded out of Barbara's mouth. "The liver," the nurse said.

The withdrawal of the machine's mouthpiece and the sudden relaxation of the nurse's efforts, the gush of the "coffee grounds," signaled the end of the attempts by medical science to save my wife's life. The nurse turned and looked at me—I was the only other person in the room. She didn't have to say anything. It seemed that Barbara also knew she had only some seconds of consciousness left. It was the conclusion of almost three years of our efforts, hers and mine, to defeat the cancer that had metastasized from a small lump in her left breast to her liver to her bone marrow to her brain. Her death—within minutes—finished the gallant and brave effort of this woman, so young at forty-eight, to maintain her life and go on to realize the artistic hope that had become essential to her. In those last instants of consciousness, however, she did not beg for our pity, she did not cry out in pain, she did not weep in self-commiseration. Angrily, she expressed bitter resentment at her fate, crying out, "Shit! Shit! Shit!" Those were her last words, and speaking them in anger was the last act of her life.

When I first met her, she was twenty-three years old, beautiful and perfect in form. She had, however, a telltale hitch in her shoulders, telling of concealed inner tensions and an unhappy history. Her youth deserved pity and her adolescence was worse. Like many pretty girls I've known, she felt worthless, felt that the only thing that gave her any value was a man's desire for her. She was worth a lot to a series of young men. Some older ones too.

She had no "higher education," no specific training, had nothing she could sell—except her youth and beauty. She was ferociously ambitious, fearless as well; she was tough and she could be ruthless. When I met her, she was taking all sorts of lessons, particularly acting lessons from Paul Mann, who emphasized a boldness in performance that more conventional Method teachers did not. She also took voice, speech, and several kinds of dance. She took these lessons devotedly. She had to get ahead, and for this purpose she was not neglectful of the advantages men's desire gave her. Including mine.

Greek and Turkish men—and I am both—will never receive a commendation from the National Organization for Women. They claim the privilege of infidelity. Women's reward is domestic sainthood. This didn't go down with Barbara.

One day years ago, she gave me a newspaper clipping, said it would make a good movie. I thought it skimpy, but when she asked me to help her turn it into a screenplay, I roughed out something in three days. It was called "The Gray World." Then she went to work on it, and it became *Wanda*, in all essentials her screenplay. It took six years to find someone who'd finance it, even though it cost "nothing," $200,000. She asked me to direct it, but I declined. I didn't see life as she did—sentimentally, I thought. So she found a man who'd work with her, photograph the action, and cut the film. Nick Proferes and Barbara were well matched. He supplied everything she lacked, and vice versa.

They made the film in a way that fascinated me, largely improvisational, departing at every turn from the script. They directed it together, she the actors, he the camera. It was a great success in Europe and won a prize in Venice. Immediately Barbara became the darling of the paparazzi. I recall her walking down the beach at Lido, the cameramen following like wild dogs, pushing each other out of the way to get at her. She was quickly acclaimed a heroine of the feminist movement, the first woman to write and direct a film about a "floater," that kind of woman, and to do it on her own. Barbara knew the subject well. In the kind of flip-flop that characterizes our culture, Barbara was suddenly on top of the world. She was where she'd always wanted to be, preeminent in a world she believed in, not competing in one for which she had no respect.

Now she plunged into work, writing screenplays one after another with Nick. They were of the same kind as *Wanda*, small films, devoted to the neglected side of American life, the secret side she knew well. She didn't want to compete in a field where she was dependent on "standard figures" like me. She wanted to be independent, find her own way. I didn't really believe she had the equipment to be an independent filmmaker, but she and Nick were a good combination, and I thought that by supplementing each other they might make it. I admired her because she never stopped trying. Tenacity unlocks doors. She believed her day would come.

The inferior position she was trying to leave behind was the position of women in our society. I realized that when I first met her; she'd been cunning and manipulative. She had little choice but to depend on her sexual appeal. But after *Wanda* she no longer needed to be that way, no longer wore clothes that dramatized her lure, no longer came on as a frail, uncertain woman who depended on men who had the power. Her new clothing spoke for her, saying that she sought no favors now. She dressed in the clothes directors wear in the field, trousers and leather jackets and boots.

I realized I was losing her, but I was also losing interest in her struggle as I became increasingly involved in my own family's story and made frequent trips to Greece and Turkey. I esteemed her as a brave person, and although we were no longer lovers and hadn't been for several years, we remained married. For a time I was content to protect her and reinforce her needs. Then she gave herself to a kind of spiritualism that I didn't understand or have sympathy for. She became devoted to an Indian "master" and his teachings; she believed in an afterlife and in the primacy of "inner space." She meditated regularly, twice a day, totally enclosed in an old cardboard carton in her room. It reminded me of Reich's orgone box—perhaps that's what it was. We didn't talk about it or about much else. She was careless about managing the house, let it fall apart, and I'm an old-fashioned man. She had succeeded completely in making a life independent of me. I decided to go my own way and go without her. I'd suggested this years before, but this time she agreed. I talked to my lawyer; she consulted a lawyer. We agreed it was time to divorce.

Then one day she stood naked before me, took my hand, and put it on her left breast. "Do you feel it?" she asked.

I found a lump there.

It was January of 1978. She died in September 1980, on the fifth. Here is the record of what happened in those thirty-three months.

As soon as she found the lump in her breast she did what a well-trained actress does: She researched it, read books, interviewed friends, particularly one friend, a woman who'd come through it—"at least so far." She consulted physicians, weighed their advice, came to her own conclusions. The record is notable for her desperate wavering from one course to another. What I saw when it was over was that no one, no expert oncologist, no spiritualist, has the vaguest idea of what to do about cancer. We live in the dark.

The first doctor she went to was Myron Buchman. It was an office visit, in the course of which he aspirated what he declared was a cyst in her breast. Still she was increasingly concerned that what she had in her breast was a malignancy, and she was looking for a way to deal with it that didn't call for an operation. Reading books on the subject and a magazine called *East-West*, she decided to become a vegetarian and undertake the macrobiotic diet. She came on the writings of Michio Kushi, a Japanese doctor who'd had some success treating cancerous patients with diet and acupuncture; she went to the Acupuncture Center of Massachusetts and adopted his wheat plant juice diet, which she found distasteful, and the macrobiotic diet of kale, brown rice, no meat. A consultation with Kushi drew this opinion: that her problem was not in her breast but in her liver. He said her liver was "feeble." Ginger presses were to be applied to her liver area.

During this period, she began to see someone named Gretl, a therapist and an acupuncture practitioner in New York. She also saw a doctor whom her friend Edna O'Brien recommended, a Dr. Baker. She was consulting everyone she could. She started sessions with M. Koltuv, Ph.D. I don't know exactly what took place at those sessions, but they went on and on, and my guess was that the treatment was spiritual, not physical.

By accident, she came across a book in a health food store. It made the point that a radical mastectomy was not necessary, that in England a lumpectomy was being successfully performed. This was what she longed to hear. A friend told her that a Dr. Esselstyn at the Cleveland Clinic had been successful with lumpectomies. Now she changed her course, called Dr. Esselstyn, made an appointment to see him; we went to Cleveland. He was a tall, handsome man with the voice doctors cultivate to calm patients. In my presence, he palpated her breast and, without hesitation or further testing, said, "I think we have a bit of mischief here." Then he wanted to

reinforce his finding with tests; Barbara went through them and we returned to New York.

She had an important decision to make. If she went ahead with a lumpectomy, it would mean a radical change of direction from the dietary and
spiritual course of Kushi and whatever other counterphysical advice she
was receiving. Her decision was to place herself in Dr. Esselstyn's hands.
She called him and received the news that of the tests involving the breast,
the liver, and a bone "image," the only place where cancer had been discovered was her left breast. Esselstyn advised her to come back to Cleveland
and have the lump removed from her breast as soon as possible. His tone
was optimistic. She was to remember, later, that the tests showed no sign
of liver involvement.

Certain doctors in New York—I don't know who they were—had advised her to come to them for this operation. Her repeated objection to
"New York doctors," whom she considered to be "a cabal, a clique," was that
before a breast operation they made you sign a paper giving them permission to take off the entire breast as well as any involved muscle if they
thought that was the best way to deal with whatever cancer they found.
Barbara was a raving paranoid about this group—the traditionalists, she
called them, the "establishment."

On September 5, exactly two years before her death, we went to the
Cleveland Clinic, and the "lump" was removed, as well as some nodes
under the arm. Barbara felt well afterward and pleased with her decision.
She had chosen lumpectomy rather than disfigurement. As the result of the
operation, there'd been this discovery: She had cancer not only in her
breast but in her lymph nodes. She told me that the lymph nodes could be
compared to distribution centers for the disease. So the question became
how to forestall its spread. Again she decided to go in two directions at the
same time. What followed seemed to me to be in the realm of fantasy, an
eccentric and, at times, even insane course. Barbara would swing violently
back and forth. I also felt that she was being taken advantage of by a series
of therapists and doctors, who were making her their victim—I don't know
a kinder word to describe what they began to do.

She first of all decided to follow Esselstyn's advice about radiating her
remaining lymph nodes—"just in case," she said. And she would keep a
watchful eye on her breast, which had healed nicely. But, more passionately, she sought help from a different direction.

Three weeks after her lumpectomy, she went with someone named Ser-
ena to the Cathedral of Faith. Her purpose, she said, was to bring about
general spiritual health, the recognition of real—that is, inner—power
and, through it, upward movement. The books she was reading included
The Will to Live, Seeing with the Mind's Eye, and *A Clearing in the Woods.*
I also found in her diary after her death an entry referring to a Reverend

Rinaldo, pages of his advice and wisdom, and quotes such as Luke 12:23: "Life is more than food, the body needs more than clothes."

Having chosen the psychic path, she was deep into the methods of "inner space," relating the cancer to the stresses of her life, including the stresses that she accused me of creating. For a time she blamed her cancer largely on me. Then she spread the field of responsibility, said that she'd always been tense, that her soul had always been sick, that she'd kept her emotions bottled up and they'd poisoned her body. She decided to forestall the metastasis of the cancer on all fronts, but above all through the psyche.

Now she went back to M. Koltuv, Ph.D. He told her her tension came from not releasing her feelings, that for one thing she didn't cry enough. She told me that he was able to touch her in certain places and she would burst into uncontrollable tears. She used to come home after seeing this man with her eyes hollow and dark and her face drained of blood.

At the same time she was going to Beth Israel Hospital in Boston, for radiation therapy under her arm. She rented a room in Boston so she'd have to do less traveling. There were further tests, at the recommendation of another doctor, whose name was Botnick. He advised her—and she agreed—to enter the operating room and have "plastic skewers," six of them, thrust through her breasts. On the following day, these skewers were filled with radioactive material. Barbara joked about it. "Now I'm radioactive," she said. Apparently the results were not completely satisfactory to Dr. Botnick, because he told her that he knew she was against chemotherapy but she should reconsider. "There's a new kind," he said, and recommended a Dr. Samuel Waxman in New York. Her response was: No more conventional medicine until something crops up again.

Every time she returned to New York, she went to Koltuv. Was it because of his influence that she began to have strange psychic experiences? She met a strange black woman on the street who said to her, "You're ugly! You're very ugly!" Her diary goes on: "I told Koltuv about the woman and began to cry. Then we began to work and I cried all the time. I said I wished I was dead. When he pressed my neck, I wanted him to kill me. I felt I might go on crying forever. Such pain in my body. I couldn't get it out. He said, 'Can you look at me?' I couldn't. 'Why?' he said. 'Because you'll see how hopeless I am,' I answered. Afterwards, he said he was going to work with my body, not my head. I rushed home to cook dinner." Another session with Koltuv: "I lay on a bed and cried the whole session while he held my hand. I was frustrated because I had not been able to let out my anger. Sorrow and sadness, on and on. It's always been like this. *I have to get it out.* Once more I couldn't look at him. I'd be asking for help but there is no help. There is no hope. I just wanted to disappear. Sitting up, bowed over and rocking, I cried on and on. Then I went home and fixed supper."

Botnick saw that she was not improving and again urged her to go the traditional chemotherapy route. Barbara would not. She didn't want to put poisons in her body, she said. It was her belief, she told Botnick, that the body and the soul are one, and if you poisoned the body you poisoned the soul.

A few weeks later I had a surprise, a one-hundred-eighty-degree swivel. Barbara asked me to come to a clinic in Floral Park, Long Island, pick her up, and bring her home, in case she wasn't able to make it on her own. The name of the establishment was The Oncological Associates, and it had gained some fame—or notoriety—because of a controversial treatment. My surprise came from this being another kind of chemotherapy, stronger, more potent, more "chemical," a treatment I'd have expected Barbara to call poisonous and reject. She told me what the injections she would receive contained: laetrile, enzymes, several vitamins, and a penetrating agent, which left the patient with a persisting foul odor. Barbara was to smell bad for weeks. It was further recommended to each patient that he or she take enemas of strong black coffee daily. Barbara did and said she found them energizing.

I didn't understand her. It all sounded like doctors' "mischief" to me. When I protested that she was admitting poisons into her system, the very thing she'd been most against, she told me that there was an intravenous "drip" given afterward, which contained counteragents to gentle the poisons. With all this, a nutritionist who worked out of the place was preparing still another dietary program for her. I made no further comment. I was frightened, but I knew there was no stopping Barbara now.

I took the Long Island Rail Road to Floral Park at the appointed hour, walked three blocks, and entered the establishment. There wasn't the usual entrance security, only a secretary in a side office—beyond which I saw a large waiting room full of sickly old people apparently waiting for their appointments. My first impression was of a smell—heavy, penetrating, and sickening, part medicinal, part the odor of human putrefaction. They were dying and they knew it. Unless—unless there was a medical miracle.

Then Barbara came prancing through the crowd. She'd been concerned that she might require help, even some support, to get home, but she looked way up on top. Perhaps it was the contrast with the others in the waiting room or her determination not to slide down into the slough where the dying waited. I saw the spark of hope in her eyes; they were bright, near feverish, and what made them gleam was: Perhaps this is it! Perhaps I'll find it at last! Perhaps this will do it for me!

She asked me if I'd like to meet the man who ran the place; he'd asked to see me. I said, Lead the way. As we walked, she told me that miracles had been performed there. I didn't remark that I'd seen no evidence of miracles among the people in the waiting room. It all seemed to me to be another ill-advised and out-of-control gamble on her part. Now a new "savior" had her. Where did she find them? Or they her? She was making me furious. I didn't know how much longer I could take it. Or the bills. Then I saw the bounce in her step and, when she turned to speak to me, the desperate gleam of hope in her eyes. I knew that if it was shit, I'd have to eat it. I didn't have a choice. Besides, no one had found a cure for cancer. It was still all guesswork. Perhaps this *was* it.

The head of the place, Donald Cole, was waiting for us in his office; he looked like a road company musical comedy leading man, a tall fellow with an engaging manner, and the reason he did was because that is what he was—or had been: a singing actor. Cole, Barbara told me, was a stage name. He greeted me with more than professional warmth and even some deference. He knew all about me and admired me, as many people do until they meet me, reacting at first to my media reputation. He'd given up our profession and found this outlet for his enterprise, talent, and cunning. To judge from the crowd in his waiting room and the size of the bills I was to receive, he was doing well. We had the usual long chat about show business ("It's not what it used to be!"), which he missed, but he was doing so much better now that he couldn't complain. He smiled fondly at Barbara and assured me that his "wonder drug" treatment would help her as it had hundreds of others. I noticed that Barbara thought I should be more cordial to her savior, and I did my best.

"Where did he learn all that chemical science?" I asked her on the way home. "Certainly not on Forty-fifth Street between Broadway and Eighth Avenue." She said, "Maybe it's from his partner"—a woman named Pung, Juanita Pung. As we rode the bumps of the Long Island Rail Road, she informed me that she'd committed herself to commuting for treatment to Cole and Pung six days a week for six weeks. I said, "Fine." I didn't know what to do.

Then she made another swivel, one hundred and eighty degrees in the opposite direction. She attended a Macrobiotic Conference in Amherst, Massachusetts, the "star" of which was Michio Kushi. She was able to pull a private talk with the big man, a consultation that made a strong impression on her. Devoutly she quoted Kushi in her diary: "Why did you come to this earth? Because you wanted to come. When you wanted to come, you changed and arrived as a human baby. But our life doesn't begin with mother's egg and father's sperm. That's biological life. Our roots are in heaven like a puppet with strings connected." This was comforting to her. I swallowed what I thought. At any rate, she was moving away from the singing chemist and his partner, Pung, because she wrote: "I am now totally committed to macrobiotics." Kushi had been impressed with Barbara and was having a new diet prepared for her. He said again that her problem was her liver.

But this single-minded devotion did not endure. She returned to the Reverend Rinaldo, who said to her, "You have prospects for a complete recovery. You are full of healthy vibrations." Naturally she thought the man wise. At the same time, she was going to a psychotherapist for psychological testing several times a week. And M. Koltuv, Ph.D., continued to help her release her pent-up emotions in a flood of tears as he held her hand. She also saw a psychiatrist whose name was Louis Ross, but apparently she wasn't sure he was "the right way," because the desperation dance continued. Who was Dr. Charles Slavetu with an office in Glen Cove, and what treatment did he administer? Who was Dr. George Krikelian—yes, an Armenian, but what did he do? She made a note of his comment: "Response rate 25%, Terminal temporary remission." Terminal temporary—what the hell does that mean? Who was Dr. Miles Galen? I was never to find out. Apparently he'd performed a cataract operation. Dr. Basek? An ear doctor. Did she have a problem with her ear? I hadn't noticed. Why did she go to Dr. Carnival, chiropractor to George Balanchine? And to Dr. Sam Getlen of Trenton? When did she go to Trenton? Who was Dr. Shisuko? And Dr. Revici of the Institute of Applied Biology? What did he find? No word on that.

It was like a novel by Gogol. She was trying everything and anything, floundering on a desperate course, with these experts leading her on. And oh, the setbacks and the disappointments! If I asked questions or sought information, she thought I was criticizing her and resented it. "I know you don't believe in anything," she'd say, and walk away. But I wasn't critical of her. What I wanted was to kill those doctors. I thought the bastards were holding out promises of progress and cure, keeping her patronage and my money, but—but then I asked myself, What *was* the solution? What should she do? What would I—or anyone "sensible"—be doing in her place? What she had was life-threatening and progressing, and it was her body, not mine. She was trying to stop the disease that was eating her, stop it before it got to her vitals. Who has the right to be critical while watching a life-and-death struggle?

At the same time she was keeping up her professional life. She conducted an acting class twice a week and was beloved by her pupils. She coached Chris Reeve for his part in *Superman*, something I wouldn't have known how to do. Barbara thought she was overpaid at fifty dollars a session. She was working with a dramatist on his play, *Come Back to the 5 and Dime, Jimmy Dean, Jimmy Dean*. That was its name. I thought it a piece of mid-South pizza with a little of everything in it. When she sensed what I didn't dare say, that my reaction was negative, she became defensive and worked harder on it. She was going to direct it, she said—in a voice that challenged my doubt.

Then, in July of 1979, it became evident that the cancer had metastasized to her liver and perhaps elsewhere. You could see that it had; she'd begun to stoop, and the área of her body where the liver is located was enlarged. She walked with difficulty and seemed to be deteriorating rapidly. This was a disaster for her. It meant that the macrobiotic diet, the psychotherapy, the radiotherapy, the wonder drug laetrile, everything she'd done in Floral Park, Long Island, and Amherst, Massachusetts, in Boston and New York, had not worked. But you couldn't blame the doctors for not having a cure. No one had a cure. You could only regret that they'd given her false hopes. Or *were* false hopes worse than none? She'd been prepared for this, read many books, listened to every kind of expert, and the threat of metastasis had been constantly on her mind. Now it had happened.

She wanted to know the facts. We decided to go back to the Cleveland Clinic and see Dr. Esselstyn, who'd done the lumpectomy, to get his opinion. Barbara had gone to her other "healers" with an adventurous spirit and some optimism, perhaps only because she was guiding her own course as well as being flattered by close attention, but she had no choice now but to trust herself completely to someone else's judgment, a concession that was anathema to her. In Dr. Esselstyn's office she looked like a girl who'd been summoned before her high school principal to face a discipline charge and was ready to pay whatever penalty he'd ask. Esselstyn, a tall, spare man, had the most confidence-evoking manner I've seen in a doctor and the softest hands to palpate his lady patients. He touched Barbara in a few places, smiling at her, a sympathetic god, but he didn't have to do much before ordering a program of tests that would take up every hour of the next three days: a liver scan, chest X-rays, an X-ray of the thoracic region, a bone scan of the entire body, an EKG to check the functioning of her heart, a bone marrow biopsy, a CAT scan, a brain scan; they covered every area where he suspected there might be "involvement." Through test after test, I trailed after her, sitting by the door so I'd be there waiting when she came out. The activity comforted her; she was being a "good girl," doing what she'd been told. We went to a movie after the first day of it, but she didn't have the energy even for that, so we left and returned to the motel and had dinner in our room.

When we went back for the results, I read the news on the kindly face of the plump nurse who attended Esselstyn's examination room. Esselstyn was waiting for us and was very kind. He drew a sketch of the liver, then made it her liver by drawing crosses all over the larger lobe. They marked involvement. He said that lobe was "gone." The smaller lobe had involvement too—he drew a few x's there—but there was enough left, he said, for her to go on. He didn't say for how long. He added that there was some involvement in the bone marrow, but he thought it could be treated. How? Up until this time he'd indicated that he didn't favor chemotherapy; now he urged it. The liver, he said, cannot be operated on; chemo was the only course available. I looked at Barbara. No reaction, her face masked as ever, guarded. Later she told me she'd been remembering that Kushi had told her the first time they'd met that her problem was the liver, not her breast.

"The liver is the seat of the violent passions," he'd said. "They're stored there." Barbara had agreed. "Yes," she said to me, "all my anger is stored there."

She gave up her fight against chemotherapy and the introduction of its poisons into her bloodstream. "Do whatever you want to me," she said to Dr. Esselstyn. Then she said, "How long do I have?" asking it plainly, a point of information. Esselstyn did what would have been acceptable for most women in Cleveland. He took her husband aside and asked me if he should tell her the truth. Before I could answer, Barbara, who'd been studying his drawing of her liver, said, "Tell me exactly, please." Esselstyn walked to her and spoke as though she were going to relay what he said to another patient, not as if she was the patient. "Two to three years," he said. I saw no reaction. She made no comment. "I believe," he went on, "we should start the treatment here immediately, this afternoon. I'll arrange for it. Then you can continue in New York. Dr. Waxman—you mentioned him. He's a good man."

Waxman was a doctor Barbara had seen a year before. He'd urged her then to take chemotherapy from him, and she'd refused, saying, "What poisons the body poisons the soul." Now she said to Esselstyn, "Whatever you think best." She didn't seem frightened or anxious. She'd accepted her powerlessness and apparently her death. She didn't beg for falsehoods. An hour later, a doctor on Esselstyn's staff gave her the first chemo injection. I found a chance to take him aside and ask the same question: How long did she have? "In four weeks," he said, "she'll be either cured or dead. It's the liver, you know."

We packed her bags and I told her I loved her, but I didn't embrace her, even as a friend. She didn't respond. We'd been estranged for years, unfaithful, unrelating. Up until now I'd been thinking of her behavior in the face of the disease as erratic and irrational. Now I thought of what she'd been doing as an evidence of courage. I was filled with admiration. Though I did not believe that anyone, anywhere, knew what to do about cancer, had seen that even in this clinic, considered the best in the field, one doctor had said two or three years and recommended what he'd previously rejected, and another, who'd stuck in the first needle, said four weeks—maybe; maybe not—what else could Barbara reasonably have done except study what knowledge there was, consider all possibilities, and come to her own conclusions? I began to feel love for her again, not as a wife—that was long gone—but as a person I esteemed and for whom I would do, as I did do from that day on, anything in every way I could.

On the train ride east, this woman who'd read every book available about her problem for so many months spent the time looking out the window as long as there was light, then sat back and closed her eyes. She seemed at ease and, in the quiet, rather smaller. We didn't speak.

The next day we met with Dr. Samuel Waxman, a neat, decent man. His waiting room was full of terminal patients, many of them with a characteristic stale odor. But Barbara, now on display again, was spirited and bright, youth and hope among the dying. That was the irony: Once she'd accepted that she was going to die, she felt relieved, and the best of her spirit revived. I knew that if courage could beat it, hers would.

Waxman put her on a regular schedule of chemotherapy, and in a few weeks he said to me that he'd never seen anyone respond to the treatment better than Barbara. Where her body had bulged over her sick liver, it now relaxed and returned to its original shape. Waxman's outlook was optimistic, almost cheerful. He said to Barbara, "I believe I'm going to be able to help you." To me he said, "I only wish she'd come here sooner." He didn't use the word "cure"—no oncologist does—only "remission." Waxman admired her too.

Soon her hair began to fall out in great combfuls, as she'd been warned it would. Remember, this was an actress, and she hadn't given that up. We went shopping for wigs on Fifty-seventh Street. She had one from her role in *After the Fall,* but it seemed too theatric. She was looking for something the same color as her own blond hair. In the next weeks, we bought five, some completely satisfactory. She kept trying them on and asking me how I liked each one and I said, "Good," but she'd look at me impatiently. "You don't care how I look," she said. In the end she wore the "Marilyn Monroe" one when she went out at night. She didn't want to lose what she'd worked so hard to gain. To wear around the house, she knit herself a skullcap.

On the seventh of September, Barbara, in high spirits, gave me a birthday party. Her energy was not normal, but she could still rise to an occasion, and she did. No one guessed that she was sick—I assured her of this when she asked me later. Whoever was in New York that I'd worked with in the theater or in films was there. The house was jammed; there weren't enough places to sit down. The food was rich and plentiful, and strong drink was being poured. Barbara moved everywhere among the guests, that evening's leading lady. Bob Anderson was there and told me later that he didn't notice she had a wig on. Harold Clurman, who was also to die of cancer within a year, was clowning all over the place in his own style, and Paddy Chayevsky, another man I loved, who'd been consulting me about a play he was writing on the Hiss case, sat with his special friend, Bob Fosse. Paddy was to die within a year too, but they were all jolly that night, with Barbara watching over them. Everyone admired her and flattered her; it was just what she needed. I whispered in her ear that she was never going to die.

On the eighteenth, we went to the White House at the invitation of Jimmy Carter, and Barbara looked beautiful and moved as gracefully as ever; not a sign of distress. I forgot about the wig. She flirted demurely with Jimmy, flashed her eyes at him, told him she was from the South, too,

and admired him more than any other President. He called for a photographer, and a picture was taken of us together—Rosalynn too—along with Archbishop Iakovas of the Greek Orthodox Church to sanctify the occasion.

By now her own hair was thin and scraggly, like the hair of a newborn babe, and she decided to shave it all off; she'd look better that way, and it was braver and more dramatic. Should she give up hope that it would ever come back? She knew it would not as long as she continued on the chemicals. So once again she began to look for an alternate treatment; even if the chemo was holding ground for her, keeping the cancer back, she believed there must be something better. She came upon a book describing what the Simontons were doing in Texas to treat terminal cancer cases with spiritual therapy. It was what she'd been looking for. She asked if we could go there and take part in it. I said of course, I'd go with her. But the Simontons were full up and wouldn't have an opening for almost a year. They recommended a Dr. John McBride, who had a camp for terminal cancer patients in Payson, Arizona. Barbara called there and we were immediately accepted. Yes, her husband could accompany her; it would be preferable.

She was delighted; it was what she believed in and it would also be a kind of adventure. The first thing she did was buy "western" clothes, and when she tried them on for me to approve, she showed me that her belly was down; she had to give Waxman and his injections credit for that, but it was somewhat grudging. Still there it was: Putting the poisons in her bloodstream had made some sort of normal life possible for her. We had two excellent weeks at the McBride camp. She was the prettiest girl there, and that was the most important thing. The therapy of the camp was simple; it consisted of identity and worth support, meditation, and psychological preparation for death—although that was not stated so plainly. The program was not a cure; it had to do with accepting death as a normal thing. McBride believed in the afterlife and in the primacy of the spirit, so he and Barbara got along. By the end of those two weeks under the sun, she looked brown and wonderful and had good energy, especially in the daytime when she was with the others. She was a clown around the long dinner table, teasing and laughing, but she'd droop when we were alone at night; she didn't have to pretend with me. We made many friendships among the terminal cases, but such friendships don't endure.

She felt that McBride's program, which consisted of fortifying the ego, easing tensions, and bolstering the body's own immune system, was close to the solution she'd been looking for. She wanted to return for more, but it didn't happen that we could. She came back to New York altered. The experience in Arizona had proved to her that disease could be treated through the energies of the spirit, by giving the body's powers a chance. Even when we heard, a week later, that the man who'd been quartered next to us had died, it proved nothing to Barbara. He'd come to the right way too late, she said. She was going to do only life-supporting things from now on. She was going to hold off death by living life. She began to look once again for alternatives to chemotherapy. I noticed that she didn't tell Dr. Waxman what she'd been searching for or where we'd been.

I did. I thought he should know.

At the same time, she was putting her house in order—just in case. The first thing she did was take Leo aside and tell him calmly about the cancer and that she might die soon. Leo took it in—and just as she would have, showed no reaction.

As a result of what happened at McBride's, she pushed ahead as if her life were going to go on undiminished, without a terminal date. She wanted to do over the house we lived in on West Sixty-eighth Street and took me to a home nearby that had been remodeled according to the designs of a Japanese architect. She wanted to engage this man to plan remodeling for our disordered brownstone. Would I pay for him to make plans? I said I would. He was a retiring little fellow, but his plans were bold, consisting of gutting what we had and building a new home within the shell. Their realization would cost, by his own estimate, about $600,000. This was a relief, because I was able to tell Barbara that the plans were handsome but they'd have to wait until I had another big book—I hadn't had one after *The Arrangement*. She rolled up the plans and kept them, waiting for the day.

In the spirit of moving ahead full steam, and as if she were going to live as long as anyone else, she proceeded with her plan to direct the play about the group of girls obsessed with the memory of Jimmy Dean. The Hudson Guild, an off-Broadway group, would produce the play with her. Anxious to do a fine job—it was her material!—she felt she'd benefit by a trip to the territory where the action of the play took place, there make a lot of notes and take photographs. Would I go with her? We caught a plane to El Paso—where she satisfied a long-held desire to buy a pair of cowboy boots from Tony Lama; they were in vogue that year—rented a car, and drove here and there in the backcountry. I took pictures of anything she pointed to—locations, objects, people, clothes. We had a marvelous time, she in high spirits all the way through, and she began to call me what she used to long ago—"Dad," spoken affectionately. Suddenly, for the first time in years, there was no tension between us.

Back in New York, she found that the money was up for the show, and she could begin casting. Before she got altogether involved, she wanted to visit her aunts and her mother and, in another state, her father. These might be final visits, but we didn't take them that way; we had a party together, especially with her father, whom I liked and who liked me. After a heavy meal of ham, black-eyed peas, and sweet potatoes, we relaxed with his pistols, shooting at targets in the backyard. When I saw what Barbara had come out of, that backcountry culture, I appreciated what it had cost her to get out on her own. She'd been on uncertain terms with both parents, so she was patching up old alienation. We also went to a reunion of her high school class, where she was the girl everyone wanted to dance with and the only one, so she boasted, who'd kept her figure. She introduced me to an old boyfriend, a great big guy, much younger than I, then went off dancing with him. She was radiating happiness because everyone was telling her how beautiful she looked—no one suspected the wig—and they all believed her to be a movie star, since they'd seen her photograph in the local paper, properly identified with credits, and with me, the escort-husband, at her side.

Waiting for rehearsals, she resumed her acting classes, and it was easy for her to gather all her old pupils again. The class members not only idolized her but were devoted to her methods. Many of them took notes, and after Barbara died, I was presented with a copy, a record of everything she'd said and done. The class continued until the end of June, and I went to pick her up after the last one. She'd had a very successful session, it seemed, and the actors expressed their appreciation by applauding her—I could hear it outside the building where I was waiting. They all came out together, a jolly crowd, she surrounded and embraced, again and again, in gratitude. I believe that many of them now knew she had cancer and that this might be the last time they'd see her. I can still see her face, flushed pink, and her eyes, wild with joy, dazzling, and her wig, a little askew but still on.

In the fall the rehearsals of the Jimmy Dean play began. Barbara had a cast she liked with a single exception: a "name" actress she'd picked blind. There are often difficulties when a new director guides a new cast, but Barbara's, with this person, exceeded the ordinary. The woman mumbled to herself so that no one could hear what she said or understand what she was up to, even those with whom she was playing a scene. Barbara spoke a plain theatre language, but nothing she said got through. I watched one rehearsal, and my impression was that the actress preferred not to be directed. So when Barbara asked what she should do, I said, "Fire the bitch!"

Which Barbara did at the end of the first week. Then she had to quickly find a replacement. She wasn't able to, not anyone she wanted in the role. So when her producer, who still didn't know she had cancer, urged her to take over the part herself while he directed, she agreed. I don't know what kept her going. Backcountry grit. She gave a glowing performance, incandescent with the delight she was feeling because she was still able to work. There was a tender sisterhood among the actresses now; they all loved being with Barbara. The play got a cold reception from the critics, but I went night after night in time to see the final moments, when Barbara and two other girls "put over" a song. I thought she was adorable and understood why I'd stayed by her through all those dry years. Then I took her home through the cold January midnight and had to help her into the house and support her up the stairs.

After the play closed, she was exhausted, but not so exhausted that she didn't respond to the offer of a German TV group that wanted to make a documentary about her. *Wanda*, already forgotten in the United States, was much admired in Europe. She prepared a thorough and careful presentation of herself, knowing that it was her last chance to make a record of her life. She even went back to work at the barre with her ballet teacher, Maestro Celli. He held her hand as she did her pliés. Barbara wanted to demonstrate the kind of training she believed all actors should have. The film turned out to be an excellent summation of her life but more vividly a tribute, made unconsciously, to her character.

When the German TV crew flew home, leaving behind memories of devotion, she gave up. She was out of gas, and the tank was not refilling. She'd sleep hour after hour during the day, and I'd watch the black thing stealing closer. Ironically, it was the first time in her life that she had an unassailable sense of her own worth. She'd struggled for that and she'd gained it. Despite the disease, she'd lived those last months as she wished. The disease had destroyed only her body. She deserved the miracle she didn't get.

Toward the end of July, I went with her to Dr. Waxman's office, where she'd been getting her chemotherapy shots. Waxman didn't need a prolonged examination to see that she was weakening fast. While she dressed, he took me aside and asked, "Shall I tell her?" He wanted her to enter the hospital immediately; there she'd have continuous care. She came out of the examination room looking sprightly; she always did when people were watching. Waxman told her what he wanted her to do. "Tests," he said. It was a blow; her face froze. She asked, could she delay entering until she'd done certain things she wanted to do about the house?

Back home, exhausted, she rested on the bed with her two dogs. I begged her not to move for the rest of the day. She decided the dogs must have baths before she left home, so she bathed them both. Again I insisted she not move any more that day, then went to get her a warming drink. When I returned, twenty minutes later, I found the crazy woman on top of a table, putting up the new roller shade she'd bought a few days before.

Then she did give out. I watched over her as she slept. She had to go to the bathroom several times during the night, and, afraid she might keel over, I went with her. That was it, the end of her strength. She was glad to get into hospital care. I had a cot placed across from her bed so I could sleep close by. I was her day and night nurse.

This was the first of three stays in the hospital. The rest did her good. She felt a little strength coming back and urged Dr. Waxman to allow her to go home. He agreed, and we did go home, but on the very next day she was willing to go back into the hospital. This time we were there almost two weeks.

Toward the end of this stay, there was a painful scene. Barbara said, with an urgency that surprised me, that she had to speak to Dr. Waxman right away. When I got him to her bed, she told him that she didn't want to take any more chemicals into her body. They hadn't benefited her, she said; in fact, she wished she'd never taken any. In what she said there was an accusation: His treatment had failed. That was the truth, she said, and now she wanted the truth from him. It had failed, hadn't it? Dr. Waxman, since she'd asked for the truth, as she always had, said, "I can't help you anymore."

It is a devastating thing for a doctor to watch a patient under his care die. Perhaps Dr. Waxman shouldn't have said what he did. The accusation— that's what it certainly was—had come from a woman hysterical from ex- haustion and fear, regret and danger. But there was the apprehension, which must live in the minds and feelings of all oncologists, that they still don't know how to deal with cancer, and the treatment they rely on and "push" all too often does not work. In that sense, the stain of death, when it comes, is on their hands. I don't know how doctors survive that. Dr. Waxman, an unfailingly kind man, must have regretted cutting Barbara loose as he did. But again and again she'd demanded the truth and nothing less. From that instant on, he was continuously solicitous with her, but I also thought him depressed and guilty. It had to have hurt him terribly, that year of unsuccessful chemotherapy—the treatment Esselstyn in Cleveland had regarded as Waxman's specialty. "She started too late with me," he said to me and said it again, holding his ground. But I didn't go for that.

Again she pleaded to go home. But this time the context of what she asked was that she wanted to die at home. He couldn't refuse this request. We were home four days this time. She kept fussing with her papers and the scripts she'd written with Nick Proferes, moving them around her study. This activity seemed aimless to me, but I'd find out later that it wasn't.

It was during these days that I began to notice something happening that frightened me more than anything before. I looked up the word "seizure" in my *Merck Manual*. "A recurrent paroxysmal disorder of cerebral function characterized by sudden brief attacks of altered consciousness, motor activ- ity, sensory phenomenon or inappropriate behavior."

The cancer had reached her brain.

These attacks were minor at first, then increasingly violent. When she came "out" of them, she begged me not to inform Dr. Waxman, because she was afraid he'd put her back into the hospital. But then she had an attack that was so grotesque it reminded me of a scene in *The Exorcist*. I was frightened because she didn't seem to come out of this one whole. I called Waxman. It was a hot Sunday afternoon, and he was in the country, but he immediately drove in and, after one look, urged her to let him put her back under professional care. She was too weak to argue. Many weeks before, we'd both been invited to the Deauville Film Festival; *Wanda* would be shown there. Our departure from New York's Kennedy was to be on September 5; our plane space was booked. Barbara had insisted she could make it, and still did after the seizures. We arranged for a wheelchair and a nurse to meet the plane. A room with a balcony in the sun was reserved. Friends were informed of our arrival time.

What meant the most to Barbara during those last days in the hospital was a visit from our son, Leo. He came in, looking intent, asked me to leave the room, and closed the door. Twenty minutes later, he left without saying a word. Nor did she tell me what had taken place between them, but I could see that whatever he'd found to say had given her comfort. I was proud of him.

At the Cleveland Clinic, Dr. Esselstyn had told her that she had two, perhaps three years to live. She died a year and three months from the day when I admired her for demanding the truth from him. Once she'd accepted the inevitability of what was coming, she'd done everything she wanted to do and done it as if she were still in good health, carried on right up until the last six weeks. I learned from her something of how to die well, which is by living to the very end as if one weren't going to die.

She told a friend who came to visit near the end that the last year of her life had been her best. Maybe it was. There was no love between us, as that word is understood in reference to husband and wife. But from me there was admiration and devotion, and from her, hard-won trust. Those are exceptional qualities and perhaps more important than "love." We were friends. That's a good word too.

Her heart stopped on the fifth of September, the day we were booked to fly to Paris—Deauville. Her death was announced from the stage at the Festival.

A S   B A R B A R A   lay dying on the seventh floor of the Klingenstein Pavilion, Harold Clurman lay two floors below, stricken with cancer of the pancreas and carrying a malignant tumor in his liver. Harold would outlive Barbara by only three days. Despite our conflicts over the years, some bitter, he and Barbara were the people closest to me. From the day I came to the Group Theatre as an apprentice, Harold had been my mentor, the man from whom I'd learned the most; he changed my life. I've had other close friends who've died; the one I miss most is Harold.

I would hurry two flights down the back stairs to see him when Barbara fell asleep. There was such a contrast between the two rooms! During the last five weeks of her life, I and her collaborator, Nick Proferes, were the only people Barbara allowed to enter her sickroom and know her condition. The news of her death surprised even her family. Harold always had visitors come to share what they'd been told might be his last days. He lay there like a dying god attended by his worshippers, or like a babe whose mother had tucked him in, then lingered, whispering loving thoughts, stroking his head (as all the girls there did and I did), staying close by until he was asleep.

But while Barbara knew precisely where the tumors killing her were growing, Harold had been told that what he had was hepatitis and that it would pass. His doctor hadn't trusted him with the facts. How he'd explained to Harold why he was paralyzed from the waist down, I can't imagine. Nor can I imagine how Harold believed it—if he had—as long as he did. There'd been a lively and sometimes acrimonious debate among the people closest to him about whether or not to tell him what he was suffering from. His companion of the time was certain that he should be told, so that he could "come to terms with his life." But she was in the minority. Most of his friends felt that the one fact Harold could not come to terms with was the fact that he would soon be dead.

They were wrong. Harold was prepared for what was coming. Even though he'd held certain hopes that were unfulfilled, he was not embittered or reengaged in lost battles. On the contrary, his was the happiest death I've witnessed.

How had this happened? How had he come to this ease of mind?

Gathered around him, sometimes four or five at a time, were the stalwarts of the army he'd once led. Aides-de-camp were two majestic black nurses, the strongest people in the room, whose duty it was to roll him from one side to the other every twenty minutes and to make sure he took his antibiotics—he'd also contracted pneumonia. Harold would overcome the pneumonia; it was the least of his problems, although the strain of fighting it left him weaker. But even then, with breath that gurgled, he didn't seem angry at his fate, as Barbara did. Was this because he'd had such success as a director of plays and even greater respect as a dramatic critic? Perhaps. But more likely it was because he was dying as he'd have chosen, surrounded by comrades in art who still looked up to him as their leader and who, each one, remembered something Harold had said or done that was significant for him or her. Harold enjoyed the devoted assembly around his bed. It was like a continuous cast reunion, morning, noon, and evenings, of everyone he'd worked with. He was doing what he'd always done, gathering an artistic family around him, a "group." Fond old stories were retold, memories revived, personal gossip relished, anecdotes plumbed for meaning. And always jokes, at which everyone would laugh—Harold too. It was a kind of party.

When I entered his room, he was overjoyed to see me; he'd been waiting for me. I sat at the side of his bed and he took my hand. His grip was soft but warm, and he held me close for a long time, looking into my face as if he was printing my image on his memory. At each of my visits, he asked me, "How's Barbara?" "She's fine," I would lie, guessing that he didn't know she was two floors above. He'd become especially fond of Barbara, had inscribed a book for her, "For darling Barbara, with passionate thoughts." I believe what he wanted to know was why she hadn't come to see him. Harold wanted everyone he liked to come close to him now.

Just as the other visitors had recollections from years gone by that were important for them, so had I. We'd come through a great deal together— and survived as friends. The thirties were a time for prophets, and Harold was ours. He came out of the wilderness of the Lower East Side to change his world, that of the theatre. Speaking with a fervor just short of hysteria to young actors hungry for an artistic faith, he brought them together into a Group Theatre and gave them the possibility of a life in art worth living. He made the Group a cause, and it became, for eight long years, *my* cause. I'd left the Yale Drama School a boy without direction, who'd learned there how to build a set and paint it, hang lights and focus them, but little more. I'd learned to work with my hands and my back. To the extent that I be- came an artist, I had Harold to thank first. He did the same for many other young theatre people.

What he preached to us had the force and the absoluteness of a revolu- tionary pronouncement: We would destroy the old theatre, we would re- build our own. Once accepted, this dogma, like a conspiratorial oath written in blood, allowed no backing off. It seemed that the core effort of his life was to gather people around him and hold them there. When an actor left the Group to go where he could make more money—i.e., Holly- wood—his act was regarded as a mortal sin not only by other members but also by himself. The actor felt guilty. But Harold still thought of the de- parted as a Group member, who'd temporarily wandered in the wrong di- rection and whom Harold would in time bring back to the right path. He pursued them, didn't write them off; sinners can be redeemed.

A childless man, Harold had married twice but, it seemed to this bour- geois, irregularly. I've always thought of him as more feminine than mas- culine. This is not a sexual implication—women were his pleasure—but in his soul I thought him a "mother," who lived through participating in the lives of his sons and daughters, the people he'd found, supported with his advice, fortified with his praise, educated with his analyses, and inspired by his passion. Not having a family, he built a family of believers, those he'd enlisted in the service of the cause that was his cause. Their achievements were his pride, their failures his concern. He had a larger-than-life family.

During the hours when I paid him visits, I sat around his bed with a number of devoted actresses and actors with whom we'd both worked. They all came in homage. I saw young directors there and playwrights who, Harold was certain, had a future. He kept wondering why Lee Strasberg had not come by, had not even called. Whatever Harold thought of Lee at the end ("corrupted"), they had once been as close as people can get and shared what may have been the best of their lives. "Surely he knows I'm sick," Harold said to me. "Everyone knows."

Harold yearned to see his first wife, Stella Adler, and sent for her to come east from Beverly Hills. He's phoned earlier to inform Stella that he was paralyzed from the waist down and couldn't walk; her immediate response had been "Can you still write?" When he heard that she'd arrived in the city and was on her way to the hospital, he had one of the nurses shave his haggard face, comb his thin, limp hair, and dress him in a fresh hospital robe. Stella entered, bearing flowers. Very soon they were in a heated discussion on Henrik Ibsen, about whose work Harold had written a book. Stella, having read it, held some conflicting views and stated them flamboyantly. This stimulated Harold and revived the last of his energy. He was delighted and grateful for her visit. When she left, Stella complained to a friend that Harold was not looking people in the eye when he spoke to them and that he'd make a better impression if he did. It was a comment an acting teacher might offer. At the same time Harold was saying to a visitor who'd observed the encounter, "Isn't she beautiful? Yes, yes, as beautiful as ever!" Later that day he was to assure Bob Whitehead that despite his paralysis, he would direct again. "I'll do it on crutches," he said. But this confidence didn't last.

Harold also sent for Juleen Compton, his estranged second wife. He boasted that she was coming all the way from California because of her feeling for him. It would become evident that she had a supplementary motive. Finding his will, she discovered that he proposed to divide his modest wealth equally among Stella, Juleen, and his stepdaughter, Ellen. This outraged Juleen, which is understandable since she had no reason not to believe that she was the sole, legal, and enduring wife and, as such, entitled to the largest cut. Harold claimed they'd been divorced but didn't have a scrap of paper to prove it. He'd either been too lazy or too indifferent to do anything legally valid about a decree. Juleen confronted the dying man in his bed. Friends waiting in the hall report overhearing a dispute in full voice. In time the issue was settled more favorably to Juleen. It was said that this episode caused the only depression in Harold's spirits during his final days, but I prefer to believe that having always had "trouble with his women" (as close friends put it), Harold found a perverse pleasure in the contest he'd stirred up. It reminded him, I would guess, of his earlier, livelier days, and when it was over, he boasted again of how Juleen had come all the way from California just to be at his bedside.

He also boasted of the telegrams he'd received wishing him well, and in particular of one letter from Oliver Smith, the designer, which he quoted to me twice. "You are the only genius I have ever known," Oliver had written.

It is difficult to imagine an autobiography he might have written, since his total concern in life seemed to have been for other people of talent. He wrote one book that he subtitled "Instead of an Autobiography"; it was not about himself but a memoir—that is, a book about those he'd admired for one reason or another, and in which he told why he favored them. All the artists whose work he'd observed and enjoyed were his family. In the theatre, this "family" extended from Tel Aviv to Tokyo. Harold learned how to convey his directorial message to people who didn't speak English and gain their admiration for his brilliance.

I believe that what he disliked most—dreaded!—was separation. What his life in the theatre meant to him was the opposite: communality. He died in a group.

What was the cause for which he fought? I've read all that he wrote—he was the seminal dramatic critic of our time—but his purpose might be expressed in a briefer and simpler way than he ever did. He believed that the theatre should illuminate people's lives so they would be more decent, more aware, more understanding, and more loving. He thought of life as a quest. In a famous quote, he said, "I believe men and women may not be perfectible, but they must act as if they were." He believed in what I believe in: effort, the effort to be worthy of human possibilities.

All this was his good side. He was at times as vain and selfish as the rest of us—but by comparison with his virtues, his faults were as nothing.

The last time I saw him, when it was time for me to leave his room—to check on Barbara again—I freed my hand from his and passed his to an actress sitting close by. Harold gave me a gentle smile, but he didn't speak. He always felt sad when anyone left the room. Did he believe he might not see that person again? In the last two or three weeks, Harold must have guessed what he had, known that he was going to die, and determined to accept the inevitable. He used to say in days gone by that the mark of a man's maturity was how he dealt with his death. He dealt with his as he must have wished.

When he died, so I've been told (I was not at his bedside but across the river in Jersey, where I'd taken Barbara's body to be cremated), Harold went down without a protest, like a survivor of a shipwreck who'd been clinging to a raft on a sea once turbulent, now calm; weakened by the long struggle, his strength depleted, he finds he cannot hold on longer, in fact doesn't want to, for the dark sea is quiet now and even inviting, so he lets

go his grasp and slips into the deep. I didn't see him unhappy, not once during those last days. While Barbara had gone down screaming her rage at what had cut her life short, I felt that Harold was ready, even willing to go.

I admired them both. Equally. I learned something from each of them.

A great debate raged: Should Harold be cremated or buried? His up-to-date cousin Richard urged that he be cremated, but the old-fashioned side won and Harold was buried close by the Adler cemetery plot in Brooklyn. On the way to the gravesite, the funeral procession of no more than fifteen people, so I've been told, had to pass the grave of the great Jacob P. Adler, the head of the Adler clan and the greatest Yiddish theatre star. Marking this grave was a monument on top of which a magnificent stone eagle (in Yiddish: *adler*) had been mounted and at the foot, a skull (*Hamlet* was one of Adler's famous performances). Once Harold's coffin had been lowered into its grave and the mourners had turned to leave, Stella broke off from the others and fell on her knees before her father's stone, embraced it, and began to weep. This took some time; the procession waited. Onlookers described Stella's grief as the climax of the day's devotion. Enslaved to Stella as he had been all his life, Harold would have understood. And perhaps he'd have smiled.

. . .

A   F E W   days after the cremation, I went back to New Jersey to pick up the container holding Barbara's ashes. I didn't know where to put it, walked through the empty house, trying to decide. Leo had gone back to school, so the place would be deserted except during the day, when my secretary, Eileen, and our housekeeper, Anna, came in. They'd begun to sort out Barbara's clothes, but it would be a year before Leo would agree to send them to Barbara's relatives in North Carolina. So her closets remained as Barbara had left them. The house seemed spooky, and it was cavernous. I went into the room adjoining our bedroom, which Barbara had used as a study. I'd rarely entered there, because she'd made it obvious she preferred I didn't. I decided to put the ashes on a shelf near the box in which she'd spent so many hours meditating.

The room was a jumble of the remnants of her life. Along one wall stood two large, glass-front bookshelves, one holding curios gathered over the years, which she'd believed could eventually be sold to bring her son some wealth; the other, her most valued books, the wisdom of her Master, Maharaj Charan Singh, by whose words she'd guided her life. On a shelf I found three shoe boxes containing diaries she'd kept and tapes of consultations she'd had with various spiritual guides. There must have been thirty of these tapes, stuffed with advice that I'd considered exploitations of Barbara's uncertainties. In the farthest corner there was an old dentist's cabinet, which Molly had picked up years before, taken over by Barbara when she'd moved in with me. Here were more tapes, these bound tight with string. In a back drawer, I found a packet of notebooks sealed with Scotch tape. Apparently she'd wanted to keep these secret.

Next to her typewriter were three piles of Xeroxed manuscripts, completed screenplays she'd written with Nick Proferes. I'd watched how hard she and Nick had worked, month after month. They'd submitted their projects for financing, obtained encouragement but nothing practical—that is, money. I was reminded of Molly and the first pages of the plays I'd found after her death, pages 1–9, 1–12, 1–8, starts made in confidence, abandoned in despair, a record of heartbreak. At least Barbara, with Nick's help, had pushed her efforts through to a presentable form. But then wouldn't the final defeat have been more painful? I recalled Molly sitting on the floor of her study playing solitaire and the sound of Barbara's slow, inexpert typing late at night. How had they upheld their morale? How had they survived? Well, they didn't and they hadn't.

I felt a sympathy now that I'd never been able to express to Barbara. With this feeling, I picked up the notebooks she'd placed in the back of the dentist's cabinet. Were they to be kept permanently private? In that case, wouldn't she have destroyed them? I remembered her last two days at home and how she'd spent hours in that room, fussing with her papers. Anything she'd wanted destroyed, she would have destroyed at that time. She must have left these records for me to find. Perhaps the notebooks or the tapes contained a message, something she wanted done after her death.

I undid the tightly bound pack of notebooks and began to read. They were what I thought they might be: her emotional history, her disappointment with our relationship, and the accounts of what illumination she'd gained from the various doctors, therapists, and advisers to whom she'd turned. None of this surprised me—then I had a shock.

I opened a small, flat packet, ripping off the Scotch tape and pulling the contents free. I unfolded a single-page letter from Nick Proferes, which I can't quote because of the law governing the use of other people's letters. It was apparently a response to a suggestion from her that they move on to a more permanent relationship.

From that letter I reconstructed a tragedy. Without hope that our bond might improve, she'd proposed that she and Nick declare their connection in love as well as in work and that their union be made open. Barbara's letter was not there, of course, but to guess from Nick's reply, it must have been charged with hope for a new future. Nick's refusal was a sad letter, written in an uncertain longhand, and it gave no reasons, only an unequivocal rejection of the hope Barbara had expressed.

Now, years later, sitting in the dead woman's dark study, I reconsidered her point of view. She'd needed a man whom she could respect, and also a man interested in her future as a filmmaker. I realized how much Nick must have meant to her, for they were in complete sympathy with regard to subject matter, taste, and technique. I couldn't blame her for trying to get it all. She was a woman who had difficulty asking for the least favor, so his rejection must have been a terrible blow. I didn't know what had happened between them, but putting everything personal aside, Nick was a fine fellow and I'm sure he had his good reasons just as she'd had hers. That was the terrible part of it: There was no one to blame.

I recalled days at that time when she'd suddenly gone sickly white and retreated to the bedroom, spending most of her time asleep. When I'd asked her what was wrong, she'd only shake her head. Now I could guess. Nick's rejection had left her stranded in a hopeless marriage, one she couldn't leave unless she had someone to go to. Months passed in this despair. She'd seemed increasingly without will and listless, resorting to what many demoralized people do, oversleeping. She must have faced the fact that despite our no longer being lovers, I continued to look after her. She may even have been forced to feel some gratitude toward me—and at the same time resented that gratitude.

Here in this spooked room were other accounts in diaries and on tape, which I now read and listened to. They detailed the advice of therapists and philosophers she'd consulted and how she'd reacted to it, swinging one way, then the other, as she'd finally come to the conclusion that her cancer had psychic roots and determined to heal herself by psychic rather than chemical therapy. The number of experts she'd turned to, the variety of their opinions, the fantastic disorder of their suggestions and recommendations, astonished me and astonishes me now. But here was an irony: Despite my disrespect for most of their advice, I was beginning to believe that a long series of unhappy events in this woman's life from the time she was a neglected child—small deaths, I've called them—had cleared the path for her cancer, that there were spiritual causes for her physical collapse. Since the M.D.s with their needles and knives had not found the cause or the cure to what killed Barbara, perhaps I should look where she'd looked, to inner, "intimate" events.

I thought of my mother's doctors, two in Port Chester, New York, two in Beverly Hills, California, fashionably dressed, politely spoken, wearing the tan of good health, art lovers, theatre and film enthusiasts, sporting the impressive manners of the profession's elite. They hadn't known what she had until it was too late and didn't have any idea what to do about it when they did know. Dr. Gold's only suggestion was that I should allow Mother to "die graciously"—which has some correspondence to what Dr. Sam Waxman had finally been forced to say to Barbara: "I can't help you anymore. You're on your own now." This after many months of treatment. So I came to the conclusion that doctors don't know much more than you or I do. They can say whatever they wish, experiment and announce their conclusions, get handsome grants, win prizes and have their photographs in *The New York Times*—but they don't impress me.

I'd begun to shift sides, to look at the evidence I myself had for what might cause the physical dissolution of a person. I'd watched it with Molly when her children had left home and she was free at last and had the opportunity she'd waited for all her life "to do my own work" and at last realize her dream of writing for the theatre. Instead she'd spent day after day on that damned Swedish rug, playing solitaire, then going to her typewriter with an idea, starting a play, going along for some pages until, with her razor-sharp intellect, she rejected whatever she'd written, so cooling each flare-up of hope. I'd seen the strain in her mounting. "I'm not going to make it, Gadg!" she'd said, and "My brain's no good, Gadg!" The despair I'd seen on that girl's face! Is it any wonder that something broke in that brain and destroyed it?

I recalled Steinbeck's last years, recalled his hopes: *The Winter of Our Discontent* ("an exhausted voice"), *Travels with Charley* ("pleasant but trivial"), his dispatches from the front ("a liberal betrays himself"), the Nobel Prize ("should have gone to someone else"). Measure hurt if you can. I've called them small deaths. But John had taken them and gone on and on— or so it seemed—until his heart, pushed to endure beyond its capacity to endure, gave out. The cause of his death at sixty-six? What's the mystery? John drove himself to death to preserve his "self" undiminished. But he never yielded his pride. Only the good ones go down that way.

Nick Ray, who died of cancer everywhere in his system, including his brain, was a proud man too. He'd become demoralized by a series of commercial failures and the resulting professional shame in the movie world. Like many others, he'd resorted to drugs, then failed even more miserably with his last films and in his disordered personal life. Finally, in desperate straits, knowing he was soon to die, proud to a degree that made it impossible for him to back off, he'd participated in a film about his own death, which was the ultimate defiance of death. Since that was the only drama left in his life, he'd put it on film. There he'd died as himself.

Harold Clurman? The man who'd inspired more people in the contemporary American theatre than any other man waited all his life for one reward, a position as head of a permanent acting company in New York. He'd seen it go to me and watched from the sidelines as I failed. Here at last was his chance. "We'll have a company one day; don't give up hope," he said to the actors devoted to him. When I resigned my post at the Repertory Theatre, he asked close friends like Ed Albee, Lenny Bernstein, Art Miller, and many others, including me, to send telegrams to the Lincoln Center people, urging, even demanding, that he be given the job I'd had. Of everybody in the world, he was the one for this position, we all knew that—except the men around George Woods and John Rockefeller. They passed him by. He lives still through what he wrote, the best and the final record of our time in the theatre. But he didn't get the one thing he wanted most.

Perhaps the most painful defeat of all was the one suffered by Clifford Odets. Consider how for years he was hailed as the leading playwright of his generation, how he was revered—a new voice, the spokesman for the common man!—and how he'd become shit to kick for the people who'd previously hero-worshipped him. He'd hidden away in Beverly Hills with the two children his wife had left for him to raise. There he'd failed again, and I'd seen the humiliation he'd eaten. For his final years, all he could get for work was "dialogue jobs" on scripts other men had written, to splash a bit of his sparkle on a dull gray movie. I don't ask sympathy for him, only that you imagine the pain he must have felt and the open wound it caused. I saw and heard the scorn heaped on him for his "friendly" testimony before HUAC, a stand, if not wrong, certainly wrong for him. I knew him well enough to know that he was not equipped, as I was, to stand up under a public beating, that he needed, more than any man should, to have people respect him as their hero—something I could, as I finally had to, get along without.

These were six people I knew well and loved. Having studied their lives, I knew that their spirit had been, bit by bit, torn down, fragmented, and destroyed. They'd been left without those essential defenses that might have protected them against a surrender of hope. So I came to my own theory about what brings on a mortal disease, a notion (it's not more than a notion; it's not "scientific") that doctors will consider foolish or, at best, halfbaked. But they should be cautious about challenging speculation. They've not found the cause—or a reliable treatment—for cancer or for high blood pressure or for the disintegration of a heart due to "stress."

I've seen it demonstrated in person after person close to me, more than the six I've been describing. There is a vital core inside a human being where his or her self-esteem lives. When that core is crushed, the person may not let it be seen because of pride or fear or ignorance or bewilderment, but a terrible thing has happened: That person's body defenses have been rendered ineffective and have given up guarding the body and resisting disease. That's the road to the grave.

The flesh and the spirit are interdependent. Something mysterious and devastating happens in a person when he or she, consciously or unconsciously, doesn't care about continuing as him- or herself. The soul passes the message on, and the body's protective force—the immune system, it's called—slowly surrenders the body to the malignancy, which has waited for this opening. The human organism is one piece, and its core is what used to be called the spirit, sometimes the holy spirit, for it is indeed holy. That is what has to survive, and when it doesn't, we don't survive. In this way, man kills himself.

What I say to myself now, as I move into the years of danger, is that while

At a journalists' party in Istanbul

there is a terrible attrition inevitable in life, and there are enemies too, the important thing is to fortify and uphold one's sense of worth. I determined that no one would ever hurt me again, not in a vital spot; that I would endure any trial, survive any pain, ignore any rejection, and do my best to live by my own standards, not hang my life on the esteem of others (the first commandment of the film and theatre world), not need their praise or need to achieve the accomplishments they expected from me and feel defeated when I didn't. No matter what hurt my body might suffer, I'd not give in to what might wound my spirit.

Harold Clurman liked to quote Sarah Bernhardt, especially two words: "despite everything." Following the operation that cost her a leg, she wrote a friend: "I accept the loss of a limb but I refuse to remain impotent. The force of art bears me up. Work is my life. I will continue with my stage engagements—despite everything." P. T. Barnum sent an agent to offer her a large sum of money to display her leg. Her response was: "Which leg?"

When I was young, I believed myself unfortunate in many respects. Now I see that my handicaps were a blessing; they made me tougher, more hardy, more resilient. Hurt so often, I could not be hurt again. Lacking what others had, I had to find my own capabilities and develop talents that were hidden. I learned to meet the cost and go on, to ask forgiveness and pay the penalty. The struggles I've known made my achievements taste sweeter. Since talent is so often the scar tissue over a wound, perhaps I had more than most men. Study those you admire for what they've accomplished, and you may be able to identify the painful and costly events that made them despair for a time but that, in the end, they had to thank for the fortitude of spirit that made it possible for them to achieve what they did. A philosopher said, "What doesn't kill me makes me stronger." I've come to believe that everything worth achieving is beyond one's capacity— or seems so at first. The thing is to persist, not back off, fight your fight, pay your dues, and carry on. Effort is all; continue and you may get there— despite everything.

I I M A G I N E that, from time to time, you've thought my book unfair, ugly, and hateful. Here and there it is vulgar too, but that's a word from which I don't shrink. I've tried to tell the truth about the people I've known but especially about myself. I believe I've been harder on myself than on anybody else. One thing you can't make me believe is that most people behave better than I did. I've traveled the country, seen their faces and studied them, talked and listened, read the daily papers, become familiar with TV (including the commercials, which tell it all), become a fan of our sports and a student of what's revealed there. The human kind is . . . well, it does the best it can—most of the time. I don't hold people's faults against them; I ask their tolerance for mine.

NICK AND CHRIS

MAYA AND ZOE

AMANDA AND EILEEN

THE FOUR BROTHERS

WILLA, AMANDA, AND ZOE, AND ALL MY CHILDREN:
CHRIS, NICK, JUDY, LEO, AND KATIE

THE CLAN, THAT SUMMER

Now I am what an English critic recently called "an extinct volcano." (Isn't it remarkable how we remember the unkind judgments and not the generous ones?) However, I am still alive and am still curious. Sometimes, like an old barracuda, I lie nose to the incoming tide, waiting to see what it may bring. Other times I'm like a kid, running here and there to see all the sights before it gets dark. I've never wished for the day to end. But talent, like beauty, fades. Unlike beauty, it goes without our seeing it go. We don't dare look into the terrible mirror within us, so we don't acknowledge that what we once had is lost.

S. N. Behrman, one of our fine writers of the comedy of ideas, used to bemoan not the loss of his talent—right to the end, his mind was prickly— but what he called vitality. How much of what's called talent, he used to say, derives from that astonishing foolhardiness that comes with energy! For nearly all of us that kind of fervor is an experience we know only in youth: insatiable appetite, spread-eagle curiosity, no end of time, a mind and a heart open to any experience, fearlessness in general.

Later in life we take naps in the afternoon.

Is it helpful for us to be kind to ourselves? To others, of course. But when we're alone, which is most of the time, isn't it better to face the facts of life as it moves on, and death as it comes, without self-favoring, to acknowledge simply: That's the way it is.

The trees in the forest are members of their silent jungle. They crowd each other out of the sun's rays, kill each other, then replace each other. The birds leave before winter; they know what's coming. There's a season of spring and there's a season of death. The rest is romance.

People keep coming to me now, saying, "Did you hear?" "Hear what?" I ask. But I know what; I can tell by their faces. I've also read the obit page that morning. "So-and-so died," they say. Sometimes the bearer of these sad tidings waits for me to shed a tear and say a word. But what the hell is there to say? Or ask? Did they lead a good life? I've formed my opinion on that long before. Did they improve our lot in some way? Did they make good children? Did they leave the world satisfied with themselves, and if so, how did that happen? Important questions, but too impertinent to ask anyone except myself.

When the dead person had achieved some importance in theatre or films, I'm sometimes asked to attend a memorial service and speak. Generally I refuse—graciously, I hope. I don't like memorial services. If praise is the purpose, it should have been offered while the person was alive. I didn't go to Tennessee Williams's memorial service, because I expected it would be a lachrymose affair and that a lot of people would be showing off their grief. I couldn't take that. But I did write something to be read there:

Ever since Tennessee Williams died, I've been hearing nothing but how unhappy his life was and how particularly wretched his last years.

Of course, his powers declined as he went through his sixties; that's true of all men. Tennessee was poet enough to accept that. But don't feel sorry for him. The man lived a life full of the most profound pleasures, and he lived it precisely as he chose. That is allowed to few of us. The talent he had was completely realized in plays that will not disappear from our boards, our memories, or our feelings. Who of us in the theatre can say they've lived a life of work as adventurous as his and as continuous in achievement—which is certainly the deepest kind of pleasure. Imagine yourself in his skin on the morning when he wrote some of the lines we all know so well. Or watching a performance of *The Glass Menagerie* and recognizing his family transmuted into art. Think of the respect he's been given and deserves and the adulation which he enjoyed. Who in our time was ever more universally admired? We should not be gathering to mourn this man, we should not be shedding public tears and making sad noises. We should celebrate his life. It was a triumph! Let us now and here thank our supreme good fortune for having had him and having had him for as long as we did. Tennessee Williams built his own monument. There's nothing left for us to do except admire the race for having produced such a man. And perhaps, whenever and wherever talent comes into our view, give it the respect and support it deserves. That's how we can best remember him.

I'VE GIVEN strict instruction to the people close to me that no memorial shindig be put on in my behalf. I've had more than my share of praise, some deserved, some not. My remains won't lie easier because a pal struggles to his feet and speaks about me. My dust doesn't need flattery.

I've known two ceremonies for the dead that I admired, and I admired them because they were celebrations, not orgies of hysterics, breast-beating, and overpraising a dead person. One was in India, just outside Old Delhi, and I watched from the time they sat the old lady, whose life they were celebrating, in her favorite chair on the makings of a great bonfire. I was invited to add a few pieces of kindling, then I watched the flames consume her, sat by patiently with the members of her family and her friends until the ashes were powder, then were gathered and emptied into the flood of a river close by, along with all the flowers that had been brought to the place. It was beautiful, it was final, and it cleared the earth of a carcass.

The other memorial service I admired I did not attend, but it was described to me several times by people who were there—for it impressed them too. When one of film director Jack Ford's "regulars" died, he invited everyone who'd lived with this fellow, including his dog, his horse, and his remaining relatives, along with everyone who'd worked with him, to a ranch-style party, which started in the afternoon and continued until morning. A great fire was built, meat roasted, liquor consumed, and stories told about the dead man. There was much laughter, which cleared the air of mawk and cleansed the soul. Some went home before dawn, others wrapped themselves in blankets and slept by the fire. The dead man was now dead—every which way.

I've put aside money in my will to hold one hell of a party when I'm gone—but no speeches. I want everyone I've known invited, even my "enemies," if they're still alive. There will be door prizes—all my old sweaters, scarves, skullcaps, shirts, sport coats, ties and trinkets, raingear and boots, my dictionaries and my thesaurus and those of my books my children don't want. I hope everyone goes away with something he likes. It's always fun to scrounge. A lot of people know funny stories about me, some of which are true, some exaggerated, some altogether false—but what the hell! Let the liquor flow, let everyone get drunk on decent drink. And no tears. I've had one hell of a life, and I will go down, when I go down, satisfied.

AND HERE'S the end. I had an unexpected blessing: my wife Frances. We've been married five years, and before that we were "seeing each other" for two years. I didn't believe it was possible, not at my age. I was seventy-two then, seventy-eight now and still at it. For the first time in my life, I

have no impulse to look elsewhere. When I'm in lively company, my eyes don't shift. I suppose one cause for fidelity is advancing years, but in my case it's because of the way Frances is. She's what used to make me buckle—a homemaker, a husband-tender. And she is not competitive in any way, even though she writes books herself.

So the rebel is dead. Something has happened that I thought would never happen: I'm settled. I'll say it before you do, I'm a bourgeois slob. I'm eager to come home every night, and I call for her when I come through the door. I treasure the quiet and good order of the home she's made for me. My final confession is to myself: I love her most of any human being, and I know how damned lucky I am.

So there you are: I'm happy—on the whole. I had to add that last because something in my gut still warns me that while I'm no longer treacherous, life is. All Anatolians expect the worst—especially when things are going well. I live on guard against fate and fortune and don't take the subway.

A philosopher is quoted: "You are born in a clear field, you die in a dark woods." The other way around for me. Were I to run into Seven-Eleven, the god of the crapshoot, I'd ask only that I should die before those I love do. And if I were lucky enough to have a visit from the good fairy and she offered me three wishes, I'd thank her, say "I have everything I want now," refuse the treasures I once craved, and ask for only one thing—more years.

INDEX

Abbott, George, 191
acting, actors, 139–46, 190, 530–1
  American vs. British, 610–11
  books on, 142
  in classics, 145, 610
  crying in, 147–9, 258
  difficulties of life devoted to, 141, 190
  directing and, 50, 90, 142, 143, 192, 256,
    314, 380, 520, 530–1, 541, 628
  form vs. content in, 144–5
  great performances in, 145–6
  habitats of, 273
  indicating in, 143
  as innate capacity, 139–40
  Lighton on emotion in, 251–2
  Method, 50, 63, 81, 90, 139, 144, 154,
    611
  Olivier's approach to, 143–4
  as sexual act, 166
  stage vs. screen, 256–7
  Strasberg and, 63, 64–7, 143, 145, 148,
    154, 300, 610–11, 647, 701, 706–8,
    714
  teaching, 142–3
  see also art, artists
Actors' Equity, 458, 473–4
Actors Studio, 66, 125, 302–3, 321, 341,
  439–40, 466–7, 485, 487, 526, 539,
  574, 592, 611, 628, 635, 711, 713–14,
  782
  acting as taught at, 50, 144, 186, 439–40,
    585
  Crawford in, 302
  genesis of, 290–303
  Kazan's resignation from Board, 631–3,
    702
  Lewis and, 302
  Lincoln Center project and, 585–7, 608–
    9, 615, 650
  roles cast from members of, 316, 342,
    489, 498, 630

  Strasberg on Kazan's betrayal of, 607,
    608, 609, 615, 630–1
Actors Studio Theatre, 631, 653, 700, 702–
  13
  first productions of, 703
  Lincoln Center Repertory Theatre com-
    pared with, 703
  revolving company of, 703–4
  Strasberg and, 712–13
  The Three Sisters produced by, 704,
    705–6, 708
Adler, Buddy, 598–9
Adler, Ellen, 812
Adler, Jacob P., 191, 814
Adler, Luther, 86, 111, 122, 160, 161, 175,
  184, 191
  in *Golden Boy,* 163, 164
Adler, Stella, 108–9, 122, 169–70, 191,
  211, 296, 301, 322, 538, 693
  Clurman and, 60, 108, 121, 149, 153,
    154, 156, 161, 163, 296, 320–1, 812
  Group Theatre and, 119, 153
  Strasberg vs., 119, 143, 154
Africa, Kazan's trip to, 742–3
African Queen, The, 511, 514
After the Fall (Miller), 659–60, 662, 663,
  666–9, 725,
  Barbara Loden Kazan in, 635, 690, 692,
    693, 764, 803
  casting of, 610, 628, 630, 635
  critical response to, 685–6, 689–90
  Kazan's criticisms of, 629–30
Agriculture, U.S. Department of, 232
Albee, Edward, 648–9, 818
All About Eve, 388
Allen, Dede, 658
All My Sons (Miller), 319–23, 329, 366,
  426
All Quiet on the Western Front, 160
America America (film), 550, 635–45, 658,
  660, 700, 702, 733

America America (*cont.*)
　casting of, 628–9
　critical reaction to, 685–6
　filming in Greece for, 645, 651–2
　financial failure of, 719
　funding of, 627–8, 639–40
　ground-kissing scene in, 647
　Joe Kazan as subject of, 547, 615, 628
　Molly Kazan and, 615–16, 660–1, 678,
　　741
　Turkish censorship of, 635–6, 640–1,
　　642, 643, 644–5
America America (Kazan), 43, 353, 741
　Joe Kazan as subject of, 317
　publication of, 616, 661
American Federation of Labor, 411, 412,
　506
American in Paris, An, 455–6
American Tragedy (Dreiser), 150
Anatolia, 14, 15, 317, 548
　marriage in, 94
Anderson, Robert, 27, 219, 495, 503, 506,
　610, 746, 803
　Tea and Sympathy and, 488, 489, 499–
　502
Anderson, Max, 300, 301
Anderson, Phyllis, 501, 508
Andersson, Bibi, 758
Andrews, Dana, 316
Ankara, 550, 552–4, 589, 618, 635, 637
Anna and the King of Siam (Leonowen),
　264, 267, 292, 369, 510
Anna Christie (O'Neill), 540
Anna Karenina, 305, 384
Antalya, 617, 621, 622
ANTA Washington Square Theatre, 611–
　12, 683, 689, 698
Ardrey, Robert, 168, 169, 182, 213, 214,
　238
Arent, Arthur, 232
Arlen, Harold, 189
Aronson, Boris, 178, 181, 219, 300, 582
Arrangement, The (film), 749–53, 755,
　761–2, 763, 764
　casting of, 749–53
Arrangement, The (Kazan), 36, 730–3, 741,
　744, 745–8, 749, 764, 787, 805
　Athena Kazan and, 747, 748
　as autobiography, 732–3
　as best-seller, 746–7
　George Kazan in, 732
　Molly Kazan vs. character in, 731–2
　reviews of, 747

Stein's editing of, 745–6
art, artists:
　arrogance and, 299–300, 658–9
　collaboration of, 322
　money and, 533
　pain and, 5, 353
　promiscuity and, 178
　selfishness of, 83
　seven deadly virtues in, 299
　success and, 125–6
　versatility in, 668
　Williams's view of, 353
　see also acting, actors
Arthur, Jean, 256
Astor Theatre, 528, 529
As Young as You Feel, 403
Athena Productions, 652
Athens, 547, 567, 579, 582, 628–9, 651,
　733
Atkinson, Brooks, 321, 583
Austen Riggs institute, 573
Awake and Sing! (Odets), 102, 110, 113,
　123, 133, 153, 154, 182, 663
　Clurman's direction of, 120, 121–3
　Strasberg and, 113, 119–20

Baby Doll, 561–5
　Cardinal Spellman's attack on, 561, 563–
　4
Baker, Carroll, 561, 562
Baker, George Pierce, 48, 49
Baker's Wife, The, 145
Balanchine, George, 322
Baldwin, James, 43, 582–3, 702–3, 704–5,
　709, 711, 747
Ball, Bill, 694
Ball, Lucille, 305
Ballard, Lucinda, 339, 384
Bankhead, Tallulah, 123, 157–8, 197, 219,
　224, 305, 320, 545
　Kazan's confrontations with, 201–2, 207–
　8, 212–13, 215
　Marches hated by, 207, 220–1
　in *The Skin of Our Teeth,* 201, 206–13,
　220–1, 223
Barber, Phil, 50, 100
Bard, Katharine, 169–70
Barrie, J. M., 224
Barry, Philip, 213
Barrymore, Ethel, 375

Barrymore, Lionel, 305
Batista y Zaldívar, Fulgencio, 124
Baxley, Barbara, 705–6
Baxter, Alan, 48, 58, 59, 76, 78, 82
    Molly Kazan and, 52, 53–4, 78
Bay, Howard, 234
Bayar, Celal, 552, 621, 625
Beatty, Warren, 602, 603, 604, 605, 670
Beaumont, Vivian, 611
Vivian Beaumont Theatre, 586, 611–14,
    615
Bechet, Sidney, 110, 381
Beckett, Samuel, 364
Begley, Ed, 316, 319
Behrman, S. N., 71, 239–40, 241, 264,
    272, 296–8, 690–1, 692, 822
Bein, Albert, 81
Bel Geddes, Barbara, 294, 540–1, 543
Bellow, Saul, 273
Bennett, Michael, 338
Bentley, Eric, 364
Bergman, Ingmar, 273, 755
Bergman, Ingrid, 229
Berle, Milton, 715
Berlin, Irving, 290
Berliner Ensemble, 532
Berman, Pandro, 306, 307, 308, 310–11,
    312
Bernhardt, Sarah, 820
Bernstein, Leonard, 527, 818
Best Years of Our Lives, The, 476
Bevan, Frank Poole, 50
Bevan, Margo, 50
Biak, 276–8
Bickford, Charles, 168–9, 170, 181
Bicycle Thief, The, 629
Big Night, 75, 76
Bing, Rudolf, 696
Blau, Herbert, 698–9
Bliss, Anthony A., 696
Bloomgarden, Kermit, 162, 170, 295, 327,
    338, 440, 592
    Death of a Salesman and, 359–61
    Kazan snubbed by, 461, 471
Blues for Mr. Charlie (Baldwin), 704, 709,
    711
Blues in the Night, 190, 197
Bogart, Humphrey, 89, 146, 158, 184, 456
Bone, Harold, 216
Bonus Army, 101
Boomerang, 316–18, 319, 321, 322, 331,
    378
    casting of, 316

Boone, Richard, 663, 664
Botnick, Dr., 797–8
Bottom of the River, The
    (Schulberg), 488
Boulting, Ingrid, 765, 766, 774, 776, 779,
    781
Boyer, Charles, 245, 249
Brando, Marlon, 27, 135, 141, 255, 256,
    300, 386, 456, 534, 539, 592, 659,
    750–1, 767
    Academy Award won by, 529
    The Arrangement and, 749–53, 764
    Dean's admiration of, 538
    on Kazan's HUAC testimony, 470–1,
        515, 516
    in On the Waterfront, 145–6, 500, 516,
        517, 518, 520, 521, 523, 524–6, 527,
        750
    in A Streetcar Named Desire, 330–1,
        341–2, 343–6, 350, 351–2
    Tandy and, 343–5
    in Viva Zapata!, 428–30
    Williams and, 341–2, 344
Brecht, Bertolt, 104, 154, 155, 322, 323,
    613
Breen Office, 254, 401, 417, 432, 433,
    434
Brennan-Gibson, Margaret, 183
Brewer, Roy, 410–13, 414, 426
Bridge on the River Kwai, The, 770
Bridges, Harry, 411
Bright, Jack, 44
Bromberg, Joseph (J. Edward), 115, 153,
    243–4, 468
    death of, 432
    as leader of Communist Party cell, 120–
        1, 128, 129, 458
Brook, Peter, 322, 338, 364
Brooks, Mel, 759
Brown, Arthur "Brownie," 492–3
Brown, Clarence, 305, 389
Brown, Kay, 508, 650
Brown, Pamela, 337
Brustein, Robert, 694, 699–700
Buchman, Myron, 795
Burke, Michael, 698
Burning Bright (Steinbeck), 786
Burstyn, Ellen, 143, 713
Burton, Richard, 545
Bury the Dead (Shaw), 426, 449
But for Whom Charlie (Behrman), 690–1,
    692, 703
Butler, Samuel, 30

Café Crown (Kraft), 191–2, 193, 201
Cagney, James, 146, 184, 185–7, 189, 535
    acting style of, 186–7
    Kazan advised by, 187
Calhern, Louis, 244
Callahan, Gene, 639, 651, 776
Callas, Maria, 145
Camille (Dumas), 65, 145
Camino Real (Williams), 485, 488, 489,
    494–8, 499, 502, 503, 545, 598
    casting of, 498
    theme of, 495–7
    Williams on, 496–7
Canby, Vincent, 756
Cannes Film Festival, 756–9
Cantor, Eddie, 51
Capa, Robert, 175, 197, 249, 788
Capone, Al, 174
Carnovsky, Morris, 175, 181, 192, 211
Carroll, Madeleine, 228, 229
Carroll, Paul Vincent, 194
Carter, Jimmy, 803–4
Carter, Rosalynn, 804
Caruso, Enrico, 145
Case of Clyde Griffiths, The (Piscator), 150-
    1, 154
Casey Jones (Ardrey), 168–70, 171, 296,
    301
casting, 536
    sexual attraction and, 229
    see also specific productions
Cathedral of Faith, 796
Catholic Church, Catholicism, 417, 421,
    432, 716
Cat on a Hot Tin Roof (Williams), 540–4,
    545
Cézanne, Paul, 273
Changeling, The (Middleton and Rowley),
    610, 691, 693, 694, 703, 706, 718, 724
Chapin, Schuyler, 696
Chaplin, Charlie, 300, 378
Chayevsky, Paddy, 403, 803
Chekhov, Anton, 146, 704, 705
Patrice Chereau Theatre, 611, 613
Children's Hour, The (Hellman), 294
Christians, Mady, 432, 467
Chrysalis (Porter), 89, 90, 91, 93
Churchill, Winston, 294
CinemaScope, 506, 511, 529
Cirkus Brumbach, 477–8
Citizen Kane, 133, 783
City for Conquest, 184–8
Civilian Conservation Corps, 107, 155
Clash by Night (Odets), 320

Cleveland Clinic, 796, 801
Clift, Montgomery, 205, 210, 574, 598,
    599, 600
    automobile accident of, 597
Clurman, Harold, 27, 66–7, 78, 118–19,
    141, 143, 147, 152, 161, 168, 169, 170,
    181, 211, 273, 471, 489, 648, 659, 676,
    693, 706, 718, 785, 818, 820
    at *All My Sons* rehearsals, 320
    Awake and Sing! and, 121–3
    background of, 121
    in break with Strasberg, 120, 154
    Brecht and, 323
    as director, 64, 121–3, 813
    Group Theatre and, 62, 105, 160, 498
    hero-worship of, 70, 150, 162
    illness and death of, 809–14
    Kazan interviewed by, 56–7
    Kazan's partnership with, 295–6, 298,
        318–24
    on Kazan's talent, 81, 154, 424
    Lincoln Center Repertory Theatre and,
        693
    Odets and, 88–9, 182–3, 319–20
    Stella Adler and, 60, 108, 121, 149, 153,
        154, 156, 161, 163, 296, 320–1, 812
    A Streetcar Named Desire and, 351–2,
        353
    theatre as viewed by, 65, 813
    Truckline Café and, 300–1
Cobb, Lee J., 146, 175, 500
    in *Death of a Salesman*, 356, 359, 362–3
Cohen, Alexander, 714
Cohn, Harry, 227, 228, 229, 253, 408, 409–
    14, 420, 421, 509
    on *The Hook*, 409
    on Miller's abandonment of *The Hook*,
        414
    "Miss Bauer" and, 409–10
    On the Waterfront screened for, 527–
    8
Colbert, Claudette, 305
Cole, Donald, 799
Cole, Ed, 50
Colleran, Bill, 599
Collins, Richard, 445–6
Columbia Pictures, 408, 409, 475, 487,
    509, 527, 628
*Come Back to the 5 and Dime, Jimmy
    Dean, Jimmy Dean* (Gracyk), 800, 805,
    806–7
Commonweal, 493
Communist Party of America, 127–33, 231,
    399, 432, 444–5, 567

Kazan's decision to name members of, 456–63

Kazan's membership in, 44, 101, 104, 128–33, 231, 294, 399, 420, 444–5, 737

on La Guardia, 108, 128

as worldwide conspiracy, 449

Compton, Juleen, 812

Confessions (Rousseau), 595

Conklin, Peggy, 170

Constantinople, 13, 14, 19, 20, 21

Conway, Curt, 467

Cooper, Gary, 184, 187, 535

Cooper, Merian, 389

Copland, Aaron, 121, 181, 659

Cornell, Katharine, 235

Corridan, John, 493

Counterattack, 441, 476, 566–7

Kazan attacked in, 474–5

Countess from Hong Kong, 751

Covici, Pat, 785

Coward, Noël, 85

Crabtree, Paul, 467

Crawford, Cheryl, 56, 57, 75, 80, 82, 103, 119, 120, 121, 154, 302, 360, 574, 631, 633, 650, 676, 704, 705, 708, 709, 711

Lincoln Center project and, 585–6, 587, 608, 609

One Touch of Venus and, 233, 234, 235

resignation from Group Theatre by, 156–7

Strasberg's estrangement from, 712

Crawford, Joan, 77

Crime Doctor, 133

Cronyn, Hume, 339–40, 345–6, 569, 742–4

Kazan's trips with, 743–4

Tandy and, 343–4

Crowther, Bosley, 437, 452

Crucible, The (Miller), 367, 449–50, 472

Cukor, George, 305, 565

Curtis, Tony, 778

Daily Variety, 390

Daily Worker, 111, 321

Kazan attacked in, 469

Dakin, Walter Edwin, 348

Dancigars, Oscar, 401, 418–19

Dantine, Helmut, 261

Danton's Death (Büchner), 699

Dark at the Top of the Stairs, The (Inge), 513, 572–3, 601

Darvas, Lili, 443

Dassin, Jules, 389

Daubney, Peter, 709

Daves, Delmer, 392

Davis, Bette, 146, 184

Davis, Frank, 307

Dead End, 158, 230, 237

Dean, Alexander, 49–50, 90

directing views of, 49–50

Dean, James, 141, 313, 534–9, 790

Angeli and, 537, 538

Brando admired by, 538

effects of success on, 535

father of, 535

in *Giant,* 538

Harris and, 538

Massey and, 535–6

narcissism of, 537–8

youth legend of, 538, 805

death, 614, 773, 782–4, 818–19

Death of a Salesman (Miller), 74, 115, 146, 162, 301, 338, 355–68, 373, 402, 426, 502, 530, 667

Crawford's rejection of, 360

Kazan's initial reaction to, 355–6

and Kazan's perception of his father, 357–8

Loman character in, 356–8

spectral house in, 361–2

success of, 359–60

theme of, 358–9

title of, 360–1

Waiting for Lefty compared with, 115

Death of Ivan Ilyich, The (Tolstoi), 614

Deauville Film Festival, 809

Deep Are the Roots (d'Usseau and Gow), 293, 294, 295

De Havilland, Olivia, 514

De Mille, Agnes, 235, 300

De Mille, Cecil B., 456

Communists pursued by, 387–93

De Niro, Robert, 141, 146, 715, 765, 766–7, 768, 769, 770, 772, 773, 774, 779, 780, 781

Kazan's coaching of, 766–7

Kazan's criticisms of, 773

Spiegel's doubts about, 768, 769, 771, 773

Dennis, Sandy, 709, 711

Depression, Great, 53, 319

George Kazan and, 97–9

de Rochemont, Louis, 316

De Sica, Vittorio, 629
Desperate Hours, The, 470
Devil in Massachusetts, The (Starkey),
    449
deVincenzo, Tony Mike, 499–500
Dickens, Charles, 583
DiMaggio, Joe, 455, 539
Dimitroff, Georgi, 112, 120
directing, directors, 49–50, 90, 145, 364,
    497, 502, 525
  actors and, 50, 90, 142, 143, 192, 256,
    314, 380, 520, 530–1, 541, 628
  actresses and, 342, 368–9
  cinematographers and, 185
  commercial, 168
  commitment in, 498–9
  family life and, 676
  famous, techniques of, 254–5
  hypocrisy in, 73, 530–31
  money and, 412–13
  restraint in, 191–2
  scripts and, 159
  stage vs. screen, 380–1
  as storytellers, 380
  versatility in, 150–1
Disston, Colonel, 280
Dmytryk, Edward, 445–6
Donohue, Roger, 521
Dougherty, Jim, 404–5
Douglas, Kirk, 752–3, 764, 775
Dowling, Constance, 194, 198, 252, 274,
    276, 619
  Boyer and, 245, 249
  Capa and, 175–6, 249
  death of, 274
  Goldwyn and, 216, 228–31, 236–8, 244,
    245, 267
  Kazan's affair with, 166–7, 178, 188–90,
    194–6, 197, 199, 202–4, 211, 216–17,
    222, 225, 232, 233, 241–2, 244, 246,
    248–9, 259, 261, 263, 264–8, 271–2,
    415
Dowling, Doris, 238, 264, 274
Draddy, Greg, 139
Draddy, Vin, 34, 37, 139
Drama Critics prize, 321
Dramatists Guild of America, 301, 530,
    544, 582, 758
Dreiser, Theodore, 150, 151, 227
Dunaway, Faye, 669, 753–4, 755, 764
Dunn, Jimmy, 257, 263
Dunnigan's Daughter (Behrman), 264, 272,
    276, 296–7
  casting of, 297, 298

Dunnock, Mildred, 530, 562, 598
Durante, Jimmy, 305
d'Usseau, Arnaud, 293, 294, 295
Dutton, George Burwell, 47

Eagels, Jeanne, 51
Eagle, S. P., *see* Spiegel, Sam
East of Eden (film), 331, 463, 534–9, 546,
    572, 574, 598, 790
  Dean's casting in, 534–5
  Kazan promised final cut on, 529
  Massey in, 535–6
  preview of, 538
East of Eden (Steinbeck), 529
Eddy, Nelson, 236
Ed Sullivan Show, The, 133
Egghead, The (Kazan), 569–71
Eisenstein, Sergei, 101, 105, 583
Maxine Elliott Theatre, 80, 95
Erkenbrecher family, 422–3
Esselstyn, Dr., 795–6, 801, 808, 809

Face in the Crowd, A, 566–9, 599, 618
Fairbanks, Douglas, Jr., 593
Farmer, Frances, 80, 88, 163, 164, 172,
    462
Farrow, John, 389–90, 393
Faulkner, William, 273
Fausse Suivante, La (Marivaux), 613
Feldman, Charles, 312–13, 383, 385, 408,
    413, 432, 433, 437, 453
  love life of, 402–3
  A Streetcar Named Desire and, 416–17
Fellini, Federico, 256, 273
Fervent Years, The (Clurman), 120
Fields, W. C., 313
Figueroa, Gabriel "Gabby," 397–8, 400,
    414, 456
Fitelson, Bill, 327–8, 329, 331, 453, 457–
    8, 679
  America America and, 639, 640
Fitzgerald, F. Scott, 761
Five Alarm Waltz (Prumbs), 370
Flaubert, Gustave, 83, 273, 583
Fleming, Victor, 251, 255, 257, 311
Flight into Egypt (Tabori), 453
Flynn, Errol, 184, 186, 535
Fonda, Henry, 158, 186

Fonda, Jane, 325
Ford, John, 251, 312, 381, 382, 392, 393,
    468, 480
  directing style of, 254–5
  famous story about, 312
  Kazan advised by, 255–6
  memorial party thrown by, 823–4
  Pinky and, 373–4, 486
Forty Days of Musa Dagh, The (Werfel),
    240
Fosse, Bob, 338, 364–5
France, Kazan's films admired in, 605, 685,
    702, 756
Freedman, Harold, 168, 169, 213, 296,
    298
Fried, Eddie, 172, 174
Fried, Walter, 319, 320, 338, 359, 360
From the Ashes: Voices from Watts, 295
Frontier Films, 105, 469
Fuller, Sam, 254

Galento, Two-Ton Tony, 521
Galileo (Brecht), 322
Gang, Martin, 390
Gangbusters, 133
Garbo, Greta, 145, 146, 305, 403
Gardner, Ava, 710
Garfield, John ("Julie"), 88, 153, 157, 163,
    164, 229, 303, 337, 341, 382, 453, 455
  in *Gentleman's Agreement*, 332, 334
  HUAC and, 440–1, 445, 446
Garfield, Roberta, 441
Garland, Judy, 145, 305
Garner, Peggy Ann, 257–8, 259, 262, 263
Gazzara, Ben, 540
Gentleman's Agreement (film), 229, 253,
    254, 328, 331–4, 340, 373, 387, 420,
    506, 510
  crucial scene in, 332
  as "liberal" film, 333
Gentleman's Agreement (Hobson), 250–1,
    322
Gentle People, The (Shaw), 77, 180–1
Gentle Woman (Lawson), 108–9, 128
George White's Scandals, 51
Germany, East, 481, 482
Germeer, 555–6, 557, 589, 591–2, 621
Germinal (Zola), 264
Giallelis, Stathis, 629
Giant, 538
Gibbons, Cedric, 312

Gill, Major General William H., 282–6,
    289
Gillenson, Lew, 288
Gilliatt, Penelope, 712
Gilman, Richard, 694
Gilmore, Frank, 473, 474
Gilmore, Margalo, 474
Girls on Parade, 278, 279
Glass Menagerie, The (Williams), 175, 326,
    348, 417, 823
Goat Song (Werfel), 240
Gold, Herbert, 769–70, 771, 772, 773,
    774, 775, 776, 817
Gold Eagle Guy (Levy), 110–11, 112, 118,
    119, 120
Golden Boy (Odets), 80, 124, 161–4, 168,
    170, 172, 342, 362
  Kazan in, 163–4, 166, 184, 202
Goldwyn, Samuel, 158, 190, 227–30, 253
  Dowling and, 216, 228–31, 236–8, 244,
    245, 267
Good Soldier Schweik, The, 154
Gordon, Ruth, 123, 196, 201
Gorelik, Mordecai "Max," 105, 162,
    321
Gow, James, 293, 294, 295
Grahame, Gloria, 479
Grant, Cary, 255
Grapes of Wrath, The, 395, 506, 509
Graziano, Rocky, 715
Greece, Greeks, 684
  America America and, 651
  men in, 629
  Turks and, 13–14, 16, 550–1, 555, 556,
    591, 733
Green, Paul, 154, 155
Greenville, Miss., 562
Griffith, D. W., 381
Grossmünster church, 269
Group Theatre, 56–67, 69–70, 82, 89, 102,
    105, 109, 118–20, 123, 144, 156, 291,
    352, 498, 505, 610, 666, 676, 811
  communism in, 104, 110–11, 112, 120–
    1, 127–32, 134, 150, 399, 444, 446–7,
    453, 457–60
  dissolution of, 142, 182
  first success of, 104, 109
  Kazan's introduction to, 56–61, 137, 424,
    810
  Kazan's reconstitution of, 160–4
  Molly Kazan and, 77–9, 327
  Shubert's visit to, 78–80
  SKKOB collective in, 112
  Stella Adler as problem in, 153, 154

Group Theatre (cont.)
  Strasberg and Crawford's resignations
    from, 156–7
  Strasberg's dominance of, 61–2, 78
  Strasberg's fall in, 123
  summer camps of, 58–67, 100, 101, 102,
    140, 152–7
Guthrie, Tyrone, 330, 338

Hadjidakis, Manos, 655, 658–9
Hagen, Uta, 352
Hall, Peter, 338
hamals, 550, 556, 620, 639, 641, 645
Hamlet (Shakespeare), 140, 347, 501
Hammerstein, Oscar, 300, 785
Hanna Theatre, 570
Harriet (Ryerson and Clements), 222–4,
    225, 231, 235, 243
Harris, Jed, 123, 147, 191, 193, 196, 206–
    7, 211, 239, 370, 442
Harris, Julie, 141, 535, 538–9, 703
Harrity, Dick, 262, 263
Hart, Moss, 125, 254, 331–2, 334
Hathaway, Henry, 251, 252, 255
Hawks, Howard, 251, 381
Hayes, Helen, 222, 231, 235, 243
  Kazan's artistic challenge to, 223–4
Haywood, William "Big Bill," 101
Hazlitt, William, 145
Heavenly Express, The (Bein), 81
Helburn, Theresa, 82, 84, 89, 103
Hellman, Lillian, 136, 294, 319, 324–5,
    382–3, 441–2, 472, 592
  HUAC and, 442, 460, 461–2
Helpern, Milton, 681–2
Hemingway, Ernest, 300
Hepburn, Katharine, 304, 305, 306, 307,
    310, 311, 316, 382
  Tracy and, 314
Hitchcock, Alfred, 186, 255
Hitler, Adolf, 231, 457
Hoboken, N.J., 488, 492–3, 515, 519, 520–
    1, 523, 533, 766
Hobson, Laura, 250, 322
Hoffman, Dustin, 141, 765
Hoffman, Irving, 361
Hoguet, Robert, 695, 696, 698
Hollandia, 218, 270, 274–6, 278, 284, 285
Holliday, Judy, 475
Hollywood, 227, 250, 265, 451
  communism in, 102

Kazan's escape from, 272
Kazan's first trip to, 157
studio heads in, 227–8, 229
Hollywood Reporter, 186, 188, 245, 249,
    258, 271, 272, 292, 361
  Kazan's HUAC testimony reported in,
    453, 454, 455
Holm, Celeste, 334
Hook, Sidney, 457
Hook, The (Miller), 375, 377, 378, 381,
    387, 401, 403, 408, 409, 420, 487
  Brewer's attack on, 410–12, 426
  Miller's abandonment of, 413–15, 420,
    426
Hoover, J. Edgar, 452
Hopkins, Arthur, 140
Horney, Karen, 165–6, 584
House Committee on Un-American Activi-
    ties (HUAC), 421, 432, 440–3, 448–
    66, 630, 818
  Kazan's testimony before, 134, 293, 323,
    339, 383, 387, 420, 448–9, 452, 455–
    64, 466, 566, 685
Houseman, John, 198, 202, 214, 216, 238,
    262, 269, 790
House of Connelly, The (Green), 53, 57, 60
HUAC, see House Committee on Un-
    American Activities
Hudson Guild, 805
Hughes, Howard, 408, 479
Humphrey, Hubert H., 704
Hunter, Kim, 342, 344, 435
Hurwitz, Leo, 469
Huston, John, 232, 390, 511, 751
  Spiegel's party for, 514
Huston, Walter, 146
Hyde, Johnny, 247–8, 404
  death of, 403
  Monroe's relationship with, 405–6
Hyman, Elliot, 628, 639

Ibsen, Henrik, 359
Iceman Cometh, The (O'Neill), 321
I Led Three Lives (Philbrick), 452
India, 735–7, 823
Informer, The, 468, 470
Inge, William, 27, 299, 572–4, 595, 610,
    719
  Splendor in the Grass and, 601–2, 604–5
Inspector General, The (Gogol), 66–7
International Alliance of Theatrical and

Stage Employees, 104–5, 407, 410, 754
Irving, Jules, 698–9
Istanbul, 548–51, 556, 620, 641
Ives, Burl, 468, 541–2, 543, 544

Jacks, Bobby, 477
Jacobowsky and the Colonel (Werfel and Behrman), 71, 239, 242–3, 297
Jacobs, Moe, 104
Jaffe, Leo, 515
Jaffe, Sam, 470
James, Jacqueline, 26, 34
Japan, Japanese, 618, 735, 736, 737–8
Pearl Harbor attacked by, 61, 192, 232
soldiers, 275–7
Javits, Jacob, 673
J.B. (MacLeish), 582–4, 592, 682–3
Jerome, V. J., 108, 127, 128, 450, 457, 487
Johnny Johnson, 155–6, 233
Johnson, Albert, 193, 209
Johnson, Lyndon B., 699, 787–8
Johnson, Malcolm, 487
Johnstone, Anna Hill, 639, 662, 770–1
Jones, Harmon, 317, 403–4, 408
Jonson, Ben, 216
Joy, Jason, 417–19, 432
Joyce, James, 206
Juilliard School of Music, 275, 607, 608, 695
Julius Caesar, 470

Kalmenson, Ben, 686
Kanin, Garson, 123
Karajosifoglou, Anna (grandmother), 15, 19
Karlweis, Oscar, 71, 242–3, 244
Kaufman, Boris, 519, 521, 522–5, 562
Kaufman, George S., 125, 147, 347
Kavundju, Osman, 553–6, 557, 559, 589, 617, 620, 621, 623–6, 627
double life of, 622–3
Kazan's trip to Antalya with, 621–4
Kaye, Danny, 216, 228, 230, 232, 233, 236
Kayseri, 13, 14, 16, 17, 71, 553–5, 556, 557, 559, 589–90, 615, 616, 619, 620, 628
toilets in, 551, 552–3

Kazan, Athena Shishmanoglou (mother), 9–10, 13–31, 33, 40, 42, 51–2, 70, 90–1, 203, 211, 317, 347, 456, 597, 747–9, 768–78
America America and, 686
The Arrangement and, 747, 748
Barbara Kazan and, 763, 764
in "beautiful brown eyes conspiracy," 27, 29, 30–31
California trip of, 762–3
cancer of, 769–76
death of, 773–8
family background of, 13–17
George Kazan's relationship with, 10–11, 25, 31, 51, 103, 358, 624–5, 748, 749
household moved by, 624
Lucy Palymyra and, 22–4
Molly Kazan and, 54, 91, 195, 198, 271
reading as habit of, 15, 25, 748–9
stomach operation of, 747–8
stroke of, 759–60
Kazan, Avraam (brother), 10, 21, 546, 652
Kazan, Avraam Elia "Joe" (uncle), 14, 21, 70, 91, 93, 436
in *Boomerang*, 317–18
death of, 318
as subject of *America America*, 317, 547, 615, 628
Kazan, Barbara Loden (second wife), 571–3, 599–60, 603, 616–20, 683, 722–32, 735–44, 747, 749–50, 779, 800
as actress, 668–9, 692
in *After the Fall*, 635, 668–9, 673–4, 690, 692, 693
The Arrangement and, 32, 749–50, 763, 764
Athena Kazan and, 761, 763, 764, 769, 776, 778
casting director assaulted by, 588–9
Come Back to the 5 and Dime, Jimmy Dean, Jimmy Dean and, 805, 806–7
courage of, 743
documentary about, 807
illness and death of, 792–809, 810, 811, 813–15, 817
Kazan's affair with, 7, 572, 619, 673, 718, 722–9, 737–41, 764
Kazan's marriage to, 742–4, 763–4, 773, 795
Lewis and, 653, 668
Molly Kazan and, 572, 653–4, 664, 668, 669, 679, 723
papers left after death by, 815–16

Kazan, Barbara Loden (*cont.*)
  pregnancy of, 616
  Proferes and, 763, 816
  spiritual pursuits of, 794, 796–8, 799–800
  Wanda made by, 793–4
Kazan, Berry (uncle), 92
Kazan, Chris (son), 262, 263, 267, 271, 424, 756, 759
  birth of, 180
  The Visitors written by, 754
Kazan, Elia:
  as actor, 64, 65, 106, 112, 114, 137–8, 139, 140, 147–9, 163–4, 180, 182–3, 184–8, 189, 190, 424
  anger of, 3–4, 8, 96, 210–12, 485, 587–8, 590–3, 719
  arrogance of, 90, 122, 142, 149, 299, 546
  as assistant stage manager, 82, 84–5, 89, 103
  birth of, 21
  Chicago mob and, 172–4, 178
  childhood of, 9–12, 24–29, 138–9
  at college, 38–48, 424
  contradictory reputations of, 606
  disruption courted by, 7, 571–2
  double life of, 6, 177, 178, 370, 574, 595, 601, 721
  early directing experiences of, 168–70, 181–2, 191–2
  fantasy life of, 41, 72, 139
  first jobs of, 29
  first sexual experiences of, 52, 53
  in "Groupstroi" apartment, 85
  in high school, 26–9, 34–6
  in Hollywood, 272–3, 323, 324, 334
  intimidating facial expression of, 3–4, 5, 6, 485
  as "miracle man," 223, 224
  nickname of, 5, 89, 100, 106, 594
  as outsider, 48, 495
  own life as dramatic material for, 353–4
  present life of, 820, 822
  professional bottoming-out of, 491
  psychoanalysis of, 7–9, 239, 242, 267, 268–9, 370, 448, 584, 587–8, 594, 717, 719–20, 722–4, 739
  radio work of, 133, 156
  reading as passion of, 25–6, 27, 28, 30, 34, 42, 139
  on self as director, 219, 363–4
  self-doubt of, 124–5, 245–6
  success's effects on, 8, 224–6, 363, 373

  theatre quit by, 684, 700
  traits of, 217–19
  unforgiving nature of, 111, 484
  vaudeville enjoyed by, 43–4
  as waiter, 42, 43, 65
  war experiences of, 192, 204, 232, 242, 270–89
  weeping scene of, 147–9
  Williams College applied to by, 26–31
  as workaholic, 260–1, 738–9
  working-class cap worn by, 106, 125, 131–2
  on writing his autobiography, 32, 595, 614, 687
  at Yale Drama School, 48–55, 424
Kazan, Elia (grandfather), 16–17, 20
Kazan, Evanthia (grandmother), 16, 92, 546–7
  Kazan's visits to, 30
  stories of, 547
Kazan, Frances (third wife), 3, 38, 219, 615, 686–7, 824–5
Kazan, Frank (uncle), 91
Kazan, George (brother), 31, 747, 771, 772, 775, 776, 777
Kazan, George (father), 9–12, 18–25, 29–31, 70, 71–2, 90–5, 198, 224, 271, 317, 347, 355, 357–8, 535, 556, 557, 590–1, 642–3, 676, 733, 748, 749, 778
  The Arrangement and, 732
  Athena Kazan's relationship with, 10–11, 17–21, 25, 31, 358, 749
  death of, 624–5
  Death of a Salesman and Kazan's perception of, 356–8
  Depression and, 97–9
  family brought to America by, 22
  on father, 20
  favorite phrases of, 42, 372
  as *gevur*, 642–3
  illnesses of, 9–10, 18–19, 103, 624, 625
  Kazan as failure to, 29–30, 49, 317, 357, 424
  Kazan's admission to Williams and, 31
  Kazan's fear of, 3–4, 9, 10, 25
  Molly Kazan and, 91, 93–4, 198
  Stellio Yeremia and, 556–7, 559
Kazan, George, Inc., Oriental Rugs and Carpets, 4, 18, 21–2, 29–30, 93, 535
Kazan, Jennifer (niece), 625
Kazan, John (uncle), 92, 94
Kazan, Judy (daughter), 167, 190, 259, 262, 271, 569
  birth of, 155

Molly Kazan's death and, 652–3, 675
pregnancy of, 657
Kazan, Katharine (daughter), 351, 633, 775
Kazan, Leo (son), 4, 358, 653, 741, 763,
    768, 778, 805, 815
  birth of, 5–6, 635
  Kazan's first conversation with, 729
Kazan, Michael (uncle), 92
Kazan, Molly Day Thacher (first wife), 73–
    4, 90, 102, 213–14, 238, 241, 508, 518,
    597, 633–5, 649–50, 652–8, 660, 731–
    2,
  abortion of, 67–9, 74, 85
  America America and, 616, 660–1, 678,
    741
  Barbara Loden Kazan and, 572, 653–4,
    668, 669, 723
  Baxter and, 52, 53–4, 78
  Central Park apartment chosen and dec-
    orated by, 6, 634–5, 636–7, 654–5
  country home of, 188, 190, 366, 634
  death of, 674–82, 691, 717, 719, 720–2,
    732
  devotion of, 36, 54–5, 95–6, 633, 722
  divorces requested by, 195, 232, 425,
    638
  family of, 73–4, 92, 422–3
  Grossmünster church compared to, 269
  Group Theatre and, 77–80, 128
  illness of, 652–3
  as Kazan's acceptance by America, 569
  as Kazan's adviser, 8, 65, 74, 193, 293,
    316, 348, 356, 376, 378, 424, 437, 486,
    518, 547, 572, 573, 580, 587, 616, 647,
    721, 722, 784
  Kazan's HUAC testimony and, 447, 462–
    5, 468
  Kazan's infidelities and, 5–6, 38, 166,
    167, 176, 188–9, 194–5, 199–200,
    271–4, 370, 425, 601, 637–8, 650,
    651–2, 672–3, 721–2
  Kazan's marriage to, 93–6, 167, 239,
    268–9, 293, 334, 423, 424–5, 454,
    533, 569, 633–4, 649, 650, 651, 672–3,
    717–18, 721, 723
  Kazan's parents and, 90–1, 269, 764
  Kazan's resentment of, 424–5, 438
  Kazan's romance with, 53–5, 70–1, 77–
    8, 82–3, 86, 167, 614–15
  loneliness of, 637–8, 650
  Miller and, 319, 426, 449, 450
  New Theatre and, 109, 449–50
  nickname of, 422
  92nd Street home set up by, 238
  Odets and, 78, 86–7, 91, 423, 652, 664
  poem for JFK written by, 670–2, 673,
    674
  pregnancies of, 36, 67–71, 147, 170, 172,
    292, 314
  psychoanalysis of, 238–9, 634
  requiem service for, 676–7
  as saint, 67, 202
  self-doubts of, 637–8, 648, 649–50
  solitaire played by, 6, 569, 648, 654,
    655–6, 684, 817
  Strasberg and, 78, 650, 653
  in Theatre Union, 105
  in Turkey, 547–53
  U.S. praised by, 677
  Viva Zapata! and, 428, 431–2
  at Voice of America, 214, 262, 269
  wedding of, 95
  Williams and, 162, 327, 339, 352, 426
  writing career of, 100, 569–71, 633, 635,
    638, 646–9, 670–2, 674, 684, 815, 817
Kazan, Nick (son), 293, 314, 778
Kazan, Seraphim (uncle), 19, 22, 91–2
Kean, Edmund, 145
Kearney, Bernard, 446, 447, 449, 453
Kelly, Gene, 791
Kelly, Grace, 229
Kelman, Harold, 584, 586, 587–8, 589,
    591, 592, 719–20, 722–4, 727
Kemal, Mustafa, 552, 554, 621
Kemper, Victor, 779
Kempton, Murray, 470
Kennedy, Arthur, 187, 188, 319, 472
Kennedy, John F., 669–70
  death of, 669–72, 677, 678
  Molly Kazan's poem for, 670–2, 673
Kennedy, Robert, 673, 677
Kerr, Deborah, 229, 503–4, 506, 545
  in *Tea and Sympathy*, 503–4
Kerr, Jean, 543
Kerr, Walter, 543, 686
Keys, Vernon, 391
King, Ernest, 61
King, Martin Luther, Jr., 295, 752
Kingdom, Frank, 467
King Lear (Shakespeare), 146
Kingsley, Sidney, 100, 104, 712
Kirkland, Alexander, 110–11
Klein, Herb, 449–50
Klune, Ray, 417–19, 420
Knickerbocker Holiday, 236
Knight, Shirley, 705, 709
Knute Rockne, All American, 185
Koltuv, M., 795, 797, 800

Kook, Eddie "Kookie," 354, 360
Kraber, Tony, 472, 475, 684–5
  HUAC testimony of, 469, 475
  Molly Kazan's death and, 679–80
Kraber, Wilhelmina, 685
Kraft, Hy, 191
Krawitz, Herman, 696–7
Krim, Arthur, 88
Kruskal, Joe, 749
Kurosawa, Akira, 146, 273
Kushi, Michio, 795, 799, 801–2

Labor for the Wind (Shaw), 302
La Guardia, Fiorello, 108, 554, 623
Lancaster, Burt, 342
Lang, Fritz, 392
Langner, Lawrence, 240, 241, 243, 298
Lasky, Victor, 476
Lastfogel, Abe, 226, 233, 247, 263, 264,
  266, 267, 285, 292, 401, 453, 490–1,
  529
  The Hook and, 403, 408, 409, 414
  On the Waterfront and, 508–11, 516–17
Lastfogel, Frances, 247, 490, 509
Last Tycoon, The (film), 380, 765–81
  Boulting in, 774, 779
  casting of, 765–6
  excerpts from Kazan's diary during, 768–
  78
  final scene in, 781
Last Tycoon, The (Fitzgerald), 761, 762
Lawrence, D. H., 348
Lawrence of Arabia, 514, 770
Lawson, John Howard, 82, 108–9, 110,
  128, 399–400, 450, 487
Lazar, Irving "Swifty," 769, 773
Lazar, Mary, 773
Lean, David, 514, 774, 780
Ledbetter, Huddie "Leadbelly," 109
Lee, Will, 278
Leeds, Herbert, 389
Left Wing Communism: An Infantile Dis-
  order (Lenin), 60
Legion of Decency, 417, 421, 432–7
Leigh, Vivien, 144, 343, 385–6
Leland, James, 652, 674–5, 680–2
Lenin, V. I., 102
Lenya, Lotte, 165
LeRoy, Mervyn, 310
Let's Make Love, 667
Letter to Three Wives, A, 388

Levy, Melvin, 110–11, 118
Lewin, Michael, 473–4
Lewis, Robert, 114, 142, 143, 153, 155,
  181, 291, 321, 341, 600
  in Actors Studio, 302, 321
  Barbara Kazan and, 653, 668
Leyte, 274, 275, 276, 278–9
Life, 747
Life with Father, 422
Lighton, Bud, 246–7, 252, 253, 257, 258,
  259, 261, 263, 264, 274, 283, 305,
  307–9, 311, 321, 404, 455
  film style of, 250–1, 253
  Kazan's HUAC testimony and, 455
  marriages of, 252
Lighton, Hope, 253
Lighton, Louis D., 233
Lillie, Beatrice, 123
Lincoln Center, 611, 612–14
  all-white board of, 703
  Kazan's doubts about, 586
Lincoln Center Repertory Theatre, 364,
  585–8, 596, 607–14, 627, 629, 656,
  684, 687–700, 703, 718, 751
  After the Fall produced by, 659–60, 662,
  666–9, 689–9, 690, 692
  Barbara Loden Kazan and, 728
  But for Whom Charlie produced by,
  690–1, 692, 703
  The Changeling produced by, 691, 693,
  703
  Danton's Death produced by, 699
  Kazan's loyalty to, 691
  Kazan's resignation from, 698
  Kelman on, 719–20
  Marco Millions produced by, 690
  Miller and, 687, 699
  Molly Kazan and, 656
  Schuman and, 695–6, 696–7, 698
  Tartuffe produced by, 694
  Whitehead and, 687, 698, 699
Little, Stuart, 670, 671
Little Carnegie Theatre, 756
Litvak, Anatole "Tola," 184, 185–8
Litvinov, Maxim, 136
Living Newspaper, 232
Loden, Barbara, see Kazan, Barbara Loden
Loeb, Phil, 473
Logan, Josh, 327, 328
Lombard, Carole, 229
Los Angeles, 160, 416
Los Angeles Times, 514
Losey, Joseph, 757, 758
Ludwig, Salem, 278

Lunceford, Jimmie, 189
Lupino, Ida, 392

MacArthur, Douglas, 274–5, 276, 285, 287
MacLeish, Archibald, 8, 450, 582, 583, 610
Maguire, Charles, 562, 604,
    America America and, 635, 639, 644–5,
        651
    On the Waterfront and, 519–24
Maguire, Jessie, 523
Mahler, Gustav, 240
Mailer, Norman, 690
Malcolm X, 295
Malden, Karl, 255, 300, 319, 342, 470, 489,
    501, 561, 569, 677, 679
Maltz, Albert, 101–2, 105, 421, 423, 456–
    7, 472
    on art and communism, 399, 400
Mamoulian, Rouben, 392
Mandaville, Molly, 420
Manila, 276, 279–89, 290, 301
Mankiewicz, Herman, 389–90
Mankiewicz, Joseph L., 393, 436, 456,
    460–1
    on Screen Directors Guild loyalty oath
        controversy, 387–93
Mankiewicz, Rosemary, 388
Mann, Paul, 143
Mann, Thomas, 594–5
Mannix, Eddie, 227
Man on a Tightrope, 476–84, 506, 510,
    511, 520
    Cirkus Brumbach in, 477–8
    commercial failure of, 492, 510
    Zanuck's cutting of, 490–2
Mantle, Burns, 104, 321
March, Florence Eldridge, 196–7, 201,
    205, 207, 210, 212, 214, 215, 220, 478,
    484
    anti-communist attacks on, 441
    letter to Molly Kazan from, 213–14
March, Fredric, 196–7, 206, 207, 208, 210,
    212, 214, 215, 221, 478, 484
    anti-communist attacks on, 441
    in Man on a Tightrope, 478
    revenge taken on Bankhead by, 221
March, Liska, 630–1, 632
Marching Song (Lawson), 109
Marco Millions (O'Neill), 690
Marivaux, Pierre Carlet de Chamblain de,
    613

Marotta, Joe, 521, 522
Marshall, George, 281, 389
Marshall Plan, 461
Martin, Mary, 234–5, 243, 337
Marx, Groucho, 711
Marx, Karl, 128
Massey, Raymond, 535–6, 538
Mastroianni, Marcello, 739
Mattei Affair, The, 758
Matthau, Walter, 568
Maugham, W. Somerset, 30, 239
Mauriello, Tami, 254, 521–2
Mayer, Louis B., 227, 228, 229, 253, 312,
    327, 345
Mayo, Virginia, 236, 237, 238
McBride, John, 804, 805
McCandless, Stanley, 50
McCarthy, Angela "Anna," 815
McCarthy, Joseph, 442, 583
McCarthy, Kevin, 709
McClintic, Guthrie, 235
McGuire, Dorothy, 229, 252, 263, 331,
    332, 334, 382
McLean, Barbara, 340
Meany, George, 506
Meisner, Sanford, 143, 153
Memoirs (Williams), 494
men:
    clothing of, 28
    feminine characteristics in, 27
    in Greece, 629
    infidelities sought by, 369
    in Turkey, 14, 618
Menderes, Adnan, 620–1, 625
Mengers, Sue, 769
Men in White (Kingsley), 100, 101, 103,
    104–5, 108, 109, 111
Menjou, Adolphe, 480, 484
Menotti, Gian-Carlo, 638
Mercer, Johnny, 189
Merchant, Vivien, 767–8
Merck Manual, The, 680, 808
Mercury Theatre, 133, 193
Meredith, Burgess, 704, 709
Merlo, Frank, 442, 495
    Williams and, 349
Merry Go Round (Maltz and Sklar), 101
Metcalf, Colonel, 280
Method acting, 50, 63, 81, 90, 139, 144,
    154, 611
Metro-Goldwyn-Mayer, 233, 304, 312, 510
Metropolitan Opera, 585
Mexican Hayride, 278
Meyerhold, V. E., 65, 66, 145, 322, 613

Meyerhold, V. E. (*cont.*)
  Soviets' termination of, 450
Midsummer Night's Dream, A (Shakespeare), 364
Mielziner, Jo, 27, 54, 338–9, 345, 361–2, 503, 542–3, 586, 613, 657, 662
Milestone, Lewis, 157, 158–60
Milford, Gene, 526
Miller, Arthur, 299, 318–21, 358–9, 365–8, 371, 410–16, 420, 421, 605, 650, 656, 659–60, 666–8, 673–4, 687, 690, 746
  in breakup with first wife, 426, 438–9
  conflicts of, 401–2
  The Crucible envisioned by, 449–50
  The Hook abandoned by, 413–15, 420
  Kazan's relationship with, 319, 320, 365–6, 460–1, 471–2, 486, 487, 508, 529, 530, 629–30
  Lincoln Center Repertory Theatre and, 586, 698, 699, 718, 818
  Molly Kazan and, 319, 426, 449, 450
  Monroe's marriage to, 427, 539–40, 565, 667–8, 673
  Monroe's romance with, 178, 408–9, 415–16, 426, 427, 439, 630
  parsimonious nature of, 366
  success enjoyed by, 365–7
  Williams compared with, 348, 356, 361, 365
  Willy Loman and, 356, 366, 367
Miller, Gilbert, 222, 224, 231
Miller, Marilyn, 51
Miller, Mary, 367, 368, 371, 402, 414, 415, 426, 438–9
Henry Miller's Theatre, 222
Misfits, The, 540
Mitchum, Robert, 779
Mittelmann, Bela, 238–9, 268–9, 448, 460, 471, 516, 584
  on Kazan-Dowling relationship, 242
  on Kazan's HUAC testimony, 448
  Molly Kazan and, 239
Molière, 613
Monroe, Marilyn, 404–9, 413, 598–9, 630, 635, 669, 673–4, 690, 706
  background of, 404–5, 407
  DiMaggio and, 454–5, 539
  Hyde's relationship with, 247–8, 403, 404, 405–6
  Kazan's relationship with, 407–8, 427, 454–5, 669
  Miller's marriage to, 427, 539–40, 565, 667–8, 673

  Miller's romance with, 178, 408–9, 415–16, 426, 427, 439, 540, 630
  as "Miss Bauer," 409–10
  Paula Strasberg on sets with, 564–5
  Strasberg and, 427, 539–40, 564–5, 713, 715
Marilyn Monroe Theatre, 715
Montand, Yves, 667
Moore, Terry, 479–80
Moreau, Jeanne, 771, 780
Mostel, Zero, 383
Mother Courage (Brecht), 347
Mount Argaeus, 616
movies:
  casting of, 536
  composers for, 658
  forewords of, 411
  theatre vs., 377
  time in, 380–1
Muni, Paul, 184
Munich, 476–7, 482
Murdoch, Rupert, 227
Murphy, Richard, 316, 378, 379
Myerberg, Michael, 192–3, 196–7, 201–2, 203, 206, 207, 209, 210, 212, 213, 214–15, 221

Nachbaur, Jean, 757
Nash, Ogden, 233
Nation, The, 470
Nelson, Bug-eye, 110
Neurotic Personality of Our Time, The (Horney), 165–6, 584
Newman, Paul, 141, 544, 703, 709
  on Kazan's resignation from Actors Studio, 632–3
New Masses, 116, 399, 456–7
New Republic, The, 147, 316, 351
New Rochelle, N.Y., 26
New Rochelle High School, 28, 36
New Rochelle Public Library, 28, 33, 139
Newsday, 787, 788
Newsweek, 693
New Theatre, 109, 118, 128, 423, 447, 459
  Communist Party confrontation with, 449–50
New Theatre League, 106, 112
New York City Ballet, 585
New York *Daily News*, 321, 706
New Yorker, The, 234

New York *Herald Tribune*, 321, 564, 670–1
  Kazan attacked in, 474
New York Journal-American, 453
New York Philharmonic Orchestra, 585
New York *Post*, 467, 470, 471, 564, 632,
  706, 788
New York Review of Books, 747
New York Times, 160, 224, 265, 324, 436,
    437, 438, 442, 452, 511, 614, 625, 632,
    633, 686, 698, 706, 748, 817
  Kazan's Actors Studio article in, 632
  Kazan's HUAC testimony and, 465, 466,
  468
  Steinbeck's Nobel Prize and, 786–7
New York Times Magazine, 299
Nichols, Louis, 452
Nichols, Mike, 299, 338, 467, 761, 765
Nicholson, Jack, 765
Nietzsche, Friedrich, 471
Night Music (Odets), 182–4, 316
Night of 100 Stars, 714–15
Nixon, Raphael, 445–8
Nixon, Richard M., 251, 583
Nizer, Louis, 441
Nolan, Lloyd, 263
Norris, Frank, 227
North, Alex, 339, 416, 433, 435
Nugent, Elliott, 230

O'Brien, Margaret, 305
O'Casey, Sean, 102
Odets, Betty, 441
Odets, Clifford, 27, 85, 86, 105, 112–13,
    153, 157–63, 172, 175, 182–3, 211,
    240, 352, 475, 505, 659, 662–5,
  acclaim of, 80, 116, 120, 123–6, 273, 818
  artistic influence of, 663
  Clurman and, 88–9, 182–3, 319–20
  Communist Party and, 120, 125
  decline of, 135, 663
  HUAC testimony of, 134–5, 441, 818
  illness and death of, 88–9, 662–4, 750,
    783, 818
  Kazan's HUAC testimony and, 445, 446,
    462–3, 465, 471
  marriages of, 87–9, 90, 91
  Molly Kazan and, 78, 86–7, 91, 423,
    652, 664
  Strasberg's insult to, 119–20, 123
Oenslager, Don, 50
Office of Strategic Services, 232, 242

Of Human Bondage (Maugham), 30
O'Hara, John, 213
Oklahoma! (Rodgers and Hammerstein),
  234
Olivier, Laurence, 143–4, 338, 385–6, 565
Onassis, Aristotle, 14
O'Neill, Eugene, 494, 540, 605, 703
One Touch of Venus (Weill, Perelman and
    Nash), 233–5, 236, 243
  problems of, 234
On the Waterfront, 145, 254, 363, 410,
    471, 499–500, 514–29, 530, 533, 568,
    574, 666, 750, 752, 761, 766, 770
  Brando in, 517, 523, 524–6
  cost of, 520, 527
  glove scene in, 525–6
  Kazan's bodyguard on, 521, 522
  New York skyline in, 519
  parallels with Kazan's life in, 500
  prizefighters in, 521–2
  Spiegel and, 510–11, 517, 519–20, 523–4
  studio rejections of, 509–10
  success of, 517, 528–9
  taxi scene in, 524–5
  Zanuck's rejection of, 508–9
Oresteia (Aeschylus), 145
orgone box, 706, 708, 794
Osato, Sono, 235
Osborn, Paul, 331, 370, 534, 546, 572, 596
Oswald, Gerd, 477
Our Town (Wilder), 192, 193, 206
Overgaard, Andy, 444–5, 446

Pacino, Al, 141, 143, 715
Page, Geraldine, 545, 653, 702, 705, 709
Pagnol, Mariel, 563
Palymyra, Lucy, 22–4, 25, 71
Panic (MacLeish), 450
Panic in the Streets, 378–83, 428, 441, 480,
  510
  shooting of, 378–9
Papp, Joseph, 611
Paradise Lost (Odets), 133, 147–50, 156,
  163, 184
  Kazan in, 147
Parc Oteli, 548, 624
Patricola, Tom, 51
Pavese, Cesare, 274
"Pearl, The" (Steinbeck), 397, 401
Pearl Harbor, Japanese attack on, 61, 192,
  232

Peck, Gregory, 331, 332, 333, 334, 382
Peer Gynt (Ibsen), 303
People of the Cumberlands, 105, 263
People's Worker, 411, 412
People's World, 566
Perelman, S. J., 233, 234
Period of Adjustment (Williams), 595, 596
Perkins, Osgood, 84–5, 89, 90
Perry, Eleanor, 747
Pescados, 105
Peters, Jean, 403
Philbrick, Herbert, 452
Philippines, 270–89, 290–2
   tribute to Roosevelt in, 279, 281
Pidgeon, Walter, 305
Pinchot, Rosamund, 370
Pinebrook Country Club, 152–7
Pinky, 251, 374–6, 377, 382, 387, 506, 509
   Barrymore in, 375
   Ford's quitting of, 486
Pinter, Harold, 761, 765, 767–8, 770, 771,
   774, 775, 779, 780, 781
   marital problems of, 767–8
Piscator, Irwin, 150, 151
Planned Parenthood, 657
Platt, Louise, 370
Playwrights Company, 296, 501
Plummer, Christopher, 582
Plunkett, Walter, 306–8, 309, 316
Poros, 581, 582
Portrait of a Madonna (Williams), 339–40
Posada, José Guadalupe, 443, 497
Pound, Ezra, 300
Powell, William, 305
Power, Tyrone, 251
Preminger, Otto, 383, 513
Prince, Harold, 338
Prince Valiant, 508
Proferes, Nick, 754, 763, 779, 794, 808,
   810, 815
   Barbara Kazan and, 763, 816
Proust, Marcel, 144, 273
Public Enemy, The, 186
Pulitzer Prize, 104, 226, 408, 409, 546,
   582, 583
Pure in Heart, The (Lawson), 82, 84, 91

Raft, George, 184
Raging Bull, 146
Raimu, Jules, 145
Rainer, Luise, 87–8, 153, 157
Ray, Nick, 109, 238, 262, 269, 273, 538,
   817–18
   career of, 790–1
   death of, 789–92, 817–18
Reagan, Ronald, 184–5, 218, 566, 670
Rebel Without a Cause, 538, 790
Redgrave, Michael, 182, 711
Reed, Florence, 205, 207, 208, 210, 214
Reeve, Christopher, 800
Reflections in a Golden Eye, 751
Reich, Wilhelm, 706, 794
Reis, Mae, 443, 467
Relais Bisson, 730
Remick, Lee, 141, 598
Revere, Anne, 334
Richard III (Shakespeare), 146
Rinaldo, Reverend, 796–7, 799–800
Rivoli Theatre, 452
Robards, Jason, 141, 667, 669, 691, 693,
   725
   Kazan criticized by, 692–3
Robbins, Jerry, 468
Roberts, Marguerite, 305
Robinson, Earl, 232
Rockefeller, John D., III, 575, 578, 579,
   585, 586, 607, 608, 609, 687, 695, 696,
   697, 698, 818
Rocket to the Moon (Odets), 175, 181
Rodgers, Richard, 300, 785
Rodriguez y Gonzalez, Pancho, 334, 344,
   348, 349
Rogell, Al, 391
Rooney, Mickey, 305
Roosevelt, Franklin D., 55, 99, 132–3, 251,
   279, 280, 281, 596–7, 669
Roosevelt and Hopkins, 476
Rose Tattoo, The (Williams), 373, 383, 414
Rossen, Robert, 469, 483
Rostova, Mira, 600
Rousseau, Jean Jacques, 595, 687
Russell, Theresa, 765–6, 770, 771, 772

Quiet City (Shaw), 181, 182
Quigley, Martin, 434–6, 564
Quinn, Anthony, 352
   in *Viva Zapata!,* 428, 429–30

Saarinen, Eero, 586, 611, 613, 657
Saint, Eva Marie, 523, 525
St. Clement's Protestant Episcopal
   Church, 670, 676
Saint-Denis, Michel, 608

St. James Theatre, 171
Sands, Diana, 709
Schaffner, Franklin, 774
Schall, Ekkehard, 532
Schenck, Joseph, 407
Schenck, Nicholas, 312
Schlesinger, Arthur, 470
Schreiber, Lew, 264, 418, 419
Schulberg, B. P., 180, 227, 492
Schulberg, Budd, 27, 421, 492–4, 506–11,
    515, 516, 517–18, 528, 529, 560, 567–
    9, 746
    Communist Party and, 399–400, 445–6,
        456, 468, 471, 566
    in Hoboken, 488, 492–3, 499–500,
        521
    Kazan's first meeting with, 486–9
    waterfront script written by, 487–8
    Watts riot and, 295
    Zanuck and, 507
Schulberg, Geraldine Brooks, 569
Schulberg, Vicki, 487, 517–18
Schuman, William, 694–5, 696–7, 698
Scorsese, Martin, 146
Scott, Elaine Anderson,
    see Steinbeck, Elaine
Scott, George C., 709, 710, 712
Screen Directors Guild of America, 387–
    93, 436, 754, 758–9
screenplays:
    direct experience and, 493–4
    pacing of, 517
Screen Writers Guild, 159
Sea of Grass, The, 304–16, 377, 382
    blizzard scene in, 313
    costumes for, 307–8
    horses in, 306, 308–9
    rear projection film used in, 310–11
Seaton, George, 391
Selznick, David O., 227, 253, 327
    on producing, 337–8
Selznick, Irene, 327–9, 331, 334–6, 338–
    42, 344, 345, 347, 453
Seven Descents of Myrtle, The (Williams),
    495
Shadow, The, 133
Shakespeare, William, 150, 364, 501, 582,
    610, 613
Shamroy, Leon, 258–9
Shanahan, Eileen, 687, 742, 815
Shanghai Gesture, The, 205
Shank, Anna B., 28, 35, 597
    Kazan encouraged by, 26–7, 29, 35, 71
    letter to Kazan from, 26

Shaw, Irwin, 77, 180–1, 302, 449, 769
    Molly Kazan and, 426
Sheridan, Ann, 186
Sherwood, Robert, 296, 476–7, 491, 501
Shishmanoglou, Isaak (grandfather), 14–17,
    21, 590
Shishmanoglou, Murda (great-grandfather),
    14
Shishmanoglou, Odysseus (uncle), 15, 19–
    21
Shishmanoglou, Sultana (great-grand-
    mother), 14
Shishmanoglou, Vassiliki "Queenie" (aunt),
    22
Shubert, Lee, 79–80
Sidney, Sylvia, 181
Silent Partner, The (Odets), 87–8, 153–4
Silvera, Frank, 471
Simon, Abe, 521
Sinatra, Frank, 390, 515–17, 519
Sing Out, Sweet Land! (Kerr and Kerr),
    543
Sismanson, Evangelos, 30
Sister Carrie, 144
Skin of Our Teeth, The (Wilder), 192, 205–
    10, 217, 219–21, 223, 225, 305, 345,
    478, 479, 597
    Aronson on, 219
    Bankhead in, 206–13, 220–1
    first performance of, 209–13
    Kazan chosen for, 192–3
    meaning of, 197
    public reactions to, 219
    review of, 216
SKKOB, 112
Skouras, Spyros, 227, 472, 507, 509, 597,
    601, 628
    background of, 451
    Kazan praised by, 263
    Kazan's HUAC testimony and, 451–2,
        455, 460
Slesinger, Tess, 307
Smith, Art, 467
Smith, Bessie, 145
Smith, Betty, 233, 245
Smith, Oliver, 813
Sokolow, Anna, 443, 497, 668
Sokolsky, George, 471, 476
    exposure of Kazan's past threatened by,
        453, 455
Sothern, Ann, 785
Soviet Union, 132, 231
Spellman, Francis Cardinal, 434, 442, 716
    Baby Doll attacked by, 561, 563–4

Spiegel, Sam (S. P. Eagle), 73, 229, 510–11, 518, 529–30, 730
  Brando obtained by, 515–16
  Kazan's anger with, 770, 777
  Lastfogel and, 516
  The Last Tycoon and, 761, 762, 765–75, 777–81
  late night calls of, 523
  Mengers's snubbing of, 769
  as mythological figure, 513–14
  as negotiator, 514–15
  On the Waterfront and, 510–11, 514, 517, 523–4, 526–7, 530
  Russell and, 765–6, 772
Splendor in the Grass, 5, 601–5, 635
  Barbara Loden Kazan in, 603
  casting of, 602–3
  drowning scene in, 604
  Inge and, 601–2, 604, 605
Spoleto Festival of Two Worlds, 638, 645, 646
Stanislavski, Konstantin, 65, 106, 145
Stanley, Kim, 705, 710, 711
Stark, Ray, 628, 639
Starkey, Marion, 449
Steiger, Rod, 524, 525
Stein, Gertrude, 300
Stein, Sol, 616, 661, 741
  The Arrangement and, 744, 745–6
Steinbeck, Elaine, 373, 395, 593, 594, 784, 785, 787, 788
Steinbeck, Gwyn, 784, 785
Steinbeck, John, 5, 273, 529, 539, 545, 546, 596, 728, 784–8, 817
  cross-country journey of, 787
  Dean approved by, 534
  death of, 784, 788, 792, 817
  depression of, 593
  on filmmaking in Mexico, 397
  Kazan advised by, 594
  marriages of, 784, 785
  Nobel Prize of, 786–7, 817
  plays and musicals written by, 785–6
  psychoanalysis attacked by, 594
  spinal surgery of, 786
  Viva Zapata! script written by, 373, 393, 395–7, 456, 784, 785
  as war correspondent, 787–8, 817
  writing warm-up of, 261
  Zanuck's snubbing of, 395
Steiner, Ralph, 105, 652, 655
Sterling Farms, 58
Stevens, George, 381, 389, 393, 456, 510, 779

on filmmaking, 340
Stevens, Liz, 779
Stewart, James, 183, 232
Stimson, Henry, 281
Stone, Lewis, 305
Stormie Seas, 580, 581, 582, 586
Stowe, Harriet Beecher, 222, 224
Strand, Paul, 105
Strasberg, Anna, 715
Strasberg, Lee, 66–7, 80–2, 85–6, 113, 151, 153–5, 211, 302–3, 439–40, 574, 676, 701–15, 790
  ambivalence of, 111–12
  Baldwin's telling off of, 704–5
  Clurman and, 62, 120, 154, 320, 812
  Crawford's estrangement from, 712
  death of, 715
  dignity brought to actors by, 141–2, 714
  Group Theatre dominated by, 61–2, 78
  Kazan interviewed by, 56–7
  on Kazan's betrayal of Actors Studio, 607, 608, 609, 630–1
  Kazan's HUAC testimony and, 464, 465
  Lincoln Center Repertory Theatre and, 585–6, 587, 608–9, 615, 633, 650, 701
  Molly Kazan and, 78, 650, 653
  Monroe and, 427, 539–40, 564–5, 713
  at *Night of 100 Stars*, 714–15
  Odets insulted by, 119–20, 123
  resignation from Group Theatre by, 156
  Russian theatre explored by, 66
  second marriage of, 713
  Stella Adler and, 119, 143, 154
  teaching of, 63, 64–7, 143, 145, 148, 154, 300, 610–11, 647, 706–8, 714
  Tone and, 75–7
  Torn and, 702, 704–5
Strasberg, Paula, 85, 121, 129, 153, 439, 464, 465, 564–5, 600, 638, 653, 712
  Kazan's infidelities revealed to wife by, 193–4, 638
Lee Strasberg Institute, 713–14, 715
Streetcar Named Desire, A (film), 144, 312, 380, 383–7, 401, 402, 421, 428, 443, 453, 454, 455–6, 516
  censorship problems of, 401, 417, 432–7, 438
  four minutes cut from, 416–17
  set of, 384
  studio protests to Kazan during, 312–13
Streetcar Named Desire, A (Williams), 74, 96, 115, 183, 301, 327–31, 334–54, 359, 361, 364, 502, 544
  Brando in, 341–2, 343–6, 351

casting of, 337, 339–40, 341–2
  Clurman and, 351–2, 353
  Irene Selznick and, 327
  Kazan's reservations about, 328
  opening of, 345
  other productions of, 330–1
  rehearsals of, 342–4
  Waiting for Lefty compared with, 115
  Williams's life reflected in, 347–51, 352
Success Story (Lawson), 59, 64, 74, 76, 77,
    78, 82, 85, 86, 89, 95, 111
Sullavan, Margaret, 337
Summer and Smoke (Williams), 545
Superman, 800
Susann, Jacqueline, 746
Sutter's Bakery, 129
Sweet Bird of Youth (Williams), 544–5
  casting of, 545
  television screen device in, 544
"Sweet Georgia Brown" (Bernie, Pinkard,
    and Casey), 45
Sweet Thursday (Steinbeck), 785
Syndicate of Film Technicians and Work-
    ers, 397, 398

Tacloban, 276, 280, 290
Taksim, 548
Tamiris, Helen, 65, 75, 232
Tandy, Jessica, 340, 344–5, 346–7, 385,
    742–4
  Brando and, 343–4
  Williams and, 346
Tartuffe (Molière), 694
Tavenner, Frank, 445, 469
Taylor, Elizabeth, 305, 545, 597
Taylor, Laurette, 175
Taylor, Robert, 305
Tea and Sympathy (Anderson), 301, 488,
    489, 499, 501–6, 507, 719
  casting of, 489
  final scene of, 504–5
  Kazan's revitalization of, 505
  Kerr in, 503–4
Ten Blocks on the Camino Real (Williams),
    443
Tennessee Valley Authority, 560, 596
Tenney Committee, 446
Thacher, Alfred Beaumont, 422
Thacher, Molly, *see* Kazan, Molly Day
    Thacher
Thalberg, Irving, 227

theatre, 364–5
  Broadway, 502
  Clurman's views on, 65, 813
  collaboration in, 322, 362
  communism in, 132
  failures in, 183
  film vs., 377
  friendship in, 183–4, 192
  naturalism and, 613
  subtext in, 66
  success in, 363
  themes in, 10, 505–6
Theatre Collective, 105
Theatre Guild, 84, 239
Theatre of Action, 105, 106–8, 128, 131,
    154, 155, 168, 225, 467
  communal living in, 107–8
  Communist Party line followed by, 108
  improvisation in, 107
  socialist criticism meetings in, 108
Theatre Union, 105, 128, 399, 423
They Live by Night, 790
This Is the Army, 290
Three Sisters, The (Chekhov), 704, 705–6,
    708, 711–12
  critical reactions to, 708
  London cast of, 709
  London reception of, 711–12
  New York cast of, 705–6
  television film of, 708–9
Thunder Rock (Ardrey), 182
Till, Emmett, 702–3
Times (London), 711
Toledano, Eduard, 49
To Live, 146
Tolstoi, Leo, 17, 271, 614
Tone, Franchot, 75–7, 78, 82, 120, 318,
    319
Torn, Rip, 653, 702, 703, 704–5, 709
Toscanini, Arturo, 300, 659
Townsend, Ruby, 760, 761, 762, 763, 768,
    769, 772, 774, 776, 777
Toy Theatre, 52
Tracy, Spencer, 247, 304, 305, 308, 309,
    310, 311, 313–14, 382, 584
Travels with Charley (Steinbeck), 787, 817
Treasure of the Sierra Madre, The, 146
Tree Grows in Brooklyn, A (film), 249, 252,
    253, 257–9, 267–8, 277–8, 280, 285,
    304, 307, 314, 452, 790
  Army showing of, 277–8
  casting of, 257–8
  Garner in, 257–8
  success of, 263

Tree Grows in Brooklyn, A (Smith), 233, 245
Trenton Six, 487, 488
Trilling, Steve, 184, 433, 436
Truckline Café (Anderson), 300–1, 341, 342
Turkey, Turks:
  Barbara Kazan in, 616–20
  Greeks and, 13–14, 16, 556, 591
  hamals in, 550
  Kazan's second trip to, 589–93
  men in, 14, 618
  political trial in, 620–1, 625–6
  women in, 589–90
Turner, Lana, 247
Twentieth Century–Fox, 233, 306, 318, 451, 475, 509, 510, 628
  Kazan's downfall at, 489–90
27 Wagons Full of Cotton (Williams), 562

Viva Zapata!, 254, 375, 377, 378, 381, 382, 383, 387, 395–401, 403, 417–20, 431, 433, 448, 471, 480, 506, 510
  Brando in, 428–9
  Crowther's review of, 452
  filming of, 427–32
  meeting on communism in Mexico and, 417–19
  Mexican location desired for, 397
  negotiations with Zanuck for, 394–7
  official Mexican position on, 400
  Quinn in, 428, 429–30
  script for, 373, 393, 395–7, 456, 784, 785
  Skouras's anxiety over, 451
  Zanuck's suggestions for, 396, 417
Vizzard, Jack, 432–3
Voice of America, 214, 262
Voice of the Turtle, The, 669

United Artists, 515, 756–7
United States:
  foreign vs. native appreciation of, 647
  Molly Kazan on, 677
  Odets on, 352
Up in Arms, 228, 236, 237–8, 244

Vakhtangov, Yevgeny, 145, 322, 613
Valentine, Marjorie, 35–6, 37
Van Fleet, Jo, 598
Variety, 216, 696, 758
Vassar *Miscellany*, 55
vaudeville, 43–4
Velde, Harold R., 446
Venice Film Festival, 436
Victoria Theatre, 539
Vietnam War, 787–8
View from the Bridge, A (Miller), 470
Visconti, Luchino, 350
Visitors, The, 754–9
  Cannes exhibition of, 757–8
  casting of, 754
  Kazan's bank loan for, 755, 757
  Losey and, 757, 758
  New York audience reactions to, 756
  non-union crew of, 754
  reviews of, 756
  Screen Actors Guild and, 758–9

Wagner, Robert, 602, 603
Waiting for Lefty (Odets), 112–17, 123, 118–19, 147, 156, 163, 449, 538, 664
  durability of, 115
  Kazan in, 106, 112, 114
  Kazan attacked with line from, 468–9
Wald, Jerry, 233, 410
Waldorf Peace Conference, 426
Wallace, Henry, 567
Wallach, Eli, 498, 561
Walsh, Raoul, 251
Wanda, 793–4, 807, 809
Wanger, Walter, 157
War and Peace (Tolstoi), 17, 199, 200, 271
Warner, Jack, 184, 253, 312, 313, 403, 416–17, 433, 434, 436, 437, 447, 535, 596
  East of Eden and, 529, 534
  on Harris, 538
  Kazan and Miller accused of subversion by, 421
  A Streetcar Named Desire and, 417
Warner Brothers, 184–5, 227, 228, 233, 385–7, 435, 510, 529, 534, 602, 628, 645, 686, 749
  America America funded by, 640
  Kazan's office at, 749
Warton, John, 512
Washington Square Theatre, 629
Wasserman, Lew, 401
Waterfront Crime Commission, 499
Waters, Ethel, 374, 376

Waxman, Samuel, 802–3, 805, 807, 808, 809, 817
Wayne, David, 403
Wayne, John, 374
Way of All Flesh, The (Butler), 30
Webb, Clifton, 251
Webber, Julie, 35
Webber, Marguerite, 35
Weill, Kurt, 72, 104, 154, 155, 156, 233–4, 235
Weisbart, David, 416–17, 433, 435
Weisbart, Gladys, 433
Welch, Constance, 50
Welles, Orson, 133–4, 135, 191, 193, 251, 273, 659
  death of, 783
Wellman, William, 251, 254, 255
Wenders, Wim, 789, 791
Werfel, Alma Mahler, 240–1
Werfel, Franz, 71, 239–41
Wexler, Haskell "Pete," 639, 640, 643
Wharton, Carly, 191, 192
Wharton, John, 508, 529
What Every Woman Knows (Barrie), 224
What Makes Sammy Run? (Schulberg), 399, 456, 487, 506
Whitehead, Robert, 6, 7, 580, 586, 587, 608–12, 629, 630, 633, 653–7, 686–9, 691, 693–5, 698, 699, 702, 703, 718, 728, 812
  background of, 688
  Lincoln Center and, 696, 697–8
  Woods's dislike of, 688–9
Widmark, Richard, 254–5, 378
Wilder, Billy, 238, 249, 264
  on Miller-Monroe match, 565
Wilder, Thornton, 192–3, 196, 197, 209, 219, 220–1, 339, 345
  on direction, 206
  Pulitzer Prize won by, 226
Wild River, 596–601, 605
  Barbara Loden Kazan in, 599–600
  casting of, 597–600
  love scenes in, 599
  Remick in, 599
Wilkerson, William, 455
Williams, Esther, 305
Williams, Rose, 348
Williams, Tennessee, 27, 273, 331, 334–7, 340, 373, 383, 384, 443, 453, 454, 485, 488, 494–8, 540–6, 659, 663, 719, 746, 783, 822–3
  artists as viewed by, 353

autobiography of, 494
Baby Doll and, 562, 564
Bel Geddes and, 540, 541
Blanche compared with, 347–51
Brando adored by, 341–2, 344
on Camino Real, 496–7
censorship of A Streetcar Named Desire and, 433, 434, 436
children desired by, 442
on desire, 369
in disagreements over Cat on a Hot Tin Roof, 541–4
dual nature of, 347–8
importance of work to, 261
Kazan's Lincoln Center offer and, 587
Kazan's refusal of play by, 595–6
Kazan's writing encouraged by, 353–4
letters to Kazan from, 326, 328, 329–30
memorial service for, 822–3
Merlo and, 349
Miller compared with, 348, 356, 361, 365
Molly Kazan and, 162, 327, 339, 352, 426
on mornings, 336
nightmares of, 351
as outsider, 494–5
Pancho and, 334, 344, 348, 349
on A Streetcar Named Desire, 352
on Tandy, 346
Williams College, 27, 29, 30–1, 39–45, 46–8, 49, 424, 619
Willkie, Wendell, 251
Winkler, Henry, 142
Winter of Our Discontent, The (Steinbeck), 261, 786, 817
Winter's Tale, A (Shakespeare), 51
women, 27, 369–70
  clothing of, 28
  fat teenagers as, 541
  flirtatious, 349
  German, 483
  in Germeer, 555
  Mastroianni on, 739
  seducing, 404
  sexual adventures desired by, 37–8
  surrounding film directors, 619
  in Turkey, 14, 589–90
  unfulfilled desires in marriages of, 369
Wood, Audrey, 322, 327, 331, 501–2, 545
Wood, Natalie, 602–4, 605
Woods, George, 607–8, 609, 612, 613, 687–9, 694–5, 696, 697, 698, 818

Woodward, Joanne, 703
Woolley, Monty, 403
World Theatre Festival, 709, 712
World War I, 22, 72
World War II, 61, 192, 232
Wyatt, Jane, 316
Wykagyl Country Club, 29, 49
Wyler, William, 144, 158, 228, 391, 392, 393
  on directing, 497
Wynn, Ed, 51

Yale Drama School, 12, 48, 53, 90, 399, 424, 508, 678, 811
  faculty of, 49–50
  Kazan at, 48–55, 424
  mannered acting taught at, 50–1
Yale University, 422
Yank, 262, 263, 288
Yearling, The (Rawlings), 311
Yeremia, Stellio, 547–55, 557–9, 642, 733–4, 735
  in Athens, 733
  George Kazan and, 556–7, 559
Yeremia, Vili, 557–9, 558–9
Young, Stark, 147
Young Go First, The (Martin, Scudder and Freidman), 107

Zanuck, Darryl F., 227–9, 232, 249–54, 267, 321, 340, 375, 378, 387, 395–7,
401, 417–21, 432, 436–7, 452, 490, 526, 527, 529, 666, 783, 785
  Boomerang script and, 316
  croquet party of, 394–6
  demise of Kazan's relationship with, 496, 508–12, 596
  as family man, 252–3
  film editing of, 259, 434
  film style of, 250–1, 253, 331
  Gentleman's Agreement and, 322
  The Golden Warriors and, 506–7
  The Hook refused by, 403
  importance of work to, 260
  Kazan esteemed by, 263, 264, 272, 292, 317, 334, 373–4
  Kazan's first meeting with, 249–50
  Kazan's HUAC testimony and, 420, 455, 470, 472
  Kazan's respect for, 331
  Man on a Tightrope and, 476, 477, 479, 489, 490–2
  On the Waterfront rejected by, 508–9
  Schulberg's meetings with, 507
  on social issues in films, 332–3
  son fired by, 252–3
  Steinbeck snubbed by, 395
  telegrams to Kazan from, 431–2
  vanity of, 253
  Viva Zapata! and, 419–20, 428, 434
Zanuck, Darrylin, 490
Zanuck, Richard, 252
Zanuck, Virginia, 229, 490
Zapata, Emiliano, 373, 397, 427, 784
  see also Viva Zapata!
Zeta Psi fraternity, 42
Zola, Emile, 264
Zolotow, Sam, 633

PHOTOGRAPHIC CREDITS

A NOTE ON THE TYPE

This book was set in Caledonia, a typeface designed by
W. A. Dwiggins (1880–1956). It belongs to the family of
printing types called "modern face" by printers—a term used
to mark the change in style of type letters that occurred about
1800. Caledonia borders on the general design of Scotch
Roman, but is more freely drawn than that letter.

Typography by Graphic Composition, Athens, Georgia
Printed and bound by Halliday Lithographers, West Hanover,
Massachusetts
Designed by Iris Weinstein